WHO'S WHO IN TELEVISION AND CABLE

WHO'S WHO IN TELEVISION AND CABLE

STEVEN H. SCHEUER, EDITOR

Robert Pardi, Managing Editor
Charles Witbeck, Hollywood Editor

Facts On File Publications
460 Park Avenue South
New York, N.Y. 10016

JUN 1 8 1984

WHO'S WHO IN TELEVISION AND CABLE

Copyright © 1983 by Steven H. Scheuer & Associates

Published by Facts On File, Inc.
460 Park Avenue South, New York, N.Y. 10016

Library of Congress Cataloging in Publication Data
Main entry under title:

Who's who in television and cable.

   1. Television personalities—United States—Biography.
I. Steven H. Scheuer & Associates.
PN1992.4.A2W44 1983   791.45'092'2 [B]   82-12045
ISBN 0-87196-747-2

Printed in the United States of America

10 9 8 7 6 5 4 3 2 1

For Nikki—for so much!

Acknowledgments

My special thanks to Managing Editor Robert Pardi for his invaluable writing, editorial and organizational skills. Also to my staff associate John Goudas for his helpful editorial contributions and to my associate, Peter Neuman, for his assistance in preparing the manuscript. Others who have helped in the preparation of this reference work include Dan Cook, Sharon Patton, Joanna Thompson, Janice Pello and Patricia Baiardi.

Preface

This is the first edition in a new series of reference books covering the burgeoning television, cable and video industries, including motion pictures. These increasingly intertwined fields are among the most rapidly growing businesses in the United States and throughout the world.

This biographical encyclopedia provides a comprehensive guide to well over 2,000 individuals in the TV, video and cable industries.

Establishing the criteria for inclusion in this "Who's Who" was a difficult and sometimes frustrating task. Due to the constraints of both space and time, various deserving candidates have been omitted—some TV station management personnel, for example, as well as TV and film agents in New York and Hollywood.

A majority of the entries are devoted to the leading executives of the three commercial networks—ABC, CBS and NBC—public television and the major national cable services, such as Home Box Office and the Cable News Network. I have also included information about hundreds of on-air television journalists, actors and actresses and dozens of important executives employed by local TV stations in New York, Washington and Los Angeles.

The biographical material herein was accurate, to the best of my knowledge, as of August 1983. Most of the entries have been based on questionnaires filled out by the respondents.

My thanks to all these organizations and individuals who assisted in the compilation of this data. I would greatly appreciate corrections and suggestions for additional entrants in future editions.

Steven H. Scheuer

About the Author

Steven H. Scheuer is the editor and publisher of TV KEY, the most widely syndicated TV newspaper column in America, appearing daily in over 200 newspapers. Mr. Scheuer and his staff in New York and Hollywood also provide a new editorial service called CABLE KEY, which previews cable television programming.

He conceived the idea of previewing television shows and has written numerous critically acclaimed books, including *Movies on TV, The Movie Book,* and *The Television Annual,* a reference work reporting on both programming and public policy issues. Mr. Scheuer is considered to be one of the most knowledgeable critics in the country. *Time* magazine called him "the most influential TV critic." *Access* magazine, published by the National Citizens Committee for Broadcasting, called Mr. Scheuer the best TV critic in the country reporting on questions of television and the public interest.

He is the executive producer and moderator of "All About TV," an award-winning weekly series shown on public and cable TV stations. Mr. Scheuer was the television critic of the CBS Radio Network for three years, where he previewed TV programming and commented on public policy issues. In 1979, he created and served as an executive producer of "The Television Annual," broadcast on the ABC TV network.

He is a partner in TELEKEY Associates, a company that markets an electronic television program guide, and is also the president of Cine-Tel Database, Inc., a corporation that is developing a worldwide computer database about motion pictures and television.

Mr. Scheuer is a native New Yorker and a graduate of Yale University. He has done graduate work at the London School of Economics and Political Science, at Columbia University, and at New York University. He has served on the faculty of the New School for Social Research and is a founding member of the Communications Media Committee of the American Civil Liberties Union. He is a vice president of International Film Seminars, a member of the Society of Fellows of the Aspen Institute, and a member of the Royal Television Society and the International Institute of Communications. Mr. Scheuer has been active in many political campaigns, including those of his brother, Representative James H. Scheuer of New York.

He participates in many sports and is a nationally ranked squash tennis player.

AAGAARD, KENNETH J.
V.P., NBC, Sports Operations

c/o NBC, 30 Rockefeller Plaza, New York, NY 10020
b. December 6, 1946. Evanston, IL.

EDUCATION: University of Iowa, B.A., Radio/TV/Film, ('69).
CAREER HIGHLIGHTS: Operations Dir. at WMAQ, Chicago ('69); joined NBC as Mgr. Broadcast Operations ('77); Mgr., Sports Operations ('79); Operations Prod., NBC Sports ('81); appointed V.P., Sports Operations ('82).
ACHIEVEMENTS & AWARDS: N.A.
PERSONAL: Resides in Closter, NJ with wife, Patti; sons Michael and Christopher.

AARON, BETSY
Correspondent, ABC, News

c/o ABC, 7 W. 66th St., New York, NY 10023
b. November 11. Forest Hills, NY.

EDUCATION: American University, B.A., History
CAREER HIGHLIGHTS: Researcher, ABC Radio, Washington, DC ('60); Researcher, ABC News, New York ('62); Reporter, WFIL-TV (now WPVI-TV), Philadelphia ('63); Reporter/Writer/Prod., WABC-TV, New York ('65); Prod., "ABC Evening News" ('70); Correspondent, ABC News, Chicago ('75); Correspondent, CBS News, Atlanta ('76); Writer/Co-Anchor, CBS News magazine for teenagers, "30 Minutes," New York ('79); Correspondent, NBC News assigned to "NBC Magazine" ('80); Correspondent, ABC News, New York ('82); Correspondent, ABC News assigned to "Nightline" ('83).
ACHIEVEMENTS & AWARDS: Dupont-Columbia citation ('82).
PERSONAL: N.A.

AARON, CHLOE
Independent Prod./TV Exec.

c/o PBS, 609 Fifth Ave., New York, NY 10017
b. October 9, 1938.

EDUCATION: Occidental College, B.A.; George Washington University, M.A.
CAREER HIGHLIGHTS: Freelance Writer; Dir. of Public Media for Natl. Endowment of the Arts; Sr. V.P., Programming, PBS ('76–'80); Pres., Chloe Aaron Productions.
ACHIEVEMENTS & AWARDS: Member, NATAS; Trustee Committee on Film for Museum of Modern Art.
PERSONAL: N.A.

ABEL, ELIE
Professor of Communications, Stanford University

1590 Dana Ave., Palo Alto, CA 94303
b. October 17, 1920. Montreal, Canada.

EDUCATION: Columbia University, M.S.; University of Western Ontario, LL.D.; McGill University, LL.D.
CAREER HIGHLIGHTS: Asst. City Editor, *Montreal Gazette* ('45); Foreign Correspondent, North American Newspaper Alliance ('46); UN Correspondent, Overseas News Agency ('47); Natl. and Foreign Correspondent, *N.Y. Times* ('49); Chief of Washington Bureau, *Detroit News* ('59); State Dept. Correspondent, NBC News ('61); Chief of London Bureau, NBC News ('65); Diplomatic Correspondent, NBC News ('67); Godfrey Lowell Cabot Professor and Dean, Graduate School of Journalism, Columbia University ('70); Harry and Norman Chandler Professor of Communications, Stanford University ('79); Chairman, Dept. of Communications, Stanford University ('83).

ACHIEVEMENTS & AWARDS: Overseas Press Club awards ('69, '70); Peabody award ('68); shared Pulitzer Prize ('57). Author of *The Missile Crisis* ('66); *Roots of Involvement: The U.S. in Asia*, with W. Averell Harriman.

PERSONAL: N.A.

ABERNATHY, JAMES L.
V.P., Corporate Affairs, ABC, Inc.

c/o ABC, 1330 Ave. of the Americas, New York, NY 10019

b. January 23.

EDUCATION: Brown University.

CAREER HIGHLIGHTS: Mgr., Corporate Information, CBS ('67); Assoc. Dir., Investor Relations ('71); Corporate V.P. in Charge of Investor Relations and Corporate Public Relations, Warner Communications, Inc. ('72); V.P., Investor Relations, ABC, Inc. ('74); V.P., Corporate Relations, ABC, Inc. ('77); V.P., Corporate Affairs, ABC, Inc. ('79).

ACHIEVEMENTS & AWARDS: N.A.

PERSONAL: N.A.

ABERNATHY, ROBERT
Correspondent, NBC, News

c/o NBC, 30 Rockefeller Plaza, New York, NY 10020

b. January 23. Geneva, Switzerland.

EDUCATION: Princeton University, B.A. and M.A.

CAREER HIGHLIGHTS: Joined NBC ('52); transferred to NBC News, Washington, DC ('53); Reporter, NBC News, London ('55); Correspondent, NBC News, New York ('58); Writer/Narrator, "Update," a weekly NBC series for high school students ('61); Correspondent, NBC News, Washington, DC ('63); Anchor/Correspondent/Commentator, KNBC-TV, Los Angeles ('66); Washington Correspondent for NBC's "Today" program ('77); Correspondent, NBC News, Washington, DC ('80).

ACHIEVEMENTS & AWARDS: Thomas Alva Edison mass media award for the best history for young people for his book *Introduction to Tomorrow* ('66).

PERSONAL: Daughter, Jane.

ABRAHAM, SETH
Sr. V.P., HBO, Sports Programming and Programming Operations

c/o HBO, 1271 Ave. of the Americas, New York, NY 10020

b. August 20, 1947.

EDUCATION: University of Toledo, B.A., Journalism; Boston University, M.A., Journalism.

CAREER HIGHLIGHTS: Stringer for *N.Y. Times*, Boston Bureau; Acct. Exec., Hill & Knowlton ('73); Special Asst. to Pres., Major League Baseball Promotion Corp. ('75); joined HBO as Dir. of Sports Operations ('78); Dir. and then V.P., Sports Programming ('80); Sr. V.P., Sports Programming and Programming Operations.

ACHIEVEMENTS & AWARDS: N.A.

PERSONAL: Resides in New York City with wife, Lynn.

ABRAMS, FLOYD
Attorney, Cahill, Gordon & Reindel

c/o Cahill, Gordon & Reindel, 80 Pine St., New York, NY 10005

b. N.A.

EDUCATION: Cornell University ('56); Yale Law School ('60).

CAREER HIGHLIGHTS: Abrams is one of the most distinguished attorneys in communications law, with special expertise in free speech and first amendment issues. Throughout the last decade, he has represented newspapers, broadcasters, and journalists in a variety of cases. He was co-counsel in the Pentagon Papers case and has argued in the Supreme Court in the cases *Nebraska Press Assn.* v. *Stuart*, *Landmark Communications* v. *Virginia*, *Smith* v. *Daily Mail*, *Nixon* v. *Warner Communications*, *Herbert* v. *Lando*, *Metromedia* v. *San Diego*, and *CBS* v. *FCC*. Abrams is a partner in the New York law firm of Cahill, Gordon & Reindel and a Lecturer in Law at the Columbia University School of Law. He was Visiting Lecturer at the Yale Law School ('74–'80), where he taught a course in constitutional law. He taught at the Columbia Graduate School of Journalism ('80) and was designated an Assoc. in Journalism.

ACHIEVEMENTS & AWARDS: Ross essay prize of the American Bar Assn. for his study of the Ninth Amendment to the U.S. Constitution ('67); First Amendment prize from the American Jewish Congress ('78). He has served as the Chairman of the Committee on Freedom of Speech and Chairman on Freedom of Expression of the Litigation Section of the American Bar Assn.

PERSONAL: Resides in New York City with wife, Efrat.

ADAMS, EDIE
Actress

c/o SAG, 7750 Sunset Blvd., Los Angeles, CA 90046

b. April 16, 1931. Kingston, PA.

EDUCATION: Juilliard School of Music; Columbia School of Drama.

CAREER HIGHLIGHTS: Stage credits include *Wonderful Town* ('52) and *L'il Abner* ('56); Her films include *The Apartment*, *It's a Mad, Mad, Mad, Mad, Mad World*, and *Love With the Proper Stranger*. Appeared in the TV series "Take a Good Look" and "Here's Edie" and her TV movies include *Evil Roy Slade*, *Superdome*, and *Fast Friends*.

ACHIEVEMENTS & AWARDS: N.A.

PERSONAL: Was married to the late comedian/ comedy writer Ernie Kovacs.

ADAMS, JACQUELINE
Correspondent, CBS, News

c/o CBS, 524 W. 57th St., New York, NY 10019

b. Boston, MA.

EDUCATION: Principia College, B.A.; Harvard Graduate School of Business Administration, M.B.A.

CAREER HIGHLIGHTS: Staff, *Christian Science Monitor* ('69); Reporter/Anchor, WNAC-TV (now WNEV-TV), Boston ('71); Reporter, WBBM-TV, Chicago ('78); Reporter, CBS News, Washington, DC ('79); Correspondent, CBS News, Washington, DC ('81); named Capitol Hill Correspondent for CBS News ('82).

ACHIEVEMENTS & AWARDS: N.A.

PERSONAL: N.A.

ADATO, PERRY MILLER
Prod./Dir., WNET-TV, New York

c/o WNET-TV, 356 E. 58th St., New York, NY

b. December 22.

EDUCATION: New School for Social Research, Manhattan

CAREER HIGHLIGHTS: She began as Film Consultant to the UN Dept. of Social Affairs; Prod./Dir. *Dylan Thomas—The World I Breathe* ('68); Co-Prod., *The Film Generation* ('69); other films include *Gertrude Stein—When This You See, Remember Me* ('70) *The Great Radio Comedians* ('72), and *An Eames Celebration* ('74); Exec. Prod. Prod./Dir., series, "The Originals—Women in Art," "Frankenthaler —Toward a New Climate" ('78), "Georgia O'Keefe" ('77), "Picasso—A Painter's Diary"

('80), and "Carl Sandburg—Echoes and Silences" ('82); responsible for "Great Performances 10th Anniversary Celebration," PBS.

ACHIEVEMENTS & AWARDS: Emmy award, outstanding achievement in cultural documentaries for *Dylan Thomas—The World I Breathe"* ('68); Diplome d'Excellence, Montreal Festival; American Film Festival—Blue Ribbon award; silver Hugo award; and American Film Festival—Red Ribbon award for *An Eames Celebration* ('73); Directors Guild award for documentary achievement and Christopher award for "Georgia O'Keefe" ('77, '78); Directors Guild award and CINE Golden Eagle award for "Picasso—A Painter's Diary" ('80); Pinnacle award and Directors Guild award for "Carl Sandburg—Echoes and Silences."

PERSONAL: Resides in Westport, CT, with her husband, Neil, and their two daughters; Laurie and Michelle.

ADELSON, MERV
Chairman of the Board, Lorimar Productions,

c/o Lorimar Productions, 3970 Overland Ave., Culver City, CA 90230
b. October 23. Beverly Hills, CA.

EDUCATION: Menlo College, Business Administration.

CAREER HIGHLIGHTS: A diverse business career that eventually led to founding Lorimar with Lee Rich began when Adelson was a child in Beverly Hills, CA. Experience in his father's grocery store was later put to use when he opened the first 24-hour supermarket in Las Vegas in the mid-fifties. Formed partnership with Irwin Molasky and soon initiated developments including Sunrise Hospital, the largest in Nevada; shopping malls; and high-rise office complexes; began development of Rancho La Costa ('63); went on to develop more than 6,000 acres of prime real estate in California. Teamed with Lee Rich to form Lorimar ('68) and currently serves as Chairman of the Board.

ACHIEVEMENTS & AWARDS: Pres., Rancho La Costa, Inc.; Pres., La Costa Cable and Community TV Antenna System.

PERSONAL: Resides in Malibu, CA, with wife, Gail; children, Gary, Andy, and Ellen.

AGREE, ARNOLD H.
V.P., ABC, Taxes

c/o ABC, 1330 Ave. of the Americas, New York, NY 10019
b. N.A.

EDUCATION: City College of New York; Brooklyn College Law School.

CAREER HIGHLIGHTS: Mgr., Taxes, 20th Century Fox Film Corp. ('56); Dir., Taxes, 20th Century Fox Film Corp. ('66); Asst. Secretary, Domestic and Foreign Tax Affairs, 20th Century Fox ('68); Dir., Taxes, ABC ('72); V.P., Taxes ('76).

ACHIEVEMENTS & AWARDS: N.A.

PERSONAL: Resides in New York City.

AGRESS, ELLEN SHAW
V.P., Business Planning, NBC

c/o NBC, 30 Rockefeller Plaza, New York NY 10020
b. May 20. New York, NY.

EDUCATION: University of Michigan, B.A., Political Science ('68); Harvard Law School, J.D. ('71)

CAREER HIGHLIGHTS: Assoc., Hale & Dorr law firm, Boston ('71); Assoc., Paul, Weiss, Rifkind, Wharton & Garrison law firm, New York ('72); Staff Attorney, Citizens Communication Center, Washington, DC ('73); Assoc., Moore, Berson & Lifflander law firm, New York ('75); Asst., General Attorney, NBC ('78); General Attorney, NBC ('81); V.P., Business Planning, NBC ('83).

ACHIEVEMENTS & AWARDS: N.A.

PERSONAL: Resides in New York City with husband, Harry; daughter, Emily; son, Adam.

AGRONSKY, MARTIN
Newsman/Documentary Prod.

1232 31st St., N.W., Washington, DC 20007
b. January 2, 1915. Philadelphia, PA.

EDUCATION: Rutgers University ('36).
CAREER HIGHLIGHTS: NBC Foreign Correspon-
dent, ABC Washington Correspondent, and
CBS Documentary Prod. ('52–'69). Anchor,
Post-Newsweek   Stations;   Commentator,
PTV's Eastern Educational Network; also,
Host, "Agronsky and Company" on PBS.
ACHIEVEMENTS & AWARDS: N.A.
PERSONAL: N.A.

AGUILAR, CARLOS
Reporter, CBS, News

c/o CBS, 7800 Beverly Blvd., Los Angeles, CA
90036
b. February 11, 1947. San Antonio, TX.

EDUCATION: San Antonio College, A.A.; Trin-
ity University, B.A.
CAREER HIGHLIGHTS: Reporter, KWEX-TV, Los
Angeles, KTLA-TV, Los Angeles, KTRK-TV,
Houston, and WOAI-TV (now KMOL-TV),
San Antonio, TX; Assignment Editor, KMOL-
TV, San Antonio ('74); Investigative Reporter,
KENS-TV, San Antonio ('75); Reporter, CBS
News, Los Angeles ('82).
ACHIEVEMENTS & AWARDS: N.A.
PERSONAL: Wife, Teri; daughters, Tina and
Rita.

ALDA, ALAN
Actor/Writer/Dir.

c/o CBS, 51 W. 52d St., New York, NY 10019
b. January 28, 1936. New York, NY.

EDUCATION: Fordham   University,   English;
Cleveland Playhouse.
CAREER HIGHLIGHTS: Alda has evolved from a
personable light comedian into a triple-threat
powerhouse as director, writer, and star of
"M*A*S*H." He performed on stage in Rome
and on TV, with his father, actor Robert Alda.
The Owl and the Pussycat, in which he starred
on Broadway, was a major breakthrough.
Other stage credits include *Purlie Victorious,
Fair Game for Lovers*, and *The Apple Tree*. His
motion picture debut was in *Gone Are the
Days*, he has also starred in *Jenny, Paper Lion,
Same Time, Next Year, California Suite*, and *The
Seduction of Joe Tynan*, for which he wrote the
screenplay. He more recently wrote, di-
rected, and starred in *The Four Seasons*, which
he will produce as a CBS series ('83–'84).
Many sequences in both the album and the
TV special "Free to be . . . You and Me," were
directed by Alda, who also performed in
them.
ACHIEVEMENTS & AWARDS: Emmy awards for
acting in, writing, and directing episodes of
"M*A*S*H"; Directors Guild and Writers
Guild awards; the Hollywood Women's Press
Golden Apple, the American Academy of
Humor award, and the TV Critics Circle
award. Honorary doctorates from Fordham
University, Emerson College, Drew Univer-
sity, and St. Peter's College.
PERSONAL: Wife, Arlene; three daughters, Eve,
Elizabeth, and Beatrice.

ALLEN, DEBBIE
Actress

c/o William Morris Agency, 151 El Camino
Dr., Beverly Hills, CA 90212
b. January 16. Houston, TX.

EDUCATION: Howard University, B.A.
CAREER HIGHLIGHTS: TV credits include "Three
Girls Three," *Roots: The Next Generation*, and
the TV special "Ben Vereen: His Roots." A
noted stage actress, Allen has appeared on
Broadway in the musicals *Purlie, Raisin*, and
the revival of *West Side Story*. Appeared in a

supporting role in the feature film *Ragtime.* Doubled as actress and choreographer in NBC's "Fame."

ACHIEVEMENTS & AWARDS: Drama Desk award for *West Side Story.*

PERSONAL: Resides in both New York City and Los Angeles.

ALLEN, IRWIN
Film and TV Prod.

c/o Warner Bros., 4000 Warner Blvd., Burbank, CA 91522
b. June 12, 1916. New York, NY.

EDUCATION: Columbia University; City College of New York.

CAREER HIGHLIGHTS: The undisputed king of catastrophe, Allen has produced a string of big-screen and little-screen disaster films that have been anything but disastrous at the box office and in the ratings. Prod. of the TV series "Voyage to the Bottom of the Sea" and "Code Red." Prod./Dir. of the TV series "Time Tunnel," "Lost in Space," and "Land of the Giants." Motion pictures include *The Poseidon Adventure* and *The Swarm.*

ACHIEVEMENTS & AWARDS: N.A.

PERSONAL: N.A.

ALLEN, STEVE
Host/Writer/Composer

15201 Burbank Blvd., Van Nuys, CA 91401
b. December 26, 1921. New York, NY.

EDUCATION: N.A.

CAREER HIGHLIGHTS: Allen is TV's most gifted all-around talent—writer, performer, talk show host, and song composer. Although he does everything extremely well, he should be given special credit for popularizing the late-night talk show format. He remains a rarity— a genuinely funny, spontaneous wit. Hosted "What's My Line?" "The Steve Allen Show," "I've Got a Secret," and "Meeting of Minds." Original host of NBC's "Tonight Show." Motion pictures include *Down Memory Lane* and *The Benny Goodman Story.* He is a prolific author and composer of thousands of songs. His many books include the classic *The Funny Men,* the most perceptive record of TV comedians of the fifties

ACHIEVEMENTS & AWARDS: N.A.

PERSONAL: Wife, actress Jayne Meadows.

ALLISON, CYNTHIA
Co-Anchor, KNBC, "News 4 LA"

c/o KNBC, 3000 W. Alameda Ave., Burbank, CA 91523
b. July 21.

EDUCATION: University of Southern California, B.A., Journalism.

CAREER HIGHLIGHTS: Writer/Reporter, WRAU, ABC affiliate in Peoria, IL ('75); Reporter/ Anchor, KSD-TV, St. Louis ('77); General Assignment Reporter and Co-Anchor, KNBC, Los Angeles ('78).

ACHIEVEMENTS & AWARDS: Two Greater Los Angeles Press Club awards for best feature reporter ('82).

PERSONAL: Resides in Studio City, CA.

ALTEMEYER, PAUL
Prod., NBC News, "Monitor"

c/o NBC, 30 Rockefeller Plaza, New York, NY 10020
b. October 29. Boston, MA.

EDUCATION: Harvard University, B.A. ('60); Columbia Graduate School of Journalism, M.S. ('61)

CAREER HIGHLIGHTS: Joined the NBC News Investigative Unit and produced numerous stories for "NBC Nightly News," Segment Three reports, and "Today" ('76); Prod./Reporter for "NBC Reports: Passport to the Unknown"

('77); spent four years as Prod./Correspondent with ABC; rejoined NBC News ('82).

ACHIEVEMENTS & AWARDS: Emmy for producing "Mission: Mind Control" ('80).

PERSONAL: N.A.

ALTER, ROBERT H.
Pres., Cabletelevision Advertising Bureau

c/o Cabletelevision Advertising Bureau, 767 Third Ave., New York, NY 10017

b. December 28.

EDUCATION: University of Iowa.

CAREER HIGHLIGHTS: Exec. V.P., Radio Advertising Bureau, where he served for more than 20 years; Pres., Cabletelevision Advertising Bureau.

ACHIEVEMENTS & AWARDS: N.A.

PERSONAL: Wife, Lucille; four daughters. Resides in Hastings-on-Hudson, NY.

AMES, BOB
Controller, V.P., Accounting, Alan Landsburg Productions

c/o Alan Landsburg Productions, 1554 S. Sepulveda Blvd., Los Angeles, CA 90025

b. April 6, 1938. Austin, MN.

EDUCATION: Austin Junior College, A.A., Business Administration.

CAREER HIGHLIGHTS: Worked on MGM payroll ('67); Asst. Controller, V.P., Ivan Tors Films, Los Angeles and Miami ('68); Controller, V.P., Accounting, Alan Landsburg Productions ('72).

ACHIEVEMENTS & AWARDS: Member, Motion Pictures Controllers Assn.

PERSONAL: N.A.

AMLEN, SEYMOUR
V.P., ABC, Entertainment

c/o ABC, 1330 Ave. of the Americas, New York, NY 10019

b. April 28, 1928. New York, NY.

EDUCATION: University of Missouri, B.A. ('49); Ohio State University, M.A. ('50).

CAREER HIGHLIGHTS: Research Analyst, Kenyon & Eckhardt ('51); Research Analyst, ABC TV ('55); Supervisor of Audience Measurement, ABC TV ('56); Mgr., Program Research ('58); Dir., Program Research ('64); V.P., Research ('72); V.P. and Asst. to Pres., ABC Entertainment ('75); V.P., Program Planning ('76); V.P., ABC Entertainment ('80).

ACHIEVEMENTS & AWARDS: N.A.

PERSONAL: Resides in New York City with wife, Elinor; daughter, Jennifer; son, David.

AMSTER, LINDA
V.P. Network Sales. CBS

c/o CBS, 7800 Beverly Blvd., Los Angeles, CA 90036

b. December 22. New York, NY.

EDUCATION: Hunter College.

CAREER HIGHLIGHTS: Started career at Popofsky Advertising, New York ('74); Media Buyer, D'Arcy, MacManus & Masius ('76); V.P./Dir. of Network TV, Western Intl. ('78); joined NBC as Acct. Exec., Burbank ('82); promoted to V.P., West Coast Sales' NBC; V.P., Network Sales, CBS ('83).

ACHIEVEMENTS & AWARDS: Member, Hollywood Radio and TV Society; Ad Club of Los Angeles.

PERSONAL: Single, resides in Sherman Oaks, CA.

ANASTOS, ERNIE
Anchor, WABC-TV, News

c/o WABC-TV, 7 Lincoln Sq., New York, NY 10023

b. N.A.

EDUCATION: Northeastern University; Columbia University Graduate School.

CAREER HIGHLIGHTS: Began career as a News Reporter, for radio and TV stations in Chicago and Boston before nailing down a regular position as Anchor, WPRI-TV, Providence, RI ('76); Correspondent/Anchor, WABC-TV, New York ('78).

ACHIEVEMENTS & AWARDS: Author, *TWIXT: Teens Yesterday and Today.*

PERSONAL: Resides in New York City.

ANCIER, GARTH RICHARD
Dir., Current Comedy Programs, NBC, Entertainment

c/o NBC, 3000 W. Alameda Ave., Burbank, CA 91523
b. September 3, 1957. Perth Amboy, NJ.

EDUCATION: Princeton University, B.A., Political Science ('79).

CAREER HIGHLIGHTS: Reporter, WBUD-AM and WBJH-FM, NBC affiliates ('72); Chairman and Chief Exec. Officer, Focus on Youth Radio Network ('74); Associate, Comedy Development, NBC Entertainment ('79); Asst. to the Pres. and Mgr., East Coast Development, NBC Entertainment ('80); Mgr., Current Comedy Programs, NBC Entertainment ('81); Dir., Current Comedy Programs, NBC Entertainment ('81).

ACHIEVEMENTS & AWARDS: N.A.

PERSONAL: Single, resides in Los Angeles.

ANCONA, EDWARD, JR.
Dir., Film and Tape Production, NBC

c/o NBC, 3000 W. Alameda Ave., Burbank, CA 91523
b. June 11, 1921. Albuquerque, NM.

EDUCATION: University of New Mexico, B.A., Electrical Engineering, B.A., Music.

CAREER HIGHLIGHTS: Engineer, RCA's Film Recording Dept., Hollywood ('46); Special Assignment with the Motion Picture Research Council to develop, install, and operate a sophisticated color telecine system ('56); Color Coordinator, Film Production Dept., NBC ('61); Color Coordinator, "Bonanza" ('65); Dir., Film and Tape Production, NBC '81).

ACHIEVEMENTS & AWARDS: Emmy for work as a color coordinator on "Bonanza" ('65).

PERSONAL: Married, resides in Hollywood. Two children, Ted and Francesa.

ANDERSON, BONNIE MARIE
News Correspondent, NBC

c/o NBC, 1666 79th St. Cswy., Suite 603, Miami, FL 33141
b. October 22, 1955. Havana, Cuba.

EDUCATION: Colegio Nueva Granda, Bogota, Colombia; Northwestern University, B.S., Journalism; University of Barcelona (Spain).

CAREER HIGHLIGHTS: Reporter, *Today*, Cocoa, FL ('77); Reporter, *Miami Herald* ('78); entered broadcast journalism as Reporter, WPLG-TV, Miami ('80); joined NBC News as Florida-based Correspondent ('81).

ACHIEVEMENTS & AWARDS: Finalist for Pulitzer Prize in feature writing for story "The Execution of My Father" ('80).

PERSONAL: Resides in Florida.

ANDERSON, DONALD E.
V.P. and General Mgr., HBO, Western Region

c/o HBO, 2049 Century Park E., Suite 4170, Los Angeles, CA 90067
b. November 19, 1938.

EDUCATION: N.A.

CAREER HIGHLIGHTS: Held engineering positions with Hughes Aircraft Co., Los Angeles, and TRW Systems, Inc., Los Angeles; headed Audio-Video Communications, Inc. ('70); Dir. of Govt. Relations, Natl. Cable TV Assn., Washington, DC ('72); Mgr., Affiliate Development, HBO ('74); established HBO's Regional Office in San Francisco ('76); named Western Region General Mgr., HBO ('76); V.P. and General Mgr., Western Region, HBO ('78).

ACHIEVEMENTS & AWARDS: Member, Board of Dirs., California Community TV Assn.

PERSONAL: Resides in Los Angeles; two sons, Donald and Brian.

ANDERSON, JON
TV Critic, *Chicago Tribune*

c/o *Chicago Tribune,* Tribune Tower, Chicago,
    IL 60611
b. March 13, 1936.

EDUCATION: Mount Allison University ('55);
McGill University Law School ('59).
CAREER HIGHLIGHTS: Editor/Correspondent,
Time magazine ('60); General Mgr., Second
City Center for the Public Arts, Chicago ('66);
Staff Reporter, *Chicago Sun-Times* ('67); Co-
Writer, "Jon and Abra" column, which ap-
peared in the *Chicago Daily News* ('69); Pres.,
City Publications, and Publisher, *Chicagoan*
magazine ('73); Natl. Arts Critic, Time Can-
ada ('75); Editorial Dir. and Management Su-
pervisor, Foote, Cone & Belding Public Re-
lations ('76),
ACHIEVEMENTS & AWARDS: N.A.
PERSONAL: N.A.

ANDERSSON, DON
V.P., Cable Health Network, Affiliate
Relations

c/o Cable Health Network, 1211 Ave. of the
    Americas, 20th Floor, New York, NY 10036
b. May 15, 1924.

EDUCATION: Boston University, B.S. and M.S.
CAREER HIGHLIGHTS: V.P., Planning and Research, Ntl. Cable TV Foundation; V.P., Cable Relations, Turner Broadcasting; V.˜., Affiliate Relations, Cable Health Network.
ACHIEVEMENTS & AWARDS: N.A.
PERSONAL: N.A.

ANGOTTI, JOSEPH
General Mgr., NBC, News, London and West
Europe

c/o NBC, 30 Rockefeller Plaza, New York, NY
    10020
b. December 14. Gary, IN.

EDUCATION: Indiana University, B.A. and
M.A., Journalism,
CAREER HIGHLIGHTS: News Dept., WHAS-TV,
Louisville, KY ('62); Writer/Prod., WMAQ-
TV, Chicago ('66); joined NBC as Prod. ('68);
Prod., "NBC Nightly News" ('74); Prod. of
NBC's political coverage ('76); Exec. Prod.,
"NBC Nightly News" ('76); Exec. Prod., Spe-
cial Programming, NBC ('79); General Mgr.,
NBC News, London and West Europe ('83).
ACHIEVEMENTS & AWARDS: N.A.
PERSONAL: Wife, Karen; three sons.

ANNENBERG, WALTER H.
Pres., *TV Guide*

c/o *TV Guide,* P.O. Box 750, Radnor, PA 19088
b. March 13, 1908, Milwaukee, WI.

EDUCATION: University of Pennsylvania Wharton School of Business.
CAREER HIGHLIGHTS: Owner of *TV Guide, Seventeen,* and the *Daily Racing Form.* Headed a
media conglomerate including Triangle Stations and the newspapers *Philadelphia Inquirer*
and *Philadelphia Daily News* until former President Nixon appointed him Ambassador to
the Court of St. James. Founder and Pres.,
Annenberg Schools of Communication at the
University of Southern California and the
University of Pennsylvania.
ACHIEVEMENTS & AWARDS: N.A.
PERSONAL: N.A.

ANTONOWSKY, MARVIN
Pres., Marketing and Research, Columbia
Pictures

c/o Columbia Pictures, 300 Colgems Sq.,
    Burbank, CA 91505
b. January 31, 1929.

EDUCATION: City College of New York, B.B.A.
('49), M.B.A. ('50)
CAREER HIGHLIGHTS: Research Exec. for Advertising Agencies; Research Exec., ABC; Program Development, NBC; V.P., Programming, NBC ('73); Program Chief, NBC ('75);
V.P., Universal TV; Sr. V.P., Columbia Pictures ('79), Pres., Marketing and Research,
Columbia Pictures ('80).
ACHIEVEMENTS & AWARDS: N.A.
PERSONAL: N.A.

ARCHER, NICHOLAS (Nicholas Occiogrosso)
V.P., ABC, TV News Services

c/o ABC, 7 W. 66th St., New York, NY 10023
b. January 14, 1928. Brooklyn, NY.

EDUCATION: Brooklyn College, B.A., History; Drake School of Journalism.

CAREER HIGHLIGHTS: Copy Boy and Editorial Asst., *N.Y. Journal American* ('45); Asst. Editor and Reporter, Paramount News ('48); Reporter, Telenews ('52); Reporter, then Editor and Exec. Editor, Hearst Metrotone News ('54); Assignment Mgr., ABC News ('63); promoted through ranks to Dir., News Services, and currently serves as V.P., TV News Services.

ACHIEVEMENTS & AWARDS: V.P., New York Working Press Assn.; Chairman, Program Steering Committee, NANBA.

PERSONAL: Wife, Nora; children, Michael and Nicholas.

ARDEN, EVE (Eunice Quedens)
Actress

c/o SAG, 7750 Sunset Blvd., Hollywood, CA 90046
b. April 30, 1912. Mill Valley, CA.

EDUCATION: N.A.

CAREER HIGHLIGHTS: Filmdom's finest second string comedienne brought her brittle wise-cracking style to TV and TV responded by making her a first-rank star in "Our Miss Brooks." She later starred in "The Mothers-in-Law." Broadway roles in *Let's Face It* and *Ziegfeld Follies of 1936*. Motion pictures include *Mildred Pierce, Cover Girl, Anatomy of a Murder, Voice of the Turtle,* and *Grease*.

ACHIEVEMENTS & AWARDS: N.A.

PERSONAL: N.A.

ARLEDGE, ROONE
Pres., ABC, News and Sports

c/o ABC, 7 W. 66th St. New York, NY 10023
b. July 8, 1931. Forest Hills, NY.

EDUCATION: Columbia University, B.A. ('52) Columbia School of International Affairs.

CAREER HIGHLIGHTS: Distinguished for his creative and insightful approach to sports programming and production, Arledge successfully applied these talents to news when he introduced a novel approach to network news with the creation of "World News Tonight." He went on to develop notable news programs such as "20/20," "Nightline," "Closeup," "This Week With David Brinkley," "Viewpoint," and numerous special event and special report broadcasts. First entered broadcasting with Dumont Network ('52); joined NBC as Stage Mgr./Dir./Prod. for News, Entertainment, and Special Events ('54); moved to ABC as Prod., NCAA football ('60). Created "ABC's Wide World of Sports" ('61); named V.P., ABC Sports ('64); appointed Pres., ABC Sports ('68); named Pres., ABC News and Sports ('77). Developed and applied numerous techniques and broadcast practices, including slow-motion, stop-motion, and split-screen techniques; use of hand-held cameras, end zone, and isolated cameras for football; use of cranes for panoramic shots; and the use of transcontinental satellites to bring international events into American homes.

ACHIEVEMENTS & AWARDS: Has received 26 Emmy awards since 1965 (25 for sports programming, one for news); four Peabody awards; grand prize, Cannes Film Festival; live TV reporting, Broadcast pioneers award; Ohio State University award; Natl. Headliners award; Man of the Year, New York Athletic Club; founders award, Intl. Council,

NATAS; special citation, New York City Baseball Federation; Man of the Year, B'nai B'rith Sports Lodge, New York ('75); brotherhood award, Natl. Conference of Christians and Jews ('75); Missouri Honor Medal, distinguished service to journalism ('77); distinguished achievement award, Journalism Assn. of University of Southern California ('81). Former Member, President's Council on Physical Fitness; Chairman, Sports Commission.

PERSONAL: Resides in Manhattan with his wife, Anne.

ARLEN, GARY H.
Pres., Arlen Communications

c/o Arlen Communications, Suite 600 E, 7315 Wisconsin Ave., Bethesda, MD 20814
b. 1945. Cleveland, OH.

EDUCATION: Northwestern University, M.A.

CAREER HIGHLIGHTS: Active in the communications industry in Washington, DC, for more than a decade as a Consultant, Editor, and Media Analyst specializing in the marketing, financial, technical and legal aspects of emerging communications technologies. Founding Editor of several video, pay TV and satellite publications. Columnist and Contributing Editor, *Washington Journalism Review*, *Radio Electronics*, and *Video Business* magazines. Also, Editor and Publisher, *International Videotex Teletext News* and *Teleservices Report* trade newsletters. Currently Pres., Arlen Communications.

ACHIEVEMENTS & AWARDS: N.A.
PERSONAL: N.A.

ARLEN, MICHAEL
Writer, *The New Yorker*

c/o *The New Yorker*, 25 W. 43rd St., New York, NY 10036
b. 1930. London, England.

EDUCATION: Harvard University.

CAREER HIGHLIGHTS: Reporter, *Life* magazine ('52); Reporter, *Holiday, Esquire, McCall's,* and the *N.Y. Times* ('56). Began contributing to *The New Yorker* ('58); took over the magazine's TV column, "The Air" ('66).

ACHIEVEMENTS & AWARDS: Author, *Living Room War* ('69); *Exiles* ('76); *An American Verdict* ('73); *Passage to Ararat* ('76); *The View from Highway One* ('76); *The Camera Age* ('81).

PERSONAL: N.A.

ARMEL, PAULA
Dir., Affiliate Services, Hearst/ABC Video Services

c/o Hearst/ABC, 555 Fifth Ave., New York, NY 10017
b. February 1, 1949. Brussels, Belgium.

EDUCATION: University of Colorado; University of Lancaster (England); San Francisco State University.

CAREER HIGHLIGHTS: Acct. Exec., Dailey & Assoc. advertising agency ('75); Sales Mgr., Advertising Dept., San Francisco and Pacific Northwest Representative. *Ms.* magazine ('77); Development Assoc., American Film Institute, Los Angeles ('78); Dir., Affiliate Services, Hearst/ABC Video Services, New York ('81).

ACHIEVEMENTS & AWARDS: Member, New York Women in Cable.

PERSONAL: Resides in New York City.

ARNAZ, DESI
Actor/Prod.

c/o SAG, 7750 Sunset Blvd., Hollywood, CA 90046
b. March 2, 1917. Santiago, Cuba.

EDUCATION: Colegio Delores, Jesuit Prep School.

CAREER HIGHLIGHTS: A kind of Cuban Maurice Chevalier, Arnaz really was a one-man goodwill committee for Latin-American relations. His keen business acumen helped make Desilu one of the top production houses in Hollywood. Exec. Prod. and Co-Star, "I Love Lucy." Formed Desilu Production Co. ('51); Founder/Pres., Desi Arnaz Productions ('65); Exec. Prod., "The Mothers-in-Law." Motion pictures include *Too Many Girls, Father Takes a Wife,* and *The Escape Artist.*

ACHIEVEMENTS & AWARDS: Emmy award for producing outstanding comedy series, "I Love Lucy" ('53).

PERSONAL: N.A.

ARNOLD, DANNY
Writer/Prod.

c/o William Morris Agency, 151 El Camino
   Dr., Beverly Hills, CA 90212
b. January 23, 1925. New York, NY.

EDUCATION: N.A.

CAREER HIGHLIGHTS: Writer for "The Rosemary
   Clooney Show" and "The Tennessee Ernie
   Ford Show"; Prod. and Story Editor for "The
   Real McCoys," "Bewitched," and "That
   Girl"; Exec. Prod., "My World and Welcome
   to It." Creator/Exec. Prod., "Barney Miller."

ACHIEVEMENTS & AWARDS: Emmy awards for
   best comedy series, for "Barney Miller" and
   "My World and Welcome to It."

PERSONAL: N.A.

ARONSON, HERMAN
**V.P., Operations and Creative Services,
Advertising and Promotion, East Coast,
CBS, Entertainment**

c/o CBS, 51 W. 52d St., New York, NY 10019
b. January 7, 1938.

EDUCATION: CBS School of Management.

CAREER HIGHLIGHTS: Joined CBS as a member
   of the Office Services Dept.. ('58); served in
   the Advertising, Promotion, and Design
   Depts. in the following divisions for CBS:
   CBS TV Stations Division ('60); WCBS-TV,
   New York ('63); CBS TV ('64); CBS Broadcast
   Group ('73); CBS, Inc. ('78). Dir., Operations,
   Advertising and Promotion, CBS Entertain-
   ment ('80); Dir., Operations and Creative Ser-
   vices, Advertising and Promotion, East
   Coast, CBS Entertainment ('82); V.P., Opera-
   tions and Creative Services, Advertising and
   Promotion, East Coast, CBS Entertainment
   ('83).

ACHIEVEMENTS & AWARDS: N.A.

PERSONAL: Resides in Tenafly, NJ, with wife,
   Judith; sons, Phillip, Seth, and Jonnathan.

ARRANTS, ROD
Actor

c/o "Search for Tomorrow," NBC, 30
   Rockefeller Plaza, New York, NY 10020
b. September 5. Los Angeles, CA.

EDUCATION: Raymond College; University of
   California at Berkeley; University of the Pacific.

CAREER HIGHLIGHTS: Popular soap opera actor
   who began in daytime TV on "The Young and
   the Restless," moving to "For Richer and
   Poorer" and "Lovers and Friends." Has also
   appeared in such primetime series as "Mannix" and "The Streets of San Francisco," as
   well as in numerous TV movies. After joining
   the cast of "Search for Tomorrow" ('78), he
   became a hit on the show as Travis Sentell.

ACHIEVEMENTS & AWARDS: N.A.

PERSONAL: Resides in Brooklyn Heights, NY,
   with wife, Patricia, and sons, Dylan and
   Zachary.

ARTHUR, BEATRICE
Actress

c/o Tandem Productions, 1901 Ave. of the
   Stars, Los Angeles, CA 90067
b. May 13, 1926. New York, NY.

EDUCATION: Dramatic Workshop of the New
   School for Social Research.

CAREER HIGHLIGHTS: With a voice pitched
   somewhere between a foghorn and a moose's
   mating call, Arthur brightened Broadway for
   years before becoming TV's resident liberated
   lady in "Maude." Critically acclaimed as Vera
   Charles in both the stage and screen versions
   of *Mame*, Arthur also appeared on stage in
   Fiddler on the Roof and *The Owl and the Pussycat*. Became an instant hit as a guest star on
   "All in the Family," which prompted Norman Lear to spin off her own "Maude" series.
   After some time off, she returned to TV as the
   star of "Amanda's."

ACHIEVEMENTS & AWARDS: Tony award for
   Mame, Genii award from the Southern California Chapter of American Women in Radio
   and TV, Emmy award for "Maude."

PERSONAL: Resides in Pacific Palisades, CA,
   with her husband, the noted director Gene
   Saks, and their two sons, Matthew and
   Daniel.

ASHLEY, TED
Vice Chairman, Warner Communications

c/o Warner Communications, 75 Rockefeller
Plaza, New York, NY 10020
b. August 3. Brooklyn, NY.

EDUCATION: City College of New York, B.A.,
Accounting.
CAREER HIGHLIGHTS: After a meteoric rise
through the ranks starting with his very first
job, Ashley was recognized by the mid-fifties
as one of the wisest talent agents and pack-
agers in the business. He played very influential roles in TV and later in the movie industry for three decades. He began his career
as an office boy at William Morris Agency;
moved up through ranks, ending at Ashley-
Steiner-Famous Agency; he was named head
of Warner Bros. after Ashley-Steiner was
taken over by Warner Communications and
the latter conglomerate purchased Warner
Bros. ('69); He then became Chairman and
Chief Exec. Officer, and after a brief retirement he served as Vice Chairman, Warner
Communications ('82).
ACHIEVEMENTS & AWARDS: N.A.
PERSONAL: Married, resides in New York City.

ASNER, ED
Actor

c/o CBS, 7800 Beverly Blvd., Los Angeles, CA
90036
b. November 15, 1929. Kansas City, MO.

EDUCATION: University of Chicago.
CAREER HIGHLIGHTS: A busy actor who moved
to Hollywood ('61), Asner was a regular on
"Slattery's People" and had numerous guest
parts in other TV series. Became well-known
for his Lou Grant role in "The Mary Tyler
Moore Show" and later in his own series,
"Lou Grant." Other memorable parts came in
the popular mini-series *Rich Man, Poor Man*
and *Roots*. TV movie credits include *Family
Man, The Good Doctor, The Huey Long Story,
The Gathering,* and *Hey, I'm Alive.* Co-starred
with Paul Newman in the *Fort Apache, The
Bronx* feature. More recent roles were in
showtime's *A Case of Libel* and CBS's *Anatomy
of an Illness.*
ACHIEVEMENTS & AWARDS: Six Emmy awards
for his acting in "The Mary Tyler Moore
Show" ('71, '72, '75), "Rich Man, Poor Man"
('76), "Roots" ('77), and "Lou Grant" ('78).
Two Television Critics' Circle awards, a Gold-
en Globe award, and a Man of the Year in
Broadcasting award from the Hollywood
Radio and TV Society. Pres. SAG ('80).
PERSONAL: Resides in Bel Air, CA, with wife,
Nancy; children, Matthew, Liza, and Kate.

ASSENZIO, RICHARD
**Administrator, Sports Program Planning,
NBC, Sports**

c/o NBC, 30 Rockefeller Plaza, New York, NY
10020
b. March 24, 1955.

EDUCATION: St. John's University, B.S., Com-
munications Arts ('77).
CAREER HIGHLIGHTS: Intern, NBC and WNBC-
TV, New York ('77); Audience Services and
Information Coordinator, NBC NFL program
('78); Administrator, Sports Program Plan-
ning, NBC Sports ('83).
ACHIEVEMENTS & AWARDS: N.A.
PERSONAL: Resides in Westbury, NY.

ASTOR, STEPHEN
**V.P., Columbia Pictures TV,
Advertising/Promotion**

c/o Columbia Pictures TV, Columbia Plaza,
Burbank, CA 91505
b. April 6, 1949. New Orleans, LA.

EDUCATION: University of California at Santa
Barbara, B.A., History; University of California at Los Angeles, M.S., Journalism.

CAREER HIGHLIGHTS: Warner Bros. Publicist ('74); moved to UA as Asst. West Coast Publicity Coordinator ('75); Dir. of Advertising/ Promotion for 20th Century Fox TV ('76); joined Columbia Pictures TV as V.P., Advertising/Promotion ('81).
ACHIEVEMENTS & AWARDS: N.A.
PERSONAL: N.A.

ATTAWAY, FRITZ E.
V.P., Administrative Affairs, Motion Picture Assn. of America

c/o Motion Picture Assn. of America, 1600 I St., N.W., Washington, DC 20036
b. July 12, 1946. Detroit, MI

EDUCATION: College of Idaho, B.A.; University of Chicago, J.D.
CAREER HIGHLIGHTS: Before joining the Motion Picture Assn. of America, he served as Attorney/Adviser in the Cable TV Bureau of the FCC, where he was involved in numerous rulemaking proceedings concerning cable TV and pay TV. He joined the Motion Picture Assn. of America ('76); became V.P. ('78). The association is an assembly of 10 of the largest producers and distributors of film in the world.
ACHIEVEMENTS & AWARDS: N.A.
PERSONAL: Married, resides in Arlington, VA.

AUBREY, JAMES
Independent Prod.

c/o Aubrey Co., 8934 Keith Ave., Los Angeles, CA 90069
b. 1918.

EDUCATION: Princeton University (cum laude).
CAREER HIGHLIGHTS: Salesman, KNX-Radio and KNXT, Los Angeles ('48); General Mgr., CBS Pacific Network; Mgr., Network Programs, CBS TV ('56); V.P., Programming, ABC; V.P., Creative Services ('58); Pres., CBS ('59); Pres., MGM; currently Independent Prod.
ACHIEVEMENTS & AWARDS: N.A.
PERSONAL: N.A.

AUERBACH, DAVID
Exec. V.P., Alan Landsburg Productions

11811 W. Olympic Blvd., Los Angeles, CA 90064
b. August 20, 1954.

EDUCATION: Boston University, B.S., Broadcasting and Film.
CAREER HIGHLIGHTS: Dir. of Development, Aaron Spelling Productions ('76); Assoc. Prod., "The Love Boat" series ('77); Assoc. Prod., "B.A.D. Cats," "Dynasty," "I'm a Big Girl Now," and "Making a Living" ('81–'82); Prod., "Cagney and Lacey" ('82); Exec. Prod., "Weekend Sports Wrap-Up" and "Pick the Pros" ('82).
ACHIEVEMENTS & AWARDS: N.A.
PERSONAL: N.A.

AUG, STEPHEN
Correspondent, ABC, News

c/o ABC, 7 W. 66th St., New York, NY 10023
b. 1936.

EDUCATION: New York University, B.A. ('56); Columbia School of Journalism M.A. ('58).
CAREER HIGHLIGHTS: Reporter/Editor, AP, Denver, New York, and Washington, DC ('61); Reporter, *Washington Star* ('69); Editor-in-Charge, Business Section, *Washington Star* ('78); Correspondent, ABC News, Washington, DC ('81).
ACHIEVEMENTS & AWARDS: Co-Author; *Who's Watching the Airways?—The Dangerous Games of the FAA* ('72). Received the INGAA award.
PERSONAL: Married, three children.

AURELIO, RICHARD
**Sr. V.P., Warner Amex Cable
Communications, Government Affairs**

c/o Warner Amex, 1211 Ave. of the Americas,
New York, NY 10036
b. North Providence, RI.

EDUCATION: Boston University, B.S., Journalism.
CAREER HIGHLIGHTS: Started as a Reporter, for
many different New England area newspapers; Reporter, *Newsday* ('55); News Editor,
Newsday ('58); Press Secretary and Administrative Asst. to U.S. Senator Jacob Javits ('62);
V.P., Public Affairs, Edward Gottlieb & Assoc., New York ('68); Deputy Mayor of New
York City ('72); Pres., Daniel J. Edelman of
New York, Inc. ('74); Sr. V.P., Government
Affairs, Warner Amex Cable Communications ('79).
ACHIEVEMENTS & AWARDS: Honorary Degree
from Johnson and Wales College.
PERSONAL: N.A.

AXELROD, JONATHAN
**Exec. V. P., Columbia Pictures TV,
Worldwide Production**

8960 St. Ives, Los Angeles, CA 90069
b. July 9, 1950. New York, NY.

EDUCATION: University of California at Los Angeles, B.A.
CAREER HIGHLIGHTS: Worked with Upland
Agency as Agent in charge of writers and
directors ('77); moved to ABC TV as Exec.
Prod., Movies for TV ('78); V.P., Dramatic
Development ('79); V.P. and Sr. Exec., in
Charge of Primetime Development ('80); left
for Columbia Pictures TV as Sr. V.P. ('81);
promoted to Exec. V.P., Worldwide Production ('82).
ACHIEVEMENTS & AWARDS: N.A.
PERSONAL: N.A.

AXTHELM, PETE
Sportscaster, NBC

c/o NBC, 30 Rockefeller Plaza, New York, NY
10020
b. August 27.

EDUCATION: Yale University.
CAREER HIGHLIGHTS: Began journalism career
as horse racing Writer and Columnist, *N.Y.
Herald Tribune;* joined *Sports Illustrated* as Staff
Writer; moved to *Newsweek* as Sports Editor
('68); joined NBC sports ('80) and provides
special commentary during NFL, horse racing, and Wimbledon tennis coverage.
ACHIEVEMENTS & AWARDS: Author of five
books, including *The City Game.*
PERSONAL: Resides in Manhattan.

AZEVEDO, HELEN
Exec. Prod., Estrada Productions

1875 Century Park E., Los Angeles, CA 90067
b. January 24, 1945. New York, NY.

EDUCATION: City College of New York; Middlebury College; Columbia University; New
York University; University of Lisbon (Portugal); San Diego State University.
CAREER HIGHLIGHTS: Asst. Prod. for numerous
TV commercials ('60); Independent Prod./
Dir. and Packager for Informational Films,
Odyssey Corp. ('71); Unit Production Mgr.,
ABC ('75); Personal Mgr. for Erik Estrada
('77–present); Exec. Prod., Estrada Productions ('80–present). Exec. Prod. *Honeyboy*
('82); Independent Prod. in association with
Orion TV ('83).
ACHIEVEMENTS & AWARDS: N.A.
PERSONAL: Resides in Hollywood with husband, Paul Gale.

B

BABBIN, JAQUELINE
Prod./Writer

c/o ABC, 1330 Ave. of the Americas, New
York, NY 10019
b. N.A.

EDUCATION: N.A.
CAREER HIGHLIGHTS: Before her involvement
with the acclaimed soap opera "All My Children," she established a fine reputation as
one of the most competent story editors and
drama producers in the industry. She started
her career as Play Adapter for David Susskind; Prod. "Dupont Show of the Week"
('62); Prod., ABC, "Wide World of Entertainment" ('70); Prod., CBS series "Beacon Hill"
('75); Prod., TV movie *Sybil* ('76); Prod., daytime serial "All My Children" ('82).
ACHIEVEMENTS & AWARDS: N.A.
PERSONAL: N.A.

BACH, CATHERINE
Actress

c/o "The Dukes of Hazzard," CBS, 51 W. 52d
St., New York, NY 10019
b. March 1. Warren, OH.

EDUCATION: Dupree Dance Academy.
CAREER HIGHLIGHTS: Bit parts in such films as
*The Widow, The Midnight Man, Thunderbolt and
Lightfoot,* and *Hustle,* as well as TV series
guest spots in "Police Woman," "Matt
Helm," "Strange New World," and "Police
Story" before gaining prominence as the
shapely and scantily clad Daisy Duke in "The
Dukes of Hazzard."
ACHIEVEMENTS & AWARDS: N.A.
PERSONAL: Resides in San Fernando Valley,
CA

BACHRACH, CHARLES L.
Sr. V.P. and Assoc. Broadcast Dir., Ogilvy & Mather, Network and Programming

c/o Ogilvy & Mather, 2 E. 48th St., New York,
NY 10017
b. N.A.

EDUCATION: Ithaca College, B.S., TV/Radio
('68).
CAREER HIGHLIGHTS: Assoc. Prod., MPO
Sports; Unit Mgr., NBC TV; Media Planning,
Ogilvy & Mather ('69); Buyer, Spot TV Dept.,
Ogilvy & Mather ('70); Broadcast Acct. Exec.,
Ogilvy & Mather ('71); Broadcast Acct. Super-
visor, Ogilvy & Mather ('72); V.P., Ogilvy &
Mather ('75); Sr. V.P. and Assoc. Broadcast
Dir., Ogilvy & Mather ('78).
ACHIEVEMENTS & AWARDS: N.A.
PERSONAL: Resides in Hartsdale, NY, with his
wife and daughter.

BACKE, JOHN D.
Chairman of the Board, Universal Communications

c/o Universal Communications, 515 Madison
Ave., New York, NY 10022
b. 1933.

EDUCATION: N.A.
CAREER HIGHLIGHTS: Joined General Electric
('57); Pres., General Learning Corp. subsidi-
ary of General Electric and Time, Inc.
('66–'72); Pres., CBS Publishing Group ('73);
Pres., CBS, Inc. ('76); Currently serves as
Pres. of Tomorrow Entertainment Co., a TV
production company, and Pres. and Chief
Exec. Officer, Universal Communications,
which acquired WRGB-TV, Schenectady, NY.
ACHIEVEMENTS & AWARDS: N.A.
PERSONAL: N.A.

BACKUS, JIM
Actor

8810 Sunset Blvd., Los Angeles, CA 90069
b. February 25, 1913. Cleveland, OH.

EDUCATION: American Academy of Dramatic
Arts.
CAREER HIGHLIGHTS: Radio announcer and ra-
dio actor; voice of Mr. Magoo in TV and film
cartoons. Motion pictures include *Bright Vic-
tory, Pat and Mike,* and *Rebel Without a Cause.*
TV series include "I Married Joan" ('52) "Hot
Off the Wire" ('60), and "Gilligan's Island"
('64). Among his TV movies are *Getting Away
From It All* ('72), *The Girl Most Likely To . . .*
('73), and *Miracle on 34th Street* ('73).
ACHIEVEMENTS & AWARDS: N.A.
PERSONAL: N.A.

BAER, ARTHUR H., JR.
Pres., Rainbow Programming Services

c/o Rainbow Programming Services, 100
Crossways Park W., Woodbury, NY 11797
b. October 31.

EDUCATION: Columbia College, B.A.; Colum-
bia University, M.B.A.
CAREER HIGHLIGHTS: Pres., MBS Management
Consultants ('72); Marketing Dept., McKin-
sey & Co. ('73); V.P., Standard Brands ('77);
Pres., Rainbow Programming Services ('83).
ACHIEVEMENTS & AWARDS: N.A.
PERSONAL: Resides in New York City with his
wife and two children.

BAER, J. A.
**V.P., Business Affairs, CBS, Entertainment,
New York**

c/o CBS, 51 W. 52d St., New York, NY 10019
b. St. Louis, MO.

EDUCATION: Middlebury College, B.A. ('67);
Duke University Law School, J.D. ('70).
CAREER HIGHLIGHTS: Attorney, Columbia Pic-
tures Industries; Talent in Program Negoti-
ator, CBS TV ('76); Dir., Business Affairs, CBS
Entertainment, New York ('79); V.P., Busi-
ness Affairs, CBS Entertainment, New York
('80).
ACHIEVEMENTS & AWARDS: N.A.
PERSONAL: Resides in Westport, CT, with wife,
Adelle; daughter, Jennifer; son, Arthur.

BAERWALD, SUSAN
Dir., Mini-Series, NBC, Entertainment

c/o NBC, 3000 W. Alameda Ave., Burbank,
CA 91523
b. June 18, 1944. Long Branch, NJ.

EDUCATION: Sarah Lawrence College, B.A.
('66).
CAREER HIGHLIGHTS: Production Asst., "That's
Life" ('69); Production Asst., "Kraft Music
Hall" ('70); Script Reader, Warner Bros. ('73);
Administrator, Paper Bag Players children's
theater, New York ('76); Script Reader, UA
('77); Story Analyst, Bob Banner Assoc. ('79);
Head of Development, Gordon-Eisner Pro-
ductions ('79); Story Assoc., NBC ('80); Mgr.,
Mini-Series, NBC Entertainment ('80); Dir.,
Mini-Series, NBC Entertainment, West Coast
('82).
ACHIEVEMENTS & AWARDS: N.A.
PERSONAL: Resides in Brentwood, CA, with
husband, Paul, and sons, Joshua and Sam-
uel.

BAFFICO, JIM
Independent Prod.

c/o NBC, 30 Rockefeller Plaza, New York, NY
10020
b. N.A.

EDUCATION: University of Nebraska, B.A. and
M.A., Directing Theater; University of Michigan, Ph.D., Directing Theater.

CAREER HIGHLIGHTS: Theater Dir., Carnegie Mellon Theater Co., Pittsburgh; Exec. Prod., "The Doctors" ('79); Prod., "Another World" ('80); Independent Prod.

ACHIEVEMENTS & AWARDS: N.A.

PERSONAL: N.A.

BAILEY, JOSEPH
Writer

Children's Television Workshop, 1 Lincoln Plaza, New York, NY 10023
b. April 1.

EDUCATION: N.A.

CAREER HIGHLIGHTS: Writer for "Sesame Street," "The Muppet Show," "Big Bird in China," "John Denver and the Muppets," "The Robert Klein Show," "Hot Hero Sandwich," "Christmas Eve on Sesame Street," "The Muppet Meeting Films," three Sesame Street Live musicals, TV pilots, feature treatments, industrials, record albums, and lyrics.

ACHIEVEMENTS & AWARDS: Two Emmy awards, two Emmy nominations, Writers Guild nominations.

PERSONAL: N.A.

BAILEY, WENDELL
V.P., Natl. Cable TV Assn., Science and Technology Dept.

c/o Natl. Cable TV Assn., 1724 Massachusetts Ave., N.W., Washington, DC 20036
b. September 9, 1946. Kentucky.

EDUCATION: University of Maryland.

CAREER HIGHLIGHTS: Private Line Communications Specialist, AT&T ('67); Engineer, MCI Telecommunications Corp., Washington, DC ('73); Mgr., Engineering, Planning, and Coordination, MCI Telecommunications Corp., Washington, DC ('76); V.P., Science and Technology Dept., Natl. Cable TV Assn. ('81).

ACHIEVEMENTS & AWARDS: N.A.

PERSONAL: Resides in Fort Washington, MD, with his wife and daughter.

BAIN, CONRAD
Actor

c/o "Diff'rent Strokes," NBC, 3000 W. Alameda Ave., Burbank, CA 91523
b. February 4. Lethbridge, Alberta, Canada.

EDUCATION: American Academy of Dramatic Arts.

CAREER HIGHLIGHTS: Moved from the stage to TV on "Studio One," "The Defenders," "Look Up and Live," "Grandpa Goes to Washington," "The Waverly Wonders," and "Maude." Fit into NBC's plans as the adult to play off Gary Coleman in the youngster's series vehicle, "Diff'rent Strokes" ('77).

ACHIEVEMENTS & AWARDS: N.A.

PERSONAL: Resides in Brentwood, CA, with wife, Monica; daughter, Jennifer; sons, Mark and Kent.

BAKER, MARGERY CLAIRE
Sr. Broadcast Prod., CBS News

c/o CBS, 524 W. 57th St., New York, NY 10019
b. May 5, 1948.

EDUCATION: Barnard College, A.B.; Columbia University, M.S.

CAREER HIGHLIGHTS: Field Prod., CBS News, Los Angeles ('71); Broadcast Prod., CBS News, New York ('73); "CBS Morning News" with Richard Threlkeld and Lesley Stahl ('76); V.P., Public Affairs Broadcast, CBS News ('78); Sr. Broadcast Prod., "CBS Morning News" ('82).

ACHIEVEMENTS & AWARDS: N.A.

PERSONAL: N.A.

BAKER, WARREN
Dir., Programs, NBC, TV Stations Division

c/o NBC, 3000 W. Alameda Ave., Burbank, CA 91523
b. February 3. Buffalo, NY.

EDUCATION: Ohio State University, B.S., Psychology, and M.A., Administration and Counseling Psychology.
CAREER HIGHLIGHTS: Exec., Avco Broadcasting Corp., Cincinnati ('66); Staff Dir., KNBC-TV, Los Angeles ('73); Exec. Prod., KNBC-TV, Los Angeles ('75); Dir., Programs, KNBC-TV, Los Angeles, ('76); Dir., Programs, NBC TV Stations Division ('83).
ACHIEVEMENTS & AWARDS: Two local Emmy awards; two Iris awards from the Natl. Assn. of TV Program Executives; V.P., ATAS.
PERSONAL: Resides in Sepulveda, CA, with his wife and their two children.

BAKER, WILLIAM F.
Pres. and Chairman, Westinghouse Broadcasting and Cable, TV Group and Group W Satellite Communications

c/o Group W, 90 Park Ave., New York, NY 10016
b. September 20, 1942.

EDUCATION: Case Western Reserve University, B.A., M.A., and Ph.D.
CAREER HIGHLIGHTS: Occupied various positions in radio and TV in Cleveland and New York in the sixties; joined Scripps-Howard Broadcasting, first as Exec. Prod., WEWS-TV, Cleveland, where he was Creator/Prod., "Morning Exchange" program ('71); Program Mgr., WEWS-TV ('74); Asst. General Mgr., WEWS-TV, Cleveland ('76); V.P. and General Mgr., WJZ-TV, Baltimore ('78); Pres. and Chief Exec. Officer, Group W Productions ('79); Pres., TV Group, Westinghouse Broadcasting and Cable ('79); continuing to serve as Pres. of the TV Group, named Chairman, Group W Satellite Communications ('81).
ACHIEVEMENTS & AWARDS: Member, TV Information Office, NAB; honorary doctorate from St. John's University. Co-Author, *Telecommunications Management* ('83).
PERSONAL: Wife, Jeannemarie; two children.

BALDWIN, GERALD
Prod., Hanna-Barbera Productions

c/o Hanna-Barbera Productions, 3400 Caheunga Blvd., Hollywood, CA 90068
b. 1930. New York, NY.

EDUCATION: Chouinard Institute.
CAREER HIGHLIGHTS: Began in the field of cartoons with "Mr. Magoo" ('58); joined Hanna-Barbera Productions as an Animator on "Quick Draw McGraw" ('59); moved to Jay Ward Productions as Dir., "Bullwinkle" ('61); worked for Depatie-Freleng as Dir., "Dr. Seuss" specials; Prod. of highly successful cartoon "The Smurfs."
ACHIEVEMENTS & AWARDS: N.A.
PERSONAL: Resides in Sunland, CA, with wife, Frances; two children.

BALKAN, DAVID H.
Writer/Prod., Horizon Entertainment, Development

1900 Ave. of the Stars, Los Angeles, CA 90067
b. February 7, 1944. Hartford, CT.

EDUCATION: University of Connecticut, B.A., English.
CAREER HIGHLIGHTS: Copywriter, Doyle, Dane, Bernbach ('71); Prod., ABC On Air Advertising ('73); Freelance Screenwriter, "All in the Family," "Laugh-In," "Six Million Dollar Man," "Ellery Queen," "The Hardy Boys," "McCloud," "Kingston," 'Hart to Hart" ('74–'79); Prod. under contract to Filmways; Prod., several TV movies for the three major networks ('79–'82); Exec. V.P. and Partner, Horizon Entertainment, broad-based entertainment company specializing in network TV, cable, and features.
ACHIEVEMENTS & AWARDS: N.A.
PERSONAL: Wife, Donna; children, Jeremy and Ashley. Resides in Los Angeles.

BALL, LUCILLE
Actress/Comedienne

c/o CBS, 7800 Beverly Blvd., Los Angeles, CA 90036
b. August 6, 1911. Jamestown, NY.

EDUCATION: Chautagua Institute of Music; John Murray Anderson Drama School.

CAREER HIGHLIGHTS: "I Love Lucy" is the longest running comedy show in history because, for more than 30 years, fans have been loving Lucille Ball, a worthy successor to the silent screen comics. Her slapstick genius and pixilated innocence have made her the queen of TV comedy. She landed her first Hollywood role in Eddie Cantor's *Roman Scandals*, which led to a studio contract. During filming of *Too Many Girls*, ('40), she met and married Desi Arnaz. She got her first significant break in *The Big Street*, which set her on the road to movie stardom. She also starred in her own radio show, "My Favorite Husband." "I Love Lucy," which is still being broadcast in worldwide syndication, made its debut in '51. Following this sitcom, she continued in series television with "The Lucy Show" and "Here's Lucy." She starred in the film version of the Broadway musical hit *Mame* ('73). After retiring from series television ('74), she has continued starring in a limited series of specials.

ACHIEVEMENTS & AWARDS: Emmy awards for best comedienne ('52), best continuing performance by an actress ('55, '66).

PERSONAL: Husband, Gary Morton; daughter, Lucie, and son, Desi IV. Resides in Beverly Hills, CA.

BALLARD, KAYE
Actress

c/o Richard Francis, 328 S. Beverly Drive, #A, Beverly Hills, CA 90212
b. November 20, 1926.

EDUCATION: N.A.

CAREER HIGHLIGHTS: Stage appearances include *Molly*, *Carnival*, and *Minnie's Boys*. Films include *The Ritz* and *The Girl Most Likely*. TV appearances include "Laugh-In," "The Mothers-in-Law," "The Dream Merchants," and the PBS special "Alice in Wonderland" ('83).

ACHIEVEMENTS & AWARDS: N.A.

PERSONAL: N.A.

BALSAM, MARTIN
Actor

300 Central Park W., New York, NY 10024
b. November 4, 1919. New York, NY.

EDUCATION: New School for Social Research.

CAREER HIGHLIGHTS: Made his professional acting debut in "The Play's the Thing" ('41) and worked regularly in theater, films, and TV. His TV appearances began ('48) on such programs as "Studio One," "Alfred Hitchcock Presents," and "Playhouse 90." Guested on numerous shows, and became a regular for two years on "Archie Bunker's Place." Recent TV movie credits include *Raid on Entebbe*, *The Love Tapes*, *Siege*, *The Seeding of Sarah Burns*, *Contract on Cherry Street*, *The Millionaire*, *Rainbow*, *House on Garibaldi Street*, *Aunt Mary*, and *The People Against Jean Harris*.

ACHIEVEMENTS & AWARDS: Academy Award for best supporting actor in *A Thousand Clowns* ('65); Tony for *You Know I Can't Hear You When the Water's Running* ('67); Obie for *Cold Storage* ('78).

PERSONAL: Resides in New York City with wife, Irene. His daughter is actress Talia Balsam.

BANNER, BOB
Independent Prod.

8687 Melrose Ave., Los Angeles, CA 90069
b. August 15, 1921. Ennis, TX.

EDUCATION: Northwestern University, B.A.

CAREER HIGHLIGHTS: Joined "The Fred Waring Show" ('48); then "Garroway-at-Large" ('49); Dir., "Omnibus" ('52); Prod. and Dir., "The Dinah Shore Show" ('54–'58) and "The Garry Moore Show" ('58–'64). He then went on to concentrate on specials including "Julie and Carol at Carnegie Hall" ('62) "Perry Como's Christmas in Mexico," and "Peggy Fleming at Sun Valley." His syndicated shows range from "Please Stand By" ('78) to "Solid Gold" ('81).

ACHIEVEMENTS & AWARDS: Peabody award and Emmy for "The Dinah Shore Show" ('57).

PERSONAL: Resides in Los Angeles.

BANNER, JONATHAN
Pres. and Publisher, *View*

c/o *View*, 150 E. 58th St., New York, NY 10155
b. June 2, 1950.

EDUCATION: University of Buffalo ('72).

CAREER HIGHLIGHTS: Natl. Sales Mgr., *The Real Paper*, Boston; Advertising Dir., *Crawdaddy*; Exec. Publisher, *Circus* magazine; Acct. Exec., Young & Rubicam advertising agency, New York. Conceived and developed *View* magazine, which is devoted to cable TV programming ('79). Pres. and Publisher, *View* ('80).

ACHIEVEMENTS & AWARDS: N.A.

PERSONAL: N.A.

BANTA, GLORIA
V.P., Paramount TV, Comedy Development

c/o Paramount TV, 5555 Melrose Avenue, Los Angeles, CA 90038
b. September 8.

EDUCATION: University of Denver, Music.

CAREER HIGHLIGHTS: In partnership with Pat Nardo, Banta wrote for the series "The Mary Tyler Moore Show" ('72–'74) and "Rhoda" ('75); they also wrote "Rookie of the Year" and the "Lily Tomlin Special." Banta moved to Paramount as Exec. Story Consultant, "Julie Farr, M.D." ('78); and Co-Prod., "Angie" ('79). Co-Prod., Witt-Thomas Productions, "It's a Living" ('82); Filmways, Writer, "Cagney and Lacey" ('82); returned to Paramount TV as V.P., Comedy Development ('82).

ACHIEVEMENTS & AWARDS: Writers Guild award for "Lily Tomlin Special."

PERSONAL: Resides in San Fernando Valley, CA.

BARBERA, JOSEPH R.
Prod., Animated TV Cartoons, Hanna-Barbera Productions

c/o Hanna-Barbera Productions, 3400 Cahuenga Blvd., Hollywood, CA 90068
b. March 24. New York, NY.

EDUCATION: New York University; American School of Banking.

CAREER HIGHLIGHTS: Salesman Joseph Barbera and his partner Bill Hanna pioneered TV animation, learning to cut costs to fit the medium. At MGM, the partners created "Tom and Jerry" ('38). Hanna-Barbera Productions began ('57) with "Ruff and Ready," "Yogi Bear," "Huckleberry Hound," and "The Flintstones," forerunners for more than 200 cartoons, topped by the current Saturday morning hit "The Smurfs." Other cartoon hits include "Fred and Barney" ('74) and "Scooby-Doo" ('69), in addition to the children's films *Last of the Curlews* ('72) *The Runaways* ('73) *Charlotte's Web* ('79), *Heidi's Song* ('82), and the primetime drama *The Gathering* ('77).

ACHIEVEMENTS & AWARDS: Three Emmy awards for *Last of the Curlews* ('72), *The Runaways* ('73), *The Gathering* ('77). Pres., Huntington Hartford Theater, Hollywood. Member, Advisory Board, Children's Village; St. Joseph's Medical Center; and Greater Los Angeles Visitors and Convention Bureau.

PERSONAL: Resides in Los Angeles

BARISH, SHERLEE
Pres., Broadcast Personnel Agency

c/o Broadcast Personnel Agency, 527 Madison Ave., New York, NY 10022
b. May 31, 1926. Asheville, NC.

EDUCATION: Florida State University, B.A. ('47)

CAREER HIGHLIGHTS: Realtor ('47); Secretary, WIRK-AM/TV, West Palm Beach, FL ('52); Program Dir., WIRK-AM/TV, West Palm Beach ('54); Sales Dept., Official Films, New York ('55); V.P., Sales, Official Films, New York ('59); Founder and Pres., Broadcast Personnel Agency, New York ('61). One of the most important agents in the country for news executives and on-air news personnel.

ACHIEVEMENTS & AWARDS: N.A.

PERSONAL: Single, resides in New York City.

BARKER, BOB
Host, CBS, "The Price Is Right"

c/o CBS, 7800 Beverly Blvd., Los Angeles, CA 90036
b. December 12. Darrington, WA.

EDUCATION: Drury College (summa cum laude).

CAREER HIGHLIGHTS: Suntanned and forever genial, Barker has been a game show sex symbol to America's housewives from "Truth or Consequences" to "The Price Is Right." Started at KTTS-Radio, Springfield, IL, as News Writer, Announcer, and Disc Jockey; moved to WWPG, Palm Beach, FL. Moved to Los Angeles and started "The Bob Barker Show" on KWIK-Radio in Burbank; first TV assignment was hosting "Your Big Moment," and later "Talent in High." Hosted Ralph Edwards's "Truth or Consequences" ('56–'74) and shortly thereafter became host of the updated "Price Is Right" game show. Barker has served as master of ceremonies for both the "Miss Universe Beauty Pageant" and the "Miss USA Beauty Pageant" since '66, and has narrated the Rose Bowl parade for CBS since '69.

ACHIEVEMENTS & AWARDS: Member, Board of Trustees, Morris Animal Foundation.

PERSONAL: Resides in Los Angeles.

BARKLEY, DEANNE
Prod., ComWorld Productions

c/o ComWorld Productions, 15301 Ventura Blvd., Sherman Oaks, CA 91403
b. New Orleans, LA.

EDUCATION: Northwestern University.

CAREER HIGHLIGHTS: Began at NBC New Orleans affiliate WDSU-TV in public affairs, then wrote for Dick Cavett's morning shows and produced the Virginia Graham and Helen Gurley Brown talk shows. Moved to Robert Stigwood Productions ('74), as Prod., *The Virginia Hill Story, All Together Now,* and *Death Scream.* Joined NBC TV as V.P., Program Development, West Coast ('75); became V.P., Dramatic Programs ('76); V.P., Motion Pictures and Mini-Series ('77). Joined Osmond Productions ('80), ComWorld ('82), before becoming Independent Prod., responsible for more than 200 hours of programming at NBC and ABC.

ACHIEVEMENTS & AWARDS: Author of the novel *Freeway* ('78).

PERSONAL: Resides in Brentwood, CA; six children.

BARNATHAN, JULIUS
Pres., ABC, Broadcast Operations and Engineering

c/o ABC, 7 W. 66th St., New York, NY 10023
b. January 22, 1927. New York, NY.

EDUCATION: Brooklyn College, B.A.; Columbia University, M.S.

CAREER HIGHLIGHTS: One of the pioneering figures in TV technology and new production equipment and techniques. Dir. of Media Research, Kenyon & Eckhardt ('52); ABC TV Dir. of Research ('54); V.P. for Affiliate Relations, ABC ('59); Pres. of Owned Stations, V.P., ABC and General Mgr., ABC TV Network ('62); V.P. in Charge of Broadcast Operations and Engineering, ABC ('65); Pres., Broadcast Operations and Engineering ('76).

ACHIEVEMENTS & AWARDS: Emmy awards for Summer Olympics ('76) and Winter Olympics ('80); SMPTE citation for outstanding service ('78); distinguished alumni award, Brooklyn College ('79); NAB engineering award ('82); honorary doctorate of science, Gallaudet College ('82). Member, Phi Beta Kappa ('51); Member, Technical Committee, European Broadcasting Union ('65–'82); Member, Royal TV Society ('70–'82); Board of Governors, New York NATAS ('76–'80); Member, Exec. Committee, NANBA ('79–'82); Member of Board, Intl. Council, NATAS ('82).

PERSONAL: Resides in Roslyn Harbor, NY, with wife, Lorraine; children, Joyce, Daniel, and Jacqueline.

BARNES, GORDON
Meteorologist, Cable News Network, Weather

c/o Cable News Network, 1050 Techwood Dr., N.W., Atlanta, GA 30318
b. April 12, 1932. Bermuda.

EDUCATION: N.A.

CAREER HIGHLIGHTS: Worked as an Operations Representative, Flight Dispatcher, Asst. Op-

erations Mgr. for the Middle and Far East, and Operations Mgr. for West Africa, Pan American Airways ('48–'60); Freelance Weather Consultant, WFLA-TV/Radio, Tampa; Weatherman, WCBS-TV, WCBS-Radio, CBS Radio Network, CBS News Apollo space shot specials ('66–'76); On-Air Meteorologist, WDVM-TV ('76); On-Air Meteorologist, CBS, "Morning With Charles Kuralt"; Anchor, weather reports, regular member of "Daybreak program," Cable News Network ('82).
ACHIEVEMENTS & AWARDS: N.A.
PERSONAL: N.A.

BARNETT, JOAN
V.P., Creative Affairs, Alan Landsburg Prod.

c/o Alan Landsburg Prod., 1554 S. Sepulveda Blvd., CA 90025
b. New York, NY.

EDUCATION: N.A.
CAREER HIGHLIGHTS: Began with Alexander H. Cohen as Company Mgr. for Broadway shows including *Home, Good Evening, Words and Music, Ulysses in Nighttown* and as Assoc. Prod. on Tony awards telecasts, network specials, and TV movies ('69). Formed Otto-Barnett Assoc. with Linda Otto and oversaw casting of more than 50 TV pilots and 30 TV movies and mini-series for all three networks ('75); Prod., three movies for TV: *Torn Between Two Lovers, Marathon,* and *The Jayne Mansfield Story* ('78). Joined NBC Entertainment as V.P., Motion Pictures for TV ('80); V.P., Creative Affairs, Alan Landsburg Prod.
ACHIEVEMENTS & AWARDS: N.A.
PERSONAL: Resides in Los Angeles.

BARONE, JOAN S.
Prod., CBS, News

c/o CBS, 2020 M St., N.W., Washington, DC 20036
b. May 24. San Francisco, CA.

EDUCATION: Mills College, B.A.; Harvard University.
CAREER HIGHLIGHTS: Political Researcher, *Washington Post* ('70); Researcher, CBS News, Washington, DC ('73); Assoc. Prod., "Face the Nation" ('74); Prod., "Face the Nation" ('79).

ACHIEVEMENTS & AWARDS: N.A.
PERSONAL: Resides in Washington, DC, with husband, Michael, and daughter, Sarah.

BARR, TONY
V.P., Current Dramatic Program Production, CBS, Entertainment

c/o CBS, 6121 Sunset Blvd., Los Angeles, CA 90028
b. March 14.

EDUCATION: Washington University, B.S., Education and Drama.
CAREER HIGHLIGHTS: Served as Assoc. Prod. and Prod. of various series including "Playhouse 90" and "Climax"; Co-Prod., "Dime With a Halo"; V.P., Current Primetime Series, ABC ('76); Dir., Current Dramatic Programming, CBS Entertainment ('79); V.P., Current Dramatic Program Production, CBS Entertainment ('82).
ACHIEVEMENTS & AWARDS: Founder and operator of the Film Actors' Workshop; Board Member, NATAS.
PERSONAL: Resides in Van Nuys, CA, with wife, Annette; daughter, Susan; sons, John and David.

BARRET, EARL
Writer/Prod./Dir.

c/o Elliot Wax, 9255 Sunset Blvd., Los Angeles, CA 90069
b. October 17, 1934. Canton, OH.

EDUCATION: California State University, B.A.
CAREER HIGHLIGHTS: Story Editor, "The Governor and J.J." ('69); Prod., "The Partners"

('70); Prod., "The Sandy Duncan Show" ('71); Story Editor, "Viva Valdez" ('75); Story Editor, "Welcome Back Kotter" ('77); Prod., "San Pedro Bums" ('78); Exec. Prod./Dir./Writer, "Too Close for Comfort" ('80).
ACHIEVEMENTS & AWARDS: N.A.
PERSONAL: N.A.

BARRETT, MARVIN GALBRAITH
Dir., Alfred I. Dupont-Columbia University Survey and Awards in Broadcast Journalism

35 Claremont Ave., New York, NY 10027
b. May 6, 1920. Des Moines, IA.

EDUCATION: Harvard College, B.A. ('42); Drake University, M.A., ('76).
CAREER HIGHLIGHTS: Contributing Editor, *Time* magazine ('48); Radio-TV Editor, *Newsweek* ('54); Exec. Editor, *Show Business Illustrated* ('61); Editor/Managing Editor, *Show* magazine ('61); Editor, *Atlas* magazine ('65); Sr. Staff Assoc. in Journalism and Lecturer in Journalism, Columbia University ('69–present); Dir., Alfred I. Dupont-Columbia University Survey and Awards in Broadcast Journalism ('68–present). Under Barrett's aegis, the Dupont-Columbia awards quickly became the most prestigious awards in broadcast journalism.
ACHIEVEMENTS & AWARDS: N.A.
PERSONAL: Wife, Mary; four children.

BARRETT, PETE (Paul W. Barrett)
V.P. and Dir., ABC TV Network Natl. Advertising

c/o ABC, 1330 Ave. of the Americas, New York, NY 10019
b. August 29, 1944. Shreveport, LA.

EDUCATION: University of North Carolina, B.A., English.
CAREER HIGHLIGHTS: Mgr., Advertising, WABC-TV ('69); Dir., Creative Services, KMOX, St. Louis ('73); Dir., Advertising, ABC TV Network ('75); Dir., Advertising Services for ABC TV Network ('77); promoted to V.P. and Natl. Advertising Dir. ('81).
ACHIEVEMENTS & AWARDS: N.A.
PERSONAL: N.A.

BARRIS, CHUCK
Game Show Prod./TV Host

6430 Sunset Blvd., Hollywood, CA 90028
b. June 3, 1929. Philadelphia, PA.

EDUCATION: University of Miami; Drexel Institute of Technology.
CAREER HIGHLIGHTS: The creator of tasteless and highly successful game shows, Barris is known to try anything—and usually comes out on top. He left the NBC Management Trainee Program ('55) and moved into sales of teleprompters before helping to promote the Ingemar Johansen–Floyd Patterson heavyweight fight ('57). Joined ABC as Dir., West Coast Daytime Programs ('59); left ABC to form Chuck Barris Productions ('65) and ended up selling the network his creations, including "The Dating Game" ('65), "The Newlywed Game" ('66), "How's Your Mother-in-Law?" ('67), "The Family Game" ('67), "The Game Game" ('69), "The New Treasure Hunt" ('74), "The Gong Show" ('76), and "The $1.98 Beauty Show."
ACHIEVEMENTS & AWARDS: N.A.
PERSONAL: Resides in West Los Angeles with daughter, Delia.

BARRY, JACK
Game Show Prod./Host

c/o Paramount TV, 5555 Melrose Ave., Los Angeles, CA 90038
b. March 20, 1918. Lindenhurst, NY.

EDUCATION: University of Pennsylvania.
CAREER HIGHLIGHTS: In the fifties, Barry produced the game shows "Tic Tac Dough," "Winky Dink," and "21." Prod., "The Joker's Wild" and "Break the Bank" ('70).
ACHIEVEMENTS & AWARDS: N.A.
PERSONAL: N.A.

BARRY, MIKE
Sports Reporter, WABC-TV

c/o WABC-TV, 7 Lincoln Sq., New York, NY 10023
b. September 10. Elgin, IL.

EDUCATION: Loras College.

CAREER HIGHLIGHTS: Newscaster, KDTH-TV, Dubuque, IA ('69); Newscaster, WOC-TV, Davenport, IA ('71); Sports Dir., WQAD-TV, Moline, IA ('73); Sports Dir., WDBO-TV, Orlando, FL ('75); Sports Dir., WFLA-TV, Tampa ('77); Sports Dir., WDIV-TV, Detroit; Sports Dir., WXYZ-TV, Detroit ('79); Sports Reporter, WABC-TV, New York ('82); Also Sportscaster, ABC Radio Network, USFL football games ('83).

ACHIEVEMENTS & AWARDS: One-time member of the Professional Golfers Assn.

PERSONAL: N.A.

BARTELME, JOE
Dir., Domestic News, NBC, News

c/o NBC, 30 Rockefeller Plaza, New York, NY 10020
b. July 4, 1930.

EDUCATION: College of St. Thomas; Northwestern University; University of Iowa, B.A. and M.A., Journalism.

CAREER HIGHLIGHTS: Reporter, KCRG-TV, Cedar Rapids, IA ('55); Reporter, WCCO-TV, Minneapolis ('60); Assoc. News Dir., WCCO-TV, Minneapolis ('60); News Dir., WCCO-TV ('67); Dir., NBC News, West Coast ('71); V.P., News, NBC TV Stations Division ('74); V.P., News Programs ('78); Exec. Prod., "Today" ('79); Prod., Special Events Programming, NBC ('80); Dir., Domestic News, NBC ('81).

ACHIEVEMENTS & AWARDS: While at WCCO-TV, recipient of six Radio-TV News Dirs. Assn. awards, a Peabody award, and a Dupont-Columbia award.

PERSONAL: N.A.

BARTON, GARY
Dir., Casting, Motion Pictures for TV, CBS, Entertainment

c/o CBS, 6121 W. Sunset Blvd., Los Angeles, CA 90028
b. Boston, MA.

EDUCATION: New York University, B.A., Theater Arts ('71).

CAREER HIGHLIGHTS: Former actor who worked in New York and Los Angeles. Casting Dir., 20th Century Fox ('78); Casting Dir., Universal Studios ('79); Assoc. Dir., Talent and Casting, CBS Entertainment ('80); Dir., Casting, Motion Pictures for TV, CBS ('80).

ACHIEVEMENTS & AWARDS: N.A.

PERSONAL: Resides in West Hollywood, CA.

BARUCH, RALPH M.
Chairman and Chief Exec. Officer, Viacom International

c/o Viacom International, 1211 Ave. of the Americas, New York, NY 10036
b. August 5, 1923. France.

EDUCATION: The Sorbonne (France).

CAREER HIGHLIGHTS: Baruch is a model of executive expertise, bridging the gap between network and cable TV. He is a former CBS executive, and his presidency at Viacom is notable for Viacom's expansion into the kinds of programming that were once considered the exclusive domain of the three major networks. Began his communications career in radio and moved to TV when he joined the Dumont TV Network ('50). Joined CBS ('54), appointed V.P. and General Mgr. ('67), and later named a CBS Group Pres. Chairman and Chief Exec. Officer of Viacom International ('78).

ACHIEVEMENTS & AWARDS: Emmy for his services as Pres. of the NATAS Intl. Council ('72–'74); the Natl. Cable TV Assn. presidents award; the Natl. Cable TV Assn. Chairman of the Year award; *View* magazine's Man of the Year award; the American Jewish Committee's human relations award ('81); Dir., IRTS; Secretary and Dir., Natl. Cable TV Assn.

PERSONAL: Wife, Jean; four children. Resides in New york City.

BASEHART, RICHARD
Actor

c/o Jack Fields, 9255 Sunset Blvd., Los
   Angeles, CA 90069
b. August 31. 1914. Zanesville, OH.

EDUCATION: N.A.
CAREER HIGHLIGHTS: Began as a radio announcer; New York stage appearances in *The Hasty Heart* and *Counter Attack;* motion pictures include *Repeat Performance, He Walked by Night, Decision Before Dawn,* and *La Strada.* Played the lead in the TV series "Voyage to the Bottom of the Sea." TV movies include *Sole Survivor, Death of Me Yet,* and *The Rebels.*
ACHIEVEMENTS & AWARDS: New York Drama Critics award for *The Hasty Heart.*
PERSONAL: N.A.

BASKIN, JOHN
Writer/Prod.

9171 Wilshire Blvd., Suite 406, Beverly Hills,
   CA 90210
b. 1944, Minneapolis, MN.

EDUCATION: University of California, B.S. University of Minnesota, M.B.A.
CAREER HIGHLIGHTS: Staff Writer, "The David Frost Revue" ('71); Staff Writer, "The Dean Martin Show" ('73); Contributing Writer, "Love, American Style," "All in the Family," "The Jeffersons," and "Good Times" ('73); Story Editor, "Good Times" ('74); Exec. Story Editor, "The Jeffersons" ('77); Prod., "Three's Company" ('78). Develops and produces pilots for Columbia Pictures TV ('79)
ACHIEVEMENTS & AWARDS: Humanitas award finalist ('76); Population Institute award finalist ('76); Los Angeles Venereal Disease Council award ('77); Humanitas award finalist ('78).
PERSONAL: Resides in Los Angeles with wife, Charlene, and children, Bradley and Alexander.

BATSCHA, ROBERT M.
Pres., Museum of Broadcasting

c/o Museum of Broadcasting, 1 E. 53d St.,
   New York, NY 10022
b. September 14, 1921. Rochester, NY.

EDUCATION: Queens College (magna cum laude), Columbia University, Ph.D., Political Science, University of Vienna (Austria).
CAREER HIGHLIGHTS: Consultant, Carl Marks & Co. and the University of Andes, Bogota, Columbia; Sr. Consultant, Organization for Economic Cooperation and Development ('72); Pres., Population Resource Center ('75). Faculty positions at Columbia University School of International Affairs and at Queens College; Pres., Museum of Broadcasting, New York ('81).
ACHIEVEMENTS & AWARDS: Member, Phi Beta Kappa. Founder, Center for Communications; Author, *Foreign Affairs News and Broadcast Journalism* ('75) and *Dissemination of Economic and Social Development Research* ('76).
PERSONAL: Resides in New York City with his wife, Francine, and their son.

BATTISTA, BOBBIE (Barbara Battista)
Anchor, Cable News Network, Headline Service

1115 Summit N. Dr., Atlanta, GA 30324
b. July 23, 1952. Iowa City, IA.

EDUCATION: Northwestern University, B.S. ('74).

CAREER HIGHLIGHTS: Started as Disc Jockey, Sales Rep. for WAKS Radio, Fuguay-Varina, North Carolina ('75); Co-Host, Program Prod. WRAL-TV, Raleigh, NC; Anchor, Cable News Network Headline Service ('81).

ACHIEVEMENTS & AWARDS: Peabody award as Writer and Asst. Prod., documentary consortium project "Fed Up with Fear."

PERSONAL: N.A.

BAUER, CHARITA
Actress

c/o "The Guiding Light," CBS, 51 W. 52d St., New York, NY 10019
b. December 20. Newark, NJ.

EDUCATION: Professional Children's School.

CAREER HIGHLIGHTS: A true veteran soap opera performer who started on the stage and radio, she joined the cast of "The Guiding Light" while it was still on radio ('50) and stayed with the show as Bert Bauer when it transferred to TV ('52). She has been with the show ever since. TV movie debut in *The Cradle Will Fall* ('83).

ACHIEVEMENTS & AWARDS: Life achievement award from NATAS.

PERSONAL: Resides in New York City.

BAUER, JAMES L.
Dir., CBS/Venture One, Business Development

c/o CBS, 524 W. 57th St., New York, NY 10019
b. March 1, 1947.

EDUCATION: Harpur College; Pace University, M.B.A.

CAREER HIGHLIGHTS: V.P., *N.Y. Times* Information Service; joined CBS ('79); Dir. of Business Development for CBS/Venture One, responsible for the development and implementation of advertising on videotext.

ACHIEVEMENTS & AWARDS: N.A.

PERSONAL: N.A.

BAUM, ROBERT
Pres. and Chief Exec. Officer, Cablentertainment

c/o Cablentertainment, 295 Madison Ave., New York, NY 10017
b. May 4.

EDUCATION: Boston University, B.S. ('61); Columbia University, Executive Action Program

CAREER HIGHLIGHTS: Natl. Sales Mgr., Vikoa ('62); formed his own investment company ('70); created Cablequities, in which he was a general partner. Pres. and Chief Exec. Officer, Cablentertainment.

ACHIEVEMENTS & AWARDS: N.A.

PERSONAL: Married, six children. Resides in New Jersey.

BAUMAN, JEROME
Exec. V.P., Cablentertainment

c/o Cablentertainment, 295 Madison Ave.,
    New York, NY 10017
b. June 24.

EDUCATION: City College of New York, B.B.A.
    ('64); New York State CPA Certificate ('67).
CAREER HIGHLIGHTS: Partner, Mann, Brown &
    Bauman. Exec. V.P., Cablentertainment ('81).
ACHIEVEMENTS & AWARDS: Member, New York
    and New Jersey State Societies of CPAs.
PERSONAL: Married, two children. Resides in
    New Jersey.

BAXTER, ELLEN
Dir.

c/o Shapiro, Taxon & Kopell, 1180 Ave. of the
    Americas, New York, NY 10036
b. N.A.

EDUCATION: University of Southern California,
    M.S.A., Cinema.
CAREER HIGHLIGHTS: Dir. (first show), "It Takes
    Two"; Assoc. Dir., "It Takes Two," "I'm a Big
    Girl Now," and "Benson." Post Prod. Super-
    visor, "Soap" (two years) and 400 episodes of
    "Mary Hartman, Mary Hartman."
ACHIEVEMENTS & AWARDS: N.A.
PERSONAL: N.A.

BAXTER BIRNEY, MEREDITH
Actress

c/o "Family Ties," NBC, 3000 W. Alameda
    Ave., Burbank, CA 91523
b. June 21. Los Angeles, CA.

EDUCATION: Interlochen Arts Academy.
CAREER HIGHLIGHTS: Her TV career was
    launched by a guest appearance ('70) on "The
    Interns" series. She starred with her future
    husband, David Birney, in the series "Bridget
    Loves Bernie" ('71–'72). Her other TV credits
    include "Family," *Dial 911, Family Man, The
    Day the Martians Landed,* "City of Angels,"
    Beulah Land, Little Women, and *What Really
    Happened to the Class of '65.* On the stage, she
    starred with her husband in *Talley's Folly* and
    Guys and Dolls, and she also starred in *Butter-
    flies Are Free* and *Vanities.* Her film credits are
    Ben, Stand Up and Be Counted, and *All the Pres-
    ident's Men.* Currently stars in the series
    "Family Ties."
ACHIEVEMENTS & AWARDS: N.A.
PERSONAL: Husband, actor David Birney; chil-
    dren, Teddy, Eva, and Kate. Resides in Santa
    Monica, CA.

BAZELL, ROBERT
Science Correspondent, NBC, News

c/o NBC, 30 Rockefeller Plaza, New York, NY
    10020
b. August 21. Pittsburgh, PA.

EDUCATION: University of California at Berke-
    ley, B.A., ('67); University of Sussex (En-
    gland), graduate study, Biology ('69); Univer-
    sity of California at Berkeley, Ph.D. study,
    Immunology.
CAREER HIGHLIGHTS: Researcher, Lawrence
    Radiation Laboratory, ('68); Writer, News and
    Comment section, *Science* magazine, ('71); Re-
    porter, *N.Y. Post* ('72); Reporter, WNBC-TV
    ('76); joined NBC News ('76); Science Corre-
    spondent, "NBC Nightly News" and "To-
    day" ('78).
ACHIEVEMENTS & AWARDS: Fellow of the Natl.
    Institutes of Health.
PERSONAL: Wife, Margot; two children.

BEADLE, DAVID
Weekend Anchor, Cable News Network

c/o Cable News Network, 1050 Techwood Dr.,
    N.W., Atlanta, GA 30318
b. March 29, 1952. San Francisco, CA.

EDUCATION: University of California at Berkeley, B.A., History (magna cum laude, '73) and M.J., Journalism Regents Fellowship, University of California at Berkeley ('74).
CAREER HIGHLIGHTS: Weekend Anchor, WINK-TV, Fort Myers, FL ('74); Weekday Anchor, WEAR-TV Pensacola-Mobile, AL ('76); Sr. Prod., WDSU-TV New Orleans ('79); Weekend Anchor, Cable News Network ('81).
ACHIEVEMENTS & AWARDS: Member, American Mensa Ltd. ('67).
PERSONAL: Married, two children.

BEAHRS, DICK
V.P., Marketing Services, Information and Analysis, HBO

c/o HBO, 1271 Ave. of the Americas, New York, NY 10020
b. March 28, 1945.

EDUCATION: University of California at Berkeley, B.A., History; Adelphi University, M.B.A.
CAREER HIGHLIGHTS: Dir., Sports Illustrated Enterprises ('69); Dir., New Product Sales, HBO ('79); Sales Dir., Cinemax ('80); V.P., Marketing Services, Information and Analysis, HBO ('82).
ACHIEVEMENTS & AWARDS: N.A.
PERSONAL: Resides in Darien, CT, with wife, Carolyn, and their four children.

BEARD, JOHN
Co-Anchor, KNBC, "LA at 6"

c/o KNBC, 3000 W. Alameda Ave., Burbank, CA 91523
b. N.A.

EDUCATION: East Carolina University, B.A., Broadcasting/Speech.
CAREER HIGHLIGHTS: Reporter, WTSB-AM and FM, in North Carolina ('68); Hospital Corpsman, U.S. Navy ('68–'72); Reporter/Correspondent/Anchor, WITN-TV and WXII-TV, NBC in North Carolina ('72–'77); Anchor, WIVB-TV, CBS in Buffalo, NY ('77–'82); Co-Anchor, KNBC, "LA at 6."
ACHIEVEMENTS & AWARDS: N.A.
PERSONAL: Resides in Santa Monica, CA.

BECKER, ARNOLD
V.P., CBS Broadcast Group, Natl. TV Research

c/o CBS, 51 W. 52d St., New York, NY 10019
b. February 17.

EDUCATION: Queens College, B.A.; Columbia University Graduate School of Business Administration, M.B.A.
CAREER HIGHLIGHTS: Joined CBS TV Research ('59); Asst. Dir. of TV Network Research ('69); Dir. of TV Network Research ('75); V.P., CBS Broadcast Group ('77).
ACHIEVEMENTS & AWARDS: N.A.
PERSONAL: Married; daughter, Nancy.

BECKHAM, PAUL D.
V.P. and Controller, Turner Broadcasting System

c/o Turner Broadcasting System, 1050 Techwood Dr., N.W., Atlanta, GA 30318
b. October 28, 1943. Greenville, SC.

EDUCATION: Georgia State University.
CAREER HIGHLIGHTS: Joined Turner Broadcasting System as a Corporate Controller ('71); named V.P. and Controller ('73).
ACHIEVEMENTS & AWARDS: N.A.
PERSONAL: Wife, Cheryl; daughter, Debbie; son, Mike.

BEDELL, J. ROBERT
Dir., Affiliate Relations and Marketing, Time, Inc., *TV-Cable Week*

c/o *TV-Cable Week*, 1271 Ave. of the Americas, New York, NY 10020
b. April 28, 1944. Hudson, OH.

EDUCATION: Princeton University; Wharton Business School.
CAREER HIGHLIGHTS: Dept. Mgr., Avon Products ('67); Dir., U.S. Marketing, Canada Dry Corp. ('71); Dir., Natl. Sales, Planning and Development, HBO ('77); V.P., Marketing and Public Relations, HBO ('79); Dir. Affiliate Relations and Marketing, *TV-Cable Week* ('83).
ACHIEVEMENTS & AWARDS: N.A.
PERSONAL: Resides in New York City.

BEDELL, SALLY
Cultural News Reporter, *N.Y. Times*

c/o N.Y. Times, 229 W. 43d St., New York,
NY 10036
b. May 27, 1948, Bryn Mawr, PA.

EDUCATION: Wheaton College, B.A. ('70); Columbia Graduate School of Journalism, M.S. ('73).
CAREER   HIGHLIGHTS: Reporter / Researcher, *Time* magazine; Staff Writer, *TV Guide*; Cultural News Reporter, specializing in TV, *N.Y. Times* ('82).
ACHIEVEMENTS & AWARDS: Author, *Up the Tube: Prime Time TV and the Silverman Years*.
PERSONAL: N.A.

BEESEMYER, RICHARD L.
V.P., General Mgr., Owned TV Stations, ABC

c/o ABC, 1330 Ave. of the Americas, New
York, NY 10019
b. January 13, 1925. Los Angeles, CA.

EDUCATION: University of Southern California, B.S., Business Administration.
CAREER HIGHLIGHTS: Acct. Exec., KHJ-TV, Los Angeles ('53); Acct. Exec., KNXT, ('56); Sales Mgr., KNXT ('60); Mgr., ABC Spot Sales, Los Angeles ('62); General Sales Mgr., WABC-TV ('65); General Mgr/V.P., WABC-TV ('69); moved to network as V.P., Affiliate Relations, ABC TV ('73); promoted to V.P., TV Network ('78); assumed title of V.P., General Mgr., Owned TV Stations ('81).
ACHIEVEMENTS & AWARDS: N.A.
PERSONAL: N.A.

BEGLEITER, RALPH J.
Washington, DC, Correspondent, State Dept., Cable News Network

c/o Lon Babby, Williams & Connolly, 1000
Hill Bldg., Washington, DC 20006
b. April 17, 1949. New York, NY.

EDUCATION: Brown University, B.A., Political Science ('71); Columbia University, M.S., Journalism ('72).
CAREER HIGHLIGHTS: Contributing Writer, *N.Y. Times*, Providence, RI ('70); Writer/Editor, ABC Radio Networks, New York (summer relief '69–'71); Writer/Reporter, WJAR-AM-TV, Providence ('71); News Dir./Reporter, WBRU-FM, Providence ('67); Writer/Reporter, WICE-AM, Providence ('69); Editor/Writer, WTOP-AM-TV, Washington, DC ('72); Reporter, WTOP-AM-TV, Washington, DC ('74); Washington, DC, Correspondent, State Dept., CNN ('81).
ACHIEVEMENTS & AWARDS: Natl. Press Club award for consumer journalism ('79); Education Writers Assn. award ('80); UPI award for in-depth reporting ('80); AP award for documentary reporting ('79, '80); AP award for human interest reporting ('79); Maryland State Teachers Assn. award for documentary ('79); Columbia University alternate Pulitzer Fellowship ('72). Member, Phi Beta Kappa ('71).
PERSONAL: Resides in Potomac, MD, with wife, Barbara Ann, and son, Joel Andrew.

BEL GEDDES, BARBARA
Actress

c/o "Dallas," CBS, 7800 Beverly Blvd., Los
Angeles, CA 90036
b. October 31, 1922. New York, NY

EDUCATION: N.A.
CAREER HIGHLIGHTS: Fans of "Dallas" may not have seen her distinguished Broadway performances, but they can recognize an exceptional actress who brings dignity and conviction to her nighttime soap opera. She made her Broadway debut in *Out of the Frying Pan* and continued in such plays as *The Moon Is Blue*, *The Living Room*, *Cat on a Hot Tin Roof*, *Burning Bright*, *The Sleeping Prince*, *Silent Night, Lonely Night*, *Mary, Mary*, *Finishing Touches*, *Luv*, *Everything in the Garden*, and *Deep Are the Roots*. Made her film debut in *The Long Night*, followed by *I Remember Mama*, *Panic in the Streets*, *Vertigo*, and *The Five Pennies*. Starred on TV in Alfred Hitchcock's *Lamb to the Slaughter* and Thornton Wilder's *Our Town* before landing on "Dallas" as Miss Ellie.
ACHIEVEMENTS & AWARDS: Emmy as best dramatic actress for "Dallas." Author/Illustrator of two children's books, *I Like To Be Me* and *So Do I*.
PERSONAL: Resides in Putnam Valley, NY; two daughters, Susan and Betsy.

BELL, DALE
V.P. and Exec. Prod., WQED

c/o WQED, 4802 Fifth Ave., Pittsburgh, PA
15213
b. May 28, 1938. Mount Kisco, NY.

EDUCATION: Princeton University, B.A., Modern Languages and Drama
CAREER HIGHLIGHTS: Worked as Prod., for WNET ('65); was Assoc. Prod., *Woodstock* ('70); continued with theatrical features as Asst. Dir. on *Mean Streets* ('73) and Assoc. Prod. on *The Groove Tube* ('74). Turned to TV as Prod. of the National Geographic specials "The Tigris Expedition" ('77) and "The Voyage of the Hokulea" ('79); became Exec. Prod. of "Previn and the Pittsburgh" series and Exec. Prod. on "Here Come the Muppets" series ('79); named Exec. Prod., "Kennedy Center Tonight" with credits including "A Copeland Celebration," "A Salute to Duke," "Sarah in America," "Lionel Hampton and Friends," and "Firebird" ('80). Currently works with "Kennedy Center Tonight" while serving as V.P. and Exec. Prod., WQED, Pittsburgh.
ACHIEVEMENTS & AWARDS: Academy Award, *Woodstock* ('70); IFPA, ("The Tigris Expedition" ('79) and "Firebird" ('82); Chicago Film Festival ; "A Copeland Celebration," ('81).
PERSONAL: Resides in Pittsburgh with wife, Linda; sons, Jonathan, David, and Andrew.

BELL, STEVE
Anchor, ABC, News

c/o ABC, 1717 DeSales St., N.W.,
Washington, DC 20036
b. December 9, 1935. Oskaloosa, IA.

EDUCATION: Central College, B.A.; Northwestern University, M.S., Journalism.
CAREER HIGHLIGHTS: ABC News New York Correspondent ('67); covered 1968 conventions and primaries for ABC Radio ('68); Combat Correspondent ('70); Campaign Correspondent ('72) Chief Correspondent and Bureau Chief, Hong Kong ('73); White House Correspondent ('74); appointed Anchor of news segments and Interviewer, "Good Morning America" ('75); continues in this position with additional anchor responsibilities for "ABC News This Morning." One of few journalists allowed into Hanoi for final release of American POWs.
ACHIEVEMENTS & AWARDS: Emmy nomination for "The People of People's China ('73); Overseas Press Club award; Headliners Club award.
PERSONAL: Wife, Joyce; daughters, Allison and Hilary.

BELLISARIO, DONALD P.
Writer/Prod.

c/o Universal Studios, Universal City, CA
91608
b. August 8. Charleroi, PA.

EDUCATION: Pennsylvania State University, B.A.
CAREER HIGHLIGHTS: Spent 14 years in advertising as Creative Dir., Bloom Agency ('58); TV Commercial Dir., ('72); Exec., Universal TV; Writer, "Switch" ('76), "Delvecchio" ('76), "Kojak" ('77); Story Editor and later Prod., "The Rockford Files" and "Baa Baa Black Sheep" ('76); Prod., "Battlestar Galactica" ('78); created "Magnum, P.I." with Glen Larson and was Prod./Writer ('80); Creator/Prod./Writer, "The Brass Monkey" ('82).
ACHIEVEMENTS & AWARDS: N.A.
PERSONAL: Resides in Hollywood Hills, CA, with wife, Lynn, and son, Michelangelo. Four children by a previous marriage.

BELLOWS, JAMES
Exec. Prod., ABC News

c/o ABC News, 1330 Ave. of the Americas,
New York, NY 10019
b. N.A.

EDUCATION: N.A.

CAREER HIGHLIGHTS: Editor of the *N.Y. Herald Tribune* ('62), *Los Angeles Times* ('66), *Washington Star* ('74), *Los Angeles Herald Examiner* ('81), and Managing Editor of "Entertainment Tonight"; Exec. Prod. Managing Editor "ABC News Magazine" ('83–'84 season).

ACHIEVEMENTS & AWARDS: Former Director of American Society of Newspaper Editors.

PERSONAL: N.A.

BENDIK, ROBERT
TV Prod.

c/o Times-Mirror Cable TV, 2381 Morse Ave. Irvine, CA 92714

b. February 8, 1917. New York, NY.

EDUCATION: New York University.

CAREER HIGHLIGHTS: Dir., Special Events, CBS ('46); Prod., "The Dave Garroway Show Today," "Bob Hope's 25 Years of *Life* Show," and "The First Look" series. Prod., "The American Sportsman" for ABC and "The Great American Dream Machine" for NET; Co-Prod., Dick Cavett's "Feeling Good"; Pres. of Bendik Assoc., Educational and Audio-Visual Systems; Consultant to Warner Qube Cable and Times-Mirror Cable TV.

ACHIEVEMENTS & AWARDS: Emmy for "The Great American Dream Machine." Member, Board of Governors, New York ATAS.

PERSONAL: N.A.

BENJAMIN, BURTON
Sr. Exec. Prod., CBS, News

c/o CBS, 524 W. 57th St., New York, NY 10019

b. October 9, 1917. Cleveland, OH.

EDUCATION: University of Michigan.

CAREER HIGHLIGHTS: Reporter for the Newspaper Enterprise Assoc. ('40); Writer/Prod./Dir., RKO-Pathe ('46); Freelance Writer for magazine articles, TV scripts, and films ('46–'57); Exec. Prod., "The 20th Century," "The 21st Century," "World War I," and "You Are There"; Exec. Prod., "CBS Evening News With Walter Cronkite" ('75); Sr. Exec. Prod., Documentary Broadcasts ('77); V.P.,

Dir. of News, CBS, ('78); Sr. Exec. Prod., hard news broadcasts ('81).

ACHIEVEMENTS & AWARDS: Emmy awards for producing "Solzhenitsyn" ('74); CBS Reports, "The Rockefellers" ('73); CBS Reports, "The Mexican Connection" ('72); "Justice Black and the Bill of Rights" ('70); recipient of eight Emmy awards, a Peabody, two Ohio State University awards, and the American Bar Assn. gavel award.

PERSONAL: Resides in Scarborough, NY, with his wife, Anne, and their two daughters.

BENNETT, BRUCE R.
V.P., General Mgr., Cox Cable
Communications, Central Division

c/o Cox Cable Communications, 219 Perimeter Center Parkway, Atlanta, GA 30346

b. April 21, 1942. Atlanta, GA.

EDUCATION: Duke University, B.A., Economics ('65); Georgia State University, M.B.A., Management ('71).

CAREER HIGHLIGHTS: Manufacturing Supervisor, Dupont, NC ('65); Planning Officer, First Natl. Bank, Atlanta ('66); V.P., Southland Investment Corp., Atlanta ('71); Admin. V.P., Ray Lang, Inc., Atlanta ('72); V.P./General Mgr., Central Division, Cox Cable Communications ('76).

ACHIEVEMENTS & AWARDS: N.A.

PERSONAL: N.A.

BENNETT, JAMES S.
V.P. and General Mgr., KNXT-TV, Los
Angeles

c/o KNXT-TV, 6121 Sunset Blvd., Los Angeles, CA 90028

b. June 1, 1947.

EDUCATION: University of California at Berkeley, B.A., Political Science and Journalism; Harvard Business School, M.B.A.

CAREER HIGHLIGHTS: Planning Analyst, CBS TV Stations Division, New York; Dir., Administration, KCBS-Radio, San Francisco; Dir. of Planning and Administration, WBBM-TV, Chicago ('74); Dir., Broadcasting, WBBM-TV ('76); Station Mgr., KNXT-TV, Los Angeles ('80); V.P. and General Mgr., KNXT-TV ('81).

ACHIEVEMENTS & AWARDS: N.A.

PERSONAL: Resides in Los Angeles with wife, Carolyn, and one child.

BENNETT, ROBERT MARTIN
Pres., Metromedia TV, and Sr. V.P., Metromedia, Inc.

c/o 5 TV Place, Needham Branch, Boston, MA 02192

b. April 17, 1927.

EDUCATION: Stonehill College; University of Southern California; University of California.

CAREER HIGHLIGHTS: Under Bennett's leadership, Metromedia (which recently signed a partnership deal with HBO) has picked up two popular series, "Fame" and "Too Close for Comfort," that the networks had dropped. His other ongoing improvement program involves the upgrading of local news operations at Metromedia stations. He began his career as sales Rep., Metromedia, New Jersey ('52); V.P., Sales, Metromedia, New Jersey ('58); V.P., Dir. of Sales, KTTV, Los Angeles ('65); V.P., General Mgr., WTTG, Washington, DC ('66); V.P., General Mgr., WNEW, New York ('69); V.P., Dir., BBI; General Mgr., WCVB ('71); Exec. V.P., Dir., BBI ('76); Pres., Dir., BBI Communications; Pres., BBI Productions; General Mgr., WCVB ('79–'82); Pres., Metromedia TV, and Sr. V.P., Metromedia, Inc.

ACHIEVEMENTS & AWARDS: Peabody award for stationwide performance; 78 regional Emmy awards. Created BBI Communications; created BBI Productions. Member, Board of Trustees, Emerson College; Founding Pres., NATAS, Boston Chapter.

PERSONAL: Wife, Marjie; children, Kelly and Casey.

BENSLEY, RUSS
Exec. Prod., CBS, News

c/o CBS, 524 W. 57th St., New York, NY, 10019

b. June 12, 1930. Chicago, IL.

EDUCATION: Northwestern University Medill School of Journalism, B.S. ('51) and M.S. ('52).

CAREER HIGHLIGHTS: Bensley came to CBS News after working as Writer/Prod./Newscaster, WBBM-TV, CBS, Chicago; joined CBS News as a Writer, New York ('60); Prod./Dir., "Eyewitness" series ('61); Mgr., CBS News Bureau, Chicago ('63); Prod., "CBS Evening News With Walter Cronkite" ('64); Exec. Prod., "CBS Evening News With Walter Cronkite" ('71–'72); Dir. of Special Events, CBS News Special Coverage ('71–'81); Exec. Prod., weekend editions, "The CBS Evening News," "The CBS Sunday Night News" ('82–'83).

ACHIEVEMENTS & AWARDS: Received Emmy awards as Exec. Prod., "Watergate: The White House Transcripts", and Prod., "The World of Charlie Company"; Overseas Press Club award; Emmy for the three-part series "The U.S./Soviet Wheat Deal: Is There a Scandal? ('72).

PERSONAL: Married to the former Patricia Bannon, three children. Resides in New Rochelle, NY.

BENSON, HUGH
Prod.

222 North Canon Dr., Beverly Hills, CA 90069

b. September 7, 1917. New York, NY.

EDUCATION: University of Southern California.

CAREER HIGHLIGHTS: Asst. to Ed Sullivan and Marlo Lewis for four years, "The Ed Sullivan Show" ('47); Asst., Warner Bros. ('55); Prod., UA, *For Those Who Think Young* ('66); Prod., Cinema Center Films ('69–'71); Exec. Prod., TV Development, Screen Gems ('66); Exec. Prod., TV, "Nightmare Honeymoon," *Logan's Run*, MGM ('72); Prod. on Staff, Pilots and Long Form, Columbia Pictures TV ('75–'82). TV movies produced include: *Contract on Cherry Street, Child Stealers, Confessions of a Lady Cop, The Dream Merchants, The Blue and the Gray,* and *Shadow Riders.*

ACHIEVEMENTS & AWARDS: N.A.

PERSONAL: Son, Jeff.

BENTON, JOE
Correspondent, ABC, News

c/o ABC, 7 W. 66th St., New York, NY 10023
b. April 18, 1945.

EDUCATION: University of North Carolina, B.A.; American University, M.A., Broadcast Journalism ('73).
CAREER HIGHLIGHTS: Production Asst., WTOP-Radio and TV, Washington, DC ('71); Reporter, WJXT-TV, Jacksonville, FL ('73); Washington-based Correspondent for the Post-Newsweek Stations ('75); Correspondent, ABC News ('80).
ACHIEVEMENTS & AWARDS: N.A.
PERSONAL: Resides in Falls Church, VA, with his wife and their two children.

BERADINO, JOHN
Actor

c/o "General Hospital," ABC, 4151 Prospect Ave., Los Angeles, CA 90027
b. May 1. Los Angeles, CA.

EDUCATION: University of Southern California.
CAREER HIGHLIGHTS: Began career as a professional baseball player, first with St. Louis Browns and later with the Cleveland Indians. Turning to acting, Beradino landed roles in "The New Breed," "I Led Three Lives," and "The Untouchables" before finding a 20-year home as Dr. Steve Hardy on the hit soap opera "General Hospital" ('63). Had supporting parts in the TV movies *Do Not Fold, Spindle or Mutilate, Moon of the Wolf,* and *Don't Look Back.*
ACHIEVEMENTS & AWARDS: N.A.
PERSONAL: Resides in Beverly Hills, CA, with his wife, Marjorie; two children, Katherine and John.

BERG, ILENE AMY
Exec. Prod., Motion Pictures for TV, ABC, Entertainment, West Coast

c/o ABC, 4151 Prospect Ave., Los Angeles, CA 90027
b. September 9. New York, NY.

EDUCATION: University of Rochester, B.A., English.
CAREER HIGHLIGHTS: Production Asst., WABC-TV, New York for its "Eyewitness News" reports ('72); Writer/Assoc. Prod., ABC's "Good Night America" ('74); Line Prod., WNET-TV, New York, Membership Week; Prod., WCBS-TV, New York, on public affairs show "...With Jeanne Parr" ('76); Supervisor, Broadcast Publicity, ABC, New York ('77); Mgr., Broadcast Publicity, ABC, New York ('78); Program Exec., Current Comedy Series, ABC Entertainment, West Coast ('79); Exec. Prod., Motion Pictures for TV, ABC Entertainment, West Coast ('81).
ACHIEVEMENTS & AWARDS: N.A.
PERSONAL: Resides in Los Angeles.

BERGER, MARILYN
Correspondent, ABC, News

c/o ABC, 7 W. 66th St., New York, NY 10023
b. August 23.

EDUCATION: Cornell University, B.A., History and Government; Columbia University School of Journalism, M.A.
CAREER HIGHLIGHTS: Correspondent, *Newsday,* Long Island, NY ('65); Correspondent, *Washington Post,* Washington, DC ('70); Correspondent, NBC News, Washington, DC ('76); Moderator/Host/Editor on a variety of PBS programs ('78); Correspondent, ABC News, New York ('82).
ACHIEVEMENTS & AWARDS: N.A.
PERSONAL: Married to Don Hewitt, Exec. Prod., "60 Minutes."

BERGER, RICHARD L.
Pres., Walt Disney Productions (Subsidiary)

c/o Walt Disney Productions, 500 S. Buena Vista St., Burbank, CA 91521
b. October 25, 1939.

EDUCATION: University of California at Los Angeles.
CAREER HIGHLIGHTS: Started as an Accountant at Fox ('66); became Asst. to Pres. of 20th Century Fox TV and moved up to V.P. of Programs ('73). Left Fox briefly to work for CBS as V.P., Programming ('76), where he supervised the development of "The Incredible Hulk" and "Dallas." Returned to Fox as V.P., Domestic Production ('77), and was appointed V.P., Worldwide Production ('79). Promoted to Sr. V.P. ('80). Before leaving Fox, he was closely involved in the productions of the films *The Rose, Brubaker, The Final Conflict, Six Pack,* and *Porky's.*
ACHIEVEMENTS & AWARDS: N.A.
PERSONAL: N.A.

BERGER, RICK
Program Exec., Motion Pictures for TV, CBS, Entertainment, West Coast

c/o CBS, 7800 Beverly Blvd., Los Angeles, CA 90036
b. May 3.

EDUCATION: University of Southern California, B.A., Cinema and TV.
CAREER HIGHLIGHTS: Joined CBS through the CBS Management Training Program ('80); Mgr., Comedy Program Development ('81); Program Exec., Motion Pictures for TV, CBS Entertainment, West Coast ('82).
ACHIEVEMENTS & AWARDS: 1980 Rod Serling award.
PERSONAL: N.A.

BERGMAN, JULES
Science Editor, ABC, News

c/o ABC, 7 W. 66th St., New York, NY 10023
b. March 21.

EDUCATION: City College of New York; Indiana University; Columbia College; Columbia University Graduate School of Journalism ('60).
CAREER HIGHLIGHTS: Worked for *Time* ('49) and as Writer/Newscaster for WFDR, New York ('50). After becoming Asst. Dir. of News, he began specializing in science and joined ABC News as Writer ('52). He became the first full-time network Science Editor in the U.S. ('61). Bergman reports for "World News Tonight," "Good Morning America," "20/20," and ABC documentaries, and has covered all 30 manned spaceflights in the U.S. space program, as well as all space shuttle missions to date.
ACHIEVEMENTS & AWARDS: Emmy ('74) for narration and co-writing, "Closeup on Fire"; Aviation/Space Writers award ('76, '77). Member, Natl. Assn. of Science Writers; Aerospace Writers Assn.; American Institute of Aeronomics and Astronauts; Wings Club. Author of *90 Seconds to Space—The Story of the X-15* and the updated *Anyone Can Fly.*
PERSONAL: Resides in New York City.

BERGMANN, DOUGLASS
Assoc. Dir., Talent and Program Acquisitions, Business Affairs, CBS, Entertainment, West Coast

c/o CBS, 7800 Beverly Blvd., Los Angeles, CA 90036
b. January 21.

EDUCATION: Georgetown University School of Foreign Service, B.S.; Boston College, M.B.A., Finance; CBS School of Management.
CAREER HIGHLIGHTS: Intl. Banking Officer, Union Bank, Los Angeles ('75); Corporate Lending Officer, Irving Trust Co., New York and Los Angeles ('77); Asst. Dir., Planning, Business Affairs, CBS ('80); Talent and Program Negotiator, Business Affairs, CBS Entertainment ('81); Assoc. Dir., Talent and Program Acquisitions, Business Affairs, CBS Entertainment, West Coast ('82).
ACHIEVEMENTS & AWARDS: N.A.
PERSONAL: N.A.

BERK, ANN
V.P., Advertising, Promotion, and Publicity, NBC, TV Stations

c/o NBC, 30 Rockefeller Plaza, New York, NY 10020
b. March 19. New York, NY.

EDUCATION: Cornell University.
CAREER HIGHLIGHTS: Promotion Copywriter, NBC Radio ('66); Mgr., Advertising and Promotion, NBC Radio Network and the NBC Owned Radio Stations ('67); Mgr., Advertising and Promotion, WNBC-TV, New York ('69); Program Dir. and Dir., Broadcast Operations, WNBC-TV, New York ('75); Station Mgr., WNBC-TV, New York ('77); Station Mgr., WRC-TV, Washington, DC, ('79); V.P., Advertising, Promotion, and Publicity, NBC TV Stations ('83).
ACHIEVEMENTS & AWARDS: Outstanding creativity award at the U.S. TV Commercial Festival for promotion campaign introducing the two-hour "NewsCenter 4" ('71); Matrix award from the New York Women in Communications ('77). Author of the novel, *Fast Forward.*
PERSONAL: Daughter, Melinda.

BERKOWITZ, BOB
Correspondent, ABC, News

c/o ABC, 7 W. 66th St., New York, NY 10023
b. May 15, 1950. New York, NY.

EDUCATION: University of Denver, B.A., Psychology and Communications.
CAREER HIGHLIGHTS: Talk Show Host for both KGMC-AM (now KWBZ), Denver, and KGO-AM, San Francisco ('74); Political Correspondent, AP Radio, Washington, DC ('75); Correspondent, Cable News Network, Washington, DC ('80); Correspondent, ABC News ('82).
ACHIEVEMENTS & AWARDS: Overseas Press Club award ('77); medal of honor from the Freedom Foundation ('79).
PERSONAL: N.A.

BERLE, MILTON (Milton Berlinger)
Actor

c/o Sagebrush Enterprises, 151 El Camino Blvd., Beverly Hills, CA 90212
b. July 12, 1908. New York, NY.

EDUCATION: N.A.
CAREER HIGHLIGHTS: Mister TV, Berle did more to popularize the medium in its infancy than any other performer. No one has ever been funnier in comedy sketch material, and Uncle Miltie can still steal any show in which he appears. He starred in "Texaco Star Theater" ('48). Berle's TV dramatic roles include "Doyle Against the House," and he had comedy guest roles on "F Troop" and "Make Room for Granddaddy." For ABC TV he appeared in a variety series, "The Milton Berle Show." TV movies include *Evil Roy Slade* ('72) and *The Legend of Valentino* ('75). Films include *Let's Make Love* and *The Oscar.* Appeared on PBS's American Playhouse in *Family Business.*
ACHIEVEMENTS & AWARDS: Member of ASCAP who has written more than 300 songs. Special Emmy for lifetime achievement ('78); *Look* magazine *TV* award ('51).
PERSONAL: Wife, Ruth; daughter, Vicki; son, Billy.

BERMAN, CHRIS
Sports Anchor, ESPN

c/o ESPN, ESPN Plaza, Bristol, CT 06010
b. May 10, 1955. New York, NY.

EDUCATION: Brown University, B.A., History ('77).
CAREER HIGHLIGHTS: General Announcer, WERI-AM-FM ('77); Sports Talk Show Host, WNVR-AM, Waterbury, CT ('78); Weekend Sports Anchor, WVIT-TV, Hartford, CT ('79);

joined ESPN as Anchor, Sportscenter and Weekly NFL Show ('79).
ACHIEVEMENTS & AWARDS: N.A.
PERSONAL: Resides in Naugatuck, CT.

BERMAN, STEVE
Dir., Comedy Program Development, CBS, Entertainment

c/o CBS, 7800 Beverly Blvd., Los Angeles, CA 90036
b. March 22.

EDUCATION: Ohio University, B.A., Playwriting; Annenberg School of Communications, University of Southern California, M.A. Communications Management
CAREER HIGHLIGHTS: Paul Shulman Co.; Columbia Studios; Paramount Pictures; ABC TV; Program Exec., CBS ('78); Mgr., Comedy Program Development, CBS Entertainment ('81); Dir., Comedy Program Development, CBS Entertainment ('82).
ACHIEVEMENTS & AWARDS: N.A.
PERSONAL: N.A.

BERNARD, RON
V.P., Showtime Entertainment, Finance and Administration

c/o Showtime, 1633 Broadway, New York, NY 10019
b. February 26, 1943. New York, NY.

EDUCATION: Syracuse University, B.S.; Columbia University, M.B.A.
CAREER HIGHLIGHTS: Treasurer, Viacom Intl. ('78); V.P., Finance and Administration, Showtime Entertainment ('80).
ACHIEVEMENTS & AWARDS: N.A.
PERSONAL: N.A.

BERNAU, CHRISTOPHER
Actor

c/o "The Guiding Light," CBS, 51 W. 52d St., New York, NY 10019
b. June 2, 1940. Santa Barbara, CA.

EDUCATION: University of California.
CAREER HIGHLIGHTS: A hard-working stage actor, Bernau landed his first daytime TV role as Philip Todd in the gothic soap opera "Dark Shadows." He joined the cast of "The Guiding Light" ('77) and developed a popular and central character as the womanizing cad Alan Spaulding.
ACHIEVEMENTS & AWARDS: N.A.
PERSONAL: Resides in New York City.

BERNSTEIN, CARL
Prod., Principal Correspondent, ABC, Special Reporting Projects

c/o ABC, 1717 DeSales St., N.W., Washington, DC 20036
b. February 14, 1944.

EDUCATION: University of Maryland.
CAREER HIGHLIGHTS: Before joining the *Washington Post* ('66), Bernstein was a reporter for the *Elizabeth Journal* in New Jersey. He joined ABC News as the Washington, DC Bureau Chief ('80). His reporting of the Watergate scandal with his colleague, Bob Woodward, first uncovered the White House connection to the break-in of the Democratic Natl. Committee headquarters at the Watergate complex ('72) during the presidential campaign. Their pursuit of the events surrounding the break-in and the subsequent White House cover-up led to the first resignation of an American president and the indictment of his

top aides. The two reporters detailed their investigative efforts in *All the President's Men*, which became a national best-seller and was the basis for a movie of the same name. That book was followed by a second best-seller, *The Final Days*, which chronicled the end of the Nixon administration. He is now Washington Correspondent for Special Reporting Projects, ABC ('82).

ACHIEVEMENTS & AWARDS: Pulitzer Prize, *Washington Post* ('72); George Polk memorial award.

PERSONAL: Resides in northwest Washington, DC.

BERNSTEIN, INA
V.P. Casting, Motion Pictures, ABC, Entertainment

c/o ABC, 4151 Prospect Ave., Los Angeles, CA 90027
b. July 16.

EDUCATION: New York University, B.A. and M.A., Motion Picture Production.

CAREER HIGHLIGHTS: Sr. Agent, MCA; Sr. Agent, Ashley Steiner Agency; Sr. Agent, Ashley Famous Agency; V.P., Talent and TV Packaging, IFA; V.P., Talent and TV Packaging, ICM ('74); V.P., Casting, Motion Pictures, ABC Entertainment ('80).

ACHIEVEMENTS & AWARDS: N.A.

PERSONAL: Resides in Beverly Hills, CA, with husband Jules Sharr.

BERNTSEN, GEORGE J.
V.P., Feature Films and Late Night Programming, CBS, Entertainment

c/o CBS, 6121 Sunset Blvd., Los Angeles, CA 90028
b. March 22, 1933. Brooklyn, NY.

EDUCATION: St. Francis College, B.B.A., Management.

CAREER HIGHLIGHTS: Has spent entire career with CBS. Began as Accounting Supervisor, Network Billing ('55); Mgr., Business Affairs, Special Projects ('70); Program Dept., Dir., Feature Films ('77); promoted to V.P., Feature Films and Late Night Programming ('81).

ACHIEVEMENTS & AWARDS: N.A.

PERSONAL: Parents are George and Margaret Berntsen, of Brooklyn, NY.

BERRESFORD, THOMAS E.
Treasurer, NBC, Inc., West Coast

c/o NBC, 3000 W. Alameda Ave., Burbank, CA 91523
b. December 22, 1938. Beaver, PA.

EDUCATION: University of Arizona, B.S., Business Administration.

CAREER HIGHLIGHTS: Began career at NBC, Inc. as Regional Mgr., Station Relations; promoted to Dir., Treasury Operations and Financial Planning ('80) and Treasurer, West Coast ('82).

ACHIEVEMENTS & AWARDS: Member, Motion Picture and TV Controllers Assn. ('80–'82).

PERSONAL: N.A.

BERRY, JIM
Reporter, Weekend News Anchor, WJLA-TV, Washington, DC, News

c/o WJLA-TV, 4461 Connecticut Ave., N.W., Washington, DC 20008
b. December, 1955. Chicago, IL.

EDUCATION: Northwestern University School of Journalism.
CAREER HIGHLIGHTS: News and Sports Reporter, WEAW-AM, WNUR-FM, Evanston, IL ('77); Prod. and Weekend News Anchor, WBTV-TV, Charlotte, NC ('78); General Assignment Reporter and Weekend News Anchor ('81).
ACHIEVEMENTS & AWARDS: N.A.
PERSONAL: N.A.

BERRY, PAUL
Reporter/Anchor/Host, WJLA-TV, Washington, DC, News

c/o WJLA-TV, 4461 Connecticut Ave., N.W., Washington, DC 20008
b. February 15, 1944. Detroit, MI.

EDUCATION: Broadcast Training Program, Armed Forces Radio and TV Services.
CAREER HIGHLIGHTS: Reporter/Anchor, WXYZ-TV, Detroit; Reporter, WJLA-TV, Washington, DC ('72); instituted WJLA-TV News 7 program, "Crimesolvers," "Seven on Your Side (SOS)" ('79).
ACHIEVEMENTS & AWARDS: Honored with the mayor's award, Chesapeake AP Broadcasters award, Metropolitan Washington mass media award; NATAS Washington Chapter community service award, for "Seven on Your Side" ('82); Ted Yates award ('82).
PERSONAL: N.A.

BERRY, KEN
Actor

c/o "Mama's Family," NBC, 3000 W. Alameda Ave., Burbank, CA 91523
b. November 3. Moline, IL.

EDUCATION: N.A.
CAREER HIGHLIGHTS: Guest roles on the series "Oh, Susannah," "The Dick Van Dyke Show," "The Carol Burnett Show," and "Dr. Kildare." Star of TV's "F Troop" and "Mayberry, RFD." Co-star of the series "Mama's Family."
ACHIEVEMENTS & AWARDS: N.A.
PERSONAL: Children, John and Jennifer. Resides in North Hollywood, CA.

BERTINELLI, VALERIE
Actress

c/o "One Day at a Time," CBS, 7800 Beverly Blvd., Los Angeles, CA 90036
b. April 23, 1960. Wilmington, DE.

EDUCATION: N.A.
CAREER HIGHLIGHTS: Wanted to become an actress at an early age and managed to land a few parts in commercials before answering a "cattle call" audition for Norman Lear's "One Day at a Time" ('75). Since then, Bertinelli has honed her craft, blossoming into a talented actress. Other TV credits include a "CBS Festival of Lively Arts for Young People" presentation, "The Magic of David Copperfield," and the TV movies *Young Love, First Love, The Promise of Love, The Princess and the Cabbie,* and *I Was a Mail Order Bride.*
ACHIEVEMENTS & AWARDS: Golden Globe award for best supporting actress in a TV series for "One Day at a Time" ('81).
PERSONAL: Resides in Los Angeles with husband, Eddie Van Halen, guitarist for the rock group Van Halen.

BESCH, ANDREW F.
Dir. of Marketing, USA Network

c/o USA Network, 1271 Ave. of the Americas, New York, NY 10020
b. December 9, 1947.

EDUCATION: Bates College, B.A.
CAREER HIGHLIGHTS: Branch Mgr. and Eastern Sales Rep. for Paramount Pictures Corp.; V.P. and East Coast Sales Mgr., Heritage Enterprises; V.P., Sales and Exec. Prod., Finley Communications. Dir. of Marketing, USA Cable Network ('83).
ACHIEVEMENTS & AWARDS: N.A.
PERSONAL: N.A.

BETZ, PAT
V.P., Story Dept., NBC, Entertainment, West Coast

c/o NBC, 3000 W. Alameda Ave., Burbank, CA 91523
b. Chicago, IL.

EDUCATION: University of Iowa.
CAREER HIGHLIGHTS: Production Planning Dept., MGM Studios; Script Supervisor, MGM Studios; Asst. Dir., MGM; Dir., MGM; moved to RKO and Universal, working on more than 70 feature films; joined NBC as Program Mgr., West Coast ('60); Exec. Prod., CBS ('68); Mgr., Film Program Operations, NBC ('71); Dir., Film Programs, NBC ('75); V.P., Film Programs, NBC ('75); V.P., Current Dramatic Programs, NBC ('77); V.P., Story Dept., NBC Entertainment, West Coast ('78).
ACHIEVEMENTS & AWARDS: N.A.
PERSONAL: Resides in Valencia, CA, with his wife.

BEUTEL, BILL
Anchor, WABC-TV, New York, NY, News

c/o WABC-TV, 7 Lincoln Sq., New York, NY 10023
b. December 12. Cleveland, OH.

EDUCATION: Dartmouth College; Case Western Reserve University; New York University; University of Michigan Law School.
CAREER HIGHLIGHTS: Began at WGAR-AM, Cleveland; moving on to WEWS-TV, Cleveland; joined WCBS-AM, New York ('60); named News Anchor, WABC-TV, New York ('62); Bureau Chief, ABC News, London ('68); prepared ABC documentary, "The Eye of the Storm" ('70); rejoined WABC-TV as Anchor, "Eyewitness News" ('70); worked concurrently as a Commentator, ABC Entertainment Radio Network ('70–'76).
ACHIEVEMENTS & AWARDS: Peabody award for "The Eye of the Storm" ('70)
PERSONAL: Resides in New York City, four children.

BIAS, FRANK
V.P., Science and Technology, Viacom Intl.

c/o Viacom Intl., 1211 Ave. of the Americas, New York, NY 10036
b. October 1, 1919. Des Moines, IA.

EDUCATION: Iowa State University, B.S., Electrical Engineering.
CAREER HIGHLIGHTS: Maintained various engineering positions with General Electric ('41-'69); Assoc. Dir., Cable Technology, CBS TV ('69); V.P., Engineering, Viacom Communications ('70); V.P., Science and Technology, Viacom Intl. ('79).
ACHIEVEMENTS & AWARDS: Member, NCTA, SCTE.
PERSONAL: Resides in Ossining, NY. Wife, Jean; daughters, Carolyn and Elaine.

BIERBAUER, CHARLES J.
Defense Correspondent, Cable News Network

c/o Cable News Network, 2133 Wisconsin Ave., N.W., Washington, DC 20007
b. July 22, 1942. Allentown, PA.

EDUCATION: Pennsylvania State University, B.A., Russian, and B.A. and M.A., Journalism.
CAREER HIGHLIGHTS: East European Correspondent, Group W News, Vienna ('69); Bonn Bureau Chief, Group W News, Bonn, ('70); Foreign Editor, Group W News, London ('74); Reporter, KYW-TV, Philadelphia

('76); ABC Moscow Bureau Chief and Correspondent ('78); ABC Bonn Bureau Chief and Correspondent ('80) Defense Correspondent, Cable Network News ('81).

ACHIEVEMENTS & AWARDS: Shared Overseas Press Club award to Group W correspondents for coverage of Mideast War ('73). Alumni Fellow, Pennsylvania State University ('80).

PERSONAL: Resides in Potomac, MD, three children, Alec, Kari, and Craig.

BILLOCK, JOHN
V.P., Marketing, HBO

c/o HBO, 1271 Ave. of the Americas, New York, NY 10020

b. August 25, 1948.

EDUCATION: Wesleyan University, B.A., English and Religion; Boston University, M.B.A., Finance and Marketing.

CAREER HIGHLIGHTS: Product Mgr., Colgate-Palmolive Co., New York ('75); Marketing Mgr., HBO ('78); Mgr., New Market Development ('79); Dir., Marketing ('79); V.P., Marketing, HBO ('82).

ACHIEVEMENTS & AWARDS: Member, Cable TV Administration and Marketing Society.

PERSONAL: Resides in Scarsdale, NY, with wife, Ann, and two sons.

BINDER, STEVE
Dir., Binder Productions

c/o Binder Productions, 666 N. Robertson Ave., Los Angeles, CA 90069

b. December 12, 1942. Los Angeles, CA.

EDUCATION: University of Southern California, B.A.

CAREER HIGHLIGHTS: Prod., "The Mac Davis Show" ('75); Prod., "The Barry Manilow Show" ('76); Prod., "The Shields and Yarnell Show" ('77); Dir., "TAMI ('78); Dir., "Give 'Em Hell, Harry" ('79); Dir., "The Star Wars Holiday Special" ('80); Prod., "Stanley" ('81); Prod., "An Innocent Love" ('81); Prod., "Diana Ross Special" ('81); Dir., "Debby Boone's One Step Closer" ('82); Dir., "Jane Fonda's Celebrity Comedy Fashion Show" ('82); Dir., "The Emmy Awards" ('82).

ACHIEVEMENTS & AWARDS: Emmy for "The Barry Manilow Show" ('76).

PERSONAL: Resides in Beverly Hills, CA.

BIONDI, FRANK J., JR.
Pres., HBO

c/o HBO, 1271 Ave. of the Americas, New York, NY 10020

b. January 9, 1945. Livingston, NJ.

EDUCATION: Princeton University, B.A.; Harvard University Business School, M.B.A.

CAREER HIGHLIGHTS: Founded and was principal of a financial consulting firm. Dir. of Business Analysis, Teleprompter Corp. ('73); Asst. Treasurer and Assoc. Dir. of Business Affairs, Children's Television Workshop ('74); joined HBO as Dir. of Entertainment Program Planning ('78); then became V.P., Programming Operations ('79); appointed Exec. V.P., Planning Administration ('82); Pres., HBO ('83). Under his leadership, HBO has joined forces with Metromedia Inc. for a distribution and film–financing partnership, beginning in 1983.

ACHIEVEMENTS & AWARDS: N.A.

PERSONAL: N.A.

BIRNEY, DAVID
Actor

c/o ICM, 8899 Beverly Blvd., Los Angeles, CA
90048
b. April 23, 1944. Washington, DC

EDUCATION: Dartmouth College, B.A.; University of California at Los Angeles, M.A.
CAREER HIGHLIGHTS: Lead roles with the American Shakespeare Festival, the Lincoln Center Repertory Theater, the New York Shakespeare Festival, and the Mark Taper Forum. He had roles in stage productions ranging from the classics *Romeo and Juliet, Hamlet,* and *Richard II* to the musical comedies *Guys and Dolls, Camelot,* and *My Fair Lady.* He starred ('71–'72) in the series "Bridget Loves Bernie," during which he met his future wife, actress Meredith Baxter Birney. Later, he had the title role in the series "Serpico" ('76) and starred in such mini-series as "The Adams Chronicles," "Testimony of Two Men," and "Jacqueline Susann's Valley of the Dolls," and the TV movies *The Five of Me, Ohms,* and *High Midnight.* His feature films include *Oh God, Book II* and *Trial by Combat.* He appeared in the TV drama "St. Elsewhere."
ACHIEVEMENTS & AWARDS: N.A.
PERSONAL: Wife, actress Meredith Baxter Birney; children, Teddy, Eva, and Kate. Resides in Santa Monica, CA.

BISSONETTE, PAUL A.
V.P., Turner Broadcasting System,
  Advertising and Promotion

c/o Turner Broadcasting System, 1050
  Techwood Dr., N.W., Atlanta, GA 30318
b. April 24, 1947. Buffalo, NY.

EDUCATION: Canisius College, B.A., English; Syracuse University, M.A., Journalism.
CAREER HIGHLIGHTS: Mgr., WUTV ('71); Promotion Mgr., WGR-TV ('72); Creative Services Dir., KYW-TV ('73); Dir., Communications and Advertising, WCBS-TV ('76); Promotion Dir., News, CBS, Inc. ('78); V.P., Advertising and Promotion, Turner Broadcasting System ('81).
ACHIEVEMENTS & AWARDS: N.A.
PERSONAL: Wife, Larissa; daughter, Maya; son, Bo.

BIVKINS, DAVID K.
V.P., Finance and Administration, NBC TV

c/o NBC, 30 Rockefeller Plaza, New York, NY
10020
b. September 10. Oklahoma.

EDUCATION: Massachusetts Institute of Technology, B.S., Mathematics ('64), M.S., Civil Engineering and Ph.D., Operations Research ('69).
CAREER HIGHLIGHTS: Developer, Resource Allocations Models for industrial clients, Abt Associates, Inc., Cambridge, MA ('69); Production Planner, Mathematica, Princeton, NJ ('70); Systems Analyst, NBC, New York ('71); Mgr., Special Financial Projects, NBC ('73); Mgr., Nighttime Pricing and Financial Evaluation, NBC ('73); Dir., Pricing and Financial Evaluation, NBC ('75); Dir., Business Administration, NBC ('76); Dir., Financial Forecasting and Administration, NBC TV ('79); V.P., Finance and Administration, NBC TV ('83).
ACHIEVEMENTS & AWARDS: N.A.
PERSONAL: Resides in Princeton Junction, NJ, with his wife, Bonnie, and their two children, David Jr. and Laura.

BIXBY, BILL
Actor

c/o "Goodnight, Beantown," 7800 Beverly
  Blvd., Los Angeles, CA 90036
b. January 22, 1934.

EDUCATION: San Francisco City College; University of California at Berkeley.

CAREER HIGHLIGHTS: Beginning as a talented juvenile in "My Favorite Martian," Bixby made television magic as "The Magician" and then returned as one of the most colorful heroes of the seventies in "The Incredible Hulk." His motion picture credits include *Lonely Are the Brave, Irma La Douce,* and *Under the Yum Yum Tree.* After co-starring in "My Favorite Martian" ('63–'66) he starred in "The Courtship of Eddie's Father" for three years. He also starred in "Steambath" and hosted the children's show "Once Upon a Classic" on public TV, and returned to series TV in "Goodnight, Beantown."

ACHIEVEMENTS & AWARDS: Emmy nomination and Directors Guild nomination for *Rich Man, Poor Man.*

PERSONAL: N.A.

BLACK, MAXENE
Correspondent, WABC-TV, Eyewitness News

c/o WABC-TV, 7 Lincoln Sq., New York, NY 10023
b. Rye, NY.

EDUCATION: Boston Emerson College, B.A., Communications.

CAREER HIGHLIGHTS: General Assignment Reporter and Anchor, WKRC-TV and WDTN-TV, Ohio ('78); General Assignment Reporter, WCAU-TV; Correspondent and Interviewer, WABC-TV.

ACHIEVEMENTS & AWARDS: AP award.

PERSONAL: Resides in Glenville, CT.

BLACKBURN, DAN
Correspondent, NBC News

c/o NBC, 3000 W. Alameda Blvd., Los Angeles, CA 91523
b. November 6. Xenia, OH.

EDUCATION: Purdue University, B.S., Political Science ('61).

CAREER HIGHLIGHTS: Reporter and Editor, WNEW Radio, New York; WBBM/CBS Radio, Chicago; WOWO Radio, Fort Wayne, IN, and other radio and TV stations in Indiana, Illinois, and Iowa. Joined Metromedia News, Washington, DC ('65–'70); Political Reporter and Anchor, KNX/CBS News, Los Angeles

('71); NBC News TV-Radio Correspondent based in Los Angeles ('75).

ACHIEVEMENTS & AWARDS: Golden mike award of the Southern California Broadcasters and grand award of the Los Angeles Press Club ('75) for spot news coverage.

PERSONAL: N.A.

BLACKMORE, ROBERT
V.P., NBC TV Network, Sales

c/o NBC, 30 Rockefeller Plaza, New York, NY 10020
b. April 9.

EDUCATION: University of Southern California.

CAREER HIGHLIGHTS: Acct. Exec., KFEL, Denver, and Angeles advertising agency; Sales Supervisor, NBC Films; Network Acct. Exec., NBC; NBC Dir., Participating Program Sales ('70); V.P., Eastern Sales ('73); V.P., Sales, NBC TV Network ('75).

ACHIEVEMENTS & AWARDS: Member, IRTS; Board of Dir., Sales Executives Club of New York.

PERSONAL: Wife, Joan; children, Robin and Karyn.

BLACKSTONE, JOHN
Correspondent, CBS, News

c/o CBS, 68 Knightsbridge, London, England SW1
b. Toronto, Ontario, Canada.

EDUCATION: York University; Carleton University School of Journalism.

CAREER HIGHLIGHTS: Newswriter, CFRA Radio in Ottawa, Canada ('71); Reporter, *Ottawa Citizen* ('72); Reporter, CBOT-TV, Ottawa ('73); Writer/Editor/Reporter, CBC ('74); Reporter, CBS News, London ('80); Corespondent, CBS News, London ('82).

ACHIEVEMENTS & AWARDS: N.A.

PERSONAL: N.A.

BLACKWOOD, NINA
Video Jockey, Warner Amex Satellite Entertainment Co., MTV: Music Television

c/o MTV, Warner Amex, 1211 Ave. of the Americas, New York, NY 10036
b. September 12. Cleveland, OH.

EDUCATION: Lee Strasberg Institute.
CAREER HIGHLIGHTS: Began as an actress with roles in feature films such as *One From the Heart* and *Vice Squad.* Served as moderator of the syndicated radio series "Woman to Woman" and performed promotional duties for WMMS Radio, Cleveland. Serves as MTV's late night/early morning video jockey ('81).
ACHIEVEMENTS & AWARDS: N.A.
PERSONAL: Resides in New York City.

BLACQUE, TAUREAN
Actor

c/o "Hill Street Blues," 3000 W. Alameda Ave., Burbank, CA 91523
b. May 10. Newark, NJ.

EDUCATION: American Musical and Dramatic Academy.
CAREER HIGHLIGHTS: TV guest spots on "Kaz," "Paris," "The White Shadow," "Taxi," and "Good Times." Motion pictures include *House Calls* and *Rocky II.* Series regular as Detective Neal Washington on "Hill Street Blues."
ACHIEVEMENTS & AWARDS: N.A.
PERSONAL: Sons, Shelby and Rodney.

BLAKE, CHARLES
Dir. of Design, NBC

c/o NBC, 30 Rockefeller Plaza, New York, NY 10020
b. December 24, 1941.

EDUCATION: State University of New York at Farmingdale.
CAREER HIGHLIGHTS: Art Dir., Ted Barash advertising agency ('69); Art Dir., Avon Products ('70); Sr. Designer, NBC ('75); Mgr., TV Network Marketing Design, NBC ('76); Dir. of Design, NBC ('80); V.P., Print and Design, NBC TV ('81); Dir. of Design, NBC ('83).
ACHIEVEMENTS & AWARDS: N.A.
PERSONAL: Resides in New York City with wife, Sandra; daughter, Gabrielle; and son, Gavin.

BLAKE, ROBERT
Actor

c/o Operation Prime Time/20th Century Fox TV, 10201 W. Pico Blvd., Los Angeles, CA 90064
b. September 18, 1933. Nutley, NJ.

EDUCATION: N.A.
CAREER HIGHLIGHTS: Once one of the Little Rascals, Blake brought a lifetime of acting experience to "Baretta" and made a run-of-the-mill character seem unhackneyed and fresh. Worked as a Hollywood stuntman before becoming a full-fledged actor in movies and television. Motion pictures include *Town Without Pity, PT-109, In Cold Blood, Busting,* and, for TV, *Blood Feud* ('83).
ACHIEVEMENTS & AWARDS: N.A.
PERSONAL: Divorced.

BLAKEMORE, BILL
Bureau Chief, ABC News, Rome

c/o ABC, 1330 Ave. of the Americas, New York, NY 10019
b. Chicago, IL.

EDUCATION: Wesleyan University.
CAREER HIGHLIGHTS: Since he was named ABC News Bureau Chief ('80), he has traveled extensively with Pope John Paul II to Poland,

Mexico, Ireland, the U.S., Africa, France, and other countries. Before his Rome assignment, he was an ABC News Correspondent assigned to Beirut and then to London. Joined ABC News ('70) as a Sound Technician in Beirut.

ACHIEVEMENTS & AWARDS: Two Overseas Press Club awards for coverage of Cyprus and Lebanon.

PERSONAL: N.A.

BLANC, MEL
Voice Specialist

c/o Warner Bros. TV, 4000 Warner Blvd., Burbank, CA 91505
b. May 30, 1908. San Francisco, CA.

EDUCATION: Lincoln High School (Portland, OR).

CAREER HIGHLIGHTS: A brilliant master of voices who has been entertaining children and adults alike with voice portrayals in Warner Bros. and Hanna-Barbera cartoons. He started as a freelance musician in the twenties and trained his incredible vocal cords to spout a variety of noises and dialects. Blanc is sole voice for Warner Bros. Looney Tunes cartoons, which feature Bugs Bunny, Daffy Duck, Porky Pig, Elmer Fudd, Sylvester, Tweetie Pie, Foghorn Leghorn, Pepe LePew, Speedy Gonzalez, and many others. In the long-running Hanna-Barbera favorite, "The Flintstones," Blanc worked as the voice of Barney Rubble.

ACHIEVEMENTS & AWARDS: N.A.
PERSONAL: N.A.

BLANCHARD, BOB
Consumer Reporter, WABC-TV, Eyewitness News

c/o WABC-TV, 7 Lincoln Sq., New York, NY 10023
b. March 18.

EDUCATION: University of Rhode Island, Journalism.

CAREER HIGHLIGHTS: General Assignment Reporter, WPRI-TV, Providence, RI; Consumer Reporter, WPRI-TV, Providence ('79).

ACHIEVEMENTS & AWARDS: AP award as best New England feature reporter ('81); ASPCA Man of the Year.

PERSONAL: Resides in New York City.

BLANK, BEN
Dir., ABC, News Graphics

c/o ABC, 7 W. 66th Street, New York, NY 10023
b. November 26, 1921. San Francisco, CA.

EDUCATION: Cooper Union.

CAREER HIGHLIGHTS: Graphics Dir., CBS News, working on "Evening News With Doug Edwards," "Evening News With Walter Cronkite," special events including spaceflights, elections, conventions ('50–'62); moved to ABC News to work on "Evening News," "20/20," "World News Tonight," "Closeup," special events, conventions and elections ('82).

ACHIEVEMENTS & AWARDS: Originated generic news graphics, was the first to use courtroom artists, and pioneered in the use of special effects and simulation for spaceflight coverage. Has won various Clio awards.

PERSONAL: Wife, Miki; children, Edward, Karen, and Jody.

BLANK, MATTHEW
V.P., Marketing, Cinemax, and Market Development, HBO

c/o HBO, 1271 Ave. of the Americas, New York, NY 10020
b. July 10, 1950.

EDUCATION: Wharton Business School, B.S., Finance; Baruch College, M.B.A., Marketing.

CAREER HIGHLIGHTS: Sales Analyst, Philip Morris ('72); Asst. Product Mgr., Philip Morris ('74); Product Mgr., American Express Co., New York ('75); Affiliate Marketing Mgr., HBO ('76); Asst. Dir., Marketing, HBO ('78); Dir., Creative Services and Communications, HBO ('79); Dir., Cinemax Marketing, HBO ('80); V.P., Marketing, Cinemax, and Market Development, HBO ('82).

ACHIEVEMENTS & AWARDS: N.A.

PERSONAL: Resides in New York City with wife, Susan.

BLAUG, GEORGE
V.P., Dir., MGM-UA TV Distribution, Intl. Operations

c/o MGM-UA TV, 1350 Ave. of the Americas, New York, NY 10019
b. December 26, 1925. The Hague, Holland.

EDUCATION: New York University.
CAREER HIGHLIGHTS: Asst. Mgr., Columbia Pictures, Holland ('54); European Sales Mgr., Screen Gems ('58); V.P., European Sales, Columbia Pictures TV, London ('68); V.P., Dir. of Intl. Operations, Columbia Pictures TV, Los Angeles ('78); V.P., Dir. of Intl. Operations, UA TV Intl., New York ('81); V.P., Dir. of Intl. Operations, MGM-UA TV Distribution, New York ('82).
ACHIEVEMENTS & AWARDS: N.A.
PERSONAL: N.A.

BLESSINGTON, JOHN
V.P., Personnel, CBS, Broadcast Group

c/o CBS, 51 W. 52d St., New York, NY 10019
b. March 29, 1933.

EDUCATION: St. Mary's University, B.A.; Fairfield University, M.A.
CAREER HIGHLIGHTS: Dir., Educational Relations, CBS TV ('79); V.P., Educational and Community Services, CBS Broadcast Group ('81); V.P., Personnel, CBS Broadcast Group ('82).
ACHIEVEMENTS & AWARDS: Honorary doctorates from St. John's University and Elizabethtown College.
PERSONAL: N.A.

BLINN, WILLIAM
Writer/Prod.

c/o NBC, 30 Rockefeller Plaza, New York, NY 10020
b. N.A.

EDUCATION: N.A.
CAREER HIGHLIGHTS: Writer, the TV movie *Brian's Song*; Co-Prod., "The Rookies"; Exec. Prod., NBC's "Fame" ('81).
ACHIEVEMENTS & AWARDS: Emmy for outstanding writing for *Brian's Song* ('71).
PERSONAL: N.A.

BLOCK, CURT
V.P., NBC, Press, East Coast

c/o NBC, 30 Rockefeller Plaza, New York, NY 10020
b. June 27, 1938. New York, NY.

EDUCATION: Hofstra College, B.A., Psychology.
CAREER HIGHLIGHTS: Sports Writer, UPI ('63); Sports Publicist, ABC ('67); Sr. Sports Editor, NBC ('69); Administrator, Business and Trade Publicity, NBC ('70); Mgr., Program and Trade Publicity ('75); Dir., Program and Trade Publicity ('76); Dir., Press and Publicity ('77); V.P., Press, East Coast ('81).
ACHIEVEMENTS & AWARDS: N.A.
PERSONAL: Resides in Manalapan, NJ, with wife, Barbara; children, Brian and Jennifer.

BLOCK, WILLARD
Pres., Viacom World Wide Ltd.

c/o Viacom, 1211 Ave. of the Americas, New York, NY 10036
b. March 18, 1930. Brooklyn, NY.

EDUCATION: Columbia College.
CAREER HIGHLIGHTS: Intl. Sales Dir., CBS Enterprises ('60); V.P., Intl. Sales, CBS ('67); Pres., Viacom Enterprises ('71); V.P., Intl. MCA TV ('74); V.P. and General Mgr., Taft, H-B Intl. ('76); concurrently started Willard Block Ltd. ('76); Pres., Viacom Enterprises ('79); Pres., Viacom World Wide Ltd. ('82).
ACHIEVEMENTS & AWARDS: N.A.
PERSONAL: Resides in Hewlett, NY. Wife Roberta; daughters, Deborah and Leslie; son, Andrew.

BLOOM, HERB
Deputy Bureau Chief, Satellite News Channel, Washington, DC, Bureau

c/o Satellite News Channels, 41 Harbor Plaza Dr., P.O. Box 10210, Stamford, CT 06904
b. September 14, 1941.

EDUCATION: Yale University, M.A.
CAREER HIGHLIGHTS: Assoc. Prod., "The David Susskind Show" ('66); Public Affairs Prod./News Editor, WABC-TV New York ('65); and Public Affairs Prod., WGBH-TV, Boston ('63). Named Deputy Bureau Chief for Satellite News Channel Washington, DC, Bureau ('82).
ACHIEVEMENTS & AWARDS: N.A.
PERSONAL: N.A.

BLOOMBERG, STUART JAMES
V.P., ABC Entertainment, Comedy and Variety Series Development

c/o ABC, 2040 Ave. of the Stars, Los Angeles, CA 90067
b. July 20, 1949. Youngstown, OH.

EDUCATION: Georgetown University, B.A.; University of Southern California, M.A.
CAREER HIGHLIGHTS: Segment Prod., NBC's 50th anniversary show ('75); Staff Writer, "Cos," Bill Cosby series, ABC ('76); Writer, "TV: The Fabulous '50's," NBC ('77); Writer, ABC's silver anniversary show ('77); Dir., Variety Series, Specials and Late Night, ABC ('79); V.P., Variety Series, Specials and Late Night Programming, ABC ('80); V.P., Comedy and Variety Series Development, ABC ('82).
ACHIEVEMENTS & AWARDS: N.A.
PERSONAL: Wife, Mary Farrell; children, Lily Bloomberg, Kate and Sarah Farrell.

BLYSTONE, RICHARD M.
Correspondent, Cable News Network, London Bureau

c/o Cable News Network, 31 Foley St., London W1, England
b. October 5, 1936. Elmira, NY.

EDUCATION: Amherst College; Rutgers University.

CAREER HIGHLIGHTS: Correspondent for AP in Atlanta, New York, Saigon, Bangkok, and London ('65); named Chief London Correspondent, Cable News Network ('80).
ACHIEVEMENTS & AWARDS: Edward R. Murrow Fellow, Council on Foreign Relations, New York ('77, '78)
PERSONAL: Wife, Helle; children, John, Julia, and Daniel.

BLYTON, JOHN
Chief Exec., RKO-Nederlander, Intl. Division, London

c/o RKO-Nederlander, 1440 Broadway, New York, NY 10018
b. September 8, 1933.

EDUCATION: Hounslow College.
CAREER HIGHLIGHTS: Controller of Program Management, London Weekend TV; appointed Chief Exec. of the Intl. Division, RKO-Nederlander, London ('83).
ACHIEVEMENTS & AWARDS: N.A.
PERSONAL: N.A.

BOCHCO, STEVEN
Writer/Prod.

c/o NBC, 3000 W. Alameda Ave., Burbank, CA 91523
b. December 16, 1943.

EDUCATION: Carnegie Tech.
CAREER HIGHLIGHTS: After years of success with conventional cops and robbers shows, Bochco became tired of walking that beat, and he co-created the original and influential police series "Hill Street Blues." Co-Writer, pilot for "Six Million Dollar Man"; Prod., "Delvecchio" and "Paris"; Co-Creator and Exec. Prod., "Hill Street Blues." Writer/Prod., of NBC's "Bay City Blues" ('83).
ACHIEVEMENTS & AWARDS: Emmy awards for writing and producing "Hill Street Blues."
PERSONAL: Married to "Hill Street Blues" star Barbara Bosson.

BODE, KEN
News Correspondent, NBC

c/o NBC, 2000 Merchandise Mart, Chicago, IL
60654
b. March 30. Chicago, IL.

EDUCATION: University of South Dakota, B.A.
('61); University of North Carolina, M.A. ('63)
and Ph.D. ('65).
CAREER HIGHLIGHTS: Research Dir., Commission on Party Structure and Delegate Section,
Natl. Democratic Party ('69); Dir., Center for
Political Reform; Dir., Project on Presidential
Nominations, 20th Century Fund Task Force
('72); Political Editor, *New Republic* ('75);
joined NBC News as News Correspondent
('79)
ACHIEVEMENTS & AWARDS: Articles published
in the *Journal of Politics, American University
Law Review,* the *N.Y. Times, New Republic, Pol-
itics Today,* and *Playboy.*
PERSONAL: Wife, Margo; children, Matilda and
Josephine.

BOGGS, BILL
Host, WNEW-TV, "Midday"

c/o WNEW-TV, Metromedia, 205 E. 67th St.,
New York, NY 10021
b. July 11. Philadelphia, PA.

EDUCATION: University of Pennsylvania, B.A.,
M.A.
CAREER HIGHLIGHTS: Started as a Public Relations Writer for the Armstrong Cork Co.,
then managed and produced the comedy
team of Tom Patchett and Jay Tarses. KYW-
TV3 cast him to play "Mr. Weekend" on the
show "McLean and Company" ('70). He also
hosted and produced "Gap Rap," a weekly
talk show, and co-produced the summer season at the John B. Kelly Playhouse in the Park
('71). Created "Southern Exposure With Bill
Boggs" at WGHP-TV in High Point, NC,
which was the region's first early morning
talk show ('72–'74). He was named host of
"Midday" ('75). He is also host of WNEW-TV
"Big Apple Minutes" and has appeared in the
NBC soap opera "Another World."
ACHIEVEMENTS & AWARDS: Author of the novel
At First Sight, ('80); Emmy award for out-
standing discussion/interview program.
PERSONAL: Single. Named one of New York's
Ten Most Eligible Bachelors by the *N.Y.
Times.*

BOGROW, PAUL
Dir., CBS, Prime Time, Program Practices

c/o CBS, 7800 Beverly Blvd., Los Angeles, CA
90036
b. N.A.

EDUCATION: Columbia University, M.A.; Har-
vard University, Ph.D.
CAREER HIGHLIGHTS: Mgr., Program Practices
Dept. ('73); Dir., Prime Time, Program Prac-
tices, CBS ('77)
ACHIEVEMENTS & AWARDS: N.A.
PERSONAL: Wife, Christina. Resides in Pasa-
dena, CA.

BOLEN, LIN
Head of Creative Affairs, Inter-Media Entertainment

c/o Inter-Media Entertainment, 1350 Ave. of
the Americas, New York, NY 10019
b. N.A.

EDUCATION: N.A.
CAREER HIGHLIGHTS: V.P., NBC, Daytime Pro-
gramming ('72); Independent Prod.; head of
Creative Affairs, Inter-Media Entertainment.
ACHIEVEMENTS & AWARDS: N.A.
PERSONAL: N.A.

BOMBECK, ERMA
On-Air Personality, ABC, "Good Morning America"

c/o "Good Morning America," 1 Lincoln
Plaza, New York, NY 10023
b. Dayton, OH.

EDUCATION: University of Dayton, B.A.

CAREER HIGHLIGHTS: Cub Reporter, *Dayton Journal Herald;* Reporter, *Kettering-Oakwood Times;* rejoined *Journal Herald* and was syndicated; currently writes syndicated column, "At Wit's End," and appears as "Housewife-at-Large" on "Good Morning America."

ACHIEVEMENTS & AWARDS: Headliner award ('69); Mark Twain award, presented annually to nation's top humorist. Member, Theta Sigma Phi and Sigma Delta Chi; published six best-selling books.

PERSONAL: Resides in Paradise Valley, AZ, with husband and three children.

BONANNI, JACK (John S. Bonanni)
V.P., Station Mgr., WABC-TV,

c/o WABC-TV, 7 Lincoln Sq., New York, NY 10023
b. September 20. Philadelphia, PA.

EDUCATION: Fordham University School of Business, B.A., Marketing.

CAREER HIGHLIGHTS: Sales Rep. *Life* magazine; Acct. Exec., ABC TV ('72); Sales Mgr. and General Sales Mgr., WABC-TV ('74); V.P., Station Mgr., WABC-TV.

ACHIEVEMENTS & AWARDS: Member, IRTS.

PERSONAL: Wife, Diane; children, Jon, Cynthia, and Gregory. Resides in Chappaqua, NY.

BONERZ, PETER
Actor

c/o Creative Artists, 1888 Century Park, East Los Angeles, CA 90067
b. August 6. Portsmouth, NH

EDUCATION: Marquette University, B.A.

CAREER HIGHLIGHTS: Best known for his portrayal of the orthodontist on "The Bob Newhart Show," Bonerz also was the authoritative boss in ABC's comedy "Nine to Five." His film credits include *Funnyman, A Session With the Committee, Fuzz, Medium Cool, Catch-22,* and *The Serial.* On TV, he has been active as both an actor and a director.

ACHIEVEMENTS & AWARDS: N.A.

PERSONAL: Married, two sons.

BOOKE, SORRELL
Actor

c/o "The Dukes of Hazzard," CBS, 7800 Beverly Blvd., Los Angeles, CA 90036
b. January 4. Buffalo, NY.

EDUCATION: Yale School of Drama; Columbia University.

CAREER HIGHLIGHTS: A strong stage performer with a multitude of dialects who turned to TV and logged more than 150 guest appearances on such shows as "Route 66," "All in the Family," "Soap," and "What's Happening!" culminating in a regular role as the blundering Boss Hogg on "The Dukes of Hazzard."

ACHIEVEMENTS & AWARDS: N.A.

PERSONAL: Resides in San Fernando Valley, CA.

BORNSTEIN, STEVEN
V.P., ESPN, Programming

c/o ESPN, ESPN PLAZA, Bristol, CT 06010
b. N.A.

EDUCATION: University of Wisconsin, B.S., Film ('74).

CAREER HIGHLIGHTS: Prod., WOSU-TV, Columbus, OH ('77); Exec. Prod., WOSU-TV, Columbus ('78); Mgr., Program Coordination, ESPN ('80); Dir., Program Acquisition and Planning, ESPN ('81); Dir., Programming, ESPN ('81); V.P., Programming, ESPN ('83).

ACHIEVEMENTS & AWARDS: Three local Emmy awards in Ohio.

PERSONAL: Resides in Farmington, CT, with his wife, Sharon, and their daughter, Cori.

BOSH, STEVE
Co-Anchor, WPIX-TV, News

c/o WPIX-TV, 11 WPIX Plaza, New York, NY 10017
b. December 21, 1940.

EDUCATION: North Allegheny High School; Denver University.

CAREER HIGHLIGHTS: Spent four years as a Writer and Reporter for radio stations including KBTR, Denver; News Team, KOA-TV, Denver; Anchor, KDKA-TV, Pittsburgh; Co-

Anchor, "Six O'Clock News," WCBS-TV; Co-Anchor, WPIX-TV, "Action News" ('77).
ACHIEVEMENTS & AWARDS: N.A.
PERSONAL: Resides in New York City, three children, David, Jenny, and Billy.

BOSLEY, TOM
Actor

c/o"Happy Days," ABC, 2040 Ave. of the Stars, Los Angeles, CA 90067
b. October 1.

EDUCATION: DePaul University.
CAREER HIGHLIGHTS: Starred on Broadway in *Fiorello, Nowhere To Go But Up, A Murder Among Us, Natural Affection, Catch Me If You Can,* and *The Education of H*y*m*a*n K*a*p*l*a*n*. Motion picture debut in *Love With the Proper Stranger* ('62), followed by *The World of Henry Orient, Divorce, American Style,* and *Yours, Mine and Ours*. Has appeared in more than 500 TV shows, with running roles in "The Debbie Reynolds Show," "The Dean Martin Show," and "The Sandy Duncan Show," and has created such notable characterizations as Teddy in the Hallmark Hall of Fame's *Arsenic and Old Lace,* Sen. George Norris in *Profiles in Courage,* and Ben Franklin in the mini-series *The Rebels*. TV movie credits include *Testimony of Two Men, Focus, Miracle on 34th Street, The Triangle Factory Fire, With This Ring,* and *Death Trap*. Hosted "That's Hollywood." Other TV credits include the pilots for "Night Gallery," "Marcus Welby, M.D.," "Love, American Style," "The Streets of San Francisco," "The Love Boat," and "Joanie Loves Chachi."
ACHIEVEMENTS & AWARDS: Tony, Drama Critics Circle, ANTA, and Newspaper Guild awards for his performance in *Fiorello*; Intl. Laurel Wreath award as an outstanding newcomer for *Love With the Proper Stranger* ('62).
PERSONAL: Married, resides in Beverly Hills, CA.

BOSSON, BARBARA
Actress

c/o "Hill Street Blues," NBC, 3000 W. Alameda Ave., Burbank, CA 91523
b. November 1. Bellvernon, PA.

EDUCATION: Carnegie Tech.
CAREER HIGHLIGHTS: Feature films include *Capricorn One* and *Bullitt*. Co-star of the series "Richie Brockelman" and "Sunshine." Plays Fay Furillo in "Hill Street Blues."
ACHIEVEMENTS & AWARDS: N.A.
PERSONAL: Husband is Writer/Prod. Steven Bochco; daughter, Melissa; son, Jess. Resides in Santa Monica, CA.

BOURGHOLTZER, FRANK
Correspondent, NBC, News

c/o NBC, 3000 W. Alameda Ave., Burbank, CA 91523
b. October 26, 1919. New York, NY.

EDUCATION: Indiana University.
CAREER HIGHLIGHTS: Worked for the *Wall Street Journal* ('43); White House Correspondent, NBC News ('46); Bureau Chief, NBC News, Paris ('53); Bureau Chief, NBC News, Bonn ('55); Bureau Chief, NBC News, Vienna ('57); State Dept. Correspondent, NBC News ('58); Bureau Chief, NBC News, Moscow ('61); Correspondent, NBC News, Paris ('65); Correspondent, NBC News, Los Angeles ('69).
ACHIEVEMENTS & AWARDS: Overseas Press Club award ('65).
PERSONAL: Wife, Shena; son, Andrew.

BOWAB, JOHN
Dir.

c/o Shapiro, Taxon & Kopell, 1180 Ave. of the Americas, New York, N.Y. 10036
b. December 22, 1933.

EDUCATION: Providence College, B.A.
CAREER HIGHLIGHTS: Dir. of "Groucho" for HBO; pilot, "Why Us?" produced by Carson & Co.; pilot, "Century Hill," produced by Embassy Productions; pilot, "Brian and Sylvia," produced by Embassy Productions. Dir. of multiple episodes of "Benson," "The Baxters," "Bosom Buddies," "The Facts of Life," "It Takes Two," "Soap," and "It's a Living." Stage credits include *Mame, She Loves Me,* and *Forty Carats*
ACHIEVEMENTS & AWARDS: N.A.
PERSONAL: N.A.

BOWEN, JERRY
Correspondent, CBS, News

c/o CBS, 7800 Beverly Blvd., Los Angeles, CA 90036
b. Ames, IA.

EDUCATION: Iowa State University; University of Minnesota.
CAREER HIGHLIGHTS: Reporter, KSI-TV, Ames, IA ('63); Reporter, KSTP-TV, Minneapolis ('68); Reporter/Anchor/Prod., WCCO-TV, Minneapolis ('69); Reporter, CBS News, Chicago ('77); Correspondent, CBS News, Rome ('77); Correspondent, CBS News, Los Angeles ('79).
ACHIEVEMENTS & AWARDS: N.A.
PERSONAL: Wife, Valrae; sons, Nathan and Spencer.

BOYER, PHILIP B.
V.P. and General Mgr., ABC Owned TV Stations, Product Development and Planning

c/o ABC, 1345 Ave. of the Americas, New York, NY 10019
b. December 13, 1940. Portland, OR.

EDUCATION: Sacramento State University, B.A., Communications.

CAREER HIGHLIGHTS: Head of Production and Program Depts., Eugene, OR ('60–'65); Program Dir., KCRA-TV, Sacramento, CA ('65); Program Dir., KNBC-TV, Los Angeles ('72–'74). Began at ABC as V.P./General Mgr., WABC-TV, New York ('79); V.P., Programming, ABC Owned TV Stations ('81); V.P. and General Mgr., Product Development and Planning, ABC Owned TV Stations ('81).
ACHIEVEMENTS & AWARDS: Several local Emmy awards while at WLS, Chicago, and WABC, New York ('77–'81). Center for Quality TV citation ('73); Natl. Assn. for Retarded Children citation ('73); Gabriel award for station programming that recognizes needs and aspirations of ethnic communities ('73). Pres., NATPE ('77).
PERSONAL: N.A.

BRADEN, THOMAS W.
Co-Host, Cable News Network, "Crossfire"

c/o Cable News Network, 1050 Techwood Dr., N.W., Atlanta, GA 30318
b. February 22, 1918. Dubuque, IA.

EDUCATION: Dartmouth University, B.A. and honorary M.A.; Franklin College, Lit.D.
CAREER HIGHLIGHTS: Asst. Prof. of English, Dartmouth University; moved to *N.Y. Herald Tribune* ('48); Exec. Dir., Museum of Modern Art, New York ('49); Asst. to Dir., CIA ('51); Publisher, *Blade Tribune,* Oceanside, CA ('54); Pres., California State Board of Education ('59); Syndicated Columnist ('68); Co-host, Cable News Network, "Crossfire".
ACHIEVEMENTS & AWARDS: Co-Author, with Stewart Alsop, *Sub Rosa, the Story of the OSS* ('46). Author *Eight Is Enough* ('75).
PERSONAL: Wife, the former Joan Ridley; eight children.

BRADLEY, ED
Co-Editor, CBS, "60 Minutes"

c/o CBS, 51 W. 52d St., New York, NY 10019
b. June 22, 1941. Pennsylvania.

EDUCATION: Cheyney State College, B.S., Education ('64).

CAREER HIGHLIGHTS: Reporter, WDAS Radio, Philadelphia ('63); Reporter, WCBS Radio ('67); joined CBS News as a Stringer, Paris Bureau ('71); Saigon Bureau ('72–'74); Correspondent ('73); moved to Washington Bureau ('74); White House Correspondent ('76); Anchor, "The CBS Sunday Night News" ('76–'81); Principal Correspondent, CBS Reports ('78); Co-Editor, "60 Minutes" ('81).

ACHIEVEMENTS & AWARDS: Emmy awards, Dupont awards, Overseas Press Club awards, Peabody award, George Polk award, Ohio State University awards.

PERSONAL: N.A.

BRADSHAW, THORNTON F.
Chairman of the Board and Chief Exec. Officer, RCA Corp.

c/o RCA, Dept. of Corporate Affairs, 30 Rockefeller Plaza, New York, NY 10112
b. August 4, 1917. Washington, DC.

EDUCATION: Harvard   University,   B.A., M.B.A., and Ph.D.

CAREER HIGHLIGHTS: Consultant, Cresap, McCormick & Paget, New York ('52); Asst. General Mgr., Atlantic Refining Co., now Atlantic Richfield ('56); moved up the ranks to Exec. V.P. of Atlantic ('62); Pres., Atlantic Refining Co. ('64); Dir., RCA Corp. ('72); Chairman of the Board and Chief Exec. Officer, RCA Corp. ('81).

ACHIEVEMENTS & AWARDS: Has served on many distinguished boards and committees.

PERSONAL: N.A.

BRADY, PAMELA
Dir., Subscriber Information Services, HBO

c/o HBO, 1271 Ave. of the Americas, New York, NY 10020
b. N.A.

EDUCATION: Queens College, B.A., English Literature.

CAREER HIGHLIGHTS: Rights and Permission Asst., Time-Life Books, New York ('74); Copywriter, Time-Life Books ('75); Mgr., Subscriber Services, HBO ('77); Dir., Subscriber Information Services, HBO ('83).

ACHIEVEMENTS & AWARDS: N.A.
PERSONAL: Resides in West Hills, NY, with her husband, William.

BRADY, RAY
Correspondent, CBS, News

c/o CBS, 524 W. 57th St., New York, NY 10019
b. April 3.

EDUCATION: Fordham University.

CAREER HIGHLIGHTS: Reporter, Business News, WCBS-AM, New York ('72); Reporter, Business News, WCBS-TV ('76); Correspondent, CBS News, assigned to "CBS Morning News" but still providing reports for the "CBS Evening News" ('77).

ACHIEVEMENTS & AWARDS: N.A.
PERSONAL: Resides in New York City with wife, Mary, and two children.

BRAND, JOSHUA
Writer/Prod., MTM Enterprises

c/o MTM Enterprises, 4024 Radford Ave., Studio City, CA 91604
b. November 29, 1950. New York, NY.

EDUCATION: City College of New York, B.A.; Columbia University, M.A.

CAREER HIGHLIGHTS: Story Editor, "The White Shadow" ('80); Co-Creator/Prod., "St. Elsewhere" ('82).

ACHIEVEMENTS & AWARDS: Humanitas award finalist ('81).
PERSONAL: N.A.

BRANDT, YANNA KROYT
Prod./Writer/Dir.

1349 Lexington Ave., New York, NY 10028
b. September 6, 1933. Berlin, Germany.

EDUCATION: Vassar College, B.A. ('53); Columbia University, M.S. ('54).

CAREER HIGHLIGHTS: Assoc. Prod./Writer, NBC ('66); Prod., NET "Vibrations," "Boulez" ('71–'73); Exec. Prod./Creator, "High Feather," PBS, NBC ('79–'81); Exec. Prod., "Vegetable Soup," PBS, NBC ('73–'77); Prod./ Writer, "The Nutcracker" with Mikhail Baryshnikov, CBS ('77); Prod., "A House Divided," PBS, and Prod./Creator, ABC "FYI" ('80–'83).

ACHIEVEMENTS & AWARDS: Emmy awards ('80, '81, '82); Gabriel award, Academy of Pediatrics award ('82); Intl. Film Festival Golden Eagle award ('81).

PERSONAL: Husband, Nathan; two children.

BRANT, TIM
Sports Dir., WJLA-TV, Washington, DC

c/o WJLA-TV, 4461 Connecticut Ave., N.W., Washington, DC 20008
b. February 26. Washington, DC

EDUCATION: University of Maryland ('72).

CAREER HIGHLIGHTS: Morning Sportscaster, WMAL-AM, Washington, DC ('76); Sports Dir., WJLA-TV, Washington, DC ('79); also well-known as a Play-by-Play Announcer for ACC basketball and preseason Washington Redskin football games.

ACHIEVEMENTS & AWARDS: Named one of the Outstanding Young Men of America by the Jaycees of America ('76); Sportscaster of the Year, Black United Fund ('82); honored for Most Readable Lips on TV by the Alexander Graham Bell Assn. for the Deaf.

PERSONAL: Resides in Gaithersburg, MD, with wife, Janet, and three children.

BRAVER, RITA
Reporter, CBS, News

c/o CBS News, 2020 M St., N.W., Washington, DC 20036
b. Washington, DC.

EDUCATION: University of Wisconsin.

CAREER HIGHLIGHTS: Joined CBS News as a News Desk editor, Washington, DC ('72); Assoc. Prod., "The CBS Morning News" ('74–'76); Prod., CBS News, Radio ('73–'74); Assoc. Prod., "The CBS Evening News" ('76); CBS News Reporter, Justice Dept. ('83).

ACHIEVEMENTS & AWARDS: N.A.

PERSONAL: N.A.

BRAVERMAN, CHUCK
Prod./Dir.

1237 Seventh St., Santa Monica, CA 90401
b. N.A.

EDUCATION: McGill University, B.S.

CAREER HIGHLIGHTS: Created special montage films for ABC and CBS; created series of specials "What's Up America" for Showtime Cable. His many TV shows include "American Time Capsule," "Oscar's First Fifty Years," "The Sixties," "Televisionland," and "Getting Married."

ACHIEVEMENTS & AWARDS: Directors Guild nomination; local Emmy awards for "The Televison Newsman" and "Breathe a Sigh of Relief."

PERSONAL: N.A.

BRAYTON, MARIAN
V.P. Dramatic Specials, CBS, Entertainment

c/o CBS, 6121 Sunset Blvd., Los Angeles, CA 90028
b. April 18, 1939. Toledo, OH.

EDUCATION: University of Nebraska, B.A. ('61)

CAREER HIGHLIGHTS: Worked for the *Kirkus Review* and Tony Bill Productions, before being named Exec. Prod. of the Motion Pictures for TV Dept., CBS ('78); Dir., Motion Pictures for TV, CBS ('79); V.P., Dramatic Specials, CBS Entertainment ('82).

ACHIEVEMENTS & AWARDS: N.A.

PERSONAL: Single, resides in West Hollywood, CA.

BRAZZIL, WILLIAM R.
V.P., Wometco Enterprises, Broadcasting

c/o Wometco Enterprises, 316 N. Miami,
  Miami, FL 33128
b. January 25, 1919. Fort Worth, TX.

EDUCATION: Texas Christian University.
CAREER HIGHLIGHTS: Before joining Wometco
  ('56), was Eastern Regional Sales Mgr., NBC
  TV Network; Sales Mgr., KSTP-TV,
  Minneapolis-St. Paul; Sales Mgr. and Prod.
  Mgr., WMCT, Memphis. V.P. in Charge of
  Broadcasting, Wometco ('83).
ACHIEVEMENTS & AWARDS: Named Man of the
  Year ('75) by American Women in Radio and
  TV; recipient of two Emmy awards.
PERSONAL: Wife, Camille; three children.

BRESNAN, WILLIAM
Chairman and Chief Exec. Officer, Group W
  Cable

c/o Group W Cable, 888 Seventh Ave., New
  York, NY 10106
b. December 5, 1933. Mankato, MN.

EDUCATION: Winona State College.
CAREER HIGHLIGHTS: Cable Engineer ('58);
  Chief Engineer of American Cablevision ('65);
  Pres., H&B Cablevision Co. ('68); V.P., Tele-
  prompter; Chief Operating Officer, Tele-
  prompter ('72); Chairman and Chief Exec. Of-
  ficer, Group W Cable ('81).
ACHIEVEMENTS & AWARDS: N.A.
PERSONAL: N.A.

BREWSTER, ALLEN
Mgr., Recording and Post-Production, NBC,
  Operations and Technical Services

c/o NBC, 3000 W. Alameda Ave., Burbank,
  CA 91523
b. Los Angeles, CA.

EDUCATION: San Bernardino Valley College.
CAREER HIGHLIGHTS: Video Tape Engineer,
  NBC, Burbank ('70); Asst. Editor, "The Flip
  Wilson Show" ('72); Editor, "The Midnight
  Special" ('74); Supervising Editor, "NBC—
  The First 50 Years" ('76); Editor, On-Air
  Promotion, NBC ('79); Mgr., Recording and
  Post-Production, Operations and Technical
  Services, NBC, Burbank ('83).
ACHIEVEMENTS & AWARDS: Emmy for editing,
  "NBC—The First 50 Years" ('76).
PERSONAL: Single, resides in Montclair, CA.

BRIGGS, FRED
Correspondent, NBC, News

c/o NBC, 30 Rockefeller Plaza, New York, NY
  10020
b. May 31, 1932. Chicago, IL.

EDUCATION: University of Louisville.
CAREER HIGHLIGHTS: Disc Jockey, WSON-AM,
  Henderson, KY ('52); Prod./Anchor, WSB-
  TV, Atlanta ('60); Reporter, WKYC-TV,
  Cleveland ('65); Reporter, NBC News ('66);
  Correspondent, NBC News, Chicago ('70);
  Correspondent, NBC News, Berlin ('75); Cor-
  respondent, NBC News, Chicago ('79).
ACHIEVEMENTS & AWARDS: Radio-TV News Dir.
  Assn. award ('64).
PERSONAL: Wife, Dorothy; son, Lowell.

BRILLIANT, ANDREW P.
V.P. and General Counsel, ESPN

c/o ESPN, 355 Lexington Ave., New York, NY
  10017
b. November 15, 1946. Boston, MA.

EDUCATION: University of Virginia, B.A., English ('68); Boston College Law School, J.D.
  ('73).
CAREER HIGHLIGHTS: Attorney for the FCC,
  Washington, DC ('73); Assoc. Counsel, HBO

('76); Chief Counsel, Operations, HBO ('79);
V.P. and General Counsel, ESPN ('80).
ACHIEVEMENTS & AWARDS: N.A.
PERSONAL: Wife, Beverly; daughters, Diana
and Natalie

BRINKLEY, DAVID
Anchor, "This Week With David Brinkley,"
ABC, News

c/o ABC, 1717 DeSales St., N.W. Washington,
DC 20036
b. July 10, 1920. Wilmington, NC.

EDUCATION: University of North Carolina;
Vanderbilt University.
CAREER HIGHLIGHTS: With his acerbic wit and
unique writing style, Brinkley achieved national prominence when producer Reuven
Frank (now president of NBC News) teamed
him with Chet Huntley. That was the heyday
of NBC, when even Walter Cronkite couldn't
beat the Huntley-Brinkley team. He has reported on every U.S. president since Franklin
Roosevelt and on major national events ranging from the *Apollo 11* moon landing to Watergate, events following the assassinations of
John F. Kennedy, Robert F. Kennedy, and
Martin Luther King Jr.. Served as NBC Sr.
Political Correspondent and Co-anchor during the past seven presidential elections, covering primaries, both of the parties' political
conventions, and election night returns.
Brinkley had been NBC News Correspondent
('43); teamed with Huntley as Co-anchor,
"The Huntley-Brinkley Report" ('56); Co-
anchor, NBC Nightly News With John Chancellor ('76); Anchor, "NBC Magazine With
David Brinkley" ('80). Brinkley joined ABC
News ('81); he contributes to special projects

and election coverage, and hosts "This Week
With David Brinkley," one of the best network TV shows, with numerous newsbreaks
to its credit.
ACHIEVEMENTS & AWARDS: Received every major broadcasting award, including 10 Emmy
awards and two Peabody awards.
PERSONAL: Resides in Washington, DC.

BRISKMAN, LOUIS J.
V.P. and Secretary, Westinghouse
Broadcasting and Cable, Group W

Westinghouse Broadcasting and Cable, 90
Park Ave., New York, NY 10016
b. January 13.

EDUCATION: University of Pittsburgh, B.A.;
Georgetown University Law Center, J.D.
CAREER HIGHLIGHTS: Joined Group W Cable
('81), after serving as Counsel for six years
with Group W's parent, Westinghouse Elec-
tric Corp. He became V.P. and General Coun-
sel, Group W ('82) and V.P. and Secretary,
Westinghouse Broadcasting and Cable ('83).
ACHIEVEMENTS & AWARDS: N.A.
PERSONAL: N.A.

BROCKINGTON, JACKIE
General Assignment Weather Reporter,
WRC-TV 4 NBC, News

c/o WRC-TV, 4001 Nebraska Ave., N.W.,
Washington, DC 20016
b. N.A.

EDUCATION: N.A.
CAREER HIGHLIGHTS: Began as interviewer,
WFRV-TV, Green Bay, WI; next Anchor,
weekend weather forecast, Host, talk show,
WLUK-TV, Greenbay ('77); Weekend
Weathercaster, WDVM-TV; Weekend Weath-
er Reporter, General Assignment Reporter,
WRC-TV ('80).
ACHIEVEMENTS & AWARDS: Named one of 10
Outstanding Black Women in the Washing-
ton Area by Unique Enterprises.
PERSONAL: Resides in Bethesda, MD with her
two daughters.

BROCKMAN, MICHAEL S.
V.P., Daytime and Children's Programs, CBS, Entertainment

c/o CBS, 6121 Sunset Blvd., Los Angeles, CA 90028
b. November 19, 1938. Brooklyn NY.

EDUCATION: Ithaca College, B.S. ('63).
CAREER HIGHLIGHTS: V.P., Daytime Programs, ABC ('74); V.P., Tape Production and Administration, ABC ('77); V.P., Daytime and Children's Programs, NBC ('77); V.P., Programs, Lorimar Productions ('80); Creative Consultant to Pres., ABC Motion Picture Division ('81); V.P., Daytime and Children's Programs ('82)
ACHIEVEMENTS & AWARDS: N.A.
PERSONAL: Wife, Wendy; daughter, Laura; son, David.

BRODER, DICK
Prod., Playboy Channel, Playboy Comedy Shorts

c/o Playboy Channel, 9046 Sunset Blvd., Los Angeles, CA 90069
b. April 4, 1944. Detroit, MI.

EDUCATION: Monterey Peninsula College.
CAREER HIGHLIGHTS: Production Exec., "Tony Orlando and Dawn," CBS ('73); Exec. Prod., "The Marilyn McCoo and Billy Davis Jr. Show" ('76); Prod., "Popclips," Warner Amex Satellite Communications Co. ('80); Prod. Consultant, Showtime Entertainment ('81); Prod., Playboy Comedy Shorts, Playboy Channel ('82).
ACHIEVEMENTS & AWARDS: N.A.
PERSONAL: Resides in Los Angeles.

BRODKIN, HERBERT
Prod., Titus Productions

c/o Titus Productions, 211 E. 51st St., New York, NY 10022
b. November 9, 1912.

EDUCATION: N.A.
CAREER HIGHLIGHTS: For two decades, Brodkin has produced a remarkable series of high-quality TV dramas. Works closely with the writers of his projects, which are often bold, issue-oriented dramas. Prod., shows for "Studio One," "Motorola Hour," and "Playhouse 90"; Prod., the TV series "The Defenders," "Shane," "The Nurses," and "Coronet Blue." Prod., original TV dramas for CBS including "The People Next Door." Also, prod. the TV movie *The Missiles of October*, the mini-series *Holocaust* ('78), and the drama *Skokie* ('81).
ACHIEVEMENTS & AWARDS: Emmy awards for producing "The Defenders" and *Holocaust*.
PERSONAL: N.A.

BRODSKY, LINDA G.
V.P., Public Relations, BroadBand Communications

c/o BroadBand Communications, 375 Park Ave., New York, NY 10022
b. June 23.

EDUCATION: University of Pennsylvania, B.A., Journalism ('62).
CAREER HIGHLIGHTS: Served in many public relations posts in the cable industry ('64). Joined TeleVision Communications Corp. to establish the firm's first Public Relations Dept. ('71); V.P., Public Relations, Warner Cable Corp. ('73); V.P., BroadBand Communications ('75).
ACHIEVEMENTS & AWARDS: Founder and Pres. ('80, '81), New York Women in Cable; Board Member, Natl. Women in Cable.
PERSONAL: Resides in New York City.

BROGLIATTI, BARBARA SPENCER
Sr. V.P., Embassy Communications, Worldwide Publicity, Promotion and Advertising

c/o Embassy Communications, Ave. of the Stars, Los Angeles, CA 90067
b. January 8, 1946. Los Angeles, CA.

EDUCATION: University of California, B.A.
CAREER HIGHLIGHTS: Publicist, CBS TV Press Information ('69); Dir. of Publicity, Tandem Productions and TAT Communications Co., "All in the Family," "Mary Hartman, Mary Hartman," "The Jeffersons," and "Good Times" ('74); Corporate V.P., Media Affairs, Tandem Productions and TAT Commu-

nications Co., "One Day at a Time," and "Maude" ('77); Sr. V.P., Worldwide Publicity, Promotion and Advertising, Embassy Communications, "Archie Bunker's Place," "The Facts of Life," "Diff'rent Strokes," "The Jeffersons," "One Day at a Time," "Gloria," "Silver Spoons," and "Square Pegs." Embassy Pictures: *The Soldiers, The Challenge, Zapped!, Deadly Force,* and *Spinal Tap.*

ACHIEVEMENTS & AWARDS: Trustee, First V.P., and Chairman, Negotiating Committee ('81), Publicists Guild.

PERSONAL: N.A.

BROKAW, JOANNE
V.P., Educational and Community Services, CBS, Broadcast Group

c/o CBS, 51 W. 52d St., New York, NY 10019
b. September 29, 1939.

EDUCATION: University of Wisconsin, B.S.; Manhattanville College, M.A., Humanities.

CAREER HIGHLIGHTS: Dir., Educational and Community Services, CBS Broadcast Group ('82); V.P., Educational and Community Services, CBS Broadcast Group ('83).

ACHIEVEMENTS & AWARDS: N.A.
PERSONAL: N.A.

BROKAW, TOM
Correspondent, NBC News

c/o NBC, 30 Rockefeller Plaza, New York, NY 10020
b. Yankton, SD.

EDUCATION: University of South Dakota, Political Science

CAREER HIGHLIGHTS: Began broadcast journal-

ism career at KMTV, Omaha ('62), then moved to WSB-TV, Atlanta, reporting on major civil rights stories for NBC News as well as anchoring the late evening news. He joined NBC News in Los Angeles ('66). Became White House Correspondent ('73), and Principal Correspondent of the "Today" program ('76). Sole Anchor for "NBC Nightly News" ('82).

ACHIEVEMENTS & AWARDS: Joseph Quinn memorial award ('82).

PERSONAL: Wife, Meredith; three daughters.

BRONSON, MICHAEL
Dir., Metropolitan Opera Assn., Media Dept.

c/o Metropolitan Opera Assn., 520 W. 27th St. New York, NY 10001
b. August 8, 1938.

EDUCATION: City College of New York.

CAREER HIGHLIGHTS: Technician, Stage Mgr., Green Mansions Hotel's summer stock theater ('60); Asst. Stage Mgr., Metropolitan Opera Studio ('61); Asst. Technical Administrator, Metropolitan Opera Studio ('66); Business and Technical Administrator ('72); Business Dir. of the Metropolitan Opera ('78); Dir. of the Metropolitan Opera Assn.'s Media Dept. and Exec. Prod. of the PBS series "Live From the Met" ('83).

ACHIEVEMENTS & AWARDS: N.A.
PERSONAL: N.A.

BROOKMAN, MICHAEL S.
Consultant, ABC, Motion Picture Division, Cable TV

c/o ABC, 7800 Beverly Blvd., Los Angeles, CA 90036
b. November 19, 1938. Brooklyn, NY.

EDUCATION: Ithaca College, B.S., Radio/TV.

CAREER HIGHLIGHTS: V.P., Daytime Programs, ABC TV ('74); V.P., Daytime and Children's Programs, NBC TV ('77); V.P., Programs, Lorimar Productions ('80); Consultant, ABC Motion Picture Division, Cable TV, ('81).

ACHIEVEMENTS & AWARDS: Member, NATAS; listed in *Who's Who in America* ('80, '82); Member, Alpha Epsilon Rho Radio/TV Fraternity.

PERSONAL: Wife, Wendy; children, Laura and David.

BROOKS, JAMES L.
Prod.

31708 Broadbeach Rd., Malibu, CA 90265
b. May 9, 1940. Brooklyn, NY.

EDUCATION: New York University.
CAREER HIGHLIGHTS: Known as one of TV's best story minds. Co-Creator, "Room 222," "The Mary Tyler Moore Show," "Rhoda," "Taxi," "The Associates," and "Lou Grant." Brooks began as a Writer, CBS News ('64), and went west to work for Wolper Productions ('65). When "Room 222" was launched ('68), Brooks also served as Story Editor along with Gene Reynolds. Since then Brooks's career has sizzled, proving that quality, honesty, and humor can be commercially successful.
ACHIEVEMENTS & AWARDS: Emmy awards for "Room 222" ('69) "The Mary Tyler Moore Show" ('70, '75); and "Taxi" ('78). Peabody awards for "The Mary Tyler Moore Show" ('77) and "Lou Grant" ('78). Golden Globe awards for "Taxi" ('78, '79, '80); Writers Guild award, for outstanding script, "Cindy" ('78); Humanitas prize for "Taxi" episode entitled "Blind Date" ('79). Member, Writers Guild, Academy of TV Arts and Sciences; SAG.
PERSONAL: N.A.

BROOKS, TIMOTHY H.
Dir., Program Research, NBC

c/o NBC, 30 Rockefeller Plaza, New York, NY 10020
b. April 18, 1942.

EDUCATION: Dartmouth College, B.A.; Syracuse University, M.S.
CAREER HIGHLIGHTS: Asst. Production/Promotion Dir., WTEN-TV, Albany, NY; Research Analyst, WCBS-TV, New York; Sr. Research Analyst, NBC Owned Stations Division ('70); Mgr., Daytime Research, NBC TV ('72); Mgr., Nighttime Program Research, NBC ('75); Assoc. Dir., Research and Marketing, TV Advertising Representatives ('76); Mgr., Audience Measurement Analysis, NBC ('77); Dir., TV Network Research, NBC ('78); Dir., Program Research, NBC ('82). Also serves as an Adjunct Professor of Communication Arts for C.W. Post Center, Long Island University.
ACHIEVEMENTS & AWARDS: Co-author, *The Complete Directory to Prime-Time Network TV Shows,*

1946–Present, which won an American Book award ('80).
PERSONAL: Resides in Long Island, NY.

BROOKSHIER, TOM
Sports Broadcaster, CBS, Sports

c/o CBS, 51 W. 52d St., New York, NY 10019
b. December 16, 1931. Roswell, NM.

EDUCATION: University of Colorado.
CAREER HIGHLIGHTS: A star defensive back for the Philadelphia Eagles before turning to broadcasting, Brookshier was a Sportscaster, WCAU-TV, Philadelphia ('61–'77); Host of the syndicated "Sports Illustrated" and Co-Host of "This Is the NFL." Joined CBS Sports as an Analyst on their coverage of the NFL football ('64).
ACHIEVEMENTS & AWARDS: N.A.
PERSONAL: Resides in Gladwyne, PA, with wife, Barbara; daughters, Linda Kay and Betsy; son, Tommy Jr.

BROWER, STUART
V.P., On-Air Promotion, ABC, Entertainment

995 Brental Rd., Pasadena, CA 91105
b. September 29, 1945. Long Beach, CA.

EDUCATION: University of Southern California, B.A., Telecommunications; Michigan State University, M.A., Broadcasting.
CAREER HIGHLIGHTS: CBS TV Promotion Dept. ('70); moved to ABC TV as Production Mgr. and Staff Prod., in On-Air Promotion Dept. ('71); Assoc. Prod. of "Happy Days Anniversary Special" ('76); Creative Dir., Sullivan & Assoc. ('76); Co-Founder, Beck, Brower & Davidson ('80); returned to ABC as V.P., On-Air Promotion, ABC Entertainment ('81). Also, Sr. Lecturer, University of California School of Journalism ('72–present).
ACHIEVEMENTS & AWARDS: Contributed to *Strategies in Broadcast Promotion* ('82).
PERSONAL: N.A.

BROWN, HILARY
Correspondent, ABC, News

c/o ABC, 7 W. 66th St., New York, NY 10023
b. Ottawa, Canada.

EDUCATION: University of Western Ontario;
University of British Columbia.

CAREER HIGHLIGHTS: Production Asst., CBC
('63); Anchor, CBC ('65); Head of Publicity,
Guggenheim Museum, New York ('69);
Parliamentary Correspondent, CJOH-TV, Ottawa, Canada ('70); Freelance Journalist
working in Teheran ('72); Reporter, ABC
News, London ('73); Correspondent, ABC
News, Paris ('76); Correspondent, NBC
News, Tel Aviv ('77); Pentagon Correspondent, NBC News, Washington, DC ('80); Correspondent, ABC News, New York ('81).

ACHIEVEMENTS & AWARDS: N.A.

PERSONAL: Husband, John Bierman; son,
Jonathan.

BROWN, JIM
Entertainment Editor, NBC, "Today"

c/o NBC, 3000 W. Alameda Ave., Burbank,
CA 91523
b. Los Angeles, CA.

EDUCATION: Pasadena City College; Stanford
University.

CAREER HIGHLIGHTS: His experience includes
working as a Newscaster/Writer, KOGO-
Radio, San Diego ('56); News Dir., KGB-
Radio, San Diego ('60–'64); Newscaster/
Writer, KPOL-Radio ('62–'64); Field Reporter,
KNXT ('64); Newsman, KNBC News ('72).

ACHIEVEMENTS & AWARDS: TV/Radio Miror
gold medal award, Golden Mike, Sigma Delta

Chi distinguished award, and Los Angeles
area Emmy for individual achievement.

PERSONAL: Resides in Glendale, CA, with his
wife and two children.

BROWN, LES
Editor-in-Chief, Channels magazine

131 N. Chatsworth, Larchmont, NY 10538
b. 1928.

EDUCATION: Roosevelt University, B.A.,
English.

CAREER HIGHLIGHTS: Brown has long been one
of the best informed reporters on industry
and trade issues in the whole TV field. In his
current role as editor of the valuable and pioneering Channels magazine, Brown is arguably the best informed TV critic now writing
about what he calls "the new television": that
is, the issues arising from today's rapidly
changing telecommunications technology
and the public policy issues posed by some of
those technologies. His positions include
Chicago Bureau Chief for Variety; Variety
Radio/TV Editor; TV Reporter, N.Y. Times;
Editor-in-Chief of magazine Channels of Communication.

ACHIEVEMENTS & AWARDS: NATPE Award;
Louis Cowan award from the Aspen Institute
('79).

PERSONAL: Wife is the former Jean Slaymaker;
they have three children.

BROWN, PHYLLIS GEORGE
Co-Host, "NFL Today," CBS, Sports

c/o CBS Sports, 51 W. 52 St., New York, NY
10019
b. Denton, TX.

EDUCATION: North Texas State University;
Texas Christian University.

CAREER HIGHLIGHTS: First joined CBS Sports as
Co-Host, "The NFL Today" ('75); hosted CBS
series "People" ('78); Co-Host, along with
Bert Parks, of "The Miss America Pageant,"
and Co-Host of "Candid Camera" with Alan
Funt; returned as Co-Host of "The NFL
Today" ('80) after a two-year absence; par-
ticipates as a host of the Macy's Thanksgiving
Day Parade.

ACHIEVEMENTS & AWARDS: First gained recognition as Miss America ('71); recipient of the Jack Quinlan Award for Sports Broadcasting Excellence ('83).

PERSONAL: Resides in Lexington, KY with husband John Y. Brown, the Governor of Kentucky, and son Lincoln.

BROWN, RICK
Anchor, Turner Broadcasting System CNN2, News

c/o Turner Broadcasting System, 1050 Techwood Dr., N.W., Atlanta, GA 30318
b. May 24, 1944. Santa Monica, CA.

EDUCATION: University of Saskatoon, B.A., Education ('73).

CAREER HIGHLIGHTS: Began his broadcasting career at CKBI-Radio and TV, Prince Albert, Saskatchewan ('75); Writer, CKBI-Radio; Asst. News Dir., Evening News Anchor, CKBI-Radio ('77); Anchor, Late News Package, Back-Up Anchor for "Eyewitness News at Six," CFRN-TV ('78–'81); Anchor, CFRN-TV News ('80); Anchor, Turner Broadcasting System CNN2, News ('81).

ACHIEVEMENTS & AWARDS: N.A.

PERSONAL: N.A.

BROWNE, L. VIRGINIA
Writer, CBS, "The Guiding Light"

c/o "The Guiding Light," CBS, 51 W. 52d St., New York, NY 10019
b. New Jersey.

EDUCATION: Montclair State College; University of Wisconsin.

CAREER HIGHLIGHTS: Writer for "Knots Landing" and Showtime's "A New Day in Eden"; Writer, "Days of Our Lives ('78); Writer, "Another World" ('80); Principal Writer, "The Guiding Light" ('82).

ACHIEVEMENTS & AWARDS: N.A.

PERSONAL: Resides in New York City.

BRUNING, RICHARD
V.P., United Satellite Communications, Finance

c/o United Satellite Communications, 1345 Ave. of the Americas, New York, NY 10105
b. November 29, 1940.

EDUCATION: Yale University; Harvard University, M.B.A.

CAREER HIGHLIGHTS: Asst. Treasurer, TransAmerica Corp.; V.P. and Treasurer, UA; V.P., Finance, United Satellite Communications New York.

ACHIEVEMENTS & AWARDS: N.A.

PERSONAL: N.A.

BRUNNER, BOB
Prod., Warner Bros., TV

c/o Warner Bros. TV, 4000 Warner Blvd., Burbank, CA 91522
b. August 3, 1934. Yonkers, NY.

EDUCATION: School of Visual Arts.

CAREER HIGHLIGHTS: It was Brunner who thought up the name Fonzie on "Happy Days." Writer and later Prod., "Happy Days" ('78). With partner Arthur Silver, Creator, "Brothers and Sisters" ('79); "Working Stiffs" ('79), and "Bad News Bears" ('80). Supervising Prod., "Love, Sidney" ('80) and Prod., "Private Benjamin" (82).

ACHIEVEMENTS & AWARDS: N.A.

PERSONAL: Resides in San Fernando Valley, CA, with wife, Ann; three children.

BRUSTIN, MICHELE
V.P., Drama Development, NBC, Entertainment, West Coast

c/o NBC, 3000 W. Alameda Ave., Burbank, CA 91523
b. Baltimore, MD.

EDUCATION: University of Maryland, B.A., English Literature.

CAREER HIGHLIGHTS: Exec. Dir., Illinois Arts Council ('76); Assoc., Drama Dept., NBC ('78); Mgr., Current Drama Programs ('79); Dir., Drama Development, NBC Entertainment ('81); V.P., Drama Development, NBC Entertainment, West Coast ('82).

ACHIEVEMENTS & AWARDS: N.A.

PERSONAL: Resides in West Los Angeles, CA, with her husband, Arnold.

BUCHANAN, MICHAEL
V.P., CBS, Press Information

c/o CBS, 6121 Sunset Blvd., Los Angeles, CA 90028
b. November 1, 1928. San Diego, CA.

EDUCATION: University of California at Los Angeles, B.A. ('53).

CAREER HIGHLIGHTS: Joined CBS Radio ('55); Publicist, Press Information Dept., CBS ('55); Mgr., Press Information ('64); Asst. Dir., Press Information ('66); Dir., Press Information, Los Angeles ('67); V.P., Press Information, CBS ('78).

ACHIEVEMENTS & AWARDS: N.A.

PERSONAL: Resides in Flintridge, CA; sons, Douglas and Eric.

BUCHANAN, PATRICK JOSEPH
Co-Host, Cable News Network, "Crossfire"

1017 Savile Lane, McLean, VA 22101
b. November 2, 1938. Washington, DC

EDUCATION: Columbia School of Journalism, B.A., English and Philosophy ('62).

CAREER HIGHLIGHTS: Editorial Writer, *St. Louis Globe-Democrat* ('62); Exec. Asst. to former V.P. Richard M. Nixon ('66); Special Asst. to the Pres., The White House, Washington, DC ('69); Syndicated Columnist; NBC Radio Commentator, WRC Radio, Washington DC; Talk Show Co-host, Cable News network, "Crossfire" ('75).

ACHIEVEMENTS & AWARDS: Winner, Freedom Foundation's George Washington medal ('75); Morality in Media award ('77). Author, *The New Majority* ('73); *Conservative Votes, Liberal Victories* ('75).

PERSONAL: Wife, the former Shelley Scarney.

BUCHANAN, R. E. (Buck)
Exec. V.P./U.S. Media Dir., J. Walter Thompson, USA

c/o J. Walter Thompson, 466 Lexington Ave., New York, NY 10017
b. March 17, 1919. Auburn, IN.

EDUCATION: Northwestern University, B.S. ('40).

CAREER HIGHLIGHTS: Moderator, Northwestern Reviewing Stand, Mutual ('46); Dir., Broadcast Public Relations ('48); TV Prod., Client Broadcast Representation, Young & Rubicam, New York ('49); T.V. Prod., J. Walter Thompson, New York ('56); Exec. V.P., J. Walter Thompson USA.

ACHIEVEMENTS & AWARDS: Chairman, AAAA, Media Policy Committee ('80–'82); Media Directors Council; Treasurer, V.P. ('80–present); Member, IRTS; Member, Broadcast Pioneers.

PERSONAL: Wife, Lee; daughters, Heather and Holly.

BUCHIN, JOHN
Correspondent, WABC-TV, Eyewitness News

c/o WABC-TV, 7 Lincoln Sq., New York, NY 10023
b. New York, NY.

EDUCATION: University of Pennsylvania, B.A.

CAREER HIGHLIGHTS: Reporter, WTNH-TV ('79); Freelance Reporter, WCBS-TV ('80); Theater and Arts Reporter, KDKA-TV, Pittsburgh ('81); Correspondent, Eyewitness News, WABC-TV.

ACHIEVEMENTS & AWARDS: N.A.

PERSONAL: Resides in Manhattan.

BUCK, JACK
Commentator, CBS, Sports

c/o CBS, 51 W. 52d St., New York, NY 10019
b. Holyoke, MA.

EDUCATION: Ohio State University.

CAREER HIGHLIGHTS: Joined KMOX-AM, St. Louis, as Announcer on St. Louis Cardinals baseball broadcasts, and Sports Dir. ('54), a position he has held ever since. Commentator on NFL broadcasts, CBS ('70); joined NBC Sports hosting "Grandstand," and broadcasting the network's NFL games ('75). Re-joined CBS Sports ('82).

ACHIEVEMENTS & AWARDS: N.A.

PERSONAL: Resides in St. Louis with wife, Carol.

BUNIM, MARY-ELLIS
Exec. Prod., CBS, Proctor & Gamble Productions, "As the World Turns"

402 E. 76th St., New York, NY 10021
b. July 9, 1946. Northampton, MA.

EDUCATION: Fordham University.

CAREER HIGHLIGHTS: Assoc. Prod., "Search for Tomorrow" ('74); Exec. Prod., "Search for Tomorrow" ('75); Exec. Prod., "As the World Turns" ('81).

ACHIEVEMENTS & AWARDS: N.A.

PERSONAL: Married; resides in New York City. Daughter, Juliana.

BURGESS, CHET
News Anchor and Reporter, Cable News Network, Atlanta Bureau

125 Elysian Way, N.W., Atlanta, GA 30327
b. September 12, 1946. Grand Junction, CO.

EDUCATION: Washington and Lee University, B.A. (magna cum laude, '74).

CAREER HIGHLIGHTS: News Stringer, *Roanoke Times*, Roanoke, VA ('72); Chief, Shenandoah Bureau, *Roanoke Times* ('73); News Dir., WJMA-Radio, Orange, VA ('74); Reporter/Anchor, WTAR-AM, Norfolk, VA ('76); News Anchor/Prod., WTAR-TV ('77); News Editor, Cable News Network, Atlanta ('80); News Anchor, Cable News Network, Atlanta ('81).

ACHIEVEMENTS & AWARDS: U.S. Navy achievement medal ('69); Region II Mark of Excellence award in radio reporting, Sigma Delta Chi ('72); Member, Phi Beta Kappa ('74); named outstanding journalism graduate, Washington and Lee University, by Sigma Delta Chi ('74); outstanding coverage of a spot news story, the Virginia AP Broadcasters ('76); Pres., Tidewater Chapter, SPJ/SDX, Norfolk, VA ('73–'74); Vestry/Council, Church of the Holy Apostles, Anglican/Roman Catholic, Norfolk ('73–'74).

PERSONAL: Wife, the former Bonnie Yates; son, Chet, IV.

BURGHEIM, RICHARD A.
Managing Editor, Time, Inc., *TV-Cable Week*

c/o *TV-Cable Week*, 1271 Ave. of the Americas, New York, NY 10020
b. July 5, 1933. St. Louis, MO.

EDUCATION: Harvard University ('55).

CAREER HIGHLIGHTS: Staff, *Time* magazine ('60); Assoc. Editor, *Time* magazine; Sr. Editor, *People* magazine ('74); Asst. Managing Editor, *People* ('80); Exec. Editor, *People* ('81). In charge of Editorial Development, *TV-Cable Week* ('81); Managing Editor, *TV-Cable Week* ('82).

ACHIEVEMENTS & AWARDS: Served on Emmy, Tony and other industry award juries.

PERSONAL: N.A.

BURK, J. ROBERT, JR.
V.P., Keycom Electronic Publishing, Technical Services

c/o Schaumburg Corporate Center, 1501 Woodfield Rd., Suite 110, Schaumburg, IL 60195
b. January 12.

EDUCATION: University of Denver, B.S., Mathematics.

CAREER HIGHLIGHTS: Staff Consultant, Applied Data Research ('66); Xerox Engineering Project Mgr. ('72); Product Mgr., Telephone Industry Computer Products, Honeywell ('76); V.P., Keycom Electronic Publishing, Technical Services ('82).

ACHIEVEMENTS & AWARDS: Member, Assn. for Computing Machinery, Institute of Electronics Engineers, and the American Natl. Standards Institute–Data Base Task Group.

PERSONAL: N.A.

BURKE, DAVID
Prod., NBC News, 'Monitor"

c/o NBC, 30 Rockefeller Plaza, New York, NY 10020
b. July 28, 1936. Waterbury, CT.

EDUCATION: Yale University, English, B.A. ('58); Yale School of Drama.

CAREER HIGHLIGHTS: Writer, Prod., and Production Mgr. for network and Syndicated TV

Programming. Has also been associated with HBO's "Sneak Preview," CBS News's "21st Century," series and documentary production for ABC News and CBS News. Associated with CBS News as Prod./Writer for "60 Minutes" (79–'82); Prod., NBC News, "Monitor" ('82).
ACHIEVEMENTS & AWARDS: N.A.
PERSONAL: N.A.

BURKE, DAVID W.
V.P. and Asst. to Pres., ABC, News

c/o ABC, 7 W. 66th St., New York, NY 10023
b. April 3, 1936. Brookline, MA.

EDUCATION: Tufts University, B.A., Economics; University of Chicago School of Business, M.S., Economics.
CAREER HIGHLIGHTS: Served as Asst. to Secretary of Commerce and Secretary of Labor and served as Exec. Secretary to Pres. Lyndon Johnson's Advisory Council on Labor-Management Policy ('61–'65); became legislative Asst. to Sen. Edward Kennedy ('65); Adm. Asst. to Sen. Kennedy ('66); joined Dreyfus Corp. as V.P. for Administration and Development ('71); appointed Secretary to New York Gov. Hugh Carey ('75); moved to ABC News as V.P. and Asst. to Pres.
ACHIEVEMENTS & AWARDS: N.A.
PERSONAL: Resides in Pelham Manor, NY, with wife, Beatrice; children, David Jr., Terence, Brendan, Owen, and Kathleen.

BURKE, DENISE W.
Dir., ABC, Inc., Awards and Special Projects

c/o ABC, 1330 Ave. of the Americas, New York, NY 10019
b. March 24, 1947. Bridgeport, CT.

EDUCATION: N.A.
CAREER HIGHLIGHTS: Public Relations Dept., ABC, Inc. ('67); Pepsi-Cola ('73); American Can ('74); returned to ABC in Owned TV Stations Division ('76); Mgr., Awards, ABC, Inc. ('77); promoted to Dir., Awards and Special Projects.
ACHIEVEMENTS & AWARDS: N.A.
PERSONAL: Resides in Mount Kisco, NY.

BURKE, KELLY
General Assignment Reporter, WRC-TV, NBC

c/o WRC-TV, 4001 Nebraska Ave., N.W., Washington, DC 20016
b. November 1, 1946. Detroit, MI.

EDUCATION: University of Detroit, B.A.
CAREER HIGHLIGHTS: General Assignment Reporter, WEWS-TV, Cleveland; Newscaster, Armed Forces Radio and TV Broadcast System; Radio Disc Jockey, WBIA-AM, Augusta, GA; Reporter, WKYZ-TV, Detroit; joined WRC-TV ('75).
ACHIEVEMENTS & AWARDS: Emmy award-winning reporter. Recipient of the San Francisco State University award for broadcast and media excellence and a variety of AP and UPI regional awards.
PERSONAL: Wife, Trisha; two children. Resides in Poolesville, MD.

BURKS, RUPERT
Dir. of Systems, ABC Video Enterprises, TeleFirst Entertainment Recording Service

c/o ABC, 1330 Ave. of the Americas, New York, NY 10019
b. June 8, 1936. Tennessee.

EDUCATION: Louisiana State University.
CAREER HIGHLIGHTS: Mgr., Rockwell Data Reduction Lab; Pres. of his own data processing consulting firm, Synalysis; Mgr. of Applications Software, Wynn Oil Co.; Mgr. of Systems and Applications Programming for Natl. Subscription's "On TV," Los Angeles; Dir. of Systems, TeleFirst Entertainment Recording Service of ABC Video Enterprises ('83).
ACHIEVEMENTS & AWARDS: Co-Author, *Fundamentals of Reliability Mathematics* and *Systems Analysis*
PERSONAL: N.A.

BURNETT, CAROL
Actress/Comedienne

c/o CBS, 7800 Beverly Blvd., Los Angeles, CA 90036
b. April 26, 1936. San Antonio, TX.

EDUCATION: University of California at Los Angeles.

CAREER HIGHLIGHTS: The heiress to Lucille Ball's comedy throne. Burnett's musical comedy clowning and talent for parody made her 13-year series the finest variety program in TV history before Burnett proved herself all over again in TV dramas such as *Friendly Fire.* She first appeared on Garry Moore's daytime TV show ('56), then made her nightclub debut at New York's Blue Angel, resulting in guest spots with Jack Paar and Ed Sullivan. She became a regular on Garry Moore's evening TV show ('59) and made her impressive stage debut in the musical *Once Upon a Mattress.* She has since starred in two TV versions of the musical and in nine other TV specials. Her movies include *Who's Been Sleeping in My Bed, Pete 'n' Tillie, The Front Page,* and *Annie.* She starred with Dick Van Dyke in *Same Time, Next Year* ('77) breaking all house records at the Huntington Hartford Theater in Los Angeles. She co-starred with Elizabeth Taylor in the HBO dramatic special *Between Friends* and appears occasionally as Eunice in the series "Mama's Family."

ACHIEVEMENTS & AWARDS: Among her numerous honors, she has received five Emmy awards, three *TV Guide* awards, five Golden Globe awards, and a Peabody award.

PERSONAL: Husband, Joe Hamilton, who was executive producer of "The Carol Burnett Show"; three daughters, Carrie, Jody, and Erin.

BURNHAM, BRUCE N.
V.P., Cox Cable Communications, Market Development

c/o Cox Cable Communications, 219 Perimeter Center Parkway, Atlanta, GA 30346
b. September 7, 1938. Hartford, CT.

EDUCATION: Middlebury College, B.A., English ('60); Queens College and Tulane University, Business Administration.

CAREER HIGHLIGHTS: District Operations Mgr., AT&T Operations, Atlanta ('70–'72); Branch Mgr., Stromberg-Carlson Communications ('72); General Mgr., Home Theater Operations/MDS, Cox Cable Communications ('75); Dir. of Franchising then V.P. Franchising, Cox Cable Communications ('78); V.P. Market Development, Cox Cable Communications ('80).

ACHIEVEMENTS & AWARDS: AT&T Pacemaker as top office of the year, Miami ('70).

PERSONAL: N.A.

BURNS, ALAN
Prod./Writer

4024 Radford Ave., Studio City, CA 91604
b. 1935. Baltimore, MD.

EDUCATION: University of Oregon, B.A.

CAREER HIGHLIGHTS: NBC Story Dept. ('56); Writer, Jay Ward Productions ('62); Writer, "The Smothers Brothers Show" ('64), "He and She" ('67), "Get Smart" ('68); Writer/Prod., "Room 222" ('69); Creator/Prod., "The Mary Tyler Moore Show" ('79), "Rhoda" ('74); Creator, "Friends and Lovers" ('74); Co-Creator, "Lou Grant" ('77). Also wrote the screenplays for *A Little Romance* and *Butch and Sundance: The Early Years.*

ACHIEVEMENTS & AWARDS: Emmy awards for outstanding comedy writer ('68, '70), best comedy series, "The Mary Tyler Moore Show" ('76, '77). Writers Guild awards for "The Mary Tyler Moore Show" and "Room 222."

PERSONAL: Wife, Irene, two children, Eric and Matthew

BURNS, ERIC
Midwest Correspondent, NBC, "Today"

c/o NBC, 30 Rockefeller Plaza, New York, NY 10020
b. August 29, 1945. Ambridge, PA.

EDUCATION: Westminster College, B.A., English ('67).

CAREER HIGHLIGHTS: Host. WQED-TV, Pittsburgh ('70); Host, WIIC-TV, Pittsburgh ('71); Reporter/Anchor, KMSP-TV, Minneapolis ('74); Correspondent, NBC News, Cleveland ('76); Correspondent, NBC News, Chicago ('76); Midwest Correspondent, NBC-TV's "Today" ('77).

ACHIEVEMENTS & AWARDS: N.A.

PERSONAL: Single.

BURNS, GEORGE (Nathan Birnbaum)
Comedian/Actor

790 N. Maple Dr., Beverly Hills, CA 90201
b. January 20, 1896. New York, NY.

EDUCATION: N.A.
CAREER HIGHLIGHTS: Burns, the straight man to
the gloriously scatterbrained Gracie Allen, is
now enjoying a second career as sexy octo-
genarian and masterful monologist making
frequent TV appearances and performing in
occasional one-man shows. Motion pictures
include *Damsel in Distress, The Big Broadcast,
The Sunshine Boys, Going in Style, International
House, Oh God, Just You and Me, Kid,* and *Oh
God! Book II."* TV co-star of "The Burns and
Allen Show" ('50–'58); starred in the comedy
series "Wendy and Me" ('64). TV Movies include *The Comedy Company* ('78).
ACHIEVEMENTS & AWARDS: Academy Award as
best supporting actor for *The Sunshine Boys.*
PERSONAL: Burns was married for many years
to the late Gracie Allen, who was his comedy
partner, most notably on TV's "The Burns
and Allen Show."

BURNS, JOHN B.
V.P., Sales Operations, Showtime
Entertainment

c/o Showtime, 1633 Broadway, New York, NY
  10019
b. October 27, 1944. Orange, NJ.

EDUCATION: Guilford College; University of
North Carolina School of Law.
CAREER HIGHLIGHTS: Asst. Gen. Mgr., Dir. of
Administration, Otis Elevator Group ('77);
Marketing Mgr., Intl. Paper ('80); V.P., Sales
Operations, Showtime Entertainment ('81).
ACHIEVEMENTS & AWARDS: N.A.
PERSONAL: Resides in New York City.

BURNS, RED
Prof. and Dir., New York University,
Alternate Media Center

c/o New York University, School of the Arts,
  725 Broadway, New York, NY 10003
b. Ottawa, Canada.

EDUCATION: N.A.
CAREER HIGHLIGHTS: With a broad background
in film and TV, Burns has been involved in
the development of cable TV and interactive
telecommunications systems. She recently
completed a field trial of broadcast teletext in
association with WETA-TV, Washington,
DC. Burns co-directed a Dept. of Health, Education, and Welfare funded project to develop uses of telecommunications to serve the
developmentally disabled. She also directed
the implementation of the internationally
acclaimed two-way cable TV project in Reading, PA. Burns has played an active role in
national communications policy process
through testimony to the House Subcommittee on the rewrite of the Communications
Act and to the FCC.
ACHIEVEMENTS & AWARDS: Appointed Chairman of the Graduate Program in Interactive
Telecommunications, New York University.
PERSONAL: Resides in New York City.

BURR, RAYMOND
Actor

c/o Lester Salkow, 8780 Sunset Blvd., Los
  Angeles, CA 90069
b. May 21, 1917. New Westminster, Canada.

EDUCATION: Stanford University; Columbia
University; University of California; University of Chungking.
CAREER HIGHLIGHTS: Star of the TV series
"Perry Mason" ('57) and "Ironside" ('70); appeared in the mini-series *Centennial* ('78). His
major motion pictures include *Rear Window*
and *A Place in the Sun.*
ACHIEVEMENTS & AWARDS: Emmy awards for
best lead actor for "Perry Mason" ('58, '60).
PERSONAL: N.A.

BURRINGTON, DAVID
Correspondent, NBC, News

c/o NBC, 30 Rockefeller Plaza, New York, NY
  10020
b. March 11, 1931. Rapid City, SD.

EDUCATION: University of Minnesota, B.A.,
Journalism, and M.A., American Studies.

CAREER HIGHLIGHTS: Reporter, KSTP-TV, Minneapolis; Reporter, WRCV-TV, Philadelphia; Reporter, KNBC-TV, Los Angeles ('64); Correspondent, NBC News, Saigon ('66); Correspondent, NBC News, Paris ('69); Correspondent, NBC News, Tel Aviv ('71); Correspondent, NBC News, Rome ('74); Correspondent, NBC News, Madrid ('77); Correspondent, NBC News, Cairo ('78); Correspondent, NBC News ('79); Correspondent, NBC News, San Francisco ('81).
ACHIEVEMENTS & AWARDS: N.A.
PERSONAL: N.A.

BURROWS, JAMES
Exec. Prod./Dir., Charles/Burrows Productions

c/o Charles/Burrows Productions, in association with Paramount Pictures Corp., 5555 Melrose Ave., Los Angeles, CA 90038
b. December 30, 1940. Los Angeles, CA.

EDUCATION: Oberlin College, B.A.; Yale School of Drama, M.F.A. ('65).
CAREER HIGHLIGHTS: Dialogue Coach for the short-lived "O.K. Crackerby!" series ('65); launched New York stage career, moving from Stage Mgr. to Dir. of various plays; returned to California to continue work in the theater and took reins as Dir., "The Mary Tyler Moore Show," which led to many more directorial assignments including "The Bob Newhart Show" ('74); "Phyllis" ('75); "Laverne and Shirley" ('76); "Lou Grant" ('77); "On Our Own" ('77); "We've Got Each Other" ('77); the TV movie *Best of Friends* ('77); 75 episodes of "Taxi" ('78–'81); "Best of the West" ('80); "The Two of Us" ('80). Dir. of the theatrical feature *Partners* ('82). Co-Creator/ Exec. Prod./Dir., "Cheers" ('82); Dir., NBC "Night Court" ('83–84).
ACHIEVEMENTS & AWARDS: Two Emmy awards for direction of "Taxi" ('80, '81).
PERSONAL: Wife, Linda; daughter, Katherine Sarah.

BURTON, AL
Exec. V.P., Embassy TV, Creative Affairs

c/o Embassy Communications, 1901 Ave. of the Stars, Los Angeles, CA 90067
b. April 9, 1928. Chicago, IL.

EDUCATION: Northwestern University, B.A., Speech ('48).
CAREER HIGHLIGHTS: Creator/Prod./Dir., series including "The Oscar Levant Show," "Hollywood A-Go-Go," and "Johnny Mercer's Musical Chairs." Dir., "Do You Trust Your Wife?" which starred Johnny Carson. Joined Norman Lear to create and develop series that later became "Mary Hartman, Mary Hartman" ('74); became Dir. of Development when Lear formed TAT with Jerry Perenchio ('74); Creative Supervisor on "Mary Hartman, Mary Hartman" and spinoffs "Fernwood 2Night," and "America 2Night"; named Exec. V.P., Creative Affairs, Embassy TV with overall creative supervisory responsibilities for company projects, and serves as Prod. Supervisor on the long-running network hits "One Day at a Time," "Diff'rent Strokes," "The Jeffersons," and "The Facts of Life," as well as "Silver Spoons," "Gloria," and "Square Pegs." An accomplished musician and songwriter, he teamed to compose themes for "Diff'rent Strokes" and "The Facts of Life."
ACHIEVEMENTS & AWARDS: Nominated for three Emmy awards honored by Natl. Conference of Christians and Jews ('79); California Governor's Committee for the Employment of the Handicapped ('81). Member, Caucus for Prods., Writers, and Dirs.; Directors Guild; Writers Guild; AFTRA; NATAS; Academy of Magical Arts.
PERSONAL: Resides in Beverly Hills, CA, with wife, Sally; daughter, Jennifer.

BUTCHER, TED
V.P., Film Production, ABC, TV

c/o ABC, 4151 Prospect Ave., Los Angeles, CA 90027
b. October 3, 1929.

EDUCATION: Los Angeles City College.
CAREER HIGHLIGHTS: Film Production, MGM ('48); First Asst. Dir., 20th Century Fox ('64); later named Asst. Head of TV Production,

20th Century Fox; joined ABC as V.P., Film Production.

ACHIEVEMENTS & AWARDS: N.A.

PERSONAL: Resides in Beverly Hills, CA, with wife, Audrey.

BUTLER, ROBERT
Dir.

c/o ICM, 8899 Beverly Blvd., Los Angeles, CA 90048
b. N.A.

EDUCATION: N.A.

CAREER HIGHLIGHTS: TV credits include *Night of the Juggler*, Columbia; *A Question of Guilt*, CBS-Lorimar; *In the Glitter Palace*, NBC; *James Dean* NBC; *Blue Knight*, NBC; *Dark Victory*, CBS-Universal, and the TV series "Remington Steele." Prod./Dir. for the ABC series "The Concrete Eye" ('83–'84)

ACHIEVEMENTS & AWARDS: N.A.

PERSONAL: N.A.

BUTLER, ROBERT C.
Exec. V.P., NBC, Finance

146 Rensselaer Rd., Essex Falls, NJ 07021
b. August 29, 1930. Newark, NJ.

EDUCATION: University of Notre Dame, B.S.; University of Pennsylvania Wharton School, M.B.A.

CAREER HIGHLIGHTS: Internal Auditor, Sylvania Electric Products ('55); Purchasing Mgr., Sylvania Intl. ('60); V.P. and Treasurer, Isotypes ('66); V.P., Financial Analysis, RCA ('72); V.P., Controller (Chief Accounting Officer), RCA ('76); Exec. V.P., Finance, NBC ('79).

ACHIEVEMENTS & AWARDS: N.A.

PERSONAL: Wife, Eileen; sons, Christopher, John, and Thomas.

BYRNE, MARY
Pres., Mary Byrne Assoc.

Mary Byrne Assoc., 30 W. 60th St., New York, NY 10023
b. February 9.

EDUCATION: Manhattanville College/University of Washington, B.A.; University of Florence (Italy)/Middletown College, M.A.; Columbia Teachers College.

CAREER HIGHLIGHTS: Reeves Communications Corp. ('76); V.P., Visual Scope TV ('80); heads Mary Byrnes Assoc. ('82), an international TV-film packaging group. Currently working on the North American representation of the "Heart of the Dragon," an NBC two-hour primetime special, which will also be a ten-hour PBS series.

ACHIEVEMENTS & AWARDS: On behalf of its clients, Visual Scope won, by shows or programs they sponsored, more than 40 Emmy and other awards.

PERSONAL: N.A.

BYRNES, JIM
Writer/Prod.

c/o Lew Weitzman & Assoc., 9171 Wilshire Blvd., Beverly Hills, CA 90024
b. August 31, 1943. Ames, IA.

EDUCATION: N.A.

CAREER HIGHLIGHTS: Asst. Story Editor, "Daniel Boone" ('66), "Gunsmoke" ('68); Writer, "Streets of San Francisco," "Movin'," "The Waltons," "Lancer" ('68–'75); Creator/Writer/Prod. of pilot for "How the West Was Won" ('75); Writer/Prod. MTM Enterprises ('76–'79); Writer/Prod. of the mini-series *The Sacketts* ('78); Writer/Prod., *Shadow Riders*, CBS ('82).

ACHIEVEMENTS & AWARDS: Writers Guild award for "Gunsmoke"; Western Writers of America awards for "Gunsmoke" ('74, '75) and "The Macahans" ('76).

PERSONAL: Divorced, father of two sons, Sean and Chad. Lives in Encino, CA.

CAESAR, SID
Performer

9255 Sunset Blvd., Los Angeles, CA 90069
b. September 8, 1922. Yonkers, NY

EDUCATION: N.A.
CAREER HIGHLIGHTS: One of the most influential performers in the history of TV comedy. The emperor of early TV comedy, Caesar was an accomplished mimic and expert sketch comic who popularized sophisticated comedy. His manic energy sparked some of the finest comedy writers of our generation, including Mel Brooks, Neil Simon, Larry Gelbart, and Woody Allen. Signed for *Broadway Revue* by Max Liebman, ('49), Star of "Your Show of Shows" on NBC-TV ('50) and "Caesar's Hour" ('54). Formed Shelbrick Corp., TV ('59). Star of TV series, "As Caesar Sees It" ('62) and "The Sid Caesar Show" ('63). Starred in the Broadway musical comedy *Little Me* ('62). Motion pictures include *It's a Mad, Mad, Mad, Mad World, The Spirit Is Willing, The Busy Body, Guide for the Married Man, Airport 1975, Silent Movie, Grease, The Cheap Detective*, and *History of the World—Part I.*
ACHIEVEMENTS & AWARDS: In *M.P. Daily's* TV poll, voted best comedian (tied, '51; '52) with Imogene Coca, and best comedy team ('53). Five Emmy awards ('57); Sylvania award ('58).
PERSONAL: N.A.

CAFFERTY, JACK
Reporter/Anchor/Host, WNBC-TV, New York, News

c/o WNBC-TV, 30 Rockefeller Plaza, New York, NY 10020
b. December 14, 1942. Reno, NV.

EDUCATION: University of Nevada, Pre-Med.
CAREER HIGHLIGHTS: Program Host, KBET-AM, Reno, NV ('60); moved to KOLO-TV, Reno ('62); KCBN-AM, Reno ('64); Operations Mgr. and News Anchor, KCRL-TV, Reno ('66); Weekend Anchor, WDAF-TV, Kansas City, MO ('68); Reporter/Weekday Anchor, WDAF-TV, Kansas City ('69); News Dir./Anchor, WHO-TV, Des Moines ('74); Reporter/Anchor and Co-Host of the station's "Live at Five" news and interview program, WNBC-TV, New York ('77).
ACHIEVEMENTS & AWARDS: N.A.
PERSONAL: N.A.

CAFFREY, KENNETH E.
Sr. V.P. and Exec. Dir., Oglivy & Mather, Media

c/o Ogilvy & Mather, 2 E. 48th St., New York, NY 10017
b. N.A.

EDUCATION: N.A.
CAREER HIGHLIGHTS: Started as Media Planner, Ogilvy & Mather ('63); V.P., Ogilvy & Mather ('68); Sr. V.P., Ogilvy & Mather ('74); Member, Ogilvy & Mather's Council of Directors ('78, '79); Co-Dir., Media Dept., Ogilvy & Mather; Sr. V.P. and Exec. Dir. Media Operations, Ogilvy & Mather ('79).

ACHIEVEMENTS & AWARDS: N.A.

PERSONAL: Resides in Scarsdale, NY, with his wife, Joan and their three children.

CAIN, BOB (Robert O. Cain)
News Correspondent/Anchor, Cable News Network, Atlanta Bureau

c/o Cable News Network, 1050 Techwood Dr., N.W., Atlanta, GA 30318
b. August 11, 1934. O'Neill, NE.

EDUCATION: Creighton University; Brown University.

CAREER HIGHLIGHTS: Entered broadcast journalism with KSWI, Council Bluffs, IA ('52). News Dir., KOIL-Radio, Omaha, ('56); Newscaster, WHK-Radio, Cleveland ('60); Anchor/Reporter, WJAR-TV, WPRI, Providence, RI ('63); Correspondent, NBC News, New York ('71); Anchor, Cable News Network, Atlanta Bureau ('80).

ACHIEVEMENTS & AWARDS: Toastmaster's gavel award, Providence, RI ('66); Peabody award for NBC News "Second Sunday" series on "Communism in the '70's" ('75).

PERSONAL: Resides in Atlanta with wife, Anne. Four children, Stephanie, Robert, Julie, and John.

CAIN, VERNON W.
V.P., Sales and Planning, Keycom Electronic Publishing

c/o Schaumburg Corporate Center, 1501 Woodfield Rd., Suite 110, Schaumburg, IL 60195
b. January 5, 1947. Bisbee, AZ.

EDUCATION: Northern Arizona University, B.S., Marketing Management; Roosevelt University, M.B.A.

CAREER HIGHLIGHTS: Division Marketing Manager, Central Telephone, Nevada; Asst. V.P. Marketing and Public Relations for Central Telephone Co.; V.P., Sales and Planning, Keycom Electronic Publishing.

ACHIEVEMENTS & AWARDS: N.A.

PERSONAL: N.A.

CAIRD, ROBERT N.
V.P., Affiliate Sales, Disney Channel

c/o Disney Channel, 500 S. Buena Vista, Burbank, CA. 91505
b. September 7, 1938. Greenwich, Ct.

EDUCATION: Boston University, B.A., Communications ('65); Thunderbird School for International Management, M.A. ('67).

CAREER HIGHLIGHTS: Asst. Marketing Mgr., American Cyanamid Co., ('67); Marketing Mgr., American Can Co. ('70); Product Mgr., American Express Co. ('74); V.P., Marketing, HBO ('76); Sr. V.P., Marketing, Entertainment Channel ('82); V.P., Affiliate Sales, Disney Channel ('83).

ACHIEVEMENTS & AWARDS: N.A.

PERSONAL: N.A.

CALABRESE, PETER ROBERT
V.P., NBC, Specials, Variety Series and Late Night Programming

c/o Lee Gables, ICM, 8899 Beverly Blvd., Los Angeles, CA 90048
b. April 22, 1943. Hoboken, NJ.

EDUCATION: Jersey City State College, B.A.

CAREER HIGHLIGHTS: Production Asst., "The Ed Sullivan Show" ('64); Dir., "Treasure Isle" ('68); Dir., "The Virginia Graham Show" ('70); Dir., various specials and series with Bill Russell, Rod Serling, and Robert Young ('71); Dir., "The Mike Douglas Show" ('73); Dir., "Tom Jones Special," "Englebert Humperdinck Special," "Ben Vereen Show" and "The Smothers Brothers Show" ('75); Dir., "Tony Orlando and Dawn," and Exec. Prod., "Barry White Special" and "Roberta Flack Special" ('76); Prod./Dir., "Photoplay Awards" for

ABC and "Everyday" series for Westinghouse ('78); joined NBC as V.P., Specials, Variety Series and Late Night Programming ('80).

ACHIEVEMENTS & AWARDS: N.A.

PERSONAL: Resides in Bel Air, CA; son, Nicholas.

CALMAN, JEFFREY
Dir., Warner Bros., Sales Development

c/o Warner Bros., 75 Rockefeller Plaza, 13th Floor, New York, NY 10019
b. March 8, 1949. New York, NY.

EDUCATION: Columbia University, B.A. ('71); New York University, M.A. ('74); University of Pennsylvania, M.B.A. ('80).

CAREER HIGHLIGHTS: Mgr., Planning and Development, Warner Bros. ('80); Dir., Sales Development ('81).

ACHIEVEMENTS & AWARDS: Author *The Mormon Tabernacle Choir* ('79).

PERSONAL: N.A.

CAMPANELLA JR., ROY
Dir./Prod./Writer, Morningstar Productions, Universal TV

c/o Universal TV, 100 Universal City Plaza, Universal City, CA 91608
b. N.A.

EDUCATION: Harvard University, B.A., Anthropology ('70); Columbia University, M.B.A.

CAREER HIGHLIGHTS: Dir./Cameraman/Editor of documentaries, WGBH-TV, Boston ('71); Film and Videotape Editor, CBS News ('73); Writer/Dir., "Pass/Fail" for PBS ('78); Program Exec., Motion Pictures for TV and Mini-Series, CBS Entertainment ('79); Dir., "Lou Grant" and "Simon and Simon" ('81). Formed his own production company, Morningstar Productions, based at Universal Studios ('82).

ACHIEVEMENTS & AWARDS: Best picture and best drama award for the Black Filmmakers Hall of Fame for "Pass/Fail" ('79).

PERSONAL: N.A.

CAMPBELL, ARCH
Feature Reporter and Theater Critic, WRC-TV, Washington, DC

c/o WRC-TV, 4001 Nebraska Ave., N.W., Washington, DC 20016
b. April 25, 1946. San Antonio, TX.

EDUCATION: University of Texas at Austin, B.A. and M.A., Journalism.

CAREER HIGHLIGHTS: Began as an Announcer, KITY-FM, San Antonio, TX, and KTBC-AM/FM/TV, Austin, TX; next worked as a Radio Announcer and News Reporter, WFAA-TV; Feature Reporter and Theater Critic, WRC-TV, Washington, DC ('75).

ACHIEVEMENTS & AWARDS: N.A.

PERSONAL: Married, resides in Chevy Chase, MD.

CAMPBELL, JOYCE B.
V.P. and Station Mgr., WETA-TV

c/o WETA-TV, Box 2626, Washington, DC 20013
b. N.A.

EDUCATION: Stanford University, B.A.; San Francisco State University, M.A.

CAREER HIGHLIGHTS: Asst. to the Dir. of Instructional Television, KQED-TV, San Francisco ('59); Exec. Secretary to the General Mgr., KQED-TV ('61); Prod./Dir., KQED-TV, San Francisco ('66); Production Dir., KUID-TV, University of Idaho ('72); Program Dir., KUID-TV, University of Idaho ('74); Station Mgr., KUID-TV, University of Idaho ('77); Programming Dir., WETA-TV, Washington, DC ('78); V.P., Programming, WETA-TV, Washington, DC ('79); V.P. and Station Mgr., WETA-TV, Washington, DC ('82).

ACHIEVEMENTS & AWARDS: N.A.

PERSONAL: N.A.

CANDIDO, JOSEPH
Dir., Compliance and Practices, NBC, West Coast

c/o NBC, 3000 W. Alameda Ave., Burbank, CA 91523
b. Albany, NY.

EDUCATION: State University of New York at Brockport, B.S., Broadcast Communications and English (cum laude, '78); Albany Law School, J.D. ('81).

CAREER HIGHLIGHTS: Legal Intern, Harris, Beach, Wilcox, Rubin & Levy law firm, Rochester, NY ('78); Sales Supervisor, ASC Hospital Supply, Albany, NY ('78); Compliance Policy Mgr., NBC ('82); Mgr., Compliance and Practices, NBC, West Coast ('83)

ACHIEVEMENTS & AWARDS: N.A.

PERSONAL: Single, resides in Sherman Oaks, CA.

CANNELL, STEPHEN J.
Writer/Prod., Cannell Productions

c/o Cannell Productions, 780 N. Gower, Los Angeles, CA 90038
b. 1942. Pasadena, CA

EDUCATION: University of Oregon.

CAREER HIGHLIGHTS: Sold "Mission Impossible" script ideas to Desilu ('66–'73); Head Writer, "Adam 12" ('70). Wrote scripts for "Toma" ('73), "The Rockford Files" ('74–'80), "Baretta" ('75), and "City of Angels" ('76). Created and produced "Baa Baa Black Sheep" ('76); "Stone" ('79); "Tenspeed and Brown Shoe" ('79); "The Greatest American Hero" ('81); "The A-Team" ('83); "Rolling Thunder" ('83); and "The Rousters" ('83)

ACHIEVEMENTS & AWARDS: Mystery Writers of America award for screenplay *Stone* ('79); Writers Guild award for best dramatic episode for the pilot of "Tenspeed and Brown Shoe" ('80); Intl. Film and TV Festival of New York, silver award for "The Greatest American Hero" ('81).

PERSONAL: Resides in Pasadena, CA, with wife and children.

CAPICE, PHILIP
Exec. Prod. and Pres., Lorimar Productions

c/o Lorimar Productions, 3970 Overland Ave., Culver City, CA 90230
b. June 24, 1931.

EDUCATION: Dickinson College, B.A.; Columbia University Graduate School of Dramatic Arts, M.F.A.

CAREER HIGHLIGHTS: As Dir. of Special Programs at CBS and Exec. Prod. for Lorimar, Capice has been associated with some of the best TV specials and TV movies, including "The Barbara Streisand Specials," *The Autobiography of Miss Jane Pittman, Sybil, Green Eyes,* and *Helter Skelter.* Began in TV Dept., Benton & Bowles, and moved through the ranks to become V.P. of Programming Development, Dir. of Special Programs, CBS TV ('68). Moved to Lorimar as Sr. V.P. in Charge of TV ('74); Co-Exec. Prod. on Lorimar Productions *Eric* and *The Blue Knight;* Pres. of Lorimar TV, and served as Co-Exec. Prod. on *Studs Lonigan* and *Married: The First Year;* Exec. Prod., "Eight Is Enough" and "Dallas."

ACHIEVEMENTS & AWARDS: Emmy for *Sybil;* two consecutive Peabody awards for *Sybil* and *Green Eyes;* Christopher award for *Long Journey Back,* two People's Choice awards for "Eight Is Enough," and "Dallas."

PERSONAL: N.A.

CAPPLEMAN, CHARLES
V.P., CBS, Facilities and Engineering

c/o CBS, 51 W. 52d St., New York, NY 10019
b. N.A.

EDUCATION: College of William and Mary.

CAREER HIGHLIGHTS: CBS Stage Mgr. ('54); Dir., Program Production Services at Television City ('69); General Mgr., Program Production Services at Television City ('77); V.P., Facilities and Engineering, CBS ('80).

ACHIEVEMENTS & AWARDS: N.A.

PERSONAL: Wife, Jane; three daughters, one son. Resides in Tarzana, CA.

CAPRON, CHRISTOPHER
Head of Current Affairs Programmes, TV, BBC

c/o BBC, 12 Cavendish Place, London, England W1
b. N.A.

EDUCATION: Wellington College; Trinity Hall, Cambridge (England).

CAREER HIGHLIGHTS: Joined BBC TV Current Affairs Dept. ('67); Editor, "Newsday" ('74); Editor, "Tonight" ('76); Editor, "Panorama"

('77); Asst. Head of Current Affairs for BBC TV ('79); Head of Current Affairs Programmes, BBC TV ('81).

ACHIEVEMENTS & AWARDS: News features award for "The Friends Who Put Fire in the Heavens;" investigative journalism Emmy for "Who Killed Georgi Markov?"

PERSONAL: Married, two children

CARAS, ROGER
Correspondent, ABC News

c/o ABC, 1330 Ave. of the Americas, New York, NY 10019
b. May 24, 1928. Methuen, MA

EDUCATION: N.A.
CAREER HIGHLIGHTS: An expert on the animal world, Caras joined ABC News ('74) as the only network news correspondent exclusively covering pets, wildlife, and the environment. Provides reports for ABC's "World News Tonight," "20/20," and ABC News "Nightline." Also hosts a radio show, "The Living World," which airs daily on the ABC Radio Network.
ACHIEVEMENTS & AWARDS: Certificate of appreciation from the Humane Society of the U.S.; special awards from the New York State and Long Island Veterinary Medical Societies; the Joseph Wood Krutch medal for "significant contributions to the improvement of quality of life on earth"; honorary doctor of letters degree, Rio Grande College, Ohio ('79). Author of more than 40 books on animals and the outdoors.
PERSONAL: Wife, Jill Langdon Barclay, who is president of the Animal Rescue Fund; two children.

CARDEA, FRANK
Co-Exec. Prod./Prod./Writer

c/o Schenck/Cardea Productions, Burbank Studios, Columbia Plaza E., Room 137, Burbank, CA 91505
b. August 17. Connecticut.

EDUCATION: La Salle College, B.S., Accounting and Finance
CAREER HIGHLIGHTS: Assoc. Prod. of the mini-series Washington Behind Closed Doors; Exec. in Charge of Prod. of the mini-series Shogun;

Writer/Prod./Creator (with George Schenck), "Sawyer and Finn," and "O'Malley" for NBC, "Hard Knocks" for ABC, and "Bring 'Em Back Alive" for CBS.
ACHIEVEMENTS & AWARDS: N.A.
PERSONAL: Wife, Judy; resides in Los Angeles.

CAREY, CARL (Bud)
V.P., General Mgr., WNBC-TV, New York

c/o WNBC-TV, 30 Rockefeller Plaza, New York, NY 10020
b. N.A.

EDUCATION: N.A.
CAREER HIGHLIGHTS: Acct. Exec., Spot Sales, NBC ('76); Natl. Sales Mgr., WNBC-TV ('77); Dir. of Sales, KNBC; Station Mgr., KNBC, Los Angeles ('79); V.P., General Mgr., WNBC-TV ('82).
ACHIEVEMENTS & AWARDS: Served on the Board of Dirs. of the Los Angeles Urban League and Burbank Chapter of the Salvation Army.
PERSONAL: N.A.

CAREY, MacDONALD
Actor

c/o "Days of Our Lives," NBC, 30 Rockefeller Plaza, New York, NY 10020
b. March 15, 1913. Sioux City, IA.

EDUCATION: University of Wisconsin; University of Iowa.
CAREER HIGHLIGHTS: Broadway roles in Lady in the Dark and Anniversary Waltz. Major motion pictures include Dream Girl, Wake Island, Variety Girl, and The Great Gatsby. TV movies include Gidget Gets Married, Who is the Black Dah-

lia, Ordeal, and *Stranger in Our House.* Regular on the daytime drama "Days of Our Lives."

ACHIEVEMENTS & AWARDS: Two Emmy awards as best actor in daytime drama for "Days of Our Lives."

PERSONAL: N.A.

CAREY, PHILIP
Actor

c/o "One Life To Live," ABC, 1330 Ave. of the Americas, New York, NY 10019
b. July 15, 1925. Hackensack, NJ.

EDUCATION: University of Miami.

CAREER HIGHLIGHTS: Veteran actor who started in motion pictures under contract with Warner Bros. and Columbia Pictures and appeared in *The Long Gray Line, Pushover, Operation Pacific, Springfield Rifle, Fighting Mad,* and *Mr. Roberts.* Primetime series credits include "Bengal Lancers," "Philip Marlowe," "Laredo," "The Untamed World," "All in the Family," "Little House on the Prairie," "Police Woman," "Gunsmoke," and "The Bionic Woman." In a departure from his previous work, he joined the cast of "One Life To Live" ('80) as the rich and powerful Texan, Asa Buchanan, a central character on the show.

ACHIEVEMENTS & AWARDS: N.A.

PERSONAL: N.A.

CARLSON, LARRY
V.P., HBO, Advertising and Promotion

c/o HBO, 1271 Ave. of the Americas, New York, NY 10020
b. May 14, 1948.

EDUCATION: Long Beach City College; University of California at Long Beach.

CAREER HIGHLIGHTS: Mgr. with American Television and Communications Corp. ('69); Gen. Mgr., Laurel Cablevision, Connecticut ('76); Gen. Mgr., Durham Cablevision, North Carolina ('77); Gen. Mgr., Moraga Cablevision, California ('78). Joined HBO as Regional Dir., San Francisco Office ('78); transferred to New York as Dir., Natl. Sales Planning and Development ('80); promoted to V.P., Advertising and Promotion ('82), responsible for the de-

velopment and implementation of all marketing programs.

ACHIEVEMENTS & AWARDS: Member, Natl. Assn. of MDS Services Companies

PERSONAL: Resides in Sag Harbor, NY, with wife, Jody.

CARPENTER, TED
Editor, TELEKEY

2917 Covington Rd., Silver Spring, MD 20910
b. September 8, 1945. Halifax, Nova Scotia, Canada.

EDUCATION: Tufts University, B.A., English Literature ('68).

CAREER HIGHLIGHTS: Exec. Dir., Broadside Video, Tennessee and Virginia ('72); Exec. Dir., Natl. Citizens Committee for Broadcasting ('75); Sr. Staff Member, Carnegie Commission on the Future of Public Broadcasting ('77); Designer and Editor of software for the FILETEX system and TELEKEY; Pres., Electronic Publishing Systems, as well as being Partner/Editor of TELEKEY Associates ('79).

ACHIEVEMENTS & AWARDS: N.A.

PERSONAL: Resides in Silver Spring, MD, with his wife and their four children.

CARPER, JEAN
Health Reporter, Cable News Network, Washington Bureau

1018 W. Peachtree St., N.W., Atlanta, GA 30309
b. January 3. Washington, D.C.

EDUCATION: Ohio Wesleyan University, B.A.

CAREER HIGHLIGHTS: Carper's experience includes health reporting, KYW-TV, Philadelphia, WDVM-TV, Washington, DC; Natl. Consumer Reporter, Group W–Westinghouse Broadcasting System; Health Reporter, Cable News Network, Washington, DC ('80).

ACHIEVEMENTS & AWARDS: Author of nine books on health topics; Contributor to *Washington Post,* Editorial Section, "Outlook"; has written articles for *Newsweek, Reader's Digest, Consumer Report, Changing Times,* and *Saturday Review.*

PERSONAL: N.A.

CARR, MARTIN
Exec. Prod., PBS

c/o PBS, 609 Fifth Ave., 11th Floor, New York, NY 10017
b. N.A.

EDUCATION: Williams College.
CAREER HIGHLIGHTS: Carr has experience as a producer, writer, and director in every major type of programming, from dramas, operas, ballets, and concerts to soap operas and cultural and news documentaries. He served as Exec. Prod., "The 10 O'Clock News" at WNEW-TV, New York and Prod., "20/20" for ABC News. Major productions include "CBS Reports: Hunger in America," "The Search for Ulysses," "Gauguin in Tahiti," NBC News's "Migrant" and "This Child is Rated X." Currently involved in a number of PBS documentary productions, including "The Smithsonian Series."
ACHIEVEMENTS & AWARDS: Four Emmy awards; three Peabody awards; Robert F. Kennedy award; the Gavel award; the Sidney Hillman Foundation award; several Writers Guild awards, and Christopher award.
PERSONAL: N.A.

CARROLL, BOB, JR.
Prod./Writer

c/o Robinson-Weintraub, 554 S. San Vicente Blvd., Suite 3, Los Angeles, CA 90048
b. McKeesport, PA.

EDUCATION: St. Petersburg Junior College.
CAREER HIGHLIGHTS: Staff Writer, CBS Radio, Hollywood ('42–'48); Writer, "My Favorite Husband," CBS Radio series ('48–'51); Writer/Creator, "I Love Lucy" TV series ('51–'57); Writer, "Lucy-Desi Hour" shows ('58–'61); Writer/Creator, "The Lucy Show" ('62–'64); Writer/Creator, "The Mothers-in-Law" ('66–'68); Writer, "Here's Lucy" ('70–'73); Prod./Writer, "Lucille Ball Special" ('76); Prod./Writer, "Alice" ('76–'79); Exec. Prod., "Alice" ('79–'82); Exec. Prod., "Private Benjamin" ('81–'82).
ACHIEVEMENTS & AWARDS: Sylvania award for TV writing ('52); Golden Globe award for "Alice" ('79).
PERSONAL: Daughter, Christina.

CARSEY, MARCIA
Independent Prod.

c/o Carsey-Werner Productions, 1130 Westwood Blvd., Los Angeles, CA 90024
b. November 21, 1944. South Weimouth, ME.

EDUCATION: University of New Hampshire, B.A.
CAREER HIGHLIGHTS: Program Supervisor, William Esty Ad Agency; Story Editor, "Tomorrow Entertainment"; ABC Program Exec. ('74); V.P., Prime Time Series for ABC ('79); Currently the co-founder and chief executive of Carsey-Werner Productions (with partner Tom Werner). Their recent productions include the ABC shows "Love and Marriage ('83–'84), "Weekends" ('83–'84) and "Oh, Madeline" ('83–'84).
ACHIEVEMENTS & AWARDS: N.A.
PERSONAL: N.A.

CARSON, JOHNNY
Host, "The Tonight Show Starring Johnny Carson"

c/o NBC, 3000 W. Alameda, Ave., Burbank, CA 91523
b. October 23, 1925. Corning, IA.

EDUCATION: University of Nebraska.
CAREER HIGHLIGHTS: TV's "Tonight Show" host delivers ad libs with unrivalled aplomb and has made the insomniac's world a happier place with his informal chitchat with guests. Carson's hilarious opening monologues have become a barometer for American manners and mores and will probably give social anthropologists of the future a good indication of what contemporary America finds funny. His first show at KNXT, Los Angeles, was "Carson's Cellar" ('50). He

hosted his own primetime network show, "Earn Your Vacation" ('54), and appeared on "The Morning Show" as substitute host for Jack Paar. He hosted ABC TV's daytime game show "Who Do You Trust?" ('57) before NBC hired him ('58) as a permanent host on "The Tonight Show."

ACHIEVEMENTS & AWARDS: His numerous awards include Hasty Pudding Club Man of the Year; the Entertainer of the Year award from AGVA; Friars Club Man of the Year Award.

PERSONAL: Grew up in Nebraska. Resides in Beverly Hills, CA; three children, Chris, Ricky, and Cory.

CARSWELL, DONALD
Sr. V.P., Financial Planning and Analysis, NBC

c/o NBC, 30 Rockefeller Plaza, New York, NY 10020
b. October 25, 1929.

EDUCATION: Harvard University, B.A. ('50); Harvard Business School, M.B.A. ('52).

CAREER HIGHLIGHTS: Joined NBC as Comptroller Trainee ('56); Business Mgr., Design Art and Scenic Production, NBC ('57); Mgr., Operating Reports and Analysis, Facilities Dept., NBC ('59); Mgr., Financial Analysis ('60); Mgr., Pricing and Financial Evaluation ('61); Dir., Pricing and Financial Evaluation ('62); V.P., Financial Planning ('68); V.P., Business Affairs ('69); V.P., Business Affairs and Production Operations ('75); V.P., Finance and Administration, NBC ('79); Sr. V.P., Financial Planning and Analysis, NBC ('83).

ACHIEVEMENTS & AWARDS: Member, Harvard Club; Vice-Chairman, Board of the Brooklyn Botanic Garden.

PERSONAL: Resides in New York City with wife Lois; three children.

CARTER, CLAIRE
Co-Anchor, WPIX-TV, News

c/o WPIX-TV, 11 WPIX Plaza, New York, NY 10017
b. N.A.

EDUCATION: N.A.

CAREER HIGHLIGHTS: Co-Host, afternoon talk show, Feature Reporter, WNAC, Midday News; Host, "Bostonia," WNAC-TV, Boston; Co-Host, "AM/Philadelphia," Philadelphia; Co-Anchor, "INN: Midday Edition," WPIX-TV New York ('81).

ACHIEVEMENTS & AWARDS: N.A.

PERSONAL: N.A.

CARTER, HODDING
Anchor and Chief Correspondent, PBS, "Inside Story"

c/o Frank Goodman Assoc., 1776 Broadway, New York, NY 10019
b. N.A.

EDUCATION: Harvard University.

CAREER HIGHLIGHTS: Editor and Publisher of the Greenville (MS) Delta-Democrat Times; Asst. U.S. Secretary of State during the Carter administration ('77); Anchor and Chief Correspondent of "Inside Story," PBS ('81). Writes a twice-monthly column for the Wall Street Journal.

ACHIEVEMENTS & AWARDS: N.A.

PERSONAL: Married to Patricia Derian, former top official with the Carter Administration.

CARTER, LYNDA
Actress/Prod.

c/o Lynda Carter Productions, P.O. Box 5973, Sherman Oaks, CA 91413
b. July 24, 1951. Phoenix, AZ.

EDUCATION: N.A.

CAREER HIGHLIGHTS: Appeared in the "Wonder Woman" series ('75–'79); four TV musical-variety specials ('80–'82); three TV movies, The Last Song, Born To Be Sold, and Hotline ('80–'82); world personal appearance tours ('76–'82).

ACHIEVEMENTS & AWARDS: Mexico's Ariel award as international entertainer of the year ('80); Emmy for "Lynda Carter—Celebration"; Gold Poster award ('80).

PERSONAL: N.A.

CARTER, NELL
Singer/Actress

c/o "Gimme a Break," NBC, 3000 W. Alameda Ave., Burbank, CA 91523
b. September 13, Birmingham, AL.

EDUCATION: N.A.
CAREER HIGHLIGHTS: This deliciously uninhibited Broadway belter is a kind of modern day Sophie Tucker, a red-hot mama with sassy delivery and dynamic presence. Broadway appearances in *Dude, Don't Bother Me, I Can't Cope, Jesus Christ Superstar*, and *Ain't Misbehavin'*. Regular star of the daytime serial "Ryan's Hope." Film credits include *Hair, Back Roads*, and *Modern Problems*. Star of "Gimme a Break."
ACHIEVEMENTS & AWARDS: Drama Desk, Obie, Theater World and Tony awards for best supporting actress in a musical for *Ain't Misbehavin'*.
PERSONAL: Husband, Georg Krynicki; resides in Studio City, CA.

CARTER, SPENCER P.
Mgr. of Employee Relations, Westinghouse Broadcasting and Cable, Group W Cable

c/o Group W Cable, 888 Seventh Ave., New York, NY 10106
b. November 27, 1943. North Carolina.

EDUCATION: University of Missouri School of Journalism, B.J.
CAREER HIGHLIGHTS: Employee Communications Specialist, Westinghouse Steam Turbine Plant, Charlotte, NC; Dir. of Communications, Blue Ridge Electric Membership Corp., Lenoir, NC; Mgr. of Employee Relations, Group W Cable, New York ('83).

ACHIEVEMENTS & AWARDS: N.A.
PERSONAL: N.A.

CARTER, VIRGINIA L.

c/o TAT Communications, 1901 Ave. of the Stars, Los Angeles, CA 90067
b. November 18, 1936. Quebec, Canada.

EDUCATION: McGill University, B.S.; University of Southern California, M.S.
CAREER HIGHLIGHTS: Physicist and Member, Technical Staff, Aerospace Corp. of Southern California ('63); Pres., Los Angeles Chapter, NOW ('69); Norman Lear's Staff Asst.; V.P., Creative Affairs for TAT and Embassy Productions ('73).
ACHIEVEMENTS & AWARDS: V.P., Women's Lobby, Inc.; Member, Womens Equity Action League, NATAS. Emmy ('82); Peabody award ('82).
PERSONAL: Resides in Redondo Beach, CA.

CASEY, FRANK
Newscaster, WPIX-TV, News

c/o WPIX-TV, 11 WPIX Plaza, New York, NY 10017
b. January 29, 1940.

EDUCATION: Virginia State College ('65).
CAREER HIGHLIGHTS: His first job was as Unit Supervisor, New York Dept. of Social Service; News Trainee, WPIX-TV ('69); Reporter, WPIX-TV ('69); Host, Channel 11, "Black Pride"; Newscaster, WPIX-TV, "Action News" ('70).
ACHIEVEMENTS & AWARDS: N.A.
PERSONAL: Married, resides in Teaneck, NJ.

CASEY, JOHN
Sr. V.P., United Satellite Communications, Operations

c/o United Satellite Communications, 1345 Ave. of the Americas, New York, NY 10105
b. January 1, 1943.

EDUCATION: Merrimac College, B.S.; Georgetown University, Ph.D., Economics.

CAREER HIGHLIGHTS: V.P., CBS; Pres. and General Mgr., Field Services Division, Western Union; Sr. V.P., Operations, United Satellite Communications, New York.
ACHIEVEMENTS & AWARDS: N.A.
PERSONAL: N.A.

CASO, LAURENCE A.
Dir., Daytime Programs, CBS, Entertainment, New York

c/o CBS, 51 W. 52d St., New York, NY 10019
b. Chappaqua, NY.

EDUCATION: Syracuse University Newhouse School of Communications, B.S. ('72); Indiana University, M.S. ('73).
CAREER HIGHLIGHTS: Company Mgr., Berkshire Theater Festival, Stockbridge, MA ('72); Program Development Exec., CBS, Los Angeles ('75); Assoc. Dir., Program Development, CBS, New York ('78); Dir., Special Programs, CBS, New York ('81); V.P., Programs, Disney Channel ('82); Consultant, Daytime Program Dept., ABC Entertainment ('83); Dir., Daytime Programs, CBS Entertainment, New York ('83).
ACHIEVEMENTS & AWARDS: N.A.
PERSONAL: Resides in Bedford Hills, NY, with his wife, Patricia.

CASO, PATRICIA
Exec. Prod., WABC-TV, New York, "The Morning Show"

c/o WABC-TV, 7 Lincoln Sq., New York, NY 10023
b. August 3. Connecticut.

EDUCATION: Syracuse University School of Public Communications, B.S., Social Work/Radio-TV.
CAREER HIGHLIGHTS: Production Asst., "For Women Only," WBZ-TV, Boston ('71); Production Asst., "Drugs and Kids," WCNY-TV, Syracuse, NY ('72); Prod./Dir., KDKA-TV, Pittsburgh ('74); Prod., KNBC-TV, Los Angeles ('76); Prod., "A.M. Los Angeles," KABC-TV, Los Angeles ('77); Prod., "A.M. New York," ('78); Assoc. Prod. and Field Prod., "Tomorrow With Tom Snyder," NBC ('79); Unit Prod., "Entertainment Tonight,"

Paramount TV, Los Angeles ('81); Exec. Prod., "The Morning Show," WABC-TV, New York ('83).
ACHIEVEMENTS & AWARDS: N.A.
PERSONAL: Resides in Bedford Hills, NY, with her husband, Laurence.

CASSUTT, MICHAEL
Dir., Prime Time, CBS Broadcast Group, Program Practices

c/o CBS, 7800 Beverly Blvd., Los Angeles, CA 90036
b. N.A.

EDUCATION: University of Arizona, B.A., Radio/TV.
CAREER HIGHLIGHTS: Program Dir., KHYT-TV, Tucson, AZ; Editor, Program Practices, CBS ('80); Mgr., Administration, Program Practices, CBS ('82); Dir., Prime Time, CBS Broadcast Group, Program Practices, Hollywood ('83).
ACHIEVEMENTS & AWARDS: N.A.
PERSONAL: Resides in Studio City, CA, with his wife, Cynthia.

CASTELLI, LOUIS P.
Dir., In-House Productions Hearst/ABC Daytime (HAVES)

c/o Hearst/ABC, 555 Fifth Ave., New York, NY 10017
b. August 4, 1946. Bogota, Colombia.

EDUCATION: Northwestern University, Ph.D.
CAREER HIGHLIGHTS: Host/Prod., "Ecos Latinos," Chicago, WMAQ-TV/NBC ('74–'75); Host, "Contigo," Chicago, WMAQ-TV/NBC ('75–'77); Asst. Professor and Head of TV Production, Radio, TV, and Film Dept., Northwestern University ('75–'82); Writer, Head Story Consultant, "33 Brompton Place," a soap opera for SHO Cable, ABA Production Co. ('81–'82); Dir. of In-House productions, Hearst/ABC Daytime (HAVES) ('82).
ACHIEVEMENTS & AWARDS: Author, *David Lean: A Guide to References and Resources.*
PERSONAL: N.A.

CATES, GILBERT
Prod./Dir.

119 W. 57th St., Suite 915, New York, NY
10019
b. June 6, 1934.

EDUCATION: Syracuse University.
CAREER HIGHLIGHTS: Prod./Dir., "International
Showtime" ('62); Prod., *I Never Sang for My
Father* special for CBS; Prod., Arthur Miller's
After the Fall for NBC; Dir. theatrical film ver-
sion of *I Never Sang for My Father* ('70). Motion
pictures also include *The Promise* and *Summer
Wishes, Winter Dreams.*
ACHIEVEMENTS & AWARDS: N.A.
PERSONAL: Brother of Prod./Dir. Joseph Cates.

CATES, JOSEPH
Dir., Musical Specials

c/o Cates Co., 9200 Sunset Blvd., Los
Angeles, CA 90069
b. 1924.

EDUCATION: New York University.
CAREER HIGHLIGHTS: Broadway Prod. of *A Day
in the Death of Joe Egg* and *What Makes Sammy
Run*; Dir. of musical specials starring Anne
Bancroft, Ethel Merman and Gene Kelly; Dir.,
NBC's "International Showtime"; Dir., TV
country music specials; Dir. of the specials
"Dames at Sea," "Elvis Remembered," and
"A Johnny Cash Christmas."
ACHIEVEMENTS & AWARDS: Emmy awards for
outstanding musical program for "Annie:
The Women in the Life of a Man" and
"S'Wonderful, S'Marvelous, S'Gershwin."
PERSONAL: Brother of Prod./Dir. Gilbert Cates.

CATLIN, ROBERT L.
**Sr. V.P., Showtime Entertainment,
Marketing**

c/o Showtime, 1633 Broadway, New York, NY
10019
b. October 6, 1934. Easton, PA.

EDUCATION: Colgate University, B.A. Psychol-
ogy ('56)
CAREER   HIGHLIGHTS: Salesman/Sales   Mgr./
Product Mgr., Vick Chemical Co. ('59); Acct.
Exec., Benton & Bowles ('65); Dir., Adver-
tising, TWA ('68); V.P., Marketing Devel-
opment, American Airlines ('69); V.P.
Marketing/Advertising, Chase Manhattan
Bank ('75); Exec. V.P., Board Member, N.W.
Ayer ('77); Sr. V.P., Marketing, Showtime En-
tertainment ('82).
ACHIEVEMENTS & AWARDS: N.A.
PERSONAL: Wife, Jennie; children, Michael and
Holly.

CAUTHEN, HENRY J.
**Pres. and General Mgr., South Carolina
Educational TV Network**

c/o South Carolina Educational TV Network,
Drawer L, Columbia, SC 29250
b. October 23, 1931. Charleston, SC.

EDUCATION: University of South Carolina; University of Georgia; University of Houston.
CAREER HIGHLIGHTS: One of the most creative
and influential executives in public TV.
Prod./Dir., WIS-TV, Columbia, SC ('54); Dir.
of Production and Engineering, South Carolina Educational TV Network ('58); Pres. and
General Mgr., ('65).
ACHIEVEMENTS & AWARDS: Vice Chairman,
Board of Dirs., PBS; inducted into South Carolina Broadcasters Hall of Fame.
PERSONAL: Wife, Jeanette; daughter, Laurie;
son, Kelley.

CAVAZZINI, JAMES J.
V.P., ESPN, Affiliate Marketing

c/o ESPN, 355 Lexington Ave., New York, NY
10017
b. July 31, 1944. New York, NY.

EDUCATION: Iona College, B.A.; Seton Hall
University, master's.
CAREER HIGHLIGHTS: Dir., Regulatory Econom-
ics, Western Union ('68); Dir. of Financial
Analysis, General Mgr. of the Movie Chan-
nel, V.P. Program Operations, Warners Cable
Corp. ('75); V.P. Affiliate Marketing, ESPN
('79–).
ACHIEVEMENTS & AWARDS: Chairman, Cable
Advertising Bureau Affiliate Information
network.
PERSONAL: Wife, Geraldine; two sons. Resides
in Stamford, CT.

CAVETT, DICK
Talk Show Host/Commentator

c/o Daphne Productions, 1790 Broadway, New York, NY 10019
b. November 19, 1937.

EDUCATION: Yale University.
CAREER HIGHLIGHTS: Comedy Writer for Jack Paar and Johnny Carson; Host, "This Morning," ABC ('68); Host, primetime series, "The Dick Cavett Show," ABC ('69); Host, "Dick Cavett, Late Night". Host, PBS specials and the talk show "The Dick Cavett Show" WNET-PBS ('77); Commentator, HBO's "Remember When."
ACHIEVEMENTS & AWARDS: Three Emmy awards.
PERSONAL: Married to actress Carrie Nye.

CERVAMI, ANTHONY
V.P., Affiliate Relations, NBC, TV

c/o NBC, 30 Rockefeller Plaza, New York, NY 10020
b. N.A.

EDUCATION: Queens College; Columbia College.
CAREER HIGHLIGHTS: Started with NBC as a Page ('49); Sales Service Statistician, NBC ('51); Service Representative, Sales Service, NBC ('54); Mgr., Service Representatives, NBC ('55); Regional Mgr., NBC Station Relations ('57); Dir., Affiliate Relations Operations, NBC ('77) V.P., Affiliate Relations Operations, NBC ('79); V.P., Planning/ Affiliate Services, NBC ('80); V.P., Affiliate Relations, NBC.
ACHIEVEMENTS & AWARDS: N.A.

PERSONAL: Resides in New Hyde Park, NY, with wife Joan; sons, Richard, Michael, and David.

CESLIK, CAROLYN
Dir., Children's Programs, CBS, Entertainment, East Coast

c/o CBS, 51 W. 52d St., New York, NY 10019
b. October 15, 1942.

EDUCATION: CBS Management Workshop.
CAREER HIGHLIGHTS: Children's and Variety Program Development, Dancer Fitzgerald Sample advertising agency, New York; joined CBS ('75); Administrator, Children's Programs, CBS ('78); Mgr., Children's Programs, CBS Entertainment, New York ('79); Dir., Children's Programs, CBS Entertainment, New York ('80).
ACHIEVEMENTS & AWARDS: N.A.
PERSONAL: Resides in Floral Park, NY, with husband, Joseph.

CHAAPEL, EARL
Pres., Darbo Productions

c/o Darbo Productions, 9142 Calahena Blvd., Los Angeles, CA 90016
b. September 14, 1941.

EDUCATION: Northwestern University.
CAREER HIGHLIGHTS: Worked in the Mailroom, Paramount Studios; Freelance Production Asst. Worked on numerous TV and feature films before starting his own Darbo Productions ('72); served as Exec. Prod. for "Darbos on Parade."
ACHIEVEMENTS & AWARDS: N.A.
PERSONAL: N.A.

CHALOM, MARC
V.P., Production and Operations, and Exec. Dir. of Production, Daytime, (HAVES) Hearst/ABC

c/o Hearst/ABC, 555 Fifth Ave., New York, NY 10017
b. September 3, 1952. Alexandria, Egypt.

EDUCATION: Fairleigh Dickinson University and Wroxton College, B.A.; New York University, M.A.

CAREER HIGHLIGHTS: PBS Location Scout and Asst. Production Mgr., *The Adams Chronicles* ('75); Production Coordinator, "Dance in America" ('76); Production Mgr., "The MacNeil/Lehrer Report" ('77); Production Mgr., WNET-PBS for election specials, Bill Moyers programming, and "Healthline" ('78); Independent Prod. of commercials ('79); returned to TV as Production Mgr., "3-2-1 Contact!" ('79); joined NBC as Production Supervisor, "Betcha Don't Know" ('80); Dir., Program Operations, "Sesame Street" ('81); Prod., syndicated series "The Uncle Floyd Show" and Assoc. Prod., CBS Cable's "Songs of Innocence" ('81); joined Hearst/ABC as V.P., Production and Operations, Daytime and (HAVES) Exec. Dir. of Production, Daytime (HAVES) ('82). Instructor at The New School ('77–'80).

ACHIEVEMENTS & AWARDS: Emmy awards for "The MacNeil/Lehrer Report" ('77) and "3-2-1 Contact!" ('80).

PERSONAL: N.A.

CHAMBERLAIN, RICHARD
Actor

c/o Creative Management Associates, 8899 Beverly Blvd., Los Angeles, CA 90048
b. May 31, 1935. Los Angeles, CA.

EDUCATION: N.A.

CAREER HIGHLIGHTS: Once a blond Adonis as TV's Dr. Kildare, Chamberlain surprised everyone with an acclaimed performance in TV's *Hamlet* and then reaffirmed his stardom in the highly rated mini-series *Centennial*,

Shogun, and *The Thorn Birds*. Starred in BBC adaptation of Henry James's "Portrait of a Lady" and the TV movies *The Count of Monte Cristo* and *The Man in the Iron Mask*.

ACHIEVEMENTS & AWARDS: Three Photoplay gold medals and a Golden Globe award for "Dr. Kildare"; Golden Globe award for *Shogun*.

PERSONAL: Single, resides in Los Angeles.

CHAMBERLAIN, WARD B., JR.
Pres. and General Mgr., WETA-TV/FM, Washington, DC

c/o WETA, P.O. Box 2626, Washington, DC 20013
b. August 4, 1921. New York, NY.

EDUCATION: Princeton University, B.A. ('46); Columbia University, LL.B. ('48).

CAREER HIGHLIGHTS: Began career practicing law in New York ('49); Asst. Counsel, Mutual Security Agency, Washington, DC ('51); Assoc. Counsel, Defense Materials Procurement Agency, Paris and London ('53); Assoc. Counsel, General Dynamics Corp., New York ('54); V.P. and General Counsel, Intl. Exec. Services Corp., New York ('65); V.P., Corp. for Public Broadcasting, New York ('68); Exec. V.P., WNET-TV, New York ('70); Pres., PACT ('72); Sr. V.P., PBS ('73); Pres. and General Mgr., WETA-TV ('75).

ACHIEVEMENTS & AWARDS: Board of Dirs., PBS, Eastern Educational TV Network; Member, Natl. Assn. of Educational Broadcasters. Received John Phillips award ('76), from Phillips Exeter Academy.

PERSONAL: Resides in Washington, DC with his wife, Lydia, a widely exhibited painter, and his two daughters.

CHAMBERS, ERNEST
Prod./Writer

c/o NBC, 3000 W. Alameda Ave., Burbank, CA 91523
b. December 28.

EDUCATION: Columbia University.

CAREER HIGHLIGHTS: Co-writer, "Tony Orlando and Dawn"; Freelance Prod./Writer;

Supervising Prod., "Love, Sidney" ('82); pilot shows for "Pump Boys and Dinettes" and "Battle of the Beat."
ACHIEVEMENTS & AWARDS: N.A.
PERSONAL: N.A.

CHAMBERS, EVERETT
Prod./Dir./Writer

c/o William Morris Agency, 1277 Sunset Plaza Dr., Los Angeles, CA 90069
b. August 19, 1926. Montrose, CA.

EDUCATION: New School for Social Research; Los Angeles City College.
CAREER HIGHLIGHTS: Prod., numerous TV shows and features ('60–'80), including the following series: "Johnny Staccato," "The Dick Powell Theater," and "Columbo" for NBC; "The Lloyd Bridges Show" for CBS; and "Peyton Place" for ABC. TV movies include *Night Slaves, Trouble Comes to Town, Can Ellen Be Saved, Twin Detectives,* and *The Girl Most Likely To...* Feature films include *Tess of the Storm Country* for 20th Century Fox and *The Lollipop Cover* for Continental Films.
ACHIEVEMENTS & AWARDS: Best film and best actor awards from the Chicago Film Festival for *The Lollipop Cover. The Kiss,* which he directed, was nominated for an Academy Award as best short film. "Columbo" received best drama award from the Chicago Film Festival, five Emmy nominations for best series, and three Golden Globe awards. *Trouble Comes to Town* received best drama award from the Atlanta Film Festival.
PERSONAL: Daughter, Alicia.

CHANCELLOR, JOHN
Correspondent, NBC, News

c/o NBC, 30 Rockefeller Plaza, New York, NY 10020
b. July 14, 1927. Chicago, IL.

EDUCATION: De Paul Academy; University of Illinois.
CAREER HIGHLIGHTS: After serving in the army, he worked as a Copy Boy, Reporter, and Feature Writer, *Chicago Sun-Times* ('47); started broadcasting career at WMAQ-TV, NBC, Chicago ('50); assigned to Vienna as Central European Correspondent ('58); Chief of Moscow Bureau ('60); host of "Today" program ('61); European Correspondent, Chief of Berlin Bureau ('63); Chief White House Correspondent ('64); Reporter, NBC News, Republican and Democratic conventions ('56, '64, '68); Co-Anchor, conventions ('72, '76, '80); Co-Anchor, NBC News coverage of election night ('72, '76, '80); Co-Anchor, presidential inaugurations ('73, '77, '81); Chief Reporter and Writer, "NBC Nightly News" ('71–'76); Anchor, "NBC Nightly News" ('80); Correspondent, NBC News.
ACHIEVEMENTS & AWARDS: Awarded the distinguished communications medal ('82); honored by the New York Chapter, NATAS ('81); received a distinguished achievement award for broadcasting from the University of Southern California Journalism Alumni Assn., and a Missouri honor award for distinguished service in journalism. He has twice won an Overseas Press Club award for best radio interpretation of foreign affairs and was the first working journalist to hold the post of Dir., Voice of America ('65–'67)
PERSONAL: N.A.

CHANDLER, ROBERT
Sr. V.P., CBS, News

c/o CBS, 530 W. 57th St., New York, NY 10019
b. September 25, 1928. Chicago, IL.

EDUCATION: City College of New York, B.S.S.
CAREER HIGHLIGHTS: Chandler played an important role in determining the content of "60 Minutes," along with producer Don Hewitt. Began his journalistic career as Variety TV/Radio Reporter, then became CBS News Head of Information Services ('63); V.P., Administration, CBS; Asst. to Pres., CBS News; V.P. and Dir., Public Affairs Broadcasts, CBS News; Sr. V.P., CBS News.
ACHIEVEMENTS & AWARDS: N.A.
PERSONAL: N.A.

CHAPMAN, ROBIN
Co-Anchor, WJLA-TV, Washington, DC, News

c/o WJLA-TV, 4461 Connecticut Ave., N.W., Washington, DC 20008
b. March 18, 1950.

EDUCATION: University of California at Santa Barbara, B.A.; University of California at Los Angeles, M.A.
CAREER HIGHLIGHTS: Reporter/Photographer, KVQA-TV, Tucson, AZ ('73); Reporter/Anchor, KGW-TV, Portland, OR ('74); Reporter/Anchor, KRON-TV, San Francisco ('78); Anchor, KGW-TV, Portland ('79); Co-Anchor, WJLA-TV, Washington, DC ('81).
ACHIEVEMENTS & AWARDS: N.A.
PERSONAL: N.A.

CHARLES, GLEN
Exec. Prod./Writer

c/o Paramount Studios, 5555 Melrose Ave., Los Angeles, CA 90038
b. Henderson, NV.

EDUCATION: University of Redlands, B.A., English; San Francisco State University.
CAREER HIGHLIGHTS: Started as an advertising copywriter, but moved to Hollywood with brother Les to sell their comedy scripts to any producer who would look at them. After a few initial rejections, the comedy writing brothers received an acceptance from "The Mary Tyler Moore Show" and were hired by MTM Enterprises as staff writers for "Phyllis" ('75). The Charles brothers later served as Writers/Prods. of "The Bob Newhart Show" ('77); Head Writers/Co-Prods., "Taxi" ('78); Exec. Prods./Writers, "Cheers" ('82).
ACHIEVEMENTS & AWARDS: Three Emmy awards for "Taxi" scripts.
PERSONAL: N.A.

CHARLES, LES
Exec. Prod./Writer

c/o Paramount Studios, 5555 Melrose Ave., Los Angeles, CA 90038
b. Henderson, NV.

EDUCATION: University of Redlands, B.A., English
CAREER HIGHLIGHTS: Started as an English teacher, but left his job to co-write comedy scripts with his brother Glen. Their first acceptance was from "The Mary Tyler Moore Show," and they were hired by MTM Enterprises as staff writers for "Phyllis" ('75). The Charles brothers later served as Writers/Prods. of "The Bob Newhart Show" ('77); Head Writers/Co-Prods., "Taxi" ('78); Exec. Prods./Writers, "Cheers" ('82).
ACHIEVEMENTS & AWARDS: Three Emmy awards for "Taxi" scripts.
PERSONAL: N.A.

CHARLES, NICK
Sportscaster/Reporter, Cable News Network, Sports

c/o Cable News Network, 1050 Techwood Dr., N.W., Atlanta, GA 30318
b. June 30, 1946, Chicago, IL.

EDUCATION: Columbia College, B.A., Communications.
CAREER HIGHLIGHTS: Sports Dir., WICS-TV, Springfield, IL ('70); Sports Dir., WJZ-TV, Baltimore ('72); Sports Dir., WRC-TV, Washington, DC ('76); Sports Dir./Reporter WTOP-AM, Commentator on NASL soccer, Washington Diplomats, WTTG-TV and NHL

hockey Washington Capitols, WDCA-TV ('79); Sportscaster/Reporter, Cable News Network ('80).
ACHIEVEMENTS & AWARDS: Maryland Sportscaster of the Year ('74, '75); Chesapeake AP award for an investigative series on horse racing.
PERSONAL: Wife, Charlotte; son, Jason; daughter, Melissa.

CHARNIN, MARTIN
Dir., TV and Broadway Musicals

c/o Beam One Ltd., 850 Seventh Ave., New York, NY 10019
b. November 24, 1934. New York, NY.

EDUCATION: Cooper Union, Art.
CAREER HIGHLIGHTS: Prod./Dir. of the Anne Bancroft special "Annie: The Women in the Life of a Man" ('70); Prod., "George M" and "Dames at Sea" for NBC ('71); Prod., "S'Wonderful, S'Marvelous, S'Gershwin" for NBC ('72); Creator and Dir. of the Broadway hit *Annie*.
ACHIEVEMENTS & AWARDS: Emmy awards for best variety special ('70, '72); Peabody award ('73); Tony awards for best director, best lyricist, for *Annie*.
PERSONAL: N.A.

CHARREN, PEGGY
Pres., Action for Children's Television

46 Austin St., Newtonville, MA 02160
b. N.A.

EDUCATION: Connecticut College, ('49).

CAREER HIGHLIGHTS: As founder and president of Action for Children's Television, Charren has, throughout the 1970s and early 1980s, been a widely admired figure among all the groups and individuals concerned with public interest and public policy questions in both TV and radio. Many major changes in childrens programming—both voluntary and legislated—are the direct result of Charren's astute handling of ACT's affairs for the past decade. In the past few years ACT has honored outstanding TV programs on commercial TV, public TV, and cable. Charren has lectured on children's TV and public policy throughout the world and served as a member of the Second Carnegie Commission study which studied the role of public TV in the U.S.
ACHIEVEMENTS & AWARDS: Regis College honorary doctor of laws degree; American Academy of Pediatrics distinguished public information service award; National Organizations Advisory Council for Children award; Massachusetts Radio and TV Assn. public service award; Natl. Conference of Christians and Jews pioneer award.
PERSONAL: Husband, Stanley; two children. Resides in Newton Centre, MA, and Chilmark, MA, in the summer.

CHASE, BARRY OLIVER
Dir., PBS, News and Current Affairs Programs

c/o PBS, 475 L'Enfant Plaza, S.W., Washington, DC 20024
b. December 12, 1945. Springfield, MA.

EDUCATION: Yale University, B.A. ('67); Harvard Law School, J.D. ('70)
CAREER HIGHLIGHTS: Started as Assoc. Wilmer, Cutler & Pickering law firm ('70); Assoc. General Counsel, PBS ('76); Dir., News and Current Affairs Programs, PBS ('78).
ACHIEVEMENTS & AWARDS: N.A.
PERSONAL: N.A.

CHASE, CHRIS
Host, "TV Tonight," Cable News Network, New York Bureau

c/o William Morris Agency, 151 El Camino Dr., Beverly Hills, CA 90212
b. January 12. New York, NY.

EDUCATION: N.A.

CAREER HIGHLIGHTS: Contributed humor pieces to the "CBS Morning News" ('80), went on to become TV Critic and Host of "TV Tonight" for Cable News Network. Also writes movie column for *N.Y. Times.*

ACHIEVEMENTS & AWARDS: Four books, *How To Be a Movie Star* ('75); *Life Is a Banquet,* with Rosalind Russell ('76); *The Times of My Life,* with Betty Ford ('78); *The Great American Waistline* ('81).

PERSONAL: N.A.

CHASE, DAVID
Writer/Prod.

c/o Creative Artists Agency, 1888 Century Park E., Suite 1400, Los Angeles, CA 90067
b. August 22, 1945. Mount Vernon, NY.

EDUCATION: New York University, B.A., Stanford University, M.A.

CAREER HIGHLIGHTS: Staff Writer, "The Magician" series, Paramount TV; Story Editor, "The Night Stalker" series and "Switch" series, Universal TV; Prod./Writer, "The Rockford Files" series and *Off the Minnesota Strip,* Universal TV.

ACHIEVEMENTS & AWARDS: Emmy for producing best show, dramatic series; Emmy for outstanding achievement, anthology drama, Writers Guild award for outstanding achievement, anthology drama.

PERSONAL: Wife, Denise; one daughter, Michele.

CHASE, REBECCA
Correspondent, ABC, News

c/o ABC, 7 W. 66th St., New York, NY 10023
b. N.A.

EDUCATION: University of Illinois, B.S., Psychology.

CAREER HIGHLIGHTS: Research Asst., *Atlanta Journal* and *Atlanta Constitution* ('71); Research Asst./Writer, Southern Regional Education Board ('72); News Dir., Georgia Statewide Radio News Network ('73); Reporter, WXIA-TV, Atlanta ('74); Correspondent, ABC News, Atlanta ('79).

ACHIEVEMENTS & AWARDS: Two local Emmy awards as well as awards from the AP, UPI, and Sigma Delta Chi.

PERSONAL: Married, resides in Atlanta.

CHASE, SYLVIA
Correspondent, ABC, "20/20"

c/o ABC, 1330 Ave. of the Americas, New York, NY 10019
b. February 23, 1938. Northfield, MN.

EDUCATION: University of California at Los Angeles, B.A., English.

CAREER HIGHLIGHTS: Reporter, KNX-AM, Los Angeles ('69); Reporter, Assignment Desk, CBS News ('71); Reporter/Prod., CBS News ('72); Correspondent, CBS News ('74); Correspondent and Co-Anchor, "ABC News Weekend Report" ('77); Correspondent, ABC News "20/20" ('80).

ACHIEVEMENTS & AWARDS: Two Emmy awards for outstanding achievement in broadcast journalism; Natl. Press Club citation.

PERSONAL: Resides in New York City.

CHASIN, ROBERT
V.P. in Charge of Business Affairs, Columbia Pictures TV

c/o Columbia Pictures TV, Columbia Plaza, Burbank, CA 91505
b. September 3.

EDUCATION: University of California at Los Angeles, B.A. and J.D., Law.

CAREER HIGHLIGHTS: Exec., Frankovich Productions ('69); Dir. Business Affairs, Columbia Pictures TV ('77); V.P., Business Affairs, Columbia Pictures TV ('79); V.P. in Charge of Business Affairs, Columbia Pictures TV ('82).

ACHIEVEMENTS & AWARDS: N.A.

PERSONAL: N.A.

CHAVEZ, JOHN A.
Mgr., Special Projects, ABC, Entertainment

c/o ABC, 2040 Ave. of the Stars, Los Angeles,
CA 90067
b. Richmond, CA.

EDUCATION: San Francisco State University
('73).
CAREER HIGHLIGHTS: On-Air Promotion Mgr.,
KGO-TV, San Francisco ('74); On-Air Promo-
tion Prod., KABC-TV, Los Angeles ('75);
Mgr., Special Projects, West Coast for ABC
Public Relations ('79); Mgr., Special Projects,
ABC Entertainment ('83).
ACHIEVEMENTS & AWARDS: Gold Medal from
the Intl Film and TV Festival for ABC public
relations documentary on the making of In-
side the Third Reich.
PERSONAL: Resides in Los Angeles.

CHEATHAM, MARIE
Actress

c/o "Search for Tomorrow," NBC, 30
Rockefeller Plaza, New York, NY 10020
b. June 2. Oklahoma City, OK.

EDUCATION: Baylor University, M.A.
CAREER HIGHLIGHTS: Primetime credits in-
clude, "Hawaii Five-O," "The FBI," "Gun-
smoke," "Kojak," and "Ben Casey." A regu-
lar on "Days of Our Lives," now appears on
"Search for Tomorrow." Recent New York
City stage credits include Christmas on Mars.
ACHIEVEMENTS & AWARDS: N.A.
PERSONAL: N.A.

CHECKLAND, MICHAEL
Dir. of Resources, TV, BBC

c/o BBC, 12 Cavendish Place, London,
England W1
b. March 13, 1936.

EDUCATION: University of Oxford (England).
CAREER HIGHLIGHTS: Auditor, Parkinson
Cowan Ltd.; Accountant, Thorn Electronics
('62); Sr. Asst., Cost Dept., BBC ('64); Sr. Cost
Accountant, BBC ('64); Head of the Central
Finance Unit, BBC ('67); Chief Accountant,
Central Finance Services, BBC ('69); Chief Ac-
countant, BBC TV ('71); Controller, Finance,
BBC ('76); Controller, Planning and Resource
Management, TV, BBC ('77); Dir. of Re-
sources, TV ('82).
ACHIEVEMENTS & AWARDS: N.A.
PERSONAL: Married, with two sons and one
daughter.

CHERMAK, CY
Series Prod.

c/o NBC, 3000 W. Alameda Ave., Burbank,
CA 91523
b. September 20, 1929. Bayonne, NJ.

EDUCATION: Brooklyn College; Ithaca College.
CAREER HIGHLIGHTS: Exec. Prod., "Ironside";
Exec. Prod., "Kolchak—The Night Stalker"
('74); Exec. Prod., "CHIPs" ('77).
ACHIEVEMENTS & AWARDS: N.A.
PERSONAL: N.A.

CHERNIN, PETER
V.P., Program Development, Showtime
Entertainment

c/o Showtime, 1633 Broadway, New York, NY
10019
b. N.A.

EDUCATION: University of California at Berke-
ley.
CAREER HIGHLIGHTS: Publicity and Promotion,
St. Martin's Press; Advertising Publicist and
Editor, Warner Books; Writer, David Gerber
Productions; V.P., Program Development,
Showtime Entertainment.
ACHIEVEMENTS & AWARDS: N.A.
PERSONAL: N.A.

CHERTOK, HARVEY
V.P., Time-Life TV, Advertising and Promotions

c/o Time-Life TV, 1271 Ave. of the Americas, New York, NY 10020
b. October 29, 1932. New York, NY.

EDUCATION: New York University.
CAREER HIGHLIGHTS: Supervisor, Advertising, UA Assoc. ('59); Dir., Advertising and Sales Promotion, Seven Arts Assoc. ('61); V.P., Advertising and Publicity, Warner Bros. Seven Arts ('68); Pres., Children's Movie of the Month ('69); V.P., Special Projects, American Film Theater ('73); V.P., Advertising and Publicity, Time-Life TV ('75); V.P., Advertising and Promotions, Time-Life TV ('78).
ACHIEVEMENTS & AWARDS: N.A.
PERSONAL: N.A.

CHESTER, GIRAUD
Exec. V.P., Goodson-Todman Productions

c/o Goodson-Todman Productions, 375 Park Ave., New York, NY 10022
b. N.A.

EDUCATION: University of Wisconsin, Ph.D.
CAREER HIGHLIGHTS: Taught Speech at Cornell University and Queens College. Program Dept., NBC ('54); V.P., ABC Daytime Programming ('58); Exec., Ted Bates Agency; V.P., Program Administration, NBC; Exec. V.P., Goodson-Todman Productions, where he has played a major role in sustaining the game show empire built by Goodson-Todman.
ACHIEVEMENTS & AWARDS: N.A.
PERSONAL: Wife, Marjorie; two children. They live in Manhattan and Easthampton, N.Y.

CHILD, JULIA
On-Air Personality, ABC, "Good Morning America"

c/o "Good Morning America," 1 Lincoln Plaza, New York, NY 10023
b. August 15, 1912. Pasadena, CA.

EDUCATION: Smith College, B.A.
CAREER HIGHLIGHTS: Served in OSS during World War II; joined State Dept. and was assigned to U.S. Embassy in Paris, where she learned French cooking and opened cooking school; returned to U.S. and created "The French Chef" on PBS ('63), which became one of the most popular and longest running series in PBS history; joined ABC's "Good Morning America" as French chef ('80).
ACHIEVEMENTS & AWARDS: Numerous awards for "The French Chef," including Peabody award for distinguished achievement in TV; first educational TV personality to win an Emmy. Published six best-selling cookbooks.
PERSONAL: Resides in Cambridge, MA, and Santa Barbara, CA, with husband, Paul.

CHIRKINIAN, FRANK
Exec. Prod./Prod., CBS, Sports

c/o CBS, 51 W. 52d St., New York, NY 10019
b. June 3. Philadelphia, PA.

EDUCATION: University of Pennsylvania; Columbia Institute.
CAREER HIGHLIGHTS: Started as an Assistant Dir., WCAU-TV, Philadelphia ('50); Prod., Masters Tournament, Tournament Players Championship, Memorial Tournament, World Series of Golf ('59–'83); Executive Prod., U.S. Open Tennis Championships ('83).

ACHIEVEMENTS & AWARDS: N.A.
PERSONAL: N.A.

CHOMSKY, MARVIN
Dir.

c/o Plant Cohen, 9777 Wilshire Blvd., Beverly
Hills, CA 90212
b. May 23, 1929. New York, NY.

EDUCATION: Syracuse University, B.S.; Stan-
ford University, M.A.
CAREER HIGHLIGHTS: Directed TV's "The Wild
Wild West" ('66); "Gunsmoke" ('68); "Star
Trek" ('73). TV films and mini-series include
Victory at Entebbe ('75), *Roots* ('77), *Holocaust*
('78), *Attica* ('80), *I Was a Mail Order Bride* ('82),
and *Inside the Third Reich.*
ACHIEVEMENTS & AWARDS: Emmy awards for
Holocaust and *Attica;* Directors Guild award
('82).
PERSONAL: N.A.

CHRISTENSEN, BRUCE L.
Pres., Natl. Assn. of Public TV Stations

c/o Natl. Assn. of Public TV Stations, 955
L'Enfant Plaza, S.W., Washington, DC
20024
b. Ogden, UT.

EDUCATION: University of Utah, B.A. ('68);
Northwestern University, M.A.
CAREER HIGHLIGHTS: Prod. and Sportswriter,
WGN-AM/TV; Correspondent, KSL-AM/TV;
Dir. of Broadcast Services, Brigham Young
University ('75); Dir. of Media Services and
General Mgr., KUED-TV, KUER-FM at the
University of Utah ('79); Pres., Natl. Assn. of
Public TV Stations ('82).
ACHIEVEMENTS & AWARDS: Board of Dirs., PBS.
PERSONAL: Resides in Arlington, VA, with his
wife, Barbara, and their four children.

CHRISTIAN, SPENCER
**Weathercaster/Sportscaster/Reporter,
  WABC-TV, New York, News**

c/o WABC-TV, 7 Lincoln Sq., New York, NY
10023
b. July 23, 1947. Virginia.

EDUCATION: Hampton University, B.A., En-
glish.
CAREER HIGHLIGHTS: Reporter, WWBT-TV,
Richmond, VA ('71); Host/Weathercaster,
WBAL-TV, Baltimore ('75); Weathercaster/
Sportscaster/Reporter, WABC-TV, New York
('77). Also fills in as a Weathercaster, "Good
Morning America."
ACHIEVEMENTS & AWARDS: N.A.
PERSONAL: Resides in Closter, NJ, with his
wife and two children.

CHRISTIANSON, PEGGY
V.P., Disney Channel, Program Development

c/o Disney Channel, 500 S. Buena Vista St.,
Burbank, CA 91521
b. N.A.

EDUCATION: California State University at
Northridge.
CAREER HIGHLIGHTS: Before joining the Disney
Channel, she worked as an Educational Film
Prod., Walt Disney Educational Media Co.;
and then as Head, Production Dept., Disney
Telecommunications and Non-Theatrical Co.
Joined Disney Channel as Dir., Program De-
velopment ('82) and was promoted to V.P.,
Program Development ('82).
ACHIEVEMENTS & AWARDS: N.A.
PERSONAL: N.A.

CHRISTOPHER, KEVIN
**Host, Turner Broadcasting System,
  "Winners"**

c/o Turner Broadcasting System, 1050
Techwood Dr., N.W., Atlanta, GA 30318
b. Point Pleasant, NJ.

EDUCATION: Loyola University.

CAREER HIGHLIGHTS: Actor in TV commercials; Boy in *The Fantasticks;* appeared in *Grease;* played title role in the national tour of *Pippin;* starred in the national tour of *Jacques Brel Is Alive and Well and Living in Paris* ('75–'81). Sports Anchor, Turner Broadcasting System, Evening News; Feature Commentator, Turner Broadcasting System, sports features ('80). Host and Field Prod., "Winners" magazine show ('81).

ACHIEVEMENTS & AWARDS: N.A.

PERSONAL: N.A.

CHRISTOPHER, WILLIAM
Actor

c/o CBS, 7800 Beverly Blvd., Los Angeles, CA 90036

b. October 20. Evanston IL.

EDUCATION: Wesleyan University.

CAREER HIGHLIGHTS: Acting debut in *My Three Angels,* appeared off Broadway in *The Hostage.* On TV, he was a semi-regular in "Gomer Pyle, USMC," "Hogan's Heroes," "That Girl," "The Andy Griffith Show," "The Patty Duke Show," "The Man From Shiloh," and "Alias Smith and Jones." He is best known as Father Mulcahy in "M*A*S*H" and "After M*A*S*H" ('83). Motion picture credits include *The Fortune Cookie, With Six You Get Eggroll, The Shakiest Gun in the West,* and *Hearts of the West.*

ACHIEVEMENTS & AWARDS: N.A.

PERSONAL: Wife, Barbara; two sons, John and Edward. Resides in Pasadena, CA.

CHUNG, CONNIE
Anchor/Correspondent, NBC, News

c/o KNXT-TV, 6121 Sunset Blvd., Los Angeles, CA 90028

b. 1946. Washington, DC

EDUCATION: University of Maryland, B.A., Journalism.

CAREER HIGHLIGHTS: Newswriter, and later Reporter, WTTG-TV, Washington, DC ('69); Correspondent, CBS News ('71); Anchor, KNXT-TV, Los Angeles ('76); NBC, Anchor, "Early Today," Saturday Anchor, "NBC Nightly News," and NBC News Correspondent, New York ('83).

ACHIEVEMENTS & AWARDS: Honored by the Natl. Assn. of Media Women ('73); Outstanding Women of America ('75). Local Emmy for outstanding anchorperson ('78); Mark Twain trophy from the California AP and TV and Radio Assn. ('79); award for best TV reporting from Los Angeles Press Club.

PERSONAL: N.A.

CICERO, JOSEPH S.
V.P., Financial Administration and Control, NBC, Entertainment, West Coast

c/o NBC, 3000 W. Alameda Ave., Burbank, CA 91523

b. Chicago, IL.

EDUCATION: University of Illinois.

CAREER HIGHLIGHTS: Accountant, WMAQ-TV, Chicago ('55); Payroll Accountant, NBC, Burbank ('59); promoted to Payroll Supervisor and Supervisor, Show Costs and Billing; Accounting and Financial Planning; named Dir., Business Affairs, Network Programs and Production, West Coast, NBC ('73); V.P., Financial Administration and Control, NBC Entertainment, West Coast ('79).

ACHIEVEMENTS & AWARDS: N.A.

PERSONAL: Resides in Studio City, CA, with wife, Del; daughters, Karen, Sharon, and Suzanne; son, Matthew.

CICHOCKI, RONALD
V.P. and General Mgr., Times Mirror, Security Communications

5 Mason St., Irvine, CA 92714

b. April 4, 1942. Chicago, IL.

EDUCATION: Marquette University, B.A., History/Philosophy ('66).

CAREER HIGHLIGHTS: District Mgr., Flint Laboratories ('67); District Sales Mgr., Abbott Medical Electronic Co. ('75); Division Mgr., Codman & Shurtleff ('76); V.P., Times Mirror Cable TV ('81); V.P. and General Mgr., Times Mirror Security Communications ('81).

ACHIEVEMENTS & AWARDS: Member, Cable TV and Marketing Society.

PERSONAL: N.A.

CLAIBORNE, JIM
V.P., Financial Analysis, Columbia Pictures
TV

c/o Columbia Pictures TV, Columbia Plaza,
  Burbank, CA 91505
b. August 19.

EDUCATION: Long Island University.
CAREER HIGHLIGHTS: Began with Columbia Pic-
  tures TV in the Accounting Dept.; Exec. Asst.
  to the Exec. V.P. of Administration; Dir. of
  Financial Analysis, Columbia Pictures TV
  ('78); V.P., Financial Analysis ('79).
ACHIEVEMENTS & AWARDS: N.A.
PERSONAL: N.A.

CLANCY, MARTIN
Prod., ABC, News

c/o ABC, 7 W. 66th St., New York, NY 10023
b. August 21, 1942.

EDUCATION: Iona College, B.A. ('64); Columbia
  University, M.S. ('66)
CAREER HIGHLIGHTS: Following graduation, he
  joined the faculty of the School of Journalism
  for a year. Exec. Prod. of News, WTOP-TV,
  Washington, DC ('68); Washington Prod.,
  NET ('70); Exec. Prod., Natl. Public Affairs
  Center for Television ('72); Washington Prod.,
  "Bill Moyers' Journal" ('73); Writer/Prod., "A
  Matter of Justice: Lawyers and the Public In-
  terest," PBS ('75); Correspondent/Prod.,
  "USA: People and Politics," WNET/New
  York, WETA/Washington ('76); Washington
  Prod., "CBS Morning News" ('77); founding
  Prod., "Sunday Morning," CBS News ('79);
  Prod., ABC News "20/20" ('80).
ACHIEVEMENTS & AWARDS: Local Emmy,
  WTOP-TV, Washington, DC ('70); Emmy for
  producing "The Pentagon Papers" ('72);
  Emmy, NPACT's Watergate hearing coverage
  ('72); George Polk award, outstanding TV re-
  porting, Watergate coverage ('73).
PERSONAL: Resides in Bronxville, NY, with his
  wife, the former Mary Dee Britt, and their
  son, Tyrone.

CLARK, BOB
Correspondent, ABC, News

c/o ABC, 7 W. 66th St., New York, NY 10023
b. Omaha, NE

EDUCATION: University of Minnesota, M.A.,
  Journalism ('48).
CAREER HIGHLIGHTS: Began career at the De-
  troit Bureau of the Intl. News Service ('49);
  Reporter, *Washington Star* ('52); White House
  Correspondent, Intl. News Service, Washing-
  ton, DC ('56); Correspondent, ABC News,
  Washington, DC ('61). In addition to his re-
  porting duties, he was named Chief Corre-
  spondent for "Issues and Answers" public
  affairs program ('75–'81).
ACHIEVEMENTS & AWARDS: N.A.
PERSONAL: N.A.

CLARK, DICK
Performer/Prod.

c/o NBC, 30 Rockefeller Plaza, New York, NY
  10020
b. November 30, 1929. Mount Vernon, NY.

EDUCATION: Syracuse University.
CAREER HIGHLIGHTS: Eternally youthful Clark
  has danced from "American Bandstand" to a
  new arena where he profits from TV's mis-
  takes in the "TV's Censored Bloopers" spe-
  cials. Staff Announcer, WOLF Station, Syr-
  acuse ('50); Announcer, WFIL, Philadelphia
  ('52); TV Host, "American Bandstand," ABC
  TV; Host, "Dick Clark's World of Talent" and
  "Missing Links." Motion pictures include
  The Young Doctors and *Because They're Young*.
  Exec. Prod., "American Music Awards" and
  "Elvis." Currently produces "TV's Censored
  Bloopers."
ACHIEVEMENTS & AWARDS: American Music
  awards; Academy of Country Music award.
PERSONAL: N.A.

CLARK, KEN
Natl. Media Reporter, *Chicago Tribune*

c/o *Chicago Tribune*, 220 E. 42d St., Room 2708,
  New York, NY 10017
b. April 20, 1932.

EDUCATION: University of Colorado, B.A., Journalism.
CAREER HIGHLIGHTS: UPI TV Reporter; Natl. Media Reporter, *Chicago Tribune* ('83).
ACHIEVEMENTS & AWARDS: N.A.
PERSONAL: Married, two children.

CLARK, MICHAEL J.
V.P., Showtime Entertainment, Program Development

c/o Showtime, 10900 Wilshire Blvd., Los Angeles, CA 90024
b. July 22, 1942. Dayton, OH.

EDUCATION: Pennsylvania State University.
CAREER HIGHLIGHTS: Worked in Network TV Dept., BBD&O ('66); Dir., Network TV, Erwin Wasey advertising agency ('69); Dir., Sales, ABC Sports ('72); V.P., Development, Transworld Intl. ('76); V.P., Program Development, Showtime Entertainment ('79).
ACHIEVEMENTS & AWARDS: N.A.
PERSONAL: Wife, Patty; daughter, Shannon; son, Peter.

CLARK, SCOTT
Sportscaster, WRC-TV, Washington, DC

c/o WRC-TV, 4001 Nebraska Ave., N.W., Washington, DC 20016
b. Lima, OH.

EDUCATION: Bowling Green University, B.A., Broadcast Journalism.
CAREER HIGHLIGHTS: Sports Prod./Reporter, WKYC-AM, Lima, OH; News Reporter and Asst. Sports Dir., WLIO-TV, Lima; Asst. Sports Dir., WTOL-TV, Toledo ('78); Sportscaster, WRC-TV, Washington, DC ('81).

ACHIEVEMENTS & AWARDS: N.A.
PERSONAL: Resides in Gaithersburg, MD, with wife, Lynn.

CLARK, SUSAN
General Assignment Reporter, WRC-TV

c/o WRC-TV, 4001 Nebraska Ave., N.W., Washington, DC 20016
b. N.A.

EDUCATION: Southwestern at Memphis University, B.A., History; University of London (England), M.A.
CAREER HIGHLIGHTS: Began career as Copywriter, WCNX-Radio, Middletown, CT; News Reporter/Anchor, WWCO-Radio News, Waterbury, CT, and WELI-Radio, New Haven, CT; Weather Reporter, WTNH-TV, New Haven ('77–'79); News Reporter and Weekend Weather Forecaster, WCAU-TV, Philadelphia; General Assignment Reporter, WRC-TV ('79).
ACHIEVEMENTS & AWARDS: Emmy award.
PERSONAL: Husband, Richard. Resides in Germantown, MD.

CLARKE, JIM
Investigative Reporter, WJLA-TV

c/o WJLA-TV, 4461 Connecticut Ave., N.W., Washington, DC 20008
b. Appalachia, KY.

EDUCATION: Fordham University, B.S., Communication Arts.
CAREER HIGHLIGHTS: Joined WJLA-TV ('62) and produced reports on drug abuse, draft dodgers and deserters, child abuse, and high school violence, and uncovered the exclusive on leakage of the toxic chemicals PCBs, which triggered a congressional investigation to tighten controls.
ACHIEVEMENTS & AWARDS: A multiple Emmy award winner, he received three ('81)—two for his report "DCDC" and one for his news series "Keep the Coal Rollin'." Also received the Headliner award; two Metropolitan Area mass media awards; the Natl. Press Club's consumer reporting award and the Ted Yates award from NATAS, Washington Chapter.
PERSONAL: N.A.

CLAXTON, WILLIAM
Prod./Dir.

c/o NBC, 3000 W. Alameda Ave., Burbank,
CA 91523
b. October 22, 1914.

EDUCATION: N.A.
CAREER HIGHLIGHTS: Prod./Dir. of the series "High Chaparral,", "Bonanza," "The Rookies," "Little House on the Prairie" and "The Twilight Zone." His motion pictures include *Desire in the Dust* and *God Is My Partner*.
ACHIEVEMENTS & AWARDS: N.A.
PERSONAL: N.A.

CLOHERTY, JACK
Reporter, WRC-TV, Washington, DC, News

c/o WRC-TV, 4001 Nebraska Ave.,
Washington, DC 20016
b. Chicago, IL.

EDUCATION: University of Montana, B.S.
CAREER HIGHLIGHTS: Researcher and Reporter for columnist Jack Anderson ('72); began his own newspaper column "The Investigators" for the *Los Angeles Times* ('74); Reporter, WRC-TV, Washington, DC ('78).
ACHIEVEMENTS & AWARDS: Recipient of a local Emmy, a George Polk award, the Ohio State University award, the Investigative Reporter's award, an Editor's Gold Medallion, and regional AP and UPI awards.
PERSONAL: Resides in Chevy Chase, MD, with wife, Barbara, and their daughter.

CLOUD, HAMILTON S., II
V.P., NBC, Current Comedy Programs

c/o NBC, 3000 W. Alameda Ave., Burbank,
CA 91523
b. November 11, 1952. Los Angeles, CA.

EDUCATION: Yale University, B.A.
CAREER HIGHLIGHTS: Entered broadcasting as Dir., Black Programming, and On-Air Personality, WYBC-FM, New Haven, CT ('73); moved to WEZN, Bridgeport, CT, as Engineer and On-Air Personality ('73); became Production Dir., WELI, New Haven ('73). Joined Westinghouse Broadcasting as Man-agement Trainee at KFWB-Radio ('75); named Production and Public Affairs Dir., KFWB ('76); named Assoc. Prod., Children's and Public Affairs Programs, KABC-TV ('77). Entered NBC as Program Assoc., Motion Pictures and Mini-Series ('78); named Mgr., Motion Pictures for TV ('79); became Dir. ('80); appointed V.P., Current Comedy Programs ('82).
ACHIEVEMENTS & AWARDS: N.A.
PERSONAL: N.A.

COATES-WEST, CAROLE
Dir., Current Drama Programs, NBC, Entertainment

c/o NBC, 3000 W. Alameda Ave., Burbank,
CA 91523
b. December 23, 1952. Glendale, CA.

EDUCATION: California State University at Northridge, B.A., Theater Arts/Film.
CAREER HIGHLIGHTS: Assoc. Prod., Penland Productions ('76); Development Assoc., Carliner Productions ('78); Assoc. Prod., "The Phoenix" ('78); Mgr., Drama Development, NBC ('80); Mgr. Current Drama Programs ('81); Dir., Current Drama Programs, NBC Entertainment ('82).
ACHIEVEMENTS & AWARDS: N.A.
PERSONAL: Resides in Van Nuys, CA, with husband, Douglas.

COCA, IMOGENE
Actress

c/o Marvin Weiss, 11620 Wilshire Blvd., Los Angeles, CA 90025
b. November 18, 1908. Philadelphia, PA.

EDUCATION: N.A.
CAREER HIGHLIGHTS: Critics have dubbed her face "The Mask of Comedy." From "Your Show of Shows" onward, this petite comedienne has graced TV with a wicked sense of parody mixed somehow with an unworldly innocence. Starred in many New York revues before teaming with Sid Caesar on "Your Show of Shows" ('50–'54); later went to star in the series "The Imogene Coca Show" and "It's About Time;" has guested on many shows including the soap opera "One Life To Live."

ACHIEVEMENTS & AWARDS: Best actress Emmy ('51).

PERSONAL: N.A.

COCHRAN, JOHN
Correspondent, NBC, News

c/o NBC, 30 Rockefeller Plaza, New York, NY 10020
b. Montgomery, AL.

EDUCATION: University of Alabama, B.A.; University of Iowa, M.A.

CAREER HIGHLIGHTS: Reporter for radio, TV, and the *Birmingham News;* Freelance Reporter in Southeast Asia during Vietnam War ('68); Reporter/Anchor, WSOC-TV, Charlotte, NC ('69); Reporter, WRC-TV, Washington, DC ('71); joined NBC News ('72); covered Congress, the White House and Pentagon for six years; transferred to London Bureau ('78); filed reports from Poland during crisis. Was only American TV network correspondent in Poland for three weeks following the outbreak of the Polish crisis; secured the first uncensored interview by a Western journalist with Polish Deputy Prime Minister Rakowski; broke the story that Prime Minister Pinkowski was to be replaced by Defense Minister Jaruzelski.

ACHIEVEMENTS & AWARDS: N.A.
PERSONAL: N.A.

COHEN, AARON M.
V.P., Grey Advertising—Broadcasting

c/o NBC, 30 Rockefeller Plaza, New York, NY 10020
b. Brooklyn, NY.

EDUCATION: Baruch College, M.B.A.

CAREER HIGHLIGHTS: Mgr. Participating Program Sales, NBC ('68); Mgr., Daytime Sales, NBC ('71); Dir., Daytime Program Sales, NBC ('72); V.P., Marketing, NBC ('73); V.P., Eastern Sales, NBC TV ('75); V.P., Programs, East Coast, NBC ('75); V.P., Program Administration, NBC TV ('77); V.P., Grey Advertising—Broadcasting.

ACHIEVEMENTS & AWARDS: Member IRTS
PERSONAL: Resides in Valley Stream, NY, with wife, Marcia, and children, Craig, Stuart, and Dana.

COHEN, ALEXANDER H.
Theater and TV Prod.

c/o Shubert Theater, 225 W. 44th St., New York, NY 10036
b. July 24, 1920. New York, NY.

EDUCATION: Columbia University.

CAREER HIGHLIGHTS: Has produced more than 50 plays and musicals on Broadway and in London's West End, including *Home, The School for Scandal, Hamlet, Anna Christie, Comedians, A Day in Hollywood/A Night in the Ukraine, The Price, Plaza Suite,* and *1776.* For TV he has produced the annual Tony award presentations as well as many other specials including "CBS: On the Air" and "Night of 100 Stars."

ACHIEVEMENTS & AWARDS: Drama Critics Circle awards for best play, *The Homecoming* ('67) and *Home* ('71). Member, Board of Governors, Actors Fund of America; Board of Governors, League of New York Theaters and Producers.

PERSONAL: Wife, Hildy Parks; two sons, Christopher and Gerald; daughter, Barbara.

COHEN, BARBARA
Washington, DC, Mgr. of Political Coverage, NBC, News

c/o NBC, 4001 Nebraska Ave., N.W., Washington, DC 20016
b. 1945. Akron, OH.

EDUCATION: Swarthmore College, B.A., English Literature ('67); Columbia University, M.S., Journalism ('69).

CAREER HIGHLIGHTS: Natl. Editor and later Managing Editor, *Washington Star* ('69); V.P., News and Information Programming, Natl. Public Radio, Washington, DC ('80); Washington, DC, Mgr. of Political Coverage, NBC News ('83).

ACHIEVEMENTS & AWARDS: Columbia University journalism alumni award ('82).

PERSONAL: N.A.

COHEN, BERNARD I.
Prod., ABC News, "20/20"

c/o ABC, 77 W. 66th St., New York, NY 10023
b. September 3, 1929. New York, NY.

EDUCATION: University of Florida and University of Tampa, B.A. ('52).

CAREER HIGHLIGHTS: White House Prod. and Prod. for many overseas presidential trips ('64–'82); Sports, Political and Feature Prod., ABC Evening News ('75–'79); Prod., ABC News, "20/20."

ACHIEVEMENTS & AWARDS: Dartmouth University Tuck award for economic reporting ('79).

PERSONAL: N.A.

COHEN, ELLIS
Exec. Writer/Prod.

c/o CBS, 7800 Beverly Blvd., Los Angeles, CA 90036

b. September 15, 1945.

EDUCATION: Baltimore College; University of Southern California.

CAREER HIGHLIGHTS: Dir., Public Relations, Jewish Community Center of Baltimore ('69); Creator and Editor in Chief, *TV/New York* magazine, nationwide TV magazine ('72); TV Prod., "The New York Area Emmys" and WOR-TV Prod. ('73); TV Movie Prod. of *Aunt Mary*, CBS ('79).

ACHIEVEMENTS & AWARDS: Member, Producers Guild, ATAS, and NATAS. Exec. Prod., Democratic Convention Gala.

PERSONAL: N.A.

COHEN, FRED
V.P., HBO Enterprises

c/o HBO, 1271 Ave. of the Americas, New York, NY 10020

b. April 29, 1944.

EDUCATION: University of Michigan, B.A.; Stanford University, M.A., Film.

CAREER HIGHLIGHTS: Special Asst. to H. Rex Lee, Commissioner, FCC, and later to Dean Burch, Chairman, FCC, Washington, DC ('69); Dir. of Cultural Programming and Intl. Coordination, PBS, Washington, DC ('74). Created and presided over own consulting and TV distribution company, Fred Cohen & Assoc., Washington, DC ('77); Dir. Co-Productions, HBO ('80); V.P., HBO Enterprises, New York ('83).

ACHIEVEMENTS & AWARDS: N.A.

PERSONAL: Resides in New York City with his wife, Eileen.

COHEN, HARVEY
Dir., Warner Amex Satellite Entertainment Co., Management Information Systems

c/o Warner Amex Satellite Entertainment Co., 1211 Ave. of the Americas, New York, NY 10036

b. February 14, New York, NY

EDUCATION: Baruch College, B.A.; St. John's University, M.B.A.

CAREER HIGHLIGHTS: Mgr., Data Processing Audit, CBS, Inc., New York ('79); Asst. Dir., Management Information Systems, CBS Cable ('80); Asst. Dir., Management Information Systems, Warner Amex Satellite Entertainment Co., New York ('82); Dir., Management Information Systems, Warner Amex Satellite Entertainment Co., New York ('83).

ACHIEVEMENTS & AWARDS: N.A.

PERSONAL: Resides in New York City.

COHEN, JANE E.
V.P., TV, NAB

c/o Natl. Assn. of Broadcasters, 1771 N St., N.W., Washington, DC 20036

b. February 11, 1954. New York, NY.

EDUCATION: N.A.

CAREER HIGHLIGHTS: Research Technician, Women's Medical College of Pennsylvania; Program Dir., WPHL-TV and WPBS-FM, Philadelphia; Mgr., Community Affairs Programs, WRC-TV, Washington, DC ('72); Dir. of Programs, WRC-TV, Washington, DC ('74); V.P., TV, NAB ('77).

ACHIEVEMENTS & AWARDS: N.A.

PERSONAL: N.A.

COHEN, JOSEPH M.
Pres., Madison Square Garden Network

c/o Madison Square Garden Network, 1
   Pennsylvania Plaza, New York, NY 10119
b. March 3, 1947.

EDUCATION: University of Pennsylvania, B.S.
   ('68); Wharton School, University of Pennsylvania, M.B.A. ('70)
CAREER HIGHLIGHTS: Oversees the four compo-
   nents of the Madison Square Garden Network. These include syndication of events on
   commercial stations, production and distribution of cable TV programming to more
   than 12 million homes nationwide, and the
   national distribution of a variety of programs,
   such as the National Invitation Tournament,
   as well as the coast-to-coast satellite transmission of New York Knickerbocker and Ranger
   games on WOR-TV in New York. Also under
   his direction is the Hughes TV Network, providing transmission and production services
   for most of the major league baseball teams
   and the majority of clubs in both the NBA and
   the NHL.
ACHIEVEMENTS & AWARDS: Concert Facility
   Manager of the Year, *Billboard* magazine ('75,
   '77). Has written several articles on contemporary music and cable TV for a number of
   publications, including *Variety.*
PERSONAL: Wife, Rita; three daughters, Aren,
   Marianne, and Johanna.

COHEN, MARK H.
Sr. V.P., ABC TV and ABC, Inc.

c/o ABC, 1330 Ave. of the Americas, New
   York, NY 10019
b. March 27, 1932. Boston, MA.

EDUCATION: University of Maine, B.A. ('54);
   Syracuse University, M.S. ('58).
CAREER HIGHLIGHTS: Extensive career with
   ABC began in Station Clearance Dept. ('58);
   Network Sales ('61); Dir., Sales ('61); V.P.,
   Sales Planning ('67); appointed V.P., Busi-
   ness Analysis and Planning, ABC TV Net-
   work ('68); V.P. and Assoc. Dir., Planning
   ('70). Added responsibilities as Assoc. Dir.,
   Planning, Business, and Financial Develop-
   ment ('72); V.P., Planning and Development
   ('74); V.P., Finance and Planning ('75); pro-
   moted to Sr. V.P. of the Dept. ('76). Named
   Sr. V.P., ABC TV ('79); appointed V.P., ABC,
   Inc. while maintaining Sr. V.P., ABC TV re-
   sponsibilities ('81).
ACHIEVEMENTS & AWARDS: Member, Exec.
   Committee, University of Maine Alumni
   Assn. ('81–'82); Board of Governors, IRTS
   ('81–'84).
PERSONAL: Resides in Armonk, NY, with wife,
   Jane; children, Beth, Cathy, and Jonathan.

COHEN, MARSHALL
V.P., Warner Amex Satellite Entertainment
Co., Programming and Marketing Services

c/o Warner Amex, 1211 Ave. of the Americas,
   New York, NY 10036
b. N.A.

EDUCATION: Pennsylvania State University,
   B.A.; University of Florida, M.A.
CAREER HIGHLIGHTS: Researcher, Hamilton &
   Staff; Mgr., Louis Harris & Assoc.; Dir., Pro-
   gramming, Movie Channel, Warner Amex
   ('80); V.P., Programming, Movie Channel,
   Warner Amex ('81); V.P., Programming and
   Marketing Services, Warner Amex ('83).
ACHIEVEMENTS & AWARDS: N.A.
PERSONAL: Resides in New York City.

COHEN, THOMAS A.
Pres., Hammermark Productions

c/o Alan C. Freeland, Cooper, White, Cooper,
   100 California St., San Francisco, CA 94111
b. September 19, 1946. San Francisco, CA.

EDUCATION: Colorado College; New York University Film School; University of California
   at Berkeley.

CAREER HIGHLIGHTS: Prod./Dir., "Final Arbiter" ('74); Dir. "Grand Prix Tennis" on PBS ('75, '77); Dir., "World Press" on PBS ('75); Prod./Dir., KQED-TV, San Francisco ('70); Pres., Hammermark Productions ('78).
ACHIEVEMENTS & AWARDS: Jane A. Harrah award for "Final Arbiter" ('74).
PERSONAL: Wife, Jane; children, Sally and Molly.

COLE, LARRY
Sr. V.P. and Dir., Ogilvy & Mather, Media Services

c/o Ogilvy & Mather, 2 E. 48th St., New York, NY 10017
b. April 16. New York, NY.

EDUCATION: New York University.
CAREER HIGHLIGHTS: Started as a Media Research Asst., Ogilvy & Mather ('57); became Media Research Supervisor ('59); Sr. V.P. ('74); Media Dir. ('78); Dir. of Media Services ('79).
ACHIEVEMENTS & AWARDS: N.A.
PERSONAL: Married, two children.

COLEMAN, CHARLES E.
Dir., Financial Planning and Control, NBC Enterprises

c/o NBC, 30 Rockefeller Plaza, New York, NY 10020
b. February 20. Brooklyn, NY.

EDUCATION: University of Dayton, B.A., History ('67).
CAREER HIGHLIGHTS: Asst. Editor, Film Operations, NBC ('69); Network Production Administrator, NBC ('76); Sr. Production Administrator, NBC ('79); Dir., Production Control and Administration, NBC Enterprises ('82); Dir., Financial Planning and Control, NBC Enterprises, New York ('83).
ACHIEVEMENTS & AWARDS: N.A.
PERSONAL: Resides in Bergenfield, NJ, with his wife, Patricia.

COLEMAN, DABNEY
Actor

c/o "Buffalo Bill," NBC, 3000 W. Alameda Ave., Burbank, CA 91523
b. January 2. Austin, TX.

EDUCATION: N.A.
CAREER HIGHLIGHTS: Started on the "That Girl" series ('67) and later went on to many guest roles before landing a regular role in the syndicated "Mary Hartman, Mary Hartman" serial. He continued in the Lear productions of "Forever Fernwood" and "Fernwood 2Night" and moved on to such feature films as *North Dallas Forty, How To Beat the High Cost of Living, Melvin and Howard, Modern Problems, Nine to Five, On Golden Pond, Tootsie* and *War Games.* Currently stars on NBC's "Buffalo Bill."
ACHIEVEMENTS & AWARDS: N.A.
PERSONAL: Resides in Los Angeles.

COLEMAN, GARY
Actor

c/o "Diff'rent Strokes," 3000 W. Alameda Ave., Burbank, CA 91523.
b. February 8, 1968. Zion, IL.

EDUCATION: N.A.
CAREER HIGHLIGHTS: Series star, "Diff'rent Strokes." Motion pictures include *On the Right Track* and *Jimmy the Kid;* TV movies include *The Kid From Left Field, Scout's Honor,* and *The Kid With the Broken Halo.* Guest appearances on "The Jeffersons" and "Good Times."
ACHIEVEMENTS & AWARDS: N.A.
PERSONAL: Resides in Zion, IL, and in Cheviot Hills, CA, with his parents, Willie and Sue Coleman.

COLEMAN, JOHN
Pres., Weather Channel

c/o Weather Channel, 2840 Mount Wilkinson
   Pkwy., Atlanta, GA 30339
b. October 15, 1937. Champaign, IL.

EDUCATION: University of Illinois, B.S., Jour-
nalism/Radio/TV.
CAREER HIGHLIGHTS: Spent 11 years at WLS-
TV, Chicago, where he developed leading TV
weather department in the U.S.; gained
prominence as Natl. Weathercaster on ABC's
"Good Morning America"; went on to con-
ceive and develop the Weather Channel in
conjunction with Landmark Communications ('82). Serves as President and Meteorologist of the 24-hour weather cable service
while continuing to work with "Good Morning America."
ACHIEVEMENTS & AWARDS: Local Chicago
Emmy ('75); NWA Corp. award, ABC ('80);
American Meteorological Society award as
Broadcast Meteorologist of the Year ('83).
PERSONAL: N.A.

COLHOUR, DONALD
Dir., Special Projects, ABC, Entertainment

c/o ABC, 2040 Ave. of the Stars, Los Angeles,
   CA 90067
b. Ellsworth, KS.

EDUCATION: University of Kansas.
CAREER HIGHLIGHTS: Mail Clerk, ABC ('69);
Production Clerk, ABC ('70); Supervisor, Ad-
ministrative Services, ABC ('76); Unit Mgr.
assigned to ABC Entertainment Specials and
ABC News Special Events Programs ('78);
Mgr., Special Projects, ABC Entertainment
('81); Dir., Special Projects ('83).
ACHIEVEMENTS & AWARDS: N.A.
PERSONAL: Resides in Los Angeles.

COLLINGWOOD, CHARLES
Former Correspondent, CBS

47 E. 64th St., New York, NY, 10021
b. June 4, 1917. Three Rivers, MI.

EDUCATION: University of Oxford.
CAREER HIGHLIGHTS: Collingwood was a CBS
correspondent since 1941. During World War
II he worked under Edward R. Murrow. After
the war he was CBS White House Correspondent and UN Correspondent, and became the
Chief European Correspondent stationed in
London ('64). During the '50s Collingwood
worked as a Special Asst. to Averell Harriman
and then to the Dir. for Mutual Security in
Washington, D.C. He was host of the award-
winning series "Vietnam Perspective" ('65–
'69) and became the first network correspondent to be admitted to North Vietnam ('68).
Collingwood has also hosted many public affairs series produced by CBS. He was the subject of several interviews on the award-winning public TV series "All About TV" hosted
by Steven H. Scheuer. Collingwood retired in
1982.
ACHIEVEMENTS & AWARDS: Peabody award;
Natl. Headliners Club award; Commander,
Order of the British Empire ('75).
PERSONAL: Married for many years to the late
actress Louise Albritton.

COLLINS, BRUCE D.
**Dir. of Operations, Cable Satellite Public
Affairs Network**

400 N. Capitol St., N.W., Suite 155,
   Washington, DC 20001
b. 1951. Albany, NY.

EDUCATION: Cornell University, B.S., Indus-
trial and Labor Relations ('73).
CAREER HIGHLIGHTS: Member, Congressional
Campaign Staff ('74); Legislative Asst., Con-
gressional Washington, DC, Office ('75); Dir.
of Congressional District Office ('76); Dir. of
Field Operations, Natl. Cable TV Assn. ('78);
Dir. of Govt. Relations, Natl. Cable TV Assn.
('80); Dir. of Operations, Cable Satellite Pub-
lic Affairs Network ('82).
ACHIEVEMENTS & AWARDS: N.A.
PERSONAL: N.A.

COLLINS, CARRIE
**Assoc. Prod., Cable Satellite Public Affairs
Network**

400 N. Capitol St., N.W., Suite 155,
   Washington, DC 20001
b. July 22, 1955. Margate, England

EDUCATION: Mount Holyoke College, B.A. ('77).

CAREER HIGHLIGHTS: Admin. Asst., New England Congressional Caucus, U.S. House of Representatives ('77); Asst. Dir. ('78); Deputy Dir. ('80); Assoc. Prod., Cable Satellite Public Affairs Network ('82).

ACHIEVEMENTS & AWARDS: N.A.

PERSONAL: N.A.

COLLINS, JOAN
Actress

c/o "Dynasty", ABC, 1330 Ave. of the Americas, New York, NY 10019
b. May 23, 1933. London, England.

EDUCATION: Royal Academy of Dramatic Arts.

CAREER HIGHLIGHTS: The queen bee of "Dynasty," Collins has brought glamour back to primetime, along with a style of florid emoting that hasn't been seen since Joan Crawford's reign at Warner Bros. Made her debut in the British film *I Believe in You* and has worked steadily ever since in both movies and TV. Notable TV credits include *Paper Dolls, The Moneychangers,* the Hallmark Hall of Fame production of *The Man Who Came to Dinner,* and the popular "Star Trek" episode entitled "The City on the Edge of Forever." Joined the cast of "Dynasty" in its second year ('82) as the vengeful ex-Mrs. Carrington.

ACHIEVEMENTS & AWARDS: Author, *The Joan Collins Beauty Book* and the autobiography *Past Imperfect.*

PERSONAL: N.A.

COLLINS, PAT
Reporter, WJLA-TV, News

c/o WJLA-TV, 4461 Connecticut Ave., N.W., Washington, DC 20008
b. Washington, DC.

EDUCATION: Notre Dame University, B.A., English ('68)

CAREER HIGHLIGHTS: Reporter, *Washington Daily News* ('71); Reporter, *Washington Star* ('72); Reporter, WDVM-TV, WAshington, DC ('73); Reporter, WLS-TV, Chicago ('80); Reporter, WJLA-TV, WAshington, DC ('83).

ACHIEVEMENTS & AWARDS: Four local Emmy awards.

PERSONAL: Married, three children.

COLLINS, PETER
Correspondent, ABC, News

c/o ABC, 7 W. 66th St., New York, NY 10019
b. N.A.

EDUCATION: Georgetown University, B.S., Foreign Service

CAREER HIGHLIGHTS: Reporter, WTOP-TV/AM, Washington, DC; various positions with the Voice of America, Washington, DC ('68); Radio Stringer, ABC News, the BBC, and the Voice of America ('71); Correspondent, CBS News ('75); Correspondent, ABC News, Miami ('82).

ACHIEVEMENTS & AWARDS: N.A.

PERSONAL: N.A.

COLLINS, STEPHEN
Actor

c/o Universal TV, 100 Universal City Plaza, Universal City, CA 91608
b. October 1, 1947. Des Moines, IA.

EDUCATION: Amherst College.

CAREER HIGHLIGHTS: TV debut in "Dan August"; first Broadway appearance in *Moonchildren.* His first motion picture was *All the President's Men.* He starred in *Star Trek: The Motion Picture,* and in the PBS biography "Edith Wharton: Looking Back."

ACHIEVEMENTS & AWARDS: N.A.

PERSONAL: Resides in New York City and Los Angeles.

COLLOFF, ROGER
V.P., Policy and Planning, CBS Broadcast Group

c/o CBS, 524 W. 57th St., New York, NY 10019
b. February 1. Asbury, NJ.

EDUCATION: Brown University; Yale University, Law
CAREER HIGHLIGHTS: Legislative Asst. to Sen. Walter Mondale ('72); Special Asst. to Secretary of Energy James Schlesinger; Dir. of Govt. Affairs, CBS, Inc. ('75); V.P. and Asst. to the Pres., CBS News ('79); V.P., Dir., Public Affairs Broadcasts, CBS News ('81); V.P., Policy Planning, CBS Broadcast Group ('83).
ACHIEVEMENTS & AWARDS: N.A.
PERSONAL: N.A.

COLMAN, HENRY
Prod./Writer

423 Linnie Canal, Venice, CA 90291
b. September 15, 1930. Altoona, PA.

EDUCATION: University of Michigan; Columbia University.
CAREER HIGHLIGHTS: Assoc. Prod., "Robert Montgomery Presents" ('51); Program Development, "The Theatre Guild" ('55); Dir., Program Development, General Artists Corp. ('58); Assoc. Prod., "Dr. Kildare" ('61); Assoc. Prod., "Peyton Place" ('63); Exec. Prod., CBS TV, Hollywood ('65); V.P., Current Programs, Paramount TV (70); V.P., Current Programs, Screen Gems ('72); Prod./Packager, Pantera Productions in association with Filmways ('74); Prod., "The Love Boat" ('76).
ACHIEVEMENTS & AWARDS: N.A.
PERSONAL: Resides in Venice, CA.

COMPTON, ANN
Correspondent, ABC, News

c/o ABC, 1717 DeSales St., N.W., Washington, DC 20036
b. N.A.

EDUCATION: Hollins College, B.A. ('69).
CAREER HIGHLIGHTS: Reporter and Anchor, WDBJ-TV, Roanoke, VA ('69); joined ABC News as Radio Network News Anchor ('73); Anchor, "News Brief" and "Good Morning America"; reported on presidential administrations, and national political conventions; Congressional Correspondent ('79); named White House Correspondent.
ACHIEVEMENTS & AWARDS: Member, Board of Trustees, Washington Journalism Center; elected to Exec. Board, White House Correspondents Assn. ('77).
PERSONAL: Resides in Washington, DC, with husband, Dr. William Hughes, and two sons.

COMPTON, FORREST
Actor

c/o "The Edge of Night," ABC, 1330 Ave. of the Americas, New York, NY 10019
b. September 15. Reading, PA.

EDUCATION: Swarthmore College, B.A.; Yale University Drama School, M.A., Fine Arts.
CAREER HIGHLIGHTS: Had numerous supporting roles in many TV series in the sixties, including "Hogan's Heroes," "That Girl," "Mannix," "The FBI," "The Fugitive," "Dan August," and "Mayberry, RFD." A regular on "Gomer Pyle, USMC" as the camp's colonel, he also had recurring roles in the soap operas "Bright Promise" and "The Brighter Day." Joined the cast of "The Edge of Night" ('71) as Mike Karr.
ACHIEVEMENTS & AWARDS: N.A.
PERSONAL: Resides in New York City with wife, Jeanne.

COMPTON, JAMES M.
Correspondent, NBC, News

c/o NBC, 30 Rockefeller Plaza, New York, NY 10020
b. Portland, OR.

EDUCATION: Reed College, B.A., History; Columbia University Graduate School of Journalism, M.S.
CAREER HIGHLIGHTS: Reporter, KING-TV, Seattle, WA ('66); News Anchor, KING-TV ('68); City Editor and later Managing Editor, *Rome Daily American*, Italy ('70); Investigative Reporter, KGW-TV, Portland, OR ('73); Washington Bureau Chief, King Broadcasting Co.

('77); Correspondent, NBC News, Cairo ('79); Correspondent, NBC News, London ('81).
ACHIEVEMENTS & AWARDS: N.A.
PERSONAL: N.A.

CONBOY, JOHN
Exec. Prod. "Capitol," John Conboy Productions

c/o CBS, Television City, Los Angeles, CA 90036
b. June 19. Binghamton, NY.

EDUCATION: Carnegie-Mellon University, B.A., Drama.
CAREER HIGHLIGHTS: Brought his theater background as a stage manager to soap operas, stressing good actors and slick, classy production values for daytime TV serials. "Love Is a Many Splendored Thing" was his first soap, and "Capitol" his most recent. Production Asst., WCBS-TV; Assoc. Prod., WCBS-TV; Stage Mgr., Broadway musicals touring companies; Stage Mgr./Assoc. Dir., nightime and dramatic programs for ABC; Prod., CBS, "Love Is a Many Splendored Thing"; Exec. Prod., Columbia Pictures TV, "The Young and the Restless" ('73); started John Conboy Productions, produced three daytime specials, movie of the week, and the daytime serial "Capitol."
ACHIEVEMENTS & AWARDS: Eight Emmy awards.
PERSONAL: Resides in Los Angeles and Palm Springs, CA.

CONLIN, NOREEN P.
V.P., Columbia Pictures TV, Daytime

13577 Valleyheart Drive North, Sherman Oaks, CA 91423
b. December 11, 1946. New York, NY.

EDUCATION: Hunter College.
CAREER HIGHLIGHTS: Assoc. Prod., "Victor Awards" ('75–'81); ABC TV Co-Prod., "Kids Are People Too" ('77); moved to NBC as Dir., Daytime Programming ('79); joined Columbia Pictures TV as V.P., Daytime ('81).
ACHIEVEMENTS & AWARDS: Emmy for outstanding childrens entertainment series for "Kids Are People Too" ('78–'79).
PERSONAL: N.A.

CONNAL, SCOTTY (Allan B. Connal)
Exec. V.P and Chief Operating Officer, ESPN

c/o ESPN, ESPN Plaza, Bristol, CT 06010
b. July 21, 1928. New York, NY.

EDUCATION: Columbia University; University of Heidelberg.
CAREER HIGHLIGHTS: Began as Page at NBC ('47); moved through Radio, TV Production Services, and Production Supervisor of network variety shows to become Unit Mgr., NBC News. Served as overall Unit Mgr. for 1964 political conventions; named Exec. Prod., NBC Sports ('64); promoted to V.P., Production Operations. Joined ESPN as Sr. V.P. ('79); appointed Exec. V.P. and Chief Operating Officer ('82).
ACHIEVEMENTS & AWARDS: Emmy for the World Series telecast ('75).
PERSONAL: Wife, Mathilde (Til); children, Christine, Susan, Bruce, Cathy, Diane, Linda, Allan, and Scott.

CONNELL, DAVID D.
V.P., Children's Television Workshop

c/o Children's Television Workshop, 1 Lincoln Plaza, New York, NY 10023
b. October 6, 1931. Cleveland, OH.

EDUCATION: University of Michigan, B.B.A., M.A.
CAREER HIGHLIGHTS: Exec. Prod., "Captain Kangaroo"; V.P., Children's Television Workshop ('68); helped create "Electric Company" for public television; Exec. Prod., "Out to Lunch," ABC ('75); Exec. Prod., "Sign-On," CBS TV ('81); V.P. and Exec. Prod., Children's Television Workshop.

ACHIEVEMENTS & AWARDS: Five Emmy awards for children's programming for "Sesame Street."

PERSONAL: N.A.

CONNELLY, RICHARD J .
V.P., ABC TV, Public Relations

c/o ABC, 1330 Ave. of the Americas, New York, NY 10019
b. July 27, 1934.

EDUCATION: University of Notre Dame, B.A.
CAREER HIGHLIGHTS: Joined ABC in 1965; currently V.P., Public Relations, ABC TV.
ACHIEVEMENTS & AWARDS: N.A.
PERSONAL: N.A.

CONNOR, MICHAEL
Correspondent, ABC, News

c/o ABC, 7 W. 66th St., New York, NY 10023
b. N.A.

EDUCATION: Holy Cross College, B.A., English Literature.
CAREER HIGHLIGHTS: Reporter, *Wall Street Journal* ('70); joined ABC News ('77); Correspondent, ABC News "Closeup" Documentary Unit ('78); Business Correspondent, ABC News, New York ('80).
ACHIEVEMENTS & AWARDS: Emmy for ABC News "Closeup" entitled "The Killing Ground" ('79); Dupont-Columbia award for "Arson: Fire for Hire" ('79).
PERSONAL: Resides in New York City with wife, Noni.

CONRAD, MICHAEL
Actor

c/o "Hill Street Blues," NBC, 3000 W. Alameda Ave., Burbank, CA 91523
b. October 16. New York, NY.

EDUCATION: City College of New York; the New School Drama Workshop.
CAREER HIGHLIGHTS: After a stint in the army, this actor got his start in summer stock and touring stage productions. Left the stage for guest roles on "Naked City," "The Defenders," "Route 66," "Soap," "Paris," and as Mike Stivic's uncle on "All in the Family." A regular on the soap opera "The Edge of Night" and the short-lived Judd Hirsch detective series "Delvecchio," Conrad currently co-stars in "Hill Street Blues" as Sergeant Esterhaus.
ACHIEVEMENTS & AWARDS: Emmy for best supporting actor in "Hill Street Blues."
PERSONAL: Resides in Malibu, CA, with wife, Sima.

CONRAD, ROBERT
Actor

c/o Shapiro & Assoc., 15301 Ventura Blvd., Sherman Oaks, CA 91403
b. March 1, 1935. Chicago, IL.

EDUCATION: Northwestern University.
CAREER HIGHLIGHTS: The macho leading man of "Hawaiian Eye," "The Wild, Wild West," and other series, Conrad branched out from his handsome hero image into solid acting stints in mini-series such as *Centennial*. Starting with guest roles in "Maverick," "The Lawman" and "77 Sunset Strip," Conrad co-

starred in "Hawaiian Eye" ('58–'62); "The Wild, Wild, West" ('65–'70); and the short-running entries "The D.A.," "Assignment Vienna," "Baa Baa Black Sheep," "The Duke," and "A Man Called Sloane." Recent TV movies include *Breaking Up Is Hard To Do* and *Confessions of a Married Man.*
ACHIEVEMENTS & AWARDS: N.A.
PERSONAL: Resides in Encino, CA.

CONRAD, WILLIAM
Prod./Dir./Actor

c/o William Morris Agency, 151 El Camino Dr., Beverly Hills, CA 90212
b. Sept. 27, 1920.

EDUCATION: Fullerton College.
CAREER HIGHLIGHTS: Prod./Dir. of "Klondike" series; star of "Cannon" series ('60); star of "Nero Wolfe" series. Voice-overs for major TV commercials. Prod/Dir. of "77 Sunset Strip" and Prod. of the films *Two on a Guillotine, First to Fight,* and *An American Dream.* Will star in NBC's series "Yazoo" ('83–'84).
ACHIEVEMENTS & AWARDS: N.A.
PERSONAL: N.A.

CONSIDINE, DENNIS J.
V.P., Development, Orion TV

11541 Laurel Crest Dr., Studio City, CA 91604
b. November 23, 1943. New York, NY.

EDUCATION: University of California at Berkeley, B.A., Psychology; Graduate Facility, New School for Social Research, M.A., Psychology.
CAREER HIGHLIGHTS: Asst. Mgr., Program Analysis, CBS, New York ('70); Dir., Program Analysis, CBS ('72); Asst. Dir., Program Development, CBS, ('76); Exec. Prod., Program Development, CBS, West Coast ('78); Dir., Specials, NBC, Burbank ('79); Dir., Motion Pictures for TV, NBC, Burbank ('80); V.P., Prime Time and Late Night TV, NBC, New York ('81); V.P., Development, Orion TV ('82).
ACHIEVEMENTS & AWARDS: N.A.
PERSONAL: N.A.

CONVY, BERT
Host, CBS, "Tattletales"

c/o CBS, 7800 Beverly Blvd., Los Angeles, CA 90036
b. July 23, 1934. St. Louis, MO.

EDUCATION: University of California at Los Angeles, B.A.
CAREER HIGHLIGHTS: Starred in numerous New York stage productions, including *Nowhere To Go But Up* and *Cabaret,* and became familiar to audiences as a regular panelist on "To Tell the Truth" and "What's My Line?" Moved to Hollywood ('72) and landed many guest roles on "Charlie's Angels," "The Love Boat," and "Fantasy Island." He had a recurring role in the failed "Snoop Sisters" series and co-starred in the TV movies *The Dallas Cowboys Cheerleaders, The Man in the Santa Claus Suit, Valley of the Dolls, Help Wanted: Male* and *Ebony, Ivory and Jade.* Hosted the game show "Tattletales" and starred in "It's Not Easy," ABC ('83).
ACHIEVEMENTS & AWARDS: N.A.
PERSONAL: Resides in Pacific Palisades, CA, with his wife and their three children.

CONWAY, ELAINE
Dir., Talent Relations and Creative Services, NBC

c/o NBC, 30 Rockefeller Plaza, New York, NY 10020
b. December 16. Rochester, MN.

EDUCATION: College of Saint Teresa.
CAREER HIGHLIGHTS: Statistical Supervisor, Capital Research Co. ('69); Budget Administrator, Operations and Engineering Dept., NBC, Burbank ('76); Unit Mgr., NBC ('77); Sr. Unit Mgr., NBC Entertainment ('81); Dir.,

Talent Relations and Creative Services, NBC, New York ('82).

ACHIEVEMENTS & AWARDS: N.A.

PERSONAL: Single, resides in New York City.

CONWAY, THOMAS A.
V.P. and Chief Financial Officer, Entertainment Channel, Finance and Administration

1133 Ave. of the Americas, New York, NY 10036
b. June 7. New York, N.Y.

EDUCATION: Fordham College, B.A. ('64); Columbia Graduate Business School, M.B.A. ('66).

CAREER HIGHLIGHTS: V.P., Finance, WNET/13 ('72); V.P., Finance and Administration, and Chief Financial Officer, Entertainment Channel ('81).

ACHIEVEMENTS & AWARDS: N.A.

PERSONAL: Wife, Catherine; three children.

COOK, FIELDER
Dir.

c/o Phil Gersch Agency, 222 N. Canon Dr., Beverly Hills, CA 90210
b. March 9, 1923. Atlanta, GA.

EDUCATION: Washington and Lee University, B.A.

CAREER HIGHLIGHTS: Dir., "Lux Video Theater" ('50); Dir., "Kraft TV Theater" ('53); Dir., "Kaiser Aluminum Hour" ('56); Dir., "Playhouse 90," "U.S. Steel Hour," "Studio One." Dir. pilots of "Ben Casey," "The Eleventh Hour" "Going My Way," "Mr. Roberts," "The Waltons," and "Beacon Hill." Dir., *Patterns, Home Is the Hero, How To Save a Marriage and Ruin Your Life, Prudence and the Pill, The Hideaway, Teacher, Teacher,* and *Will There Really Be a Morning.*

ACHIEVEMENTS & AWARDS: N.A.

PERSONAL: Wife, Sarah; two children.

COOK, STANTON
Publisher, Tribune Co.

c/o Tribune Co., 435 N. Michigan Ave., Chicago, IL 60611
b. July 3, 1925.

EDUCATION: Northwestern University, B.A., Engineering.

CAREER HIGHLIGHTS: Production Mgr. ('60) and Production Dir. ('66), *Chicago Tribune;* Exec. V.P. ('67) and Chief Exec. Officer ('70), *Chicago Tribune.* Second Vice Chairman, *Chicago Tribune* ('74). Pres., Tribune Co., including the Cable TV Division ('82). Also, Dir. of the Federal Reserve Bank of Chicago.

ACHIEVEMENTS & AWARDS: N.A.

PERSONAL: N.A.

COOKE, ALISTAIR
TV Host/Journalist

Nassau Point, Cutchogue, NY 11935
b. November 20, 1908.

EDUCATION: Yale University and Harvard University, Drama Fellowship.

CAREER HIGHLIGHTS: This British journalist has been commentator, "Omnibus" series ('52); Creator, NBC series "America: A Personal History of the United States"; American Correspondent, *The Guardian* ('72); Commentator, BBC radio series "Letter From America"; Host, PBS series "Masterpiece Theatre."

ACHIEVEMENTS & AWARDS: Emmy for outstanding achievement for "Masterpiece Theatre" ('74).

PERSONAL: N.A.

COOKE, JOHN
Pres., Times-Mirror Satellite Programming

c/o Times-Mirror Satellite Programming, 2951
E. 28th St., Suite 2000, Santa Monica, CA
90405
b. December 11, 1941.

EDUCATION: University of California at Los An-
geles, B.A., History ('64); University of
Southern California, M.B.A. ('73).
CAREER HIGHLIGHTS: CPA, Coopers & Lybrand
('73); Dir., Budgets and Forecasts, Times-Mir-
ror Co. ('76); V.P., New Business, Times-
Mirror Cable TV ('79); Sr. V.P., Times-Mirror
Satellite Programming ('80); Exec. V.P., ('81);
Pres., Times-Mirror Satellite Programming
('82).
ACHIEVEMENTS & AWARDS: N.A.
PERSONAL: N.A.

COOKERLY, THOMAS B.
**Pres., Albritton Communications Co.,
Broadcast Division**

4461 Connecticut Ave., N.W., Washington,
DC 20008
b. N.A.

EDUCATION: Duke University, B.A., Business
Administration.
CAREER HIGHLIGHTS: Began his broadcast ca-
reer with WBT-WBTV, Charlotte, NC; V.P.,
Jefferson-Pilot Broadcasting; Managing Dir.,
WBTV, Jefferson Productions; General Mgr.,
WJLA-TV ('71–'83); Exec. V.P., WJLA-TV
('76–'78); Pres., Broadcast Division, Albritton
Communications Co., licensee of WJLA-TV,
Washington, DC ('78–'83).
ACHIEVEMENTS & AWARDS: Past Chairman of
the TV Bureau of Advertising and Washing-
ton Area Broadcasters; serves on the Exec.
Committee, Federal City Council; Chairman,
Board of Governors of ABC Affiliates.
PERSONAL: Married, four children.

COONEY, JOAN GANZ
Pres., Children's Television Workshop

c/o Children's Television Workshop, 1 Lincoln
Plaza, New York, NY 10023
b. November 30, 1929. Phoenix, AZ.

EDUCATION: University of Arizona, B.A., Education.
CAREER HIGHLIGHTS: Because she conceived of
the vastly successful and influential children's series "Sesame Street," Cooney had a
major influence not only on children's programming for public TV, but to a lesser degree on commercial TV here and abroad.
"Sesame Street" is broadcast in various versions throughout the world. She began her
career as a reporter, *Arizona Republic;* Publicist for NBC; Prod., documentaries for public
TV. She designed the research project for
"Sesame Street' ('66); Prod., "The Electric
Company"; prod., commercial TV specials;
Exec. Dir., Children's Television Workshop
('68); Pres., Children's Television Workshop.
ACHIEVEMENTS & AWARDS: American Women
in Radio and TV silver satellite award; Natl.
Assn. of TV and Radio Announcers Award;
NATAS governors award; NAEB distin-
guished service award; AJC Stephen Wise
award; Harrison Foundation award. Ohio
State University award; Natl. Institute of So-
cial Sciences gold medal.
PERSONAL: Married to Peter Peterson, an in-
vestment banker with Lehman Bros.

COOPER, HAL
Prod./Writer

c/o Major Talent Agency, 2651 Hutton Dr.,
Beverly Hills, CA 90210
b. Far Rockaway, NY.

EDUCATION: University of Michigan.
CAREER HIGHLIGHTS: Cooper broke into TV as
Dir. "Search for Tomorrow," ('51); moved to
California and was Dir., "I Dream of Jeannie"
('62–'70); followed by episodes of "Hazel,"
"Mayberry, RFD," "That Girl," "The Odd
Couple," "The Courtship of Eddie's Father,"
"The Mary Tyler Moore Show," and "All in
the Family." Writer/Prod., "Maude" ('72–
'78); currently Prod., "Love, Sidney."
ACHIEVEMENTS & AWARDS: N.A.
PERSONAL: Resides in Beverly Hills, CA.

COOPER, KAREN
Program Exec., CBS, Entertainment

c/o CBS, 6121 Sunset Blvd., Los Angeles CA 90028
b. January 5, 1945.

EDUCATION: N.A.
CAREER HIGHLIGHTS: Assoc., CBS TV Story Dept. ('67); Sr. Reader, Story Dept., CBS ('69); Asst. Story Editor, Story Dept., CBS ('72); Exec. for Comedy and Drama, Program Dept., CBS ('74); Mgr., Comedy Development, CBS ('75); Dir., Comedy Development, CBS ('77); V.P., Program Development, Filmways TV ('79); Program Exec., CBS Entertainment, West Coast ('82).
ACHIEVEMENTS & AWARDS: N.A.
PERSONAL: N.A.

COOPERMAN, ALVIN
Independent Prod.

146 Central Park W., New York, NY 10023
b. July 24, 1923. Brooklyn, NY.

EDUCATION: New York University.
CAREER HIGHLIGHTS: Assoc. Prod., "Wide Wide World" for NBC; Exec. Prod., "Producer's Showcase"; Exec. Dir., Shubert Theater; Pres., Madison Square Garden Prods.; Chairman, Athena Communications Corp.; Consultant, NBC's Big Event; V.P., Special Programs for NBC; Independent Prod.
ACHIEVEMENTS & AWARDS: Emmy for outstanding classical program ('80).
PERSONAL: N.A.

CORCORAN, JOHN
Entertainment Reporter, Telepictures

c/o Telepictures, 291 S. La Cienaga Blvd., Beverly Hills, CA 90211
b. July 27, 1943.

EDUCATION: N.A.
CAREER HIGHLIGHTS: Contributing Editor, *Washingtonian* magazine; TV Critic, *National Observer*; Entertainment Critic, WRC-Radio, Washington, DC; Entertainment Editor, WJLA-TV, Washington, DC; Entertainment Reporter, Telepictures.

ACHIEVEMENTS & AWARDS: Local Emmy for writing and hosting "Don't Go Out Tonight" ('80); two more local Emmy awards for co-producing, writing and hosting "The Plight Before Christmas" ('81). Author of *True Grits: A Handbook for Survival in Jimmy Carter's America* ('77).
PERSONAL: Married, two children. Resides in Bethesda, MD.

CORDTZ, DAN
Economics Editor, ABC, News

c/o ABC, 7 W. 66th St., New York, NY 10023
b. May 1, 1927. Gary, IN.

EDUCATION: Stanford University, B.A.
CAREER HIGHLIGHTS: Reporter, *Cleveland Plain Dealer*; 11 years with *Wall Street Journal* as Detroit Bureau Chief, Paris Correspondent, Senate Correspondent and Page One Editor; eight years as Writer and two as Washington Editor for *Fortune*; joined ABC News ('74) as only network correspondent covering economic stories exclusively; currently Economic Editor ABC News.
ACHIEVEMENTS & AWARDS: Nine Janus awards; Martin Gainsbrugh award; judges award of the North American Consumer Film Festival for "Japanese Imports" report for "20/20"; 1980 media award for economic understanding from Amos Tuck Business School for "1979: Stretching the Shrinking Dollar."
PERSONAL: N.A.

CORNET, ROBERT J.
V.P., NBC, Educational Services/Corporate Communications

c/o NBC, 30 Rockefeller Plaza, New York, NY 10020
b. November 2, 1944. St. Louis, MO.

EDUCATION: Florida State University, B.A., English ('66) and M.A., English ('67); Pennsylvania State University, Ph.D., English ('72).
CAREER HIGHLIGHTS: Asst. Prof. of English, University of Tennessee, Chattanooga ('67); Communications Officer, Hamilton County, TN ('75); Mgr., Educational Services, Miller Brewing ('78); Mgr., Educational Services/Corporate, Philip Morris ('80); joined NBC as

Dir., Educational Services/Corporate Communications ('80); named V.P. of Dept. ('81).

ACHIEVEMENTS & AWARDS: Named among Outstanding Young Men of America, by the U.S. Jaycees ('79); IABC gold quill award of merit for speechwriting ('80).

PERSONAL: N.A.

CORONA, ROBERT J.
Division Mgr., MGA-UA TV, Distribution Sales

c/o MGM-UA TV, 1350 Ave. of the Americas, New York, NY 10019

b. July 25, 1951. New York, NY.

EDUCATION: University of Pittsburgh, B.A.

CAREER HIGHLIGHTS: Acct. Exec., Station Clearance for ABC ('76); Dir., Western Division, Distribution Sales, MGM-UA TV ('79).

ACHIEVEMENTS & AWARDS: N.A.

PERSONAL: Wife, Dorothy.

CORPORA, THOMAS
Atlanta Bureau Chief, NBC, News

c/o NBC, Atlanta News Bureau, P.O. Box 467, Atlanta, GA 30301

b. February 18, 1937. Los Angeles, CA.

EDUCATION: Pasadena City College; University of California at Santa Barbara; Columbia University.

CAREER HIGHLIGHTS: News Asst., NBC News, New York ('59); Reporter, UPI, Albuquerque, Santa Fe, and Fresno ('62); News Writer, NBC News ('65); UPI Saigon Reporter ('70); Reporter "Newsroom," WETA, Washington, DC ('71); returned to NBC as News Desk Editor and "Today" News Writer ('72); Bureau Chief, Saigon ('73); Bureau Chief, Tokyo ('74); Field Prod., Atlanta ('78); appointed Bureau Chief, Atlanta ('80).

ACHIEVEMENTS & AWARDS: N.A.

PERSONAL: N.A.

CORPORON, JOHN R.
Pres., Independent Network News

c/o Independent Network News, 11 WPIX Plaza, New York, NY 10017

b. March 1, 1929. Acadia, KS.

EDUCATION: Kansas University, B.A., Journalism, and M.A., Political Science.

CAREER HIGHLIGHTS: Reporter and Bureau Chief, UPI, Baton Rouge and New Orleans; Dir. of News, WDSU-TV, WDSU-Radio; V.P. of News and Public Affairs, Metromedia TV; Dir. of News, WNEW-TV, New York; V.P. and General Mgr., WTOP-TV, Washington, DC; Head, Newsweek Broadcasting Service; V.P., News, WPIX; Exec. Prod. and Founder, Independent Network News; Pres., Independent Network News ('83).

ACHIEVEMENTS & AWARDS: Served as Pres., the Independent TV News Assn.; developed the acclaimed "Action News," a program of local and national news which has twice been cited by the New York Chapter, NATAS, as the outstanding news broadcast in the nation's number one market ('80, '82).

PERSONAL: Married, two children. Resides in Brooklyn, NY.

CORWIN, M. J.
V.P., Program Production Operations, NBC, Operations and Technical Services, West Coast

c/o NBC, 3000 W. Alameda Ave., Burbank, CA 91523

b. April 14. Boston, MA.

EDUCATION: University of California at Los Angeles; Boston University.

CAREER HIGHLIGHTS: Assoc. Dir., NBC, New York ('50); Dir., NBC ('51); Operations Supervisor, NBC ('53); Mgr., Operations, NBC West Coast ('54); Dir., Broadcast Facilities and Operations, NBC West Coast ('68); V.P., Program Production Operations, NBC West Coast ('80). Also serves as a Full Professor, Radio/TV Dept., California State University at Northridge.

ACHIEVEMENTS & AWARDS: N.A.

PERSONAL: Resides in Northridge, CA, with wife, Paula; daughters, Diane and Wendy Ann; sons, Mark and Stephen.

COSBY, BILL
Actor/Comedian

c/o Jemmin, Inc., 1800 Highland Ave., Los
  Angeles, CA 90028
b. July 12, 1938. Philadelphia, PA.

EDUCATION: Temple University; University of
  Massachusetts.
CAREER HIGHLIGHTS: One of the few black entertainers to have more than one major TV
  series to his credit, he is a comic, actor, commercial pitchman, talk show host, and concert hall soloist. TV guest spots include appearances on "The Electric Company," "To
  All My Friends on Shore," and "Top Secret";
  Writer/Dir., Natl. Educational TV. Starred in
  the series "I Spy" and "Cos" and hosts "The
  New Fat Albert Show," an animated children's show.
ACHIEVEMENTS & AWARDS: Three Emmy
  awards as best actor for "I Spy"; six Grammy
  awards for his comedy albums; image award
  from the NAACP.
PERSONAL: Wife, Camille; daughters, Erika,
  Erinn, Ensa, and Evin; son, Ennis.

COSELL, HOWARD
Sports Commentator, ABC, Sports

c/o ABC, 1330 Ave. of the Americas, New
  York, NY 10019
b. March 21, 1920. Winston-Salem, NC.

EDUCATION: N.A.
CAREER HIGHLIGHTS: Cosell's multifaceted career started at ABC Radio ('53) and now includes a wide variety of roles on TV. He is a
  Regular Commentator on ABC's NFL "Monday Night Football" and a Color Commentator on ABC's "Monday Night Baseball." He
  is also the Primary Commentator on ABC's
  coverage of championship boxing events.
  Host for a variety of ABC Sports specials, including "Battle of the Network Stars." Ac-
  knowledged as the pioneer of TV sports journalism, he is the Host and Sr. Prod., "ABC
  SportsBeat," the only network TV show devoted solely to sports journalism. He retains
  an active voice in radio as Host, "Speaking of
  Sports," on the ABC Contemporary Radio
  Network.
ACHIEVEMENTS & AWARDS: Emmy award for
  NFL "Monday Night Football" series; Poynter Fellow at Yale University. Author of *Cosell
  by Cosell*. Conducts lectures at Yale University
  for a course entitled "Big Time Sports in Contemporary America."
PERSONAL: Wife, Emmy; two daughters; four
  grandchildren. Resides in Manhattan.

COSGROVE, DANIEL J.
V.P., Media Sales, Group W Productions

c/o Group W Productions, 90 Park Ave., New
  York, NY 10016
b. August 14. New York, NY.

EDUCATION: Iona College, B.S.; New York Uni-
  versity Graduate School of Business, M.B.A.
CAREER HIGHLIGHTS: Acct. Exec., Dancer-
  Fitzgerald-Sample advertising agency ('66);
  Group Supervisor, Time Buying Services
  ('69); Special Representative, TvAR, now
  Group W Television Sales ('71); promoted to
  Acct. Exec. ('72); Group Sales Mgr., TvAR
  ('74); V.P. and General Sales Mgr., TvAR
  ('76); added the responsibility of being New
  York Sales Mgr. ('79); V.P. and New York
  Sales Mgr., Group W Productions ('79); V.P.,
  Media Sales, Group W Productions ('81).
ACHIEVEMENTS & AWARDS: N.A.
PERSONAL: Resides in Harrison, NY, with
  wife, Kathleen, and their daughter.

COSTELLO, MARJORIE
Editor, *Videography*

c/o *Videography*, 475 Park Ave. S., New York,
  NY 10016
b. February 6, 1950. New York, NY.

EDUCATION: Smith College, B.A. ('72); Boston University School of Public Communications, M.S. ('74).
CAREER HIGHLIGHTS: Mgr., Video Services, Windsor Total Video, New York ('75); Prod./ Writer, Marsteller ('79); Editor, *Videography* magazine ('80).
ACHIEVEMENTS & AWARDS: N.A.
PERSONAL: N.A.

COTTON, BILL
Managing Dir., BBC, Direct Broadcasting by Satellite

c/o BBC, 12 Cavendish Pl., London, England W1
b. April 23, 1928.

EDUCATION: Ardingly College.
CAREER HIGHLIGHTS: Freelance Prod., BBC ('56); Asst. Head of Light Entertainment, BBC ('62); Head of Variety, BBC ('69); Head of Light Entertainment Group, BBC ('74); Controller, BBC-1 ('77); Deputy Managing Dir., TV, BBC ('77); Vice-Chairman, BBC Enterprises ('80); Dir. of Development, BBC ('82); Chairman of BBC Enterprises and Dir. of Programmes ('82); Managing Dir., Direct Broadcasting by Satellite ('83).
ACHIEVEMENTS & AWARDS: OBE award ('76); Fellow of the Royal TV Society ('83).
PERSONAL: N.A.

COWEN, EUGENE S.
V.P., ABC, Washington, DC

c/o ABC, 1717 DeSales St., N.W., Washington, DC 20036
b. May 1, 1925. New York, NY.

EDUCATION: Syracuse University, B.A. ('49); Syracuse University, M.A. ('54).
CAREER HIGHLIGHTS: Staff Reporter, *Syracuse Herald Journal* ('48–'52); News Secretary for Rep. Frances F. Bolton ('53); Information Officer, Dept. of HEW ('56–'68); Asst. to U.S. Sen. Hugh Scott ('58–'68); Deputy Asst. to Pres. Nixon ('69–'71); named V.P., Washington, ABC ('71).
ACHIEVEMENTS & AWARDS: Air Medal, Air Corps ('45); Member, Phi Beta Kappa ('49); Dir., NAB ('72–'82).
PERSONAL: N.A.

COWGILL, BRIAN
Chief Exec., Thames TV

c/o BBC, 630 Fifth Ave., New York, NY 10020
b. England.

EDUCATION: N.A.
CAREER HIGHLIGHTS: Programming Exec., BBC; Head, News and Public Affairs, BBC; Chief Exec., Thames TV.
ACHIEVEMENTS & AWARDS: N.A.
PERSONAL: N.A.

COWLES, SYMON B.
V.P., ABC, Creative Services

c/o ABC, 1330 Ave. of the Americas, New York, NY 10019
b. August 30, 1926. New York, NY.

EDUCATION: City College of New York, B.S. and M.A.
CAREER HIGHLIGHTS: Began in various advertising positions at Warner Bros. ('54); Dir., Advertising and Promotion, WCKT, Miami ('58) Dir., Advertising and Promotion, Metromedia ('59); Dir., Advertising and Publicity, ABC O&O Division ('62); V.P., Sales Development and Promotion, ABC TV Network ('68); V.P., Creative Services, ABC ('74).
ACHIEVEMENTS & AWARDS: Member, Board of Dirs., Broadcast Promotion Assn. ('81–'82); Contributing Editor, *Strategies in Broadcast Promotion* ('82).
PERSONAL: Resides in Glen Ridge and Sea Girt, NJ, with wife, Christine; children, Stephen and Lisa.

COX, NELL
Prod./Dir./Writer

1629 Georgina Ave., Santa Monica, CA 90403
b. N.A.

EDUCATION: N.A.
CAREER HIGHLIGHTS: Has been making films since '60. Starting as an Editor, she was later Pres., Nell Cox Films, New York ('68–'77). Directed episodes of "M*A*S*H," "Falcon Crest," "Lou Grant," "Nine to Five," "The Waltons," "CBS Halloween Special," "Freestyle Series," "Visions Series," PBS.
ACHIEVEMENTS & AWARDS: Christopher award ('76).
PERSONAL: N.A.

COX, RICHARD
Pres., CBS, Cable Division

c/o CBS, 51 W. 52d St., New York, NY 10019
b. August 21, 1929. New York, NY.

EDUCATION: Fordham University.
CAREER HIGHLIGHTS: Began with Young & Rubicam as V.P., Radio/TV Programming; V.P. in Charge of Radio/TV, Doyle, Dane, Bernbach ('66); Pres., Young & Rubicam Ventures, DCA Productions ('79); formed DCA-TV ('79); Pres., CBS Cable Division, CBS Broadcast Group ('81).
ACHIEVEMENTS & AWARDS: Obie Award ('70).
PERSONAL: Married, four children.

COX, TONY (Winston H. Cox)
Pres., HBO Network Group

c/o HBO, 1271 Ave. of the Americas, New York, NY 10020
b. September 14, 1941. Summit, NJ.

EDUCATION: Princeton University ('63); Harvard Business School, M.B.A. ('65).
CAREER HIGHLIGHTS: Asst. to Comptroller and Dir. of Budgets and Financial Analysis, Time, Inc. ('65); Business Mgr., *Life* ('71); joined magazine Development Group which created and introduced *People* and *Money* ('73); Asst. to the Group V.P. for Magazines ('75); Dir. of Affiliate Services, HBO ('76); V.P., Affiliate Relations ('77); V.P., Sales and Marketing ('79); Sr. V.P., Sales and Marketing ('80); Exec. V.P., Operations, overseeing sales and marketing, public relations, and studio and network operations ('82); Pres., HBO Network Group ('83).
ACHIEVEMENTS & AWARDS: N.A.
PERSONAL: Resides in Summit, NJ, with wife, Barbara, and two children.

COYLE, HARRY
Dir., NBC, Sports

c/o NBC, 30 Rockefeller Plaza, New York, NY 10020
b. January 7, 1922. Ridgewood, NJ.

EDUCATION: New Jersey State College (now William Paterson College).
CAREER HIGHLIGHTS: One of Coyle's most notable directorial feats was catching Carlton Fisk's reaction to his game-winning home run in the historic sixth game of the 1975 World Series. Coyle began his career as a Dir. for the Dumont Network ('47); joined NBC Sports in the same capacity ('54). He hasn't stopped directing since, providing marvelous pictures on all of NBC Sports major events including the Rose Bowl, major league baseball, NCAA basketball, tennis, pro golf, and NFL football.
ACHIEVEMENTS & AWARDS: Six Emmy awards for sports direction.
PERSONAL: Wife, Romona.

COYLE, WILLIAM
V.P., Operations, Warner Amex Cable Communications, Dallas

c/o Warner Amex, 75 Rockefeller Plaza, New York, NY 10019
b. December 6, 1934.

EDUCATION: Southern Methodist University School of Business.
CAREER HIGHLIGHTS: Operated his own real estate development firm; Rockwell Intl.; Office Products Branch Mgr., Xerox Corp. ('77); V.P., Operations, Warner Amex of Dallas.
ACHIEVEMENTS & AWARDS: N.A.
PERSONAL: N.A.

CRAIG, DEAN K.
Dir., Program Preparation, NBC, Entertainment

c/o NBC, 3000 W. Alameda Ave., Burbank, CA 91523
b. June 9.

EDUCATION: Pomona College, B.A., English; Yale University Drama School.
CAREER HIGHLIGHTS: Stage Mgr., NBC, West Coast ('58); Program Mgr., KNBC-TV, Los Angeles ('52); Unit Mgr., NBC ('58); initiated the West Coast Telesales Dept. for NBC ('59); Mgr., Daytime Programs ('65); Mgr., Specials and Late Night Programs, West Coast, NBC Entertainment ('80); Dir., Variety Programs, West Coast, NBC ('81); Dir., Program Preparation, NBC Entertainment ('82).
ACHIEVEMENTS & AWARDS: Member, Board of Governors, ATAS.
PERSONAL: Resides in Chatsworth, CA, with wife, Candy; daughters, Eden and Bronwen; son, Matthew.

CRAMER, DOUGLAS
Prod., Aaron Spelling Productions

c/o Aaron Spelling Productions, 10201 W. Pico Blvd., Los Angeles, CA 90064
b. August 22, 1931. Louisville, KY.

EDUCATION: Northwestern University; Sorbonne (France); Cincinnati University.
CAREER HIGHLIGHTS: ABC Program Exec.; Head of Paramount TV; Independent Prod.; Exec. Prod., "Bridget Loves Bernie"; Prod. TV movies QB VII and Cage Without a Key; Exec. Prod., "Strike Force," "Dynasty," "At Ease," "Hotel" ('83), and "Shooting Stars" ('83) for Aaron Spelling Productions.
ACHIEVEMENTS & AWARDS: N.A.
PERSONAL: N.A.

CRANE, ALBERT H., III
V.P., EXTRAVISION, CBS

c/o CBS, 51 W. 52d St., New York, NY 10019
b. September 7, 1942.

EDUCATION: Trinity College, B.A., Economics; Syracuse University, M.S., Communications;

Wharton School of Finance and Commerce, M.B.A., Marketing.
CAREER HIGHLIGHTS: Sales Analyst, CBS ('68); Mgr. of Daytime Sales Analysis ('70); Acct. Exec., CBS ('71); Dir. of Daytime Sales ('77); V.P., Eastern Sales ('78); V.P., Primetime Sales ('79); V.P., EXTRAVISION, CBS TV ('82).
ACHIEVEMENTS & AWARDS: N.A.
PERSONAL: Resides in Bronxville, NY, with wife, Mary Ella, daughter, Mary, and son, Albert.

CREDLE, GARY
V.P., Warner Bros. TV, Production

c/o Warner Bros. TV, 4000 Warner Blvd., Burbank, CA 91522
b. N.A.

EDUCATION: N.A.
CAREER HIGHLIGHTS: Produced the TV movie Hotline, CBS, and was Exec. in Charge of Prod. for the theatrical feature On the Brink. Prod., the telefeatures The Baby Brokers, NBC, and Callie and Son, CBS. Prod., the TV movie Mysterious Two, NBC; and Staff Production Mgr./Assoc. Prod. on TV movies such as The Jayne Mansfield Story, Island of Beautiful Women, and Torn Between Two Lovers, for CBS; and The Triangle Factory Fire and Marathon, for NBC.
ACHIEVEMENTS & AWARDS: N.A.
PERSONAL: N.A.

CREECH, KATHRYN H.
V.P., Hearst/ABC Video, Affiliate Relations

c/o Hearst/ABC, 555 Fifth Ave., New York, NY 10017
b. September 8, 1951. Washington, DC.

EDUCATION: University of Virginia; George Mason University, B.A.
CAREER HIGHLIGHTS: Creech spent eight years with the NCTA, beginning as Research Coordinator ('71); Research Dir. ('73); Dir., Research and Planning ('74); V.P., Research and Planning ('75); Sr. V.P. ('78); moved to Hearst/ABC Video Services as V.P., Affiliate Relations, with special focus on Daytime network.

ACHIEVEMENTS & AWARDS: Founding Board Member, Women in Cable; Member, NCTA Convention Committee. Idell Kaitz award ('83).

PERSONAL: Resides in Manhattan with husband, Victor.

CRILE, GEORGE, III
Correspondent/Prod., CBS, News

c/o CBS, 524 W. 57th St., New York, NY 10019
b. San Diego, CA.

EDUCATION: Trinity College; Georgetown University School of Foreign Service.

CAREER HIGHLIGHTS: Crile was the producer and off-camera reporter for the controversial 1983 documentary on Gen. William C. Westmoreland, and he has had a notable career with CBS as producer of other CBS News Reports. Reporter for syndicated columnist Drew Pearson ('69); Reporter, *Gary Post-Tribune*, Indiana ('70); Pentagon Correspondent, Knight-Ridder Newspapers ('72); Contributing Editor, *Harper's* magazine ('73); Washington Editor, *Harper's* magazine ('75); Prod./Reporter, CBS News, assigned to the CBS Reports Unit ('76); Correspondent/Prod., CBS News ('81).

ACHIEVEMENTS & AWARDS: Emmy award and Peabody award for CBS Reports "The Battle for South Africa" ('78); American Film Festival blue ribbon award and Writers Guild award for CBS Reports "The CIA's Secret Army" ('77).

PERSONAL: Resides in Manhattan.

CRIQUI, DON
Sportscaster, NBC, Sports

c/o NBC, 30 Rockefeller Plaza, New York, NY 10020
b. Buffalo, NY.

EDUCATION: St. Joseph's Institute; University of Notre Dame.

CAREER HIGHLIGHTS: Sports Dir., WSBT-TV/AM, South Bend, IN; Asst. to Frank Gifford, WCBS-TV, New York ('65); TV Commentator, for the New York Knicks ('66); worked NFL telecasts for CBS Sports ('67–'79); Sports Dir., WOR-AM, New York ('68–present); Sportscaster, NBC Sports ('79).

ACHIEVEMENTS & AWARDS: N.A.

PERSONAL: Resides in Essex Falls, NJ, with wife, Molly, and their five children.

CRISLER, RICHARD CARLETON
Pres., R. C. Crisler & Co.

c/o R. C. Crisler & Co., 580 Walnut St., Cincinnati, OH 45202
b. November 3, 1907. Cincinnati, OH.

EDUCATION: Yale University, B.A.

CAREER HIGHLIGHTS: Guaranty Trust Co., New York, Cleveland and Cincinnati ('29); V.P. and Partner, Field Richards Co., Cincinnati ('35); Exec. V.P. and later Pres., Transit Radio ('49); Pres., R. C. Crisler & Co. ('52).

ACHIEVEMENTS & AWARDS: N.A.

PERSONAL: Wife, Lucy; three sons.

CRIST, JUDITH
Film Critic, *TV Guide*

c/o *TV Guide*, Triangle Publications, 100
  Matson Ford Rd., Radnor, PA 19088
b. March 22, 1922. New York, NY.

EDUCATION: Hunter College, B.A. ('41); Columbia University, M.S., Journalism.
CAREER HIGHLIGHTS: Reporter, *N.Y. Herald
Tribune* ('45–'60); Theater Critic, *Herald Tribune* ('58); Arts Editor, *Herald Tribune* ('60);
Film Critic, *Herald Tribune* ('63); Film Critic,
TV Guide ('65–present). Also reviewed films
for *New York* magazine ('68–'75); *Saturday Review* ('75–'77, '80–present).
ACHIEVEMENTS & AWARDS: George Polk award
('51); Page One award ('55); New York Newspaper Women's Club award ('55, '59, '63, '65,
'67); Hunter College Hall of Fame ('73).
PERSONAL: N.A.

CROFOOT, TERRY
Dir., KABC-TV, Los Angeles, News

c/o KABC-TV, 4151 Prospect Ave., Los
  Angeles, CA 90027
b. Portland, OR.

EDUCATION: San Diego State University, B.A.,
Journalism ('68).
CAREER HIGHLIGHTS: Night Bureau Chief, UPI,
San Diego, CA ('65); Field Reporter/News
Prod./Assignment Editor, KGTV-TV San Di-
ego ('69); News Assignment Mgr., KNXT-TV,
Los Angeles ('75); Dir. of News Operations,
KABC-TV, Los Angeles ('77); Exec. Prod.,
Early News, KABC-TV ('78); Asst. News Dir.,
KABC-TV ('80); News Dir., KABC-TV ('81).
ACHIEVEMENTS & AWARDS: N.A.
PERSONAL: Resides in Woodland Hills, CA,
with wife, Elizabeth, and their two children.

CRONKITE, WALTER
Special Correspondent, CBS, News

c/o CBS, 51 W. 52d Street, New York, NY
  10019
b. November 4, 1916. St. Joseph, MO.

EDUCATION: University of Texas.
CAREER HIGHLIGHTS: Once voted the most
trusted man in America, Cronkite set the

standard for TV news anchoring and was val-
ued by viewers for his objective but reassur-
ing manner. One of broadcasting's most honored journalists, he has spent more than 30
years as a CBS newsman. Joined CBS News
('50), covering virtually every major news
event. Anchor, "The CBS Evening News"
('62–'81); Anchor and Reporter, "Walter
Cronkite's Universe" ('80–'82). Cronkite,
who is also a CBS Director, will earn $1 mil-
lion a year for the next seven years as a CBS
Special Correspondent and Assignment Consultant.
ACHIEVEMENTS & AWARDS: Recipient of every
major award in broadcast-journalism. Most
recent awards include NAB distinguished
service award ('82); Presidential Medal of
Freedom; Dupont-Columbia award; American Educators award ('83); Emmy awards for
individual achievement ('65); NATAS Trustees award ('81).
PERSONAL: Married to the former Mary Elizabeth Maxwell; three children, Nancy Elizabeth, Mary Kathleen, and Walter III.

CROSBY, JOHN
V.P., Casting, ABC, Entertainment

c/o ABC, 2040 Ave. of the Stars, Los Angeles,
  CA 90067
b. Liverpool, England.

EDUCATION: California State University.
CAREER HIGHLIGHTS: Joined CBS as Asst. to
V.P. in Charge of Casting ('68); Casting
Agent for Kurt Frings ('70); Agent, ICM ('72);
created John Crosby & Assoc. talent agency
('77); named V.P., Casting, ABC Entertain-
ment ('82).
ACHIEVEMENTS & AWARDS: N.A.
PERSONAL: Resides in Los Angeles.

CROTHERS, JOEL
Actor

c/o "The Edge of Night," ABC, 1330 Ave. of
  the Americas, New York, NY 10019
b. January 28, 1941. Cincinnati, OH.

EDUCATION: Harvard University, B.A., English
(magna cum laude).

CAREER HIGHLIGHTS: Began in New York as a child actor on such early shows as "Studio One," "Playhouse 90," "Kraft Theater," and "Goodyear Playhouse." A veteran of soap operas, Crothers had feature roles on "Dark Shadows," "The Secret Storm," and "Somerset" before settling on "The Edge of Night" ('77).

ACHIEVEMENTS & AWARDS: Member, Phi Beta Kappa.

PERSONAL: N.A.

CRUTCHFIELD, ROBERT
V.P., Publicity/Advertising, Lorimar Productions

c/o Lorimar Productions, 3970 Overland Ave., Culver City, CA 90230
b. July 10, 1937. Wichita, KS.

EDUCATION: Lon Morris College.

CAREER HIGHLIGHTS: Worked as a Unit Publicist for films and TV ('61–'74); Dir. of Publicity, MTM Enterprises ('74); V.P., Publicity/Advertising, Lorimar Productions ('80).

ACHIEVEMENTS & AWARDS: N.A.

PERSONAL: N.A.

CRUZ, FRANK
Co-Anchor, KNBC News 4, News

c/o KNBC, 3000 W. Alameda Ave., Burbank, CA 91523
b. Tucson, AZ.

EDUCATION: University of Southern California, B.A., History, and M.A., Latin Studies.

CAREER HIGHLIGHTS: Chairman of Mexican-American Studies, Sonoma State College and California State University at Long Beach; after an extensive career in education he entered the TV industry as a Reporter, KABC-TV; Host/Narrator, "Chicano," KNBC-TV ('71–'72); presented a half hour TV program, "The Legacy of the Mexican War, 1846–48, and Its Significance to the Chicano," KNXT-TV ('71); Co-Anchor, weekend editions, KNBC News 4, Los Angeles ('83).

ACHIEVEMENTS & AWARDS: Ruben Salazar award for investigative reporting ('73); Golden Eagle award for his outstanding achievements in and contributions to the TV industry ('80). Co-Author, *Latin Americans: Past and Present* ('72). Served as Pres., California Chicano News Media Assn. Professional memberships include Alpha Mu Gama foreign language honorary society ('64) and Phi Alpha Theta honorary history society ('65).

PERSONAL: Resides in Fountain Valley, CA, with his wife, Bonnie, and their three children, Heather, Francisco, and Vanessa.

CRYSTAL, LESTER M.
Exec. Prod., "MacNeil/Lehrer Report"

c/o WNET/13, 356 W. 58th St., New York, NY 10019
b. September 13, 1934. Duluth, MN.

EDUCATION: Northwestern University, B.A. and M.S., Journalism.

CAREER HIGHLIGHTS: Worked as Regional Mgr. in Chicago for NBC News ('65); moved to "The Huntley-Brinkley Report" as Assoc. Prod. ('67); Prod. on program ('68); Field Prod., Europe, based in London for NBC News ('70); returned to U.S. as Exec. Prod., "Nightly News" ('73); Exec. V.P., NBC TV News ('76); Pres., NBC News ('77). Took on responsibilities of Sr. Exec. Prod., Political Coverage and Special Programs ('79); V.P., Affiliate News Services, Exec. Prod., "MacNeil/Lehrer Report."

ACHIEVEMENTS & AWARDS: Emmy awards for "An Investigation of Teenage Drug Addiction —Odyssey House" segment on "The Huntley-Brinkley Report" ('69–'70); "Reports on World Hunger" for "Nightly News" ('73–'74); Dupont award for "Human Rights —A Soviet-American Debate" and "The Struggle for Freedom" ('76–'77); daytime Emmy award for "Ask NBC News" ('79–'80).

PERSONAL: Resides in Scarsdale, NY, with wife, Toby; children, Bradley, Alan, and Elizabeth.

CULHANE, DAVID
Correspondent, CBS, News

c/o CBS, 524 W. 57th St., New York, NY 10019
b. 1930. Chicago, IL.

EDUCATION: University of Michigan, Master's, English Literature.

CAREER HIGHLIGHTS: London Correspondent, *Baltimore Sun*; host for "International Magazine" produced in London for Natl. Educational TV; Chief Political Reporter, *Baltimore Evening Sun*; joined CBS News as a Correspondent ('67), covering everything from politics to social change and the arts.

ACHIEVEMENTS & AWARDS: Peabody and Emmy awards for CBS Reports, "Hunger in America" ('68).

PERSONAL: Four children, Stephen, Philip, Maximilian, and Christiane.

CULLEN, BILL
Game Show Host

c/o CBS, 7800 Beverly Blvd., Los Angeles, CA 90036
b. February 18, 1920. Pittsburgh, PA.

EDUCATION: University of Pittsburgh.

CAREER HIGHLIGHTS: Although stricken with polio as a child, Cullen was not deterred from a successful broadcasting career that has spanned 40 years. Started as a Disc Jockey in his native Pittsburgh, Cullen moved to New York to become a Staff Announcer with CBS Radio ('44); Writer, "Easy Aces" and "The Danny Kaye Show"; met Bill Todman, who formed Goodson-Todman Productions with Mark Goodson, and became Game Show Host for that company ever since, hosting more than 25 different series including "The Price Is Right," "Eye Guess," "Three on a Match," "To Tell the Truth," "I've Got a Secret," "Winning Streak," "The $25,000 Pyramid," "The Love Experts," and "Child's Play."

ACHIEVEMENTS & AWARDS: N.A.

PERSONAL: Resides in Bel Air, CA, with wife, Ann.

CULLETON, KATHLEEN
Dir., Administration, Advertising and Promotion, CBS, Entertainment, West Coast

c/o CBS, 7800 Beverly Blvd., Los Angeles, CA 90036
b. N.A.

EDUCATION: Syracuse University, B.S., Accounting and TV/Radio; CBS School of Management.

CAREER HIGHLIGHTS: Staff Auditor, East Coast Internal Audit Dept., CBS, New York ('76); held various financial positions within CBS Entertainment ('78); Dir., Financial Planning, CBS Theatrical Films ('80); Dir., Administration, Advertising and Promotion, CBS Entertainment, West Coast ('82).

ACHIEVEMENTS & AWARDS: N.A.

PERSONAL: N.A.

CULP, ROBERT
Actor

c/o DHKPR, 7319 Beverly Blvd., Los Angeles, CA 90067
b. August 16, 1930. Berkeley, CA.

EDUCATION: Washington University; San Francisco State University.

CAREER HIGHLIGHTS: Major motion pictures include *PT-109*, *Sunday in New York*, *Bob and Carol and Ted and Alice*. TV guest appearances in "Police Story," *Roots: The Next Generation*, and *Killjoy*. TV series star of "Trackdown," "I Spy," and "The Greatest American Hero."

ACHIEVEMENTS & AWARDS: Obie award for best actor in *He Who Gets Slapped* ('56). Wrote, directed, produced, and narrated "Operation Breadbasket," the first hard-news documentary acquired by any network from an outside source.

PERSONAL: Wife, Candace Celeste Wilson; daughter, Samantha.

CURLE, CHRIS
Broadcast Journalist/News Anchor, Cable News Network

c/o Cable News Network, 1050 Techwood Dr., N.W., Atlanta, GA 30318
b. February 17, 1947. Denver, CO.

EDUCATION: University of Texas, B.S.
CAREER HIGHLIGHTS: Reporter, KTRK-TV, Houston ('69); Freelance Reporter, London and Bonn ('72); Anchor, WJLA-TV, Washington, DC ('75); Anchor "Take Two," Cable News Network ('80).
ACHIEVEMENTS & AWARDS: Local Emmy nominations and awards for People in the News documentaries ('75–'80); Sigma Delta Chi award ('78).
PERSONAL: Husband, Don Farmer, also with Cable News Network.

CURRAN, JOHN
Sr. V.P., Dir. of Network Buying and Programming, Doyle, Dane, Bernbach

c/o Doyle, Dane, Bernbach, 437 Madison Ave., New York, NY 10022
b. June 15, 1935.

EDUCATION: City College of New York.
CAREER HIGHLIGHTS: Began his career at Reach-McClinton Agency as a Network TV Buyer ('56); joined McCann-Erickson to handle all network negotiations ('59); V.P. in Charge of TV Programming, Cline Maxon Agency ('66); Sr. V.P., Dir. of Network Buying and Programming, Doyle, Dane, Bernbach ('68).
ACHIEVEMENTS & AWARDS: N.A.
PERSONAL: N.A.

CURRLIN, LEE
Sr. V.P., NBC, East Coast Programs

c/o NBC, 30 Rockefeller Plaza, New York, NY 10020
b. New York, NY.

EDUCATION: City College of New York; Hofstra University.
CAREER HIGHLIGHTS: Held various positions in the Radio/TV Dept., William H. Weintraub agency and Kenyon & Eckhardt; moved to Benton & Bowles as V.P. in Charge of Programming; joined CBS TV as Dir. of Marketing ('68); V.P., Special Projects, Network Sales ('69); V.P., Sales Planning and V.P., Programming, CBS TV Stations Division. He joined NBC as V.P., Broadcast Planning ('78); V.P., Program Planning, NBC Entertainment ('79); Sr. V.P., Program Planning, NBC Entertainment ('79); Sr. V.P., East Coast Programs ('82).
ACHIEVEMENTS & AWARDS: N.A.
PERSONAL: Resides in Rockville Centre, NY, with wife, Helen, and five children.

CURTAN, DEBORAH A.
Mgr., Casting, NBC, Entertainment

c/o NBC, 3000 W. Alameda Ave., Burbank, CA 91523
b. Denver, CO.

EDUCATION: University of Northern Colorado, B.A., Elementary Education ('71).
CAREER HIGHLIGHTS: Acct. Mgr., Bayly Co., Denver ('71); Agent, Wormser, Helfond & Joseph ('75); Mgr., Casting, NBC Entertainment ('80).
ACHIEVEMENTS & AWARDS: N.A.
PERSONAL: Single, resides in Hollywood.

CURTIN, VALERIE
Actress

c/o "Nine to Five," ABC, 2040 Ave. of the
Stars, Los Angeles, CA 90067
b. March 31. New York, NY.

EDUCATION: N.A.

CAREER HIGHLIGHTS: Made her TV debut in an
episode of ABC's "Happy Days," and appeared in numerous episodes of comedy series. Played a waitress in *Alice Doesn't Live
Here Anymore* ('74) and a political worker in
All the President's Men ('75). After these films
she wrote an episode of "The Mary Tyler
Moore Show" with Mary Kay Place. They
later wrote for the "Phyllis" series. Collaborated with writer Barry Levinson on the script
of *And Justice for All* ('78), the screenplay for
Inside Moves ('80) *and Best Friends* ('82). Series
star of "Nine to Five."

ACHIEVEMENTS & AWARDS: Academy Award
nomination for best original screenplay for
And Justice for All.

PERSONAL: Resides in Encino, CA.

CURTIS, DAN
Prod., Dan Curtis Productions

c/o Dan Curtis Productions, 5541 Marathon,
Hollywood, CA 90038
b. August 12. Bridgeport, CT.

EDUCATION: Syracuse University.

CAREER HIGHLIGHTS: Made a breakthrough in
soap opera by producing the first gothic soap,
"Dark Shadows." Kept upgrading his product with a number of made for TV features,
culminating with the huge multipart mini-
series based on Herman Wouk's *The Winds of
War* ('83). Used golfing background to enter
producing ranks with "CBS Golf Classic"
('66); produced TV movies *The Night Stran-
gler, Frankenstein, The Norliss Tapes, The Night
Stalker, The Picture of Dorian Gray, The Strange
Case of Dr. Jekyll and Mr. Hyde* ('73); *Scream of
the Wolf, Shadow of Fear, Dracula, The Invasion of
Carol Enders, Melvin Purvis: G-Man, The Turn of
the Screw, Come Die With Me, Nightmare at 43
Hillcrest, The Great Ice Rip-Off, Trilogy of Terror*
('74); *The Kansas City Massacre* ('75); *Dead of
Night, The Curse of the Black Widow* ('77); and
When Every Day Was the Fourth of July ('78).

Produced NBC series "Supertrain" ('79) and
"The Long Days of Summer" ('80).

ACHIEVEMENTS & AWARDS: Emmy for achievement in sports for "CBS Golf Classic" ('65).

PERSONAL: Resides in Beverly Hills with wife,
Norma; daughters, Cathy and Tracy.

CUSACK, PETER
V.P., ABC, Human Resources

c/o ABC, 1330 Ave. of the Americas, New
York, NY 10019
b. N.A.

EDUCATION: Cornell University, B.S., Industrial and Labor Relations ('56); New York University, LL.B. ('62).

CAREER HIGHLIGHTS: Wage and Salary Admin-
istrator, Sperry & Hutchinson Co. ('63);
Corporate Dir. of Personnel, Borden ('67);
Corporate Dir. of Personnel, Ciba-Geigy
Corp. ('70); Staff V.P., Personnel, Pan Ameri-
can World Airways ('73); V.P., Personnel,
ABC ('74); V.P., Human Resources, ABC,
Inc. ('81).

ACHIEVEMENTS & AWARDS: Recipient of the
Judge William B. Groat award for distinguished achievement in industrial relations.

PERSONAL: Resides in Croton-on-Hudson, NY
with his wife, Suzanne, and their children,
Michele, Heather, Crispin, and Timothy.

D

DAILEY, IRENE
Actress

c/o "Another World," NBC, 30 Rockefeller
Plaza, New York, NY 10020
b. September 12, 1920. New York, NY.

EDUCATION: New York University.
CAREER HIGHLIGHTS: Theater credits include
Tomorrow With Pictures and *The Subject Was
Roses*. Motion pictures include *No Way To Treat
a Lady* and *Five Easy Pieces*. Regular on the
daytime drama "Another World."
ACHIEVEMENTS & AWARDS: Drama Critics Circle
award for *The Subject Was Roses*; Emmy as best
actress in a daytime series ('79).
PERSONAL: N.A.

DALE, AL
Correspondent, ABC, News

c/o ABC, 7 W. 66th St., New York, NY 10023
b. N.A.

EDUCATION: Mercer University, B.A., History.
CAREER HIGHLIGHTS: Reporter/Anchor, WBTV-
TV, Charlotte, NC; Reporter/Anchor, KPIX-
TV, San Francisco; Reporter, WBBM-TV, Chi-
cago; Correspondent, ABC News, Atlanta
('78); Correspondent, ABC News, London
('82).
ACHIEVEMENTS & AWARDS: Emmy ('81).
PERSONAL: N.A.

D'ALEO, JOSEPH S., JR.
Dir. of Meteorology, Weather Channel

c/o Weather Channel, 2840 Mount Wilkinson
Pkwy., Atlanta, GA 30339
b. June 3, 1946. Brooklyn, NY.

EDUCATION: University of Wisconsin, B.S. and
M.S., Meteorology; New York University and
Georgia Institute of Technology, doctoral
study.
CAREER HIGHLIGHTS: Meteorologist for CBS
Weather ('71); Pres., Sentry Weather Services
('75); founded Great American Weather Cal-
endar Co. and served as Pres. ('78); joined
ABC's "Good Morning America" as Meteoro-
logist ('80); moved to the Weather Channel as
Dir. of Meteorology ('81). Asst. Professor,
Lyndon State College ('74–'80).
ACHIEVEMENTS & AWARDS: Shared Natl.
Weather Assn. award to ABC Weather for
most significant contribution to meteorology
('81).
PERSONAL: N.A.

DALVI, AJIT
Dir. of Marketing, Cox Cable
Communications

c/o Cox Cable Communications, 219 Perimeter
Center Parkway, Atlanta, GA 30346
b. May 27, 1942. India.

EDUCATION: Bombay University (India), B.A.,
Sociology; Indian Institute of Management
(India), M.B.A.
CAREER HIGHLIGHTS: Marketing Research,
Coca-Cola USA, Atlanta ('71); Brand Mgr.,
Fresca, Coca-Cola USA, Atlanta ('77); Sr.
Brand Mgr., Tab, Coca-Cola, USA, Atlanta
('79); Brand Dir., Coca-Cola, Coca-Cola USA,
Atlanta ('80); Dir. of Marketing, Cox Cable
Communications, Atlanta ('82).
ACHIEVEMENTS & AWARDS: N.A.
PERSONAL: N.A.

DALY, ROBERT
**Co-Chairman and Chief Exec. Officer,
Warner Bros.**

c/o Warner Bros., 4000 Warner Blvd.,
Burbank, CA 91505
b. December 8, 1936.

EDUCATION: Brooklyn College.
CAREER HIGHLIGHTS: Accounting Dept., CBS
('55); V.P., Business Affairs, CBS; Exec. V.P.,
CBS TV ('76); Pres., CBS Entertainment ('77);
Co-Chairman and Chief Exec. Officer, War-
ner Bros.
ACHIEVEMENTS & AWARDS: N.A.
PERSONAL: N.A.

DALY, TYNE
Actress

c/o Marilyn Reiss, Cramer & Reese, 9100
Sunset Blvd., Suite 240, Los Angeles, CA
90069
b. February 21. Madison, WI.

EDUCATION: Brandeis University.
CAREER HIGHLIGHTS: Appeared in the daytime
drama "General Hospital"; guest roles on
"Judd for the Defense," "Ironside," "Medical
Center," and "Lou Grant." TV movies in-
clude *A Matter of Life and Death, The Women's
Room,* and *The Entertainer;* feature films in-
clude *The Enforcer, John and Mary, Play It As It
Lays, Speedtrap, Telefon,* and *Zoot Suit.* Series
lead as Mary Beth Lacey in "Cagney and
Lacey."
ACHIEVEMENTS & AWARDS: N.A.
PERSONAL: Husband, Georg Stanford Brown;
daughters, Elizabeth and Kathryne. Reside in
Los Angeles.

DAMON, STUART
Actor

c/o "General Hospital," ABC, 4151 Prospect
Ave., Los Angeles, CA 90027
b. February 5. Brooklyn, NY.

EDUCATION: Brandeis University, B.A., Psychology.
CAREER HIGHLIGHTS: Co-starred in the TV musical production of "Cinderella" with Lesley
Ann Warren ('65). Moved to England to star
in various British series for 11 years, including "The Champions" ('66). After returning
to the U.S., he was signed as Dr. Alan Quar-
termaine on the soap opera "General Hospital" ('77). He co-starred in the TV movie *Fantasies* ('81).
ACHIEVEMENTS & AWARDS: N.A.
PERSONAL: Resides in Hancock Park, CA, with
wife Deidre, daughter, Jennifer, and son,
Christopher.

DAMSKI, MEL
Dir.

c/o Phil Gersh Agency, Canon Dr., Beverly
Hills, CA 90210
b. July 21, 1946. Bronx, NY.

EDUCATION: Colgate University, B.A.
CAREER HIGHLIGHTS: Reporter, *Suffolk Sun* ('68);
Reporter, *Newsday* ('69); Dir., five "Lou
Grant" episodes in first season ('77); Dir. of
the TV movies *Long Journey Back, Child Stealer,
American Dream* ('79), *A Perfect Match, Word of
Honor* ('80), *For Ladies Only, Invasion of Privacy*
('81), and *Attack on Fear,* and the feature film
Yellowbeard ('82).
ACHIEVEMENTS & AWARDS: Emmy nominations
for "Lou Grant" ('79) and *American Dream*
('80).
PERSONAL: N.A.

DANAHER, KAREN
Program Dir., NBC, Movies for TV

c/o NBC, 3000 W. Alameda Ave., Burbank, CA 91523
b. February 18, 1947. New York, NY.

EDUCATION: Hunter College, B.A.
CAREER HIGHLIGHTS: Assoc. Prod./Editor, documentaries/industrials, Don Lane Pictures, New York ('69); Post-Production Supervisor/Assoc. Dir., TV, CBS News ('79); Mgr., Motion Pictures for TV, NBC ('79); Dir., Motion Pictures for TV, NBC: *Kent State, Acorn People, Bitter Harvest, Child Bride of Short Creek, Living Proof, Hank Williams, Jr., Death of a Centerfold, G. Gordon Liddy, Kid With a Broken Halo, Born Beautiful,* and *Jacobo Timerman: Prisoner Without a Name, Cell Without a Number.*
ACHIEVEMENTS & AWARDS: N.A.
PERSONAL: N.A.

DANCY, JOHN
Correspondent, NBC, News

c/o NBC, 30 Rockefeller Plaza, New York, NY 10020
b. August 5, 1936. Jackson, TN.

EDUCATION: Union University, B.A., English; Case Western Reserve University.
CAREER HIGHLIGHTS: Correspondent, NBC News, Berlin ('73); Correspondent, NBC News, London ('75); Sr. White House Correspondent, NBC News, Washington, DC ('78); Correspondent covering the U.S. Senate, NBC News, Washington, DC ('82).
ACHIEVEMENTS & AWARDS: National Emmy award; Dupont-Columbia award for excellence in broadcast journalism; Overseas Press Club citation for excellence.
PERSONAL: Wife Ann; four children.

DANDRIDGE, PAUL
Reporter, KABC-TV, News

c/o KABC-TV, 4151 Prospect Ave., Los Angeles, CA 90027
b. March 24. Jersey City, NJ.

EDUCATION: Manhattan College, B.A., Economics ('65).
CAREER HIGHLIGHTS: Reporter, WRGB-TV, Albany, NY ('68); Reporter, WCBS-TV, New York ('70); Reporter/Anchor, KNBC-TV, Los Angeles ('75); Reporter, KABC-TV, Los Angeles ('82).
ACHIEVEMENTS & AWARDS: N.A.
PERSONAL: Resides in Los Angeles with his wife, Linda.

DANIEL, ANN
V.P., Dramatic Series Development, ABC, Entertainment

c/o ABC, 4151 Prospect Ave., Los Angeles, CA 90027
b. Santa Barbara, CA.

EDUCATION: University of California at Los Angeles, B.A., Film and Social Psychology; University of Southern California, M.A.
CAREER HIGHLIGHTS: Prod./Developer, Nontheatrical features, Walt Disney Productions; Program Exec., Current Comedy Series, ABC Entertainment ('79); Mgr., Dramatic Development, ABC ('79); Dir., Dramatic Series Development, ABC ('80); V.P., Dramatic Series Development, ABC Entertainment ('81).
ACHIEVEMENTS & AWARDS: N.A.
PERSONAL: Resides in Los Angeles.

DANIELS, BILL
Chairman, Daniels & Associates
c/o Daniels & Associates, Third and Milwaukee Sts., Denver, CO
b. July 1, 1920. Greeley, CO.

EDUCATION: New Mexico Military Institute.
CAREER HIGHLIGHTS: Known as "the Father of Cable Television," Mr. Daniels is credited with bringing many newspapers and broadcasters into the cable industry. Between 1952 and 1958 Daniels maintained a lucrative oil insurance practice while building cable systems in Wyoming and New Mexico. His cable systems firm was incorporated in Denver in

1958. As a brokerage, Daniels & Associates has handled more than two thirds of all deals in the industry for over 25 years.

ACHIEVEMENTS & AWARDS: Humanitarian of the Year Award, Denver ('73); owner of Home Savings of America; former Pres., Natl. Cable TV Assn.; Member, Board of Dirs., Cable-TV Industries.

PERSONAL: N.A.

DANIELS, RALPH
V.P., Broadcast Standards, NBC

c/o NBC, 30 Rockefeller Plaza, New York, NY 10020
b. December 22, 1927. San Francisco, CA.

EDUCATION: Pomona College, B.A.; University of California, graduate study.

CAREER HIGHLIGHTS: Moved up the ladder at the CBS TV Stations Division from Acct. Exec. in the Sales Dept. to V.P. and Station Mgr., WCBS-TV, New York, and eventually Pres. of the CBS Owned Stations ('56–'71); joined NBC as V.P., Broadcast Standards ('75).

ACHIEVEMENTS & AWARDS: Mass media award for editorial services from the Natl. Conference of Christians and Jews ('68); Member, Board of Dirs., Intl. Radio and TV Foundation.

PERSONAL: Resides in Larchmont, NY; wife, Rosemary; daughters, Katherine, Elizabeth, and Margaret.

DANIELS, WILLIAM
Actor

c/o "St. Elsewhere," 3000 W. Alameda Ave., Burbank, CA 91523
b. March 31, 1927. Brooklyn, NY.

EDUCATION: Northwestern University, B.A., Theater Arts.

CAREER HIGHLIGHTS: Broadway credits include *1776*, *Zoo Story*, and *A Little Night Music*. His motion pictures include *The Graduate*, *Two for the Road*, *The Parallax View*, *Oh God!*, *1776*, and *Black Sunday*. TV co-star of "Captain Nice," "Freebie and the Bean," and "The Nancy Walker Show." His TV movies and miniseries include *The Bastard*, *Blind Ambition*, and

A Case of Rape. Series regular as Dr. Mark Craig in "St. Elsewhere."

ACHIEVEMENTS & AWARDS: N.A.

PERSONAL: Wife, actress Bonnie Bartlett; children, Michael and Robert.

DANN, MIKE (Michael H. Dann)
Sr. Program Adviser, ABC Video Enterprises

c/o ABC, 1330 Ave. of the Americas, New York, NY 10019
b. N.A.

EDUCATION: University of Michigan, Economics.

CAREER HIGHLIGHTS: During his tenure at CBS in the late fifties and through much of the sixties, Dann was a pivotal figure in determining what got on and stayed on the CBS air. His candor and caustic wit were widely known throughout the industry. His career began as U.S. Army News Correspondent ('42–'45); joined NBC ('48); CBS, V.P. for Programs ('58); Network V.P. for Programs ('63); Sr. V.P. for Programs ('66). He spearheaded the Children's Television Workshop's move into cable and other software activities; Consultant to Warner Cable planning programming for Qube ('74); developed new concepts for the Disney Corp. for Epcot; Sr. Program Adviser, ABC Video Enterprises ('80). Also, Visiting Lecturer in American Studies and Guest Fellow of Yale University ('73–'78).

ACHIEVEMENTS & AWARDS: Author of articles and lectures on the communications field.

PERSONAL: Married; resides in New York City.

DANNHAUSER, WILLIAM
Dir., Special Programs, NBC, Programming

c/o NBC, 30 Rockefeller Plaza, New York, NY 10020
b. Englewood, NJ.

EDUCATION: Rutgers University; University of Colorado.

CAREER HIGHLIGHTS: Began career at NBC in the mailroom ('50); Studio Supervision, NBC ('51); Unit Mgr. ('54); Sr. Unit Mgr. ('57); Mgr., News Unit Mgrs. ('61); Administrator, Budgeting, Business Affairs Dept. ('62); Mgr.,

Business Affairs Dept. ('63); Dir., Business Affairs Dept. ('67); Dir., Special Programs, NBC ('75).

ACHIEVEMENTS & AWARDS: N.A.

PERSONAL: Resides in New City, NY, with wife, Marilyn; children, Lori, Bill Jr., and Jamie.

DANTAS, REGINA
V.P., Metromedia Producers Corp., Program Acquisitions

c/o Metromedia Producers Corp., 485 Lexington Ave., New York, NY 10017
b. N.A.

EDUCATION: N.A.

CAREER HIGHLIGHTS: Dir., Program Acquisitions, TV Globe; Dir., Sales and Acquisitions, Taft Broadcasting Group ('76); V.P./General Mgr., Sales and Acquisitions, Taft Broadcasting Group ('78); V.P., Intl. Sales, Viacom ('80); V.P./Managing Dir., CBS Cable ('81); V.P., Program Acquisitions, Metromedia Producers Corp. ('83).

ACHIEVEMENTS & AWARDS: N.A.

PERSONAL: N.A.

DANZA, TONY
Actor

c/o Artists Agency, 1000 Santa Monica Blvd., Suite 305, Los Angeles, CA 90067
b. April 21. Brooklyn, NY.

EDUCATION: University of Dubuque.

CAREER HIGHLIGHTS: TV movies include *Murder Can Hurt You*; feature films include *Going Ape*

and *Hollywood Knights*. Was a series regular as Tony Banta in "Taxi."

ACHIEVEMENTS & AWARDS: N.A.

PERSONAL: Single, resides in Los Angeles.

DARION, SIDNEY
Dir., ABC, Cultural Affairs

276 Riverside Dr., New York, NY 10025
b. June 2, 1923. New York, NY.

EDUCATION: University of Missouri, B.A.

CAREER HIGHLIGHTS: Joined ABC News as Staff Writer ('53); named Prod./Writer ('61); Exec. Prod. of Special Events Unit ('64); Exec. Prod. of "ABC Evening News" ('66); moved to Documentary Unit as Prod. ('69); Mgr., TV Cultural Affairs, ABC TV News and Exec. Prod. of "Directions" ('71); promoted to Dir. of same dept. while maintaining responsibility for "Directions" ('81).

ACHIEVEMENTS & AWARDS: Dupont citation for "Directions" ('79–'80); Emmy award for best religious series on network TV for "Directions" ('80–'81); five additional Emmy nominations before '79.

PERSONAL: Resides in Manhattan; married with two children.

DAVENPORT, GEORGE LEWIS
V.P., Cox Cable Communications, Eastern Division

c/o Cox Cable Communications, 219 Perimeter Center Parkway, Atlanta, GA 30346
b. January 23, 1922. Mosier, OR.

EDUCATION: Arkansas State University ('43); Muskingum College ('44).

CAREER HIGHLIGHTS: General Mgr., The Dalles TV Company, The Dalles, OR ('54); Regional Mgr., Clatsop TV, Astoria, OR ('62); Regional Mgr., Cox Cablevision Corp., Astoria, OR ('64); V.P. Eastern Division, Cox Cable Communications ('72).

ACHIEVEMENTS & AWARDS: N.A.

PERSONAL: N.A.

DAVIDSON, JOHN
Host, ABC TV Network, "That's Incredible!"

c/o ABC, 2040 Ave. of the Stars, Los Angeles, CA 90067
b. December 13, 1941. Pittsburgh, PA.

EDUCATION: Denison University, B.A., Philosophy

CAREER HIGHLIGHTS: After singing for his supper on numerous variety shows, Davidson has made a second career just by talking on "That's Incredible!" He appeared on the New York stage in *The Fantasticks*, *Foxy*, and *Oklahoma*. Motion pictures include *The Happiest Millionaire* and *Concorde, Airport '79*. Host of two primetime variety shows, "The John Davidson Show" and "The Entertainers." Host of "That's Incredible!"

ACHIEVEMENTS & AWARDS: N.A.

PERSONAL: N.A.

DAVIES, JOHN HOWARD
Head of Light Entertainment Group, TV, BBC

c/o BBC, 12 Cavendish Place, London, England W1
b. London, England.

EDUCATION: Imperial Services College; Grenoble University.

CAREER HIGHLIGHTS: Production Asst., BBC ('67); Prod./Dir. on such BBC series as "The World of Beachcomber," "All Gas and Gaiters," "The Goodies," "Steptoe and Son," "Monty Python's Flying Circus," "The Good Life," and "Fawlty Towers"; appointed Head of Light Entertainment Group, TV, BBC ('78).

ACHIEVEMENTS & AWARDS: N.A.

PERSONAL: Married, one son and one daughter.

DAVIS, CURTIS W.
Dir. of Programs for ARTS, Hearst/ABC

c/o Clyde Taylor, Curtis Brown Ltd., 575 Madison Ave., New York, NY 10022
b. June 14, 1928. New Haven, CT.

EDUCATION: Columbia University, B.A. ('49).

CAREER HIGHLIGHTS: Production Mgr., W-N Recorder Corp., New York ('49); Production Asst./Production Mgr., Louis de Rochemont Assoc., New York ('53); Assoc. Dir. for Film, Council for the Humanities, Boston ('58); Prod./Exec. Prod., Natl. Educational TV, New York ('59); Dir., Cultural Programs, Natl. Educational TV, New York ('65); Head of own prod. company, Intl. Poorhouse, New York ('72); Exec. Prod./Dir. of Program Services, ARTS, ABC Video Enterprises, New York ('81–'82), Dir. of Programs, ARTS, Hearst/ABC.

ACHIEVEMENTS & AWARDS: Emmy awards, best drama series, "NET Playhouse" ('69); best music program, "Cinderella" ('70); best music program, "Leopold Stokowski" ('71). Prix Anik (Canada), special award, "The Music of Man." Co-Author, with Yehudi Menuhin, of *The Music of Man*; author of biography, *Leopold Stokowski* ('84).

PERSONAL: Wife, Julie; children, James and Melissa.

DAVIS, DAVID
Prod.

c/o ICM, 8899 Beverly Blvd., Los Angeles, CA 90048
b. N.A.

EDUCATION: N.A.

CAREER HIGHLIGHTS: Dir., "Dobie Gillis"; Co-Prod., "The Mary Tyler Moore Show"; Exec. Prod., "Rhoda"; Exec. Prod., "The Bob Newhart Show"; Co-Creator and Exec. Prod., "Taxi."

ACHIEVEMENTS & AWARDS: N.A.

PERSONAL: N.A.

DAVIS, MADELYN
Prod./Writer

c/o Robinson-Weintraub, 554 S. Vicente Blvd., Los Angeles, CA 90048
b. Indianapolis, IN.

EDUCATION: Indiana University, B.A.

CAREER HIGHLIGHTS: One of Lucille Ball's top writers (along with Bob Carroll Jr.) for 30 years, Davis wrote some of the best "I Love Lucy" scripts, which have since become classics. After "Lucy," went on to become Co-

Prod. with Co-Writer Carroll. Exec. Prod. with Carroll on "Private Benjamin."

ACHIEVEMENTS & AWARDS: Sylvania award for TV writing ('52); Woman of Achievement award from Women in Communications ('57); Woman of the Year, *Los Angeles Times* ('57); achievement award, Kappa Kappa Gamma ('60); distinguished alumni award, Indiana University ('72); Golden Globe award for "Alice" ('79).

PERSONAL: Married to Dr. Richard M. Davis; children, Brian, Charlotte, Lisa, Ned, and Michael Martin.

DAVIS, PETER
Writer/Prod.

320 Central Park W., New York, NY 10025
b. January 2, 1937.

EDUCATION: Harvard University, B.A. ('57).

CAREER HIGHLIGHTS: ABC Newswriter; Assoc. Prod., NBC News; Documentary Prod. and Writer for CBS (including "The Selling of the Pentagon") ('65); Prod., the motion picture documentary *Hearts and Minds* ('74). His six-part documentary "Middletown" aired on PBS ('82).

ACHIEVEMENTS & AWARDS: Won the Academy Award for best documentary for *Hearts and Minds*. Emmy award for outstanding documentary ('69). Author of the nonfiction book *Hometown*.

PERSONAL: N.A.

DAVIS, SAMMY, JR.
Entertainer

9000 Sunset Blvd., Los Angeles, CA 90069
b. December 8, 1925. New York, NY.

EDUCATION: N.A.

CAREER HIGHLIGHTS: The triple threat of TV song and dance, Davis has been an all-around entertainer since childhood and can still add variety to the few variety specials left on TV. Broadway appearances in *Mr. Wonderful* and *Golden Boy*. Guest appearances on TV specials and series, most notably "All in the Family." His TV movies include *The Pigeon* ('69), *The Trackers* ('71), and *Poor Devil* ('73). Major motion pictures include *Porgy and Bess* and *Cannonball Run*.

ACHIEVEMENTS & AWARDS: N.A.

PERSONAL: Wife, Altovise.

DAVIS, SID
V.P., NBC News, Washington, DC

c/o NBC, 4001 Nebraska Ave., Washington, DC 20016
b. Youngstown, OH.

EDUCATION: Ohio University, B.S., Journalism.

CAREER HIGHLIGHTS: Anchor and News Dir., WKBN-TV, Youngstown, OH ('56); moved to Group W as White House Correspondent ('60); Washington, DC, Bureau Chief ('68); joined NBC as Dir. of News, Washington, DC ('77); V.P./Washington, DC, Bureau Chief ('79); V.P., NBC News, Washington, DC ('82).

ACHIEVEMENTS & AWARDS: Sigma Delta Chi's outstanding male journalism graduate ('52).

PERSONAL: Wife, Barbara; children, Lawrence Jay and Morse R.

DAWSON, FREDERIC C.
Chairman of the Board, Chief Exec. Officer, and Treasurer, Diaspora Communications

c/o Diaspora Communications, 225 Central Park W., Suite 1123, New York, NY 10024
b. N.A.

EDUCATION: Northwestern University, B.S.; Stanford Business School, M.B.A.

CAREER HIGHLIGHTS: Trust Investment Officer, American Natl. Bank and Trust Co. of Chicago ('76); Investment Adviser, Forstmann-Leff Assoc., New York ('79); Chairman of the Board, Chief Exec. Officer, and Treasurer, Diaspora Communications.

ACHIEVEMENTS & AWARDS: N.A.

PERSONAL: N.A.

DAWSON, LEN
Sportscaster, NBC

c/o NBC, 30 Rockefeller Plaza, New York, NY 10020
b. N.A.

EDUCATION: N.A.

CAREER HIGHLIGHTS: During his final 10 years as an NFL quarterback, served as Sports Dir. of KMBC-TV and Radio, Kansas City, MO, and did two evening sports reports and four radio shows daily and a weekly 30-minute show. Joined NBC Sports as Football Analyst ('76); has served as Contributing Analyst during Super Bowl XV and Fiesta Bowl ('82) coverage; also Co-Host, HBO's weekly "Inside the NFL" show.

ACHIEVEMENTS & AWARDS: N.A.

PERSONAL: Resides in Kansas City, MO; two children.

DAWSON, MIMI WEYFORTH
Commissioner, FCC

c/o FCC, 1919 M St., N.W., Washington, DC 20554
b. August 31, 1944. St. Louis, MO.

EDUCATION: Washington University, B.A., Government ('66)

CAREER HIGHLIGHTS: Legislative Asst. to U.S. Rep. James Symington ('69); Legislative Asst. and Press Secretary to U.S. Rep. Richard Ichord ('73); Press Secretary, U.S. Senator Robert Packwood ('73); Legislative Dir., Senator Packwood ('75); Administrative Asst. and Chief of Staff, Senator Packwood ('76); Coordinator, Senate Republican Committee and Senate Republican Conference ('78); FCC Commissioner ('81).

ACHIEVEMENTS & AWARDS: N.A.

PERSONAL: N.A.

DAWSON, RICHARD
Host, "Family Feud," ABC TV

c/o ABC, 2040 Ave. of the Stars, Los Angeles, CA 90067
b. November 20. Gosport, England.

EDUCATION: N.A.

CAREER HIGHLIGHTS: TV guest star on "The Match Game," "McCloud," "McMillan and Wife," and "Hollywood Palace." Series regular on "The Dick Van Dyke Show," "Hogan's Heroes," and "Laugh-In." Motion pictures include *King Rat* and *Devil's Brigade*. Game show host on ABC's "Family Feud."

ACHIEVEMENTS & AWARDS: Emmy award as outstanding host of a game or participation show ('77).

PERSONAL: Resides in Beverly Hills, CA, with sons, Mark and Gary.

DAWSON, TED
Sportscaster, KABC-TV, "Eyewitness News"

c/o KABC-TV, 4151 Prospect Ave., Los Angeles, CA 90027
b. N.A.

EDUCATION: University of Utah, Business Administration ('65)

CAREER HIGHLIGHTS: After graduation from college, started at KUTV-TV, Salt Lake City as a Documentary Newswriter, then joined KTVS-TV, Dodge City, KS. Sportscaster, KOLO-TV and Radio in Reno, NV; promoted to News Dir. Hosted radio program in Portland, OR, entitled "Calling All Sports" and worked at KOIN-TV, Portland as Sports Dir. and On-Air Reporter before joining KNXT, Los Angeles. Sportscaster, KABC-TV ('78).

ACHIEVEMENTS & AWARDS: Named Sportscaster of the Year by the Los Angeles Press Club and the AP ('77).

PERSONAL: Wife, Joyce; sons, Jeff, Sean, and Matthew.

DAY, JAMES
TV Consultant and Professor, Brooklyn College

Suite 300, 1 Lincoln Plaza, New York, NY 10023
b. N.A.

EDUCATION: University of California at Berkeley, B.A., Economics ('41); Stanford University.

CAREER HIGHLIGHTS: Day has enjoyed a distinguished career in public TV as a TV Exec. and Consultant in addition to being Host/Interviewer for such WNET-TV, New York, series as "Conversations With...," "Afterword," and "Day at Night," produced by Publivision. He began his broadcasting career as a Civilian Radio Specialist during the Allied Occupation of Japan ('49); Deputy Dir., Radio

Free Asia, San Francisco ('51); Pres., KQED-TV, San Francisco ('53); Pres., Natl. Educational TV, New York ('69); Pres., WNET-TV, New York ('71); Pres., Publivision, and Prof. of Television, Brooklyn College ('73).

ACHIEVEMENTS & AWARDS: Robert C. Kirkwood award for community service ('66); American Academy of Achievement ('68); Paul Niven award for excellence in electronic journalism ('70); Member, Board of Dirs., Children's Television Workshop.

PERSONAL: Resides in New York City.

DEALY, JOHN T.
V.P., ABC, Corporate Legal Affairs

c/o ABC, 1330 Ave. of the Americas, New
   York, NY 10019
b. N.A.

EDUCATION: Harvard College; Harvard Law School.

CAREER HIGHLIGHTS: Attorney, Dewey, Ballantine, Bushby, Palmer & Wood law firm, New York ('64); Asst. General Counsel, Anchor Corp., Elizabeth, NJ ('72); Assoc. General Counsel, Cooper Laboratories, Bedford Hills, NY ('73); Asst. Secretary, ABC, Inc. ('75); V.P., Corporate Legal Affairs, ABC, Inc. ('76).

ACHIEVEMENTS & AWARDS: N.A.

PERSONAL: Resides in Bronxville, NY, with his wife, Connie, and their two children.

DEAN, MORTON
Anchor, Newsbreak, CBS

c/o CBS, 51 W. 52d Street, New York, NY
   10019
b. N.A.

EDUCATION: Emerson College, B.A.

CAREER HIGHLIGHTS: News Dir., Herald Tribune Radio Network; General Assignment Reporter, WBZ, Boston ('61); Correspondent, WCBS-TV, New York ('64); Correspondent, CBS News ('67); Anchor, "The CBS Sunday Night News" ('75–'76); Weekend Anchor, "The CBS Evening News" ('76); Anchor, Sunday to Tuesday editions of "Newsbreak."

ACHIEVEMENTS & AWARDS: UPI golden mike award, Emmy.

PERSONAL: Lives in Stamford, CT, with wife, Valerie, and children.

deBOER, LEE
V.P., Cinemax, Programming

c/o Cinemax, 1271 Ave. of the Americas, New
   York, NY 10020
b. May 8, 1952.

EDUCATION: University of Wisconsin, B.A., Radio/TV/Film.

CAREER HIGHLIGHTS: Research Dir., TeleRep ('75); joined HBO as Dir. of Research and Development ('77); Dir. of Programming, Tiered Services ('79); Dir. of Programming, Cinemax ('80); V.P., Cinemax Programming, with responsibilities for family programming for HBO and managing HBO Program Services ('82).

ACHIEVEMENTS & AWARDS: N.A.

PERSONAL: Resides in Manhattan with wife, Sophia.

DE CORDOVA, FREDERICK
Prod., NBC

c/o NBC, 3000 W. Alameda Ave., Burbank,
   CA 91523
b. 1910. New York, NY.

EDUCATION: Northwestern University.

CAREER HIGHLIGHTS: Prod./Dir., Warner Bros. Pictures ('43); Prod., Universal Studios ('48); Dir., "My Three Sons" ('65); Dir., "The George Burns and Gracie Allen Show" ('53); Prod., "The Jack Benny Show" ('63); Prod./Dir., "The Tonight Show" ('70–'83).

ACHIEVEMENTS & AWARDS: Emmy awards for "Tonight Show" ('76, '77, '78)

PERSONAL: Wife, Janet; resides in Beverly Hills, CA.

DE GUERE, PHILIP
Prod.

c/o Universal Studios, Universal City, CA
   91608
b. N.A.

EDUCATION: Stanford University

CAREER HIGHLIGHTS: Creator/Prod., "Simon and Simon" ('82). Began as a writer for Universal ('67), writing teleplays for "Run for Your Life" ('68) and "The Name of the Game" ('69). Tried the documentary field for five years and returned to Universal to write "Baretta" and *The Last Convertible*. Story Consultant, "The Bionic Woman," ('75); Co-Prod., "City of Angels" ('76); Supervising Prod., "Baa Baa Black Sheep." Created "Whiz Kids" ('81).

ACHIEVEMENTS & AWARDS: N.A.

PERSONAL: Resides in Los Angeles.

DEKNATEL, JANE
V.P., HBO, Made-for-Pay Motion Pictures

c/o HBO, Suite 4170, 2049 Century Park E., Los Angeles, CA 90067
b. December 15, 1942.

EDUCATION: University of Southampton, Social Studies; Simmons College, M.B.A.

CAREER HIGHLIGHTS: CBS Corporate Affairs Staff; Dir., Docudrama, CBS Broadcast Group ('77); Dir. and V.P., Motion Pictures for TV and Mini-Series, NBC ('78); V.P., Development, Susskind Co. ('80); joined HBO as V.P., Made-for-Pay Motion Pictures ('81).

ACHIEVEMENTS & AWARDS: Member, Women in Film, American Film Institute, and NATAS.

PERSONAL: Resides in Santa Monica, CA; two daughters, Alison and Caroline.

DE LAMADRID, GIL
Feature Reporter, WNEW-TV, "Midday"

c/o WNEW-TV, 205 E. 67 St., New York, NY 10021
b. Ponce, Puerto Rico.

EDUCATION: Hunter College.

CAREER HIGHLIGHTS: Dir. of Advertising Services and Program Prod., WADO-Radio, for three years; became a member of the NewsCenter 4 team, NBC TV ('75); Feature Reporter, WNEW-TV's "Midday" ('77). Has appeared on TV programs and in motion pictures, both in the U.S. and Puerto Rico.

ACHIEVEMENTS & AWARDS: The Golden Goddess award, Puerto Rican public ('72).

PERSONAL: N.A.

DELANEY, STEVE
Correspondent, NBC, News

c/o 4001 Nebraska Ave., N.W., Washington, DC 20016
b. August 30, 1938. Dobbs Ferry, NY.

EDUCATION: Belmont Abbey College, B.A., English ('60).

CAREER HIGHLIGHTS: He started working at a radio station, WCGC, Belmont, NC; moved to WSOC-TV, Charlotte, NC; News Dir., WSOC-TV, Charlotte; Legislative Reporter, WKYC-TV, NBC, Cleveland ('67); Prod., late evening news program, WKYC-TV, Cleveland ('68); General Assignment Reporter, WKYC-TV, Cleveland ('69); covered stories for NBC News network programs ('70); News Correspondent, NBC, "First Tuesday" ('70); Correspondent, NBC, Atlanta ('73); Correspondent, NBC, Tel Aviv ('74); Correspondent, NBC, Athens ('77); General Assignment Reporter, NBC, Washington, DC ('78).

ACHIEVEMENTS & AWARDS: N.A.

PERSONAL: Married, son, Sean.

DEMARCO, FRED
Station Mgr., NBC, WMAQ-TV, Chicago

c/o WMAQ-TV, Merchandise Mart, Chicago, IL 60654
b. December 25, 1942. New York, NY.

EDUCATION: Curry College, B.S., Business Administration ('65); Adelphi University, M.B.A., Finance ('67).

CAREER HIGHLIGHTS: Joined NBC as an Exec., Accounting Dept. ('67); served in numerous positions in the Broadcast Operations and Communications Dept., New York ('69); Dir. of Operations and Engineering, Business Affairs, WRC-TV, Washington, DC ('76); Business Mgr., WMAQ-TV ('78); Station Mgr. ('80).

ACHIEVEMENTS & AWARDS: Member, Board of the Illinois Broadcasters Assn.; NATAS.

PERSONAL: Resides in Wheaton, IL, with wife, Rikki, and children, Ken, Lori, and Jennifer.

DENISON, SUSAN
V.P., Marketing, Showtime Entertainment

c/o Showtime, 1633 Broadway, New York, NY 10019
b. April 12, 1946. Waterbury, CT.

EDUCATION: Connecticut College, B.A.; University of Rochester, M.A.; Harvard University, M.B.A.
CAREER HIGHLIGHTS: Asst. Product Mgr. and later Product Mgr., Richardson-Vicks ('73); Product Group Supervisor, Clairol ('77); Dir., Marketing, Showtime Entertainment ('79); promoted to V.P., Marketing ('81).
ACHIEVEMENTS & AWARDS: N.A.
PERSONAL: N.A.

DENOFF, SAM
Prod./Writer, Writers Guild West

c/o Writers Guild West, Hollywood, CA 90046
b. N.A.

EDUCATION: N.A.
CAREER HIGHLIGHTS: Wrote comedy material for Sid Caesar, Dick Shawn, and Steve Allen ('55); Writer, "The Andy Williams Show" ('59), "The Joey Bishop Show," and "McHale's Navy" ('60); Writer/Story Editor, "The Dick Van Dyke Show" ('62); Prod., "The Dick Van Dyke Show" ('66); Creator, "That Girl" ('66); Writer/Prod., "The Bill Cosby Special" ('68); Creator/Prod., "The Funny Side" ('71), "The Don Rickles Show" ('72), "Lotsa Luck" ('73); Prod., "On Our Own" ('77), "Turnabout" ('79), and "Harper Valley PTA" ('80).
ACHIEVEMENTS & AWARDS: Emmy awards for writing "The Dick Van Dyke Show" ('64, '65); Emmy for writing Sid Caesar special ('67); Writers Guild award for Sid Caesar special ('67); Emmy for best variety special, "The Bill Cosby Special" (68).
PERSONAL: N.A.

DERROUGH, NEIL E.
Pres., CBS TV Stations Division

c/o CBS, 51 W. 52d St., New York, NY 10019
b. N.A.

EDUCATION: San Jose State University.
CAREER HIGHLIGHTS: Joined CBS as Natl. Sales Rep., KCBS-AM, San Francisco ('62); Acct. Exec., CBS Radio Spot Sales, Detroit; transferred to WEEI-AM, Boston, as Asst. Sales Mgr.; promoted to General Sales Mgr. Returned to KCBS as V.P. and General Mgr. ('67). Appointed V.P. and General Mgr., WCBS-AM, New York ('71); V.P., CBS Owned AM Stations ('73); V.P. and General Mgr. WBBM-TV, Chicago ('74); transferred to WCBS-TV in same capacity ('77); named Pres., CBS TV Stations ('82).
ACHIEVEMENTS & AWARDS: Named outstanding alumnus, San Jose State University ('69); Member, New York State Broadcasters Assn., Governmental Affairs Committee, and Communications Industry Council.
PERSONAL: N.A.

DESMONI-HORNE, MADDY
Program Exec., Motion Pictures for TV, CBS, Entertainment, West Coast

c/o CBS, 7800 Beverly Blvd., Los Angeles, CA 90036
b. Queens, NY.

EDUCATION: Attended school in New York.
CAREER HIGHLIGHTS: Administrative Asst., Programming Services, CBS, New York ('72); Supervisor, Program Services, CBS, New York ('76); Production Coordinator, Motion Pictures for TV and Mini-Series, CBS, Los Angeles ('79); Program Exec., Motion Pic-

tures for TV, CBS Entertainment, West Coast ('82).
ACHIEVEMENTS & AWARDS: N.A.
PERSONAL: N.A.

DESPAIN, DAVE
Managing Editor/Host, "Motorweek Illustrated," WTBS

c/o WTBS, 1050 Techwood Dr., N.W., Atlanta, GA 30318
b. Fairfield, IA.

EDUCATION: Parsons College.
CAREER HIGHLIGHTS: Publicity Mgr., American Motorcycle Assn. ('72); Communications Dir., American Motorcycle Assn. ('76); Publisher, *American Motorcyclist* ('76); Managing Editor/Host, "Motorweek Illustrated" WTBS ('82).
ACHIEVEMENTS & AWARDS: N.A.
PERSONAL: N.A.

deVARONA, DONNA
Commentator, NBC, Sports

c/o NBC, 30 Rockefeller Plaza, New York, NY 10020
b. San Diego, CA.

EDUCATION: University of California at Los Angeles.
CAREER HIGHLIGHTS: Joined NBC to do swimming commentary on "Sportsworld" ('78); also files reports on NBC Sports NFL pregame show and covers a variety of women's reports on "Sportsworld."
ACHIEVEMENTS & AWARDS: Championship swimmer, youngest member of the U.S. Olympic team at age 13; won Gold Medal in Tokyo in first ever 400-meter individual medley ('64); set various world records in swimming ('60-'65).
PERSONAL: Resides in New York City.

DE VITO, DANNY
Actor

c/o "Sunday Funnies," NBC, 3000 W. Alameda Ave., Burbank, CA 91523
b. November 17. Neptune, NJ

EDUCATION: Academy of Dramatic Arts.
CAREER HIGHLIGHTS: Film roles include *Goin' South*, *One Flew Over the Cuckoo's Nest*, and *Goin' Ape*; TV movies include *Valentine*. Was a series regular on "Taxi." Star of "Sunday Funnies," NBC ('83).
ACHIEVEMENTS & AWARDS: Emmy as best supporting actor for "Taxi" ('81).
PERSONAL: Wife, actress Rhea Perlman, who co-stars in NBC's "Cheers." Resides in Los Angeles.

DE WITT, JOYCE
Actress

c/o "Three's Company," ABC, 2040 Ave. of the Stars, Los Angeles, CA 90067
b. April 23. Wheeling, WV

EDUCATION: Ball State University, B.A.; University of California at Los Angeles, M.F.A.
CAREER HIGHLIGHTS: Musical special appearances on "The Steve Martin Special" and "Cheryl Ladd's Souvenir Special." Guest roles on "The Love Boat," "The Tony Randall Show," and "Most Wanted." Series regular on "Three's Company."
ACHIEVEMENTS & AWARDS: Clifton Webb scholarship.
PERSONAL: Resides in southern California.

DIAMOND, JEFFREY L.
Segment Prod., ABC, "20/20"

c/o ABC, 77 W. 66th St., New York, NY 10023
b. May 6, 1950. Detroit, MI.

EDUCATION: Lehigh University, B.A., History
('72).
CAREER HIGHLIGHTS: Desk Asst., ABC News
('72); Researcher, Special Events, ABC News
('74); Production Assoc., ABC, Evening News
('74); Assoc. Prod., ABC, Evening News ('77);
Editorial "Show" Prod., ABC, Weekend
News ('78); Segment Prod., ABC, "20/20"
('79).
ACHIEVEMENTS & AWARDS: Emmy and Judges
awards for "VW Beetle: The Hidden Danger"
('80); Emmy nomination for "The Rites of Passage" ('81); Natl. Press Club, consumer journalism citation for "Pickup Trucks, The Safety
Factor" ('81).
PERSONAL: Wife, Amy; son, Aaron.

DICK, DAVID
Correspondent, CBS, News

c/o CBS, 524 W. 57th St., New York, NY
10019
b. Cincinnati, OH.

EDUCATION: University of Kentucky, B.A. and
M.A., English.
CAREER HIGHLIGHTS: Joined CBS News as a Re-
porter ('66) after seven years as Reporter,
Documentary Prod., and News Editor with
WHAS and WHAS-TV, Kentucky. Named a
Correspondent ('69), reported out of various
bureaus including Atlanta and Latin Amer-
ica. Assigned to the Dallas Bureau ('79).
ACHIEVEMENTS & AWARDS: Emmy award ('72),
for report on attempt to assassinate George
Wallace on "CBS News With Walter Cron-
kite."
PERSONAL: Wife, Eulalie; children, Samuel,
Deborah, Catherine, and Nell.

DICKINSON, ANGIE
Actress

c/o Blake Agency Ltd., 409 N. Camden Dr.,
Beverly Hills, CA 90212
b. September 30, 1931. Kulm, ND.

EDUCATION: Immaculate Heart College; Glendale College.
CAREER HIGHLIGHTS: Major films include *Rio
Bravo, Ocean's Eleven, The Chase, Captain Newman, M.D.,* and *Dressed To Kill.* TV films include *A Sensitive, Passionate Man, The Love
War, Thief, Pearl,* and *Overboard.* TV series star
of "Police Woman" and, more recently, "Cassie and Company."
ACHIEVEMENTS & AWARDS: N.A.
PERSONAL: Daughter, Nikki.

DIEKHAUS, GRACE
Prod.

c/o CBS, 530 W. 57th St., New York, NY
10019
b. May 25.

EDUCATION: Columbia University.
CAREER HIGHLIGHTS: Line Prod., "60 Minutes";
Sr. Prod., "Who's Who"; Exec. Prod., "Maga-
zine"; Sr. Prod., CBS Reports; Principal
Prod., "60 Minutes" ('82).
ACHIEVEMENTS & AWARDS: N.A.
PERSONAL: N.A.

DIGNAM, ARTHUR F.
**V.P., NBC News, Finance and
Administration**

c/o NBC, 30 Rockefeller Plaza, New York, NY
10020
b. March 20, 1946. Jamaica, NY.

EDUCATION: Fordham University, B.S., Accounting; New York University, M.B.A., Finance.

CAREER HIGHLIGHTS: Audit Mgr., Arthur Young & Co., ('67–'78); 1st Lt., U.S. Army ('68–'70); Dir., Auditing, NBC Finance ('78–'79); V.P., Finance and Administration, NBC News ('82).

ACHIEVEMENTS & AWARDS: N.A.

PERSONAL: Wife, Joan; children, Lori, Melissa, and Matthew. Resides in North Merrick, NY.

DILLER, JOHN C.
Exec. V.P. and Chief Exec. Officer, Entertainment Channel

c/o Entertainment Channel, 1133 Ave. of the Americas, New York, NY 10036
b. June 2, 1938. Greenport, NY.

EDUCATION: Georgetown University, B.A. ('60); Yale University Law School ('63).

CAREER HIGHLIGHTS: V.P., Legal Affairs, Madison Square Garden Corp. ('69). Entered private legal practice serving as a business adviser to cable TV clients ('75). Exec. V.P. and Chief Exec. Officer, Entertainment Channel ('80).

ACHIEVEMENTS & AWARDS: N.A.

PERSONAL: Resides in Laurel, NY, with wife, Holly, and children, Raegan and Corey.

DISHELL, WALTER D.
Health and Medical Reporter, KNBC, "News 4 LA"

c/o KNBC, 3000 W. Alameda Ave., Burbank, CA 91523
b. N.A.

EDUCATION: University of Michigan, M.D. ('64).

CAREER HIGHLIGHTS: Medical Adviser, "M*A*S*H," "Trapper John," and "House Calls"; Medical Editor, "Women's Page"; Health and Medical Reporter, KNBC "News 4 LA."

ACHIEVEMENTS & AWARDS: N.A.

PERSONAL: Married; three children. Resides in Tarzana, CA.

DOBBS, GREG
Correspondent, ABC, News, London

c/o ABC, 8 Carburton St., London W1, England
b. N.A.

EDUCATION: University of California at Berkeley, B.A.; Northwestern University, M.S., Journalism.

CAREER HIGHLIGHTS: Summer Intern, KGO-TV, San Francisco ('66); Reporter, KGO-TV, San Francisco; Editor, ABC Radio Network News, Chicago; Assignment Editor, WLS-TV, Chicago; Field Prod., ABC News, Chicago; Correspondent, ABC News, Chicago ('73); Correspondent, ABC News, London ('77).

ACHIEVEMENTS & AWARDS: Distinguished service award from Society of Professional Journalists ('80); Emmy for national news ('82).

PERSONAL: N.A.

DOBSON, KEVIN
Actor

c/o "Knots Landing," CBS, 7800 Beverly Blvd., Los Angeles, CA 90036
b. March 18, 1944. Jackson Heights, NY

EDUCATION: New York University; Neighborhood Playhouse.

CAREER HIGHLIGHTS: TV series co-star of "Kojak," had title role in TV series "Shannon." TV movies include *Transplant, Orphan Train, Hardhat and Legs, Reunion,* and *Mark I Love You.* TV series star of "Knots Landing."

ACHIEVEMENTS & AWARDS: U.S. Jaycees Outstanding Young Men in America award for professional achievement and community service.

PERSONAL: Wife, Susan; two children. Resides in Studio City, CA.

DOBYNS, LLOYD
Anchor, NBC, "Monitor"

c/o NBC, 30 Rockefeller Plaza, New York, NY 10020
b. Newport News, VA.

EDUCATION: Washington and Lee University, B.A., Journalism ('57).

CAREER HIGHLIGHTS: Dobyns is known for his dry wit and for writing his own exceptional copy. NBC News Correspondent in Paris ('72); wrote and anchored "Weekend," the NBC News magazine that won two Peabody awards ('74–'79). Reporter/Writer for two NBC White Papers, "If Japan Can...Why Can't We?" ('80) and "America Works When America Works" ('81). Wrote and narrated NBC special, "An American Adventure—The Rocket Pilots" ('81). Co-Anchor, "NBC News Overnight" ('82), left to become Anchor of the new NBC News magazine, "Monitor" ('83).

ACHIEVEMENTS & AWARDS: A number of programs on which Dobyns has worked have won awards; two Peabody awards for "Weekend," Dupont award, Gainsburgh awards for two NBC White Papers.

PERSONAL: Resides in Manhattan with wife, Patricia; two daughters and two sons.

DODD, KIRK
V.P., NBC Entertainment, Finance and Administration

c/o NBC, 30 Rockefeller Plaza, New York, NY 10020
b. Ohio.

EDUCATION: Rutgers University; Harvard Business School, M.B.A. ('75).

CAREER HIGHLIGHTS: Joined the Comptrollers Dept., Irving Trust Co. ('72); Assoc., TV Network Business Affairs Dept., NBC ('75); Administrator, Financial Analysis then Mgr., Sports Pricing and Special Financial Projects. Mgr., Special Sales Pricing ('77); Dir., Financial Evaluation ('78); V.P., NBC Entertainment, Finance and Administration.

ACHIEVEMENTS & AWARDS: N.A.

PERSONAL: Single; resides in Greenville, NJ.

DOLAN, PATRICK FRANCIS
Correspondent, Cable News Network

6266 Melody Lane, Dallas, TX 75231
b. June 17, 1951. Cleveland, OH.

EDUCATION: Columbia University, B.A., English Literature.

CAREER HIGHLIGHTS: Reporter, WSAV-TV, Savannah, GA ('78); Reporter/Prod. WTVH-TV, Syracuse, NY ('79); Correspondent, Cable News Network ('80).

ACHIEVEMENTS & AWARDS: Honored by the Georgia AP ('78).

PERSONAL: N.A.

DOMINUS, JEROME
V.P., CBS TV Network, Sales Planning

c/o CBS, 51 W. 52d St., New York, NY 10019
b. 1938. New York, NY.

EDUCATION: Lafayette College ('59).

CAREER HIGHLIGHTS: Joined CBS TV Network ('65), holding various executive positions, including Acct. Exec.; Mgr., Sales Administration; and Dir., Daytime Sales. Named V.P., Eastern Sales ('77), and V.P., Natl. Sales Mgr. then V.P., Sales Planning ('80).

ACHIEVEMENTS & AWARDS: N.A.

PERSONAL: Married, three children.

DONAHUE, PHIL
On-Air Personality, WGN

c/o WGN, 2501 W. Bradley Plaza, Chicago, IL 60618
b. 1936.

EDUCATION: N.A.

CAREER HIGHLIGHTS: Hosted "The Phil Donahue Show," local morning talk show, WLWD-TV, Dayton, OH ('67), which was syndicated nationally ('69); moved to Chicago and changed show's name to "Donahue" ('76); regular contributor to the "Today" show on NBC ('79–'82); currently hosts his own syndicated talk show.

ACHIEVEMENTS & AWARDS: Peabody award; Broadcaster of the Year award, IRTS; four national Emmy awards for "Donahue," four Emmy awards for outstanding host of a talk, service, or variety series; author of *Donahue: My Own Story.*

PERSONAL: Married to actress Marlo Thomas; resides in Winnetka, IL, and New York City.

DONALDSON, SAM
Correspondent, ABC, News

c/o ABC, 7 W. 66th St., New York, NY 10023
b. March 11, 1934.

EDUCATION: University of Texas, B.A.

CAREER HIGHLIGHTS: Known as one of TV's most perceptive interviewers, Donaldson can be abrasive, but only because of his determination to present a full picture of the news. As a guest panelist for question-and-answer sessions on programs such as "This Week With David Brinkley," Donaldson exhibits the thorough preparation and conscientiousness that have earned him a deserved reputation for incisiveness. Moderator/Anchor, WTOP-TV, Washington, DC; Capitol Hill Correspondent, ABC News, Washington, DC; White House Correspondent, ABC News, Washington, DC; Anchor, ABC "Sunday Evening News."

ACHIEVEMENTS & AWARDS: N.A.

PERSONAL: N.A.

DONVAN, JOHN
News Correspondent, ABC News, London

c/o ABC, 8 Carburton St., London W1, England
b. Yonkers, NY.

EDUCATION: Dartmouth College, B.A., English Literature; Columbia School of Journalism, M.A. ('80).

CAREER HIGHLIGHTS: Started his broadcast journalism career as a reporter for WLS-Radio, Connecticut ('78). Moved to WMTW-TV as a Reporter/Anchor with WMTW-TV, Maine. He was assigned to the ABC News Tel Aviv Bureau ('82) after working three years as a radio correspondent based in London.

ACHIEVEMENTS & AWARDS: Lowell Thomas award from the Overseas Press Club for an ABC News radio special on the Sadat assassination ('82).

PERSONAL: N.A.

DOTSON, BOB
Correspondent, NBC, News

c/o NBC, 30 Rockefeller Plaza, New York, NY 10020
b. October 3, 1946. St. Louis, MO.

EDUCATION: Kansas University, B.S., Journalism and Political Science ('68); Syracuse University, M.S., TV/Radio ('69).

CAREER HIGHLIGHTS: Reporter/Photographer, KMBC-TV, Kansas City, MO ('67); Reporter/Photographer, WKY-TV, Oklahoma City, now KTVY-TV ('69); Dir., Special Projects, WKY-TV, Oklahoma City ('71); Reporter, WKYC-TV, Cleveland ('75); Reporter, NBC News, Dallas ('77); Correspondent, ABC News, Atlanta, also filing reports for the "Cross Country" segment of the "Today" program ('79).

ACHIEVEMENTS & AWARDS: A local Emmy and a Robert F. Kennedy award for the outstanding regional TV program of 1974, "Through the Looking Glass Darkly," while at WKY-TV, Oklahoma City.

PERSONAL: Wife, Linda; daughter, Amy.

DOUGAN, DIANA LADY
Coordinator for Intl. Communication and Information Policy, U.S. State Dept.

4300 Parkview Dr., Salt Lake City, UT 84117
b. January 13, 1943. Dayton, OH.

EDUCATION: University of Maryland, B.A. ('64); University of Utah; Harvard University.
CAREER HIGHLIGHTS: Public Relations Consultant, Washington, DC, and New York ('64); CATV Marketing and Promotion Dir., Time, Inc. ('66); Dir. of the Corp. for Public Broadcasting, Washington, DC ('76); appointed by Pres. Reagan as Coordinator for Intl. Communication and Information Policy, U.S. State Dept. ('83).
ACHIEVEMENTS & AWARDS: Peabody award.
PERSONAL: Resides in Salt Lake City, UT, with her husband, J. Lynn, and their children, Gavin and Elena.

DOUGLAS, MIKE (Michael Delaney Dowd Jr.)
Talk Show Host

c/o Cable News Network, 1050 Techwood Dr., N.W., Atlanta, GA 30318
b. 1925.

EDUCATION: N.A.
CAREER HIGHLIGHTS: The heart throb of the senior citizen set, Douglas has enjoyed several decades of popularity as a talk show host. Syndicated Talk Show Host, Group W Westinghouse; interview show, Cable News Network; Independent Prod.
ACHIEVEMENTS & AWARDS: Emmy ('67).
PERSONAL: N.A.

DOUTHIT, RANDALL
Exec. Prod., Cable News Network

2133 Wisconsin Ave., N.W., Washington, DC 20007
b. November 15, 1949. Newburgh, OR.

EDUCATION: B.S., M.A.
CAREER HIGHLIGHTS: Prod./Dir., News, KGW-TV, Portland, OR ('70); Prod./Dir., Children's Programming, KING-TV, Seattle, WA ('75); became Prod., News ('77); Sr. Prod., "Seattle Today" ('79); moved to WABC-TV, New York as Prod., "Good Morning New York" ('80); Sr. Prod. "Freeman Reports" on Cable News Network ('81); Exec. Prod., "Crossfire" for Cable News Network ('82).
ACHIEVEMENTS & AWARDS: Peabody award for "How Come" ('75); two local Emmy awards.
PERSONAL: Married, two children.

DOW, DAVID
Correspondent, CBS, News

c/o CBS, 7800 Beverly Blvd., Los Angeles, CA 90036
b. December 8, 1937. Auburn, CA.

EDUCATION: Stanford University, B.A.
CAREER HIGHLIGHTS: Reporter, *San Diego Union* ('59); Reporter, *Sacramento Bee* ('64); Reporter and Prod., KOVR-TV, Sacramento, CA ('66); Political Correspondent for several California radio and TV stations owned by McClatchy Broadcasting ('67). Joined CBS News as a Reporter and Assignment Editor, New York ('72). Named a Correspondent ('75) and reassigned to Latin America. Based in the Los Angeles Bureau ('78).
ACHIEVEMENT & AWARDS: Stanford University Professional Journalism Fellowship ('71).
PERSONAL: Wife, Dr. Nancy Edwards; children Mary and Mark.

DOW, HAROLD
Co-Anchor/Interviewer, Correspondent, CBS, News

c/o CBS, 524 W. 57th St., New York, NY 10019
b. Hackensack, NJ

EDUCATION: University of Nebraska at Omaha

CAREER HIGHLIGHTS: Reporter/Co-Anchor/Talk Show Host, KETV-TV, Omaha, NE; News Anchor, WPAT-FM, Paterson, NJ; Reporter, KCOP-TV, Los Angeles; Anchor/Reporter, Theta Cable TV, Santa Monica, CA ('71); Broadcast Assoc., CBS News, Los Angeles ('72); Reporter, CBS News ('73); Correspondent, CBS News ('77); Co-Anchor/Interviewer, "CBS News Nightwatch" ('82).

ACHIEVEMENTS & AWARDS: Operation PUSH excellence in journalism award ('76).

PERSONAL: Resides in Upper Saddle River, NJ, with wife, Kathleen, and children, Joelle and Danica.

DOWNS, HUGH
Host, ABC, "20/20"

c/o William Morris Agency, 1350 Ave. of the Americas, New York, NY 10019
b. February 14, 1921. Akron, OH.

EDUCATION: Bluffton College; Wayne State University; Columbia University.

CAREER HIGHLIGHTS: An extensive career in TV began as Staff Announcer, WLOK, Lima, OH ('39); Staff Announcer, WWJ, Detroit ('40); Announcer and Emcee, WMAQ, Chicago ('43); NBC Co-Host, "Home Show" ('54). Joined NBC's "Tonight Show" as Announcer and Substitute Host for Jack Paar ('57); Host, NBC's long-lived game show "Concentration" for 10 years ('58–'68) while simultaneously hosting "Today" ('62–'71). Left the network to host PBS's "Over Easy" ('77–'80); joined ABC as Host, "20/20" ('78).

ACHIEVEMENTS & AWARDS: Honorary doctorates from St. John's University, Westminster College, Arizona State University, Bluffton College. Churchill Fellow, Westminster College; Chairman, U.S. Committee for UNICEF; Pres. and Chairman, Natl. Space Institute; Consultant to the Center for the Study of Democratic Institutions. Emmy award ('81) for "Over Easy". Books published include *Yours Truly* ('60), *Shoal of Stars* ('67), *Rings Around Tomorrow* ('70), *Potential* ('73), *Thirty Dirty Lies About Old* ('79), and *The Best Years Book* ('81).

PERSONAL: N.A.

DREILINGER, DAVID A.
V.P., General Counsel and Secretary, Viacom Intl.

c/o Viacom, 1211 Ave. of the Americas, New York, NY 10036
b. October 13, 1947. New York, NY.

EDUCATION: Syracuse University; Syracuse University School of Law; New York University.

CAREER HIGHLIGHTS: Joined Viacom Intl. as an Attorney ('78); promoted to General Counsel ('80); named Deputy General Counsel, Entertainment Group, Viacom Intl. ('81); V.P., General Counsel and Secretary ('82).

ACHIEVEMENTS & AWARDS: N.A.

PERSONAL: N.A.

DREXLER, MICHAEL
Exec. V.P., Dir. of Media and Programming, Doyle, Dane, Bernbach

c/o Doyle, Dane, Bernbach, 437 Madison Ave., New York, NY 10022
b. November 2, 1938.

EDUCATION: Long Island University, B.S.; New York University.

CAREER HIGHLIGHTS: Senior V.P., Dir. of Media, Ogilvy & Mather; joined Doyle, Dane, Bernbach ('74); Exec. V.P., Dir. of Media Programming, Doyle, Dane, Bernbach.

ACHIEVEMENTS & AWARDS: Pres., Media Dirs. Council.

PERSONAL: N.A.

DRINKWATER, TERRY
Correspondent, CBS, News

c/o CBS, 6121 Sunset Blvd., Los Angeles, CA 90028
b. Denver, CO.

EDUCATION: Pomona College, B.A., Government, History, and Economics ('58); University of California at Berkeley, M.A., Political Science and Journalism ('59).

CAREER HIGHLIGHTS: Writer/Editorial Asst., KNXT-TV, Los Angeles ('56); Founder and Station Mgr., KPFK-FM, Los Angeles ('59); Prod./News Writer, KTLA-TV, Los Angeles ('61); Member of CBS News's West Coast Election Unit ('63); Mgr., Los Angeles Bureau, CBS News ('65); Correspondent, CBS News, Los Angeles ('65); added responsibility of anchoring the Western Edition of "The CBS Evening News" when it premiered ('79).

ACHIEVEMENTS & AWARDS: Received local Emmy.

PERSONAL: Wife Judith; two children, Croft and Angela.

DUCLON, DAVID W.
Writer/Producer (freelance)

c/o Tony Ludwig, Creative Artists, 1888 Century Park E., Los Angeles, CA 90067
b. April 27, 1950. Rockford, IL.

EDUCATION: Drake University; University of Southern California.

CAREER HIGHLIGHTS: Four years as Story Editor, "The Odd Couple" ('70); Story Editor, "Happy Days" ('75); Exec. Script Consultant, "Laverne and Shirley" and "Bustin' Loose" ('76); Prod., "The Ted Knight Show" ('77); Prod., "Makin' It" ('78); Supervising Prod.,

"Working Stiffs," and Prod., "Laverne and Shirley" ('79); Prod., "The Jeffersons" ('80); Exec. Prod., "The Jeffersons" ('81); currently Exec. Prod., "Silver Spoons" ('82).

ACHIEVEMENTS & AWARDS: N.A.

PERSONAL: Wife, Deborah.

DUFFY, JAMES E.
Pres., ABC TV Network

c/o ABC, 1330 Ave. of the Americas, New York, NY 10019
b. April 2, 1926, Decatur, IL.

EDUCATION: Beloit College, B.A., English.

CAREER HIGHLIGHTS: News background as Reporter, *Beloit Daily News*, and Announcer, WBNB-Radio ('48); joined ABC as Press Representative ('49); Asst. Publicity Mgr., ABC ('52); Dir., Advertising and Promotion ('52); moved into sales area as Acct. Exec., Central Division, ABC Radio Network ('53); ABC TV Network Central Division Acct. Exec. ('55); Dir. of Sales, Central Division ABC Radio Network ('57); Natl. Dir. of Sales for ABC Radio Network ('60); V.P. of Sales ('61); Exec. V.P. and Natl. Dir. of Sales for Network ('62). Moved into ABC TV Network as V.P. in Charge of Sales ('63); Pres., ABC TV Network ('70).

ACHIEVEMENTS & AWARDS: Honorary doctorate of laws ('74); Communicator of the Year award from Sales and Marketing Exec. Intl. ('74); Natl. Asthma Center's Man of the Year ('76); Golden 44 award, Los Angeles Chamber of Commerce, for outstanding corporate citizenship ('77); Illinois State Broadcaster of the Year ('78); Marketing Man of the Year, Chicago Sales and Marketing Execs. Club ('82).

PERSONAL: Resides in Darien, CT, with wife, Deanna; children, Jay, Marcia, and Corinne.

DUFFY, PATRICK
Actor

c/o "Dallas," CBS, 7800 Beverly Blvd., Los
Angeles, CA 90036
b. March 17, 1949. Townsend, MN.

EDUCATION: University of Washington.
CAREER HIGHLIGHTS: Appeared in TV series including "Switch" and "Charlie's Angels";
star of "Man From Atlantis." His TV movies
include *The Stranger Who Looks Like Me*, *Hurri-
cane*, and *Cry for the Strangers*. TV star of the
series "Dallas."
ACHIEVEMENTS & AWARDS: N.A.
PERSONAL: Wife, Carlyn; two children.

DUGOW, IRIS
V.P., HBO, Original Programming, West
Coast

c/o HBO, Suite 4170, 2049 Century Park E.,
Los Angeles, CA 90067
b. April 1, 1947. Los Angeles, CA.

EDUCATION: University of California at Berkeley, B.A., Political Science; University of California at Los Angeles Graduate School.
CAREER HIGHLIGHTS: Assoc. Prod., ABC Sports
('73); Segment Prod., ABC's "A.M. America"
('75); Dir. of Premium Programming, Qube
('76); joined HBO as Dir. of Special Programming ('78); V.P., Special Programming ('79);
named V.P., Original Programming, West
Coast ('81).
ACHIEVEMENTS & AWARDS: N.A.
PERSONAL: Resides in Los Angeles.

DUITSMAN, DOUG
V.P., Columbia Pictures TV, Publicity and
Promotion

c/o Columbia Pictures TV, Columbia Plaza,
Burbank, CA 91505
b. January 25. Sioux Falls, SD.

EDUCATION: Pepperdine University.
CAREER HIGHLIGHTS: Sportscaster, KGMB-TV,
Honolulu ('53); Writer, Walt Disney Produc-
tions ('56); joined NBC TV as Mgr., Press and
Publicity ('58); moved to Columbia Pictures
TV as V.P., Publicity and Promotion ('70).
ACHIEVEMENTS & AWARDS: Recipient of first
Publicists Guild award for best conceived and
executed publicity campaign for movie or TV
program, for *Brian's Song* ('71); Member,
Board of Governors, ATAS ('74–present); Of-
ficer, ATAS ('78–'81); Chairman, Awards
Committee, ATAS ('81–'82).
PERSONAL: Rheba; daughters, Karen and Joni.

DUKE, ROBIN
Repertory Player

c/o "Saturday Night Live," NBC, 30
Rockefeller Plaza, New York, NY 10020
b. March 13, 1954. Toronto, Ontario.

EDUCATION: University of Toronto.
CAREER HIGHLIGHTS: Appeared on many Cana-
dian TV shows and commercials before join-
ing the Second City Improvisational Troupe
as a Performer/Writer ('76); joined "Saturday
Night Live" ('81).
ACHIEVEMENTS & AWARDS: N.A.
PERSONAL: Resides in both New York City and
Toronto, Ontario.

DUKE ASTIN, PATTY
Actress

c/o William Morris Agency, 151 El Camino
Dr., Beverly Hills, CA 90212
b. December 14, 1947. New York, NY.

EDUCATION: N.A.

CAREER HIGHLIGHTS: Began acting career at age 8 in TV commercials and as a film extra. Gained notoriety at age 12 for her Broadway performance as Helen Keller in *The Miracle Worker* and later reprised her role in the feature film. As a teenager, she starred as look-alike cousins in "The Patty Duke Show," and thereafter continued a career as a brilliant actress in films, TV shows, and TV movies. Her feature films include *Billie, Valley of the Dolls, You'll Like My Mother,* and *The Swarm.* Had recent TV movie leading roles in *Whatever Happened to Rosemary's Baby, Black Widow, Having Babies III, Family Upside Down, Hanging by a Thread, Women in White, The Babysitter, The Women's Room,* and *The Miracle Worker,* in which she played Annie Sullivan. Most recently starred as Molly Quinn in the ABC comedy series "It Takes Two."

ACHIEVEMENTS & AWARDS: Academy Award for *The Miracle Worker;* Emmy awards for *My Sweet Charlie, The Captains and the Kings;* and *The Miracle Worker;* two Golden Globe awards.

PERSONAL: Married to actor/director John Astin; five sons.

DULLAGHAN, JAMES R.
**Sr. V.P., ESPN, Production Operations and
Administration**

c/o ESPN, ESPN Plaza, Bristol, CT 06010
b. August 18, 1936. New York, NY.

EDUCATION: Iona College, B.A., Economics.

CAREER HIGHLIGHTS: Research Writer, *N.Y. Daily News* ('56); Film Editor, Ross Gaffney Productions ('61); started at NBC as Documentary Editor ('62) and rose to Dir., Business Affairs, Sports Division ('76). Joined ESPN as V.P., Production Operations and Administration ('79); Sr. V.P. ('81).

ACHIEVEMENTS & AWARDS: N.A.

PERSONAL: Daughter, Denise.

DUNHAM, CORYDON B.
Exec. V.P. and General Counsel, NBC

c/o NBC, 30 Rockefeller Plaza, New York, NY
10020
b. November 14, 1927. Yonkers, NY.

EDUCATION: Bowdoin College, B.A. ('48); Harvard Law School, LL.B. ('51).

CAREER HIGHLIGHTS: Spent 14 years as Assoc., Cahill, Gordon, Reindel & Ohl ('51); joined NBC as Asst. General Attorney ('65); V.P. and General Attorney ('68); V.P. and General Counsel ('71); named Exec. V.P. and General Counsel ('76).

ACHIEVEMENTS & AWARDS: Articles on media regulation, First Amendment rights, and fairness doctrine published in legal and trade journals. Member, Exec. Committee, Board of Dirs., American Arbitration Assn.; Board of Dirs., United Way of Greenwich, CT; Exec. Committee, Camp Backet, YMCA; Communications Law Committee, Section of Science and Technology, American Bar Assn.; Assn. of the Bar of the City of New York; Federal Communications Bar Assn.; Founding Member, World Assn. of Lawyers.

PERSONAL: Resides in Greenwich, CT, with wife, Janet; sons, Cory and Chris.

DUNNING, BRUCE
Correspondent, CBS, News, Peking

c/o CBS, 524 W. 57th St., New York, NY
10019
b. Rahway, NJ.

EDUCATION: Princeton University, B.A. ('62);
Columbia University, M.S., Journalism ('63);
the Sorbonne (France, '67–'68).

CAREER HIGHLIGHTS: Freelance Reporter, CBS
News in Paris ('68); based in Saigon ('70); CBS
News Corresponent ('72); based in Southeast
Asia ('75); assigned to Peking Bureau ('81).

ACHIEVEMENTS & AWARDS: Overseas Press Club
award for report "Back From Danang" ('75);
member of the CBS News team honored by
the Overseas Press Club for radio coverage of
the fall of Cambodia and Vietnam ('75).

PERSONAL: N.A.

DUNPHY, JERRY
Anchor, KABC-TV, "Eyewitness News"

c/o KABC-TV, 4151 Prospect Ave., Los
Angeles, CA 90027
b. Milwaukee, WI.

EDUCATION: University of Wisconsin; Northwestern University, Medill School of Journalism.

CAREER HIGHLIGHTS: Entered TV broadcasting
at WTVH-TV, ('53). Peoria, IL, as News Dir.
('53). Successively, he was with KEDD in
Wichita, KS; WXIX in Milwaukee; and WBBM
in Chicago before moving to the CBS station
KNXT in Hollywood ('60). Joined KABC-TV
('75). A veteran journalist whose background
includes extensive experiences in all news
media as a writer, reporter, and newscaster.

ACHIEVEMENTS & AWARDS: Emmy awards from
ATAS, Los Angeles; golden mikes from the
Radio and TV News Assn. of Southern Cali-
fornia; the John Swett award; the Ohio State
University award; the Greater Los Angeles
Press Club award.

PERSONAL: Married; resides in Encino, CA.

DUNSMORE, BARRIE
Correspondent, ABC, News

c/o ABC, 1717 DeSales St., N.W.,
Washington, DC 20036
b. Saskatchewan, Canada.

EDUCATION: Regina College.

CAREER HIGHLIGHTS: Reporter for Canadian radio; Prod./Dir./Anchor, news for Canadian
TV stations. Joined ABC as Correspondent
('65); Paris Bureau ('66); named Rome Bureau
Chief ('68); hosted Canada's leading public
affairs program, "W-5" ('74); returned to ABC
as Military Correspondent ('75); named Diplomatic Correspondent, travels with Secretary of State, files reports for "World News
Tonight" on State Dept. activities and from
hot spots around the globe.

ACHIEVEMENTS & AWARDS: N.A.

PERSONAL: N.A.

DUSSAULT, NANCY
Actress

c/o D. L. Taffner Ltd., 5900 Wilshire Blvd.,
Los Angeles, CA 90036
b. June 30, 1936. Pensacola, FL.

EDUCATION: Northwestern University, B.A.,
Music.

CAREER HIGHLIGHTS: Began professional career
in many New York musical revues and off
Broadway productions as a singer/actress;
moved on to star in many notable Broadway
shows including *Do Re Mi, Bajour,* and *Side by
Side by Sondheim.* A regular on "The New Dick
Van Dyke Show," she spent a short time as a
co-host of "Good Morning America" with
David Hartman. Guest-starred on TV specials
and "Barney Miller" before landing role as
Muriel Rush on "Too Close for Comfort."

ACHIEVEMENTS & AWARDS: N.A.

PERSONAL: Maintains residences in New York
City and Los Angeles.

DWYER, ARTHUR A.
**V.P., Cox Cable Communications, Marketing
and Programming**

219 Perimeter Center Parkway, Suite 500,
Atlanta, GA 30346
b. June 13, 1942. Chelsea, MA.

EDUCATION: University of Missouri, M.A.,
Communications/Advertising ('68).

CAREER HIGHLIGHTS: Advertising/Public Relations Specialist, General Electric, Philadelphia ('68); Marketing Mgr. VALOX, General
Electric, Pittsfield, MA ('78); Dir., Corporate
Communications, Cox Cable Communica-

tions, Atlanta ('80); V.P., Marketing and Programming, Cox Cable Communications, Atlanta ('80).

ACHIEVEMENTS & AWARDS: Board of Dirs., Cable Advertising Bureau; Pres., Cable TV Administration and Marketing Society ('82).

PERSONAL: N.A.

DWYER-DOBBIN, MARY ALICE
V.P., Programming and Exec. Prod.,
Hearst/ABC (HAVES)

c/o Hearst/ABC, 555 Fifth Avenue, New York, NY 10017

b. December 22. St. Louis, MO.

EDUCATION: Visitation Academy; Webster College, B.A.; Catholic University of America, M.F.A.

CAREER HIGHLIGHTS: Production Asst., Bob Stewart Productions ('68); Assoc. Prod., Rankin-Bass Productions, working on "Festival of Family Classics" and "The Red Baron" ('70); joined ABC as Mgr., Daytime Programming ('74); Dir., Children's Programs ('76). Joined NBC as Dir., Daytime and Children's Programs ('77); V.P., Children's Programming and Exec. Prod., "How to Watch TV," "When You Turn off Your Set, Turn on a Book" ('79); moved to Hearst/ABC as V.P. Programming and Exec. Prod, Daytime ('81).

ACHIEVEMENTS & AWARDS: TV Critics Circle award for excellence in children's programming ('77); AWRT/*Good Housekeeping* magazine award ('79). Published article on teenagers and the elderly in *TV and Teens: Experts Look at the Issues,* Action for Children's Television ('82)

PERSONAL: Married to Leon Dobbin; resides in Manhattan.

E

EATON, BOB
Los Angeles Bureau Chief, NBC News

c/o NBC, 3000 W. Alameda Ave., Burbank, CA 91523
b. October 5, 1941. Cambridge, MA.

EDUCATION: Northwestern University, B.S. ('63).
CAREER HIGHLIGHTS: News writer, WCCO-Radio, Minneapolis ('63); Cameraman/Reporter, WHAS-TV, Louisville, KY ('64); WMAQ, Chicago ('65); joined NBC News, Chicago as Deskman and Field Prod. ('67). Field Prod., NBC News, Los Angeles ('69); West Coast Prod., "NBC Nightly News" ('72); left network to become News Dir., KNBC ('74); returned to NBC as Dir. of News, Los Angeles ('77); West Coast Prod., "NBC Magazine" ('79); currently Bureau Chief, NBC News, Los Angeles.
ACHIEVEMENTS & AWARDS: Emmy award for "Heart Transplant" segment on "Prime Time Sunday" ('80).
PERSONAL: N.A.

EATON, HUGH MITCHELL, JR.
V.P. and General Mgr., Weather Channel

c/o Weather Channel, 2840 Mount Wilkinson Pkwy., Atlanta, GA 30339
b. August 6, 1932. Roanoke, VA.

EDUCATION: Virginia Polytechnic Institute, B.S., Business Administration ('59); CPA ('61); Harvard University School of Business, Manager Development Program, ('71).
CAREER HIGHLIGHTS: Joined Times-World Corp. as Admin. Asst. to Treasurer ('62); Asst. to the Pres./Finance ('66); Financial Analyst, Landmark Communications ('70). Appointed Dir. of Management Information ('71); Corporate Treasurer ('73); V.P., Personnel ('76); joined Landmark's Weather Channel as V.P. and General Mgr. ('81).

ACHIEVEMENTS & AWARDS: Teaching positions in accounting at Virginia Polytechnic Institute; University of Virginia at Lynchburg; Old Dominion University. Member, American Society of Personnel Administrators; Natl. Personnel Relations Assn.
PERSONAL: Married, three children.

ECKHERT, JULIE
Correspondent, WABC-TV, Eyewitness News

c/o WABC-TV, 7 Lincoln Sq., New York, NY 10023
b. Terre Haute, IN.

EDUCATION: University of Minnesota, B.S. and M.A.
CAREER HIGHLIGHTS: Reporter, *Minneapolis Tribune* and WWTC-Radio Minneapolis; Prod./Anchor, KMSP-TV; ABC News Midwest Bureau Correspondent; Correspondent, WABC-TV ('81).
ACHIEVEMENTS & AWARDS: N.A.
PERSONAL: Resides in Westchester, NY.

EDWARDS, DOUGLAS
Anchor, CBS, "For Our Times";
"Newsbreak," and "Mid-Day News"

c/o CBS, 51 W. 52nd St., New York, NY 10019
b. July 14, 1917. Ada, OK.

EDUCATION: University of Alabama; Emory University; University of Georgia Evening College.
CAREER HIGHLIGHTS: Reporter, WAGF, Dothan, AL; Asst. News Editor, *Atlanta Journal* and its radio station, WSB; named News Editor ('40); joined CBS Radio News and appeared on "Report to the Nation" and "The World Today" ('42); Chief of CBS News Paris Bureau; "Douglas Edwards With the News" (48–'62);

141

anchor, CBS News weekday five-minute broadcasts ('62–'80); Anchor, Morning Edition, "Newsbreak" and "For Our Times" ('82). Edwards anchored CBS News first gavel-to-gavel TV coverage of a political convention in 1948, and his debut with CBS TV News marked the first time a major newsman made the transition from radio to TV. Currently he is on CBS "Mid-Day News."

ACHIEVEMENTS & AWARDS: Peabody award.

PERSONAL: N.A.

EDWARDS, RALPH
Prod.

1717 N. Highland, Hollywood, CA 90028
b. June 13, 1913. Merino, CO.

EDUCATION: University of California, B.A., English ('35).

CAREER HIGHLIGHTS: A veteran of radio who was in on the ground floor when TV came along. He made the best of it, coming up with such long-running winners as "Truth or Consequences" and "This Is Your Life." Wrote copy for Oakland radio station at age 15; became Announcer, KFRC, San Francisco ('35); moved to New York as CBS Staff Announcer ('37). Conceived and sold the radio show "Truth or Consequences" ('40) and created "This Is Your Life" for radio ('48); both shows went on to become TV staples ('52). Also produced "Place the Face" ('53–'55); "It Could Be You" ('56–'61); "$100,000 Name That Tune" ('76–'80); "Cross-Wits" ('76–'80); Exec. Prod., "The People's Court" ('82).

ACHIEVEMENTS & AWARDS: Emmy awards for "Truth or Consequences" ('50); "This is Your Life" ('53; '54); First Carbon Mike award; honorary doctor of law, Pepperdine University ('75); Heart of Gold award, Los Angeles, American Heart Assn. ('75); Honorary Chairman, Federal Savings Bond Drive ('76); presidential citation, New York NATAS ('78).

PERSONAL: Resides in Beverly Hills, CA, with wife, Barbara Jean; three children, Christine, Gary, and Lauren.

EDWARDS, STEVE
Co-Host, KNXT-TV, "2 on the Town"

c/o KNXT-TV, 6121 Sunset Blvd., Los Angeles, CA 90028
b. New York, NY.

EDUCATION: University of Miami; University of Houston.

CAREER HIGHLIGHTS: News Anchor and Talk Show Host, KTRH-AM, Houston; Prod./Host and News Anchor, KHOU-TV, Houston; Host and Entertainment Critic, WLS-TV, Chicago ('75); Host, "The Steve Edwards Show" and "2 on the Town," Entertainment Critic for KNXT-TV, Los Angeles ('78); concurrently served as Host of the syndicated "Entertainment This Week."

ACHIEVEMENTS & AWARDS: Numerous local Emmy awards in Chicago and Los Angeles.

PERSONAL: Married, two children.

EGAN, TRACY
Correspondent, WABC-TV, Eyewitness News

c/o WABC-TV, 7 Lincoln Sq., New York, NY 10023
b. Schenectady, NY.

EDUCATION: Union College, B.A., Political Science

CAREER HIGHLIGHTS: Reporter and Anchor, PTR-Radio, Albany, NY; Reporter and Anchor, WAST-TV, Albany and WRGB-TV, Schenectady, NY; Correspondent, WABC-TV, Eyewitness News.

ACHIEVEMENTS & AWARDS: N.A.

PERSONAL: Husband, Neil Goldstein; daughter, Bridget.

ELIASBERG, PHYLLIS
Consumer Reporter, WABC-TV

c/o WABC-TV, 7 Lincoln Sq., New York, NY 10023
b. July 23, 1939. Brooklyn, NY.

EDUCATION: University of Chicago; Goucher College; New York University School of Law.

CAREER HIGHLIGHTS: Directing Attorney, Los Angeles. Neighborhood Legal Services ('73); Consumer Reporter, KNXT-TV, Los Angeles;

Consumer Reporter, WXYZ-TV, Detroit ('79); Consumer Reporter, WABC-TV, New York, "The 5 O'Clock Eyewitness News" and "Good Morning, New York" ('81).

ACHIEVEMENTS & AWARDS: Emmy nomination for best consumer reporter ('77).

PERSONAL: Three sons, James, David, and Jonathan. Resides in New York City.

ELKES, TERRENCE A.
Pres., Viacom Intl.

1211 Ave. of the Americas, New York, NY 10036
b. April 28, 1934. New York, NY.

EDUCATION: University of Michigan, LL.D.

CAREER HIGHLIGHTS: Attorney, Norwich Pharmacal Co. ('58); V.P., General Counsel, Parsons & Whittemore ('65); V.P., General Counsel and Secretary, Viacom Intl. ('72); Exec. V.P. in charge of pay TV and the company's financial, legal, and human resources, Viacom Intl. ('76); Pres., Viacom Idtl. ('78).

ACHIEVEMENTS & AWARDS: Member, New York City Bar Assn., IRTS.

PERSONAL: N.A.

ELLERBEE, LINDA
News Anchor/Corresondent, NBC, "NBC News Overnight"

c/o NBC, 30 Rockefeller Plaza, New York, NY 10020
b. Bryan, TX.

EDUCATION: Vanderbilt University.

CAREER HIGHLIGHTS: Trade Magazine Reporter, Chicago; Newscaster and Disc Jockey,

WVON-Radio, Chicago ('64); Program Dir., KSJO, San Francisco ('67–'68); covered state legislature for KJNO Juneau and the AP ('69–'72); AP Reporter, Dallas, hired by KHOU-TV ('73); moved to WCBS-TV as General Assignment Reporter; named NBC Washington Correspondent ('75); Principal Reporter and Co-Anchor, NBC News magazine "Weekend" ('78); Co-Anchor, "NBC News Overnight" ('82).

ACHIEVEMENTS & AWARDS: N.A.

PERSONAL: N.A.

ELLIOTT, BUD (R. Elliott Stambaugh)
Prod./Anchor, CNN-2

1634 Ponce de Leon Ave., N.E., Atlanta, GA 30307
b. December 4, 1948.

EDUCATION: Colorado State University, B.A., History.

CAREER HIGHLIGHTS: Started as a News Announcer, KOA-Radio, Denver ('64). Moved to KCSU-FM Radio, Fort Collins; KADE-Radio, Boulder, CO; KMGH-TV, Denver; KBTV-TV, Denver; KHOW-Radio and KIMN-Radio, Denver. Became News Dir., KWBZ-Radio, Denver ('80) and joined WAPE-Radio, Jacksonville, FL as News Dir. ('81). Presently at CNN-2 as Prod./Anchor.

ACHIEVEMENTS & AWARDS: Pres., AP Broadcasters of Colorado ('76, '77).

PERSONAL: N.A.

EMMERICH, JOZIE (Joann Ammerich)
V.P., ABC, Daytime Programs, East Coast

c/o ABC, 1330 Ave. of the Americas, New York, NY 10019
b. September 1. St. Louis, MO.

EDUCATION: Catholic University of America, B.A. and M.A. ('71).

CAREER HIGHLIGHTS: Staff member at Olney Theater, MD ('68); St. Albans Repertory Theater Exec. Staff ('70); TV and Commercials Dept., Intl. Famous Agency ('72); joined CBS as Asst. Prod., "As the World Turns" ('75); joined ABC as Mgr., Daytime Programs, East Coast ('76); Dir., Daytime Programs, East Coast ('77); named V.P., Daytime Programs, East Coast ('80).

ACHIEVEMENTS & AWARDS: Listed in *Who's Who Among Students in American Colleges and Universities* ('64); *Outstanding Young Woman of America* ('78); Member, NATAS, American Film Institute.
PERSONAL: N.A.

ENBERG, DICK
Sportscaster, NBC

c/o NBC, 30 Rockefeller Plaza, New York, NY 10020
b. N.A.

EDUCATION: Central Michigan University ('57); Indiana University, Ph.D., Health Science ('61).
CAREER HIGHLIGHTS: Joined NBC Sports ('75); has handled Super Bowl XV, NCAA Natl. Collegiate Basketball championships ('76–'81), primetime boxing, regular season and post-season NFL coverage; major league baseball, including league championship series ('79 and '81), Rose Bowl ('79–'82); tennis coverage, and a variety of events for NBC's "Sportsworld."
ACHIEVEMENTS & AWARDS: Natl. Sportscaster of the Year, Natl Sportscasters and Sportswriters Assn. ('79, '80, '81); Emmy for outstanding sports personality in play-by-play ('81).
PERSONAL: N.A.

ENGEL, CHARLES
Pres., MCA Pay TV, New Programming

c/o MCA, 100 Universal City Plaza, Universal City, CA 91608
b. N.A.

EDUCATION: N.A.
CAREER HIGHLIGHTS: Mgr., Program Development, ABC TV ('64); Exec. Prod., "It Takes a Thief" ('68). V.P., Universal TV Movies of the Week and ABC Suspense Movies ('72), including the Emmy winner *That Certain Summer*. Exec. V.P., Universal TV ('80). Pres., MCA Pay TV, New Programming ('81).
ACHIEVEMENTS & AWARDS: N.A.
PERSONAL: N.A.

ENGLER, NOEL
V.P., Advertising and Promotion, NBC

c/o NBC, 3000 W. Alameda Ave., Burbank, CA 91523
b. December 25, 1935. Orange, NJ.

EDUCATION: Florida Southern College, B.A.
CAREER HIGHLIGHTS: Started at NBC as a Guide, Guest Relations Dept., New York ('59); Promotional Services Coordinator, Advertising Dept., NBC ('61); Writer/Prod., Promotional Sports for NBC and Affiliates ('62); Mgr., Production, On-Air Advertising ('69); Dir., On-Air Promotion ('76); V.P., On-Air Promotion ('81); V.P., Advertising and Promotion, NBC, West Coast ('82).
ACHIEVEMENTS & AWARDS: Member, ATAS; American Film Institute. Clio award for best promotional announcement, for 1964 Summer Olympics.
PERSONAL: Resides in Bell Canyon, CA, with wife, Dieta, and two children, Grant and Christina.

ENGLISH, JIM
V.P., Program Planning, Showtime Entertainment, Program Dept.

c/o Showtime Entertainment, 1633 Broadway, New York, NY 10019
b. N.A.

EDUCATION: Catholic University of America, B.A., Psychology.
CAREER HIGHLIGHTS: Mgr., Film Dept., and Asst., Program Dir., WJLA-TV, Washington, DC ('73); joined HBO, moving up to Dir. of Programming, HBO Program Services; entered Program Dept. at Showtime Entertainment ('81); promoted to V.P., Program Planning ('82).
ACHIEVEMENTS & AWARDS: N.A.
PERSONAL: Resides in Brooklyn, NY, with his wife.

ENGLUND, GEORGE
Exec. Prod./Dir./Actor, George Englund Productions

73 Market St., Venice, CA 90291
b. June 22, 1926. Washington, DC.

EDUCATION: University of California at Los Angeles.

CAREER HIGHLIGHTS: Prod./Dir. for many theatrical films; Prod., *See How She Runs*, TV movie; Prod./Dir., *A Christmas To Remember*, TV movie; Prod., *The Streets of L.A.*, TV movie; Exec. Prod./Dir., *Dixie: Changing Habits*, TV movie.

ACHIEVEMENTS & AWARDS: N.A.

PERSONAL: N.A.

ENRIQUEZ, RENE
Actor

c/o "Hill Street Blues," 3000 W. Alameda Ave., Burbank, CA 91523
b. November 25. San Francisco, CA.

EDUCATION: San Francisco State College; American Academy of Dramatic Arts.

CAREER HIGHLIGHTS: His film credits include *Midnight Cowboy, Popi,* and *Bananas.* Series regular on "Hill Street Blues."

ACHIEVEMENTS & AWARDS: N.A.

PERSONAL: Resides in Studio City, CA.

ENTELIS, AMY R.
Prod., ABC, News

c/o ABC, 7 W. 66th St., New York, NY 10023
b. March 10, 1951. New York, NY.

EDUCATION: Vassar College, B.A.; Columbia University Graduate School of Journalism, M.S.

CAREER HIGHLIGHTS: Considered one of the ablest young producers in TV journalism. Prod., "All About TV" on PBS ('76); Writer, AP Broadcast Division ('79); Assoc. Prod./

Researcher, ABC News's "20/20" ('79); Prod., "ABC News World News Tonight" ('81).

ACHIEVEMENTS & AWARDS: Gainsburgh award, for excellence in economic news coverage.

PERSONAL: Married, one child.

EPSTEIN, JON
Exec. Prod.

c/o Universal TV, 100 Universal City Plaza, Universal City, CA 91608
b. New York, NY.

EDUCATION: Lehigh University, B.A.

CAREER HIGHLIGHTS: One of Universal's prolific producers whose output is generally in the detective genre, such as "McMillan and Wife" and "Switch." Prod./Dir., radio soap opera ('48–'49); Story Editor ('53–'54); Head, TV Story Dept. ZIV-TV ('54–'55); Asst. Exec. Prod. ZIV-TV ('55–'57); Exec. Prod., "Rough Riders," ABC, "Mackenzie's Raiders," syndicated ('57–'58); Exec. Prod., UA-TV ('61–'63); Prod., "Kraft Suspense Theater" ('64–'65); Prod., "Tarzan," "Rat Patrol" ('66–'67); Prod., Screen Gems, for the series "The Flying Nun," The Young Rebels," and movies of the week ('68–'71); Exec. Prod. and Prod. for the Universal series "McMillan and Wife," *Rich Man, Poor Man,* "Switch."

ACHIEVEMENTS & AWARDS: N.A.

PERSONAL: N.A.

ERBE, BONNIE G.
Correspondent, NBC, News

c/o NBC, 30 Rockefeller Plaza, New York, NY 10020
b. New York, NY.

EDUCATION: Barnard College, B.A., English ('74); Columbia University Graduate School of Journalism, M.A. ('75).

CAREER HIGHLIGHTS: Started as Stringer, New York Bureau, *Washington Post,* while also working as Reporter, WXLO-FM, New York ('74); Co-Anchor/Reporter, WLIW-TV, Garden City, NY ('74); Newswriter/Part-Time Reporter, WINS-AM, New York ('74); Broadcast Dir./Reporter/Washington Bureau Chief, Capitol Hill News Service, Washington, DC

('75); Reporter/Assignment Editor, Independent TV News Assn. ('76); Reporter, WTVT-TV, Tampa, FL ('77); Reporter, WDVM-TV, Washington, DC ('80); Correspondent, NBC News, Atlanta ('81).
ACHIEVEMENTS & AWARDS: N.A.
PERSONAL: Fluent in Spanish, French, and Italian.

ERICKSON, LAUREL M.
Reporter, KNBC, "News 4 LA"

c/o KNBC, 3000 W. Alameda Ave., Burbank, CA 91523
b. N.A.

EDUCATION: Moorhead State College ('70).
CAREER HIGHLIGHTS: Prod. and General Assignment Editor, WDSM-TV, Duluth, Minn.; Weekend Prod. and Assignment Editor, KSTP-TV News, Minnesota; Prod./Assignment Editor/Reporter, KTAR-TV News, NBC, Phoenix; joined KNBC as General Assignment Reporter ('76); currently Nightside Reporter, "News 4 LA."
ACHIEVEMENTS & AWARDS: N.A.
PERSONAL: Resides in Santa Monica, CA.

ERLICHT, LEWIS H.
Pres., ABC, Entertainment

c/o ABC, 2040 Ave. of the Stars, Century City, CA 90067
b. New York, NY.

EDUCATION: Long Island University, B.A., Psychology.
CAREER HIGHLIGHTS: ABC TV Spot Sales Research ('62); Mgr., Research, ABC TV Spot Sales ('65); WABC-TV Sales Mgr. ('69); General Sales Mgr. ('72); WLS-TV General Mgr. ('74); V.P., East Coast, ABC Entertainment ('77); V.P. and General Mgr., ABC Entertainment ('78); appointed V.P. and Asst. to Press. ('79); Sr. V.P. and Asst. to Pres. ('80); Sr. V.P., Prime Time, ABC Entertainment ('81); Pres., ABC Entertainment ('84).
ACHIEVEMENTS & AWARDS: N.A.
PERSONAL: Resides in Los Angeles with wife, Willie, and sons, Paul and Jamie.

ERLICK, EVERETT H.
Exec. V.P. and General Counsel, ABC

c/o ABC, 1330 Ave. of the Americas, New York, NY 10019
b. September 12, 1921. Birmingham, AL.

EDUCATION: Vanderbilt University, B.A. ('42); Yale University Law School, LLD. ('48).
CAREER HIGHLIGHTS: Worked with New York law firm of Engel, Judge & Miller ('48); joined legal staff of Young & Rubicam ('51). Associate Dir., Media Dept. ('55); elected to V.P., Media ('58); transferred to Radio/TV Dept. ('58). Joined ABC as V.P. and General Counsel ('61); named to ABC Board of Dirs. ('62); Group V.P. ('68); appointed Sr. V.P. while maintaining General Counsel responsibilities ('72); Exec. V.P. and General Counsel ABC Inc. ('83).
ACHIEVEMENTS & AWARDS: Grover C. Cobb award, NAB ('80); Member, Pres. John F. Kennedy's Business Advisory Committee on Desegregation ('63); Pres. Lyndon B. Johnson's Natl. Citizens Committee for Community Relations ('64); Natl. Committee for Immigration Reform ('65); Campaign Committee, American Cancer Society ('65–present); Natl. Chairman, Parents Committee, Duke University ('74–'75); Board of Advisers, Everglades Protection Assn. ('80); Pres.'s Assn. Duke University ('82). Member, New York Bar.
PERSONAL: Resides in Rye, NY, with wife, Nancy Ruth; son, James; daughter, Lorre.

ESCHELBACHER, DAVID
Dir., ABC, TV Production

c/o ABC, 38 W. 66th St., New York, NY 10023
b. September 20, 1930. New York, NY.

EDUCATION: Pace College, B.A., Business Administration.
CAREER HIGHLIGHTS: Mailroom Clerk, ABC ('52); moved to Property Dept. ('53); various positions in Production Services, culminating in Asst. Dir. ('53–'68); Dir., ABC, TV Production ('69).
ACHIEVEMENTS & AWARDS: Emmy award for technical excellence for 1980 Winter Olympics.
PERSONAL: Wife, Rose; resides in Manhattan.

ESTRADA, ERIK
Actor

c/o Special Artists Agency, 9155 Sunset Blvd.,
  Los Angeles, CA 90069
b. March 16. New York, NY.

EDUCATION: N.A.
CAREER HIGHLIGHTS: TV's first Hispanic sex
  symbol managed to sustain a hit series primarily through his own macho appeal. TV
  guest star for "Hawaii Five-O," "Police
  Woman," and "Six Million Dollar Man." TV
  movies include *Honey Boy* and *Fire.* Was the
  series star of "CHiPs."
ACHIEVEMENTS & AWARDS: N.A.
PERSONAL: Divorced; resides in the San Fernando Valley area of Los Angeles.

EUBANKS, BOB
Host, NBC, "Dream House"

c/o "Dream House," NBC, 3000 W. Alameda
  Ave., Burbank, CA 91523
b. January 8. Flint, MI.

EDUCATION: Pierce Junior College; California
  State University at Northridge.
CAREER HIGHLIGHTS: Disc Jockey, KACY, Ox-
  nard, CA ('58); Disc Jockey, KRLA, Los An-
  geles ('60); Host, "The Newlywed Game"
  ('67); "Rhyme and Reason," "The Diamond
  Head Game," and "All Star Secrets." Cur-
  rently Host of the game show "Dream
  House," on NBC.
ACHIEVEMENTS & AWARDS: N.A.
PERSONAL: Resides in Los Angeles.

EVANS, LINDA
Actress

c/o "Dynasty," ABC, 1330 Ave. of the
  Americas, New York, NY 10019
b. November 18. Hartford, CT.

EDUCATION: N.A.
CAREER HIGHLIGHTS: Motion pictures include
  The Klansman, Avalanche Express, and *Tom
  Horn;* TV movies include *Female Artillery* and
  Standing Tall; TV series star of "The Big Val-
  ley," *Bare Essence,* and "Dynasty."
ACHIEVEMENTS & AWARDS: N.A.
PERSONAL: Resides in Los Angeles.

EVEY, STUART W.
V.P. and General Mgr., Getty Oil Co.,
Diversified Operations division

c/o Getty Oil Co., 3810 Wilshire Blvd., Los
  Angeles, CA 90010
b. February 26, 1933. Havre, MT.

EDUCATION: University of Washington, B.A.
CAREER HIGHLIGHTS: Traffic Trainee, Getty Oil
  Co., San Francisco ('58); Control Supervisor,
  Getty Oil Co.: General Services Supervisor,
  Getty Oil Co.; Administrative Asst. to the
  Exec. V.P., Getty Oil Co. ('64); Exec. Asst. to
  the Exec. V.P. and Chief Exec. Officer ('65);
  Mgr., Public Relations and Real Estate, Getty
  Oil Co. ('69); Mgr., Administration, Getty Oil
  Co. ('71); V.P. of Corporate Administration
  ('72); V.P. and General Mgr., Real Estate and
  Forest Products Division ('77); division re-
  named Diversified Operations Division, over-
  seeing TV programming activities including
  ESPN ('79).
ACHIEVEMENTS & AWARDS: N.A.
PERSONAL: Resides in North Hollywood, CA,
  with wife, Shirley, and two daughters.

FABER, GEORGE D.
Dir. of Communications, Viacom Enterprises, West Coast

c/o Viacom Enterprises, 10900 Wilshire Blvd., Los Angeles, CA 90024
b. June 17, 1921. Minneapolis, MN.

EDUCATION: Northwestern University, B.A. ('44).

CAREER HIGHLIGHTS: News Announcer, WMFD, Wilmington, NC ('55); News Editor/On-Air Newsman, CBS News, Chicago ('53–'56); Midwest Mgr./On-Air News, CBS Newsfilm, CBS News, Chicago ('56–'61); Mgr., Publicity, CBS Films, Los Angeles ('61–'65); Intl. Mgr., CBS TV Films, West Coast ('65–'71); Intl. Mgr., West Coast, Viacom Enterprises ('71–'75); Dir., Communications, Client Relations, Viacom, West Coast ('75).

ACHIEVEMENTS & AWARDS: Emmy nomination for coverage of Our Lady of Angels School fire, CBS News, Chicago ('46). Columnist and author *Behind the Mike*, series of newspaper columns ('39–'41).

PERSONAL: Married.

FABRAY, NANETTE
Actress

c/o "One Day at a Time," CBS, 7800 Beverly Blvd., Los Angeles, CA 90036
b. October 27, 1920. San Diego, CA.

EDUCATION: Los Angeles City College.

CAREER HIGHLIGHTS: Wide-eyed Fabray is still working hard on "One Day at a Time" and remains as delightfully wacky as she was in her Sid Caesar salad days. Starred on Broadway, in films, and in such TV shows as "Caesar's Hour" and "Yes, Yes, Nanette." Became a panelist on many game shows and appeared as a guest in series and specials before joining the cast on "One Day at a Time."

ACHIEVEMENTS & AWARDS: Tony award and Donaldson award as best musical actress in *High Button Shoes* ('48); two emmy awards as best comedienne, "Caesar's Hour" ('55, '56); Emmy for best suporting actress, "Caesar's Hour" ('55); Woman of the Year of the Radio and TV Editors of America ('55).

PERSONAL: Her niece is actress Shelley Fabares.

FARMER, DON (Donald E. Farmer)
Anchor, Cable News Network, "Take Two"

c/o Martin Krall, 1800 M St., Washington, DC
20036
b. September 27, 1938. St. Louis, MO.

EDUCATION: University of Missouri, B.A.,
Journalism.
CAREER HIGHLIGHTS: Reporter, *St. Louis Globe-
Democrat* ('60); Reporter/Newscaster, WRCV-
TV, Philadelphia (to '65); Correspondent,
ABC News, based in New York, Chicago
('65–'80); Anchor, "Take Two" Cable News
Network.
ACHIEVEMENTS & AWARDS: Overseas Press Club
award for coverage of Turkish invasion of Cy-
prus ('74); Headliners award for coverage of
mine disaster in Hazelton, PA ('64); Emmy
nomination for coverage of aftermath of De-
troit riots ('67); Secretary/Treasurer, Natl.
Correspondents Assn., Capital ('78)
PERSONAL: Wife, Chris Curle, is co-anchor of
"Take Two"; children, Laurie and Jamie.

FARMER, KIPLYN R.
Exec. V.P., Southern Satellite Systems

8252 S. Harvard, Tulsa, OK 74136
b. August 26, 1948. Higginsville, MO.

EDUCATION: Central Missouri State College,
B.A. ('71).
CAREER HIGHLIGHTS: Started as Staff An-
nouncer, KLEX-Radio, Lexington, MO ('66);
Floor Mgr., KCMO-TV ('69); Program Dir.,
St. Joseph Cablevision ('71); Prod./Dir.,
KTEW-TV ('72). Marketing Consultant,
United Video, Tulsa ('73); Coordinator of Sub-
scriber Services, United Cable TV Corp. ('74);
Dir. of Marketing, Westar TV Corp. (Western

Union) ('75); V.P., Southern Satellite Systems
('77); Pres. and General Mgr., Satellite TV
Systems, a subsidiary of Southern Satellite
Systems in Ann Arbor, MI ('80); Exec. V.P.,
Southern Satellite Systems ('82).
ACHIEVEMENTS & AWARDS: Emmy for outstand-
ing technical achievement ('80). Member of
CTAM, NATPE, STVA.
PERSONAL: Wife, Mary Lynn; children, Chris
and Kelly. Resides in Tulsa.

FARR, JAMIE
Actor

c/o "After M*A*S*H," CBS, 7800 Beverly
Blvd., Los Angeles, CA 90036
b. July 1, 1934. Toledo. OH.

EDUCATION: Pasadena Playhouse.
CAREER HIGHLIGHTS: Regular TV roles in "Dear
Phoebe," "The Red Skelton Show," "The
Danny Kaye Show," and "The Chicago
Teddy Bears." TV guest star on "The Gong
Show, "The Love Boat," and "Barnaby
Jones." TV films include *Murder Can Hurt You*
and *Amateur Night at the Dixie Bar and Grill.*
Series regular as Corporal Klinger on the
long-running "M*A*S*H" and "After
M*A*S*H" ('83).
ACHIEVEMENTS & AWARDS: N.A.
PERSONAL: Married; son, Jonas; daughter,
Yvonne. Resides in Bell Canyon, CA.

ton, DC ('61); General Counsel, U.S. Senate Democratic Policy Committee ('69); General Counsel to House of Representatives Speaker Tip O'Neill ('77); Chairman, FCC ('77); Partner, Mintz, Levin, Cohen, Ferris, Glovsky and Popero law firm, Washington, DC ('81).

ACHIEVEMENTS & AWARDS: N.A.

PERSONAL: Wife, Patricia; children, Caroline and Sabrina.

FIELD, FRANK
Health and Science Editor, WNBC-TV, "News 4 New York"

c/o WNBC-TV, 30 Rockefeller Plaza, New York, NY 10020
b. 1923. New York, NY.

EDUCATION: Brooklyn College, B.A. ('44); Columbia University, B.S. ('49); Massachusetts College of Optometry, Dr. of Optometry ('60).

CAREER HIGHLIGHTS: Meteorologist, Army Air Force; Base Weather Officer, Massachusetts Institute of Technology; Meteorology Instructor, Homestead AFB, Florida; Meteorologist, U.S. Weather Bureau, New York ('47); General Mgr., Weather Fotocast Co. ('50); Pres., International Weather Corp. ('56); Consulting Meteorologist, New York State Dept. ('58); Co-Host, "Not for Women Only" ('75); Newscast Reporter, WNBC, on a variety of health and science related topics ('59–'82).

ACHIEVEMENTS & AWARDS: Several Emmy awards, Peabody award; two honorary doctor of science degrees for experimental biology, Worcester Foundation, St. John's University; WNBC-TV, six Emmys, "What Man Shall Live and Not See Death?" Author of many books, including *Taking It Off With Frank,* and *Dr. Frank Field's Weather Book.* Member, American Meteorological Society. First professional meteorologist to report the weather on TV in New York.

PERSONAL: Married; resides in New York City.

FIELD, LYNN
Program Exec., Motion Pictures for TV, CBS, Entertainment, West Coast

c/o CBS, 7800 Beverly Blvd., Los Angeles, CA 90036
b. New York, NY.

EDUCATION: University of Southern California, B.A., Broadcast Management.

CAREER HIGHLIGHTS: Joined the CBS Management Training Program ('80); Marketing Specialist, CBS ('80); Assoc. Program Exec., Motion Pictures for TV, CBS Entertainment ('81); Program Exec., Motion Pictures for TV, CBS Entertainment, West Coast ('82).

ACHIEVEMENTS & AWARDS: N.A.

PERSONAL: N.A.

FIELD, SALLY
Actress

c/o William Morris Agency, 151 El Camino Dr., Beverly Hills, CA 90212
b. November 6, 1946. Pasadena, CA.

EDUCATION: N.A.

CAREER HIGHLIGHTS: Doffing her flying nun's habit and hanging up her Gidget surfboard, Field gave TV one of its finest acting displays in *Sybil*. The former ingenue is now a grown-up actress whose occasional TV appearances *(All the Way Home)* are always welcome. Series lead, "Gidget" ('65); "The Flying Nun" ('67); "The Girl With Something Extra." TV movies include *Maybe I'll Come Home in the Spring* ('71), *Marriage: Year One* ('71), *Home for the Holidays* ('72), *Hitched* ('73), and *Sybil* ('76). Theatrical films include *Norma Rae, Smokey and the Bandit, Smokey and the Bandit II, Absence of Malice, The End,* and *Kiss Me Goodbye.*

ACHIEVEMENTS & AWARDS: Emmy award as best actress for *Sybil* ('76); Academy Award as best actress for *Norma Rae* ('79).

PERSONAL: N.A.

FIELD, STORM
Anchor, WABC-TV

c/o WABC-TV, 7 Lincoln Sq., New York, NY 10023

b. N.A.

EDUCATION: McGill University, B.S.; Massachusetts College of Optometry, Ph.D.

CAREER HIGHLIGHTS: Science/Medical Editor for TV News Service ('75); Medical/Science Editor for WPIX-TV, New York ('76); Co-Anchor/Weather Anchor, WABC-TV; Health/Medical/Science Editor, WABC-TV.

ACHIEVEMENTS & AWARDS: One to One award for coverage of human rights; awards for Arthritis Foundation and the American Cancer Society. Honorary mayor, Clark and Westfield Township, NJ. Moderator, Senate Subcommittee and Distinguished Scientist Seminars.

PERSONAL: Father is eminent health and science editor Frank Field.

FIELDER, RICHARD
Writer/Prod. (Freelance)

c/o H.N. Swanson, Inc., 8523 Sunset Blvd., Los Angeles, CA 90069

b. April 13, 1927. Philadelphia, PA.

EDUCATION: Temple University, Columbia University, B.Sc.; University of Pennsylvania.

CAREER HIGHLIGHTS: Writer "Studio One," "Kraft Television Theater" ('57–'58); Writer, "Four Star Playhouse," "Dupont Show," "Zane Grey Theater," "Chrysler Theater," "Rawhide," "Alcoa Presents" ('59–'66); Writer, "Alfred Hitchcock," "The Virginian," "Cimarron Strip" ('67–'69); Writer, "Gunsmoke," "The Waltons," "Marcus Welby, M.D.," "CBS Theater," "Born Free," ('70–'75); wrote many movies for TV; Prod., "Seven Brides for Seven Brothers" ('82–'83).

ACHIEVEMENTS & AWARDS: Western Heritage award, Writers Guild awards.

PERSONAL: Married to Tavia Arnold; children, Carolina, Angela, Mary Beth, Michele, Renee, Richard Jr., John, and Tavia Ann.

FILERMAN, MICHAEL
Exec. Prod. (Freelance)

c/o Lorimar Productions, 3970 Overland Ave., Culver City, CA 90230

b. Chicago, IL.

EDUCATION: University of Illinois, B.A., Communications ('60).

CAREER HIGHLIGHTS: Worked with CBS TV Network for five years as General Program Exec. and Dir. of Daytime TV ('67); Paramount TV, Dir. of Program Development ('74); joined Playboy Productions as Pres. of Program Development ('72); to Lorimar as Prod. ('76). Currently serves as Co-Exec. Prod., "Knots Landing" and "Falcon Crest."

ACHIEVEMENTS & AWARDS: N.A.

PERSONAL: N.A.

FINE, DELIA
Prod., WABC-TV, New York, "The Morning Show"

c/o WABC-TV, 7 Lincoln Sq., New York, NY 10023

b. Evanston, IL.

EDUCATION: Northwestern University.

CAREER HIGHLIGHTS: Began as an actress in regional stage productions in the midwest; then moved on to manage Tiffany's Chicago jewelry store, where she was responsible for publicity; Sr. Assoc. Prod., "A.M. Chicago," WLS-TV, Chicago ('79); Prod., Cable News Network "Freeman Reports" segment, New York ('81); Prod., "The Morning Show," WABC-TV, New York ('83).

ACHIEVEMENTS & AWARDS: N.A.

PERSONAL: Resides in Riverside, CT, with her husband.

FINEHOUT, ROBERT
V.P., Modern Talking Picture Service

c/o Modern Talking Picture Service, 45
Rockefeller Plaza, New York, NY 10020
b. September 16, 1921. New York, NY.

EDUCATION: University of North Carolina,
B.A., Journalism ('46).
CAREER HIGHLIGHTS: Started in public relations
at Fred Elkdean Organization ('49); V.P.,
Sales Mgr., Assn. Films ('50–'77); V.P., Mod-
ern Talking Picture Service, Modern Satellite
Network, Programming ('78–present); Con-
tributing Editor, *Business Screen* magazine and
editor "Back Stage.
ACHIEVEMENTS & AWARDS: Freedoms Founda-
tion award for creation of series, "Films for
Freedom"; special recognition, V.P. Hubert
Humphrey for TV series "Discovering Amer-
ica."
PERSONAL: Wife, Jane; daughters, Deborah,
Pamela, and Andrea.

FINELL, ALYCE
Prod./Writer

301 E. 79th St., New York, NY 10021
b. Bay Shore, NY.

EDUCATION: Syracuse University, B.S., Radio/
TV.
CAREER HIGHLIGHTS: Program Supervisor and
various production positions, Bob Stewart
Productions, Griffin Productions, Talent
Assoc., Goodson-Todman Productions,
NBC, ABC, CBS TV ('60s–'70s); Pres., L'Etoile
Productions, Prod. and Writer, "An Evening
With the Royal Ballet" hosted by Rudolf Nur-
eyev; Prod., "Friends of . . .", Metromedia
TV; Prod., "A.M. New York" ABC TV; Con-
cept Originator and Creative Consultant,
"Looking Through Super Plastic Elastic Gog-
gles," NBC TV ('70s). Pres., Finell Enter-
prises, Dir. of Development and Supervising
Prod., Hearst/ABC, TV Consultant, Elan
Films Intl. ('80s).
ACHIEVEMENTS & AWARDS: Emmy for "Friends
of . . ." celebrity talk series ('77). Co-Founder,
the Hunza Foundation.
PERSONAL: N.A.

FINKEL, GEORGE
Sports Prod./Dir., NBC

110 Brentwood Drive, Mount Laurel, NJ 08054
b. July 29, 1936. Paris, France.

EDUCATION: University of Michigan, B.A.,
Speech.
CAREER HIGHLIGHTS: Started at WTVO, Rock-
ford, IL as Announcer/Dir. ('60); Operations
Mgr., WFIE-TV, Evansville, IN ('62); Prod./
Dir., WFIL-TV, Philadelphia ('64); Opera-
tions Mgr./Prod., WPHL-TV, Philadelphia
('65); promoted to Mgr., Sports Operations.
Joined NBC as freelancer, later joined staff of
Sports Dept. ('71). Production work with
NBC Sports, including Prod. and Co-Prod. of
four Super Bowls; two World Series; six
NCAA basketball finals; two Stanley Cup
hockey series; 1980 Olympic gymnastics
finals.
ACHIEVEMENTS & AWARDS: Emmy for produc-
ing telecast of Super Bowl XIII ('79).
PERSONAL: Wife, Lynn; children, Mike and
Lori.

FINNEGAN, BILL
Prod.

c/o Finnegan Assoc., 4225 Coldwater Canyon,
Studio City, CA 91604
b. 1928. Michigan.

EDUCATION: Loyola University; New York University; University of California at Los Angeles.
CAREER HIGHLIGHTS: His career in films began
in Los Angeles ('53), and he served in various
production capacities for every major studio
and each of the three major networks. Has
worked as an Asst. Dir., Production Mgr.,
and Dir. on various productions for more
than 25 years and for every major film company. Production Supervisor *Little Big Man*
and *A Man Called Horse*. Prod. *Support Your
Local Sheriff* and its sequel, *Support Your Local
Gunfighter* for UA. His most recent feature
film was *Bobby Deerfield*.
ACHIEVEMENTS & AWARDS: N.A.
PERSONAL: Wife, Pat; four children.

FINNEGAN, PAT
Prod.

c/o Finnegan Assoc., 4225 Coldwater Canyon, Studio City, CA 91604
b. N.A.

EDUCATION: University of California at Los Angeles.
CAREER HIGHLIGHTS: Started working in TV as a Production Asst. in New York on "Your Show of Shows." Formed Finnegan Assoc. with her husband ('77). Prod., *Stranger in Our House, Vacation in Hell*, and *The Choice*. Exec. Prod., *World War III*, an NBC mini-series.
ACHIEVEMENTS & AWARDS: N.A.
PERSONAL: Husband, Bill; four children.

FISCHER, LARRY
V.P., Advertising Sales, Madison Square Garden Network

c/o Madison Square Garden Network, 2 Pennsylvania Plaza, New York, NY 10001
b. April 16, 1950.

EDUCATION: Case Western Reserve University, B.A. ('71).
CAREER HIGHLIGHTS: Associated in a marketing capacity with many New York radio stations. Local Sales Mgr., WNBC-AM, New York; Sales Development Mgr., WNBC-AM; V.P., Advertising Sales, Madison Square Garden Network ('81).
ACHIEVEMENTS & AWARDS: N.A.
PERSONAL: N.A.

FISCHER, WILLIAM P.
V.P., Columbia Pictures TV, Live and Tape Production

1977 N. Dracena Dr., Los Angeles, CA 90027
b. June 17, 1941. New York, NY.

EDUCATION: Rutgers University, M.B.A. ('64).
CAREER HIGHLIGHTS: Exec. V.P., Kelly & Morey, Denver ('70); Partner, Somerset Management Group, Los Angeles ('72); Asst., Columbia Pictures TV ('76); Prod. Exec., Columbia Pictures TV ('77); Dir., Video Tape Production, Columbia Pictures TV ('78); V.P., Live and Tape Production, Columbia Pictures TV ('81).
ACHIEVEMENTS & AWARDS: Trustee, Directors Guild Producers Training Program; Member, ATAS; Society of Motion Picture and TV Engineers ('77); ATAS, Awards Committee ('80).
PERSONAL: Daughter, Lauren. Brother, Joseph Fischer, is Pres., MGM-UA Entertainment.

FISHBECK, GEORGE
Meteorologist, KABC-TV, Los Angeles, News

c/o KABC-TV, 4151 Prospect Ave., Los Angeles, CA 90027
b. New Jersey.

EDUCATION: University of New Mexico, B.A. and M.A.
CAREER HIGHLIGHTS: Weathercaster, KOB-TV, Albuquerque, NM; Meteorologist, KABC-TV, Los Angeles ('72); also prepares educational shows on weather and science for PBS.
ACHIEVEMENTS & AWARDS: Emmy for educational program "It's About Time" ('75); honorary doctorate from the University of Albuquerque.
PERSONAL: N.A.

FISHER, SANFORD H.
Pres. and Chief Exec. Officer, Corp. for Entertainment and Learning

c/o Corp. for Entertainment and Learning, 515 Madison Ave., New York, NY 10022
b. December 1.

EDUCATION: Lafayette College; New York University School of Law.

CAREER HIGHLIGHTS: Attorney, Nat'l. Labor Relations Board, Washington, DC ('66); Staff Attorney, CBS Law Dept. ('70); Dir., Program Development and Business Affairs, CBS TV Stations Division ('73); formed Fish Communications ('77); merged with Corp. for Entertainment and Learning ('78). Serves as Pres. and Chief Exec. Officer, overseeing the production of such shows as "Sports Probe" on the USA Network and "Working" on Nickelodeon.

ACHIEVEMENTS & AWARDS: Member, Planning Committee of the NCTA's Natl. Cable Programming Conference.

PERSONAL: N.A.

FITCH, DENNIS
V.P., Advertising, ABC, Entertainment

c/o ABC, 4151 Prospect Ave., Los Angeles, CA 90027

b. Santa Cruz, CA.

EDUCATION: University of San Francisco.

CAREER HIGHLIGHTS: Traffic Clerk, Cox Broadcasting Co., San Francisco ('66); Dir., Publicity, Advertising and Promotion, KGO-TV, San Francisco ('72); Dir., Creative Services, KRON-TV, San Francisco ('79); Dir. of Natl. Advertising, West Coast, ABC TV ('82); Dir., Advertising, ABC Entertainment ('82); V.P., Advertising, ABC Entertainment ('83).

ACHIEVEMENTS & AWARDS: N.A.

PERSONAL: Resides in Los Angeles with wife, Marge, daughter, Denise, and son, David.

FITZGERALD, GLEN J.
Dir., Affiliate Advertising, NBC, Entertainment

c/o NBC, 3000 W. Alameda Ave., Burbank, CA 91523

b. New York, NY.

EDUCATION: Mercy Teachers College, B.S., History.

CAREER HIGHLIGHTS: Started as a Page with NBC ('74); Page Supervisor, NBC ('74); Coordinator, Sales Service, NBC Radio Network ('74); Regional Administrator, Sales Service, NBC ('75); Mgr., Station Advertising, NBC,

New York ('78); Dir., Affiliate Advertising, NBC Entertainment, Burbank ('83).

ACHIEVEMENTS & AWARDS: N.A.

PERSONAL: Resides in Sherman Oaks, CA, with his wife, Jennifer, and their daughter, Jaclyn.

FLAHERTY, JOE
Writer/Performer, "SCTV Network"

c/o SCTV, 110 Lombard St., Toronto, Ontario, Canada M5C-IM3

b. June 21. Pittsburgh, PA.

EDUCATION: Second City Workshops in Chicago and Toronto, Canada.

CAREER HIGHLIGHTS: Feature films include *1941*, *Used Cars*, and *Stripes*. Assoc. Prod./Head Writer, original "SCTV Network" ('76); Writer/Performer, "SCTV Network."

ACHIEVEMENTS & AWARDS: Emmy award for achievement in comedy/variety writing for "SCTV."

PERSONAL: N.A.

FLAHERTY, JOSEPH A.
V.P., CBS Broadcast Group, Engineering and Development

c/o CBS, 524 W. 57th St., New York, NY 10019

b. December 25.

EDUCATION: University of Rockhurst, Physics.

CAREER HIGHLIGHTS: Began his TV career at WDAF-TV in Kansas City, MO ('52); served with the U.S. Army Signal Corps ('53); TV Engineer, NBC TV, New York ('55). Joined CBS ('57); promoted to General Mgr. ('67) and subsequently appointed V.P., Engineering and Development. He is responsible for all TV engineering and development activities for the CBS Broadcast Group, including planning and coordinating the development of new equipment, and for the installation of technical facilities.

ACHIEVEMENTS & AWARDS: Emmy award citation for CBS minicam color camera ('69); David Sarnoff gold medal for progress in TV engineering ('74); technical Emmy award for electronic news gathering ('75); Montreux achievement gold medal ('79).

PERSONAL: Resides in Port Washington, NY.

FLEISCHMAN, STEPHEN
Prod., ABC, "ABC News Closeup"

c/o ABC, 1330 Ave. of the Americas, New York, NY 10019
b. February 19, 1919.

EDUCATION: Haverford College, B.A. ('40).

CAREER HIGHLIGHTS: Before joining ABC News Documentary Unit, Fleischman had been a Prod./Dir., CBS News and Public Affairs; Exec. Prod., "Mission Possible," a three-part series on ecology and environment ('70); Developed and Prod., "To All the World's Children" ('70); Prod., "The Cherokee Shaft: The Story of Mines and Men" ('71); Writer/Prod. "Assault on Privacy" ('72); Prod., ABC News Documentary Unit, including eight "ABC News Closeups" ('64–'78); Prod. "ABC News Closeup" ('78).

ACHIEVEMENTS & AWARDS: Dupont-Columbia broadcast journalism award for "The Gene Merchants" for "ABC News Closeup" ('82–'83).

PERSONAL: N.A.

FLEMING, PAMELA S.
Program Dir., C-SPAN

22005 Foxlair Rd., Gaithersburg, MD 20879
b. June 23, 1943. Lima, OH.

EDUCATION: College of William and Mary, B.A. ('65); University of Maryland.

CAREER HIGHLIGHTS: Professional Model ('65); English Teacher, Lima, OH ('68); English/Art/Journalism Teacher, Maryland ('73); Press Secretary for Congressman Tom Evans ('81); Sr. Prod., Program Dir. C-SPAN ('81).

ACHIEVEMENTS & AWARDS: Kappa Delta Pi, honorary teachers fraternity ('65).

PERSONAL: Husband, William; two children.

FLETCHER, MARTIN
Prod./Correspondent, NBC, News

c/o NBC, 73 Ave. des Champs Elysees, Paris #8, France
b. London, England.

EDUCATION: University of Bradford.

CAREER HIGHLIGHTS: Writer, VisNews ('70); Writer, BBC's "9 O'Clock News" ('71); Cameraman/Writer and Field Prod., VisNews ('73); Correspondent, NBC News, Johannesburg, South Africa ('77); Prod./ Correspondent, NBC News, Paris ('80).

ACHIEVEMENTS & AWARDS: N.A.

PERSONAL: N.A.

FLICKER, THEODORE
Writer/Dir.

1801 Ave. of the Stars, Los Angeles, CA 90067
b. June 6, 1930.

EDUCATION: Royal Academy of Dramatic Arts (RADA), Bard College.

CAREER HIGHLIGHTS: Flicker got his start as an improvisational comic with the group The Establishment and carried over the same offbeat style to his direction of such feature films as *The President's Analyst, The Troublemaker,* and *Up in the Cellar.* He brought the same comic stylishness to such TV films as *Playmates, Guess Who's Sleeping in My Bed, Just a Little Inconvenience,* and *Last of the Good Guys.* Also, Writer/Dir., "The Dick Van Dyke Show,"

"The Andy Griffith Show," "The Rogues," "I Dream of Jeannie," and "Night Gallery." Co-Creator, "Barney Miller."
ACHIEVEMENTS & AWARDS: N.A.
PERSONAL: N.A.

FLOCK, JEFF
Chief Midwest Correspondent, Cable News Network

c/o Chicago Merchandise Mart, Suite 409, Chicago, IL 60654
b. March 16, 1958. Lakewood, NJ.

EDUCATION: Boston University, B.S., Broadcast Journalism.
CAREER HIGHLIGHTS: Morning Drive Anchor and Consumer Affairs Reporter, WBUR-FM, Boston ('78); Freelance Reporter, Natl. Public Radio, covered visit of Pope John Paul II to Boston ('79–'80); Anchor, "Prime Time News" WBUR-FM ('80); Writer/Prod., Cable News Network, Atlanta ('80); Prod., Cable News Network coverage of assassination of Anwar Sadat, royal wedding of Prince Charles, attempted assassination of Pope John Paul II ('81); Chief Midwest Correspondent, Cable News Network.
ACHIEVEMENTS & AWARDS: N.A.
PERSONAL: Wife, Gretchen.

FLOOD, ANN
Actress

c/o "The Edge of Night," ABC, 1330 Ave. of the Americas, New York, NY 10019
b. November 12. Jamaica, NY.

EDUCATION: N.A.
CAREER HIGHLIGHTS: Broadway appearances in *Kismet* and *Holiday for Lovers*. TV appearances in "West Point," "Matinee Theater," and "Annapolis." Soap opera star of "From These Roots" and "The Edge of Night."
ACHIEVEMENTS & AWARDS: N.A.
PERSONAL: Husband, Herbert A. Granath; four children. Resides in Manhattan.

FLYNN, DONALD L.
Asst. to Pres., ABC TV

c/o ABC, 1330 Ave. of the Americas, New York, NY 10019
b. April 5, 1934. New Rochelle, NY.

EDUCATION: St. Michael's College, B.A.; Fordham Law School, LL.D.
CAREER HIGHLIGHTS: ABC Trainee ('59); left to practice law ('61); returned to ABC TV as Dir., Sales Contracts ('63); V.P., Business Affairs ('67); appointed Asst. to Pres., ABC TV ('78).
ACHIEVEMENTS & AWARDS: N.A.
PERSONAL: Resides in Manhattan with wife and two daughters.

FLYNN, JOHN P.
Mgr., Broadcast Technical Training, NBC, Operations and Technical Services

c/o NBC, 3000 W. Alameda Ave., Burbank, CA 91523
b. Chicago, IL.

EDUCATION: Iona College, B.A., Physics; Notre Dame University, M.S., Physics.
CAREER HIGHLIGHTS: Project Mgr., Jet Propulsion Laboratory with the Ford Aerospace and Communications Corp., Pasadena, CA; Mgr., Special Projects Design, Tratec/McGraw-Hill, Culver City, CA; Mgr., Broadcast Technical Training, NBC, Operations and Technical Services ('83).
ACHIEVEMENTS & AWARDS: N.A.
PERSONAL: Resides in Glendale, CA.

FLYNN, STEPHEN
V.P., Sales Service, NBC

c/o NBC, 30 Rockefeller Plaza, New York, NY 10020
b. New York, NY.

EDUCATION: Dartmouth College.
CAREER HIGHLIGHTS: Promotion Asst., Sales Dept., NBC ('47); after a series of advancements, named Mgr., Sales Service, NBC ('53); Dir., Sales Service ('58); V.P., Sales Service, NBC ('70).
ACHIEVEMENTS & AWARDS: Member, IRTS.

PERSONAL: Resides in Wilton, CT, with wife, Mary; three children, Stephen, Louise, and Bart.

FOGARTY, JOSEPH R.
Commissioner, FCC

c/o FCC, 1919 M St., N.W., Washington, DC 20554
b. January 12, 1931. Newport, RI.

EDUCATION: Holy Cross, B.A. ('53); Boston College Law School, J.D. ('59).
CAREER HIGHLIGHTS: Considered one of the most knowledgeable of the FCC commissioners in the past several decades, and one of the few commissioners genuinely concerned with public interest and public policy questions. Entered private law practice ('59–'66); joined the law firm of Enos & McCarthy, Lowell, MA ('67); Staff Counsel and Communications Counsel, U.S. Senate Committee on Commerce ('66); Commissioner, FCC ('76).
ACHIEVEMENTS & AWARDS: N.A.
PERSONAL: N.A.

FORD, PETER SHANN
Anchor/Correspondent, Cable News Network

c/o Geller Media Management, 250 W. 57th St., New York, NY 10019
b. August 20, 1950. Miles, Australia.

EDUCATION: University of Queensland, Australia, Economics and Law.
CAREER HIGHLIGHTS: News Anchor and Correspondent, Seven Network, Sydney, Australia; Co-Prod. and Anchor, news specials and documentaries, for the New England Network, Tamworth, Australia (to '81); Anchor, Cable News Network Headline Service, since its inception ('82).
ACHIEVEMENTS & AWARDS: N.A.
PERSONAL: N.A.

FORREST, HERBERT E.
Pres., Federal Communications Bar Assn.

c/o Steptoe & Johnson, 1250 Connecticut Ave., N.W., Washington, DC 20036
b. September 20, 1923. New York, NY.

EDUCATION: George Washington University, B.A. ('48); George Washington University Law School, J.D. ('52).
CAREER HIGHLIGHTS: Plate Printer, U.S. Bureau of Engraving and Printing ('42); Law Clerk to Chief Judge Bolitha J. Laws, U.S. District Court, Washington, DC ('52); joined law firm of Welch & Morgan ('55); Partner, Steptoe & Johnson law firm and Pres., Federal Communications Bar Assn. ('65).
ACHIEVEMENTS & AWARDS: N.A.
PERSONAL: Wife, Marilyn; sons Glenn and Andrew.

FORSYTHE, HENDERSON
Actor

c/o "As the World Turns," CBS, 51 W. 52d St., New York, NY 10019
b. September 11. Macon, MO.

EDUCATION: Culver-Stockton College; University of Iowa.
CAREER HIGHLIGHTS: Appeared in numerous stage productions in regional theater and on Broadway; TV credits include "U.S. Steel Hour," "Hallmark Hall of Fame," "From These Roots," "The Edge of Night," and "As the World Turns" a soap opera which he has been with since '60.
ACHIEVEMENTS & AWARDS: Tony award as best supporting actor in a musical for *The Best Little Whorehouse in Texas*. Certificate of merit from NATAS ('83).
PERSONAL: Resides in Tenafly, NJ, with wife, Dorothea; two grown sons, Eric and Jason.

FORSYTHE, JOHN
Actor

c/o "Dynasty," ABC, 4151 Prospect Ave., Los
    Angeles, CA 90027
b. January 29, 1918. Penn's Grove, NJ.

EDUCATION: N.A.
CAREER HIGHLIGHTS: The matinee idol looks
    have grown more interesting with age, and
    whether he's the good "Bachelor Father" or
    the bad daddy of "Dynasty," Forsythe has
    always been worth watching. Appeared in
    numerous stage productions and feature
    films; featured on early TV shows such as
    "Studio One," "Philco Playhouse," "Kraft
    Theater," and "Robert Montgomery Pre-
    sents." Starred in "Bachelor Father" ('57–'62);
    "To Rome With Love" ('69). Host of the syn-
    dicated "World of Survival"; the voice of
    Charlie in the series "Charlie's Angels"; cur-
    rently has leading role as Blake Carrington on
    ABC's "Dynasty."
ACHIEVEMENTS & AWARDS: N.A.
PERSONAL: Resides in Bel Air, CA, with wife,
    Julie; three children.

FOSTER, CHRISTINE
V.P., Program Development, Westinghouse
Broadcasting Co., Group W Productions

c/o Group W Productions, 70 Universal City
    Plaza, Universal City, CA 91608
b. N.A.

EDUCATION: Immaculate Heart College, B.A.
    (magna cum laude); University of California
    at Los Angeles, M.A., Journalism.
CAREER HIGHLIGHTS: Dir., Research and Devel-
    opment, Metromedia Producers Corp., su-
    pervising film and editorial research of

"Jacques Cousteau" and "National Geographic" specials ('68); Dir., Development
and Production Services, Wolper Organization ('71); Mgr., Film Programs, NBC ('76);
V.P., Movies for TV and Mini-Series, Columbia Pictures TV ('77); V.P., Program Development, Group W Productions ('81).
ACHIEVEMENTS & AWARDS: N.A.
PERSONAL: N.A.

FOSTER, PHIL
Actor

c/o Paramount TV, 5555 Melrose Ave., Los
    Angeles, CA 90038
b. March 29, 1914. Brooklyn, NY.

EDUCATION: N.A.
CAREER HIGHLIGHTS: Guest star of TV shows
    including "The Tallulah Bankhead Show"
    and "The Odd Couple." Regular on the series
    "Laverne and Shirley." Motion pictures in-
    clude *Conquest of Space*.
ACHIEVEMENTS & AWARDS: N.A.
PERSONAL: N.A.

FOUHY, EDWARD
V.P. and Washington Bureau Chief, ABC,
News

c/o ABC, 1717 DeSales St., N.W.,
    Washington, DC 20036
b. N.A.

EDUCATION: N.A.
CAREER HIGHLIGHTS: Joined CBS News ('66);
    Saigon Bureau Chief ('67); Prod., "CBS Eve-
    ning News With Walter Cronkite" ('69);
    moved to NBC News as Prod., "NBC Nightly
    News" ('74); Dir. of NBC News, Washington,
    DC; returned to CBS as Evening News Prod.
    ('77); V.P. and Washington Bureau Chief
    ('78); V.P. and Dir. of News, CBS, New York
    ('81); moved to ABC News as V.P. and Wash-
    ington Bureau Chief ('82) with responsibili-
    ties for broadcast origination of ABC News
    "World News Tonight," "Nightline," "Good
    Morning America" News, "This Week With
    David Brinkley," and other regularly sched-
    uled programming.
ACHIEVEMENTS & AWARDS: Two Emmy awards
    for individual achievement ('74).
PERSONAL: N.A.

FOWLER, JOHN
Exec. V.P., Warner Amex Cable Communications

c/o Warner Amex Cable Communications, 75 Rockefeller Plaza, New York, NY 10019
b. Youngstown, OH.

EDUCATION: Yale University; University of Pennsylvania Law School.

CAREER HIGHLIGHTS: A specialist in railroad reorganization and real estate law, he became General Counsel to the Dept. of Transportation ('81). Before that, he served as V.P. and Chief Financial Officer, Reading Co. of Philadelphia. Named Exec. V.P., Warner Amex Cable Communications ('83).

ACHIEVEMENTS & AWARDS: N.A.

PERSONAL: Wife, Jill; son, Evan.

FOWLER, MARK S.
Chairman, FCC

c/o FCC, 1919 M St., N.W., Washington, DC 20554
b. October 6, 1941. Toronto, Ontario.

EDUCATION: University of Florida College of Law.

CAREER HIGHLIGHTS: Part-Time Announcer, WABR-Radio, Winter Park, FL ('56); Announcer, WDVH-Radio, Gainesville, FL ('59); Announcer, WKEE-AM/FM, Huntington, WV ('63); Announcer/Sales Representative, WMEG-Radio, Melbourne, FL ('64); Associate, Smith & Pepper communications law firm, Washington, DC ('70); Co-Founder, Fowler & Meyers communications law firm ('75–present); Counsel to the Virginia Assn. of Broadcasters ('78); Communications Coun-

sel for Ronald Reagan's presidential campaigns ('75–'76 and '79–'80); Chairman, FCC.

ACHIEVEMENTS & AWARDS: N.A.

PERSONAL: Resides in Arlington, Va, with wife, Jane; son, Mark Jr.; daughter, Claire.

FOX, SONNY
Prod.

c/o Sonny Fox Productions, 1447 N. Kings Rd., Los Angeles, CA 90069
b. June 17, 1925.

EDUCATION: New York University, B.A.

CAREER HIGHLIGHTS: TV Host for "Let's Take a Trip" ('55) and "The $64,000 Challenge"; V.P., NBC Children's Programming; Prod., Alan Landsburg Productions; Independent Prod. He recently produced "The Golden Age of Television Series," which included teleplays or kinescopes of such highly acclaimed fifties TV dramas as "Marty," "Days of Wine and Roses," and "Requiem for a Heavyweight," as well as recent interviews conducted by Fox with the original stars and creators of those programs.

ACHIEVEMENTS & AWARDS: Three presidential Emmy awards; Eleanor Roosevelt humanitarian award. Past Chairman, NATAS.

PERSONAL: N.A.

FOX, STEVE
Correspondent, ABC, News

c/o ABC, 7 W. 66th St., New York, NY 10023
b. N.A.

EDUCATION: Dartmouth College, B.A., Government.

CAREER HIGHLIGHTS: Reporter/Photographer, *Santa Monica Journal*, California; Writer/Prod./Reporter/Anchor, KMJ-TV, Los Angeles; Host, "Evening Magazine," KPIX-TV, Los Angeles ('75); Reporter, ABC News, Los Angeles ('79); Correspondent, ABC News, Washington ('81).

ACHIEVEMENTS & AWARDS: Received two Golden Mike awards while at KMJ-TV. Emmy for his participation in the development of the first "Evening Magazine," known in many markets as "P.M. Magazine."

PERSONAL: N.A.

FOXWORTH, ROBERT
Actor

c/o "Falcon Crest," CBS, 7800 Beverly Blvd., Los
    Angeles, CA 90036
b. Houston, TX.

EDUCATION: Mellon University.
CAREER HIGHLIGHTS: Motion pictures include
    *Treasure of Matecumbe, Omen II, The Astral Fac-
    tor,* and *The Black Marble.* TV appearances in-
    clude "The Storefront Lawyers" and "Falcon
    Crest."
ACHIEVEMENTS & AWARDS: N.A.
PERSONAL: N.A.

FRAME, PETER W.
Exec. V.P., HBO, Affiliate Relations

c/o HBO, 1271 Ave. of the Americas, New
    York, NY 10020
b. February 28, 1941.

EDUCATION: Middlebury College; Boston Uni-
    versity School of Public Communications;
    Columbia University.
CAREER HIGHLIGHTS: Unit Production Mgr.,
    CBS News Special Events Group ('68); Dir.,
    Marketing Sales for the cable TV operations of
    CBS ('70); General Mgr., Operations, Triangle
    Publications ('71); Dir., Marketing Services
    Development, HBO ('74); Dir., Program-
    ming, HBO ('74); Dir., Natl. Sales ('75); V.P.
    and Eastern Regional General Mgr. ('78);
    V.P., Regional Operations ('79); V.P., Affili-
    ate Relations, HBO ('80); Exec. V.P., Affiliate
    Relations, HBO ('83).
ACHIEVEMENTS & AWARDS: N.A.
PERSONAL: Resides in New York City.

FRANCIS, FRED
Correspondent, NBC, News

c/o NBC, Heussallee #20, Bonn 53, West
    Germany
b. Boston, MA.

EDUCATION: Miami Community College.
CAREER HIGHLIGHTS: Reporter/Cameraman,
    WBLW-TV, Miami, now WPLG-TV ('66); In-
    vestigative Crime Reporter, WVCG-Radio,
    Miami ('69); Investigative Reporter, WTVJ-
    TV, Miami ('70); Reporter, NBC News, Miami
    ('75); Correspondent, NBC News, West Ger-
    many ('79).
ACHIEVEMENTS & AWARDS: Dupont-Columbia
    award ('74).
PERSONAL: Wife, Carol; three children.

FRANCIS, GENIE ANN
Actress

c/o ICM, 8899 Beverly Blvd., Los Angeles, CA
    90048
b. May 26, 1962. Englewood, NJ.

EDUCATION: N.A.
CAREER HIGHLIGHTS: Already an accomplished
    and talented actress, she got her start with a
    guest shot on ABC's "Family" at age 14, and
    soon after became a regular on the soap opera
    "General Hospital" as the beleagured Laura
    Webber Baldwin Spencer. After leaving
    "General Hospital" ('82), Francis was a very
    hot commodity, first signing with CBS to do
    TV movies including *Bare Essence,* and later
    with NBC ('83) to do the TV series of the same
    name.
ACHIEVEMENTS & AWARDS: N.A.
PERSONAL: Daughter of actor Ivor Francis. Sin-
    gle, resides in suburban Los Angeles.

FRANK, REUVEN
Former Pres., NBC, News

c/o NBC, 30 Rockefeller Plaza, New York, NY 10019
b. December 7, 1920. Montreal, Canada.

EDUCATION: City College of New York, B.S. ('42); Columbia University, M.S., Journalism ('47).
CAREER HIGHLIGHTS: Began as Reporter, *Newark Evening News* ('47); promoted to Night City Editor ('49); joined staff of NBC News ('50). Experimented with weekly half-hour news form, organized coverage of 1956 political conventions, where he teamed Chet Huntley and David Brinkley; went on to originate and produce "The Huntley-Brinkley Report" ('56). Named Exec. Prod. of program and changed it from 15-minute to 30-minute format ('63); promoted to V.P., NBC News, while maintaining role in political conventions and election coverage ('66); named Exec. V.P. ('67). Appointed Pres., NBC News ('68); named Sr. Exec. Prod., NBC News Special Programs ('73); reappointed to Pres., NBC News ('82).
ACHIEVEMENTS & AWARDS: Sigma Delta Chi award ('55); Robert Sherwood award ('58, '59); George Polk award ('61); Columbia journalism award for distinguished service ('61). Emmy awards, best news program ('58, '59, '60, '61, '62, '64), best documentary program ('63) best program of the year, "The Tunnel" ('63), the only news program to receive this award. Man of the Year Award, Missouri Broadcasters Assn. ('71); Dupont award ('80); Gainsburgh award ('80); Headliners award ('81); Humanitas award ('82). Poynter Fellow, Yale University ('70).
PERSONAL: Resides in Tenfly, NJ, with wife, Bernice; children, Peter and James.

FRANKEL, ERIC C.
Dir., Warner Bros. TV, Pay-TV Marketing

75 Rockefeller Plaza, New York, NY 10019
b. May 16, 1958.

EDUCATION: Syracuse University, B.S. ('79).
CAREER HIGHLIGHTS: Prod. Asst., WOUR-FM ('76); Cable TV Salesman, Upstate Cable ('79); Concert Coordinator, Syracuse University ('79); Supervisor, Advertising/Publicity, Warner Bros. TV ('80); Manager ('81); Dir., Pay-TV Marketing ('82).
ACHIEVEMENTS & AWARDS: Member, Cable TV Marketing Assn.; Member, IRTS; Member, NATAS ('80–present).
PERSONAL: N.A.

FRANKENHEIMER, JOHN MICHAEL
Dir.

c/o Jeff Berg, ICM, 8899 Beverly Blvd., Los Angeles, CA 90048
b. 1930. New York, NY.

EDUCATION: Williams College, B.A. ('51)
CAREER HIGHLIGHTS: Actor ('50–'51). Dir., CBS TV: "You Are There," "Danger," "Climax," "Studio One," and "Playhouse 90." Dramas include *Forbidden Area, The Comedian, The Last Tycoon, Clash by Night, The Days of Wine and Roses, Old Man, For Whom the Bell Tolls.* Movies include *Young Stranger, The Browning Version, Turn of the Screw, The Young Savages, Birdman of Alcatraz, All Fall Down, The Train, Seven Days in May, The Fixer, I Walk the Line, The Iceman Cometh, The French Connection II, Black Sunday,* and *Prophecy.*
ACHIEVEMENTS & AWARDS: Christopher award ('54); Emmy for *The Comedian* ('58); Acapulco Film Festival award ('62).
PERSONAL: Married, two children.

FRANKLIN, BONNIE
Actress

c/o "One Day at a Time," CBS, 7800 Beverly
  Blvd., Los Angeles, CA 90036
b. January 6, 1944. Santa Monica, CA.

EDUCATION: University of California at Los Angeles and Smith College, B.A., English.
CAREER HIGHLIGHTS: This bouncy actress has
  brightened the lives of single working moth-
  ers with her exploits on the long-running
  "One Day at a Time." New York stage appearances in *Dames at Sea* and *Applause*. Her
  TV movies include *Your Place or Mine*, *Portrait
  of a Rebel*, and *The Law*. Series star of "One
  Day at a Time."
ACHIEVEMENTS & AWARDS: Theatre World
  award; Outer Critics Circle award for *Applause*.
PERSONAL: Resides in Encino, CA.

FRANKLIN, ELLEN
Dir., Current Comedy Programs, ABC,
Entertainment

c/o ABC, 2040 Ave. of the Stars, Los Angeles,
  CA 90067
b. New York, NY.

EDUCATION: Cornell University, B.A., Sociology ('74); State University of New York at Buffalo, M.A., Sociology.
CAREER HIGHLIGHTS: Analyst, ABC TV Research ('76); Mgr., Program Research, ABC
  ('79); Program Exec., Current Comedy Programs, ABC Entertainment ('81); Dir., Current Comedy Programs, ABC Entertainment
  ('83).
ACHIEVEMENTS & AWARDS: N.A.
PERSONAL: Resides in Los Angeles.

FRANKLIN, JOE
Host, WOR-TV, New York, "The Joe
Franklin Show"

c/o WOR-TV, 1440 Broadway, New York, NY
  10019
b. N.A.

EDUCATION: N.A.
CAREER HIGHLIGHTS: Host and Interviewer,
  "The Joe Franklin Show" ('53). During the
  long run of his show, Franklin has become
  known for his knowledge of TV trivia and for
  showcasing new performers.
ACHIEVEMENTS & AWARDS: Author of *Down
  Memory Lane*.
PERSONAL: N.A.

FRANKOVICH, PETER
Dir., Motion Pictures for TV, CBS,
Entertainment, West Coast

c/o CBS, 6121 Sunset Blvd., Los Angeles, CA
  90028
b. N.A.

EDUCATION: University of Oregon, B.A. ('65).
CAREER HIGHLIGHTS: Story Editor with an inde-
  pendent production company; Program
  Exec., CBS ('76); Exec. Prod., CBS Entertain-
  ment ('77); Dir., Motion Pictures for TV, CBS
  Entertainment, West Coast ('78).
ACHIEVEMENTS & AWARDS: N.A.
PERSONAL: Resides in Los Angeles with wife,
  Judy; daughter, Elissa; son, Gregory.

FRANSECKY, ROGER
V.P., Corporate Affairs, HBO

c/o HBO, 1271 Ave. of the Americas, New
  York, NY 10020
b. November 22, 1940.

EDUCATION: State University of New York, B.S.
  and M.S.; University of Cincinnati, Ph.D.,
  Psychology.
CAREER HIGHLIGHTS: Professor and Chairman,
  Communication Arts Dept., University of
  Cincinnati ('69); Sr. Consultant to CBS on
  children's programming and program practices ('73); headed his own media consulting
  and production company in New York ('78);

V.P., Public Affairs, Group W Cable ('80); V.P., Corporate Affairs, HBO ('82).

ACHIEVEMENTS & AWARDS: Chairs the Committee on Cable and the New Technologies, NATAS.

PERSONAL: Resides in Dobbs Ferry, NY, with wife, Nancy and their children.

FRAZIER, STEPHEN
Correspondent, NBC, News

c/o NBC Japan, NTV, Yobancho, Bekkan Bldg. 5-6, Chiyoda-ku, Tokyo 102, Japan
b. N.A.

EDUCATION: Williams College ('74).

CAREER HIGHLIGHTS: General Assignment Reporter, Co-Anchor, News, WNYS-TV (now WIXT-TV), Syracuse, NY ('74); Anchor, Weekend News, WJZ-TV, Baltimore ('77); Correspondent, NBC News, Northeast Bureau ('80); Correspondent, NBC News, Tokyo ('82).

ACHIEVEMENTS & AWARDS: N.A.

PERSONAL: Wife, Cynthia.

FREEDMAN, LEWIS
TV Drama Prod.

c/o Corp. for Public Broadcasting, 1111 16th St., N.W., Washington, DC 20036
b. N.A.

EDUCATION: N.A.

CAREER HIGHLIGHTS: Prod., "Camera Three," CBS ('56); V.P., Programming, WNDT; Dir. of Cultural Programming, Public Broadcasting Laboratory; Prod., "Hollywood Television Theater" ('70); Prod., CBS Mini-Series ('72); Head of Program Fund, a division of the Corp. for Public Broadcasting ('80).

ACHIEVEMENTS & AWARDS: N.A.

PERSONAL: N.A.

FREEMAN, AL, JR.
Actor

c/o "One Life to Live," ABC, 1330 Ave. of the Americas, New York, NY 10019
b. March 21, 1934. San Antonio, TX.

EDUCATION: University of Massachusetts, Master's, Education.

CAREER HIGHLIGHTS: Broadway appearances in *Blues for Mr. Charlie, Golden Boy, Look to the Lilies,* and *The Dozens.* TV appearances on "Kojak," "The Mod Squad," "The Defenders," and *Roots: The Next Generation.* TV movies include *My Sweet Charlie.* Daytime soap regular on "One Life to Live."

ACHIEVEMENTS & AWARDS: Emmy award as outstanding actor in daytime drama ('79).

PERSONAL: Wife, Sevara. Resides in Manhattan.

FREIDMAN, SEYMOUR
Sr. V.P., Columbia Pictures TV

c/o Columbia Pictures TV, Columbia Plaza, Burbank, CA 91505
b. August 17, 1917. Detroit, MI.

EDUCATION: Magdalene College, University of Cambridge, B.S. ('36)

CAREER HIGHLIGHTS: Joined Columbia as Apprentice Film Editor ('39); moved up the ladder from Asst. Dir. to Production Mgr., Screen Gems, now Columbia Pictures TV ('55); V.P. ('68); Sr. V.P., Columbia Pictures TV ('78).

ACHIEVEMENTS & AWARDS: N.A.

PERSONAL: Resides in Beverly Hills, CA, with wife, Jacquie.

FRICKE, JOHN
Anchor, Cable News Network, Sports

c/o Cable News Network, 1050 Techwood Dr., Atlanta, GA 30318
b. June 2, 1960, Chicago, IL.

EDUCATION: DeKalb Central.

CAREER HIGHLIGHTS: Reporter, *Decatur News-Sun,* Decatur, GA ('79); Reporter, WGST-AM ('80); Prod./Reporter on Sports, WTBS ('80); moved to Cable News Network Headline News as Sports Dir. ('81); Sports Anchor, Cable News Network ('82).

ACHIEVEMENTS & AWARDS: N.A.

PERSONAL: N.A.

FRIEDMAN, PAUL
Prod., ABC, News

c/o ABC, 1330 Ave. of the Americas, New
   York, NY 10019
b. N.A.

EDUCATION: N.A.
CAREER HIGHLIGHTS: Exec. Prod., WNBC-TV,
   New York ('74); Exec. Prod., "Today" show
   ('76); Executive Prod., NBC's "Prime Time
   Sunday" ('79); Prod., ABC News ('82).
ACHIEVEMENTS & AWARDS: N.A.
PERSONAL: N.A.

FRIEDMAN, RONALD
**V.P., Cable Health Network (HAVES),
Marketing**

16A Algonquin Lane, Stratford, CT 06497
b. April 6, 1942. Brooklyn, NY.

EDUCATION: Brooklyn College, B.A.; New York
   University Graduate School of Business Ad-
   ministration, M.B.A.
CAREER HIGHLIGHTS: Sr. Marketing Research
   Supervisor, Batten, Barton, Durstine & Os-
   born ad agency ('64); Acct. Exec., McCann-
   Erickson ad agency ('69); Sr. Acct. Exec.,
   Ogilvy & Mather ad agency ('71); Mgr., Mar-
   keting Planning and Advertising, American
   Airlines ('73); V.P., Planning, Analysis and
   Administration, American Express Co., Card
   Division ('81); V.P., Marketing, Cable Health
   Network (HAVES) ('82).
ACHIEVEMENTS & AWARDS: N.A.
PERSONAL: Wife, Valerie.

FRIEDMAN, SONYA
Host, USA Cable Network, "Sonya"

c/o USA Cable Network, 208 Harristown Rd.,
   Glen Rock, NJ 07452
b. N.A.

EDUCATION: Wayne State University, Ph.D.,
   Psychology ('67)
CAREER HIGHLIGHTS: Before hosting her own
   series, "Sonya," she was seen as a guest on a
   number of network and syndicated TV
   shows. The most prominent of these appearances was as resident psychologist on ABC's

"A.M. America." Other TV credits include
Special Correspondent, ABC Evening News;
Local Host, "The Baxters," a Norman Lear
production; and guest appearances with
Mike Douglas and Lou Gordon, and on
"A.M. New York" and "A.M. Detroit." Host
of Detroit's afternoon radio talk show on
WXYZ ('78).
ACHIEVEMENTS & AWARDS: Woman of the Year
   award from the Business and Professional
   Women of Birmingham ('69); outstanding
   achievement of the year award from Ameri-
   can Women in Radio and TV ('80); local
   Emmy award for best interview/discussion
   show.
PERSONAL: N.A.

FRIEDMAN, STEVE
Exec. Prod., NBC, "Today"

c/o NBC, 30 Rockefeller Plaza, New York, NY
   10020
b. July 22, 1946. Chicago, IL.

EDUCATION: University of Illinois, B.S., Jour-
   nalism.
CAREER HIGHLIGHTS: Newswriter, KNBC ('69);
   Special Projects Prod. ('74); Prod., 5 O'clock
   News ('75); named West Coast Prod., "To-
   day" ('77); New York Prod., "Today" ('79);
   named Exec. Prod. ('80).
ACHIEVEMENTS & AWARDS: Four Los Angeles lo-
   cal Emmy awards for producing (two in '75;
   two in '76).
PERSONAL: Resides in Manhattan with wife,
   Beverly, and daughter, Louisa.

FRIENDLY, ANDREW
Prod., Parkinson Friendly Productions

c/o Parkinson Friendly Productions, Suite 814,
   1717 N. Highland Ave., Hollywood, CA
   90028
b. N.A.

EDUCATION: University of Southern California
   Film School.
CAREER HIGHLIGHTS: Prod./Writer, "Tomor-
   row," NBC ('76); Prod./Writer, "Prime Time
   Sunday," NBC ('79); Prod./Writer of the three
   NBC primetime specials featuring Tom

Snyder ('79); Prod., "Speak Up America," NBC ('80); Prod./Writer, "30th Anniversary This is Your Life" ('81); Creator/Prod./Writer of the first 52 "Entertainment Tonight" programs for Paramount ('81); Prod., "World of Entertainment," syndicated for MGM-UA ('82); Prod./Writer of Paramount pilot "Taking Advantage" ('82); Prod./Writer of the new "This is Your Life" pilot ('82); Prod. of syndicated pilot "Being Your Best" ('83); Prod. of the syndicated "$1,000,000 Pet of the Year" special ('83); Prod. of the stage production "The Magic of David Copperfield" ('83). Productions currently in development include the TV movies *The Rolf Benischke Story* and *The Grandma Mafia*, the special "The British Invasion," and a Richard Pryor concert film.

ACHIEVEMENTS & AWARDS: N.A.

PERSONAL: N.A.

FRIENDLY, ED
Prod.

1041 N. Formosa Ave., Los Angeles, CA 90046
b. April 8, 1922. New York, NY.

EDUCATION: Manlius School.

CAREER HIGHLIGHTS: Producer of the long-running, skillfully mounted "Little House on the Prairie," which has outdistanced all the competition for a decade. Previously was Radio Dir., BBD&O; Dir., Sales, ABC; V.P. in Charge of Special Programs, NBC. Co-Creator/Prod., "Laugh-In" ('67).

ACHIEVEMENTS & AWARDS: Emmy award for "Laugh-In"; Golden Globe award.

PERSONAL: N.A.

FRIENDLY, FRED W.
Broadcasting Exec. and Professor Emeritus

c/o Columbia University School of Journalism, 116th St. and Broadway, New York, NY 10027
b. October, 1921. Providence, RI.

EDUCATION: Nichols College ('36).

CAREER HIGHLIGHTS: This pivotal and distinguished figure in TV news and public affairs worked very closely with Edward R. Murrow on virtually all of Murrow's TV shows during Murrow's years at CBS. Friendly's resignation from the presidency of CBS News in 1966 was one of the few times in American TV history that a top executive quit his job on a matter of principle—Friendly vigorously objected to CBS's refusal to broadcast live important Senate coverage of testimony about the Vietnam War in favor of a rerun of an "I Love Lucy" episode. Shortly after resigning from CBS, Friendly became the Ford Foundation's top official dealing with public TV. During the sixties and seventies the Ford Foundation contributed more than $200 million to the support and development of public TV. Another enduring Friendly legacy is the creation of the Media and Society Seminars, several of which were broadcast, in edited versions, (late '82 and early '83) on CBS. Friendly's most important positions include the following: Prod. and Journalist, WEAN-AM, Providence, RI ('37); Prod., News and Documentaries, NBC ('47); Exec. Prod., "See It Now," "CBS Reports," CBS News ('50–'64); Pres., CBS News ('64); Professor, Journalism, and Chairman, Broadcast Program, Columbia University ('68); Professor Emeritus, Columbia Graduate School of Journalism ('81).

ACHIEVEMENTS & AWARDS: Author, *The Good Guys, and the Bad Guys and the First Amendment*; Co-Author, with Edward R. Murrow, *See It Now*.

PERSONAL: Resides in Riverdale, NY with his wife, Ruth; six children. His son Andy is a TV and motion picture producer with Parkinson-Friendly Productions.

FRIES, CHARLES
Pres., Charles Fries Productions

4024 N. Radford Ave., Studio City, CA 91604
b. September 30, 1928. Cincinnati, OH.

EDUCATION: Ohio State University, B.A.

CAREER HIGHLIGHTS: V.P. in Charge of Production Administration, Screen Gems ('60); V.P. in Charge of Feature Film Production, Columbia Pictures ('68); Exec. V.P. in Charge of Production, Metromedia Producers Corp., Jacques Cousteau and Jane Goodall "National Geographic" specials ('70); Pres., Charles Fries Productions ('74). Prod., *A Rumor of War, Cat People, Rage, A Cry for Love, High Noon, Part II, For the Love of It, . . . And Your Name Is Jonah, The Martian Chronicles, Intimate Strangers, A Love Affair: The Eleanor and Lou Gehrig Story, The Word, The Amazing Spiderman,* and *Baby I'm Back.*

ACHIEVEMENTS & AWARDS: Christopher award/ Cine Eagle, *Bitter Harvest;* Christopher award, *. . . And Your Name Is Jonah.* Governor, ATAS; Pres., Alliance of TV Film Producers.

PERSONAL: N.A.

FRITTS, EDWARD O.
Pres., NAB

c/o NAB, 1771 N St., N.W., Washington, DC 20036
b. N.A.

EDUCATION: University of Mississippi.

CAREER   HIGHLIGHTS: Announcer,   WENK, Union City, TN. Affiliated with his father in ownership of WPAD and WDDJ, Paducah, KY. Pres. and Owner, Fritts Broadcasting, Indianola, MS, which includes WNLA, Indianola, MS; WELO and WZLQ of Tupelo, MS; KMAR, Winnsboro, LA; KCRI, West Helena, AR; KCRI-FM, Helena, AR. Past Chairman, NAB's Small Market Radio Committee, Chairman, NAB's Joint Board of Dirs. ('81); elected Pres., NAB ('82).

ACHIEVEMENTS & AWARDS: N.A.

PERSONAL: Wife, Martha; daughters, Kimberly and Jennifer; son, Timothy.

FRITZ, ALLEN
Treasurer, Cablentertainment

c/o Cablentertainment, 295 Madison Ave., New York, NY 10017
b. N.A.

EDUCATION: Wagner College, B.S., Economics.

CAREER HIGHLIGHTS: Officer and later Corporate Lending Officer, Chase Manhattan Bank ('62); Asst. V.P., Chase Manhattan Bank ('73); V.P., Corporate Lending Officer, Natl. Bank of North America ('74); Treasurer, Vikoa, Inc. cable TV system operator ('75); Treasurer, Cablentertainment ('81).

ACHIEVEMENTS & AWARDS: N.A.

PERSONAL: Resides in New Jersey with his wife and two children.

FRITZ, JACK W.
Pres. and Chief Exec. Officer, John Blair & Co.

717 Fifth Ave., New York, NY 10022
b. April 22, 1927. Battle Creek, MI.

EDUCATION: University of Michigan, B.A.

CAREER HIGHLIGHTS: Began his business career as a member of the Midwest Consumer Products Marketing Unit, Lever Bros. Co. ('49); entered broadcasting as an Acct. Exec., ABC Spot Sales, Detroit ('50); Product Mgr., Lever Bros., Pepsodent Division, New York ('51); Acct. Exec., TV Sales Division, John Blair & Co., New York ('54); V.P. and Mgr., Blair TV Station Division, New York Sales Office ('65); V.P. and General Mgr., Blair TV Station Division ('66); V.P. and General Mgr. of Broadcasting ('68); Pres. and Chief Exec. Officer, John Blair & Co. ('72).

ACHIEVEMENTS & AWARDS: N.A.

PERSONAL: Wife, Marilyn; three children.

FRONS, BRIAN
V.P., Daytime Programs, NBC, Entertainment

c/o NBC, 3000 W. Alameda Ave., Burbank, CA 91523
b. N.A.

EDUCATION: State University of New York at Fredonia, B.A., History; Syracuse University School of Public Communications, M.S., TV/ Radio ('78).

CAREER HIGHLIGHTS: Immediately after graduating from Syracuse, Frons was selected by CBS to enter its Exec. Training Program ('78); Assoc., Daytime Programs Dept., CBS, New

York ('79); Mgr., Daytime Programs, CBS ('80); Dir., Daytime Programs, CBS, New York ('81); V.P., Daytime Programs, NBC Entertainment, Burbank ('83).
ACHIEVEMENTS & AWARDS: N.A.
PERSONAL: Single, resides in Los Angeles.

Dir. of Special Programming and Sports ('76); V.P. in Charge of Specials and Sports ('77); V.P., Programming ('79); named Sr. V.P. ('80); Exec. V.P., Programming ('82); Pres., HBO Entertainment Group ('83).
ACHIEVEMENTS & AWARDS: N.A.
PERSONAL: N.A.

FRYE, ROBERT E.
Exec. Prod., ABC, "World News Tonight"

c/o ABC, 7 W. 66th St., New York, NY 10023
b. December 20, 1939. Syracuse, NY.

EDUCATION: Hobart College, Political Science.
CAREER HIGHLIGHTS: Joined ABC News as Co-ordinator, News Operations ('66); moved to CBC as Sr. Prod., "Weekend News" ('69); joined WETA as Prod., daily "Newsroom" ('70); Prod., "Evening Edition With Martin Agronsky" ('71); Dir., Communications Programs, Appalachian Regional Commission; Washington, DC, Bureau Chief, TV News, Inc.; returned to ABC as Prod., news segments for "A.M. America" ('74); remained in same position when "Good Morning America" premiered ('75); Prod., "ABC News With Harry Reasoner" ('75); Sr. Prod., London, "World News Tonight" ('78); Sr. Prod., numerous documentary specials; Exec. Prod., "ABC News This Morning" and "Good Morning America" news ('82); Exec. Prod., ABC, "World News Tonight" ('83).
ACHIEVEMENTS & AWARDS: Dupont-Columbia, Peabody, George Polk, and Investigative Reporters awards, Exec. Prod., "America Held Hostage: The Secret Negotiations" ('82).
PERSONAL: Resides in Ridgewood, NJ, with wife, Doris; children, Sarah and Robert E. Jr.

FULTON, EILEEN
Actress

c/o "As the World Turns," CBS, 51 W. 52d St., New York, NY 10019
b. September 13. Asheville, NC.

EDUCATION: Greensboro College.
CAREER HIGHLIGHTS: Off Broadway credits include *Sabrina Fair, Any Wednesday,* and *The Fantasticks.* TV guest spot on "Fantasy Island." Soap opera star of "As the World Turns."
ACHIEVEMENTS & AWARDS: N.A.
PERSONAL: Resides in New York City.

FUCHS, MICHAEL J.
Pres., HBO Entertainment Group

c/o HBO, 1271 Ave. of the Americas, New York, NY 10020
b. March 9, 1946. New York, NY.

EDUCATION: Union College, B.A., Political Science; New York University Law School, J.D.
CAREER HIGHLIGHTS: Law Assoc., specializing in entertainment; Dir. of Business Affairs, William Morris Agency ('75); joined HBO as

FURNESS, BETTY
Consumer Reporter, NBC

c/o NBC, 30 Rockefeller Plaza, New York, NY 10020
b. January 3, 1916. New York, NY.

EDUCATION: N.A.

CAREER HIGHLIGHTS: Started out in movies ('32–'38); moved to theater ('40–'44); first worked in TV doing commercials for Westinghouse ('49–'60). Entered news and information broadcasting with CBS Radio's "Dimension of a Woman's World" and "Ask Betty Furness" ('62–'67); served as Special Asst. to the Pres. for Consumer Affairs ('67–'69); chaired the New York State Consumer Protection Board ('70–'71); appointed New York City Consumer Affairs Commissioner ('73). Joined WNBC-TV as Consumer Reporter ('74); Consumer Reporter, "Today" ('76). Maintains dual role for both "News 4 New York," WNBC, and "Today."

ACHIEVEMENTS & AWARDS: Pres., New York Chapter, NATAS ('61–'63); Consumers Union, Board Member and Officer ('69–present); *Ladies' Home Journal* Woman of the Year in Business ('76); Peabody award for "Buyline: Betty Furness" ('77). Local Emmy awards for "Buyline: Betty Furness" ('77, '78, and '79). AWRT pinnacle award, TV News ('82); Sigma Delta Chi award for public service in TV journalism for "Adoptions" series ('82).

PERSONAL: Married to Leslie Midgley, former CBS News and Documentary Prod., currently V.P., Special Programs, NBC News.

FYFFE, BILL
V.P. and General Mgr., WABC-TV, New York

c/o WABC-TV, 7 Lincoln Sq., New York, NY 10023
b. N.A.

EDUCATION: Northwestern University.

CAREER HIGHLIGHTS: Began at WEAW-Radio, Evanston, IL; News Dir., WXYZ-TV, Detroit ('64); News Dir., WLS-TV, Chicago ('68); News Dir., KABC-TV, Los Angeles ('72); V.P., News, ABC Owned TV Stations ('77); V.P. and Station Mgr., WLS-TV, Chicago ('79); V.P. and General Mgr., WABC-TV, New York ('81).

ACHIEVEMENTS & AWARDS: Natl. Headliners award for coverage of Detroit riots ('68); Los Angeles Press Club grand award, Peabody award, California AP awards while at KABC-TV.

PERSONAL: Resides in New York City with wife, Nancy.

GAFFNER, HAINES B.
Pres., LINK Resources

c/o LINK Resources, 215 Park Ave. So., New
  York, NY 10017
b. N.A.

EDUCATION: University of Washington, B.S.,
  Business.
CAREER HIGHLIGHTS: Intl. Marketing Mgr.
  based in numerous foreign countries;
  Founder and Pres., FIND/SVP information
  brokerage firm; V.P., Business Intl. and
  Quantum Science Corp.; Founder and Pres.
  of LINK Resources, market research and
  management consulting organization.
ACHIEVEMENTS & AWARDS: Chairman, Informa-
  tion Industry Assn. Business Operations
  Council.
PERSONAL: N.A.

GAFFNEY, RICKIE
Prod./Writer

7225 Shoup Ave., Los Angeles, CA 91307
b. Attleboro, MA.

EDUCATION: Ohio University, B.S.
CAREER HIGHLIGHTS: Worked as both a Free-
  lance Prod. and Prod. of local programming
  in Philadelphia, Baltimore, Boston, San Fran-
  cisco, and Washington, D.C. Sr. Assoc.
  Prod., "The Mike Douglas Show/Entertain-
  ment Hour" ('78); Assoc. Prod., "Entertainer
  of the Year Awards" ('81); Line Prod., "The
  Larry King Show" pilot ('82); Prod., "Just
  Men!" ('83).
ACHIEVEMENTS & AWARDS: N.A.
PERSONAL: N.A.

GALBRAITH, BILL
Dir., News Operations, CBS, News

c/o CBS, 2020 M St., N.W., Washington, DC
  20036
b. Columbus, OH.

EDUCATION: University of Washington.
CAREER HIGHLIGHTS: Desk Assistant, UPI ('47);
  Reporter, UPI, Washington, DC ('51); Desk
  Editor, CBS News, Washington, DC ('60); As-
  signment Editor, CBS News ('64); Exec. Edi-
  tor, CBS News ('75); Dir., News Operations,
  CBS News, Washington, DC ('83).
ACHIEVEMENTS & AWARDS: N.A.
PERSONAL: N.A.

GALLAGHER, HELEN
Actress

c/o "Ryan's Hope" ABC, 1330 Ave. of Americas,
  New York, NY 10019
b. July 19, 1926. New York, NY.

EDUCATION: N.A.
CAREER HIGHLIGHTS: Broadway appearances
  include *The Seven Lively Arts, Billion Dollar
  Baby, Make a Wish, Pal Joey, Hazel Flagg,* and
  No, No Nanette. TV series star of soap opera,
  "Ryan's Hope."
ACHIEVEMENTS & AWARDS: Tony for best sup-

porting actress in a musical, *Pal Joey*; Tony for best actress in a musical, *No, No Nanette*; Emmy awards for best daytime actress, "Ryan's Hope" ('76 and '77).

PERSONAL: N.A.

GANZ, LOWELL
Producer (Freelance)

c/o ABC, 2040 Ave. of the Stars, Los Angeles, CA 90067

b. August 31, 1948. Bronx, NY.

EDUCATION: Queens College.

CAREER HIGHLIGHTS: Writer, "The Odd Couple" ('72); Prod., "Happy Days" ('74); Prod., "Laverne and Shirley" ('76); Creator/Prod./Writer, pilot for "Busting Loose" ('76); Writer, "The Ted Knight Show" ('78); Exec. Prod., "Makin' It" ('79); Writer/Consultant, "Joanie Loves Chachi" ('81–'82).

ACHIEVEMENTS & AWARDS: N.A.

PERSONAL: Resides in West Hollywood, CA, with wife, Jeanne.

GARAGIOLA, JOE
Sportscaster, NBC, Sports

c/o NBC, 30 Rockefeller Plaza, New York, NY 10020

b. February 12, 1926. St. Louis, MO.

EDUCATION: N.A.

CAREER HIGHLIGHTS: Nine-year career in baseball as a Natl. League catcher ('46); TV play-by-play for St. Louis Cardinals ('55); NBC Sports Game of the Week baseball telecasts ('61); Host, "Today" ('67); NBC Game Show Host, Radio Commentator, Host of "The Baseball World of Joe Garagiola."

ACHIEVEMENTS & AWARDS: Peabody and Freedom Foundation awards for journalistic excellence for "The Baseball World of Joe Garagiola," ('73).

PERSONAL: Resides in Paradise Valley, AZ, with wife, Audrie, and three children.

GARCHER, DENNIS
V.P. and General Mgr., Home Box Office, Eastern Region

c/o HBO, 1271 Ave. of the Americas, New York, NY 10020

b. April 3, 1945. Youngstown, OH.

EDUCATION: N.A.

CAREER HIGHLIGHTS: Marketing Analyst, GTE Data Services, Tampa, FL ('69); V.P. and General Mgr., Channel 100, Los Angeles ('74); Regional Mgr., Mid-Atlantic Region, HBO ('76); Regional Mgr., Florida Region, HBO ('77); Regional Dir., Southeast Region HBO, Atlanta ('79); V.P. and General Mgr., Central Region, HBO ('80); V.P. and General Mgr., Eastern Region, HBO, New York ('80).

ACHIEVEMENTS & AWARDS: N.A.

PERSONAL: Resides in New York City; daughter, Lorraine.

GARCIA, DAVID
Sr. Correspondent, KNXT-TV, News

c/o KNXT-TV, 6121 Sunset Blvd., Los Angeles, CA 90028

b. Temple, TX.

EDUCATION: Baylor University, B.A., Journalism.

CAREER HIGHLIGHTS: Reporter/Anchor, KTEM-Radio, Temple, TX ('60); Reporter/Weekend Anchor, WFAA-AM/TV, Dallas ('65); Correspondent, ABC Radio, Washington, DC ('68); White House Correspondent, ABC News, Washington, DC ('78); Latin American Bureau Chief, ABC News, Miami ('79); Sr. Correspondent, KNXT-TV, Los Angeles ('82).

ACHIEVEMENTS & AWARDS: N.A.

PERSONAL: N.A.

GARNER, JAMES
Actor

c/o NBC, 3000 W. Alameda Ave., Burbank, CA 91523
b. April 7, 1928. Norman, OK.

EDUCATION: New York Berghof School of Drama.
CAREER HIGHLIGHTS: Although he played Maverick twice, there's nothing recycled about Garner's skill as a rugged leading man or his light comic touch, qualities best combined on "The Rockford Files." Motion pictures include *Grand Prix, Move Over Darling, Health, The Children's Hour, The Americanization of Emily,* and *The Skin Game.* TV series star of "Maverick," "The Rockford Files," and "Bret Maverick."
ACHIEVEMENTS & AWARDS: Emmy as outstanding Series actor for "The Rockford Files" ('77).
PERSONAL: Wife, Lois Clarke; two daughters, Kimberly and Greta (Gigi). Resides in Brentwood, CA.

GARRELS, ANNE
Correspondent, ABC, News

c/o ABC, 1717 DeSales St., Washington, DC 20036
b. N.A.

EDUCATION: Middlebury College; Harvard University, B.A., General Studies ('72).
CAREER HIGHLIGHTS: Editor, Weidenfeld and Nicolson Publishing; Researcher/Prod., ABC News ('75); Production Assoc., Special Events Unit; Reporter ('78); Correspondent based in Moscow ('80); returned to Washington, DC, Bureau.
ACHIEVEMENTS & AWARDS: N.A.
PERSONAL: N.A.

GARRETT, EDWARD
V.P., NBC, Finance and Administration, Operations and Technical Services

c/o NBC, 30 Rockefeller Plaza, New York, NY 10020
b. 1929.

EDUCATION: Temple University, B.S.
CAREER HIGHLIGHTS: Division V.P., Finance, RCA, Somerville, NJ, before joining NBC; V.P., NBC, Finance and Administration, Operations and Technical Services.
ACHIEVEMENTS & AWARDS: Member, Natl. Assn. of Accountants; Treasurer and Member, Board of Trustees of the Somerset County Community College, also serves as Chairman, Finance Committee.
PERSONAL: Wife, Dorothy; three children, Susan, Donald, and Nancy. Resides in Somerville, NJ.

GARTIN, SANDY RUSSEL
Dir., ABC, Children's Programming

151 W. 86th St., New York, NY 10024
b. Norwich, CT.

EDUCATION: University of Connecticut; City College of New York; Manhattan Center for Advanced Psychoanalytic Studies.
CAREER HIGHLIGHTS: Worked on various shows, including "The Garry Moore Show," "The Play of the Week," "The Doctors," "The Secret Storm," "The U.S. Steel Hour," "Henry Winkler Meets Shakespeare," "Lena Horne and Arthur Fiedler at Carnegie Hall," "Peggy Fleming in Holiday on Ice." Developed children's programming for NBC and ABC; named Dir., Children's Programming, for both ABC and NBC; named Dir., Children's Programming, ABC, with responsibilities for ABC Afterschool Specials, "Kids Are People Too," "Schoolhouse Rock," and "Dear Alex and Annie."
ACHIEVEMENTS & AWARDS: Numerous awards for ABC Afterschool Specials.
PERSONAL: Son, Christopher; daughter Pamela.

GARVEY, CYNDY
Co-Host, WABC-TV, New York, "The Morning Show"

c/o WABC-TV, 7 Lincoln Sq., New York, NY 10023
b. Detroit, MI.

EDUCATION: Michigan State University, B.S., Education and Science ('71).
CAREER HIGHLIGHTS: Co-Host, "A.M. Los Angeles," KABC-TV, Los Angeles ('79); Co-Host, "Games People Play" on NBC; Co-Host, "The Morning Show," WABC-TV, New York ('83).
ACHIEVEMENTS & AWARDS: N.A.
PERSONAL: Divorced from baseball star Steve Garvey; resides in New York City with her two daughters, Whitney and Krisha.

GATTI, ROSA M.
V.P., ESPN, Communications/Public Relations

c/o ESPN, ESPN Plaza, Bristol, CT 06010
b. June 27, 1950. Philadelphia, PA.

EDUCATION: Villanova University, B.A., French.
CAREER HIGHLIGHTS: Asst. Sports Information Dir.; Sports Information Dir., Villanova University ('73); Sports Information Dir., Brown University ('76); Dir., Communications, ESPN ('80); V.P., Communications, ESPN ('81).
ACHIEVEMENTS & AWARDS: First female sports information director of a major university in the U.S. V.P., College Sports Information Dirs. of America ('79–'80). One-year term as Pres., Eastern College Athletic Conference Sports Information Dirs. Assn.
PERSONAL: N.A.

GAY, JOHN
Writer

c/o Creative Artists, 1636 San Onofre Dr., Pacific Palisades, CA 90272
b. April 1, 1924. Whittier, CA.

EDUCATION: American Academy.
CAREER HIGHLIGHTS: Writing credits include TV screenplays for *All My Darling Daughters, The Red Badge of Courage, Things in Their Season, The Amazing Howard Hughes, Kill Me If You Can, Transplant, The Court Martial of George Armstrong Custer, A Tale of Two Cities, Berlin Tunnel 21, The Bunker, The Hunchback of Notre Dame, Ivanhoe, A Piano for Mrs. Cimino,* and *Witness for the Prosecution.*
ACHIEVEMENTS & AWARDS: Two Christopher awards ('78, '80).
PERSONAL: N.A.

GEARY, ANTHONY
Actor

c/o "General Hospital," ABC, 4151 Prospect Ave., Los Angeles, CA 90027
b. May 29. Coalville, UT.

EDUCATION: University of Utah.
CAREER HIGHLIGHTS: A run-of-the-mill actor until he hit it big on "General Hospital" as half of the popular Luke and Laura, lovers-on-the-run team. Began by making guest appearances on such shows as "Starsky and Hutch," "Barnaby Jones," "The Streets of San Francisco," "Six Million Dollar Man," "Mannix," "The Mod Squad," "Room 222," and "Marcus Welby, M.D." Lead role in TV movie *Intimate Agony* ('83); starred in serials "Bright Promise" and "The Young and the

Restless" before making a big splash as Luke Spencer on "General Hospital."

ACHIEVEMENTS & AWARDS: Emmy as outstanding actor in a daytime drama for "General Hospital" ('81).

PERSONAL: N.A.

GEER, HAL
V.P., Warner Bros. Cartoons

c/o Warner Bros., 4000 Warner Blvd., Burbank, CA 91522
b. September 13, 1916. Oronogo, MO.

EDUCATION: University of Southern California, B.A. ('53).

CAREER HIGHLIGHTS: Army Air Corps Motion Picture Cameraman ('42); Color Technician, Warner Bros. ('46); Color Technician and Asst. Film Editor, Walt Disney Productions ('50); Film Editor, UPA, Ziv and Screen Gems ('60); Film Editor, Hanna-Barbera and Universal ('65); Prod. Mgr., Post Production Supervisor/Writer/Dir./Exec. Prod., Warner Bros. Cartoons, Commercials and Industrial Films.

ACHIEVEMENTS & AWARDS: Clio and Hugo awards for ITT commercial.

PERSONAL: Son, Wally; daughter, Nancy.

GEER, STEPHEN
Correspondent, ABC, News

c/o ABC, 7 W. 66th St., New York, NY 10023
b. N.A.

EDUCATION: Columbia University.

CAREER HIGHLIGHTS: Anchor/Correspondent, WTOP-TV, Washington, DC ('67); Correspondent, ABC News, Washington, DC ('73); Correspondent, ABC News ('79).

ACHIEVEMENTS & AWARDS: Washington, DC, local Emmy award ('66).

PERSONAL: N.A.

GEISS, TONY
Writer

c/o Children's Television Workshop, 1 Lincoln Plaza, New York, NY 10023
b. N.A.

EDUCATION: N.A.

CAREER HIGHLIGHTS: Writer, "The David Frost Show" ('70–'72); Prod., "The John Bartholomew Tucker Show" for WCBS-TV; joined Children's Television Workshop ('74) as Head Writer, "Feeling Good." Has written network TV comedy for such stars as Robert Klein, Dick Cavett, and Bill Cosby. Writer, PBS's "We Interrupt This Week"; Contributing Editor on the best-seller *The 1980's: A Look Backward*. Created the Honkers for "Sesame Street."

ACHIEVEMENTS & AWARDS: Local Emmy for individual achievement ('65).

PERSONAL: N.A.

GELBART, LARRY
Writer

c/o Writers Guild West, 8955 Beverly Blvd., Los Angeles, CA 90048
b. February 25, 1928.

EDUCATION: N.A.

CAREER HIGHLIGHTS: Prolific comedy creator who worked with TV's comic giants in the fifties and later returned to TV with a still-adventurous comic spirit that developed the long-running "M*A*S*H" and the innovative series "United States." He began as a comedy writer for Bob Hope and Sid Caesar; Broadway credits include *Sly Fox* and *A Funny Thing Happened on the Way to the Forum*. Creator/Writer of the experimental series "United States." Motion pictures include *Tootsie, Oh God!* and *Rio*. Creator/Writer of TV's "M*A*S*H" series. Creator of the new CBS series "After M*A*S*H."

ACHIEVEMENTS & AWARDS: Tony award for *A Funny Thing Happened on the Way to the Forum*. Emmy for comedy writing, "M*A*S*H."

PERSONAL: N.A.

GELINE, ROBERT J.
Dir., Teletext, NBC

c/o NBC, 30 Rockefeller Plaza, New York, NY 10020
b. N.A.

EDUCATION: University of Wisconsin, B.A., Psychology; Northwestern University, M.S., Journalism.

CAREER HIGHLIGHTS: Press Secretary for U.S. Rep. Henry S. Reuss of Wisconsin; Management Consultant/Correspondent/Editor, *Business Week*; City Hall Reporter, *N.Y. Daily News*; Special Assignment Correspondent, *Time* magazine, New York ('78); Dir., Teletext, NBC, overseeing the network's first experiment with teletext ('81).

ACHIEVEMENTS & AWARDS: N.A.

PERSONAL: N.A.

GELLER, HENRY
Dir., Washington Center for Public Policy Research

c/o Washington Center for Public Policy Research, 1767 K St., N.W., Washington, DC 20006

b. February 14, 1924. Springfield, MA.

EDUCATION: University of Michigan, B.S. ('43); Northwestern Law School, J.D.

CAREER HIGHLIGHTS: One of the most knowledgeable and influential communications lawyers, specializing in all areas of public interest law and public policy issues. Geller served as Law Clerk to Illinois Supreme Court Justice Walter V. Schaffer ('50). Most of his career was spent at the FCC where he served in various positions. Appointed General Counsel ('64); Special Asst. to the Chairman ('70). Pursued communications law and research interests at the Rand Corp. ('73); Communications Fellow with the Aspen Institute Program on Communications and Society ('75); Asst. Secretary for Communications and Information and Administrator of the Natl. Telecommunications and Information Administration in the U.S. Dept. of Commerce ('77); Currently serves as the Dir., Washington Center for Public Policy Research, which focuses on telecommunications policy issues and research, part of Duke University's Institute of Policy Sciences and Public Affairs ('81).

ACHIEVEMENTS & AWARDS: National Civil Service award ('70).

PERSONAL: N.A.

GELLER, ROBERT
Pres. and Exec. Prod., Learning in Focus

c/o Learning in Focus, 310 Madison Ave., New York, NY 10017

b. N.A.

EDUCATION: New York University, M.A.; Cornell University.

CAREER HIGHLIGHTS: Exec. Prod., "The American Short Story" film series for TV; Exec. Prod. of series at screening of "Sky Is Gray" at the Kennedy Center; Exec. Prod. of NBC's dramatic special *Too Far To Go*, based on works by John Updike.

ACHIEVEMENTS & AWARDS: Peabody award, "The American Short Story" series ('80). First Chairman and Advisory Board Member of Robert Redford's Sundance Institute, a project designed to create professional film opportunities for young and disadvantaged film artists.

PERSONAL: Married; two children.

GERALDI, JODEPH M.
Dir., Advertising Operations, NBC

c/o NBC, 30 Rockefeller Plaza, New York, NY 10020

b. Brooklyn, NY.

EDUCATION: Baruch College.

CAREER HIGHLIGHTS: Field Auditor, Crane Co. ('67); Jr. Accountant, Mobil Oil Corp. ('69); Financial Analyst; Mobil Oil Corp. ('72); Sales Accounting, Union Carbide Co. ('74); Jr. Auditor, Financial Auditing Dept., NBC ('75); Sr. Auditor, Financial Auditing Dept., NBC ('75); Administrator, Overhead, Business Affairs, NBC TV ('78); Administrator, Advertising Budgets, NBC ('78); Mgr., Advertising Business Affairs, NBC ('79); Mgr., Advertising Budgets and Administration ('79); Dir., Advertising Finance and Administration ('81); Dir., Advertising Operations, NBC ('82).

ACHIEVEMENTS & AWARDS: N.A.

PERSONAL: Resides in New York City.

GERBER, DAVID
Exec. Prod.

20303 W. Washington Blvd., Culver City, CA 90230
b. Brooklyn, NY.

EDUCATION: University of the Pacific at Stockton, B.A.
CAREER HIGHLIGHTS: V.P. in Charge of Sales, 20th Century ('65); moved into production with credits that include "The Ghost and Mrs. Muir" ('70), "Cade's County" ('71), "Police Story" ('73), "Police Woman" ('74). Named V.P., Columbia Pictures TV ('74); formed David Gerber Co. ('76). Productions since then include "Today's FBI" series ('79); *Beulah Land* mini-series ('80); "Seven Brides for Seven Brothers" series ('82).
ACHIEVEMENTS & AWARDS: Christopher award, Nosotron award, and NAACP award for outstanding drama, "Follow the North Star" ('72); best dramatic series, "Police Story" ('75).
PERSONAL: Married to actress Laraine Stephens.

GERBER, MICHAEL H.
V.P., Viacom Enterprises, Business Affairs

c/o Viacom, 1211 Ave. of the Americas, New York, NY 10036
b. February 6, 1944. Brooklyn, NY.

EDUCATION: St. John's University.
CAREER HIGHLIGHTS: Various executive positions with Columbia Pictures Industries ('69); V.P., Corporate Affairs, Allied Artists Pictures Corp. ('74); V.P., Business Affairs, Viacom Enterprises ('80).
ACHIEVEMENTS & AWARDS: N.A.
PERSONAL: N.A.

GERBNER, GEORGE
Professor of Communications, Dean, Annenberg School of Communications, University of Pennsylvania

c/o University of Pennsylvania, 3620 Walnut St., Philadelphia, PA
b. N.A.

EDUCATION: University of California at Berkeley, B.A.; University of Southern California, M.S. and Ph.D.
CAREER HIGHLIGHTS: On staff of *San Francisco Chronicle*; taught at Institute of Communications Research, University of Illinois, University of Southern California, El Camino College, and John Muir College in California. Directed U.S. and multinational mass communication research projects for the Natl. Science Foundation, the U.S. Office of Education, UNESCO, the Intl. Sociological Assn., Intl. Research and Exchanges Board, President's Commission on the Causes and Prevention of Violence, and the Surgeon General's Scientific Advisory Committee on TV and Social Behavior, as well as other organizations.
ACHIEVEMENTS & AWARDS: Communicator of the Year award, B'nai B'rith Communications Lodge ('81); media achievement award of excellence of the Philadelphia Bar Assn. ('81); Broadcast Preceptor award, Broadcast Communications, Art Dept., San Francisco State University. Publications include *The World According to Television, Exploring TV's Hold on Viewers, TV Changing Our Lives,* and *Education and the Challenge of Mass Culture.*
PERSONAL: N.A.

GERSHMAN, LAWRENCE E.
Pres., MGM-UA, TV Distribution

c/o MGM-UA TV, 1350 Ave. of the Americas, New York, NY 10019
b. March 21, 1936. Brooklyn, NY.

EDUCATION: Pennsylvania State University; Fordham University School of Law.
CAREER HIGHLIGHTS: Mgr., NBC Spot Sales ('71); Sales Mgr. WNBC-TV, New York ('73); Station Mgr., WNBC-TV ('75); V.P., Intl., Viacom Enterprises ('77); Exec. V.P., Worldwide Syndication ('80); Pres., MGM-UA TV Distribution ('81).
ACHIEVEMENTS & AWARDS: Dir. of the TV Bureau of Advertising; Dir. of Intl. Council.
PERSONAL: Resides in New York City with wife, Rosanna, and two children.

GERSON, ALAN H.
V.P., NBC, Law, Broadcast Administration

c/o NBC, 30 Rockefeller Plaza, New York, NY 10020
b. November 30, 1946. Brooklyn, NY.

EDUCATION: State University of New York at Plattsburgh, B.A., Political Science; Fordham University Law School, J.D.
CAREER HIGHLIGHTS: Practicing Attorney ('71); joined NBC as Attorney ('73); named Dir., Compliance and Practices ('75); V.P., Compliance and Practices ('78); V.P., Law, Broadcast Administration, NBC ('81). Adjunct Professor, Graduate School of Communications, New York Institute of Technology ('81).
ACHIEVEMENTS & AWARDS: Federal Communications Bar Assn.; American Bar Assn.
PERSONAL: Resides in Douglaston, NY, with wife, Gerri; children, Jennifer and Daniel.

GETZ, ROBERT
Prod.

524 W. 57th St., New York, NY 10019
b. N.A.

EDUCATION: Goodman Memorial Theatre, Theater Arts and Communications.
CAREER HIGHLIGHTS: Production Supervisor, daytime TV pilots "The Guest Room," CBS ('74); "Trio for Lovers," CBS ('74); "Women in Chains," Paramount ('74). Game show pilot "Musical Chairs," CBS ('74); "Captain Kangaroo" and "Special Events." Assoc. Prod., "Search for Tomorrow" ('80).
ACHIEVEMENTS & AWARDS: N.A.
PERSONAL: N.A.

GIAQUINTO, JOSEPH E.
V.P., ABC, Affiliate Development Planning

c/o ABC, 1330 Ave. of the Americas, New York, NY 10019
b. August 12, 1926. Brooklyn, NY.

EDUCATION: Attended school in New York.
CAREER HIGHLIGHTS: ABC Mailroom ('43); Supervisor, Accounting Dept. ('44); Manager, TV Station Clearance ('55); Dir., TV Station Clearance ('62); moved into Affiliate Relations as Dir. ('66); V.P., Operations for Affiliate Relations ('68); V.P., Station Planning ('70); V.P., Affiliate Planning ('76); assumed responsibilities as V.P. for Special Projects ('79); appointed V.P., Affiliate Development Planning, ABC TV Network ('81).
ACHIEVEMENTS & AWARDS: N.A.
PERSONAL: Resides in Searingtown, NY, with wife, Helen; children, Helen and Thomas; two grandchildren.

GIARRAPUTO, LEONARD T.
V.P., Sales, Westinghouse Broadcasting Company, Group W Productions

c/o Group W, 90 Park Ave., New York, NY 10016
b. January 13, 1930.

EDUCATION: Columbia University.
CAREER HIGHLIGHTS: Sales Dept., Metromedia, New York ('59); Acct. Exec., WNEW-TV, New York ('61); Natl. Sales Mgr., WNEW-TV ('63); V.P., WNEW-TV ('64); General Sales Mgr., WNEW-TV ('65); Exec. V.P. and Asst. Publisher, *Playbill* magazine ('69); V.P., Dir. of Sales, Post-Newsweek Stations ('70); Exec. V.P., Post-Newsweek Stations ('73); V.P., Sales, Group W Productions, New York ('81).
ACHIEVEMENTS & AWARDS: N.A.
PERSONAL: Wife, Edna; two children.

GIBBS, MARLA
Actress

c/o "The Jeffersons," CBS, 7800 Beverly Blvd., Los Angeles, CA 90036
b. June 14, 1946. Chicago, IL.

EDUCATION: N.A.

CAREER HIGHLIGHTS: As a not-quite tamed domestic on "The Jeffersons," Gibbs wrings more laughs out of a single line than many series stars can get with entire scenes. Her TV guest spots include "Doc" and "Barney Miller." Regular on "The Jeffersons," with a brief time out to star in the short-lived "Checkin' In."

ACHIEVEMENTS & AWARDS: N.A.

PERSONAL: Resides in Los Angeles. Children, Jordan, Dorian, and Angela.

GIBSON, CHARLES
Correspondent, ABC, News

c/o ABC, 1717 DeSales St., N.W., Washington, DC 20036
b. N.A.

EDUCATION: Princeton University, B.A.

CAREER HIGHLIGHTS: Washington Prod. for RKO Network ('66); News Dir., WLVA-TV and Radio, Lynchburg, VA; Anchor and Reporter, WMAL-TV ('70); Reporter, TV News, Inc. ('74); joined ABC News ('75); White House Correspondent ('76); Congressional Correspondent ('81).

ACHIEVEMENTS & AWARDS: Two nominations for local Emmy awards, outstanding reporting, Washington, DC ('73); Natl. Journalism Fellow, Natl. Endowment for the Humanities ('73).

PERSONAL: N.A.

GIFFORD, FRANK
Commentator, ABC, Sports

c/o ABC, 1330 Ave. of the Americas, New York, NY 10019
b. August 16, 1930.

EDUCATION: University of Southern California.

CAREER HIGHLIGHTS: An All-American football star at the University of Southern California, Gifford was drafted number one by the New York Giants ('52). While still a player, he joined CBS Sports ('59); moved to ABC Sports ('71) where he became Play-by-Play Announcer, "Monday Night Football." Major contributor to the network's Olympic coverage ('72, '76, '80); appears regularly on "Superstars" and "Good Morning America."

ACHIEVEMENTS & AWARDS: Named most valuable player in NFL ('56). Emmy award ('77). Member, Pro Football Hall of Fame; Member, Boards of the Natl. Society of Multiple Sclerosis and the Special Olympics.

PERSONAL: Resides in Greenwich, CT, with wife, Astrid.

GIGANTE, PAULA M.
Regional Dir., NBC, Affiliate Relations

c/o NBC, 30 Rockefeller Plaza, New York, NY 10020
b. New York, NY.

EDUCATION: Syracuse University, B.S., Advertising and Marketing ('78); Pace University, M.B.A. ('83).

CAREER HIGHLIGHTS: Production Assoc., "NewsCenter 4," WNBC-TV, New York ('77); Prod. Asst., "Weekend," NBC News ('78); Asst. Clearance Representative, Sales Services Dept., NBC ('79); Program Clearance Representative, Sales Services Dept., NBC ('80); Sr. Research Analyst, NBC ('81); Regional Dir., Affiliate Relations, NBC ('83).

ACHIEVEMENTS & AWARDS: N.A.

PERSONAL: Resides in New York City.

GIGGANS, JIM
Reporter, KNBC-TV, Los Angeles, News

c/o KNBC, 3000 W. Alameda Ave., Burbank, CA 91523
b. Seattle, WA.

EDUCATION: University of Washington, B.A., Political Science ('64); the Sorbonne (France), La Faculte de Droit et Sciences Economics and L'Institut de Sciences Politiques, M.A., International Politics ('66).

CAREER HIGHLIGHTS: Writer, ABC News, New York ('68); Dir., ABC News ('69); Prod., ABC News, New York ('70); Correspondent, ABC News, Saigon ('70); Correspondent, ABC News, Paris ('73); Morning Anchor/Reporter, KNXT-TV, Los Angeles ('76); Reporter, KNBC-TV, Los Angeles ('81).

ACHIEVEMENTS & AWARDS: Award for outstanding Vietnam coverage from the Natl. Assn. of Media Women ('73).

PERSONAL: Resides in Pacific Palisades, CA, with wife, Patricia, and their two children.

GILBERT, JON C.
Assoc. Dir. of Labor Relations, ABC, West Coast

c/o ABC, 4151 Prospect Ave., Los Angeles, CA 90027
b. Oakland, CA.

EDUCATION: University of California at Los Angeles; Pepperdine University School of Law.
CAREER HIGHLIGHTS: Joined MCA ('71), working his way up to Managing Dir. for the Universal Amphitheater; Attorney, ABC West Coast Dept. of Labor Relations and Legal Affairs ('81); Assoc. Dir. of Labor Relations, ABC, West Coast ('83).
ACHIEVEMENTS & AWARDS: Member, California Bar Assn.
PERSONAL: Resides in Los Angeles.

GILBERT, MELISSA
Actress

c/o Writers and Artists Agency, 11726 San Vicente Blvd., Los Angeles, CA 90049
b. May 8, 1964. Los Angeles, CA.

EDUCATION: N.A.
CAREER HIGHLIGHTS: Joined "Little House on the Prairie," at the age of nine and has remained with the show ever since. During that time she has starred in such TV films as *The Miracle Worker, The Diary of Anne Frank,* and *Splendor in the Grass.*
ACHIEVEMENTS & AWARDS: N.A.
PERSONAL: Resides in San Fernando Valley, CA.

GILLESPIE, HENRY
Corporate V.P., Turner Broadcasting System, and Chairman of the Board, Turner Programming Services

c/o Turner Broadcasting System, 1050 Techwood Drive, N.W., Atlanta, GA 30318
b. December 3, 1929.

EDUCATION: New York University, B.A.; Harvard Business School.
CAREER HIGHLIGHTS: NBC Page; Southeast Sales Mgr., Atlanta, NBC Radio Recording; Southeast Sales Mgr., Screen Gems ('54); Pres., CBS and Viacom Enterprises for 21 years; Pres., Columbia Pictures TV Distribution; Pres., Gillespie Co. Los Angeles ('80); currently Corporate V.P., Turner Broadcasting System, and Chairman of the Board of Turner Programming Services.
ACHIEVEMENTS & AWARDS: Served on the Boards of Dirs. of the Natl. Assn. of Independent TV Prods. and Distributors, the Natl. Assn. of TV Programming Execs., and the TV Bureau of Advertising.
PERSONAL: N.A.

GILLMAN, BRUCE
V.P., Viacom Cable, Human Resources

P.O. Box 13, Pleasanton, CA 94566
b. December 31, 1946.

EDUCATION: Ohio State University, B.S., Industrial Management ('68).
CAREER HIGHLIGHTS: Various industrial relations positions, Goodyear Tire and Rubber Co. ('68–'75); Dir. of Industrial Relations, Arcata Natl. Corp. ('76); Labor Relations Consultant, Modern Management Methods ('78); Dir. of Industrial Relations, Viacom Cable; promoted to V.P. of Human Resources ('82).
ACHIEVEMENTS & AWARDS: N.A.
PERSONAL: Wife, Kimberly; children, Leslie and Brad.

GILMOUR, SANDY
Correspondent, NBC, News

c/o NBC, Quian Men Hotel, Rms. 805–807, Peking, China
b. Montclair, NJ.

EDUCATION: University of Utah; Downing College, Cambridge (England).
CAREER HIGHLIGHTS: Reporter, KALL-AM, Salt Lake City ('65); Reporter, AP, Louisville, KY ('66); Reporter/Documentary Prod., KCPX-TV, Salt Lake City ('68); Reporter, KMOX-TV, St. Louis ('73); Reporter, KUTU-TV, Salt Lake City ('75); Correspondent, NBC News, Houston ('79); Correspondent, NBC News, Peking ('81).
ACHIEVEMENTS & AWARDS: N.A.
PERSONAL: Wife, Karen.

GIRARD, STEPHEN
Sr. V.P., Creative Affairs, Columbia Pictures TV

c/o Columbia Pictures TV, Columbia Plaza, Burbank, CA 91505
b. August 10, 1938.

EDUCATION: University of North Carolina, B.A. ('60).
CAREER HIGHLIGHTS: Partner, Gerard/Flaherty Agency; V.P., Programming Dept., Columbia Pictures TV ('80); V.P., Creative Affairs ('81); Sr. V.P., Creative Affairs, Columbia Pictures TV ('82).
ACHIEVEMENTS & AWARDS: N.A.
PERSONAL: Resides in Los Angeles with wife, Marcia, and daughters, Nicole and Cassidy.

GIRVAN, GARRETT J.
Chief Financial Officer, Viacom Cable

c/o Viacom Cable, P.O. Box 13, Pleasanton, CA 94566
b. July 22, 1945. Darby, PA.

EDUCATION: La Salle College, B.S. ('67); New York University, M.B.A. ('77).
CAREER HIGHLIGHTS: Captain, U.S. Marine Corps ('68); Audit Mgr., Price Waterhouse ('71); Audit Mgr., Asst. Controller, Dir. of Planning, Shaklee Corp. ('78); Chief Financial Officer, Viacom Cable ('82).
ACHIEVEMENTS & AWARDS: CPA ('73).
PERSONAL: Wife, Paula; children, Monica, Carey, and Garrett M. Resides in Danville, CA.

GISH, C. EDWIN
V.P., On-Air Promotion, CBS, Entertainment

c/o CBS, 6121 Sunset Blvd., Los Angeles, CA 90028
b. April 12. Twin Falls, ID.

EDUCATION: N.A.
CAREER HIGHLIGHTS: V.P. and Creative Dir., Gish-Sprague & Assoc. advertising agency; Exec. Prod., Allied Cinema Talents; Promotion Mgr., Motion Pictures Made for TV and Mini-Series, CBS Entertainment ('78); Dir., On-Air Promotion, CBS ('80); V.P., On-Air Promotion, CBS Entertainment, Los Angeles ('82).
ACHIEVEMENTS & AWARDS: N.A.
PERSONAL: N.A.

GITTER, RICHARD P.
V.P., NBC, Broadcast Standards, East Coast

240 E. 76th St., New York, NY 10021
b. March 2, 1942. Brooklyn, NY.

EDUCATION: New York University, B.A. ('63); New York University School of Law, J.D. ('66).
CAREER HIGHLIGHTS: UA Staff Attorney ('68); moved to ABC in same capacity ('69); Legal Counsel, WNET ('71); Dir., Broadcast Standards, ABC ('73); promoted to V.P. ('76);

moved to NBC as V.P., Broadcast Standards, East Coast ('80).

ACHIEVEMENTS & AWARDS: New York State Moot Court Justices Assn. ('74); Member, NAB Radio Code Review Board ('77); named in *Who's Who in American Law* ('79); Member, NATAS, IRTS.

PERSONAL: Resides in Manhattan.

GLASER, ROBERT L.
Pres., Viacom Enterprises

1211 Ave. of the Americas, New York, NY 10036
b. January 9, 1929. Chicago, IL.

EDUCATION: University of Miami, B.A., History ('50).

CAREER HIGHLIGHTS: Acct. Exec., ABC Films ('59); Acct. Exec., CBS Films ('60); Acct. Exec., Metro TV Sales ('61); Midwest Daytime Sales Mgr., ABC TV ('64); Midwest Sales Mgr., RKO-TV Representative ('66); General Sales Mgr., WOR-TV, New York ('68); V.P. and General Mgr., WOR-TV ('70); Pres., RKO-TV ('72); Pres., Viacom Enterprises ('82).

ACHIEVEMENTS & AWARDS: Governor's award, New York ATAS ('72); Dir., United Cerebral Palsy ('75–'82); Treasurer, Independent TV Assn.

PERSONAL: Resides in Connecticut with wife, Nancy; three sons, Robert, Geoffrey and Douglas.

GLASS, CHARLES
Correspondent, ABC, News

c/o ABC, P.O. Box 1135168, Gefinor Ctr. 1602, Block B, Beirut, Lebanon
b. Los Angeles, CA.

EDUCATION: University of Southern California, B.A., Philosophy ('72).

CAREER HIGHLIGHTS: Freelance Reporter, ABC Radio, *Time* magazine, *Christian Science Monitor, Chicago Daily News, London Guardian,* based in Beirut ('72); Freelance journalist, London ('77); Assoc. Prod., "Weekend World," London ('78); Editor, *Near East Business,* London ('79); Correspondent, *Newsweek* magazine, London ('81); Correspondent, ABC News, Beirut ('83).

ACHIEVEMENTS & AWARDS: Overseas Press Club award ('76).

PERSONAL: N.A.

GLASS, RON
Actor

c/o 1800 Ave. of the Stars, Suite 660, Los Angeles, CA 90067
b. July 10, 1945. Evansville, IN.

EDUCATION: University of Evansville.

CAREER HIGHLIGHTS: Guest appearances on "The Streets of San Francisco," "Maude," "Sanford and Son," "Hawaii Five-O," "Good Times," and "All in the Family." TV movies include *Switch, Beg, Borrow or Steal,* and *Shirts/Skins.* A series regular on "Barney Miller" ('75–'82) and "The New Odd Couple" ('82).

ACHIEVEMENTS & AWARDS: N.A.
PERSONAL: N.A.

GLEASON, JACKIE
Actor

c/o Marks, Gould & Cohen, 411 Hackensack Ave., Hackensack, NJ 07601
b. February 16, 1916. Brooklyn, NY.

EDUCATION: N.A.

CAREER HIGHLIGHTS: Starred in the TV series "The Life of Riley," "The Jackie Gleason Variety Show," "The Honeymooners" ('55), and the revived hour-long show of "The Honeymooners'' (late '60's). Motion pictures include *Skidoo, Papa's Delicate Condition, Gigot, Smokey and the Bandit, The Sting II, The Toy,* and *The Hustler.* Starred in the HBO special *Mr. Halpern and Mr. Johnson.*

ACHIEVEMENTS & AWARDS: Tony award for *Take Me Along.*
PERSONAL: N.A.

GLEASON, MICHAEL
Writer/Exec. Prod.

c/o Lou Pitt, ICM, 8899 Beverly Blvd., Los Angeles, CA 90048
b. January 14, 1938. Brooklyn, NY.

EDUCATION: American Academy of Dramatic Arts.
CAREER HIGHLIGHTS: Followed the accepted route from writer to producer, working on all sorts of shows, including comedy, westerns, medical series, and adventure shows. Writer of many hit shows including ''Maverick'' ('60), ''Laramie,'' ''Rawhide'' ('61), ''My Favorite Martian,'' ''Mr. Novak'' ('63), ''Peyton Place'' ('65–'69), ''Marcus Welby, M.D.'' ('71). Writer/Prod., ''McCloud,'' ''Six Million Dollar Man'' ('73); Writer/Exec. Prod., *Rich Man, Poor Man* ('76); Writer/Exec. Prod./Co-Creator, ''Remington Steele'' ('82).
ACHIEVEMENTS & AWARDS: Two Emmy nominations; two Writers Guild nominations.
PERSONAL: Married to actress Lynne Randall; son, William; daughters, Carol, Courtney, Julie, Jackie, Jessica, and Jennifer. Resides in Encino, CA.

GLENN, CHRISTOPHER
Co-Anchor, CBS ''Nightwatch,'' CBS

c/o CBS, 51 W. 52d St., New York, NY 10019
b. New York.

EDUCATION: University of Colorado, B.A. ('59).
CAREER HIGHLIGHTS: Newsman for Armed Forces Broadcasting, Korea and New York ('60–'61); Radio Press Intl., New York ('61); WICC-Radio in Bridgeport, CT ('63–'64); Managing Editor, Metromedia News Network, Washington, DC ('70–'71); Reporter/Editor, Documentary Prod., WNEW-Radio,

New York ('64–'70); Prod., radio special events broadcasts; Narrator ''In the News,'' CBS ('71); named Reporter ('72); CBS News Correspondent ('76); Co-Editor, ''30 Minutes'' ('78); Co-Anchor, CBS ''Nightwatch'' ('82).
ACHIEVEMENTS & AWARDS: N.A.
PERSONAL: N.A.

GLICKSMAN, FRANK
Exec. Prod.

c/o 20th Century Fox, 10201 W. Pico, Los Angeles, CA 90067
b. New York, NY.

EDUCATION: University of California at Los Angeles.
CAREER HIGHLIGHTS: Producer who found his niche in the medical profession, TV style. First big hit was ''Medical Center,'' followed by ''Trapper John, M.D.'' Started in Mailroom, MGM Studios ('47); Studio Publicist, then Story Analyst ('51); Story Editor, ''Climax'' ('54); West Coast Story Editor, CBS. Moved to 20th Century Fox as Story Editor ('59); Prod. ''12 O'Clock High'' ('64) and ''The Long, Hot Summer'' ('65); returned to MGM to produce ''Medical Center'' ('68); ''Trapper John, M.D.'' ('79); collaborated with James Fitzhand to sell the novel, *The Unicorn Affair* ('80).
ACHIEVEMENTS & AWARDS: N.A.
PERSONAL: Resides in Beverly Hills, CA, with family.

GLIEBER, FRANK
Broadcaster, CBS, Sports

c/o CBS, 51 W. 52d St., New York, NY 10019
b. Milwaukee, WI.

EDUCATION: Northwestern University, B.S., Radio/TV.
CAREER HIGHLIGHTS: Sports Announcer, WRR-AM, Dallas ('56); Sports Broadcaster, KRLD-TV, Dallas, now KDFW-TV ('59); joined CBS Sports to do play-by-play for the NFL telecasts ('63); Sports Dir., WJW-TV, Cleveland ('66); added responsibilities with CBS Sports

broadcasting golf tournaments ('67); returned to KRLD, Dallas ('68), continuing with CBS Sports.

ACHIEVEMENTS & AWARDS: Chosen Texas Sportscaster of the Year by the Natl. Sportwriters and Sportscasters Assn.

PERSONAL: Resides in Dallas with wife, Kathy; children, Lynn, John, Robin Kay, Frank Craig, and Mitchell.

GLUCKSMAN, MARGIE
Dir., Talent and Casting, CBS, Entertainment, West Coast

c/o CBS, 6121 Sunset Blvd., Los Angeles, CA 90028
b. Omaha, NE.

EDUCATION: Brooklyn College.

CAREER HIGHLIGHTS: Worked as a Theatrical Agent for many years in New York City, including work with the William Morris Agency. Dir., Talent and Casting, CBS Entertainment, New York ('78); Dir., Talent and Casting, CBS Entertainment, West Coast ('79).

ACHIEVEMENTS & AWARDS: N.A.
PERSONAL: Resides in Los Angeles.

GOLDBERG, BERNARD
Correspondent, CBS, News

c/o CBS, 1800 Century Blvd., N.E., Atlanta, GA 30345
b. New York, NY.

EDUCATION: Rutgers University, B.A.

CAREER HIGHLIGHTS: Joined CBS News as Prod. based in Atlanta ('72); Reporter, CBS News ('74); Correspondent, CBS News, San Francisco ('76); Correspondent, CBS News, New York ('81); Correspondent, CBS News, Atlanta ('82).

ACHIEVEMENTS & AWARDS: N.A.
PERSONAL: N.A.

GOLDBERG, GARY D.
Prod./Writer, Paramount Studios, TV

c/o Paramount Studios, 5451 Marathon Blvd., Hollywood, CA 90038
b. June 25, 1944. Brooklyn, NY.

EDUCATION: Brandeis University; San Diego State University.

CAREER HIGHLIGHTS: Writer, "The Bob Newhart Show" ('76); Writer/Story Editor, "The Tony Randall Show" ('76); Writer/Co-Prod., "The Tony Randall Show" ('77); Writer/Co-Prod., "Lou Grant" ('78); Writer/Story Editor, "M*A*S*H" ('78); Creator/Prod., "Last Resort" ('80); Creator/Exec. Prod., "Making the Grade" ('82); Creator/Exec. Prod., "Family Ties" ('82).

ACHIEVEMENTS & AWARDS: Writers Guild Award for best episodic comedy, "M*A*S*H" episode, "Baby It's Cold Outside" ('78); Emmy award, best drama series, "Lou Grant" ('79); Humanitas and Peabody awards for "Lou Grant" ('79).

PERSONAL: Wife, Diana; daughter, Shana.

GOLDBERG, JEAN V.
Dir., Marketing Research, MGM-UA, TV Distribution

c/o MGM-UA, 1350 Ave. of the Americas, New York, NY 10019
b. Wappingers Falls, NY.

EDUCATION: University of Wisconsin at Oshkosh.

CAREER HIGHLIGHTS: Media Analyst, A.C. Nielsen Co. ('64); Sr. Analyst, Papert, Koenig & Lois ('66); TV Research Mgr., Avco Radio-TV Sales ('67); Sr. Research Analyst, Ted Bates Advertising Agency ('71); Group Research Mgr. Petry TV Sales ('72); Mgr., Research and Development, Viacom Enterprises ('74); Dir., Research and Development, Viacom Enterprises ('76); Dir., Marketing Research, MGM-UA TV Distribution ('80).

ACHIEVEMENTS & AWARDS: Member, American Women in Radio and TV; NATAS, Radio-TV Research Council.

PERSONAL: Resides in New York City.

GOLDBERG, LEONARD
Prod., Leonard Goldberg Co.

c/o MGM Thalberg Bldg., Room 255, Culver City, CA 90230
b. January 24, 1934. New York, NY.

EDUCATION: Wharton School of Business, B.S., Economics; University of Pennsylvania.

CAREER HIGHLIGHTS: NBC Supervisor of Special Projects ('57); Head, Daytime TV Programming, BBD&O. ('61); Mgr., Program Development, ABC ('63); Dir., Program Development ('64); V.P., Daytime Programming, ABC ('65); V.P., Network TV Programming, created the form of weekly, original movies for TV ('66); Head, Production, Screen Gems ('69). Formed Spelling/Goldberg Productions ('72); produced many TV series hits, among them "Starsky and Hutch," "Charlie's Angels," "Family," "Hart to Hart," "Fantasy Island"; formed the Leonard Goldberg Co./Mandy Films ('82).

ACHIEVEMENTS & AWARDS: Peabody award for *Brian's Song*; NAACP image award; the Film Advisory Board's award of excellence; Braille Institute first annual award for distinguished contribution to public understanding of blindness; Critics Circle award; three Humanitas awards. Member, 1984 Olympics Committee, Hollywood ATAS; Hollywood Radio and TV Society.

PERSONAL: Resides in Beverly Hills, CA, with wife, Wendy, and daughter, Amanda.

GOLDBERG, RALPH E.
V.P. and Asst. to Pres., CBS, News

c/o CBS, 524 W. 57th St., New York, NY 10019
b. May 18.

EDUCATION: University of Michigan, B.A.; Columbia University Law School.

CAREER HIGHLIGHTS: Regarded as one of the commercial network's top lawyers in many aspects of communications law. Attorney, CBS ('61); Asst. General Attorney, CBS ('69); General Attorney ('70); Assoc. General Counsel, CBS Broadcast Group ('77); V.P. and Asst. to Pres., CBS News, ('82).

ACHIEVEMENTS & AWARDS: N.A.

PERSONAL: N.A.

GOLDEN, JEROME B.
V.P. and Secretary, ABC

c/o ABC, 1330 Ave. of the Americas, New York, NY 10019
b. N.A.

EDUCATION: City College of New York.

CAREER HIGHLIGHTS: Law clerk, Paramount Pictures ('39); Attorney, United Paramount Theatres, and later ABC. Has served as Secretary of ABC ('58–present) and V.P. of ABC ('59–present).

ACHIEVEMENTS & AWARDS: N.A.

PERSONAL: Resides in New York City; two sons.

GOLDEN, STAN
V.P. Intl. Syndication, Alan Landsburg Productions

11811 W. Olympic Blvd., Los Angeles, CA 90064
b. October 30, 1953. Boston, MA.

EDUCATION: University of Denver, B.S. and B.A., Finance.

CAREER HIGHLIGHTS: V.P., Intl. Syndication, Alan Landsburg Productions ('77)

ACHIEVEMENTS & AWARDS: N.A.

PERSONAL: N.A.

GOLDEN-GOTTLIEB, PHYLLIS
Dir., Comedy Development, Walt Disney Productions

c/o Walt Disney Productions, 500 S. Buena Vista St., Burbank, CA 91521
b. Sharon, MA.

EDUCATION: University of Massachusetts.

CAREER HIGHLIGHTS: Appeared regularly on "A.M. Los Angeles" ('76); Prod. of Specials and Documentaries, KTTV-TV, Los Angeles ('77); Production Exec., "The Facts of Life" ('79); Production Exec., MGM TV ('81); Dir., Comedy Development, Walt Disney Productions ('82).

ACHIEVEMENTS & AWARDS: N.A.

PERSONAL: Resides in Sherman Oaks, CA; daughter, Cathy; son, Jimmy.

GOLDENSON, LEONARD H.
Chairman of the Board and Chief Exec. Officer, ABC, Inc.

c/o ABC, 1330 Ave. of the Americas, New York, NY 10019
b. December 7, 1905. Scottsdale, PA.

EDUCATION: Harvard College, LL.D.; Harvard Law School.

CAREER HIGHLIGHTS: One of the key executives in the history of commercial network TV, Goldenson played a pivotal role in guiding ABC to a highly competitive position with CBS and NBC. Under his guidance, ABC has been the most adventurous of the three networks, moving into the new areas of telecommunications including cable and pay-per-view services. And Goldenson can share credit for ABC's having more total revenue in 1982 than any other communications company. He joined Paramount Pictures ('33); assumed full responsibility for Paramount Pictures' 1,700 motion picture theaters ('38); V.P., Paramount Pictures, Inc.; named Dir. ('42); Pres. and Chief Exec. Officer, and Dir. of United Paramount Theaters ('50); American Broadcasting–Paramount Theaters formed with Goldenson as Pres. ('53); parent company's name changed to ABC, Inc., Goldenson named Chairman of the Board and Chief Exec. Officer ('65).

ACHIEVEMENTS & AWARDS: Active in humanitarian and civic endeavors. Co-Founder of United Cerebral Palsy Assn. ('50). Trustee, Children's Cancer Research Foundation; Dir., Daughters of Jacob Geriatric Center. Pres. medal, B'nai B'rith; IRTS gold medal ('64); gold medal of achievement, Poor Richard's Club of Philadelphia; distinguished service award, NEB ('65).

PERSONAL: Married to the former Isabelle Weinstein. Resides in Mamaroneck, NY; two daughters, Loreen Arbus, who is married to Norman Fox, and Maxine.

GOLDIN, MARION
Sr. Prod., Program Development and Sr. Prod. and Asst. to the Exec. Prod., ABC News, "20/20"

c/o ABC, 7 W. 66th St., New York, NY 10023
b. N.A.

EDUCATION: Barnard College, B.A., Government and Political Science; Harvard University, M.A., History.

CAREER HIGHLIGHTS: Assoc. Prod., CBS News ('64); Segment Producer, CBS News "60 Minutes" ('72); Sr. Prod., Program Development and Sr. Prod. and Asst. to the Exec. Prod., ABC News "20/20" ('82).

ACHIEVEMENTS & AWARDS: N.A.

PERSONAL: Married, resides in suburban Maryland, but divides time between Washington, DC and New York City.

GOLDMAN, ROBERT T.
V.P., ABC, Administration

c/o ABC, 1330 Ave. of the Americas, New York, NY 10019
b. New York, NY.

EDUCATION: Brooklyn College, B.A.; Harvard Graduate School of Business Administration, M.B.A.

CAREER HIGHLIGHTS: Joined the ABC Management Training Program ('58); Treasurer, ABC TV Spot Sales Division ('61); Asst. to the Pres., ABC Owned TV Stations ('62); General Mgr., ABC News ('65); V.P., ABC News ('66); V.P., Planning and Analysis, ABC, Inc. ('69); V.P., Finance, ABC ('70); V.P., Administration, ABC, Inc. ('73).

ACHIEVEMENTS & AWARDS: N.A.

PERSONAL: Resides in New York City with his wife, Judith; three children.

GOLDSHOLL, BOB
Sports Reporter, Independent Network News, Weekend Reports

c/o Independent Network News, 11 WPIX Plaza, New York, NY 10017
b. N.A.

EDUCATION: New York University, Journalism.
CAREER HIGHLIGHTS: Played two seasons minor league baseball in New York Giants organization ('50s). Color Commentator/Interviewer, New Jersey Nets. Handled sports events for ESPN. Sports Reporter, Independent Network News, Weekend Reports.
ACHIEVEMENTS & AWARDS: N.A.
PERSONAL: N.A.

GOLDSTEIN, CHARLES A.
V.P., NBC TV, Film Production

19463 Hatton Street, Reseda, CA 91335
b. February 23, 1946. Los Angeles, CA.

EDUCATION: Los Angeles Valley College and University of California at Los Angeles, Communications and Film.
CAREER HIGHLIGHTS: Joined ABC TV as Film Editor ('65); Supervisor, Production/Post-Production, ABC TV, On-Air Advertising ('67); Paramount Pictures Asst. Post-Production Supervisor ('71); Dir. of Editorial Operations, Universal Pictures ('73); V.P., Post-Production, Columbia Pictures TV ('76); joined NBC TV as V.P. Film Production ('81).
ACHIEVEMENTS & AWARDS: Member, 776 ('65); Member, ACE ('80)
PERSONAL: Wife, Sharon; children, Lisa and Jimmy.

GOLDSTEIN, MORTON N.
Dir., ABC, Production, Tape Shows, West Coast

4151 Prospect Avenue, Hollywood, CA 90027
b. September 18, 1933. Chicago, IL.

EDUCATION: University of Illinois, B.A., Journalism/TV Production.
CAREER HIGHLIGHTS: Dir. of University of Illinois TV station ('54); Dir., Medical TV Shows at Walter Reed Medical Center while in U.S.

Army ('55–'57); Asst. Dir., TV Dept., Myerhoff Ad Agency ('57); Production Dept., CBS TV ('58); moved to ABC TV as Hollywood Unit Mgr. ('67); appointed Dir., Production, Tape Shows, West Coast. Also, Assoc. Professor, California State University, TV Production and Direction.
ACHIEVEMENTS & AWARDS: N.A.
PERSONAL: Resides in Sepulveda, CA.

GOMEZ, CHARLES
Correspondent, CBS, News

c/o CBS, 45 N.W. Third St., Miami, FL 33128
b. Miami, FL.

EDUCATION: University of Miami, B.A., Communications; Columbia University Graduate School of Journalism, M.A.
CAREER HIGHLIGHTS: Reporter, *Miami Herald* ('71); Reporter, *N.Y. Post* ('74); Reporter/Weekend Anchor, WPLG-TV, Miami ('75); Reporter, WBBM-TV, Chicago ('76); Reporter, CBS News, Washington, DC ('79); Correspondent, CBS News, Miami ('81).
ACHIEVEMENTS & AWARDS: Ernesto Lecuona award for reporting while at WPLG-TV ('75); Sigma Delta Chi award for news writing under deadline pressure.
PERSONAL: N.A.

GOODCHILD, PETER
Head of Science Features Dept., TV, BBC

c/o BBC, 12 Cavendish Place, London, England W1
b. N.A.

EDUCATION: University of Oxford (England).
CAREER HIGHLIGHTS: BBC Trainee ('63); Dir., "The Science of Man" ('65); Editor, "Horizon" ('69); Editor, Special Features, BBC ('78); Head of Science Features Dept., TV, BBC ('80).
ACHIEVEMENTS & AWARDS: "Horizon" series won the Society of Film and TV Arts award, the TV Guild award, and the Mullard award.
PERSONAL: Resides in Berkshire, England, with his wife and their two daughters.

GOODMAN, MARK
Video Jockey, Warner Amex Satellite Entertainment Co., MTV: Music Television

c/o MTV, Warner Amex, 1211 Ave. of the Americas, New York, NY 10036
b. N.A.

EDUCATION: N.A.
CAREER HIGHLIGHTS: Disc Jockey, WMMR-FM, Philadelphia ('77); Disc Jockey, WPLJ-FM, New York ('79); Video Jockey, MTV: Music Television ('81).
ACHIEVEMENTS & AWARDS: N.A.
PERSONAL: Resides in New York City.

GOODMAN, MAURICE
V.P., NBC, Broadcast Standards, West Coast

c/o NBC, 3000 W. Alameda Ave., Burbank, CA 91523
b. October 23, 1928. Phoenix, AZ.

EDUCATION: Carroll College.
CAREER HIGHLIGHTS: Joined NBC, Broadcast Standards, West Coast ('63); left network to become Authors' Rep., Dick Hyland Agency ('65); Freelance Writer ('66); returned to NBC as V.P., Broadcast Standards, West Coast ('72).
ACHIEVEMENTS & AWARDS: Member, Writers Guild West, Los Angeles Press Club, Mystery Writers of America, Elks Club, Beta Pi Epsilon, and Pi Kappa Delta.
PERSONAL: Wife, Yvonne; daughter, Danielle Nicolle.

GOODMAN, WALTER
Book Reviewer and Media Writer, *N.Y. Times*

c/o *N.Y. Times*, 229 W. 43d St., New York, NY 10036
b. August 22, 1927. New York, NY.

EDUCATION: Reading University (England), M.A.
CAREER HIGHLIGHTS: Author of several hundred articles for numerous magazines, in addition to many books. His first assignment with the *N.Y. Times* was as Editor, Arts and Leisure, and Deputy Editor, *N.Y. Times Magazine*. He also served on the Editorial Board ('74); moved to WNET-TV, New York as Exec.

Editor and Dir. of Humanities Programming ('79); named Sr. Writer, for *Newsweek* magazine ('82); rejoined the *N.Y. Times* as TV and Media Critic ('82). Currently, Book Reviewer and Media Writer.
ACHIEVEMENTS & AWARDS: Author, *A Percentage of the Take, The Committee, All Honorable Men*, and *The Clowns of Commerce*.
PERSONAL: Married, two sons.

GOODSON, MARK
Prod.

c/o Goodson-Todman Productions, 375 Park Ave., New York, NY 10152
b. January 24, 1915. Sacramento, CA.

EDUCATION: University of California at Berkeley, B.A.
CAREER HIGHLIGHTS: A leading developer of quiz and game shows since TV's inception. Known primarily for game shows, he is rightfully considered the dean of TV's game show producers. Originated first game show, "Pop the Question," at KFRC, San Francisco ('39); created first network show for ABC, "Appointment With Life" ('43); wrote and directed drama episodes, "Kate Smith Variety With Life" ('43); wrote and directed drama episodes, "Kate Smith Variety Hour" ('43). Goodson-Todman partnership began with the sale of "Winner Takes All" for CBS Radio ('46); they created "What's My Line," "I've Got a Secret," "The Price Is Right," "Match Game," and "Family Feud."
ACHIEVEMENTS & AWARDS: Natl. TV award of Great Britain; three Emmy awards; Sylvania award. Present Member and former Pres., New York Chapter, ATAS; Dir., New York City Center of Music and Drama; Board of Dirs., American Film Institute.
PERSONAL: N.A.

GORDON, BARRY
V.P., Business Affairs, ABC, West Coast

c/o ABC, 4151 Prospect Ave., Los Angeles, CA 90027
b. N.A.

EDUCATION: University of California at Los Angeles (summa cum laude); University of California at Berkeley School of Law.
CAREER HIGHLIGHTS: Legal Staff, Capitol Records, Los Angeles; Legal Staff, Paramount Pictures Corp.; joined CBS, Los Angeles, as an Attorney, and eventually promoted to Negotiator for CBS TV; V.P., Business Affairs, Filmways TV Productions ('68); Dir. of Negotiations/Business Affairs, Capitol Records ('70); Dir., Business Affairs, ABC West Coast ('71); V.P., Business Affairs, ABC West Coast ('81).
ACHIEVEMENTS & AWARDS: N.A.
PERSONAL: Resides in South Pasadena, CA.

GORDON, CHRIS
Co-Anchor, WJLA-TV, Washington, DC, News

c/o WJLA-TV, 4461 Connecticut Ave., N.W., Washington, DC 20008
b. Utica, NY.

EDUCATION: University of Rochester; Cornell University Law School.
CAREER HIGHLIGHTS: Reporter, WTOP-AM, Washington, DC ('75); Reporter, WSFB-TV, Hartford ('76); Reporter, WDVM-TV, Washington, DC ('77); Co-Anchor, "News 7 at Noon," WJLA-TV, Washington, DC ('80).
ACHIEVEMENTS & AWARDS: N.A.
PERSONAL: N.A.

GORDON, DAVID
Sr. V.P., United Satellite Communications, Marketing and Sales

c/o United Satellite Communications, 1345 Ave. of the Americas, New York, NY 10105
b. 1939.

EDUCATION: Wesleyan University, B.A.; Columbia University, M.B.A.
CAREER HIGHLIGHTS: Marketing Dir., Alberto Culver; General Mgr., Chicago Subscription TV; V.P., Oak Communications; Sr. V.P., Marketing and Sales, United Satellite Communications, New York.
ACHIEVEMENTS & AWARDS: N.A.
PERSONAL: N.A.

GORDON, JANE
Editor, *View* Magazine

c/o *View* Magazine, 150 E. 58th St., New York, NY 10155
b. N.A.

EDUCATION: Emerson College, B.S., Mass Communications ('76); Brooklyn Law School, J.D. ('85).
CAREER HIGHLIGHTS: Marketing Assoc., Sanyo Electric ('77); Editor, Fairchild Publications ('78); Managing Editor, *View* magazine ('80); Exec. Editor, *View* ('82); Editor, *View* ('83).
ACHIEVEMENTS & AWARDS: N.A.
PERSONAL: N.A.

GORMAN, KENNETH F.
Pres., Viacom Entertainment Group

10900 Wilshire Blvd., Los Angeles, CA 90024
b. N.A.

EDUCATION: N.A.
CAREER HIGHLIGHTS: With Viacom since its inception ('71). Moved up the ladder from Dir. of Financial Planning to Asst. Controller, Controller, and Sr. V.P. ('79). His career began with the Equitable Life Assurance Society of America as a Contract Specialist, Annuities and Pension. He moved to NBC as a Financial Analyst ('61); then joined CBS as Dir. of Analysis ('64). When Viacom became a separate entity, Gorman became Dir. of Financial Planning. Currently Pres., Viacom Entertainment Group.
ACHIEVEMENTS & AWARDS: N.A.
PERSONAL: Wife, Patricia; children, Kathleen and Michael. Resides in Manhasset, NY.

GOSSETT, LOUIS, JR.
Actor

c/o William Morris Agency, 151 El Camino Dr., Beverly Hills, CA 90212
b. May 27. Brooklyn, NY.

EDUCATION: New York University.
CAREER HIGHLIGHTS: Series appearances in "The Defenders," "East Side, West Side," and "The Nurses." Major motion pictures include *Skin Game*, *The Choirboys*, *The Deep*, and *An Officer and a Gentleman*. TV movies and miniseries include *Roots*, *Don't Look Back*, and *Benny's Place*, and *Sadat*. Was the TV series star of "The Powers of Matthew Star."
ACHIEVEMENTS & AWARDS: Academy Award as best supporting actor for *An Officer and a Gentleman*.
PERSONAL: N.A.

GOTTLIEB, JEROME
Exec. V.P., MGM-UA TV

c/o MGM-UA TV, 10202 W. Washington Blvd., Culver City, CA 90230
b. September 4, 1942. Brooklyn, NY.

EDUCATION: Hamilton College, B.A. ('64); New York University Law School, J.D.
CAREER HIGHLIGHTS: Attorney for Screen Gems ('71); Dir., Business Affairs, Columbia Pictures TV ('74); joined Business Affairs Dept., William Morris Agency ('76); V.P., Business Affairs, Viacom Intl. ('78); V.P., Business Affairs, Universal TV ('80); appointed Exec. V.P., MGM-UA TV ('82).
ACHIEVEMENTS & AWARDS: N.A.
PERSONAL: Married to Deborah Capogrosso; children, Benjamin and Jonathan.

GOULD, CHERYL
Sr. Prod., NBC News, "NBC News Overnight"

c/o NBC, 30 Rockefeller Plaza, New York, NY 10020
b. N.A.

EDUCATION: Princeton University; the Sorbonne (France).
CAREER HIGHLIGHTS: Reporter, WOKR-TV, Rochester, NY ('76); Field Prod./Radio Reporter, NBC News, Paris ('77); Assoc. Prod., "NBC Nightly News" ('81); Prod., "NBC News Overnight" ('82); Sr. Prod., "NBC News Overnight." ('83).
ACHIEVEMENTS & AWARDS: N.A.
PERSONAL: N.A.

GOWDY, CURT
Host, ABC TV Network, "The American Sportsman"

c/o ABC, 1330 Ave. of the Americas, New York, NY 10019
b. 1919.

EDUCATION: University of Wyoming.
CAREER HIGHLIGHTS: A former star athlete at the University of Wyoming, he is noted for his colorful, authoritative sports commentary on TV and radio. He started his sports broadcasting career in Cheyenne, WY, and has handled play-by-play on seven Super Bowls, 14 World Series, and 12 Rose Bowls, as well as baseball's All-Star Game, college and pro football games, college and pro basketball games, and the East-West grid game. Host of "The American Sportsman" for all of its 18 seasons.
ACHIEVEMENTS & AWARDS: Two Emmy awards

for outstanding edited sports series, "The American Sportsman" ('80–'81; '78–'79); Hall of Fame of the Natl. Sportscasters and Sportswriters Assn. ('81); Peabody award for television entertainment ('70). Gowdy's native state of Wyoming has named a state park in his honor, Curt Gowdy State Park.

PERSONAL: Wife, Jerre; three children, Cheryl, Curt Jr., and Trevor. Resides in Wellesley Hills, MA.

GRAD, PETER
Sr. V.P., Development, 20th Century Fox, TV

P.O. Box 900, Beverly Hills, CA 90213
b. March 22, 1940. New Jersey.

EDUCATION: University of Pennsylvania, B.S., Economics.
CAREER HIGHLIGHTS: Dir. of Development, Paramount TV ('77); V.P., Development, Columbia Pictures TV ('79); Sr. V.P., Development, 20th Century Fox ('80).
ACHIEVEMENTS & AWARDS: N.A.
PERSONAL: Wife, Laurie; son, Nicholas.

GRADE, MICHAEL
Pres., Embassy TV

c/o 100 Universal City Plaza, Bldg. 426, Universal City, CA 91608
b. March 8, 1943. London, England.

EDUCATION: St. Dunstan's College (England).
CAREER HIGHLIGHTS: Sports Journalist, *London Daily Mirror* ('60–'66); formed London Management ('68); Creative Head of Entertainment, London Weekend TV ('73); Dir., Programming, London Weekend TV ('77); Pres., Embassy TV ('82).
ACHIEVEMENTS & AWARDS: Emmy awards for "Upstairs Downstairs." Member, Royal TV Society, held position on Council of British Academy of Film and TV.
PERSONAL: Son of Sir Lew Grade, long-time top impresario in the British entertainment industry.

GRADINGER, EDWARD BARRY
Chief Operating Officer, 20th Century Fox, TV

c/o 20th Century Fox TV, P.O. Box 900, Beverly Hills, CA 90213
b. June 1, 1940. Brooklyn, NY.

EDUCATION: New York University, B.A.; Brooklyn Law School, LL.B.
CAREER HIGHLIGHTS: Dir., Business Affairs, ABC ('71); V.P., East Coast Operations, Columbia Pictures TV ('74); Sr. V.P., Business Affairs, ABC ('75); Chief Operating Officer, 20th Century Fox TV and Group Exec. V.P., Columbia Pictures TV ('80).
ACHIEVEMENTS & AWARDS: N.A.
PERSONAL: Wife, Daryl; daughter, Jackie; son, Gary.

GRAHAM, FRED
Law Correspondent, CBS, News

c/o CBS, 524 W. 57th St., New York, NY 10019
b. Little Rock, AR.

EDUCATION: Vanderbilt Law School LL.B. ('59); Oxford University, Diploma in Law ('60)
CAREER HIGHLIGHTS: Reporter, *Nashville Tennessean* ('56); Press Secretary to Mayor Edmund Orgill of Memphis ('58); practiced law in Nashville ('60); Chief Counsel, Senate Judiciary Subcommittee on Constitutional Amendments ('63); Special Asst. to Secretary of Labor W. Willard Wirtz ('63); Supreme Court Correspondent, *N.Y. Times* ('65); CBS News Law Correspondent ('72).
ACHIEVEMENTS & AWARDS: Three Emmy awards ('73); Peabody award. Author of *The Self-Inflicted Wound, Press Freedom Under Pressure, The Alias Program.*
PERSONAL: N.A.

GRALNICK, JEFF
Exec. Prod. of Political Broadcasts

c/o ABC, 7 West 66th St., New York, NY 10023
b. April 3, 1939. New York, NY.

EDUCATION: New York University, B.S., Marketing ('69).
CAREER HIGHLIGHTS: News career began with CBS News, serving in various field productions and reporting capacities, including Vietnam ('69–'70); joined ABC News as Field Prod. ('71); covered Sadat visit to Israel in capacity of Exec. Prod., Special Events, ABC ('78); given additional title of V.P. ('79); named V.P. and Exec. Prod., "World News Tonight" ('79); Exec. Prod. of Political Broadcasts ('83).
ACHIEVEMENTS & AWARDS: Emmy award for best program for post-election special ('80).
PERSONAL: N.A.

GRANATH, HERBERT A.
Pres., ABC, Video Enterprises

c/o ABC, 1330 Ave. of the Americas, New York, NY 10019
b. N.A.

EDUCATION: Fordham University, B.S.
CAREER HIGHLIGHTS: Acct. Exec., ABC Radio Network ('60); Eastern Sales Mgr., ABC Radio Network ('63); V.P., ABC Radio Network ('66); V.P. and Dir. of Sales, ABC Radio Network ('67); V.P., Sports Sales, ABC TV Network ('70); V.P., Program Development and Marketing, ABC Sports ('75); Sr. V.P., Trans World Intl. ('75); V.P., ABC, Inc., and Asst. to the Pres., ABC, Inc. ('76); V.P. in Charge of ABC Video Enterprises ('82); Pres., ABC, Video Enterprises ('83).
ACHIEVEMENTS & AWARDS: Past Pres., Veteran's Bedside Network, currently on Board of Advisers; First V.P., Carnegie Hill Cooperative; Member, Advisory Council of Fordham University; Member, IRTS.
PERSONAL: Resides in Darien, CT, with wife, Ann Flood, an actress on "The Edge of Night"; four children, Kevin, Brian, Peter, and Karen.

GRANDE, GEORGE
Sr. Announcer, ESPN

c/o ESPN, ESPN Plaza, Bristol, CT 06010
b. October 9, 1946. New Haven, CT.

EDUCATION: University of Southern California, B.A., History/Telecommunications ('69).
CAREER HIGHLIGHTS: Worked concurrently at WNHC-Radio, New Haven, CT, and WERI-Radio, Westerly, RI, in News/Sports/Sales ('69); Anchor, WTNH-TV, New Haven ('73); Sports Anchor, WCBS-TV, New York ('77); joined ESPN as Sr. Announcer ('79).
ACHIEVEMENTS & AWARDS: Connecticut Sportscaster of the Year ('80–'81).
PERSONAL: Wife, JoAnne; son, Geoffrey.

GRANT, B. DONALD (Bud)
Pres. and Sr. V.P., CBS, Entertainment and
CBS Broadcast Group

c/o CBS, 7800 Beverly Blvd., Los Angeles, CA
90036
b. February 7, 1932. Baltimore, MD.

EDUCATION: Johns Hopkins University, B.S.,
Business Administration, and Ph.D.

CAREER HIGHLIGHTS: Grant's rise to the CBS
presidency was well-grounded in his prominent track record in successful daytime
scheduling maneuvers. Joined NBC in Exec.
Training Program ('56); worked in several
depts. including "Project 20" and "Today,"
and held positions including Mgr., Nightline
Programs and Mgr., Daytime Programs before being named Natl. Dir., Daytime Programs ('67). Left NBC to become V.P., Daytime Programs at CBS TV ('72); promoted to
V.P., Programs ('76); assumed title of V.P.,
Programs, CBS Entertainment when CBS res-
tructured operations ('77). Named Pres., CBS
Entertainment Division ('80); also appointed
Sr. V.P., CBS Broadcast Group ('82).

ACHIEVEMENTS & AWARDS: Man of the Year,
Beverly Hills Chapter of B'nai B'rith ('81);
honorary doctorate of humane letters, Co-
lumbia College ('82). Member, ATAS;
Trustee, NATAS; Board of Dirs., Hollywood
Radio-TV Society; Advisory Board, School of
Arts and Sciences, Johns Hopkins University.

PERSONAL: Children, David and Katie.

GRAUMAN, WALTER
Prod./Dir., Warner Bros. TV

c/o Warner Bros. TV, 4000 Warner Blvd.,
Burbank, CA 91522
b. March 17. Milwaukee, WI.

EDUCATION: University of Wisconsin; University of Arizona.

CAREER HIGHLIGHTS: Dir. "The Untouchables,"
"Naked City," "The Twilight Zone," "The
Fugitive," "Empire," "The Blue Light,"
"Eleventh Hour," "Felony Squad," "Daugh-
ter of the Wind," "Lancer," *Dead Men Tell No
Tales*, "Manhunter" pilot, *Are You in the House
Alone?*, "Barnaby Jones," *Golden Gate Mur-
ders*, *To Race the Mind*, *Pleasure Palace*.
Prod./Dir., *Valley of the Dolls*, CBS; *Illusions*,
CBS; *Bare Essence* mini-series and NBC series.
Motion pictures include *Lady in a Cage*, *A Rage
to Live*, and *The Last Escape*.

ACHIEVEMENTS & AWARDS: Directors Guild and
NATAS nominations.

PERSONAL: Resides in Los Angeles.

GRAVES, PETER
Actor

c/o ABC, 2040 Ave. of the Stars, Los Angeles,
CA 90067
b. March 18, 1926. Minneapolis, MN.

EDUCATION: University of Minnesota.

CAREER HIGHLIGHTS: TV movies include *Call to
Danger*, *Scream of the Wolf*, *Dead Man on the
Run* and *The Rebels*. TV mini-series appear-
ance in *The Winds of War*. TV series star of
"Fury," "Whiplash," "Court Martial," and
"Mission Impossible."

ACHIEVEMENTS & AWARDS: N.A.

PERSONAL: Wife, Joan; three daughters.

GRAY, ANN MAYNARD
V.P., ABC, Business Planning

c/o ABC, 1330 Ave. of the Americas, New
York, NY 10019
b. N.A.

EDUCATION: University of Michigan, B.A.;
New York University Graduate School of
Business, M.B.A., finance.
CAREER HIGHLIGHTS: Began working in the Fi-
nance Depts., Chemical Bank and Chase
Manhattan Bank in New York; Asst. to the
Treasurer, ABC ('73); Asst. Treasurer, ABC
('74); Treasurer, ABC ('76); V.P. and Trea-
surer, ABC ('79); V.P., Business Planning,
ABC, Inc. ('81).
ACHIEVEMENTS & AWARDS: N.A.
PERSONAL: N.A.

GRAY, LINDA
Actress

c/o "Dallas," CBS, 7800 Beverly Blvd., Los
Angeles, CA 90036
b. September 12, 1940. Santa Monica, CA.

EDUCATION: N.A.
CAREER HIGHLIGHTS: Guest roles in "Mc-
Cloud," "Switch," and "Marcus Welby,
M.D."; TV movie credits include *Haywire*,
High Ride, *The Wild and the Free*, and *Not in
Front of the Children*. Series regular on the syn-
dicated "All That Glitters" and "Dallas."
ACHIEVEMENTS & AWARDS: Chosen Woman of
the Year by the Hollywood Radio and TV, So-
ciety ('82).
PERSONAL: Resides in Canyon County, CA;
two children.

GREEN, JAMES
Prod., Exec. Prod. (Freelance)

c/o Universal TV, 100 Universal City Plaza,
Universal City, CA 91608
b. November 14, 1942. Los Angeles, CA.

EDUCATION: California State University at San
Francisco, B.A.
CAREER HIGHLIGHTS: Program Exec., ABC TV
('67–'76); formed Green/Epstein Productions,
producing movies of the week for TV net-
works. Movies include *Black Market Baby* ('76),
Breaking Up Is Hard To Do ('78), *Money on the
Side* ('82), and *I, Desire* ('82) for ABC; *Fast
Friends* for NBC; and *A Shining Season* ('80)
and *Fallen Angel* ('81) for CBS.
ACHIEVEMENTS & AWARDS: Emmy nomination,
Freedom Foundation awards, George Wash-
ington medal, Mary Ellen award from the So-
ciety for Prevention of Cruelty to Children;
gold medal, Chicago Intl. Film Festival, for
Fallen Angel; Christopher award for *A Shining
Season*.
PERSONAL: Wife, Cathy; daughter, Jamie.

GREEN, PAUL
V.P., BBD&O Advertising

c/o BBD&O, 383 Madison Ave., New York,
NY 10017
b. March 5, 1950. New York, NY.

EDUCATION: Ohio University, B.S. ('72).
CAREER HIGHLIGHTS: ABC TV ('72–'76); V.P.,
BBD & O Advertising.
ACHIEVEMENTS & AWARDS: American Assn. of
Advertising Agencies, Subcommittee on Ca-
ble TV ('81–'83).
PERSONAL: Wife, Sheryl. Resides in East Mead-
ow, NY.

GREENBERG, ALICE
**Sr. V.P., Assoc. Dir., Ogilvy & Mather,
Broadcast**

2 E. 48th St., New York, NY 10017
b. N.A.

EDUCATION: N.A.
CAREER HIGHLIGHTS: V.P., Dir. of Daytime Net-
work, BBD&O; joined Ogilvy & Mather as
Broadcast Acct. Supervisor ('75). Became a Sr.

V.P. ('80), with responsibilities that involve her in work on all broadcast accounts, from negotiation to programming and syndication.

ACHIEVEMENTS & AWARDS: Active in the Heart Fund and American Cancer Society.

PERSONAL: Resides in Manhattan.

GREENBERG, PAUL W.
Exec. Prod., NBC, News

c/o NBC, 30 Rockefeller Plaza, New York, NY 10020
b. April 6, 1933. New York, NY.

EDUCATION: University of Michigan, B.A., Columbia University, M.S.

CAREER HIGHLIGHTS: Prod., WIIC, Pittsburgh ('57); ABC News Prod. for strip shows and special events ('61); CBS News Prod. for evening news and documentaries ('64); left for NBC News to be Prod. on special events and nightly news ('78); currently Exec. Prod., "NBC Nightly News."

ACHIEVEMENTS & AWARDS: Emmy awards for "CBS Evening News" ('72, '73).

PERSONAL: Wife, Alice; children, Seth and Judith.

GREENBURG, EARL D.
Prod.

1807 Nichols Canyon Rd., Los Angeles, CA 90046
b. September 27, 1946. Philadelphia, PA.

EDUCATION: University of Pennsylvania, B.A.; University of Pennsylvania Law School, J.D.

CAREER HIGHLIGHTS: Started with the law firm of David Berger, P.A. ('70); became Deputy Attorney General, Pennsylvania ('74); Attorney, Atlantic Richfield ('77); Dir., Compliance and Practices Dept., NBC; V.P., Compliance and Practices Dept., NBC ('80); V.P., Daytime Programming Dept., NBC ('81). Currently Independent Prod., in association with Columbia Pictures TV.

ACHIEVEMENTS & AWARDS: Emmy, for "The Regis Philbin Show" ('82).

PERSONAL: Daughter, Meredith; son, Ari.

GREENE, BOB
Contributing Correspondent, ABC News, "Nightline"

c/o ABC News, 7 W. 66th St., New York, NY 10023
b. Columbus, OH.

EDUCATION: Northwestern University, B.S., Journalism.

CAREER HIGHLIGHTS: General Assignment Reporter, *Chicago Sun-Times* ('69); Columnist, *Chicago Sun-Times* ('71); Columnist, *Chicago Tribune* ('78). In addition to his daily *Chicago Tribune* column, he is a Contributing Editor, *Esquire* magazine, and Contributing Correspondent, ABC News "Nightline" ('81).

ACHIEVEMENTS & AWARDS: Natl. Headliner award ('77); distinguished achievement award from the Journalism Alumni Assn. of the University of Southern California ('81).

PERSONAL: Resides in Chicago.

GREENE, DAVID
Dir.

c/o David Greene Productions, 4225 Coldwater Canyon, Studio City, CA 91604
b. February 22, 1921. England

EDUCATION: Attended school in England.

CAREER HIGHLIGHTS: Settled in the U.S. ('72). Wrote the screenplay and directed *Godspell*, and directed the films, *The Count of Monte Cristo, Gray Lady Down,* and *Hard Country.* Recently, Co-Prod./Dir. for TV's *World War III, Rehearsal for Murder,* and *Take Your Best Shot.* Other TV directorial achievements are *The Choice, Friendly Fire, Roots, Rich Man, Poor Man,* and *The People Next Door.*

ACHIEVEMENTS & AWARDS: Four Emmy awards for direction, for *The People Next Door* ('70); *Rich Man, Poor Man* ('76); *Roots* ('77); and *Friendly Fire* ('79).

PERSONAL: N.A.

GREENFIELD, JEFF
Special Correspondent, ABC, News

c/o ABC, 7 W. 66th St., New York, NY 10023
b. New York, NY.

EDUCATION: University of Wisconsin; Yale Law School.

CAREER HIGHLIGHTS: Greenfield's lucid commentary for TV's "Sunday Morning Show" under Shad Northshield's aegis marked a rare occasion when all the commercial networks permitted honest coverage of the medium. Worked as an aide to the late Sen. Robert F. Kennedy; was Asst. to former New York City Mayor John Lindsay; Asst. to consultant David Garth; Freelance Writer on TV for *N.Y. Times Magazine, New York* magazine, UPI, and the *Columbia Journalism Review;* panelist on William F. Buckley Jr.'s "Firing Line," and the PBS broadcast "We Interrupt This Week"; Media Commentator for the "Morning Show," CBS ('79–'82); Special Correspondent, CBS News ('79–'83); Special Correspondent, ABC ('83), including "Good Morning America."

ACHIEVEMENTS & AWARDS: Author or Co-Author, eight books, including *The Real Campaign, Playing To Win: An Insider's Guide to Politics, Jeff Greenfield's Book of Books, The Advance Man, A Populist Manifesto, No Peace, No Place, The World's Greatest Team,* and *Television: The First Fifty Years.*

PERSONAL: Married, two children.

GREENWALD, SHELLEY
Sr. Attorney, NBC, Law Dept.

c/o NBC, 30 Rockefeller Plaza, New York, NY 10020
b. N.A.

EDUCATION: Lehigh University, B.A.; New York University School of Law, J.D.

CAREER HIGHLIGHTS: Asst. Corp. Counsel, Law Dept., City of New York ('78); Assoc., Solomon & Rosenbaum, Drechsler & Leff law firm ('80); Sr. Attorney, NBC Law Dept. ('83).

ACHIEVEMENTS & AWARDS: N.A.

PERSONAL: Resides in New York City.

GREENWOOD, BILL
Correspondent, ABC, News

c/o ABC, 1717 DeSales St., N.W.,
  Washington, DC 20036
b. N.A.

EDUCATION: American University, B.A.

CAREER HIGHLIGHTS: Washington Bureau Reporter, UPI; Public Affairs Dir., Natl. Educational Radio Network (now NPR); Congressional and Political Reporter, Mutual Broadcasting System; named V.P. and News Dir. ('74); Reporter and Host, "Newsmakers" WCBS-TV ('76); ABC News Reporter ('79); White House Correspondent ('80); named Congressional Correspondent ('81).

ACHIEVEMENTS & AWARDS: Media merit award, Assn. of Trial Lawyers ('76); Emmy for outstanding reporting ('78); Emmy nomination ('79); New York City Firefighters award ('79). Past Pres.; Congressional Radio-TV Correspondents Assn.; Natl. Press Club; Past Chairman, Congressional Radio-TV Galleries; Past Member, White House Correspondents Assn.

PERSONAL: Wife, Marsha; daughter, Kelly.

GREGORY, BETTINA
Correspondent, ABC, News

c/o ABC, 7 W. 66th St., New York, NY 10023
b. N.A.

EDUCATION: Smith College; Webber-Douglas Academy of Dramatic Art, London; Pierce College, Athens, Greece B.A., Psychology and English (summa cum laude).

CAREER HIGHLIGHTS: Freelance Reporter, *N.Y. Times;* Freelance Newscaster, NBC Radio Network; Reporter and Anchor, WCBS-AM, New York; Correspondent, ABC News, American FM Radio Network ('74); Military Affairs Correspondent, ABC News, Washington, DC ('77); Correspondent, ABC News, London ('78); White House Correspondent, ABC News, Washington, DC ('79); Sr. General Assignment Correspondent ('80).

ACHIEVEMENTS & AWARDS: Front Page award from the Newswoman's Club of New York ('76); Women at Work broadcast award for excellence ('79); Clarion award for investigative reporting ('79).

PERSONAL: Married, resides in Arlington, VA.

GREGORY, NICK
Meteorologist, Cable News Network, Weather

c/o Cable News Network, 1050 Techwood Dr., Atlanta, GA 30318
b. April 24, 1960. Chicago, IL.

EDUCATION: Lyndon State College, B.S., Meteorology.
CAREER HIGHLIGHTS: Asst. Meteorologist, WCBS-TV, New York ('77); Asst. Meteorologist, NBC's "Today" Show ('80); Meteorologist, WTLV-TV, Jacksonville, FL ('81); Meteorologist, Cable News Network ('81).
ACHIEVEMENTS & AWARDS: Member, American Meteorological Society.
PERSONAL: N.A.

GRENIER, JACQUES
Correspondent, ABC, News

c/o ABC, P.O. Box 4516, Johannesburg 2000, South Africa
b. N.A.

EDUCATION: Laval University, B.A.; University of Western Ontario.
CAREER HIGHLIGHTS: Reporter, CBC-TV, Ottawa, Canada; Correspondent, CFCF-TV, Montreal; Correspondent, CJOH-TV, Ottawa; Correspondent, CTV-TV, Quebec; Prod., ABC News, London and Paris ('79); Correspondent, ABC News, Paris ('80); Correspondent, ABC News, Johannesburg, South Africa ('82).
ACHIEVEMENTS & AWARDS: N.A.
PERSONAL: N.A.

GRIFFIN, MERV
Host, "The Merv Griffin Show"

c/o Guttman & Pam Ltd., 120 El Camino Dr., Beverly Hills, CA 90212
b. July 6, 1925. San Mateo, CA.

EDUCATION: University of San Francisco; Stanford University.
CAREER HIGHLIGHTS: Recording star and band singer. Motion pictures include *By the Light of the Silvery Moon* and *So This Is Love.* Created the quiz show "Jeopardy" and produced "Wheel of Fortune" and "Dance Fever." Network talk shows on NBC and CBS. Host of the syndicated talk show "The Merv Griffin Show," which specializes in theme shows focusing on a particular idea, topic, or personality. Of all talk show hosts, Griffin is the most persistent and the most adept at getting reluctant guests to say what they were most determined not to say.
ACHIEVEMENTS & AWARDS: Four Emmy awards.
PERSONAL: Resides in Carmel Valley, CA.

GRILES, EDD
V.P., Horizon Entertainment

c/o Horizon Entertainment, 919 Third Ave., New York, NY 10022
b. November 18, 1945. New York, NY.

EDUCATION: School of Visual Arts.
CAREER HIGHLIGHTS: Art Supervisor, Doyle, Dane, Bernbach ('65); Creative Dir., NHL ('73); Exec. V.P., People and Properties ('76); V.P., Horizon Entertainment ('83).
ACHIEVEMENTS & AWARDS: N.A.
PERSONAL: Resides in New York City.

GRIMES, J. WILLIAM
Pres. and Chief Exec. Officer, ESPN

c/o ESPN, ESPN Plaza, Bristol CT, 06010
b. March 7, 1941. Wheeling, WV.

EDUCATION: West Virginia Wesleyan College, B.A., English; St. John's University School of Law.
CAREER HIGHLIGHTS: Joined CBS Radio ('68); Dir., Sales, WCAU-AM, Philadelphia ('71); V.P. and General Mgr., CBS Radio Spot Sales ('72); V.P. and General Mgr., WEEI-AM, Boston ('73); V.P., AM Stations, CBS Radio ('74); V.P., Personnel, CBS, Inc.('77); Sr. V.P., AM and FM Stations ('79); V.P., CBS Broadcast Group ('81); Exec. V.P. and Chief Exec. Officer, ESPN ('81); Pres. and Chief Exec. Officer, ESPN ('82).
ACHIEVEMENTS & AWARDS: Dir., NAB ('79–'80).
PERSONAL: N.A.

GRIMSBY, ROGER
Anchor, WABC-TV, "Eyewitness News"

c/o WABC-TV, 7 Lincoln Sq., New York, NY 10023
b. Duluth, MN.

EDUCATION: St. Olaf College; Columbia University Graduate School.
CAREER HIGHLIGHTS: News Correspondent, KMOX-TV, St. Louis; News Dir., KGO-TV, San Francisco ('61); Investigative Reporter and News Anchor, WABC-TV ('68).
ACHIEVEMENTS & AWARDS: Two New York local Emmy awards for outstanding documentary and for individual craft; two New York local Emmy awards for outstanding investigative reporting.

PERSONAL: Resides in Manhattan. Recently signed million dollar a year contract with Channel 7 to co-anchor "Eyewitness News."

GRINKER, CHARLES
Vice Chairman and Creative Dir., Corp. for Entertainment and Learning

c/o Corp. for Entertainment and Learning, 515 Madison Ave., New York, NY 10022
b. May 30, 1933.

EDUCATION: New York University ('56).
CAREER HIGHLIGHTS: Prod., NBC Radio's "Monitor" series ('57); Prod., Project 20 Unit, NBC-TV ('61); Prod. of numerous TV specials in the sixties and seventies including "The World of Jacqueline Kennedy," "The World of Bob Hope," and "The World of Sophia Loren"; Exec. Prod., "Creativity With Bill Moyers" ('81); Co-Host of family game shows on the cable network Entertainment Channel ('82); Vice-Chairman and Creative Dir., Corp. for Entertainment and Learning ('82).
ACHIEVEMENTS & AWARDS: Emmy for "Creativity With Bill Moyers."
PERSONAL: N.A.

GRISCOM, TOM
Sr. V.P., WSM, Inc., Broadcasting

c/o WSM, Inc., Nashville Network, 2806 Opryland Dr., Nashville, TN 37214
b. Nashville, TN.

EDUCATION: Vanderbilt University, bachelor's.
CAREER HIGHLIGHTS: Joined WSM-TV as Sales Asst. ('51), then became an Acct. Exec., WSM-TV; appointed Sales Mgr. ('58), named V.P. and General Mgr. ('68). He is responsible for the Nashville Network cable TV project as well as for WSM-AM and WSM-FM radio stations.
ACHIEVEMENTS & AWARDS: Printer's Ink silver medal for outstanding service to the community and advertising; Founder and Past Pres., Nashville Better Business Bureau.
PERSONAL: N.A.

GROSS, HERBERT
V.P. and Asst. to the Pres., CBS, Entertainment

c/o CBS, 6121 Sunset Blvd., Los Angeles, CA 90028
b. N.A.

EDUCATION: City College of New York, B.A., Business Administration ('53); and M.B.A. ('58).

CAREER HIGHLIGHTS: Sr. Research Analyst, McCann-Erickson advertising agency ('59); Mgr., Media Research, Dancer-Fitzgerald-Sample advertising agency ('60); Mgr., Coverage and Analysis, CBS Research Dept., New York ('62); Mgr., Sales Development, CBS; Dir., Sales Development, CBS TV Network Sales; Acct. Exec., CBS TV Network Sales, New York; Dir., Daytime Sales; Dir., Sports Sales; Dir., Nighttime Sales; Dir., CBS Sports ('76); V.P., Sales Planning, CBS TV ('77); V.P. and Dir., Sports Programming, CBS Sports ('80); V.P. and Asst. to the Pres., CBS Entertainment, Los Angeles ('81).

ACHIEVEMENTS & AWARDS: N.A.

PERSONAL: Married, four children.

GROSS, MARY
Repertory Player

c/o "Saturday Night Live," NBC, 30 Rockefeller Plaza, New York, NY 10020
b. March 25, 1953. Chicago, IL.

EDUCATION: Second City Workshop in Chicago.

CAREER HIGHLIGHTS: Member, Chicago's Second City Troupe; Repertory Player, "Saturday Night Live" ('81).

ACHIEVEMENTS & AWARDS: N.A.

PERSONAL: Resides in Chicago.

GROSS, PETER A.
Pres., Time, Inc., Video Group, Development and Information Services

c/o Time/Life, Inc., 1271 Ave. of the Americas, New York, NY 10020
b. March 30, 1943. New York, NY.

EDUCATION: Yale University, B.A.; University of Pennsylvania, LL.B.

CAREER HIGHLIGHTS: Associate, Dewey, Ballantine, Bushby, Palmer & Wood ('69–'73); Corporate Counsel, Teleprompter Corp. ('73); V.P. and General Counsel, HBO ('74); General Counsel, Time, Inc., Video Group ('80–'81); Pres., Time, Inc., Video Group Development and Information Services Division; Chairman, Time-Life Video; Chairman, Time Video Information Services ('82).

ACHIEVEMENTS & AWARDS: N.A.

PERSONAL: Wife, Madelyn; children, Daniel, Matthew, and Gabriel. Resides in Montclair, NJ.

GROSSMAN, LAWRENCE K.
Pres., NBC, News

c/o PBS, 475 L'Enfant Plaza, S.W., Washington, DC 20024
b. June 21, 1931.

EDUCATION: Columbia University, B.A. ('52); Harvard Law School ('53).

CAREER HIGHLIGHTS: Began media career on staff of *Look* magazine ('53); joined Advertising Division, CBS TV ('56); V.P. in Charge of Advertising, NBC ('62). Grossman left commercial TV to form his own advertising and production company, Lawrence K. Grossman, Inc., specializing in serving media and public service clients, including NBC,

CBS, *Ladies' Home Journal,* Teleprompter, Council on the Aging, the Agency for Intl. Development, the Ford Foundation, WNET-TV, Children's Television Workshop, and PBS ('66). He became founding Pres. of Forum Communications ('68); became Pres. and Chief Exec. Officer, PBS ('76). Since Grossman became president, public TV has become a leader in broadcast journalism. "Frontline," virtually the only primetime weekly documentary series, premiered in 1983. Other noteworthy PBS innovations are "Inside Story" and the expansion of "The MacNeil/Lehrer Report" to an hour, thereby making PBS the first TV network with an hour newscast. Under Grossman, PBS has moved vigorously into continuing education with PBS's new Adult Learning Program Service providing telecourses to more than 600 colleges and universities. A number of new technology endeavors include Confersat, a PBS satellite video conference service, and PBS Video, a videocassette-making service. Grossman's foresight and expertise helped sustain PBS and enlarge its audience in the early 1980's despite severe budget problems.
ACHIEVEMENTS & AWARDS: N.A.
PERSONAL: Married, resides in Bethesda, MD.

GROSSMAN, MICHAEL J.
V.P. in Charge of Business Affairs, Columbia Pictures TV

c/o Columbia Pictures TV, 300 ColGems Sq., Burbank, CA 91505
b. November 29, 1942. New York, NY.

EDUCATION: Princeton University; Brandeis University; Harvard Law School.
CAREER HIGHLIGHTS: Sr. Attorney, NBC ('67); Dir., Business Affairs, NBC ('70); V.P., Talent and Program Administration ('76); entered private law practice ('78); V.P. in Charge of Business Affairs, Columbia Pictures TV ('82).
ACHIEVEMENTS & AWARDS: N.A.
PERSONAL: Resides in Tarzana, CA; wife, Leslie; daughter, Rachel; sons, Adam and Jonathan.

GROSSMAN, SANDY
Dir., CBS, Sports

c/o CBS, 51 W. 52d St., New York, NY 10019
b. June 12, 1935. New Jersey.

EDUCATION: University of Alabama, B.A.
CAREER HIGHLIGHTS: The network's top sports director and a master at his craft. Started career at CBS as Usher ('57); moving to clerical positions before joining the Public Affairs Dept., WCBS-TV, New York ('58); later Production Asst. at the station before moving to CBS Sports ('63). Moved quickly up the ranks, establishing himself as the front-line director, especially for football and basketball telecasts. Dir., Super Bowl X and Super Bowl XVI.
ACHIEVEMENTS & AWARDS: Emmy for his direction of Super Bowl XIV.
PERSONAL: Resides in Union, NJ, with wife, Faith; four children.

GROTH, ROBIN
Correspondent, ABC, News

c/o ABC, 2040 Ave. of the Stars, Los Angeles, CA 90067
b. N.A.

EDUCATION: University of Washington; Scripps College.
CAREER HIGHLIGHTS: Asst. Managing Editor, Conde Nast Publications ('69); Reporter and Co-Anchor, Weekend News, KING-TV, Seattle, WA ('71); Reporter, KNBC-TV, Los Angeles ('76); Correspondent, ABC News, Los Angeles ('81).
ACHIEVEMENTS & AWARDS: Sigma Delta Chi award for reporting ('74); local Emmy ('79); Los Angeles Press Club award ('79).
PERSONAL: Resides in Los Angeles.

GRUMBLES, WILLIAM H.
V.P. and General Mgr., HBO, Central Region

c/o HBO, 1271 Ave. of the Americas, New York, NY 10020
b. June 17, 1949.

EDUCATION: Southern Methodist University

CAREER HIGHLIGHTS: Regional Controller, Teleprompter, based in Atlanta ('71); System Mgr., responsible for running three Teleprompter Cable Systems in Texas ('73); Supervisor for Special Projects in Florida ('76); District Mgr., Houston, in charge of eight cable systems for Teleprompter ('77). Joined HBO, establishing the company's Central Regional Office in Kansas City, MO ('78); Dir. HBO's South Central Region, Dallas ('79); named V.P. and General Mgr., Central Region, which covers 1,200 affiliates ('80).

ACHIEVEMENTS & AWARDS: N.A.

PERSONAL: Wife, Fran.

GUEST, JEAN
V.P., Talent and Casting, CBS, Entertainment

c/o CBS, 6121 Sunset Blvd., Los Angeles, CA 90028

b. New York, NY.

EDUCATION: New York University.

CAREER HIGHLIGHTS: Dir., ANTA ('54); Theatrical Agent ('68); Assoc. Dir. of the Theater Communications Group ('75); Dir., Talent, CBS, New York ('76); V.P., Talent and Casting, CBS Entertainment, Los Angeles ('78).

ACHIEVEMENTS & AWARDS: N.A.

PERSONAL: Married to Peter Haden Guest, former UN Secretariat official. Three children; Christopher, an actor and Emmy Award-winning writer; Nicholas, an actor; and Elissa, a writer.

GUIDA, ORLANDO C.
Treasurer/V.P., USA Cable Network, Finance and Administration

c/o USA Cable Network, 208 Harristown Rd., Glen Rock, NJ 07452

b. N.A.

EDUCATION: University of Rhode Island, B.S., Accounting; Columbia University School of Business.

CAREER HIGHLIGHTS: Staff Accountant, progressing to Sr. Auditor, Arthur Andersen & Co., New York ('57–'64); Dir., Business Affairs, NBC, News Division, New York ('71); Treasurer/V.P. Finance and Administration, USA Cable Network ('80).

ACHIEVEMENTS & AWARDS: N.A.

PERSONAL: Wife, Elaine; daughter, Paula; sons Carl and Andrew.

GUIDA, TONY
Chief Political Correspondent and Weekend Anchor, WCBS-TV

c/o WCBS-TV, 530 W. 57th St., New York, NY 10019

b. N.A.

EDUCATION: Holy Cross College.

CAREER HIGHLIGHTS: General Assignment Reporter, NBC: Reporter for WNBC-News Center 4: Chief Political Correspondent and Weekend Anchor for WCBS-TV.

ACHIEVEMENTS & AWARDS: N.A.

PERSONAL: N.A.

GUILLAUME, ROBERT
Actor

c/o "Benson," ABC, 2040 Ave. of the Stars, Los Angeles, CA 90067
b. November 30. St. Louis, MO.

EDUCATION: St. Louis University; Washington University.

CAREER HIGHLIGHTS: Broadway roles in *Purlie* and *Golden Boy*. TV guest roles on "Sanford and Son," "The Jeffersons," and "The Love Boat." TV series star of "Soap" and "Benson."

ACHIEVEMENTS & AWARDS: Emmy award for "Soap."

PERSONAL: Two sons, Kevin and Jacques. Resides in Tarzana, CA.

GUMBEL, BRYANT C.
On-Air Personality, Co-Anchor "Today," NBC

c/o NBC, 30 Rockefeller Plaza, New York, NY 10020
b. September 29, 1948. New Orleans, LA.

EDUCATION: De LaSalle Institute; Bates College, B.A., History.

CAREER HIGHLIGHTS: Sportscaster, KNBC-TV, Los Angeles ('72); Hosted "Prep Sports World" ('73–'76); Host and Prod., "Olympic Reflections" ('76); Sports Dir. ('77); simultaneously hosted NFL coverage for NBC TV ('75–'82); NBC baseball coverage, "Major League Baseball: An Inside Look" ('78–'81); Super Bowls XI, XIII, and XV ('77, '79, '81); NBC's World Series coverage ('80); Tournament of Roses parade, NBC ('76–'82); Macy's Thanksgiving Day parade, NBC ('77–'81).

Joined NBC as Host, "Games People Play" ('80); appointed Host, "Today" ('82).

ACHIEVEMENTS & AWARDS: Local Emmy as sportscaster ('75, '76); local Emmy, as producer, best sports special ('76); Los Angeles Golden Mike award, best sportscaster ('76, '77, '78). Honorary Board Member, Sister Cities, Intl. ('81–present); honorary Dir., Xavier University ('82).

PERSONAL: Wife, June; son, Bradley Christopher.

GUMBEL, GREG
Sportscaster

172 N. Franklin St., Suite 300, Chicago, IL 60606
b. May 3, 1946. New Orleans, LA.

EDUCATION: Loras College, B.A., ('67).

CAREER HIGHLIGHTS: Asst. Advertising Dir., H.C. Lython & Co., Chicago ('67); Sportscaster, WMAQ-TV, NBC, Chicago ('73); Sportscaster, ESPN, Bristol, CT ('81).

ACHIEVEMENTS & AWARDS: Emmy, Chicago area ('76–'77, '77–'78); Cable Sports Personality of the Year, *On Cable* magazine ('82).

PERSONAL: Resides in Connecticut with his wife, Mary, and one daughter.

GUNN, HARTFORD N., JR.
V.P., Satellite TV Corp., Program Development

c/o Satellite TV Corp., 1301 Pennsylvania
  Ave., N.W., Suite 300, Washington DC
  20004
b. N.A.

EDUCATION: N.A.

CAREER HIGHLIGHTS: One of the most important and admired executives in the history of
  public TV. Founder and Pres., PBS ('70); Vice
  Chairman, PBS, Washington, DC ('77); Sr.
  V.P., KCET-TV, Los Angeles ('80); Sr. Consultant, Satellite TV Corp. ('82); V.P., Program Development, Satellite TV Corp. ('83).

ACHIEVEMENTS & AWARDS: Eastern Educational
  Network dedication of "Hartford N. Gunn,
  Jr., Satellite Terminal", Hartford, CT ('78);
  Natl. Assn. of Educational Broadcasters distinguished service award ('77); honorary doctor of laws degree, Central Michigan University ('75); Ralph Lowell Medal for outstanding
  contributions to public television ('73).
  Named one of 11 Outstanding Men of the
  Year by the Boston Junior Chamber of Commerce ('62).

PERSONAL: N.A.

GUTHRIE, JAMES F.
Sr. V.P., Treasurer, Times Mirror Cable TV

c/o Times Mirror Cable TV, 2381 Morse Ave.,
  Irvine, CA 92714
b. N.A.

EDUCATION: University of Redlands, B.A. ('66);
  University of Southern California, M.B.A.
  ('69).

CAREER HIGHLIGHTS: Sr. Consultant, Arthur
  Andersen & Co. ('69); Controller, V.P.,
  Naugles, Inc. ('73); Sr. V.P., Chief Financial
  Officer, Grace Restaurant Co. ('81); Sr. V.P.,
  Treasurer, Times Mirror Cable TV ('82).

ACHIEVEMENTS & AWARDS: N.A.

PERSONAL: N.A.

GUTOWSKI, ROBERT M.
V.P., ESPN, Programming

c/o ESPN, ESPN Plaza, Bristol, CT 06010
b. March 9, 1948. New York NY.

EDUCATION: Hofstra University, B.B.A.

CAREER HIGHLIGHTS: Began at NBC as Page
  ('70); named Sales Service Representative
  ('70); appointed Acct. Exec. for "Today" and
  "Tonight" ('74); moved to Mgr., Sports Sales
  ('75); promoted to Dir. ('78). Joined ESPN as
  V.P., Programming ('81).

ACHIEVEMENTS & AWARDS: N.A.

PERSONAL: Resides in Cold Spring Harbor,
  NY, with wife Laura; children, Christian and
  Tara.

HABER, LES
Exec. Prod., Les Haber Productions

c/o Les Haber Productions, 350 E. 52d St.,
Suite 6-D, New York, NY 10022
b. N.A.

EDUCATION: Adelphi University, B.A., Marketing and Advertising ('66); Adelphi University, M.B.A., Marketing Management ('68).

CAREER HIGHLIGHTS: Media Buyer/Planner, Benton & Bowles ('66); Asst. to the Exec. Prod., Bob Stivers Productions ('67); Assoc. Prod., Showcase Productions ('68); Assoc. Prod., NBC ('70); V.P., Music Production Consultants ('71); Production Supervisor, Pop Film ('72); Prod., Cartridge TV ('73); Program Supplier, Videomation ('73); V.P., Direction Plus ('73). Created own production company, Les Haber Productions ('76); added responsibilities as Dir., Special Program Development, HBO ('78).

ACHIEVEMENTS & AWARDS: His production company's "Marvin Hamlisch: They're Playing My Song" was honored with ACE award from the Natl. Cable TV Assn. and gold award from the Intl. Film and TV Society ('82).

PERSONAL: N.A.

HABIB, GEORGE
Dir., Unit Mgrs., NBC

c/o NBC, 3000 W. Alameda Ave., Burbank, CA 91523
b. N.A.

EDUCATION: Wayne University, Theater and Speech.

CAREER HIGHLIGHTS: First worked as an actor on radio shows including "The Lone Ranger" and "The Green Hornet"; Announcer, national radio show "The Answer Man"; Radio Operator/Mechanic, Control Tower Operator, Middle East Air Force Command ('42–'46); Stage Mgr., Actor, "G.I. Hamlet"; Stage Mgr., Fulton Theatre, New York ('49); Dir., "Gangbusters" ('50); Assoc. Prod., "The Eddie Cantor Show," "The Fred Allen Show," Bob Hope specials, "Saturday Nite Revue," and "The Colgate Summer Comedy Hour"; Unit Mgr., NBC ('55); Prod., news show, "Today in the West"; Sr. Unit Mgr.; Mgr., Unit Mgrs., West Coast ('60); Dir., Unit Mgrs., West Coast, NBC TV Network ('68–'80).

ACHIEVEMENTS & AWARDS: N.A.

PERSONAL: Resides in Woodland Hills, CA, with his wife, Margaret.

HACKEL, DAN
Anchor, Cable News Network

c/o Cable News Network, 1050 Techwood Dr., N.W., Atlanta, GA 30318
b. Jacksonville, FL.

EDUCATION: Columbia University, M.S., Journalism

CAREER HIGHLIGHTS: Correspondent, ABC News, Washington, DC ('66); Editorial Dir., WMAL-AM-FM-TV, Washington, DC ('68); Anchor, Mutual Radio Networks, Washington, DC ('72); Asst. Prof. of Broadcasting, University of Florida, Gainesville ('78); joined Cable News Network Correspondent, Tel Aviv; Anchor, Atlanta ('80).

ACHIEVEMENTS & AWARDS: N.A.

PERSONAL: N.A.

HAGMAN, LARRY
Actor

c/o "Dallas," CBS, 7800 Beverly Blvd., Los
Angeles, CA 90036
b. September 21, 1931. Fort Worth, TX.

EDUCATION: Bard College.
CAREER HIGHLIGHTS: Hagman's wily J. R.
Ewing, the perpetual fox in the "Dallas"
chicken coop, is a villain so irresistible that it's
hard to remember Hagman's earlier TV days
as good Major Nelson on "I Dream of Jean-
nie." New York stage appearances include
Career, Comes a Day, The Beauty Part, and *A
Priest in the House.* Motion picture credits in-
clude *Failsafe, The Cavern, Harry and Tonto, The
Group, Stardust, Superman,* and *S.O.B.* Starred
in many movies of the week, including *The
President's Mistress, Last of the Good Guys,
Battered, Deadly Encounter,* and *Intimate
Strangers.* He was a regular on "The Edge of
Night" ('62) and starred in four TV series: "I
Dream of Jeannie," "The Good Life," "Here
We Go Again," and "Dallas."
ACHIEVEMENTS & AWARDS: N.A.
PERSONAL: Resides in Malibu, CA, with wife
Maj; son, Preston, and daughter, Heidi, who
is an actress. His mother is actress Mary
Martin.

HAID, CHARLES
Actor

c/o "Hill Street Blues," NBC, 3000 W.
Alameda Ave., Burbank, CA 91523
b. June 2. San Francisco, CA.

EDUCATION: Carnegie Tech, B.F.A., Theater
Arts.
CAREER HIGHLIGHTS: Feature films include *Al-*

tered States. Co-starred in the series "Kate
McShane" and "Delvecchio." His TV movies
include *Twirl, Divorce Wars,* and *Working.* Co-
producer of the documentary *Who Are the
De Bolts and Where Did They Get 19 Kids?* Series
regular on "Hill Street Blues."
ACHIEVEMENTS & AWARDS: N.A.
PERSONAL: Resides in Studio City, CA.

HAIMOVITZ, JULES
V.P., Viacom Intl.

Viacom Intl., 1211 Ave. of the Americas, New
York, NY 10036
b. December 25, 1950.

EDUCATION: Brooklyn College, Mathematics,
B.A. and M.A.
CAREER HIGHLIGHTS: Began as Sr. Research An-
alyst and moved up to Mgr., Operations and
Statistical Research, ABC TV Network ('71);
became Dir., Planning, Pay TV Viacom ('76);
Sr. V.P. Showtime Entertainment ('79); V.P.,
Viacom Intl. ('81).
ACHIEVEMENTS & AWARDS: N.A.
PERSONAL: Wife, Betsey; resides in Manhattan.

HAINES, LARRY
Actor

c/o "Search for Tomorrow," NBC, 30
Rockefeller Plaza, New York, NY 10020
b. August 3.

EDUCATION: City College of New York.
CAREER HIGHLIGHTS: Broadway appearances in
Promises, Promises, Twigs, and *Tribute.* TV
guest spots on "The Defenders," "Kojak,"
"Maude," and "Doc"; a regular on the soap
opera "Search for Tomorrow."
ACHIEVEMENTS & AWARDS: Two Emmy awards
for his continued performance in "Search for
Tomorrow."
PERSONAL: N.A.

HAINES, MARK
Correspondent, WABC-TV, "Eyewitness News"

c/o WABC-TV, 7 Lincoln Sq., New York, NY 10023
b. N.A.

EDUCATION: Denison University, B.A., History

CAREER HIGHLIGHTS: Capitol Cities Communications Broadcast Group ('69); Newscaster, KPOL-AM-FM, Los Angeles and Washington, DC News Bureau ('73); Investigative Reporter and Co-Anchor, WPRI-TV, Providence, RI ('76); Correspondent, WABC-TV, "Eyewitness News" ('82).

ACHIEVEMENTS & AWARDS: UPI award for best news story ('77).

PERSONAL: Wife, Barbara.

HAINES, RANDA
Dir., CBS TV Network

c/o CBS, 7800 Beverly Blvd., Los Angeles, CA 90036
b. New York, NY.

EDUCATION: American Film Institute.

CAREER HIGHLIGHTS: Studied with Lee Strasberg; started as a struggling actress, then spent 10 years as a script supervisor in film and television production. First professional directing assignment for PBS, "Under This Sky," then "The Jilting of Granny Weatherall." Has directed two episodes of "Hill Street Blues" and one of "Knots Landing." Dir., "Just Pals."

ACHIEVEMENTS & AWARDS: N.A.

PERSONAL: N.A.

HALEY, JACK, JR.
Exec. Prod./Dir.

1443 Devlin Dr., Los Angeles, CA 90060
b. October 25, 1933. Los Angeles, CA.

EDUCATION: Loyola University, Los Angeles, B.S., English.

CAREER HIGHLIGHTS: He worked with Wolper Productions, Co-Prod., *The Race for Space*; Prod. and Co-Writer, "A Funny Thing Happened on the Way to the White House," "A Funny Thing Happened on the Way to Hollywood." Prod./Dir./Co-Writer, "The Hidden World," for National Geographic, and the TV specials "The Best of Brass," "With Love, Sophia," "Monte Carlo," "C'est La Rose," "Frank Sinatra Jr. With Family and Friends," "Movin' With Nancy" ('67); Dir., feature film, *Norwood* ('70); Dir., *The Love Machine* ('71); Prod./Dir./Writer, *That's Entertainment!* ('74); Co-Prod., with Ronald Lyon, "50 Years of MGM" ('75). Named Pres., 20th Century Fox TV ('75); Co-Prod., "America Salutes Richard Rogers" ('75); Prod., "Life Goes to the Movies," "Bob Hope's World of Comedy," "Life Goes to War: Hollywood and the Home Front" ('76); Prod./Co-Author, "Entertainment Tonight" ('81); Prod./Dir., "American Movie Awards," "Hollywood: The Gift of Laughter," and "Ripley's Believe It or Not" ('82). Prod., Academy Awards shows ('70, '74, '79).

ACHIEVEMENTS & AWARDS: San Francisco Film Festival award for best documentary for *The Race for Space* ('59); Peabody and Venice Film Festival silver lion awards for "The Hidden World" ('67); Emmy for directing "Movin' With Nancy" ('67).

PERSONAL: Resides in Hollywood. Son of actor Jack Haley.

HALL, BRUCE
Correspondent, CBS, News

c/o CBS, 524 W. 57th St., New York, NY 10019
b. March 11, 1941. Oakland, CA.

EDUCATION: University of Missouri, B.A., Journalism.

CAREER HIGHLIGHTS: Anchor, KODE-TV, Joplin, MO ('63); Anchor, KFVS-TV, Cape Girardeau, MO ('65); Assignment Editor, WJXT-TV, Jacksonville, FL ('67); Reporter/Assignment Editor, CBS News, New York ('71); Reporter, CBS News, Atlanta ('72); Correspondent, CBS News, Atlanta ('77).

ACHIEVEMENTS & AWARDS: N.A.

PERSONAL: Wife, Susan; daughter, Sherry; son, Jeff.

HALL, DAVID
General Mgr., Nashville Network

c/o Nashville Network, 2806 Opryland Dr.,
Nashville, TN 37214
b. N.A.

EDUCATION: Vanderbilt University, BSEE ('72).
CAREER HIGHLIGHTS: Staff, WSM-TV, Nashville
('66); placed in charge of the construction,
installation of the sound and lighting systems
for the Opryland theme park ('71); placed in
charge of construction of the Opry House
broadcasting studio ('73); Chief Engineer,
Opryland theme park ('75); named General
Mgr., Opryland Productions ('77); General
Mgr., Nashville Network ('83).
ACHIEVEMENTS & AWARDS: Member, NATPE,
ITA, ITVA, Natl. Cable TV Assn., CMA and
the Tennessee Film, Tape, and Music Commission.
PERSONAL: N.A.

HALL, DEIDRE
Actress

c/o "Days of Our Lives," NBC, 3000 W.
Alameda Ave., Burbank, CA 91523
b. Milwaukee, WI.

EDUCATION: N.A.
CAREER HIGHLIGHTS: Disc Jockey, WQXT-AM,
Palm Beach, FL; made guest appearances on
"The Streets of San Francisco," "Joe Forrester," "Columbo," "Night Gallery," "Emer-
gency!" and "SWAT." Starred in "The Young
and the Restless" for three years before assuming the popular role of Marlena on "Days
of Our Lives."
ACHIEVEMENTS & AWARDS: N.A.
PERSONAL: N.A.

HALL, MONTY
TV Personality

c/o Hatos-Hall Productions, 6725 Sunset
Blvd., Hollywood, CA 90028
b. August 25, 1923. Canada.

EDUCATION: University of Manitoba, B.S.
CAREER HIGHLIGHTS: Emcee and Prod. of the
Canadian show, "Who Am I"; worked on
NBC Radio's Monitor; Emcee, "Strike It
Rich," "Video Village," and "Your First Im-
pression"; Game Show Host, "Let's Make a
Deal."
ACHIEVEMENTS & AWARDS: N.A.
PERSONAL: N.A.

HALLBERG, GARTH R.
Sr. V.P., J. Walter Thompson, Cableshop

466 Lexington Ave., New York, NY 10017
b. January 31, 1944. Albany, NY.

EDUCATION: M.S., Journalism, ('69); Columbia
University, M.B.A. ('70).
CAREER HIGHLIGHTS: Has held various account
management positions at J. Walter Thompson
('70). Sr. V.P., Cableshop, J. Walter Thomp-
son.
ACHIEVEMENTS & AWARDS: N.A.
PERSONAL: N.A.

HALPERT, SAUL
Political Editor/Reporter, KNBC

c/o KNBC, 3000 W. Alameda Ave., Burbank,
CA 91523
b. N.A.

EDUCATION: University of California, B.A., Social Science; University of California at Los Angeles, M.J.

CAREER HIGHLIGHTS: Writer and Prod., News and Documentary Programs, ABC Radio and TV; Prod., News and Documentary Programs, Field Reporter and Urban Affairs Editor, KNXT, Los Angeles; Political Editor/Reporter, KNBC ('73).

ACHIEVEMENTS & AWARDS: Community service award from the San Fernando Valley Interfaith Council and the John Swett award from the California Teachers Assn. Certificate of merit from the Los Angeles Human Relations Commission, Sigma Delta Chi award.

PERSONAL: N.A.

HAMBRICK, JOHN
Reporter/Anchor, WNBC-TV, New York, News

c/o WNBC-TV, 30 Rockefeller Plaza, New York, NY 10020
b. N.A.

EDUCATION: N.A.

CAREER HIGHLIGHTS: Reporter/Weekend Anchor, KDFX-TV, Witchita Falls, TX ('64); Reporter/Weekend Anchor, KHOU-TV, Houston ('65); Reporter/Anchor, WCPO-TV, Cincinnati ('66); News Prod./Reporter/Anchor, WEWS-TV, Cleveland ('67); Anchor/Managing Editor, News, KABC-TV, Los Angeles ('75); Reporter/Anchor, KRON-TV, San Francisco ('77); Reporter/Weekend Anchor, WNBC-TV, New York ('80).

ACHIEVEMENTS & AWARDS: Award for best investigative TV reporting from the Long Island Press Club ('80).

PERSONAL: Married, resides in Purchase, NY; three children.

HAMBRICK, MIKE
Co-Anchor, WRC-TV, Weekend News

c/o WRC-TV, 4001 Nebraska Ave. N.W., Washington, DC 20016
b. N.A.

EDUCATION: East Texas State University.

CAREER HIGHLIGHTS: Anchor, weeknight news

for KPNX-TV, Phoenix; Primary Anchor, WBAL weeknight news; Prod., news and information magazine, "Our American Exchange"; Co-Anchor, Channel 4 weekend news, WRC-TV 4 ('82).

ACHIEVEMENTS & AWARDS: N.A.

PERSONAL: N.A.

HAMBURG, MORTON
Communications Lawyer, Netter, Dowd & Alfieri

660 Madison Ave., New York, NY 10021
b. January 7, 1931. Brooklyn, NY.

EDUCATION: New York University.

CAREER HIGHLIGHTS: Partner, Goldstein, Judd & Gurfein, New York ('59); Partner, More, Berson, Hamburg & Bernstein ('69); Partner, Sinscheimer, Sinscheimer & Dubin ('73); Adjunct Professor, Communications Law, New York University School of Law ('72); Exec. V.P. and Dir., JAG Communications ('82).

ACHIEVEMENTS & AWARDS: Author, *All About Cable—Legal and Business Aspects of Cable and Pay Television.*

PERSONAL: Resides in New York City with his wife, Joan Hamburg of WOR-AM, and their children, Elizabeth and John.

HAMEL, VERONICA
Actress

c/o "Hill Street Blues," NBC, 3000 W. Alameda Ave., Burbank, CA 91523
b. November 20. Philadelphia, PA.

EDUCATION: Temple University.

CAREER HIGHLIGHTS: Appearances on "Dallas"

and "The Rockford Files." TV movies included *The Gathering* and *The Gathering II.* Appeared in the mini-series, *Beyond the Valley of the Dolls.* Series regular on "Hill Street Blues."
ACHIEVEMENTS & AWARDS: N.A.
PERSONAL: Single, resides in Brentwood, CA.

HAMILTON, JOE
Prod.

c/o EBM, 132 S. Rodeo Dr., Beverly Hills, CA 90212
b. January 6, 1929. Los Angeles, CA 90212.

EDUCATION: Los Angeles Conservatory of Music and Arts.
CAREER HIGHLIGHTS: From the early New York days of "The Garry Moore Show," Hamilton spotted Carol Burnett's potential for superstardom, and guided her career toward that goal. Along the way he also married the lady. Prod., "The Garry Moore Show" ('59); "Julie and Carol at Carnegie Hall" ('62); "Carol and Company" ('63); "The Sammy Davis Show" ('66); "The Carol Burnett Show" ('67–'78); "6 Rms Riv Vu" ('73); "Sills and Burnett at the Met" ('76).
ACHIEVEMENTS & AWARDS: The Golden Rose for "Julie and Carol at Carnegie Hall"; five Emmy awards for "The Garry Moore Show" and "The Carol Burnett Show."
PERSONAL: Three daughters, Carrie, Jody, and Erin; resides in Beverly Hills, CA, and Maui, HI.

HAMILTON, NANCY E.
Dir. of Operations, Westinghouse Broadcasting Co., Group W Productions

c/o Group W Productions, 70 Universal City Plaza, Universal City, CA 91608
b. Crawfordsville, IN.

EDUCATION: Hanover College; Indiana University.
CAREER HIGHLIGHTS: Unit Mgr., MetroTape West ('75); Mgr., Studio Operations, Metro-Tape West ('78); Dir. of Operations, MetroTape West, a division of Metromedia, Los Angeles ('79); Dir. of Operations, Group W Productions, Los Angeles ('80).
ACHIEVEMENTS & AWARDS: N.A.
PERSONAL: Resides in Los Angeles.

HAMLIN, JOHN
V.P., Special Programs, ABC, Entertainment

c/o ABC, 4151 Prospect Ave., Los Angeles, CA 90027
b. New York, NY.

EDUCATION: N.A.
CAREER HIGHLIGHTS: V.P. in Charge of Programming, West Coast, Benton & Bowles; V.P., Variety Programs, NBC; V.P., Specials, NBC, West Coast ('74); Prod., "Happy Birthday Bob" and "The 36 Most Beautiful Girls in Texas" ('78); Dir., Special Programs, West Coast, ABC ('79); V.P., Special Programs, ABC Entertainment ('82).
ACHIEVEMENTS & AWARDS: N.A.
PERSONAL: Resides in Santa Monica, CA.

HAMMER, ROBERT
V.P., CBS, Facilities and Engineering

c/o CBS, 51 W. 52d St., New York, NY 10019
b. Brooklyn, NY.

EDUCATION: Rensselaer Polytechnic Institute.
CAREER HIGHLIGHTS: Technical Mgr., Recording Services and Mgr., Technical Planning Operations Dept., CBS ('50); Dir. of Technical Services/Operations, CBS ('62); General Mgr., CBS TV Network Operations ('72); V.P., Facilities and Engineering, CBS ('80).
ACHIEVEMENTS & AWARDS: N.A.
PERSONAL: Wife, Helen; three daughters, one son. Resides in Searington, NY.

HAMNER, EARL, JR.
Atlanta Bureau Chief, NBC, News

c/o NBC, 3000 W. Alameda Ave., Burbank, CA 91523
b. February 18, 1937. Los Angeles, CA.

EDUCATION: Pasadena City College; University of California at Santa Barbara; Columbia University.
CAREER HIGHLIGHTS: News Asst., NBC News, New York ('59); Reporter, UPI, Albuquerque, Santa Fe, and Fresno ('62); News Writer, NBC News ('65); UPI Saigon Reporter ('70); Reporter "Newsroom," WETA, Washington DC ('71); returned to NBC as News Desk Editor and "Today" News Writer ('72); Bureau Chief, Saigon ('73); Bureau Chief, Tokyo ('74); Field Prod., Atlanta ('78); appointed Bureau Chief, Atlanta ('80).
ACHIEVEMENTS & AWARDS: N.A.
PERSONAL: N.A.

HANNA, WILLIAM
Prod., Animated TV Cartoons, Hanna-Barbera Productions

c/o Hanna-Barbera Productions, 3400 Cahuenga Blvd., Hollywood, CA 90068
b. July 14, 1911. Melrose, NM.

EDUCATION: Compton College.
CAREER HIGHLIGHTS: With partner Joseph Barbera, he created "Tom and Jerry" at MGM ('38). The two men then formed Hanna-Barbera Productions and were responsible for the cartoons, "Ruff and Ready," "Yogi Bear," "Huckleberry Hound," "The Flintstones," and "The Smurfs." Hanna-Barbera Productions also made the full-length cartoons *Last of the Curlews*, *The Runaways*, *Charlotte's Web*, and *Heidi's Song*.
ACHIEVEMENTS & AWARDS: Three Emmy awards for *Last of the Curlews* ('72), *The Runaways* ('73), and *The Gathering* ('77).
PERSONAL: Resides in North Hollywood, CA, with wife, Vi. Two children, seven grandchildren.

HANSON, JANE
Reporter, WNBC-TV, New York, News

c/o WNBC-TV, 30 Rockefeller Plaza, New York, NY 10020
b. N.A.

EDUCATION: University of Minnesota, B.A., Broadcast Journalism.
CAREER HIGHLIGHTS: Reporter/Anchor, noontime news telecast, KSFY-TV, Sioux Falls, SD ('73); Reporter/Anchor, WMT-TV, Cedar Rapids, IA ('74); Reporter, WNBC-TV, New York ('79).

ACHIEVEMENTS & AWARDS: Named Correspondent of the Year by the New York City Police Detectives ('81).
PERSONAL: Resides in Secaucus, NJ.

HANSON, TERRY
Exec. Prod., Turner Broadcasting System, Sports

4606 Eberline Ct., Stone Mountain, GA 30083
b. June 16, 1947. East St. Louis, IL.

EDUCATION: St. Benedict's College, Southeast Missouri State University.
CAREER HIGHLIGHTS: Assoc. Prod., "Football Saturday," WTBS, Atlanta ('79); promoted to Exec. Prod., WTBS Sports, ('81).
ACHIEVEMENTS & AWARDS: N.A.
PERSONAL: Wife, Patricia; children, Amy, Joseph, and Elizabeth.

HARBERT, TED (Edward W. Harbert III)
Dir., ABC, Program Planning and Scheduling, Entertainment

c/o ABC, 2040 Ave. of the Stars, Los Angeles, CA 90067
b. June 15, 1955.

EDUCATION: Boston University, B.S., Broadcasting and Film ('77).
CAREER HIGHLIGHTS: Joined ABC Entertainment as Feature Film Coordinator ('77); Supervisor, Feature Film and Late Night Program Planning ('79); Asst. to V.P., Program Planning and Scheduling ('79); Dir., Program Planning and Scheduling ('81).
ACHIEVEMENTS & AWARDS: N.A.
PERSONAL: Resides in Los Angeles with wife, Julie Ann, Assoc. Dir., Programming, "On TV," Los Angeles.

HARDY, JOE
Exec. Prod., ABC, "Ryan's Hope"

c/o "Ryan's Hope," ABC, 1330 Ave. of the Americas, New York, NY 10019
b. March 8, 1929. Carlsbad, NM.

EDUCATION: New Mexico Highlands University, B.A. and M.A.; Yale University School of Drama, M.F.A.
CAREER HIGHLIGHTS: Prod., daytime serials "Love of Life," "A Time for Us," and "Love Is a Many Splendored Thing." Dir. of Broadway productions *Child's Play, Streets of New York, Night of the Iguana, The Real Inspector Hound, What the Butler Saw,* and *You're a Good Man, Charlie Brown.* TV movie credits include *Not in Front of the Children, Dream House, The Users,* and *The Seduction of Miss Leona.* Prod., *Shadow of a Gunman, Man of Destiny,* and *The Lady's Not for Burning* for PBS. Named Exec. Prod. of ABC soap opera "Ryan's Hope" ('83).
ACHIEVEMENTS & AWARDS: Tony award and Drama Desk award for *Child's Play.*
PERSONAL: Resides in New York City.

HARMON, PHIL
V.P. in Charge of Production, Madison Square Garden Network

c/o Madison Square Garden Network, 4 Pennsylvania Plaza, New York, NY 10001
b. January 23.

EDUCATION: New York University, TV/Motion Pictures.
CAREER HIGHLIGHTS: Worked in production and promotion for ABC Sports; Prod., variety of sports programs for the NHL and the NFL; Exec. V.P., W&W Films, New York ('72); V.P. in Charge of Production, Madison Square Garden Network ('82).
ACHIEVEMENTS & AWARDS: N.A.
PERSONAL: N.A.

HARPER, CHRIS
Correspondent, ABC, News

c/o ABC News, 7 W. 66th St., New York, NY 10023
b. Boise, ID.

EDUCATION: University of Nebraska; Northwestern University Graduate School of Journalism.

CAREER HIGHLIGHTS: Reporter, AP, Chicago; Reporter, *Newsweek*, Chicago ('75); Beirut Bureau Chief, *Newsweek* ('78); Correspondent and Cairo Bureau Chief, ABC News, Cairo ('80); Correspondent, ABC News ('82).

ACHIEVEMENTS & AWARDS: N.A.

PERSONAL: N.A.

HARPER, PAT
Co-Anchor, WPIX, "Action News" and Independent Network News

c/o WPIX-TV, 11 WPIX Plaza, New York, NY 10017
b. N.A.

EDUCATION: Pine Manor; Columbia University.

CAREER HIGHLIGHTS: Commentator, WBBM-TV, Chicago; moved from Chicago to Philadelphia as a member of the WFIL-TV news staff, where she specialized in reporting hard news. Joined WPIX as the first woman in New York to co-anchor a TV news show on a regular basis. Joined Independent Network News as Co-Anchor ('80).

ACHIEVEMENTS & AWARDS: N.A.

PERSONAL: Resides in New York City.

HARRINGTON, PAT
Actor

c/o "One Day at a Time," CBS, 7800 Beverly Blvd., Los Angeles, CA 90036
b. August 13, 1929. New York, NY.

EDUCATION: Fordham University, B.S., Philosophy and Government, and M.A., Political Philosophy.

CAREER HIGHLIGHTS: Joined NBC as a Mailroom Clerk ('53); moved into Sales Dept., NBC ('54); Natl. TV Sales, NBC ('55). Through an invitation from Jonathan Winters, who was a guest host on "The Jack Paar Show," Harrington appeared ('57) as a comedy character named Guido Panzini, which became his trademark. He became a regular on "The Jack Paar Show" and "The Steve Allen Show" ('59); featured role as the son-in-law on "The Danny Thomas Show" ('59); made guest appearances on many series, including "Mr. Deeds Goes to Town," "Hawaii Five-0," "Owen Marshall, Counselor at Law," and "The Love Boat," and TV-movies such as *The Critical List, Benny and Barney*, and *Brothers*. Currently co-stars as Dwayne Schneider on "One Day at a Time."

ACHIEVEMENTS & AWARDS: N.A.

PERSONAL: Resides in West Los Angeles, CA, with wife, Marjorie, and their four children.

HARRIS, BOB
Weatherman, WPIX

c/o WPIX, 11 WPIX Plaza, New York, NY 10017
b. December 26, 1939. Bronx, NY.

EDUCATION: Columbia University; College of the City of New York; Hunter College; University of Buffalo.

CAREER HIGHLIGHTS: Wrote weather column for the *N.Y. Times;* designed weather column, *The Record,* New Jersey. Staff Weatherman, CBS Radio Network; Weatherman, WOR, New York; Weekend Weatherman, WNEW-TV; Weatherman, INN, "Action News," WPIX. Also, Consultant, Long Island Railroad; teacher of course in weather for New School for Social Research in New York City.

ACHIEVEMENTS & AWARDS: Married, resides in Oakland, NJ.

HARRIS, JULIE
Actress

c/o "Knots Landing," CBS, 51 W. 52d St., New York, NY 10019
b. December 2, 1925. Grosse Pointe Park, MI.

EDUCATION: Yale University School of Drama.
CAREER HIGHLIGHTS: A great stage actress whose forays into TV drama (*Little Moon of Alban; Victoria Regina*) are among the medium's proudest achievements. Her Lily Mae on "Knots Landing" is so richly detailed one wishes the camera would never leave her. Broadway roles include *The Member of the Wedding, I Am a Camera, The Lark, Little Moon of Alban, A Shot in the Dark, Forty Carats,* and *The Belle of Amherst.* Motion pictures include *The Member of the Wedding, East of Eden, You're a Big Boy Now, Harper,* and *The Haunting.* TV movies include *How Awful About Allan, House on Greenaple Road,* and *The Greatest Gift.* TV special appearances include roles in *A Doll's House, The Holy Terror, Little Moon of Alban,* and *Victoria Regina.* TV series roles in "Thicker Than Water," "The Family Holvak," and "Knot's Landing."

ACHIEVEMENTS & AWARDS: Tony, Donaldson, and New York Drama Critics Circle awards for *I Am a Camera.* Tony awards also for *The Lark, Forty Carats, The Last of Mrs. Lincoln,* and *The Belle of Amherst.* Emmy awards for *Little Moon of Alban* and *Victoria Regina.*
PERSONAL: Son, Peter.

HARRISON, BARBARA
Co-Anchor, WRC-TV, Washington, DC, Weekend News

c/o WRC, 4001 Nebraska Ave., N.W., Washington, DC 20016
b. N.A.

EDUCATION: N.A.
CAREER HIGHLIGHTS: Started as Weekday News Anchor, KDFW-TV, Dallas, and Weekend News Anchor, KGO-TV, San Francisco; Reporter, WRC-TV, Washington, DC ('81); Co-Anchor, Weekend News, WRC-TV, Washington, DC ('82).
ACHIEVEMENTS & AWARDS: N.A.
PERSONAL: N.A.

HART, ALAN
Controller, BBC-1, BBC

c/o BBC, 12 Cavendish Place, London, England W1
b. Pinner, Middlesex, England.

EDUCATION: N.A.
CAREER HIGHLIGHTS: Journalist, *Newcastle Evening Journal* ('57); Journalist, *London Evening News* ('58); Editorial Asst., "Sportsview" ('59); BBC Sports Prod. based in Manchester ('62); Asst. Editor, "Sportsview" ('64); Editor, "Sportsview" ('64); Editor, "Grandstand" ('67); Prod., "Sports Review of the Year" ('65); Head of Sport BBC TV ('77); Controller, BBC-1 ('81).
ACHIEVEMENTS & AWARDS: N.A.
PERSONAL: Resides in Chalfont St. Peter, Buckinghamshire, England, with his wife and their three children.

HART, JOHN
Correspondent, NBC, News

c/o Ralph Mann, Agent, ICM, 40 W. 57th St.,
New York, NY 10019
b. February 1, 1932. Denver, CO.

EDUCATION: Westmont College, B.A.; University of California at Los Angeles, M.S.

CAREER HIGHLIGHTS: Began as News Dir., WSJV-TV, Elkhart, IN ('56); moved to same position at KPOL, Los Angeles ('57); Newswriter, KNXT, Los Angeles ('60); promoted to Special Assignment Reporter ('61); named Chief, CBS Stations Bureau, Washington, DC ('64); appointed CBS News Correspondent, Atlanta, Saigon, Washington, DC ('65); transferred to "CBS Morning News" as Washington, DC, Anchor ('69); moved to New York in same capacity ('70); Correspondent, CBS Special Broadcasts and Analyst, "CBS Morning News" ('73). Moved to NBC as Natl. Affairs Correspondent ('75); added responsibility of Anchor, "NBC Saturday Night News" ('76); named Chief European Correspondent for NBC ('79); appointed Anchor, "NBC Sunday Night News," with additional duties as Correspondent, "Special Segment" and documentaries ('82).

ACHIEVEMENTS & AWARDS: Emmy awards ('73, '79).

PERSONAL: N.A.

HARTER, JOHN
Co-Anchor/Reporter, WJLA-TV, Washington, DC, News

c/o WJLA-TV, 4461 Connecticut Ave., N.W.,
Washington, DC 20008
b. Washington, DC.

EDUCATION: American University
CAREER HIGHLIGHTS: Co-Anchor/Reporter, early morning newscasts, WJLA-TV, Washington, DC.
ACHIEVEMENTS & AWARDS: N.A.
PERSONAL: N.A.

HARTMAN, DAVID
On-Air Personality, ABC, "Good Morning America"

c/o ABC, 1 Lincoln Plaza, New York, NY 10023
b. May 19, 1935. Pawtucket, RI.

EDUCATION: Duke University, B.A., Economics; Amerian Academy of Dramatic Arts.

CAREER HIGHLIGHTS: This low-key, noncombative interviewer has won millions of viewers for ABC. He explored the fields of radio and TV during college; as an actor, his TV credits include "The Virginian," "The Bold Ones," and "Lucas Tanner." He formed Rodman-Downs Ltd., a production company, and served as Exec. Prod. and Narrator, "David Hartman: Birth and Babies" ('74); joined "Good Morning America" as Host when show began ('75). He continues in that same role while maintaining involvement in Rodman-Downs productions, "David Hartman: Gamblers...Winners and Losers" ('77), "David Hartman: New Beginnings" ('78), "David Hartman: "The Shooters" ('80).

ACHIEVEMENTS & AWARDS: Golden eagle award of the Council on Intl. Non-Theatrical Events for "David Hartman: "The Shooters" ('80).

PERSONAL: Married to the former Maureen Downey, a TV producer; children, Sean, Brian, and Bridget.

HARTZ, JIM
TV Host, "Over Easy"

c/o PBS, 475 L'Enfant Plaza, S.W.,
   Washington, DC 20024
b. N.A.

EDUCATION: University of Tulsa.
CAREER HIGHLIGHTS: News Reporter and An-
   chor, WNBC, New York; Co-Host, "Today
   Show" ('74); Reporter, NBC "Today Show"
   ('76); Co-Anchor, WRC-TV, Washington, DC.
   Host of "Over Easy," PBS.
ACHIEVEMENTS & AWARDS: N.A.
PERSONAL: N.A.

HARVEY, PAT (Patricia Lynn Harvey)
Newscaster, WNEM-TV

c/o WNEM-TV, 107 N. Franklin, Saginaw, MI
   48607
b. November 13, 1954.

EDUCATION: University of Detroit; Saginaw
   Valley State College.
CAREER HIGHLIGHTS: Radio and TV Host,
   WGPR-TV and Radio, Detroit ('76); Commu-
   nity Affairs Asst., WJBK-TV, Detroit ('77);
   Booth Announcer, WJBK-TV, Storer Broad-
   casting, Detroit ('78); News Anchor/Reporter/
   Prod., WNEM-TV, Saginaw-Flint-Bay City,
   MI ('79).
ACHIEVEMENTS & AWARDS: Named Miss Black
   Michigan ('75). Spirit of Detroit award for
   community service ('75).
PERSONAL: N.A.

HASSELHOFF, DAVID
Actor

c/o "Knight Rider," NBC, 3000 W. Alameda
   Ave., Burbank, CA 91523
b. July 17. Baltimore, MD.

EDUCATION: California Institute of the Arts.
CAREER HIGHLIGHTS: Began acting in many regional theaters before being plucked by noted
   casting Director Joyce Selznick to appear on
   TV. Had guest roles in "Police Story," "The
   Love Boat" and the TV movie *Griffin and Phoenix*. Appeared on "The Young and the Restless" for seven years as Snapper Foster before
   moving to primetime and "Knight Rider."
ACHIEVEMENTS & AWARDS: People's Choice
   award ('82).
PERSONAL: Single, resides in Los Angeles.

HAYES, BILL
Actor

c/o "Days of Our Lives," NBC, 3000 W.
   Alameda Ave., Burbank, CA 91523
b. Chicago, IL.

EDUCATION: DePauw University, B.A.; Northwestern University, M.A.

CAREER HIGHLIGHTS: Once a featured singer on "Your Show of Shows," he moved on to soap opera stardom. Cast member of "Days of Our Lives" ('70).

ACHIEVEMENTS & AWARDS: N.A.

PERSONAL: Resides in North Hollywood, CA, with wife, Susan Seaforth Hayes, who also stars on "Days of Our Lives."

HAYES, JONATHAN
Pres., Westinghouse Broadcasting Company, Group W Satellite Communications

c/o Group W Satellite Communications, 41 Harbor Plaza Dr., P.O. Box 10210, Stamford, CT 06904

b. Washington, DC

EDUCATION: Johns Hopkins University, B.A., Political Science.

CAREER HIGHLIGHTS: Trainee, Group W ('64); Acct. Exec., Group W TV Sales, New York; General Sales Mgr., WJZ-TV, Baltimore ('69); General Sales Mgr., KYW-TV, Philadelphia ('73); V.P. and General Mgr., KDKA-TV, Pittsburgh ('75); Pres., Group W Satellite Communications ('81).

ACHIEVEMENTS & AWARDS: N.A.

PERSONAL: Wife, Beth; children, Christopher and Tory.

HAYES, SUSAN SEAFORTH
Actress

c/o "Days of Our Lives," NBC, 3000 W. Alameda Ave., Burbank, CA 91523

b. N.A.

EDUCATION: N.A.

CAREER HIGHLIGHTS: Has been acting since age 4, and has appeared in numerous films, stage productions, and TV shows. Most famous for her role as Julie Williams on "Days of Our Lives." Recently initiated a soap opera workshop with her husband, Bill Hayes.

ACHIEVEMENTS & AWARDS: N.A.

PERSONAL: Married castmate Bill Hayes ('74), and they now reside in North Hollywood, CA.

HAYS, KATHRYN
Actress

c/o "As the World Turns," CBS, 51 W. 52d St., New York, NY 10019

b. Princeton, IL.

EDUCATION: Northwestern University.

CAREER HIGHLIGHTS: A hard-working actress who has had featured roles in films such as *Counterpoint, The Savage Land, Yuma, Ride Beyond Vengeance,* and *Lady Bug, Lady Bug.* TV credits include "The Road West," "High Chapparral," and "Star Trek" before settling in the daytime serial "As the World Turns" in the role of Kim Andropolous ('72).

ACHIEVEMENTS & AWARDS: N.A.

PERSONAL: Resides in New York City; daughter, Sherri.

HEADLINE, WILLIAM
Washington, DC, Bureau Chief, Turner Broadcasting System, Cable News Network

c/o Cable News Network, 1050 Techwood Dr., N.W., Atlanta, GA 30318

b. December, 1931. Cleveland, OH.

EDUCATION: Ohio Wesleyan University.

CAREER HIGHLIGHTS: Dir., Research, Lou Harris & Assoc.; Voting Analyst, CBS News ('64); Asst. V.P., CBS News, New York ('69); Asst. News Dir., CBS News, Washington, DC ('74); Washington, DC, Bureau Chief, Cable News Network ('83).

ACHIEVEMENTS & AWARDS: N.A.

PERSONAL: Married, three children.

HEALEY, DIANE
V.P., NBC TV, Corporate Affiliate Relations

c/o NBC, 30 Rockefeller Plaza, New York, NY 10020
b. N.A.

EDUCATION: University of Pennsylvania; University of Sussex; Harvard School of Business, M.A., M.B.A.
CAREER HIGHLIGHTS: Acct. Exec., Charles River Broadcasting, WRCB-AM/FM, Boston; Assoc., Press Department ('75); Station Service Representative for NBC's Radio NIS; Dir., Regional Affiliate Relations, nine Plains States ('77–'79); V.P., Corporate Affiliate Relations, NBC TV ('82).
ACHIEVEMENTS & AWARDS: N.A.
PERSONAL: N.A.

HEALY, JOHN T.
V.P., Product Development and Acquisitions, ABC, Video Enterprises

c/o ABC, 1330 Ave. of the Americas, New York, NY 10019
b. N.A.

EDUCATION: Brooklyn College.
CAREER HIGHLIGHTS: Joined ABC as Assoc. Dir. of Corporate Planning ('70); Dir. of Planning and Development ABC ('72); V.P., Planning and Administration, ABC Leisure ('74); V.P., Corporate Planning ('76); V.P., Product Development and Acquisitions, ABC Video Enterprises ('79).
ACHIEVEMENTS & AWARDS: N.A.
PERSONAL: Resides in Manhattan.

HECHT, KEN
Prod. (Freelance)

c/o Warner Bros., 4000 Warner Blvd., Burbank, CA 91505
b. April 4, 1947. Miami, FL.

EDUCATION: University of Miami, B.B.A.
CAREER HIGHLIGHTS: Exec. Story Editor, "The Love Boat" ('80); Supervising Prod., "Love, Sidney" ('81); Exec. Prod. "Private Benjamin" ('82).
ACHIEVEMENTS & AWARDS: Nominated for two Emmy awards.
PERSONAL: N.A.

HEITZER, HARRY
V.P., Business Affairs, Music Operations, CBS, Entertainment

c/o CBS, 7800 Beverly Blvd., Los Angeles, CA 90036
b. Philadelphia, PA.

EDUCATION: University of California at Los Angeles, B.A., Theater Arts.
CAREER HIGHLIGHTS: Messenger, CBS, Los Angeles ('56); Asst. in Story Dept., CBS ('57); Assoc., Facilities Operations, CBS ('60); Mgr., Business Affairs Dept., CBS ('68); Dir., Business Affairs, Music Operations, CBS Entertainment, Los Angeles ('80).
ACHIEVEMENTS & AWARDS: N.A.
PERSONAL: Resides in Studio City, CA, with wife, Robbi.

HEKTOEN, JEANNETTE
Dir., NBC, Guest Relations, East Coast

c/o NBC, 30 Rockefeller Plaza, New York, NY 10020
b. October 1. Gary, IN

EDUCATION: Munster High School ('69).
CAREER HIGHLIGHTS: Variety of jobs at WLS-TV, Chicago, then worked for six years as Exec. Asst. to Roone Arledge at ABC. Joined NBC as Mgr., Talent, East Coast ('78), Dir., NBC, Guest Relations, East Coast.
ACHIEVEMENTS & AWARDS: Member, NATAS.
PERSONAL: Married.

HELLER, JOEL
Exec. Prod. and Dir., CBS News, Children's Programming

c/o CBS, 524 W. 57th St., New York, NY 10019
b. N.A.

EDUCATION: Syracuse University, B.A., Liberal Arts ('53), and M.S., TV ('54).

CAREER HIGHLIGHTS: Starting out in the CBS mailroom, Heller became a Reporter and Researcher, "The Hidden Revolution" ('56); introduced short individualized segments in children's programming with "In the Know" ('70); Exec. Prod., "What's It All About" ('72); responsible for "30 Minutes" ('78); Prod., "Razzmatazz" ('77); Exec. Prod. of Children's Broadcasts, CBS News ('71); Dir., Children's Programs, CBS News ('79).

ACHIEVEMENTS & AWARDS: Ohio State University award ('80), Peabody award ('79); Action for Children's Television award ('79) for "30 Minutes". "Razzmatazz" received daytime Emmy award as outstanding children's informational special ('79). Daytime Emmy for outstanding instructional information program short ('83).

PERSONAL: Resides in Chappaqua, NY, with wife, Pat, and their three daughters.

HEMION, DWIGHT
Prod./Dir., Hemion-Smith Productions

c/o Hemion-Smith Productions, 9255 Sunset Blvd., Los Angeles, CA 90069
b. 1926. New Haven, CT.

EDUCATION: Royal London University (England); the Sorbonne (France).

CAREER HIGHLIGHTS: Associate Dir., ABC TV ('46); Dir., "The Tonight Show" ('50), "The Perry Como Show" ('66), "The Sound of Burt Bacharach" ('70), "Barbra Streisand Special" ('73). Formed Hemion-Smith Productions ('75), which is responsible for such glossy TV specials as "America Salutes Richard Rodgers" ('76), "Bette Midler—The Divine Miss M" ('77), "Ben Vereen...His Roots" ('77), "Steve and Edie Celebrate Irving Berlin" ('78), and "Baryshnikov on Broadway" ('79).

ACHIEVEMENTS & AWARDS: Emmy awards for outstanding musical program ('65, '77, '78, '79). Also, Emmy awards for directorial achievement ('69, '74, '76, '77).

PERSONAL: Resides in Beverly Hills, CA, with wife, Katherine; two children.

HEMSLEY, SHERMAN
Actor

c/o "The Jeffersons," 51 W. 52d St., New York, NY 10019
b. February 1, 1938. Philadelphia, PA.

EDUCATION: Philadelphia Academy of Dramatic Arts.

CAREER HIGHLIGHTS: Stage appearances include *Purlie* on Broadway and *Don't Bother Me I Can't Cope* on tour. Series star of "The Jeffersons" as George Jefferson.

ACHIEVEMENTS & AWARDS: N.A.

PERSONAL: Single; resides in Los Angeles.

HENDREN, RON
Reporter, "Observer"; Co-Host,
"Entertainment Tonight," KNBC, "News 4
LA"

c/o KNBC, 3000 W. Alameda Ave., Burbank,
CA 91523
b. Southern Pines, NC.

EDUCATION: University of North Carolina at
Chapel Hill.
CAREER HIGHLIGHTS: Visiting Lecturer in Jour-
nalism, University of Maryland; Political
Commentator, public TV and WRC-TV; na-
tionally syndicated Political Reporter, *Los
Angeles Times;* Television Critic, for NBC's
"Today." Hosts his own syndicated radio
program, "TV Tonight," and co-hosts "Enter-
tainment Tonight."
ACHIEVEMENTS & AWARDS: N.A.
PERSONAL: Resides in Oxnard, CA, with wife,
Jeanne.

HENINBURG, GUSTAV
Co-Host, WNBC-TV, "Positively Black"

c/o WNBC-TV, 30 Rockefeller Plaza, New
York, NY 10020
b. Tuskegee, AL

EDUCATION: Hampton College.
CAREER HIGHLIGHTS: Head of Newark Urban
Coalition; formed the Natl. Sports Committee
in support of the NAACP Legal Defense and
Educational Pact; founder of the Natl. Negro
Business and Professional Committee; ini-
tiated the pre-alumni program of the United
Negro College Fund. Co-Host, WNBC-TV's
"Positively Black."

ACHIEVEMENTS & AWARDS: Chairman of the
Board, Newark Construction Trades and
Training Corp.; Chairman, Architects Com-
munity Design Center; Chairman, Public
Housing Task Force of Newark.
PERSONAL: Father of a boy and girl. Resides in
Maplewood, NJ.

HENNER, MARILU
Actress

b. April 6. Chicago, IL.

EDUCATION: University of Chicago.
CAREER HIGHLIGHTS: Starred in the national
company of *Grease,* which led to Broadway
roles; on TV she appeared in *Dream House on
West 71st Street,* "The Paper Chase," *Seventh
Avenue, Leonard,* and *Off Campus* before hit-
ting it big on "Taxi."
ACHIEVEMENTS & AWARDS: N.A.
PERSONAL: Resides in Los Angeles.

HENRY, CHUCK
Anchor/Reporter, KABC-TV,News

c/o KABC-TV, 4151 Prospect Avenue, Los
Angeles, CA 90027
b. N.A.

EDUCATION: Brigham Young University, Communications ('65)
CAREER HIGHLIGHTS: He began his broadcasting career as the morning Anchor, all-news
radio station KHVH, Honolulu; then became
a Reporter/Anchor, KHVH-TV; Field Re-
porter/Co-Anchor, weekend "Eyewitness
News", KABC-TV ('71); Anchor, weekday 5
P.M. "Eyewitness News," KABC-TV ('74);

Reporter/Documentary Writer, WMAQ-TV, Chicago ('78); Anchor/Reporter, KABC-TV "Eyewitness News," Los Angeles ('82).

ACHIEVEMENTS & AWARDS: Three Emmy awards—one for his special on the election of Mayor Jane Byrne, "City Hall, Here I Come"; another for his coverage of the Los Angeles SLA shootout ('71); and a third for his Channel 7 "Firetrap" series ('77).

PERSONAL: Wife, Kay, four children.

HENSON, JIM
Entertainer

c/o Solters/Roskin/Friedman, 9255 Sunset Blvd., Los Angeles, CA 90069
b. September 24, 1936. Greenville, MS.

EDUCATION: University of Maryland.

CAREER HIGHLIGHTS: A performer, writer, director and producer, Jim Henson is a versatile and potent force in today's entertainment industry. Although the public has come to connect the Henson name with a certain type of puppet entertainment, Henson's career has encompassed everything from experimental animated films to ice shows and a Las Vegas extravaganza. WRC-TV offered him a spot for the show "Sam and Friends" ('55). His Muppet creations were given guest spots on "The Tonight Show," "The Ed Sullivan Show," and other programs, including a regular spot for Rowlf the dog on "The Jimmy Dean Show." The Muppets became series regulars on "Sesame Street" and later on "The Muppet Show." Characters such as Big Bird, Oscar the Grouch, Kermit, and Miss Piggy became international stars. Henson's feature films include *The Muppet Movie*, *The Great*

Muppet Caper, and *Dark Crystal*. He recently launched a new series, "Fraggle Rock," on HBO.

ACHIEVEMENTS & AWARDS: Emmy awards for "The Muppet Show" and "Sesame Street."

PERSONAL: Wife, Jane; three daughters, two sons.

HERMAN, GEORGE
Economics Correspondent, CBS, News

c/o CBS, 524 W. 57th St., New York, NY 10019
b. N.A.

EDUCATION: Dartmouth College, B.A., Mathematics (cum laude, '41); Columbia University Graduate School of Journalism.

CAREER HIGHLIGHTS: Announcer, WQXR-AM, New York ('42); joined CBS News ('44); Night News Editor, CBS Radio Network ('45); Far Eastern Bureau Mgr., CBS News ('51); White House Correspondent, CBS News ('53); Moderator, "Face the Nation," CBS News ('69); named Economics Correspondent, CBS News ('74).

ACHIEVEMENTS & AWARDS: Christopher award ('70).

PERSONAL: N.A.

HERRLING, ANTHONY C.
Mgr., Public Relations, ABC, Video Enterprises

c/o ABC, 1330 Ave. of the Americas, New York, NY 10019
b. N.A.

EDUCATION: Columbia College, B.A., Urban Studies/Political Science.

CAREER HIGHLIGHTS: Joined the CBS News Special Projects Library, New York ('74); Mgr., Creative Services, CBS Broadcast Group Audience Services ('78); Assoc. Editor, *Broadcasting* magazine ('79); Mgr., Public Relations, ABC Video Enterprises ('83).

ACHIEVEMENTS & AWARDS: N.A.

PERSONAL: Resides in New York City with wife, Jane.

HERTZ, ARTHUR H.
Exec. V.P. and Chief Exec. Officer, Treasurer, Chief Financial Officer, and Dir., Wometco Enterprises

c/o Wometco Enterprises, 400 N. Miami Ave., Miami, FL 33128
b. N.A.

EDUCATION: University of Miami, B.B.A.
CAREER HIGHLIGHTS: Accountant, Wometco ('56); Controller, Wometco ('60); V.P., Wometco ('64); Sr. V.P. and Dir., Wometco ('71); Exec. V.P. and Treasurer, Wometco ('81); Chief Exec. Officer, Wometco ('83).
ACHIEVEMENTS & AWARDS: N.A.
PERSONAL: Resides in Coral Gables, FL, with his two sons, Stephen and Andrew.

HERZOG, FRANK
Sports Dir., WJLA-TV

c/o WJLA-TV, 4461 Connecticut Ave., N.W., Washington, DC 20008
b. March 1. Great Bend, KS.

EDUCATION: American University, B.S., Political Science.
CAREER HIGHLIGHTS: Announcer/Reporter, KGKL-Radio, San Antonio, TX ('67); News Correspondent, WOAI-AM/TV, San Antonio ('68); Weekend Sportscaster, WDVM-TV, Washington, DC ('69); Sports Broadcaster, announcing games of the NBA Washington Bullets ('75); added the responsibility of announcing games of the NFL Washington Redskins ('79); Weekend Sportscaster, WDVM, Washington, DC ('69); Sports Dir., WJLA-TV, Washington, DC ('83).
ACHIEVEMENTS & AWARDS: N.A.
PERSONAL: Resides in Maryland with his wife, Sharon-Lynne, and their three daughters.

HEWITT, DON
Exec. Prod., CBS, News

c/o CBS, 524 W. 57th St., New York, NY 10019
b. December 14, 1922. New York, NY.

EDUCATION: New York University.
CAREER HIGHLIGHTS: Pioneering innovative figure in TV journalism for 30 years. His dominant role in the development of "60 Minutes" helped change the course of TV journalism. Hewitt began his journalism career as Head Copy Boy, *N.Y. Herald Tribune* ('42); War Correspondent, in the European and Pacific theaters during World War II ('43); Night Editor-Associated Press, Memphis Bureau ('45); Editor, *Pelham Sun,* New York ('46); Night Telephoto Editor, Acme News Pictures; joined CBS News as Assoc. Dir., "Douglas Edwards With the News" ('48); Prod. Dir., "Douglas Edwards With the News" ('48–'62); Exec. Prod., "CBS Evening News With Walter Cronkite"; Exec. Prod., "Town Meeting of the World" ('65); Co-Prod., "Victory in Europe: 20 Years After" ('65); Prod./Dir., "Eyewitness of History"; Exec. Prod., "Hunger in America"; Prod./Dir., Kennedy-Nixon TV debate ('60); Exec. Prod., "60 Minutes" ('68).
ACHIEVEMENTS & AWARDS: Recipient of seven Emmy awards; named Broadcaster of the Year by IRTS ('80); and has also received the George Polk memorial award; Columbia-Dupont award; University of Missouri distinguished service journalism award; and two Peabody awards.
PERSONAL: Married to ABC News Correspondent Marilyn Berger.

HEWITT, STEVEN W.
Dir., Special Programs, CBS, Entertainment

c/o CBS, 6121 Sunset Blvd., Los Angeles, CA 90028
b. New Rochelle, NY.

EDUCATION: North Carolina School of the Arts, B.A., Theater.
CAREER HIGHLIGHTS: Worked in Programming Dept., Teleprompter Corp., New York; Programming Dept., HBO, New York; Creative Dir., East Coast Advertising and Promotion, CBS Entertainment ('77); Exec. Prod., West Coast Specials, CBS ('79); Dir., Special Programs, CBS Entertainment ('80).

ACHIEVEMENTS & AWARDS: N.A.

PERSONAL: Resides in Santa Monica, CA, with wife, Pamela, and their son.

HEYWORTH, JIM (James O. Heyworth)
Deputy V.P., Video Group, Time, Inc.

c/o HBO, 1271 Ave. of the Americas, New York, NY 10020

b. N.A.

EDUCATION: Yale University; University of Chicago, M.B.A.

CAREER HIGHLIGHTS: Marketing Mgr., *Time* ('67); Asst. Business Mgr., Time-Life Broadcast, then responsible for Time, Inc.'s cable and TV operations; named Business Mgr., Time-Life Cable ('72); V.P. and Treasurer, HBO ('73); Sr. V.P., Finance and Development ('76); Sr. V.P., Operations ('78); appointed Exec. V.P. ('79); elected Pres. and Chief Operating Officer, HBO, and V.P., Time, Inc. ('80); designated Chief Exec. Officer, HBO ('81). Currently Deputy V.P. of Time's Video Group.

ACHIEVEMENTS & AWARDS: N.A.

PERSONAL: Resides in Manhattan with wife, Christine, and three sons.

HICKEY, JIM
Correspondent, ABC, News

c/o ABC, 7 W. 66th St., New York, NY 10019

b. N.A.

EDUCATION: Western Michigan University, B.A., Speech/Journalism ('69).

CAREER HIGHLIGHTS: Reporter/Anchor/Editor/Prod., WKZO-TV, Kalamazoo, MI; Reporter/Editor/Cameraman/Anchor, WTVM-TV, Columbus, GA ('72); Reporter/Anchor, WSB-TV, Atlanta ('74); Reporter/Anchor and New Jersey Bureau Chief, KYW-TV, Philadelphia ('76); Correspondent, ABC News, Chicago ('80).

ACHIEVEMENTS & AWARDS: Received AP award while at WSB-TV, Atlanta; a New Jersey Bar award and an American Bar Assn. award while at KYW-TV, Philadelphia.

PERSONAL: N.A.

HICKEY, NEIL
New York Bureau Chief, *TV Guide*

25 Fifth Ave., New York, NY 10003

b. August 16. Baltimore, MD.

EDUCATION: Loyola College, B.A.

CAREER HIGHLIGHTS: One of the few really knowledgeable reporters covering American television. Has written numerous excellent series on public policy issues and new developments in telecommunications. Joined *TV Guide* ('64).

ACHIEVEMENTS & AWARDS: N.A.

PERSONAL: Resides in New York City and Carmel, NY, with wife, Lisa.

HICKOX, S. BRYAN
Pres., Hickox/Daniel Productions

4000 Warner Blvd., Prod. 4, Room 16, Burbank, CA 91522

b. July 15, 1938. New York, NY.

EDUCATION: Occidental College, B.S.

CAREER HIGHLIGHTS: His 25 years in broadcasting and production began at the local broadcast level in Arizona and throughout California, where he produced and directed more than 400 commercials, followed by positions in sales, sales management, production management, line producing, producing, and executive producing for major network TV series, pilots, and movies. His current work includes "Wizards and Warriors," CBS; "Secret Agent Boy," CBS Children's Special; *The Shooting*, CBS; *No Place To Hide*, CBS; *Jake's Way*, CBS; *Thou Shalt Not Kill*, NBC and *Thou Shalt Not Commit Adultery*, NBC.

ACHIEVEMENTS & AWARDS: Recipient of more than 220 awards.

PERSONAL: Wife, Donna; daughter, Heather.

HILL, ANDREW
V.P. in Charge of Movies and Mini-Series, Columbia Pictures TV

c/o Columbia Pictures TV, Columbia Plaza, Burbank, CA 91505

b. N.A.

EDUCATION: University of California at Los Angeles.

CAREER HIGHLIGHTS: Educational Research Analyst, ABC Circle Films ('77); V.P., Development, Movies and Mini-Series, Henry Jaffe
Enterprises ('79); V.P. in Charge of Movies
and Mini-Series, Columbia Pictures TV ('82).
ACHIEVEMENTS & AWARDS: N.A.
PERSONAL: Resides in Rancho Park, CA, with
his wife and two children.

HILL, BENNY
Comedian/TV Writer/Performer

c/o WOR-TV, 1440 Broadway, New York, NY
10018
b. January 21, 1925. Southampton, England.

EDUCATION:
CAREER HIGHLIGHTS: TV appearances on Brit-
ish television's "Showcase" and "The Service
Show." Motion pictures include *Who Done It,
Light Up the Sky*, and *Chitty Chitty Bang Bang*.
TV series star of the internationally syndi-
cated "Benny Hill Show."
ACHIEVEMENTS & AWARDS: *Daily Mail* award
('54).
PERSONAL: N.A.

HILL, JIM
Sports Anchor, KNXT-TV

c/o KNXT-TV, 6121 Sunset Blvd., Los
Angeles, CA 90028
b. San Antonio, TX.

EDUCATION: Texas A&I, B.S., Journalism.
CAREER HIGHLIGHTS: Disc Jockey, KINE-Radio,
Kingsville, TX ('67); Pro Football Player, San
Diego Chargers and concurrently worked as a
Sports Reporter for KCST-TV, San Diego, CA
('68); Sports Reporter, WBAY-TV, Green Bay,
WS, and Defensive Back for the Green Bay
Packers ('71); Weekend Sports Anchor,
KGTV-TV, San Diego ('73); Weekend Sports
Reporter, KNXT-TV, Los Angeles ('76);
Sports Anchor and Host of "Sunday Sports
Final," KNXT-TV, Los Angeles ('77).
ACHIEVEMENTS & AWARDS: California AP TV
and Radio Assn. award ('78).
PERSONAL: N.A.

HILL, PAMELA
V.P. and Exec. Prod., "Closeup" Unit, ABC, News

c/o ABC, 7 W. 66th St., New York, NY 10023
b. Indiana.

EDUCATION: Bennington College, B.A.; Uni-
versity of Glasgow (Scotland), graduate
study; University of Mexico.
CAREER HIGHLIGHTS: Rockefeller Presidential
Campaign; Foreign Affairs Analyst for Henry
Kissinger ('61); NBC News ('65); Dir. of NBC
White Paper; moved to ABC as Prod./Dir./
Co-Writer, "Fire!" ('73); named V.P. and
Exec. Prod. of ABC News and TV Documentaries with overall responsibilities for "Closeup" Unit ('79).
ACHIEVEMENTS & AWARDS: Worked on Emmy
award-winning programs while at NBC, including "United States Foreign Policy,"
"Summer '67: What We Learned," and Peabody award-winning "Organized Crime in
America." For directing "Pollution Is a Matter
of Choice," she won two Emmy awards and
a Dupont. "Fire!" won two Emmy awards for
best documentary and best direction and the
Peabody, Dupont, and Natl Press Club
awards. "Closeup," in '82 alone, garnered
some 10 prestigious awards. Hill wrote *United
States Foreign Policy: 1945–1965*; her photographs have appeared in numerous magazines and in *Catching Up With America*.
PERSONAL: Married to Tom Wicker, *N.Y. Times*
columnist.

HILL, SANDY
Co-Anchor, KNXT, Channel 2 News, "Live at Five"

c/o KNXT/CBS, 6121 Sunset Blvd., Los
Angeles, CA 90028
b. Centralia, WA.

EDUCATION: University of Washington, B.A.,
Spanish.
CAREER HIGHLIGHTS: Began as Reporter/News-
writer/Prod., KIRO-TV, Seattle, WA. First
woman to co-anchor early evening news at
KNXT. Reported for "20/20," "American
Sportsman," ABC's "Wide World of Sports."
Co-Host, ABC's "Good Morning America";

News Reporter, CBS Sports, Saturday/Sunday ('81–'82).
ACHIEVEMENTS & AWARDS: N.A.
PERSONAL: N.A.

HIRSCH, JUDD
Actor

c/o Artists Agency, 1000 Santa Monica Blvd., Suite 305, CA 90067
b. March 15. New York, NY.

EDUCATION: City College of New York.
CAREER HIGHLIGHTS: Hirsch's hilarious arsenal of slow burns followed by staccato outbursts could serve as textbook examples for anyone trying to master comic timing. Starred on Broadway in *Chapter Two* and *Talley's Folly*, and has guest-starred on many TV shows, including "The Mary Tyler Moore Show," "Medical Story," "The Last Resort," and "Rhoda." Appeared in the feature films *King of the Gypsies, Serpico, Ordinary People,* and *Without a Trace.* TV movies include *The Legend of Valentino, Fear on Trial, Sooner or Later,* and *The Law.* Star of the TV series "Delvecchio" and later "Taxi."
ACHIEVEMENTS & AWARDS: Emmy for his portrayal of Alex Rieger in "Taxi" ('81).
PERSONAL: Single, keeps residences in both New York and Los Angeles.

HOBAN, BRUCE
Dir., Research, Warner Amex Cable Communications

c/o Warner Amex, 75 Rockefeller Plaza, New York, NY 10019
b. N.A.

EDUCATION: N.A.
CAREER HIGHLIGHTS: Sales System Dir., WXYS and WRIF-Radio, Detroit; Dir. of Research and Systems Development, ABC Radio; V.P./Dir. of Research, Cable Advertising Bureau; Dir., Research, Warner Amex Cable Communications ('83).
ACHIEVEMENTS & AWARDS: N.A.
PERSONAL: N.A.

HOCKEMEIR, J. CURT
Dir., Cox Cable Communications, Market Development Operations

219 Perimeter Center, Atlanta, GA 30346
b. May 15, 1948. Carrollton, MO.

EDUCATION: University of Missouri, B.S. ('70).
CAREER HIGHLIGHTS: Publicist, General Electric, Schenectady, NY ('70); Advertising Copywriter ('71); Acct. Supervisor, General Electric, Erie, PA ('72); Acct. Supervisor, General Electric, Washington, DC ('74); Mgr., Plastics Programs, Advertising and Sales Promotion, General Electric, Pittsfield, MA ('76); Dir., Corporate Advertising, Cox Cable Communications ('80); Dir., Market Development Operations, Cox Cable Communications ('82).
ACHIEVEMENTS & AWARDS: N.A.
PERSONAL: N.A.

HOFFMANN, BETTYE K.
V.P., NBC, Program Information Resources

c/o NBC, 30 Rockefeller Plaza, New York, NY 10020
b. May 5, 1926. Tewksbury, MA.

EDUCATION: New York University, B.A.
CAREER HIGHLIGHTS: Exec. Secretary, NBC ('52); named Mgr., Audience Services ('68); Dir., Audience Services ('72); V.P., Information Services ('73); appointed V.P., Program Information Resources ('77).
ACHIEVEMENTS & AWARDS: Member, AWRT, New York Chapter; Exec. V.P. ('81); Pres. ('82).
PERSONAL: Resides in Croton-on-Hudson, NY.

HOGAN, GERALD
V.P., Turner Broadcasting System, Sales

c/o Turner Broadcasting System, 1050
   Techwood Dr., Atlanta, GA 30318
b. November 30, 1949. Chicago, IL.

EDUCATION: St. Ambrose College, B.A.
CAREER HIGHLIGHTS: Acct. Exec., Leo Burnett
   Co. ('69) and WTCG, now WTBS ('71); Local
   Sales Mgr., WTBS ('72) and General Sales
   Mgr. ('78). Joined Turner Broadcasting Sys-
   tem as V.P., Sales ('80).
ACHIEVEMENTS & AWARDS: N.A.
PERSONAL: N.A.

HOLLADAY, DOUGLAS S.
V.P., Weather Channel

2840 Mount Wilkinson Parkway, Suite 200,
   Atlanta, GA 30339
b. December 21, 1946. East Orange, NJ.

EDUCATION: University of Virginia, M.B.A.
CAREER HIGHLIGHTS: Started on the staff of
   Landmark Communications ('76); Circulation
   Dir., *Virginian Pilot Ledger Star* ('78); Dir.,
   Management Information ('78); Dir., Special
   Projects ('80); Dir., Cable Marketing ('82);
   V.P., Weather Channel ('82).
ACHIEVEMENTS & AWARDS: N.A.
PERSONAL: Resides in Atlanta with wife, Mary,
   and son, Whit.

HOLLIDAY, POLLY
Actress

c/o Richard Dinkins & Co., 5550 Wilshire
   Blvd., Los Angeles, CA 90036
b. July 2. Jasper, AL.

EDUCATION: Alabama State College.
CAREER HIGHLIGHTS: Turned "kiss my grits"
   into a national catch phrase and turned a
   waitress cliche into a comic Texas landmark as
   memorable as the Alamo. Acting career
   started in varied stage productions and pro-
   gressed to the film *All the President's Men;* won
   the part of Flo in an audition for the "Alice"
   series ('76); was given her own "Flo" series
   and later substituted for an injured Eileen
   Brennan in the "Private Benjamin" series
   ('82).
ACHIEVEMENTS & AWARDS: Two Golden Globe
   awards for her portrayal of Flo on "Alice."
PERSONAL: Resides in New York City.

HOLLIMAN, JOHN
**White House Correspondent, Cable News
Network, Washington, DC, Bureau**

2133 Wisconsin Ave., Washington, DC 20007
b. October 23, 1948. Atlanta, GA.

EDUCATION: University of Georgia.
CAREER HIGHLIGHTS: Began career at various
   small radio stations in Georgia before landing
   a job as Anchor/Reporter, WSB-AM, Atlanta
   ('70); Correspondent/Anchor, Metromedia
   Radio ('72); Agricultural Editor/Correspon-
   dent, AP Radio Network, Washington, DC
   ('74); Correspondent/Anchor, Cable News
   Network ('80); named White House Correspondent ('82).
ACHIEVEMENTS & AWARDS: Peabody award for
   the documentary "The Garden Plot."
PERSONAL: Resides in Washington, DC

HOLLY, JAMES
**Exec. V.P. and General Mgr., Times Mirror
Videotex Services**

c/o Times Mirror Videotex Services, 1375
   Sunflower Ave., Costa Mesa, CA 92626
b. February 21, 1938. Clinton, MA.

EDUCATION: Holy Cross College, B.S., Market-
   ing ('60); Harvard Business School, M.B.A.
   Marketing, ('65).
CAREER HIGHLIGHTS: Special Asst. to General
   Mgr., American Express Co. ('65); Dir., Uni-
   Serve Corp. ('67); V.P., TRW Information Ser-

vices ('68); Exec. V.P. and General Mgr., Times Mirror Videotex Services ('80).
ACHIEVEMENTS & AWARDS: N.A.
PERSONAL: N.A.

HOOKS, WILLIAM G.
Sr. V.P., HBO, Regional Operations

c/o HBO, 1271 Ave. of the Americas, New York, NY 10020
b. July 6, 1943.

EDUCATION: Boston University; Southern Methodist University; Brown University.
CAREER HIGHLIGHTS: Regional Marketing Mgr., Teleprompter Corp., now Group W Cable, New York ('70); Regional Marketing Dir., Warner Cable Corp., New York ('73); Marketing Mgr., HBO ('74); opened company's Regional Office in Dallas ('76); General Mgr., Central Region ('77); promoted to V.P. ('78); V.P. and General Mgr., HBO's Eastern Region ('79); V.P., Marketing Administration and Communications ('80); V.P., Regional Operations, HBO ('82); Sr. V.P., Regional Operations, HBO ('83).
ACHIEVEMENTS & AWARDS: N.A.
PERSONAL: Resides in Upper Saddle River, NJ, with wife, Elaine, and three children.

HOOKSTRATTEN, ED
Attorney and Agent

9012 Beverly Blvd., Los Angeles, CA 90048
b. N.A.

EDUCATION: University of Southern California ('53); Southwestern Law School.
CAREER HIGHLIGHTS: Hookstratten represents many of the top names in news, entertainment and sports. A topflight agent, he has landed some of the most lucrative contracts for clients such as Tom Brokaw, Bryant Gumbel, Merlin Olsen, and Joey Bishop. Before forming his own agency, he also worked with the law firm of Raoul Magana.
ACHIEVEMENTS & AWARDS: N.A.
PERSONAL: Resides in Bel Air, CA.

HOOPER, GEORGE A.
V.P., NBC, Audience Research

c/o NBC, 30 Rockefeller Plaza, New York, NY 10020
b. June 29, 1931. Akron, Ohio

EDUCATION: Ohio Wesleyan University, B.A.; Columbia Graduate School of Business, M.S.
CAREER HIGHLIGHTS: Career at NBC began as Stage Mgr. ('53); several promotions through Mgr., Station Sales and Clearance ('62); Dir., Research, NBC TV Stations; currently V.P., Audience Research.
ACHIEVEMENTS & AWARDS: N.A.
PERSONAL: N.A.

HOOVER, JULIE TARACHOW
V.P., ABC, Standards and Practices, East Coast

c/o ABC, 1330 Ave. of the Americas, New York, NY 10019
b. New York, NY.

EDUCATION: Bryn Mawr College, B.A.
CAREER HIGHLIGHTS: Dir., Audience Information and Awards, ABC, Inc., Public Relations ('73); Dir., East Coast, Broadcast Standards and Practices ('76); appointed V.P. of same dept. ('80).
ACHIEVEMENTS & AWARDS: Member, IRTS; AWRT.
PERSONAL: Resides in Mount Kisco, NY, and Manhattan.

HOPE, BOB (Leslie Townes Hope)
Comedian

c/o NBC, 3000 W. Alameda Ave., Burbank, CA 91523
b. May 29, 1903. Eltham, England.

EDUCATION: N.A.
CAREER HIGHLIGHTS: TV's durable king of comedy, whose longevity and multimedia track record will probably never be matched. He is a consistent star who made the transition from radio to TV, with many movies in between. New York stage appearances include *Roberta, Red, Hot and Blue,* and *Ziegfeld Follies.* Star of his own radio series for 18 years on

NBC Radio. Motion pictures include *College Swing, Thanks for the Memory, Ghost Breakers, Caught in the Draft, Let's Face It, Paleface, Fancy Pants, Here Come the Girls, Seven Little Foys, Bachelor in Paradise,* and a number of *Road* pictures with Bing Crosby. NBC TV star of top-rated specials, especially USO Christmas shows for more than 34 years.

ACHIEVEMENTS & AWARDS: Among his numerous awards are *Look* magazine film achievement award ('48); Independent Motion Picture Prods. award ('48); top comedy performance, *Independent Film Journal* ('52–'53) and the Headliner of the Year award, Greater Los Angeles Press Club ('64). For more than a decade ('42–'57), Hope was among the top ten box-office draws in the motion picture industry.

PERSONAL: Wife, the former Dolores Reade; children, Tony, Linda, Nora, and Kelley. Resides in Toluca Lake, CA.

EDUCATION: Harvard Business School, M.B.A.

CAREER HIGHLIGHTS: Joined Norman Lear and Jerry Perenchio ('72) and rose quickly through the ranks; became Head, Business Affairs; Exec. V.P. and Chief Operating Officer responsible for company's financial and business operations; Pres. ('78). also served as Exec. Prod., "One Day at a Time," "The Jeffersons," "Archie Bunker's Place" and added new shows, "Diff'rent Strokes" and "The Facts of Life." Named Chairman and Chief Exec. Officer, Embassy Communications with total responsibility for Embassy Communications, Embassy TV, Tandem Productions, Embassy Telecommunications, and Embassy Pictures. Horn now works for Embassy as an independent.

ACHIEVEMENTS & AWARDS: N.A.

PERSONAL: N.A.

HORGAN, SUSAN BEDSOW
Prod., CBS, "As the World Turns"

c/o CBS, 51 W. 52d St., New York, NY 10019
b. November 24, 1947. Chicago, IL.

EDUCATION: University of California at Irvine, B.A. ('69).

CAREER HIGHLIGHTS: Spent first six years after graduation trying to find work as an actress; during that time she also served as a Production Secretary and Asst. to the Prod. on ABC's "One Life To Live" ('71); Asst. to the Prod., "The Guiding Light" ('77); promoted to Assoc. Prod. ('78); moved to "As the World Turns" in the same capacity ('79); and promoted to her current position as Prod., "As the World Turns" ('79).

ACHIEVEMENTS & AWARDS: N.A.

PERSONAL: Married; resides in New York City.

HORN, ALAN
Ind. Prod., Embassy Communications

c/o Embassy Communications, 1901 Ave. of the Stars, Los Angeles, CA 90067
b. N.A.

HORNER, VIVIAN
V.P., Warner Cable

c/o Warner Cable, 75 Rockefeller Plaza, New York, NY 10019
b. N.A.

EDUCATION: Ohio State University, English Literature, B.A. and M.A.; University of Rochester, Linguistics, M.S., and Psycholinguistics, Ph.D.

CAREER HIGHLIGHTS: Dir., "Electric Company" for Children's Television Workshop; joined Warner Cable, where she mounted Nickelodeon, the cable network for children; created Pinwheel, a channel for preschoolers ('76); V.P. of Program Development, Warner Cable ('79). As V.P. at Warner Cable, she piloted the "Video-Jukebox," a forerunner of MTV, developed the first WA interactive disc for Qube, and initiated co-ventures to produce narrowcast pay-per-view videocassettes.

ACHIEVEMENTS & AWARDS: Member, Board of Dirs., C-Span.; Nat'l. Pres., Women in Cable ('82).

PERSONAL: N.A.

HOROWITZ, DAVID
Consumer Advocate/Reporter, NBC TV

9012 Beverly Blvd., Los Angeles, CA 90048
b. New York, NY.

EDUCATION: Bradley University, B.A.; Northwestern University; Columbia University, M.S.J.

CAREER HIGHLIGHTS: Broke ground for consumer advocacy coverage on TV newscasts aimed at educating consumers about their rights. Prod., ABC Radio News ('62); Writer/Reporter, NBC News "Huntley-Brinkley Report" ('63); Far East Correspondent, NBC News ('64); Los Angeles Reporter, NBC News ('66); Consumer Reporter, KNBC ('70); Creator/Host, "David Horowitz Consumer Byline" ('76); Creator/Host "Fight Back With David Horowitz" ('79); Consumer Advocate, "Today" show ('82); Consumer Reporting Specialist, NBC TV News ('82).

ACHIEVEMENTS & AWARDS: Emmy awards ('73, '76, '77, '82). Also awards from the U.S. Consumer Product Safety Commission and the Society of Consumer Affairs Professionals. Author of *Fight Back! And Don't Get Ripped Off;* syndicated columnist.

PERSONAL: Married to Suzanne McCambridge, two daughters; resides in Los Angeles.

HOROWITZ, EDWARD D.
Sr. V.P., Network Operations and Corporate Development, HBO

c/o HBO, 1271 Ave. of the Americas, New York, NY 10020
b. November 16, 1947.

EDUCATION: City College of New York; Columbia University, M.B.A.

CAREER HIGHLIGHTS: Held various engineering positions at numerous local cable companies before joining HBO as a Field Engineer ('74);

promoted to Mgr. of Transmission Development ('75); Mgr. of Affiliate Relations ('76); Mid-Atlantic Regional Mgr. ('77), and subsequently Mid-Atlantic and New York Metro Regional Dir.; V.P. ('79); General Mgr. of Central Region ('79); V.P., Studio and Network Operations, overseeing the national satellite communications network and studio operations ('80); Sr. V.P., Network Operations and Corporate Development ('83).

ACHIEVEMENTS & AWARDS: Member, Institute of Electrical and Electronics Engineers; society of Cable TV Engineers; Society of Broadcast Engineers; Natl. Cable TV Assn.

PERSONAL: Resides in Short Hills, NJ, with wife, Susan, and son, David.

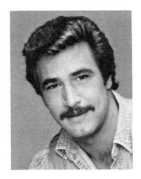

HORSLEY, LEE
Actor

c/o "Matt Houston," ABC, 2040 Ave. of the Stars, Los Angeles, CA 90067
b. May 15. Muleshoe, TX.

EDUCATION: University of North Colorado.

CAREER HIGHLIGHTS: Appeared in productions of *Oklahoma, Fiddler on the Roof, Kismet,* and *The Lion in Winter,* then went to New York and Hollywood. Starred in the movie *The Sword and the Sorcerer* before becoming the star of "Matt Houston."

ACHIEVEMENTS & AWARDS: N.A.

PERSONAL: Wife, Stephanie; one daughter. Resides in Los Angeles.

HOTTELET, RICHARD C.
UN Correspondent, CBS, News

c/o CBS, 524 W. 57th St., New York, NY
10019
b. 1917.

EDUCATION: Brooklyn College, B.A.

CAREER HIGHLIGHTS: Hottelet's journalism career began as a Reporter, UPI, Berlin ('38); worked for the U.S. Office of War Information in London, North Africa, and Italy ('42); joined Edward R. Murrow's CBS News London Bureau ('44). After assignment in Moscow, he returned to the U.S. ('46); opened CBS News Bureau in Bonn ('51); assigned to the UN ('60). Special CBS News broadcasts include "Where We Stand," "Years of Crisis," "The Correspondents' Reports," and "Face the Nation."

ACHIEVEMENTS & AWARDS: N.A.

PERSONAL: Married to the former Ann Delafield; two children.

HOUGH, STANLEY
Dir., CBS TV Movies and Mini-Series

c/o CBS, 4024 N. Radford, Studio City, CA
91604
b. July 23, 1920. Los Angeles, CA.

EDUCATION: Loyola University.

CAREER HIGHLIGHTS: Exec. Production Mgr., 20th Century Fox ('55); V.P., Production, 20th Century Fox ('60); Independent Prod., feature films, TV series, TV movies ('72); Dir., CBS TV Movies and Mini-series ('81).

ACHIEVEMENTS & AWARDS: NAACP image award; Christopher award.

PERSONAL: N.A.

HOUSEMAN, JOHN (Jacques Haussmann)
Actor/Author/Prod./Dir./Teacher

c/o ABC, 1330 Ave. of the Americas, New
York, NY 10019
b. September 22, 1902. Bucharest, Rumania.

EDUCATION: Clifton College.

CAREER HIGHLIGHTS: Houseman's ominous voice is one of the most recognizable on TV. He started his career as a prominent Broad-

way Dir./Prod., who formed the Mercury Theater with Orson Welles. Joined David O. Selznick, Inc. as V.P., and then became Prod. of the motion pictures *Lust for Life*, *The Bad and the Beautiful*, *Executive Suite*, and *All Fall Down*. Exec. Prod., "Playhouse 90." As an actor, his TV movies include *Fear on Trial*, *Captains and Kings*, and *Aspen*. He also appeared in the mini-series *The Winds of War*. Motion pictures include *The Paper Chase*, *Ghost Story*, and *The Fog*. Network series star of "The Paper Chase." New episodes of "The Paper Chase" are being produced ('83) for Showtime.

ACHIEVEMENTS & AWARDS: Academy Award as best supporting actor for *The Paper Chase*.

PERSONAL: Wife, Joan Courtney; two sons. Resides in Southern California.

HOWARD, CHUCK
V.P. in Charge of Program Production, ABC, Sports

c/o ABC, 1330 Ave. of the Americas, New
York, NY 10019
b. N.A.

EDUCATION: Duke University.

CAREER HIGHLIGHTS: Joined ABC Sports ('60) and moved up the production ladder to one of the top executive positions in the company. Has been involved with nearly all major productions of ABC Sports, including NCAA football, Monday night baseball, the Kentucky Derby, U.S. Open Golf, the Indianapolis 500, the World Series, and seven telecasts of the Olympic Games.

ACHIEVEMENTS & AWARDS: Eight Emmy awards for sports programs.

PERSONAL: Resides in Pound Ridge, NY, with wife, Carolyn; daughters, Dana, Dawn, and Caroline; son, Christopher.

HOWARD, RON
Actor

c/o ABC, 2040 Ave. of the Stars, Los Angeles,
CA 90067
b. March 1, 1954. Duncan, OK.

EDUCATION: University of Southern California; Los Angeles; Valley College.

CAREER HIGHLIGHTS: Perhaps the best child actor of his day, Howard has developed into a pleasant leading man and a comedy director who bears watching. TV career began with appearances on "The Red Skelton Show," "GE Theater," "The Twilight Zone," and "Dobie Gillis." Motion pictures include *The Journey, The Music Man, The Shootist, American Graffiti,* and *Eat My Dust.* Wrote and directed the film *Grand Theft Auto* and directed *Night Shift.* Since childhood, he has starred in three series: "The Andy Griffith Show," "The Smith Family," and "Happy Days." Also, Prod./Dir., NBC's "Littleshots" ('83).
ACHIEVEMENTS & AWARDS: N.A.
PERSONAL: Wife, Cheryl Alley.

HOWELL, JOSH
Investigative Reporter

c/o WABC-TV, 1330 Ave. of the Americas, New York, NY 10019
b. Newport, RI.

EDUCATION: George Washington University, B.S.; Harvard University, M.A.
CAREER HIGHLIGHTS: Newswriter/Prod./On-Air Reporter, WBAL-TV ('74); Investigative Reporter, WABC-TV.
ACHIEVEMENTS & AWARDS: AP Broadcasters Assn. award ('76); three Edward R. Murrow awards ('77–'78); New York local Emmy for best investigative reporting ('78).
PERSONAL: N.A.

HOWLAND, BETH
Actress

c/o "Alice," CBS, 7800 Beverly Blvd., Los Angeles, CA 90036
b. May 28, 1947. Boston, MA.

EDUCATION: N.A.
CAREER HIGHLIGHTS: New York stage appearances in *Company, George M, Your Own Thing,* and *A Tribute to Stephen Sondheim.* TV guest appearances on "Little House on the Prairie," "The Mary Tyler Moore Show," "Cannon," "Eight Is Enough," "The Love Boat," and "The Rookies." Series star of "Alice" as Vera.
ACHIEVEMENTS & AWARDS: Golden Globe nomination for best actress in a TV series.
PERSONAL: Daughter, Holly. Resides in Los Angeles.

HUBERT, DICK
Chairman, Gateway Productions

c/o Gateway Productions, 304 E. 45th St., New York, NY 10017
b. June 30, 1938.

EDUCATION: Amherst College.
CAREER HIGHLIGHTS: Writer/Prod., ABC News; Exec. Prod., Group W, Inc.; formed Gateway Productions, specializing in documentaries for PBS; Independent Prod. of TV documentaries. Among his public affairs specials are "Fire Trap," "The Blue Minority," and "The Shame of Welfare."
ACHIEVEMENTS & AWARDS: Peabody award, Sidney Hillman award, and the mass media award of the Natl. Conference of Christians and Jews, for his Group W production, "One Nation Indivisible."
PERSONAL: N.A.

HUDSON, BETTY
V.P., NBC, Corporate Relations

c/o NBC, 30 Rockefeller Plaza, New York, NY 10020
b. July 16, 1949. Atlanta, GA.

EDUCATION: University of Georgia, A.B.J., Advertising and Public Relations.

CAREER HIGHLIGHTS: Copywriter, WCBD-TV, Charleston, SC ('72); Dir. of Promotion, WCIV-TV ('75); Dir. of Advertising and Promotion, WAVE-TV, Louisville, KY ('76); Dir. of Advertising and Promotion, WSB-TV, Atlanta ('77); joined NBC as V.P., Corporate Projects ('79); named V.P., Corporate Relations ('81).

ACHIEVEMENTS & AWARDS: Charleston Ad Club award ('76); Outstanding Young Careerist, State of South Carolina, Business and Professional Women's Club ('76); two Louisville Ad Club awards ('78); John E. Drewry award, Most Outstanding Young Graduate, University of Georgia School of Journalism ('82). Chairperson, NBC Affiliate Promotion Committee ('77–'79); Board Member, Atlanta Chapter, NATAS ('78); Co-Chairman, Learning Center Committee, Junior League of New York City ('82); Board Member, TV Information Office and IRTS ('81–present).

PERSONAL: Resides in New York City.

HUDSON, ROCK (Roy Fitzgerald)
Actor

c/o Chasin-Park-Citron Agency, 10889 Wilshire Blvd., Los Angeles, CA 90024
b. November 17, 1924. Winnetka, IL.

EDUCATION: New Trier High School.
CAREER HIGHLIGHTS: Whether movie idol or TV

star, Hudson exhibits the same dependability and strength, qualities as solid as his name. Has made more than 60 motion pictures, beginning with *Fighter Squadron* ('48); later appearing in *Magnificent Obsession, One Desire, All That Heaven Allows, Giant, Pillow Talk, Lover Come Back, Come September, Darling Lili, Pretty Maids All in a Row*, and *The Mirror Crack'd*. TV credits include *Wheels, Once Upon a Dead Man, World War III, The Martian Chronicles*, and the TV series "McMillan and Wife" ('71–'76) and "The Devlin Connection" ('82).

ACHIEVEMENTS & AWARDS: M.P. *Herald-Fame* Poll, top box office star ('57–'65).

PERSONAL: Single, resides in Beverly Hills, CA.

HULL, RON
Dir., Program Fund, Corp. for Public Broadcasting

c/o Corp. for Public Broadcasting, 1111 16th St., N.W., Washington, DC 20036
b. N.A.

EDUCATION: Dakota Wesleyan University, B.A.; Syracuse University School of Public Communications, M.S., Television/Radio; University of Nebraska-Lincoln, Ed.D.

CAREER HIGHLIGHTS: Joined KUON-TV, Lincoln, NE ('55); Program Mgr., Nebraska Educational TV Network, since it began ('63); took a leave of absence to serve as TV Adviser for the State Dept. to the government of South Vietnam ('66); Prod./Dir., "Vietnam Beyond the Fury" documentary for PBS ('72); served on the President's Committee on the Arts ('79); Dir., Program Fund, Corp. for Public Broadcasting ('82).

ACHIEVEMENTS & AWARDS: Member and former Chairman, PBS Public TV Library Program Selection Committee.

PERSONAL: Wife, Naomi; four children.

HUME, BRIT
Correspondent, ABC, News

c/o ABC, 1717 DeSales St., N.W., Washington, DC 20036
b. N.A.

EDUCATION: University of Virginia.

CAREER HIGHLIGHTS: Reporter, *Baltimore Evening Sun;* Reporter, UPI; Reporter, *Hartford Times;* worked as an Investigative Reporter for syndicated columnist Jack Anderson ('69); Consultant, ABC News, assigned to the "Closeup" Documentary Unit ('72); Reporter, ABC News ('77); Correspondent, ABC News, Capitol Hill ('79); Chief Senate Correspondent, ABC News ('81).

ACHIEVEMENTS & AWARDS: Author, *Death and Mines* ('71); *Inside Story* ('74).

PERSONAL: Resides in Bethesda, MD, with his wife and their three children.

HUMI, PETER JOHN
Prod./Correspondent, Cable News Network, Rome

c/o Cable News Network, Via dei Robilant I, Rome 00194, Italy
b. December 29, 1955. Rome, Italy.

EDUCATION: University of London, B.A., History and Italian; University of Florence, University of Venice.

CAREER HIGHLIGHTS: Freelance Newsroom Asst., UPITN Newsfilm Agency, London ('77); Freelance Satellite Prod./Writer, UPITN ('78); Staff Member, UPITN, London; Satellite Prod./Eurovision News; Exchange Editor/Sports Prod. ('79); Prod./ Correspondent, Cable News Network, Rome ('82).

ACHIEVEMENTS & AWARDS: N.A.

PERSONAL: N.A.

HUNT, JOHN
V.P., Assoc. Dir., Ogilvy & Mather, Media Research

c/o Ogilvy & Mather, 2 E. 48th St., New York, NY 10017
b. N.A.

EDUCATION: Fordham University; New York University, Graduate School of Business.

CAREER HIGHLIGHTS: Joined Ogilvy & Mather ('67); elected V.P. ('80). Primarily works with the Broadcast Dept. as a Network Analyst. Also tracks long-term trends in TV and services the broadcast groups in the agency's branch offices.

ACHIEVEMENTS & AWARDS: Member, Ad Hoc Committee on Cable TV Measurements recently formed by CTAM and Natl. Cable TV Assn.

PERSONAL: Native of Staten Island, NY; married, with two children.

HUNTER, ALAN
Video Jockey, Warner Amex Satellite Communications Co., MTV: Music Television

c/o MTV, Warner Amex, 1211 Ave. of the Americas, New York, NY 10036
b. February 14. Mississippi.

EDUCATION: N.A.

CAREER HIGHLIGHTS: Developed a background in musical and dramatic theater with bit parts in various stage and TV productions. Selected to be one of MTV's five video jockeys when the cable channel began ('81).

ACHIEVEMENTS & AWARDS: N.A.

PERSONAL: N.A.

HUNTER, NATALIE
V.P., Strategic Planning, Corporate Planning and Business Development, NBC

c/o NBC, 30 Rockefeller Plaza, New York, NY 10020
b. N.A.

EDUCATION: Wellesley College; Massachusetts Institute of Technology, B.S.; Harvard Business School, M.A., Business Administration

CAREER HIGHLIGHTS: Consultant, McKinsey & Co.; Business Planner, American Airlines; Mgr., Finance, Philip Morris Intl.; Dir., Strategic Planning, NBC ('80); V.P., Strategic Planning, Corporate Planning and Business Development, NBC ('83).

ACHIEVEMENTS & AWARDS: N.A.

PERSONAL: Married, resides in New York City.

HUSKY, RICK
Prod./Writer

c/o Columbia Pictures TV, Producer 7, #12, Burbank, CA 91505
b. May 6, 1940. Philadelphia, PA.

EDUCATION: Arkansas State University, B.S.

CAREER HIGHLIGHTS: Has written more than 100 pilots, TV movies and episode scripts. Developed "Cade's County" ('70); "SWAT" ('74); "T.J. Hooker" ('82). Prod., "The Mod Squad" ('72), "The Rookies" ('73), "SWAT" ('75), "Charlie's Angels" ('78), and "T.J. Hooker" ('82).

ACHIEVEMENTS & AWARDS: N.A.

PERSONAL: N.A.

HUSTED, AL
Dir., Hearst/ABC, Public Relations

c/o Hearst/ABC, 555 Fifth Ave., New York, NY 10017
b. October 1, 1938. Elkhart, IN.

EDUCATION: Ithaca College; Northwestern University

CAREER HIGHLIGHTS: Prod./Dir./Announcer, WTVO, Rockford, IL ('60); U.S. Army, Information Specialist ('62); NBC Press Dept., Coordinator of Information, Enterprises Division ('65); Press Agent, Johnny Carson, "Tonight Show" ('68); Dir. of Publicity, "Tonight Show" ('66); "The Dick Cavett Show," Dir. of Media Relations ('70); Freelance Public Relations and Photographer ('72); V.P., March Five Public Relations ('76); Dir., Public Relations, Hearst/ABC ('82).

ACHIEVEMENTS & AWARDS: N.A.

PERSONAL: N.A.

HYMEN, SARALEE
V.P., Cabletelevision Advertising Bureau, Marketing

c/o Cabletelevision Advertising Bureau, 767 Third Ave., New York, NY 10017
b. Chicago, IL.

EDUCATION: Indiana University at Bloomington.

CAREER HIGHLIGHTS: Dir. of Station Relations and Asst. to the Pres., Radio Advertising Bureau; Natl. Accts. Mgr., ABC Radio. Currently V.P., Marketing, Cabletelevision Advertising Bureau.

ACHIEVEMENTS & AWARDS: N.A.

PERSONAL: N.A.

HYSLOP, AL
V.P., Children's Television Workshop, "Sesame Street"

c/o Children's Television Workshop, 1 Lincoln Plaza, New York, NY 10023
b. California.

EDUCATION: Attended school in England. American Theatre Wing and the Martha Graham Dance Co.

CAREER HIGHLIGHTS: Began his career in the theater, as actor, director, and stage manager for numerous productions in London and New York. Joined CBS TV in New York, and moved on to Robert Keeshan Assoc. as V.P. and Prod., "Captain Kangaroo." He joined Children's Television Workshop as a Consultant in Intl. Production ('77). Served as Exec. Prod. for the second season of CTW's "3-2-1 Contact."

ACHIEVEMENTS & AWARDS: Emmy, 10th anniversary shows, "Sesame Street," taped in Puerto Rico.

PERSONAL: N.A.

I

IANNUCCI, SALVATORE J.
Exec. V.P., Embassy Communications

1901 Ave. of the Stars, #666, Los Angeles, CA 90067
b. September 24, 1927. Brooklyn, NY.

EDUCATION: New York University, B.A., Political Science ('49); Harvard Law School, J.D. ('52).

CAREER HIGHLIGHTS: Started career as Staff Attorney ('52); joined CBS TV Network, New York as V.P., Business Affairs ('54); then became Pres., Capitol Records ('69); V.P. and Corporate Dir., Entertainment Division, Playboy Enterprises, Los Angeles ('71); Partner, Jones, Day, Reavis & Pogue ('75); Pres., Filmways Entertainment, Los Angeles ('79). Exec. V.P., Embassy Communications ('82).

ACHIEVEMENTS & AWARDS: N.A.

PERSONAL: Wife, Aileen; daughter, Helene; sons, Thomas and Peter. Resides in Los Angeles.

IGER, ROBERT
Dir., Program Planning, ABC Sports, "Wide World of Sports"

c/o ABC, 1330 Ave. of the Americas, New York, NY 10019
b. N.A.

EDUCATION: Ithaca College, B.S., Communications.

CAREER HIGHLIGHTS: Reporter/Weathercaster, WCIC-TV, Ithaca, NY ('72); Studio Coordinator, ABC ('74); Operations Supervisor, ABC Sports ('76); Program Controller, ABC Sports ('77); Mgr., Program Planning, ABC Sports "Wide World of Sports" ('78); Dir., Program Planning, ABC Sports "Wide World of Sports" ('80).

ACHIEVEMENTS & AWARDS: N.A.

PERSONAL: Resides in New York City with wife, Susan, and their two daughters, Kate and Amanda.

ILLES, ROBERT
Prod./Writer (Freelance)

c/o Bernie Weintraub, 2916 Waverly Dr., Los Angeles, CA 90039
b. May 17, 1948. Downey, CA.

EDUCATION: University of Southern California, B.A., Telecommunications.

CAREER HIGHLIGHTS: Writer, CBS, "The New Bill Cosby Show" ('72–'73); Writer, Lily Tomlin special "Lily" ('73, '74); Writer, "The Smothers Brothers Show" ('74–'75); Story Editor, "One Day at a Time" ('76–'77); writer, "The Carol Burnett Show" ('77–'78); Writer/Prod., "Flo" ('79–'80); "Private Benjamin" (81–'82); and "Silver Spoons" ('82).

ACHIEVEMENTS & AWARDS: Emmy awards for "Lily" and "The Carol Burnett Show."

PERSONAL: Wife, Barbara Pariot.

ILOTT, PAMELA
V.P. of Cultural and Religious Broadcasts, CBS, News

c/o CBS, 524 W. 57th St., New York, NY 10019
b. N.A.

EDUCATION: Durham University.

CAREER HIGHLIGHTS: Joined CBS News as Script Editor ('54); named Prod., "Lamp Unto My Feet" ('54); Exec. Prod., "Lamp Unto My Feet" and "Look Up and Live" ('57). Currently oversees production of the CBS religious broadcasts as V.P. of Cultural and Religious Broadcasts.

ACHIEVEMENTS & AWARDS: Awarded the gold medal of the Patriarch of Antioch by the Syrian Orthodox Church ('65); Peabody award for her accomplishments on "Lamp Unto My Feet" and "Look Up and Live" ('73); honored by the Broadcasting and Film Commission of the Natl. Council of Churches and the North American Chapter of the World Assn. for Christian Communication ('74). Also received numerous Emmy, Sylvania, and Gabriel awards.
PERSONAL: N.A.

ILSON, SAUL
Writer/Prod.

c/o Writers' Guild of America, 8955 Beverly Blvd., Beverly Hills, CA 90048
b. N.A.

EDUCATION: N.A.
CAREER HIGHLIGHTS: Co-Writer, with Ernest Chambers, "Tony Orlando and Dawn" series; NBC Exec. for Variety and Comedy Development; Prod., "The Billy Crystal Comedy Hour" for NBC; Prod. for Columbia Pictures. Also Prod., "The Lynda Carter Special," "The Beatrice Arthur Special," "For Members Only," CBS, and "There Goes the Neighborhood," NBC.
ACHIEVEMENTS & AWARDS: N.A.
PERSONAL: N.A.

INDELLI, JOSEPH D.
Sr. V.P., Columbia Pictures TV

c/o Columbia Pictures TV, 300 Colgems Sq., Burbank, CA 91505
b. January 23, 1940. Chicago, IL.

EDUCATION: Vanderbilt University, B.A., History.
CAREER HIGHLIGHTS: Sales Representative, Proctor and Gamble ('64); Sales Representative, MGM TV ('68); V.P., Sales, Metromedia Production Corp. ('76); moved over to Columbia Pictures TV in same capacity ('80); appointed Sr. V.P., Columbia Pictures TV ('82).
ACHIEVEMENTS & AWARDS: N.A.
PERSONAL: Resides in Pacific Palisades, CA, with wife, Mary.

INDERFURTH, RICK
Correspondent, ABC, News

c/o ABC, 1717 DeSales St., N.W., Washington, DC 20036
b. N.A.

EDUCATION: University of North Carolina, B.A., Political Science; Strathclyde University (Scotland), Fulbright Scholar; Princeton University, M.A.
CAREER HIGHLIGHTS: Staff Member, U.S. Select Committee on Intelligence ('75); Member, Carter-Mondale Transition Team ('76); Special Asst. to the Asst. for Natl. Security Affairs ('77); Deputy Staff Dir., Political and Security Affairs, the Senate Committee on Foreign Affairs ('79); Pentagon Correspondent, ABC News, Washington, DC ('81).
ACHIEVEMENTS & AWARDS: N.A.
PERSONAL: N.A.

INGALLS, DON
Writer/Prod.

c/o Shapiro-Lichtman, 2 Century Plaza, Suite 1320, 2049 Century Park E., Los Angeles, CA 90067
b. July 29, 1927. Humboldt, NE.

EDUCATION: George Washington University.
CAREER HIGHLIGHTS: Writer/Prod., "Have Gun, Will Travel" ('58); "Travels of Jamie McPheeters" ('62); "The Virginian" ('63); "Honey West" ('65); "Serpico" ('76); "Kingston Confidential" ('77). Freelance writing credits include "Police Story," "Bonanza," "Gunsmoke," "The Big Valley," "Marcus Welby, M.D.," "Night Gallery," and the "Sixth Sense." Feature films include *Secret Agent, Duel at Shiloh, Airport '75,* and *Who's Got the Body?* Currently Writer/Prod., "Fantasy Island."
ACHIEVEMENTS & AWARDS: N.A.
PERSONAL: Resides in Ventura, CA.

ISAACS, CAROL
Mgr., Administration, Program Practices, CBS, Broadcast Group

c/o CBS, 7800 Beverly Blvd., Los Angeles, CA 90036
b. N.A.

EDUCATION: Baruch College, B.B.A., Marketing.

CAREER HIGHLIGHTS: Commercial Clearance Editor, Program Practices Dept., CBS, New York ('69); Editor, Daytime and Prime Time Depts., CBS, Hollywood ('73); Mgr., Administration, Program Practices, CBS Broadcast Group, Hollywood ('83).

ACHIEVEMENTS & AWARDS: N.A.

PERSONAL: Resides in Los Angeles.

ISAACS, DAVID
Writer

c/o William Morris Agency, 151 El Camino Dr., Beverly Hills, CA 90212
b. October 26, 1949. New York, NY.

EDUCATION: University of Miami.

CAREER HIGHLIGHTS: Freelance Writer for "The Jeffersons," "Joe and Sons," "M*A*S*H," "The Tony Randall Show," "The Practice," ('75); Story Editor, "M*A*S*H" ('77); Exec. Script Consultant, "M*A*S*H" ('78); Prod., 20th Century Fox ('79); Prod., Lorimar Productions ('81); Co-Prod., "Cheers" ('82).

ACHIEVEMENTS & AWARDS: Emmy and Writers Guild awards for the "Goodbye Radar" episode of "M*A*S*H" ('80).

PERSONAL: N.A.

ISAACS, JEREMY
Chief Exec., Channel 4 TV Co.

c/o Channel 4 TV, 60 Charlotte St., London W1P 2AX
b. September 28, 1932.

EDUCATION: Merton College.

CAREER HIGHLIGHTS: Prod., Granada TV ('58); Prod., Associated-Rediffusion ('63); Prod., BBC's "Panorama" ('65); Controller of Features, Associated Rediffusion ('67); Controller, Thames TV ('68); Prod., "The World at War" for Thames TV ('74); Dir. of Programmes, Thames TV ('74); Prod., "A Sense of Freedom," ITV ('79); Chairman, BFI Production Board ('79); Chief Exec., Channel 4 TV, London ('81).

ACHIEVEMENTS & AWARDS: Desmond Davis award; George Polk award.

PERSONAL: Resides in London, England.

ISACSSON, PAUL
Sr. V.P., CBS, Broadcast Group

c/o CBS, 51 W. 52d St., New York, NY 10019
b. N.A.

EDUCATION: Fordham University.

CAREER HIGHLIGHTS: Researcher, Ratings Analysis Dept., NBC; Mgr., Audience Measurement, Young & Rubicam; Member, TV and Program Dept., Wells, Rich, Greene; Acct. Exec., CBS TV Sales Dept. ('68); Dir., Nighttime Sales, CBS; V.P., Eastern Sales, CBS; V.P., Sales Planning, CBS; V.P., Sales, CBS TV ('77); Sr. V.P., CBS Broadcast Group ('82).

ACHIEVEMENTS & AWARDS: N.A.

PERSONAL: N.A.

ISELIN, JOHN JAY
Pres., Educational Broadcasting Corp., WNET/13, New York

356 W. 58th Street, New York, NY 10019
b. December 8, 1933. Greensville, SC.

EDUCATION: Harvard University, M.A. and Ph.D. ('56).

CAREER HIGHLIGHTS: Sr. Writer, *Congressional Quarterly* ('60); Sr. Editor, National Affairs, *Newsweek* magazine ('61); Pres., Educational Broadcasting Corp. ('73).

ACHIEVEMENTS & AWARDS: On *Times* list of 200 rising young American leaders ('74); Research Fellow, Brookings Institution ('60).

PERSONAL: Wife, Josephine; five children. Resides in New York City.

ISENBERG, GERALD
Prod., Jozak Co.

c/o Guttman & Pam Ltd., 120 El Camino Dr., Beverly Hills, CA 90212
b. Boston, MA.

EDUCATION: Bowdoin College, B.A. ('61); Harvard Business School, M.B.A. ('64).

CAREER HIGHLIGHTS: Asst. to the Pres., Columbia Pictures ('64); Asst. to V.P. in Charge of West Coast Production, Columbia Pictures, Hollywood ('67); Exec. in Charge of Feature Film Production ('68); Exec. Prod., Metromedia Producers Corp. ('71). Formed own production company, the Jozak Co. ('73). With his own production company, Exec. Prod., *It Couldn't Happen to a Nicer Guy* ('73); *Winner Take All* ('73); *James Dean* ('74); *Having Babies* ('76); *Secrets* ('76); *The Secret Life of Joan Chapman* ('77); *The Defection of Simas Kudirka* ('77); *Having Babies II* ('77); *Having Babies III* ('78) *Ski Lift to Death* ('78); *Murder at the Mardi Gras* ('78); *The Gift* ('79); *Flesh and Blood* ('79); and *Letters From Frank* ('79). Exec. Prod./Dir., *Seizure* ('79); Exec. Prod., "Fame" series ('82).

ACHIEVEMENTS & AWARDS: N.A.

PERSONAL: Resides in Bel Air, CA, with wife, Carole, and their two sons, Joshua and Zachary.

ISHIMINE, JOANNE
Reporter/Weekend Anchor, KABC-TV, News

c/o KABC-TV, 4151 Prospect Ave., Los Angeles, CA 90027
b. N.A.

EDUCATION: University of California at Los Angeles, B.A., English.

CAREER HIGHLIGHTS: A member of KABC-TV "Eyewitness News" staff for 10 years, Ishimine began as a General Assignment Field Reporter for "Eyewitness News." She is a frequent Anchor, Channel 7's local "Eyewitness News" insert of ABC TV's weekday program "Good Morning America," and has hosted KABC-TV's early morning public affairs talk show, "Daybreak LA"; Prod., two "mini-documentaries."

ACHIEVEMENTS & AWARDS: N.A.

PERSONAL: Resides in North Hollywood, CA.

J

JACKSON, GREG
Correspondent, ABC, News

c/o ABC, 7 W. 66th St., New York, NY 10023
b. N.A.

EDUCATION: Whitman College, B.A.; Columbia Graduate School of Journalism, M.A., Journalism.
CAREER HIGHLIGHTS: Reporter, *Idaho Daily Statesman*; News Dir./Anchor, KTVB-TV, Boise, ID; Prod., ABC News Public Broadcast Library ('66); Correspondent, ABC News ('68); Independent Prod. ('75); Exec. Prod., "Healthline," PBS ('78); Off-Camera Interviewer on CBS Cable's "Signature" series ('81); Host, ABC News "The Last Word" ('82), until the show was cancelled ('83); now Off-Camera Correspondent for "One to One."
ACHIEVEMENTS & AWARDS: Emmy for ABC documentary "Portrait of Whitney Young" ('67). His "Healthline" series won the Blakeslee award ('81). Author, *Getting Into Broadcast Journalism: A Guide to Careers in Radio and TV News*.
PERSONAL: N.A.

JACKSON, J. J.
Video Jockey, Warner Amex Satellite Entertainment Co., MTV: Music Television

c/o MTV, Warner Amex, 1211 Ave. of the Americas, New York, NY 10036
b. November 25.

EDUCATION: N.A.
CAREER HIGHLIGHTS: Disc Jockey, KLOS-FM, Los Angeles; Contributing Reporter, providing interviews of rock stars for "Eyewitness News," on KABC-TV, Los Angeles; Disc Jockey, KWST-FM, Los Angeles; Video Jockey, MTV: Music Television ('81).

ACHIEVEMENTS & AWARDS: N.A.
PERSONAL: Resides in New York City.

JACKSON, KATE
Actress

c/o William Morris Agency, 151 El Camino Dr., Beverly Hills, CA 90212
b. October 29, 1949. Birmingham, AL.

EDUCATION: University of Mississippi; Birmingham University; American Academy of Dramatic Arts.
CAREER HIGHLIGHTS: The most intelligent of Charlie's winged associates, Jackson did yeoman service in several series before developing into a capable actress specializing in TV and theatrical movies that benefit immeasurably from her presence. Her first professional acting job was on the gothic soap opera "Dark Shadows," and she landed guest spots on "Movin' On" and "The Jimmy Stewart Show." Spent four years as a regular on "The Rookies" before the "Charlie's Angels" series. TV movie credits include *Charlie's Angels, Death at Love House, Satan's School for Girls, The New Healers, James at 15, Topper,* and *Thin Ice.* Also the star of the series "Scarecrow and Mrs. King" ('83).
ACHIEVEMENTS & AWARDS: N.A.
PERSONAL: Resides in Beverly Hills, CA.

JACKSON, KEITH
Sportscaster, ABC

c/o ABC, 1330 Ave., of the Americas, New
York, NY 10019
b. N.A.

EDUCATION: N.A.
CAREER HIGHLIGHTS: Sports Announcer, Uni-
versity of Washington and Washington State
University; Anouncer, KOMO-TV, Seattle,
WA; Commentator for ABC Sports, including
NCAA football and major league baseball;
Commentator for ABC's "Wide World of
Sports."
ACHIEVEMENTS & AWARDS: N.A.
PERSONAL: N.A.

JACOBS, DAVID
Prod., Lorimar Productions

c/o Lorimar Productions, 3970 Overland Ave.,
Culver City, CA 90230
b. Baltimore, MD.

EDUCATION: N.A.
CAREER HIGHLIGHTS: A fiction and short story
writer ('60s), Jacobs went west and conquered
by thinking up "Dallas" and nasty J. R. Ewing. Next came "Knots Landing," which he
currently produces. His latest creation is
"Loving Friends and Perfect Couples," a soap
opera for the Showtime cable network.
ACHIEVEMENTS & AWARDS: N.A.
PERSONAL: Resides in Beverly Hills, CA.

JACOBS, RICK
Dir., Talent and Casting, CBS,
Entertainment, West Coast

c/o CBS, 6121 Sunset Blvd., Los Angeles, CA
90028
b. New York, NY.

EDUCATION: State University of New York at
Buffalo, B.A.; Florida State University,
M.F.A.
CAREER HIGHLIGHTS: Casting Dir. for legitimate
dramas; Casting Dir., PBS; Casting Dir. of
NBC soap opera "The Doctors"; Dir., Talent
and Casting, CBS, New York ('79); Dir., Tal-
ent and Casting, CBS Entertainment, West
Coast ('82).
ACHIEVEMENTS & AWARDS: N.A.
PERSONAL: N.A.

JAFFE, ALFRED J.
V.P./Editor, *Television/Radio Age*

c/o *Television/Radio Age,* 1270 Ave. of the
Americas, New York, NY 10020
b. N.A.

EDUCATION: Temple University, B.S.; Colum-
bia University Graduate School of Journal-
ism, M.S.
CAREER HIGHLIGHTS: Sr. Editor, "Sponsor"
('52); Managing Editor, "Sponsor" ('60); Pro-
motion Dir., Radio Advertising Bureau ('62);
Editor, "The Key Report" ('63); Editor, "Mar-
keting Forum" ('64); Editorial Dir., *Television/
Radio Age* ('67); V.P. and Editor, *Television
Radio/Age* ('81).
ACHIEVEMENTS & AWARDS: N.A.
PERSONAL: N.A.

JAFFE, HENRY
Prod., Jaffe Enterprises

c/o Jaffe Enterprises, Sunset Gower Studios,
Hollywood, CA 90028
b. New York, NY.

EDUCATION: Columbia University; Columbia
Law School.
CAREER HIGHLIGHTS: Lawyer Jaffe entered
show business through the back door, or-
ganizing the American Guild of Musical Art-

ists ('36). The following year Jaffe helped form the American Federation of Radio Artists. When a client became ill, Jaffe stepped in to manage "Producer's Showcase" ('52); "Goodyear Playhouse" ('52); and "The Alcoa Hour" ('55). Prod., "The Bell Telephone Hour" ('59–'68); "The Dinah Shore Chevy Show" ('57); "Dinah's Place" ('70); "Dinah" ('74). Jaffe coaxed Shirley Temple out of retirement for "The Shirley Temple Theater" ('69). Exec. Prod. for the TV movies *Teacher, Teacher* ('68); *Richie* ('78); *Emily* ('80), and *I Was a Mail Order Bride* ('82).

ACHIEVEMENTS & AWARDS: Emmy for *Teacher, Teacher* ('68); three Emmy awards for Dinah Shore shows ('72, '74, '75).

PERSONAL: Resides in Beverly Hills, CA.

JAFFE, STEPHEN (Steve)
Prod., Jaffe/Blakely Films

9454 Wilshire Blvd., Suite 405, Beverly Hills, CA 90212
b. February 14, 1944. San Diego, CA.

EDUCATION: University of California at Santa Barbara, B.A.; University of California at Los Angeles.

CAREER HIGHLIGHTS: Publicist, "Dragnet," "The Virginian," Universal TV ('69); Pres., Steve Jaffe Public Relations ('71), clients include Barbra Streisand, Jane Fonda, Susan Blakely, Tatum O'Neal, John Cassavettes, Donald Sutherland, Richard Dreyfuss, and Richard Pryor. Pres., Jaffe/Blakely Films ('76).

ACHIEVEMENTS & AWARDS: N.A.

PERSONAL: Wife, actress Susan Blakely.

JAMES, WATSON S.
V.P., Video Technology/Programming, Doyle, Dane, Bernbach

c/o Doyle, Dane, Bernbach, 437 Madison Ave., New York, NY 10020
b. March 16, 1944.

EDUCATION: Cornell University, B.A., Economics; Harvard Business School, M.B.A., Marketing.

CAREER HIGHLIGHTS: Began as an executive in motion picture production and distribution ('68). Acct. Management and Media, Doyle,

Dane, Bernbach ('76); Network TV Programming Exec., Doyle, Dane, Bernbach ('80); V.P., Video Technology/Programming, Doyle, Dane, Bernbach ('81).

ACHIEVEMENTS & AWARDS: Author, *Television in Transition* ('82).

PERSONAL: N.A.

JAMIESON, BOB
News Correspondent, NBC

c/o NBC, 30 Rockefeller Plaza, New York, NY 10020
b. Varna, IL.

EDUCATION: Knox College, Bradley University.

CAREER HIGHLIGHTS: Began news career while in high school as Film Lab Asst./Photographer/Reporter, WMBD-TV, Peoria ('59); KSDK-TV, St. Louis, Reporter/Anchor ('67); moved to WBBM ('68); NBC News Chicago-based Reporter ('71); named Correspondent ('73); assigned to White House ('76); "Special Segment" reports on "NBC Nightly News" ('78); assigned to New York Bureau ('79).

ACHIEVEMENTS & AWARDS: N.A.

PERSONAL: N.A.

JANKOWSKI, GENE F.
Pres., CBS Broadcast Group

c/o CBS, 51 W. 52d Street, New York, NY 10019
b. May 31, 1934. Buffalo, NY.

EDUCATION: Canisius College, B.A.; Michigan State, M.S., Communication Arts ('59).

CAREER HIGHLIGHTS: Following stints as substitute teacher and work at ad agency and radio station WBNY, Buffalo, now WYSL, joined CBS Radio Network as Acct. Exec. ('61). Promoted to Eastern Sales Mgr. ('66); moved to network TV sales ('69); named General Sales Mgr., WCBS-TV ('70); promoted to Dir., Sales ('71). Became V.P., Sales, CBS TV Stations Division ('73); named V.P., Finance and Planning ('74); promoted to V.P. and Controller, CBS, Inc. ('76); appointed V.P., Administration ('77); named Exec. V.P., CBS Broadcast Group, then elected V.P., CBS, Inc., and Dir. of Corp. ('77); Pres., CBS Broadcast Group.

ACHIEVEMENTS & AWARDS: Communications medal, Southern Baptist Radio and TV Commission.

PERSONAL: Resides in Connecticut with wife, Sally; four children.

JARRIEL, TOM
Correspondent, ABC, News

c/o ABC, 1717 DeSales St., N.W., Washington, DC 20036

b. La Grange, GA.

EDUCATION: University of Houston.

CAREER HIGHLIGHTS: Started journalism career at KPRC-TV, Houston, and moved up the ranks from Copy Boy to News Editor. Correspondent, ABC News, Atlanta ('65); Correspondent, ABC News, Washington, DC ('68); White House Correspondent, ABC News ('69); Sr. Regional Correspondent, ABC News ('78). Currently serves as a regular contributor to ABC News "20/20" and anchors "World News Tonight—The Weekend Report."

ACHIEVEMENTS & AWARDS: Natl. Headliners award for reporting on "20/20."

PERSONAL: Resides in Potomac, MD, with his wife, Joan and their three sons.

JARVIS, LUCY
Pres. and Founder, Creative Projects Inc.

45 Rockefeller Plaza, Suite 715, New York, NY 10020

b. New York, NY.

EDUCATION: Cornell University, B.S.; Columbia Teachers College, M.S.

CAREER HIGHLIGHTS: Assoc. Editor and Nutrition Editor, *McCall's* magazine; TV Editor, Pathé News; Co-Prod., "Capital Closeup"; joined NBC Creative Projects Unit ('60). Her documentaries include "The Kremlin" ('63); "The Louvre" ('64); "Khrushchev in Exile" ('67); "Dr. Barnard's Heart Transplant Operations" ('68); "Trip to Nowhere" ('70); primetime specials with Barbara Walters at ABC ('76). Other credits include "The Forbidden City," "The Royal Lovers," and "Museum Without Walls." Formed Creative Projects ('76). Prod. of the mini-series *Family Reunion* with Bette Davis ('81).

ACHIEVEMENTS & AWARDS: Emmy awards for "The Kremlin" ('63) and "The Louvre" ('64). Other awards include the Peabody, Christopher, and Ohio State Journalism awards.

PERSONAL: N.A.

JELLINEK, HERB
V.P., Production, ABC, Entertainment and Motion Pictures

c/o ABC, 4151 Prospect Ave., Los Angeles, CA 90027

b. N.A.

EDUCATION: University of Vienna; Columbia University.

CAREER HIGHLIGHTS: Joined the Cost Accounting Dept., ABC ('52); Asst. Supervisor of Cost Accounting, ABC ('55); Asst. Dir. of Sales Service, ABC TV ('58); Cost Control Administrator ('59); Dir. of Budgets and Cost Control, West Coast, ABC ('62); V.P., Controller, ABC TV ('68); V.P., Production Coordination and Administration for ABC Circle Entertainment

('71); V.P., Production Operations and Administration, ABC TV ('76); V.P., Production, ABC TV ('77); V.P., Production for ABC Entertainment and ABC Motion Pictures ('79).

ACHIEVEMENTS & AWARDS: N.A.

PERSONAL: Resides in Tarzana, CA, with wife Faye.

JENNERJAHN, MARY LOU
V.P., Asst. to the Pres., CBS, TV

c/o CBS, 51 W. 52d St., New York, NY 10019
b. N.A.

EDUCATION: St. John's University, B.A., LL.B.

CAREER HIGHLIGHTS: Counsel, FCC; Counsel, Paramount Pictures; Counsel for the Natl. General Pictures Corp.; General Counsel for the Natl Assn. of Theater Owners; joined the CBS News Business Affairs Dept. ('71); Dir., Business Affairs, CBS News, London ('75); Dir., Commercial Clearance, CBS ('77); V.P., Commercial Clearance, Program Practices, CBS Broadcast Group ('81); V.P., Asst. to the Pres., CBS TV ('83).

ACHIEVEMENTS & AWARDS: Member, New York Bar Assn.

PERSONAL: Resides in New York City.

JENNINGS, PETER
Anchor "World News Tonight," ABC News

c/o ABC, 7 W. 66th St., New York, NY 10019
b. N.A.

EDUCATION: N.A.

CAREER HIGHLIGHTS: News and Public Affairs Correspondent, Canadian TV Network; ABC Anchor, network evening news ('64); Natl

Correspondent ('68). Established and operated ABC News Bureau in Beirut ('71); Washington Co-Anchor, ABC morning program ('74); Interviewer, "Issues and Answers"; named Chief Correspondent, London ('75); currently serves as Foreign Desk Anchor of ABC's "World News Tonight." Produced numerous network documentaries, short stories, and human interest feature pieces; conducted first full-length interview seen in U.S. with Yasir Arafat; currently sole anchor on "World News Tonight" ('83–'84).

ACHIEVEMENTS & AWARDS: Lowell Thomas award of the Overseas Press Club, for "Sadat: The Aftermath," an ABC News radio special "Perspective"; Peabody award for "Sadat: Action Biography" ('74); Natl. Headliners award for coverage of Bangladesh conflict.

PERSONAL: N.A.

JENSEN, MIKE (Michael C. Jensen)
NBC News Correspondent

c/o NBC, 30 Rockefeller Plaza, New York, NY 10020
b. November 1, 1934. Chicago, IL.

EDUCATION: Harvard University, B.A., English ('56); Boston University, M.S., Journalism ('61).

CAREER HIGHLIGHTS: Joined *Boston Herald Traveler* as Reporter; named Business and Financial Editor ('61); moved to *N.Y. Times* as Financial Reporter/Editor ('69); NBC News Correspondent, specializing in business and economics ('78). Appears on "NBC Nightly News" and "Today," and is a frequent panelist on "Meet the Press."

ACHIEVEMENTS & AWARDS: AP-Managing Editors of New England award; Overseas Press Club award for national reporting ('72); Deadline Club award for best economic reporting in the New York metropolitan area ('74); Media award for economic understanding for the "Killer Inflation" segment on "NBC Nightly News" ('80); Janus award for excellence in broadcast journalism for "The Social Security Squeeze" segment on "NBC Nightly News" ('81). Published articles in many periodicals; wrote *The Financiers* ('77); contributing author to *Corporations and Their Critics* ('80).

PERSONAL: Married to the former Jane Rice Woodruff; children, Heidi and Michael Jr.

JEROME, ALBERT
Pres., NBC, TV Stations Division

c/o NBC, 30 Rockefeller Plaza, New York, NY 10020
b. July 9, 1942. New York, NY.

EDUCATION: Cornell University, B.A.; New York University, M.A., Business Administration.
CAREER HIGHLIGHTS: Automotive Sales Mgr., WCBS-TV, New York ('69); Natl. Sales Mgr., WCBS-TV ('70); Eastern Sales Mgr. based in New York for WBBM-TV, Chicago ('73); General Sales Mgr., WCAU-TV, Philadelphia ('74); Acct. Exec., NBC, New York, ('75); Natl. Sales Mgr., WMAQ-TV, Chicago ('75); V.P. and General Mgr., WNBC-TV, New York ('80); Exec. V.P., NBC TV Stations Division ('82); Pres., NBC TV Stations Division ('82).
ACHIEVEMENTS & AWARDS: N.A.
PERSONAL: Resides in Demarest, NJ, with wife, Michele, and son, Zachary. He also has two sons, Gregory and Kenneth, from a previous marriage.

JETER, FELICIA
Correspondent/Co-Anchor/Interviewer, CBS, News

c/o CBS, 524 W. 57th St., New York, NY 10019
b. Atlanta, GA.

EDUCATION: Mundelein College; Columbia University Graduate School of Broadcast Journalism; University of Southern California.
CAREER HIGHLIGHTS: Correspondent/Co-Anchor, WAGA-TV, Atlanta ('72); concurrently Prod./Host, "Basic Black," WAOK-Radio, Atlanta; Reporter/Weekend Anchor, "Newscenter 4," Co-Host, "Everywhere," KNBC-TV, Los Angeles ('74); Co-Host, NBC's "Speak Up America" ('80); Co-Anchor, "10 O'Clock News," KHJ-TV, Los Angeles ('80); Prod./Host, PBS "Great Escapes" ('81); Correspondent/Co-Anchor/Interviewer, "Nightwatch," CBS News ('82).
ACHIEVEMENTS & AWARDS: Image award from the NAACP; gubernatorial commendation from the Governor of Georgia Jimmy Carter, for journalistic excellence.
PERSONAL: N.A.

JIMIRRO, JAMES. P.
Pres., Walt Disney Productions, Walt Disney Telecommunications and Non-Theatrical Co.

c/o Walt Disney Telecommunications, 500 S. Buena Vista St., Burbank, CA 91521
b. Pittsburgh, PA.

EDUCATION: Pennsylvania State College, B.A., Radio and TV; Syracuse University, M.S.
CAREER HIGHLIGHTS: Program Dir., WPBS-Radio, Philadelphia; Dir., Intl. Sales, CBS; Dir., Intl. Sales, Viacom Intl.; Dir., Intl. Sales, Walt Disney Educational Media Co., New York ('73); Exec. V.P., Walt Disney Educational Media Co. ('74); Pres., Walt Disney Telecommunications and Non-Theatrical Co. ('82).
ACHIEVEMENTS & AWARDS: Member, Board of Dirs., Intl. Tape-Disc Assn. and the ECT Foundation.
PERSONAL: N.A.

JOBLIN, MONIA B.
Mgr., USA Network, Program Development and Scheduling

c/o USA Network, 208 Harristown Rd., Glen Rock, NJ 07452
b. N.A.

EDUCATION: Wellesley College, B.A.
CAREER HIGHLIGHTS: Assoc. Prod., "Masterpiece Theatre" and "Classic Theatre" series; Prod. of "Zoom," WGBH-TV, Boston. Prod., Calliope, USA Network film series as well as Mgr., Program Development and Scheduling.
ACHIEVEMENTS & AWARDS: Emmy award ('77).
PERSONAL: N.A.

JOHNSON, BRUCE
Pres. of HAVES (Hearst ABC/Viacom Entertainment Services)

c/o HAVES, 1211 Ave. of the Americas, New York, NY 10036
b. November 15, 1934.

EDUCATION: University of Southern California, B.S. Telecommunications; Southwestern University School of Law; Juris Doctor.
CAREER HIGHLIGHTS: V.P. and West Coast Mgr. of Metromedia; V.P. and Gen. Mgr. of KFAC-Los Angeles; V.P. and Gen. Mgr. of KLAC-Los Angeles; Pres. of the Radio Division and Chairman of the Board of RKO; Pres. and Chief Exec. Officer of Shamrock Starr Broadcasting; started his own management consulting firm, BFJ Co.; Pres. of Cable Health Network; Pres. of HAVES ('83).
ACHIEVEMENTS & AWARDS: Radio Executive of the Year Award ('78); Directorships in N.A.B. and the Southern California Broadcasters Assn.
PERSONAL: Resides in San Marino, Calif. with wife and three children.

JOHNSON, DEBORAH
Exec. Prod., NBC News, "NBC News Overnight"

c/o NBC, 30 Rockefeller Plaza, New York, NY 10020
b. N.A.

EDUCATION: Radcliffe College.
CAREER HIGHLIGHTS: Freelance Writer, Boston ('70); Reporter, AP ('73); Editor, *Mother Jones* magazine ('75); Newswriter, weekend news, KPIX-TV, San Francisco ('78); Prod., weekend news, KPIX-TV, San Francisco ('79); Prod., News, KTVU-TV, Oakland, CA ('80); Sr. Editor, "NBC Nightly News" ('81); Exec. Prod., "NBC News Overnight" ('83).
ACHIEVEMENTS & AWARDS: N.A.
PERSONAL: N.A.

JOHNSON, DAVID
V.P., ABC, Strategic Planning

c/o ABC, 1330 Ave. of the Americas, New York, NY 10019
b. N.A.

EDUCATION: Amherst College ('61); Harvard Graduate School of Business Administration, M.B.A. ('63).
CAREER HIGHLIGHTS: Cost Control Administrator, ABC ('64); Business Mgr., ABC Owned TV Stations Division ('65); Acct. Exec., WABC-TV, New York ('69); Sales Mgr., WABC-TV, New York ('74); General Sales Mgr., TV Spot Sales Division, ABC ('75); Dir. of Sales, ABC TV Spot Sales Division ('76); V.P. and General Mgr., ABC TV Spot Sales Divison ('77); V.P., ABC Owned TV Stations ('78); V.P., Strategic Planning, ABC, Inc. ('81).
ACHIEVEMENTS & AWARDS: N.A.
PERSONAL: Resides in Greenwich, CT.

JOHNSON, DOUG
Correspondent, WABC-TV, New York, News

c/o WABC-TV, 7 Lincoln Sq., New York, NY 10023
b. Canada.

EDUCATION: N.A.
CAREER HIGHLIGHTS: Anchor/News Dir., CFTO-TV, Toronto, Ontario ('60); Correspondent, WABC-TV, New York, also serving as Co-Host of the station's "Good Morning New York" ('69).
ACHIEVEMENTS & AWARDS: Uniformed Firefighters Assn. media award ('77); Emmy for individual craft achievement ('78).
PERSONAL: Resides in New York City.

JOHNSON, JOHN
Correspondent/Investigative Reporter/Part-Time Anchor, WABC-TV, New York, News

c/o WABC-TV, 7 Lincoln Sq., New York, NY 10023
b. New York, NY.

EDUCATION: City University of New York.
CAREER HIGHLIGHTS: Prod./Writer/Dir., ABC Documentary Unit; Correspondent, WABC-TV, New York ('72).
ACHIEVEMENTS & AWARDS: Christopher award for ABC Documentary "To All the World's Children"; AP Broadcasters award ('77);

Emmy ('78). Member, Assn. of Radio-TV News Analysts.

PERSONAL: Resides in New York City.

JOHNSON, KENNETH
Writer/Prod./Dir

c/o Universal Studios, 100 Universal City Plaza, Universal City, CA 91608
b. October 26, 1942.

EDUCATION: Carnegie Tech.

CAREER HIGHLIGHTS: Production Asst., CBS TV, New York; Prod./Dir., "The Mike Douglas Show," Group W, Philadelphia; Writer, "Adam-12"; Writer/Prod., "Six Million Dollar Man" and "The Bionic Woman"; Creator/Exec. Prod./Dir., "The Incredible Hulk"; Creator/Exec. Prod., "Cliffhangers"; Exec. Prod./Dir./Writer, *Senior Trip*, TV movie; and *V*, mini-series ('83). Writer/Prod. "A Death in the Family."

ACHIEVEMENTS & AWARDS: Two Emmy awards for "The Mike Douglas Show.

PERSONAL: Resides in Los Angeles.

JOHNSON, LUCY ANTEK
V.P., NBC, Daytime Children's Project Peacock Programming

c/o NBC, 30 Rockefeller Plaza, New York, NY 10020
b. July 14, 1945. New York, NY.

EDUCATION: Boston University School of Fine Arts.

CAREER HIGHLIGHTS: Asst. to Dir., "The Guide" ('68); "Nash at Nine" ('73); "Music! Music!" ('75). Entered broadcasting as Pro-

duction Assoc. and Assoc. Prod. working with producers including Joe Cates, Martin Charnin, Roone Arledge, Alan King, and David Susskind ('67–'77). Became Independent Prod., developing programming for networks and syndication ('76); joined NBC Programming as Dir., Daytime Development ('78). Dir., Specials and Late Night ('79); Dir., Development, Project Peacock ('80); promoted to V.P., Daytime Children's Project Peacock Programming ('81).

ACHIEVEMENTS & AWARDS: Member, Exec. Board, Natl. Council for Children and TV ('81).

PERSONAL: Married to Roger (Biff) Johnson.

JOHNSON, ROBERT L.
Pres., Black Entertainment TV

c/o Black Entertainment TV, 1050 31st St., N.W., Washington, DC 20007
b. N.A.

EDUCATION: University of Illinois; Princeton University.

CAREER HIGHLIGHTS: Held positions with the Corp. for Public Broadcasting and the Urban League; Press Secretary for Congressional Representative Walter Fauntroy of the District of Columbia; V.P., Government Relations, Natl. Cable TV Assn. ('76); founded and became Pres. of Black Entertainment TV cable network ('79).

ACHIEVEMENTS & AWARDS: Natl. Cable TV Assn. president's award; NAACP image award.

PERSONAL: Resides in Washington, DC with wife, Sheila.

JONES, CHARLIE
Sportscaster, NBC

c/o 3000 W. Alameda Ave., Burbank, CA
91523
b. N.A.

EDUCATION: University of Arkansas, LL.D.
('53).
CAREER HIGHLIGHTS: Sportscaster, KNAC-TV,
Fort Smith, AR ('56); Dir. of TV and Radio,
Dallas Texans ('60); Sports Dir., WFAA-TV,
Dallas ('62); joined NBC to cover AFL ('65);
continues with NFL football, major league
baseball, golf, track and field, and auto rac-
ing; was voice of Cincinnati Reds baseball
team ('73–'74).
ACHIEVEMENTS & AWARDS: N.A.
PERSONAL: Resides in La Jolla, CA, with wife,
Ann; two children.

JONES, CHARLOTTE SCHIFF
Pres., Schiff-Jones, Ltd.

1775 Broadway, New York, NY 10019
b. January 21, 1932. New York, NY.

EDUCATION: Brooklyn College, B.A.; Columbia
University, M.B.S.
CAREER HIGHLIGHTS: Began extensive produc-
tion career in TV with Screen Gems as Pro-
duction Coordinator and Prod. ('65); named
Exec. Prod., Drew Lawrence Productions,
working on TV commercials ('68). Jumped
into cable TV with Teleprompter as Dir.,
Community Programming, and Natl. Dir.,
Franchise Acquisitions; produced the Natl.
Black Political Convention for PBS while with
Teleprompter ('72); moved to Manhattan
Cable TV as Exec. V.P./Dir./Exec. Prod., "Vil-
lage Voice" and "Women in Business' series

('74). Did a one-year stint in publishing as
Assoc. Publisher, *People* ('77); returned to TV
production as Prod., "People" series on CBS
('78); worked in program development for
Time, Inc.'s Video Division ('79); joined CBS
Cable at its inception as V.P. ('80–'82); Pres.,
Schiff-Jones, Ltd. ('83).
ACHIEVEMENTS & AWARDS: Natl. Cable TV
Assn. best program awards for Natl. Black
Political Convention ('72) and "The Uncon-
vention" ('73); New York Emmy award for
"N.Y. Live" with Harrison Salisbury ('74).
Named among Top 100 Corporate Women in
Business Week ('76); gold medal of the Broad-
cast Promotion Assn. for multi-media cam-
paign, "Celebrate the Arts," ('82). Co-Chair,
Advisory Board, Negro Ensemble Co.
('71–'75); Public Affairs Advisory Committee,
Air Force Academy Education Center ('74);
Dir., New York State Cable TV Assn.
('75–'77).
PERSONAL: N.A.

JONES, CHRISTOPHER
Reporter, WNEW-TV

c/o WNEW-TV, 205 E. 67th St., New York,
NY 10021
b. New York, NY.

EDUCATION: Williams College, B.A.; Middle-
bury College, M.A., Spanish; Columbia Law
School.
CAREER HIGHLIGHTS: Freelance Writer; Writer
for *Reader's Digest;* Corporate Intl. Lawyer,
Curtis, Mallet-Prevost, Colt, Mosle; Action
Reporter, "10 O'Clock News," WNEW-TV
('70).
ACHIEVEMENTS & AWARDS: Windsor Life con-
sumerism award ('78); AP outstanding enter-
prise reporting award ('79).
PERSONAL: Resides in Manhattan.

JONES, CHUCK
Animator

6290 Sunset Blvd., Hollywood, CA 90028
b. September 21, 1912. Spokane, WA.

EDUCATION: Chouinard Art Institute.
CAREER HIGHLIGHTS: Dir., Animation, Warner
Bros. ('38); Creator/Writer/Dir./Prod., Warner

Bros. ('38–'63). Created the characters Road Runner, Pepe Le Pew, and Wiley Coyote. Independent Prod. ('68). TV specials include "The Cricket in Times Square," "Bugs Bunny in King Arthur's Court," "Raggedy Ann and Andy in the Great Santa Claus Caper," "The White Seal," and "Mowgli's Brother."

ACHIEVEMENTS & AWARDS: Cine award ('65); Peabody award ('71); Tehran Festival Film award ('77); British Film Festival tribute ('79); American Film Institute tribute ('75, '80).

PERSONAL: Resides in Los Angeles; one daughter.

JONES, KENLEY
Correspondent, NBC, News

c/o NBC, 30 Rockefeller Plaza, New York, NY 10020
b. February 24, 1935. Greenville, SC.

EDUCATION: Northwestern University, B.S., Speech ('57) and M.S., Journalism ('63).

CAREER   HIGHLIGHTS: Reporter/Cameraman, KRNT-TV, Des Moines, IA; Reporter/News Editor, WSB-TV, Atlanta ('65); Correspondent, NBC News, Saigon ('69); Correspondent, NBC News, Asia ('70); Correspondent, NBC News ('72).

ACHIEVEMENTS & AWARDS: Overseas Press Club award for best reporting from abroad ('70); distinguished broadcaster award from the South Carolina Broadcasters Assn. ('73).

PERSONAL: Wife, Margaret; daughters, Stephanie and Eleanor; son, Jason.

JONES, PHIL
News Correspondent, CBS, Capitol Hill

c/o CBS, 2020 M St., N.W., Washington, DC 20036
b. N.A.

EDUCATION: N.A.

CAREER HIGHLIGHTS: Joined CBS News as a Reporter based in the Hong Kong and Saigon Bureaus ('69). Covered Capitol Hill ('77), and has reported such major stories as congressional debates on the Panama Canal and SALT II treaties.

ACHIEVEMENTS & AWARDS: Member of the CBS News team that won an Emmy award for a series of exclusive reports on the Indochina air war, broadcast on "The CBS Evening News" ('72)

PERSONAL: N.A.

JORGENSEN, BILL
Anchor, WPIX-TV, New York, Independent Network News

c/o Independent Network News, 11 WPIX Plaza, New York, NY 10017
b. N.A.

EDUCATION: University of Illinois.

CAREER HIGHLIGHTS: News Editor, WIBC-AM, Indianapolis; News Dir., WTVN-AM/TV, Columbus, OH; News Dir., WERE-TV, Cleveland; Anchor, KYW-TV, Pittsburgh; Anchor, "The 10 O'Clock News," WNEW-TV, New York ('67); Anchor, "Action News," WPIX-TV, ('79); Anchor, Independent Network News ('80). Also, narrated 35 films produced by NASA; has appeared as himself in feature films *Nasty Habits* ('76) and *Contract on Cherry Street* ('77).

ACHIEVEMENTS & AWARDS: N.A.

PERSONAL: Resides in New York City and is the father of six children.

JOSELOFF, GORDON
Correspondent, CBS, News, Tokyo

c/o Foreign Correspondents Club, Yurakucito Denki Bldg., 1-7-1 Yurakucito, Chiyado-ku, Tokyo 100, Japan
b. New York, NY.

EDUCATION: Syracuse University, B.S., Broadcasting ('67).

CAREER HIGHLIGHTS: Started as a Stringer for UPI, *N.Y. Times*, and other publications ('66); Natl. News Desk, UPI ('69); Editor, *Overnight News*, London, UPI ('70); Correspondent, UPI, Moscow ('72); Newswriter/Reporter, CBS News ('75); Correspondent, CBS News, Moscow ('79); Correspondent, CBS News, Tokyo ('81). First American TV correspondent in Poland covering the strike in the Gdansk shipyard ('80).

ACHIEVEMENTS & AWARDS: N.A.

PERSONAL: Wife, Suzanne.

JOYCE, ED
Pres. CBS, News

c/o CBS, 524 W. 57th St., New York, NY 10019
b. December 13, 1932. Phoenix, Ariz.

EDUCATION: University of Wyoming.
CAREER HIGHLIGHTS: V.P. and Gen. Mgr. of three CBS-owned TV stations, WCBS, KNXT, and WBBM; V.P. News for CBS TV stations ('77); Exec. V.P., CBS News ('81); and Pres., CBS News ('83).

JOYELLA, JAMES A.
V.P., CBS TV, Marketing Services, Network Sales

c/o CBS, 51 W. 52d St., New York, NY 10019
b. Waterbury, CT.

EDUCATION: Fordham University, B.A. ('64).
CAREER HIGHLIGHTS: Joined CBS ('69); Dir. of Sales, WBBM-TV, CBS in Chicago ('77); V.P., General Sales Mgr., CBS Radio Network ('78); V.P., Sales, CBS, Cable Division ('81); V.P., CBS TV Marketing Service, Network Sales.
ACHIEVEMENTS & AWARDS: N.A.
PERSONAL: Resides in Norwalk, CT.

JURZYKOWSKI, CHRISTINE
Pres., Cinetudes Film Productions Ltd

c/o Cinetudes Film Productions Ltd., 295 W. 4th St., New York, NY 10014
b. N.A.

EDUCATION: Boston University, B.A.
CAREER HIGHLIGHTS: Founded Cinetudes Film Productions Ltd. ('76); founded Cinetudes Cable Programming Assn. ('81); founded Atelier Cinema Video Stages ('81); serves as Exec. Prod. over her company's commercials and public service announcements.
ACHIEVEMENTS & AWARDS: Numerous Clio awards and film festival honors.
PERSONAL: N.A.

KAATZ, RONALD B.
Sr. V.P., Dir. of Media Resources and Research, J. Walter Thompson, Chicago

c/o J. Walter Thompson, 875 N. Michigan Ave., Chicago, IL 60611
b. April 27, 1934. Kansas City, MO.

EDUCATION: Northwestern University.
CAREER HIGHLIGHTS: Mgr., Media Research, Leo Burnett Co., Chicago ('57); Dir., Sales Administration, CBS TV, Chicago ('64); Sr. V.P., Dir. of Media Resources and Research, J. Walter Thompson ('67).
ACHIEVEMENTS & AWARDS: N.A.
PERSONAL: Resides in Highland Park, IL, with wife, Suzanne; daughters, Kathy and Roberta.

KAHN, IRVING
Pres. and Chairman of the Board, Broadband Communications

375 Park Ave., Suite 3701, New York, NY 10152
b. September 30, 1917. Newark, NJ.

EDUCATION: University of Alabama.
CAREER HIGHLIGHTS: V.P. in charge of the radio and TV subsidiary of 20th Century Fox; formed Teleprompter Corp., and was an early pioneer in pay TV for Teleprompter. Developed major cable complex in southern New Jersey. Consultant to the *N.Y. Times* for Broadband Communications. Under his guidance, Teleprompter joined with Hughes Aircraft for a new microwave service, Amplitude Modulation Link. Chairman of the Board of General Optronics Corp.; Pres. and Chairman of the Board, Broadband Communications.

ACHIEVEMENTS & AWARDS: Member, Board of Dir., Natl. Cable TV Assn.
PERSONAL: N.A.

KALB, BERNARD
Correspondent, NBC, News

c/o NBC, 4001 Nebraska Ave., N.W., Washington, DC 20016
b. New York, NY.

EDUCATION: City College of New York.
CAREER HIGHLIGHTS: Reporter, *N.Y. Times* ('46); Reporter, *N.Y. Times* covering Southeast Asia ('56); Correspondent, CBS News, New York ('62); Correspondent and Southeast Asia Bureau Chief, based in Hong Kong ('63); Paris Bureau Chief, CBS News ('65); Southeast Asia Bureau Chief, CBS News ('66); Correspondent/Washington, DC, Anchor, "The CBS Morning News," CBS News, Washington, DC ('70); Foreign Affairs Correspondent, CBS News, Washington, DC ('72); State Department Correspondent, NBC News, Washington, DC ('80).
ACHIEVEMENTS & AWARDS: Overseas Press Club award for a documentary on the Vietcong ('68). Co-Author, *Kissinger* and *The Last Ambassadors*.
PERSONAL: Married; four daughters.

KALB, MARVIN
Correspondent, NBC, News

c/o NBC, 4001 Nebraska Ave., N.W.,
Washington, DC 20016
b. New York, NY.

EDUCATION: City College of New York, B.A.;
Harvard University, M.A., Russian and Chinese History.
CAREER HIGHLIGHTS: Press Attache for State
Dept., American Embassy in Moscow ('56–
'57); CBS News Moscow Correspondent ('60);
Diplomatic Correspondent based in Washington, DC ('63); NBC News Chief Diplomatic Correspondent based in Washington,
DC ('80). Appears regularly on "NBC Nightly
News" and is a permanent panel member of
"Meet the Press."
ACHIEVEMENTS & AWARDS: CBS Fellow at Columbia University; won an Emmy for his reporting from Moscow ('62–'63); received nine
Overseas Press Club awards for best foreign
affairs reporting; won the first annual Natl.
Press Club Edwin M. Hood award for diplomatic correspondents ('80). Author of five
nonfiction books; Co-Author, of two novels.
PERSONAL: N.A.

KAMEN, JEFF
Field Reporter, WPIX-11, "Action News"

c/o WPIX-TV, 11 WPIX Plaza, New York, NY
10017
b. N.A.

EDUCATION: N.A.
CAREER HIGHLIGHTS: Still Photographer ('60s),
with photos in *Newsweek* and *Parade;* Editor/
Correspondent, Radio Press Intl. Reporter/
Documentary Prod., WCFL-Radio, Chicago;

Prod., eight documentaries; Reporter,
WNEW-Radio, Chicago; Prod., eight documentaries; Reporter, WNEW-Radio; Prod/
Reporter, "The 51st State," WNET; joined
Channel 11 News Dept. ('74). Instrumental in
getting Natl. Public Radio on the air in Washington, DC.
ACHIEVEMENTS & AWARDS: N.A.
PERSONAL: Married, two children. Resides in
Jamaica Hills, NY.

KANANACK, ARTHUR
**Exec. V.P., ITC Entertainment, Business
Affairs**

c/o ITC Entertainment, 12711 Ventura Blvd.,
Studio City, CA 91604
b. New York, NY.

EDUCATION: Cornell University, Cornell Law
School, doctor of laws.
CAREER HIGHLIGHTS: Started with ABC Business Affairs, New York ('63); joined Creative
Management Associates ('66); Business Affairs 20th Century Fox ('69); V.P., Warner
Bros. ('72); V.P., Business Affairs, Warner
Bros. TV Distribution ('79); Exec. V.P., Business Affairs, ITC ('82).
ACHIEVEMENTS & AWARDS: N.A.
PERSONAL: Resides in Los Angeles.

KANDEL, MYRON (Mike)
Financial Editor, Cable News Network

c/o Cable News Network, 1 World Trade
Center, Bldg. 1 Lobby, New York, NY
10048
b. N.A.

EDUCATION: Columbia Graduate School of
Journalism, master's.
CAREER HIGHLIGHTS: Widely regarded as one of
the best financial reporters in TV. Started as
Copy Boy, *N.Y. Times;* Copy Editor/Financial
Reporter, *N.Y. Times;* Financial Editor, *Washington Star;* Foreign Correspondent, *N.Y. Herald Tribune;* Financial Editor, *N.Y. Post.*
Planned the debut of Cable News Network
('80).
ACHIEVEMENTS & AWARDS: N.A.
PERSONAL: Wife, Thelma; daughter, Bethany.
Resides in Manhattan.

KANE, ARNOLD
Prod./Writer

c/o Bernie Brillstein, 9200 Sunset Blvd., Suite 428, Los Angeles, CA 90069
b. May 21, 1935. New York, NY.

EDUCATION: Long Island University, B.A.
CAREER HIGHLIGHTS: Prod., "Pantomine Quiz" ('56); Prod., "Man in Space" ('65); Prod., "Bridget Loves Bernie" ('72); Prod., "The Diana Rigg Show" ('73); Prod., "The Montefuscos" ('75); Prod., "Alice" ('76); Prod., "On Our Own" ('77); Prod., "Turnabout" ('79); Prod., "One in a Million" ('80); Prod., "Private Benjamin" ('81).
ACHIEVEMENTS & AWARDS: N.A.
PERSONAL: N.A.

KANE, JOSH
V.P., CBS, Entertainment, Program Development, New York

c/o CBS, 51 W. 52d St., New York, NY 10020
b. February 14, 1944. Bronx, NY.

EDUCATION: Brooklyn College, B.A., Speech/Theater/Broadcasting ('64); University of California at Los Angeles and Brooklyn College Graduate TV Center.
CAREER HIGHLIGHTS: Page, NBC ('65); Correspondent and then Staff Writer, Press Dept.; Asst. Trade News Editor ('69); promoted to Mgr., Program and Trade Publicity and then Mgr., Press and Publicity ('72); Dir. of Public Information ('74); moved into programming as General Program Exec. ('76); named V.P., Programs, East Coast ('77); V.P., Theatrical Features, and Asst. to the Pres., NBC Entertainment ('81); resumed expanded post of V.P., Programs, East Coast ('81); joined CBS Entertainment as V.P., Program Development, New York ('82).
ACHIEVEMENTS & AWARDS: N.A.
PERSONAL: Resides in Neponsit, NY, with wife, Janet; children, Brian, Robin, and Alison.

KANE, PETER
Assoc. Dir., Business Affairs, Talent and Program Acquisition, CBS, Entertainment, West Coast

c/o CBS, 7800 Beverly Blvd., Los Angeles, CA 90036
b. N.A.

EDUCATION: University of California at San Diego (cum laude, '70); Georgetown University Law Center ('73).
CAREER HIGHLIGHTS: Assoc., Fulop, Rolston, Burns & McKittrick, Beverly Hills, CA ('74); Asst. U.S. Attorney in the Civil Division, Los Angeles ('76); Legal Dept., MGM ('78); joined Business Affairs Dept., CBS ('80); named Assoc. Dir., Business Affairs, Talent and Program Acquisition, CBS Entertainment, West Coast ('82).
ACHIEVEMENTS & AWARDS: N.A.
PERSONAL: N.A.

KANEGSBERG, HENRY
V.P., NBC News, Finance and Administration

c/o NBC, 30 Rockefeller Plaza, New York, NY 10020
b. N.A.

EDUCATION: New York University, master's, Finance.
CAREER HIGHLIGHTS: Began his professional career at RCA as a Financial Assoc. ('69); became Dir. of Forecasting and Performance Reporting; then joined CBS as Dir., Financial Planning ('78).
ACHIEVEMENTS & AWARDS: N.A.
PERSONAL: N.A.

KANTER, HAL
Comedy Writer/Prod.

c/o Marvin Moss Agency, 9200 Sunset Blvd., Suite 601, Los Angeles, CA 90069
b. December 18, 1918.

EDUCATION: N.A.
CAREER HIGHLIGHTS: Writer, Bob Hope's radio show; Prod./Writer/Dir., "The George Gobel Show"; Exec. Prod., "Julia"; Supervising

Prod., "Chico and the Man"; Freelance Writer/Dir. for such shows as "All in the Family." Also Dir./Writer, ABC TV Movies ('80), and Prod., Walt Disney Productions. Formed Savannah Productions ('82).

ACHIEVEMENTS & AWARDS: Emmy, best comedy writing ('54).

PERSONAL: N.A.

KAPLAN, RICK
Exec. Prod., ABC, "World News This Morning" and "Good Morning America News"

c/o ABC, 7 W. 66th St., New York, NY 10023
b. N.A.

EDUCATION: University of Illinois
CAREER HIGHLIGHTS: TV News Prod., WBBM ('69); Prod., "CBS Evening News With Walter Cronkite," CBS Morning News and CBS "Sunday Morning." Sr. Prod., "World News Tonight" ('79); Exec. Prod., "World News This Morning" and "Good Morning America News."

ACHIEVEMENTS & AWARDS: N.A.

PERSONAL: N.A.

KAPLOW, HERBERT
News Correspondent, ABC, Washington

c/o ABC, 1717 DeSales St., N.W., Washington, DC 20036
b. New York, NY.

EDUCATION: Northwestern University, master's, Journalism.
CAREER HIGHLIGHTS: Spent 21 years with NBC News as a News Writer, Radio and TV News Editor, and Correspondent; joined ABC News as a Washington, DC, Correspondent ('72), covering a variety of major national news stories. He is Frequent Host, "Directions," a religious and cultural affairs program.

ACHIEVEMENTS & AWARDS: Emmy for "Directions."

PERSONAL: Wife, Betty; three sons. Resides in Virginia.

KASHIWAHARA, KEN
Correspondent and San Francisco Bureau Chief, ABC, News

c/o ABC, 277 Golden Gate Ave., San Francisco, CA 94102
b. N.A.

EDUCATION: San Francisco State College, B.A., Broadcasting.
CAREER HIGHLIGHTS: Anchor/Political Reporter, KGMB-TV, Honolulu; Field Reporter/ Weekend Co-Anchor, "Eyewitness News," KABC-TV; joined ABC News as Southeast Asia Reporter; named Bureau Chief in Hong Kong; San Francisco Bureau Chief ('78).

ACHIEVEMENTS & AWARDS: N.A.

PERSONAL: N.A.

KATER, DAN
V.P., General Mgr., Modern Satellite Network

c/o Modern Satellite Network, 45 Rockefeller Plaza, New York, NY 10111
b. June 10, 1929. Cincinnati, OH.

EDUCATION: Ohio State University, B.S., Public Relations; Loyola University, M.B.A., Communications.
CAREER HIGHLIGHTS: Acct. Exec., McCann-Erickson ('51); Modern Talking Picture Service ('53); V.P. General Mgr., Modern Satellite Network ('82).

ACHIEVEMENTS & AWARDS: Pres. CINE, Washington, DC ('79–'80)

PERSONAL: Wife, Joyce; sons, Chris and David.

KATLEMAN, HARRIS L.
Chairman of the Board and Chief Exec. Officer, 20th Century Fox

c/o 20th Century Fox TV, 10201 W. Pico Blvd., Los Angeles, CA 90064
b. August 19. Omaha, NE

EDUCATION: University of California at Los Angeles, B.A.
CAREER HIGHLIGHTS: Dir. and Sr. Exec. V.P., Goodson-Todman Broadcasting ('55–'70); Pres., Four Star Entertainment ('70); Pres., MGM TV, Sr. V.P., MGM ('72); Exec. Prod., Bennett/Katleman Productions, Columbia

Pictures ('77); Chairman of the Board and Chief Exec. Officer, 20th Century Fox TV ('80).

ACHIEVEMENTS & AWARDS: Founding Member, ATAS; Co-Founder and Member, Board of Governors, Municipal League of Beverly Hills.

PERSONAL: Two sons, Steven and Michael; daughter, Lisa.

KATZ, JOEL
Exec. V.P., Playboy Channel

c/o Playboy Channel, 8560 Sunset Blvd., Los Angeles, CA 90069
b. N.A.

EDUCATION: Columbia Law School.

CAREER HIGHLIGHTS: Exec. V.P., Plateus Productions; Exec., MCA, ('69); Independent Prod., Hollywood ('71); Sr. V.P., Business Affairs and Administration, MGM TV ('77); Sr. V.P., Administration and Business Affairs, Playboy Channel ('82); Exec. V.P., Playboy Channel ('83).

ACHIEVEMENTS & AWARDS: N.A.

PERSONAL: Resides in Los Angeles with his wife and their two children.

KATZ, RICHARD J.
V.P., Business Affairs, Motion Pictures for TV and Mini-Series, CBS, Entertainment, West Coast

c/o CBS, 6121 Sunset Blvd., Los Angeles, CA 90028
b. Philadelphia, PA.

EDUCATION: Syracuse University, B.A. ('73); University of California at Los Angeles, J.D. ('76).

CAREER HIGHLIGHTS: Served on the Staff of the General Counsel, U.S. Copyright Office ('76); Talent and Program Negotiator, Motion Pictures for TV and Mini-Series, CBS ('78); V.P., Business Affairs, Motion Pictures for TV and Mini-Series, CBS Entertainment, West Coast ('81).

ACHIEVEMENTS & AWARDS: N.A.

PERSONAL: Single, resides in West Hollywood, CA.

KAUFER, JERRY
V.P., Viacom Intl., Creative Services

c/o Viacom Intl., 1211 Ave. of the Americas, New York, NY 10036
b. May 23, 1933. Brooklyn, NY.

EDUCATION: Brooklyn College.

CAREER HIGHLIGHTS: Mgr. of Advertising and Sales Promotion, Screen Gems ('55); Dir. of Advertising and Public Relations, Peters Griffin Woodward, Inc. ('65); Dir. of Advertising and Sales Promotion, Screen Gems/Columbia ('68); Dir. of Advertising, P.R. and Sales Promotion, Paramount TV Distribution ('73).

ACHIEVEMENTS & AWARDS: N.A.

PERSONAL: N.A.

KAUFMAN, ARVIN
Dir. of Network Movies and Mini-Series for TV, 20th Century Fox, TV

11970 Montana Ave., Los Angeles, CA 90049
b. January 15, 1950. Kansas City, MO.

EDUCATION: Arizona State University.

CAREER HIGHLIGHTS: Worked for William Morris Agency ('72); moved to Lew Weitzman & Assoc. Talent Agency ('75); Dir., Program Development ('80); Dir. of Network Movies and Mini-Series for TV ('81).

ACHIEVEMENTS & AWARDS: N.A.

PERSONAL: Resides in Los Angeles, CA.

KAUFMAN, HAL
Pres., Hal Kaufman Inc.

c/o Kaufman, Lansky, and Baker, Inc.; 656 Fifth Ave., San Diego, CA 92101
b. December 16, 1924. New York, NY.

EDUCATION: University of Texas; University of Michigan.

CAREER HIGHLIGHTS: Sr. Writer, V.P. and Dir., Broadcast Design in Production, Needham, Louis & Brorby ('56); Assoc. Creative Dir., Dir., Radio and TV and then Creative Dir., Needham, Harper & Steers ('65); V.P. and then Exec. V.P., Kaufman Lansky Advertising ('70); Program Dir. of Z Channel, Theta Cable TV ('79); Pres., Hal Kaufman, Inc., advertising consultants for TV ('81).

ACHIEVEMENTS & AWARDS: N.A.

PERSONAL: N.A.

KAUFMAN, LEONARD B.
Prod./Writer

c/o Sherill Agency, 7060 Hollywood Blvd.,
Suite 610, Hollywood, CA 90028
b. August 31, 1927. Newark, NJ.

EDUCATION: New York University.
CAREER HIGHLIGHTS: Writing credits include
"Flipper," "Hagen," "Adam-12," "Hawaii
Five-0," "Dukes of Hazzard," "Baretta,"
"Grizzly Adams," "Enos," "Private Ben-
jamin," and "Bring 'Em Back Alive." Prod.,
"O'Hara, U.S. Treasury" ('69); "Escape"
('70); "Archer" ('76); "Sam" ('78); "Grizzly
Adams" ('78); "Hawaii Five-O" ('79); *Scruples*
('80); *Beyond Westworld* ('80); "Private Ben-
jamin" ('81).
ACHIEVEMENTS & AWARDS: N.A.
PERSONAL: Resides in West Los Angeles, CA,
with wife, Doris.

KAUFMAN, SID
Dir., Technical Planning and Labor Affairs, CBS, Sports

c/o CBS, 51 W. 52d St., New York, NY 10019
b. N.A

EDUCATION: Temple University.
CAREER HIGHLIGHTS: Joined CBS as an Audio
Engineer ('50); moved up the ranks, holding
numerous positions at CBS including Dir. of
Operations, CBS News and Prod., CBS News
Special Events; Coordinating Prod., "The
NFL Today," CBS Sports; Dir. of Operations,
CBS Sports ('75); V.P., Operations, CBS Ca-
ble ('80); Dir., Technical Planning and Labor
Affairs, CBS Sports ('83).
ACHIEVEMENTS & AWARDS: Two Emmy awards.
PERSONAL: Resides in Wantagh, NY, with his
wife.

KAVANAU, TED
Exec. V.P., Cable News Network, Headline News

1 South Prado, Atlanta, GA 30309
b. March 7, 1933.

EDUCATION: City College of New York, B.A.;
Syracuse University, M.S.

CAREER HIGHLIGHTS: Prod./Dir., Public Affairs,
UBZ-TV Boston ('62); Exec. Prod., WNEW-
TV ('66); Prod., WNEW-TV, New York ('67);
Managing Editor, WPIX-TV News ('75); Con-
sultant, TV News, Metromedia TV ('78); Sr.
News Prod., Cable News Network ('79);
Managing Editor and V.P., Cable News Net-
work ('80); Exec. V.P. and Dir. of News,
Cable News Network Headline News ('81).
He also heads the Cable News Network In-
vestigative Unit in Washington, DC ('83).
ACHIEVEMENTS & AWARDS: N.A.
PERSONAL: N.A.

KAYDEN, WILLIAM
Prod./Writer, W.K. Productions, Inc./Orion TV

c/o W.K. Productions, Inc., 999 North Doheny
Dr., Los Angeles, CA 90069
b. December 31, 1926. New York, NY.

EDUCATION: University of Southern California,
B.A.
CAREER HIGHLIGHTS: Movies produced for TV
include *Missing Children: A Mother's Story*
CBS, and *To Race the Wind,* for CBS; *Lady of the
House* for NBC; and *Crazy Times* for ABC. Net-
work specials produced include "Bicen-
tennial Minutes" for CBS; four annual Emmy
award shows; "Operation Entertainment"
and "World Championship Rodeo" for NBC.
ACHIEVEMENTS & AWARDS: N.A.
PERSONAL: N.A.

KAZURINSKY, TIM
Actor/Writer, NBC, "Saturday Night Live"

c/o NBC, 30 Rockefeller Plaza, New York, NY
  10020
b. March 3, 1950. Johnstown, PA.

EDUCATION:　University of Pittsburgh.
CAREER HIGHLIGHTS:　Syndicated series "Big
  City Comedy"; Co-Author of screenplay, *My
  Bodyguard*. Motion pictures include *Neighbors*
  and *My Bodyguard*. Regular on "Saturday
  Night Live."
ACHIEVEMENTS & AWARDS:　Two best actor nom-
  inations for the Joseph Jefferson award.
PERSONAL:　Resides in Chicago.

KEEPER, GARY
Dir., Comedy Development, Paramount, TV

c/o Paramount TV, 5555 Melrose Ave., Los
  Angeles, CA 90038
b. May 3, 1951. Houston, TX.

EDUCATION:　Oberlin College, B.A., Music The-
  ater.
CAREER HIGHLIGHTS:　Supervisor, Program De-
  velopment, Paramount TV ('78); Mgr., Com-
  edy Development, Paramount TV ('79); Dir.,
  Comedy Development, Paramount TV ('80).
ACHIEVEMENTS & AWARDS:　N.A.
PERSONAL:　N.A.

KEESHAN, BOB
Actor

c/o "Captain Kangaroo," CBS, 51 W. 52d St.,
  New York, NY 10019
b. June 27, 1927. Lynbrook, NY.

EDUCATION:　Fordham University.
CAREER HIGHLIGHTS:　Innovative, pioneering
  children's programming star, whose Captain
  Kangaroo has been required viewing by generations of children. He was the original Clar-
  abelle on "The Howdy Doody Show." His
  other children's programs include "Time for
  Fun," "Tinker's Workshop," and "Captain
  Kangaroo," the longest running children's
  program in network history. Also the host of
  the radio program "The Subject Is Young People."
ACHIEVEMENTS & AWARDS:　Four Emmy awards;
  two Gabriel awards for achievement in children's programming. Named Broadcaster of
  the Year by IRTS and received the Natl. Education award for advancement of learning
  through broadcasting; Joseph O'Connor
  award.
PERSONAL:　Wife, Jeanne; three children; two
  grandchildren. Resides in Babylon, NY.

KELLER, THOMAS B.
**Sr. V.P., PBS, Washington, DC, Science and
  Technology**

c/o PBS, 475 L'Enfant Plaza, S.W., Washington,
  DC 20024
b. N.A.

EDUCATION:　N.A.
CAREER HIGHLIGHTS:　Radar Field Engineer,
  Philco Corp.; Special Projects Engineer, Wal-
  ter Reed Army Medical Center; Dir. of En-

gineering, WGBH-TV/FM in Boston and its sister station, WGBX, Boston, and WGBY, Springfield, MA. Joined PBS ('79) and is responsible for engineering work in the areas of developing communications technologies.
ACHIEVEMENTS & AWARDS: N.A.
PERSONAL: N.A.

KELLEY, CHRIS
Correspondent, CBS, News

c/o CBS, 524 W. 57th St., New York, NY 10019
b. N.A.

EDUCATION: Villanova University, Economics ('61).
CAREER HIGHLIGHTS: Reporter, Dun & Bradstreet ('64); Reporter, WICC-Radio, Bridgeport, CT ('65); News Dir., WICC-Radio, Bridgeport ('67); Radio Newswriter, CBS News ('69); News Editor, CBS News, Radio ('70); CBS News Correspondent ('72).
ACHIEVEMENTS & AWARDS: N.A.
PERSONAL: Married to CBS News Correspondent Betty Ann Bowser; two sons, Patrick and Matthew.

KELLEY, WILLIAM
V.P., Affiliate Relations Operations, NBC

c/o NBC, 30 Rockefeller Plaza, New York, NY 10020
b. Detroit, MI.

EDUCATION: Pennsylvania State University.
CAREER HIGHLIGHTS: Started as a Page for NBC ('47); moved into TV Network Operations Dept. ('48); Asst., Cooperative Advertising Sales, Stations Relations, NBC ('48); Supervisor of Radio/TV Contracts for the Dept. ('49); Regional Mgr., Affiliate Relations Operations ('53); Regional Dir. ('78); V.P., Affiliate Relations Operations, NBC ('80).
ACHIEVEMENTS & AWARDS: N.A.
PERSONAL: Resides in Tenafly, NJ, with wife, Marguerite; daughter, Susan; son, Richard.

KELLY, JIM
Sports Broadcaster, CBS

c/o CBS, 51 W. 52d St., New York, NY 10019
b. Toledo, OH.

EDUCATION: University of Toledo.
CAREER HIGHLIGHTS: This star hockey player at the University of Toledo began his broadcast career as Sports Dir., WMHE-FM, Toledo; went on to WNOB-FM and WCUY-FM in Cleveland and WKNT-AM and FM in Kent, OH. Before joining "CBS Morning News," Kelly served as Sports Anchor, "Live at 5" "Live at 11," the weekday news broadcasts on WCAU-TV, Philadelphia, where he also covered local sports events. He has done play-by-play coverage of games as well as PGA tour events for CBS Sports.
ACHIEVEMENTS & AWARDS: N.A.
PERSONAL: Married, two daughters.

KELLY, KATIE
Entertainment Critic, WABC-TV, New York, Eyewitness News

c/o WABC-TV, 7 Lincoln Sq., New York, NY 10023
b. Albion, NE.

EDUCATION: University of Missouri, B.A., Journalism/History/Literature.
CAREER HIGHLIGHTS: Public School Teacher; Production Asst., CBS TV, New York; Researcher/Writer, Time magazine ('66); Entertainment Writer, Time magazine ('68); Managing Editor, Women's World magazine ('73); TV Critic, N.Y. Post ('77); Entertainment Critic, WNBC-TV, New York ('78); Entertainment Critic, WABC-TV, New York ('83).
ACHIEVEMENTS & AWARDS: Author of three books, Wonderful World of Women's Wear Daily ('72); Garbage: The History and Future of Garbage in America ('73); My Prime Time: Confessions of a TV Watcher ('80).
PERSONAL: N.A.

KENIN, DAVID
V.P., USA Network, Programming

c/o USA Network, 208 Harristown Rd., Glen
Rock, NJ 07452
b. October 19, 1941. Portland, OR.

EDUCATION: Long Island University, B.A.;
University of Oregon, M.A.; Syracuse University, M.S.
CAREER HIGHLIGHTS: With CBS in News, CBS
Stations, and Corporate Staff for five years
('67); Operations Mgr., WHPL-TV Philadelphia ('72); Production Mgr., WFLD, Chicago
('74); V.P., Dir. of Broadcast Operations,
KMBC, Kansas City, MO ('78); moved to
KSHB, Kansas City as Station Mgr. ('81);
joined USA Network as V.P., Programming
('82).
ACHIEVEMENTS & AWARDS: N.A.
PERSONAL: N.A.

KENNEDY, ROYAL
Correspondent, ABC, News, Los Angeles

c/o ABC, 2040 Ave. of the Stars, Los Angeles,
CA 90067
b. N.A.

EDUCATION: Ohio University; Dartmouth College; Columbia University.
CAREER HIGHLIGHTS: Began her news career as
a Copy Editor/Researcher, *Playboy* magazine,
Chicago ('69); joined WDSU-TV, New Orleans ('71); moved on to WKYC-TV, Cleveland ('73) as General Assignment Reporter,
Host of a weekly public affairs program, and
Anchor for "Today" show local newscasts,
before becoming an ABC News Los Angeles
Correspondent ('78).

ACHIEVEMENTS & AWARDS: Cleveland Emmy
for outstanding individual achievement for
producing and reporting a five-part series on
rape. The same series also earned her a citation for excellence in reporting a legal issue
from the American Assn. of Trial Lawyers.
Received a San Francisco State University
journalism award for producing and reporting a series on abortion.
PERSONAL: N.A.

KENNEY, H. WESLEY
Prod./Dir.

c/o Irv Schechter, 12996 Galewood St., Studio
City, CA 91604
b. January 3. Dayton, OH.

EDUCATION: Carnegie Tech, B.F.A.
CAREER HIGHLIGHTS: Dir., "All in the Family,"
CBS, 22 episodes ('74); Dir., pilot, "Rosenthal
and Jones," CBS ('75); Exec. Prod., "Days of
Our Lives," NBC ('76); Dir., Pilot and Series
"Ladies Man," CBS ('80); Dir., "Flo," CBS
('80); Dir., pilot "Filthy Rich," CBS ('81);
Exec. Prod., "Young and the Restless," CBS
('82).
ACHIEVEMENTS & AWARDS: Emmy, best director
of the year, Daytime ('73); Emmy, "Miss
Kline We Love You," best daytime special
('73); Emmy, best director daytime series,
"Days of Our Lives" ('76); merit award, Carnegie Tech ('78).
PERSONAL: Wife, Heather; children, Nina,
Wesley III, Kara, and Kevin.

KENT, ART
V.P., Affiliate News Services, NBC, News

c/o NBC, 30 Rockefeller Plaza, New York, NY
10020
b. New York, NY.

EDUCATION: Williams College; University of
Utah.
CAREER HIGHLIGHTS: Reporter, KLUB-AM, Salt
Lake City ('59); Reporter, KCPX-TV, Salt Lake
City ('60); Anchor/News Dir., KUTV-TV, Salt
Lake City ('61); Reporter for NBC News from
Vietnam ('70); News Mgr., KSL-TV, Salt Lake
City ('71); News Dir., KTVX-TV, Salt Lake

City ('72); News Dir., WIIC-TV, Pittsburgh ('76); Mgr. of NBC News Pittsburgh Bureau ('78); Prod., NBC News ('79); Correspondent, NBC News, Tel Aviv ('80); Managing Dir., Affiliate News Services, NBC News ('82); V.P., Affiliate News Services, NBC News ('83).
ACHIEVEMENTS & AWARDS: N.A.
PERSONAL: N.A.

KENYON, SANDY (Alexander Vicary Low Kenyon)
Entertainment Correspondent, Cable News Network, Washington Bureau

c/o Cable News Network, 6290 Sunset Blvd., Los Angeles, CA 90028
b. July 23, 1956. Hanover, NH.

EDUCATION: Princeton University, B.A., History ('78).
CAREER HIGHLIGHTS: Production Asst., RHA Productions ('77); Prod/Dir., On-Air Talent—The Focus on Youth Radio Network ('77); Assoc. Prod., WNET/13, "Our Turn" pilot public affairs show ('79); Personal Asst. to Arthur Penn ('79); Writer/Prod., Cable News Network, Washington, DC, Bureau, for Anchor Bernard Shaw ('80).
ACHIEVEMENTS & AWARDS: N.A.
PERSONAL: N.A.

KERAMIDAS, GEORGE
V.P., ABC, TV Research

284 Voorhis Avenue, River Edge, NJ 07661
b. December 21, 1934. New York, NY.

EDUCATION: City College of New York, B.B.A.
CAREER HIGHLIGHTS: Began as Mgr., Network Relations, with Ted Bates advertising agency ('60); joined ABC as V.P., TV Research ('66).
ACHIEVEMENTS & AWARDS: Member, Broadcast Ratings Council; Board of Dirs., Advertising Research Foundation.
PERSONAL: N.A.

KERRIGAN, KEVIN
Reporter, WRC-TV, Washington, DC, News

c/o WRC-TV, 4001 Nebraska Ave., N.W., Washington, DC 20016
b. New York, NY.

EDUCATION: St. Lawrence University, B.A.
CAREER HIGHLIGHTS: Newswriter, WELI-AM, New Haven, CT ('77); News Reporter/Anchor, KTOK-Radio, Oklahoma City ('78); Reporter/Morning Anchor, KOCO-TV, Oklahoma City ('79); Reporter, WRC-TV, Washington, DC ('82).
ACHIEVEMENTS & AWARDS: N.A.
PERSONAL: Resides in Washington, DC.

KETCHAM, WILLIAM P.
V.P., ESPN, Consumer Marketing

355 Lexington Ave., New York, NY 10017
b. February 28, 1951. New Rochelle, NY.

EDUCATION: Rensselaer Polytechnic Institute, B.S. ('73); University of Virginia, M.B.A. ('77).
CAREER HIGHLIGHTS: Analyst, Corporate Planning, General Foods Corp. ('73); Sr. Analyst, Corporate Planning, General Foods Corp. ('74); Product Mgr., General Foods Corp. ('80); Sr. Marketing Mgr., Pepsi Co. ('82); V.P., Consumer Marketing, ESPN.
ACHIEVEMENTS & AWARDS: N.A.
PERSONAL: Wife, Renee; resides in Cos Cob, CT.

KEYES, PAUL WILLIAM
Prod./Writer

135 Screenland Dr., Burbank, CA 91505
b. March 18, 1924, Dorchester, MA

EDUCATION: Attended school in Massachusetts.
CAREER HIGHLIGHTS: Production Dir., Yankee Network ('46); Mgr., Comedy Development ('55); Writer, "The Tonight Show" with Steve Allen ('56); Writer, "The Tonight Show" with Jack Paar ('57); Head Writer, "The Wonderful World of Jack Paar" ('62); Head Writer/Co-Prod., "The Dean Martin Show" ('65); Head Writer, "Laugh-In" ('67); Prod./Head Writer,

"Laugh-In" ('68); Prod., "The Emmy Awards," "Bob Hope's Bicentennial Star Spangled Salute," "Rowan and Martin Report" and "The Don Rickles Special" ('75–'82).

ACHIEVEMENTS & AWARDS: Emmy for writing "Laugh-In" ('68); Emmy awards for producing "Laugh-In" ('69) and "The American Film Institute Salute to James Cagney" ('74).

PERSONAL: Resides in Beverly Hills, CA, with wife, Miriam.

KIBBEE, LOIS
Actress

c/o "The Edge of Night," ABC, 1330 Ave. of the Americas, New York, NY 10019
b. July 13. Wheeling, WV.

EDUCATION: N.A.
CAREER HIGHLIGHTS: Radio actress on "Gunsmoke" and "The Jack Benny Show." Broadway appearances in *A Man for All Seasons* and *Venus Is.* TV regular on the daytime series "The Edge of Night."
ACHIEVEMENTS & AWARDS: Author of *The Bennett Playbill* and *Christine.*
PERSONAL: N.A.

KIBBEE, ROLAND
Writer/Prod./Dir.

Major Talent Agency, 11812 San Vicente Blvd., Suite 510, Los Angeles, CA 90049
b. February 15, 1914. Monongahela, PA.

EDUCATION: Los Angeles City College.
CAREER HIGHLIGHTS: Radio Writer for Groucho Marx and Fred Allen; Exec. Prod., "Columbo"; Prod., "Barney Miller" ('76); Prod./Writer, "It Takes a Thief" and "The Bob Newhart Show." Also wrote screenplay for *Vera Cruz, The Devil's Disciple,* and *Top Secret Affair.*
ACHIEVEMENTS & AWARDS: N.A.
PERSONAL: N.A.

KIKER, DOUGLAS
Correspondent, NBC, News, Washington

c/o NBC, 4001 Nebraska Ave., N.W., Washington, DC 20016
b. Griffin, GA.

EDUCATION: Presbyterian College.
CAREER HIGHLIGHTS: Most of Kiker's journalistic career, spanning more than two decades, has been spent as a Washington, DC, Correspondent. He has been closely involved with the coverage of stories during some of the capital's most turbulent periods. Joined NBC News as Correspondent ('66); based in NBC News Rome Bureau ('69), reporting from almost every country in Western Europe and the Middle East. Returned to the Washington, DC, Bureau ('71), where he is currently NBC Correspondent.
ACHIEVEMENTS & AWARDS: N.A.
PERSONAL: N.A.

KINBERG, JUD
Sr. V.P., Embassy Communications, Dramatic Division

c/o Embassy Communications, 1901 Ave. of the Stars, Los Angeles, CA 90067
b. N.A.

EDUCATION: N.A.
CAREER HIGHLIGHTS: Co-Writer/Prod., feature films; Exec. Prod. "Quincy" ('77–'78); Exec. Prod., Motion Pictures for TV, ABC, *Marilyn: The Untold Story, The Victims, The Letter,* and *Starflight: The Plane That Couldn't Land,* ('79–'82); Sr. V.P., Dramatic Division, Embassy Communications ('82).

ACHIEVEMENTS & AWARDS: Emmy and Peabody awards for CBS TV series "The Seven Lively Arts"; Emmy nomination for "Quincy." British Motion Pictures Academy UN award; two awards at the Cannes Film Festival ('65).

PERSONAL: Resides in Beverly Hills, CA.

KING, EMERY
White House Correspondent, NBC, News

c/o NBC, 4001 Nebraska Ave., N.W., Washington, DC 20016
b. Gary, IN.

EDUCATION: Purdue University.

CAREER HIGHLIGHTS: Reporter, WJOB-AM, Hammond, IN ('70); Reporter, WWCM-AM, Gary, IN ('72); Reporter/Anchor, WBBM-AM, Chicago ('73); Reporter, WBBM-TV, Chicago ('77); Correspondent, NBC News, Washington, DC ('80); named White House Correspondent ('81).

ACHIEVEMENTS & AWARDS: N.A.

PERSONAL: N.A.

KING, JERRY
Bureau Chief, ABC, News, Warsaw

c/o ABC, 1330 Ave. of the Americas, New York, NY 10019
b. Ontario, Canada.

EDUCATION: Queen's University, Ontario.

CAREER HIGHLIGHTS: Two years at CKLB-AM and CKQS-FM, Ontario; Newscaster, ZBM-Radio and TV, Bermuda ('66); UPI, London and New York ('68); joined ABC News ('71). Became ABC News Bureau Chief, Warsaw ('81), after five years of covering nearly every major military conflict in the Middle East.

ACHIEVEMENTS & AWARDS: Overseas Press Club awards for radio coverage of the Turkish invasion of Cyprus ('74) and of the conflict in Lebanon ('76).

PERSONAL: N.A.

KING, JOE
Regional Dir., HBO, Los Angeles Metro, Southwest and Mountain States Regions

c/o HBO, 2049 Century Park E., Suite 4170, Los Angeles, CA 90067
b. N.A.

EDUCATION: Memphis State University, B.A., Business Management.

CAREER HIGHLIGHTS: Stockbroker, Rauscher Pierce, Dallas ('73); Sales Representative, Xerox Corp., Dallas ('76); Regional Mgr., HBO, South Central Region, in Dallas ('79); Regional Dir., HBO, South Central Region ('81); Regional Dir., Los Angeles Metro, Southwest and Mountain States Regions, Los Angeles ('83).

ACHIEVEMENTS & AWARDS: N.A.

PERSONAL: Resides in Los Angeles with his wife, Cissy, and their two children.

KING, LARRY
Talk Show Host

1101 30th St., N.W., Washington, DC 20007
b. November 19, 1933. Brooklyn, NY.

EDUCATION: N.A.

CAREER HIGHLIGHTS: Began radio career at WAHR in Miami as a Newscaster and Disc Jockey; joined staff at WKAT Radio as an On-Air Personality with a talk show broadcast from the Pumpernick Restaurant in Miami; WIOD-Radio—Surfside 6 Talk Show; regular column with *Miami Beach Sun, Miami Herald,* and *Miami News;* Mutual Broadcasting Systems all-night national radio talk show. Formerly hosted the nationally syndicated TV program "The Larry King Show."

ACHIEVEMENTS & AWARDS: N.A.

PERSONAL: N.A.

KING, PAUL
V.P., Current Programs, NBC, Entertainment

c/o NBC, 3000 W. Alameda Ave., Burbank, CA 91523
b. Los Angeles, CA.

EDUCATION: Loyola University; University of Southern California.

CAREER HIGHLIGHTS: Staff Exec., CBS ('66); Exec. Prod., Development, CBS ('67); V.P., Development, CBS; Exec., Warner Bros. TV ('77); Exec., Quinn Martin Productions ('78); V.P., Prime Time Series, NBC ('78); V.P., Drama Programs, NBC Entertainment ('80); V.P., Current Programs ('81).

ACHIEVEMENTS & AWARDS: Regent of the University of Santa Clara; Member, Writers Guild, ATAS, and the Authors League.

PERSONAL: Resides in Hancock Park, CA, with wife, Mary Ellen; eight children.

KINLEY, DAVID D.
Sr. V.P., Viacom Cable

c/o Viacom Cable, P.O. Box 13, Pleasanton, CA 94566
b. June 28, 1941. Fort Worth, TX.

EDUCATION: Principia College, B.A. ('63); Harvard Law School, LL.B. ('66).

CAREER HIGHLIGHTS: Special Asst. to Secretary of HEW ('69); Exec. Asst., Civil Division, U.S. Dept. of Justice ('71); Chief, Cable TV Bureau, FCC ('74); V.P. and Sr. V.P., American TV and Communications Corp. ('76); Sr. V.P., Viacom Cable ('80).

ACHIEVEMENTS & AWARDS: N.A.

PERSONAL: Resides in San Ramon, CA.

KINOY, ERNEST
Writer

66 Lewis Pkwy., Yonkers, NY 10705
b. April 1, 1925.

EDUCATION: Columbia University.

CAREER HIGHLIGHTS: Staff Writer, NBC Radio ('48–'60); Writer for "Alcoa Theater," "The Defenders," "Naked City," "Route 66," "Dr. Kildare," and "The Nurses." Writer, TV movies, *The President's Plane Is Missing, Theodore, The Rivalry, Irish Potato Famine, The Deadliest Season, Victory at Entebbe, The Henderson Monster, Passages, Jackie and Rachel, Skokie,* and the first two installments of the *Roots* mini-series.

ACHIEVEMENTS & AWARDS: Two Emmy awards for episodes of "The Defenders" ('63, '64); Emmy for *Roots* ('77). Member, Writers Guild.

PERSONAL: Resides in Yonkers, NY.

KITMAN, MARVIN
TV Critic, *Newsday*

c/o *Newsday*, 1500 Broadway, New York, NY 10036
b. November 24, 1929. Pittsburgh, PA.

EDUCATION: City College of New York.

CAREER HIGHLIGHTS: One of the wittiest TV newspaper critics. Freelance Writer; Sr. Copy Writer, Carl Ally advertising agency; TV Critic, *New Leader* ('67); TV Critic, *Newsday* ('69); Co-Creator of "Ball Four" TV series ('76); TV Commentary on the Saturday edition of "The 10 O'Clock News" on WNEW-TV, New York ('82).

ACHIEVEMENTS & AWARDS: Author, *The Number-One Best Seller* ('66); *You Can't Judge a Book by Its Cover* ('70); *George Washington's Expense Account* ('70); *Coward's Almanac* ('75).

PERSONAL: Resides in Leonia, NJ, with his wife, Carol, and their three children.

KLADSTRUP, DON
Correspondent, CBS, News

c/o CBS, 524 W. 57th St., New York, NY 10019
b. N.A.

EDUCATION: University of Iowa, B.A., Journalism ('65); Iowa State University, M.S., Journalism ('67); University of Minnesota, M.A., Chinese History ('70).

CAREER HIGHLIGHTS: Reporter, WOI-TV, Ames, IA ('65); Reporter, WCCO-TV, Minneapolis ('67–'75); Writer/Anchor, "Living With Death" for WCCO-TV ('73); Reporter, CBS News ('75); Correspondent, CBS News ('77).

ACHIEVEMENTS & AWARDS: Overseas Press Club award for spot reporting from abroad ('82).

PERSONAL: Wife, Petie; daughters, Regan and Kwan-li.

KLEIN, BILL
V.P., Business Affairs, CBS, Entertainment

c/o CBS, 6121 Sunset Blvd., Los Angeles, CA 90028
b. N.A.

EDUCATION: University of Pittsburgh, B.A.; Fordham University, LL.B.

CAREER HIGHLIGHTS: Assoc. Dir., Business Affairs, CBS ('69); Assoc. Dir., Business Affairs, Warner Bros. TV ('72); Dir., Business Affairs, Program Administration, CBS, Hollywood ('74); Dir., Business Affairs, Motion Pictures for TV and Mini-Series, CBS Entertainment ('77); V.P., Business Affairs, CBS Entertainment, Hollywood ('78).

ACHIEVEMENTS & AWARDS: N.A.

PERSONAL: Single, resides in Los Angeles.

KLEIN, MALCOM
Sr. V.P., Managing Dir., STAR-TV

c/o STAR-TV, 714 Washington St., Wilmington, DE 19801
b. November 22, 1927. Los Angeles, CA.

EDUCATION: N.A.

CAREER HIGHLIGHTS: Acct. Exec. and Asst. General Mgr., KABC-TV ('52); V.P., NTA Broadcasting ('59); V.P. and General Mgr., RKO-General TV ('60); V.P. Creative Services, Natl. General TV Productions ('68); Pres., Filmways TV ('72); General Mgr., Sterling Recreation Broadcast Division ('73); Sr. V.P. and Managing Dir., STAR-TV, subscription TV ('81).

ACHIEVEMENTS & AWARDS: Former Pres., American Song Festival.

PERSONAL: N.A.

KLEIN, PAUL L.
Pres., Playboy Cable Network

919 North Michigan Ave., Chicago, IL 60611
b. November 6, 1928. Brooklyn, NY.

EDUCATION: Brooklyn College, M.A., Mathematics, Philosophy.

CAREER HIGHLIGHTS: Began as a Research Analyst, Biow Co. ('53); joined Doyle, Dane, Bernbach ('55); V.P., Audience Measurement, NBC ('61); formed Computer TV, the original pay TV enterprise ('72); sold his interest to Time, Inc. Returned to NBC as V.P. of Programs, and helped initiate *Holocaust, Shogun, Centennial, Backstairs at the White House,* and *Summer of My German Soldier.* As Pres. of RKO-TV ('80), produced *The People vs. Jean Harris* for NBC and "Romance" for Showtime before joining Playboy Enterprises to become Pres., Playboy Cable Network ('82).

ACHIEVEMENTS & AWARDS: Writer about television for *TV Guide, New York* magazine; Consultant, PBS, the Ford Foundation, Lincoln Center for the Performing Arts.

PERSONAL: Wife, Janet; two children. Resides in New York City.

KLEIN, STEWART
Entertainment Editor, Metromedia, WNEW-TV, New York

c/o WNEW-TV, 205 E. 67th St., New York, NY 10021
b. Philadelphia, PA.

EDUCATION: Temple University School of Journalism.

CAREER HIGHLIGHTS: Started career as Copy Boy, *Philadelphia Inquirer,* moving on as a Reporter, *Doylestown Intelligencer;* Reporter/Editor/Columnist, *Philadelphia Daily News;* News Dir., WCAU-AM, Philadelphia; moved to New York as Newswriter/Editor/Broadcaster, ABC News and ABC Network Radio; Reporter/Critic for WNEW-AM, New York; shortly thereafter worked in same capacity on WNEW-TV. Has been providing reports and entertainment critiques on New York's Metromedia Channel 5 "10 O'Clock News" since its inception ('67).

ACHIEVEMENTS & AWARDS: Emmy for his review of Latin film *Sebastiane* ('78).

PERSONAL: Resides in New York City.

KLEINE, JOHN
Dir., Financial Affairs, Warner Bros. TV

c/o Warner Bros., 75 Rockefeller Plaza, New York, NY 10020
b. February 28, 1954. New York, NY.

EDUCATION: Queens College, B.A.; Baruch College, M.B.A.

CAREER HIGHLIGHTS: Accountant, Viacom Intl. ('76); promoted to Financial Analyst ('77); and Mgr., Financial Planning ('78); joined the Showtime Entertainment Division as Mgr., Financial Services ('79); then Mgr., Budget and Forecast ('80); moved to Warner Bros. as Business Mgr. ('81); Dir., Financial Affairs ('82).

ACHIEVEMENTS & AWARDS: N.A.

PERSONAL: Resides in New Castle, NY, with wife, Amy, and son, John.

KLEINERMAN, ISAAC
Documentary Filmmaker

11 Sandusky Rd., New City, NY 10956
b. July 21, 1916.

EDUCATION: N.A.

CAREER HIGHLIGHTS: Prod./Dir. of documentaries for NBC ('51); Prod./Dir. of documentaries for CBS, including "The Twentieth Century" series and "CBS Reports" ('57); Independent Prod. of documentaries ('76); produced the syndicated series "The Unknown War" ('78).

ACHIEVEMENTS & AWARDS: Emmy for documentary achievement ('67).

PERSONAL: N.A.

KLUGE, JOHN
Chairman, Pres., Metromedia

c/o Metromedia, 205 E. 67th St., New York, NY 10021
b. 1914. Chemnitz, Germany.

EDUCATION: Columbia University, B.A. ('37).

CAREER HIGHLIGHTS: One of the most brilliant station management executives in American TV, Kluge gave Metromedia a new concept in communications through intra-state marketing and diversification. In early '83, Met-

romedia was the highest-priced stock on the N.Y. Stock Exchange. Founded radio station WGAY in Maryland; formed the New England Fritos Corp. ('47); founded a Food Brokerage firm and later served as Marketing Consultant to packaged food producers ('51); joined Metropolitan Broadcasting Corp. and became Chief Exec. Officer ('59); Chairman and Pres. of the TV and radio station chain, Metromedia ('61).

ACHIEVEMENTS & AWARDS: Numerous awards and affiliations include Dir. of the Shubert Foundation; Exec. V.P., United Cerebral Palsy Assn.

PERSONAL: N.A.

KLUGER, BARRY D.
Dir., USA Network, Communications

c/o USA Network, 208 Harristown Rd., Glen Rock, NJ 07452
b. N.A.

EDUCATION: American University, B.A., Broadcast Journalism.

CAREER HIGHLIGHTS: Prod./Announcer, WLMD Radio, Baltimore ('73); Dir., Creative Services, Douglas Poretz & Assoc., Washington, DC ('75); Mgr., Press and Publicity, WHN-AM, New York ('76); Sr. Acct. Exec., March Five Public Relations, New York ('77); Dir. of Communications, USA Network ('81).

ACHIEVEMENTS & AWARDS: N.A.

PERSONAL: Resides in New York City with his wife, Carol.

KLUGMAN, JACK
Actor

c/o Lee Fryd, 30 Rockefeller Plaza, New York, NY 10020
b. April 27, 1922. South Philadelphia, PA.

EDUCATION: Carnegie Tech.
CAREER HIGHLIGHTS: The hard-hitting Klugman brings the same intensity to comedy and drama and has moved from being half of the Odd Couple to being odd man out on "Quincy." Broadway shows include *St. Joan, Mr. Roberts,* and *Gypsy.* Motion pictures include *Twelve Angry Men, Days of Wine and Roses, The Detective, The Split, Goodbye, Columbus,* and *Two-Minute Warning.* TV roles on "Playhouse 90," "The Defenders," "The FBI," and "Ben Casey." TV series star of "The Odd Couple" and most recently, "Quincy."
ACHIEVEMENTS & AWARDS: Emmy for outstanding single performance by an actor, "The Defenders" ('63); Emmy awards for best actor in a comedy series for "The Odd Couple" ('71, '73).
PERSONAL: Separated; children, Adam and David. Resides in Malibu, CA.

KNIGHT, TED
Actor

P.O. Box 642, Pacific Palisades, CA 90272.
b. December 7. Terryville, CT.

EDUCATION: N.A.
CAREER HIGHLIGHTS: Voiceovers for radio and TV commercials and cartoon voice actor. Radio and TV appearances on "Big Town," "Suspense," and "Lux Video Theater." TV series star of "The Mary Tyler Moore Show" and "Too Close for Comfort."

ACHIEVEMENTS & AWARDS: Emmy awards for best supporting actor in a comedy series for "The Mary Tyler Moore Show" ('72, '75).
PERSONAL: Wife, Dorothy; three children, Ted Jr., Elyse, and Eric.

KNOTTS, DON
Actor/Comedian

c/o "Three's Company," ABC, 2040 Ave. of the Stars, Los Angeles, CA 90067
b. July 21, 1924. Morgantown, WV.

EDUCATION: West Virginia University; University of Arizona.
CAREER HIGHLIGHTS: The shaky "why not" funnyman stepped out of Steve Allen's line-up of men in the street into a comic spotlight of his own on "The Andy Griffith Show" and "Three's Company." Broadway role in *No Time for Sergeants* was his big break. Series regular on "The Garry Moore Show" and "The Steve Allen Show." Motion pictures include *The Incredible Mr. Limpet, It's a Mad, Mad, Mad, Mad World, No Time for Sergeants,* and *Prize Fighter.* TV series star of "The Andy Griffith Show," "The Don Knotts Show," and "Three's Company."
ACHIEVEMENTS & AWARDS: Five Emmy awards for his portrayal of Barney Fife on "The Andy Griffith Show."
PERSONAL: Wife, Loralee; children, Tom and Karen. Resides in Beverly Hills, CA.

KOBE, GAIL
Exec. Prod., Proctor & Gamble Productions, "Guiding Light"

c/o CBS, 51 W. 52d St., New York, NY 10020
b. March 19.

EDUCATION: University of California at Los Angeles, B.A. and graduate work, Film/Broadcasting.
CAREER HIGHLIGHTS: Began as an actress in the days of live TV, appearing on such shows as daytime soap opera "Bright Promise" and nighttime soap opera "Peyton Place." Left acting to teach the craft at San Fernando Valley State College; became a Script Editor, American Film Institute; Casting Supervisor, Mark Taper Forum; Assoc. Prod., for NBC

soaper "Return to Peyton Place." Joined Lorimar Productions as Story Editor, "The Waltons" ('74); appointed Assoc. Prod., "Days of Our Lives" ('76); moved around as Prod. Supervisor, "As the World Turns," "Search for Tomorrow," and "The Edge of Night" before being named Exec. Prod., "Texas" (81). After "Texas" was cancelled, Kobe was named Exec. Prod., "Guiding Light" ('83).

ACHIEVEMENTS & AWARDS: N.A.

PERSONAL: Resides in New York City.

KOLZAK, STEVE
Mgr., NBC Entertainment, West Coast, Casting

c/o NBC, 3000 W. Alameda Ave., Burbank, CA 91523

b. West Hartford, CT.

EDUCATION: Harvard University, B.A., Dramatic Literature ('76).

CAREER HIGHLIGHTS: Casting Coordinator, Universal Studios ('77); Asst. to Mary Goldberg, Mary Goldberg Casting Co. ('78); Casting Dir., "Starsky and Hutch" series; Freelance Casting Dir.; Casting Dir., Barbara Claman, Inc.; Mgr., Casting, NBC Entertainment, West Coast ('79).

ACHIEVEMENTS & AWARDS: N.A.

PERSONAL: Resides in Venice, CA.

KOMACK, JAMES
Prod./Dir./Writer

c/o Oppenheim, Appel, Dixon & Co., 2029 Century Park E., Los Angeles, CA 90067

b. August 3, 1930. New York, NY.

EDUCATION: New York University.

CAREER HIGHLIGHTS: Writer/Dir., "My Favorite Martian;" Dir., "Tarzan"; Dir., "Get Smart"; Creator/Exec. Prod., "The Courtship of Eddie's Father"; Creator/Exec. Prod., "Chico and the Man" ('77); Creator/Exec. Prod., "An-other Day" ('78); Creator/Exec. Prod., "Welcome Back Kotter" ('79); Creator/Exec. Prod., "Me and Maxx" ('80); Exec. Supervising Prod., "Nine to Five" ('82). Also currently serves as a minister for United Life Church.

ACHIEVEMENTS & AWARDS: N.A.

PERSONAL: N.A.

KONNER, JOAN
V.P., WNET/13, Metropolitan Programming

c/o WNET/13, 356 W. 58th St., New York, NY 10019

b. February 24, 1931. Paterson, NJ.

EDUCATION: Vassar College, B.A.; Sarah Lawrence College; Columbia Graduate School of Journalism, M.A.

CAREER HIGHLIGHTS: Editorial Writer/Columnist/Reporter, *Bergen Record* ('61); joined WNDT, now WNET, as Prod./Reporter/Host of local public affairs programs ('63); Writer/Reporter, NBC News ('65); Prod/Writer for "New York Illustrated," WNBC-TV ('68); Dir. of Programs, NBC Radio Network ('73); rejoined NBC News as Prod./Writer/Dir. for documentaries ('74); joined PBS as Exec. Prod., Natl. News and Public Affairs, "The Dick Cavett Show," and news and documentaries ('77); Exec. Prod., "Bill Moyers Journal" for WNET/13 ('78); appointed V.P. Dir. of Metropolitan Programming, WNET/13 ('82).

ACHIEVEMENTS & AWARDS: Received numerous awards including four local Emmy awards; one national Emmy; award from AP Broadcasters Assn. ('68–'73); Columbia Graduate School of Journalism alumni award ('75); Front Page award for "Maryjane Grows Up" ('76); Overseas Press Club award for "New World: Hard Choices," ('76); Peabody award for "MX Debate" on "Bill Moyers Journal."

PERSONAL: Resides in Palisades, NY. Two daughters, Rosemary and Catherine.

KOPELAN, AMY DORN
Dir., ABC, Early Morning Programming, Entertainment

c/o ABC, 1330 Ave. of the Americas, New York, NY 10019

b. April 15, 1951. New Jersey.

EDUCATION: Boston University School of Public Communications, B.S.; University of Grenoble.

CAREER HIGHLIGHTS: Asst. to Prod., "Show of Faith," WBZ-TV ('70–'72); Videotape Editor, ABC ('74); Program Administrator, ABC Entertainment for News and Sports ('77); Dir., Program Administration, East Coast ('79); appointed to Dir., Early Morning Programming ('81).

ACHIEVEMENTS & AWARDS: Judge at Emmy awards for excellence in editing ('75); Broadcast Operations and Engineering certificate of excellence ('76). Member, NATAS; NABET.

PERSONAL: Resides in Manhattan and New Jersey with husband, Rick, and stepchildren, Brett and Adam.

KOPELL, BERNIE
Actor

c/o "The Love Boat," ABC, 2040 Ave. of the Stars, Los Angeles, CA 90067
b. June 21. Brooklyn, NY.

EDUCATION: New York University, Dramatic Arts.

CAREER HIGHLIGHTS: Regular on the daytime drama "Brighter Day"; recurring roles on "Get Smart," "That Girl," "The Doris Day Show," and "Bewitched." A series regular on "Needles and Pins," "When Things Were Rotten," and "The Love Boat."

ACHIEVEMENTS & AWARDS: N.A.

PERSONAL: Wife, Yolanda Veloz; resides in Tarzana, CA.

KOPLIN, MERT
Chairman, Corp. for Entertainment and Learning

c/o Corp. for Entertainment and Learning, 515 Madison Ave., New York, NY 10022
b. May 2.

EDUCATION: University of Wisconsin.

CAREER HIGHLIGHTS: Early in his career, Koplin worked as a Prod., Writer, Dir., and Actor for all three commercial networks in New York and Hollywood. Founded the Corp. for Entertainment and Learning ('63); Prod. of such series as "The Presidents," "Better World," and "The Great Ladies"; Exec. Prod., "Creativity With Bill Moyers" ('82); Exec. Prod., "A Walk Through the 20th Century With Bill Moyers" ('83).

ACHIEVEMENTS & AWARDS: Emmy for "Creativity With Bill Moyers" ('82).

PERSONAL: N.A.

KOPLOVITZ, KAY
Pres., USA Cable Network

c/o USA Cable Network, 208 Harristown Rd., Glen Rock, NJ 07452
b. April 11, 1945. Milwaukee, WI.

EDUCATION: University of Wisconsin; Michigan State University, M.S.

CAREER HIGHLIGHTS: One of the few women to occupy a top management position in cable TV. Began as Prod./Dir., WTMJ-TV, Milwaukee ('67); joined COMSAT as Public Information Officer ('68); moved to UA-Columbia Cablevision in Franchising Dept. ('73); formed Conn-Koplovitz Communications ('75); Named Pres., USA Cable Network ('77).

ACHIEVEMENTS & AWARDS: Idell Kaitz award, Natl. Cable TV Assn. ('79); Person of the Year of the University of Wisconsin Alumni Club ('82); Jerry Greene memorial award, Natl. Cable TV Assn. ('82). Chairman, Natl. Cable TV Assn. Advertising Committee ('79-'81); Chairman, Membership Committee, Women in Cable ('79-'82); Founding Board Member, Exec. Committee Member, and Treasurer, CAB ('80-'82); Member: Women's Sports Foundation ('81-'82); AWRT ('81-'82).

PERSONAL: Married to William C. Koplovitz, V.P., Corporate Development, UA-Rogers Cablesystems.

KOPPEL, TED
Anchor, ABC, News

c/o ABC, 1717 DeSales St., N.W.,
  Washington, DC 20036
b. Lancashire, England.

EDUCATION: Syracuse University, B.A.; Stanford University, M.A.

CAREER HIGHLIGHTS: This no-nonsense newsman and relentless interviewer started in broadcasting as Desk Asst./Off-Air Reporter, WMCA-Radio; joined ABC News as General Assignment Correspondent ('63); covered civil rights movement and was nightly ABC Radio Newscaster ('65); Saigon Bureau TV Reporter ('67); Miami Bureau Chief ('68); moved to Hong Kong in same capacity ('69). Appointed Chief Diplomatic Correspondent ('71) and earned reputation for quality with reports including "Second to None?," a 10-part series on national defense ('79), and "Kissinger: Action Biography" for which he was both Correspondent and Prod. ('74); Anchor, "The Saturday Evening News," while filling State Dept. responsibilities ('75); appointed Anchor and Editorial Mgr., ABC News "Nightline" when it was introduced ('80); also anchors "Viewpoint" and some special events programming.

ACHIEVEMENTS & AWARDS: Overseas Press Club awards for best TV commentary on foreign news ('74, '76); Dupont award for "Second to None?" ('79); Emmy as Co-Anchor, "Nightline" special edition on Pres. Ronald Reagan's victory ('81). Cited for outstanding work when "Nightline" and "Viewpoint" received Peabody awards for overall excellence ('82); Polk award for best TV news reporting ('82). Honorary doctor of laws, Syracuse University; honorary doctor of humanities, University of South Carolina.

PERSONAL: Resides in Potomac, MD, with wife, Grace Anne, and four children.

KORDA, RONALD
Dir., Program Scheduling and Theatrical Acquisitions, NBC, Entertainment

c/o NBC, 30 Rockefeller Plaza, New York, NY
  10020
b. New York, NY.

EDUCATION: University of Pennsylvania, B.A. (cum laude); Baruch College, M.B.A., Marketing Research

CAREER HIGHLIGHTS: Acct. Representative, Affiliate Relations Dept., ABC ('70); Analyst, Research Dept., ABC ('72); Sr. Analyst, ABC ('73); Marketing Representative, NBC ('73); Supervisor, Marketing Services, NBC TV Network Sales ('75); Mgr., Broadcast Ratings, NBC, New York ('77); Mgr., Program Planning, NBC Entertainment, New York ('79); Dir., Program Scheduling and Theatrical Acquisitions, NBC Entertainment, New York ('83).

ACHIEVEMENTS & AWARDS: N.A.

PERSONAL: Resides in Scarsdale, NY.

KOTLOWITZ, ROBERT
Public Broadcasting Programming Exec. and Exec. Prod., WNET, Programming

c/o WNET, 356 W. 58th St., New York, NY
  10019
b. November 21, 1924. Paterson, NJ.

EDUCATION: Johns Hopkins University, B.A.

CAREER HIGHLIGHTS: Joined WNET as Sr. V.P., Programming ('73). Credits as Exec. Prod. include "Brideshead Revisited" and "The Magic of Dance" ('82).

ACHIEVEMENTS & AWARDS: Emmy for "The Sleeping Beauty" ('72). Author of two critically acclaimed novels, *Somewhere Else* ('72) and *The Boardwalk* ('77).

PERSONAL: Resides in New York City with his wife.

KRASNOW, ERWIN G.
Sr. V.P. and General Counsel, NAB

5604 Surrey St., Chevy Chase, MD 20015
b. N.A.

EDUCATION: Boston University (summa cum laude, '58); Harvard Law School, J.D. ('61); Georgetown University Law Center, LL.M. ('65).

CAREER HIGHLIGHTS: On the faculty at Ohio State University's Graduate School of Communications; American University's Graduate School of Communications and Department of Communications; Temple University's School of Communications and Theater; George Washington University's Graduate School of Arts and Sciences; and Catholic University of America's Law School. Former Partner in the law firm of Kirkland & Ellis, Washington, DC ('64); Sr. V.P. and General Counsel, NAB, Washington, DC ('76).

ACHIEVEMENTS & AWARDS: Past Pres., Capitol Hill Bar Assn.; Co-Chairman, Communications Law Committee, Federal Bar Assn.; Member, Exec. Committee, Federal Communications Bar Assn.; Chairman, Communications Committee, Administrative Law Section of the American Bar Assn.

PERSONAL: N.A.

KRAUSS, MITCHELL
Correspondent, CBS, News, Cairo
c/o CBS, Flat #6, 18 Sharia Sahel Ghelelai, Cairo, Egypt
b. New York, NY.

EDUCATION: New York University ('51); University of Pennsylvania ('56).

CAREER HIGHLIGHTS: Started as Reporter, WFLN, Philadelphia, and later WQXR, New York; Dir., News and Special Events, WIP, Philadelphia ('56); V.P. and Dir. of News, Radio New York Worldwide ('60); Anchor, "Newsfront," WNET-TV, New York ('66); Exec. Prod./Host, "Another Look," WNET-TV, New York ('70); Special Correspondent and Anchor, CBS Radio Network ('72); Correspondent, CBS News, New York ('73); Correspondent, CBS News, Cairo ('81).

ACHIEVEMENTS & AWARDS: Peabody award ('64); Member, Foreign Press Assn. of Cairo.

PERSONAL: Wife, Elisabeth; daughter, Jennifer; son, David.

KREBS, JOE
General Assignment Reporter, WRC-TV

c/o WRC-TV, 4001 Nebraska Ave., N.W., Washington, DC 20016
b. N.A.

EDUCATION: St. Louis University, Law.

CAREER HIGHLIGHTS: Asst. Prosecuting Attorney for St. Louis County; Prod./Anchor/Capitol Correspondent, WFMY-TV, Greensboro, NC; Anchor, WBAL-TV, Baltimore ('73); General Assignment Reporter with emphasis on the criminal justice system, WRC-TV ('80).

ACHIEVEMENTS & AWARDS: American Bar Assn. gavel certificate of merit; local Emmy ('81).

PERSONAL: Wife, Mary Lynn; daughter, Anna. Resides in Washington, DC.

KREEK, BOB
V.P., HBO, Film Acquisition

c/o HBO, 1271 Ave. of the Americas, New York, NY 10020
b. July 22, 1948.

EDUCATION: Villanova University, B.A., Business Administration; Wharton Business School, M.B.A., Finance.

CAREER HIGHLIGHTS: Financial Analyst, United Brands ('76); Mgr. of Program Finance, HBO ('78); named Mgr., Feature Film Planning ('79); Dir. of Film Acquisition ('79); appointed V.P., Film Acquisition ('82).

ACHIEVEMENTS & AWARDS: N.A.

PERSONAL: Resides in Manhattan with wife, Sherry.

KREMER, SELMAN M.
V.P., Southern Satellite Systems

8252 S. Harvard, Tulsa, OK 74136
b. May 4, 1924. Baltimore, MD.

EDUCATION: City College of Baltimore.
CAREER HIGHLIGHTS: General Mgr., Atomic TV Co., a service company repairing TVs and installing home antennas and master antenna systems, Baltimore ('46); Dir. of Marketing Services, Jerrold Electronics Corp., CATV, MATV, hifi equipment and home TV antenna manufacturer, Philadelphia ('53); Dir. of Operations, TPT Communications Corp. ('68); Self-Employed Consultant, New York and Baltimore, ('73–'76). Presently V.P., Southern Satellite Systems and parent company Satellite Syndicated Systems, in charge of WTBS satellite service sales and new cabletext, keyfax projects.
ACHIEVEMENTS & AWARDS: In early years of his career he held posts in many trade organizations, including Natl. TV Service Man's Assn., EIA, and Natl. Cable TV Assn.
PERSONAL: Wife, Ruth; son, Frank; daughter, Julie. Resides in Tulsa, OK.

KRIEGLER, PHILIP
V.P., Public Relations, ABC, West Coast

c/o ABC, 4151 Prospect Ave., Los Angeles, CA 90027
b. N.A.

EDUCATION: University of Missouri School of Journalism.
CAREER HIGHLIGHTS: Joined ABC as a Press Representative in New York ('59); Mgr., Special Projects, ABC ('68); Mgr., Special Projects, ABC, West Coast ('71); Dir., Special Projects, ABC, West Coast ('72); Dir., Public Relations, ABC, West Coast ('74); V.P., Public Relations, ABC, West Coast ('76).
ACHIEVEMENTS & AWARDS: N.A.
PERSONAL: Resides in Van Nuys, CA; wife, Jean; daughters, Ingrid and Vicki.

KRIVEN, ALBERT
Sr. V.P., Metromedia

c/o Metromedia, 205 E. 67th St., New York, NY 10021
b. N.A.

EDUCATION: N.A.
CAREER HIGHLIGHTS: Sales Exec., Westinghouse Broadcasting; V.P. and General Mgr., KMBC-TV, Kansas City, MO ('61); Pres. Metromedia TV ('66); Sr. V.P., Metromedia.
ACHIEVEMENTS & AWARDS: N.A.
PERSONAL: N.A.

KROENCKE, MARY
Anchor, WJLA-TV, News

c/o WJLA-TV, 4461 Connecticut Ave., N.W., Washington, DC 20008
b. N.A.

EDUCATION: Central Missouri State University, B.S.
CAREER HIGHLIGHTS: Reporter/Co-Anchor, KTVX-TV, Salt Lake City, UT ('78); Anchor, WJLA-TV, Washington, DC ('83).
ACHIEVEMENTS & AWARDS: Local Emmy in Salt Lake City.
PERSONAL: N.A.

KROFT, STEVE
Correspondent, CBS, News, Dallas

c/o CBS, 3111 One Main Place, Dallas, TX 75250
b. August 22, 1944. Kokomo, IN.

EDUCATION: Syracuse University, B.S. ('67); Columbia University Graduate School of Journalism, M.S. ('75).

CAREER HIGHLIGHTS: Reporter, WSYR-TV, Syracuse, NY ('72); Reporter, WJXT-TV, Jacksonville, FL ('75); Reporter, WPLG-TV, Miami ('77); Correspondent, CBS News, New York ('80); Correspondent, CBS News, Dallas ('81).

ACHIEVEMENTS & AWARDS: Nine local Emmy awards while working at WPLG-TV; two Sigma Delta Chi awards; Ohio State University award; UPI award.

PERSONAL: N.A.

KUBEK, TONY
Sportscaster, NBC, Sports

c/o NBC, 30 Rockefeller Plaza, New York, NY 10020
b. October 12, 1935. Milwaukee, WI.

EDUCATION: Attended school in Milwaukee.

CAREER HIGHLIGHTS: New York Yankee baseball player and three-time American League All Star; joined NBC Sports as a Commentator on major league baseball ('66); also does commentary for Canadian TV and CBC.

ACHIEVEMENTS & AWARDS: Member, AFTRA.

PERSONAL: Resides in Appleton, WI, with wife and four children.

KUNHARDT, PETER W.
Prod., ABC, News, "20/20"

c/o ABC, 77 W. 66th St., New York, NY 10023
b. December 26, 1952. Los Angeles, CA.

EDUCATION: Middlebury College.

CAREER HIGHLIGHTS: Assoc. Prod., ABC News, "20/20" (79); Prod., ABC News, "20/20" ('81).

ACHIEVEMENTS & AWARDS: Emmy awards for "Saigon Evacuation" ('81) and "Hyatt Collapse" ('81).

PERSONAL: N.A.

KUR, BOB
Network News Correspondent, NBC

c/o NBC, 4001 Nebraska Ave., N.W., Washington, DC 20016
b. Newark, NJ.

EDUCATION: Ithaca College, B.S. ('70); Columbia University Graduate School of Journalism, master's ('71).

CAREER HIGHLIGHTS: General Assignment Reporter, WRC-TV ('73); NBC Correspondent, Cleveland ('76); Chicago Bureau ('77); Washington, DC, Bureau ('78). Covered Sen. Edward M. Kennedy's campaign for president, and after the convention covered V.P. Walter Mondale's activities until the November general election ('79–'80). Named NBC News's third correspondent at the State Dept. ('80); assigned to cover the House of Representatives ('82).

ACHIEVEMENTS & AWARDS: N.A.

PERSONAL: N.A.

KURALT, CHARLES
News Anchor and Correspondent, CBS

c/o CBS, 51 W. 52d St., New York, NY 10019
b. Wilmington, NC.

EDUCATION: University of North Carolina ('55).

CAREER HIGHLIGHTS: Kuralt's casual manner belies his urbanity and cultivation. His multi-award-winning "Sunday Morning" show's leisurely pace is ideal because there's time for viewers to savor his skillful reporting. Reporter/Columnist, *Charlotte News* ('55); Writer, CBS News ('56); Assignment Desk ('58); Host, CBS News series "Eyewitness" ('60); Chief Latin America Correspondent and Chief West Coast Correspondent; "On the Road" ('67); Anchor, "CBS Sunday Morning" ('79); Anchor, "Morning" ('80–'82); anchor, "CBS Sunday Morning" ('82).

ACHIEVEMENTS & AWARDS: Emmy ('81); Dupont-Columbia award; cited by Overseas Press Club citation for "Sunday Morning." Also, Peabody awards ('69, '76), Emmy for "On the Road" ('69); George Polk award for work on the Sunday and weekday editions of the morning news broadcasts ('81); IRTS Broadcaster of the Year.

PERSONAL: Resides in New York City.

KURTIS, BILL
Co-Anchor, CBS, Morning News

c/o CBS, 51 W. 52d Street, New York, NY
10019
b. September 21, 1940. Pensacola, FL.

EDUCATION: University of Kansas, B.S., Journalism ('62); Washington University School of Law at Topeka, J.D. ('66).
CAREER HIGHLIGHTS: Reporter, WIBW-Radio, Topeka, KS; Reporter/Prod. CBS News, Los Angeles Bureau ('70); named Correspondent ('71); Co-Anchor, 6 o'clock and 10 o'clock news broadcasts, WBBM-TV, Chicago, and Reporter ('73); Correspondent and Co-Anchor, with Diane Sawyer, "CBS Morning News" ('82).
ACHIEVEMENTS & AWARDS: Emmy awards, Broadcast Media award, Illinois Journalist of the Year, Sigma Delta Chi award. Member, American Bar Assn.
PERSONAL: Widower; two children, Mary Kristin and Scott Erik.

KURTZ, BOB
Sportscaster, Cable News Network

10 Columbus Circle, New York, NY
b. May 23, 1941. Norfolk, VA.

EDUCATION: Yankton College; Drake University; Northwestern University.
CAREER HIGHLIGHTS: TV Host, "Wonderful World," "Different Drummers," WBBM-TV, Chicago ('68); Sportscaster, KVIL-Radio, Dallas ('73); Sportscaster, KDFW-TV, CBS, Dallas ('71); Sports Dir., KBTV, ABC, Denver ('74); Sports Dir., WTCN, NBC, Minneapolis ('79); Sportscaster, Cable News Network ('80).
ACHIEVEMENTS & AWARDS: Colorado Sportscaster of the Year ('77, '78); USA Film Festival award for documentary of the year ('73); Emmy nomination for "Lift Every Voice," a black history series on WBBM-TV ('71); Idaho Sports Hall of Fame ('82).
PERSONAL: Golf professional; son of a clergyman. Two daughters, Beth and Kim.

KURTZ, SWOOSIE
Actress

c/o William Morris Agency, 151 El Camino Dr., Beverly Hills, CA 90212
b. September 6. Omaha, NE.

EDUCATION: University of Southern California: Academy of Music and Dramatic Art (England).
CAREER HIGHLIGHTS: Broadway credits include *Tartuffe, Fifth of July,* and *A History of the American Film.* TV series regular, "The Mary Tyler Moore Variety Show" and "Love, Sidney."
ACHIEVEMENTS & AWARDS: Drama Desk award for *A History of the American Film;* Tony, Drama Desk, and Outer Critics Circle awards for *Fifth of July.*
PERSONAL: Single; resides in New York City.

KUTNER, STEVE
V.P., United Satellite Communications, Program Acquisition

c/o United Satellite Communications, 1345 Ave. of the Americas, New York, NY 10105
b. September 8, 1937.

EDUCATION: City College of New York, B.S.; Columbia University, M.B.A.
CAREER HIGHLIGHTS: Sr. V.P., Marketing, Columbia Pictures; V.P. in Charge of Pay TV, MGM-UA; V.P., Program Acquisition, United Satellite Communications, New York.
ACHIEVEMENTS & AWARDS: N.A.
PERSONAL: N.A.

KWARTIN, LESLIE
Prod., CBS, "The Guiding Light"

c/o CBS, 51 W. 52d St., New York, NY 10019
b. April 10, 1943. Norwalk, CT.

EDUCATION: University of Connecticut, B.A., Music ('65).

CAREER HIGHLIGHTS: Catalogue Editor, RCA Records ('65); Production Asst., "The Guiding Light" ('67); Assoc. Prod., "The Guiding Light" ('71); named Prod. of the show ('77).

ACHIEVEMENTS & AWARDS: "The Guiding Light" won two daytime Emmy awards for best daytime drama under Kwartin ('80, '82).

PERSONAL: Resides in New York City.

L

LABICH, RICHARD A.
Assoc. Publisher, Time, Inc., *TV-Cable Week*

c/o TV-Cable Week, 123 Main St., White
Plains, NY 10601
b. December 28, 1938. Chicago, IL.

EDUCATION: Loyola University, B.S. ('63); Columbia University Executive Master's Degree
Programs, M.S. ('77).
CAREER HIGHLIGHTS: Joined Time, Inc., gradu-
ally moving up the ranks through a series of
executive positions in the Corporate Manufacturing and Distribution Division of Time,
Inc.'s Magazine Group ('61); Assoc. Dir., Corporate Manufacturing and Distribution Division of Time, Inc.'s Magazine Group ('80);
assigned to the groundwork of the *TV-Cable
Week* project ('81); named Assoc. Publisher,
TV-Cable Week ('83).
ACHIEVEMENTS & AWARDS: N.A.
PERSONAL: Resides in Fairfield, CT.

LABUNSKI, STEPHEN B.
Exec. Dir., IRTS

c/o IRTS, 420 Lexington Ave., New York, NY
10170
b. Poland.

EDUCATION: University of Missouri; George-
town University.
CAREER HIGHLIGHTS: Salesman, KCMO, Kan-
sas City, MO ('51); V.P. and General Mgr.,
WDGY, Minneapolis ('55); Pres., NBC Radio
('65); Exec. V.P., Merv Griffin Radio ('73);
Exec. Dir., IRTS ('78).
ACHIEVEMENTS & AWARDS: N.A.
PERSONAL: Resides in New York City with his
wife, Jeralyn.

LACHER, RICHARD S.
**Dir., Financial Administration, NBC,
Entertainment, West Coast**

c/o NBC, 3000 W. Alameda Ave., Burbank,
CA 91523
b. December 21, 1951. St. Paul, MN.

EDUCATION: Arizona State University.
CAREER HIGHLIGHTS: News Photographer,
KTAR-TV, Phoenix ('73); Acct. Exec., Radio
Sales, KXIV-Radio, Phoenix ('74); Cost and
Billing Coordinator in Broadcast Operations,
NBC, Burbank ('75); Dir., Financial Adminis-
tration, NBC Entertainment, West Coast
('81).
ACHIEVEMENTS & AWARDS: N.A.
PERSONAL: Resides in Burbank with wife,
Nancy, and daughter.

LACHMAN, BRAD
Prod.

c/o Bob Banner Assoc., 8687 Melrose Ave.,
Los Angeles, CA 90069
b. September 6, 1945. Los Angeles, CA.

EDUCATION: University of California at Los An-
geles.
CAREER HIGHLIGHTS: Writer, "The Merv Griffin
Show" ('73); Prod., "Rich Little–Olivia New-
ton-John Special" ('75); Prod., "The Don Ho
Special" ('76); Prod., "The Mike Douglas
Show" ('77); Prod., ABC's summer series
"Keep on Truckin'," and two Bob Hope
shows ('78); Prod., "Solid Gold '79" special
('79); "Solid Gold" syndicated series for Bob
Banner Assoc. ('80–'82).
ACHIEVEMENTS & AWARDS: N.A.
PERSONAL: Resides in Los Angeles.

LACHMAN, MORT
Prod./Writer/Dir.

c/o Bernie Weintraub, Robinson/Weintraub,
4115-B Warner Ave., Burbank, CA 91505
b. March 20, 1918. Seattle, WA.

EDUCATION: University of Washington.
CAREER HIGHLIGHTS: Writer/Prod./Dir., Bob
Hope specials in Hollywood and specials
from Morocco, Moscow, Middle East,
Europe, Vietnam, and Thailand; Dir./Prod.,
"Chrysler Theater," "Kraft Music Hall";
Exec. Prod., "One Day at a Time," "All in
the Family," "Archie Bunker's Place," and
"Gimme a Break," and the CBS series "Sut-
ter's Bay" ('83–'84).
ACHIEVEMENTS & AWARDS: Emmy award as
Exec. Prod., "All in the Family" ('77) and as
Dir., "The Girl Who Couldn't Lose" for "ABC
Afternoon Playbreak."
PERSONAL: Daughters, Diane and Joanne; son,
Robert.

LACK, ANDREW
Exec. Prod., CBS, News

c/o CBS, 524 W. 57th St., New York, NY
10019
b. May 16. New York, NY.

EDUCATION: Boston University School of Fine
Arts ('68); Sorbonne.
CAREER HIGHLIGHTS: One of the ablest young
producers in TV news and documentary. Was
on-air correspondent for several of his own
programs. Joined CBS as Prod., "Who's
Who" ('76); Prod., "60 Minutes" ('77); Prod.,
CBS Reports, "The Politics of Abortion" ('78),
"The Boat People" ('79), "Teddy" ('79), and
"Boys and Girls Together" ('80); Sr. Prod.,
CBS Reports, "The Defense of the United
States" ('81) and "Bittersweet Memories: A
Vietnam Reunion" ('81); Exec. Prod., CBS Re-
ports, "Central America in Revolt" ('82),
"People Like Us" ('82), "A Time to Die" ('82),
and "After the Dream Comes True" ('82);
Correspondent for CBS Reports, "The
American-Israeli Connection" ('82).
ACHIEVEMENTS & AWARDS: Seven   Emmy
awards, three Dupont-Columbia awards;
Peabody, Ohio State University, Overseas
Press Club, and American Bar Assn. awards
for his CBS Reports broadcasts.
PERSONAL: N.A.

LADD, CHERYL
Actress

c/o ABC, 2040 Ave. of the Stars, Los Angeles,
CA 90067
b. July 2. Huron, SD.

EDUCATION: Attended school in South Dakota.
CAREER HIGHLIGHTS: TV guest star on "Ben
Vereen: His Roots," "Police Woman," "Hap-
py Days," "Switch," and "Police Story." Star
of "Charlie's Angels." Star of the variety spe-
cials "Cheryl Ladd" and "The Cheryl Ladd
Special: Souvenirs." Her TV movies include
The Grace Kelly Story, Kentucky Woman, and
When She Was Bad.
ACHIEVEMENTS & AWARDS: N.A.
PERSONAL: Husband, David; daughter, Jor-
dan.

LADENDORFF, MARCIA
**News Anchor, Turner Broadcasting System,
WTBS-TV and Cable News Network**

c/o Alfred Geller, 250 W. 57th St., New York,
NY 10019
b. August 16, 1949. Hackensack, NJ.

EDUCATION: Whittier College; Arizona State
University.
CAREER HIGHLIGHTS: Began as News Film Edi-
tor and Camera Operator, KPHO-TV, Phoe-
nix ('73); moved on to WROC-TV, Rochester,
NY as Weathercaster before establishing her-
self as News Reporter ('74); switched to
WOKR-TV, Rochester, as Reporter ('76); be-
came Anchor/Prod. at WNDU-TV, South
Bend, IN ('76); then Anchor at KETV-TV,
Omaha, NE ('77); and finally landing in At-
lanta as Anchor for WTBS-TV and Cable
News Network ('80).

ACHIEVEMENTS & AWARDS: N.A.

PERSONAL: Resides in Atlanta.

LAFFERTY, MARTIN C.
Independent Prod.

219 Perimeter Center Pkwy., Atlanta, GA 30346
b. December 24, 1947. New York, NY.

EDUCATION: Williams College, B.A., English ('69); Yale School of Drama, M.F.A., Producing/Directing ('72).

CAREER HIGHLIGHTS: Freelance Prod./Dir. ('72); Asst. Prof./Resident Prod., Rutgers University ('74); Mgr., Creative Services, General Electric Co., Atlanta ('78); Dir., Programming Services, Cox Cable Communications ('80); Independent Prod.

ACHIEVEMENTS & AWARDS: Chairman, Awards for Cablecasting Excellence Awards Committee.

PERSONAL: N.A.

LAFFERTY, PERRY F.
Sr. V.P., NBC, Programs and Talent

c/o Charles Goldring, 9044 Melrose, Los Angeles, CA 90069
b. October 3, 1917. Davenport, IA.

EDUCATION: Cornell University; Yale University; Certificate of Music, Yale Music School.

CAREER HIGHLIGHTS: Prod., B. F. Goodrich's "Riddle Me This" ('47); Prod., "College of Musical Knowledge" ('49); Prod./Dir., "The Victor Borge Show" ('51) and "The Imogene Coca Show" ('52). Dir., "Robert Montgomery Presents" ('53–'56), Dir., various "Studio One" and "U.S. Steel Hour" programs ('53–'57). Prod. and Dir. of network hits including "Your Hit Parade" ('58); "The Andy Williams Show" ('59); "The Twilight Zone" and "Rawhide" ('62); "The Danny Kaye Show" ('63–'64). Joined CBS TV Network as V.P., Programs ('65); moved to NBC as Sr. V.P., Programs and Talent ('76); Sr. V.P., Programs and Talent, including responsibility for late-night programming ('83).

ACHIEVEMENTS & AWARDS: Emmy and Peabody awards for best variety show for "The Danny Kaye Show" ('64). Published *Birdies Sing and Everything* ('64) and *How To Lose Your Fear of Flying* ('80). Member, AFM, Local 802, Directors Guild, Authors League of America, Producers Guild.

PERSONAL: Wife, Frances; children, Marcie Shatner and Steven.

LAFFERTY, STEVE
V.P., Business Affairs, Showtime Entertainment

c/o Showtime, 1633 Broadway, New York, NY 10019
b. July 1, 1953.

EDUCATION: University of California at Santa Barbara; Whittier College of Law.

CAREER HIGHLIGHTS: Assoc. Dir., MTM Enterprises ('75); Dir., Business Affairs, Hanna-Barbera Productions ('78); V.P., Business Affairs, Viacom Entertainment Group ('80); V.P., Business Affairs, Showtime ('82).

ACHIEVEMENTS & AWARDS: N.A.

PERSONAL: N.A.

LAIBSON, MICHAEL D.
Prod., CBS, "As the World Turns"

c/o CBS, 51 W. 52d St., New York, NY 10019
b. October 20, 1946. Miami Beach, FL.

EDUCATION: University of California at Los Angeles, B.A. ('70).

CAREER HIGHLIGHTS: Production Asst., "Guiding Light" ('78); Asst. to the Prod., "The Guiding Light" ('79); Assoc. Prod., "The Guiding Light" ('80); Prod., "As the World Turns" ('81).

ACHIEVEMENTS & AWARDS: N.A.

PERSONAL: Resides in New York City with wife, Holly, daughter Tracy, and son, Kevin.

LAMONT, PEGGY
Dir. of Program Development, Tomorrow Entertainment

c/o Tomorrow Entertainment, 405 Lexington Ave., New York, NY 10174
b. April 8, 1949. New Jersey.

EDUCATION: Groucher College, B.A. ('71); Simmons College Graduate Program in Management ('78).

CAREER HIGHLIGHTS: Planning Analyst, CBS TV ('78); Mgr., Sales Analysis Dept., CBS TV ('80); Dir. of Program Development, Tomorrow Entertainment ('81).

ACHIEVEMENTS & AWARDS: N.A.

PERSONAL: N.A.

LAMOREAUX, E. S., III (Bud)
Exec. Prod., CBS, News

c/o CBS, 524 W. 57th St., New York, NY 10019
b. April. Mount Vernon, NY.

EDUCATION: University of Missouri School of Journalism ('55).

CAREER HIGHLIGHTS: Started in the CBS Mailroom ('58); shortly thereafter became a Newswriter, before being promoted to Prod. of Sports, CBS News. Covered all the major sports events in the sixties and early seventies, including the Olympics, World Series and Super Bowls. Was instrumental in developing the sports essay, which was first broadcast on the CBS News weekend broadcasts. In addition, served as Prod., political conventions and Apollo moon shots ('59–'72); Exec. Prod., weekend editions of the "CBS Evening News" ('72); moved to CBS Sports as Exec. Prod., boxing, NBA, and horse racing broadcasts ('75); Sr. Prod., "CBS News Sunday Morning" ('79); Exec. Prod., "CBS News Sunday Morning" ('80).

ACHIEVEMENTS & AWARDS: N.A.

PERSONAL: Resides in Mount Kisco, NY, with wife, Susan; daughters, Sheri, Melissa, and Denise.

LANDAY, JERRY M.
Correspondent, CBS, News

c/o CBS, 524 W. 57th St., New York, NY 10019
b. August 22.

EDUCATION: Syracuse University, B.S., Communications.

CAREER HIGHLIGHTS: Associated with Westinghouse Broadcasting Co., heading News Departments in Pittsburgh, Boston, and New York, and serving as Natl. News Editor in Washington, DC, Natl. Political Correspondent, and London Correspondent ('54–'69); Group W Chief Foreign Correspondent, London; covered the White House for ABC News; wrote for "The Week In Review," *N.Y. Times* ('66–'69); joined CBS News as Correspondent ('75); reports frequently on "CBS News Sunday Morning."

ACHIEVEMENTS & AWARDS: Awards from Sigma Delta Chi ('62, '63). Author of *Silent Cities, Sacred Stores, The Dome of the Rock,* and a history of the House of David. Member of the Reform Club of London.

PERSONAL: Three children, Jonathan, Woodrow, and Stephanie.

LANDERS, HAL
Prod. and Pres., Landers Productions

c/o R. Wald, 1900 Ave. of the Stars, Century City, CA 90067
b. June 26, 1928. Chicago, IL.

EDUCATION: N.A.

CAREER HIGHLIGHTS: Formed Landers Productions ('60).

ACHIEVEMENTS & AWARDS: N.A.

PERSONAL: N.A.

LANDON, MICHAEL
Actor

c/o Jay J. Eller, Esq., 1930 Century Park E., Suite 401, Los Angeles, CA 90067
b. October 31, 1937. Forest Hills, NJ.

EDUCATION: University of Southern California.

CAREER HIGHLIGHTS: From the western range of "Bonanza" to the Little Prairie, Landon has demonstrated know-how as actor and surprised everyone with his directing and producing savvy. Motion pictures include *I Was a Teenage Werewolf,* and TV movies include *The Loneliest Runner.* Series star of "Bonanza"; Writer/Dir./Star of the series "Little House on the Prairie."

ACHIEVEMENTS & AWARDS: N.A.

PERSONAL: Wife, Lynn; seven children, including adoptions. Resides in Beverly Hills, CA.

LANDSBURG, ALAN
Exec. Prod., Alan Landsburg Productions

1554 S. Sepulveda Blvd., Los Angeles, CA 90025
b. May 10, 1933. White Plains, NY.

EDUCATION: New York University, B.A.

CAREER HIGHLIGHTS: Prod./Dir., CBS TV ('58); Exec. Prod. or Prod., Wolper Productions, including, *Ten Seconds That Shook the World, The March of Time,* "National Geographic Specials," "The Undersea World of Jacques Cousteau," *Storm in Summer,* and *Black Water Gold.* Formed Alan Landsburg Productions ('70), serving as Exec. Prod. and Chairman of the Board overseeing such productions as *On Location, Small Miracle* ('73); *Fear on Trial* ('75); the syndicated "In Search of..." series; *The Savage Bees* ('76); *Ants!* ('77); *Tarantulas: The Deadly Cargo* ('77); *Ruby and Oswald* ('78); *The Triangle Factory Fire* ('78); *The Chisolms* miniseries ('78); *Terror Out of the Sky* ('78); *Torn Between Two Lovers* ('79); *Mysterious Island of Beautiful Women* ('79); *And Baby Makes Six* ('79); *Marathon* ('80); *The Jayne Mansfield Story* ('80); *Baby Comes Home* ('80); "That's Incredible!" ('80); "Those Amazing Animals" ('81); *Bill* ('82); and *A Long Way Home* ('83); and the CBS series "Sutter's Bay" ('83–'84).

ACHIEVEMENTS & AWARDS: Emmy awards for best drama, *Storm in Summer* ('70) and *Bill* ('82); Man of the Year of the Natl. Jewish Hospital and Research Center.

PERSONAL: Resides in Malibu, CA, with wife, Linda; daughter, Valerie; son, Michael.

LANGE, KELLY
Anchor, KNBC-TV, News

c/o KNBC-TV, 3000 W. Alameda Ave., Los Angeles, CA 91523
b. New York, NY.

EDUCATION: Merrimack College.

CAREER HIGHLIGHTS: Helicopter Traffic Reporter, KABC-AM, Los Angeles ('67); Reporter, KABC-TV, Los Angeles ('69); Reporter, KNBC-TV, Los Angeles ('71); Anchor and Host, for "News 4 LA," "Sunday," and "The Tournament of Roses Parade" for NBC and KNBC-TV ('74). Also serves as a substitute for the NBC Weekend News and the "Today" program.

ACHIEVEMENTS & AWARDS: Genii award from the American Women in Radio and TV and a Los Angeles Emmy for outstanding achievement as a news anchor.

PERSONAL: Resides in Los Angeles, CA.

LANNING, JERRY
Actor

c/o NBC, 30 Rockefeller Plaza, New York, NY 10020
b. May 17, 1943. Miami, FL.

EDUCATION: University of Southern California.

CAREER HIGHLIGHTS: Broadway theater credits include *Mame* and a revival of *My Fair Lady.* Soap opera star of "Texas."

ACHIEVEMENTS & AWARDS: N.A.

PERSONAL: Wife, Sherry Mathis. Resides in Manhattan.

LARGE, BRIAN
Dir.

c/o Metropolitan Opera, Lincoln Center, New York, NY 10023
b. 1941. Great Britain.

EDUCATION: Royal Academy of Music; University of London.

CAREER HIGHLIGHTS: An internationally known director of live opera on TV, Large became Chief Dir., Opera, for the BBC ('74) and is regarded as the premiere director of opera on TV. Productions have included *The Flying Dutchman* and *Owen Wingrave* for the BBC; *Electra* and *Tannhauser* for the Metropolitan Opera, and the Bayreuth Centennial *Ring of the Nibelung*.

ACHIEVEMENTS & AWARDS: N.A.

PERSONAL: N.A.

LARSON, ERIC
Publisher, *TV Guide*

c/o *TV Guide*, 4 Radnor Corp. Center, Radnor, PA 19088
b. December 30, 1924. Detroit, MI.

EDUCATION: University of Pennsylvania, B.S.

CAREER HIGHLIGHTS: Armstrong Cork Co. ('50–'53); joined *TV Guide* ('54), first as Detroit Mgr., then Promotion Dir., Advertising Mgr., Dir. of Advertising and Promotion. Named Publisher ('82).

ACHIEVEMENTS & AWARDS: N.A.

PERSONAL: N.A.

LARSON, GLEN A.
Exec. Prod.

100 Universal City Plaza, Universal City, CA 91608
b. N.A.

EDUCATION: N.A.

CAREER HIGHLIGHTS: Started out as a member

of "The Four Preps," a musical group that earned three gold records; moved from Free-lance Scriptwriter to Prod., for "It Takes a Thief." Prod., "McCloud"; Creator/Prod./Writer, "Alias Smith and Jones"; went back to "McCloud" as Exec. Prod.; Exec. Prod., "Quincy," "Hardy Boys/Nancy Drew Mysteries," "Six Million Dollar Man"; Co-Creator, pilot for "Magnum, P.I." Prod., ABC series "Automan" ('83), "Masquerade" ('83), "Trauma Center" ('83), "Crossfire" ('83), and "Manimal" ('83).

ACHIEVEMENTS & AWARDS: N.A.

PERSONAL: N.A.

LASSALLY, PETER
Prod., NBC, "The Tonight Show Starring Johnny Carson"

c/o NBC, 3000 W. Alameda Ave., Burbank, CA 91523
b. October 14.

EDUCATION: N.A.

CAREER HIGHLIGHTS: Co-Prod., "The Tonight Show Starring Johnny Carson," NBC ('80); Prod., "The Tonight Show Starring Johnny Carson," NBC ('83).

ACHIEVEMENTS & AWARDS: N.A.

PERSONAL: N.A.

LAUGHTON, ROGER
Head of Network Features, BBC

c/o BBC, 12 Cavendish Place, London, England, W1
b. May 19, 1942. Sheffield, England.

EDUCATION: Merton College, University of Oxford (England); Stanford University.

CAREER HIGHLIGHTS: Film Dir., BBC's "Nationwide" ('69); Asst. Editor, Pebble Mill ('73); Features Editor, BBC Manchester ('81); Head of Network Features ('81).

ACHIEVEMENTS & AWARDS: N.A.

PERSONAL: Married; one daughter.

LAURENCE, JOHN
Correspondent, ABC, News, London

c/o ABC, 8 Carburton St., London W1P 7DT,
England
b. Bridgeport, CT.

EDUCATION: Rensselaer Polytechnic Institute;
University of Pennsylvania.

CAREER HIGHLIGHTS: News Editor, WICC-Ra-
dio, Bridgeport, CT; News Editor, WWDC-
Radio, Washington, DC; Writer/Reporter,
WNEW-AM, New York ('62); Reporter, CBS
Radio ('65); Correspondent, CBS News, Lon-
don ('71); Correspondent, ABC News, Lon-
don ('78); Correspondent, ABC News, Los
Angeles ('79); Correspondent, ABC News,
London ('80).

ACHIEVEMENTS & AWARDS: Overseas Press Club
award ('73); numerous Emmy awards, a
Dupont-Columbia award, and a George Polk
award for his coverage of the Vietnam War for
CBS News.

PERSONAL: Wife, Joy.

LAURIE, JIM
Peking Bureau Chief, ABC, News

c/o ABC News, 7 W. 66th St., New York, NY
10023
b. N.A.

EDUCATION: American University, History,
B.A. ('70).

CAREER HIGHLIGHTS: Correspondent, NBC
News, Tokyo ('76); Correspondent, ABC
News, Hong Kong ('78). When ABC became
the first network news organization to establish a bureau in the People's Republic of China, Laurie was named Bureau Chief ('82).

ACHIEVEMENTS & AWARDS: N.A.

PERSONAL: N.A.

LAVERY, CHARLES V.
V.P., ABC Sports, Programming Planning

c/o ABC, 1330 Ave. of the Americas, New
York, NY 10019
b. January 5, 1934. New Haven, CT.

EDUCATION: Virginia Military Institute, B.A.,
English.

CAREER HIGHLIGHTS: Worked as Asst. Dir., TV
Programming, Cunningham & Walsh ('58);
moved to Young & Rubicam as V.P., Broadcast Programming and Purchasing ('64);
joined ABC Sports as V.P., Programming
Planning ('77).

ACHIEVEMENTS & AWARDS: N.A.

PERSONAL: Resides in Manhattan with wife,
Helen.

LAVIN, LINDA
Actress

c/o "Alice," CBS, 7800 Beverly Blvd., Los
Angeles, CA 90036
b. October 15, 1937. Portland, ME.

EDUCATION: College of William and Mary.

CAREER HIGHLIGHTS: America's working wom-
en applaud her waitress character, and TV
sitcom fans would rather have "Alice" serve
them comedy than anyone else. New York
stage appearances include *Last of the Red Hot
Lovers*, *Little Murders*, *The Mad Show*, *It's a
Bird, It's a Plane, It's Superman*, and Paul Sill's
Story Theater. Her TV movies include *Like
Mom, Like Me*, *The $5.20 an Hour Dream*, *A
Matter of Life and Death*, and *The Morning After*.
Guest appearances on "Family," "Rhoda,"
"Kaz," "Phyllis," and "Barney Miller."
Starred in her own variety special, "Linda in
Wonderland."

ACHIEVEMENTS & AWARDS: N.A.

PERSONAL: Resides in Malibu, CA.

LAW, LINDSAY E.
Exec. Prod.

356 W. 58th St., New York, NY 10019
b. February 21, 1949.

EDUCATION: New York University.
CAREER HIGHLIGHTS: Served as a Production Asst., Assoc. Prod., and Prod. on various films and specials; Dir. of Specials, Warner Bros. TV ('77); Exec. Prod., "American Playhouse" and "Great Performances" series on PBS.
ACHIEVEMENTS & AWARDS: N.A.
PERSONAL: N.A.

LAWENDA, JEFFREY B.
V.P., Advertising Sales and Commercial Program Development, USA Cable Network

c/o USA Cable Network, 1230 Ave. of the Americas, 18th Floor, New York, NY 10020
b. October 3, 1942. New York, NY

EDUCATION: University of Vermont, B.S., Commerce and Economics ('64).
CAREER HIGHLIGHTS: Sales Management, RKO-General ('68); Sales Management, Metromedia ('69); Sales Management, Westinghouse ('70); Sales Management, H&R Representatives ('71); New York Sales Mgr., CBS Radio Spot Sales ('73); General Sales Mgr., WCBS-AM, New York ('75); V.P., General Mgr., CBS Radio Spot Sales ('77); Publisher and Exec. V.P., *People* magazine ('79); V.P., Advertising Sales and Commercial Program Development, USA Cable Network ('80).
ACHIEVEMENTS & AWARDS: N.A.

PERSONAL: Resides in Chappaqua, NY, with wife, Bonnie; daughter, Debra, and son, David.

LAWRENCE, VICKI
Actress

c/o "Mama's Family," NBC, 3000 W. Alameda Blvd., Burbank, CA 91523
b. March 26, 1949. Inglewood, CA.

EDUCATION: University of California at Los Angeles.
CAREER HIGHLIGHTS: Regular on "The Carol Burnett Show"; guest roles on "Laverne and Shirley" and "The Tim Conway Show." Her TV movies include *Having Babies.* Co-star of the show "Mama's Family."
ACHIEVEMENTS & AWARDS: Five Emmy nominations and one Emmy award as best featured performer, comedy-variety, for "The Carol Burnett Show." Gold record for "The Night the Lights Went Out in Georgia."
PERSONAL: Resides in Los Angeles.

LAWSON, PAT
News Reporter, WRC-TV

c/o WRC-TV, 4001 Nebraska Ave., N.W., Washington, DC 20016
b. Las Vegas, NV.

EDUCATION: Howard University, B.A., Broadcast Management.
CAREER HIGHLIGHTS: Researcher, WRC-TV's "Contact 4" Consumer Unit; Announcer/Anchor, Mutual Black Network, Washington, DC; Anchor/Reporter, weekly public affairs

program, WOL-Radio; Afternoon Drive-Time Reporter, WTOP-Radio ('78); Anchor/Reporter, WBAL-TV, Baltimore ('80); News Reporter, WRC-TV ('82).

ACHIEVEMENTS & AWARDS: N.A.

PERSONAL: N.A.

LEAHY, THOMAS F.
Exec. V.P., CBS, Entertainment Division and
TV Network Division

c/o CBS, 51 W. 52d St., New York, NY 10019
b. June 30, 1937.

EDUCATION: Manhattan College, B.E.E.

CAREER HIGHLIGHTS: Joined CBS as Acct. Exec. ('62); Dir., Daytime Sales for Network ('69); V.P., Sales, CBS TV Stations ('71); moved to WCBS-TV as V.P. and General Mgr. ('73); named Pres., CBS TV Stations ('77); appointed Sr. Broadcast V.P. of Broadcast Group ('81); named Exec. V.P., CBS Broadcast Group ('81); Exec. V.P., CBS Entertainment Division and TV Network Division.

ACHIEVEMENTS & AWARDS: New York City certificate of appreciation ('76); Pres., Intl. Council of NATAS; Board of Dirs., IRTS; Member, Mayor's Mid-Town Committee, Board of Trustees, College of Mount St. Vincent's and Fordham Preparatory School.

PERSONAL: N.A.

LEAR, NORMAN
Writer/Prod./Dir., Embassy Communications

c/o Embassy Communications, 1901 Ave. of the Stars, Los Angeles, CA 90067
b. July 27, 1922. New Haven, CT.

EDUCATION: Emerson College.

CAREER HIGHLIGHTS: One of the great innovators of TV comedy, this liberal-minded writer and producer reshaped the TV sitcom from escapist fare into a thinking person's entertainment. Lear's use of touchy material was handled with finesse. Gaining experience as Co-Writer, "Ford Star Revue" and "The Colgate Comedy Hour," Lear entered into long-range partnership with Bud Yorkin. Together they produced "The Andy Williams Show" and specials with Fred Astaire, Carol Channing and other stars before repeating their success on the big screen with *Divorce American Style, Cold Turkey,* and *The Night They Raided Minsky's.* Reconquering TV, Lear built up a TV comedy empire beginning with the smash hit "All in the Family," followed by "Good Times," "The Jeffersons," and "Maude," which consolidated the Lear trademark of controversial comedy grounded in beloved characterizations. "One Day at a Time" and "Diff'rent Strokes" were equally as popular, if not as adventurous. Not content with primetime supremacy, Lear explored syndicated territory with "Mary Hartman, Mary Hartman," which was revolutionary in terms of plot lines, format, and late-night time slot. Lear has continued to be one of TV's free thinkers with the feminist comedy "All That Glitters," the audience-response gimmick of "The Baxters," and his People for the American Way, which is his personal campaign against censorship in any medium. After an absence from series TV, Lear returned (late '83) with "Good Evening, He Lied," a spoof of local TV news for NBC.

ACHIEVEMENTS & AWARDS: Three Emmy awards; the Writers Guild Valentine Davies award, the IRTS gold medal, and the Peabody award.

PERSONAL: Married to Frances Lear, a leading figure in civil liberties issues and women's rights.

LEARY, MARIAN CLAASSEN
Mgr., MGM-UA TV, Marketing Research

c/o MGM-UA, 1350 Ave. of the Americas, New York, NY 10019
b. February 13, 1955. Surabaya, Indonesia.

EDUCATION: Boston University, B.S., Business Administration ('76).

CAREER HIGHLIGHTS: Began career as a Sr. Research Analyst, Viacom Enterprises ('76); Dir., Research, Colbert TV Sales ('81); Mgr. of Marketing Research, MGM-UA TV ('82).

ACHIEVEMENTS & AWARDS: N.A.

PERSONAL: Married, resides in Rockville Centre, NY.

LECLAIR, DENISE
Anchor, Cable News Network and CNN2

c/o Cable News Network, 1050 Techwood Dr., N.W., Atlanta, GA 30318
b. May 26, 1952. Englewood, NJ.

EDUCATION: West Virginia University, B.S., Journalism.

CAREER HIGHLIGHTS: Prod./Anchor/Reporter, WFIE-TV, Evansville, IN ('75); Anchor/Reporter, WNGE-TV, Nashville ('77); Anchor/Reporter, WJAR-TV, Providence, RI ('79); Anchor, Cable News Network and CNN2 ('80).

ACHIEVEMENTS & AWARDS: Indiana Public Health Assn. and Indiana Medical Assn. TV reporting awards ('77); American Heart Assn. award of merit, ('78); AP award for in-depth reporting ('79).

PERSONAL: N.A.

LEE, JOANNA
Exec. Prod., Pres., NBC, Christiana Productions, "Search for Tomorrow"

c/o NBC, 30 Rockefeller Plaza, New York, NY 10020
b. April 7.

EDUCATION: N.A.

CAREER HIGHLIGHTS: A prolific writer for episodic TV and TV movies, Lee has also produced and directed many features. As an actress, she appeared in films including the cult classic *Plan 9 From Outer Space*. A partial list of her writing credits include the TV movies *Babe, I Want To Keep My Baby, Mary Jane Harper Cried Last Night, Cage Without a Key, Mirror, Mirror, Like Normal People,* and *The Children of Divorce*. Named Exec. Prod. of "Search for Tomorrow" ('83).

ACHIEVEMENTS & AWARDS: Emmy for best writing for a special two-hour Thanksgiving show of "The Waltons" ('74) and a Golden Globe award for *Babe* ('75).

PERSONAL: N.A.

LEE, MICHELE
Actress

c/o "Knots Landing," CBS, 7800 Beverly Blvd., Los Angeles, CA 90036
b. June 24, 1942. Los Angeles, CA.

EDUCATION: N.A.

CAREER HIGHLIGHTS: Vibrant and commanding, Lee brings an all-the-stops-pulled-out energy to her acting and brightens every scene in which she appears. Her TV movies include *Dark Victory, Only With Married Men,* and *Bud and Lou.* New York stage appearances in *Bravo Giovanni, How to Succeed in Business Without Really Trying,* and *Seesaw.* Motion pictures include *The Love Bug, How to Succeed in Business Without Really Trying,* and *The Comic.* Series star of "Knot's Landing."

ACHIEVEMENTS & AWARDS: Outer Circle Critics award, Drama Desk award, and Tony nomination for her role in the musical *Seesaw.*

PERSONAL: Resides in Los Angeles.

LEE, MIKE
Correspondent, ABC, News

c/o ABC, 7 W. 66th St., New York, NY 10023
b. Dallas, TX.

EDUCATION: University of Texas, B.S., Political Science.

CAREER HIGHLIGHTS: Asst., KHFI-TV, Austin, TX; Reporter, WFAA-TV, Dallas ('66); Reporter/Anchor, KPIX-TV, San Francisco ('68); Correspondent, CBS News ('75); Correspondent, ABC News, London ('80).

ACHIEVEMENTS & AWARDS: Four Overseas Press Club awards; Sigma Delta Chi award.

PERSONAL: N.A.

LEHRER, JIM
Anchor, Assoc. Editor, "The MacNeil/Lehrer Report"

c/o WETA, Box 2626, Washington, DC 20013
b. 1935

EDUCATION: University of Missouri.

CAREER HIGHLIGHTS: Though he may be best known for his work on "The MacNeil/Lehrer Report," he has appeared in a number of other TV presentations and is a correspondent with WETA/26 in Washington, DC, which co-produces "The MacNeil/Lehrer Report" with WNET/13 in New York. When he joined forces with Robert MacNeil for the weeknightly news program ('75), each drew upon his own style and journalistic experiences to create an informative, innovative news program. For Lehrer, this meant drawing on his knowledge in the fields of both print and broadcast journalism.

ACHIEVEMENTS & AWARDS: Emmy award and George Polk award ('74) for coverage of the Senate Watergate Committee's investigation. Has also won the American Bar Assn. silver gavel certificate of merit and the Peabody award ('74); the Lowell Thomas award of the American Platform Assn., and, with Robert MacNeil, the University of Missouri School of Journalism medal of honor. Author of *We Were Dreamers* and *Viva Max*.

PERSONAL: Wife, Kate; three daughters.

LEIBERT, PHYLLIS R.
Mgr., Daytime Research, NBC

c/o NBC, 30 Rockefeller Plaza, New York, NY 10020
b. January 10. Rockville Centre, NY.

EDUCATION: Vermont College, A.A. ('62).

CAREER HIGHLIGHTS: Secretary, *Rudder* magazine ('63); Sr. Research Analyst, ABC Radio Network ('64); Asst. to the Dir. of Research, Mutual Broadcasting System ('68); Research Mgr., Metromedia Radio Stations and Metromedia Radio Sales ('69); Dir., Research, RKO Owned Radio Stations and RKO Radio Sales ('72); Mgr., Research, NBC Radio Stations ('77); Dir., Research, NBC Radio Stations ('79); Mgr., Daytime Research, NBC TV ('83).

ACHIEVEMENTS & AWARDS: N.A.

PERSONAL: Resides in New York City.

LEIBNER, RICHARD
Talent Agent, N. S. Bienstock, Inc.

c/o N. S. Bienstock, Inc., 10 Columbus Circle, New York, NY 10019
b. 1942.

EDUCATION: University of Rochester, B.S.; New York University, M.B.A.

CAREER HIGHLIGHTS: One of the leading talent agents in the TV news business, he negotiates contracts for such network stars as Jessica Savitch, Morley Safer, Dan Rather and more than 100 other anchors, reporters, correspondents, producers, and directors. He started working for Nate Bienstock ('65), later formed N. S. Bienstock, Inc., and acquired the corporation over the next several years. Leibner's most noteworthy achievement involved his negotiation with CBS to have Dan Rather selected as Walter Cronkite's successor.

ACHIEVEMENTS & AWARDS: N.A.

PERSONAL: Wife, Carole; sons, Adam and Jonathan.

LEIDER, JERRY
Prod., ITC Entertainment

c/o ITC Entertainment, 12711 Ventura Blvd.,
Studio City, CA 91604
b. May 28, 1931. New York, NY.

EDUCATION: Syracuse University, B.A.; Bristol
University.
CAREER HIGHLIGHTS: Joined CBS TV as Dir. of
Program Sales ('64); became V.P. in Charge of
TV at Ashley Famous Agency ('66); Pres. of
Warner Bros. TV, responsible for "Kung Fu"
('72) and "Harry O" ('74), becoming V.P. of
Warner's Foreign Film Production in Rome.
Produced independent films ('77) including
The Jazz Singer, and, for ITC, *Sophie's Choice*,
and *Dark Crystal*, along with TV's *The Scarlet
and the Black* ('83) and *Jane Doe* ('83).
ACHIEVEMENTS & AWARDS: N.A.
PERSONAL: Resides in Beverly Hills, CA.

LEISER, ERNEST
Prod., V.P.

c/o CBS, 51 W. 52d St., New York, NY 10019
b. February 26, 1921.

EDUCATION: University of Chicago
CAREER HIGHLIGHTS: Prod., CBS News ('53);
Exec. Prod., "CBS News With Walter Cron-
kite" ('64); Exec. Prod., CBS Special Reports
Unit; Exec. Prod., "ABC Evening News" and
"The Reasoner Report" ('72); Prod., CBS
"All-Day Spectacular for the Bicentennial"
('76); CBS V.P. of Special Events and Political
Coverage ('79); V.P., CBS News ('81).
ACHIEVEMENTS & AWARDS: Two Peabody
awards ('56, '77); two Ohio State University
awards ('69, '77).
PERSONAL: N.A.

LELAND, JON
Mgr., On-Air Promotion, USA Network

c/o USA Network, 208 Harristown Rd., Glen
Rock, NJ 07452
b. June 21, 1947.

EDUCATION: Cornell University.
CAREER HIGHLIGHTS: News Dir., KRAB-Radio,
Seattle, WA ('70); Post-Production Super-

visor, Metromedia Prods. Corp.; Dir. of Transitional Programming, Premiere, Inc.; Field
Prod., "P.M./Evening Magazine," Group W
Productions ('81); Consultant, Warner Amex's Movie Channel ('81); Mgr., On-Air Promotion ('81).
ACHIEVEMENTS & AWARDS: N.A.
PERSONAL: Resides in Palisades, NY, with
wife, Ellen, and their son, Andrew.

LEM, CAROL
Dir., Program Planning, CBS, Entertainment

c/o CBS, 6121 Sunset Blvd., Los Angeles, CA
90028
b. November 25.

EDUCATION: Washington State University.
CAREER HIGHLIGHTS: Media Buyer, Grey Ad-
vertising; Planner and Supervisor, Doyle,
Dane, Bernbach; Acct. Exec., Needham,
Harper & Steers, Los Angeles ('77); Media
Dir., Advertising and Promotion, CBS Enter-
tainment ('78); Dir., Program Planning, CBS
Entertainment ('81).
ACHIEVEMENTS & AWARDS: N.A.
PERSONAL: Married, resides in Los Angeles.

LeMASTERS, KIM (Earle H. LeMasters)
**V.P., CBS TV, Primetime Development and
Production**

c/o CBS, 7800 Beverly Blvd., Los Angeles, CA
90036
b. November 16, 1949. San Francisco, CA.

EDUCATION: University of California at Los Angeles, B.A., History.
CAREER HIGHLIGHTS: Began at ABC TV as Mgr.,

Primetime Development ('72); Dir. of Development, Warner Bros. TV ('74); CBS TV, Dir., Drama Development ('76); moved up through ranks to V.P., Drama Development, V.P., Comedy Development, V.P., Primetime Development and currently serves as V.P., Primetime Development and Production.

ACHIEVEMENTS & AWARDS: N.A.

PERSONAL: Wife, Donna; children, Bree and Jill.

LENARD, KATHRYN
V.P., NBC, TV Stations Research

c/o NBC, 30 Rockefeller Plaza, New York, NY 10020
b. January 5, 1934. New York, NY.

EDUCATION: Brooklyn College, B.A.

CAREER HIGHLIGHTS: Dir. of Research, RKO ('72); V.P. and General Mgr., RKO Radio Sales ('75); V.P., Research, NBC Radio ('78); V.P., TV Stations Research, NBC ('81).

ACHIEVEMENTS & AWARDS: Pres., Radio and TV Research Council ('79–'80).

PERSONAL: Husband, Jay; daughters, Jennifer and Dena.

LENZ, PETER G.
Exec. Prod., WXYZ-TV, Detroit

c/o WXYZ-TV, 20777 W. Ten Mile Rd., Southfield, MI 48037
b. January 14, 1946. West Germany.

EDUCATION: Northern Illinois University, B.S., Management; Loyola University, M.B.A., Marketing.

CAREER HIGHLIGHTS: Worked as a Promotion Mgr. in Cleveland and Philadelphia ('74); Advertising Mgr., Columbus, OH ('76); Dir. Program Development and Marketing, Prod., "PM Magazine," WXYZ-TV, Detroit ('79); named Exec. Prod., "PM Magazine" ('79).

ACHIEVEMENTS & AWARDS: Emmy for "PM Magazine" ('82).

PERSONAL: N.A.

LEONARD, BILL
Prod.

c/o CBS, 524 W. 57th St., New York, NY 10019
b. April 9, 1916.

EDUCATION: Dartmouth University.

CAREER HIGHLIGHTS: Played a pivotal role at CBS News for more than 20 years and was largely responsible for the development of "CBS Sunday Morning," one of the most innovative shows in the history of broadcast journalism. Also played a major role in selecting Dan Rather to succeed Walter Cronkite as the anchor of the "CBS Evening News." Prod., CBS Radio ('46); Prod./Correspondent, CBS Reports ('59); Exec., CBS News Election Unit ('64); Exec. for all CBS Documentaries ('69); V.P., CBS Washington, DC, Bureau; Pres. of CBS News ('79) until he retired ('82).

ACHIEVEMENTS & AWARDS: Albert Lasker award; Ed Stout award; N.Y. local Emmy ('62).

PERSONAL: N.A.

LERNER, KAREN
Sr. Prod., ABC, News, "20/20"

c/o ABC, 7 W. 66th St., New York, NY 10023
b. Boston, MA.

EDUCATION: Vassar College.

CAREER HIGHLIGHTS: Reporter, *Life* magazine ('59); Correspondent for *Time* and *Life* ('62); Asst. Editor, *Newsweek* ('63); Researcher, NBC's "Today" program ('72); Prod./Reporter, NBC News ('73); Prod., NBC News "Weekend" ('74); Prod., news documentary "Hype" ('78); Sr. Prod., ABC News "20/20" ('79).

ACHIEVEMENTS & AWARDS: Chicago Film Festival award for the news documentary "Hype" ('78). Member, Phi Beta Kappa.

PERSONAL: Resides in New York City.

LESSER, SEYMOUR H.
V.P., Hearst/ABC Video Services, Administration and Finance

c/o Hearst/ABC, 555 Fifth Ave., New York, NY 10017
b. November 9, 1929. New York, NY.

EDUCATION: Pace University/City University B.B.A.; CPA, New York State ('61).

CAREER HIGHLIGHTS: Asst. Comptroller, MGM Films and TV and Music ('60); Pres. and General Mgr., Robbins Music Corp. ('67); V.P., Finance and Administration, Allied Artists Picture Corp. ('73); V.P., Finance and Administration, and Treasurer, Bulova Watch Co. ('78). Exec. Acct. Mgr., Prager & Fenton CPAs ('80); V.P., Administration and Finance, Hearst/ABC Video Services ('81).

ACHIEVEMENTS & AWARDS: Chairman, Management Planning and Control Committee, Financial Executives Institute ('78–'80).

PERSONAL: Resides in New York City with wife, Barbara, and daughters, Jill and Susan.

LETTERMAN, DAVID
Host, NBC, "Late Night With David Letterman"

c/o NBC, 30 Rockefeller Plaza, New York, NY 10020
b. April 12, 1947. Indianapolis, IN.

EDUCATION: Ball State University.

CAREER HIGHLIGHTS: Irreverent talk show host whose business executive exterior belies his offbeat, droll humor, often aimed at major personalities of show business, politics, and business. Canadian daytime show Host and TV Weatherman. Replacement Host, "The Tonight Show." Host, the daytime version of "The David Letterman Show"; Host, "Late Night With David Letterman."

ACHIEVEMENTS & AWARDS: Emmy award for the daytime "David Letterman Show."

PERSONAL: N.A.

LEVENS, PHILIP J.
V.P., ABC, Broadcast Operations

c/o ABC, 1330 Ave. of the Americas, New York, NY 10019
b. New York, NY.

EDUCATION: New York University, B.E.E.

CAREER HIGHLIGHTS: Joined CBS as Operations Engineer ('47); moved to ABC in same capacity ('48); Freelance TV Prod./Dir. for ABC, NBC, and CBS in U.S. and Europe ('55–'63); joined ABC in various management positions before being named V.P., Broadcast Operations.

ACHIEVEMENTS & AWARDS: Emmy award for technical supervision of the 1976 Summer Olympics broadcast.

PERSONAL: Resides in Massapequa, NY, with wife, Joyce; children, Beth, David, and Richard.

LEVIN, ALAN
V.P., CBS, Entertainment

c/o CBS, 7800 Beverly Blvd., Los Angeles, CA 90036
b. August 26, 1943. New York, NY.

EDUCATION: Brooklyn College; Brooklyn Law School.

CAREER HIGHLIGHTS: Assoc., Fink, Weinberger & Levin; joined Business Affairs Dept. of CBS News ('69); V.P., Business Affairs, CBS Entertainment, New York ('77); V.P., Business Affairs and Administration, CBS Entertainment ('80); V.P., CBS Entertainment, Los Angeles ('82).

ACHIEVEMENTS & AWARDS: N.A.

PERSONAL: Resides in Los Angeles with wife Adrienne and their two children.

LEVIN, ALAN M.
Independent Prod./Documentary Filmmaker

88 Claremont Ave., Maplewood, NJ 07040
b. 1936. Brooklyn, NY.

EDUCATION: Wesleyan University, B.A.

CAREER HIGHLIGHTS: Rewrite Man, Reporter, and Features Writer, N.Y. Post; Press Secretary to Sen. Harrison A. Williams; Assignment Editor, WCBS-TV; Writer/Reporter/ Prod., WABC-TV; Prod., Public Broadcast Laboratory, TV Magazine; Prod., "51st State"; Exec. Prod. of the New Jersey show and other documentaries and series, WNET, New York.

ACHIEVEMENTS & AWARDS: Dupont-Columbia award, investigative journalism, ('69); George Polk memorial award for TV reporting ('70); Emmy for writing and best documentary, "The New Immigrants" ('79); best documentary and best writing for "Sleep" ('67); Emmy for "Crisis in the Cities."

PERSONAL: Married; four children.

LEVIN, GERALD M.
Group V.P., Video, Time, Inc.

c/o Time, Inc., 1271 Ave. of the Americas, New York, NY 10020
b. May 6, 1939. Philadelphia, PA.

EDUCATION: Haverford College ('60); University of Pennsylvania Law School ('63).

CAREER HIGHLIGHTS: Levin is renowned for building HBO into the nation's largest pay-TV organization, a service offering films, specials and documentaries, many of which are now being produced directly for HBO. Practiced law in New York ('63); joined the Development and Resources Corp. ('67); General Mgr. and Chief Exec. Officer, Development and Resources Corp. ('69); Representative for Intl. Basic Economy Corp., Tehran ('71); V.P., Programming HBO ('72); Pres. and Chief Exec. Officer, HBO ('73); elected as V.P. of Time, Inc. ('75); and named Chairman, HBO ('76); elected Group V.P., Video, Time, Inc. which includes American TV and Communications Corp., HBO, USA Network, Time-Life Video and WOTV-TV, Grand Rapids, MI ('82).

ACHIEVEMENTS & AWARDS: Member of the Board of the Natl. Council for Children and TV; Dir., IRTS.

PERSONAL: Married to Barbara Riley; four children.

LEVIN, HARVEY
Reporter, KNBC, "News 4 LA"

c/o KNBC, 3000 W. Alameda Ave., Burbank, CA 91523
b. California.

EDUCATION: University of Santa Barbara, Political Science, (magna cum laude, '72).

CAREER HIGHLIGHTS: Taught at the University of Miami School of Law ('75); Civil Litigator, Richards, Watson, Dreyfuss & Gershon; Consultant, American Bar Assn. ('75–'78). On-Air Legal Editor of syndicated TV show "Women's Page"; Consultant to the syndicated show "People's Court"; Professor, Whittier College School of Law; Author, *Los Angeles Times* column, "The Law and You." Reporter, "News 4 LA," KNBC-TV.

ACHIEVEMENTS & AWARDS: Member, Phi Beta Kappa; listed in *Who's Who in American Law.*

PERSONAL: Resides in Hollywood Hills, CA.

LE VINE, DEBORAH JOY
Prod., Charles Fries Productions

c/o Charles Fries Productions, 9200 Sunset Blvd., Los Angeles, CA 90069
b. May 26, 1952.

EDUCATION: California State University at Northridge, B.A.; San Fernando State College of Law, J.D.

CAREER HIGHLIGHTS: Formed first mother/daughter law team in the country with mother Estelle Le Vine; Independent Film Prod.; Prod./Partner, for Le Vine/Robins through Charles Fries Productions.

ACHIEVEMENTS & AWARDS: N.A.
PERSONAL: N.A.

LEVINE, ELLEN
Dir., Pricing, NBC, Finance and Administration

c/o NBC, 30 Rockefeller Plaza, New York, NY 10020
b. May 19.

EDUCATION: Bryn Mawr College, B.A., Sociology ('73); Columbia Graduate School of Business, M.B.A., Finance ('79).

CAREER HIGHLIGHTS: Assoc., NBC's Management Development Program ('79); Prime Time Cost Forecasting Mgr., NBC ('80); Mgr., Nighttime and News Pricing ('81); Dir., Pricing, NBC ('83).
ACHIEVEMENTS & AWARDS: N.A.
PERSONAL: Resides in New York City with husband, Andrew Cramer.

LEVINE, IRVING R.
Network News Correspondent, NBC

c/o NBC, 30 Rockefeller Plaza, New York, NY 10020
b. August 26. Pawtucket, RI.

EDUCATION: Brown University, B.A.; Columbia University Graduate School of Journalism, M.A.
CAREER HIGHLIGHTS: Started his career with *Providence Journal-Bulletin*, Rhode Island; Bureau Chief, Intl. News Service; NBC News Correspondent in Korea ('50). Based in Rome for 10 years; Moscow, four years; Tokyo, two years; and London, one year. Named Economic Affairs Correspondent ('70).
ACHIEVEMENTS & AWARDS: Awarded honorary doctor of letters degrees by Brown University and Bryant College; Overseas Press Club award; Headliners award; Emmy citation; wrote four books and numerous magazine articles.
PERSONAL: Wife, Nancy; two sons and one daughter.

LEVINE, KEN
Writer/Prod.

c/o William Morris Agency, 151 El Camino Dr., Beverly Hills, CA 90212
b. February 14, 1950. Santa Monica, CA.

EDUCATION: University of California at Los Angeles, B.A., Psychology.
CAREER HIGHLIGHTS: Freelance Writer, "The Jeffersons," "Joe and Son."
ACHIEVEMENTS & AWARDS: N.A.
PERSONAL: N.A.

LEVINE, MICHAEL A.
Dir., Current Drama Programs, NBC

c/o NBC, 3000 W. Alameda Ave., Burbank, CA 91523
b. May 3, 1955. New York, NY.

EDUCATION: University of Southern California, B.A., Broadcasting
CAREER HIGHLIGHTS: Production Coordinator, Sullivan & Marks ('77); Asst. Production Mgr., Sullivan & Marks ('78); Prod., NBC Fall Preview Show ('79, '80, '81); Mgr., On-Air Promotion ('80); promoted to Dir., On-Air Promotion ('81); Dir., Current Drama Programs, NBC ('82).
ACHIEVEMENTS & AWARDS: Teacher at the University of Southern California and author of *Principles of Television Production.*
PERSONAL: Resides in Canoga Park, CA, with wife, Joan, and son, Jason.

LEVINE, RICHARD I.
V.P., Programs, East Coast, ABC, Entertainment

c/o ABC, 1330 Ave. of the Americas, New York, NY 10019
b. June 19, 1936. New York, NY.

EDUCATION: Union College, B.S., Psychology.
CAREER HIGHLIGHTS: Ashley Famous Agency; Sr. V.P., TV, Marvin Josephson Assoc. ('63); moved over to Dick Levine Entertainment as Personal Mgr., TV Packaging ('71); joined ABC Entertainment as V.P., Programs, East Coast ('80).
ACHIEVEMENTS & AWARDS: N.A.
PERSONAL: Single, resides in New York City.

LEVINSOHN, ROANN KIM
Dir., ABC Video Enterprises, Public Relations

c/o ABC, 1330 Ave. of the Americas, New York, NY 10019
b. March 2, 1950. Englewood, NJ.

EDUCATION: Northwestern University, B.S., Journalism; Cornell University, M.S., Communication Arts.
CAREER HIGHLIGHTS: Asst. Prod., Instructional

TV Center, Tel Aviv ('74); joined ABC, Inc., as Mgr., Editorial Services ('76); Mgr., Corporate Projects ('77); Mgr., Business Information, ABC TV ('79); appointed Dir., Public Relations, ABC Video Enterprises ('81).
ACHIEVEMENTS & AWARDS: N.A.
PERSONAL: Resides in Manhattan.

LEVINSON, RICHARD L.
Writer/Prod., Universal TV

c/o Universal TV, 100 Universal City Plaza, Universal City, CA 91608
b. August 7, 1934. Philadelphia, PA.

EDUCATION: University of Pennsylvania, B.A., Economics.
CAREER HIGHLIGHTS: Writer/Prod. at Universal ('66); Co-Pres., Levinson-Link Productions ('78). His movies of the week include *My Sweet Charlie, The Gun, That Certain Summer, The Story Teller,* and *The Execution of Private Slovik* and *Prototype* ('83). With partner William Link, he created, wrote, and produced the TV series "Mannix," "Columbo," and "Ellery Queen."
ACHIEVEMENTS & AWARDS: Two Emmy awards ('70; '72); Edgar Allan Poe awards ('80; '82); two Golden Globe awards ('72); Writers Guild award ('72). Co-Author, with William Link, of *Stay Tuned* and the Broadway musical *Merlin.*
PERSONAL: N.A.

LEVY, ALAN
Mgr. of Corporate Public Relations, HBO

c/o HBO, 1271 Ave. of the Americas, New York, NY 10020
b. November 21, 1953.

EDUCATION: Rutgers University; New York University.
CAREER HIGHLIGHTS: Staff Reporter and Photographer, *Chain Drug Review* ('78); Natl. Editor, Multichannel News ('80); Mgr., Information Services, Group W Satellite Communications for the Satellite News Channel ('82); Mgr., Corporate Public Relations, HBO ('83).
ACHIEVEMENTS & AWARDS: N.A.
PERSONAL: Resides in New York City with his wife, Mollie.

LEVY, EUGENE
Writer/Performer, NBC, "SCTV Network"

c/o SCTV; 110 Lombard St., Toronto, Ontario, Canada M5C-IM3
b. December 17. Hamilton, Canada.

EDUCATION: McMaster University.
CAREER HIGHLIGHTS: Canadian TV appearances in "The Sunshine Hour" and "Stay Tuned"; late-night CBS Special "From Cleveland." Feature films include *Running.* Writer/Performer, "SCTV Network."
ACHIEVEMENTS & AWARDS: N.A.
PERSONAL: Resides in Los Angeles.

LEVY, FRANKLIN R.
Exec. Prod.

c/o ICPR, 9255 Sunset Blvd., 8th Floor, Los Angeles, CA 90069
b. New York, NY.

EDUCATION: State University of New York.
CAREER HIGHLIGHTS: Personal management with CMA for four years; worked with Norman Rosemont for one year; worked with Tomorrow Entertainment; joined Mike Wise and formed the Production Co., a multimedia company organized to produce feature motion pictures for theatrical release, TV films, TV series. Films produced include *Child Stealer, Return Engagement, Last Hurrah, Great Expectations, Enola Gay,* and *Hawks.*
ACHIEVEMENTS & AWARDS: N.A.
PERSONAL: N.A.

LEWIN, DENNIS
V.P., Production Coordinator, ABC, Sports

c/o ABC, 1330 Ave. of the Americas, New York, NY 10019
b. December 2, 1944. Queens, NY.

EDUCATION: Michigan State University, B.A., Communication Arts.
CAREER HIGHLIGHTS: Worked on ABC's "NFL Monday Night Football" as Prod., Special Effects Unit ('70); Coordinating Prod., "Wide World of Sports" ('71) and still maintains that title while serving as V.P., Production Coordination, ABC Sports. Production career with

ABC Sports has been extensive, and includes: Co-Prod., "NFL Monday Night Football" ('71–'72); Prod., Summer Olympic Games, swimming, diving, U.S.-USSR basketball competitions ('72); Prod., Summer Olympic Games, gymnastics competition ('76); Prod., "NFL Monday Night Football" ('77–'79); Prod., "Major League Baseball All Star Games" ('78, '80, '82); Prod., Natl. League Championship Series ('78, '80); Sr. Prod., Winter Olympics ('80); Prod., World Series ('81).

ACHIEVEMENTS & AWARDS: Eight Emmy Awards.

PERSONAL: Resides in Irvington, NY, with wife, Vicki; children, Cassidy and D.J.

LeWINTER, RANDI
Dir., ABC, Daytime Programs, East Coast

c/o ABC, 1330 Ave. of the Americas, New York, NY 10019
b. May 15, 1953. Brooklyn, NY.

EDUCATION: Syracuse University, B.S.

CAREER HIGHLIGHTS: Began with Jerome Schnur Productions as Contestant Coordinator ('75); NBC Asst. to the Dir., Prime Time Development ('76); moved to ABC Entertainment as Mgr., Daytime Programs ('77); promoted to Dir., Daytime Programs, East Coast ('80).

ACHIEVEMENTS & AWARDS: Gordon J. Alderman award for excellence in creative broadcasting ('74); silver award, Broadcasters Promotion Assn., for "Hooray for Love" campaign ('82).

PERSONAL: N.A.

LEWIS, ARTHUR BERNARD
Writer/Prod.

c/o Franklin Rohner, 9255 W. Sunset Blvd., Suite 510, Los Angeles, CA 90069
b. January 15, 1926. New York, NY.

EDUCATION: Brooklyn College.

CAREER HIGHLIGHTS: Photographer, CBS TV ('52); Publicity, CBS TV ('61); Exec. Story Editor, CBS TV ('68); Dir. Program Development ('74); Freelance TV Writer ('76); Exec. Story Editor/Writer, "Dallas" ('78); Supervising Prod./Writer, "Dallas" ('81).

ACHIEVEMENTS & AWARDS: N.A.

PERSONAL: Resides in Woodland Hills, CA, with wife, Ursula; three children.

LEWIS, DREW
Chairman and Chief Exec. Officer, Warner Amex Cable Communications

c/o Warner Amex, 1211 Ave. of the Americas, New York, NY 10036
b. Pennsylvania.

EDUCATION: Haverford College, B.S. ('53); Harvard Graduate School of Business, M.B.A. ('55).

CAREER HIGHLIGHTS: Utilities Mgr., Henkel's & McCoy, Philadelphia ('55); Production Mgr. and Member of the Board of Dirs., Henkel's & McCoy ('58); V.P. and Asst. to the Chairman, National Gypsum Co., and V.P., Marketing, American Olean Tile Co., subsidiary of Gypsum, Buffalo, NY ('60); Pres. and Chairman of the Board, Simplex Wire and Cable Co., Boston ('60–'72); Pres. and Chief Exec. Officer, Snelling & Snelling, Philadelphia ('70); headed own consulting firm, Lewis & Assoc., Philadelphia ('75); Deputy Political Dir., Reagan-Bush Presidential Campaign ('80); U.S. Secretary of Transportation ('83); Chairman and Chief Exec. Officer, Warner Amex Cable Communications ('83).

ACHIEVEMENTS & AWARDS: Member, Board of Dirs., Equitable Life Assurance Society and Campbell Soup Co.

PERSONAL: Wife, Marilyn; daugther, Karen; sons, Russell and Andrew.

LEWIS, JOHN M.
Pres. and Dir., Wometco Cable TV

400 N. Miami Ave., Miami, FL 33128
b. March 29, 1931.

EDUCATION: N.A.
CAREER HIGHLIGHTS: Gulf Power Co.; V.P., Member of the Board of Governors, Burnup & Sims of Florida; joined Wometco Enterprises as mgr., Cable TV Division ('71), and also served as Pres., Wometco Home Theater.
ACHIEVEMENTS & AWARDS: N.A.
PERSONAL: Resides in Miami.

LEWIS, MILTON
Correspondent, WABC-TV, "Eyewitness News"

c/o WABC-TV, 7 Lincoln Sq., New York, NY 10023
b. New York, NY.

EDUCATION: University of Wisconsin.
CAREER HIGHLIGHTS: Investigative Journalist, *N.Y. Herald Tribune*; Correspondent, "Eyewitness News" ('67); Moderator, "Eyewitness News Conference," WABC-TV.
ACHIEVEMENTS & AWARDS: N.A.
PERSONAL: Resides in New York City.

LEWIS, RICHARD
Exec. Prod.

c/o Rowland Perkins, Creative Artists Agency, 10790 Wilshire Blvd., Los Angeles, CA 90024
b. January 2, 1920. New York, NY.

EDUCATION: Yale University, B.A.
CAREER HIGHLIGHTS: Worked at MCA (Universal TV, Revue Productions) as V.P., Exec. Prod./Prod., Creator and Pilot Prod., "Wagon Train," "M Squad," "Leave It to Beaver," "Laramie," "Checkmate," "Bachelor Father," "Restless Gun," "Wells Fargo," "Wide Country," and "Crusader" ('54–'68). Exec. Prod., "Alcoa Premiere" starring Fred Astaire, episodes of "GE Theater," "Chrysler Theater," "Schlitz Playhouse." Coordinated original world premiere two-hour movies for NBC-MCA; Prod. *The Borgia Stick* world premiere. Became partner in Bel Productions ('76–'82). Exec. Prod., "Mama Malone" series, CBS ('82–'83).
ACHIEVEMENTS & AWARDS: Christopher award for "Crusader" ('56); *TV Guide* awards for "Wagon Train" and "Checkmate" ('58, '60); Emmy nomination for "People Need People," Alcoa Premiere ('62).
PERSONAL: Wife, Marjorie; two sons, Jeffrey and Richard.

LEY, ROBERT
Anchor, ESPN

c/o ESPN, ESPN Plaza, Bristol, CT 06010
b. March 16, 1955. Perth Amboy, NJ.

EDUCATION: Seton Hall University, B.A., Communications (magna cum laude, '76).
CAREER HIGHLIGHTS: Reporter, *Herald-News*, Passaic, NJ ('74); Production Mgr., WOR-AM, New York ('75); Dir., Sports/Public Affairs, Suburban Cablevision, East Orange, NJ ('76); Anchor, ESPN ('79).
ACHIEVEMENTS & AWARDS: Award for sports programming, Natl. Cable TV Assn. ('78, '79).
PERSONAL: Resides in Bristol, CT, with wife, Barbara.

LICHT, JUDY
Correspondent, "Eyewitness News"; Co-Host "Good Morning New York," WABC-TV

c/o WABC-TV, 7 Lincoln Sq., New York, NY 10023
b. Brooklyn, NY.

EDUCATION: Syracuse University, M.A. Radio/TV.

CAREER HIGHLIGHTS: Host for news-talk shows, KMBC-TV; Consumer Editor/Reporter for WNEW-TV's "Midday"; Anchor/Reporter, WNEW-TV ('74); News Correspondent, WCBS-TV ('78); Correspondent, "Eyewitness News," WABC-TV ('81); Co-Host, "Good Morning New York," WABC-TV.

ACHIEVEMENTS & AWARDS: N.A.

PERSONAL: Married to Jerry Della Femina. Resides in Manhattan.

LIEBERTHAL, GARY B.
Sr. V.P., Syndication, Embassy Telecommunications

1901 Ave. of the Stars, Los Angeles, CA 90064
b. October 29, 1945. Asheville, NC.

EDUCATION: Cornell University, B.S.

CAREER HIGHLIGHTS: Dir. of Marketing, Time-buying Service ('70); West Coast Dir., Arbitron Corp. ('73); V.P., Syndication, TAT Communications ('76); Sr. V.P., Syndication, Embassy Telecommunications ('80).

ACHIEVEMENTS & AWARDS: N.A.

PERSONAL: N.A.

LIGHTSTONE, RONALD
V.P., Viacom Intl., Corporate Affairs

c/o Viacom Intl., 1211 Ave. of the Americas, New York, NY 10036
b. October 4, 1938. New York, NY.

EDUCATION: Columbia College, B.A. ('59); New York University School of Law, J.D. ('62).

CAREER HIGHLIGHTS: Served as V.P., General Counsel and Secretary, Viacom Intl. ('75–'80); became V.P., Business Affairs, Viacom Entertainment Group ('80); and V.P., Corporate Affairs, Viacom Intl. ('82).

ACHIEVEMENTS & AWARDS: N.A.

PERSONAL: N.A.

LINDAUER, JERRY D.
Sr. V.P., Times Mirror, Cable TV, Corporate Development

c/o Times Mirror Cable TV, 2381 Morse Ave., Irvine, CA 92714
b. February 2, 1936. Louisville, KY.

EDUCATION: Bellarmine College, B.A., History ('57); University of Texas Law School, J.D. ('72).

CAREER HIGHLIGHTS: After 20 years in the Marine Corps, became Asst. to Pres., Communications Properties ('77); V.P., Times Mirror Cable TV ('79); Sr. V.P., Corporate Development, Times Mirror Cable TV ('80).

ACHIEVEMENTS & AWARDS: Member, NCTA.

PERSONAL: N.A.

LINDEMANN, CARL, JR.
V.P. and Asst. to Pres., CBS Sports

c/o CBS, 51 W. 52d St., New York, NY 10019
b. December 15.

EDUCATION: Phillips Exeter Academy; Massachusetts Institute of Technology.

CAREER HIGHLIGHTS: Assoc. Prod., "The Kate Smith Show" ('53); Unit Mgr., "The Home Show"; Business Mgr., Program Dept.; Dir. of Daytime Programs ('57); V.P., NBC Sports ('63); V.P. and Asst. to Pres., CBS Sports ('80).

ACHIEVEMENTS & AWARDS: N.A.

PERSONAL: N.A.

LINDEN, HAL
Actor

c/o William Morris Agency, 151 El Camino
  Drive, Beverly Hills, CA 90212
b. March 20. Bronx, NY.

EDUCATION: Queens College.
CAREER HIGHLIGHTS: Linden's persuasive charm
  and nonaggressive style made him the police
  chief fans would most like to be arrested by,
  especially if it meant being locked up with the
  "Barney Miller" cast. New York stage appear-
  ances in *Bells Are Ringing, Wildcat, On a Clear
  Day, Ilya Darling,* and *The Rothschilds.* TV host
  of "FYI" informational series and the chil-
  dren's series "Animals Animals Animals."
  TV movies include *Father Figure, Mr. Inside/
  Mr. Outside,* and *How to Break Up a Happy
  Divorce.* Series star of "Barney Miller."
ACHIEVEMENTS & AWARDS: Tony award for best
  Actor in a musical for *The Rothschilds.*
PERSONAL: Wife, Frances; four children. Re-
  sides in Beverly Hills, CA.

LINDSTROM, PIA
**Arts Editor/Film and Theater Critic,
  WNBC-TV, New York, News**

c/o WNBC-TV, 30 Rockefeller Plaza, New
  York, NY 10020
b. September 20. Stockholm, Sweden.

EDUCATION: Mills College, B.A., History; Uni-
  versity of Colorado; New York University,
  M.A., History.
CAREER HIGHLIGHTS: Co-Host, "The A.M.
  Show," KGO-TV, San Francisco ('66); Report-
  er/Co-Anchor, KGO-TV, San Francisco ('67);
  Reporter, WCBS-TV, New York ('68); Report-
  er, WNBC-TV, New York ('73); Arts Editor/
  Film and Theater Critic, WNBC-TV ('75).
ACHIEVEMENTS & AWARDS: Emmy ('77); New
  York State AP Broadcasters Assn. award ('78).
PERSONAL: Daughter of the late actress Ingrid
  Bergman. Resides in New York City with hus-
  band, Joseph Daly; two sons.

LINK, WILLIAM
**Writer/Prod. and Co-Pres., Levinson/Link
  Productions**

c/o Universal TV, 100 Universal Plaza,
  Universal City, CA 91608
b. December 15, 1933. Philadelphia, PA.

EDUCATION: University of Pennsylvania, B.S.
CAREER HIGHLIGHTS: Writer/Creator/Prod.,
  "Mannix," "Columbo," "Ellery Queen,"
  "Tenafly," "My Sweet Charlie," "That Cer-
  tain Summer," *The Execution of Private Slovik,
  The Gun, The Storyteller,* and *Prototypes* ('83);
  Co-Writer of the play *Prescription: Murder;* Co-
  Pres., Levinson/Link Productions.
ACHIEVEMENTS & AWARDS: Emmy awards ('70,

'72); Golden Globe award ('72); Edgar Allan Poe award ('80, '82). Author, *Fireman,* and *An Inside Look at Prime-Time Television.*
PERSONAL: N.A.

LIPSTONE, HOWARD
Pres., Alan Landsburg Productions

11811 W. Olympic Blvd., Los Angeles, CA 90064
b. April 28. Chicago, IL.

EDUCATION: University of Southern California, B.A., Cinema.
CAREER HIGHLIGHTS: Asst. General Mgr., KTLA ('50); Dir., Film Dept., KABC-TV ('55); Exec. V.P., Ivan Tors Films and Studios ('69); Pres., Alan Landsburg Productions ('72).
ACHIEVEMENTS & AWARDS: N.A.
PERSONAL: N.A.

LIPSTONE, JANE
V.P., Alan Landsburg Productions, Public Relations

11811 W. Olympic Blvd., Los Angeles, CA 90064
b. March 8, 1931. Chicago, IL.

EDUCATION: Purdue University, B.A. ('52).
CAREER HIGHLIGHTS: Freelance Publicist, Jane Lipstone, Inc.; V.P., Advertising and Public Relations, Alan Landsburg Productions.
ACHIEVEMENTS & AWARDS: N.A.
PERSONAL: Married to Howard Lipstone; two children, Lewis and Greg.

LIPSYTE, ROBERT
Reporter/Commentator, CBS News, "Sunday Morning"

c/o CBS, 524 W. 57th St., New York, NY 10019
b. January 16, 1938. New York, NY.

EDUCATION: Columbia College, B.A. ('57); Columbia University Graduate School of Journalism, M.S. ('59).
CAREER HIGHLIGHTS: Sports Reporter/Columnist, *N.Y. Times* ('57); Columnist, *N.Y. Post* ('77); Commentator, "All Things Consid-

ered," Natl. Public Radio ('76–'81); Reporter/Commentator, CBS News's "Sunday Morning" ('82).
ACHIEVEMENTS & AWARDS: Author, *The Masculine Mystique* ('66); *Sportsworld: An American Dreamland* ('75); *Free To Be Muhammad Ali* ('78); *The Summerboy* ('83).
PERSONAL: Resides in New York City with his wife, Marjorie, and their two children.

LIPTAK, GREGORY J.
Exec. V.P., Times Mirror Cable TV

c/o Times Mirror Cable TV, 2381 Morse Ave., Irvine, CA 92714
b. January 4, 1940. Streator, IL.

EDUCATION: University of Illinois, B.S., Marketing, and M.S., Communications.
CAREER HIGHLIGHTS: V.P., Marketing, United Cable TV Corp. ('68); V.P., Marketing, Communications Properties ('75); Sr. V.P., Marketing, Communications Properties ('75); Sr. V.P., Marketing, Times Mirror Cable TV ('79); Sr. V.P., Operations ('80); named Exec. V.P. ('81). Founder and first Pres., Cable Television Administration and Marketing Society ('75); Board of Dirs. ('75–'82). Founder and first Chairman, HBO Natl. Affiliates Committee ('76); Board of Dirs., Cable TV Advertising Bureau ('81–'82).
ACHIEVEMENTS & AWARDS: NCTA, excellence in local community programming on a cable system ('69).
PERSONAL: N.A.

LISWOOD, LAURA
District Mgr., Westinghouse Broadcasting Co., Group W Cable, Seattle, WA

c/o Group W Cable, 15241 Pacific Way Highway S., Seattle, WA 98188
b. March 8.

EDUCATION: California State University, B.A.; University of California-Davis Law School, law degree; Harvard Business School, M.B.A.
CAREER HIGHLIGHTS: Region Controller, TWA, Los Angeles; General Mgr., Sales and Services, TWA, Seattle, WA; V.P. of Marketing, Continental Airlines; District Mgr., Group W Cable's, North Pacific District ('83).

ACHIEVEMENTS & AWARDS: Member, California State Bar; Board of Dirs., First Women's Bank of California.

PERSONAL: Resides in Seattle, WA.

LITKE, MARK
Correspondent, ABC, News, Hong Kong

c/o ABC, 1253 Mercury House, Fenwick St., Wanchai, Hong Kong, BCC

b. California.

EDUCATION: University of California at Berkeley, B.A., Sociology.

CAREER HIGHLIGHTS: Assignment Editor/Writer/Prod., KPIX-TV, San Francisco ('71); Reporter/Prod., KING-TV, Seattle, WA ('73); Prod., KNXT-TV, Los Angeles ('75); Writer/Photographer, various Los Angeles publications including the *Los Angeles Times* ('75); Prod., ABC News, Tokyo ('79); Correspondent, ABC News, Hong Kong ('80).

ACHIEVEMENTS & AWARDS: N.A.

PERSONAL: N.A.

LITTLE, CLEAVON
Actor

c/o NBC, 30 Rockefeller Plaza, New York, NY 10020

b. June 1, 1940.

EDUCATION: N.A.

CAREER HIGHLIGHTS: Broadway credits include *Purlie, Scuba Duba,* and *Jimmy Shine.* Feature films include *Greased Lightning, Blazing Saddles, FM,* and *John and Mary.* TV movies include *Don't Look Back* and *The Day the Earth Moved.* TV series star of "Temperature's Rising." Regular daytime serial star of "Another World."

ACHIEVEMENTS & AWARDS: Tony and Drama Desk awards as best actor in a musical, for *Purlie.*

PERSONAL: N.A.

LITTLE, TAWNY GODIN
Anchor, KABC-TV, News

c/o KABC-TV, 4151 Prospect Ave., Los Angeles, CA 90027

b. Portland, ME.

EDUCATION: Skidmore College; University of Southern California.

CAREER HIGHLIGHTS: Joined KABC-TV as Host and General Assignment Reporter ('77); Co-Anchor, Sunday Weekend Edition "Eyewitness News," KABC-TV ('78); Co-Anchor, Weekday 4 P.M. "Eyewitness News," KABC-TV ('80).

ACHIEVEMENTS & AWARDS: Crowned Miss America ('75).

PERSONAL: Married to John Schneider of CBS's "The Dukes of Hazzard."

LITTLEFIELD, WARREN
V.P., Comedy Programs, NBC, Entertainment

c/o NBC, 3000 W. Alameda Ave., Burbank, CA 91523

b. May 11, 1952. Montclair, NJ.

EDUCATION: American University; Hobart College.

CAREER HIGHLIGHTS: V.P. in Charge of Development and Production, Westfall Productions ('77); Dir., Comedy Development, Warner Bros. Studios ('79); Mgr., Comedy Development, NBC ('79); Dir., Current Comedy Programs ('80); V.P., Current Comedy, NBC ('81); V.P., Comedy Development ('81); V.P., Comedy Programs, NBC Entertainment ('83).

ACHIEVEMENTS & AWARDS: N.A.

PERSONAL: Resides in Los Angeles with his wife, Theresa, and their daughter, Emily.

LITVACK, JOHN ALAN
V.P., NBC, Current Drama Programs

1741 Pier Ave., Santa Monica, CA 90405

b. May 25, 1945. Newton, MA.

EDUCATION: Columbia University, B.A.

CAREER HIGHLIGHTS: Freelance Dir. for daytime serials, commercials ('67); Dir., Daytime Programs, CBS ('78); Dir., Current Programs,

MGM TV ('80). Joined NBC as Dir., Current Drama Programs ('80); promoted to V.P. ('82).

ACHIEVEMENTS & AWARDS: N.A.

PERSONAL: Resides in Santa Monica, CA, with wife, Murphy; children, Zachary and Cameron.

LITVACK, NEAL
Marketing Dir., HBO, Cinemax

c/o HBO, 1271 Ave. of the Americas, New York, NY 10020
b. June 9, 1955.

EDUCATION: Vassar College, B.A., Economics; Harvard Business School, M.B.A., General Management.

CAREER HIGHLIGHTS: Product Mgr., General Foods, White Plains, NY ('79); Marketing Mgr., HBO Retention ('81); Marketing Mgr., Cinemax Advertising ('82); Marketing Dir., HBO, Cinemax ('83).

ACHIEVEMENTS & AWARDS: N.A.

PERSONAL: N.A.

LLOYD, CHRISTOPHER
Actor

c/o Phil Gersh Assoc., 222 N. Canon, Beverly Hills, CA 90210
b. October 22. Stamford, CT.

EDUCATION: N.A.

CAREER HIGHLIGHTS: Broadway appearances include *Happy End* and *Red White and Maddox;* TV guest star on "Best of the West"; TV appearances on *The Word* and *Lacy and the Mississippi Queen.* Was a series regular on "Taxi."

ACHIEVEMENTS & AWARDS: N.A.

PERSONAL: N.A.

LLOYD, ROBIN
News Correspondent, NBC, Miami

1666 79th Street Cswy., #610, Miami, FL 33141
b. October 4, 1950. Winchester, VA.

EDUCATION: Princeton University, B.A.; Columbia University, M.S., Journalism.

CAREER HIGHLIGHTS: Reporter, Anchor and later News Dir., WSVI-TV and Radio Announcer, WSTX-TV ('74); Freelance Reporter, *Philadelphia Bulletin* ('76); Reporter/Anchor, King TV ('76); and for WTVJ ('79); named Correspondent, NBC News ('79).

ACHIEVEMENTS & AWARDS: Intl. Affairs Fellow, Columbia University ('76); Overseas Press Club award for "Guatemala: The Next Act" ('81).

PERSONAL: N.A.

LOBO, RICHARD
Station Mgr., WNBC-TV

c/o WNBC-TV, 30 Rockefeller Plaza, New York, NY 10020
b. October 18. Tampa, FL.

EDUCATION: University of Miami, B.A., Radio/TV/Film and Journalism ('58).

CAREER HIGHLIGHTS: Reporter/Photographer, WTVH-TV, Miami ('58); Reporter/Photographer, WCKT-TV, Miami ('59); Asst. Promotion Mgr., WTTV-TV, Tampa ('62); Reporter, WCBS-TV, New York ('63); Assignment Mgr., WCBS-TV ('66); Exec. Prod., WCBS-TV ('68); Assignment Editor, WNBC-TV, New York ('71); News Dir., WKYC-TV, Cleveland ('74); Program Dir., WMAQ-TV, Chicago ('77); Station Mgr., WNBC-TV, New York ('80).

ACHIEVEMENTS & AWARDS: Member, NAPTE; NATAS; IRTS.

PERSONAL: Resides in New York City; daughter, Laura; sons, Lance and Christopher.

LOCKHART, RAY
V.P., News Operations, NBC, News

c/o NBC, 30 Rockefeller Plaza, New York, NY 10020
b. November 26. Philadelphia, PA.

EDUCATION: N.A.
CAREER HIGHLIGHTS: Film Editor, NBC News ('54); Assoc. Dir., "The Huntley-Brinkley Report" ('59); Dir., "The Huntley-Brinkley Report" ('60); Night Mgr., NBC News ('66); Mgr., Convention Operations, NBC News ('67); Prod., Special Programming, NBC News ('69); Sr. Prod., NBC News ('72); Prod./Dir., NBC News Documentaries ('78); V.P., News Operations, NBC News ('82).
ACHIEVEMENTS & AWARDS: Directors Guild award ('78); Dupont-Columbia award ('78); Gainsburgh award ('81).
PERSONAL: Wife, Ann; five children.

LOGGIA, ROBERT
Actor/Dir.

c/o Merritt Blake, Blake-Glenn Agency, 409 N. Camden, Beverly Hills, CA 90210
b. January 3, 1930. Staten Island, NY.

EDUCATION: University of Missouri, B.A., Journalism.
CAREER HIGHLIGHTS: Guest star on most of the live TV shows of the Golden Age of the fifties. Title role in "The Nine Lives of Elfego Baca" for "Walt Disney Presents," NBC series ('57–'59); title role of "T.H.E. Cat", NBC series ('67–'69); joined director ranks with "Quincy" and has followed with episodes of "Magnum, P.I." and "Hart to Hart." Roles in *An Officer and a Gentleman, Trail of the Pink Panther, Psycho II, Scarface.*
ACHIEVEMENTS & AWARDS: N.A.
PERSONAL: N.A.

LOLLOS, JOHN S.
Sr. V.P. and Prod., Video Properties

c/o Video Properties, 33 E. 68th St., New York, NY 10021
b. N.A.

EDUCATION: Opsala College; Hunter College.
CAREER HIGHLIGHTS: Began career in theater as a director and playwright; later joined NBC as a Network Exec., Prod./Writer with the "Today" program, "The Tonight Show With Johnny Carson," and "The Hallmark Hall of Fame." Prod., 10-part Ernie Kovacs comedy series on PBS ('77); Prod., for specials on CBS Cable and Hearst/ABC Arts Cable channels. Sr. V.P. and Prod., Video Properties, creating programming for TV and cable.
ACHIEVEMENTS & AWARDS: N.A.
PERSONAL: N.A.

LOMOND, DIANE
Mgr., NBC Entertainment, West Coast, Casting

c/o NBC, 3000 W. Alameda Ave., Burbank, CA 91523
b. Los Angeles, CA.

EDUCATION: University of California at Los Angeles.
CAREER HIGHLIGHTS: Started as local TV Newswriter; Talent Coordinator, "The Art Linkletter Show"; joined Casting Dept., Ziv Studios ('61); Asst. Casting Dir., Paramount ('66), Don Fedderson Productions ('68), Warner Bros. ('71); Head of Talent, Billy Jack Productions, assisted Al Trescony, NBC's Dir., Casting ('72). Named Mgr., Casting, NBC Entertainment, West Coast ('79).
ACHIEVEMENTS & AWARDS: N.A.
PERSONAL: N.A.

LONG, JANET
Regional Dir., HBO, Mountain State Region

c/o HBO, 1271 Ave. of the Americas, New York, NY 10020
b. N.A.

EDUCATION: Mount Holyoke College, B.A., Economics; University of California at Berkeley, M.B.A., Finance.
CAREER HIGHLIGHTS: Sr. Adjuster, Liberty Mutual Insurance Co., San Francisco ('74); Acct. Officer, World Corp. Group, Citibank, N.A., New York ('77); Natl. Acct. Exec., HBO, New York ('80); Natl. Acct. Mgr., HBO ('81); Regional Dir., Mountain States Region, HBO, Denver ('83).
ACHIEVEMENTS & AWARDS: N.A.
PERSONAL: Resides in Denver.

LONG, LORETTA
Actress/Educator, Children's Television Workshop, "Sesame Street"

c/o Children's Television Workshop, 1 Lincoln
Plaza, New York, NY 10023
b. October 4.

EDUCATION: University of Massachusetts,
Ed.D., Urban Education.
CAREER HIGHLIGHTS: A former schoolteacher,
Long has portrayed Susan on the popular
children's series "Sesame Street" since the
program's inception.
ACHIEVEMENTS & AWARDS: N.A.
PERSONAL: N.A.

LONG, SHELLY
Actress, NBC

c/o "Cheers," NBC, 3000 W. Alameda Ave.,
Burbank, CA 91523
b. August 23. Fort Wayne, IN.

EDUCATION: Northwestern University.
CAREER HIGHLIGHTS: Writer, educational and
industrial films; Writer/Co-Host, Chicago information show "Sorting It Out." TV guest
star on "Family" and "The Love Boat". TV
movies include *The Cracker Factory* and *The
Promise of Love;* feature films include *Caveman*
and *Night Shift.* Regular on the series
"Cheers."
ACHIEVEMENTS & AWARDS: Three local Emmy
awards for Chicago's "Sorting It Out."
PERSONAL: Husband, Bruce Tyson.

LOPER, JAMES L.
Independent Telecommunications Consultant

735 Holladay Rd., Pasadena, CA 91106
b. September 4, 1931. Phoenix, AZ.

EDUCATION: Arizona State University, B.A.,
Journalism ('53); University of Denver, M.A.,
Radio and Television ('57); University of
Southern California, Ph.D., Communications
('67).
CAREER HIGHLIGHTS: Weekend News Editor,
KTAR Radio, Phoenix ('55); Dir. of the Edu-
cational TV and Bureau of Broadcasting, Cal-
ifornia State University at Los Angeles ('59);
V.P. and Asst. to Pres., KCET-TV, Los An-
geles ('63); Dir. of Educational Services,
KCET-TV ('64); Asst. General Mgr., KCET-TV
('65); V.P. and General Mgr., KCET-TV ('67);
Pres. and General Mgr., KCET-TV ('71); Pres.
and Chief Exec. Officer, KCET-TV ('77); left
KCET to become Independent Telecom-
munications Consultant ('82).
ACHIEVEMENTS & AWARDS: Governor's award,
Hollywood Chapter, NATAS ('75); Member,
Hollywood Radio and TV Society; ATAS; TV
Academy Foundation.
PERSONAL: Resides in Pasadena, CA, with wife
Mary, daughter, Elizabeth; son, James Jr.

LOPINTO, JOHN
Dir. of Technology Development, Time Video Information Services

c/o Time Video Information Services, 1271
Ave. of the Americas, New York, NY 10020
b. May 15. New York, NY.

EDUCATION: Manhattan College.
CAREER HIGHLIGHTS: Regional Mgr., Network
Operations Dept., HBO, before joining Time
Video Information Services as Dir. of Tech-
nology Development ('80).
ACHIEVEMENTS & AWARDS: Member, Institute
of Electrical and Electronic Engineers; Chair-
man, Natl. Cable TV Assn.'s Engineering
Subcommittee on Teletext.
PERSONAL: N.A.

LORD, ARTHUR A.
Dir. of Special Operations, NBC, News

c/o NBC, 3000 W. Alameda Ave., Burbank,
CA 91505
b. March 3, 1942. Rockaway Beach, NY.

EDUCATION: University of Florida, B.A., Journalism ('63).

CAREER HIGHLIGHTS: NBC Newswriter, Assignment Editor, and Reporter ('67); War Correspondent, Saigon ('71); appointed Southwest Bureau Chief ('73); moved to Burbank in same capacity ('79); promoted to Dir. of Special Operations, NBC News Burbank ('82).

ACHIEVEMENTS & AWARDS: Aviations Space Writers award, for writing "Beyond the Sky" ('68); Emmy for writing "Apollo: A Journey to the Moon" ('69); Emmy for producing "Heart Transplant" ('79).

PERSONAL: Resides in Tarzana, CA, with wife, Susan; children, Michael and Sharon.

LORD, WILLIAM E.
V.P. and Exec. Prod., ABC, News

c/o ABC, 7 W. 66th St., New York, NY 10023
b. December 7, 1937, Portland, ME.

EDUCATION: Boston University, B.S. and A.A.; University of Pennsylvania Annenberg School of Communications, M.A.

CAREER HIGHLIGHTS: Reporter/Writer for ABC News, Washington, DC ('61); Prod., ABC News, Washington, DC ('64); Sr. Prod., "ABC Evening News," Washington, DC ('66); V.P., ABC Washington, DC, News Bureau ('74); V.P. in Charge of ABC TV News ('76); V.P. and Exec. Prod., "Good Morning America" news ('78); V.P. and Exec. Prod., "Nightline" ('80); V.P. and Exec. Prod., "Viewpoint" ('81).

ACHIEVEMENTS & AWARDS: Emmy award ('81); Dupont award ('81); Christopher award ('82); Peabody awards for "Nightline" and "Viewpoint" ('82); Boston University distinguished alumni award ('82).

PERSONAL: Resides in Greenwich, CT, with wife, Deborah, three daughters, and a son.

LORING, GLORIA
Singer/Actress

c/o "Days of Our Lives," NBC, 3000 W. Alameda Ave., Burbank, CA 91523
b. N.A.

EDUCATION: N.A.

CAREER HIGHLIGHTS: As a singer, Loring made more than 300 guest star appearances on such shows as "The Carol Burnett Show" and "The Dean Martin Show." She appeared in the documentary special "Two Singers" with Aretha Franklin. Series regular on "Days of Our Lives."

ACHIEVEMENTS & AWARDS: N.A.

PERSONAL: N.A.

LOUGHLIN, MARY ANNE
Prod./Show Host, WTBS, Atlanta

1050 Techwood Drive, N.W., Atlanta, GA 30318
b. July 30, 1956. Biddeford, ME.

EDUCATION: Florida State University, B.S., Mass Communications ('77).

CAREER HIGHLIGHTS: Reporter, "Morning Magazine," WFSU-FM, Tallahassee, FL ('77); Prod./Anchor, "Action News," WECA, Tallahassee ('77); Prod./Host, "Nice People," WTBS, Atlanta ('81).

ACHIEVEMENTS & AWARDS: Voted most popular news personality, Tallahassee, FL ('81); woman of achievement, Atlanta chapter AWRT ('82); Georgia Emmy award nomination, talent ('82); Georgia Emmy award nomination, Prod., "Nice People."

PERSONAL: N.A.

LOVETT, JOSEPH F.
Prod., ABC News, "20/20"

11 Fifth Ave., New York, NY 10003
b. March 29, 1945. Providence, RI.

EDUCATION: Columbia College, B.A., English ('67).

CAREER HIGHLIGHTS: Editor, ABC News Documentaries, "What About Tomorrow" series ('73); Sound Editor, *Lenny*, feature film by Bob Fosse ('74); Prod., independent film *Vet-*

erans of the Abraham Lincoln Brigade ('74); Editor, "60 Minutes" and "Magazine," CBS News ('75); Editor, "CBS Reports" ('78); Prod., "Viewpoint" pilot, ABC News ('81); Prod., "20/20," ABC News ('79). Also, Lecturer, New School for Social Research ('80–'83).

ACHIEVEMENTS & AWARDS: Advocate humanitarian award for "What Do You Say When Your Kid Says He's Gay?" CBS "Magazine" ('77); One to One award for "Tools of Hope," "20/20," ABC News ('81); Operation PUSH award for "A Joyful Noise," "20/20" ABC News ('82).

PERSONAL: N.A.

LOVULLO, SAM
Prod.

45 W. 10th St., New York, NY 10011
b. Buffalo, NY

EDUCATION: Woodbury College; University of California at Los Angeles.
CAREER HIGHLIGHTS: CBS Accounting Dept.; Business Mgr. for CBS West Coast; Assoc. Prod., "The Jonathan Winters Show"; Prod., "Hee Haw"; also produced specials for the Harlem Globetrotters, Herb Alpert and John Wayne.
ACHIEVEMENTS & AWARDS: N.A.
PERSONAL: Wife, Grace; two sons and two daughters.

LOW, RICHARD H.
Exec. V.P./Dir., Young & Rubicam, Broadcast Programming and Purchasing

c/o Young & Rubicam, 285 Madison Ave., New York, NY 10017
b. February 20, 1927. Union City, NJ.

EDUCATION: University of Michigan; Columbia University, J.D., ('52).
CAREER HIGHLIGHTS: CBS News ('52); CBS TV Network ('56); joined Young & Rubicam ('62); Exec. V.P./Dir., Young & Rubicam, Broadcast Programming and Purchasing.
ACHIEVEMENTS & AWARDS: N.A.
PERSONAL: N.A.

LOWE, BARBARA E.
V.P., Research and Marketing Services, Eastman CableRep

c/o Eastman CableRep, Inc., 1 Rockefeller Plaza, New York, NY 10020
b. September 11, 1946.

EDUCATION: New York University, B.A., Political Science.
CAREER HIGHLIGHTS: Held research positions with Storer TV Sales and Corinthian Broadcasting; Research Dir., Harrington, Righter & Parsons; Dir. of Special Services, Eastman CableRep ('80); V.P., Research and Marketing Services, Eastman CableRep ('81).
ACHIEVEMENTS & AWARDS: Member, CTAM; Women in Cable, New York Chapter.
PERSONAL: N.A.

LOXTON, DAVID
Dir., TV Laboratory at WNET/13; Pres., Nicholas Films

c/o WNET/13, 356 W. 58th St., New York, NY 10019
b. January 28, 1943. Kingston, Ontario, Canada.

EDUCATION: Trinity College, Dublin, M.A. ('65).
CAREER HIGHLIGHTS: Joined WNET/13 ('72). Exec. Prod., "Nonfiction TV" series ('77). Prod./Dir., *The Lathe of Heaven* ('80); Exec. Prod., "Video/Film Review" series ('79–'80). Exec. Prod., "Bad Boys," "Vietnam: Picking Up the Pieces," "Making Television Dance," "The Police Tapes," "Health Care: Your Money or Your Life," "Super Bowl," "Gerald Ford's America," "Philobolus and Joan," "Scapemates," "Global Groove." Pres., Nich-

olas Films ('80); Prod./Dir., Nicholas Films "Flashback" series for HBO, and "People" starring Lily Tomlin for NBC.

ACHIEVEMENTS & AWARDS: Chicago Intl. Film Festival gold medal for producing "Hindenburg: Ship of Doom," for "Flashback" ('81); Chicago Intl. Film Festival certificate of merit for *The Lathe of Heaven* ('80); Christopher award as Exec. Prod., "A Lady Named Baybie" ('80); Emmy, Exec. Prod., "Presumed Innocent" ('79); Emmy, Peabody award, and Dupont-Columbia award, Exec. Prod., "Police Tapes" ('76); Christopher award, Exec. Prod., "Chinatown" ('76).

PERSONAL: Wife, Pamela; sons, William and Charles.

LUCAS, GUS
V.P., Program Planning and Scheduling, and Asst. to the Sr. V.P., Prime Time, ABC, Entertainment

c/o ABC, 4151 Prospect Ave., Los Angeles, CA 90027
b. N.A.

EDUCATION: Syracuse University ('69).
CAREER HIGHLIGHTS: Jr. Analyst, ABC ('70); Supervisor, Prime Time and Sports Audience Measurements, ABC ('72); Mgr., Audience Analysis, Prime Time and Sports ('74); Assoc. Dir. of Audience Analysis ('76); V.P., Program Planning, ABC Entertainment ('78); V.P., Program Planning and Scheduling ('79); V.P., Program Planning and Scheduling, and Asst. to the Sr. V.P., Prime Time, ABC Entertainment ('81).
ACHIEVEMENTS & AWARDS: N.A.
PERSONAL: Resides in Los Angeles with wife, Joanne; daughter, Jennifer; son, Johnny.

LUCCI, SUSAN
Actress

c/o "All My Children," ABC, 1330 Ave. of the Americas, New York, NY 10019
b. December 23. Westchester, NY.

EDUCATION: Marymount College.
CAREER HIGHLIGHTS: Daytime drama lead in "All My Children."

ACHIEVEMENTS & AWARDS: Emmy nominations as best daytime actress.
PERSONAL: N.A.

LUDWIG, FORREST
Production Mgr., NBC, Entertainment

c/o NBC, 3000 W. Alameda Ave., Burbank, CA 91523
b. August 8, 1942. Boise, ID.

EDUCATION: Glendale College.
CAREER HIGHLIGHTS: Mail Room Clerk, NBC ('63); Clerk, Staging Operations, NBC ('64); Assoc., Business Affairs Dept. ('68); Unit Mgr., NBC ('73); Sr. Unit Mgr. ('79); Production Mgr., NBC Entertainment, West Coast ('82).
ACHIEVEMENTS & AWARDS: N.A.
PERSONAL: Resides in Glendale, CA, with wife, Jeanne.

LUDWIN, RICK
V.P., Specials, NBC, Entertainment

c/o NBC, 3000 W. Alameda Ave., Burbank, CA 91523
b. Cleveland, OH.

EDUCATION: Miami (Ohio) University, B.A., Speech ('70); Northwestern University, M.A. ('71).
CAREER HIGHLIGHTS: Writer for Bob Hope, "The Mike Douglas Show" and "America 2Night"; Assoc. Prod., NBC Sports ('78); Prod., "America Alive" ('79); Dir., Variety Programs, NBC ('80); Dir., Specials and Variety Series, NBC ('81); V.P., Specials, NBC Entertainment ('83).
ACHIEVEMENTS & AWARDS:
PERSONAL: Resides in Westwood, CA.

LUMA, JOHN C.
Dir., On-Air Promotion, NBC, Advertising and Promotion, West Coast

c/o NBC, 3000 W. Alameda Ave., Burbank, CA 91523
b. May 24. Detroit, MI.

EDUCATION: Loyola University, B.A., Telecommunications and Film.

CAREER HIGHLIGHTS: Research Analyst, KNXT-TV, Los Angeles ('71); Mgr., On-Air Promotion, CBS, West Coast ('79); Mgr., On-Air Promotion, ABC, West Coast ('81); Dir., On-Air Promotion, NBC, West Coast ('83).

ACHIEVEMENTS & AWARDS: N.A.

PERSONAL: Resides in Camarillo, CA, with wife, Jeanne, and daughter, Jennifer.

LUND, CHRISTINE
Co-Anchor, KABC-TV, Los Angeles, News

c/o KABC-TV, 4151 Prospect Ave., Los Angeles, CA 90027
b. March 28. Froson Island, Sweden.

EDUCATION: Carroll College; Earlham College; Harvard University; Lake Forest College; University of Chicago.

CAREER HIGHLIGHTS: News Anchor for cable channel KFOR-TV, Chicago; News Dir., WLXT-TV, Chicago; Reporter, KGO-TV, San Francisco ('70); Reporter, KABC-TV, Los Angeles ('72); Co-Anchor, "Eyewitness News," KABC-TV, Los Angeles ('74).

ACHIEVEMENTS & AWARDS: Three Emmy awards for individual achievement ('76, '77, '78); outstanding media award from the Venereal Disease Council ('76); outstanding media achievement award from the Los Angeles Chapter, American Business and Professional Women's Assn. ('77).

PERSONAL: Resides in San Fernando Valley, CA, with husband, Dr. Stephen P. Londe.

LUND, PETER A.
V.P. and General Mgr., CBS, WCBS-TV, New York

c/o WCBS-TV, 524 W. 57th St., New York, NY 10019
b. January 12.

EDUCATION: St. Thomas College; CBS School of Management.

CAREER HIGHLIGHTS: Started as Radio Announcer and Reporter, before moving into sales and management; General Sales Mgr., WIND-AM, Chicago ('68); V.P. and General Mgr., KSDO-AM, San Diego, CA ('72); V.P.

and General Mgr., WTOP-AM, Washington, DC ('75); V.P., CBS Owned AM Stations, CBS, New York ('77); V.P., Station Services, CBS TV Stations Division, CBS ('79); V.P. and General Mgr., WBBM-TV, Chicago ('80); V.P. and General Mgr., WCBS-TV, New York ('83).

ACHIEVEMENTS & AWARDS: N.A.

PERSONAL: Resides in New York City.

LUNDEN, JOAN
On-Air Personality, ABC, Entertainment

c/o "Good Morning America," ABC TV, 1 Lincoln Plaza, New York, NY 10023
b. September 19. Sacramento, CA.

EDUCATION: Universidad de las Americas (Mexico); University of California; California State University, B.A., Liberal Arts; American River College.

CAREER HIGHLIGHTS: Co-Anchor, Consumer Reporter, and Prod. of daily noon news at KCRA-TV; moved to WABC-TV ('75); Co-Anchor, 6 P.M. Sunday newscast and simultaneously appeared on "Good Morning America" as Consumer Product Reporter ('76); Feature Reporter on "Good Morning America" ('80); named Reporter/Interviewer ('80).

ACHIEVEMENTS & AWARDS: Council of United Cerebral Palsy auxiliaries, Today's Woman ('81); Outstanding Mother of the Year, Natl. Mother's Day Committee ('82).

PERSONAL: Resides in Manhattan suburb with husband, Michael Krauss, and daughter, Jamie.

LUSTGARTEN, MARC
Pres., Cablevision Enterprises

c/o Cablevision Enterprises, 100 Crossways Park W., Suite 200, Woodbury, NY 11797
b. March 13, 1947.

EDUCATION: Pace University; New York Law School; New York University Law School.

CAREER HIGHLIGHTS: Worked in many New York law firms; served as Counsel to the Office of New York Mayor John Lindsay; served as an Attorney specializing in program acquisition for cable TV; Chief Counsel for Cablevision Enterprises; Pres., Cablevision Enterprises (Bravo Network and Sportschannel).

ACHIEVEMENTS & AWARDS: N.A.

PERSONAL: Resides in New York City with wife, Marcia, and son, Andy.

LUXENBERG, LEON
Dir., Network Relations, J. Walter Thompson, Chicago

875 N. Michigan Ave., Chicago, IL 60611
b. May 9, 1926. New York, NY.

EDUCATION: City College of New York, B.A. ('48).

CAREER HIGHLIGHTS: Statistician, Daniel Starch ('48); Research and Planning Dept., *American Weekly* magazine ('50); Dir., Sales Development, CBS Radio Network ('55); Dir., Sales Development, CBS TV, Chicago ('70); Sr. V.P., Buyer of Cable, J. Walter Thompson, Chicago ('76); Dir., Network Relations, J. Walter Thompson, Chicago.

ACHIEVEMENTS & AWARDS: N.A.

PERSONAL: Married; sons, Mitchell and Steven; daughter, Ellen.

LYMAN, DOROTHY
Actress

c/o "All My Children," ABC, 1330 Ave. of the Americas, New York, NY 10019.
b. April 18. Minneapolis, MN.

EDUCATION: Sarah Lawrence College.

CAREER HIGHLIGHTS: New York stage appearances in *House of Mirth* and *A Coupla White Chicks Sitting Around Talking*, which she also

produced and directed. Daytime serial regular on "Another World," "Search for Tomorrow," "The Edge of Night," and "All My Children." Series regular on primetime series "Mama's Family."

ACHIEVEMENTS & AWARDS: Emmy as best supporting actress in daytime drama ('81); Emmy, best actress in daytime drama ('83).

PERSONAL: Resides in New York City.

LYNCH, BILL
Correspondent, CBS, News

c/o CBS, 2020 M St., N.W., Washington, DC 20036
b. Salinas, KS. September 11.

EDUCATION: University of Kansas.

CAREER HIGHLIGHTS: Reporter, WTOP-TV, now WDVM, Washington, DC ('68); Reporter, WNEW-TV, New York ('70); Reporter/Anchor, WCBS-AM, New York ('75); Correspondent, NBC News, Washington, DC ('75); Correspondent, CBS News, Washington, DC ('81); named Pentagon Correspondent, CBS News ('82).

ACHIEVEMENTS & AWARDS: N.A.

PERSONAL: N.A.

LYNCH, PATRICIA
Prod., NBC, News, "Monitor"

c/o NBC, 30 Rockefeller Plaza, New York, NY 10020
b. N.A.

EDUCATION: College of New Rochelle; Boston College, M.A.

CAREER HIGHLIGHTS: Joined NBC News; Prod./Editor "NewsCenter 4" ('73); Prod./Writer for Segment Three, the investigative arm of "NBC Nightly News" ('77); Prod., ABC News ('79); returned to NBC News ('82).

ACHIEVEMENTS & AWARDS: Local New York Emmy ('76).

PERSONAL: N.A.

LYON, RONALD
Exec. Prod./Dir.

c/o ABC, 2040 Ave. of the Starts, Los Angeles,
CA 90067
b. N.A.

EDUCATION: Pennsylvania State University.
CAREER HIGHLIGHTS: Mailboy at KTLA-TV, Los
Angeles ('64); Creator/Prod., "There Are
Giants' for NETN ('67); moved to Media Creations Ltd., as Prod. ('69); was Assoc. Prod.
for MGM's *Slither* ('72); Co-Prod., with Jack
Haley, "50 Years of MGM" and *That's Entertainment* ('75); formed Aubrey-Lyon Productions ('76); became Pres., Raystar Productions
('80). Co-Prod., three "Ripley's Believe It or
Not" specials, which later led to the ABC
series ('81).
ACHIEVEMENTS & AWARDS: N.A.
PERSONAL: Married to dancer, model, and
photographer Linda Hall; two sons, Gregory
and Sascha.

LYONS, JEFFREY
Critic, WPIX-TV and "Sneak Previews," PBS

c/o WPIX-TV, 11 WPIX Plaza, New York, NY
10017
b. November 5, 1944.

EDUCATION: University of Pennsylvania; Syracuse Law School, J.D.; Juilliard School of Music; Lee Strasberg Theater Institute.
CAREER HIGHLIGHTS: Reporter, *Jersey Journal;*
Metropolitan Desk, *N.Y. Times;* Critic, WCBS-
Radio, New York; Film and Art Critic, WPIX,
New York. ('70). His annual ten best films list
has become a popular feature of WPIX's Year-
in-Review program. He also co-hosts the PBS
series "Sneak Previews" with Neal Gabler

('82). He appeared in the film *Deathtrap.*
ACHIEVEMENTS & AWARDS: N.A.
PERSONAL: Son of late columnist Leonard
Lyons. Resides in New York City with his
wife and son.

LYONS, SIDNEY
V.P. Business Affairs, Contract Negotiations,
CBS

c/o CBS, 6121 Sunset Blvd., Los Angeles, CA
90028
b. February 13, 1927.

EDUCATION: Northwestern University, B.S.;
Harvard Law School, LL.B.
CAREER HIGHLIGHTS: Assoc. Dir., Business Af-
fairs, CBS ('61); Mgr. of Administration, CBS
('62); Dir. of Administration, CBS ('64); Dir.,
Business Affairs, CBS, Los Angeles ('71);
V.P., Business Affairs, Motion Pictures for
TV and Mini-Series, CBS Entertainment ('78);
V.P., Business Affairs, Contract Negotia-
tions, CBS ('81).
ACHIEVEMENTS & AWARDS: Member, NATAS;
Hollywood Radio-TV Society, California Bar
Assn., Phi Beta Kappa.
PERSONAL: Resides in Woodland Hills, CA,
with wife, Dorelle, and their daughters, An-
drea and Alyson.

MAAS, JON
Dir., NBC, Entertainment, Programs, East Coast

c/o NBC, 30 Rockefeller Plaza, New York, NY 10020
b. November 19, 1957.

EDUCATION: Pratt Institute, B.F.A., Theater and Advertising.
CAREER HIGHLIGHTS: Asst. to Broadway and Film Prod. David Merrick; Story Analyst for 20th Century Fox and Orion Pictures. Joined NBC Entertainment as Dir., Programs, East Coast ('81).
ACHIEVEMENTS & AWARDS: N.A.
PERSONAL: Resides in New York City.

McBRIDE, BOB
Anchor, WRC-TV, News

c/o WRC-TV, 4001 Nebraska Ave., N.W., Washington, DC 20016
b. Chicago, IL. Sept. 8.

EDUCATION: George Washington University, B.A. and graduate work, Political Science.
CAREER HIGHLIGHTS: McBride began his journalism career at *U.S. News and World Report*; Research Dir., *Detroit Free Press*; Program Dir., WJBK-TV; News Dir., WJBK-TV; Weeknight Anchor, WBBM-TV, Chicago; General Mgr., WJBK-TV, Detroit; Anchor, WRC-TV ('82).
ACHIEVEMENTS & AWARDS: Numerous AP Natl. awards, Detroit Press Club award for excellence in journalism.
PERSONAL: Resides with his family in Potomac, MD.

McCARTHY, GARY J.
V.P., Finance and Business Affairs, Theatrical Films, CBS, Broadcast Group

c/o CBS, 7800 Beverly Blvd., Los Angeles, CA 90036
b. N.A.

EDUCATION: Hofstra University, B.B.A., Accounting; Pace University, M.B.A.; CBS School of Management.
CAREER HIGHLIGHTS: Finance Dept., CBS Publishing Group ('70); V.P., Finance, Planning and Administration, CBS Theatrical Films ('81); V.P., Finance and Business Affairs, Theatrical Films, CBS Broadcast Group ('83).
ACHIEVEMENTS & AWARDS: N.A.
PERSONAL: Resides in Los Angeles.

McCARTHY, LARK
Co-Anchor, WJLA-TV, News

4461 Connecticut Ave., N.W., Washington, DC 20008
b. January 6, 1955. Chicago, IL.

EDUCATION: Northwestern University, B.S., Journalism; Northwestern University Medill School of Journalism, M.S.
CAREER HIGHLIGHTS: She started as a City Desk Asst., *Chicago Daily News*; Washington, DC, Correspondent, WCAR-Radio, Detroit; Reporter, *Citizen Patriot*, Jackson, MI; Co-Prod., WTTW-TV, Chicago ('75); Newswriter and Morning Anchor, WJLA-TV, Washington, DC ('76); Reporter/Morning Anchor WPLG-TV, Miami; Reporter, WJLA-TV ('78); Weekend Anchor, WJLA-TV ('79); Host WJLA-TV, "Good Morning Washington" ('81); Co-Anchor/Special Assignment Reporter, WJLA-TV ('81).
ACHIEVEMENTS & AWARDS: N.A.
PERSONAL: N.A.

McCARTHY, SEAN J.
Pres., Time Video Information Services

c/o Time Video Information Services, 1271
   Ave. of the Americas, New York, NY 10020
b. June 1, 1943. Rochester, NY.

EDUCATION: St. John Fisher College, B.A.; Har-
   vard University, M.B.A.
CAREER HIGHLIGHTS: Worked in the Finance
   Dept., Time, Inc. ('71); Mgr., Corporate Intl.,
   Time, Inc. ('75); V.P., Finance, HBO ('76);
   Pres., Time Video Information Services ('81).
ACHIEVEMENTS & AWARDS: N.A.
PERSONAL: Resides in New York City.

McCARTHY, SHERYL
Correspondent, ABC, News

c/o ABC, 7 W. 66th St., New York, NY 10023
b. Birmingham, AL.

EDUCATION: Mount Holyoke College, B.A.,
   English; Columbia University, M.A., En-
   glish, and law degree.
CAREER HIGHLIGHTS: Reporter, *Boston Globe;*
   Reporter, *Baltimore Sun;* Reporter, *N.Y. Daily
   News* ('76); Correspondent, ABC News, New
   York ('82).
ACHIEVEMENTS & AWARDS: Two awards from
   the Education Writers Assn.
PERSONAL: Resides in New York City.

McCOURT, MICHAEL
**Correspondent and Bureau Chief, ABC,
   News, Johannesburg**

c/o ABC, P.O. Box 4516, Johannesburg 2000,
   South Africa
b. Fredericton, New Brunswick, Canada.

EDUCATION: University of Saskatoon (Canada).
CAREER HIGHLIGHTS: Reporter for CTV-Radio
   and TV, Toronto, Vancouver, and Ottawa
   ('66); Sr. Correspondent, CTV, Ottawa ('72);
   Washington, DC, Bureau Chief, CTV ('79);
   Correspondent, and Johannesburg, South
   Africa, Bureau Chief, ABC News ('80).
ACHIEVEMENTS & AWARDS: N.A.
PERSONAL: N.A.

McCREARY, BILL
Co-Anchor, WNEW-TV, New York, News

c/o WNEW-TV, 205 E. 67th St., New York,
   NY 10021
b. New York, NY.

EDUCATION: City College of New York; New
   York University.
CAREER HIGHLIGHTS: Reporter and later News
   Dir., WLIB. Joined WNEW-TV as Co-Anchor,
   "10 O'Clock News" ('67). In addition, he
   serves as Exec. Prod./ Managing Editor/Host
   of "Black News" on WNEW-TV ('71).
ACHIEVEMENTS & AWARDS: N.A.
PERSONAL: Resides in New York City.

MacCURDY, JEAN H.
V.P./General Mgr., Warner Bros., Cartoons

c/o Warner Bros., 4000 Warner Blvd.,
   Burbank, CA 91522
b. April 15, 1949. Palo Alto, CA.

EDUCATION: Occidental College, B.A. ('71).
CAREER HIGHLIGHTS: Mgr., Children's Pro-
   grams, NBC TV ('74); Dir. of Animation Pro-
   gramming, Warner Bros. ('79); V.P./General
   Mgr., Warner Bros. Cartoons overseeing
   "The Daffy/Speedy Show," and "The Bugs
   Bunny/Road Runner Show" ('82).
ACHIEVEMENTS & AWARDS: N.A.
PERSONAL: Resides in Burbank, CA.

McDANIEL, JAN
News Assignment Mgr., CBS, News

c/o CBS, 2020 M St., N.W., Washington, DC
   20036
b. June 27, 1952. St. Louis, MO.

EDUCATION: University of Missouri.

CAREER HIGHLIGHTS: Moderator/Prod., Public Affairs Programming, WEEI-AM, Boston ('74); Newswriter/Copy Editor, CBS Radio News, New York ('75); Assignment Editor/Field Prod., CBS Radio News ('76); Assignment Desk Editor, CBS News, Washington, DC ('76); Asst. Assignment Editor, CBS News, Washington, DC ('78); Field Prod., CBS News election night coverage ('78, '80, '82); News Assignment Mgr., CBS News, Washington, DC ('83).

ACHIEVEMENTS & AWARDS: N.A.

PERSONAL: N.A.

McDERMOTT, ANNE
Reporter, Cable News Network, Los Angeles Bureau

c/o Cable News Network, 1050 Techwood Dr., N.W., Atlanta, GA 30318
b. January 7, 1955. Cincinnati, OH.

EDUCATION: Syracuse University, B.S., Communications.

CAREER HIGHLIGHTS: Reporter/Anchor, WKTV, Utica, NY ('77); Reporter/Anchor, KID-TV, Idaho Falls, ID ('78); Reporter, Cable News Network, Atlanta Bureau ('80); Reporter Cable News Network, Los Angeles Bureau ('81).

ACHIEVEMENTS & AWARDS: N.A.

PERSONAL: Husband, Mark D. Geers. Resides in Los Angeles.

McDEVITT, F. RAYMOND
Sr. V.P., Technical Operations, Warner Amex Cable Communications, Inc.

c/o Warner Amex, 75 Rockefeller Plaza, New York, NY 10019
b. April 23, 1944.

EDUCATION: Auburn University, B.S.E.E. and M.S.E.E.

CAREER HIGHLIGHTS: Program Mgr., Harris Corp.; Dir. of the Fiber Optics Laboratory of the Electro-Optical Products Division of IT&T; V.P., Technical Operations, Warner Amex Cable Communications ('81); Sr. V.P., Technical Operations, Warner Amex Cable Communications ('83).

ACHIEVEMENTS & AWARDS: N.A.

PERSONAL: N.A.

McDONALD, GRAEME
Controller BBC 2, BBC

c/o BBC, 12 Cavendish Place, London, England W1
b. July 30, 1930.

EDUCATION: University of Cambridge (England).

CAREER HIGHLIGHTS: Dir. Trainee with Granada TV; Prod., BBC TV Drama Group ('66); Prod., "The Eleventh Hour" ('75); Head, BBC TV Drama, Series and Serials ('77); Head, BBC TV Drama Group ('81); Controller, BBC-2 ('83).

ACHIEVEMENTS & AWARDS: N.A.

PERSONAL: N.A.

McDOWALL, RODDY
Actor

c/o William Morris Agency, 151 El Camino Dr., Beverly Hills, CA 90212
b. September 17, 1928. London, England.

EDUCATION: St. Joseph's College; Hanover Academy of Dramatic Arts.

CAREER HIGHLIGHTS: Starring roles in such TV dramas as *Billy Budd, Heart of Darkness, The Power and the Glory, Miracle on 34th Street, The Thief of Baghdad.* Starred in the series "The Planet of the Apes," "Fantastic Journey," and "Tales of the Gold Monkey." Motion picture credits include *The Poseidon Adventure, The Loved One, Bedknobs and Broomsticks, That Darned Cat, Inside Daisy Clover, Funny Lady,* and *Evil Under the Sun.*

ACHIEVEMENTS & AWARDS: Emmy for his supporting role in *Not Without Honor* ('60).

PERSONAL: N.A.

McEVEETY, BERNARD
Dir.

c/o Eisenbach-Greene, 760 North La Cienega Blvd., Los Angeles, CA 90069
b. N.A.

EDUCATION: N.A.

CAREER HIGHLIGHTS: Dir. of more than 300 TV shows including "Voyagers," "Trapper John, M.D.," "Vega$," "The Rockford Files," "Jessica Novak," "McLain's Law," and "Si-

mon and Simon." TV movie credits include *Roughnecks, A Step Out of Line, Killer by Night, Hostage Heart, The Mask of Alexander, Donovan's Kid,* and Chapter 11 of the mini-series *Centennial.*
ACHIEVEMENTS & AWARDS: N.A.
PERSONAL: N.A.

McFARLAND, ROBERT
V.P., NBC, News

c/o NBC, 4001 Nebraska Ave., N.W., Washington, DC 20016
b. December 1, 1938. Burnet, TX.

EDUCATION: Southwest Texas University.
CAREER HIGHLIGHTS: Reporter, WSB-TV, Atlanta ('64); Reporter, NBC News, Cleveland ('66); News Dir., WRC-TV, Washington, DC ('68); Assoc. Prod., "The Huntley-Brinkley Report" ('69); Assoc. Prod., "NBC Nightly News" ('70); Prod./London Bureau Chief, NBC News, London ('73); Washington, DC, Prod., "NBC Nightly News" ('77); V.P., NBC News, Washington, DC ('82).
ACHIEVEMENTS & AWARDS: Four Emmy awards; two AP outstanding broadcaster awards, and numerous local citations.
PERSONAL: Resides in Burke, VA, with wife, Elizabeth, and their children, Lisa, Robert Jr., and Lane.

McGANNON, LAURA L.
Design Mgr., NBC, Advertising and Promotion, West Coast

c/o NBC, 3000 W. Alameda Ave., Burbank, CA 91523
b. November 28. Cleveland, OH.

EDUCATION: Ohio University, B.F.A. (summa cum laude, '74).
CAREER HIGHLIGHTS: Freelance Graphic Artist, Los Angeles area ('75); Asst. Art Dir., D'Arcy, McManus & Masius, Los Angeles ('76); Art Dir., D'Arcy, McManus & Masius, Los Angeles ('77); Promotion Art Dir., *Architectural Digest* and *Bon Appetit* magazines ('77); Asst. Mgr. of Design, KNXT-TV, Los Angeles ('78); Design Mgr., Advertising and Promotion, NBC, Burbank ('83).
ACHIEVEMENTS & AWARDS: N.A.
PERSONAL: Resides in Burbank.

McGOWAN, JAMES F.
V.P., CBS, Business Affairs Administration

c/o CBS, 7800 Beverly Blvd., Los Angeles, CA 90036
b. October 14. Brooklyn, NY.

EDUCATION: St. Francis College, B.A.
CAREER HIGHLIGHTS: Dir. of Administration, Business Affairs, CBS ('70); Dir. of Finance, Operations and Generations, CBS ('76); Dir. of Research and Planning, Business Affairs, CBS ('77); V.P., Business Affairs Administration, CBS ('81).
ACHIEVEMENTS & AWARDS: N.A.
PERSONAL: Wife, Cathy; three children, James, Mark, and Meredith.

McGOWAN, WILLIAM G.
Chairman and Chief Exec. Officer, MCI Communications Corp.

1275 Summer, Stamford, CT 06204
b. December 10, 1927.

EDUCATION: Kings College, B.S.; Harvard Graduate School of Business Administration, M.B.A.
CAREER HIGHLIGHTS: Owned several technology companies, including the Ultrasonic Corp., a pioneer in the development of cryogenic devices for the space program. Founded MCI ('68), the largest non-Bell coast-to-coast telecommunications network.
ACHIEVEMENTS & AWARDS: Selected Telecommunications Executive of the Year by the *Wall Street Transcript* ('79, '81).
PERSONAL: N.A.

McGRATH, BOB
Singer

c/o Children's Television Workshop, 1 Lincoln Plaza, New York, NY 10023
b. June 13.

EDUCATION: University of Michigan, B.A.; Manhattan School of Music, M.A.
CAREER HIGHLIGHTS: Singer with "The Mitch Miller Show." Regular cast member of "Sesame Street" since its inception.
ACHIEVEMENTS & AWARDS: N.A.
PERSONAL: N.A.

McGROARTY, ROBERT G.
Sr. V.P., Advertising Sales, Warner Amex Satellite Entertainment Co.

c/o Warner Amex, 1211 Ave. of the Americas, New York, NY 10036
b. August 3, 1945. Brooklyn, NY.

EDUCATION: University of Scranton, B.S., Political Science.
CAREER HIGHLIGHTS: Media Dept., Needham, Harper & Steers Advertising Agency, New York; Sales Exec., *Life* magazine; Dir. of Sales and Natl. Sales Mgr., WEEI-AM, Boston; Acct. Exec., CBS Radio Spot Sales; V.P. and General Mgr. of Natl. FM Sales, CBS; V.P., Marketing, Warner Cable Corp.; Sr. V.P., Advertising Sales, Warner Amex ('82).
ACHIEVEMENTS & AWARDS: N.A.
PERSONAL: N.A.

McGUINESS, JOHN P.
Assoc. Natl. Dir. of Credit and Collections, ABC, Inc.

c/o ABC, 1330 Ave. of the Americas, New York, NY 10019
b. March 29.

EDUCATION: Hunter College, B.A., English Literature.
CAREER HIGHLIGHTS: Credit Supervisor, Texaco; Administrative Mgr., Credit and Collections, Xerox Corp.; Sr. Credit Analyst, ABC Corporate Credit Dept., ABC ('73); Asst. Natl. Credit Mgr., ABC, Inc. ('76); Asst. Natl. Dir. of Credit and Collections, TV Operations, ABC ('81); Assoc. Natl. Dir. of Credit and Collections, ABC, Inc. ('83).
ACHIEVEMENTS & AWARDS: N.A.
PERSONAL: Resides in Toms River, NJ, with wife, Denise, and their two daughters.

McGUIRE, AL
Sportscaster, NBC

c/o NBC, 30 Rockefeller Plaza, New York, NY 10020
b. September 7, 1928. New York, NY.

EDUCATION: St. John's University, B.A., Sports Journalism.

CAREER HIGHLIGHTS: Collegiate basketball career ('49–'51); NBA career with New York and Baltimore; coached at Marquette University; nine NCAA tournaments as coach at Marquette; NCAA championship ('77). Joined NBC as College Basketball Commentator; also does half-time features and covers events for "Sportsworld"
ACHIEVEMENTS & AWARDS: N.A.
PERSONAL: Resides in Milwaukee with wife, Pat; three children.

McGUIRK, TERENCE F.
V.P., Turner Broadcasting System, Special Projects

c/o Turner Broadcasting System, 1050 Techwood Dr., N.W., Atlanta, GA 30318
b. August 21, 1951. Bay Shore, NY.

EDUCATION: Middlebury College, B.A., American History.
CAREER HIGHLIGHTS: Acct. Exec., WTBS ('72); Acct. Exec., WRET-TV, Charlotte, NC; Dir. of Cable Relations, WTBS; Dir. of Special Projects, WTBS; V.P., Special Projects, WTBS.
ACHIEVEMENTS & AWARDS: N.A.
PERSONAL: N.A.

McHUGH, NEIL R.
V.P. and General Mgr., Viacom World Wide

c/o Viacom Cablevision, 2055 Folsom St., San Francisco, CA 94110
b. August 26, 1941.

EDUCATION: University of Oregon, Business Administration; University of Washington, M.B.A.

CAREER HIGHLIGHTS: Joined Viacom Cable ('73), serving in various financial and executive positions. He participated in the initial launching of the Showtime premium program service, Viacom's cable systems ('76); was General Mgr. of Viacom's Cable System, San Francisco ('79); Sr. V.P., Operations ('80); now General Mgr., Viacom World Wide ('83).

ACHIEVEMENTS & AWARDS: Vice Chairman of the California Cable TV Assn.

PERSONAL: Married; two children.

McKAY, JIM
Host, ABC, "Wide World of Sports"

c/o ABC, 1330 Ave. of the Americas, New York, NY 10019
b. September 24, 1921. Philadelphia, PA.

EDUCATION: Loyola College.

CAREER HIGHLIGHTS: Reporter, *Baltimore Sun* newspapers; WMAR-TV as Writer, Prod., Dir., Newsman, Sports Commentator, and On-Camera Personality ('47); joined CBS, New York ('50) as Host of a TV variety show called "The Jim McKay Show," directed by Don Hewitt, now Exec. Prod. of "60 Minutes." Then Anchor for the Masters and PGA golf championships, also covering college football, horse racing, and other sports. Became Host, ABC's "Wide World of Sports" ('61).

ACHIEVEMENTS & AWARDS: Two Emmy awards ('72); George Polk memorial award for journalism; Officer's Cross of the Legion of Merit for his reporting from Munich ('72); Olympic medal from the Austrian government for his work at the Innsbruck Winter Games ('76).

PERSONAL: Wife, Margaret; two children. Resides in Westport, CT.

McKEEFE, ELLEN
Bureau Chief, NBC, News

c/o NBC, 30 Rockefeller Plaza, New York, NY 10020
b. September 16, 1944. Washington, DC.

EDUCATION: Skidmore College, B.S.

CAREER HIGHLIGHTS: Began with NBC as Assignment Editor, Network News, New York ('74); named Field Prod., NBC Network News, New York ('76); moved to Miami in same capacity ('77); relocated to Washington, DC, to do same ('79); named Bureau Chief, NBC News, Boston ('81); returned to New York as NBC News Bureau Chief ('82).

ACHIEVEMENTS & AWARDS: Emmy nomination for special segment on Iranian hostage rescue attempt ('81).

PERSONAL: Resides in Manhattan.

McKENNA, JAMES
V.P. and General Mgr., CBS, Sports

c/o CBS, 51 W. 52d St., New York, NY 10019
b. N.A.

EDUCATION: Iona College.

CAREER HIGHLIGHTS: Joined CBS ('73) and has held a variety of financial positions, primarily in the Corporate Division. Named V.P., Finance, CBS Sports ('78); V.P. and Dir., Finance and Business Planning ('81); V.P. and General Mgr., CBS Sports ('83).

ACHIEVEMENTS & AWARDS: N.A.

PERSONAL: Resides in Lawrence, NY, with his wife, Dale, and their two daughters.

McKINVEN, MARY JANE
Dir., PBS, Public Information Dept.

c/o PBS, 475 L'Enfant Plaza, S.W., Washington, DC 20024
b. N.A.

EDUCATION: Cornell University, B.A., English Literature

CAREER HIGHLIGHTS: Assoc. Editor, American Libraries ('74); Publicist, Harvard University Press ('75); Foreign Service Information Officer, U.S. Information Agency ('76); Corporate Communications Editor, *Miami Herald* ('79); Consulting Writer/Editor, Natl. Public Radio ('80); Editorial Assoc. ('82); Dir., Public Information Dept., PBS ('83).

ACHIEVEMENTS & AWARDS: N.A.

PERSONAL: N.A.

McLAGLEN, ANDREW
Dir., CBS, Entertainment

c/o CBS, 7800 Beverly Blvd., Los Angeles, CA 90036
b. July 28, 1920. London, England.

EDUCATION: University of Virginia.
CAREER HIGHLIGHTS: Directed the series "Have Gun, Will Travel," "Gunsmoke," and "Rawhide." His major motion pictures include *Shenandoah, The Way West, Fool's Parade, McClintock,* and *The Wild Geese.* Directed the TV mini-series *The Blue and the Gray.*
ACHIEVEMENTS & AWARDS: N.A.
PERSONAL: Son of well-known actor Victor McLaglen.

McLAIN, CHUCK
V.P., Warner Bros. TV

4000 Warner Blvd., Burbank, CA 91522
b. December 8, 1942. Lancaster, NH.

EDUCATION: American Academy of Arts.
CAREER HIGHLIGHTS: Actor with Broadway Cafe La Mama Theater Co. ('68); Story Editor, ICM Talent Agency ('71); Dir. of Specials, CBS TV, New York ('72–'75); V.P., Movies and Mini-series, Lorimar Productions: *Studs Lonigan, A Man Called Intrepid, Young Love, First Love, Some Kind of Miracle, Mary and Joseph,* and *Long Journey Back* ('76); V.P., TV movies and mini-series, Warner Bros., involved with *The Letter* ('82), *In Our Hands, Murder Is Easy, A Few Days in Weasel Creek,* and *A Family of Children.*
ACHIEVEMENTS & AWARDS: N.A.
PERSONAL: N.A.

McLAUGHLIN, BILL
Correspondent, CBS, News, Washington, DC

c/o CBS, 2020 M St., N.W., Washington, D.C. 20036
b. New York, NY.

EDUCATION: Fordham University.
CAREER HIGHLIGHTS: Joined CBS News as a Reporter ('66); named Correspondent, CBS News Bonn Bureau ('68); assigned to CBS News Bureaus in Saigon ('69), Beirut ('71), and Paris ('74–'77); UN Correspondent, NBC

News ('80–'83); Correspondent, CBS News, covering the State Dept. ('83).
ACHIEVEMENTS & AWARDS: N.A.
PERSONAL: N.A.

McLAUGHLIN, EMILY
Actress

c/o "General Hospital," ABC, 2040 Ave. of the Stars, Los Angeles, CA 90067
b. December 1, 1928. White Plains, NY.

EDUCATION: Middlebury College, B.A.
CAREER HIGHLIGHTS: Broadway appearances in *The Frogs of Spring* and *The Lovers.* TV guest appearances on "Studio One," "Kraft Theater," "The Twilight Zone," and "The Eleventh Hour." Soap opera star of "General Hospital."
ACHIEVEMENTS & AWARDS: N.A.
PERSONAL: Son, Robert. Resides in Van Nuys, CA.

MacLEOD, GAVIN
Actor

c/o "The Love Boat," ABC, 2040 Ave. of the
  Stars, Los Angeles, CA 90067
b. February 28. Mount Kisco, NY.

EDUCATION: Ithaca College, B.F.A.
CAREER HIGHLIGHTS: Broadway appearances in
  A Hatful of Rain and *Captains and Kings.* Mo-
  tion pictures include *I Want to Live, Compul-
  sion, The Sand Pebbles,* and *Operation Petticoat.*
  TV films include *The Intruders, Only With Mar-
  ried Men, Murder Can Hurt You,* and *Scruples.*
  Series regular on "The Mary Tyler Moore
  Show" and "The Love Boat."
ACHIEVEMENTS & AWARDS: N.A.
PERSONAL: Four children, Keith, David, Julie,
  and Meghan.

McMAHON, ED
Announcer, NBC, "The Tonight Show
  Starring Johnny Carson"

c/o NBC, 3000 W. Alameda Ave., Burbank,
  CA 91523
b. March 6, 1923. Detroit, MI.

EDUCATION: Catholic University of America,
  B.A.
CAREER HIGHLIGHTS: Johnny Carson's right-
  hand man is the best audience any talk show
  host could have. His motion pictures include
  Fun With Dick and Jane and *The Incident.* TV
  movies include *The Great American Traffic Jam*
  and *The Star Maker.* Announcer on "The Tonight Show" and host of "Star Search."
ACHIEVEMENTS & AWARDS: Man of the Year humanitarian award from the Myasthenia
  Gravis Foundation ('81).
PERSONAL: N.A.

McMAHON, JENNA
Prod./Writer

c/o George Shapiro, 41 El Camino, Beverly
  Hills, CA 90212
b. May 24, 1937. Kansas City, MO.

EDUCATION: Attended school in Missouri.
CAREER HIGHLIGHTS: Another actress whose
  career as a performer wasn't enough to satisfy
  her creative abilities, she turned to writing for
  such quality shows as "The Mary Tyler Moore
  Show" and then became one of Carol
  Burnett's staff of capable comedy writers. The
  natural progression led to her producing, as
  well as writing and directing. Writer, "The
  Mary Tyler Moore Show," "The Bob Newhart
  Show," "Maude" ('71–'72); Writer, "The
  Carol Burnett Show" ('73–'77); Co-Prod./
  Writer, "Soap" ('81); Prod./Writer/Dir.
  "Mama's Family" ('83).
ACHIEVEMENTS & AWARDS: Emmy awards for
  "The Carol Burnett Show" ('73–'74, '74–'75,
  '77–'78).
PERSONAL: N.A.

McMAHON, JOHN J.
Pres., Carson Productions

c/o NBC, 3000 Alameda Ave., Burbank, CA
  91523
b. Chicago, IL.

EDUCATION: Northwestern University, B.A.,
  English.
CAREER HIGHLIGHTS: Joined KABC in Los An-
  geles in production, promoted to General
  Mgr. of KABC and an ABC Network V.P.

('58); joined NBC as V.P., Programs, West Coast ('72); Sr. V.P., Programs and Talent, West Coast ('78); Pres., Raystar TV ('79); Pres., Carson Productions ('80).

ACHIEVEMENTS & AWARDS: N.A.

PERSONAL: Resides in Bel Air with wife, Barbara, and three children, Katy, Megan, and John Jr.

McMANUS, SEAN
V.P., Programming, NBC, Sports

c/o NBC, 30 Rockefeller Plaza, New York, NY 10020

b. February 16, 1955. New York, NY.

EDUCATION: Duke University, B.A., English and History.

CAREER HIGHLIGHTS: Prod. Asst., ABC Sports ('77); Assoc. Prod., NBC Sports ('79); Mgr. of Program Administration, NBC Sports ('80); Dir. of Program Development and Asst. to the Exec. Prod. ('81); V.P. of Program Planning and Development, NBC Sports ('82). He is the youngest V.P. in network sports TV history.

ACHIEVEMENTS & AWARDS:

PERSONAL: Resides in New York City.

McMILLON, DORIS
Correspondent, WABC-TV, "Eyewitness News"

c/o WABC-TV, 7 Lincoln Sq., New York, NY 10023

b. N.A.

EDUCATION: Wayne State University, B.A.

CAREER HIGHLIGHTS: Anchor, NBC Radio ('75); WNEW-TV Reporter/Host, "Sunday Night Extra" and "Big Apple Minutes" ('76); Correspondent, WABC-TV Eyewitness Reports ('80).

ACHIEVEMENTS & AWARDS: N.A.

PERSONAL: Resides in Long Island, NY.

McNAMARA, ROBERT
Correspondent, CBS, News

c/o CBS, 524 W. 57th St., New York, NY 10019

b. Lancaster, WI.

EDUCATION: Columbia College.

CAREER HIGHLIGHTS: Copy Boy, WBBM-TV, Chicago ('65); Reporter/Anchor, KCRG-TV, Cedar Rapids, IA ('67); Reporter/Anchor, WCCO-TV, Minneapolis ('68); Reporter, CBS News, New York ('74); Correspondent, CBS News, Bonn ('75); Correspondent, CBS News, London ('78); Correspondent, CBS News, New York ('79).

ACHIEVEMENTS & AWARDS: N.A.

PERSONAL: Wife, Jane; son, Michael.

MacNEIL, ROBERT
Exec. Editor/Co-Anchor, WNET/13, New York, "The MacNeil/Lehrer Report"

c/o Gene Nichols & Assoc., 1650 Broadway, New York, NY 10019

b. 1932. Montreal, Canada.

EDUCATION: Carleton University, B.A.

CAREER HIGHLIGHTS: Along with his Co-Interviewer, Jim Lehrer, MacNeil brings a low-key, cerebral approach to "The MacNeil/Lehrer Report," which dared to break the pattern of episodic news shows by pursuing one topic in depth on each show. Rewrite Man, Reuters News Agency, London; NBC News Correspondent overseas; NBC White House Correspondent; Co-Anchor, "Scherer-MacNeil Report," NBC ('65); BBC Commentator and Current Affairs Programs Moderator ('67); wrote and narrated documentaries for Public Broadcasting Laboratory; Host,

Narrator, and Interviewer, for PBS series "The MacNeil/Lehrer Report," WNET/13.

ACHIEVEMENTS & AWARDS: Peabody award; Dupont-Columbia University award. Author of several books, including *The Right Place at the Right Time.*

PERSONAL: N.A.

McNEILL, DONALD
Correspondent, CBS, News, Moscow

c/o American Embassy (M), Helsinki, Finland
b. November 10, 1934. St. John's, Newfoundland.

EDUCATION: Memorial University of Newfoundland, Nova Scotia Technical College, B.Sc., Engineering; University of Oxford, M.A., Politics, Philosophy, and Economics.

CAREER HIGHLIGHTS: Reporter, *Scottish Daily Express* ('60); Copy Editor, *Toronto Globe and Mail* ('61); Prod. and Correspondent, CBC ('67); Chief Political Correspondent, CBC, Ottawa ('74); Anchor and Chief Natl. Correspondent, CBC ('76); Correspondent, CBS News, Moscow ('81).

ACHIEVEMENTS & AWARDS: Rhodes scholar.

PERSONAL: N.A.

MacPHAIL, WILLIAM C.
V.P., Cable News Network, Sports

c/o Cable News Network, 1050 Techwood Dr., N.W., Atlanta, GA 30318
b. March 26, 1920. Columbus, OH.

EDUCATION: Swarthmore College, B.A.

CAREER HIGHLIGHTS: V.P. in Charge of Sports, CBS ('55); V.P., Robert Wold Co. ('75); V.P., Cable News Network, Sports ('79).

ACHIEVEMENTS & AWARDS: N.A.

PERSONAL: Brother of Lee MacPhail, president of baseball's American League.

McWETHY, JOHN F.
Chief Pentagon Correspondent, ABC, News

c/o ABC, 1717 DeSales St., N.W., Washington, DC 20036
b. February 28, 1947.

EDUCATION: DePauw University; Columbia University School of Journalism.

CAREER HIGHLIGHTS: Writer, *Congressional Quarterly*, Washington, DC ('70); Science and Technology Editor, *U.S. News and World Report* ('73); Chief White House Correspondent, *U.S. News and World Report* ('77); Correspondent, ABC News, Washington, DC ('79); Chief Pentagon Correspondent, ABC News, Washington, DC ('81).

ACHIEVEMENTS & AWARDS: Author, *Power of the Pentagon.*

PERSONAL: Wife, Laurie.

MADDEN, JERRY (Malcolm E. Madden)
Prod.

c/o Lew Sherrell, 7060 Hollywood Blvd., #610, Hollywood, CA 90028
b. Los Angeles, CA.

EDUCATION: Loyola University; Arizona State University.

CAREER HIGHLIGHTS: Unit Mgr./Assoc. Prod., "All Star Review," "Colgate Comedy Hour," "Hallmark Hall of Fame" ('50); Mgr., Prod. Services, NBC, Los Angeles ('55); Dir., Telesales and Unit Mgrs., NBC, New York ('60); Dir., Special News Projects, NBC, New York ('64); Dir., NBC European Operations ('68); V.P. in Charge, Disney on Parade ('70); Co-Producer, *You Can't Take It With You* ('80); Prod., "Alice" ('75–present).

ACHIEVEMENTS & AWARDS: Golden Globe award as Co-Prod. "Alice" ('80).

PERSONAL: Wife, Patricia; daughters, Claudia, Kathleen, and Christine.

MADDEN, JOHN
Broadcaster, Sports Commentary, CBS, Sports

c/o CBS, 7800 Beverly Blvd., Los Angeles, CA 90036
b. April 10, 1936. Austin, MN.

EDUCATION: California Polytechnic College at San Luis Obispo, B.S. ('59) and M.A. ('61).

CAREER HIGHLIGHTS: One of the most colorful and articulate sports broadcasters in the business, Madden joined CBS Sports after retiring as head coach of the Super Bowl champion Oakland Raiders ('77). His effervescent personality and insight into football have made him one of the most popular football announcers on TV.

ACHIEVEMENTS & AWARDS: Golden mike award for sports broadcasters, Touchdown Club of America ('81).

PERSONAL: Resides in Pleasanton, CA, with wife, Virginia; sons, Mike and Joe.

MADIGAN, THOMAS F.
V.P., WQED-TV, Natl. Program Development

c/o National Program Development, WQED Pittsburgh, 509 Madison Ave., New York, NY 10022
b. May 4.

EDUCATION: Trinity College.

CAREER HIGHLIGHTS: Dir. of Network TV Programming, NBC ('52); Dir. of Programming and Program Development, Ted Bates Development ('61); V.P., Intl. TV Production, Seven Arts/Warner Bros. ('66); developed and produced a closed-circuit TV Network and financial analysis series for Roger Williams Securities and Investments, Inc. ('72); Dir. of Corporate Underwriting, WNET-TV, New York ('74); V.P., Natl. Program Development, WQED/Pittsburgh based in New York ('77).

ACHIEVEMENTS & AWARDS: N.A.

PERSONAL: Resides in New York City.

MAHONEY, SHEILA
V.P. and Dir., Franchising, Cablevision Systems Corp.

c/o Cablevision Systems Corp., 1 Media Crossways, Woodbury, NY 11797
b. Yonkers, NY.

EDUCATION: Newton College; Fordham Law School.

CAREER HIGHLIGHTS: Asst. Corp. Counsel, City of New York ('67); Exec. Dir., Cable TV Information Center ('73); V.P. and Dir., Franchising, Cablevision Systems Corp. ('80).

ACHIEVEMENTS & AWARDS: Co-Author, *Keeping PACE With the New Television*.

PERSONAL: Resides in New York City.

MAIER, STEVEN PERRY
V.P., Talent and Program Acquisitions, Business Affairs, West Coast, ABC, Entertainment

c/o ABC, 4151 Prospect Ave., Los Angeles, CA 90027
b. April 9, 1947. Oak Ridge, TN.

EDUCATION: Beloit College; California Western University School of Law.

CAREER HIGHLIGHTS: Sr. Program and Talent Contract Attorney, NBC ('78); promoted to Sr. Program and Talent Negotiator ('79); V.P., Business Affairs, MGM TV ('81); V.P., Business Affairs, MGM-UA Entertainment ('82); V.P., Talent and Program Acquisitions, Business Affairs, West Coast ('83).

ACHIEVEMENTS & AWARDS: N.A.

PERSONAL: Resides in Hollywood with wife, Janet.

MAJORS, LEE
Actor

c/o "The Fall Guy," ABC, 2040 Ave. of the Stars, Los Angeles, CA 90067
b. April 23, 1940. Wyandotte, MI.

EDUCATION: Eastern Kentucky State College.

CAREER HIGHLIGHTS: From riding the range on "The Big Valley" to leaping in the air as the "Six Million Dollar Man" to falling out of buildings on "The Fall Guy," Majors is the perfect athlete/star for TV; not many stars can boast three hit series to their credit. Motion pictures include *Will Penny, The Liberation of L.B. Jones,* and *Steel.* Movies for TV include *The Ballad of Andy Crocker, Weekend of Terror, The Francis Gary Powers Story,* and *Star Flight One.* Series star of "The Big Valley," "The Man From Shiloh," "Owen Marshall, Counselor at Law," "Six Million Dollar Man," and "The Fall Guy."

ACHIEVEMENTS & AWARDS: N.A.

PERSONAL: N.A.

MALARA, ANTHONY C.
Pres., CBS, CBS TV Network

c/o CBS, 51 W. 52d St., New York, NY 10019
b. September 20.

EDUCATION: Syracuse University; CBS School of Management.

CAREER HIGHLIGHTS: Mgr. Broadcasting, WWNY-TV, Watertown, NY; V.P., Station Services, CBS TV Network Affiliate Relations ('78); V.P., Affiliate Relations ('80); promoted to V.P.. and General Mgr., CBS TV Network; Pres., CBS TV Network.

ACHIEVEMENTS & AWARDS: Past Pres., New York State Broadcasters Assn.; former Member, CBS TV Network Affiliate Advisory Board; Exec. Committee of the CBS Radio Network Affiliates Assn.

PERSONAL: N.A.

MALLARDI, MICHAEL P.
Exec. V.P. and Chief Financial Officer, ABC, Inc.

10 Charnwood Dr., Suffern, NY 10901
b. March 17, 1934. New York, NY.

EDUCATION: University of Notre Dame., B.A., Philosophy.

CAREER HIGHLIGHTS: Joined ABC, Inc., as Systems Specialist ('56); Cost Control Adm. ('57); Asst. Controller, West Coast ('59). Spent 10 years outside the network, beginning as Location Auditor, MGM ('61); Radio Press Intl. Business Mgr. ('61); Treasurer, Strauss Broadcasting Group ('65). V.P. and General Mgr., Strauss ('68); returned to ABC as V.P., Corporate Planning ('71); Pres., ABC Record and Tape Sales Corp. ('74); appointed V.P. and Chief Financial Officer, ABC, Inc. ('76); Exec V.P. and Chief Financial Officer ('83).

ACHIEVEMENTS & AWARDS: Member, Chemical Advisory Board ('80); Planning Board, Good Samaritan Hospital, Suffern, NY ('81). Trustee, Pierpont Fund ('82).

PERSONAL: Resides in Suffern, NY, with wife, Sylvia; daughters, Karen and Stephanie.

MANBY, C. ROBERT
Pres., RKO-Nederlander, RKO Pictures

c/o RKO-Nederlander, 1440 Broadway, New York, NY 10018
b. February 24, 1920.

EDUCATION: Hillsdale College, B.A. ('43); Harvard Business School, M.B.A. ('53).

CAREER HIGHLIGHTS: Began career at WJW-AM, Cleveland ('44); General Mgr., WONS-AM, Hartford, CT ('46); Program Exec., the Yankee Network, Boston ('49); Exec., General Teleradio ('53); V.P. RKO-General ('56); Pres., Show Corp. of America ('58–'75); Sr. V.P., Corporate Development, RKO-General ('76); added responsibility of Pres., RKO Pictures, Pres., Performance Properties ('78). One of the four managing partners of RKO-Nederlander Productions.

ACHIEVEMENTS & AWARDS: N.A.

PERSONAL: N.A.

MANDALA, MARK
Pres., ABC, Owned TV Stations

c/o ABC, 1330 Ave. of the Americas, New York, NY 10020
b. May 1. Los Angeles, CA.

EDUCATION: University of Southern California ('59).

CAREER HIGHLIGHTS: Began at ABC at its Los Angeles station, KABC-TV, in the Research and Promotion Depts. ('62); climbed the management ladder with positions in Spot Sales for ABC in San Francisco, Chicago, and New York. Took over as Pres., ABC Owned TV Stations after being General Sales Mgr., at ABC's KGO-TV, San Francisco.

ACHIEVEMENTS & AWARDS: N.A.

PERSONAL: Wife, Joan; three sons.

MANINGS, ALAN
Prod., CBS

c/o CBS, 7800 Beverly Blvd., Los Angeles, CA 90036
b. N.A.

EDUCATION: N.A.

CAREER HIGHLIGHTS: Comedy Writer; Exec. Prod., "Good Times" series, CBS; Co-Creator, "One Day at a Time," CBS.

ACHIEVEMENTS & AWARDS: N.A.

PERSONAL: N.A.

MANN, ABBY
Prod./Writer

c/o Writers Guild, 8955 Beverly Blvd., Los
Angeles, CA 90048
b. 1927. Philadelphia, PA.

EDUCATION: Temple University, New York
University.
CAREER HIGHLIGHTS: This noted TV playwright
began with "Studio One," "Alcoa Goodyear
Theater," "Robert Montgomery Theater" in
the early fifties. He wrote *Judgment at Nur-
emberg* for "Playhouse 90" ('58) and *A Child Is
Waiting*. Wrote *The Marcus-Nelson Murders*,
which introduced Kojak ('73). Prod. "Medical
Story" for NBC ('75), Writer/Prod., *Martin Lu-
ther King* ('78) and "Skag" ('80). Motion pic-
ture scripts include *Judgment at Nuremberg*
('61) *A Child Is Waiting* ('63); *Ship of Fools* ('65);
The Detectives ('68) and *Report to the Commis-
sioner* ('75).
ACHIEVEMENTS & AWARDS: Academy Award for
Judgment at Nuremberg ('61); Emmy for *The
Marcus-Nelson Murders* ('72).
PERSONAL: Resides in Los Angeles.

MANN, DELBERT
Dir.

c/o Caroline Productions, 401 S. Burnside
Ave., Los Angeles, CA 90036
b. January 30, 1920. Lawrence, KS.

EDUCATION: Vanderbilt University, M.F.A.;
Yale Drama School.
CAREER HIGHLIGHTS: NBC Staff Director for
"Lights Out," "Philco-Goodyear Playhouse,"
and "Producer's Showcase"; also, Dir. of
"Playhouse 90," "Ford Star Jubilee," and the
TV versions of *Marty, Our Town*, and *The Pet-
rified Forest*. Directed the films *Marty* ('54); *The
Bachelor Party* ('56); *Desire Under the Elms* ('57);
Separate Tables ('58); *Middle of the Night* ('59);
Lover Come Back ('61); *That Touch of Mink* ('62);
Dear Heart ('63); *Kidnapped* ('72). TV movies
include *Heidi* ('68); *David Copperfield* ('72); *Jane
Eyre* ('71); *A Girl Named Sooner* ('75); *Breaking
Up* ('78); *All Quiet on the Western Front* ('79);
Member of the Wedding ('82) and *Playing for
Time* ('80).
ACHIEVEMENTS & AWARDS: Directors Guild
award and Academy Award for *Marty*. Mem-
ber, Directors Guild, Producers Guild.

PERSONAL: Wife, Ann Caroline; three children,
David, Frederick, and Steven. Resides in Beverly Hills, CA.

MANNING, GORDON
V.P., NBC, News, News Programs

c/o NBC, 30 Rockefeller Plaza, New York, NY
10020
b. May 28. New Haven, CT.

EDUCATION: Boston University.
CAREER HIGHLIGHTS: Managing Editor, *Colliers*
magazine ('50); Editor, *Newsweek* ('56); V.P.
and Dir. of News, CBS ('64); Sr. V.P., CBS
('71); Exec. Prod., Special Broadcasts ('75);
Exec. Prod., NBC News political coverage
('76); V.P., News Planning ('78); V.P., Political Coverage and Special Programming ('79);
V.P., NBC News ('82).
ACHIEVEMENTS & AWARDS: Dupont-Columbia
University award; Overseas Press Club
award.
PERSONAL: N.A.

MANULIS, MARTIN
Prod., M. Manulis Productions

c/o M. Manulis Productions, P.O. Box 813,
Beverly Hills, CA 90250
b. May 30, 1915. New York, NY.

EDUCATION: Columbia University, B.A. ('35).
CAREER HIGHLIGHTS: During the fifties and six-
ties, he compiled one of the most distin-
guished records as a producer of quality dra-
mas. Managing Dir., Bahamas Playhouse
('51); Prod., CBS "Playhouse 90" ('52); Film
Prod., *Days of Wine and Roses* ('62); Prod.,
James at 15 ('79).
ACHIEVEMENTS & AWARDS: Emmy for "Play-
house 90" ('56).
PERSONAL: Wife, Katherine; three children.
Resides in Beverly Hills, CA.

MAPES, PIERSON G.
Pres., NBC, TV

c/o NBC, 30 Rockefeller Plaza, New York, NY 10020
b. September 29, 1937. New York, NY.

EDUCATION: Norwich University, B.S., Business Administration ('59).
CAREER HIGHLIGHTS: Asst. Sales Service Rep., NBC ('63); Station Information Analyst, NBC ('64); Sales Service Rep., NBC ('65); Sr. Sales Service Rep., NBC ('66); Station Sales Rep., NBC ('67); Station Relations Regional Mgr., NBC ('68); Acct. Exec., Blair TV ('72); Sales Mgr., Blair TV ('77); V.P., Blair TV ('78); V.P., Network Planning, NBC TV ('78); V.P., Affiliate Relations, NBC TV ('79); Pres., NBC TV ('82).
ACHIEVEMENTS & AWARDS: N.A.
PERSONAL: Resides in Sloatsburg, NY, with wife, Patricia.

MARAZZI, JOSEPH
Dir., Affiliate Marketing and Planning, NBC

c/o NBC, 30 Rockefeller Plaza, New York, NY 10020
b. August 9. Springfield, MA.

EDUCATION: Seton Hall University, B.A., Communications, and M.B.A.
CAREER HIGHLIGHTS: Video Tape Operator, Operations and Technical Services, NBC, New York ('73); Asst. Clearance Rep., Sales Service Dept., NBC ('75); Sales Services Rep., NBC ('77); Mgr., Station Clearance Operations ('78); Administrator, Affiliate Planning, NBC ('79); Regional Dir., Affiliate Relations Dept., NBC ('81); Dir., Affiliate Marketing and Planning, NBC, New York ('83).
ACHIEVEMENTS & AWARDS: N.A.
PERSONAL: Resides in Wayne, NJ, with wife, Louise.

MARCH, ALEX
Prod./Dir.

c/o Directors Guild, 7950 Sunset Blvd., Los Angeles, CA 90046
b. 1920. Brooklyn, NY.

EDUCATION: N.A.
CAREER HIGHLIGHTS: Dir. of pilot/TV movies, *Madigan*, *McMillan and Wife*, and *Moving Target*. Episodic TV credits include Supervising Prod./Dir., "Nurse"; and Dir., "Cassie and Company," "Trapper John, M.D.," "Barney Miller," "House Calls," "Archie Bunker's Place," "The Paper Chase," "Police Story," "Kojak," "The Odd Couple," "Rossetti and Ryan," "Turnabout," "Baretta," "Hec Ramsey," "The Monroes," "Jericho," "Shane," "Cowboy in Africa," "The Road West," "Convoy," "Madigan," "The Fugitive," "The Defenders," "NYPD," "The Untouchables," "The Nurses," "East Side, West Side," "Ben Casey," "Dr. Kildare," and "The Long Hot Summer."
ACHIEVEMENTS & AWARDS: N.A.
PERSONAL: N.A.

MARCHIANO, SAL
Sportscaster, ESPN

c/o ESPN, ESPN Plaza, Bristol, CT 06010
b. March 3, 1941. Brooklyn, NY.

EDUCATION: Fordham University, B.S.S., Communication Arts ('63).
CAREER HIGHLIGHTS: WCBS-TV ('66); WABC-TV and ABC Sports and Radio ('71); moved back to WCBS-TV ('79); joined ESPN ('80).
ACHIEVEMENTS & AWARDS: New York State Broadcasters award for "Tom Seaver Traded by Mets" ('77); New York Emmy for best 11 P.M. newscast ('80).
PERSONAL: Wife, Bernadette; daughter, Susan.

MARCUS, ANN
Writer, "Days of Our Lives"

c/o NBC, 3000 W. Alameda Ave., Los Angeles, CA 91523
b. N.A.

EDUCATION: N.A.
CAREER HIGHLIGHTS: Co-Creator, "Mary Hartman, Mary Hartman"; Co-Creator, "All That Glitters"; Writer, "Days of Our Lives."
ACHIEVEMENTS & AWARDS: N.A.
PERSONAL: N.A.

MARDEN, MICHAEL
Dir., CBS TV Network, Motion Pictures for TV and Mini-Series

c/o CBS, 7800 Beverly Blvd., Los Angeles, CA 90036
b. September 27.

EDUCATION: Princeton University ('55).
CAREER HIGHLIGHTS: Joined CBS, New York ('57); TV Program Exec., Benton & Bowles Advertising Agency; General Program Exec., CBS, New York ('66); Dir., Feature Films, "The CBS Late Movies" ('72); Dir., Motion Pictures for TV and Mini-Series, CBS, Hollywood ('76).
ACHIEVEMENTS & AWARDS: N.A.
PERSONAL: Resides in Los Angeles.

MARGULIES, LEE
Staff Writer, *Los Angeles Times*

c/o *Los Angeles Times,* Times Mirror Square, Los Angeles, CA 90053
b. September 12, 1947. Burbank, CA.

EDUCATION: University of California at Santa Barbara, B.A., Political Science ('69).
CAREER HIGHLIGHTS: General Assignment Writer and Editor, AP, Los Angeles ('70); Staff Writer specializing in covering TV trends and programming, *Los Angeles Times* ('76). Also, Sr. editor of *Emmy* magazine.
ACHIEVEMENTS & AWARDS: N.A.
PERSONAL: Wife, Linda; three children.

MARGULIES, STAN
Exec. Prod.

4000 Warner Blvd., Burbank, CA 91522
b. December 14, 1920. New York, NY.

EDUCATION: New York University.
CAREER HIGHLIGHTS: Feature Writer/Asst. Sunday Editor for *Salt Lake Tribune;* V.P. in Charge of Advertising and Publicity, Bryna Productions, an independent film company owned by Kirk Douglas. Prod., *Those Magnificent Men in Their Flying Machines* and *Moviola: The Scarlett O'Hara Wars* for TV; Exec. Prod., *The Thorn Birds* TV mini-series. Other TV productions include *The Morning After, Murder Is Easy,* and *Collision Courses.*

ACHIEVEMENTS & AWARDS: Emmy for *Roots.*
PERSONAL: Married to the former Lillian Parton; two sons and a daughter. Resides in Encino, CA.

MARINARO, ED
Actor

c/o "Hill Street Blues," NBC, 3000 W. Alameda Ave., Burbank, CA 91523

EDUCATION: Cornell University.
CAREER HIGHLIGHTS: A star running back at Cornell and runner-up for the Heisman trophy, Marinaro played pro football with the Minnesota Vikings for six years and briefly with the New York Jets and Seattle Seahawks. Turned to acting and had recurring roles in "Eischied," "Laverne and Shirley," and, currently, "Hill Street Blues." Also co-starred in the TV movie *Born Beautiful* on NBC ('82).
ACHIEVEMENTS & AWARDS: N.A.
PERSONAL: Single, resides in Beverly Hills, CA.

MARKELL, ROBERT
V.P., Mini-Series, CBS, Entertainment

c/o CBS, 6121 Sunset Blvd., Los Angeles, CA 90028
b. April 12, 1924.

EDUCATION: Northeastern University, B.S.
CAREER HIGHLIGHTS: Set Designer for CBS; Prod., "The Defenders," "NYPD" and "Bicentennial Minutes"; Exec. Prod., Dramatic Programs, CBS Entertainment, New York; V.P., Creative Services, CBS, New York ('79); V.P., Mini-Series, CBS Entertainment, Los Angeles ('81).
ACHIEVEMENTS & AWARDS: Won an Emmy for set design; three other Emmy awards for "The Defenders" and "Bicentennial Minutes."
PERSONAL: N.A.

MARKS, KENNETH
Dir., Hearst/ABC, Marketing

c/o Hearst/ABC, 555 Fifth Ave., New York, NY 10017
b. August 6, 1940. Reading, PA.

EDUCATION: Wharton School of the University of Pennsylvania, B.S., Economics ('61)
CAREER HIGHLIGHTS: Admin. Asst., CBS TV Network ('63); Advertising Sales Supervisor, *Time* magazine ('66); Advertising Mgr., *New York* magazine ('74); Advertising Dir., *N.Y. Post* ('76); V.P., Sales, *Cue/New York* magazine ('79); Assoc. Publisher, American Express Publishing Co. ('81).
ACHIEVEMENTS & AWARDS: Columnist, Media Industry Newsletter ('81); Member, Board of Dirs., Advertising Club of New York ('82).
PERSONAL: Resides in Connecticut with wife, Paula; daughter, Elizabeth Ann.

MARLAND, DOUGLAS
Writer/Dir.

c/o ABC, 1330 Ave. of the Americas, New York, NY 10019
b. N.A.

EDUCATION: American Academy of Dramatic Arts.
CAREER HIGHLIGHTS: Theatrical credits include production of *The Sound of Music, Mame, Champagne Complex, Born Yesterday, Cabaret, George M,* and *Mr. Roberts.* Film credits include *The Great Impostor, The Pleasure of His Company,* and *Toward the Light.* Writer for "Another World" and "Guiding Light." Co-Creator of "Loving," ABC soap opera, with Agnes Nixon.
ACHIEVEMENTS & AWARDS: Emmy for outstanding writing for a drama series, for "Another World" ('74).
PERSONAL: N.A.

MARLOW, JESS
Anchor, KNXT-TV, News

c/o KNXT-TV, 6121 Sunset Blvd., Los Angeles, CA 90028
b. N.A.

EDUCATION: University of Illinois.
CAREER HIGHLIGHTS: Reporter, WHBF-TV, Rock Island, IL ('59); Anchor/News Dir., KNTV-TV, San Jose, CA ('61); Anchor, KNBC-TV, Los Angeles ('66); Anchor, KNXT-TV, Los Angeles ('80).
ACHIEVEMENTS & AWARDS: Golden mike award from the Radio and TV News Assn. of Southern California ('72, '81); Los Angeles Emmy ('78).
PERSONAL: Resides in Pasadena, CA, with his wife, Phyllis.

MARMOR, HELEN
Exec. Prod., NBC, Religious Programs

c/o NBC, 30 Rockefeller Plaza, New York, NY 10020
b. March 18, 1922. Jersey City, NJ.

EDUCATION: N.A.
CAREER HIGHLIGHTS: Started out as reporter with *Bergen Record* ('41); became Editor/Writer

with AP, New York; joined NBC News ('55); moved through ranks from Newswriter/Prod. to Prod., "Today"; Prod. of instant specials, with responsibilities for all NBC News Watergate and Vietnam instant specials during sixties and seventies and civil rights movement specials; currently Exec. Prod. Religious Programs.

ACHIEVEMENTS & AWARDS: Overseas Press Club award for best TV interpretation of foreign affairs for "Peace Begins" ('73); American Bar Assn. silver gavel for Watergate coverage ('74); Emmy for the news documentary "Pope John Paul II in Poland" ('79); Chicago Film Festival certificate of merit for "A Talent for Life" ('80); Southern California Motion Picture Council golden halo award for excellence in religious programming ('82). Member, MENSA ('72–'82).

PERSONAL: N.A.

MARSH, EARLE F.
V.P., Research, Showtime Entertainment

c/o Showtime, 1633 Broadway, New York, NY 10019
b. May 17, 1945. Cleveland, OH.

EDUCATION: Northwestern University, B.S., Business Administration.

CAREER HIGHLIGHTS: Administrator of Business Development, NBC Radio Division, New York ('70); Asst. Dir. of Research, CBS TV Stations Division, New York ('70); Mgr., Broadcast Ratings, NBC, New York ('74); Mgr., Prime Time Research, New York ('76); Mgr. of Special Projects, CBS TV, New York ('78); V.P., Research, Showtime Entertainment, New York ('81).

ACHIEVEMENTS & AWARDS: Co-Author, *Complete Directory to Prime Time Network TV Shows,* two editions ('79, '81); American Book award, general reference category ('80).

PERSONAL: Single, resides in Yonkers, NY.

MARSH, JEAN
Actress

c/o "Nine to Five," ABC, 1330 Ave. of the Americas, New York, NY 10019
b. July 1. London, England.

EDUCATION: N.A.

CAREER HIGHLIGHTS: New York stage appearances in *Much Ado About Nothing* and *Whose Life Is It Anyway?* Motion pictures include *Cleopatra* and *Frenzy.* Co-Creator/Star of the British series "Upstairs, Downstairs." Regular performer on "Nine to Five."

ACHIEVEMENTS & AWARDS: N.A.

PERSONAL: Resides in Manhattan.

MARSHALL, GARRY KENT
Exec. Prod./Writer

c/o Paramount Studios, 5451 Marathon, Los Angeles, CA 90038
b. November 13, 1934. New York, NY.

EDUCATION: Northwestern University, B.A., Journalism.

CAREER HIGHLIGHTS: A prolific hit-maker with a finger on the pulse of the viewing public. Entered TV as a Writer for Jack Paar's "Tonight Show" ('60) and later for "The Joey Bishop Show." After teaming with Jerry Belson, he wrote episodes for "The Danny Thomas Show" and "The Dick Van Dyke Show" as well as for "I Spy" and "Bob Hope Presents the Chrysler Theater." They became well-known for adapting films such as *Barefoot in the Park* and *The Odd Couple* for TV series. Among the comedy shows Marshall has created or produced, are "The Little People," "Happy Days" "Blansky's Beauties," "Laverne and Shirley," "Mork and Mindy," and "Angie." He co-wrote the films *How Sweet It Is* and *The Grasshopper,* and directed the recent spoof *Young Doctors in Love.* Prod. of ABC sitcom "Herndon and Me" ('83–'84).

ACHIEVEMENTS & AWARDS: Emmy for "The Dick Van Dyke Show."

PERSONAL: Wife, Barbara; three children.

MARSHALL, JOHN
General Assignment Reporter, KNBC, "News 4 LA"

c/o KNBC, 3000 W. Alameda Ave., Burbank, CA 91523
b. July 16, 1942.

EDUCATION: University of Colorado.

CAREER HIGHLIGHTS: Newsman with radio station KBOL in Boulder, CO.; on News Staff at KIMN, Denver; Armed Forces TV Service of the U.S. Air Force; Acct. Representative, ABC TV; Reporter for KNBC, KTTV, KTLA-TV.

ACHIEVEMENTS & AWARDS: Emmy ('79).

PERSONAL: Wife, Joan; daughter, Vanessa. Resides in North Hollywood, CA.

MARSHALL, PENNY
Actress

c/o Paramount TV, 5555 Melrose Ave., Los Angeles, CA 90038
b. October 15, 1944. New York, NY.

EDUCATION: University of New Mexico.

CAREER HIGHLIGHTS: This comedienne, part Nancy Walker and part Joan Davis, gained stardom after providing sterling support on a number of her brother Garry Marshall's shows. Her TV movies include *The Feminist and the Fuzz, Let's Switch,* and *More Than Friends.* Guest appearances on "The Odd Couple," "Mork and Mindy," "Happy Days," "Saturday Night Live," and "The Mary Tyler Moore Show." Series star of "Laverne and Shirley."

ACHIEVEMENTS & AWARDS: N.A.

PERSONAL: Daughter, Tracy. Resides in Los Angeles.

MARSHALL, PETER
Host, NBC, "Fantasy"

c/o NBC, 3000 W. Alameda Ave., Burbank, CA 91523
b. March 30. Huntington, WV.

EDUCATION: N.A.

CAREER HIGHLIGHTS: Worked as a Page for NBC, New York, and later worked as an actor on Broadway and in a few theatrical features. When his acting career fizzled, Marshall found his true calling as a game show host, particularly on "The Hollywood Squares," where he emceed more than 5,000 editions, feeding lines to the likes of Paul Lynde, Charlie Weaver, George Gobel, and countless other celebrities. Hosted his own syndicated variety show and has returned to daytime TV as host of NBC's "Fantasy."

ACHIEVEMENTS & AWARDS: Five Emmy awards for hosting "The Hollywood Squares."

PERSONAL: Resides in Encino, CA, with wife, Sally; daughters, Suzanne and Jaime; sons, Peter and David.

MARSHALL, TOM
Medical Reporter WDIV-TV

c/o WDIV-TV, 550 W. Lafayette St., Detroit, MI 48226
b. November 12, 1949. Kansas City, MO.

EDUCATION: North Park College.

CAREER HIGHLIGHTS: A registered Respiratory Therapist who spent nine years in medical community. Prod. KMBC-TV's "PM Magazine," Kansas City, MO; Co-Host, "PM Magazine," WTOL-TV, Toledo ('80–'82); Co-Host, "PM Magazine," WNEW; Medical Reporter, WDIV-TV Detroit ('83).

ACHIEVEMENTS & AWARDS: N.A.

PERSONAL: N.A.

MARTIN, ANDREA
Writer/Performer, NBC, "SCTV Network"

c/o SCTV, 110 Lombard St., Toronto, Ontario, Canada M5C-IM3
b. January 15. Portland, ME.

EDUCATION: The Sorbonne (France).
CAREER HIGHLIGHTS: One of the funniest women currently working on TV, Martin is a cult figure whose caricatures of everyone from Indira Gandhi to Liza Minnelli are triumphs of satire. Appeared in the feature films *Foxy Lady* and *Soup for One,* and the stage productions *Hard Sell* and *She Loves Me.* Writer/Performer, "SCTV Network," NBC.
ACHIEVEMENTS & AWARDS: Two Emmy awards for writing.
PERSONAL: Resides in Toronto, Ontario.

MARTIN, DAVID
Correspondent, CBS, News

c/o CBS, 2020 M St., N.W., Washington, DC 20036
b. Washington, DC.

EDUCATION: Yale University.
CAREER HIGHLIGHTS: Researcher, CBS News, New York ('69); Newswriter, AP Broadcast Wire ('71); Fellow, Washington Journalism Center ('73); Reporter, AP, Washington, DC ('73); Correspondent, *Newsweek,* Washington, DC ('77); Pentagon Correspondent, CBS News, Washington, DC ('83).
ACHIEVEMENTS & AWARDS: N.A.
PERSONAL: N.A.

MARTIN, JOHN
Correspondent, ABC, News

c/o ABC, 7 W. 66th St., New York, NY 10023
b. December 3, 1931. New York, NY.

EDUCATION: San Diego State College.
CAREER HIGHLIGHTS: Copy Editor/Reporter, *San Diego Union;* Copy Editor, Intl. Edition, *N.Y. Times,* Paris; Reporter, KCRA-TV, Sacramento, CA ('67); Correspondent, ABC News, New York ('75).
ACHIEVEMENTS & AWARDS: Natl. Headliner of the year award for excellence in journalism ('80); Natl. Society of Professional Engineers first place award ('82).
PERSONAL: N.A.

MARTIN, JOHN
V.P., Programming, and Asst. to the Pres., ABC, Sports

c/o ABC, 1330 Ave. of the Americas, New York, NY 10019
b. June 2, 1942.

EDUCATION: Duke University.
CAREER HIGHLIGHTS: Production Asst., ABC Sports ('69); Asst. Coordinating Prod., "ABC's Wide World of Sports" ('70); Program Administrator, "ABC's Wide World of Sports" ('71); V.P., Program Development and Asst. to the Pres., ABC Sports ('76); V.P., Programming, and Asst. to the Pres., ABC Sports ('78).
ACHIEVEMENTS & AWARDS: N.A.
PERSONAL: Resides in Sherman, CT.

MARTIN, KIEL
Actor

c/o "Hill Street Blues," NBC, 3000 W. Alameda Ave., Burbank, CA 91523
b. July 26. Pittsburgh, PA.

EDUCATION: Trinity University; University of Miami.
CAREER HIGHLIGHTS: Feature films include *Panic in Needle Park* and *The Lolly Madonna War*. TV movies include *Raid on Short Creek*. Regular on daytime's "Edge of Night." Regular on "Hill Street Blues."
ACHIEVEMENTS & AWARDS: N.A.
PERSONAL: Divorced; daughter, Jesse. Resides in Venice, CA.

MARTIN, QUINN
Prod., QM Productions

c/o ICPR, 9255 Sunset Blvd., 8th Floor, Los Angeles, CA 90069
b. May 22, 1927. Los Angeles, CA.

EDUCATION: University of California at Berkeley.
CAREER HIGHLIGHTS: Raised in the business, Martin became a highly successful independent producer of adventure shows, usually with police themes. QM Productions was known for production values and casting, such as Robert Stack in "The Untouchables," David Janssen in "The Fugitive," Efrem Zimbalist Jr. in "The FBI," William Conrad in "Cannon," and Karl Malden in "The Streets of San Francisco." Martin wrote for "Four Star Playhouse" ('52); "The Jane Wyman Show" ('55); and "Desilu Playhouse" ('58). Prod., "The Untouchables" for Desilu in ('59) and formed his own company ('63). Prod.,

"Banyon" ('72), "Barnaby Jones" ('73), "Bert D'Angelo/Superstar," "Cannon" ('71), "Caribe" ('75), "Dan August," "The FBI" ('65), "The Fugitive" ('63), "The Invaders," "Manhunter" ('74), "Most Wanted," "The New Breed," "The Streets of San Francisco" ('76), "Quinn Martin's Tales of the Unexpected" ('77), and "12 O'Clock High."
ACHIEVEMENTS & AWARDS: Member, Board of Dirs., Hollywood Park Race Track.
PERSONAL: Resides in Beverly Hills, CA. Married; three children.

MASIUS, JOHN W.
Writer/Prod. (Freelance)

14100 Sunset Blvd., Pacific Palisades, CA 90272
b. July 30, 1950. New York, NY.

EDUCATION: University of Pennsylvania, B.S., Economics ('72); University of California at Los Angeles, M.B.A., Management in the Arts ('74).
CAREER HIGHLIGHTS: Asst. to Managing Dir., American Shakespeare Theater ('74); Production Asst., "The White Shadow"; promoted to Story Consultant ('79); named Coordinating Prod. ('80); Prod., "St. Elsewhere" ('82).
ACHIEVEMENTS & AWARDS: Emmy nomination for best dramatic series for co-producing "The White Shadow" ('81).
PERSONAL: N.A.

MASON, GEOFFREY
Prod., NBC, Sports

c/o NBC, 30 Rockefeller Plaza, New York, NY 10020
b. December 30, 1940. Englewood, NJ.

EDUCATION: Duke University, B.A., Sociology.
CAREER HIGHLIGHTS: Prod., ABC Sports, where he coordinated production for the Munich, Innsbruck, and Montreal Olympic Broadcasts ('67); joined NBC Sports as Prod. of Wimbledon tennis broadcasts and other network events ('77); V.P., NBC Sports, European Production, Paris ('78); Exec. V.P., NBC Sports, New York ('79); Prod., NBC Sports ('83).

ACHIEVEMENTS & AWARDS: Received several Emmy awards for his work on the ABC Olympics coverage and "Wide World of Sports."

PERSONAL: Resides in New York City with wife, Claudia.

MASSEY, PERRY E., JR.
V.P., NBC, Program Prod., Entertainment Division

22525 Dardenne St., Woodland Hills, CA 91364
b. June 19, 1927. Troy, NY.

EDUCATION: Emerson College, B.A.
CAREER HIGHLIGHTS: Started at NBC as Guide, Film Librarian, Film Cutter, Film Editor ('50); became Stage Mgr., "Show of Shows," "Milton Berle Show," Bob Hope specials, NBC ('53); Dir., Home Show, NBC "Wide Wide World" ('57); Commercial Prod., "Tonight Show" with Jack Paar ('58–'62); "Tonight Show" with Johnny Carson ('62–'68); Dir., Special Programs, TV NET, NBC ('72); Dir., Program Administration and Operations, TV NET, NBC ('73); V.P., Program Operations, Entertainment Division, NBC ('79); V.P., Program Production, Entertainment Division, NBC ('81).
ACHIEVEMENTS & AWARDS: N.A.
PERSONAL: Wife, Pam, sons, Craig and Bruce; daughter, Barbara.

MASUCCI, TONY
Dir., Motion Pictures for TV, NBC

c/o CBS, 6121 Sunset Blvd., Los Angeles, CA 90028
b. October 7, 1944. New York, NY.

EDUCATION: Stella Adler Studio.
CAREER HIGHLIGHTS: Began career as Prod. of TV commercials in New York, where he was V.P. and General Mgr. of Lewron, Inc. Production credits include "The Impossible Flight," "Arthur Fiedler and the Boston Pops at Carnegie Hall," "Today is Ours," and "20 Shades of Pink"; Exec. in Charge of Production for the TV division of the Robert Stigwood Organization ('78); Dir., Mini-Series, CBS Entertainment ('80); Dir., Motion Pictures for TV, NBC.
ACHIEVEMENTS & AWARDS: N.A.

PERSONAL: Married, resides in Studio City, CA.

MATER, GENE PAUL
Sr. V.P., Communications and News Practices, CBS, News

c/o CBS, 51 W. 52d St., New York, NY 10019
b. November 27, 1926. New York, NY.

EDUCATION: Polytechnic Institute of Brooklyn.
CAREER HIGHLIGHTS: Reporter/Editor, Sun-Telegram, San Bernardino, CA ('49); Assoc. Editor, Newark Star Ledger, New Jersey ('53); Asst. News Editor, World-Telegram and Sun, New York ('53); News Dir., Radio Free Europe, Munich ('59); Public Affairs Dir. and Exec. V.P., Radio Free Europe ('65); Special Asst. to Pres., CBS Broadcast Group ('70); V.P. and Asst. to Pres. ('72); Sr. V.P., Policy, CBS Broadcast Group ('82); Sr. V.P., Communications and News Practices, CBS News ('83).
ACHIEVEMENTS & AWARDS: N.A.
PERSONAL: Wife, Jeanne; sons, Richard, Gene, and Philip.

MAXWELL, ROBERT
V.P., Research, HBO

c/o HBO, 1271 Ave. of the Americas, New York, NY 10020
b. November 24, 1944.

EDUCATION: University of Missouri, B.S., Journalism; New York University, M.A. and Ph.D., Communications.
CAREER HIGHLIGHTS: Mgr., Program Research, ABC Entertainment, New York ('75); Mgr., Program Research, HBO ('78); Dir., Research, HBO ('79); V.P., Research, HBO ('82).
ACHIEVEMENTS & AWARDS: N.A.
PERSONAL: Resides in New York City.

MAYER, JERRY
Exec. Prod./Writer (Freelance)

c/o Broder-Kurland, 9046 Sunset Blvd., Suite #202, Los Angeles, CA 90069
b. September 5, 1931.

EDUCATION: Washington University.

CAREER HIGHLIGHTS: Writer, "The Jonathan Winters Show" ('69); Exec. Prod., "Tabitha" ('77); Prod., "The Facts of Life" ('79–'80); Exec. Prod., "The Facts of Life" ('81–'82); Writer, Mitzi Gaynor specials ('73–'78).

ACHIEVEMENTS & AWARDS: Nominated for two Emmy awards.

PERSONAL: N.A.

MAYER, VERA
V.P., NBC, Information and Archives

c/o NBC, 30 Rockefeller Plaza, New York, NY 10020

b. July 5. Budapest, Hungary.

EDUCATION: Columbia Graduate School, M.S. ('65).

CAREER HIGHLIGHTS: Asst. to Chief of *N.Y. Times* Bureau in Geneva ('47); Research Administrator, Cornell University Medical College ('65); Mgr., Library and Records Administration, NBC ('68); V.P., Information and Archives ('78).

ACHIEVEMENTS & AWARDS: N.A.

PERSONAL: Husband, Klaus; son, Rulon; daughter, Carla.

MAYNOR, ASA
Prod., CBS

c/o CBS, 7800 Beverly Blvd., Los Angeles, CA 90036

b. May 26.

EDUCATION: Mary Wood College, B.A., Communications.

CAREER HIGHLIGHTS: As part of the Warner Bros. stable of beautiful starlets in the late fifties, Maynor was a regular in the series "Dan Raven" and "The Racers", and appeared in more than 100 other television shows, such as "Maverick," "Cheyenne," "Tightrope," "The Lawman," and "Hawaiian Eye." She turned TV producer with *Another Woman's Child*, a TV motion picture about step-parenting ('82).

ACHIEVEMENTS & AWARDS: She put together the Emmy award-winning TV movie *Babe*.

PERSONAL: N.A.

MAZER, BILL
Sportscaster, WNEW-TV, "10 O'Clock News"

c/o Metromedia, 205 E. 67th St., New York, NY 10021

b. N.A.

EDUCATION: N.A.

CAREER HIGHLIGHTS: Sportscaster, Buffalo, NY ('48); Host, Sports Telephone Talk Show, New York ('64–'69); Host, "Reach for the Stars," NBC TV; General Interviewer, WOR-Radio; nightly interview show, WHN; Broadcaster, CBS TV, ABC TV, NBC TV. Sportscaster, "10 O'Clock News," WNEW-TV; Co-Host, "Sports Extra," WNEW-TV ('72).

ACHIEVEMENTS & AWARDS: Broadcaster of the Year, Natl. Assn. of Sportscasters and Sportswriters for three consecutive years. Wrote the best-seller *The Sports Answer Book*.

PERSONAL: Resides in Westchester County, NY, with wife, Dutch.

MEADOWS, AUDREY
Actress

c/o "Too Close for Comfort," c/o D. L. Taffner, 5900 Wilshire Blvd., Los Angeles, CA 90036

b. 1924. Wuchang, China.

EDUCATION: N.A.

CAREER HIGHLIGHTS: The caustic retort and the comic look of disdain are the trademarks of this "Honeymooners" alumna who's been away from TV too long for comfort. Broadway appearance in *Top Banana*. TV guest star on "The Carol Burnett Show," "The Red Skelton Show," "Honeymooner" specials, "Wagon Train," and "The Love Boat." Series star of "The Honeymooners" and "Too Close for Comfort."

ACHIEVEMENTS & AWARDS: Emmy as best supporting actress in a series for "The Honeymooners" ('54). Dir. of the First Natl. Denver Bank; Trustee of Pearl S. Buck Foundation.

PERSONAL: Sister of actress Jayne Meadows.

MEADOWS, JAYNE
Actress

c/o ABC, 2040 Ave. of the Stars, Los Angeles, CA 90067
b. 1925. Wuchang, China.

EDUCATION: N.A.
CAREER HIGHLIGHTS: Theatrical appearances in *Kiss Them for Me, Spring Again, Another Love Story*, and *The Gazebo*. Film appearances include *Undercurrent* and several films in *The Thin Man* series. Meadows also appeared on the TV panel show, "I've Got a Secret." Series regular on "It's Not Easy," ABC ('83).
ACHIEVEMENTS & AWARDS: N.A.
PERSONAL: Married to Steve Allen; son, William.

MEANEY, DONALD
Managing Dir. of Affiliate and Intl. Liaison, NBC, News

c/o NBC, 30 Rockefeller Plaza, New York, NY 10020
b. June 3, 1920. Newark, NJ.

EDUCATION: Rutgers University School of Journalism.
CAREER HIGHLIGHTS: Reporter, *Plainfield Courier-News*, New Jersey; Reporter, *Newark Evening News*, New Jersey; News Dir., WCTC-AM, New Brunswick, NJ; News Dir., WNJR-AM, Newark; News Writer, NBC News, New York ('52); Natl. TV News Editor, NBC News ('54); Mgr., Natl. News ('60); Mgr., Special News Programs, NBC News ('61); Dir., News Programs, NBC News ('62); General Mgr., NBC News ('65); V.P. in Charge of All Special TV Programming, NBC News ('66); V.P., TV News Programming, NBC News ('73); V.P., News, Washington, DC ('74); Managing Dir. of Affiliate and Intl. Liaison, NBC News ('79).
ACHIEVEMENTS & AWARDS: Member, North American Natl. Broadcasters Assn.
PERSONAL: Wife, Ruth; daughter, Andrea; son, Christopher.

MEISTER, DAVID L.
Sr. V.P., HBO, Cinemax and Program Services

c/o HBO, 1271 Ave. of the Americas, New York, NY 10020
b. December 9, 1939. New York, NY.

EDUCATION: Brown University, B.A.; Columbia University, M.B.A.
CAREER HIGHLIGHTS: Ad Agency Exec. for 12 years; Independent Prod.; Dir. of Broadcasting, Office of the Commissioner of Baseball ('76); joined HBO as Dir. of Sports ('78); V.P., Sports ('79); became V.P., Programming Time-Life Films ('80); returned to HBO to head Cinemax team ('81); named V.P., Cinemax and Program Services for HBO ('81); Sr. V.P., Cinemax and Program Services, HBO ('83).
ACHIEVEMENTS & AWARDS: Nominated for Edgar award as author of outstanding paperback of the year by the Mystery Writers of America for *The Gravy Train Hit* ('75).
PERSONAL: Resides in New York City with wife, Joan, and four children.

MELENDEZ, BILL
Pres., Bill Melendez Productions

438 N. Larchmont Blvd., Los Angeles, CA 90004
b. November 15, 1916. Hermosillo, Sonora, Mexico.

EDUCATION: Los Angeles City College; Chouinard Art Institute.
CAREER HIGHLIGHTS: Joined Walt Disney Productions, working on *Fantasia, Bambi*, and *Pinocchio* ('38); Leon Schlesinger Cartoons ('41); moved to UPA, Animated Prod. for *Gerald McBoing* and *Madeleine* ('48); Dir., industrial films, John Sutherland Productions ('54); founded Bill Melendez Productions ('64). Also on the faculty of the Cinema Arts Dept., University of Southern California.
ACHIEVEMENTS & AWARDS: Emmy and Peabody for "A Charlie Brown Christmas" ('65); honored by the Natl. Society of Cartoonists as best animation cartoonist of the year ('72); Emmy, "Life Is a Circus, Charlie Brown" ('81).
PERSONAL: Married, resides in Los Angeles; two sons.

MELNICK, DANIEL
Exec. Prod.

10201 W. Pico Blvd., Los Angeles, CA 90064
b. April 21, 1934. New York, NY.

EDUCATION: New York University.
CAREER HIGHLIGHTS: Program Exec., ABC ('59); Partner in David Susskind's Talent Assoc.; Prod. Chief, MGM Pictures ('72); Head of World Wide Productions, Columbia Pictures ('77); Independent Prod. ('79). Films produced include *Straw Dogs, All That Jazz, Altered States,* and *Making Love.*
ACHIEVEMENTS & AWARDS: N.A.
PERSONAL: N.A.

MELTZER, BARBARA
Dir., Network Creative Services, NBC

c/o NBC, 3000 W. Alameda Ave., Burbank, CA 91523
b. July 14. Bronx, NY.

EDUCATION: New York City Community College.
CAREER HIGHLIGHTS: Secretary for NBC Unit Mgrs., New York ('62); Asst. to the Prod., "The Tonight Show Starring Johnny Carson" ('67); Asst. to the Prod., "Jack Paar Tonight" ('72); Assoc. Prod., King-Hitzig Productions, in association with Alan King ('74); Contest Coordinator on the remake of the "$64,000 Question" ('76); Program Coordinator, "The Tonight Show Starring Johnny Carson" ('77); Sr. Talent Coordinator, Creative Services Dept., NBC, Burbank ('79); promoted to Mgr., Talent Coordinators ('80); named Dir., Network Creative Services, NBC ('81).
ACHIEVEMENTS & AWARDS: N.A.
PERSONAL: Resides in West Hollywood, CA.

MENCHEL, DONALD
Pres., MCA, TV

445 Park Ave., New York, NY 10022
b. October 26, 1932. New York, NY.

EDUCATION: Brandeis University, B.A. ('54).
CAREER HIGHLIGHTS: Started as Traffic Clerk, ABC ('56); joined Telcom Assoc., and during his 15 years with them moved from Buyer to V.P. to Exec. V.P. ('57); Dir. of Marketing, Time-Life Films ('72); moved to MCA TV as V.P. and Dir. of Sales, promoted first to Exec. V.P. and then Pres. ('75).
ACHIEVEMENTS & AWARDS: Board of Dirs, IRTS ('76–present); TV Bureau of Advertising ('77–'81).
PERSONAL: Wife, Barbara; daughters, Pamela and Terry.

MENDELSON, NANCY
Creative Dir., CBS, CBS TV Sales/Marketing Services

c/o CBS, 51 W. 52d St., New York, NY 10019
b. October 14.

EDUCATION: Pratt Institute.
CAREER HIGHLIGHTS: Assoc. Managing Editor, Fawcett Publications Gold Medal Books ('72); Creative Dir., Leo Burnett Advertising ('75); Creative Dir., FoBregGaSa & Assoc. Advertising, Honolulu ('77); Promotion Mgr., *Panorama* magazine ('79); Asst. Mgr., Print Communications, CBS ('81); Mgr., Print Communications, Marketing Services, CBS ('81); Creative Dir., CBS TV Sales/Marketing Services, CBS, New York ('83).
ACHIEVEMENTS & AWARDS: N.A.
PERSONAL: Resides in New York City.

Commentator; Spokesperson, Lipton Tea commercials.
ACHIEVEMENTS & AWARDS: N.A.
PERSONAL: N.A.

MEREDITH, BURGESS
Actor

c/o Jack Fields, 9255 Sunset Blvd., Suite 1105, Los Angeles, CA 90069
b. November 16, 1908. Cleveland, OH.

EDUCATION: Amherst College.
CAREER HIGHLIGHTS: Remembered for his marvelous performance on Broadway as Mio in Maxwell Anderson's classic, *Winterset*. He also appeared on stage in *High Tor, The Remarkable Mr. Pennypacker*, and *Teahouse of the August Moon*. Motion pictures include *Winterset, Of Mice and Men, The Story of G.I. Joe, Rocky, Rocky II, Rocky III, Such Good Friends, The Day of the Locust, Foul Play, Magic*, and *True Confessions*. TV movies include *Lock, Stock and Barrel, Johnny We Hardly Knew Ye, Tail Gunner Joe, The Last Hurrah*, and *How the West Was Won*. Series regular on "Those Amazing Animals" and "Gloria." Does many voiceovers for TV commercials.
ACHIEVEMENTS & AWARDS: Emmy award for *Tail Gunner Joe* ('77); Tony award for *A Thurber Carnival* ('60).
PERSONAL: Resides in Malibu, CA, Mount Ivy, NY, and the Cayman Islands.

MEREDITH, DON
Sports Commentator/Actor

c/o ABC, 1330 Ave. of the Americas, New York, NY 10019
b. April 10, 1938. Mount Vernon, TX.

EDUCATION: N.A.
CAREER HIGHLIGHTS: Star football quarterback; ABC Sportscaster, "Monday Night Football"; NBC Sports Commentator; Replacement Host, "The Tonight Show"; ABC Sports

MERLIS, GEORGE
Prod., "Entertainment Tonight"

1549 N. Vine St., Los Angeles, CA 90028
b. New York, NY.

EDUCATION: University of Pennsylvania; Columbia University Graduate School of Journalism.
CAREER HIGHLIGHTS: Sports Editor, *Rome Daily American* ('61); Reporter, *N.Y. World-Telegram and Sun* ('62); Asst. City Editor, *N.Y. World-Telegram and Sun* ('63); Day City Editor, *N.Y. World Journal Tribune* ('65); Dir., Editorial Training Program, *N.Y. Daily News* ('66); Publicity Representative, ABC News ('67); Prod., "The Reasoner Report ('72); Prod., "ABC Evening News" ('74); Prod., "Good Morning America" ('75); Sr. Prod. "Good Morning America" ('77); Exec. Prod., "Good Morning America" ('79); Exec. Prod., "CBS Morning News" ('81); Prod., "Entertainment Tonight" ('83). Planned new CBS primetime magazine show scheduled for '84.
ACHIEVEMENTS & AWARDS: Author, *V.P.—A Novel of Vice-Presidential Politics* ('71).
PERSONAL: Resides in New York City with his wife and two children.

MERMELSTEIN, PAULA
V.P., NBC, On-Air Promotion and Print Copy

c/o NBC, 30 Rockefeller Plaza, New York, NY 10020
b. November 8, 1947. Brooklyn, NY.

EDUCATION: Brooklyn College, B.A.
CAREER HIGHLIGHTS: Secretary at NBC ('69); published column in *Glamour* ('70); Editorial Staff of Joe Garagiola's "Memory Game" ('71); Freelance Production Asst., NBC's coverage of Thanksgiving Day parade, pilot for "Perpetual People Puzzle," and NBC election coverage promotion ('71); named Writer/Prod. for On-Air Promotion Dept. ('72); Su-

pervising Writer/Prod. ('78); appointed Dir. of Dept. ('79); promoted to V.P., On-Air Promotion and Print Copy ('79).

ACHIEVEMENTS & AWARDS: First place award, U.S. TV Commercials Festival, news promotion category, for "NBC Profile: David Brinkley" ('77).

PERSONAL: Husband, Jay James.

METCALFE, BURT
Prod./Writer/Dir., 20th Century Fox Studios

P.O. Box 900, Beverly Hills, CA 90213
b. Saskatchewan, Canada.

EDUCATION: University of California at Los Angeles, B.A., Theater Arts.

CAREER HIGHLIGHTS: "M*A*S*H" producer for five years, Metcalfe helped cast the pilot and stayed on as Assoc. Prod., schooled by Gene Reynolds and Larry Gelbart. Broke into TV as an actor on "Hennessy" ('60) and "Father of the Bride" ('61). Joined Jackie Cooper as a Casting Dir., Screen Gems, became Asst. to Harry Ackerman at Screen Gems, and moved to Universal Studios as Casting Dir. ('69). He cast "M*A*S*H" and "Anna and the King" ('70). Prod., "After M*A*S*H" ('83).

ACHIEVEMENTS & AWARDS: Resides in Los Angeles.

MEYER, BARRY M.
Exec. V.P., Warner Bros., Films and TV

4000 Warner Blvd., Burbank, CA 91522
b. November 28, 1944.

EDUCATION: University of Rochester.

CAREER HIGHLIGHTS: Dir. of ABC Business Affairs ('67); joined Warner Bros. ('71); became V.P., TV Business Affairs ('73); in charge of Warner Bros. TV programming, business affairs, and product acquisition ('78).

ACHIEVEMENTS & AWARDS: Member, NATAS.

PERSONAL: Resides in Sherman Oaks, CA, with wife, Barbara, and children, Mathew and Elizabeth.

MEYER, ROY F.
V.P., NBC TV Stations, News

c/o NBC, 4001 Nebraska Ave., N.W., Washington, DC 20016
b. September 4, 1933. Chicago, IL.

EDUCATION: Northwestern University, B.S., and M.S., Journalism.

CAREER HIGHLIGHTS: Radio Reporter and Editorial Researcher, WJBC Radio, Bloomington, IN ('61); TV Reporter, Editorial and Documentary Prod., WITI, Milwaukee ('64); News and Public Affairs Dir., WMBD AM-FM-TV, Peoria, IL ('68). News Dir., WSPD-TV, Toledo ('69). WAVE AM and TV, Louisville, KY ('72). News Adviser and Consultant, McHugh & Hoffman ('74). Appointed V.P., News, NBC TV Stations ('79).

ACHIEVEMENTS & AWARDS: N.A.

PERSONAL: Resides in Vienna, VA, with wife, Elaine; son, Scott.

MICHAEL, GEORGE
Sportscaster, WRC-TV, News

c/o WRC-TV, 4001 Nebraska Ave., N.W., Washington, DC 20016
b. St. Louis, MO.

EDUCATION: St. Louis University, B.S., Philosophy, Political Theory, and Speech.

CAREER HIGHLIGHTS: Began as Music Dir. and Disc Jockey, WMAY-Radio, Springfield, IL; Disc Jockey, WABC-Radio; Sportscaster, and the play-by-play voice of the New York Islanders hockey team; Sportscaster, WRC-TV, Channel 4 News ('80).

ACHIEVEMENTS & AWARDS: Emmy award winner. Received the Multiple Sclerosis Society bronze chest as Man of the Year in Philadelphia ('70); voted Man of the Year by the Pres., Philadelphia Chamber of Commerce ('71).

PERSONAL: N.A.

MICHAEL, WERNER
Sr. V.P., MGM TV, Programs

c/o MGM TV, 10202 W. Washington Blvd., Culver City, CA 90230
b. March 5, 1910. Detmold, Germany.

EDUCATION: University of Berlin; University of Paris, Ph.D.

CAREER HIGHLIGHTS: Radio Writer and Dir. ('38); Co-Author of two Broadway revues ('40); Dir. of French films and a Dir., Broadcast Division, Voice of America ('42); joined CBS as Prod./Dir. ('46); Asst. Program Dir. ('48); moved to Kenyon & Eckhardt as Dir., TV Dept. ('50); Prod. for Dumont Network ('52); Prod., Benton & Bowles ('56); V.P. and Dir., TV-Radio Dept., Reach, McClinton Advertising ('57); named V.P., Dir., TV Dept. of SSC&B and did consulting on TV programming and commercial production ('63); Program Exec. with ABC TV ('75); Dir., Dramatic Programs('76). Left ABC for MGM TV as Sr. V.P., Creative Affairs ('77); Exec. V.P. for Wrather Entertainment Intl. ('79); rejoined MGM TV as Sr. V.P., Programs ('80).

ACHIEVEMENTS & AWARDS: N.A.

PERSONAL: Wife, Rosemary.

MICHAELI, JOHN E.
V.P., Taft Entertainment Co., Communications

10960 Wilshire Blvd., Los Angeles, CA 90024
b. November 20. Los Angeles, CA.

EDUCATION: California State University.

CAREER HIGHLIGHTS: Started as a Publicist, MGM Studios ('65); joined Hanna-Barbera Productions in same capacity ('67); promoted to Dir. of Publicity and Advertising ('72); further promoted to V.P., Communications ('78); moved to Taft Entertainment as V.P., Communications ('82).

ACHIEVEMENTS & AWARDS: N.A.

PERSONAL: Resides in Los Angeles.

MICHAELS, LORNE
Prod./Writer

88 Central Park W., New York, NY 10023
b. November 17. Toronto, Canada.

EDUCATION: University of Toronto.

CAREER HIGHLIGHTS: Writer/Prod. at CBC; Writer, "Laugh-In"; Writer and Co-Prod., three Lily Tomlin specials and the Paul Simon special. Prod. of the landmark comedy series "Saturday Night Live." Independent Prod. and Series Developer for NBC.

ACHIEVEMENTS & AWARDS: Two Emmy awards for the Lily Tomlin specials, one Emmy for the Paul Simon special. Three Emmy awards as Prod., "Saturday Night Live."

PERSONAL: N.A.

MICHAELSON, MIKE
Exec. V.P., C-SPAN

c/o C-SPAN, 400 N. Capitol St., Washington, DC
b. April 25. Richmond, VA.

EDUCATION: University of Richmond; American University.

CAREER HIGHLIGHTS: Asst. Program Dir., WWDC, Washington, DC ('48); Superintendent for the House Radio-TV Correspondents' Gallery at the U.S. Capitol ('51–'81); Exec. V.P., C-SPAN ('81).

ACHIEVEMENTS & AWARDS: N.A.

PERSONAL: Wife, Gloria; daughter, Diane; son, Robert.

MICHELIS, JAY
V.P., Talent Relations and Creative Services, NBC, Entertainment

c/o NBC, 3000 W. Alameda Ave., Burbank, CA 91523
b. July 1. Livermore, CA.

EDUCATION: San Jose State University; Stanford University.

CAREER HIGHLIGHTS: Began career at NBC as a Page ('60); Coordinator of Audience Promotion ('61); NBC News ('62); Supervisor, Guest Relations ('65); Coordinator of Promotion, West Coast ('69); Mgr. Promotion, West Coast ('69); Dir., Promotion, New York ('71); Dir., Promotion, West Coast ('73); V.P., Talent Relations and Creative Services, NBC Entertainment ('79).

ACHIEVEMENTS & AWARDS: Member, ATAS.
PERSONAL: Resides in Pasadena, CA.

MIDGLEY, LESLIE
TV Consultant

400 E. 56th St., New York, NY 10022
b. Salt Lake City, UT.

EDUCATION: University of Utah.

CAREER HIGHLIGHTS: Journalist, *Deseret News, Louisville Courier-Journal, Chicago Times, N.Y. World Telegram, N.Y. Herald Tribune.* Assoc. Editor, *Colliers;* Foreign Editor and Managing Editor, *Look;* Prod., Sunday CBS News ('55); Prod., special broadcasts ('56); Prod., "Eyewitness" ('59); produced important broadcasts on the Vietnam War ('64); Exec. Prod., "CBS Evening News With Walter Cronkite" ('67); Exec. Prod., CBS Documentaries ('72); V.P., Special Programs, NBC News ('80); TV Consultant ('83).

ACHIEVEMENTS & AWARDS: Emmy and Peabody awards for "The Senate and the Watergate Affair," "Showdown in Iran," and "The Face of Red China."

PERSONAL: Wife, Betty Furness, Consumer Affairs Dir., WNBC-TV, New York.

MILAVSKY, J. RONALD
V.P., NBC, News and Social Research

c/o NBC, 30 Rockefeller Plaza, New York, NY 10020
b. May 19, 1933. Hartford, CT.

EDUCATION: Wesleyan University, B.A.; Columbia University, Ph.D.

CAREER HIGHLIGHTS: Research Assoc., Bureau of Applied Social Research at Columbia University ('58); Mgr., Social Research, Prudential Insurance Co. ('65); joined NBC ('69); Dir., Social Research ('74); named V.P., News and Social Research, NBC ('78).

ACHIEVEMENTS & AWARDS: Member, American Assn. of Public Opinion Research; American Sociological Assn.; published articles and chapters in various professional journals and texts. Co-Author, *Television and Aggression: A Panel Study* ('82).

PERSONAL: Resides in Baldwin, NY, with wife, Adelle; children, Joseph and Jennifer.

MILES, LARRY
Sr. V.P., Times Mirror Cable TV, Marketing and Programming

c/o Times Mirror Cable TV, 2381 Morse Ave., Irvine, CA 92714
b. February 10, 1939. Klamath Falls, OR.

EDUCATION: Sacramento State University, B.S.; Michigan State University, M.B.A.

CAREER HIGHLIGHTS: Regional Mgr., Asst. V.P., Times Mirror Cable TV ('71); V.P. and General Mgr., Hecht, Higgins & Peterson Advertising ('78); V.P., Sales, Premiere ('80); V.P., Western Division, Times Mirror Cable TV ('80); Sr. V.P., Marketing and Programming ('81).

ACHIEVEMENTS & AWARDS: N.A.
PERSONAL: Resides in Mission Viejo, CA

MILKIS, EDWARD K.
Prod., Miller-Milkis-Boyett Productions

c/o Miller-Milkis-Boyett, 5451 Marathon St., Hollywood, CA 90038
b. July 16, 1931. Los Angeles, CA.

EDUCATION: University of Southern California.

CAREER HIGHLIGHTS: Asst. Editor, ABC-TV ('52); moved to Disney Studios ('54); Asst. Editor, MGM ('57); Editor, MGM ('60); Assoc. Prod., "Star Trek" ('66); Exec. in Charge of Post Production, Paramount ('69); formed Miller-Milkis Productions ('72); which later became Miller-Milkis Productions ('72); which later became Miller-Milkis-Boyett ('79); Co-Prod. of the feature films *Silver Streak* and *Foul Play*; Exec. Prod. of the TV series "Happy Days," "Laverne and Shirley," "Petrocelli," "Angie," "Out of the Blue," "Bosom Buddies," "Goodtime Girls," and "Feel the Heat."

ACHIEVEMENTS & AWARDS: N.A.

PERSONAL: N.A.

MILLER, FRANK R.
V.P., Marketing, Westinghouse Broadcasting Co., Group W Productions

c/o Group W Productions, 70 Universal City Plaza, Universal City, CA 91608

b. July 31. Milledgeville, IL.

EDUCATION: University of Iowa.

CAREER HIGHLIGHTS: Programming and Production Exec., WMT-TV, Cedar Rapids, IA; Dir., Broadcast Operations, WAVE-TV, Louisville, KY; Station Mgr., WTVJ-TV, Miami; V.P., General Mgr. and Exec. Prod., "The Mike Douglas Show" ('77); Exec. Prod., "The John Davidson Show" ('80); V.P., Marketing, Group W Productions ('81).

ACHIEVEMENTS & AWARDS: N.A.

PERSONAL: Resides in Tarzana, CA, with wife, Genie; daughter, Karen; sons, Matthew and Andrew.

MILLER, JIM
V.P., Program Planning and Feature Films, Showtime Entertainment, Programming Dept.

c/o Showtime, 1633 Broadway, New York, NY 10019

b. November 18, 1948

EDUCATION: Columbia University, B.A., Economics.

CAREER HIGHLIGHTS: Joined Teleprompter Manhattan Cable TV ('70), performing numerous functions including News Dir. and Sports Dir. and later, Advertising Sales Mgr. ('74); Assoc. Dir. of Programming, Teleprompter Corp. ('76); Dir. of Programming, Teleprompter Manhattan Cable TV ('77); Dir. of Marketing and Programming, Teleprompter Manhattan Cable TV ('78); Dir., Program Administration, Showtime Entertainment Programming Dept. ('79); V.P., Program Planning and Feature Films, Showtime Entertainment Programming Dept ('80).

ACHIEVEMENTS & AWARDS: N.A.

PERSONAL: N.A.

MILLER, JOHN
V.P., Advertising and Promotion, West Coast, NBC, Entertainment

c/o NBC, 3000 W. Alameda Ave., Burbank, CA 91523

b. Chicago, IL.

EDUCATION: University of Kansas; Syracuse University, B.S. Public Communications (magna cum laude).

CAREER HIGHLIGHTS: Freelance Production Asst. for advertising agencies and production companies in Chicago ('72); Prod., Program Dept., WMAQ-TV, Chicago ('74); Mgr., On-Air Promotion, WMAQ-TV, Chicago ('75); Mgr., On-Air Promotion, WBBM-TV, Chicago ('76); Promotion Mgr., ('78); Dir., Affiliate Promotion Services, CBS-TV, West Coast ('80); Dir., Advertising and Promotion, CBS News, New York ('81); V.P., Affiliate Promotion Services, West Coast, NBC ('82); V.P., Advertising and Promotion, NBC Entertainment, West Coast ('83).

ACHIEVEMENTS & AWARDS: N.A.

PERSONAL: Resides in Tarzana, CA, with wife Sharon and their two sons, Bobby and Jason.

MILLER, J.P.
Writer

c/o Major Talent Agency, 11812 San Vicente, Los Angeles, CA 90049

b. December 18, 1919. San Antonio, TX.

EDUCATION: Rice University; Yale Drama School.

CAREER HIGHLIGHTS: One of the outstanding playwrights to emerge from the Golden Age of live TV drama, Miller began his career with the original dramas "Philco TV Playhouse," "Hide and Seek," "Old Tasslefoot," "The Rabbit Trap," "The Pardon Me Boy," "Playhouse 90," "Days of Wine and Roses," "CBS Playhouse," "The People Next Door," "The Unwanted," "The Lindbergh Kidnapping Case," "Gauguin," and "The Savage." His TV dramatization of the book *Helter Skelter* ranked number one in the Nielsens for the 1976 season.

ACHIEVEMENTS & AWARDS: N.A.

PERSONAL: N.A.

MILLER, RON
Pres. and Chief Exec. Officer, Walt Disney Productions

c/o Walt Disney Productions, 500 S. Buena Vista St., Burbank, CA 91521
b. April 17, 1933. Los Angeles, CA.

EDUCATION: University of Southern California.

CAREER HIGHLIGHTS: Second Asst. Dir., Disney Productions ('57); Assoc. Prod., Disney Productions ('59); Asst. to Pres., Walt Disney during Winter Olympics ('60); Assoc. Prod., Disney theatrical productions including such features as *Bon Voyage, Summer Magic, Son of Flubber, Moon Pilot, The Misadventures of Merlin Jones,* and *A Tiger Walks* ('61); Co-Prod., on Disney films *The Monkey's Uncle, That Darn Cat, Lt. Robinson Crusoe, U.S.N.* and *Monkeys, Go Home!* ('64); Prod., Disney theatrical productions beginning with *Never a Dull Moment* ('67); Exec. Prod., Disney Productions ('71); Pres., Disney Productions ('80); elected Chief Exec. Officer, Disney Productions ('83).

ACHIEVEMENTS & AWARDS: N.A.

PERSONAL: Resides in Encino, CA, with his wife, Diane. Seven children, Christopher, Joanna, Tamara, Jennifer, Walter, Ron Jr., and Patrick.

MILLER, RON
Correspondent, ABC, News

c/o ABC, 7 W. 66th St., New York, NY 10023
b. N.A.

EDUCATION: Temple University; University of Pennsylvania.

CAREER HIGHLIGHTS: Weekend Copy Boy, WCAU-TV, Philadelphia ('61); moved up the ranks to Reporter, WCAU-TV ('64); Weekend Anchor, WCAU-TV ('67); Reporter, ABC News, New York ('71); Correspondent, ABC News, South Vietnam ('71); Correspondent, ABC News, Chicago ('72).

ACHIEVEMENTS & AWARDS: Pennsylvania News Dirs. award; Pennsylvania AP award; Sigma Delta Chi award; Natl. Science Foundation award.

PERSONAL: N.A.

MILLER, SCOTT W.
Design Mgr., NBC, Advertising and Promotion, West Coast

c/o NBC, 3000 W. Alameda Ave., Burbank, CA 91523
b. Gary, IN.

EDUCATION: Art-Center College of Design.

CAREER HIGHLIGHTS: Co-Owner of a design business; Art Dir., Ebey, Utley & McManus advertising agency, Palo Alto, CA ('77); Freelance Designer and Illustrator, San Francisco ('79); Freelancer in Los Angeles area ('82); Design Mgr., Advertising and Promotion, NBC, Burbank ('83).

ACHIEVEMENTS & AWARDS: N.A.

PERSONAL: Resides in Hollywood.

MILLS, DONNA
Actress

c/o "Knots Landing," CBS, 7800 Beverly
  Blvd., Los Angeles, CA 90036
b. December 11. Chicago, IL.

EDUCATION: University of Illinois.
CAREER HIGHLIGHTS: Appeared in the TV soap
  operas "The Secret Storm" and "Love Is a
  Many Splendored Thing." Her motion pic-
  tures include *Play Misty for Me*. Her TV mov-
  ies include *Bare Essence, The Hunted Lady, The
  Bait, Fire,* and *Woman on the Run*. Star of the
  series "The Good Life." Star of "Knot's
  Landing."
ACHIEVEMENTS & AWARDS: N.A.
PERSONAL: Single; resides in Beverly Hills, CA.

MILLS, STEVE
V.P., CBS TV, Movies for TV and
  Mini-Series

c/o CBS, 7800 Beverly Blvd., Los Angeles, CA
  90036
b. Russell, KS.

EDUCATION: University of Kansas, B.A.; Ohio
  State University, M.A.

CAREER   HIGHLIGHTS: Prod./Dir.,   WBNS-TV,
  Columbus, OH and KCMO-TV, Kansas City,
  MO, ('52); Exec. Prod. an Program Mgr. ABC,
  Los Angeles, ('60); V.P., Programs, ABC,
  Hollywood, ('68); moved to CBS as Exec.
  Prod. in charge of Movies for TV, ('73); V.P.,
  Program Production, CBS ('76); V.P., Movies
  for TV, CBS ('79); became V.P., Movies for TV
  and Mini-Series, CBS ('82). Executive in
  charge of the award-winning productions
  Helter Skelter, Fear on Trial, Babe.
ACHIEVEMENTS & AWARDS: Past Member, Board
  of Governors, TV Academy; past Member,
  Board of Dirs., IRTS.
PERSONAL: Wife, Dr. Barbara Mills; four sons,
  Stuart, Creighton, Kevin, and Tobin.

MILNE, ALASDAIR
Dir. General, BBC

c/o BBC TV Centre, London, England, W12
b. October 8, 1930. Kanpur, India.

EDUCATION: Winchester University; New Col-
  lege.
CAREER HIGHLIGHTS: TV Prod., (58); Asst. Edi-
  tor, "Tonight" ('59); Editor, "Tonight," ('61);
  Asst. Head of Talks, Current Affairs ('62);
  Head of Tonight Productions ('63); Freelance
  Prod. ('65); Controller, Scotland, BBC ('68);
  Dir. of Programmes, TV, BBC ('73); Managing
  Dir., TV, BBC ('77); Deputy Dir. General,
  BBC ('81); Dir. General, BBC ('82).
ACHIEVEMENTS & AWARDS: Committee Member
  of Sir Harold Wilson's Film Industry Working
  Party.
PERSONAL: N.A.

MILTON, CHARLES H.
Sr. Prod., CBS, Sports

c/o CBS, 51 W. 52d St., New York, NY 10019
b. February 18, 1935.

EDUCATION: Louisiana State University.
CAREER HIGHLIGHTS: Joined CBS as a Mail
  Room Clerk ('57); joined the Sports Division
  ('64); has produced many major events for
  CBS Sports over the years. Named Exec.
  Prod. of the NBA broadcasts ('79); Sr. Prod. of
  NFL broadcasts ('80).
ACHIEVEMENTS & AWARDS: N.A.
PERSONAL: Wife, Pat.

MITCHELL, JANE
Correspondent, WCBS-TV, News

c/o WCBS-TV, 524 W. 57th St., New York, NY 10019
b. New York, NY.

EDUCATION: New York University, B.A., Journalism.
CAREER HIGHLIGHTS: Reporter and Weekend Anchor, WBBH-TV, Fort Myers, FL; Reporter, WTCN-TV, Minneapolis/St. Paul ('79); General Assignment Reporter, WCAU-TV ('81).
ACHIEVEMENTS & AWARDS: Honored twice by the fifth annual media awards of the Odyssey Institute ('81). UPI Broadcasters Assn. certificate of merit.
PERSONAL: N.A.

MITCHELL, JOHN H.
Pres., John H. Mitchell Co.

1801 Ave. of the Stars, Suite 312, Los Angeles, CA 90067
b. New York, NY.

EDUCATION: University of Michigan.
CAREER HIGHLIGHTS: Past Pres., Hollywood Radio and TV Society ('75–'76); Pres., Columbia Pictures TV, and Exec. V.P. and Member of the Board of Dirs. of Columbia Pictures Industries for nine years. General Chairman, Intl. Broadcasting awards ('75); currently serves as Pres., ATAS and is the Chairman of the TV Academy Forum Luncheons.
ACHIEVEMENTS & AWARDS: Recipient of the liberty award from B'nai Brith.
PERSONAL: N.A.

MIZIKER, RON
Prod., Disney Channel

c/o Disney Channel, 500 S. Buena Vista St., Burbank, CA 91521
b. October 15, 1941. Albuquerque, NM.

EDUCATION: University of Southern California.
CAREER HIGHLIGHTS: Prod. of the syndicated consumer series "Back to Basics" and a syndicated 90-minute talk-variety show for Avco Broadcasting. Created, developed, and produced network variety specials, including several Perry Como shows, "EPCOT Center . . . The Opening Celebration" and "50 Years of Golden Hits." As Independent Prod. at Disney Studios, he produced "25th Reunion of the Mousketeers" and segments for "The Wonderful World of Disney." Dir. of Show Development for Disneyland and Walt Disney World; V.P. of Programming for Disney Channel.
ACHIEVEMENTS & AWARDS: Emmy award and the Intl. TV Assn. award of excellence.
PERSONAL: N.A.

MOGUL, LAURA
Dir. of Advertising, Home View Network, ABC, Video Enterprises

c/o ABC, 1330 Ave. of the Americas, New York, NY 10019
b. June 23.

EDUCATION: University of California at Los Angeles, B.A.; Barnard College.
CAREER HIGHLIGHTS: Sr. Acct. Exec., Merchandising and Sales Promotion, Intl. Paper Co., with Ross Roy, Inc., Detroit; Marketing Services Mgr., Playcable; Dir. of Advertising for

the Home View Network, ABC Video Enterprises ('83).
ACHIEVEMENTS & AWARDS: N.A.
PERSONAL: Resides in New York City.

MONROE, BILL (William B. Monroe Jr.)
News Correspondent, NBC

28 Westpath Way, Fort Sumner, MD 20816
b. July 17, 1920. New Orleans, LA.

EDUCATION: Tulane University, B.S.
CAREER HIGHLIGHTS: UPI Correspondent, New Orleans ('41); News Dir., WNOE-Radio, New Orleans ('46); Assoc. Editor, *New Orleans Item* ('49); News Dir., WDSU, New Orleans ('54); NBC News Washington, DC, Bureau Chief ('61); Washington, DC, Correspondent, "Today" ('68); Moderator and Exec. Prod., "Meet the Press" ('75).
ACHIEVEMENTS & AWARDS: Member, Phi Beta Kappa; Peabody award ('72); Paul White award, Radio-TV News Dirs. Assn. ('78). Pres., Radio-TV News Dirs. Assn. ('62–'63); Pres., Radio-TV Correspondents Assn. ('65–'66); Member, Board of Administrators, Tulane University ('71–'82).
PERSONAL: Resides in Fort Sumner, MD, with wife, Elizabeth; daughters, Anne Lee, Arthe Vairin, Catherine Harrison, and Maria Blanc.

MONSKY, MARK
Pres., Metromedia TV News

c/o Metromedia TV, 205 E. 67th St., New York, NY 10021
b. August 28, 1941.

EDUCATION: Columbia School of Journalism.
CAREER HIGHLIGHTS: Investigative Reporter, *N.Y. Mirror, Long Island Daily Press* ('60); Prod. and Reporter, CBS Radio ('66); Managing Editor, WNEW "10 O'clock News" ('70); News Dir. of Metromedia flagship station ('74); V.P. and News Dir., WNEW's "10 O'clock News" ('82); named Pres. ('83). Pres., Independent TV News Assn., involved in establishing Metromedia's participation in the Satellite News Channel, New York.
ACHIEVEMENTS & AWARDS: For "10 O'clock News," received a dozen Emmy awards, three American Bar Assn. awards, two gold

typewriter awards from the New York Press Club; a UPI award for investigative work, and six New York State AP awards.
PERSONAL: N.A.

MONTALBAN, RICARDO
Actor

c/o "Fantasy Island," ABC, 2040 Ave. of the Stars, Los Angeles, CA 90067
b. November 25, 1920. Mexico City, Mexico.

EDUCATION: N.A.
CAREER HIGHLIGHTS: His elegance and Latin looks made Montalban the ideal choice for letting TV viewers' fantasies come true, usually in exotic locales. His motion pictures include *Fiesta, Neptune's Daughter, Battleground, My Man and I, Sweet Charity,* and *Star Trek: The Wrath of Khan.* TV films include *The Pigeon, The Face of Fear, Desperate Mission, Wonder Woman, The Mark of Zorro,* and *Fantasy Island.* TV series regular on "Fantasy Island."
ACHIEVEMENTS & AWARDS: N.A.
PERSONAL: Wife, Georgiana; two sons, Mark and Victor; two daughters, Laura and Anita. Resides in Hollywood Hills, CA.

MONTY, GLORIA
Prod.

c/o ABC, 2040 Ave. of the Stars, Los Angeles,
CA 90067
b. New Jersey.

EDUCATION: University of Iowa, B.A., Drama
and Speech; Columbia University, M.A.,
Drama.
CAREER HIGHLIGHTS: One of the few women
producers in soap operas who has become
almost as popular a name as the stars in her
shows, she is known for her ability to turn a
soap floundering in the ratings into a top daytime entry. That skill, incidentally, earns
Monty about half a million dollars annually.
She ran Old Towne Theatre in Smithtown,
NY; Dir., "Secret Storm" CBS daytime drama; Dir., "Bright Promise" daytime drama;
Dir., "This Child of Mine" daytime drama
('69); Prod., "General Hospital" ABC daytime
drama ('78). Made "General Hospital" into
the number one-rated daytime show, bringing in one quarter of profits for ABC ($50
million); introduced never-before-used lighting techniques on daytime dramas.
ACHIEVEMENTS & AWARDS: N.A.
PERSONAL: Husband, freelance writer Bob
O'Byrne.

MOONEY, ELIZABETH WILDE
Dir., Regional Affiliate Relations, NBC,
Affiliate Relations

c/o NBC, 30 Rockefeller Plaza, New York, NY
10020
b. March 10. Floral Park, NY.

EDUCATION: Fordham University.
CAREER HIGHLIGHTS: Sales Dept., NBC ('60);

Asst. to Herbert Schlosser, former Pres. and
Chief Exec. Officer, NBC ('73); Station Clear-
ance Representative, Closed Circuits, TV
Sales Service Dept., NBC ('78); Program
Clearance Representative, Prime Time, NBC
('79); Dir., Regional Affiliate Relations, NBC
('83).
ACHIEVEMENTS & AWARDS: N.A.
PERSONAL: Resides in New York City and
Westhampton Beach, NY, with husband,
Frank.

MOONEY, JAMES P.
Exec. V.P., Natl. Cable TV Assn.

c/o Natl. Cable TV Assn., 1724 Massachusetts
Ave., N.W., Washington, DC 20036
b. May 28. Rhode Island.

EDUCATION: University of Rhode Island; New
York University School of Law.
CAREER HIGHLIGHTS: Legislative Counsel, U.S.
Equal Employment Opportunity Commis-
sion, Washington, DC ('69); various Capitol
Hill staff positions, Washington, DC ('71);
Chief of Staff to the Majority Whip to the U.S.
House of Representatives ('77); V.P., Govern-
ment Relations, Natl. Cable TV Assn., Wash-
ington, DC ('81); Exec. V.P., Natl. Cable TV
Assn., Washington, DC ('81).
ACHIEVEMENTS & AWARDS: N.A.
PERSONAL: Resides in Washington, DC.

MOORE, EARLE
Lawyer

555 Madison Ave., New York, NY 10022
b. December 8, 1921. Buffalo, NY.

EDUCATION: Harvard University, B.A. and LL.B.

CAREER HIGHLIGHTS: Headed Natl. Committee for Commercial Broadcasting; in charge of Action for Children's Television ('74); in charge of Media Access Project ('76); worked for the Tri-State Media Ministry Committee for Municipal Broadcasting ('73–'75); Lawyer, New York.

ACHIEVEMENTS & AWARDS: Award from the United Church of Christ.

PERSONAL: Five children.

MOORE, ELLIS O.
V.P., ABC, Public Affairs

c/o ABC, 1330 Ave. of the Americas, New York, NY 10019
b. May 12, 1924. New York, NY.

EDUCATION: Washington and Lee University.

CAREER HIGHLIGHTS: Newspaper Reporter, *Pine Bluff Commercial,* Arkansas ('46); Reporter, *Commercial Appeal,* Memphis ('47); NBC Staff Writer ('52); V.P. for Press and Publicity ('61); Public Relations, Standard Oil ('63); V.P. in Charge of Press Relations, ABC ('66); V.P. in Charge of Public Relations, ABC ('68); V.P., Public Relations, ABC, the Broadcast Division, ABC, Inc. ('70); V.P., Public Relations, ABC, Inc. ('72); V.P., Corporate Relations, ABC, Inc. ('79); V.P., Public Affairs, ABC, Inc. ('82).

ACHIEVEMENTS & AWARDS: Natl. Headliners award ('50).

PERSONAL: Married; five children and five grandchildren. Resides in Pelham Manor, NY.

MOORE, RICK
News Anchor, Cable News Network, Headline Service

c/o Cable News Network, 1050 Techwood Dr., N.W., Atlanta, GA 30318
b. September 8, 1936. Belmont, MS.

EDUCATION: Peabody College.

CAREER HIGHLIGHTS: Staff Announcer, Reporter, then Anchor News Editor at WTVF-TV, Nashville ('60); Political Campaign Dir.,

V.P., Public Relations, Financial Firm, Nashville ('66); News Dir./Anchor, WNGE-TV, Nashville ('69); News Dir./Anchor, WLKY-TV, Louisville, KY ('72); Operations Mgr., WTSP-TV, St. Petersburg, FL ('77); News Anchor, WIFR-TV, Rockford, IL ('78); News Anchor, KBMT-TV, Beaumont, TX ('80); News Anchor, Cable News Network Headline Service ('82).

ACHIEVEMENTS & AWARDS: National Headliners award ('69); Louie award (Louisville, KY) for documentary ('75).

PERSONAL: Three children.

MOORE, THOMAS
Prod./Exec.

91 Dorchester Rd., Darien, CT 06820
b. September 17, 1918. Meridian, MS.

EDUCATION: Mississippi State University; University of Missouri.

CAREER HIGHLIGHTS: Program Chief, ABC; Pres., ABC TV; Head of Ticketron; Founder and Head, Tomorrow Entertainment, which produced *The Autobiography of Miss Jane Pitman, Larry, In This House of Brede, The Glass House, Tell Me When It Hurts,* and *Queen of the Stardust Ballroom.* Vice Chairman, Corp. for Public Broadcasting; Independent Prod.; Co-Prod., "The Body Human" specials.

ACHIEVEMENTS & AWARDS: Emmy awards ('79, '81). Member, Corp. for Public Broadcasting Board of Dirs.; Member, the University Club.

PERSONAL: Wife, Claire; two children, Jean Anne and Thomas Jr.

MOOS, JEANNE
Reporter, Cable News Network, New York

225 Henry St., New York, NY 10002
b. May 21, 1954. Pittsburgh, PA.

EDUCATION: Syracuse University, B.S., Public Communications.

CAREER HIGHLIGHTS: Reporter/Weekend Anchor, WPTZ-TV, NBC affiliate in Plattsburgh, NY ('76); Cable News Network, New York Writer promoted to Reporter, UN ('80).

ACHIEVEMENTS & AWARDS: N.A.

PERSONAL: N.A.

MORD, MARVIN S.
V.P., Research, ABC

c/o ABC, 1330 Ave. of the Americas, New
   York, NY 10019
b. January 31.

EDUCATION: N.A.
CAREER HIGHLIGHTS: Research Analyst, ABC
   ('59); Sales Exec., American Research Bureau
   ('63); Assoc., Research Dept., ABC ('67);
   V.P., Research, ABC TV ('75).
ACHIEVEMENTS & AWARDS: N.A.
PERSONAL: N.A.

MORENO, RITA
Actress

c/o William Morris Agency, 151 El Camino
   Dr., Beverly Hills, CA 90212
b. December 11, 1931. Puerto Rico.

EDUCATION: N.A.
CAREER HIGHLIGHTS: Motion pictures include
   Singin' in the Rain, *The King and I*, *Summer and
   Smoke*, *West Side Story*, *The Ritz*, *The Four Sea-
   sons*, and *Carnal Knowledge*. Broadway appear-
   ances in *The Sign in Sidney Brustein's Window*,
   Gantry, *Last of the Red Hot Lovers*, and *The Ritz*.
   TV movies include *Anatomy of a Seduction*. Se-
   ries regular on "The Electric Company" and
   "Nine to Five."
ACHIEVEMENTS & AWARDS: The only woman to
   win an Oscar, an Emmy, a Grammy, and a
   Tony. Academy Award as best supporting ac-
   tress for *West Side Story*; Tony award as best
   supporting actress for *The Ritz*. Grammy
   award for "The Electric Company" album.
   Emmy award as best supporting actress for
   "The Rockford Files."
PERSONAL: Husband, Dr. Leonard Gordon.
   Daughter, Fernanda. Resides in Pacific Pal-
   isades, CA.

MORFOGEN, ANN
Dir. of Communications, CBS, News

c/o CBS, 524 W. 57th St., New York, NY
   10019
b. February 26, 1948. Morristown, NJ.

EDUCATION: Albright College, B.A.; New York
   University; Columbia University Graduate
   School of Film.
CAREER HIGHLIGHTS: Assoc., Press Information
   Dept., "60 Minutes" and CBS News, New
   York ('70); Mgr., Press Information and Pub-
   licity, KNXT-TV, Los Angeles ('77); Dir. of
   Station Services, KNXT-TV ('78); Dir. of Sta-
   tion Services, WCBS-TV, New York ('82); Dir.
   of Communications, CBS News ('83).
ACHIEVEMENTS & AWARDS: N.A.
PERSONAL: Resides in New York City.

MORGAN, CLIFF
Head of Outside Broadcasts Group, TV, BBC

c/o BBC, 12 Cavendish Place, London,
   England W1
b. April 7, 1930. Rhonda Valley, England.

EDUCATION: University College of Wales at
   Cardiff.
CAREER HIGHLIGHTS: Sports Organizer, Wales,
   BBC ('58); Editor, "Grandstand" and "Sports-
   view" on the BBC ('61); Commentator, BBC-
   2's "Rugby Special" ('68); Editor, BBC Radio
   Sport ('73); Head of BBC Radio Outside
   Broadcasts ('75); Head of Outside Broadcasts
   Group, TV, BBC ('75).
ACHIEVEMENTS & AWARDS: Awarded the OBE
   in the Queen's Silver Jubilee Birthday Hon-
   ours List ('77).
PERSONAL: Married, two children.

WCBS-AM, New York ('74); TV News, Inc., Washington, DC ('75); Prod., NBC Radio News and Information Service, New York ('76); Dir., NBC Radio News and Information Service ('77); V.P., NBC Radio News ('78); General Mgr., Affiliate News Services, NBC News, New York ('83).

ACHIEVEMENTS & AWARDS: N.A.

PERSONAL: Resides in New York City with her husband, Jerry, and their three children.

MORGAN, HARRY
Actor

c/o CBS, 7800 Beverly Blvd., Los Angeles, CA 90036
b. April 10, 1915. Detroit, MI.

EDUCATION: University of Chicago.

CAREER HIGHLIGHTS: Several series, from "December Bride" to "M*A*S*H" have benefited from Morgan's subtle scene-stealing, which makes comic acting seem effortless. Motion pictures include *High Noon, The Ox Bow Incident, My Six Convicts, Inherit the Wind, The Shootist, The Blue Veil, The Far Country,* and *The Greatest.* TV movies include *Dragnet, The Feminist and the Fuzz, Sidekicks, The Bastard, Murder at the Mardi Gras,* and the mini-series *Roots: The Next Generation.* Regular series star on "December Bride," "Pete and Gladys," "Dragnet," "The Richard Boone Show," "M*A*S*H," and "After M*A*S*H."

ACHIEVEMENTS & AWARDS: Emmy as best supporting actor for "M*A*S*H" ('79).

PERSONAL: Wife, Eileen; four sons, Chris, Charlie, Paul, and Danny. Resides in Santa Rosa, CA.

MORING, JO
General Mgr., Affiliate News Services, NBC, News

c/o NBC, 30 Rockefeller Plaza, New York, NY 10020
b. August 7.

EDUCATION: University of Maryland ('65).

CAREER HIGHLIGHTS: Reporter/Anchor, WCUM-Radio, Cumberland, MD ('65); Reporter/Anchor, WBAL-TV, Baltimore ('67); various posts with ABC Radio News, New York ('73);

MORRIS, DELORES
Dir., Children's Programming, East Coast, ABC, Entertainment

c/o ABC, 1330 Ave. of the Americas, New York, NY 10019
b. September 7. Staten Island, NY.

EDUCATION: Hunter College, B.A., Physical Anthropology and Political Science.

CAREER HIGHLIGHTS: Began career as a teacher in New York and San Francisco and moved into TV with Children's Television Workshop doing research and developing projects. Named Dir., Children's Programming, ABC Entertainment, East Coast ('83).

ACHIEVEMENTS & AWARDS: N.A.

PERSONAL: N.A.

MOSES, HARRY
Prod., CBS News

c/o CBS, 524 W. 57th St., New York, NY 10019
b. N.A.

EDUCATION: N.A.

CAREER HIGHLIGHTS: Prod., 48 separate reports for the CBS News Magazine series "60 Minutes" ('73–'79). He served as Exec. Prod. for a CBS telefilm, "Thornwell" ('80), based on one of his "60 Minutes" segments. Since then, he has produced "The Mike Wallace Profiles," CBS Evening News Reports, and pieces for Bill Moyers's CBS News series.

ACHIEVEMENTS & AWARDS: N.A.

PERSONAL: N.A.

MOSES, JUDITH
Prod./Investigative Reporter, ABC News, "20/20"

c/o ABC, 77 W. 66th St., New York, NY 10023
b. May 16, 1940. Charleston, WV.

EDUCATION: Smith College, B.A.
CAREER HIGHLIGHTS: Researcher, "Make a Wish," ABC News ('73); Researcher, "Cuba: The People," WNET ('73); Asst. to Dir., Program Planning, WNET ('74); Assoc. Prod., "A Woman Is . . ." with Bess Myerson, WCBS ('76); Creator and Prod., "Feelings," 13-part series, PBS ('78); Prod., "20/20," ABC News ('80).
ACHIEVEMENTS & AWARDS: N.A.
PERSONAL: Husband, Harry; daughter, Anne.

MOSS, JEFFREY
Writer

c/o Children's Television Workshop, 1 Lincoln Plaza, New York, NY 10023
b. N.A.

EDUCATION: Princeton University.
CAREER HIGHLIGHTS: One of the original creators of the "Sesame Street" TV series, he served as Head Writer and Composer/Lyricist. His songs have been performed by artists ranging from Johnny Cash to the Boston Pops orchestra. His play *Sweetness* was performed at the La Mama Experimental Theater Co. in New York. Author and Co-Author of several of the best-selling Sesame Street books; Writer/Prod., 10 Sesame Street record albums.
ACHIEVEMENTS & AWARDS: Three Emmy awards; four Grammy awards; two Gold Records.
PERSONAL: N.A.

MOUNTAIN, JOHNNY
Weathercaster, KABC-TV, Los Angeles, News

c/o KABC-TV, 4151 Prospect Ave., Los Angeles, CA 90027
b. October 15.

EDUCATION: University of Tennessee; Technical Institute in Sarasota.

CAREER HIGHLIGHTS: Began work as a Disc Jockey, Knoxville radio station; News Dir., Music Dir., Sales and On-Air Personality, WBLC and WNOX-Radio ('65); "Bozo the Clown," WTVK-TV ('69); Host, "Good Morning" ('71); Weekend Weathercaster, WLS-TV, Chicago ('77); Weekend Weathercaster, KABC-TV, Los Angeles ('78).
ACHIEVEMENTS & AWARDS: N.A.
PERSONAL: Resides in West Los Angeles, CA, with wife, Martha, and their son, John.

MOYER, PAUL
Anchor/Host, KABC-TV, News

c/o KABC-TV, 4151 Prospect Ave., Los Angeles, CA 90027
b. Los Angeles, CA.

EDUCATION: University of Arizona, B.S., Economics.
CAREER HIGHLIGHTS: Reporter, KTIV-TV, Sioux City, IA; Reporter, WMBD-TV, Peoria, IL; Anchor/Reporter, KTVI-TV, St. Louis; Anchor/Reporter, KDKA-TV, Pittsburgh; Anchor/Correspondent, WCBS-TV, New York; Anchor, KNBC-TV, Los Angeles; Anchor/Host, KABC-TV, Los Angeles ('79).
ACHIEVEMENTS & AWARDS: Two Emmy awards; two AP awards and a Valley Press Club award.
PERSONAL: Single.

MOYERS, BILL
Correspondent, CBS, News

c/o CBS, 51 W. 52d St., New York, NY 10019
b. June 5, 1934. Hugo, OK.

EDUCATION: North Texas University; University of Texas.
CAREER HIGHLIGHTS: This erudite interviewer and thoughtful commentator is one of the most respected people in TV journalism. When he began his TV commentary segments for CBS Evening News ('81), Moyers was given more editorial freedom and latitude than any other network correspondent has enjoyed in recent years. His career highspots include positions as Deputy Dir. of the Peace Corps ('61); Special Asst. to Pres. Johnson ('63); Publisher, *Newsday* ('67); Editor-in-

Chief of PBS's "Bill Moyers Journal" ('71–'76 and '79–'81); Anchor and Chief Correspondent, "CBS Reports" ('76–'78); Political Analyst, CBS News, coverage of Democratic and Republican national conventions and election night ('80); Correspondent, CBS News ('81); anchored PBS series "Creativity With Bill Moyers" ('82); Host, "Our Times With Bill Moyers," CBS ('83). PBS will carry "A Walk Through the Twentieth Century," originally produced for CBS Cable ('83).

ACHIEVEMENTS & AWARDS: Earned virtually every broadcast journalism award available, including Dupont-Columbia award. Author of *Listening to America*.

PERSONAL: N.A.

MUDD, ROGER
**Reporter, "NBC
White Paper" and Senior Political
Correspondent, NBC, News**

c/o NBC, 4001 Nebraska Ave., N.W.,
  Washington, DC 20016
b. February 9, 1928. Washington, DC.

EDUCATION: Washington and Lee University, B.A. ('50); University of North Carolina, M.A. ('53).

CAREER HIGHLIGHTS: Reporter, *Richmond News Leader* ('53); News Dir., WRNL-Radio, Richmond, VA ('53); WTOP in Washington, DC ('56); Congressional Correspondent, CBS News ('61–'76); Anchor, Saturday broadcast, "CBS Evening News" ('66–'73); Anchor, Sunday broadcast, "CBS Evening News," ('70–'71); regular replacement for Walter Cronkite, "CBS Evening News" and "Walter Cronkite Reporting," CBS Radio Network ('73–'79); joined NBC News as Chief Washington Correspondent ('80); Co-Anchor, TV coverage of the presidential inauguration and return of the American hostages ('81); Co-Anchor, special live coverage on the attempted assassination of President Reagan ('81); Anchor, two "NBC White Paper" special programs ('81); Anchor, "Hear and Now," NBC Radio Network ('81); Co-Anchor, "NBC Nightly News" ('82). Currently, Reporter, "NBC White Paper" series and Senior Political Correspondent, NBC News ('83).

ACHIEVEMENTS & AWARDS: Chairman, Radio-TV Correspondents Assn. ('69–'70); Peabody awards ('70, '79); Emmy awards ('72, '73, '74, '79).

PERSONAL: Wife, Emma Jeanne; children, Daniel, Maria, Jonathan, and Matthew.

MULHARE, EDWARD
Actor

c/o "Knight Rider," NBC, 30 Rockefeller
  Plaza, New York, NY 10020
b. Cork, Ireland.

EDUCATION: N.A.

CAREER HIGHLIGHTS: New York stage appearances in *My Fair Lady, Mary, Mary, The Devil's Advocate*, and *The Marriage Go Round*. Motion pictures include *Von Ryan's Express, Our Man Flint*, and *Caprice*. Series regular on "The Ghost and Mrs. Muir" and "Knight Rider."

ACHIEVEMENTS & AWARDS: N.A.

PERSONAL: Resides in Connecticut.

MULHOLLAND, ROBERT E.
Pres. and Chief Exec. Officer, NBC

c/o NBC, 30 Rockefeller Plaza, New York, NY
    10020
b. 1934.

EDUCATION: Northwestern University, B.A.
    and M.A., Journalism.
CAREER HIGHLIGHTS: NBC Newswriter, Chi-
    cago ('61); Midwestern Field Prod., "The
    Huntley-Brinkley Report," when program ex-
    panded to half-hour ('63); European Prod. for
    NBC News ('64); Washington, DC, Prod. of
    "The Huntley-Brinkley Report" ('65). Ap-
    pointed Dir. of News, West Coast, with re-
    sponsibilities for news coverage in western
    states and for news programming where he
    started the nation's first two-hour local news
    program on KNBC, Los Angeles ('67); Prod.
    "NBC Nightly News" ('71); named Exec.
    Prod. ('72); assumed position of V.P., NBC
    News ('73); promoted to Exec. V.P.; named
    Pres., NBC TV Network ('77); became Pres.
    and Chief Exec. Officer, NBC ('81).
ACHIEVEMENTS & AWARDS: N.A.
PERSONAL: Resides in Manhattan with wife,
    Adrienne.

MUNRO, RICHARD
Pres., Time, Inc.

c/o Time, Inc., 1271 Ave. of the Americas,
    New York, NY 10020
b. January 26.

EDUCATION: Colgate University, B.A. ('57);
    Columbia University; New York University.
CAREER HIGHLIGHTS: Played an important role
    in developing HBO, and in Time, Inc.'s
    moves into video, electronic publishing, and

the magazine, *TV Cable Week*. Started with
Time & Life in the Time Magazine Circulation
Dept. ('57); *Sports Illustrated* General Mgr.,
then Publisher; Head of Time, Inc., Video
Group ('75); Dir. of Time, Inc., including
HBO ('78); Pres., Time, Inc. ('80).
ACHIEVEMENTS & AWARDS: N.A.
PERSONAL: N.A.

MURPHY, EDDIE
Comic/Actor, NBC, "Saturday Night Live"

c/o NBC, 30 Rockefeller Plaza, New York, NY
    10020
b. April 3, 1961. Brooklyn, NY.

EDUCATION: N.A.
CAREER HIGHLIGHTS: Confident and ultra-
    smooth, Murphy is the media superstar of
    the eighties—a nouveau Richard Pryor who's
    almost singlehandedly kept "Saturday Night
    Live" from fading after its initial cast had
    abandoned it. Stand-up comic at Catch a Ris-
    ing Star and the Improv. Feature film debut in
    48 Hours, followed by *Trading Places*. Regular
    on "Saturday Night Live."
ACHIEVEMENTS & AWARDS: N.A.
PERSONAL: N.A.

MUSBURGER, BRENT
Host and Managing Editor, CBS, Sports

c/o CBS, 51 W. 52d St., New York, NY 10019
b. May 26, 1940. Portland, OR.

EDUCATION: Northwestern University Medhill
    School of Journalism.
CAREER HIGHLIGHTS: A skilled knowledgeable
    professional who anchors all CBS weekend

sports shows including "CBS Sports Saturday/Sunday," "The NCAA Today," and "The NFL Today," Musburger began as a Sports Reporter and Columnist, *Chicago American*; moved on as Sports Dir., WBBM-AM, Chicago; Sports Dir., WBBM-TV, Chicago; Co-Anchor, KNXT-TV, Los Angeles; Network Weekend Sports Anchor and Play-by-Play Announcer for NBA basketball, CBS Sports ('75).

ACHIEVEMENTS & AWARDS: AP award ('65); best regular sports show award from AP ('70); Illinois Sportscaster of the Year ('70).

PERSONAL: Resides in Weston, CT, with wife, Arlene, and sons, Blake and Scott.

MUSE, REYNELDA W.
News Anchor/Reporter, CNN

c/o Daniel E. Muse, 1739 E. 29th Ave., Denver, CO 80205
b. November 16, 1946. Columbus, OH.

EDUCATION: Ohio State University, B.A., English.

CAREER HIGHLIGHTS: Staff Announcer, WOSU-Radio, Ohio State University ('66); Co-Host, Smith & Muse, KRMA-TV, Denver ('80); Host, American Skyline Series, Pacific Mountain Network and PBS Stations ('81); News Anchor/Reporter, KOA-TV, Denver ('68–'80); Principal Weekend Anchor, CNN ('80).

ACHIEVEMENTS & AWARDS: Headliner award, Women in Communications ('70); Woman of the Year, Delta Sigma Theta sorority ('73); Woman of the Year, Colorado Press Women; Barney Ford community service award ('75); American Legion media award ('78).

PERSONAL: Married, three children. Lives in Denver.

MYERS, BARBARA
Marketing Dir., HBO, Cinemax

c/o HBO, 1271 Ave. of the Americas, New York, NY 10020
b. August 6.

EDUCATION: Syracuse University, B.A., English Literature; New York University, M.B.A., Marketing and Finance.

CAREER HIGHLIGHTS: Financial Analyst, Lin-coln First Bank, Rochester, NY ('73); Planner, Domestic Merchandising, Avon Products, New York ('79); Mgr., Sales Planning, Cinemax ('81); Dir., Staff Sales Support, Cinemax ('82); Marketing Dir., Cinemax ('83).

ACHIEVEMENTS & AWARDS: N.A.
PERSONAL: N.A.

MYERS, LISA MERRYMAN
Correspondent, NBC, News

c/o NBC, 4000 Nebraska Ave., N.W., Washington, DC 20016
b. Joplin, MO.

EDUCATION: University of Missouri at Columbia, B.A., Journalism ('73).

CAREER HIGHLIGHTS: Reporter, *Columbia Missourian* ('72); Chief Tax and Economics Writer and Congressional Correspondent, Bureau of Natl. Affairs ('73); Freelance Writer, *Washington Post, Washington Star, Chicago Tribune,* and *Detroit News* ('75); Correspondent, Political Writer, *Chicago Sun-Times,* based in Washington, DC ('77); Political Correspondent, *Washington Star* ('80); Correspondent, NBC News, Washington, DC ('81).

ACHIEVEMENTS & AWARDS: N.A.
PERSONAL: N.A.

MYERS, VAN
Pres., Chief Exec. Officer, Dir., Wometco Enterprises

c/o Wometco Enterprises, 316 N. Miami, Miami, FL 33128
b. N.A.

EDUCATION: Harvard University, B.A. ('39)

CAREER HIGHLIGHTS: Joined Wometco ('40); named Sr. V.P. in Charge of Vending ('64), Exec. V.P. ('81); and Pres. and Chief Exec. Officer ('83).

ACHIEVEMENTS & AWARDS: N.A.

PERSONAL: Wife, Jane; two children. Resides in Coral Gables, FL.

MYERSON, ALAN
Dir., Playboy Channel

c/o Playboy Channel, 8560 Sunset Blvd., Los Angeles, CA 90069

b. N.A.

EDUCATION: N.A.

CAREER HIGHLIGHTS: Dir. of the motion pictures *Private Lessons* and *Steelyard Blues*. TV credits include the pilots for "The Harvey Korman Show," "Please Stand By," and "Delta House." His episodic TV credits include "Archie Bunker's Place," "Voyagers," "The Bob Newhart Show," "Knight Rider," "Rhoda," and "Welcome Back Kotter," and the TV movie *The Love Boat*. Dir., "4Play," the first sitcom produced expressly for cable TV, for the Playboy Channel.

ACHIEVEMENTS & AWARDS: N.A.

PERSONAL: N.A.

MYHRUM, ROBERT G.
Dir.

c/o Children's Television Workshop, 1 Lincoln Plaza, New York, NY 10023

b. N.A.

EDUCATION: N.A.

CAREER HIGHLIGHTS: Dir., "Sesame Street" ('71–present). Also Dir., Cerebral Palsy Telethon ('78); a CBS Young People's Concert; and a 30-part humanities series for the State University of New York. Dir. soap operas "Love of Life," "Ryan's Hope," "As the World Turns," "The Doctors," "The Secret Storm," and "A Time for Us."

ACHIEVEMENTS & AWARDS: N.A.

PERSONAL: N.A.

MYLES, STAN
Program Exec., Motion Pictures for TV, CBS, Entertainment

c/o CBS, 7800 Beverly Blvd., Los Angeles, CA 90036

b. Los Angeles, CA.

EDUCATION: California State University at Long Beach.

CAREER HIGHLIGHTS: Host, "I Am Somebody," KABC-TV, Los Angeles ('71); Mgr., Variety Programs, NBC ('75); Supervisor, Drama Development, ABC ('78); Editor, Program Practices, CBS Broadcast Group ('80); Program Exec., Motion Pictures for TV, CBS Entertainment, West Coast ('82).

ACHIEVEMENTS & AWARDS: N.A.

PERSONAL: N.A.

N

NACHMAN, JERRY
V.P., News, NBC, TV Stations Division

c/o NBC, 30 Rockefeller Plaza, New York, NY 10020
b. N.A.

EDUCATION: Youngstown State University.
CAREER HIGHLIGHTS: Started as a Copy Editor, *Pittsburgh Press*; Reporter, WCBS-AM, New York ('71); Correspondent, WCBS-TV, New York ('77); News Dir., KCBS-AM, San Francisco ('79); Exec. Prod., News, WCBS-TV ('81); V.P. and General Mgr., WRC-AM, Washington, DC ('81); V.P., News, NBC TV Stations Division ('83).
ACHIEVEMENTS & AWARDS: N.A.
PERSONAL: Resides in New York City.

NAHAN, STU
Dir. of Sports, KNBC, Sports

c/o KNBC, 3000 W. Alameda Ave., Burbank, CA 91523
b. Los Angeles, CA.

EDUCATION: McGill University.
CAREER HIGHLIGHTS: Began his broadcasting career as Asst. to Bob Kelley for radiocasts, Los Angeles Angels Pacific Coast League games ('54); became Play-by-Play Announcer, Sacramento Solons ('56); joined NBC affiliate KCRA, Sacramento, CA, as Sports Reporter ('56); provided play-by-play announcing, CBS-televised NHL game-of-the-week, Philadelphia Eagles telecasts for the NFL ('65); became Sports Dir., KABC, Los Angeles ('68–'76); covered two Winter Olympic Games, at Squaw Valley ('60) and Innsbruck ('76). Became Dir. of Sports, KNBC, Los Angeles, and also provides play-by-play commentary for local preseason Los Angeles Rams football and Los Angeles Kings hockey games ('76).
ACHIEVEMENTS & AWARDS: N.A.
PERSONAL: N.A.

NARDINO, GARY
Pres., Paramount TV

c/o Paramount Pictures Corp., 5555 Melrose Avenue, Hollywood, CA 90038
b. August 26, 1935. Garfield, NJ

EDUCATION: Seton Hall University, B.S. ('57).
CAREER HIGHLIGHTS: Joined industry as Agent ('59); became Sr. V.P., New York TV Dept., ICM; moved to William Morris Agency as V.P., New York TV Dept.; joined Paramount TV as Pres.
ACHIEVEMENTS & AWARDS: Pres., Hollywood Radio and TV Society; Member, Natl. Advisory Council, Arthritis Foundation; Natl. Council for Children and TV; Bel Air Country Club; New York Athletic Club; Burning Tree Country Club; ATAS; Alpha Kappa Psi professional business fraternity.
PERSONAL: Married to the former Florence Peluso; children, Caroline and Gary Charles Frank. Resides in Greenwich, CT, and Beverly Hills, CA.

NATHANSON, GREG
Sr. V.P., Showtime, Programming

c/o Showtime Entertainment, 1211 Ave. of the Americas, New York, NY 10036
b. April 6.

EDUCATION: University of Southern California, B.A. ('69).

CAREER HIGHLIGHTS: Started as Program Scheduler, WTTW, Chicago; joined KTLA, Research ('74); became Head of Promotion, KTLA, then Program Dir., Los Angeles ('77). V.P., Programming, Premier ('80); Sr. V.P., Programming, Showtime ('81).

ACHIEVEMENTS & AWARDS: N.A.

PERSONAL: N.A.

NATHANSON, TED
Coordinating Prod./Dir., NBC, Sports

c/o NBC, 30 Rockefeller Plaza, New York, NY 10020
b. Philadelphia, PA.

EDUCATION: N.A.

CAREER HIGHLIGHTS: Staff Dir., NBC ('53); Prod., NBC Sports ('64); Coordinating Prod., NBC Sports coverage of NFL football ('79). One of the most knowledgable and respected sports producer/directors in the business, Nathanson has covered such major sports events for NBC as Wimbledon tennis, the NCAA basketball championships, the Winter Olympics ('72), major league baseball; and NFL football, including playoffs and the Super Bowl.

ACHIEVEMENTS & AWARDS: Emmy Award for Directing the AFC championship playoffs ('77).

PERSONAL: Resides in Fairfield, CT, with his wife, Edith, and their three children.

NEDERLANDER, JAMES M.
Chairman of the Board, Nederlander Organization

c/o RKO-Nederlander, 1440 Broadway, New York, NY 10018
b. March 31, 1922.

EDUCATION: Detroit Institute of Technology.

CAREER HIGHLIGHTS: One of the four managing partners of RKO-Nederlander, a joint venture between the Nederlander Organization and RKO Pictures to supply programming for pay TV. He also operates the New York State Theater summer season presenting top names of ballet, opera, and theater in addi-

tion to supervising numerous other theaters and productions of distinguished entertainment. His Broadway productions include *Sherlock Holmes, My Fat Friend, Treemonisha, Seesaw, Applause* and *Nine*.

ACHIEVEMENTS & AWARDS: N.A.

PERSONAL: N.A.

NEDERLANDER, ROBERT E.
Pres./Dir., Nederlander Organization

c/o RKO-Nederlander, 1440 Broadway, New York, NY 10018
b. April 10, 1933.

EDUCATION: University of Michigan, B.A., Economics; University of Michigan Law School, J.D.

CAREER HIGHLIGHTS: Oversees the operations of the Nederlander theaters, the largest live-attraction theatrical chain in the U.S. He is also Pres., Nederlander Worldwide and Nederlander Brothers TV and Film Production.

ACHIEVEMENTS & AWARDS: Regent of the University of Michigan ('68–present); Partner, New York Yankees baseball club; Natl. V.P., Muscular Dystrophy Assn. Fielding H. Yost award ('55). Member, President's Club, University of Michigan.

PERSONAL: N.A.

NELSON, LINDSEY
Commentator, CBS, Sports

c/o CBS, 51 W. 52d St., New York, NY 10019
b. N.A.

EDUCATION: University of Tennessee.

CAREER HIGHLIGHTS: Began broadcasting in Knoxville, TN; moved to Liberty Broadcasting System, Dallas. Mgr. of Sports, NBC, for ten years; Radio & TV Announcer for the Mets; Announcer, CBS Sports ('63).

ACHIEVEMENTS & AWARDS: Named America's top sportscaster by Natl. Sportscasters and Sportswriters Assn. for four consecutive years ('59–'62). Honored by Overseas Press Club, Old Pros Night. Winner of the golden mike award, presented by New York Touchdown Club ('79).

PERSONAL: N.A.

NENNO, STEPHEN K.
Dir., ABC TV, Program Administration

c/o ABC, 1330 Ave. of the Americas, New
York, NY 10019
b. July 12, 1942. Los Angeles, CA.

EDUCATION: University of Southern California,
B.A., Telecommunications.
CAREER HIGHLIGHTS: KNX-Radio-TV, Los
Angeles, as Operations Asst. ('63); KHJ-TV,
Los Angeles ('65); joined ABC TV as Super-
visor, Program Unit Mgrs., Los Angeles ('68);
moved to New York as Dir., Program
Administration ('71).
ACHIEVEMENTS & AWARDS: Natl. Adviser of the
Year, Alpha Epsilon Rho ('81); Board Mem-
ber, IRTS; New York Chapter, NATAS; Alpha
Epsilon Rho ('82); Member, Advisory Board,
Seton Hall University's WSOU.
PERSONAL: N.A.

NERENBERG, SUSAN A.
Dir., Prime Time Program Development, East Coast, ABC, Entertainment

c/o ABC, 1330 Ave. of the Americas, New
York, NY 10019
b. June 13. New York, NY.

EDUCATION: Davis and Elkins College, B.A.,
English.
CAREER HIGHLIGHTS: Administrative Asst.,
Broadcast Standards, NBC ('70); Assoc., Pro-
gramming, NBC ('72); Agent in Training, Intl.
Famous Agency ('72); TV Agent, ICM ('74);
Dir., Prime Time Program Development, East
Coast, ABC Entertainment ('80).
ACHIEVEMENTS & AWARDS: N.A.
PERSONAL: Resides in New York City.

NEUFELD, MACE
Pres., Neufeld Productions

c/o Neufeld Productions, 9454 Wilshire Blvd.,
Suite 309, Beverly Hills, CA 90212
b. July 13, 1928. New York, NY.

EDUCATION: Yale University; New York University Law School.
CAREER HIGHLIGHTS: Neufeld formed an independent TV production and personal management company ('52). He produced the
first programs starring Dick Van Dyke and
the comedy team of Elaine May and Mike
Nichols for NBC ('58). Over the next quarter
century, his independent TV company and
personal management firm discovered and
developed such stars as Don Knotts, Louis
Nye, Gabe Kaplan, and Don Adams. In association with Harvey Bernhard for 20th Century Fox he was Prod., *The Omen* ('76). After
continuing with *The Omen II* and *The Final
Conflict*, he embarked full-time on independent motion picture and TV production.
Prod., for ABC's ambitious eight-hour mini-
series *East of Eden* ('81); Prod., "Cagney and
Lacey" ('81); and the TV movies *Angel on My
Shoulder* and *The American Dream.*
ACHIEVEMENTS & AWARDS: Exec. Committee
Board of Trustees, American Film Institute,
ASCAP, and the Motion Picture Academy.
PERSONAL: Married, four children.

NEUMEISTER, FRANK
Dir., Sales Service, West Coast, NBC

c/o NBC, 3000 W. Alameda Ave., Burbank,
CA 91523
b. Pittsburgh, PA.

EDUCATION: Lowell University.
CAREER HIGHLIGHTS: Show Costs Analyst, NBC
('54); Adm., Sales Service Dept., NBC ('69);
Mgr., Sales Service ('72); Dir., Sales Service
('81).
ACHIEVEMENTS & AWARDS: N.A.
PERSONAL: Resides in Sylmar, CA, with wife,
Herta.

NEUSTADT, RICHARD M.
Partner, Wiley, Johnson, & Rein Law Firm, Communications Law

1776 K St., N.W., Washington, DC 20006
b. February 4, 1948.

EDUCATION: Harvard Law School, B.A., (magna cum laude, '69); Harvard Law School, J.D.
(cum laude, '74).
CAREER HIGHLIGHTS: Regarded as one of the
nation's most outstanding young communications attorneys, he has special expertise
in the burgeoning field of electronic publishing. Political Writer for Walter Cronkite

('72); Assoc. Dir., White House Domestic Policy Staff ('77); Partner, Wiley, Johnson, & Rein law firm, (formerly Kirkland & Ellis), Washington, DC, specializing in communications law ('81).

ACHIEVEMENTS & AWARDS: Trustee, Benton Foundation. Author, *The Birth of Electronic Publishing* ('82).

PERSONAL: N.A.

NEWHART, BOB
Actor

c/o "Newhart," CBS, 7800 Beverly Blvd., Los Angeles, CA 90036
b. September 5, 1929. Chicago, IL.

EDUCATION: Loyola University.
CAREER HIGHLIGHTS: This stand-up comic's impeccable, low-key technique set the tone for two series that reflected Newhart's deft timing and dry delivery. Motion pictures include *Cold Turkey*, *Cool Millions*, and *Catch-22*. TV movies include *Thursday's Game*. Star of "The Bob Newhart Variety Show," "The Bob Newhart Show" sitcom, and "Newhart" sitcom.
ACHIEVEMENTS & AWARDS: N.A.
PERSONAL: Wife, Ginny; four children. Resides in Beverly Hills, CA.

NEWMAN, EDWIN
Correspondent, NBC, News

c/o NBC, 30 Rockefeller Plaza, New York, NY 10020
b. 1919. New York

EDUCATION: University of Wisconsin.
CAREER HIGHLIGHTS: Greatly admired by his colleagues and sadly underutilized by NBC for the past decade, Newman is one of the most graceful and witty writers to be found anywhere, on or off camera. Worked for Intl. News Service and UPI in Washington, DC ('41); joined Eric Sevareid's staff, CBS, in Washington, DC ('47); special assignments for NBC News ('49); NBC News in London, Rome, and Paris ('52–'61); based in New York, host of "Today" and "Update"; Anchor and Reporter of numerous documentaries.
ACHIEVEMENTS & AWARDS: Peabody award for Radio Commentaries; Overseas Press Club award; New York Emmy awards. Author of *Strictly Speaking: Will America Be the Death of English?* ('74); *A Civil Tongue* ('76); articles published in *Esquire*, *Harper's*, *Atlantic*, *N.Y. Times Sunday Magazine*, *TV Guide*.
PERSONAL: Wife, Rigel; one daughter. Resides in Manhattan.

NEWMAN, JACK
Writer/Prod.

c/o NBC, 3000 W. Alameda Ave., Burbank, CA 91523
b. Toledo, OH.

EDUCATION: University of Missouri, University of California at Los Angeles.
CAREER HIGHLIGHTS: Creator, "Police Story," "Petrocelli," and "Kate McShane"; Writer/Prod., "Law and Order" pilot. Founded P.A. Production Co; also, Writer/Prod., "Dr. Kildare," "Mr. Novak," and "Night Games." Independent Prod. who usually works with NBC.
ACHIEVEMENTS & AWARDS: N.A.
PERSONAL: N.A.

NEWMAN, MONTELLE G.
V.P. and General Mgr., NBC, WMAQ-TV, Chicago, IL

c/o WMAQ-TV, Merchandise Mart, Chicago, IL 60654
b. December 17. Quincy, MA.

EDUCATION: Boston University, B.S.
CAREER HIGHLIGHTS: Started in Sales Dept. of

WRC-TV, Washington, DC ('66); Spot Sales for NBC in New York and Chicago ('68); Local Sales Mgr., WNBC-TV, New York ('70); General Sales Mgr., WRC-TV ('72); Dir., Eastern Sales, NBC-TV ('75); Station Mgr., WNBC-TV ('75); Station Mgr. WRC-TV ('77); V.P. and General Mgr., WMAQ-TV ('79).

ACHIEVEMENTS & AWARDS: N.A.

PERSONAL: Resides in suburban Chicago.

NEWMAN-MINSON, LAUNA
Dir., ABC, Special Programs

c/o ABC, 2040 Ave. of the Stars, Los Angeles, CA 90067

b. Youngstown, OH.

EDUCATION: Northwestern University, B.A.

CAREER HIGHLIGHTS: Started TV Career with development of the original "Mike Douglas Show" ('61); Westinghouse Writer, Assoc. Prod., and Prod. for syndicated and network shows including "The Merv Griffin Show" ('62), "The Smothers Brothers Show" ('67), "The Glen Campbell Show" ('69), "The David Frost Show" ('70) 10 years with Dinah Shore. ABC Exec. Prod. ('80); promoted to Dir. of Special Programs.

ACHIEVEMENTS & AWARDS: N.A.

PERSONAL: Resides in Los Angeles with husband, Michael, and daughter, Whitney Anne.

NICHOLSON, NICK
Prod., ABC, "The Edge of Night"

c/o "The Edge of Night," ABC, 1330 Ave. of the Americas, New York, NY 10019

b. Buffalo, NY.

EDUCATION: N.A.

CAREER HIGHLIGHTS: Production Asst., "Lamp Unto My Feet" ('54); Production Asst., "Ford Star Jubilee" ('57); Asst. Prod., "Secret Storm" ('59); became Prod., "The Edge of Night" ('66).

ACHIEVEMENTS & AWARDS: "The Edge of Night" has received three Emmy awards under Nicholson's tenure.

PERSONAL: Resides in New York City.

NIXON, AGNES
Writer/Prod.

c/o Agnes Nixon & Assoc., 774 Conestoga Rd., Rosemont, PA 19010

b. N.A.

EDUCATION: Northwestern University.

CAREER HIGHLIGHTS: After a long and fruitful apprenticeship with soap opera pioneer Irna Phillips, Nixon displayed the same flair as her predecessor for adapting the daytime drama to meet her audience's needs. More than any other producer, Nixon introduced the element of relevance into serials and created story lines involving contemporary issues. Dialogue Writer for Daytime Drama ('50s); wrote episodes of "As the World Turns"; Head Writer for Proctor & Gamble serials; created and produced the "One Life To Live" serial ('68); created and produced "All My Children" serial ('70); wrote *The Manions of America* mini-series ('81). Creator/Prod., "Loving" ('83).

ACHIEVEMENTS & AWARDS: NATAS trustees award; *Soap Opera Digest* award.

PERSONAL: N.A.

NOBLE, GIL
Prod./Correspondent, WABC-TV

c/o WABC-TV, 7 Lincoln Sq., New York, NY 10023

b. February 22. Harlem, NY

EDUCATION: N.A.

CAREER HIGHLIGHTS: WLIB-Radio, New York ('62); Instructor, Mass Communications, Seton Hall University; Eyewitness News Correspondent, WABC-TV ('67); Managing Editor, Prod., and Host, "Like It Is" ('75).

ACHIEVEMENTS & AWARDS: Six local Emmy awards for "Like It Is"; Journalist of the Year award ('82); New York Urban League, Frederick Douglass Award ('79); NATAS governor's citation of merit ('78); recipient of more than 300 community awards. Author of *Black Is the Color of My TV Tube* ('81).

PERSONAL: N.A.

NOBLE, PAUL
Exec. Prod., WNEW-TV

c/o WNEW-TV, 205 E. 67th St., New York, NY 10021
b. December 8. New York.

EDUCATION: Cornell University, B.A., Government; Boston University, M.S., Communications.
CAREER HIGHLIGHTS: Prod./Dir., WGBH-TV, Boston ('57); Prod., Public Affairs/Politically Oriented Programs, WNEW-TV ('61); Exec. Prod., WNEW-TV ('75).
ACHIEVEMENTS & AWARDS: Emmy for "S.O.S. Save Our Schools" series ('77); certificate of merit from the American Bar Assn., for "Cost of Crime" ('76). Member, American Film Institute and Theater Historical Society.
PERSONAL: N.A.

NORTHSHIELD, ROBERT ("Shad")
Sr. Exec. Prod., CBS, News

c/o CBS, 524 W. 57 St., New York, NY 10019
b. 1922. Oak Park, IL.

EDUCATION: Knox College, B.A., Chemistry, and doctorate of humane letters.
CAREER HIGHLIGHTS: Before working at CBS, he was a Reporter, Picture Editor, and Columnist, *Chicago Sun-Times*; Assoc. Prod. of CBS's "Adventure" ('53); Prod., "Seven Lively Arts", CBS ('57); Prod., Public affairs broadcasts, ABC ('58); joined NBC ('60); Prod., NBC News coverage of special events ('60–'70); Prod., "Today" program, NBC News ('60–'77); Exec. Prod., "The Huntley-Brinkley Report" ('65–'69); Exec. Prod., election night returns ('62–'74); Exec. Prod., CBS Sports ('78); Prod., CBS news documentaries ('78); Exec. Prod., "Morning," CBS ('78); Sr. Exec. Prod., "Morning," CBS ('80–'82); Sr. Exec. Prod., "CBS News Sunday Morning" ('80). His crowning achievement in recent years has been this acclaimed "Sunday Morning" show, arguably the most civilized and urbane show in the history of American television journalism.
ACHIEVEMENTS & AWARDS: "Sunday Morning" has earned the Dupont-Columbia University award ('81), Peabody award ('79), Ohio State University award ('80), and numerous citations.

PERSONAL: Married; four sons. Resides in Croton-on-Hudson, NY.

NORVET, ROBERT
V.P., Production Facilities, Hollywood, CBS, TV

c/o CBS, 7800 Beverly Blvd., Los Angeles, CA 90036
b. Forest City, IA.

EDUCATION: Grinnell College.
CAREER HIGHLIGHTS: Production Exec., MGM Studios; Dir., Film Operations, CBS, Hollywood ('60); V.P., CBS Studio Center, Los Angeles ('67); V.P., Production Facilities, CBS TV, Hollywood ('77).
ACHIEVEMENTS & AWARDS: N.A.
PERSONAL: Wife, Mary; two sons.

NUNN, RAY
Prod., ABC, News

c/o ABC, 1330 Ave. of the Americas, New York, NY 10019
b. N.A.

EDUCATION: Yale University; Harvard Law School.
CAREER HIGHLIGHTS: Reporter and Anchor, WICD-TV, Champaign, IL; Anchor, Reporter, Prod., WJCT-TV, Jacksonville, FL; Editor, Asst. Weekend TV News Prod., CBS; Reporter, ABC News ('77); General Assignment Correspondent, ABC News ('81); Sr. Foreign Prod., London, ABC News ('83).
ACHIEVEMENTS & AWARDS: N.A.
PERSONAL: N.A.

NYKANEN, MARK
News Correspondent, NBC, "Monitor"

c/o NBC, 30 Rockefeller Plaza, New York, NY 10020
b. New York, NY.

EDUCATION: Mesa Community College.
CAREER HIGHLIGHTS: Freelance Writer ('72–'74); Writer/Researcher, *New Times Weekly*, Phoenix ('73); Freelance Prod., KDKB-Radio, Mesa, AZ ('74); Contributing Editor, *New*

Times Weekly ('74); Dir., News and Public Affairs, KDKB-Radio, Mesa ('76); Investigative Reporter, "Arizona Weekly," TV magazine, KAET-TV, PBS, Phoenix ('78); Correspondent, NBC News, Chicago ('80); Head of NBC "Monitor" Investigative Unit ('83).

ACHIEVEMENTS & AWARDS: Natl. Headliners award for outstanding public service by a radio station ('75); Natl. Headliners award for outstanding documentary by a radio station ('77); Arizona Press Club award for editorial writing.

PERSONAL: Wife, Ann.

OBER, ERIC
V.P. and General Mgr., CBS, WBBM-TV, Chicago

c/o WBBM-TV, 630 N. McClurg Ct., Chicago, IL 60611
b. N.A.

EDUCATION: Yale University, B.A., History; Columbia University, M.S., Political Science.
CAREER HIGHLIGHTS: Newswriter, WCBS-TV, New York ('68); Editor, WCBS-TV ('70); Prod., WCBS-TV ('71); Exec. Prod., WCBS-TV ('72); Asst. News Dir., WCBS-TV ('73); Dir., News, WCAU-TV, Philadelphia ('76); Dir., News, WBBM-TV, Chicago ('79); V.P. and Station Mgr., WCBS-TV ('83); V.P. and General Mgr., WBBM-TV, Chicago ('83).
ACHIEVEMENTS & AWARDS: N.A.
PERSONAL: N.A.

O'BRIEN, BOB
Reporter, WNEW-TV

c/o WNEW-TV, 205 E. 67th St., New York, NY 10021
b. Pittsburgh, PA.

EDUCATION: Xavier University.
CAREER HIGHLIGHTS: Reporter for WRAN-Radio, New York ('68); Production Asst., Writer, Editor, and Prod., WNEW-TV; Investigative Reporter, WNEW-TV.
ACHIEVEMENTS & AWARDS: Emmy for reporting; American Bar Assn. certificate of merit for WNEW-TV "Police Series."
PERSONAL: N.A.

O'BRIEN, TIM
Correspondent, ABC, News

c/o ABC, 1717 DeSales St., N.W., Washington, DC 20036
b. New York, NY.

EDUCATION: Michigan State University, B.A., Communications; University of Maryland, M.A., Political Science; Loyola University Law School, law degree.
CAREER HIGHLIGHTS: Newswriter, WILS-Radio, Lansing, MI ('62); Staff, WJIM-TV, Lansing, MI ('64); Reporter/ Anchor/Writer/Photographer/Prod., WILX-TV, Jackson, MI ('66); Reporter/Anchor/Writer, WKBD-TV, Detroit ('68); Reporter/Weekend Anchor, WTOP-TV, Washington, DC ('69); Reporter/Anchor/Writer/Prod., WDSU-TV, New Orleans ('72); Reporter, ABC News ('77); Legal Correspondent, ABC News ('79).
ACHIEVEMENTS & AWARDS: New Orleans Press Club award ('76); two certificates of merit from the American Bar Assn. ('79); Columbia-Dupont award and a gavel award from the American Bar Assn. for his ABC News Closeup report, "The Shooting of Big Man" ('79).
PERSONAL: Resides in Maryland with his wife and their two children.

O'CONNELL, KEVIN
Weather Reporter, KNBC, "News 4 LA"

c/o KNBC, 3000 W. Alameda Ave., Burbank, CA 91523
b. N.A.

EDUCATION: Buffalo State University.
CAREER HIGHLIGHTS: He began his broadcasting career as Announcer and Disc Jockey, WYSL-Radio; promoted to Program Dir.; was a popular radio Music/Talk Show Host, WBEN; hosted a weekly public affairs program, "By the People," WIVB-TV, Buffalo, NY; Weathercaster, WIVB-TV, Buffalo, NY; Weather Reporter, KNBC, "News 4 LA."
ACHIEVEMENTS & AWARDS: N.A.
PERSONAL: Married, one son.

O'CONNELL, RAYMOND T.
**V.P., NBC TV, Station Relations
Administration**

c/o NBC, 30 Rockefeller Plaza, New York, NY
10020
b. N.A.

EDUCATION: N.A.
CAREER HIGHLIGHTS: Started in the Guest Relations Dept., NBC TV, and advanced to Audience Promotion Mgr. Became Dir., NBC Station Relations ('67); promoted to V.P., Station
Relations Administration ('76).
ACHIEVEMENTS & AWARDS: N.A.
PERSONAL: Wife, Mary; children, Kevin, Kate,
and Christopher. Resides in Larchmont, NY.

O'CONNOR, CARROLL
Actor

c/o Creative Management Assoc., 8899
Beverly Blvd., Los Angeles, CA 90048
b. August 2, 1925. New York, NY.

EDUCATION: University College of Dublin; University of Montana.
CAREER HIGHLIGHTS: Carroll's remarkable portrayal of Archie Bunker on "All in the Family," which turned into "Archie Bunker's
Place" for several years, has earned him more
awards than any other actor has ever received
for a single TV characterization. Starred in
numerous stage productions in New York
and Europe and later concentrated his efforts
on feature films such as *A Fever in the Blood,
Lonely Are the Brave, Cleopatra, Waterhole No. 3,
Kelly's Heroes, Doctors' Wives,* and *Law and Dis-
order.* Performed on TV in "The U.S. Steel
Hour," "Armstrong Circle Theater," and
"Kraft Theater," and in specials *Of Thee I Sing*
and "The Carroll O'Connor Special—Three
for the Girls." Guest-starred in more than 50
series including "That Girl" before getting
lead role in "All in the Family" ('71), the forerunner of "Archie Bunker's Place" ('79). Also,
Co-Creator, "Bronk" series; and Story Editor,
"Archie Bunker's Place."
ACHIEVEMENTS & AWARDS: Named Male Star of
the Year by the American Guild of Variety
Artists ('72); Emmy awards ('72, '77, '78, '79);
Golden Globe award ('72); Peabody award
('80).

PERSONAL: Resides in Malibu, CA, with wife,
Nancy; son, Hugh.

O'CONNOR, DANIEL P.
Managing Dir., Documentaries, NBC, News

c/o NBC, 30 Rockefeller Plaza, New York, NY
10020
b. November 9, 1921. Omaha, NE.

EDUCATION: Creighton University; Catholic
University of America, M.A., Communica-
tions.
CAREER HIGHLIGHTS: Assoc. Dir. and Produc-
tion Stage Mgr. for entertainment shows,
NBC ('51); moved to NBC News as Assoc.
Prod. and Unit Mgr.; Mgr., News Programs,
NBC News ('65); Dir., Special News Pro-
grams, NBC News ('77); Managing Dir., Doc-
umentaries, NBC News ('82).
ACHIEVEMENTS & AWARDS: N.A.
PERSONAL: Resides in Roxbury, CT, with wife,
Lenka; five children.

O'CONNOR, JOHN J.
TV Critic, *N.Y. Times*

c/o *N.Y. Times,* 229 W. 43d St., New York, NY
10036
b. July 10. Bronx, NY.

EDUCATION: City College of New York: Yale
University.
CAREER HIGHLIGHTS: Arts Editor, *Wall Street
Journal* ('61); TV Critic, *N.Y. Times* ('71).
ACHIEVEMENTS & AWARDS: N.A.
PERSONAL: Cousin of actor Carroll O'Connor.

OGIENS, MICHAEL
V.P., CBS, Entertainment, Programs

c/o CBS, 51 W. 52d St., New York, NY 10019
b. June 19, 1947.

EDUCATION: N.A.
CAREER HIGHLIGHTS: Production background
with ABC TV and independent producers;
joined CBS Network as General Daytime
Programming Exec. ('72); Dir., Daytime
Programs, Hollywood ('73); became V.P.,
Daytime Programs during restructuring of

broadcast operations ('77); V.P., Daytime and Children's Programs ('79); appointed V.P., Programs, New York ('82).

ACHIEVEMENTS & AWARDS: N.A.

PERSONAL: Resides in New York City.

O'HARA, CATHERINE
Writer/Performer, "SCTV Network"

c/o SCTV, 110 Lombard St., Toronto, Ontario, Canada, M5C-IM3

b. March 4. Toronto, Canada.

EDUCATION: N.A.

CAREER HIGHLIGHTS: TV credits include "The Steve Allen Comedy Hour" and "From Cleveland." Writer/Performer, "SCTV Network."

ACHIEVEMENTS & AWARDS: N.A.

PERSONAL: Resides in Toronto, Canada.

OHLMEYER, DON
Dir./Prod., NBC, Sports

c/o NBC, 30 Rockefeller Plaza, New York, NY 10020

b. February 3, 1945. New Orleans, LA.

EDUCATION: University of Notre Dame, B.A., Communications.

CAREER HIGHLIGHTS: One of the major figures in TV sports production, he began as Assoc. TV Dir. of the Summer Olympics from Mexico City, ABC ('68); Dir. of Summer Olympics Telecast, Munich, ABC ('72); Dir. of Winter Olympics Telecast, Montreal, ABC ('76); Exec. Prod. of all NBC Sports Programming; also, Prod., "Battle of the Network Stars."

ACHIEVEMENTS & AWARDS: Seven Emmy awards for sports programming; Cine golden eagle award ('79).

PERSONAL: N.A.

OKIE, RICHARD C.
Dir., Current Drama Programs, NBC, West Coast

c/o NBC, 3000 W. Alameda Ave., Burbank, CA 915233

b. Los Angeles, CA.

EDUCATION: Yale University, B.A., English ('74).

CAREER HIGHLIGHTS: Payroll Dept., CBS TV ('76); Story Dept., CBS TV ('77); Story Dept., NBC ('78); Mgr., Current Drama Programs ('79); Dir., Current Drama Programs, NBC ('81).

ACHIEVEMENTS & AWARDS: N.A.

PERSONAL: N.A.

OLBERMANN, KEITH
Natl. Sports Correspondent, Cable News Network, Sports

c/o Cable News Network, 1050 Techwood Dr., N.W., Atlanta, GA 30318

b. January 27, 1959. New York, NY.

EDUCATION: Cornell University, B.S., Communications.

CAREER HIGHLIGHTS: Sportscaster, UPI Radio Network ('79); Sportscaster, RKO-Radio Network ('80); Sportscaster, WNEW-AM, New York ('80); while continuing with WNEW, named Natl. Sports Correspondent, Cable News Network ('82).

ACHIEVEMENTS & AWARDS: N.A.

PERSONAL: Single; resides in New York City.

O'LEARY, RICHARD A.
TV Consultant

c/o Richard A. O'Leary & Assoc., 1 E. 57th St., New York, NY 10022

b. May 5, 1926. San Francisco, CA.

EDUCATION: University of Southern California, B.S.

CAREER HIGHLIGHTS: Sales Mgr., KTTV, Los Angeles ('51); KABC-TV Acct. Exec. ('54); Sales Mgr. ('59); General Sales Mgr. ('60). Moved to WLS, Chicago, as V.P./General Mgr. ('66); Pres., ABC Owned TV Stations ('70); added responsibility for Pres., ABC Intl. TV ('72); left ABC to form Richard A. O'Leary & Assoc., a consulting, development, and marketing company ('82).

ACHIEVEMENTS & AWARDS: Former Pres., Intl. Council, NATAS; former First V.P., IRTS; Board of Dirs., TV Bureau of Advertising.

PERSONAL: Resides in New Canaan, CT, with

wife Jeanette; children, Karen, Maureen, Kevin, and Shawn.

OLIANSKY, JOEL
Writer

c/o Writers Guild, 8955 Beverly Blvd., Los Angeles, CA 90048
b. 1935. New York, NY.

EDUCATION: Hofstra University; Yale University.
CAREER HIGHLIGHTS: Writer, *Shame, Shame on the Johnson Boys* ('66); *The Law* ('75); *The Competition* ('80); and *Masada* ('81).
ACHIEVEMENTS & AWARDS: Emmy award ('71); Humanitas prize ('75); Writers Guild award ('75).
PERSONAL: N.A.

OLIVER, DON
Correspondent, NBC, News

c/o NBC, 30 Rockefeller Plaza, New York, NY 10020
b. Billings, MT.

EDUCATION: University of Montana, B.A.; Columbia University Graduate School of Journalism.
CAREER HIGHLIGHTS: Political Editor, KCRA-TV, Sacramento, CA ('63); News Dir., KREM-TV, Spokane, WA ('65); Correspondent, NBC News ('66); Correspondent, NBC News, Los Angeles ('69).
ACHIEVEMENTS & AWARDS: N.A.
PERSONAL: N.A.

OLKEN, JONATHAN
V.P., ABC Owned TV Stations, Creative Services

130 W. 75th St., New York, NY 10023
b. August 3, 1944. Cambridge, MA.

EDUCATION: Boston University, B.S., Journalism ('66)
CAREER HIGHLIGHTS: Joined WNAC-TV, Boston, as Writer/Prod. ('66); WSPD, Toledo, Mgr., Promotions ('68); Mgr., Advertising, WLS, Chicago. Moved to WABC, New York,

as Dir., Creative Services ('72); V.P., Creative Services, ABC Owned TV Stations ('81).
ACHIEVEMENTS & AWARDS: Gabriel award ('74); Clio awards ('74, '78, '80); BPA gold awards ('69, '74, '79, '80, '81, '82); New York State Broadcasters award ('79, '80, '81); CEBA awards ('78, '80, '81).
PERSONAL: N.A.

OLSEN, MERLIN
Actor/Sports Broadcaster, NBC, Sports

c/o NBC, 3000 W. Alameda Ave., Burbank, CA 91523
b. September 15, 1940.

EDUCATION: Utah State University.
CAREER HIGHLIGHTS: Talented football analyst for NBC Sports whose insightful commentaries in conjunction with Dick Enberg's play-by-play make him part of one of the top broadcast teams working on pro football. A star defensive tackle with the Los Angeles Rams ('62–'77), he joined NBC Sports as an analyst on their NFL football broadcasts ('77); doubled as an actor in "Little House on the Prairie" ('77); starred in his own series, "Father Murphy," on NBC ('81); also appeared on numerous network specials including Bob Hope programs.
ACHIEVEMENTS & AWARDS: Inducted into the Pro Football Hall of Fame ('82).
PERSONAL: Resides in Pasadena, CA, with his wife and children.

O'NEIL, CAROLYN A.
Prod./Reporter, Nutrition News, Cable News Network

c/o Cable News Network, 1050 Techwood Dr., N.W., Atlanta, GA 30318
b. July 16, 1955. Dundee, Scotland.

EDUCATION: Florida State University, B.S.; Boston University, M.A.
CAREER HIGHLIGHTS: Consumer Reporter, Warner Cable TV, Sommerville, MA ('79); Consumer Reporter/Noon Anchor, WTVX-TV, Fort Pierce, FL ('80); Prod./Reporter, Nutrition News, Cable News Network ('82).
ACHIEVEMENTS & AWARDS: Member, American Dietetic Assn.
PERSONAL: Single, resides in Atlanta.

O'NEIL, ROGER
Correspondent, NBC, News

c/o NBC, 30 Rockefeller Plaza, New York, NY 10020
b. April 17, 1945. Chicago, IL.

EDUCATION: Southern Illinois University, B.A., Radio and TV ('66).
CAREER HIGHLIGHTS: Reporter, WMDD-TV, Peoria, IL ('66); Reporter, WSAZ-TV, Huntington, WV ('67); Reporter, WAVE-TV, Louisville, KY ('71); Reporter, KPRC-TV, Houston ('77); Reporter, WMAQ-TV, Chicago ('79); Correspondent, NBC News, Chicago ('79).
ACHIEVEMENTS & AWARDS: N.A.
PERSONAL: Wife, Lynn, and daughter, Meredith.

O'NEIL, SHANE
Exec. V.P., RKO-General

c/o RKO-General, 1440 Broadway, New York, NY 10018
b. March 25, 1947. Boston, MA.

EDUCATION: New York University, Columbia Graduate School of Business.
CAREER HIGHLIGHTS: Joined RKO-General as Financial Researcher ('70); V.P., formation of the Corporate Development, RKO ('77); V.P., RKO-Pictures and Performance Properties ('78); one of four Managing Partners, RKO-Nederlander ('79); Exec. V.P., RKO-General ('82).
ACHIEVEMENTS & AWARDS: N.A.
PERSONAL: Single, resides in Manhattan.

O'NEIL, TERRY
Exec. Prod., NFL Football, CBS, Sports

c/o CBS, 51 W. 52d St., New York, NY 10019
b. N.A.

EDUCATION: University of Nortre Dame, B.S., Communications; Columbia Graduate School of Journalism, M.A.
CAREER HIGHLIGHTS: Began career as a Researcher for ABC and the 1972 Olympics; Statistician for NCAA and "Monday Night Football" broadcasts ('72); Announcer, WKPA-Radio, Pittsburgh; full-time Prod., ABC Sports ('75); Prod., Olympics ('76); Prod.

"ABC Sports Magazine" ('78); joined CBS Sports as Exec. Prod., NFL telecasts, and CBS "Sports Saturday/Sunday" ('81).
ACHIEVEMENTS & AWARDS: Two Emmy awards; author of Fighting Back, the story of Pittsburgh Steeler running back Rocky Bleier.
PERSONAL: Single, resides in Greenwich, CT.

O'NEILL, ROBERT F.
Prod., Universal TV

c/o Universal TV, 100 Universal Plaza, Universal City, CA 91608
b. N.A.

EDUCATION: Loyola University.
CAREER HIGHLIGHTS: Production Asst., Universal-Intl. Studios; Production Asst., CBS TV; Assoc. Prod., "Dr. Kildare"; Story Editor, "Mission Impossible"; Prod. for Universal on "Columbo," "Quincy," "Wheels," and Operation Prime Time special Evening in Byzantium.
ACHIEVEMENTS & AWARDS: Emmy for "Columbo."
PERSONAL: N.A.

ONORATO, AL
V.P., Casting, Columbia Pictures TV

c/o Columbia Pictures TV, Columbia Plaza, Burbank, CA 91505
b. N.A.

EDUCATION: N.A.
CAREER HIGHLIGHTS: Joined Columbia Pictures TV ('70) as Casting Dir. on such shows as "The Young Rebels," "The Good Life," "Bewitched," " Bridget Loves Bernie," "Joe Forrester," and "Police Story." Dir. of Talent, Columbia Pictures TV ('75); Head of Casting, Columbia Pictures TV ('76); V.P., Casting, Columbia Pictures TV ('79).
ACHIEVEMENTS & AWARDS: N.A.
PERSONAL: N.A.

OPOTOWSKY, STAN
Dir., Political Operations, ABC, News

c/o ABC, 7 W. 66th St., New York, NY 10023
b. April 13, 1923. New Orleans, LA.

EDUCATION: Tulane University.

CAREER HIGHLIGHTS: UPI Reporter in New Orleans, Denver, New York ('47); Reporter,
N.Y. Post ('58); Managing Editor, *N.Y. Post*
('67). Joined ABC News as Assignment Editor
('72); Dir., Operations, for Documentaries
('73); Dir., TV News Coverage ('74); promoted to Dir., Political Operations ('81).

ACHIEVEMENTS & AWARDS: Books published are
The Kennedy Government ('60); *The Longs of Louisiana* ('59); *TV: The Big Picture* ('61); *Men Behind Bars* ('72).

PERSONAL: Resides in Pleasantville, NY, with
wife, Martha; children, Peter, Anne, and
Kate.

OSERANSKY, BERNARD
V.P., CBS, Facilities and Engineering

c/o CBS, 51 W. 52d St., New York, NY 10019
b. San Bernardino, CA.

EDUCATION: Los Angeles City College; Trinity
University; San Antonio College.

CAREER HIGHLIGHTS: Asst. Production Mgr.
and Unit Production Mgr. for "Hawaii Five-
O" ('67); Production Mgr. for CBS Studio
Center ('77); General Mgr., CBS Studio Center, Hollywood ('78).

ACHIEVEMENTS & AWARDS: N.A.

PERSONAL: Wife, Edith; three daughters and
one son. Resides in Northridge, CA.

OSGOOD, CHARLES
Correspondent, CBS, News

c/o CBS, 51 W. 52d St., New York, NY 10019
b. January 9, 1933. New York.

EDUCATION: Fordham University, B.S., Economics ('54).

CAREER HIGHLIGHTS: General Manager of
WHCT, Hartford, CT; Program Dir. and
Mgr., WGMS, Washington, DC; Correspon-
dent, ABC News; Anchor/Reporter, WCBS-
Radio ('67); Correspondent, CBS News ('71);
Anchor, "CBS Sunday Night News"; Writer/
Anchor, daily CBS Radio broadcasts "News-
break" and "The Osgood File."

ACHIEVEMENTS & AWARDS: Author of two
books, *Nothing Could Be Finer Than a Crisis
That Is Minor in the Morning* ('79), *There's Noth-*

ing I Wouldn't Do If You Would Be My POSSLQ
('81).

PERSONAL: N.A.

OVADIA, AL
Dir., Affiliate Creative Services, NBC

c/o NBC, 3000 W. Alameda Ave., Burbank,
CA 91523
b. Seattle, WA.

EDUCATION: University of Washington.

CAREER HIGHLIGHTS: Started as a Page with
NBC, Burbank ('75); Page Supervisor ('76); Intern in NBC Sales Dept. ('76); Mgr. of Guest
Relations ('77); Studio Tour Mgr. ('77); Administrator, Creative Services, NBC, New
York ('78). Left NBC to start his own business
marketing specialty items pertaining to the
telecast of the 1980 Summer Olympic Games
('79). Mgr. of the Non-Theatrical Film Division, Walt Disney Productions ('80); rejoined
NBC as Dir., Affiliate Creative Services, NBC,
Burbank ('81).

ACHIEVEMENTS & AWARDS: N.A.

PERSONAL: N.A.

OVITZ, MARK
Sr. V.P., Paramount TV, Creative Affairs

c/o Paramount Pictures Corp., 5555 Melrose
Ave., Los Angeles, CA 90038
b. N.A.

EDUCATION: N.A.

CAREER HIGHLIGHTS: Affiliated with Cine Art-
ists Pictures and Avco Embassy pictures be-
fore joining Paramount as Mgr. of Program
Development ('77); Admin. Asst. to Pres.,
Paramount TV; Mgr. of Current Programs,
Paramount; Dir. of Current Programs; V.P.,
Current Programs, Paramount TV ('79); Sr.
V.P., Creative Affairs, Paramount TV ('82).

ACHIEVEMENTS & AWARDS: N.A.

PERSONAL: N.A.

OWENS, ANGELA
Reporter, WRC-TV

c/o WRC-TV, 4001 Nebraska Ave., N.W.,
Washington, DC 20016
b. N.A.

EDUCATION: Eastern College, B.A., English Literature and Philosophy; Columbia University, Journalism.

CAREER HIGHLIGHTS: Newswriter/Reporter, *Washington Informer* newspaper ('66); In-Paper Promotions Writer, *Philadelphia Evening* and *Sunday Bulletin;* Washington, DC. Correspondent for WNBC, New York; WMAQ, Chicago; WKYC, Cleveland; and KNBC, Los Angeles. Reporter, WRC-TV ('72).

ACHIEVEMENTS & AWARDS: Emmy; Capitol Press Club award

PERSONAL: Resides in northwest Washington, DC.

OZ, FRANK
Puppeteer, Creative Consultant, V.P., Henson Assoc.

c/o Solters/Roskin/Friedman, 45 W. 34th St., New York, NY 10001
b. England.

EDUCATION: N.A.

CAREER HIGHLIGHTS: Recruited by Jim Henson ('63). Known as the voices of Cookie Monster, Bert, and Grover of "Sesame Street"; Fozzie Bear, Miss Piggy, and Animal of "The Muppet Show"; and other Muppet characters. Prod., *The Great Muppet Caper,* with David Lazer; Co-Dir., *The Dark Crystal,* with Jim Henson. Portrayed Yoda in *The Empire Strikes Back,* as well as being a star performer in Henson feature films.

ACHIEVEMENTS & AWARDS: Emmy for outstanding variety series, "The Muppet Show" ('77).

PERSONAL: N.A.

P

PAGE, GEORGE H.
Dir., WNET, Program Development, Arts and Sciences Programming

c/o WNET, 356 W. 58th St., New York, NY 10019
b. March 31, 1935. Hartwell, GA.

EDUCATION: Emory University, B.A.
CAREER HIGHLIGHTS: Worked at WSB-TV, Atlanta, as Anchor, 6 and 11 P.M. news; Host, "This Week With George Page," and Prod., "Block Busting Atlanta Style" and "One in a Million" ('59). Dir., Special Projects, WGBH-TV, and Prod./Writer/Narrator, WNET, the documentaries "The Young Americans," "The Parents," "Seven Who Dared," and "Confronted" ('63); NBC News Writer/Correspondent, "The Huntley-Brinkley Report," Correspondent in Vietnam, Europe, and South America, and Prod., "We Won't Go," special on draft resistance ('66). Joined PBS, as Asst. to the Pres., Dir., Public Information, and Head, Cultural Affairs Programming ('72); Dir., Program Development and Dir., Arts and Sciences Programming ('74). In this role he has supervised development and acquisition of *The Adams Chronicles*, "Monty Python's Flying Circus," *Scenes from a Marriage*, "Bill Moyers' Journal," and "The MacNeil/Lehrer Report."
ACHIEVEMENTS & AWARDS: Radio-TV News Dirs. Assn. award for "Block Busting Atlanta Style" ('63); Blue Ribbon, Edinburgh Film Festival, for "The Young Americans" ('64); Emmy award, as executive producer of "Picasso—A Painter's Diary" ('81).
PERSONAL: Resides in Dobbs Ferry, NY.

PAISNER, BRUCE
Pres., King Features Entertainment

c/o King Features Entertainment, 235 E. 45th St., New York, NY 10017
b. N.A.

EDUCATION: Harvard Law School.
CAREER HIGHLIGHTS: Reporter, *Life* magazine; Asst. to Chairman of Time, Inc.; Pres., Time-Life Films; Independent Prod.; Pres., Kings Features Entertainment.
ACHIEVEMENTS & AWARDS: N.A.
PERSONAL: N.A.

PAIVA, JEAN
Dir. of Marketing, Cablentertainment

c/o Cablentertainment, 295 Madison Ave., New York, NY 10017
b. N.A.

EDUCATION: Fashion Institute of Technology.
CAREER HIGHLIGHTS: Marketing Mgr., American Management Assns.; Marketing Mgr., American TV Communications Corp. ('79); Dir. of Marketing and Dir. of Corporate Communications, Cablentertainment.
ACHIEVEMENTS & AWARDS: N.A.
PERSONAL: N.A.

PALEY, JANE (Jane Paley Price)
Dir., ABC, Community Relations

c/o ABC, 1330 Ave. of the Americas, New York, NY 10019
b. June 30, 1947. New York, NY.

EDUCATION: Brandeis University, B.A.; New York University, M.A.

CAREER HIGHLIGHTS: TV Prod. with Lennen & Newell advertising agency ('69); Teacher, Dalton School ('71); Asst. Dir. of Neil Simon's *The Good Doctor* ('75) and of Joseph Papp's production of *Trelawny of the Wells* ('76); Public Relations Acct. Supervisor, The Softness Group ('76); V.P., Manning Selvage & Lee ('77); joined ABC as Dir., Community Relations ('81).

ACHIEVEMENTS & AWARDS: YMCA achievement award ('80), Intl. Film and TV Festival of New York bronze award ('80), Silver Screen award, U.S. Industrial Film Festival ('81), Cine golden eagle ('81). Board of Dirs., Second Stage Theater ('79–present).

PERSONAL: Resides in Manhattan with husband, Laurence Price.

PALEY, WILLIAM S.
Founder/Chairman, CBS, Inc.

c/o CBS, 51 W. 52d St., New York, NY 10019
b. September 28, 1901. Chicago, IL.

EDUCATION: University of Chicago; University of Pennsylvania.

CAREER HIGHLIGHTS: Paley left his family's business to buy the United Independent Broadcasting Co. ('28), soon to become the Columbia Broadcasting Co. During his early years, Paley served in many executive and production roles and spent much of his time working to convince sponsors and artists of the importance of the relatively new medium. Throughout the thirties, he was successful in attracting many of the great entertainers and important advertisers of the Golden Age. Paley's purchase of the American Record Corp. ('38) gave rise to the highly successful CBS Records Inc. Alongside the successful entertainment segment of CBS, there developed a distinct and separate news department under Paley's firm guidance. The radio documentary unit that Paley established shortly after World War II became the forerunner of a long line of CBS television public affairs programs, including "Face the Nation" and "60 Minutes." Paley became Chairman and Chief Exec. Officer of CBS ('46) with Frank Stanton succeeding him as Pres. Programming became Paley's specialty and he developed innovative dramatic series such as "Studio One" and "Playhouse 90." Throughout his career in TV, Paley advocated high-quality educational programming on the major networks, a concept that has yet to be realized. The now defunct CBS Cable was established ('81) as a subscriber service devoted primarily to cultural programming and folded due to lack of support. William Paley resigned as Chief Exec. Officer ('83) but retained the position of Chairman of the Board. He remains active in a policymaking role, and has a particular interest in the new technologies. Paley became a Trustee of the Museum of Modern Art ('37), a Trustee of Columbia University ('50) and is Chairman of the Board of the Museum of Broadcasting, which he founded ('76).

ACHIEVEMENTS & AWARDS: Peabody Awards ('58, '61). First Amendment Freedoms Award from the Anti-Defamation League of B'nai Brith.

PERSONAL: Resides in New York City.

PALMER, JOHN
Anchor/Correspondent, NBC, News

c/o NBC, 30 Rockefeller Plaza, New York, NY 10020
b. Kingsport, TN.

EDUCATION: Northwestern University; Columbia University Graduate School of Journalism, M.A.

CAREER HIGHLIGHTS: Reporter/Anchor, WSB-TV, Atlanta ('61); Reporter, NBC News Midwestern Bureau, and Anchor, daily news program on WMAQ-TV ('63); New York Reporter/Anchor, WNBC-TV ('69); NBC News Correspondent, Israel ('71); assigned to Beirut ('73); based in Paris ('76); covered the White House ('79); NBC News Anchor on "Today" show ('82).

ACHIEVEMENTS & AWARDS: Edgar Bergen Fellowship; NBC-RCA Earl Godwin Memorial Fellowship; Overseas Press Club award and Natl. Headliners award ('75); Merriman Smith Memorial Fund award for excellence in presidential news coverage ('81).

PERSONAL: N.A.

PALTROW, BRUCE
Exec. Prod.

c/o MTM Enterprises, 4024 Radford Ave., Studio City, CA 91604
b. Long Island, NY.

EDUCATION: Tulane University, B.F.A. ('65).

CAREER HIGHLIGHTS: Creative writer/producer concerned with ethical issues who worked against all odds to develop one of the best-ever TV shows with a sports theme, "The White Shadow." His innovative knack continued with the much-heralded but initially low-rated "St. Elsewhere." He began as a Freelance Writer ('67); produced two off-Broadway plays ('69–'70); moved into TV as Writer/Dir. of pilots ('71). Joined MTM Enterprises ('77); Creator/Prod./Dir., "The White Shadow" ('78); Co-Prod./Dir., *A Little Sex*, his first feature film ('81). Became Exec. Prod., "St. Elsewhere" ('82).

ACHIEVEMENTS & AWARDS: N.A.

PERSONAL: Resides in Brentwood, CA, with his wife, actress Blythe Danner, and two children.

PANITT, MERRILL
Editorial Dir., Triangle Publications, *TV Guide*

c/o *TV Guide*, 4 Corporate Center, Radnor, PA 19088
b. September 11, 1917. Hartford, CT.

EDUCATION: University of Missouri School of Journalism, B.A.

CAREER HIGHLIGHTS: Writer, UPI ('38); Writer, Triangle Publications ('46–present); Administrative Asst. to Walter Annenberg; Managing Editor, *TV Guide*; Editorial Dir., *TV Guide* and *Seventeen*.

ACHIEVEMENTS & AWARDS: N.A.

PERSONAL: N.A.

PAPPAS, IKE
Correspondent, CBS, News

c/o CBS, 2020 M St., N.W., Washington, DC 20036
b. New York, NY.

EDUCATION: Long Island University.

CAREER HIGHLIGHTS: Reporter, UPI ('56); Reporter, WNEW News, New York ('58); Writer/Reporter, CBS Radio News ('64); Prod./General Assignment Reporter, CBS News for both TV and Radio ('65); Correspondent, CBS News ('67); Correspondent, CBS News, Chicago ('68); Pentagon Correspondent, CBS News, Washington, DC ('75); Labor Correspondent, CBS News, Washington, DC ('82).

ACHIEVEMENTS & AWARDS: Ohio State University award ('64); Hellenic Club award from the University of Pennsylvania; distinguished service award from Long Island University.

PERSONAL: Wife, Carolyn; three children.

PARDI, KATHLEEN
Mgr., On-Air Promotion Operations, NBC, Administration

c/o NBC, 3000 W. Alameda Ave., Burbank, CA 91523
b. Glendale, CA.

EDUCATION: California State University at Northridge, B.A., Radio, TV and Film (magna cum laude, '78).

CAREER HIGHLIGHTS: Joined NBC as a Secretary, Film Exchange Dept., Burbank ('78); moved into the On-Air Promotion Dept., NBC ('78); named Broadcast Advertising Specialist, On-Air Promotion ('79); Administrator, On-Air Production, Advertising and Promotion ('81); Mgr., On-Air Promotion ('82); Mgr., On-Air Promotion Operations, NBC, Burbank ('83).
ACHIEVEMENTS & AWARDS: N.A.
PERSONAL: Resides in Sylmar, CA, with husband, Rick.

PARIS, JERRY
Dir./Prod.

c/o Creative Artists Agency, 1888 Century
   Park E., Century City, CA 90067
b. July 25, 1925. California.

EDUCATION: New York University.
CAREER HIGHLIGHTS: Started as an actor on Broadway, in movies and on TV, co-starring on "The Dick Van Dyke Show"; started directing on the "The Dick Van Dyke Show"; went on to direct pilots that have become long-running series, including "That Girl," "The Partridge Family," "Love, American Style," "The Odd Couple," "Happy Days," and "Laverne and Shirley"; directed more than 15 movies made for TV, including *The Feminist and the Fuzz, How To Break Up a Happy Divorce,* and *House Hunting.*
ACHIEVEMENTS & AWARDS: Emmy for "The Dick Van Dyke Show"; Directors Guild award.
PERSONAL: Resides in Pacific Palisades, CA, with three children, Tony, Julie, and Andy.

PARKER, EVERETT C.
Editor-At-Large, Channels Magazine

c/o Channels Magazine, 131 N. Chatsworth,
   Larchmont, NY 10538
b. January 13, 1913. Chicago, IL.

EDUCATION: University of Chicago ('43).
CAREER HIGHLIGHTS: For more than 20 years Parker was one of the most important public interest spokesman concerning broadcasting and public policy issues. His work resulted in numerous pivotal broadcasting reforms, in-

cluding the WLBT case in Jackson, MS, where the courts recognized that individual citizens had the right to participate in legal action against broadcasters. Parker was also active in areas concerning minority employment in broadcasting, censorship, and civil liberties issues. He started as a religious broadcaster in the Midwest; founded the Joint Religious Radio Committee ('45) to aid postwar relief attempts; and assumed the post of Dir. of Communications of the United Church of Christ ('53), from which he retired on August 31, 1983; Editor-at-Large, Channels Magazine ('83).
ACHIEVEMENTS & AWARDS: Many awards from major national and religious organizations.
PERSONAL: Resides in White Plains, NY.

PARKER, JEANNE A.
Mgr., Art Services, NBC, Advertising and Promotion, West Coast

c/o NBC, 3000 W. Alameda Ave., Burbank,
   CA 91523
b. Bryn Mawr, PA.

EDUCATION: Parsons School of Design; Philadelphia Academy of Fine Art; Western Michigan University, B.S., Fine Arts; University of Iowa.
CAREER HIGHLIGHTS: Co-Owner of an interior design business, Chicago ('68); Freelance Art Designer and Prod., Los Angeles area ('70); Sr. Art Dir., B. J. Stewart Advertising, Newport Beach CA ('77); Production Mgr., Leo Monahan & Assoc., Los Angeles ('80); Mgr., Art Services, Advertising and Promotion, NBC, Burbank ('83).
ACHIEVEMENTS & AWARDS: N.A.
PERSONAL: Resides in Silverlake, CA.

PARKER, RON
Prod.

c/o ABC, 2040 Ave. of the Stars, Los Angeles,
   CA 90067
b. November 7, 1949. Hutchinson, KS.

EDUCATION: University of Kansas, B.S., Journalism ('72).
CAREER HIGHLIGHTS: Agent, Creative Management Assoc. ('72); Story Editor, Robert Fryer

Productions ('73); Production Assoc. on Broadway musical *Chicago* and Broadway play *The Norman Conquests* ('75); Dir. of Development, Producer Circle Co. ('76); Dir. of Creative Affairs, Marble Arch Productions ('77); Partner, Catalina Production Group ('80–present); Exec. Prod. *Thursday's Child*, CBS ('82); Prod., *The Fighter*, CBS ('83); Prod., *Legs*, ABC ('83).
ACHIEVEMENTS & AWARDS: N.A.
PERSONAL: N.A.

PARKIN, BRYON
Managing Dir., BBC Enterprises LTD.

c/o BBC, 12 Cavendish Place, London, England W1
b. April 1, 1932. Sheffield, England.

EDUCATION: N.A.
CAREER HIGHLIGHTS: Sr. Cost Accountant, BBC Finance Division ('68); General Mgr., BBC Enterprises ('77); Managing Dir., BBC Enterprises ('79).
ACHIEVEMENTS & AWARDS: N.A.
PERSONAL: N.A.

PARKIN, JUDD
Mgr., Mini-Series and Novels for TV, NBC, Entertainment

c/o NBC, 3000 W. Alameda Ave., Burbank, CA 91523
b. Chicago, IL.

EDUCATION: University of Illinois, B.A., English and Drama ('74).
CAREER HIGHLIGHTS: Dir., Oregon Shakespearean Festival, Ashland, OR ('74–'80); Freelance Dir., Los Angeles ('80); Story Editor, NBC Story Dept., West Coast, ('81); Mgr., Mini-Series and Novels for TV, NBC Entertainment, West Coast, ('83).
ACHIEVEMENTS & AWARDS: N.A.
PERSONAL: Resides in Los Angeles with wife, Marilyn.

PARKINSON, BOB
Prod., Parkinson/Friendly Productions

c/o Parkinson/Friendly Productions, Suite 814, 1717 N. Highland Ave., Hollywood, CA 90028
b. N.A.

EDUCATION: College of Wooster, B.A., Communications ('59).
CAREER HIGHLIGHTS: Host/Disc Jockey, WWST-AM, Wooster, OH ('55); Host/Disc Jockey, WTOD-AM, Toledo ('59); Host/Disc Jockey, WPAS-AM, Zephyrioll, FL ('62); Host/Disc Jockey, WEAM-AM, Washington, DC ('64); Host, WTTG-TV, Washington, DC ('64); Beginning in '67 his production credits include "Circus of the Stars," "National Juke Box Awards," "Celebrity Daredevils," "All American Women," "The Miss Universe Pageant," "The Miss U.S.A. Pageant," "The People's Choice Awards," and the syndicated "This is Your Life." As a Prod./Writer, his credits include "The Magic of David Copperfield," "Pageant 80," and "Music, Music, Music." His latest development projects include the TV movies *The Rolf Benischke Story* and *The Grandma Mafia* and the TV specials "The British Invasion" and "Divorce," as well as a Richard Pryor concert film.
ACHIEVEMENTS & AWARDS: Florida Broadcaster of the Year ('63); Gabriel Heatter Award ('63); Man of the Year from the Washington, DC, Jaycees.
PERSONAL: N.A.

PARRIOTT, JAMES D.
Writer/Prod./Dir. (Freelance)

Suite 1530, 1900 Ave. of the Stars, Los Angeles, CA 90067
b. November 14, 1950. Denver, CO.

EDUCATION: University of Denver, B.A.; University of California at Los Angeles, M.F.A.
CAREER HIGHLIGHTS: Prod./Writer, "The Bionic Woman" ('75–'78); Supervising Prod./Writer/Dir., "The Incredible Hulk" ('78); Supervising Prod./Writer, *The Legend of the Golden Gun*, movie of the week for NBC ('79); Co-Supervising Prod./ Co-Writer, "Nick and the Dobermans" and "Alex and the Doberman Gang," pilots for NBC ('80); Co-Exec. Prod., "Fitz and Bones" series, NBC ('81); Co-Exec.

Prod./Co-Writer, "The Seal" pilot, NBC, ('81); Exec. Prod. (pilot and series), Writer/Dir. (pilot) "Voyagers," NBC ('82).
ACHIEVEMENTS & AWARDS: N.A.
PERSONAL: Married to Diane Civita Parriott, an actress; two children. Resides in Los Angeles.

PASETTA, MARTIN A.
Dir., ICM

c/o ICM, 8899 Beverly Blvd., Los Angeles, CA 90048
b. San Francisco, CA.

EDUCATION: University of Santa Clara, B.A.
CAREER HIGHLIGHTS: Writer/Prod./Dir., KGO, Santa Clara, CA ('52); Assoc. Prod., "Dateline Hollywood." Dir., "The Smothers Brothers Comedy Hour," "The Glen Campbell Hour," "Steve 'n' Eydie." Specials include Elvis Presley Special, Frank Sinatra's "Ole Blue Eyes Is Back," "The Stars Salute Israel at 30," "Gene Kelly, An American in Pasadena," "Paul Anka in Monte Carlo," "Barry Manilow in Concert," "A Country Christmas," "All-Star Salute to Pearl Bailey," "AFI Salute to Alfred Hitchcock," and "A Gift of Song."
ACHIEVEMENTS & AWARDS: Nine Grammy awards; seven Emmy awards.
PERSONAL: Wife, Elise; three children. Resides in Bel Air, CA.

PATTERSON, V. L. ("Pat")
Pres., Cardiff Cablevision

c/o Cardiff Cablevision, 6430 S. Yosemite, Englewood, CO 80111
b. N.A.

EDUCATION: Kansas University.
CAREER HIGHLIGHTS: Served as a Radar Technician, Marine Corps. Owned and operated TV service companies in Kansas and later in Soda Springs, ID, where he helped to construct and manage and later become an owner of the local cable system. Joined Cardiff Cablevision ('70), becoming V.P., then Pres.
ACHIEVEMENTS & AWARDS: N.A.
PERSONAL: N.A.

PAUL, SOL J.
Publisher and Pres., *Television/Radio Age*

c/o *Television/Radio Age*, 1270 Ave. of the Americas, New York, NY 10020
b. Rochester, NY.

EDUCATION: Georgetown University School of Foreign Service ('39).
CAREER HIGHLIGHTS: Worked as a reporter for the *Washington Post* and was the Washington, DC, Correspondent for the Gannett Newspapers chain ('39). Feature Writer, *Broadcasting* magazine ('41); Midwest Mgr., *Broadcasting* ('42); Advertising Mgr., broadcasting, New York ('46); started *Television Age,* now *Television/Radio Age* ('53). former owner and publisher of the *Magazine of Wall Street* and the *World Radio and TV Handbook*. He is now publisher and owner of *Investment Business Forecast* and *Cableage*.
ACHIEVEMENTS & AWARDS: Member, Board of Dirs., Intl. Radio and TV Foundation.
PERSONAL: Wife, Margaret; three children, Celia, Abigail, and John.

PAULEY, JANE
Co-Anchor, NBC, "Today"

c/o NBC, 30 Rockefeller Plaza, New York, NY 10020
b. October 31, 1950. Indianapolis, IN.

EDUCATION: Indiana University, B.A., Political Science ('71).

CAREER HIGHLIGHTS: Started out in Indiana state politics; joined WISH-TV, Indianapolis, as a Reporter; moved up to Co-Anchor, mid-day new reports, and Anchor, weekend news reports; at WMAQ became the first woman ever to co-anchor a regularly scheduled news program in Chicago; featured regularly on the "Today" show ('76); named Co-Anchor of "Today".

ACHIEVEMENTS & AWARDS: N.A.

PERSONAL: Married to cartoonist Garry Trudeau.

PEARLMAN, SY
Exec. Prod., NBC, News, "Monitor"

c/o NBC, 30 Rockefeller Plaza, New York, NY 10019
b. New York, NY.

EDUCATION: Brooklyn College, B.A. ('50); New York University, M.A. ('59); Columbia Graduate School of Journalism, M.S. ('60).

CAREER HIGHLIGHTS: Served as Counter-Intelligence Agent, U.S. Army in West Germany ('53); Teacher of History, New York City Schools ('56–'59); Editor, Sunday Dept. of the N.Y. Times ('61); Freelance Reporter in Eastern Europe ('67); NBC News Radio Reporter in Czechoslovakia during '68 crisis and through the Soviet invasion; Stringer, Time magazine, in Berlin ('69); became a full-time NBC News Staff Member ('70), assignments included Bureau Chief in Tel Aviv; coverage of President Nixon's trip to Moscow; Israeli-Arab Yom Kippur War. Prod., NBC magazine series "Weekend"; Prod., NBC White Paper "America Works When America Works" ('81); Prod., "An American Profile: The Narcs"; Exec. Prod., NBC White Paper, "Facing Up to the Bomb"; Exec. Prod., NBC News Magazine series, "Monitor" ('82–).

ACHIEVEMENTS & AWARDS: Peabody award ('76); Martin R. Gainsburgh award.

PERSONAL: N.A.

PELGRIFT, KATHRYN C.
V.P., Corporate Planning and Business Development, NBC

c/o NBC, 30 Rockefeller Plaza, New York, NY 10020
b. N.A.

EDUCATION: Wellesley College; University of North Carolina; New York University Graduate School of Business Administration.

CAREER HIGHLIGHTS: Joined the Corporate Finance Dept., First Boston Corp., New York ('68); Asst. to the Exec. V.P. and Chief Exec. Officer, Intl. Paper Co. ('70); Asst. Treasurer, Intl. Paper Co. ('71); Asst. to Pres., CBS, Inc. ('72); V.P., Planning, CBS, Inc. ('74); Dir. of Finance, Philip Morris, Inc. ('77); Treasurer, Philip Morris, USA ('79); V.P., Corporate Planning, NBC ('80); V.P., Corporate Planning and Business Development ('83).

ACHIEVEMENTS & AWARDS: Member, Council on Foreign Relations.

PERSONAL: N.A.

PEPPER, PETE
Reporter, KNBC, "News 4 LA"

c/o KNBC, 3000 W. Alameda Ave., Burbank, CA 91523
b. N.A.

EDUCATION: University of Hawaii, Creative Writing (magna cum laude).

CAREER HIGHLIGHTS: Eight years military experience in the U.S. Army in which he attained the rank of Captain, Airborne Infantry. Began his journalistic career as News Dir., KCCN-Radio, Honolulu ('72); Reporter/Anchor, KHON-TV, Honolulu; Investigative Reporter, Fill-In Anchor, KGTV, San Diego, CA; Consumer Advocacy Reporter, KGTV, San Diego; correspondent, KNXT, Los Angeles, San Fernando Valley Bureau; Nightside Reporter, "News 4 LA," KNBC ('81).

ACHIEVEMENTS & AWARDS: Was awarded the Silver Star, three Bronze Stars for valor, and the Vietnamese Cross of Gallantry.

PERSONAL: Resides in North Hollywood.

PERAGINE, FRANCES
Dir. of Programming, Cinemax

c/o Cinemax, 1271 Ave. of the Americas, New York, NY 10020
b. New York, NY.

EDUCATION: Fashion Institute of Technology, B.A.

CAREER HIGHLIGHTS: Booking Agent, Paramount Pictures Corp.; Dir. of Programming, TPS ('77); Dir. of Program Operations, TPS ('78); Dir. of Operations, TPS and HBO Program Services ('79); Program Mgr. for Take II Pay Service ('80); Dir. of Acquisition and Dir. of Programming, Cinemax ('82).

ACHIEVEMENTS & AWARDS: N.A.

PERSONAL: N.A.

PERCELAY, DAVID
V.P., CBS, News

c/o CBS, 524 W. 57th St., New York, NY 10019
b. Providence, RI.

EDUCATION: Brown University, B.A., Economics; Harvard Business School, M.B.A.

CAREER HIGHLIGHTS: Planning Analyst, CBS TV Stations ('76); Mgr., Planning, CBS TV ('77); Dir., Planning, KNXT-TV, Los Angeles ('78); Dir., CBS Teletext Project, Los Angeles ('80); V.P., CBS News ('82).

ACHIEVEMENTS & AWARDS: N.A.

PERSONAL: N.A.

PERKINS, JACK
Co-Anchor, KNBC, "LA at 4"

c/o KNBC, 3000 W. Alameda Ave., Burbank, CA 91523
b. Cleveland, OH.

EDUCATION: Western Reserve University, B.A.

CAREER HIGHLIGHTS: News Dir., WEWS-TV, Cleveland; NBC News Correspondent; Correspondent, "NBC Magazine With David Brinkley," "Prime Time Saturday"; Co-Anchor, KNBC, "LA at 4."

ACHIEVEMENTS & AWARDS: Two Emmy awards.

PERSONAL: Resides in Tarzana, CA, with wife, Mary Jo, and two sons.

PERKINS, JAMES N.
Pres., Perkins-Washburn

c/o Perkins-Washburn, 6 E. 68th St., New York, NY 10021
b. August 9, 1933.

EDUCATION: Dartmouth College, B.A.

CAREER HIGHLIGHRS Publishing Exec., Times-Mirror, Playboy, Curtia Publishing, and Doubleday; founded Perkins-Bernstein, one of the leading marketing and advertising agencies specializing in the direct marketing field; founded and served as Pres., Washburn Assoc., where he created "Home Shopping Show" for cable TV and introduced the concept of the "informercial." Appointed Pres. and Chief Operating Officer, Hearst/ABC Video Services; Pres., Perkins-Washburn ('83).

ACHIEVEMENTS & AWARDS: N.A.

PERSONAL: Resides in Manhattan with wife, Judith; daughters, Karen, Susan, and Betsy.

PERLMUTTER, ALVIN
Independent Prod.

31 W. 57th St., New York, NY 10019
b. March 24, 1928.

EDUCATION: N.A.

CAREER HIGHLIGHTS: Dir., Public Affairs and Program Mgr., WNBC-TV, New York; Prod. of Documentaries, WNET, New York, including "American Dream Machine," "Black Journal," "NET Journal,"and "At Issue." V.P., NBC News Documentaries ('75); Independent Prod. ('77).

ACHIEVEMENTS & AWARDS: Emmy awards, Robert F. Kennedy award.

PERSONAL: N.A.

PERRYMAN, MACK
V.P., HBO, Programming Operations

c/o HBO, 1271 Ave. of the Americas, New York, NY 10020
b. June 2, 1947.

EDUCATION: University of Alabama, B.A.; Fordham University Graduate School.

CAREER HIGHLIGHTS: Joined ABC TV in Program Information Services ('71); named Mgr. of Program Operations, ABC Entertainment ('74); Dir., Program Administration, East Coast ('76); moved to HBO as Dir. of Scheduling ('79); additional responsibilities for intermissions programming operations ('80); appointed V.P., Programming Operations, HBO ('82).

ACHIEVEMENTS & AWARDS: Member, NATAS; IRTS.

PERSONAL: Resides in Manhattan with wife, Terry.

PERSKY, BILL
Writer/Prod./Dir.

c/o Creative Artists Agency, 1888 Century Parkway E., Los Angeles, CA 90067
b. September 9. New Haven, CT.

EDUCATION: Syracuse University, B.A.

CAREER HIGHLIGHTS: Comedy Sketch Writer for Sid Caesar, Dick Shawn, and Steve Allen ('55); Writer, "The Andy Williams Show" ('59); Writer, "The Joey Bishop Show" ('60); Writer, "McHale's Navy" ('61); Writer/Story Editor, "The Dick Van Dyke Show" ('62); Co-Prod., "The Dick Van Dyke Show" ('66); Creator/Prod./Dir., "That Girl," with partner Sam Denoff ('66); Writer/Prod., "The Bill Cosby Special" ('68); Writer for the TV specials "Pure Goldie," "Dick Van Dyke and Other Women," and "The Confessions of Dick Van Dyke" ('69–'70); Creator/Prod., "The Funny Side" ('71), "The Don Rickles Show" ('72), and, "Lotsa Luck" ('73); Dir. for such TV shows as "The Montefuscos," "The Betty White Show," "Joe & Valerie," "Busting Loose," "The Waverly Wonders," "Baby, I'm Back," "Big City Boys," "Husbands and Wives," "No Honesty," "The Practice," "Big Eddie," "The McLean Stevenson Show," "A New Kind of Family," "Love at First Sight," "Two Plus Two," "Baker's Dozen," "Filthy Rich," "Johnny Gringo," and "Sutter's Bay."

ACHIEVEMENTS & AWARDS: Four Emmy awards for writing for "The Dick Van Dyke Show" ('64, '65), "The Sid Caesar Special" ('67), and "The Bill Cosby Special" ('68); Writer's Guild award for "The Sid Caesar Special" ('67).

PERSONAL: Three daughters, Jeanne, Liza, and Dayna.

PETERSON, KATHRYN R.
V.P., Home Theater Network, Affiliate Relations and Administration

465 Congress St., Portland, ME 04101
b. February 24, 1949. Norway, ME.

EDUCATION: University of Southern Maine.

CAREER HIGHLIGHTS: Dir. of Administrative Services, Home Theater Network ('79); promoted to V.P., Administration ('80); then to V.P., Affiliate Relations and Administration ('82).

ACHIEVEMENTS & AWARDS: Member, Women in Cable; CTAM; Administrative Management Society.

PERSONAL: Resides in South Windham, ME, with husband, Thomas.

PETERSON, ROGER
Correspondent, ABC, News

c/o ABC, 1717 DeSales St., N.W., Washington, DC 20036
b. Hopkins, MN.

EDUCATION: University of Minnesota.

CAREER HIGHLIGHTS: Early broadcast jobs began in radio stations KSJB, Minot, ND; WCHK, Canton, GA; WSB, Atlanta. Moved into TV, WSB-TV, Atlanta; KSTP-TV, Minneapolis. Writer/Reporter/Anchor, WTMJ-TV, Milwaukee ('62); Reporter, WBKB-TV (now WLS-TV), Chicago ('65); Correspondent, ABC News, Saigon ('66); Bureau Chief, ABC News, Tokyo ('67); Correspondent, ABC News, New York ('69); Pentagon Correspondent, ABC News, Washington, DC ('70); Energy Correspondent, ABC News, Washington, DC ('73).

ACHIEVEMENTS & AWARDS: N.A.

PERSONAL: Resides in suburban Washington, DC, with wife, Karen.

PETERSON, SUSAN
President of Susan Peterson and Associates

b. Watersmeet, MI.

EDUCATION: Denison University ('67).

CAREER HIGHLIGHTS: Host, "Today at Twelve," WAEO-TV, Rhinelander, WI ('67); Reporter, WISN-TV, Milwaukee ('68); Public Relations

Representative, Ruder & Finn ('68); Reporter, WCCO-TV, Minneapolis ('69); Reporter and Co-Host, "Kennedy & Co.," WLS-TV, Chicago ('72); Reporter, WRC-TV, Washington, DC ('73); Reporter, CBS News, Washington, DC ('74); Reporter, CBS News, London ('75); Correspondent, CBS News ('77); Correspondent, NBC News, Washington, DC ('80); Pres. Susan Peterson and Associates ('83).
ACHIEVEMENTS & AWARDS: N.A.
PERSONAL: N.A.

Correspondent ('79). Was one of NBC News's four TV floor reporters at the national political conventions ('72, '76, '80); became Exec. V.P., NBC News ('82).
ACHIEVEMENTS & AWARDS: Peabody award, Emmy award for "First Tuesday" segment, "CBW: The Secrets of Secrecy" ('69); Emmy for reporting and writing "Some Footnotes to 25 Nuclear Years" on "First Tuesday" ('70); Emmy for "America's Nerve Gas Arsenal" on "First Tuesday" ('73).
PERSONAL: N.A.

PETINA, DOMINIC A.
Dir., On-Air Production Operations, NBC, On-Air Promotion

c/o NBC, 3000 W. Alameda Ave., Burbank, CA 91523
b. Bristol, PA.

EDUCATION: Theater School of Dramatic Arts and TV Workshop.
CAREER HIGHLIGHTS: Joined NBC as a Page, Guest Relations Dept. ('56); moved to positions as Adm., On-Air Promotion; Mgr., Broadcast Advertising; Mgr., Production and Administration, On-Air Promotion; named Dir., On-Air Production Operations, On-Air Promotion Dept. NBC, West Coast ('81).
ACHIEVEMENTS & AWARDS: N.A.
PERSONAL: Resides in Sherman Oaks, CA, with wife, Soralyn.

PETRICK, JACK
Dir. of Programming, WTBS-TV, Atlanta

c/o WTBS, 1050 Techwood Dr., N.W., Atlanta, GA 30318
b. N.A.

EDUCATION: Iowa State University, B.S., Electrical Engineering; Creighton University, M.S., Business Administration.
CAREER HIGHLIGHTS: Sales Mgr., Program Dir., Chief Engineer, KETV-TV, Omaha ('58); General Mgr., KDNL-TV, St. Louis ('70); Dir. of Programming, WTBS-TV, Atlanta ('83).
ACHIEVEMENTS & AWARDS: N.A.
PERSONAL: N.A.

PETIT, TOM
Exec. V.P., NBC, News

c/o NBC, 30 Rockefeller Plaza, New York, NY 10020
b. Cincinnati, OH.

EDUCATION: University of Northern Iowa ('53); University of Minnesota, M.A., American Studies ('58).
CAREER HIGHLIGHTS: Reporter, WOI-TV, Ames, IA ('53); NBC News Reporter, WRCV, Philadelphia ('59); NBC News Los Angeles Bureau ('62); gained nationwide attention for on-the-scene reporting of the shooting of Pres. John F. Kennedy's assassin, Lee Harvey Oswald ('63); Chief West Coast Correspondent for NET's PBL ('68); returned to NBC in Washington, DC, Bureau ('75); U.S. Senate

PFISTER, EDWARD J.
Pres., Corp. for Public Broadcasting

c/o Corp. for Public Broadcasting, 1111 16th St., N.W., Washington, DC 20036
b. New York, NY.

EDUCATION: St. Peter's College, B.A., Literature and Philosophy; Seton Hall University, M.A., Professional Education.

CAREER HIGHLIGHTS: Worked as a Reporter, *Reno Evening Gazette,* and *The Record,* Hackensack, NJ; Mgr., Information Services, and Writer/Editor, Natl. Educational TV and Radio Center, New York ('60); Dir., Information Services, and Asst. to Exec. Dir., Natl. Instructional TV Center (now the Agency for instructional TV), Bloomington, IN ('65); Dir., Public Relations and Information Services, Natl. Assn. of Educational Broadcasters, (Washington, DC ('70); Dir. of the PBS Coordinating Committee ('72); Exec. Asst. to the Chairman of the Board of PBS, Washington, DC ('73); Pres. and General Mgr., KERA-TV/FM, Dallas/Fort Worth ('76); Pres., Corp. for Public Broadcasting, Washington, DC ('81).

ACHIEVEMENTS & AWARDS: N.A.

PERSONAL: Wife, Katherine; three children, Eddie, Tony, and Terese.

PFISTER, LARRY
V.P., Time Video Information Services

c/o Time Video Information Services, 1271 Ave. of the Americas, New York, NY 10019
b. N.A.

EDUCATION: University of Tulsa.

CAREER HIGHLIGHTS: Involved in broadcasting, cable TV, and data processing for more than 25 years, he has worked as General Mgr., Broadcast Division, Harris Corp.; Dir. of Marketing and Corporate Development, Cable-Data; V.P., Mini-computer Division, Control Data; V.P., Telidon Videotex Systems; and now as V.P., Dir., Teletext Service, Time Video Information Services ('83).

ACHIEVEMENTS & AWARDS: Chairman, U.S. Videotex Industry Assn.

PERSONAL: N.A.

PHILBIN, REGIS
Co-Host, WABC-TV, New York, "The Morning Show"

c/o WABC-TV, 7 Lincoln Sq., New York, NY 10023
b. New York, NY.

EDUCATION: University of Notre Dame, B.A., Sociology.

CAREER HIGHLIGHTS: Started as a Page with NBC, New York ('58); went on to host numerous TV programs in southern California including "Philbin's People," "The Unknowns," and "Tempo" at KHJ-TV, Los Angeles, and "The Neighbors" and "Almost Anything Goes" for ABC; Reporter/Host for KABC-TV, Los Angeles for the station's "Eyewitness News" and "A.M. Los Angeles" ('74); Host, "The Regis Philbin Show" on NBC ('81); Host, "Regis Philbin's Health Styles" on the Cable Health Network ('82); Co-Host, "The Morning Show" with Cyndy Garvey on WABC-TV, New York ('83). Recorded "It's Time for Regis" record album.

ACHIEVEMENTS & AWARDS: N.A.

PERSONAL: Resides in New York City with his wife, Joy, and their two daughters, Joanna and Jennifer.

PICARD, PAUL
Prod.

4000 Warner Blvd., Burbank, CA 91522
b. Jamestown, RI.

EDUCATION: American Theatre Wing ('55).

CAREER HIGHLIGHTS: Actor ('57); Production Mgr., WNDT-TV, New York ('62–'66); Dir. of Daytime and Live Programs, ABC, responsible for "Marcus Welby, M.D.," "The Courtship of Edie's Father," "The Brady Bunch," "Love, American Style," and "Room 222" pilots ('67–'69); Exec. Prod., MGM Studios, V.P., MGM TV ('69); V.P. of Prod., American Intl. Pictures ('74); Prod., Warner Bros. TV, "The Dukes of Hazzard" ('79); *Scruples* ('81).

ACHIEVEMENTS & AWARDS: N.A.

PERSONAL: Wife, Louise Latham; one daughter.

PIERCE, FREDERICK S.
Pres. and Chief Operating Officer, ABC, Inc.

c/o ABC, 1330 Ave. of the Americas, New York, NY 10019
b. April 8, 1933. New York, NY.

EDUCATION: Baruch College, B.A.

CAREER HIGHLIGHTS: Pierce's rapid rise to the top of the ABC executive ladder was due to his outstanding managerial skills in addition to his flair for programming. His career at ABC began at age 23 as Analyst, TV Network Research Dept. ('56); promoted to Supervisor of Audience Measurements ('57); became Mgr., Audience Measurements ('58). Made Dir. of Research ('61); given additional responsibilities as Dir., Sales Development ('62); promoted to Dir., of Sales Planning and Sales Development ('62); elected V.P. and Natl. Dir of Sales for the ABC TV Network ('64). Moved to V.P., Planning, for ABC TV Network ('68); Became V.P., in Charge of Planning as Asst. to the Pres. of the ABC TV Network ('70–'72); assumed title of V.P. in Charge of ABC TV Planning and Development ('72); moved on to Sr. V.P. of ABC TV and named Pres., ABC TV and elected to Board of Dirs., ABC, Inc. ('74); added News and Broadcast Operations and Engineering to

his responsibilities ('77). Named Exec. V.P. of ABC while continuing as Pres., ABC TV ('79); reorganized ABC TV Division and at that time relinquished title of Pres., ABC TV ('81). Recently replaced Elton Rule as Pres. and Chief Operating Officer, ABC, Inc. ('83).

ACHIEVEMENTS & AWARDS: Member, Board of Dirs., ABC, Inc.; Board of Trustees, American Film Institute; Board of Dirs., Museum of Broadcasting.

PERSONAL: Resides in Manhattan with wife, Marion.

PIERCE, PONCHITTA
Host/Co-Prod., WNBC-TV, "Today in New York"

c/o WNBC-TV, 30 Rockefeller Plaza, New York, NY 10020
b. N.A.

EDUCATION: University of Southern California, B.A.; University of Cambridge (England).

CAREER HIGHLIGHTS: Began her career in journalism at *Ebony* magazine ('64): served as Special Correspondent for CBS News ('68); wrote for *McCall's* magazine and *Reader's Digest* as well as for *Newsday* and *Family Circle.* Joined WNBC as Co-Host, Channel 4's Sunday magazine series "The Sunday Show." ('73). Also, Host/Co-Prod., WNBC-TV, "Today in New York."

ACHIEVEMENTS & AWARDS: AMITA award ('74) for distinguished achievement in the field of communications arts; the Headliner award from the Natl. Theta Sigma Phi Assn. for "outstanding work in the field of broadcasting"; the New York Urban League John Russwurm award for "sustained excellence in interpreting, analyzing, and reporting the news" ('68) and the first annual *Penney-Missouri Magazine* award for excellence in women's journalism.

PERSONAL: Resides in New York City.

PIFER, ALICE
Prod., ABC, News, News Magazine Segments

c/o ABC, 77 W. 66th St., New York, NY 10023
b. November 1, 1951. Fort Wayne, IN.

EDUCATION: Michigan State University, B.A. ('73).

CAREER HIGHLIGHTS: Desk Asst., CBS News ('73); Audio Archivist, CBS Radio News ('74); Researcher, WCBS-TV News ('77); Prod., Writer, WCBS-TV News ('80); Prod., ABC News "20/20" ('81) and Prod., ABC News Magazine Segments.

ACHIEVEMENTS & AWARDS: Emmy for "Vocational Schools," WCBS-TV, Researcher ('79); New York State AP award and Emmy for "Housing Discrimination," Prod., WCBS-TV ('80); Emmy and New York State AP award for "Employment Agency Job Racket," Prod., WCBS-TV ('81); Emmy for "Census Scam," Prod., WCBS-TV ('81).

PERSONAL: N.A.

PIKE, SIDNEY
Pres., Turner Broadcasting System, Program Services

c/o Turner Broadcasting System, 1050 Techwood Dr., N.W., Atlanta, GA 30318
b. August 6, 1927. Boston, MA.

EDUCATION: Clark University.

CAREER HIGHLIGHTS: Prod./Dir., WBZ-TV, Boston ('50); Dir. Program Development, WHDH-TV, Boston ('57); Station Mgr., WQXI-TV, Atlanta ('68); V.P. and Dir. of TV Operations, WTBS ('71); promoted to Pres., Turner Program Services ('81).

ACHIEVEMENTS & AWARDS: N.A.

PERSONAL: Resides in Atlanta; wife, Lillian; two daughters, Susan and Andrea; son, Steven.

PILSON, NEAL H.
Exec. V.P. in charge of CBS Sports and CBS Radio Division

c/o CBS, 51 W. 52d St., New York, NY 10019
b. N.A.

EDUCATION: Hamilton College, B.A., History; Yale Law School, LL.B

CAREER HIGHLIGHTS: Private law practice; V.P., Metromedia Producers Corp.; Dir., Business Affairs, William Morris Agency. Joined CBS as Dir., Sports Business Affairs ('76); V.P., Business Affairs; V.P., Business Affairs and Administration; V.P. and Dir., Business Affairs and Compliance, all with CBS Sports. Named Sr. V.P., Planning and Administration, Broadcast Group ('81); appointed Pres., CBS Sports ('81); Exec. V.P. in charge of CBS Sports and CBS Radio Division.

ACHIEVEMENTS & AWARDS: N.A.

PERSONAL: N.A.

PINTAURO, FRANCIS N.
V.P., NBC, Advertising and Creative Services, East Coast

c/o NBC, 30 Rockefeller Plaza, New York, NY 10020
b. June 9, 1951. Brooklyn, NY.

EDUCATION: Manhattan College, B.A., English.

CAREER HIGHLIGHTS: Writer/Prod. at NBC ('75); Administrator, On-Air Operations ('77); Mgr., Broadcast Advertising ('78); Dir., On-Air Operations ('78); V.P., Advertising Operations ('79); V.P., Advertising and Creative Services, East Coast ('82).

ACHIEVEMENTS & AWARDS: N.A.

PERSONAL: Resides in Manhattan and Sag Harbor, NY, with wife, Kathy; son, Anthony.

PISCOPO, JOE
Repertory Player, NBC, "Saturday Night Live"

c/o "Saturday Night Live," NBC, 30 Rockefeller Plaza, New York, NY 10020
b. June 17, 1951. Passaic, NJ.

EDUCATION: Jones College, B.S., Broadcast Management.

CAREER HIGHLIGHTS: When "Saturday Night Live" regrouped after all the original cast members had decided to move on, Piscopo was one of the seven new repertory players. Since that time, nine performers have been fired and replaced, but through it all Piscopo has remained. His brilliant characterizations of Frank Sinatra, the loud abrupt "sports guy," Andy Rooney of "60 Minutes", and the constantly complaining Doug Whiner have proven his versatile acting and comedic abilities. Started as a stand-up comic and worked in numerous TV commercials before joining the cast of "Saturday Night Live."

ACHIEVEMENTS & AWARDS: N.A.

PERSONAL: Resides in New Jersey with wife, Nancy, and their son, Joey.

PITTMAN, ROBERT W.
Sr. V.P., Programming, Warner Amex Satellite Entertainment Co.

c/o Warner Amex, 1211 Ave. of the Americas, New York, NY 10036
b. N.A.

EDUCATION: N.A.

CAREER HIGHLIGHTS: Program Dir. and Disc Jockey at various radio stations in Mississippi; Research Dir., WDRQ-Radio, Detroit; Program Dir., WPEZ-Radio, Pittsburgh; Dir. of Programming, WMAQ-AM and WKQX-FM, Chicago; Program Dir., WNBC-AM, New York; Dir., Pay TV, Warner Amex, New York ('79); V.P., Programming, Warner Amex ('80); Sr. V.P., Programming, Warner Amex ('82).

ACHIEVEMENTS & AWARDS: Program Mgr. of the Year from *Billboard* ('77); Program Director of the Year ('78); Innovator of the Year for his work in the development of MTV: Music Television from *Performance* magazine ('81).

PERSONAL: N.A.

PLAKIAS, MARK
Dir. of Research, LINK

215 Park Ave. S., New York, NY 10003
b. N.A.

EDUCATION: Yale University, B.A.

CAREER HIGHLIGHTS: Involved in the development and implementation of a full-text archi-

val online database for the *Boston Globe* ('75). Joined Link ('79) as a specialist in the area of videotex and teletext, serving as Dir. of the Videotex Planning Service.

ACHIEVEMENTS & AWARDS: Chairman, Product Development Task Force for the IIA's Future Technology Committee; Member, Videotex Industry Assn.

PERSONAL: N.A.

PLANTE, JAMES F.
Director of News Services, NBC

c/o NBC, 30 Rockefeller Plaza, New York, NY 10020
b. August 5, 1945. Chicago, IL.

EDUCATION: Southern Illinois University.

CAREER HIGHLIGHTS: Reporter and Weekend Anchor, WTVW-TV, Evansville, IL ('69); Reporter and Assignment Editor, WAST, Albany, NY ('71); Weekend Anchor and State House Reporter ('72); joined ABC News Syndication Dept. as Writer, then Night Editor ('73); became Foreign Editor and periodically wrote for "ABC Weekend News" ('74); Deskman for convention and election coverage ('76); Weekend Editor for ABC News Syndication ('76); left ABC for NBC to be Dir., Domestic News ('79); appointed to Dir., NBC News Services ('81).

ACHIEVEMENTS & AWARDS: Founding Pres., Empire State Chapter, Sigma Delta Chi ('72); Chairman, Broadcast Committee, New York State Deadline Club ('78); Regional Dir. and Board of Dirs., Sigma Delta Chi.

PERSONAL: Resides in Flushing, NY, with wife, Helen; children, Deirdre, Bridget, and Nora.

PLEVEN, PATRICK A.
Dir., NBC TV, Daytime Programming

1160 Fifth Ave., New York, NY 10029
b. March 30, 1933. Paris, France.

EDUCATION: Cornell University, B.A., English ('54).

CAREER HIGHLIGHTS: Assoc. Prod., "Timex All-Star Circus" ABC TV ('60); Prod., "International Showtime", NBC TV ('60–'65); Prod., "Coliseum", CBS TV ('66); Prod., *Oh, Calcutta*, Theatrevision ('68); Programming Exec., "Good Morning America," ABC TV

('75); Mgr., Prime Time Programming Development, ABC TV ('76); Dir., Daytime Programming, NBC TV ('80).

ACHIEVEMENTS & AWARDS: N.A.

PERSONAL: Wife, Linda; children, Anick, Katell, and Liam.

POLEVOY, ROY
V.P., On-Air Promotion, ABC, Entertainment

c/o ABC, 4151 Prospect Ave., Los Angeles, CA 90027
b. N.A.

EDUCATION: City College of New York, B.A., Marketing.

CAREER HIGHLIGHTS: Spot Media Buyer, Ted Bates & Co., New York ('67); Research Dir. and Acct. Exec., CKLW-TV, Detroit/Windsor, Ontario ('68); Research Dir., WXYZ-TV, Detroit ('70); Research Dir., WLS-TV, Chicago ('70); Dir., Research and Sales Promotion, ABC Spot Sales ('72); Dir., Planning and Administration, ABC TV Spot Sales ('76); V.P., Creative Services, ABC Owned TV Stations ('78); V.P., Programming, ABC Owned TV Stations ('80); V.P., On-Air Promotion, ABC Entertainment ('80).

ACHIEVEMENTS & AWARDS: N.A.

PERSONAL: Resides in Los Angeles.

POLING, DOUG
Correspondent, CBS, Radio Network News

c/o CBS, 51 W. 52d St., New York, NY 10019
b. Toledo, OH.

EDUCATION: University of Toledo, B.A., Journalism.

CAREER HIGHLIGHTS: Reporter and News Dir., WOHO-Radio, Toledo ('58); Broadcast News Specialist with the U.S. Army ('64); Night News Editor, WGAR-Radio, Cleveland ('66); New York Correspondent, ABC News ('68); Reporter, CBS ('73); Correspondent, CBS ('77). Frequent contributor to news broadcasts on the CBS TV Network, including the children's news series "In the News."

ACHIEVEMENTS & AWARDS: N.A.

PERSONAL: N.A.

POLK, JAMES
Correspondent, NBC, News

c/o NBC, 30 Rockefeller Plaza, New York, NY 10020
b. Oaktown, IN.

EDUCATION: Indiana University, B.A., Political Science ('62).

CAREER HIGHLIGHTS: Reporter, AP ('62); Reporter, *Washington Star* ('72); Correspondent, NBC News, Washington, DC ('75).

ACHIEVEMENTS & AWARDS: Pulitzer Prize for national reporting for his Watergate coverage for *Washington Star* ('74). Sigma Delta Chi award for national reporting and the Clapper award twice for outstanding Washington investigative reporting.

PERSONAL: Resides in Arlington, VA, with his wife.

POLLACK, MORTON J.
V.P., Advertising and Promotion, CBS, Entertainment

c/o CBS, 6121 Sunset Blvd., Los Angeles, CA 90038
b. New York, NY.

EDUCATION: New York University, B.S., Marketing.

CAREER HIGHLIGHTS: Promotion Mgr., *Parents* magazine ('55); Advertising Dir., American Dairy Assn. Chicago ('64); Promotion Dir. and Creative Dir., Playboy Intl., Chicago ('67); Dir., Promotion, *Washington Post* ('70); Dir., On-Air Promotion, CBS Entertainment ('77); V.P., On-Air Promotion, CBS Entertainment ('80); V.P., Advertising and Promotion, CBS Entertainment ('82).

ACHIEVEMENTS & AWARDS: Several Andy awards from the New York Advertising Club and Addy awards from the Metropolitan Washington Advertising Club.

PERSONAL: Resides in Los Angeles with wife, Janice.

POMPADUR, MARTIN
Pres., Ziff-Davis Publishing

c/o Ziff Corp., 1 Park Ave., New York, NY 10016
b. N.A.

EDUCATION: N.A.

CAREER HIGHLIGHTS: Lawyer, private practice; ABC Corporate V.P.; ABC Asst. to the Pres.; Board Member, ABC, Inc.; Corporate Officer, Ziff-Davis Publishing; Pres., Ziff-Davis Publishing.

ACHIEVEMENTS & AWARDS: N.A.

PERSONAL: N.A.

POOLE, MARCUS LLOYD
Pres., Diaspora Communications

c/o Diaspora Communications, 175 Adams St., Brooklyn, New York, NY 11201
b. N.A.

EDUCATION: Northwestern University, B.S.; Case Western Reserve University Law School, J.D.

CAREER HIGHLIGHTS: Independent Concert Promoter, CBS, Chicago; chaired the Communications Research Committee for Justice and Business Communications ('71); Asst. Dir. of Franchises for Teleprompter Corp. ('78); Dir. of Programming Development for Teleprompter Corp., now Group W Cable ('80); currently Pres., Diaspora Communications.

ACHIEVEMENTS & AWARDS: N.A.

PERSONAL: N.A.

POOR, PETER
Sr. Prod., NBC, News, "Monitor"

c/o NBC, 30 Rockefeller Plaza, New York, NY 10020
b. N.A.

EDUCATION: Harvard University, B.A.

CAREER HIGHLIGHTS: CBS News, "60 Minutes," "CBS Reports," "20th Century," "21st Century" ('54–'75); Prod., NBC News, "Weekend" ('77); Prod., "Prime Time Sunday," "Prime Time Saturday," "NBC Magazine With David Brinkley" ('78); Prod., "Louis Rukeyser's Business Journal" ('81); Sr. Prod., NBC's "Monitor."

ACHIEVEMENTS & AWARDS: Fulbright Scholar in Italy.

PERSONAL: N.A.

POPE, LEAVITT J.
Pres. and Chief Exec. Officer, WPIX, Inc.

c/o WPIX, Inc., 11 WPIX Plaza, New York, NY 10017
b. N.A.

EDUCATION: Massachusetts Institute of Technology, Business and Engineering Administration.

CAREER HIGHLIGHTS: Pope's range of responsibilities with WPIX have covered almost the entire scope of broadcasting, including the early pioneering of New York Giants and New York Yankees baseball rights negotiations and telecasts and the original televising of sports events from Madison Square Garden. Pope began as an Administrative Asst., N.Y. Daily News ('47); Asst. to the General Mgr., WPIX ('51); Operations Mgr., WPIX ('53); V.P. in Charge of Operations, WPIX ('56); elected to the Board of Dirs., WPIX ('61); Secretary and Part-Owner, WPIX ('69); Exec. V.P. ('72); Pres. and Chief Exec. Officer, WPIX, Inc. ('75). Under Pope's direction, WPIX formed the Independent Network News ('80).

ACHIEVEMENTS & AWARDS: Founder and Chairman of the Board of the Assn. of Independent TV Stations and serves on the Steering Committee of Operation Prime Time, a consortium of more than a hundred TV stations to produce and acquire first-run primetime programming.

PERSONAL: Wife, Martha; 11 children; resides in Scarsdale, NY.

PORGES, WALTER
Sr. News Prod., ABC, "World News Tonight"

c/o ABC, 7 W. 66th St., New York, NY 10023
b. 1931.

EDUCATION: City College of New York, B.A. ('53).

CAREER HIGHLIGHTS: Newswriter, ABC News ('58); Asst. Assignment Mgr., ABC News ('65); Assoc. Prod., "ABC Evening News" ('66); Sr. Prod., "ABC World News Tonight" ('73).

ACHIEVEMENTS & AWARDS: N.A.

PERSONAL: N.A.

POSTON, TOM
Actor

c/o "Newhart," CBS, 7800 Beverly Blvd., Los
  Angeles, CA 90036
b. October 17. Columbus, OH.

EDUCATION: Bethany College; American Academy of Dramatic Arts.
CAREER HIGHLIGHTS: Began professional career
  in many Broadway productions including
  *Cyrano de Bergerac, A Funny Thing Happened on
  the Way to the Forum, Come Blow Your Horn, Bye
  Bye Birdie, Mary, Mary, King Lear*, and *Fiddler
  on the Roof*. Became prominent on TV as the
  befuddled Everyman on the early "Steve
  Allen Show" ('58); a regular panelist on "To
  Tell the Truth" for many years; also had recurring roles on "We've Got Each Other," "On
  the Rocks," and "Mork and Mindy." Had
  often appeared in "The Bob Newhart Show"
  as Newhart's prankster college buddy, and
  currently co-stars in "Newhart" as the not-so-
  handy handyman George Utley.
ACHIEVEMENTS & AWARDS: Emmy as best supporting actor for "The Steve Allen Show"
  ('58).
PERSONAL: Resides in Los Angeles with wife,
  Kay; daughter, Francesca; sons, Jason and
  Hudson.

POTTER, ALLEN M.
Exec. Prod., Procter & Gamble Productions,
  "Another World"

c/o NBC, 30 Rockefeller Plaza, New York, NY
  10020
b. September 5, 1919. Plainfield, NJ.

EDUCATION: Rutgers University.
CAREER HIGHLIGHTS: Began as an actor, shortly
after World War II, and soon moved into
radio and TV as a director. Prod., many serials including "The Brighter Day," "Our Pri-
vate World," "As the World Turns," and
"The Doctors." He was the first producer of
"Another World" ('64). Moved on to become
Exec. Prod., "How To Survive a Marriage"
and "The Guiding Light." Returned as Exec.
Prod., "Another World" ('83).
ACHIEVEMENTS & AWARDS: Emmy for outstand-
ing achievement in daytime programming for
"The Doctors" ('72); two Emmy awards for
outstanding achievement in daytime drama
for "The Guiding Light" ('80, '82).
PERSONAL: Resides in Norwalk, CT, with wife
Joan; three children, Duke, Matthew and
Julie.

POTTER, MARK
Correspondent, ABC, News, Miami

c/o ABC, 2801 Ponce de Leon Blvd., Suite 820,
  Coral Gables, FL 33134
b. Ann Arbor, MI.

EDUCATION: University of Missouri, B.S., Jour-
  nalism ('75).
CAREER HIGHLIGHTS: Cameraman, WTVW-TV,
  Evansville, IN ('75); Reporter, WCKT-TV, Mi-
  ami ('77); Reporter, WPLG-TV, Miami ('81);
  Correspondent, ABC News, Miami ('83).
ACHIEVEMENTS & AWARDS: Two local Emmy
  awards for investigative reporting; a five-part
  study on alien smuggling earned him a
  Dupont-Columbia award, a Robert F. Ken-
  nedy award, an Investigative Reporters and
  Editors award and three local Emmy awards
  ('82).
PERSONAL: N.A.

POUSSAINT, RENE
Co-Anchor, WJLA-TV, Washington, DC,
  News

c/o WJLA-TV, 4461 Connecticut Ave., N.W.,
  Washington, DC 20008
b. N.A.

EDUCATION: Sarah Lawrence College, B.A.,
  Comparative Literature; University of Califor-
  nia, M.A., African Studies.
CAREER HIGHLIGHTS: Reporter, CBS News,

Washington, DC, Midwest; Co-Anchor, WJLA-TV, Washington, DC.
ACHIEVEMENTS & AWARDS: Three Washington, DC, Emmy awards.
PERSONAL: Married to Henry Richardson.

POWELL, NORMAN S.
Dir., Motion Pictures for TV, CBS, Entertainment, West Coast

c/o CBS, 6121 Sunset Blvd., Los Angeles, CA 90028
b. 1934. Los Angeles, CA.

EDUCATION: Cornell University, B.A.
CAREER HIGHLIGHTS: Co-Creator and Co-Prod., "The Bob Crane Show"; involved with the production of "Flatbush," "Rafferty," *Washington: Behind Closed Doors*, "More Than Friends," and the "Salvage I" pilot; V.P., Production and Development, Wrather Entertainment Intl.; Dir., Motion Pictures for TV, CBS Entertainment, West Coast ('79).
ACHIEVEMENTS & AWARDS: N.A.
PERSONAL: Single, resides in Los Angeles.

POWERS, RON
Media Critic, CBS, "CBS News Sunday Morning"

c/o Geller Media Management, 250 W. 57th St., New York, NY 10019
b. November 18, 1941. Hannibal, MO.

EDUCATION: University of Missouri, B.S., Journalism ('63).
CAREER HIGHLIGHTS: Sportwriter, *St. Louis Post-Dispatch* ('63); Reporter, *Chicago Sun-Times* ('69); Radio-TV Critic, *Chicago Sun-Times* ('70); On-Air Media Commentator, WMAQ-TV, Chicago ('76); Commentator, "City Edition," WNET-TV, New York ('79); Commentator, "CBS Morning Show With Charles Kuralt" ('81); Media Critic for the syndicated "Entertainment Tonight" ('82); Media Critic, "CBS News Sunday Morning" ('83).
ACHIEVEMENTS & AWARDS: Pulitzer Prize for criticism in *Chicago Sun-Times* ('73); local Emmy for spot reporting on WMAQ-TV, Chicago ('77). Author, *The Newscasters: The News Business as Show Business* ('77), *Face Value* ('79), *Toot-Toot-Tootsie, Good-bye* ('81), and *Supertube: The Rise of Television Sports* ('84).

PERSONAL: Resides in New York City and South Kent, CT, with his wife, Honoree Fleming, and their son, Dean.

POWERS, STEFANIE
Actress

c/o "Hart to Hart," ABC, 2040 Ave. of the Stars, Los Angeles, CA 90067
b. November 2, 1942. Hollywood, CA.

EDUCATION: N.A.
CAREER HIGHLIGHTS: Her feminine allure and breezy sophistication make an ordinary night of TV viewing seem like a night on the town. Her motion pictures include *Experiment in Terror, The Interns, Die, Die My Darling, McClintock,* and *Stagecoach.* TV movies include *A Death in Canaan, Five Desperate Women, Sweet, Sweet Rachel, Hardcase, No Place to Run, Night Games,* and *Manhunter.* TV series include "The Girl From UNCLE," "Feather and Father," and "Hart to Hart."
ACHIEVEMENTS & AWARDS: Received People's Choice award ('81).
PERSONAL: Single.

PRESBREY, MICHAEL O.
Sr. V.P., Advertising Sales, ESPN

c/o ESPN, ESPN Plaza, Bristol, CT 06010
b. October 19, 1934. Mineola, NY.

EDUCATION: University of Virginia, B.S.

CAREER HIGHLIGHTS: Acct. Exec., WINS, New York ('58); Acct. Exec., WGN, Chicago ('60); Sales Dir., Spot Salesman, NBC ('61); Sales Dir. and V.P., CBS ('71); Sr. V.P., Advertising Sales, ESPN ('79).

ACHIEVEMENTS & AWARDS: N.A.

PERSONAL: Resides in Weston, CT, with wife, Mary; children, Natalie, James, and Mary.

PRESCOTT, ELEANOR
Prod., ABC, News, "20/20"

c/o ABC, 77 W. 66th St., New York, NY 10023
b. December 9, 1946. Detroit, MI.

EDUCATION: Barnard College, B.A. ('68); Columbia University, M.S.J. ('70).

CAREER HIGHLIGHTS: Writer, Newsweek ('72); Reporter, KERA-TV Dallas ('73); Writer, ABC ('73); Instructor, Journalism, Fairleigh Dickinson University, Rutherford, NJ ('75); Prod., NBC Radio, News and Information Service ('76); Writer, "Today," NBC News ('78); Prod., "Today," NBC News, Washington, DC ('78); Prod., Weekend Report, ABC News ('79); Prod., "20/20," ABC News ('80).

ACHIEVEMENTS & AWARDS: Deadline Club award for community service, NBC Radio special "Cancer" ('76); New York State Broadcasters award, NBC Radio special "Violence and the News Media" ('77); Freedom Foundation award, NBC Radio special "Violence and the News Media" ('78); Ohio State University award for NBC Radio documentary "The Pro Israel Lobby" ('79).

PERSONAL: Husband, Nicholas Garaufis.

PRESSMAN, DAVID
Dir., ABC, "One Life To Live"

c/o "One Life To Live," ABC, 1330 Ave. of the Americas, New York, NY 10019
b. October 10, 1913. Tiflis, Russia.

EDUCATION: Columbia University.

CAREER HIGHLIGHTS: Actor on Broadway in Eve of St. Mark ('42); Brooklyn, U.S.A. ('42); Dream Girl ('46); performed in local and off-Broadway productions ('46–'52). He was an acclaimed acting teacher in the fifties and six-

ties before turning to TV production. Dir., "The Defenders," "Nurses and Doctors," "Coronet Blue," "NYPD," "The Nurses," "Another World," "One Life To Live."

ACHIEVEMENTS & AWARDS: Emmy for best director of a daytime drama ('76).

PERSONAL: Resides in New York City with wife, Sasha; three sons, Gregory, Eugene, and Michael, who is a film director.

PRESSMAN, GABE
General Assignment Reporter, WNBC-TV, "Newscenter 4"

c/o WNBC-TV, 30 Rockefeller Plaza, New York, NY 10020
b. New York.

EDUCATION: Columbia University Graduate School of Journalism.

CAREER HIGHLIGHTS: Started his career with five years of reporting for the N.Y. World Telegram and Sun, followed by 17 years with WNBC-TV. Joined Channel 5's "10 O'Clock News" ('72). Returned to "Newscenter 4" ('80) as General Assignment Reporter.

ACHIEVEMENTS & AWARDS: George Polk award; four Emmy awards. Named Journalist of the Year ('77) by the New York Publicity Club, and cited as one of the outstanding journalists in the past 50 years by the Journalism Hall of Fame.

PERSONAL: N.A.

PRESTON, MARILYN
TV Critic, Chicago Tribune

c/o Chicago Tribune, Tribune Tower, Chicago, IL 60611
b. N.A.

EDUCATION: University of Illinois, B.S., Communications ('67); Northwestern University, M.S., Journalism ('68).

CAREER HIGHLIGHTS: Intern, Medill News Service ('68); Assoc. Editor, Medical World News, New York ('68); Arts Critic, Chicago Today ('69); Feature Writer, Chicago Tribune ('76); TV Critic, Chicago Tribune ('80).

ACHIEVEMENTS & AWARDS: Co-Author, Dear Dr. Jock: The People's Guide to Sports and Fitness ('80).

PERSONAL: Resides in Chicago with her husband, Barry.

PRICE, JUDY
V.P., CBS, Children's Programs and Daytime Specials

c/o CBS, 7800 Beverly Blvd., Los Angeles, CA 90036
b. November 27, 1943. Muncie, IN.

EDUCATION: N.A.
CAREER HIGHLIGHTS: Prod., KHJ-TV, Los Angeles ('65); Prod., "American Bandstand," for Dick Clark Productions ('70); joined ABC as West Coast Mgr. of Children's Programs ('76); Dir. of Children's Early Morning Programming, West Coast ('79). V.P., Children's Programming, ABC Entertainment ('81); V.P., CBS, Children's Programs and Daytime Specials ('83).
ACHIEVEMENTS & AWARDS: Member, Board of Governors, ATAS.
PERSONAL: Resides in Los Angeles, CA, with two teenage daughters.

PRINCIPAL, VICTORIA
Actress

c/o "Dallas," CBS, 7800 Beverly Blvd., Los Angeles, CA 90036
b. January 3, 1950. Fulipla, Japan.

EDUCATION: Miami Dade Junior College.
CAREER HIGHLIGHTS: Worked as a model in New York before moving to Hollywood where she appeared in the feature films *The Life and Times of Judge Roy Bean*, *The Naked Ape*,

Earthquake, I Will, I Will . . . for Now, and *Vigilante Force*. Her early TV credits include "Fantasy Island," "Love, American Style," and "Greatest Heroes of the Bible." Discontent with her acting career, she abruptly quit ('75) to become an agent for actors, writers, and producers. She was lured back to acting to star in "Dallas" ('78). Recent TV movie credits include *Not Just Another Affair* and *Pleasure Palace*.
ACHIEVEMENTS & AWARDS: N.A.
PERSONAL: Resides in Beverly Hills, CA.

PRISENDORF, ANTHONY
Reporter, WNEW-TV, New York, News

c/o WNEW-TV, Metromedia, 205 E. 67th St., New York, NY 10021
b. N.A.

EDUCATION: N.A.
CAREER HIGHLIGHTS: Reporter, *The Record*, Hackensack, NJ ('59); Reporter, *Paris Herald-Tribune* ('63); Reporter, *N.Y. Post* ('66); Reporter, NBC News, New York ('72); Reporter, "The 10 O'Clock News," WNEW-TV, New York ('76).
ACHIEVEMENTS & AWARDS: N.A.
PERSONAL: Married, two children.

PUDNEY, GARY LAURENCE
V.P., ABC, Special Projects, Entertainment

c/o ABC, 2040 Ave. of the Stars, Los Angeles, CA 90067
b. July 20, 1934. Minneapolis, MN.

EDUCATION: University of California at Los Angeles, B.A., Theater Arts/Motion Pictures.
CAREER HIGHLIGHTS: Started career as Acct. Exec. with Young & Rubicam advertising agency ('61); moved over to same position at Compton Advertising ('64) for two years before becoming West Coast Exec. Prod. for "ABC Stage '67" ('66–'67). Made Dir. of Specials and Talent, ABC TV ('69); named Dir. of Nighttime Live and Tape Production, West Coast, ABC TV ('69); promoted to V.P., Nighttime Tape Production ('72); named V.P., Variety Programs ('73). Joined Intl. Famous Agency as Exec. of Variety TV and remained in same position when agency be-

came ICM ('74); joined Youngstreet Intl. as V.P. and Exec. Prod. ('76); returned to ABC as Exec. in Charge of Talent for ABC's 25th anniversary special ('77). Named V.P., Special Projects, ABC Entertainment ('78) and given additional responsibilities as Sr. Exec. in Charge of Talent ('79).

ACHIEVEMENTS & AWARDS: Exec. Committee, ATAS ('81); Board of Dirs., Hollywood Radio and TV Society ('82); Board of Dirs., Natl. Cerebral Palsy Foundation ('82).

PERSONAL: Resides in Beverly Hills, CA.

PURVIS, ARCHIE C., JR.
V.P., ABC Video Enterprises, Video Sales

c/o ABC, 825 Seventh Ave., New York, NY 10023

b. May 24, 1939. New York, NY.

EDUCATION: Baruch School of Business, B.A., Business and Management.

CAREER HIGHLIGHTS: Acct. Mgr., General Foods; ('63); Polaroid General Sales Mgr. ('66); Exec. V.P., Lear/Purvis/Walker & Co. ('73). V.P., Universal Studios and Dir., MCA Discovision ('74); joined ABC Video Enterprises as V.P., Video Sales ('80).

ACHIEVEMENTS & AWARDS: N.A.

PERSONAL: Wife, Candace; children, Victoria and Christian.

QUARLES, NORMA
Correspondent, NBC, News, Chicago

c/o NBC, 30 Rockefeller Plaza, New York, NY 10020
b. N.A.

EDUCATION: Hunter College; City College of New York.

CAREER HIGHLIGHTS: Began her broadcast career as News Reporter and Disc Jockey, WSDM Radio, Chicago ('65); joined NBC training program, including a period with WRC-TV, Washington, DC ('66); Broadcast Journalist, WKYC-TV, NBC in Cleveland ('67–'70); transferred to WNBC-TV, New York ('70); Anchor, early morning local news broadcasts, WNBC-TV; Prod. and Reporter, "Urban Journal" series, "NewsCenter 5," WMAQ-TV, Chicago; named NBC News Correspondent, Chicago ('78–'79).

ACHIEVEMENTS & AWARDS: Film story "The Stripper" earned the Front Page award and Sigma Delta Chi's Deadline Club award for excellence in TV journalism ('73). Her "Urban Journal" series won a local Emmy award ('77).

PERSONAL: Two children, Laurence and Susan.

QUELLO, JAMES H.
Commissioner, FCC

c/o FCC, 1919 M St., N.W., Washington, DC 20554
b. April 21, 1914. Laurium, MI.

EDUCATION: Michigan State University, B.A. ('35).

CAREER HIGHLIGHTS: As an FCC Commissioner, Quello has consistently voted in favor of legislation benefiting the commercial broadcasting industry. Promotion Mgr., WJR-AM, Detroit; V.P. and General Mgr., WJR-AM, Detroit ('60); V.P., Capital Cities Broadcasting Corp. ('64); Commissioner, FCC ('74). Was previously the voice of "The Lone Ranger" on the original radio series.

ACHIEVEMENTS & AWARDS: N.A.

PERSONAL: N.A.

QUINN, JANE BRYANT
Columnist, *Newsweek* and the *Washington Post*

c/o *Newsweek*, 444 Madison Ave., New York, NY 10022
b. N.A.

EDUCATION: Middlebury College.

CAREER HIGHLIGHTS: Reporter, Co-Editor, *The Insider's Newsletter*, published by *Look* magazine; Co-Founder, Editor, and General Mgr., *McGraw-Hill Personal Finance Letter*; Columnist for *Woman's Day* magazine, the *Washington Post* and *Newsweek* magazine. Occasionally provides business reports for the "CBS Morning News."

ACHIEVEMENTS & AWARDS: John Hancock award; Janus award; Natl. Press Club award. Author, *Everyone's Money Book.*

PERSONAL: Resides with husband, David, and their two sons.

QUINN, MARTHA
Video Jockey, Warner Amex Satellite Entertainment Co., MTV: Music Television

c/o MTV, Warner Amex Satellite Entertainment Co., 1211 Ave. of the Americas, New York, NY 10036
b. May 11.

EDUCATION: New York University.

CAREER HIGHLIGHTS: Disc Jockey, WNYU-FM, New York; Announcer and Voice-Over Specialist, radio and TV national advertising campaigns; Asst. to the Music Dir., WNBC-AM, New York; Video Jockey, MTV: Music Television ('81).

ACHIEVEMENTS & AWARDS: N.A.

PERSONAL: Resides in New York City.

QUINONES, JOHN
Correspondent, ABC, News

c/o ABC, 7 W. 66th St., New York, NY 10023

b. N.A.

EDUCATION: St. Mary's University, B.A., Speech/Communications; Columbia School of Journalism, M.A.

CAREER HIGHLIGHTS: News Editor, KTRH-Radio, Houston ('75); concurrently worked as Anchor/Reporter, KPRC-TV, Houston ('75); Reporter, WBBM-TV, Chicago ('79); Reporter, ABC News, Miami ('82); Correspondent, ABC News, Miami ('83).

ACHIEVEMENTS & AWARDS: Two Emmy awards for reporting at WBBM-TV ('80).

PERSONAL: Resides in Miami.

QUIRT, JOHN
Chief Economics Correspondent, Cable News Network

Suite 1205, 10 Columbus Circle, New York, NY

b. June 26, 1939. Stoughton, WI.

EDUCATION: University of Wisconsin, B.A., Journalism; University of Minnesota.

CAREER HIGHLIGHTS: Financial Correspondent, WCBS-TV, New York ('62); Independent Contractor, Contributor to NBC News, Institutional Investor Systems, *N.Y. Times, Business Week, Money* magazine ('69); Correspondent, *Time* magazine; Assoc. Editor, *Fortune* magazine ('74); Chief Economics Correspondent, Cable News Network ('82). Also, Lecturer, California State University.

ACHIEVEMENTS & AWARDS: Adviser, University of California TV Broadcast Workshop.

PERSONAL: N.A.

RABEL, ED
Correspondent, CBS, News

c/o CBS, 524 W. 57th St., New York, NY 10019
b. Charleston, WV.

EDUCATION: Morris Harvey College, B.A., Political Science ('63).
CAREER HIGHLIGHTS: News Editor, WCHS-TV, Charleston, WV ('62); News Dir., WCHS-TV, Charleston ('63); Reporter, CBS News, New York ('66); Reporter, CBS News, Atlanta ('67); Reporter, CBS News, Saigon ('70); Correspondent, CBS News, Tel Aviv ('71); Correspondent, CBS News, Atlanta ('73); has served most recently as a Correspondent for the CBS News Documentary Unit.
ACHIEVEMENTS & AWARDS: N.A.
PERSONAL: Wife, Mary.

RAE, CHARLOTTE
Actress

c/o "The Facts of Life," NBC, 30 Rockefeller Plaza, New York, NY 10020
b. April 22, 1926. Milwaukee, WI.

EDUCATION: Northwestern University.
CAREER HIGHLIGHTS: Rae's rubber face and infectious laughter have helped her spin off from "Diff'rent Strokes" into a well-deserved show of her own, "The Facts of Life." New York stage appearances in *L'il Abner, Pickwick,* and *Morning, Noon and Night.* TV appearances on "Diff'rent Strokes" and the TV film *Queen of the Stardust Ballroom.*
ACHIEVEMENTS & AWARDS: N.A.
PERSONAL: N.A.

RAINES, DALLAS D.
Meteorologist, Cable News Network

c/o Cable News Network, 1050 Techwood Dr., N.W., Atlanta, GA 30318
b. October 15, 1953. Thomaston, GA.

EDUCATION: Florida State University.
CAREER HIGHLIGHTS: Meteorologist, WBRZ-TV, Baton Rouge, LA ('77); Meteorologist, WDSU-TV, New Orleans ('78); Meteorologist, Cable News Network ('80).
ACHIEVEMENTS & AWARDS: Voted best TV meteorologist by *New Orleans Times* ('79); Member, American Meteorological Society.
PERSONAL: Wife, Debbie, and daughter, Elizabeth.

RAMBO, DACK
Actor

c/o "All My Children," ABC, 1330 Ave. of the Americas, New York, NY 10019
b. November 13, 1941. Delano, CA.

EDUCATION: N.A.
CAREER HIGHLIGHTS: Series regular on "The New Loretta Young Show" and "Guns of Will Sonnett." Motion pictures include *Deadly Honeymoon, Wild Flowers,* and the movie of the week *Hit Lady.* TV guest appearances on "The Love Boat," "Fantasy Island," "Gunsmoke," "Cannon," and "Marcus Welby, M.D." Day-

time drama regular on "Never Too Young" and "All My Children."

ACHIEVEMENTS & AWARDS: N.A.

PERSONAL: N.A.

RANDALL, ELIZABETH
V.P., Print Advertising, West Coast, CBS, Entertainment

c/o CBS, 6121 Sunset Blvd., Los Angeles, CA 90028

b. New York, NY.

EDUCATION: University of Wisconsin; New York University.

CAREER HIGHLIGHTS: Chief Writer for game show "Reach for the Stars"; Advertising and Promotion Mgr., NBC Radio Division; Sr. Writer/Prod., ABC Sales Development ('71); served as Creative Dir., for an audiovisual production firm specializing in sales promotion ('73); V.P., Advertising, Omega Watch Co. ('75); Mgr., Advertising and Promotion, East Coast, for Specials and Daytime Programs, CBS ('77); Dir., Print Advertising, West Coast, CBS ('78); V.P., Print Advertising, West Coast, CBS Entertainment ('83).

ACHIEVEMENTS & AWARDS: The department under her direction received a number of awards for advertising and design excellence, including several from *Art Design* magazine.

PERSONAL: N.A.

RANDALL, TONY
Actor

c/o Diamond Artists, 119 W. 57th St., New York, NY 10019

b. February 26, 1920. Tulsa, OK.

EDUCATION: Northwestern University; Columbia University.

CAREER HIGHLIGHTS: Randall does it all with grace, style, and uncommon skill—TV series, talk show guest appearances, commercials, hosting opera specials, documentary voice-overs, etc. Stage credits include *The Corn Is Green, Oh Men, Oh Women,* and *Inherit the Wind.* TV movies include *Kate Bliss and the Ticker Tape Kid.* Motion pictures include *Oh Men, Oh Women, Will Success Spoil Rock Hunter, No Down Payment, The Mating Game, Pillow Talk,* and *Lover Come Back.* TV star of "Mister Peepers," "The Tony Randall Show," "The Odd Couple," and "Love, Sidney."

ACHIEVEMENTS & AWARDS: Emmy as best actor in a comedy series for "The Odd Couple" ('75).

PERSONAL: Wife, Florence. Resides in New York City, on Central Park W.

RANDLES, WILLIAM
Sr. V.P., Cablentertainment

c/o Cablentertainment, 295 Madison Ave., New York, NY 10017

b. N.A.

EDUCATION: N.A.

CAREER HIGHLIGHTS: Tower Communications ('57); joined Vikoa ('67) and became V.P. of Operations ('70). Regional Mgr., American TV Communications Corp. ('71); joined Cablentertainment ('76); Sr. V.P., Cablentertainment.

ACHIEVEMENTS & AWARDS: Member, CTAM, and Pres., Ohio Cable TV Assn.

PERSONAL: Resides with his wife and children in Zanesville, OH.

RAPPAPORT, JOHN H.
Prod./Writer

c/o Broder/Kurland Agency, 9046 Sunset
  Blvd., Los Angeles, CA 90069
b. August 26, 1940. Chicago, IL.

EDUCATION: Indiana University, B.A.
CAREER HIGHLIGHTS: Staff Writer, "Laugh-In"
  ('69–'73); Staff Writer, "Lily Tomlin Special"
  ('73); Story Editor, "All in the Family"
  ('73–'74); Story Editor, "Maude" ('73–'74);
  Exec. Script Consultant, "The Odd Couple"
  ('74–'75); Prod./Writer, pilots for CBS, ABC,
  NBC ('76–'78); Supervising Prod.,
  "M*A*S*H" ('79–'83).
ACHIEVEMENTS & AWARDS: Seven Emmy nominations; three Writers Guild nominations for
  best comedy script; four People's Choice
  awards as producer of best TV comedy;
  Golden Globe award as producer of best TV
  comedy; two Humanitas awards as producer
  of "M*A*S*H" episodes.
PERSONAL: Wife, Lee; three children, Stacy,
  Jamie, and Scott.

RASKY, HARRY
Prod./Dir./Writer, Harry Rasky Productions

c/o CBC, P.O. Box 500, Station A, Toronto,
  Ontario, M5W 1E6
b. N.A.

EDUCATION: University of Toronto.
CAREER HIGHLIGHTS: Rasky is an internationally acclaimed maker of films and TV programs. He has produced, directed and
  written films for all major TV networks in the
  U.S., Canada, and England. Some of his
  works include "Being Different" ('81), "Hom-
  age to Chagall" ('76), "The Spies Who Never
  Were" ('81), "The Song of Leonard Cohen"
  ('81), and "Arthur Miller on Home Ground"
  ('81). Currently serves as Pres., Harry Rasky
  Productions.
ACHIEVEMENTS & AWARDS: Author, *Nobody
  Swings on Sunday—The Many Lives and Films of
  Harry Rasky*. Winner of 100 international
  prizes and citations, including an Academy
  Award, *TV Guide* award, Sylvania award,
  Writers Guild award, and the New York Intl.
  Film and TV Festival grand prize.
PERSONAL: Wife, Arlene; two children, Adam
  and Holly.

RASMUSSEN, WILLIAM F.
V.P., Satellite Syndicated Systems, Corporate Development

8252 S. Harvard St., Tulsa, OK 74136
b. October 15, 1932. Chicago, IL.

EDUCATION: De Pauw University, B.A., Eco-
  nomics ('54); Rutgers University, M.B.A.
  ('60).
CAREER HIGHLIGHTS: Rasmussen's biggest
  coup was turning a small Connecticut sports
  cable outfit, ESPN, into one of the largest,
  most widely watched cable networks. He got
  the broadcasting bug as a freelance Sports
  Announcer in New England ('63); became
  Sports Dir., News Dir., and Co-Anchor, with
  WWLP-TV, Springfield, MA ('65); joined the
  New England Whalers, now the Hartford
  Whalers, as Communications Dir. ('74);
  Founder, Pres., Chairman of the Board,
  ESPN, headquartered in Bristol, CT ('78);
  Chairman of the Board, Enterprise Radio, an
  all-sports radio network based in Avon, CT
  ('80); joined Satellite Syndicated Systems as
  V.P., Corporate Development ('81).
ACHIEVEMENTS & AWARDS: N.A.
PERSONAL: Wife, Lois; children, Scott, Glenn,
  and Lynn.

RATHER, DAN
Anchor and Managing Editor, "CBS Evening News"

c/o CBS, 524 W. 57th St., New York, NY
  10019
b. 1931. Wharton, TX.

EDUCATION: N.A.
CAREER HIGHLIGHTS: Known for his impeccable
  deportment and conservative but casual

wardrobe, this formidable news journalist regained the high ratings position CBS had long held under his predecessor, Walter Cronkite. Joined CBS News as Southwest Bureau Chief ('62); Anchor, weekend editions of "CBS Evening News"; Chief, CBS News Bureaus in London and Saigon; White House Correspondent; Anchor, "CBS Reports"; Co-Editor, "60 Minutes"; Anchor and Managing Editor, "CBS Evening News" ('81). Also reports on the CBS Radio Network.

ACHIEVEMENTS & AWARDS: Six Emmy awards; Distinguished Achievement for Broadcasting award ('74); elected a Fellow of the Society of Professional Journalists ('80); Overseas Press Club award ('82); Bob Considine award ('83).

PERSONAL: Resides in New York City with his wife, Jean.

RATNER, VIC
Correspondent, ABC, News

c/o ABC, 1717 DeSales St., N.W.,
Washington, DC 20036
b. New York, NY.

EDUCATION: University of Pennsylvania, B.S. and M.S., Communications.

CAREER HIGHLIGHTS: News Announcer, WJBR-AM, Wilmington, DE ('58); News Announcer, WFIL-AM, Philadelphia ('58); Reporter/Announcer, WVOX-AM, New Rochelle, NY ('59); Reporter, Herald-Tribune Radio Network ('60); Reporter/Announcer, WMMM, Westport, CT ('60); News Editor, Radio Press Intl., New York ('61); News Writer/Assignment Editor/Reporter, WFIL-AM, Philadelphia ('62); New York Bureau Chief, Radio Press Intl. ('63); Reporter, WMCA-AM, New York ('66); News Dir., WMCA-AM, New York ('69); Correspondent, ABC Radio Network ('73); Correspondent, ABC News, Washington, DC ('74).

ACHIEVEMENTS & AWARDS: Ohio State University award; Natl. Headliner award.

PERSONAL: Resides in Chevy Chase, MD, with wife, Judith; two children.

RAYBURN, GENE
Comedian/Announcer/Host

c/o CBS, 7800 Beverly Blvd., Los Angeles, CA 90036
b. December 22. Christopher, IL.

EDUCATION: Knox College.

CAREER HIGHLIGHTS: Appeared in "The Rayburn and Finch Show," WNEW-Radio, New York; Resident Cast Member of Steve Allen's "Tonight Show"; Game Show Host, "Dough-Re-Mi" and "The Match Game."

ACHIEVEMENTS & AWARDS: N.A.

PERSONAL: N.A.

RAYE, MARTHA
Singer/Dancer/Comedienne

c/o CBS, 7800 Beverly Blvd., Los Angeles, CA 90036
b. August 27, 1916. Butte, MN.

EDUCATION: N.A.

CAREER HIGHLIGHTS: Vaudeville and nightclub performer; starred on "All-Star Revue" ('51). Starred in "The Martha Raye Show" ('54). Guest-starred on "The Steve Allen Show," "The Milton Berle Show," "The Bob Hope Show," and "The Carol Burnett Show." She made her TV dramatic debut on "McMillan and Wife" ('75). Also appeared on the TV children's show "The Bugaloos" ('70). Currently, Raye appears as Vic Tayback's mother on CBS's "Alice." Raye's film career started in '34 and her movies include *Rhythm on the Range, Artists and Models, Pin-Up Girl, Monsieur Verdoux*, and *Jumbo*. Excellent pop singer during her TV variety career. Now widely seen doing TV commercials.

ACHIEVEMENTS & AWARDS: N.A.

PERSONAL: N.A.

RAYVID, JAY
Sr. V.P. and Exec. Dir., WQED, PBS, Children's and Family Consortium

c/o WQED, 4802 Fifth Ave., Pittsburgh, PA 15213
b. February 27, 1932. New York, NY.

EDUCATION: University of Miami, B.A., Liberal Arts.
CAREER HIGHLIGHTS: PBS Prod. and Exec. Prod., PBS, whose extensive credits include "A Mother Janek" ('65); "The Place and Ofoeti" ('66); "The 39th Witness' ('67); "NET Playhouse" ('69); "Turned-On Crisis" ('71); "Harry S. Truman: Plain Speaking" ('76); "Previn and the Pittsburgh" ('76–'78); "Once Upon a Classic" ('76–'80); "A Connecticut Yankee in King Arthur's Court" ('78); "The People's Business" ('82). Currently serves as Exec. Dir., PBS Children's and Family Consortium; Project Dir., "Moving Right Along" and Sr. V.P., WQED.
ACHIEVEMENTS & AWARDS: NET award of excellence ('66, '67); Emmy awards ('69, '76, '80, '81); Peabody award ('71, '78); Corp. for Public Broadcasting award ('71); Treasurer, Transitional Services ('77–'80); Chairman of the Board, Transitional Services ('80–'82); Board of Dirs., Pennsylvania Assn. of Broadcasters ('81–'82).
PERSONAL: Resides in Pittsburgh. Wife, Lynn; daughters, Rachel and Lisa.

REASONER, HARRY
Co-Editor, "60 Minutes," CBS, News

c/o CBS, 524 W. 57th St., New York, NY 10019
b. 1923. Dakota City, IA.

EDUCATION: Stanford University; University of Minnesota.
CAREER HIGHLIGHTS: Reasoner has survived both reporting the Vietnam War and a celebrated on-air feud with Barbara Walters; he remains one of TV's most admired journalists. Drama Critic, Minneapolis Times ('46–'48); Newswriter, WCCO-TV, Minneapolis ('50); News Dir., KEYD-TV; joined CBS News in New York ('56); Anchor, "CBS Evening News," ('63); original Co-Editor, "60 Minutes," with Mike Wallace ('68); Anchor, "ABC Evening News" ('70); rejoined CBS News ('78); Co-Editor "60 Minutes," Reporter, for some "CBS Reports" broadcasts, Anchor, "The Reasoner Report," on CBS Radio Network.
ACHIEVEMENTS & AWARDS: Emmy for individual achievement ('65); Emmy, News Broadcaster of the Year ('74); Overseas Press Club award ('74). Honor medal, University of Missouri School of Journalism ('70); Peabody award ('67); Emmy as writer of "What About Ronald Reagan?" ('67–'68); University of Southern California Journalism Alumni Assn. distinguished achievement award ('69). Author of Before the Colors Fade and the novel Tell Me About Women.
PERSONAL: N.A.

REDA, LOUIS J.
Prod./Packager/Personal Mgr.

44 N. Second St., Easton, PA 18042
b. January 31, 1925. Tuckahoe, NY.

EDUCATION: N.A.
CAREER HIGHLIGHTS: Co-Prod., "The Amazing World of Kreskin" ('71), "Kreskin's Japanese Special" ('77), and Just Jesse feature film ('77); Exec. Prod., "The Misadventures of Ichabod Crane" ('79), and the CBS mini-series The Blue and the Gray ('82).
ACHIEVEMENTS & AWARDS: Author, Moments: The Pulitzer Prize Photographs ('78); The Best of Will Rogers ('80); Will Rogers Treasury ('81); Reflections of the Civil War ('81); The Constitution ('82); The Declaration ('82); The Blue and the Gray ('82).
PERSONAL: N.A.

REDEKER, BILL
Correspondent, ABC, News

c/o ABC, 7 W. 66th St., New York, NY 10023
b. Mason City, IA.

EDUCATION: N.A.
CAREER HIGHLIGHTS: Instructor at Arizona State University; Reporter, KTAR-TV, Phoenix ('72); Reporter, KABC-TV, Los Angeles ('74); Correspondent, ABC News, Los Angeles ('76); Tokyo Bureau Chief, ABC News ('78); Correspondent, ABC News,

Washington, DC ('80); Correspondent, ABC News "Nightline" ('82).

ACHIEVEMENTS & AWARDS: N.A.

PERSONAL: N.A.

REDGRAVE, LYNN
Actress

c/o Box 1207, Topanga, CA 90290
b. March 8, 1943. London, England.

EDUCATION: N.A.

CAREER HIGHLIGHTS: Broadway stage appearances in *Black Comedy* and *My Fat Friend*. Motion pictures include *Smashing Time, The Virgin Soldiers, The National Health, The Deadly Affair*, and *Georgy Girl*. TV movies include *Turn of the Screw, Sooner or Later, Gauguin/The Savage, The Seduction of Miss Leona*, and the mini-series *Centennial*. Co-Host on the interview show "Not for Women Only." Series star of "House Calls" and "Teachers Only."

ACHIEVEMENTS & AWARDS: N.A.

PERSONAL: Husband, John Clark; two children. Resides in Beverly Hills, CA. Sister of actress Vanessa Redgrave; daughter of the great English actor Michael Redgrave.

REDMAN, C. DANA
V.P., ESPN, Research and Measurement

c/o ESPN, Sports Channel, Bristol, CT 06010
b. June 9, 1935. Boston, MA.

EDUCATION: Dartmouth College, B.A. and M.B.A.

CAREER HIGHLIGHTS: Mgr. of Media Analysis, Benton & Bowles ('59); Assoc. Media Dir., Kenyon & Eckhardt ('65); Dir. of Daytime Sales, CBS TV Network ('69); Media Dir., Compton ('77); V.P., Research, NBC Owned Stations ('79); V.P., Research and Measurement, ESPN ('80).

ACHIEVEMENTS & AWARDS: N.A.

PERSONAL: N.A.

REDPATH, JOHN, JR.
Sr. V.P. and General Counsel, HBO, Legal Dept.

c/o HBO, 1271 Ave. of the Americas, New York, NY 10020
b. March 14, 1944.

EDUCATION: Princeton University, B.A., Politics; University of Michigan, J.D.; New York University, LL.M., Taxation.

CAREER HIGHLIGHTS: Assoc., Dewey, Ballantine, Bushby, Palmer & Wood law firm ('74); Assoc. Counsel, Film Programming, HBO ('78); Chief Counsel, Programming, HBO ('79); Asst. General Counsel, HBO ('80); V.P. and General Counsel, HBO ('81); Sr. V.P. and General Counsel, HBO ('83).

ACHIEVEMENTS & AWARDS: N.A.

PERSONAL: Resides in New York City with wife, Suzanne.

REINA, JAMES L.
Dir., ABC, News Special Projects

c/o ABC, 1330 Ave. of the Americas, New York, NY 10019
b. May 29, 1924. New York, NY.

EDUCATION: Manhattan College, B.B.A.

CAREER HIGHLIGHTS: Accounting Dept., NBC ('49); Supervisor, Budgets and Pricing ('51); Sr. Unit Mgr. ('54); Assoc. Prod. on freelance basis and with NBC ('61). Joined ABC as Mgr. of Unit Mgrs. ('66); Dir. of Administration, ABC News ('69); named Dir. of Special Projects, ABC News ('72).

ACHIEVEMENTS & AWARDS: N.A.

PERSONAL: Resides in Edison, NJ; married to actress Gloria Cromwell; sons, Joseph, Thomas, and John.

REISBERG, RICHARD S.
Pres., MGM-UA TV Productions

10202 W. Washington Blvd., Culver City, CA 90230
b. New York, NY.

EDUCATION: Michigan State University; Fordham Law School.

CAREER HIGHLIGHTS: V.P., Business Affairs, Viacom ('71); Pres., Viacom Productions ('79); Pres., UA TV Production ('81); Pres., MGM-UA TV Productions ('82).

ACHIEVEMENTS & AWARDS: N.A.

PERSONAL: Married; two children. Resides in Encino, CA.

REISS, JEFFREY C.
Pres. and Chief Exec. Officer, Cable Health Network

c/o Cable Health Network, 1211 Ave. of the Americas, New York, NY 10020
b. April 14, 1942. Brooklyn, NY.

EDUCATION: Washington University, B.A. ('63).
CAREER HIGHLIGHTS: Worked in Literary Dept., General Artists Corp., now ICM ('65); taught with Project Apex, New York University ('66); continued as high school teacher in public schools ('67); joined Tandem Productions as Story Editor ('68); formed Kleiman-Reiss Productions ('69); named Dir. of Programming, Cartridge TV ('70); joined ABC Entertainment as Dir. of Feature Films ('73); left to help start Showtime and serve as Pres. ('76); named Exec. V.P., Viacom Entertainment Group ('80); founded Reiss Video Development Corp. ('81); appointed Pres. and Chief Exec. Officer, Cable Health Network ('81).
ACHIEVEMENTS & AWARDS: Natl. Cable TV Assn. award for excellence in pay cable program production ('79); AMA Effie award for advertising effectiveness in print and broadcasting. Authored chapter on pay TV programming entitled "Strategies for Winning Television and Radio Audiences" ('80).
PERSONAL: Resides in Manhattan with wife, Ellen, who is daughter of Norman Lear.

RENICK, JEANE
V.P., CBS Entertainment, Daytime Programs

c/o CBS, 51 W. 52d St., New York, NY 10019
b. April 2.

EDUCATION: University of California at Los Angeles; Ohio State University.
CAREER HIGHLIGHTS: Mgr., CBS Daytime Programs ('76); Dir., Daytime Programs, Hollywood ('77); East Coast Dir., Daytime Programs ('78); V.P., Daytime Programs, CBS Entertainment ('80).
ACHIEVEMENTS & AWARDS: N.A.
PERSONAL: N.A.

RENICK, RALPH A.
V.P., Wometco TV News Operations and News Dir., WTVJ, Miami

400 N. Miami Ave., Miami, FL 33128
b. 1928. New York, NY.

EDUCATION: University of Miami.
CAREER HIGHLIGHTS: His 6 P.M. nightly news program, "The Ralph Renick Report," is the nation's longest continuous running news report and the highest-rated local news program in south Florida. He is also V.P., Wometco TV News Operations in addition to his post as News Dir., WTVJ, Miami. One of the nation's best local TV newsmen.
ACHIEVEMENTS & AWARDS: Numerous awards for local news reporting.
PERSONAL: Widower; five daughters, one son.

REO, DON
Writer/Prod.

c/o Robinson-Weintraub, 554 S. San Vicente, Los Angeles, CA 90048
b. January 28, 1946. Providence, RI.

EDUCATION: N.A.
CAREER HIGHLIGHTS: Staff Writer, "Laugh-In" ('70); Writer, episodes of "All in the Family," and "The Mary Tyler Moore Show" ('72), Exec. Script Consultant, "We'll Get By"; Co-Prod./Writer, "Cher" ('74); Co-Prod./Writer, "M*A*S*H" ('75); Co-Prod./Writer, "Rhoda" ('76); Exec. Prod./Writer, "Private Benjamin" ('81); Prod./Writer, "The George Hamilton Show" pilot ('83).
ACHIEVEMENTS & AWARDS: Peabody award for "M*A*S*H" ('76); Critics Circle award for "M*A*S*H" ('76). Author, *Legacy of Thunder* ('79).

PERSONAL: Wife, Judith D. Allison; three children. Resides in Los Angeles.

RESING, GEORGE
Sr. V.P., Westinghouse Broadcasting and Cable, Group W Productions

c/o Group W Productions, Universal City Plaza, Universal City, CA 91608
b. N.A.

EDUCATION: N.A.
CAREER HIGHLIGHTS: Station Mgr. WQXI-TV and Program Mgr. WLS-TV; V.P., Programming, Avco Broadcasting; Program Mgr., KPIX-TV ('73) and General Mgr., KPIX-TV; V.P., Group W TV Group; Sr. V.P., Group W Productions ('79).
ACHIEVEMENTS & AWARDS: N.A.
PERSONAL: N.A.

RESNICK, NOEL
Assoc. Dir., Children's Programs, West Coast, ABC, Entertainment

c/o ABC, 2040 Ave. of the Stars, Los Angeles, CA 90067
b. May 19. Chicago, IL.

EDUCATION: University of California at Los Angeles.
CAREER HIGHLIGHTS: Freelance Writer/Prod., working on various industrial and educational films ('74); Staff Support, ABC Entertainment ('76); Supervisor, Children's Programs, ABC ('78); Production Mgr., Children's Programs, ABC ('80); Assoc. Dir., Children's Programs, West Coast, ABC Entertainment ('83).
ACHIEVEMENTS & AWARDS: N.A.
PERSONAL: Resides in Los Angeles.

RETTIG, RICHARD
Dir., Administration, Advertising and Creative Services, NBC

c/o NBC, 3000 W. Alameda Ave., Burbank, CA 91523
b. May 10, 1943. Los Angeles, CA.

EDUCATION: University of San Francisco; Wabash College.

CAREER HIGHLIGHTS: Started at NBC as a Page, Guest Relations Dept. ('63); Promotion Specialist, NBC Advertising Dept. ('67); Administrator, NBC Advertising Dept. ('68); Prod., On-Air Promotion Operations ('79); Mgr., On-Air Promotion Operations ('80); Mgr., On-Air Promotions, Comedy-Variety Programs, NBC ('81); Mgr., On-Air Promotion, Dramatic Programs ('82); Dir., Administration, Advertising and Creative Services, NBC, Burbank ('83).
ACHIEVEMENTS & AWARDS: N.A.
PERSONAL: Resides in Saugus, CA, with wife, Elizabeth; daughter, Jennifer; sons, James and Daniel.

REVARD, JAMES
Dir., CBS, Prime Time, Program Practice

c/o CBS, 7800 Beverly Blvd., Los Angeles, CA 90036
b. N.A.

EDUCATION: San Francisco State University.
CAREER HIGHLIGHTS: Joined Program Practices, CBS ('66); Dir., Prime Time, Program Practices, CBS ('75).
ACHIEVEMENTS & AWARDS: N.A.
PERSONAL: Wife, Elaine. Resides in Van Nuys, CA.

REYNOLDS, ART
V.P., Disney Channel, Sales and Marketing

c/o Disney Channel, 500 S. Buena Vista St., Burbank, CA 91521
b. May 10, 1940.

EDUCATION: N.A.

CAREER HIGHLIGHTS: Eight years with Time, Inc., New York; V.P., Walt Disney Telecommunications ('73); three years at Oak Media Development Corp. as V.P. of Marketing and Programming; rejoined Disney as V.P., Sales and Marketing, Disney Channel.
ACHIEVEMENTS & AWARDS: N.A.
PERSONAL: N.A.

REYNOLDS, GENE
Prod., MTM Enterprises

c/o MTM Enterprises, Studio Center, Studio City, CA 91604
b. April 4, 1920, Cleveland, OH.

EDUCATION: University of California at Los Angeles, B.A. ('47).
CAREER HIGHLIGHTS: Began acting career at age 10 as an extra in the "Our Gang" comedies and "Babes in Toyland"; signed an MGM contract to perform in *Boys Town, Love Finds Andy Hardy, Gallant Sons,* and *The Santa Fe Trail.* Casting Dir., NBC ('53); Dir., "Hennessey" ('59); Dir., "Peter Gunn" ('60); Dir., "Father of the Bride" ('61); Dir., "The Andy Griffith Show" ('61); Dir., "My Three Sons" ('62)r., "Hogan's Heroes" ('65); Creator/Prod., "Room 222" ('69); Prod./Dir., "Anna and the King" ('72); Prod./Dir., "M*A*S*H" ('72); Prod./Exec. Prod., "Lou Grant" ('77).
ACHIEVEMENTS & AWARDS: Emmy for "Room 222" ('69); Emmy for "Lou Grant" ('79).
PERSONAL: Resides in Hollywood.

REYNOLDS, JOHN
General Mgr., Co-Productions, BBC

c/o BBC, 12 Cavendish Place, London, England W1
b. August 26, 1941.

EDUCATION: N.A.
CAREER HIGHLIGHTS: Sub-Editor, BBC Radio News ('64); Asst. Prod., BBC TV Current Affairs ('67); Prod., Current Affairs and Sports Programmes, BBC, New York ('71); Sr. Prod., "Midweek," Deputy Editor, "Tonight" ('75); Editor, Special Projects, BBC ('79); Editor, "Money Programme" ('82); General Mgr., Co-Production, BBC TV ('83).
ACHIEVEMENTS & AWARDS: N.A.
PERSONAL: N.A.

RICE, ALLAN LEONARD
V.P., 20th Century Fox, Network Business Affairs

c/o 20th Century Fox, 10201 W. Pico Blvd., Los Angeles, CA 90064
b. February 8, 1932. Boston, MA.

EDUCATION: Northeastern University, B.S.
CAREER HIGHLIGHTS: Business Affairs Dept., Screen Gems TV, Columbia Pictures ('59–'73). Currently V.P., Network Business Affairs, 20th Century Fox.
ACHIEVEMENTS & AWARDS: Member, Writers Guild ('72–present); Member, ATAS ('65–present).
PERSONAL: N.A.

RICE, MICHAEL
Sr. Fellow, Aspen Institute

717 Fifth Ave., New York, NY 10022
b. November 3, 1941.

EDUCATION: Harvard University; University of Oxford (England).
CAREER HIGHLIGHTS: One of the outstanding public TV executives before his tenure at Aspen Institute. His expertise in the new communications technologies and the major public policy issues made him a valuable addition to the Aspen Institute. Radio Mgr., TV Program Mgr., V.P. and General Mgr. for WGBH ('65); Dir. of the Communications Program and Sr. Fellow of the Aspen Institute, which addresses the uses and effects of mass media in society ('78). Also Pres., Michael Rice Media ('83).
ACHIEVEMENTS & AWARDS: N.A.
PERSONAL: N.A.

RICH, JOHN
Dir.

c/o Major Talent Agency, 11812 San Vicente, Los Angeles, CA 90049
b. 1925. Rockaway Beach, NY.

EDUCATION: University of Michigan, B.A. and M.A.

CAREER HIGHLIGHTS: Dir., "The Eve Arden Show" ('57); Dir., "The Dick Van Dyke Show" ('60); Dir., "All in the Family" ('72); Dir., "Clarence Darrow" starring Henry Fonda ('74); Prod. and Dir., "On the Rocks" ('75), Exec. Prod., "Benson" ('80).

ACHIEVEMENTS & AWARDS: Emmy for directing "The Dick Van Dyke Show" ('62); Directors Guild award for "All in the Family" ('72); Golden Globe award ('72); Emmy for Directing "All in the Family" ('72); Christopher award ('74).

PERSONAL: Wife, Andrea; three children. Resides in Los Angeles.

RICH, LEE
Pres., Lorimar Productions

c/o Lorimar Productions, 3970 Overland Ave., Culver City, CA 90203
b. Cleveland, OH.

EDUCATION: Ohio University, B.A.

CAREER HIGHLIGHTS: V.P., Benton & Bowles; Prod., Mirisch-Rich TV ('65); Prod., *The Big Red One* and *Who Is Killing the Great Chefs of Europe?*; Prod., Leo Burnett Agency. Formed Lorimar Productions ('69). Exec. Prod., TV series "Dallas," "Flamingo Road," "Eight Is Enough," "Knots Landing," and "The Waltons"; TV movies *Helter-Skelter, Sybil, Studs Lonigan,* and *Skag*.

ACHIEVEMENTS & AWARDS: Emmy for "The Waltons" ('72). Honorary doctorate in communications, Ohio University, 1982.

PERSONAL: N.A.

RICH, TRACY S.
Sr. General Attorney, NBC, Law

c/o NBC, 3000 W. Alameda Ave., Burbank, CA 91523
b. January 30, 1949.

EDUCATION: University of California at Davis.

CAREER HIGHLIGHTS: Clerk, California State Supreme Court; Assoc., Gibson, Dunn & Crutcher; Supervising Attorney, California Public Defender's Office; Corporate Attorney, Morrison & Foerster; Sr. Counsel, Law Dept., NBC, West Coast ('81); Asst. General Attorney, Law Dept., NBC, West Coast ('82); Sr. General Attorney, Law Dept., NBC, West Coast ('83).

ACHIEVEMENTS & AWARDS: N.A.

PERSONAL: Resides in Los Angeles.

RICHARDSON, BARRIE
V.P., Press Information, CBS, Entertainment

c/o CBS, 51 W. 52d St., New York, NY 10019
b. New York, NY.

EDUCATION: Columbia College, B.A. ('49).

CAREER HIGHLIGHTS: Mgr., Press Information, CBS-TV ('66); Dir., Publicity and Advertising, MGM TV ('76); V.P., Press Information, CBS ('72); V.P., Press Information, CBS Entertainment ('77).

ACHIEVEMENTS & AWARDS: N.A.

PERSONAL: N.A.

RICHARDSON, LINDA
V.P. and Dir., Elkar Productions and Silver Leopard Productions

c/o Elkar Productions, 11 Sandusky Rd., New City, NY 10956
b. Kankankee, IL.

EDUCATION: Northwestern University, B.S., Speech.

CAREER HIGHLIGHTS: Prod., WCIX-TV, Miami ('67); Feature Writer, Cosmo Public Relations, Tokyo ('69); Public Relations Mgr., Scripps-Howard's Newspaper Enterprise Assn. ('72); Freelance Journalist and Screenwriter ('75); Screenwriter for 20-hour documentary series "The Unknown War"; Principal of Elkar Productions; V.P. and Dir., Silver Leopard Productions ('82).

ACHIEVEMENTS & AWARDS: N.A.

PERSONAL: N.A.

RICHMAN, JOAN
V.P. and Dir., Special Events, CBS, News

c/o CBS, 524 W. 57th St., New York, NY
  10019
b. April 10, 1939. St. Louis, MO.

EDUCATION: Wellesley College.
CAREER HIGHLIGHTS: Researcher, CBS News
  ('61); Sr. Researcher, CBS News ('63); Re-
  searcher, Special Events Unit, CBS News
  ('65); Assoc. Prod., Special Events Unit ('66);
  Prod., Special Events Unit ('68); Sr. Prod.,
  "The Reasoner Report," ABC News ('72);
  Exec. Prod., "CBS Sports Spectacular" ('75);
  Exec. Prod., weekend editions of "CBS
  Evening News" ('76); V.P. and Dir., Special
  Events, CBS News ('81).
ACHIEVEMENTS & AWARDS: Emmy ('71); Wel-
  lesley College alumnae achievement award.
PERSONAL: Resides in New York City.

RICHTER, RICHARD
Sr. Prod., ABC, Documentary Unit, News

c/o ABC, 7 W. 66th St., New York, NY 10023
b. November 17, 1929.

EDUCATION: Queens College, B.A. ('51).
CAREER HIGHLIGHTS: Reporter, Newsday ('52);
  Reporter, Rewriteman, and Asst. City Editor,
  N.Y. World Telegram and Sun ('53); CBS News
  Writer, News Editor, and Prod., "Douglas
  Edwards With the News," "The CBS Sunday
  News With Walter Cronkite," "The Saturday
  News With Robert Trout," and "Eyewitness"
  ('59); awarded CBS News Fellowship for ad-
  vanced study at Columbia University with
  concentration on Africa ('60); four-year hiatus
  from journalism working with Peace Corps
  programs ('63); Deputy Dir. of Peace Corps in
  Kenya ('65); Prod. and Exec. Prod., NET's
  PBL ('68); Prod., ABC's "Evening News"
  ('69); Exec. Prod.; became first Sr. Prod. of
  News for "A.M. America" and "Good Morn-
  ing America"; returned to "Evening News"
  as Sr. Prod. ('76); assumed position of Sr.
  Prod. of ABC News Documentary Unit ('78).
  Has served as Sr. Prod. for more than 40 ABC
  News "Closeup" documentaries; was Sr.
  Prod. of "Fidel Castro Speaks," TV's first in-
  depth look at Castro since the U.S. and Cuba
  broke off relations.
ACHIEVEMENTS & AWARDS: N.A.
PERSONAL: N.A.

RICHTER, ROBERT
Prod., Robert Richter Productions

c/o Robert Richter Productions, 330 W. 42d
  St., New York, NY 10036
b. N.A.

EDUCATION: Reed College, B.A.; Columbia
  University, M.A.; University of Iowa, M.F.A.
CAREER HIGHLIGHTS: Prod./Dir./Writer/Report-
  er/Host, University of Iowa/NET ('53); Dir. of
  Public Affairs, Oregon Educational and Public Broadcasting Service ('57); Pacific Northwest Reporter, N.Y. Times ('62); Prod./Dir./
  Writer, CBS News ('63); Independent Documentary Prod. for CBS, ABC, PBS, and other
  organizations ('68–present). Some of his
  works include "For Export Only: Pesticides
  and Pills," "Gods of Metal," "A Plague on
  Our Children," "Linus Pauling, Crusading
  Scientist," "Incident at Brown's Ferry," and
  "Vietnam: An American Journey." Latest feature length documentary called "In Our
  Hands," about the huge anti-nuclear march
  in New York City on June 12, 1982.
ACHIEVEMENTS & AWARDS: Dupont-Columbia
  award; two Emmy awards ('67, '68); Peabody
  award ('67); Golden CINE eagles ('70, '73, '74,
  '75); American Film Festival blue ribbon ('65)
  and red ribbon ('81, '82); New York Intl. Film
  & TV Festival gold medals ('70, '74) and silver
  medal ('75).
PERSONAL: Resides in New York City.

RIISNA, ENE
Prod./Dir., ABC News, "20/20"

c/o ABC, 7 W. 66th St., New York, NY 10023
b. July 27, 1942. Tallinn, Estonia.

EDUCATION: University of Toronto, B.A. and
  M.A.
CAREER HIGHLIGHTS: Exec. Prod., "Woman,"
  WCBS daily talk show ('71); Freelance Prod./
  Dir./Writer, Canadian Broadcasting, PBS
  ('72–'76); Prod./Dir., "Violence in America"
  NBC ('76); Prod./Dir., ABC "Closeup" ('78);
  Prod., ABC News, "20/20" ('78).
ACHIEVEMENTS & AWARDS: N.A.
PERSONAL: N.A.

RINGO, MARILYN
News Dir./Prod., Turner Broadcasting System

c/o Turner Broadcasting System, 1050
Techwood Dr., N.W., Atlanta, GA 30318
b. September 12, 1949. Kingston, NY.

EDUCATION: University of Florida, M.A., Journalism and Communications.

CAREER HIGHLIGHTS: Guest Relations Coordinator, NBC, New York ('71); Film/Tape Coordinator, NBC, New York ('72); Public Affairs Director/Asst. News Dir., WCJB-TV, Gainesville, FL ('75); Host/Prod., "Between the Lines," "Open Up," Turner Broadcasting System ('79); Co-Anchor "TBS Weekend News" ('80). Field Prod./Reporter, "Nice People," Turner Broadcasting System ('81); currently Sup./Anchor, "TBS Newswatch"; fill-in Anchor, Cable News Network Headline News; Booth Announcer, Turner Broadcasting System; Host, "Between the Lines," Turner Broadcasting System.

ACHIEVEMENTS & AWARDS: Georgia UPI first place public affairs show for producing "Between the Lines" ('80).

PERSONAL: Husband, James E.; daughter, Alison Elizabeth. Resides in Atlanta.

RINTELS, DAVID W.
Prod./Writer, NBC

c/o NBC, 3000 W. Alameda Ave., Burbank,
CA 91523
b. Boston, MA.

EDUCATION: Harvard University, B.A. (magna cum laude).

CAREER HIGHLIGHTS: Sportswriter, *Boston Herald-American* ('58); Reporter/News Dir., WVOX-Radio, Westchester County, NY ('59);

Researcher, NBC ('61); Writer, "The Defenders" ('62); Writer, "Slattery's People" ('65); Writer, "Run for Your Life" ('70); Writer, "The Young Lawyers" ('70); Writer of the Broadway play and TV adaptation of *Clarence Darrow* ('74); Writer, *Fear on Trial* ('76); Prod./Writer, *Gideon's Trumpet* ('80); Prod., *The Oldest Living Graduate*, NBC Live Theater ('80); Prod., *All the Way Home*, NBC Live Theater ('81); Prod., *Member of the Wedding*, NBC Live Theater ('82).

ACHIEVEMENTS & AWARDS: Writer's Guild award for "A Continual Roar of Musketry" ('70); Emmy award for *Clarence Darrow* ('75); Emmy, Writers Guild and American Bar Assn. awards for *Fear on Trial*.

PERSONAL: Resides in Los Angeles.

RIORDAN, DAN
V.P., Broadcast Dir., J. Walter Thompson, Detroit

17000 Executive Plaza, Dearborn, MI 48126
b. September 20, 1935. New York, NY.

EDUCATION: Fordham College, B.S. ('60).

CAREER HIGHLIGHTS: Media Asst., NCK Ltd. ('61); Media Buyer, Grey Advertising ('63); Mgr., Business Affairs, Doyle, Done, Bernbach ('64); V.P., Mgr. Nighttime Purchasing, Young & Rubicam ('67); Broadcast Dir., J. Walter Thompson ('76).

ACHIEVEMENTS & AWARDS: N.A.

PERSONAL: Wife, Eileen; four children.

RISSIEN, EDWARD L.
Independent Prod.

760 N. La Cienega Blvd., Los Angeles, CA
90069
b. Des Moines, IA.

EDUCATION: Grinnell College; Stanford University.

CAREER HIGHLIGHTS: Prod., Four Star Productions ('58); Prod., Screen Gems ('60); Program Exec., ABC-TV ('60); V.P., Bing Crosby Productions ('63); V.P., Filmways Productions ('67); Prod., Warner Bros. ('70); Exec. V.P., Playboy Productions ('72); Consultant to Playboy and Independent Prod., *Minstrel*

Man, *A Whale for the Killing*, and *The Death of Ocean View Park*.

ACHIEVEMENTS & AWARDS: Member, Board of Dirs., Screen Prods. Guild.

PERSONAL: N.A.

RITCHIE, DANIEL
Chairman and Chief Exec. Officer,
Westinghouse Broadcasting Co., Group W

c/o Group W, Westinghouse Broadcasting Co., 90 Park Ave., New York, NY 10016
b. September 19, 1931.

EDUCATION: Harvard Graduate School of Business, M.B.A.

CAREER HIGHLIGHTS: Exec. V.P., Learning and Leisure Time Industries ('74); Pres., Corporate Staff and Strategic Planning, Group W ('78); Pres. and Chief Operating Officer and Pres. and Chief Exec. Officer ('79); Chairman and Chief Exec. Officer, Group W ('81).

ACHIEVEMENTS & AWARDS: N.A.

PERSONAL: Lives in New Jersey.

RITTER, JOHN
Actor

c/o "Three's Company," ABC, 2040 Ave. of the Stars, Los Angeles, CA 90067
b. September 17. Burbank, CA.

EDUCATION: University of Southern California.

CAREER HIGHLIGHTS: Recognized as one of the best young light comedians on TV today, Ritter has made "Three's Company" more ingratiating than it otherwise would have been. TV guest star on "Dan August," Hawaii Five-O," "Medical Center," "M*A*S*H,"

"Phyllis," "Rhoda," and "The Rookies." TV movies include *The Night That Panicked America, Leave Yesterday Behind, Pray TV*, and *The Comeback Kid*. Motion pictures include *They All Laughed, Americathon*, and *Hero at Large*. TV star of "Three's Company."

ACHIEVEMENTS & AWARDS: N.A.

PERSONAL: Wife, Nancy; son, Jason; daughter, Carly. Resides in Los Angeles.

RIVERA, GERALDO
Investigative Reporter

c/o ABC, 1330 Ave. of the Americas, New York, NY 10019
b. July 4, 1943. New York, NY.

EDUCATION: University of Arizona; Columbia School of Journalism.

CAREER HIGHLIGHTS: This controversial reporter has acquired the aura of a one-man crusade against social injustice. He began his career as a lawyer before joining the WABC-TV Eyewitness News Team; Contributor to ABC's "Good Morning America"; Host, for a series of late-night specials, "Good Night America"; created the local documentary "Willowbrook: The Last Disgrace"; Special Correspondent for the TV newsmagazine "20/20."

ACHIEVEMENTS & AWARDS: Six Emmy awards, of which four are local awards.

PERSONAL: N.A.

RIVERA, HENRY M.
Commissioner, FCC

c/o FCC, 1919 M St., N.W., Washington, DC 20554
b. September 25, 1946. Albuquerque, NM.

EDUCATION: University of New Mexico, B.A. and J.D.

CAREER HIGHLIGHTS: Pres., Young Lawyers Division, New Mexico State Bar ('76); State Delegate, American Bar Assn. Young Lawyers Division ('77); V.P., Albuquerque Bar Assn. ('78); Partner, Sutin, Thayer & Browne, Albuquerque ('79); Commissioner, FCC ('81).

ACHIEVEMENTS & AWARDS: Bronze Star for service in Vietnam ('68–'70).

PERSONAL: N.A.

RIVERS, JOAN
Comedienne, Host, NBC

c/o NBC, 3000 W. Alameda Ave., Burbank, CA 91532

b. 1935. Brooklyn, New York.

EDUCATION: Barnard College.

CAREER HIGHLIGHTS: Early in her career, Rivers was a fashion coordinator. Turning to the stage, she began constructing sketches for "Candid Camera" and also wrote comedy material for Phyllis Diller and Zsa Zsa Gabor. In addition to being a crowd-pleasing nightclub performer, she directed the movie *Rabbit Test* ('78). Now frequently a guest host for Johnny Carson's "Tonight Show," she is known for her rapid-fire jokes and blunt comedic style.

ACHIEVEMENTS & AWARDS: Member, Phi Beta Kappa.

PERSONAL: Husband is producer Edgar Rosenberg; one daughter.

ROBERTS, ALEC
Reporter, WPIX, "Action News"

c/o WPIX-TV, 11 WPIX Plaza, New York, NY 10017

b. February 2, 1950.

EDUCATION: New York University, B.A.

CAREER HIGHLIGHTS: Radio Reporter, WLIR-FM, Long Island; Anchor, WVIR-TV, Charlottesville, VA; Investigative Reporter, WRGB, Schenectady, NY.

ACHIEVEMENTS & AWARDS: AP Broadcasters award.

PERSONAL: N.A.

ROBERTS, PERNELL
Actor

c/o "Trapper John, M.D.," CBS, 7800 Beverly Blvd., Los Angeles, CA 90036

b. May 18. Waycross, GA.

EDUCATION: University of Maryland.

CAREER HIGHLIGHTS: Whether seated tall in the saddle on "Bonanza" or looming large behind a desk on "Trapper John, M.D.," Roberts's forceful presence makes him a sort of TV Sean Connery. New York stage appearances in *The Lovers, A Clearing in the Woods,* and *Macbeth.* Major motion pictures include *Desire Under the Elms, The Sheepman, The Silent Gun, The Bravos,* and *The Night Rider.* TV series star of "Bonanza" and "Trapper John, M.D."

ACHIEVEMENTS & AWARDS: N.A.

PERSONAL: Wife, Cara. Resides in Malibu, CA.

ROBERTSON, PAT (Marion Gordon Robertson)
Pres., Christian Broadcasting Network

c/o Christian Broadcasting Network Center, Virginia Beach, VA 23463

b. March 22, 1930.

EDUCATION: Washington and Lee University, B.A. ('50); Yale University Law School, J.D. ('55); New York Theological Seminary, M.Div. ('59).

CAREER HIGHLIGHTS: Founder and Pres., Christian Broadcasting Network ('60); Host, "The 700 Club" TV program ('68); Founder and Chancellor, CBN University, a graduate level school offering master's programs in communication, education, business administration, biblical studies and public policy. Ordained Southern Baptist clergyman ('61).

ACHIEVEMENTS & AWARDS: Intl. Clergyman of the Year, Religion in Media ('81); Man of the Year, Intl. Committee for Goodwill ('81); bronze halo, Southern California Motion Picture Council ('82); humanitarian award, Food for the Hungry ('82).

PERSONAL: Wife, Adelia (Dede); children, Timothy, Elizabeth, Gordon, and Ann.

ROBINS, DEBBIE
Prod., Charles Fries Productions

c/o Charles Fries Productions, 9200 Sunset Blvd., Los Angeles, CA 90069
b. November 14, 1956. New York, NY.

EDUCATION: Kenyon College, B.A.

CAREER HIGHLIGHTS: Asst. to Theatrical Mgrs. Tyler Gatchell and Peter Neufeld, New York; Asst. Prod., Ladd Co., Los Angeles; Prod./Partner, Le Vine/Robins through Charles Fries Productions.

ACHIEVEMENTS & AWARDS: N.A.

PERSONAL: Married.

ROBINSON, MAX
Anchor, ABC, News

c/o ABC, 190 N. State St., Chicago, IL 60601
b. May 1, 1939. Richmond, VA.

EDUCATION: Oberlin College.

CAREER HIGHLIGHTS: Began in TV as Studio Dir. at WDVM, CBS Washington, DC, affiliate ('65); became News Correspondent, WRC-TV, Washington, DC ('66); Anchor, WDVC "Eyewitness News," Washington, DC ('69). Appointed Natl. Desk Anchor/Journalist, ABC "World News Tonight" to serve as Chicago-based Co-Anchor ('78).

ACHIEVEMENTS & AWARDS: Co-founder, Assn. of Black Journalists, and used own funds to begin first internship for blacks in broadcasting in Washington, DC; awards ('81) include College of William and Mary heritage award for excellence in journalism; Martin Luther King, Jr. memorial drum major for justice award; Detroit distinguished recognition award from City Council; cited by Natl. Assn. of Black Journalists and Natl. Assn. of Media Women. His awards ('82) include Avi-

ation and Space Writers Assn. Robert S. Ball memorial award.

PERSONAL: Resides in Chicago; wife, the former Beverly Hamilton; children, Mark, Michael, Maureen, and Malik.

RODGERS, JONATHAN
Exec. Prod., Weekend Evening News Shows, CBS, News

c/o CBS, 524 W. 57th St., New York, NY 10019
b. California.

EDUCATION: University of California at Berkeley, B.A., Journalism ('67); Stanford University, M.A., Communications ('72).

CAREER HIGHLIGHTS: Writer/Reporter, *Sports Illustrated* ('67); Assoc. Editor, *Newsweek* ('68); Writer/Prod., WNBC-TV, New York ('73); Reporter, WKYC-TV, Cleveland ('75); News Mgr., WBBM-TV, Chicago ('76); Exec. Prod., "Channel 2 News," KNXT-TV, Los Angeles ('78); News. Dir., KNXT-TV, Los Angeles ('80); Station Mgr., KNXT-TV, Los Angeles ('81); Exec. Prod., "CBS News Nightwatch," CBS News, New York ('83); Exec Prod., Weekend Evening News Shows, CBS News ('83).

ACHIEVEMENTS & AWARDS: Michele Clark Fellowship for Minority Journalists at the Columbia University Graduate School of Journalism.

PERSONAL: N.A.

RODMAN, ELLEN
Dir., NBC, Inc., Corporate Informational Services

c/o NBC, 30 Rockefeller Plaza, New York, NY 10020
b. July 5.

EDUCATION: Simmons College, B.S.; Columbia University, M.A.; New York University, Ph.D.

CAREER HIGHLIGHTS: Theatrical experience with the Boston Children's Theater and Tufts College Arena Summer Theater; Dir. of Theater Arts, at several private schools and for the city of Medford, MA. Freelance Writer, *N.Y. Times, N.Y. Daily News,* and *McCall's* magazine. Co-Author, *The New York Times Guide to Children's Entertainment in New York, New Jersey and Connecticut* ('76); Dir., Children's Informational Services, including NBC's Parent Participation TV Workshops; Dir., NBC, Corporate Informational Services.

ACHIEVEMENTS & AWARDS: Member, American Theater Assn., Children's Theater Assn. of America.

PERSONAL: Married; two children. Resides in New York City.

RODOMISTA, ROD H.
V.P., Tape Production, East Coast, ABC

c/o ABC, 1330 Ave. of the Americas, New York, NY 10020
b. October 31, 1916. New York, NY.

EDUCATION: N.A.

CAREER HIGHLIGHTS: Mgr., Studio and Production Services, NBC ('51); Mgr., Staging Services, CBS ('60); worked for the World's Fair in New York ('63); Exec. Dir., Hollywood Pavilion ('65); Unit Mgr., ABC TV ('66); V.P. and General Mgr. of Lewron TV ('71); General Mgr. of Vega Assn. ('73); Dir. of Production Administration and Operations, ABC, East Coast ('74); V.P., Tape Production, East Coast, ABC ('81).

ACHIEVEMENTS & AWARDS: N.A.

PERSONAL: Resides in Oceanside, NY, with wife, Betty.

ROGERS, FRED
Host

4802 Fifth Ave., Pittsburgh, PA 15213
b. 1928. Latrobe, PA.

EDUCATION: University of Pittsburgh.

CAREER HIGHLIGHTS: Rogers's gentle manner on TV and his thoughtful prosocial attitudes have been one of the few highlights in American children's TV programming. Network Floor Dir. for "The Kate Smith Hour" and "Your Hit Parade." Creator and Host, "Mister Rogers Talks With Parents" and "Old Friends . . . New Friends." Host of the long-running children's series "Children's Corner" and "Mister Roger's Neighborhood."

ACHIEVEMENTS & AWARDS: Emmy, three American Film Festival prizes, the Gabriel award, the Ralph Lowell award, Action for Children's Television award, Peabody award, and a *Saturday Review* TV award.

PERSONAL: N.A.

ROGERS, MELODY
Host, KNXT-TV, "2 on the Town"

c/o KNXT-TV, 6121 Sunset Blvd., Los Angeles, CA 90028
b. N.A.

EDUCATION: Northwestern University; Chicago Conservatory of Music and Drama.

CAREER HIGHLIGHTS: Started as an actress in numerous stage productions. Rogers also appeared on the TV series "Buck Rogers in the 25th Century" and "Nobody's Perfect." While based in Chicago, she served as a Weather Reporter with WBBM-TV and later became Co-Host, "2 On the Town," with Steve Edwards, after reading a newspaper article about a job opening ('80).

ACHIEVEMENTS & AWARDS: N.A.

PERSONAL: Resides in Hollywood.

ROGGIN, FRED
Reporter, KNBC, "News 4 LA"

c/o KNBC, 3000 W. Alameda Ave., Burbank, CA 91523
b. N.A.

EDUCATION: Phoenix College, Broadcasting.

CAREER HIGHLIGHTS: Sports Anchor, KPNX-TV, Phoenix; Sports Dir., KVUE-TV, Austin, TX; Sports Dir., KBLU-Radio and KYEL-TV, Yuma, AZ; radio and TV work for KIKO-Radio, Globe, AZ; reports on KNBC's "Sports

4 LA''; appears on "News 4 LA.''
ACHIEVEMENTS & AWARDS: N.A.
PERSONAL: Resides in North Hollywood, CA.

ROHRBECK, JOHN H.
**V.P. and General Mgr., WRC-TV,
Washington, DC**

c/o WRC-TV, 4001 Nebraska Ave., N.W.,
Washington, DC 20016
b. N.A.

EDUCATION: University of Washington.
CAREER HIGHLIGHTS: Station Mgr., KNBC-TV,
Los Angeles; V.P. and General Mgr., WRC-
TV, Washington, DC ('78).
ACHIEVEMENTS   &   AWARDS: Regional   Co-
Chairman, Natl. Conference of Christians
and Jews; Member, Exec. Committee, Duke
Ellington School for the Performing Arts.
PERSONAL: Resides in Washington, DC, with
wife, Joan, and son, Douglas.

ROJAS, GLORIA
**Correspondent, WABC-TV, "Eyewitness
News"**

c/o WABC-TV, 7 Lincoln Sq., New York, NY
10023
b. April 1. New York, NY.

EDUCATION: N.A.
CAREER HIGHLIGHTS: General Assignment Re-
porter, WCBS-TV ('68); Reporter, WLS-TV,
Chicago, and WNEW-TV, New York; "Eye-
witness News" Reporter, WABC-TV ('74).
ACHIEVEMENTS   &   AWARDS: New York Press
Club byline award ('79).
PERSONAL: Resides in New Jersey.

ROLAND, JOHN
Anchor, Metromedia, WNEW-TV, New York

c/o WNEW-TV, 205 E. 67th St., New York,
NY 10021
b. Pittsburgh, PA.

EDUCATION: California   State   University   at
Long Beach.
CAREER HIGHLIGHTS: Began broadcasting ca-
reer as a Researcher/Newswriter, KNBC-TV,

Los Angeles; News Assignment Editor, NBC,
West   Coast;   Reporter,   KTTV-TV,   Los
Angeles; Reporter, WNEW-TV, New York
('69);   Reporter/Co-Anchor,   WNEW's   "10
O'Clock News" ('72); Anchor, "10 O'Clock
News" ('79).
ACHIEVEMENTS & AWARDS: Public service award
from the American Federation of Government Employees for a series of reports on the
easy entry for many illegal aliens; Emmy for
newswriting ('78).
PERSONAL: Resides in New York City with
wife, Susan.

ROLLIN, BETTY
Correspondent, ABC, News

c/o ABC, 1330 Ave. of the Americas, New
York, NY 10019
b. January 3, 1936, New York.

EDUCATION: Fieldston Ethical Culture School;
Sarah Lawrence College.
CAREER HIGHLIGHTS: Features Editor and Staff
Writer, *Vogue*; Sr. Editor, *Look*; Reporter,
NBC newsmagazine "First Tuesday" ('71);
Theater Critic, WNBC-TV, New York ('72);
NBC Northeast Bureau Correspondent ('73);
Contributing Correspondent for ABC News
"Nightline" ('82).
ACHIEVEMENTS & AWARDS: Author of five books
including *First, You Cry*, a personal story
about her mastectomy, which was made into
a TV movie, starring Mary Tyler Moore.
PERSONAL: Resides in Manhattan with hus-
band, Dr. Harold M. Edwards.

ROONEY, ANDY
Writer/Prod., CBS, News

c/o CBS, 524 W. 57th St., New York, NY
10019
b. January 14, 1920. Albany, NY.

EDUCATION: Colgate University.
CAREER HIGHLIGHTS: Rooney began his versatile writing career as a Writer, for Arthur
Godfrey ('49–'55); "The Garry Moore Show,"
CBS Radio Network ('59–'65); collaborated
with CBS News Correspondent Harry Reasoner on many notable CBS News specials in
the sixties; Writer, script for the first Telstar

transatlantic satellite broadcast ('65); Writer, two CBS News specials, "Of Black America" ('68) and "Harry and Lena" ('75); Writer/ Prod./Dir., series of one-hour CBS broadcasts. His broadcasts became a regular feature on "60 Minutes" ('78). In addition to working with CBS News, Rooney writes a column three days a week for the Tribune Co. Syndicate.

ACHIEVEMENTS & AWARDS: Six-time winner of the Writers Guild award for best script of the year. Two Emmy awards for his essays "A Few Minutes With Andy Rooney" ('79, '81), and a Peabody award for "Mr. Rooney Goes to Washington." He has also written five books: *The Story of the Stars and Stripes, Air Gunner, Conqueror's Peace, The Fortunes of War,* and *A Few Minutes With Andy Rooney.*

PERSONAL: Wife, Marguerite; four children.

ROSE, JUDD
Correspondent, ABC, News, Los Angeles

c/o ABC, 2040 Ave. of the Stars, Los Angeles, CA 90067
b. Chicago, IL.

EDUCATION: University of California at Los Angeles; New York University; Santa Monica College.

CAREER HIGHLIGHTS: Desk Asst., ABC Radio News, New York ('73); Writer, AP Broadcast Wire, New York ('74); Writer/Reporter, KFWB-AM, Los Angeles ('78); Reporter, KNBC-TV, Los Angeles ('79); Reporter, KABC-TV, Los Angeles ('80); Correspondent, ABC News, Los Angeles ('82).

ACHIEVEMENTS & AWARDS: Los Angeles Valley Press Club award ('79); AP Broadcasters award ('79).

PERSONAL: Resides in Los Angeles.

ROSE, REGINALD
Writer

20 Wedgewood Rd., Westport, CT 06880
b. 1920. New York, NY.

EDUCATION: City College New York.

CAREER HIGHLIGHTS: One of the most gifted and prolific of TV dramatists during the Golden Age of television in New York in the

fifties, he is the author of *Twelve Angry Men* ('54); and creator of "The Defenders" ('61–'65), one of the best drama series in the history of TV. Motion picture screenplays include *Crime in the Streets, Twelve Angry Men, Baxter!, Somebody Killed Her Husband, The Wild Geese, The Sea Wolves,* and *Whose Life Is It Anyway?* Plays include *Black Monday, Twelve Angry Men,* and *The Porcelain Year.* Books include *Six TV Plays* and *The Thomas Book.*

ACHIEVEMENTS & AWARDS: Emmy awards ('54, '62, '63).

PERSONAL: Wife, Ellen; four children. Resides in Connecticut.

ROSEMONT, NORMAN
Prod.

c/o Viacom, 1211 Ave. of the Americas, New York, NY 10036
b. December 12, 1924.

EDUCATION: Attended school in New York City.

CAREER HIGHLIGHTS: Prod. of the TV musical shows *Brigadoon, Carousel,* and *Kismet.* Prod., on many distinguished TV dramatic specials and movies for TV, including *The Man Without a Country, Miracle on 34th Street, The Red Badge of Courage, The Man in the Iron Mask, Captains Courageous, Les Miserables, All Quiet on the Western Front, Little Lord Fauntleroy,* and *A Tale of Two Cities.*

ACHIEVEMENTS & AWARDS: N.A.

PERSONAL: N.A.

ROSENBAUM, R. ROBERT
Sr. V.P., Paramount Pictures, TV Production

c/o Paramount, 5555 Melrose Ave., Los Angeles, CA 90038
b. August 24, 1928. Uniontown, PA.

EDUCATION: B.A., University of Southern California.

CAREER HIGHLIGHTS: N.A.

ACHIEVEMENTS & AWARDS: N.A.

PERSONAL: Resides in Los Angeles CA with wife Jane; two daughters, Julie and Amy.

ROSENBERG, GRANT
V.P., Paramount TV, Dramatic Development

5451 Marathon St., Hollywood, CA 90038
b. N.A.

EDUCATION: University of California at Davis,
B.A.
CAREER HIGHLIGHTS: Sr. Research Assoc., NBC
('76); V.P., Market Research, Paramount TV
('78); V.P., Dramatic Development, Para-
mount TV ('81).
ACHIEVEMENTS & AWARDS: N.A.
PERSONAL: Married; resides in Los Angeles.

ROSENBERG, HOWARD
TV Columnist, *Los Angeles Times*

c/o *Los Angeles Times*, Times Mirror Square,
Los Angeles, CA 90053
b. June 10, 1942. Kansas City, MO.

EDUCATION: Oklahoma University, B.A., His-
tory; University of Minnesota, M.A., Political
Science.
CAREER HIGHLIGHTS: Editor, *White Bear Weekly
Press* ('65); General Assignment Reporter,
Moline Dispatch ('66); General Assignment/
Political Reporter, *Louisville Times* ('68); TV
Critic, *Louisville Times* ('70); TV Columnist, *Los
Angeles Times* ('78).
ACHIEVEMENTS & AWARDS: N.A.
PERSONAL: Wife, Carol; child, Kirsten.

ROSENBERG, META
Prod./Writer

c/o Ziegler-Diskant Agency, 9255 Sunset
Blvd., Los Angeles, CA 90069
b. June 5.

EDUCATION: N.A.
CAREER HIGHLIGHTS: Personal Mgr. for James
Garner; Exec. Prod. for "Nichols," "The
Rockford Files," and "Bret Maverick"; served
as Prod. and Writer, "Tenspeed and Brown-
shoe." Other TV credits include *Portrait of
Elizabeth, Quickie Nirvana*, and *The Queen of
Peru*.
ACHIEVEMENTS & AWARDS: N.A.
PERSONAL: N.A.

ROSENCRANS, ROBERT M.
Pres. and Chief Exec. Officer, Rogers UA Cablesystems

c/o Rogers UA Cablesystems, 315 Post Rd.
W., Westport, CT 06881
b. March 26, 1927.

EDUCATION: Columbia College, B.A.; Columbia University Graduate School of Business,
B.S.
CAREER HIGHLIGHTS: One of the pioneering
and most influential figures in the growth of
cable TV over the past two decades. Pres. and
Chief Exec. Officer, Rogers UA Cablesystems, Westport, CT.
ACHIEVEMENTS & AWARDS: NCTA-Larry Boggs
award for outstanding contributions to the
advancement of the cable TV industry ('80);
first chairman of C-SPAN.
PERSONAL: Resides in Greenwich, CT, with his
wife and their four children.

ROSENFELD, JAMES H.
Sr. Exec. V.P., Finance, Operations and Development

c/o CBS, 51 W. 52d St., New York, NY 10019
b. July 29. Boston, MA.

EDUCATION: Dartmouth College.
CAREER HIGHLIGHTS: Radio Announcer during
college; Exec. Trainee, NBC ('54); NBC Acct.
Exec.; Advertising Mgr. for Polaroid; V.P.,
Marketing Dir. for Airequipt; joined CBS
Network as Acct. Exec. ('65). Named Dir.,
Daytime Sales ('67); Dir., Eastern Sales ('69);
V.P., Eastern Sales ('72); V.P., Sales Adminis-
tration and Marketing ('75); V.P. and Net-
work Sales Mgr. ('77); Pres., CBS TV Network
('77); appointed Exec. V.P., Broadcast Group;
Sr. Exec. V.P., Finance, Operations and De-
velopment.
ACHIEVEMENTS & AWARDS: Honorary doctorate
of commercial science, St. Johns' University
('81); first V.P. and Board Member, IRTS;
Member, NATAS; New York State Motion
Picture and TV Advisory Board. Member of
the Board, Advertising Council of New York;
New York Heart Assn.; Natl. Board of Junior
Achievement; Alumni Trustee, Roxbury Latin
School, Boston.
PERSONAL: N.A.

ROSENTHAL, ARNIE
Exec. V.P., TeleFrance USA Ltd.

c/o TeleFrance USA Ltd., 1966 Broadway,
New York, NY 10023
b. July 18, 1951.

EDUCATION: New York Institute of Technology, masters, Communication Arts.

CAREER HIGHLIGHTS: Co-Founder and Head of Sales for the English Channel, USA Cable Network. Independent Prod., WSNL-TV, and headed own production company, Shamus Productions, which produced "The Big Giveaway," cable TV's first game show. Created the syndicated TV game show "It's Rock 'n' Roll." Dir. of Marketing, TeleFrance USA ('80); Exec. V.P., TeleFrance USA.

ACHIEVEMENTS & AWARDS: N.A.

PERSONAL: N.A.

ROSENTHAL, JANE
Dir., Motion Pictures for TV, CBS, Entertainment

c/o CBS, 6121 Sunset Blvd., Los Angeles, CA 90028
b. N.A.

EDUCATION: Brown University; New York University.

CAREER HIGHLIGHTS: Research Staff, CBS Sports ('76); Editor, Program Practices, CBS Entertainment ('77); Assoc. Program Dept., CBS ('78); Program Exec. for Mini-Series, CBS Entertainment, Los Angeles ('78); Assoc. Dir., Motion Pictures for TV, CBS Entertainment ('79); Dir., Motion Pictures for TV, CBS Entertainment ('81).

ACHIEVEMENTS & AWARDS: N.A.

PERSONAL: Single, resides in Los Angeles.

ROSNER, RICK
Prod./Creator

c/o NBC, 3000 W. Alameda Ave., Burbank, CA 91523
b. May 8, 1941. Englewood, NJ.

EDUCATION: LeHigh University, B.A.

CAREER HIGHLIGHTS: Prod., "The Mike Douglas Show" ('67); "The Della Reese Show" ('69); "The Steve Allen Show" ('71); "Jerry Lewis Telethon" ('74); Writer/Prod., NBC movie of the week *Sky Heist* ('75); V.P., Variety Programs, NBC ('76); Creator/Exec. Prod. "CHiPs," NBC ('77); "240-Robert," ABC ('79); "Just Men!," NBC ('82); "Lottery!," ABC ('83).

ACHIEVEMENTS & AWARDS: N.A.

PERSONAL: Resides in Lake Arrowhead and Marina del Rey, CA.

ROSS, BRIAN
Correspondent, NBC, News

c/o NBC, 30 Rockefeller Plaza, New York, NY 10020
b. Chicago, IL.

EDUCATION: University of Iowa.

CAREER HIGHLIGHTS: Reporter, KWWL-TV, Waterloo, IA; Reporter, WCKT-TV, Miami ('72); NBC Reporter for WKYC-TV, Cleveland ('74); NBC News Correspondent, based in New York ('76).

ACHIEVEMENTS & AWARDS: Peabody award for investigative reporting; Dupont-Columbia award for reports on the Teamsters Union; Sigma Delta Chi award and a Natl. Headliner award for five-part series on the Teamsters Union ('76); Natl. Headliner award for "The New Mob" ('77); Emmy for "Migrants" ('80); Natl. Headliner award for coverage of Abscam ('81).

PERSONAL: N.A.

ROSS, MARION
Actress

c/o "Happy Days," ABC, 2040 Ave. of the
Stars, Los Angeles, CA 90067
b. October 25, 1928. Albert Lea, MN.

EDUCATION: San Diego State College.
CAREER HIGHLIGHTS: Motion pictures include
*The Glenn Miller Story, Lust for Life, Teacher's
Pet, Operation Petticoat,* and *Grand Theft Auto.*
Daytime serial regular on "Paradise Bay." TV
guest roles in "Petrocelli," "Hawaii Five-O,"
"Mannix," "The Untouchables," and "Perry
Mason." TV movies include *The Survival of
Dana, The Burning,* and *Pearl.* Series star of
"Happy Days."
ACHIEVEMENTS & AWARDS: N.A.
PERSONAL: Two children, Ellen and Jim.

ROSS, MICHAEL
Prod./Dir./Writer, NRW Productions

c/o Elliott Wax, 9255 Sunset Blvd., Los
Angeles, CA 90069
b. August 4, 1924. New York, NY.

EDUCATION: City College of New York, B.S.
CAREER HIGHLIGHTS: Program Editor, "Cae-
sar's Hour" ('54); Comedy Dir. "The Perry
Como Show" ('55); Comedy Supervisor,
"The Garry Moore Show" ('63); Story Editor,
"All in the Family" ('71); Prod., "All in the
Family" ('74); Creator/Exec. Prod., "The Jef-
fersons" ('75); Creator/Exec. Prod., "Three's
Company" ('77).
ACHIEVEMENTS & AWARDS: Emmy for best com-
edy writing for "All in the Family" ('73).
PERSONAL: N.A.

ROSS, RICHARD
**Dir., USA Network, Broadcast
Administration**

c/o USA Network, 208 Harristown Rd., Glen
Rock, NJ 07452
b. N.A.

EDUCATION: University of Miami, B.A.; New
York University, masters, Communications.
CAREER HIGHLIGHTS: Sr. Facilities Adminis-
trator, CBS, and Asst. Mgr. of News, CBS

('74); Mgr. of Network Operations, including
coordination of international and domestic
communications for the news, CBS; Dir.,
Broadcast Administration, USA Network.
ACHIEVEMENTS & AWARDS: N.A.
PERSONAL: N.A.

ROSSEN, ELLEN
Prod., ABC News "20/20"

c/o ABC, 77 W. 66th St., New York, NY 10023
b. October 13, 1946. Los Angeles, CA.

EDUCATION: Sarah Lawrence College, B.A.
('68).
CAREER HIGHLIGHTS: Assoc. Prod., WNEW-
TV, New York ('69); Prod./Writer, WCVB-TV,
Boston ('71); Prod./Writer, TV News, Inc.
('73); Prod./Writer, WABC, "Eyewitness
News" ('75); Prod., "World News Tonight,"
ABC ('78).
ACHIEVEMENTS & AWARDS: New York Press
Club award, writer, WABC-TV ('76); Emmy
for program segment on "20/20" ('81).
PERSONAL: N.A.

ROTH, PETER
**V.P., Current Programming, ABC,
Entertainment**

c/o ABC, 4151 Prospect Ave., Los Angeles,
CA 90027
b. N.A.

EDUCATION: University of Pennsylvania; Tufts
University.
CAREER HIGHLIGHTS: Theatrical Consultant for
Myron Sanft & Co., New York, Prod. of in-
dustrial shows; Dir., Development, Chil-
dren's Programming, Filmways TV Produc-
tions ('74); Mgr., Children's Programs, West
Coast, ABC ('76); Dir., Children's Programs,
West Coast ABC ('76); Dir., Current Drama
Programs ('79); V.P., Current Programming,
ABC Entertainment ('81).
ACHIEVEMENTS & AWARDS: N.A.
PERSONAL: Resides in Los Angeles with wife,
Andrea, and daughter, Erica.

ROTH, RICHARD
Correspondent, CBS, News, Rome

c/o CBS, 524 W. 57th St., New York, NY 10019
b. New York, NY.

EDUCATION: Union College, B.A., English; Columbia University Graduate School of Journalism, M.S.

CAREER HIGHLIGHTS: Reporter/Anchor, WROW-Radio, Albany, NY ('68); Legislative Correspondent, WTEN-TV, Albany, NY ('69); Reporter/Assignment Editor, CBS Radio News, New York ('72); Reporter, CBS News, Chicago ('73); Correspondent, CBS News, Chicago ('74); Correspondent, CBS News, Washington, DC ('76); Correspondent, CBS News, Rome ('81).

ACHIEVEMENTS & AWARDS: AP Broadcasters award for best spot news coverage ('70).

PERSONAL: N.A.

ROZENZWEIG, BARNEY
Exec. Prod., CBS

5150 Wilshire Blvd., Suite 500, Los Angeles, CA 90034
b. December 23, 1937. Los Angeles, CA.

EDUCATION: University of Southern California, B.A. ('59).

CAREER HIGHLIGHTS: Prod., "Daniel Boone" series, NBC ('67), "One of My Wives Is Missing," ABC ('75), "American Dream" pilot, ABC ('81), *East of Eden* mini-series, ABC ('81), "Modesty Blaise" pilot, ABC ('82); Exec. Prod., "Cagney and Lacey" dramatic series, CBS ('82).

ACHIEVEMENTS & AWARDS: Atlanta Film Festival award for best low budget feature for *Who Fears the Devil* ('72); Golden Globe award for best TV movie or mini-series for *East of Eden* ('82).

PERSONAL: Wife, Barbara; four daughters. Resides in Los Angeles.

RUBENS, WILLIAM S.
V.P., NBC, Research

c/o NBC, 30 Rockefeller Plaza, New York, NY 10020
b. December 25, 1927. Brooklyn, NY.

EDUCATION: City College of New York, B.B.A.

CAREER HIGHLIGHTS: Research Asst., Harry B. Cohen Advertising ('51); ABC Statistician ('53); Supervisor, Ratings ('55); Mgr. Audience Measurement ('58). Joined NBC as Dir., Marketing for Owned Stations ('64); V.P., Audience Measurement ('70); V.P., Research and Corporate Planning ('73); appointed V.P. Research ('77).

ACHIEVEMENTS & AWARDS: Pres., Radio and TV Research Council ('65–'66); Chairman of the Board, Advertising Research Foundation ('80); Trustee, Marketing Science Institute ('80); Co-Author, *Television and Aggression: A Panel Study* ('82).

PERSONAL: Resides in Roslyn, NY, with wife, Ruth; son, Steven.

RUBIN, ALBERT
V.P., ABC TV

c/o ABC, 1330 Ave. of the Americas, New York, NY 10019
b. May 1, 1940. Brooklyn, NY.

EDUCATION: Brooklyn College, B.A., Economics.

CAREER HIGHLIGHTS: Sales Service Dept. ('61); Jr. Analyst, Research Dept. ('63); Daytime Availabilities Coordinator ('64). Mgr., Daytime Sales Planning for one year ('65); named Asst. Mgr., Nighttime Sales Planning, ABC TV Network ('66); Dir., Revenue and Business Analysis ('69); Dir., Business Analysis and Financial Planning ('72); V.P., ABC TV in same area ('74); V.P. Financial Planning and Controls for ABC TV Network and ABC Entertainment ('77); became V.P., ABC TV ('81).

ACHIEVEMENTS & AWARDS: N.A.

PERSONAL: Resides in Suffern, NY, with wife, Ina; two children, Nancy and Daniel.

RUBIN, JAY
Editor, *Cablevision* Magazine

c/o *Cablevision* Magazine, 101 Park Ave., 4th Floor, New York, NY 10178
b. March 5, 1952. Quincy, MA.

EDUCATION: Syracuse University, B.A.

CAREER HIGHLIGHTS: Correspondent, *Patriot Ledger*, Quincy, MA ('74); various staff positions in New York and Washington, DC, *Broadcasting* magazine ('75); New York Bureau Chief, *Broadcasting* magazine ('82); editor, *Cablevision* magazine.

ACHIEVEMENTS & AWARDS: N.A.

PERSONAL: N.A.

RUBIN, ROBERT H.
V.P., Programming for Cable, Westinghouse Broadcasting Co., Group W Productions

c/o Group W Productions, 645 Madison Ave., New York, NY 10022
b. N.A.

EDUCATION: Brooklyn College, B.A.; Brown University, M.A.

CAREER HIGHLIGHTS: Prod. of the NBC game show "Jeopardy!" ('64–'75); Dir., Program Development, Premium Program Dept. ('77); V.P., Programming for Cable, Group W Productions ('79).

ACHIEVEMENTS & AWARDS: N.A.

PERSONAL: Resides in New Rochelle, NY, with his wife; two children.

RUBINSTEIN, ALLAN
Exec. V.P., Chief Operating Officer, Madison Square Garden Network

c/o Madison Square Garden Network, 4 Pennsylvania Plaza, New York, NY 10001
b. December 11, 1939.

EDUCATION: Brooklyn College, B.A. ('61); New York University Graduate School of Business, M.B.A. ('64).

CAREER HIGHLIGHTS: Public Accounting, Arthur Young & Co.; Treasurer and Controller,

Madison Square Garden; V.P. of Finance, Madison Square Garden Network; Exec. V.P. and Chief Operating Officer, Madison Square Garden Network.

ACHIEVEMENTS & AWARDS: N.A.

PERSONAL: Wife, Anita; two daughters, Jill and Robyn.

RUCKER, BOB
Correspondent, Cable News Network, San Francisco Bureau

74 Crestline Dr., San Francisco, CA 94131
b. July 12, 1954. Chicago, IL.

EDUCATION: Northern Illinois University, B.S.

CAREER HIGHLIGHTS: Reporter/Anchor, WHO-TV, Des Moines ('76); Natl. News Prod./Reporter, Newsweek Broadcasting ('77); Anchor/Medical Correspondent/Reporter, KYW-TV, Philadelphia ('78); Correspondent, Cable News Network, San Francisco ('82).

ACHIEVEMENTS & AWARDS: Honored by the Northwest Broadcasters Assn. ('78) and the Philadelphia Press Assn. ('82).

PERSONAL: N.A.

RUDD, HUGHES
Correspondent, ABC, News

c/o ABC, 7 W. 66th St., New York, NY 10023
b. September 14, 1921. Wichita, KS.

EDUCATION: Stanford University; University of Missouri; University of Minnesota.

CAREER HIGHLIGHTS: Reporter *Kansas City Star* ('46); moved to *Minneapolis Tribune* ('50); joined CBS News ('59); Moscow Bureau Chief ('65); Sr. Correspondent in Germany ('66);

Anchor, "CBS Morning News" ('73); reported for "CBS Reports" and "Morning" ('77); left for ABC News as New York Correspondent, reporting on "World News Tonight" and other ABC news programs including "20/20" and "Good Morning America" ('79).

ACHIEVEMENTS & AWARDS: N.A.

PERSONAL: N.A.

RUDRUD, JUDY L.
V.P., Cardiff Publishing Co.

c/o Cardiff Publishing Co., 3900 S. Wadsworth Blvd., Denver, CO 80235

b. N.A.

EDUCATION: University of North Dakota, B.A., Speech Communications.

CAREER HIGHLIGHTS: V.P., Cardiff Publishing Co., and Publisher, *Cable Television Business* magazine (formerly TVC). Also serves as Group Publisher of *Communications* and *Global Communications* magazines. Joined Cardiff Publishing ('77).

ACHIEVEMENTS & AWARDS: First V.P. of Women in Cable's Rocky Mountain Chapter ('81); Member, Natl. Board of Dirs., Women in Cable and its Exec. Committee.

PERSONAL: N.A.

RUKEYSER, BUD, JR. (M. S. Rukeyser Jr.)
Exec. V.P., NBC, Public Information

c/o NBC, 30 Rockefeller Plaza, New York, NY 10020

b. April 15, 1931.

EDUCATION: University of Virginia.

CAREER HIGHLIGHTS: Joined NBC as Staff Writer, Press Dept. ('58); Press Editor, News and Public Affairs ('59); Mgr. Business and Trade Publicity ('59); Dir., News Information, Washington, DC ('62); Dir., Program Publicity and later Dir., Press and Publicity ('62); V.P., Press and Publicity ('63); V.P., Corporate Information ('72); Exec. V.P., Public Information ('77); V.P./Dir. of Communications, Newsweek, Inc. ('80); returned to NBC as Exec. V.P., Public Information ('81).

ACHIEVEMENTS & AWARDS: N.A.

PERSONAL: Resides in Manhattan with wife, Phyllis; daughters, Jill and Patricia. Brothers, Louis, well known for PBS's "Wall Street Week" and William, managing editor of *Fortune*.

RUKEYSER, LOUIS
Host, "Wall Street Week"

c/o Maryland Center for Public Broadcasting, Owings Mills, MD 21117

b. January 30, 1933.

EDUCATION: Princeton University Woodrow Wilson School of Public and International Affairs.

CAREER HIGHLIGHTS: Chief Political Correspondent and Chief Asian Correspondent, *Baltimore Sun*. Paris Correspondent, Economic Editor, Radio and TV Commentator, ABC TV and Radio. Writer, syndicated column on economics for the McNaught Syndicate. Public TV Host, "Wall Street Week," a program that has made him America's most popular economic commentator.

ACHIEVEMENTS & AWARDS: Two Overseas Press Club awards; two Freedom Foundation awards ('73, '78); 1980 New York Financial Writers Assn. award; the G. M. Loeb award, and honorary degrees from many universities. Author of the book *How To Make Money in Wall Street.*

PERSONAL: Married; three daughters. Resides in Greenwich, CT.

RULE, ELTON H.
Dir. of ABC, Inc.

c/o ABC, 1330 Ave. of the Americas, New York, NY 10019
b. 1917. Stockton, CA.

EDUCATION: Sacramento College.

CAREER HIGHLIGHTS: Rule's ascendancy at ABC is based on a solid background as an executive responsible for dramatic improvements in the position of the ABC owned stations. V.P., General Mgr. KABC-TV; Pres., ABC TV Network ('68); Group V.P. of ABC Companies ('69); Board of Dirs. of ABC, Inc. ('70); Pres. of ABC ('70); Pres. and Chief Operating Officer, ABC, Inc., and named to the Exec. Committee of the Corp. ('72); Vice Chairman of the Board, ABC, Inc. ('83); Dir. of ABC, Inc. ('84).

ACHIEVEMENTS & AWARDS: UCLA School of Medicine's Board of Visitors, Advisory Board of the Exec. Committee of the Institute of Sports Medicine and Athletic Trauma, Board of Dirs., United Way; Governors' Award, ATAS ('81); IRTS gold medal ('75).

PERSONAL: Wife, Betty; three children, Cindy Dunne, Christie, and James. Resides in Scarsdale, NY.

RUNGE, BLANCHE
Dir., Administration, NBC, Entertainment

c/o NBC, 3000 W. Alameda Ave., Burbank, CA 91523
b. Los Angeles, CA.

EDUCATION: University of California at Los Angeles.

CAREER HIGHLIGHTS: Editor, Broadcast Standards Dept., NBC; Researcher, Story Dept., NBC; Exec. Asst. to Sr. V.P., Programs, NBC, West Coast; Dir., Administration, West Coast, NBC Entertainment ('79).

ACHIEVEMENTS & AWARDS: N.A.

PERSONAL: Resides in Los Angeles.

RUSH, ALVIN
Pres., MCA TV

c/o MCA TV, 445 Park Ave., New York, NY 10022
b. June 24.

EDUCATION: Columbia College, B.A.; Columbia University Law School.

CAREER HIGHLIGHTS: Talent Agent and Packager for MCA and Creative Management Assoc.; Sr. V.P., NBC, Program and Sports Administration; Exec. V.P., NBC TV; Pres., MCA TV ('80).

ACHIEVEMENTS & AWARDS: N.A.

PERSONAL: N.A.

RUSH, HERMAN
Pres., Columbia Pictures TV

c/o Columbia Pictures TV, Columbia Plaza, Burbank, CA 91505
b. June 20, 1929. Philadelphia, PA.

EDUCATION: Temple University, B.A.

CAREER HIGHLIGHTS: Served as V.P., Sales for Official Films ('51); Pres. of Flamingo Films ('57); V.P., General Artists ('61); formed Herman Rush Assoc. and served as Exec. Prod. of various series and TV movies ('72); V.P., Creative Management Assoc., with additional responsibilities as Pres., TV Division; named Pres., Marble Arch TV Productions ('79); joined Columbia Pictures TV as Pres. ('81).

ACHIEVEMENTS & AWARDS: Trustee, Sugar Ray

Robinson Youth Foundation ('67–'74); Member, Steering Committee, Producers and Writers Caucus ('82); Exec. Committee, Board of Governors, NATAS ('82); Hollywood Radio and TV Society ('82).
PERSONAL: Wife, Joan; children, Mandie and James.

RUSHNELL, SQUIRE D.
V.P., ABC, Long Range Planning and Children's TV, Entertainment

c/o ABC, 1330 Ave. of the Americas, New York, NY 10019
b. N.A.

EDUCATION: Syracuse University.
CAREER HIGHLIGHTS: Exec. Prod., "Bob Kennedy/Contact," WBZ-TV, which went on to achieve the highest ratings in the market's history in its time period ('64); Consultant, Westinghouse Broadcasting, and helped establish various talk shows; developed "Kennedy and Company" at WLS to compete with "Today" in that market ('69); named Program Dir., WLS ('71); joined ABC as V.P., Program Services for Owned TV Stations ('73) and was involved in children's and morning programming; Exec.-in-Charge of "Good Morning America" ('78–'81). As V.P., Long Range Planning and Children's TV, he is responsible for all ABC children's programming including "ABC Schoolhouse Rock," "ABC Afterschool Specials," and "ABC Weekend Specials." Created "Kids Are People Too" and initiated "Open House Week for Children's TV" and the programming of ABC's "nutrition commercials."
ACHIEVEMENTS & AWARDS: N.A.
PERSONAL: Two teenage daughters.

RUSHTON, MATTHEW
V.P., Catalina Production Group Ltd., Development

c/o Catalina Production Group Ltd., 15301 Ventura Blvd., Suite 221, Sherman Oaks, CA 91403
b. February 19, 1952, Phoenix, AZ.

EDUCATION: Occidental College, B.A.; University of California at Los Angeles.
CAREER HIGHLIGHTS: Dir. of Development, Production Company/Martin Poll Productions ('79); Assoc. Prod., *For Ladies Only*, NBC TV ('81); Assoc. Prod., *Thursday's Child*, CBS TV ('82); Prod., *Journey's End*, Showtime Pay TV ('82); Prod., *The Wager*, for Catalina Production Group/Stonehenge Prods. ('83); V.P., Development, Catalina Production Group Ltd.
ACHIEVEMENTS & AWARDS: N.A.
PERSONAL: N.A.

RUSSELL, MICHAEL
Publicist, Disney Productions

c/o Disney Productions, 500 S. Buena Vista St., Burbank, CA 91521
b. 1955. Los Angeles, CA.

EDUCATION: Pasadena Community College, A.A., Journalism; University of Southern California, B.A., ('78).
CAREER HIGHLIGHTS: Joined Walt Disney Studios as a Publicist ('78); Mgr., Disney TV Publicity ('79); Dir., TV Publicity, Disney Studios ('79).
ACHIEVEMENTS & AWARDS: N.A.
PERSONAL: Married, resides in Los Angeles.

RUTHSTEIN, ROY
V.P., ABC, Entertainment Research

c/o ABC, 7 W. 66th St., New York, NY 10023
b. March 11, 1947. New York, NY.

EDUCATION: City College of New York, B.B.A.
CAREER HIGHLIGHTS: Librarian, Direct Mail Advertising ('68); J. Walter Thompson Research Analyst ('69); joined ABC TV as Sr. Research Analyst ('70) with responsibilities including Supervisor, Daytime, Late Night and Weekend Children's Research; Mgr. of same; Mgr., Marketing and Operations Research; Dir., Audience Research. Named V.P., Entertainment Research ('82).
ACHIEVEMENTS & AWARDS: N.A.
PERSONAL: Wife, Lynne; daughters, Stacey Michelle and Andrea Joy.

RUTZ, DANIEL C.
Medical News Correspondent, Cable News Network

c/o Cable News Network, 1050 Techwood Dr., N.W., Atlanta, GA 30318
b. August 30, 1950.

EDUCATION: University of Wisconsin at Platteville, B.S. Speech/Broadcast.
CAREER HIGHLIGHTS: Anchor/Reporter, KDUB-TV, Dubuque, IA ('71); Documentary Prod., "New Kidney; New Life" ('79); Anchor/Reporter, WMTV, Madison, WI ('71); News Operations Mgr., WMTV, Madison ('80); Medical News Correspondent Prod., "News From Medicine," and Co-Anchor "Health-week," Cable News Network ('81).
ACHIEVEMENTS & AWARDS: Wisconsin Kidney Foundation public service award ('79).
PERSONAL: Wife, Anne Neufeld; daughter, Christine Louise.

RYAN, BOB
Meteorologist, WRC-TV, Washington, DC, News

c/o WRC-TV, 4001 Nebraska Ave., N.W., Washington, DC 20016
b. N.A.

EDUCATION: State University of New York.
CAREER HIGHLIGHTS: Researcher and Consultant, Arthur D. Little Co., Cambridge, MA; Meteorologist, NBC's "Today" program ('78); Meteorologist, WRC-TV, Washington, DC ('80).
ACHIEVEMENTS & AWARDS: Member, American Meteorological Society; American Assn. for the Advancement of Science. Selected best local TV weatherman by readers of *The Washington Magazine*.
PERSONAL: Resides in McLean, VA, with wife, Olga, and their son.

RYAN, TIM
Sports Broadcaster, CBS, Sports

c/o CBS, 51 W. 52nd St., New York, NY 10019
b. Winnipeg, Canada.

EDUCATION: University of Notre Dame.
CAREER HIGHLIGHTS: Reporter, *Toronto Star*; Re-porter, CFO-TV, Toronto, Ontario, TV and Radio Announcer for the California Golden Seals of the NHL ('67); Co-Anchor/Sportscaster, WPIX-TV, New York ('70); Hockey Broadcaster, NBC-TV; Sports Broadcaster, CBS Sports ('77).
ACHIEVEMENTS & AWARDS: N.A.
PERSONAL: Resides in Larchmont, NY, with wife, Lee, and their four children.

RYDER, JEFFREY C.
V.P., NBC, Daytime Programs, East Coast

c/o NBC, 30 Rockefeller Plaza, New York, NY 10020
b. July 4, 1952. Cooperstown, NY.

EDUCATION: Rider College, B.A.
CAREER HIGHLIGHTS: Asst. Casting Dir., "Hawaii Five-0" ('77); Mgr., Casting, NBC Network ('78); Dir., Casting, NBC Network ('79); Dir., Mini-series and Novels for TV, NBC ('80); V.P., NBC ('81).
ACHIEVEMENTS & AWARDS: N.A.
PERSONAL: N.A.

SABINSON, ALLEN C.
V.P., NBC, Entertainment, Program Administration

c/o NBC, 3000 W. Alameda Ave., Burbank, CA 91523
B. N.A.

EDUCATION: Brandeis University, B.A., English Literature.

CAREER HIGHLIGHTS: Joined NBC as Sr. Correspondent, Audience Services Dept.; became Administrator, Audience Services Dept.; Facilities Scheduling Coordinator in Operations and Engineering Division ('76); Analyst ('77); promoted to Administrator in Corporate Business Affairs; Administrator, Financial Evaluation; Mgr., Program Commitments and Prime-Time Forecasting, then Dir. Became V.P., NBC Entertainment, Program Administration ('81).

ACHIEVEMENTS & AWARDS: N.A.

PERSONAL: Resides in Hollywood Hills, CA.

SAFER, MORLEY
Co-Editor, CBS, "60 Minutes"

c/o CBS, 51 W. 52d St., New York, NY 10019
b. Toronto, Canada.

EDUCATION: University of Western Ontario.

CAREER HIGHLIGHTS: Correspondent/Prod., CBC; joined CBS News, London ('64); opened CBS News Saigon Bureau ('65) and spent two tours in Vietnam; CBS London Bureau Chief ('67–'70); joined CBS "60 Minutes" ('70). His droll writing style and expert investigative skills have kept Safer at the pinnacle of T.V. journalism for over a decade.

ACHIEVEMENTS & AWARDS: Three Overseas Press Club awards, the Paul White award, Peabody award, George Polk memorial award for two tours in Vietnam as Correspondent; many of his "60 Minutes" segments won

awards, including the Howard W. Blakeslee award of the American Heart Assn. for "Heart Attack"; American Cancer Society's second annual media award for "Marixa" ('77–'78); Emmy awards for outstanding program achievement for "Pops" and "Teddy Kollek's Jerusalem" ('78–'79).

PERSONAL: N.A.

SAGAN, CARL
Host, Co-Writer, Carl Sagan Productions, "Cosmos"

c/o Ben Kubasik, Inc., 30 E. 42d St., New York, NY 10017
b. November 9, 1934. Brooklyn, NY.

EDUCATION: Cornell University.

CAREER HIGHLIGHTS: Sagan is widely recognized for his efforts to popularize scientific enterprise through his books, lectures, and TV appearances. In conjunction with the TV premiere of "Cosmos," Random House published Sagan's hardcover book, Cosmos, ('80) which has been a long-time best-seller. Author or Co-Author of some 300 scientific papers on genetics, astrophysics, planetary science, and extraterrestrial communication. Co-Founder and first Pres., The Planetary Society, a group of people who wish to further the exploration of space.

ACHIEVEMENTS & AWARDS: "Cosmos" received a Peabody award, three Emmy awards, the Academy of Family Films and Family TV award for best TV series ('80), and the American Council for Better Broadcasting citation for highest quality TV programming ('80–'81). Recipient of the NASA medal for exceptional scientific achievement ('72); the Intl. Astronautics prize, the Prix Galabert ('73); and, twice, the NASA medal for distinguished public service ('77, '81).

PERSONAL: N.A.

SAGANSKY, JEFF
Sr. V.P., Series Programming, NBC

c/o NBC, 3000 W. Alameda Ave., Burbank, CA 91523
b. January 26, 1952. Boston, MA.

EDUCATION: Harvard College, B.A. ('74); Harvard Business College, M.B.A. ('76).

CAREER HIGHLIGHTS: Broadcast Administration, CBS ('76); Assoc., Film Program Development, NBC ('77); Mgr., Film Programs, NBC ('77); Dir., Dramatic Development ('78); V.P., Development, David Gerber Co. ('79); V.P., Series Development, NBC ('81); Sr. V.P., Series Programming, NBC ('83).

ACHIEVEMENTS & AWARDS: N.A.

PERSONAL: Single, resides in Sherman Oaks, CA.

SAGER, CRAIG
Anchor, Cable News Network, Sports

3064 Spring Hill Rd., Smyrna, GA 30080
b. June 29, 1951. St. Charles, IL.

EDUCATION: Northwestern University.

CAREER HIGHLIGHTS: Reporter, WXLT-TV, Sarasota, FL ('72); News Dir., WSPB-Radio, Sarasota, FL ('73); Weathercaster, WTSP-TV, St. Petersburg, FL ('75); Sports Dir., WINK-TV Fort Myers, FL ('76); Sports Dir., KMBC-TV, Kansas City, MO ('79); Anchor, Cable News Network Sports ('81).

ACHIEVEMENTS & AWARDS: N.A.

PERSONAL: Wife, Lisa.

ST. JOHNS, KATHLEEN
V.P., Columbia Pictures TV, Creative Affairs

c/o Columbia Pictures TV, Columbia Plaza, Burbank, CA 91506
b. March 22, 1954.

EDUCATION: University of California at Los Angeles, B.A.; Loyola Law School, J.D.

CAREER HIGHLIGHTS: Practiced law before joining Columbia Pictures TV. Dir. of Movies and Mini-Series ('81); Dir. of Current Programs, ('82). Currently heads a new Columbia TV division, Creative Affairs, overlooking new programming for independents, fourth network, first-run syndication, and late-night programming.

ACHIEVEMENTS & AWARDS: N.A.

PERSONAL: Resides in Los Angeles.

STE. MARIE, STEPHEN B.
V.P., Marketing, Viacom, Cable

P.O. Box 13, Pleasanton, CA 94566
b. November 29, 1948. New York, NY.

EDUCATION: Georgia Tech University, B.S., Industrial Management ('70); Pace University, M.B.A.('77).

CAREER HIGHLIGHTS: District Mgr., Anheuser Busch ('71); Brand Management, Standard Brands ('73); Group Marketing Mgr., Pepsico ('78); V.P., Marketing, Viacom Cable ('81).

ACHIEVEMENTS & AWARDS: N.A.

PERSONAL: Resides in Piedmont, CA, with wife, Jennifer, and three children.

SALANT, RICHARD
Pres. and Chief Exec. Officer, Natl. News Council

c/o NBC, 30 Rockefeller Plaza, New York, NY 10020
b. April 14, 1914. New York, NY.

EDUCATION: Harvard College; Harvard Law School.

CAREER HIGHLIGHTS: Associate and then Partner, Roseman, Goldmark, Colin & Kave ('46); Pres., CBS News Division ('61); V.P. and Special Asst. to the Pres. of CBS News ('64); Pres., CBS News Division ('66); Member, Board of Dirs., CBS; Vice Chairman, Board of

Dirs., NBC; Pres. and Chief Exec. Officer, Natl. News Council.

ACHIEVEMENTS & AWARDS: N.A.

PERSONAL: N.A.

SALINGER, PIERRE
Chief Foreign Correspondent, ABC, News

c/o ABC, 7 W. 66th St., New York, NY 10023
b. June 14, 1925.

EDUCATION: University of San Francisco, B.A., History.

CAREER HIGHLIGHTS: West Coast and Contributing Editor, *Collier's* Magazine ('55); Press Secretary, for Pres. John F. Kennedy ('60); Press Secretary, for Pres. Lyndon B. Johnson ('63); appointed U.S. Senator for California finishing the term of the late Sen. Clair Engle ('64); V.P., Natl. General Corp.; V.P., Continental Airlines; V.P., Continental Air Services; Pres., Fox Overseas Theaters Corp.; Contributing Correspondent, ABC News, Paris ('77); Full-Time Correspondent, ABC News, Paris ('78); Paris Bureau Chief, ABC News ('79); Chief Foreign Correspondent, ABC News ('83).

ACHIEVEMENTS & AWARDS: Dupont-Columbia award; Natl. Headliners award; Overseas Press Club award; Cornelius Ryan award; McQuade memorial award.

PERSONAL: Resides in Paris.

SALKOWITZ, SY
Pres., Viacom Productions

c/o Viacom Productions, Studio Center, Studio City, CA 90024
b. April 21, 1926. Philadelphia, PA.

EDUCATION: Yale University; University of California at Los Angeles.

CAREER HIGHLIGHTS: Freelance Writer on numerous TV shows and movies ('54–'74); V.P., 20th Century Fox TV ('74); Pres., 20th Century Fox TV ('76); Pres., Sy Salkowitz Productions ('79); Prod., "The New FBI" ('81); Pres., Viacom Productions ('82). Member, Board of Dirs., Writers Guild ('65–'70); Trustee, Writers Foundation ('65–'82); Member, Board of Governors, TV Academy ('70–'74); Member, Advisory Panel, California State Film Commission ('79–'82); Member, Advisory Panel, Natl. Endowment for the Humanities ('79–'82).

ACHIEVEMENTS & AWARDS: Golden Eagle CINE award ('71); Edgar Allen Poe award, Mystery Writers Assn. ('74).

PERSONAL: Resides in Malibu, CA.

SALLAN, BRUCE
Exec. Prod., Motion Pictures for TV, ABC, Entertainment

c/o ABC, 4151 Prospect Ave., Los Angeles, CA 90027
b. Los Angeles, CA.

EDUCATION: University of California at Santa Cruz, B.A. ('73); University of California at Los Angeles, M.B.A. ('75).

CAREER HIGHLIGHTS: Assoc. Prod., TV movie, *The Defection of Simas Kudirka, Act of Love*; Prod., *Secrets, Having Babies,* and *With This Ring*; Co-Exec. Prod., *Berlin Tunnel 21*; while at Cypress Point Productions, developed *Golda* mini-series; Dir. of Development, Jozak Co. ('75); V.P., Creative Affairs, Cypress Point Productions ('78); V.P. of West Coast TV for Highgate Pictures ('81); Exec. Prod., Motion Pictures for TV, ABC Entertainment ('82).

ACHIEVEMENTS & AWARDS: N.A.

PERSONAL: Resides in Los Angeles.

SALTZMAN, JOSEPH
Head, "Entertainment Tonight," Special Enterprise Unit

c/o "Entertainment Tonight," 6922 Hollywood Blvd., Suite 407, Los Angeles, CA 90028
b. N.A.

EDUCATION: N.A.

CAREER HIGHLIGHTS: Freelance Journalist, reporting on the media for such publications as *TV Guide, Los Angeles Times, San Francisco Chronicle, San Francisco Examiner, Newsday, EMMY* magazine, and *USA Today;* Sr. Prod./ Writer, KNXT-TV, Los Angeles ('73); named Head of "Entertainment Tonight" Special Enterprise Unit, which provides reports on trends and current issues in the entertainment industry ('83).

ACHIEVEMENTS & AWARDS: Chairman of the Broadcasting Dept., University of Southern California; five regional Emmy awards; two Edward R. Murrow awards; four Golden Mike awards; and a Dupont-Columbia award.

PERSONAL: N.A.

SAMUELS, STU
V.P., Motion Pictures for TV, ABC,
Entertainment

c/o ABC, 4151 Prospect Ave., Los Angeles, CA 90027
b. N.A.

EDUCATION: Hofstra University.

CAREER HIGHLIGHTS: Natl. Programming Editor, *TV Guide* ('73); Dir., Program Development, Warner Bros. TV ('74); Program Exec. assigned to the Motion Pictures for TV Division ('77); Exec. Prod., Motion Pictures for TV ('78); V.P., Motion Pictures for TV, ABC Entertainment ('80).

ACHIEVEMENTS & AWARDS: N.A.

PERSONAL: Resides in Sherman Oaks, CA, with wife, Lois, daughter, Julie, and son, Joshua.

SAND, BARRY
Prod., NBC

c/o NBC, 30 Rockefeller Plaza, New York, NY 10020
b. Brooklyn, NY.

EDUCATION: University of Pennsylvania.

CAREER HIGHLIGHTS: Prod., "A.M. New York," WABC-TV, New York; Prod., "The Mike Douglas Show" and "The David Frost Show"; Story Editor for Norman Lear; Prod., NBC TV, "SCTV Comedy Network," "The David Letterman Show."

ACHIEVEMENTS & AWARDS: N.A.

PERSONAL: Married, resides in New York City.

SAND, LAUREN JOY
Dir., Late Night Development, CBS,
Entertainment

c/o CBS, 7800 Beverly Blvd., Los Angeles, CA 90036
b. N.A.

EDUCATION: University of California at Berkeley, B.A., Rhetoric and Art; University of California at Los Angeles, M.A., Journalism.

CAREER HIGHLIGHTS: Newswriter/Reporter, KHON-TV, Honolulu; Researcher for Hollywood producers and writers including Danny Arnold and David Rintels; Writer, Alan Landsburg Productions ('79); Mgr., Program Development, Broadcast Standards and Practices, ABC ('80); Dir., Late Night Development, CBS Entertainment, Los Angeles ('82).

ACHIEVEMENTS & AWARDS: N.A.

PERSONAL: Resides in Los Angeles.

SANDERS, DAVE
Sportscaster, ESPN

c/o ESPN, ESPN Plaza, Bristol, CT 06010
b. April 1, 1950. Dayton, OH.

EDUCATION: University of Miami, B.A., Mass Communications.

CAREER HIGHLIGHTS: Sports Dir., WVUM-Radio ('68); Asst. Sports Dir., WSM-TV and Radio, Nashville ('72); Sportscaster, WHIO-TV, Dayton, OH ('74); Sports Dir. WOI-TV, Ames/Des Moines('78); Sports Dir., KMTV,

Omaha ('80); joined ESPN as Sportscaster ('82).
ACHIEVEMENTS & AWARDS: N.A.
PERSONAL: N.A.

SANDERS, MARLENE
Correspondent/Prod., CBS, News

c/o CBS News, 524 W. 57th St., New York, NY 10019
b. January 10, 1931. Cleveland, OH.

EDUCATION: Ohio State University.
CAREER HIGHLIGHTS: Prod., Writer, and Reporter for WNEW-TV ('55); Asst. Dir. of News and Public Affairs for WNEW-Radio, New York. Joined ABC News as a Correspondent and Anchor ('64) until she was named a Documentary Prod. ('72). Became a Correspondent/Prod. in the documentary area, CBS News ('78). Anchor, Saturday edition of "Newsbreak" on the CBS TV Network; frequently anchors CBS News broadcasts on the CBS Radio Network. Regular Contributor to the CBS News broadcasts "CBS News Sunday Morning" and "Magazine."
ACHIEVEMENTS & AWARDS: Three Emmy awards and a Christopher award. Named Broadcast Woman of the Year by American Women in Radio and TV ('75). Silver satellite award presented by AWRT ('77).
PERSONAL: Husband, Jerome Toobin; son, Jeff. Resides in New York City and Sherman, CT.

SANDRICH, JAY
Dir.

c/o Ron Meyer, 1888 Century Park E., Los Angeles, CA 90067
b. February 24, 1932. Los Angeles, CA.

EDUCATION: University of California at Los Angeles, B.A., Theater Arts.
CAREER HIGHLIGHTS: Dir., "The Mary Tyler Moore Show" ('70); Dir., "Soap" ('77); Dir., pilots for "The Bob Newhart Show," "Phyllis," "The Tony Randall Show," "WKRP in Cincinnati," and "Side by Side." Dir. of the theatrical feature *Seems Like Old Times.*
ACHIEVEMENTS & AWARDS: Two Emmy awards for direction on "The Mary Tyler Moore

Show" ('71, '73); Directors Guild award for a Lily Tomlin variety special.
PERSONAL: N.A.

SANFORD, ISABEL
Actress

c/o "The Jeffersons," CBS, 7800 Beverly Blvd., Los Angeles, CA 90036
b. August 29, 1917. New York, NY.

EDUCATION: N.A.
CAREER HIGHLIGHTS: New York stage appearances in *The Amen Corner* and *The Egg and I.* Motion pictures include *Pendulum, The New Centurions, Guess Who's Coming to Dinner* and *Love at First Bite.* TV guest roles on "The Mod Squad," "All in the Family," "The Carol Burnett Show," "Bewitched," and "Supertrain." TV series star of "The Jeffersons."
ACHIEVEMENTS & AWARDS: Emmy as best actress in a comedy series for "The Jeffersons."
PERSONAL: Widow, three children. Resides in Los Angeles.

SANO, AL (Alfred R. Sanno)
Sr. V.P., Dir., Network Programming Local TV and Broadcast Services, Clyne Maxon

383 Madison Ave., New York, NY 10017
b. August 25, 1925. New York, NY.

EDUCATION: Dartmouth College, B.A. ('46).
CAREER HIGHLIGHTS: Started at Macy's in Exec. Training Program and became Merchandise Buyer ('46); Training Program at Young & Rubicam, Media Buyer ('48); joined BBDO as Media Supervisor ('51); V.P., Dir. of Media

Planning, McCann Erickson ('53); V.P., Dir. of Marketing, Clyne Maxon ('65); Sr. V.P., Dir., Network Programming Local TV and Broadcast Services ('67).
ACHIEVEMENTS & AWARDS: N.A.
PERSONAL: Wife, Linda; daughters, Lisa and Laura.

SARGENT, HERB
Writer/Prod.

c/o William Lazarow, 119 W. 57th St., New York, NY 10019
b. N.A.

EDUCATION: N.A.
CAREER HIGHLIGHTS: One of the most experienced and gifted comedy producer-writers in the history of American TV. Worked as a Writer/Prod. on such TV specials as "Annie— The Women in the Life of a Man," "The Jack Lemmon Special," Burt Bacharach specials, "The George Siegel Show," Alan King specials, and "Funny Girl to Funny Lady." Writer, "Saturday Night Live" and Exec. Prod./Writer, NBC's "The News Is the News," which had a brief run ('83).
ACHIEVEMENTS & AWARDS: Four writing Emmy awards ('70, '74, '76, '77).
PERSONAL: Resides in New York City.

SARGENT, JOSEPH
Dir.

c/o Shapiro-Lichtman Agency, 2 Century Plaza, Suite 1320, 2049 Century Park E., Los Angeles, CA 90067
b. July 23, 1925. Jersey City, NJ.

EDUCATION: New School for Social Research.
CAREER HIGHLIGHTS: Dir. of the TV movie *The Spanish Portrait, The Challenge, The Immortal, Longstreet, Wheeler & Murdock, Man on a String, Maybe I'll Come Home in the Spring, Tribes, The Marcus-Nelson Murders, A Time for Love, Interrupted Journey, Amber Waves, Freedom, Genesis,* and *Nightmare,* and the miniseries *The Manions of America.*
ACHIEVEMENTS & AWARDS: Emmy award for directing *The Marcus-Nelson Murders;* Peabody award for *Amber Waves.* Directors Guild

award; named best director, San Sebastian Film Festival, for the theatrical feature *The Taking of Pelham 1-2-3.*
PERSONAL: N.A.

SARGENT, TONY
Correspondent, ABC, News

c/o ABC, 1717 De Sales St., N.W., Washington, DC 20036
b. N.A.

EDUCATION: Washington and Lee University, B.A., Modern Humanities; Columbia University Graduate School of Journalism, M.S.
CAREER HIGHLIGHTS: Writer/Editor, UPI, Chicago ('62); joined CBS News in a variety of positions ('63); Correspondent, CBS News ('68); Correspondent, ABC News, Washington, DC ('77).
ACHIEVEMENTS & AWARDS: N.A.
PERSONAL: Resides in Arlington, VA.

SARNOFF, THOMAS
Exec. V.P., Venturetainment Corp.

4433 Lakeside Dr., Burbank, CA 91505
b. February 23, 1927. New York, NY.

EDUCATION: Princeton University; Stanford University.
CAREER HIGHLIGHTS: ABC Floor Mgr., ('49); NBC Asst. Dir. of Finance and Operations ('52); Exec., NBC Business Affairs; Exec. V.P., NBC West Coast; V.P., Administration ('60); Exec. V.P. ('65); Dir., Valley Country Cable TV ('69); Pres., NBC Entertainment Corp. ('72); Pres., Sarnoff Intl. Enterprises ('77); Pres., Sarnoff Entertainment Corp. ('81); Exec V.P., Venturetainment Corp. ('81).
ACHIEVEMENTS & AWARDS: Past Chairman of the Board, NATAS.
PERSONAL: Grandson of RCA founder David Sarnoff.

SASS, ERIC L.
V.P., PBS, Program Development

c/o PBS, 475 L'Enfant Plaza, S.W.,
  Washington, DC 20024
b. January 12, 1946. New York, NY.

EDUCATION: University of Maine, B.A.
CAREER HIGHLIGHTS: Exec. Prod., Public Affairs, Maine ETV Network ('68); Prod./Dir., Public Affairs WJCT-TV/FM, Jacksonville, FL ('70); Dir. of Development, WJCT ('76); V.P., Development, WJCT ('78); Dir., Future Funding, PBS ('78); Dir., Development, PBS ('79); V.P., Marketing and New Techniques ('80); V.P., Programming ('81); V.P., Program Development ('82).
ACHIEVEMENTS & AWARDS: Member, Board of Dirs., Natl. Urban League ('75-'78).
PERSONAL: Wife, Eveleen; sons, Jeff and Michael.

SASSER, DUFFY A., II
V.P., NBC, Operations and Engineering

c/o NBC, 30 Rockefeller Plaza, New York, NY
  10020
b. 1945. Clovis, NM.

EDUCATION: University of New Mexico, B.B.A. and J.D.
CAREER HIGHLIGHTS: Dir., Legal and Engineering Services for SIN ('76); V.P., Operations and Engineering, NBC TV Stations ('80).
ACHIEVEMENTS & AWARDS: N.A.
PERSONAL: Resides in Stamford, CT, with wife, Vera; four children.

SAUDEK, ROBERT
Dir. and Exec.

4 Plateau Circle E., Bronxville, NY 10708
b. N.A.

EDUCATION: Harvard University.
CAREER HIGHLIGHTS: V.P., ABC; Dir. of "TV Radio Workshop" ('51); Dir. of the series "Omnibus" and "Profiles in Courage"; founded Robert Saudek Assoc.; Former Pres., New York's Museum of Broadcasting.
ACHIEVEMENTS & AWARDS: Pres., Radio Executives Club; Member, Phi Beta Kappa.
PERSONAL: N.A.

SAUERESSIG, DEAN G.
Assoc. Natl. Dir. of Credit and Collections, ABC

c/o ABC, 1330 Ave. of the Americas, New
  York, NY 10019
b. N.A.

EDUCATION: Pace University, B.S., Business Administration.
CAREER HIGHLIGHTS: Asst. Credit Mgr., Olivetti Underwood Corp.; Asst. Credit Mgr., Zenith Radio Corp.; Sr. Credit Analyst, Corporate Credit Dept., ABC ('75); Asst. Credit Mgr., ABC ('76); Asst. Natl. Dir. of Credit and Collections ('80); Assoc. Natl. Dir. of Credit and Collections ('83).
ACHIEVEMENTS & AWARDS: N.A.
PERSONAL: Resides in Brooklyn, NY, with wife, Priscilla.

SAUTER, VAN GORDON
Exec. V.P. in charge of CBS, News and CBS Television Stations Division

c/o CBS News, 524 W. 57th St., New York,
  NY 10019
b. September 14, 1935.

EDUCATION: Ohio University, B.A.
CAREER HIGHLIGHTS: As Pres., CBS News, Sauter introduced important changes including those involving the style and format of "CBS Morning News." He also hired Bill Kurtis to succeed Charles Kuralt. Reporter, *Standard Times*, New Bedford, MA, *Detroit Free Press*,

and *Chicago Daily News;* joined CBS Chicago affiliate, WBBM-AM as News and Program Dir. ('68); Exec. Prod., CBS News, Radio, New York ('70); moved to Chicago as News Dir., WBBM-TV ('72); CBS Paris Bureau Chief ('75); V.P., Program Practices, CBS TV Network ('76). Moved to KNXT, Los Angeles, as V.P. and General Mgr. ('77); returned to New York with appointment as Pres., CBS Sports ('80); named Deputy Pres., CBS News; Pres., CBS News; Exec. V.P. in charge of CBS News and CBS Television Stations Division.

ACHIEVEMENTS & AWARDS: Co-Author, *Nightmare in Detroit: A Revolution and Its Victims* and *Fabled Land, Timeless River.* Member, Radio and TV News Dirs. Assn.

PERSONAL: N.A.

SAWYER, DIANE
Co-Anchor, "CBS Morning News"

c/o CBS, 51 W. 52d St., New York, NY 10019
b. December 22. Glasgow, KY.

EDUCATION: Wellesley College, B.A. ('67).

CAREER HIGHLIGHTS: Clearly the dominant player on the "CBS Morning News," this brainy journalist rose to prominence with her dogged reporting on the Three Mile Island crisis. Boasting a background that includes such traditional female roles as being an American Junior Miss ('63) and a local weathercaster in Louisville, KY, Sawyer has clearly come a long way to be the only woman on the network dawn patrol to garner heavy journalistic assignments, a clear challenge to early morning male supremacy. She is magnetic and industrious, and her teamwork with Bill Kurtis has given CBS its first healthy ratings for "CBS Morning News" in three decades. Her career began with a stint as Reporter, WLKY-TV, Louisville ('67); then, Press Aide, Nixon Administration ('70); Nixon-Ford Transition Team ('74); Asst. to Pres. Nixon in the writing of his memoirs ('75); Reporter, CBS News ('78); Correspondent ('80); State Dept. Correspondent ('80); Co-Anchor "Morning" with Charles Kuralt ('81); Co-Anchor, "CBS Morning News," with Bill Kurtis ('82).

ACHIEVEMENTS & AWARDS: N.A.

PERSONAL: Lives in New York City.

SCALI, JOHN
Sr. Correspondent, ABC, News

c/o ABC, 1717 DeSales St., N.W., Washington, DC 20036
b. April 27, 1918. Canton, OH.

EDUCATION: Boston University.

CAREER HIGHLIGHTS: ABC News State Dept. and Diplomatic Correspondent ('61); appointed Special Consultant for Foreign Affairs and Communications by Pres. Richard M. Nixon ('71); Permanent U.S. Representative to the UN ('73); ABC News Sr. Correspondent ('75).

ACHIEVEMENTS & AWARDS: AFTRA created the John Scali award ('64).

PERSONAL: Wife, Denise. Resides in Washington, DC.

SCAMARDELLA, ROSE ANN
Anchor, WABC-TV, "The 5 O'Clock Eyewitness News"

c/o WABC-TV, 7 Lincoln Sq., New York, NY 10023
b. New York.

EDUCATION: Marymount College, B.A.; New York University, M.A., Sociology.

CAREER HIGHLIGHTS: Commissioner at New York City Commission on Human Rights; 11 P.M. Co-Anchor, WABC-TV; Anchor, WABC-TV "The 5 O'Clock Eyewitness News."

ACHIEVEMENTS & AWARDS: N.A.

PERSONAL: Married to Mark Niedhammer, WABC-TV Technical Dir.

SCARBOROUGH, CHUCK
Co-Anchor, WNBC-TV, New York, News

c/o WNBC-TV, 30 Rockefeller Plaza, New York, NY 10020
b. November 4, 1943. Pittsburgh, PA.

EDUCATION: University of Mississippi, B.S.

CAREER HIGHLIGHTS: Anchor, WLOX-TV, Biloxi, MS ('66); Reporter/Anchor, WDAM-TV, Hattiesburgh, MS ('68); Managing Editor/Anchor, WAGA-TV, Atlanta ('69); Reporter/Anchor, WNAC-TV, Boston ('72); Co-Anchor, WNBC-TV, New York ('74).

ACHIEVEMENTS & AWARDS: Six AP awards; four Emmy awards; Skyline Foundation award; Aviation and Space Writers award ('78, '79); Author, novels *Stryker* and *The Myrmidon Project*.

PERSONAL: Married to Anne Ford.

SCHAAP, DICK
Sports Correspondent, ABC, News

c/o ABC, 7 W. 66th St., New York, NY 10023
b. N.A.

EDUCATION: Cornell University; Columbia University Graduate School of Journalism.

CAREER HIGHLIGHTS: Sports Editor, *Newsweek* magazine, New York ('60); Sr. Editor, *Newsweek* ('62); City Editor, *N.Y. Herald-Tribune* ('64); Co-Host, "The Joe Namath Show" ('69); Sports Anchor, WNBC-TV, New York ('70); Sports Correspondent, "NBC Nightly News" and the "Today" program ('77); Sports Correspondent, ABC News ('80).

ACHIEVEMENTS & AWARDS: Shared horse racing's Eclipse award for his coverage of the Marlboro Cup ('79); author of 22 books, including *Instant Replay*.

PERSONAL: Resides in New York City with wife, Trish.

SCHADLER, JAY
Correspondent, ABC, News

c/o ABC, 7 W. 66th St., New York, NY 10023
b. N.A.

EDUCATION: Michigan State University, B.A., Political Science (cum laude); Syracuse University School of Public Communications, M.A., Mass Communication Theory and Communication Law (magna cum laude); Syracuse University School of Law, law degree.

CAREER HIGHLIGHTS: Reporter/Weekend Anchor/Prod., WZZM-TV, Grand Rapids, MI ('79); Reporter, KSTP-TV, Minneapolis ('81); Correspondent, ABC News, Atlanta ('82).

ACHIEVEMENTS & AWARDS: AP Broadcast Reporter of the Year in Michigan ('81).

PERSONAL: N.A.

SCHADLOW, JEFFREY H.
V.P., Marketing and Research, 20th Century Fox, TV

c/o 20th Century Fox TV, 10201 W. Pico Blvd., Los Angeles, CA 90035
b. February 19, 1948. New York, NY.

EDUCATION: Pace University.

CAREER HIGHLIGHTS: Research Analyst, ABC TV ('69); Promotion Writer, ABC TV ('71); Marketing Specialist, NBC TV ('74); Mgr., Merchandising and Sales Development, NBC ('75); Dir., Advertising Promotion, Arbitron ('78); Dir. of Research, 20th Century Fox TV ('81); V.P., Marketing and Research, 20th Century Fox TV ('82).

ACHIEVEMENTS & AWARDS: N.A.

PERSONAL: Resides in Westwood, CA, with wife, Barbara.

SCHAEFER, GEORGE
Prod./Dir.

1801 Ave. of the Stars, Los Angeles, CA 90067
b. December 16, 1920. Wallingford, CT.

EDUCATION: Lafayette College; Yale School of Drama.

CAREER HIGHLIGHTS: Illustrious Prod./Dir. of live TV in the fifties. For three decades, his name has been a hallmark of TV dramatic excellence because of his intelligent adaptations of classic and contemporary plays, which he revisualized for the TV screen. Prod./Dir., *First You Cry, Blind Ambition, The Last of Mrs. Lincoln, Sandburg's Lincoln, Love Story, Do Not Go Gentle Into That Good Night, My Father and My Mother, Macbeth, The Bunker, Our Town*, 56 Hallmark Hall of Fame programs, and "Right of Way" for HBO.

ACHIEVEMENTS & AWARDS: Eight Emmy awards; four Directors Guild awards; Peabody, Sylvania, and Tony awards.

PERSONAL: Resides in Beverly Hills, CA, with his wife, Mildred.

SCHAFFNER, FRANKLIN JAMES
Dir./Prod.

c/o Chasin-Park-Citron Agency, 9255 Sunset Blvd., Los Angeles, CA 90067
b. May 30, 1920. Tokyo, Japan.

EDUCATION: Franklin and Marshall College.

CAREER HIGHLIGHTS: Began his directing career with CBS TV in New York with "Studio One," "Ford Theater," "Person to Person With Edward R. Murrow." Directed *Twelve Angry Men, The Caine Mutiny Court Martial,* and "A Tour of the White House." Motion pictures include *The Stripper, The Best Man, The War Lord, Patton, Nicholas and Alexandra, Papillon, Islands in the Stream,* and *The Boys From Brazil.*

ACHIEVEMENTS & AWARDS: Emmy awards ('54, '55, '62); Sylvania award ('53); Academy Award, Directors Guild award ('71).

PERSONAL: Wife, Helen; two children, Jenny and Kate. Resides in Los Angeles.

SCHANZER, KENNETH D.
Exec. V.P., NBC, Sports

c/o NBC, 30 Rockefeller Plaza, New York, NY 10020
b. May 16, 1945. Brooklyn, NY.

EDUCATION: Colgate University, B.A.; Columbia Law School, J.D.

CAREER HIGHLIGHTS: Legislative Counsel, NAB ('73–'76); Campaign Mgr. for John Heinz for U.S. Senate ('76); joined NBC as Dir., Government Relations ('76); named Sr. V.P., Government Relations, NAB ('80); returned to NBC as V.P., Talent and Program Negotiations, NBC Sports ('81); Exec. V.P., NBC Sports ('83).

ACHIEVEMENTS & AWARDS: N.A.
PERSONAL: N.A.

SCHAPIRO, ANGELA P.
Pres., Angela P. Schapiro Assoc.

1133 Ave. of the Americas, New York, NY 10036
b. August 18, 1942. Beaconsfield, England.

EDUCATION: University College; London University; Institute of International Affairs.

CAREER HIGHLIGHTS: Various positions in advertising, Market Research Exec. and Media Dir., London ('64); Independent Prod., England ('67); Documentary Prod., Cappy Productions ('68); Exec. Asst. to the Chairman of the Board, Athena Communications ('72);

concurrently, Pay-TV Sales Dir., Warner Bros.; Program Dir., Warner Cable Star Channel; Member, Qube Task Force, Warner Communications ('74–'76); V.P., General Mgr., Columbia Pictures Pay TV ('76); V.P., Programming, Cinemax and Program Services, HBO, and Pres. of Telemation Program Services ('78); Sr. V.P., the Entertainment Channel, Business Affairs and Operations; Pres., Angela P. Schapiro Assoc.

ACHIEVEMENTS & AWARDS: Founding Dir., Women in Cable ('79); Member, NATAS, IRTS.

PERSONAL: Husband, Benson H. Begun.

SCHAUB, WARREN D.
V.P., ABC, Finance

c/o ABC, 1330 Ave. of the Americas, New York, NY 10019
b. N.A.

EDUCATION: Rutgers University.

CAREER HIGHLIGHTS: Dir. of Taxes, Natl. Sugar Refining Co. ('62); Dir. of Taxes, Mack Trucks ('66); Dir. of Taxes, ABC, Inc. ('70); Controller, ABC, Inc.('71); V.P. and Controller, ABC, Inc. ('74); V.P., Finance, ABC, Inc. ('75).

ACHIEVEMENTS & AWARDS: N.A.

PERSONAL: Resides in Upper Saddle River, NJ, with his wife, Patricia; four children.

SCHECHNER, WILLIAM
Co-Anchor, NBC News, "Overnight"

c/o NBC, 30 Rockefeller Plaza, New York, NY 10020
b. Newark, NJ.

EDUCATION: Oberlin College; Columbia University.

CAREER HIGHLIGHTS: Journalism career began at the *Bergen Record,* New Jersey ('65). Public Affairs Dir. and Prod. of documentaries, WBAI ('68). Program Dir., Host of his own morning show, and Prod. of documentaries, KPFA ('71). General Assignment Reporter, KQED, San Francisco, then joined KPIX, Group W TV station in San Francisco. Became NBC News Correspondent based in the Atlanta Bureau ('81). Co-Anchor, "Overnight" ('82).

ACHIEVEMENTS & AWARDS: Two Emmy awards from the San Francisco Chapter, NATAS.
PERSONAL: Wife, Danice; daughter, Lilah.

SCHEFFER, STEPHEN J.
Exec. V.P., HBO Film Programming

c/o HBO, 1271 Ave. of the Americas, New York, NY 10020
b. January 27, 1939.

EDUCATION: U.S Naval Academy; Harvard Business School, M.B.A.
CAREER HIGHLIGHTS: Columbia Pictures ('66); MGM ('69); Exec. V.P., Polydor Records ('72); Asst. to Chairman, Allied Artists ('75); joined Time-Life Films as Dir., Film Acquisition ('77); V.P., Film Operations; V.P., Programming; named V.P., Film Programming, HBO ('80); Exec. V.P., Film Programming, HBO ('83).
ACHIEVEMENTS & AWARDS: N.A.
PERSONAL: Resides in Scarsdale, NY, with wife, Lenore, and two sons.

SCHEIMER, LOU
Animation Cartoon Executive

18107 Sherman Way, Reseda, CA 91335
b. Pittsburgh, PA.

EDUCATION: Carnegie Institute of Technology.
CAREER HIGHLIGHTS: Founded Filmation Studios ('62); went into partnership with Norm Prescott, and their talents were soon evidenced when "Superman" made the Saturday morning network lineup ('65); "Archie" and "Batman" series followed ('68); continued success with animated cartoons on network TV, including "Fat Albert" ('72); "Star Trek" and "Isis" ('75); "Shazam" ('76); "Space Academy" ('77); and "Tarzan" ('78). Filmation animation features have included *Journey Back to Oz* ('76); *Oliver Twist*, and *Treasure Island* ('81).
ACHIEVEMENTS & AWARDS: N.A.
PERSONAL: Resides in San Fernando Valley, CA, with wife, Jay; children, Lane and Erika.

SCHEINFELD, JOHN
Mgr., Dramatic Development, Paramount TV

c/o Paramount TV, 5555 Melrose Ave., Los Angeles, CA 90038
b. October 20, 1952. Highland Park, IL.

EDUCATION: Oberlin College, B.A; Northwestern University, M.F.A.
CAREER HIGHLIGHTS: Instructor of Radio, TV, and Film, Northwestern University ('77); Dir. of Advertising and Promotion, WISN AM-FM-TV, Milwaukee ('78); Supervisor of Comedy Development, Paramount TV ('81); Mgr. of Dramatic Development, Paramount TV ('82).
ACHIEVEMENTS & AWARDS: N.A.
PERSONAL: N.A.

SCHELL, TOM
Correspondent, ABC, News, Los Angeles

c/o ABC, 2040 Ave. of the Stars, Los Angeles, CA 90067
b. August 11, 1935. Steubinville, OH.

EDUCATION: College of Steubinville.
CAREER HIGHLIGHTS: Reporter, WEIR-AM, Weirton, WV ('52); Reporter, WSTV-AM, Steubinville, OH ('53); Reporter, WCPO-TV, Cincinnati ('55); Reporter, WLW-TV, Cincinnati ('61); Correspondent, ABC News, Los Angeles ('64).
ACHIEVEMENTS & AWARDS: Member, Radio-TV News Dirs. Assn.
PERSONAL: Resides in Glendale, CA, with his wife, Betty, and their three children.

SCHENCK, GEORGE
Prod./Writer

c/o Schenck/Cardea Productions, Burbank Studios Columbia Plaza E., Room 137, Burbank, CA 91505
b. February 12. New York, NY.

EDUCATION: University of Southern California, B.A. and M.A., Cinema.
CAREER HIGHLIGHTS: Writer of TV show episodes of "Bonanza," "Love, American Style," "Branded," "Hondo," "Barnaby Jones," "Wild, Wild West." Writer of TV

movies including *The Phantom of Hollywood*, CBS; *Night Train to Terror*, ABC; *Death Moon*, CBS. Writer of the feature films *Futureworld*, *Superbeast*, *Barquero*, *More Dead Than Alive*, and *Kill a Dragon*. Writer/Prod./Creator, with Frank Cardea, of "Sawyer and Finn," NBC ('81); "O'Malley," NBC ('81); "Hard Knocks," ABC ('81); "Bring 'Em Back Alive" series, CBS ('82).

ACHIEVEMENTS & AWARDS: N.A.

PERSONAL: Wife, Ginna; sons, Kirk and Jeff. Resides in Encino, CA.

SCHERICK, EDGAR J.
Prod.

5746 W. Sunset Blvd., Hollywood, CA 90028
b. New York, NY.

EDUCATION: Harvard University, B.A. (magna cum laude).

CAREER HIGHLIGHTS: Independent Prod., who worked his way up the ladder from the Dancer-Fitzgerald-Sample advertising agency ('53); moving to CBS Sports ('55), and later to ABC Sports, where he was involved in the creation of "Wide World of Sports" ('57); moving on to ABC Sales ('60); promoted to V.P. in Charge of Programming, responsible for "The FBI," "Hollywood Palace," "Bewitched," "Peyton Place," and "Batman." Became an Independent Prod. ('67), and was involved in theatrical films including *Take the Money and Run, Sleuth, The Heartbreak Kid, The Stepford Wives, I Never Promised You a Rose Garden, For Love of Ivy*, and *Ring of Bright Water*. TV movie credits include *Raid on Entebbe* ('78), *Circle of Children* ('79), *Little Gloria . . . Happy at Last* ('82), and the NBC Project Peacock Specials.

ACHIEVEMENTS & AWARDS: Member, Phi Beta Kappa.

PERSONAL: Resides in Beverly Hills, CA, with son, Bradford. Sons, Gregory and J.J., and daughter, Christine, are in college.

SCHEUER, LAURA
Attorney, CBS

c/o CBS, 51 W. 52d St., New York, NY 10019
b. September 20.

EDUCATION: Swarthmore College; Harvard Law School (with honors).

CAREER HIGHLIGHTS: Considered one of the ablest young communications lawyers working in commercial network TV. Started as a Clerk in the 5th Circuit, moved on to a position with the Webster & Sheffield law firm; Attorney, CBS Broadcast Group, Legal Dept. ('82).

ACHIEVEMENTS & AWARDS: N.A.

PERSONAL: Daughter of Congressman James Scheuer.

SCHICK, ELLIOT
Prod.

c/o CBS, 7800 Beverly Blvd., Los Angeles, CA 90036
b. December 24, 1924. Brooklyn, NY.

EDUCATION: Brooklyn College; New School for Social Research.

CAREER HIGHLIGHTS: Prod./Dir. of TV Shows, Nova Productions ('50); Editor, "Candid Camera" ('53); Prod. and Dir. of Commercials and Documentaries, Fred Niles, Inc., and Hollywood Film Commercials, Inc. ('56); Asst. Dir. for such TV series as "Time Tunnel," "Star Trek," and "12 O'Clock High," as well as such features as *Hombre, Bloody Mama*, and *Billy Jack*. Supervising Prod. for the films *Futureworld* and *Cooley High*, and Exec. in Charge of Prod. for *The Deer Hunter*. Prod. of "Private Benjamin" series for CBS and *Pippin* for cable TV.

ACHIEVEMENTS & AWARDS: N.A.

PERSONAL: N.A.

SCHIEFFER, BOB
Anchor/Correspondent, CBS, News

c/o CBS, 2020 M St., N.W., Washington, DC 20036
b. Austin, TX.

EDUCATION: Texas Christian University, B.A., Journalism.

CAREER HIGHLIGHTS: Reporter, *Fort Worth Star-Telegram*; News Anchor, WBAP-TV, Dallas-Fort Worth; joined CBS News ('69); Pentagon Correspondent ('70–'74); Anchor, "CBS Sunday Night News" ('73–'74); White House Correspondent, ('74–'79); Anchor, Saturday edition of "The CBS Evening News" ('76–present); Anchor, "Morning" ('79–'80); Natl. Correspondent ('80).

ACHIEVEMENTS & AWARDS: Sigma Delta Chi, Texas Assn. Press Broadcasters, AP Managing Editors, and Emmy awards.

PERSONAL: N.A.

SCHILLACI, PETER P.
Dir. of Wide World of Learning and Product Development, ABC, Video Enterprises

c/o ABC, 1330 Ave. of the Americas, New York, NY 10019
b. August 13, 1927. Chicago, IL.

EDUCATION: University of Illinois; Loyola University, Ph.B.; Aquinas Institute, M.A., Philosophy, and M.A., Theology; College of St. Thomas, Rome, Ph.D.

CAREER HIGHLIGHTS: Taught metaphysics and philosophy of art for five years ('61); taught film at Fordham University and was part of Marshall McLuhan's research team ('67). Writer/Prod., "Film and Society," wrote 30 half-hour programs for New York State Dept. of Education ('69); Exec. Dir. of Media Education, McGraw-Hill's Contemporary Films Division ('72); Dir. of Marketing and Advertising, Macmillan Films ('75); joined ABC as Dir. of Wide World Learning and Product Development for ABC Video Enterprises and Exec. Prod. of various series, including "Wellness Lifestyles" and "Sports Medicine" ('79). Also, Film Critic and Editor, *Man Media Newsletter* ('72–'82); Exec. Prod. "Schooldisc," an ABC/NEA joint project to develop interactive videodisc curricula for fourth to sixth grade school children.

ACHIEVEMENTS & AWARDS: Published books including *Movies and Morals* ('62); *Films Deliver* ('69); *Luis Bunuel and the Death of God* ('72); *Life Goes to the Movies* ('73).

PERSONAL: Resides in Port Washington, NY, with wife, Patricia.

SCHILLER, LAWRENCE
Prod.

c/o William Morris Agency, P.O. Box 5345, Beverly Hills, CA 90212
b. December 28, 1936. New York, NY.

EDUCATION: N.A.

CAREER HIGHLIGHTS: Started as a Photo-Journalist for *Look, Life,* and the *Saturday Evening Post* ('59); Dir. of the noted documentary *The Man Who Skiied Down Mount Everest* ('74); Prod./Dir., *Sunshine,* CBS TV movie ('75); Prod., *Hey, I'm Alive,* ABC TV movie ('76); as well as *The Trial of Lee Harvey Oswald* ('77), *The Winds of Kitty Hawk* ('78), *Marilyn—The Final Days* ('80), and *The Patricia Neal Story* ('80).

ACHIEVEMENTS & AWARDS: Academy Award for feature length documentary *The Man Who Skiied Down Mount Everest* ('74).

PERSONAL: Resides in Beverly Hills, CA with wife, Stephanie, two sons, Anthony and Cameron Austin. Three children by a previous marriage, Suzanne, Marc, and Howard.

SCHLATTER, GEORGE H.
Exec. Prod./Prod./Dir./Writer

8321 Beverly Blvd., Los Angeles, CA 90048
b. December 31, 1929. Birmingham, AL.

EDUCATION: Missouri Valley College; George Pepperdine University.

CAREER HIGHLIGHTS: Both as producer and director, Schlatter has been responsible for more than 1,000 hours of TV series and specials involving such personalities as Frank Sinatra, Dinah Shore, Judy Garland, and Lucille Ball. Other credits include Grammy awards shows ('64–'70); "Laugh-In" ('67–'73); Diana Ross special, Goldie Hawn special,

Cher specials and series ('75); "Laugh-In" specials, Shirley MacLaine special ('77); "Real People" series ('79–'83); "Goldie and Liza Together" ('80); and "Speak Up America" ('80–'81),

ACHIEVEMENTS & AWARDS: Received 19 Emmy nominations, three Emmy awards, Golden Globe award, Image award. Named IRTS Man of the Year; received Directors Guild award.

PERSONAL: Married to actress Jolene Brand; two daughters.

SCHMERTZ, HERBERT
V.P. and Dir., Mobil Oil Corp., Corporate and Governmental Public Relations

c/o Mobil, 150 E. 42d St., New York, NY 10017

b. March 22, 1930. Yonkers, NY.

EDUCATION: Union College, B.A. ('52); Columbia University, LL.B. ('55).

CAREER HIGHLIGHTS: As the executive responsible for Mobil's broadcasting activities for many years, Schmertz exercised enormous influence on public and commercial TV. Mobil funded many shows on public TV, most notably "Masterpiece Theatre" on Sunday evenings, and pioneered in syndicating high-quality programs such as *Nicholas Nickleby*, which aired on many major network affiliates. A list of Schmertz's most important positions includes General Counsel for the Federal Mediation and Conciliation Service ('61); Mgr., Corporate Labor Relations, Mobil Oil Corp. ('66); Mgr., Corporate Planning Coordination, Mobil ('68); V.P., Public Affairs, Mobil ('69) Pres., Mobil Shipping and Transportation Co. ('73); Board of Dirs., Mobil Oil Corp. ('76); Board of Mobil Corp. ('79); currently serves as Dir. of the Mobil Corp. and V.P. and Dir. of Mobil Oil Corp., Corporate and Governmental Public Relations.

ACHIEVEMENTS & AWARDS: Member of the President's Commission on Broadcasting to Cuba. Co-Author, *Takeover*.

PERSONAL: Resides in New York City.

SCHNEIDER, ALFRED R.
V.P., ABC, Inc.

c/o ABC, 1330 Ave. of the Americas, New York, NY 10019

b. April 25, 1926. New York, NY.

EDUCATION: Hamilton College, B.A.; Harvard Law School, LL.B.

CAREER HIGHLIGHTS: Business Affairs Dept. of ABC ('53); CBS TV Network Exec. Asst. to Pres. ('55); ABC V.P., Administration ('60); V.P., ABC, and Asst. to Exec. V.P., ABC, Inc. ('62); appointed V.P., ABC, Inc. ('72).

ACHIEVEMENTS & AWARDS: Sr. Member, NAB TV Code Review Board; Board of Dirs., Council of Better Business Bureaus, and Member, Exec. Committee; served three terms on Board of Governors, IRTS and as Secretary.

PERSONAL: Resides in Larchmont, NY, with wife, Jane, a sculptor; children, Leland J., Jeffry, and Elizabeth Sue.

SCHNEIDER, DICK
Prod./Dir.

110 W. 57th St., New York, NY 10019

b. March 7. Cazadero, CA.

EDUCATION: College of the Pacific.

CAREER HIGHLIGHTS: Prod./Dir., NBC ('50). Freelance Prod./Dir. of the following specials since '68; "The Rose Parade"; "NBC Star Salute"; Doc Severinsen Christmas special; "Stars and Stripes Show With Bob Hope"; "Rose Queen Pageant"; "Orange Parade"; "Ringling Brothers Circus"; Emmy award shows; Sammy Davis special; "The Tonight Show" and the Oscar award show.

ACHIEVEMENTS & AWARDS: Pres., of New York Chapter, NATAS

PERSONAL: N.A.

SCHNEIDER, JOHN A.
Pres. and Chief Exec. Officer, Warner Amex Satellite Entertainment Co.

c/o Warner Amex, 1211 Ave. of the Americas, New York, NY 10036

b. December 4, 1926. Chicago, IL.

EDUCATION: University of Notre Dame, B.S.

CAREER   HIGHLIGHTS: WGN-AM,   Chicago;

Exec., CBS, Chicago and New York ('50); V.P. and General Mgr., WCAU-TV, Philadelphia ('58); V.P. and General Mgr., WCBS-TV, New York ('64); Pres., CBS TV, and V.P. and Dir., CBS, Inc. ('65); Pres., CBS Broadcast Group ('66); Exec. V.P., CBS, Inc. ('69); reappointed Pres., CBS Broadcast Group ('71); full-time Exec. Consultant, Warner Communications ('79); Pres. and Chief Exec. Officer, Warner Amex Satellite Entertainment Co. ('80).

ACHIEVEMENTS & AWARDS: Trustee and Member, Exec. Committee, University of Notre Dame; Exec. Committee, American Film Institute. Holds honorary degrees from Trinity University and the University of Notre Dame.

PERSONAL: N.A.

SCHNEIER, FREDERICK
Sr. V.P., Viacom Enterprises, Program Acquisitions and Motion Pictures

c/o Viacom, 1211 Ave. of the Americas, New York, NY 10036
b. May 31, 1927. New York, NY.

EDUCATION: New York University, B.S. ('51), and M.B.A. ('53).

CAREER HIGHLIGHTS: Exec. V.P., Show Corp. ('58); V.P., TV Programs, RKO-General ('72); V.P., Hemdale Leisure Co. ('73); Sr. V.P., Program Acquisitions and Motion Pictures, Viacom Enterprises ('79).

ACHIEVEMENTS & AWARDS: N.A.

PERSONAL: Wife, Joyce.

SCHNURMAN, NED
Exec. Prod., PBS, "Inside Story"

c/o Frank Goodman Assoc., 1776 Broadway, New York, NY 10019
b. N.A.

EDUCATION: Columbia University School of Journalism.

CAREER HIGHLIGHTS: Reporter, *Newark Evening News,* New Jersey; News Editor, *International Herald Tribune,* Paris; News Dir., WNET-TV, New York ('62); Exec. Prod. for Special Projects at Natl. Educational TV; City Editor, WCBS-TV, New York; Founding Assoc. Dir., Natl. News Council; Exec. Prod., PBS's "Inside Story."

ACHIEVEMENTS & AWARDS: Awarded the Ford Fellowship in international reporting ('63).

PERSONAL: N.A.

SCHOENBRUN, DAVID
News Analyst, WPIX-TV, Independent Network News

c/o WPIX-TV, 220 E. 42d St., New York, NY 10017
b. March 15, 1915. New York, NY.

EDUCATION: City College of New York, B.A.

CAREER HIGHLIGHTS: Freelance Writer ('39); Editor, French broadcasts of the Voice of America ('41); Reporter, CBS News, Paris ('45); Correspondent, CBS News, Washington, DC ('60); Correspondent, ABC News ('63–'79); News Analyst, Independent Network News, WPIX-TV, New York ('81).

ACHIEVEMENTS & AWARDS: Decorated, Croix de Guerre, Legion d'Honneur (France); Author, *As France Goes* ('66); *Three Lives of Charles De Gaulle* ('66); *Vietnam* ('68); *The New Israelis* ('73); *Triumph in Paris* ('76); and *Soldier of the Night* ('80).

PERSONAL: Wife, Dorothy; daughter, Lucy.

SCHORR, DANIEL
Sr. Washington Correspondent, Turner Communications Corp., Cable News Network

c/o Cable News Network, Washington, 2133 Wisconsin Ave., N.W., Washington, DC 20007
b. August 31, 1916. New York, NY.

EDUCATION: City College of New York, B.S.S.

CAREER HIGHLIGHTS: Before joining CBS News, Schorr was a Correspondent, *Christian Science Monitor* and *N.Y. Times*; started at CBS as Staff Correspondent, Washington, DC ('53–'55); Correspondent, CBS Bureau, Moscow ('57); headed CBS News Bureau, Germany and Eastern Europe ('60); returned as Natl. Correspondent, Washington, DC ('66); Economic Reporter, Washington, DC, CBS ('71); investigated Watergate ('72–'74); coverage of abuses within the CIA leading to national controversy and his resignation from CBS ('76); Commentator, National Public Radio, and several public and independent TV stations ('79); Sr. Washington Correspondent, Turner Communications Corp., Cable News Network ('80).

ACHIEVEMENTS & AWARDS: Distinctions have included First Amendment award of Sigma Delta Chi; the Profiles in Courage award of the John F. Kennedy Chapter of B'nai B'rith; and the Natl. Headliners' award. In addition, he was awarded the Grand Cross of Merit, Germany, the highest decoration West Germany has given a journalist and the decoration of Officer of Orange-Nassau from Queen Juliana, Netherlands.

PERSONAL: Married Lisbeth Bamberger ('67); they have two children.

SCHOUMACHER, DAVID
Correspondent, WJLA-TV, Washington, DC, News

c/o WJLA-TV, 4461 Connecticut Ave., N.W., Washington, DC 20008
b. Chicago, IL.

EDUCATION: Northwestern University Medill School of Journalism, B.S. and M.S.

CAREER HIGHLIGHTS: Reporter and News Broadcaster, WKY-TV, Oklahoma City; News Dir., KTIV-TV, Sioux City, IA ('61); Network Correspondent, CBS News, ABC News ('63–'75); Correspondent, WJLA-TV, Washington, DC ('76).

ACHIEVEMENTS & AWARDS: N.A.
PERSONAL: N.A.

SCHUBECK, JOHN
Co-Anchor, KNBC, "News 4 LA"

c/o KNBC, 3000 W. Alameda Ave., Burbank, CA 91523
b. Detroit, MI.

EDUCATION: University of Michigan, B.A., Radio and TV; Loyola University, law degree.

CAREER HIGHLIGHTS: Newscaster, WJR-Radio, Detroit; Anchor, WRCV-TV, Philadelphia ('62); Anchor, KNBC ('65); WABC-TV, New York, Anchor of 5 P.M. Newscast as well as Drama/Film Critic, News Correspondent, and Moderator. Rejoined KNBC ('74).

ACHIEVEMENTS & AWARDS: N.A.
PERSONAL: N.A.

SCHULTE, STEPHAN WILLIAM
V.P., Showtime Entertainment, Operations and Production Services

40 W. 67th St., New York, NY 10023
b. May 14, 1944. Brooklyn, NY.

EDUCATION: University of Vermont.

CAREER HIGHLIGHTS: Started as Film Traffic Controller, ABC, Net Film Dept. ('69); rose to Mgr., Film Production ('73); joined Showtime Entertainment as Dir. of Operations ('78), and became V.P., Operations and Production Services ('79).

ACHIEVEMENTS & AWARDS: N.A.
PERSONAL: N.A.

SCHWAB, SHELLY
Sr. V.P., MCA TV, Marketing

c/o MCA TV, 445 Park Ave., New York, NY 10022
b. Brooklyn, NY.

EDUCATION: New York University, B.S., Marketing.

CAREER HIGHLIGHTS: Sales Mgr., N.Y. Daily News ('58); Sales Exec., WCBS-TV, New York ('68); Sales Mgr., CBS Records, Atlanta and New York ('70); Station Mgr., WAGA-TV, Atlanta ('73); Sr. V.P., Marketing, MCA TV ('78).

ACHIEVEMENTS & AWARDS: Actively involved with the Leukemia Society.

PERSONAL: Wife, Blanche; daughter, Kerry; sons, Kyle and Kevin.

SCHWARTZ, DOROTHY
V.P., Primetime Sales, CBS TV, Sales Dept.

c/o CBS, 51 W. 52d St., New York, NY 10020
b. N.A.

EDUCATION: New York University, B.A.; Columbia University Teachers College, M.A.

CAREER HIGHLIGHTS: Asst. to V.P., Marschalk Co. advertising agency ('61); moved up the ranks to V.P., Network Programs before leaving Marschalk ('71); Mgr., Sales Development and Eastern Sales Mgr. of the NBC Radio Network, New York ('71); Mgr., Daytime Sales, NBC ('73); Dir. of Advertising, Heublein ('75);

Acct. Exec., CBS TV Sales ('77); V.P., Prime-time Sales, CBS-TV ('82).
ACHIEVEMENTS & AWARDS: N.A.
PERSONAL: Resides in New York City.

SCHWARTZ, MICHAEL
Dir. of Marketing Services, Time Video Information Services

c/o Time Video Information Services, 1271 Ave. of the Americas, New York, NY 10020
b. N.A.

EDUCATION: Boston University; City College of New York.
CAREER HIGHLIGHTS: Before joining Time Video Information Services, Schwartz held managerial positions in marketing and advertising research at Ogilvy & Mather and the General Foods Corp. As Dir. of Marketing Services for Time Video Information Services, he is responsible for consumer marketing and research.
ACHIEVEMENTS & AWARDS: N.A.
PERSONAL: N.A.

SCHWARTZMAN, ANDREW JAY
Exec. Dir., Media Access Project

c/o Media Access Project, 1609 Connecticut Ave., N.W., Washington, DC 20009
b. October 4, 1946.

EDUCATION: University of Pennsylvania, B.S. and J.D.
CAREER HIGHLIGHTS: Staff Counsel, United Church of Christ ('71); Counsel, Office of General Counsel of the U.S. Dept. of Energy ('74); Exec. Dir., Media Access Project, which represents organizations concerned that the print and broadcast media represent them fairly to the general public.
ACHIEVEMENTS & AWARDS: Member, American Bar Assn., Natl. Organization for Women.
PERSONAL: N.A.

SCOTT, DREW
Correspondent, Independent Network News, Washington Bureau

c/o Independent Network News, 11 WPIX Plaza, New York, NY 10017
b. Los Angeles, CA.

EDUCATION: Orange Coast College.
CAREER HIGHLIGHTS: Reporter, ZBM, Hamilton, Bermuda; WOR-TV, New York ('72); Freelance Writer, Editor, and Reporter ('76); Correspondent, Independent Network News, Washington Bureau ('80).
ACHIEVEMENTS & AWARDS: N.A.
PERSONAL: Resides in Fort Washington, MD, with his wife and four children.

SCOTT, MARVIN
Co-Anchor, Independent Network News

c/o Independent Network News, 11 WPIX Plaza, New York, NY 10017
b. N.A.

EDUCATION: New York University.
CAREER HIGHLIGHTS: Reporter, *Herald-Tribune*; WABC-TV, New York; Mutual Broadcasting Co.; Reporter/Weekend Anchor, WNEW-TV, New York ('72); Co-Anchor, Independent Network News, Midday Edition ('80).
ACHIEVEMENTS & AWARDS: Emmy award ('77); New York State AP Broadcasters award ('79).
PERSONAL: Resides in New York City.

SCOTT, WILLARD H., JR.
On-Air Personality, NBC

c/o NBC, 4001 Nebraska Ave., N.W., Washington, DC 20016
b. March 7, 1934. Alexandria, VA.

EDUCATION: American University, B.A., Philosophy and Religion.

CAREER HIGHLIGHTS: "Today's" weathercaster who is also the resident clown. Scott found a unique role to play in morning TV, and he does it better than anyone. "The Joy Boys" radio show, WRC, Washington, DC ('53–'72); Weather and On-Air stint at WRC-TV and WRC-AM ('67–'80); joined NBC as Weathercaster for "Today" ('80).

ACHIEVEMENTS & AWARDS: Humanitarian in Residence, Natl. Society of Fund Raisers ('75); Washingtonian of the Year ('79); published autobiography, *The Joy of Living* ('82).

PERSONAL: Wife Mary; daughters, Mary and Sally.

SCULLY, VIN
Sportscaster, NBC, Sports

c/o NBC, 30 Rockefeller Plaza, New York, NY 10020

b. November 29, 1927. New York, NY.

EDUCATION: Fordham University.

CAREER HIGHLIGHTS: Began his professional broadcasting career as a Staff Announcer, radio station WTOP, Washington, DC; joined the Dodgers broadcast team, Los Angeles ('58); joined CBS Sports for NFL play-by-play assignments and hosting duties for professional golf coverage ('75); Broadcaster, NBC Sports ('82).

ACHIEVEMENTS & AWARDS: Winner of the Frick award recognizing major contributions to the game of baseball ('82); two-time winner of the Natl. Sportscaster of the Year award ('66, '78); Peabody award for excellence in broadcasting ('82).

PERSONAL: N.A.

SEAMANS, BILL
Correspondent and Bureau Chief, ABC, News

c/o ABC, 7 W. 66th St., New York, NY 10023

b. N.A.

EDUCATION: Brown University, B.A., Economics; Columbia School of Journalism.

CAREER HIGHLIGHTS: Ten years as Writer/Editor, CBS News ('52); ABC News Prod. ('63);

Prod., pool TV coverage of Democratic Natl. Convention ('72); has reported on every major conflict in Israel since '67 war; currently serves as Tel Aviv Bureau Chief.

ACHIEVEMENTS & AWARDS: Overseas Press Club award for radio coverage of the Cyprus invasion ('74); Overseas Press Club award for "Rabin: Action Biography" ('74).

PERSONAL: N.A.

SEAMANS, IKE
News Correspondent, NBC

c/o NBC, Piazza del Collegio, Romano 1-A, Rome, Italy

b. May 4, 1938. Greenwood, MS.

EDUCATION: West Virginia University, B.A., Political Science ('61).

CAREER HIGHLIGHTS: Army Information Officer and Broadcaster for Armed Forces Radio; Feature Reporter for *Stars and Stripes* (mid-'60's); Correspondent for WTVJ-TV, Miami ('69); joined NBC News as Miami Correspondent ('79); NBC News Correspondent based in Rome ('82).

ACHIEVEMENTS & AWARDS: Ohio State University award for "Israel After the War: Before the Peace" ('72).

PERSONAL: Wife, Mary Stacy; children, Stacy, Ryan, and Reid.

SEARLE, ROBERT A.
Pres., V.P., and Dir., Cardiff Communications, Cardiff Publishing Co.

6430 S. Yosemite, Englewood, CO 80111

b. N.A.

EDUCATION: N.A.

CAREER HIGHLIGHTS: Editor and Publisher, *Cable Television Business*; Pres., Natl. Cable TV Institute; Pres., Cardiff Publishing Co., V.P., and Dir., Cardiff Communications, overseeing the publication of *Cable Television Business* magazine, formerly *TVC* magazine.

ACHIEVEMENTS & AWARDS: Founded the Denver Cable Club; Member, Cable TV Pioneers Club.

PERSONAL: N.A.

SEGAL, JOEL M.
Sr. V.P., Ted Bates Advertising

c/o Ted Bates Advertising, 1515 Broadway, New York, NY 10036
b. September 2, 1933. New York, NY.

EDUCATION: Cornell University, B.A.; Columbia University, M.B.A., Marketing.

CAREER HIGHLIGHTS: Asst. Media Dir., Benton & Bowles ('60); Dir., TV Network Sales Presentations, NBC ('63); began as Network Negotiator, Ted Bates Advertising, and rose to Sr. V.P. ('65).

ACHIEVEMENTS & AWARDS: N.A.

PERSONAL: Wife, Alix; two sons, Mark and Gregg.

SEGELSTEIN, IRWIN
Vice Chairman, NBC, Inc.

101 Central Park W., New York, NY
b. May 1, 1925. New York, NY.

EDUCATION: City College of New York, B.S. ('45).

CAREER HIGHLIGHTS: V.P., TV/Radio Program Dept., Benton & Bowles ('47); V.P., Program Administration, CBS TV Network ('65); Pres., CBS Records Division ('73); joined NBC ('76); several promotions through present position as Vice Chairman.

ACHIEVEMENTS & AWARDS: N.A.

PERSONAL: N.A.

SEGURA, DEBI
Anchor, Cable News Network, Sports

c/o Cable News Network, 1050 Techwood Dr., N.W., Atlanta, GA 30318
b. Los Angeles, CA.

EDUCATION: N.A.

CAREER HIGHLIGHTS: Sports Correspondent for Cable News Network based in Los Angeles ('80); moved to New York Bureau ('81); transferred to the Atlanta Headquarters as Sports Anchor ('82).

ACHIEVEMENTS & AWARDS: N.A.

PERSONAL: Married to Lou Dobbs.

SEIDEL, ERIC M.
Correspondent, Cable News Network, Washington, DC Bureau

7242 Greentree Rd., Bethesda, MD 20817
b. April 10, 1947. Washington, DC.

EDUCATION: University of Missouri, B.A., Journalism.

CAREER HIGHLIGHTS: Reporter/Anchor, WRAN-Radio, Dover, NJ ('69); Reporter/Anchor, WCAU-Radio, CBS, Philadelphia ('72); News Dir., WGST Newsradio/WPCH-FM, Atlanta ('75); News Mgr., WJLA-TV, Washington, DC ('80); Correspondent, Cable News Network, Washington, DC, Bureau ('82).

ACHIEVEMENTS & AWARDS: Various Regional (Southeast) Sigma Delta Chi awards ('76–'79); Georgia UPI newsleader award; national Sigma Delta Chi award for radio reporting ('78); Georgia AP Broadcasters Assn. Pacemaker award ('79). Board Member, Atlanta Chapter, Sigma Delta Chi ('76–'78); Pres., Georgia AP Broadcasters Assn. ('77–'78); Secretary/Treasurer, Atlanta Press Club ('78–'79).

PERSONAL: Wife, Marlene; daughters, Lisa and Meredith.

SELF, WILLIAM
Pres., CBS, Theatrical Films

c/o CBS, 7800 Beverly Blvd., Los Angeles, CA
90036
b. June 21, 1921. Dayton, OH.

EDUCATION: University of Chicago.
CAREER HIGHLIGHTS: Exec. Prod., "The Twi-
light Zone" ('60); Exec. Prod., 20th Century
Fox TV and V.P. in Charge of Production,
20th Century Fox; Pres., Fox TV and V.P.,
20th Century Fox Film Corp. ('69); Pres., Wil-
liam Self Productions ('75); V.P., Programs,
CBS TV Network ('76); V.P. of Motion Pic-
tures for TV, CBS ('77); Pres., CBS Theatrical
Films ('82).
ACHIEVEMENTS & AWARDS: N.A.
PERSONAL: N.A.

SELLECK, TOM
Actor

c/o "Magnum, P.I.," CBS, 7800 Beverly Blvd.,
Los Angeles, CA 90036
b. January 29. Detroit, MI.

EDUCATION: University of Southern California.
CAREER HIGHLIGHTS: From Marlboro man to
"Magnum, P.I.," Selleck has an unabashedly
masculine appeal, the sort of Clark Gable
quality that elicits passion from women and
admiration from men. Motion pictures include *Coma, Myra Breckinridge,* and *High Road
to China.* TV guest star on "Bracken's World"
and "The Rockford Files." TV movies include
*The Sacketts, Gypsy Warriors, Boston and Kil-
bride, The Shadow Riders, The Movie Murderer,
Returning Home, Most Wanted, Superdome,* and
Divorce Wars. TV star of "Magnum, P.I."

ACHIEVEMENTS & AWARDS: N.A.
PERSONAL: Maintains homes in Los Angeles
and Honolulu.

SENDLER, DAVID ALAN
Co-Editor, *TV Guide*

c/o *TV Guide,* 4 Corporate Center, Radnor, PA
19088
b. December 12, 1938. White Plains, NY.

EDUCATION: Dartmouth University, B.A.; Co-
lumbia University, M.S.
CAREER HIGHLIGHTS: Sr. Editor, *Parade* ('74);
Managing Editor, *TV Guide* ('75); Exec. Edi-
tor, *TV Guide* ('79); Editor, *Panorama* ('80); Co-
Editor, *TV Guide.*
ACHIEVEMENTS & AWARDS: N.A.
PERSONAL: N.A.

SENIE, KEVIN D.
Sr. V.P. and Treasurer, HBO

c/o HBO, 1271 Ave. of the Americas, New
York, NY 10020
b. June 7, 1947.

EDUCATION: University of Michigan, B.A.,
Economics; Harvard University, M.B.A., Fi-
nance.
CAREER HIGHLIGHTS: Financial Analyst, Time,
Inc. ('73); Asst. Treasurer, HBO ('76); pro-
moted to Dir., Sales Planning and Develop-
ment ('79); moved back to Time, Inc., as Dir.,
Business Development ('80); returned to
HBO as V.P., Finance and Administration,
and Treasurer ('81); Sr. V.P. and Treasurer,
HBO ('83).
ACHIEVEMENTS & AWARDS: N.A.
PERSONAL: Resides in Westport, CT, with wife,
Ann Marie, and daughter, Jessica.

SEPKOWITZ, IRV
Sr. V.P., Business Affairs, Lorimar
Productions

c/o Lorimar Productions, 3970 Overland Ave.,
Culver City, CA 90230
b. July 28, 1936. Wichita Falls, TX.

EDUCATION: University of California at Los Angeles.

CAREER HIGHLIGHTS: Attorney in Business Affairs, Ashley Famous Agency ('65); Literary Agent ('68); Dir., Business Affairs, CBS ('72); V.P., Business Affairs, Lorimar Productions ('78); Sr. V.P., Business Affairs, Lorimar Productions ('80).

ACHIEVEMENTS & AWARDS: N.A.

PERSONAL: Wife, Joyce; daughter, Amy; son, Matthew.

SERAFIN, BARRY
Correspondent, ABC, News

c/o ABC, 7 W. 66th St., New York, NY 10023
b. Coquille, OR.

EDUCATION: Washington State University, B.A., Radio/TV/Speech.

CAREER HIGHLIGHTS: Started in radio; Prod./ Dir. at KOAP-TV, Portland, OR; Reporter/ Anchor at CBS-owned KMOX, St. Louis ('68); spent ten years at Washington, DC, Bureau, CBS News, covering labor issues, Dept. of HEW, political campaigns and conventions, and anchoring presidential news conferences and speeches ('69); joined ABC News as Natl. Correspondent covering political economic issues ('81).

ACHIEVEMENTS & AWARDS: Emmy for "CBS News Special Report: Watergate: The White House Transcripts" ('74).

PERSONAL: Married to the former Lynn Van Camp; two daughters.

SERIO, DOM
V.P. and General Mgr. of Studio Production and Operations, HBO

c/o HBO, 1271 Ave. of the Americas, New York, NY 10020
b. December 10, 1939.

EDUCATION: New York City Community College.

CAREER HIGHLIGHTS: Worked as an Electronics Technician, Mgr. of a trucking company, and Cameraman, ABC, before becoming a Technical Dir. for Sterling Manhattan Cable Co. ('68); Technical Supervisor, HBO ('72); Dir., Operations, HBO ('75); General Mgr. in Charge of Studio and Originations Operations ('78); V.P. and General Mgr. of Studio Production and Operations ('81).

ACHIEVEMENTS & AWARDS: Member, Society of Motion Picture and TV Engineers; NATAS.

PERSONAL: Resides in Maspeth, NY, with wife, Lorraine and children, Denise and Nicholas.

SERMERSHEIM, GAIL
V.P. and General Mgr., HBO, Southern Region

c/o HBO, 1271 Ave. of the Americas, New York, NY 10020
b. May 13, 1943.

EDUCATION: Indiana University.

CAREER HIGHLIGHTS: Started with the Telesis Corp., Evansville, IN, as Sales Mgr., eventually moving up to Dir. of Marketing ('66); named Southeast Regional Mgr., HBO ('78); V.P. and General Mgr., HBO, Southern Region ('81).

ACHIEVEMENTS & AWARDS: Founder and second Pres., Cable TV Administration and Marketing Society; Board of Dirs., Women in Cable; recipient of the Idell Katz award for outstanding contributions to the cable TV industry from the Natl. Cable TV Assn.('80).

PERSONAL: Resides in Atlanta.

SEVAREID, ERIC
Consultant, CBS, News

c/o CBS, 524 W. 57th St., New York, NY 10019
b. November 26, 1912. Velva, ND.

EDUCATION: University of Minnesota ('35).

CAREER HIGHLIGHTS: One of the most admired figures in American broadcast journalism, Sevareid joined CBS as a member of the original news team assembled by the late Edward R. Murrow ('39); first newsman to report that France was about to capitulate to the Germans ('40). War Correspondent, China ('43); War Correspondent, London ('45); Chief Washington, DC, Correspondent, Washington, DC, Bureau ('46); European Correspondent ('59); Commentator, "The CBS Evening News" ('63); Natl. Correspondent, CBS News ('64); interview series, CBS News, "Conversations with Eric Sevareid" ('75); Consultant, CBS News ('77).

ACHIEVEMENTS & AWARDS: Recipient of three Peabody awards for news interpretation ('50, '64, '67); two Emmy awards for his coverage of the resignation of Vice President Spiro Agnew and the death of Lyndon B. Johnson; two Overseas Press Club awards; and the Harry S. Truman award ('81); and numerous other awards. Inducted into the Hall of Fame of the Washington, DC, Chapter, Sigma Delta Chi ('74), received many honorary degrees. He's the author of an autobiography entitled *Not So Wild a Dream.*

PERSONAL: Wife, Suzanne St. Pierre, Prod., CBS News.

SEVERINO, JOHN C.
Pres., ABC TV

c/o ABC, 1330 Ave. of the Americas, New York, NY 10019
b. November 29, 1936. New Haven, CT.

EDUCATION: University of Connecticut, B.A.

CAREER HIGHLIGHTS: Acct. Exec., WCSH-TV, Portland, ME ('63); same capacity for WBZ-AM, Boston ('64); joined ABC as Acct. Exec. at WABC ('65). Moved into spot sales in New York and Chicago for the network ('66); Sales Mgr. of the Chicago affiliate, WLS ('68); General Sales Mgr. of WLS, Chicago ('68); General Sales Mgr., ABC's Detroit station WXYZ ('69); V.P. and General Mgr., WLS ('70); transferred in same capacity to KABC, Los Angeles ('74); named Pres., ABC TV ('81).

ACHIEVEMENTS & AWARDS: Chicago Conference for Brotherhood award; Dante award, Chicago Area Joint Civic Committee of Italian-Americans; distinguished alumni award, University of Connecticut; Latinos media award. Pres., Hollywood Radio and TV Society; Trustee, NATAS ('82); Board of Dirs., California Broadcasters Assn.; Member: Los Angeles Better Business Bureau; Greater Los Angeles Visitors and Convention Bureau; Los Angeles Advisory Board of United Cerebral Palsy; Advisory Council, Dept. of Radio and TV, California State University.

PERSONAL: Wife, Sally Ann; sons, J. Mark and David.

SEVERINSEN, DOC
Music Dir., NBC, "The Tonight Show Starring Johnny Carson"

c/o NBC, 3000 W. Alameda Ave., Burbank, CA 91523
b. July 7, 1927. Arlington, OR.

EDUCATION: N.A.

CAREER HIGHLIGHTS: Joined NBC in New York ('49) as a Staff Musician working for Steve Allen, Dinah Shore, Kate Smith, and Eddie Fisher. Became a member of "The Tonight Show" orchestra ('62) and the Music Dir. for "The Tonight Show" ('67).

ACHIEVEMENTS & AWARDS: N.A.

PERSONAL: N.A.

SHAIMAN, LARRY
Reporter, WRC-TV, Washington, DC, News

c/o WRC-TV, 4001 Nebraska Ave., N.W., Washington, DC 20016
b. St. Louis, MO.

EDUCATION: Vanderbilt University, B.A., History; University of Missouri, M.A., Journalism.

CAREER HIGHLIGHTS: Reporter, WPLG-TV, Miami ('73); Reporter, KYW-TV, Philadelphia ('76); Reporter, WKYC-TV, Cleveland ('79); Reporter, WRC-TV, Washington, DC ('81).

ACHIEVEMENTS & AWARDS: Named AP best feature reporter in Florida ('74).

PERSONAL: Resides in Washington, DC.

SHAKER, TED
Exec. Prod., CBS, Sports

c/o CBS, 51 W. 52d St., New York, NY 10019
b. N.A.

EDUCATION: Allegheny College.

CAREER HIGHLIGHTS: Started at CBS as a Shipping Clerk ('73); Clerk for CBS News ('73); Asst. Prod., CBS News ('74); Assoc. Prod. for CBS Sports, "The NFL Today" ('78); promoted to Prod. ('80); further promoted to Exec. Prod. ('82); added responsibilities included the NCAA pre- and post-game shows; named Exec. Prod., NBA basketball telecasts ('83).

ACHIEVEMENTS & AWARDS: N.A.

PERSONAL: Resides in Rowayton, CT.

SHALES, TOM
TV Editor, Chief TV Critic, *Washington Post*

c/o Washington Post Writers Group, 1150 15th St., N.W., Washington, DC 20017
b. 1948. Elgin, IL.

EDUCATION: American University.

CAREER HIGHLIGHTS: Joined *Washington Post* as a Writer, Style Section ('72); named Chief TV Critic ('77) and appointed TV Editor ('79).

ACHIEVEMENTS & AWARDS: N.A.

PERSONAL: N.A.

SHALIT, GENE
On-Air Personality, NBC

c/o NBC, 30 Rockefeller Plaza, New York, NY 10020
b. 1932. New York, NY.

EDUCATION: University of Illinois.

CAREER HIGHLIGHTS: Joined NBC "Today" show as Book Reviewer ('69); became featured regular on "Today" providing movie reviews and interviews with top stars; added

responsibility as Host, of multi-part PBS series, "Mystery" ('80).

ACHIEVEMENTS & AWARDS: N.A.

PERSONAL: N.A.

SHARP, ROGER
Correspondent, WABC-TV, "Eyewitness News"

c/o WABC-TV, 7 Lincoln Sq., New York, NY 10023
b. N.A.

EDUCATION: Michigan State University, B.A., Journalism.

CAREER HIGHLIGHTS: Award-winning News Dir., KOTV, Tulsa, WEWS, Cleveland, and WTVT, Tampa. ABC Newswriter and Correspondent ('61); Freelance for RKO-General ('64); Exec. News Editor, CBS News; Correspondent, WABC-TV.

ACHIEVEMENTS & AWARDS: N.A.

PERSONAL: N.A.

SHATNER, WILLIAM
Actor

c/o "T. J. Hooker," ABC, 2040 Ave. of the Stars, Los Angeles, CA 90067
b. March 22, 1931. Montreal, Canada.

EDUCATION: McGill University, B.A.

CAREER HIGHLIGHTS: Always in charge of the situation, Shatner remains imperturbable whether driving his squad car on "T. J. Hooker" or flying the Enterprise in outer space on "Star Trek." Motion pictures include *Judgment at Nuremberg, The Intruder, Fright, Star Trek,* and *Star Trek: The Wrath of Khan.*

Broadway roles in *The World of Suzie Wong* and *A Shot in the Dark*. TV movies include *Sole Survivor, Vanished, The People, Go Ask Alice, Pioneer Woman, The Barbary Coast, The Bastard,* and *Little Women*. TV star of "T. J. Hooker" and "Star Trek."

ACHIEVEMENTS & AWARDS: N.A.

PERSONAL: Wife, actress Marcy Lafferty; three daughters from a previous marriage.

SHAW, BERNARD
Anchor/Correspondent, Cable News Network, Washington, DC, Bureau

17 Pine Ave., Takoma Park, MD 20912
b. May 22, 1940. Chicago, IL.

EDUCATION: University of Illinois.
CAREER HIGHLIGHTS: Anchor/Reporter, WYNR Radio, Chicago ('64); Newswriter WFLD-TV, Chicago ('65); Anchor and Education Reporter WIND-AM, Chicago ('66); White House Correspondent, Group W ('68); Correspondent, CBS News, Washington, DC Bureau ('71); Correspondent, ABC News ('77); Capitol Hill Correspondent, ABC News ('79); Principal Washington Anchor, Cable News Network ('80).
ACHIEVEMENTS & AWARDS: N.A.
PERSONAL: Wife, Linda; children, Amar Edgar and Anil Louise.

SHAYNE, ALAN
Pres., Warner Bros. TV Programming

9371 Beverlycrest Dr., Beverly Hills, CA 90216
b. Boston, MA.

EDUCATION: N.A.
CAREER HIGHLIGHTS: Acted on Broadway and on TV, then joined David Susskind's Talent Assoc. for eight years as Head of Casting and subsequently Prod., *House Without a Christmas Tree, Thanksgiving Treasure, Addie and the King of Hearts,* and *The Easter Promise* for CBS. Created "The Snoop Sisters" for NBC with Helen Hayes and Mildred Natwick. Worked as V.P., Creative Affairs, Warner Bros. ('72–'74); V.P., Talent, CBS ('75); Pres., Warner Bros. TV Programming ('75).
ACHIEVEMENTS & AWARDS: Christopher award for *House Without a Christmas Tree.*
PERSONAL: N.A.

SHEA, TIMOTHY M.
Project Mgr., Group W Cable, Chicago

c/o Group W Cable, Westinghouse Broadcasting and Cable, 888 Seventh Ave., New York, NY 10106
b. N.A.

EDUCATION: Worcester Polytechnic Institute; University of Pittsburgh; American University at Cairo; University of Massachusetts.
CAREER HIGHLIGHTS: Experience in project management at Westinghouse Electric Corp., Raytheon Corp., Bechtel Corp., and Holyoke Gas and Electric Co. before being named Chicago Project Mgr., Group W Cable ('83).
ACHIEVEMENTS & AWARDS: Holyoke Gas and Electric scholarship; official commendation from the Korea Electric Co., and a special Westinghouse management incentive award.
PERSONAL: N.A.

SHEAHAN, JOHN
Correspondent, CBS, News

c/o CBS, 524 W. 57th St., New York, NY 10019
b. Worcester, MA.

EDUCATION: Syracuse University; Carnegie Tech; University of Munich.
CAREER HIGHLIGHTS: News Dir., WORC-Radio; Freelance Reporter for Group W, the CBC, and UPI; Staff Prod./Reporter and CBS News Correspondent ('70).
ACHIEVEMENTS & AWARDS: N.A.
PERSONAL: N.A.

SHENKER, NEIL
Dir., Business Affairs, HBO, West Coast

c/o HBO, 1271 Ave. of the Americas, New York, NY 10020
b. New York, NY.

EDUCATION: New York University, B.A., English; Brooklyn Law School, J.D.
CAREER HIGHLIGHTS: Attorney, Motion Picture Division, Columbia Pictures, Burbank; Literary Agent, ICM, Los Angeles; Dir., Business Affairs, West Coast, NBC ('81); Dir., Business Affairs, West Coast, HBO ('83).
ACHIEVEMENTS & AWARDS: N.A.
PERSONAL: Resides in North Hollywood, CA.

SHEPARD, GARY
Correspondent, CBS, News

c/o CBS, 524 W. 57th St., New York, NY
10019
b. N.A.

EDUCATION: Boston University, B.A., History
('61)
CAREER HIGHLIGHTS: Writer/News Editor/Asst.
News Dir., WBZ-TV, Boston ('61); Reporter/
Anchor, WCAU-AM, Philadelphia ('64);
Writer/Reporter, CBS News ('66); Reporter,
CBS News ('69); Correspondent, CBS News,
New York ('71); Correspondent, CBS News,
Los Angeles ('80).
ACHIEVEMENTS & AWARDS: Natl. Safety Council
public service award ('68).
PERSONAL: Wife, Candace; sons, Jamie and
Christopher.

SHEPARD, STEVE
Correspondent, ABC, News

c/o ABC, 1717 De Sales St., N.W.,
Washington, DC 20036
b. N.A.

EDUCATION: Yale University, B.A.
CAREER HIGHLIGHTS: Announcer at WNAC-TV,
Boston ('71); named Reporter ('74); General
Assignment Reporter, WBBM-TV, Chicago
('78); joined ABC News as General Assign-
ment Reporter, Washington, DC, Bureau, re-
porting for "World News Tonight," "Night-
line," "Good Morning America" and ABC
Radio ('80).
ACHIEVEMENTS & AWARDS: Local Chicago
Emmy ('79).
PERSONAL: Married, two children.

SHEPHARD, HARVEY
Sr. V.P., Programs, CBS, Entertainment

c/o CBS, 6121 W. Sunset Blvd., Los Angeles,
CA 90028
b. 1937. New York, NY.

EDUCATION: City College of New York ('58).
CAREER HIGHLIGHTS: Assoc. Media Dir., Lennen & Newel advertising agency, New York
('64); Mgr., Audience Measurement, CBS
('67); Dir., Audience Measurement ('69); Dir.,

Program Projects ('73); V.P., Program Planning ('75); V.P., Programs, CBS Entertainment, New York ('77); V.P., Program Administration, CBS Entertainment, Los Angeles
('78); V.P., Programs ('80); Sr. V.P., Programs, CBS Entertainment ('82).
ACHIEVEMENTS & AWARDS: N.A.
PERSONAL: Resides in Los Angeles; two
daughters, two sons.

SHERLOCK, MICHAEL
**V.P., Finance and Administration, NBC,
Sports**

c/o NBC, 30 Rockefeller Plaza, New York, NY
10020
b. Syracuse, NY.

EDUCATION: St. Peter's Prep; LeMoyne Col-
lege.
CAREER HIGHLIGHTS: V.P., Administration, the
Hertz Corp.; V.P., Business Affairs and Ad-
ministration, NBC News ('77); V.P. in Charge
of Production Administration, NBC ('79);
V.P., Finance and Administration, NBC
Sports ('80).
ACHIEVEMENTS & AWARDS: N.A.
PERSONAL: Resides in Hasbrouck Heights, NJ,
with his wife, Ann, and their four children.

SHERR, LYNN
Correspondent, ABC, News

c/o ABC, 7 W. 66th St., New York, NY 10023
b. N.A.

EDUCATION: Wellesley College, B.A.
CAREER HIGHLIGHTS: Reporter and Editor for
Conde Nast Publications ('63); Reporter and
News Feature Writer for AP; WCBS-TV; On-
Air Correspondent for WNET and WETA and
principal Reporter/Anchor of PBS magazine
series "USA: People and Politics"; Corre-
spondent and Prod. of WNET's "The 51st
State Host, several "Woman Alive!" editions
on PBS; joined ABC ('77); reports the ABC
News/*Washington Post* Poll results and is a
Contributor, "World News Tonight"; Natl.
Correspondent, ABC.
ACHIEVEMENTS & AWARDS: Special Commend-
ation, AWRT, for "Women, Work and Sexual
Harassment," special assignment series on

"World News Tonight" ('79); Ohio State University award for "USA: People and Politics" golden award for journalism, Philadelphia's Golden Slipper Club ('80). Co-authored two books, published articles in various periodicals.

PERSONAL: Married to Lawrence Hilford.

SHORE, GARY
Meteorologist, WJLA-TV, Washington, DC, News

c/o WJLA-TV, 4461 Connecticut Ave., N.W., Washington, DC 20008
b. N.A.

EDUCATION: New York University, B.A., Meteorology; Pennsylvania State University, M.S., Meteorology.

CAREER HIGHLIGHTS: Meteorologist, KJRH-TV, Tulsa; Meteorologist, KARD-TV, Wichita, KS; Chief Meteorologist, WJLA-TV, Washington, DC ('82).

ACHIEVEMENTS & AWARDS: N.A.

PERSONAL: N.A.

SHULMAN, ROGER
Writer/Prod.

c/o Lew Weitzman, 9171 Wilshire Blvd., Suite 406, Beverly Hills, CA 90210
b. September 1, 1943. San Francisco, CA.

EDUCATION: University of California at Berkeley, B.A., and J.D., Law.

CAREER HIGHLIGHTS: Staff Writer, "The David Frost Revue" ('71); Staff Writer, "The Dean Martin Show" ('73); wrote episodes of "Love, American Style," "All in the Family," "The Jeffersons," "Good Times" ('73–'74); Story Editor, "Good Times" ('74–'76); Exec. Story Editor, "The Jeffersons" ('77–'78); Prod., "Three's Company" ('78–'79); Creator/Prod., pilots for "Fisherman's Wharf," "Dear Teacher," and "The High Five," Columbia Pictures TV ('79–'82).

ACHIEVEMENTS & AWARDS: Humanitas award finalist ('76, '78); Population Institute award finalist ('76); Los Angeles Venereal Disease Council award ('77).

PERSONAL: Wife, Donna; children, Darcy and Stephanie. Resides in Los Angeles.

SIDEL, ELLY
Dir. of Special Projects, Motion Pictures for TV and Mini-Series, CBS, Entertainment, East Coast

c/o CBS, 6121 Sunset Blvd., Los Angeles, CA 90028
b. Brooklyn, NY.

EDUCATION: Bennington College, B.A., Literature.

CAREER HIGHLIGHTS: Talent Agent, Wender & Assoc. ('70); Editor, Sr. Editor, Bantam Books ('72); V.P., Production, 20th Century Fox, East Coast ('79); Dir. of Special Projects, Motion Pictures for TV and Mini-Series, CBS Entertainment, East Coast ('81).

ACHIEVEMENTS & AWARDS: N.A.

PERSONAL: Resides in Manhattan; two children.

SIDER, DON
Managing Editor/V.P., Time Video Information Services

c/o Time Video Information Services, 1271 Ave. of the Americas, New York, NY 10020
b. January 11, 1933. Chicago, IL.

EDUCATION: University of Miami, B.A.

CAREER HIGHLIGHTS: Editor, Newsfeatures and Sunday Magazine, *St. Petersburg Times* ('56–'66). At Time, Inc., as *Time* magazine correspondent, Caribbean, Vietnam, Washington, DC; Bureau Chief in Detroit; News Editor in Washington, DC; Editor and V.P., Time, Inc., subsidiary, Pioneer Press, Publisher of 24 weeklies around Chicago; participant in launches of *Money* and *People* magazines; Managing editor/V.P., Time Video Information Services, teletext project.

ACHIEVEMENTS & AWARDS: Roy Howard award won by Pioneer Press effort to expose drug trafficking in Cook County forest preserves ('71)

PERSONAL: Three children, Todd, Dean, and Darby.

SIE, JOHN J.
Sr. V.P., Showtime Entertainment, Sales and Planning

c/o Showtime Entertainment, 1633 Broadway, New York, NY 10019

b. April 12, 1936. Kiang-Si, China.

EDUCATION: Manhattan College, M.E.E. ('57); Polytechnic Institute of Brooklyn, M.E.E. ('58).

CAREER HIGHLIGHTS: Sr. Member, RCA Technical Staff ('58); Pres., Micro State Electronics, subsidiary of Raytheon ('60); Consultant to aerospace industry ('70); V.P. and General Mgr., CATV Division, Jerrold Electronics ('72); Sr. V.P., Showtime Entertainment, in Sales and Planning Dept. ('77).

ACHIEVEMENTS & AWARDS: David Sarnoff Research Fellowship ('59); Board Member, CTAM ('79, '82); Robert H. Beisswenger memorial award, Natl. Cable TV Assn. ('82).

PERSONAL: Resides in Watchung, NJ, with wife, Anna; children, Deborah, James, Michelle, Allison, and Susan.

SIEBERT, CHARLES
Actor

c/o "Trapper John, M.D.," CBS, 7800 Beverly Blvd., Los Angeles, CA 90036.

b. May 9. Kenosha, WI.

EDUCATION: Marquette University.

CAREER HIGHLIGHTS: Broadway debut in *Jimmy Shine* ('68); daytime serial work in "Search for Tomorrow," "As the World Turns," and "Another World." Recurring roles in "One Day at a Time" and "The Blue Knight"; TV movies include *The Miracle Worker* and *The Seeding of Sarah Burns*. Series regular on "Trapper John, M.D."

ACHIEVEMENTS & AWARDS: N.A.

PERSONAL: Three children; resides in Pacific Palisades, CA.

SIEGEL, ANDREW M.
Sr. V.P., MBA-UA TV, Creative Affairs

10201 W. Washington Blvd., Culver City, CA 90230

b. November 18, 1941. Los Angeles, CA.

EDUCATION: University of California at Los Angeles, B.A. History.

CAREER HIGHLIGHTS: Production Asst. at 20th Century Fox ('66); Directors Guild Training Program ('67); joined ABC as Mgr., Movies of the Week ('72); Dir., Comedy Development ('73); V.P., Current Programs ('76); V.P., Comedy Development, CBS TV ('76); left for MTM Enterprises in same capacity ('80); joined UA TV as V.P., Creative Affairs ('82); appointed Sr. V.P., Creative Affairs for MGM-UA TV ('82).

ACHIEVEMENTS & AWARDS: N.A.

PERSONAL: Wife, Sharon; children, David, Julie, Holly, and Elizabeth.

SIEGEL, JOEL
Entertainment Critic, ABC

c/o ABC, 1 Lincoln Plaza, New York, NY 10023

b. Los Angeles, CA.

EDUCATION: University of California at Los Angeles, B.A.

CAREER HIGHLIGHTS: Held various positions including Radio Newscaster, Book Reviewer for *Los Angeles Times*, Freelance Writer, *Rolling Stone* and *Sports Illustrated*, Gag Writer for Sen. Robert Kennedy; Ad Agency Exec.; joined WCBS-TV as Feature Reporter and hosted "Joel Siegel's New York" on WCBS Radio ('72); WABC-TV Entertainment Critic ('76); began doing some work for the network's "Good Morning America" while maintaining responsibilities at WABC-TV.

ACHIEVEMENTS & AWARDS: Five Emmy awards; public service award, Anti-Defamation League of B'nai B'rith ('77); New York State AP Broadcasters award ('77). Wrote book of the Broadway musical *The First* about Jackie Robinson, which was nominated for a Tony award ('82).

PERSONAL: Resides in Manhattan.

SIEGENTHALER, ROBERT
V.P. and Exec. Prod., Special Events Coverage, ABC, News

c/o ABC, 7 W. 66th St., New York, NY 10023
b. N.A.

EDUCATION: Xavier University.
CAREER HIGHLIGHTS: During a 21-year career with ABC News, has held major executive posts including Exec. Prod., Evening News; Exec. Prod., Special Events; Exec. Prod. of Instant News Specials and of "America Held Hostage," the forerunner of "Nightline." Represented ABC News in three-network pool coverage as Chairman of Pool Committee for Pres. Richard M. Nixon's trip to China ('72); Pool Prod. for Nixon impeachment hearings ('74); Writer/Prod. of more than 24 documentaries including "America Lives—American Honor" ('72); "Years of Anguish, Day of Peace" ('73) and "Lessons Learned, Prices Paid" ('75); named Exec. Prod. of News Specials ('80); appointed V.P., ABC News ('82); maintains responsibilities as Exec. Prod. of ABC News Special Events Coverage.
ACHIEVEMENTS & AWARDS: N.A.
PERSONAL: Resides in Harrington Park, NJ, with wife, Anita.

SIEGLER, SCOTT MERRILL
Sr. V.P., Warner Bros. TV, Creative Affairs

c/o Warner Bros. TV, 4000 Warner Blvd., Burbank, CA 91505
b. February 15, 1947. Columbus, OH.

EDUCATION: Union College, B.A.; University of Toronto, M.A.; Brandeis University, M.F.A.
CAREER HIGHLIGHTS: Prod./Writer/Dir. for WGBH TV Documentary Unit ('72); did same for WAVE-TV, Louisville, KY ('73); moved to WKYC, Cleveland, in same capacity ('77). Asst. Prod., *The Manitou*, for Avco-Embassy ('78); Assoc. Prod. with Mel Simon Productions on *Cloud Dancer* ('79); joined NBC TV as Mgr., Current Drama ('79). Moved to CBS as Dir., Drama Development ('80); V.P., Comedy Development ('82). Left network for Warner Bros. TV as Sr. V.P., Creative Affairs ('82).
ACHIEVEMENTS & AWARDS: Emmy award for best documentary ('74).
PERSONAL: N.A.

SIKKING, JAMES B.
Actor

c/o "Hill Street Blues," NBC, 3000 W. Alameda Ave., Burbank, CA 91523
b. March 5. Los Angeles, CA.

EDUCATION: University of California at Los Angeles, B.A.
CAREER HIGHLIGHTS: Regular on the daytime drama "General Hospital"; co-star of the series "Turnabout." Motion pictures include *Ordinary People, Outland, The Electric Horseman,* and *The New Centurions*. TV series regular on "Hill Street Blues."
ACHIEVEMENTS & AWARDS: N.A.
PERSONAL: N.A.

SILBERLING, ROBERT M.
V.P., Motion Pictures for TV, CBS, Entertainment

c/o CBS, 7800 Beverly Blvd., Los Angeles, CA 90036
b. Brooklyn, NY.

EDUCATION: University of California at Los Angeles, B.A., Theater Arts.
CAREER HIGHLIGHTS: Motion Picture Project Supervisor, U.S. Information Agency; T&L Productions; Program Exec. and Dir., "ABC Suspense Movie," "Movie of the Week"; Dir., Current Prime Time Comedy Programs, ABC Entertainment; joined CBS as Dir., Comedy Program Development ('76); appointed V.P., Dramatic Program Development ('77); V.P., Motion Pictures for TV ('82).
ACHIEVEMENTS & AWARDS: N.A.
PERSONAL: Resides in Studio City, CA; wife and two children.

SILVERMAN, FRED
Exec.

c/o Intermedia Entertainment, 10210 Washington Blvd., Culver City, CA 90210
b. September, 1937. New York, NY.

EDUCATION: Syracuse University, Ohio State University.
CAREER HIGHLIGHTS: During his reign at NBC, Silverman was unable to improve NBC's ratings slump, but he must be remembered as

the program planning master who helped bring ABC into first place in the ratings race, and who previously had been responsible for many of CBS's biggest hits. In addition to developing pilot projects for network TV, Silverman is developing a new cable channel called Magicable and is promoting a talk show personality, Alan Thicke, set to compete against Johnny Carson's "Tonight Show." The only man to run all three network's Entertainment Divisions, he was Dir. of CBS Daytime Programming ('63). Became Head of Programming ('70) and is credited with the development of "Kojak," "All in the Family," "M*A*S*H," "The Waltons," "Maude," "Rhoda," "Good Times," and "The Jeffersons." Pres., ABC Entertainment ('75) Pres. and Chief Exec. Officer, NBC, Inc. ('78). Formed his own independent production company, Intermedia Entertainment ('82), producing TV pilots in conjunction with MGM TV ('83); also producing the NBC series "We Got It Made" ('83).

ACHIEVEMENTS & AWARDS:　N.A.

PERSONAL:　Wife, Cathy; children, Melissa and William. Resides in Manhattan and Beverly Hills, CA.

SILVERMAN, PETE
Exec. Prod., Madison Square Garden Network

c/o Madison Square Garden Network, 4 Pennsylvania Plaza, New York, NY 10001
b. April 11, 1947.

EDUCATION:　Georgetown University, B.A.; Emory College, M.A. ('70).

CAREER HIGHLIGHTS:　Exec. Prod., the Philadelphia Flyers game announcer responsible for

the production of Canada Cup ('81) and two NHL All-Star games. Spent four years as an announcer on Flyers games and has broadcast a number of other sporting events. Also hosted a nightly radio sports show following Flyer and Philadelphia Phillies baseball games when he served as the Sports Dir., WCAU-Radio. Currently Exec. Prod., Madison Square Garden Network, responsible for the game-by-game presentation of all live sports events telecast on the Madison Square Garden Network.

ACHIEVEMENTS & AWARDS:　N.A.

PERSONAL:　N.A.

SILVESTRI, JOHN
V.P. Sales, Hearst/ABC

c/o Hearst/ABC, 555 Fifth Ave., New York, NY 10017
b. Detroit, MI.

EDUCATION:　Wayne State University, B.A. and M.A.

CAREER HIGHLIGHTS:　Worked in Advertising and Public Relations Depts. at Uniroyal ('65); Sales Mgr., WWJ Radio-TV ('68); Dir., TV Net Sales, NBC ('71); V.P. Sales, Hearst/ABC ('81).

ACHIEVEMENTS & AWARDS:　N.A.

PERSONAL:　Married, three children. Resides in Wheaton, IL.

SIMMONS, RICHARD
Host, "The Richard Simmons Show"

c/o WABC-TV, 7 Lincoln Plaza, New York, NY 10023
b. New Orleans, LA.

EDUCATION:　Florida State University.

CAREER HIGHLIGHTS:　Marketing Dir., Coty and Dina Merrill Toiletries; Co-Owner, Beverly Hills Restaurant–Exercise Studio and now Teacher, at his Anatomy Asylum studio. Host, "The Richard Simmons Show," a popular syndicated exercise and nutrition program. Flamboyant, exuberant style made his show a big hit in the early eighties among daytime audiences.

ACHIEVEMENTS & AWARDS:　Author of *Not Just Another Head of Lettuce* and *Never Say Diet.*

PERSONAL:　Resides in Beverly Hills, CA.

SIMMONS, SUE
Reporter/Anchor, WNBC-TV, "Live at Five"

c/o WNBC-TV, 30 Rockefeller Plaza, New
    York, NY 10020
b. New York.

EDUCATION: N.A.
CAREER HIGHLIGHTS: Began as a Reporter,
    WTNH-TV in New Haven, CT ('73). Moved to
    WBAL-TV, Baltimore ('74). Joined WRC-TV,
    Washington, DC ('76) as a Reporter and Host
    of two public affairs series. Joined WNBC-TV
    ('80) as Co-Anchor of the station's early news-
    cast, "Live at Five," as well as its 11 P.M.
    report.
ACHIEVEMENTS & AWARDS: Emmy at WBAL-TV;
    award for outstanding performance by a
    news commentator from the New York Cul-
    tural Center ('81).
PERSONAL: Resides in New York City.

SIMON, ALBERT J.
V.P., Tape Production, ABC, West Coast

c/o ABC, 4151 Prospect Ave., Los Angeles,
    CA 90027
b. N.A.

EDUCATION: N.A.
CAREER HIGHLIGHTS: Unit Mgr., ABC ('63);
    Freelance Assoc. Prod., "Hollywood Palace,"
    "Tom Jones," and the "Julie Andrews Spe-
    cial" ('69); Dir., Tape Production, Columbia
    Pictures TV ('72); Freelance Assoc. Prod. for
    the John Denver specials, *Victory at Entebbe*
    and "CBS on the Air, 50th Anniversary Spe-
    cial" ('75); V.P., Tape Production, West
    Coast, ABC ('78).
ACHIEVEMENTS & AWARDS: N.A.
PERSONAL: N.A.

SIMON, ANNE
Sideline Reporter and Feature Contributor,
ABC, Sports

c/o ABC, 1330 Ave. of the Americas, New
    York, NY 10019
b. N.A.

EDUCATION: State University of Buffalo.
CAREER HIGHLIGHTS: Writer/Sports Reporter,
    WKBW-TV, Buffalo, NY ('78); Sports Re-
    porter, WWL-TV, New Orleans ('81); Sideline
    Reporter and Feature Contributor, ABC
    Sports ('82).
ACHIEVEMENTS & AWARDS: N.A.
PERSONAL: N.A.

SIMON, ARTHUR
Dir., Marketing, Warner Amex Cable
Communications, Commercial Services

c/o Warner Amex Cable Communications, 75
    Rockefeller Plaza, New York, NY 10019
b. March 16, 1951.

EDUCATION: Brooklyn College.
CAREER HIGHLIGHTS: Mgr., Marketing, Xerox;
    Mgr. of Data Communications Services for
    Manhattan Cable TV; Dir., Marketing, Com-
    mercial Services, Warner Amex Cable Com-
    munications ('83).
ACHIEVEMENTS & AWARDS: N.A.
PERSONAL: N.A.

SIMON, RONALD C.
Curator, Museum of Broadcasting

c/o Museum of Broadcasting, 1 E. 53d St.,
    New York, NY 10022
b. February 23, 1951.

EDUCATION: Dickinson College, B.A., English
    Literature ('73); Columbia University, M.F.A.
CAREER HIGHLIGHTS: Freelance Writer ('75);
    News Asst., WNYC-TV, New York ('75); Re-
    searcher, NBC, New York ('76); Media Coor-
    dinator, First Boston Corp., New York ('77);
    Special Projects Supervisor/Asst. Curator,
    Museum of Broadcasting, New York ('78);
    Mgr., Public Relations, Museum of Broad-
    casting ('80); Curator, Museum of Broadcast-
    ing, New York ('82).

ACHIEVEMENTS & AWARDS: N.A.
PERSONAL: Resides in New York City.

SIMONS, SUSAN
Mgr., Daytime Programs, NBC, Entertainment, West Coast

c/o NBC, 3000 W. Alameda Ave., Burbank, CA 91523
b. Lincoln, NE.

EDUCATION: San Fernando Valley State College.
CAREER HIGHLIGHTS: Production Asst. on the game show "You Don't Say" ('66); Production Asst., "It Takes Two" ('69); Assoc. Prod., "It's Your Bet"; Production Asst., "The Don Knotts Variety Show"; Production Asst. for the Bob Hope specials, including the ones originating from Vietnam ('71); worked on game shows such as "Hollywood Squares" for Heatter-Quigley Productions ('73); Administrator, Compliances and Practices, NBC ('74); Mgr., Compliances and Practices, NBC ('78); Mgr., Daytime Programs, NBC Entertainment, West Coast ('80).
ACHIEVEMENTS & AWARDS: N.A.
PERSONAL: Single, resides in Burbank.

SIMPSON, CAROLE
Correspondent, ABC, News

c/o ABC, 1717 DeSales St., N.W., Washington, DC 20036
b. N.A.

EDUCATION: N.A.
CAREER HIGHLIGHTS: WBBM and WCFL-Radio, Chicago; General Assignment Reporter and Anchor, WMAQ ('70); NBC News Washington, DC, Correspondent ('75); joined ABC as General Assignment Correspondent, Washington, DC ('82).
ACHIEVEMENTS & AWARDS: N.A.
PERSONAL: N.A.

SIMPSON, JIM
Sportscaster, ESPN

7501 Radnor Rd., Bethesda, MD 20817
b. December 20, 1927. Washington, DC.

EDUCATION: George Washington University; University of California at Los Angeles.
CAREER HIGHLIGHTS: WTOP, Washington, DC ('50); WRC, Washington, DC ('52); CBS Play-by-Play Commentator for Football ('62); same position at ABC ('60) and then NBC ('64); joined ESPN as Play-by-Play Announcer and Talk Show Host ('79).
ACHIEVEMENTS & AWARDS: Three local Emmy awards at WTOP and WRC; NAB award as best sportscaster, Washington, DC.
PERSONAL: Wife, Sara; five children.

SINGER, ALEXANDER
Dir.

c/o ICM, 8899 Beverly Blvd., Los Angeles, CA 90048
b. N.A.

EDUCATION: N.A.
CAREER HIGHLIGHTS: Has directed features including *A Cold Wind in August, Psyche '59, Love Has Many Faces, Glass Houses*; episodes of "Cagney and Lacey," "Knots Landing," "The Secrets of Midland Heights," "Dallas," "Lou Grant," "Police Story," "The Bold Ones," "Quincy," "Logan's Run," "Police Woman," and "Paris"; pilots of "Falcon Crest," "Spanner's Reef," "Time Travellers," "Dr. Durant," and "Bunko"; and two movies for TV, *Million Dollar Heist* and *Man Undercover*.
ACHIEVEMENTS & AWARDS: Emmy awards for

directing episodes of "Lou Grant," "The Bold Ones," and "Police Story."

PERSONAL: N.A.

SINGER, AUBREY
Managing Dir., BBC, TV

c/o BBC, 12 Cavendish Place, London, England W1
b. January 21, 1927. Bradford, England.

EDUCATION: Giggleswick School.
CAREER HIGHLIGHTS: Production Asst., TV Outside Broadcasts, BBC ('49); Prod., BBC, Scotland ('52); BBC Sales, New York ('53); Prod., BBC Outside Broadcasts ('56); Head of Features Group, BBC ('67); Controller, BBC-2 ('74); Managing Dir., BBC Radio ('78); Managing Dir., TV, and Deputy Dir. General, BBC ('82).
ACHIEVEMENTS & AWARDS: N.A.
PERSONAL: Married, four children.

SINGER, CARLA
V.P., Dramatic Program Development, CBS, Entertainment

c/o CBS, 51 W. 52d St., New York, NY 10019
b. N.A.

EDUCATION: Brandeis University, B.A.; Hebrew University (Israel), M.A.
CAREER HIGHLIGHTS: Worked in various capacities for KDKA-TV, Pittsburgh, BBC and CBC; Prod. "Everyday" for Group W Productions ('78); Dir., Dramatic Program Development, CBS Entertainment ('80); promoted to V.P. ('82).
ACHIEVEMENTS & AWARDS: N.A.
PERSONAL: Single, resides in Los Angeles.

SINGER, DULCY
Exec. Prod., Children's Television Workshop, "Sesame Street"

c/o Children's Television Workshop, 1 Lincoln Plaza, New York, NY 10023
b. New York, NY.

EDUCATION: Mount Holyoke College.
CAREER HIGHLIGHTS: Her TV career began at CBS, where she was a Member, Production Staff, "The Garry Moore Show," "The Entertainers," and "The Secret Storm"; Assoc. Prod., Public Broadcasting Laboratory; Assoc. Prod., "Sesame Street"; Prod., "Christmas Eve on Sesame Street."
ACHIEVEMENTS & AWARDS: Emmy for outstanding children's program ('79).
PERSONAL: N.A.

SINGER, MAURICE
V.P., HBO, Pre-Production Acquisition

c/o HBO, 2049 Century Park E., Suite 4170, Los Angeles, CA 90067
b. June 8, 1941.

EDUCATION: University of Vermont, B.A.
CAREER HIGHLIGHTS: Dir. of Production, Group W Films; V.P. in Charge of Studio Affairs and Sr. Exec. in Charge of Creative Affairs, Columbia Pictures; Pres. of Maurice Singer Productions, an independent movie production and development company; joined HBO as V.P., Pre-Production Acquisition ('82).
ACHIEVEMENTS & AWARDS: N.A.
PERSONAL: Resides in Beverly Hills, CA, with wife, Judith.

SINGER, STEVE
Prod., ABC, News Documentary Unit

c/o ABC, 7 W. 66th St., New York, NY 10023
b. N.A.

EDUCATION: Cornell University, B.A.
CAREER HIGHLIGHTS: He began his news career at the *Cornell University Daily Sun* ('61–'64); Reporter, *Boston Herald* ('67); Reporter/Photographer, *Rockland County Journal-News,* New York ('67); Press Aide, U.S. Rep. John G. Dow, New York ('68); Reporter, Photog-

rapher, *Riverside Press-Enterprise*, California ('69); Reporter, *Houston Chronicle* ('69); Prod. and Investigative Reporter, KERA-TV, Dallas; Prod. and Writer, "CBS Reports" Documentary Unit; Prod., ABC News "Closeup" Documentary Unit ('80).

ACHIEVEMENTS & AWARDS: Documentary *The Killing Ground* earned an Academy Award nomination ('80), two Emmy awards and the Prince Rainier prize at the Monte Carlo Film Festival; *A Thirst in the Garden*, a documentary for which he was producer, writer, and reporter, won the Peabody award. Twice honored by the Dallas Press Club for best documentary and won a first and second place award in the best local documentary category at the Chicago Intl. Film Festival. Named a Walter Lippmann Fellow in economics by the Ford Foundation.

PERSONAL: Resides in Brooklyn, NY.

SIRKIN, BOB
Correspondent, ABC, News, Atlanta

c/o ABC, 7 W. 66th St., New York, NY 10023
b. N.A.

EDUCATION: Morris Harvey College; University of Maryland.

CAREER HIGHLIGHTS: Reporter/Anchor, WHNB-TV, Hartford, CT; WBTV and WBT-Radio, Charlotte, NC ('71); KDFW-TV, Dallas ('72); WFAA-TV, Dallas ('73); named ABC News Correspondent, Atlanta ('77).

ACHIEVEMENTS & AWARDS: Katie award, Dallas Press Club ('74); Texas Medical Assn. award ('76); Dupont award ('77); Dallas Press Club award of excellence for investigative reporting and spot news coverage ('77).

PERSONAL: Married, two children.

SISK, JOHN (John J. Sisk Jr.)
Sr. V.P. and Dir., J. Walter Thompson, Network Negotiations

466 Lexington Ave., New York, NY 10017
b. July 26, 1929. New York.

EDUCATION: Iona College, B.A. ('51).

CAREER HIGHLIGHTS: Time Buyer, Al Paul Lefton Co. ('53); Network Buyer, Kudner Agency ('54); Sr. V.P. and Dir., Network Negotiations, J. Walter Thompson ('56).

ACHIEVEMENTS & AWARDS: N.A.

PERSONAL: Wife, Margaret; two daughters. Resides in Bayside, Queens.

SKAGGS, CALVIN
V.P., Prod., Learning in Focus

c/o Learning in Focus, 310 Madison Ave., New York, NY
b. N.A.

EDUCATION: Duke University, M.A. and Ph.D., English.

CAREER HIGHLIGHTS: Professor of English and Cinema, Drew University ('70–'75); Dir., off-Broadway plays; Assoc. Prod. and Literary Adviser, six hour-long films for TV in "The American Short Story" series I; Series Prod. and Literary Adviser for the eight hour-long films in "The American Short Story," series II; V.P., Prod., Learning in Focus.

ACHIEVEMENTS & AWARDS: Editor, *The American Short Story*, vol. I–II, Dell Publishing Co.

PERSONAL: Married; two children.

SKLOVER, THEODORA K.
Consultant Prod.

433 E. 51st St., New York, NY 10022
b. N.A.

EDUCATION: Bennington College, B.A., Social Science.

CAREER HIGHLIGHTS: Consultant, New York Cultural Council, Creative Artists Public Service Program ('68); Founder and Exec. Dir., Open Channel ('71); Exec. Dir., Governor of the State of New York's Office for Motion Picture and TV Development ('76); Consultant Prod. for WNET-TV, New York; New York University; Brooklyn Academy of Music; and the Boston Redevelopment Authority ('81).

ACHIEVEMENTS & AWARDS: N.A.

PERSONAL: N.A.

SLAKOFF, MORTON A.
V.P., MCA TV, Creative Services

445 Park Ave., New York, NY.
b. February 13, 1934. Philadelphia, PA.

EDUCATION: Pennsylvania State University, B.A.; University of Iowa, M.A.

CAREER HIGHLIGHTS: Merchandising Mgr. for the Triangle Stations, Philadelphia ('57); Mgr., Sales Promotion, WNTA TV ('59); Dir. of Advertising, Promotion, NBC Films ('61); Dir., Advertising, Promotion, MPC ('66); Dir. of Advertising, Promotion, Time-Life Films ('69); Dir., Creative Services, Viacom ('71); V.P., Creative Services, Metromedia TV ('77); V.P., Creative Services, MCA TV ('81).

ACHIEVEMENTS & AWARDS: Member, Board of Dirs., Broadcasters Promotion Assn.

PERSONAL: Resides in New York City; wife, Rhoda; daughter, Susan; son, Marc.

SLATER, GERALD
Exec. V.P., WETA-TV/AM, Washington, DC

c/o WETA, Box 2626, Washington, DC 20013
b. June 4, 1933.

EDUCATION: New York University, B.S., Business Administration ('55).

CAREER HIGHLIGHTS: Administrator, Planning and Scheduling, CBS ('57); Network Supervisor, CBS ('58); Production Supervisor, CBS ('62); Mgr. of News Production Services, CBS News ('64); Dir. of Operations, Public Broadcasting Laboratory ('67); Project Specialist, Communications, Ford Foundation ('69); General Mgr., PBS ('70); V.P., Broadcasting, PBS ('73); Exec. V.P., WETA-TV/AM, Washington, DC ('75).

ACHIEVEMENTS & AWARDS: N.A.

PERSONAL: Resides in Washington, DC.

SLATTERY, JOHN
Correspondent, WABC-TV, "Eyewitness News"

c/o WABC-TV, 7 Lincoln Sq., New York, NY 10023
b. Springfield, MO.

EDUCATION: Xavier University, B.A., Economics.

CAREER HIGHLIGHTS: Staff Announcer, WSWT, Peoria, IL ('72); Reporter for WCBS and WMAY; General Assignment Reporter for WCIA-TV, Urbana, IL, and WCAU-TV, Philadelphia ('75); Correspondent, WABC-TV, New York.

ACHIEVEMENTS & AWARDS: Awards from the Pennsylvania AP Broadcasters and the Philadelphia Press Assn. for best spot news coverage.

PERSONAL: Married; two children. Resides in Westchester, NY.

SMALL, WILLIAM J.
Pres./Chief Operating Officer, UPI

c/o UPI, 220 E. 42d St., New York, NY 10017
b. September 20, 1926.

EDUCATION: University of Chicago, master's.

CAREER HIGHLIGHTS: Washington Bureau Mgr., CBS News ('62); Sr. V.P., Dir. of News, CBS ('74); V.P., Washington, CBS, Inc. ('78). Joined NBC as Pres. ('79), responsible for the NBC News "Nightly News" broadcast, the daily "Today" program, other TV news and documentary programs, and an extensive radio news network.

ACHIEVEMENTS & AWARDS: The Wells memorial key award; the Paul White memorial award of RTNDA, and the Natl. Headliners award.

PERSONAL: Married; two daughters.

SMILEY, CHARLES A., JR.
V.P. and Asst. to Sr. V.P., ABC, TV and Theatrical Affairs, Entertainment

c/o 2040 Ave. of the Stars, Century City, CA 90068
b. 1943. Louisville, KY.

EDUCATION: University of Michigan, B.S. ('64); Brooklyn Law School, LL.D. ('68).

CAREER HIGHLIGHTS: Sr. Counsel for Proctor & Gamble's Operating Division ('69); Sr. Attorney for Entertainment, CBS Law Dept. ('70); ABC Sports Dir., Legal and Business Affairs ('73); named V.P. ('76); V.P. and Asst. to the Sr. V.P., TV and Theatrical Affairs, ABC Entertainment ('79), with responsibilities for business negotiations for all primetime and late-night programming and talent, mini-series, made for TV movies, and late-night network projects.

ACHIEVEMENTS & AWARDS: Black Achiever in Industry award, Harlem Branch of YMCA of Greater New York ('74); Pres., Huntington Branch, NAACP ('74); Trustee, Fraternity of Recording Execs., New York; listed in *Who's Who in Black America* ('75). Member of the Ohio Bar ('69); U.S. Patent Bar ('70); New York State Bar ('71); Guest Lecturer at New York University School of Law ('74); Lehman College ('75).

PERSONAL: Resides in Brentwood, CA, with wife, Barbara; children, Chad and Brooke.

SMITH, ANTHONY
Dir., British Film Institute

c/o British Film Institute, 127 Charing Cross Rd., London WC2H0EA
b. N.A.

EDUCATION: University of Oxford (England), B.A. ('60).

CAREER HIGHLIGHTS: Prod., BBC current affairs programs ('60–'71). Editor, BBC "Twenty Four Hours" ('68–'71). Joined British Film Institute as Dir. ('79). After leaving the BBC and before assuming the top position with the British Film Institute, Smith wrote numerous books and dozens of articles dealing with print and broadcast media. He produced and moderated an excellent documentary for the BBC in the early 80's called "Goodbye Gutenberg."

ACHIEVEMENTS & AWARDS: Leverhulme Fellowship ('71–'75).

PERSONAL: N.A.

SMITH, APRIL
Prod./Writer, CBS, Entertainment

c/o CBS, 7800 Beverly Blvd., Los Angeles, CA 90036
b. New York, NY.

EDUCATION: Boston College; Stanford University.

CAREER HIGHLIGHTS: Writer, "James at 15" ('78); Writer, "Family" ('79); Writer, "Lou Grant" ('80); Writer/Story Editor, "Lou Grant" ('81); Prod./Writer, "Cagney and Lacey" ('82).

ACHIEVEMENTS & AWARDS: N.A.

PERSONAL: Resides in Los Angeles.

SMITH, DORRANCE
Exec. Prod., ABC, News

1800 Old Meadow Road, McLean, VA 22102
b. May 25, 1951. Houston, TX.

EDUCATION: Claremont Men's College, B.A.

CAREER HIGHLIGHTS: Asst. to the Prod., ABC Sports ('73); Mgr., Program Planning, "Wide World of Sports" ('74); Staff Asst. to Pres. Gerald Ford ('75–'77). Returned to ABC as Prod., ABC News ('77); Exec. Prod., Week-end News ('79); named Exec. Prod., "This Week With David Brinkley" ('81).

ACHIEVEMENTS & AWARDS: N.A.

PERSONAL: Resides in McLean, VA.

SMITH, DOW C.
V.P. and Station Mgr., WJLA-TV, Washington, DC

c/o WJLA-TV, 4461 Connecticut Ave., N.W., Washington, DC 20008
b. June 23, 1940.

EDUCATION: University of the Pacific, B.A., Business Administration; University of Missouri School of Journalism, M.A.

CAREER HIGHLIGHTS: Prod., KOVR-TV, Sacramento, CA; Exec. Prod., WBBM-TV, Chicago; Assignments Mgr., KNXT-TV, Los Angeles; Asst. News Dir., KPIX-TV, San Francisco; News Dir., WPLG-TV, Miami ('77); Exec. News Dir., WJLA-TV, Washington, DC ('80); V.P., WJLA-TV ('81); V.P. and Station Mgr., WJLA-TV ('82).

ACHIEVEMENTS & AWARDS: N.A.

PERSONAL: Resides in Potomac, MD, with wife, Bonnie; four children.

SMITH, GARY
Prod., Smith-Hemion Productions

c/o Smith-Hemion Productions, 9255 Sunset
Blvd., Los Angeles, CA 90048
b. January 7, 1935.

EDUCATION: Carnegie-Mellon University, B.A.
('56).
CAREER HIGHLIGHTS: Art Dir., "The Andy Williams Show," "The Perry Como Show" ('59);
Art. Dir. and Assoc. Prod., "The Judy Garland Show." Prod. of "Hullaballoo" series;
formed the Yorkshire Production Co. with
partner Dwight Hemion and produced 100
TV specials as well as "Kraft Music Hall." As
part of Smith-Hemion Productions, he produced such specials as "Barbra Streisand and
Other Musical Instruments," "Ann-Margret
Smith," "Ann-Margret Olson," a new musical version of "Peter Pan with Mia Farrow,"
"America Salutes Richard Rodgers," "The
Bette Midler Special," "Elvis Presley in Concert," and "Baryshnikov on Broadway,"
among many others.
ACHIEVEMENTS & AWARDS: Christopher awards
for "Peter Pan" ('76), "Baryshnikov on Broad-
way" ('79), and "Uptown: A Musical Comedy
History of Harlem's Apollo Theater." Emmy
award for art direction for "Kraft Musical
Hall" ('61) and five Emmy awards for out-
standing musical special for "Singer Presents
Burt Bacharach" ('70), "Barbra Streisand and
Other Musical Instruments ('73), "Bette Mid-
ler, Ol' Red Hair Is Back" ('77), "Steve and
Eydie Celebrate Irving Berlin" ('78), and
"Baryshnikov on Broadway" ('79).
PERSONAL: N.A.

SMITH, HARRY E.
V.P., New Venture Development, CBS, Inc.

c/o CBS, 51 W. 52d St., New York, NY 10019
b. N.A.

EDUCATION: Purdue University, B.S., Engineering ('50).
CAREER HIGHLIGHTS: Mgr., Marketing and Advertising, General Electric ('50); V.P., Marketing, Electronic Video Recording Division,
CBS, Inc. ('70); Dir., Technology, CBS ('73);
V.P., Technology, CBS ('74); V.P., Planning,
CBS, Inc. ('77); V.P., New Venture Development, CBS, Inc. ('82).

ACHIEVEMENTS & AWARDS: N.A.
PERSONAL: Resides in Ridgewood, NJ.

SMITH, HOWARD K.
News Commentator and Host, ABC, News

c/o ABC, 1330 Ave. of the Americas, New
York, NY 10019
b. May 12, 1914. Ferriday, LA.

EDUCATION: Tulane University ('36); Heidel-
berg University ('36); University of Oxford
(Rhodes Scholar, '39).
CAREER HIGHLIGHTS: Began working for UPI,
Copenhagen ('39); worked for UPI, Berlin
('40); Correspondent, CBS News, Berlin ('41);
Chief European Correspondent, CBS ('41);
Washington, DC, Correspondent, CBS News
('57); Chief Correspondent and Mgr., CBS
News, Washington, DC, Bureau ('61); Reporter and Anchor, ABC TV and Radio Networks ('61); News Commentator, ABC ('79);
Host, "ABC News Closeup" ('79). Retired
('79).
ACHIEVEMENTS & AWARDS: Peabody award
('60); Emmy for writing "CBS Reports: The
Population Explosion" ('61); Overseas Press
Club award for TV interpretation of foreign
affairs ('67); Paul White memorial award ('61);
Dupont commentator award ('62); first journalist to interview Pres. Richard M. Nixon
live in a one-to-one format ('71); only journalist to address the House of Representatives,
special congressional honoree for his contribution to American journalism; author of
*Last Train From Berlin, The State of Europe,
Washington, D.C.*
PERSONAL: Wife, Benedicte; two children, Jack
and Catherine.

SMITH, JACLYN
Actress

c/o ABC, 2040 Ave. of the Stars, Los Angeles,
Ca 90067
b. October 26, 1947. Houston, TX.

EDUCATION: Trinity University.
CAREER HIGHLIGHTS: The most ravishing of
"Charlie's Angels," Smith has kept her TV
stardom alive by shrewdly choosing roles
within her range, such as that in *Rage of An-*

gels. Guest star "The Rookies," "McCloud," and "Switch." Series star of "Charlie's Angels." TV movies include *Escape From Bergen County, Night Kill, The Users*, and *Rage of Angels*.

ACHIEVEMENTS & AWARDS: N.A.

PERSONAL: Resides in Beverly Hills, CA.

SMITH, JACQUELINE
V.P., ABC, Daytime Programs, Entertainment

c/o ABC, 1330 Ave. of the Americas, New York, NY 10019

b. May 24, 1933. Philadelphia, PA.

EDUCATION: Antioch College.

CAREER HIGHLIGHTS: Has had major impact in ABC's emergence as the leader in daytime network TV; also initiated CBS Children's Film Festival. Writer/Prod., KPIX; Dir. of On-Air Promotion, WPIX-TV; joined CBS TV Network as Exec. Prod., Daytime Programs ('63); Dir. of Special Projects for Warner Bros. ('71); Dir. Special Programs, CBS TV Network, Hollywood ('74); V.P., Daytime Programs, ABC Entertainment ('77). Under her supervision, the first public service series on network TV, "FYI" was added to ABC's daytime schedule.

ACHIEVEMENTS & AWARDS: Under her supervision, ABC daytime programs won 10 Emmy awards ('81–'82); inducted into YWCA Academy of Woman Achievers ('82).

PERSONAL: Resides in Manhattan; two children.

SMITH, JERRY
Exec. V.P., Home Theater Network, Marketing

c/o Home Theater Network, 90 Park Ave., New York, NY 10016

b. New York, NY.

EDUCATION: Middlebury College, B.A.; Carnegie-Mellon University, M.F.A.

CAREER HIGHLIGHTS: Acct. Exec., 20th Century Fox TV ('62); Sr. V.P., Natl. Sales Mgr., ABC Films ('65); Partner/Stockholder, Worldvision Enterprises ('73); Pres., Smith TV Assoc.

('81); Exec. V.P., Marketing, Home Theater Network ('82).

ACHIEVEMENTS & AWARDS: Member, NATPE.

PERSONAL: N.A.

SMITH, JOE
Pres. and Chief Exec. Officer, Warner Amex Cable Communications, Home Entertainment Network

c/o Warner Amex, 75 Rockefeller Plaza, New York, NY 10019

b. Chelsea, MA.

EDUCATION: Yale University.

CAREER HIGHLIGHTS: Began as a Disc Jockey, Virginia and Pennsylvania, before becoming a hit as a Disc Jockey, WMEX-AM, Boston ('57); Publicist, Warner Bros. Records, New York ('60); Natl. Promotion Mgr., Warner Bros. Records ('61); V.P., Warner Bros./Reprise Records ('68); Exec. V.P. and General Mgr., Warner Bros./Reprise ('70); Pres., Warner Bros./Reprise Records ('72); Chairman, Elektra/Asylum/Nonesuch Records ('75); Pres. and Chief Exec. Officer, Home Entertainment Network, Warner Amex Cable Communications ('83).

ACHIEVEMENTS & AWARDS: Honored as Promotion Man of the Year for three years in a Galvin Poll.

PERSONAL: N.A.

SMITH, PATRICIA FALKEN
Head Writer/Exec. Story Consultant/Prod.

c/o Showtime, 1633 Broadway, New York, NY 10019

b. Montevideo, MN.

EDUCATION: Pasadena Playhouse, Writing and Theater Arts.

CAREER HIGHLIGHTS: Head Writer, "Showtime," pilot for 90-minute series; Exec. Story Consultant/Head Writer, "General Hospital," ABC; Head Writer, "Days of Our Lives," NBC; Exec. Story Consultant, "Playhouse 90," CBS; Exec. Story Consultant and Head Writer, "Bonanza," "Father of the Bride," and "National Velvet," NBC. Exec. Story Consultant, Alcoa-Goodyear Playhouse, Ford, and Celebrity Playhouse. Freelance

Writer, TV episodes of "Perry Mason," "Shane," and "Rawhide."

ACHIEVEMENTS & AWARDS: Emmy for best writing for "Days of Our Lives" ('76).

PERSONAL: N.A.

SMITH, RICHARD B.
Pres., Satellite Program Network

8252 S. Harvard St., Tulsa, OK 74136
b. March 15, 1934. Independence, MO.

EDUCATION: Central Missouri University, B.S., Business Administration ('56).

CAREER HIGHLIGHTS: Held several key positions with AT&T ('58); joined United Computing Systems ('68); then Western Union ('75); moved to Satellite Syndicated Systems as Exec. V.P., handling finance, investments, and administration ('79); assumed additional responsibilities of engineering and operations including transportable earth stations ('80); appointed Pres., Satellite Program Network ('82).

ACHIEVEMENTS & AWARDS: N.A.

PERSONAL: Resides in Tulsa, OK, with wife, Margi; children, Bret, Betsy, and Greg.

SMITH, ROBERT C.
Managing Editor, *TV Guide*

c/o *TV Guide*, Radnor, PA 19088
b. March 12, 1940. Sioux Center, IA.

EDUCATION: Drake University; University of Iowa; University of Chicago.

CAREER HIGHLIGHTS: Sr. Editor, *Today's Health*, Chicago ('71); Assoc. Travel Editor, *Saturday Review*, San Francisco ('72); Managing Editor,

Columbia Journalism Review, New York ('74); Managing Editor, *TV Guide* ('79).

ACHIEVEMENTS & AWARDS: N.A.

PERSONAL: N.A.

SMITH, SUKI (Sue Laniado Smith)
Advertising/Sales Promotion Mgr., MGM-UA TV

c/o MGM-UA TV, 1350 Ave. of the Americas, New York, NY 10019
b. September 29, 1950. Orange, NJ.

EDUCATION: University of Maryland, B.A. ('72).

CAREER HIGHLIGHTS: Asst. to Publicity Dir., Walker Publishing Co. ('72); Admin. Asst. to Art Dir., Fieldcrest Mills ('74); Creative Dir., Bill Gold Advertising ('77); Freelance Film Advertising, Suki Laniado, Inc. ('81); Mgr., Advertising and Sales Promotion MGM-UA TV ('82).

ACHIEVEMENTS & AWARDS: N.A.

PERSONAL: Husband, Hy. Resides in New York City.

SMITH BROWNSTEIN, ELIZABETH
Editorial/Research Director, Smithsonian World

c/o Smithsonian World, 1752 N St., N.W., Washington, DC 20036
b. July 24, 1930.

EDUCATION: Wellesley College, B.A.; London School of Economics, M.Sc., Economics.

CAREER HIGHLIGHTS: Dir., New York Office, The Experiment in Intl. Living ('60); Assoc. Prod., Evening Edition, PBS ('71); Program Mgr./Prod., WETA ('76); Program Development Mgr., WETA ('78); Editorial/Research Director for the series "Smithsonian World."

ACHIEVEMENTS & AWARDS: Cine Golden Eagle, Chris bronze plaque for "Adventures in Art With Julie Harris," for which she was Writer/Exec. Prod.

PERSONAL: Single. Resides in Washington, DC.

SMYLIE, BEN B.
V.P., Information Products, Keycom Electronic Publishing

c/o Schaumburg Corporate Center, 1501 Woodfield Rd., Suite 110 W., Schaumburg, IL 60195
b. N.A.

EDUCATION: De Paul University; San Antonio College; University of Texas.
CAREER HIGHLIGHTS: Mgr. of Atex Operations ('79); Mgr. of Technical Services, *Chicago Sun Times* ('79); V.P. and Gen. Mgr. Field Electronic Publishing ('81); V.P., Information Products, Keycom Electronic Publishing.
ACHIEVEMENTS & AWARDS: Member, Institute of Electrical and Electronic Engineers and Institute of Optical Electronic Engineers.
PERSONAL: N.A.

SNOW, RONALD
Mgr., Creative Services, 20th Century Fox TV

10746 Francis Place, #112, Los Angeles, CA 90034
b. November 23, 1953. Detroit, MI.

EDUCATION: University of Michigan, B.A., Radio, TV, and Film.
CAREER HIGHLIGHTS: Acct. Exec., Wilding Communications; Freelance Writer/Prod., On-Air Promotion, NBC TV, CBS TV; Mgr., Creative Services, 20th Century Fox TV.
ACHIEVEMENTS & AWARDS: N.A.
PERSONAL: N.A.

EDUCATION: Goddard College, B.A. ('51); Yale University, M.F.A. ('54).
CAREER HIGHLIGHTS: Asst. Dir. of Studio Operations, CBS TV, New York; V.P., Programming and Operations, WOR-TV, New York ('70); V.P., Programming, Madison Square Garden Cable Network, New York ('80).
ACHIEVEMENTS & AWARDS: N.A.
PERSONAL: N.A.

SNYDER, JIMMY ("Jimmy the Greek")
Sports Analyst, CBS, Sports, "The NFL Today"

c/o CBS, 51 W. 52d St., New York, NY 10019
b. September 9, 1919. Steubenville, OH.

EDUCATION: N.A.
CAREER HIGHLIGHTS: The CBS Sports resident handicapper of football games and horse races, Snyder is famous for setting the odds on most major events, be they sports events or political events. Worked as a professional gambler in the thirties and forties before working for some Las Vegas hotels and his own public relations business. Serves as an Analyst, CBS Sports ('75).
ACHIEVEMENTS & AWARDS: N.A.
PERSONAL: Resides in Durham, NC, with his wife, Joan; daughter, Stephanie; sons, Anthony and Jamie.

SNOWDEN, GEORGE
V.P., Programming, Madison Square Garden Network

c/o Madison Square Garden Network, 4 Pennsylvania Plaza, New York, NY 10001
b. November 7, 1929.

SNYDER, TOM
Anchor, WABC-TV, "Eyewitness News"

c/o WABC-TV, 7 Lincoln Sq., New York, NY 10023
b. May 12, 1936. Milwaukee, WI.

EDUCATION: Marquette University.

CAREER HIGHLIGHTS: Known as a brash, irreverent interviewer, willing to ask tough, biting questions. After several years on the "Tomorrow Show," the ratings began to lag and Snyder is back where he began his career, in local TV news. Snyder worked in a variety of broadcasting jobs including WSAV-TV, Savannah, GA; WAII-TV, Atlanta; KTLA-TV, Los Angeles, and KYW-TV, Philadelphia. He became Host, "Tomorrow Coast to Coast," NBC TV ('73); moved to New York and became Anchor, 6 P.M. "NewsCenter 4" ('74–'77); returned to Burbank and continued hosting "Tomorrow Coast to Coast"; Anchor, NBC-TV, "Prime Time" ('79); Anchor, WABC-TV, "Eyewitness News," 11 P.M. ('82).

ACHIEVEMENTS & AWARDS: Emmy award as host of "Tomorrow" ('74); named Big Apple Newscaster of the Year for "NewsCenter 4."

PERSONAL: N.A.

SOBEL, REBECCA
Correspondent, NBC, News

c/o NBC, 30 Rockefeller Plaza, New York, NY 10020
b. Brooklyn, NY.

EDUCATION: School of American Ballet; University of California at Los Angeles.

CAREER HIGHLIGHTS: She started as a Reporter, *Hollywood Citizen-News* ('69); Assoc. Prod., evening news broadcast, KTLA, Los Angeles ('71); News Assignment Editor, KHJ TV, Los Angeles ('72); Reporter, WXYZ-TV, Detroit ('73); On-Air Reporter, WCAU-TV, Philadelphia ('76–'78); Co-Anchor, Newscast, WNET, New York; General Assignment Correspondent, NBC News, Washington, DC ('79); Correspondent, NBC News, Pittsburgh ('81).

ACHIEVEMENTS & AWARDS: Detroit Press Assn. Golden Mike award for her reporting on the Jimmy Hoffa case ('76). Author, *The Disappearance of Jimmy Hoffa* ('76).

PERSONAL: Two children, Michael and Jessica.

SOHMER, STEVE (Stephen T. Sohmer)
Sr. V.P., NBC, Entertainment

c/o NBC, 3000 W. Alameda Ave., Burbank, CA 91523
b. December 16, 1941. Savannah, GA.

EDUCATION: Yale College ('62); Doubleday Fellow in Creative Writing, Columbia University ('64–'65).

CAREER HIGHLIGHTS: V.P., Creative Dir., Newspaper Advertising Bureau ('62); formed Steve Sohmer, Inc. ('71); joined CBS TV Network as V.P., Advertising and Promotion ('77); moved to NBC TV as V.P., Advertising and Creative Services; Sr. V.P., NBC Entertainment, in charge of daytime, children's, and other special programming ('83).

ACHIEVEMENTS & AWARDS: Numerous advertising awards, including Clio ('80). Published novel, *The Way It Was* ('66) and *Where the Fun Is*, a guidebook for Pan Am ('67).

PERSONAL: Single, one daughter. Resides in Los Angeles.

SOLOMON, MARK
Prod.

c/o Robinson/Weintraub, 554 S. San Vicente, Los Angeles, CA 90048
b. November 1, 1947, Hartford, CT.

EDUCATION: University of Connecticut, B.F.A.

CAREER HIGHLIGHTS: Freelance Writer, scripts for three episodes of "House Calls," "Semi-Tough," "Detective School," "Me, on the Radio," "Pottsville," and two episodes of "Alice" ('78–'80). Script Consultant, "Alice," and wrote more than 20 "Alice" episodes ('80); Exec. Story Editor, "Alice" ('81); Prod., "Alice" ('82).

ACHIEVEMENTS & AWARDS: N.A.

PERSONAL: Wife, Cary. Resides in Woodland Hills, CA.

SOLSON, STANLEY J.
V.P., Warner Bros. TV, Pay TV Marketing

c/o Warner Bros. TV, 75 Rockefeller Plaza, New York, NY 10019
b. August 16, 1933. Brooklyn, NY.

EDUCATION: New York University, M.B.A. ('63).

CAREER HIGHLIGHTS: Sr. Analyst, Corporate Planning Dept., NBC ('60); Dir., Research, Columbia Pictures ('67); Pres., TWC Communications, Division of Computer Television, Time, Inc. ('73); Sr. Consultant, Natl. Economic Research Assoc. ('75).

ACHIEVEMENTS & AWARDS: N.A.

PERSONAL: Son, Joshua.

SOMERS, SUZANNE
Actress

c/o SAG, 7750 Sunset Blvd., Hollywood, CA 90046

b. October 16, 1946. San Bruno, CA.

EDUCATION: Lone Mountain College.

CAREER HIGHLIGHTS: This best-selling poster girl jiggled her way to stardom before she walked out on her megahit "Three's Company" and concentrated on variety specials geared to showcase her Las Vegas-type abilities. Motion pictures include *American Graffiti, Yesterday's Hero,* and *Nothing Personal.* TV credits include "One Day at a Time," "Lotsa Luck," "Starsky and Hutch," "The Rockford Files," and "The Love Boat." TV movies include *Happily Ever After, Zuma Beach, The Princess and the Lumberjack,* and *Ants.* Series star of "Three's Company." Star of musical variety specials for CBS.

ACHIEVEMENTS & AWARDS: N.A.

PERSONAL: Husband, Alan Hamel; one son from a previous marriage. Resides in southern California.

SOMERSET-WARD, RICHARD
Head of Music and Arts, BBC

c/o BBC, 12 Cavendish Place, London, England W1

b. May, 1942.

EDUCATION: University of Cambridge (England).

CAREER HIGHLIGHTS: General Trainee, BBC ('63); Sr. Prod., Oversea Regional Service, BBC ('65); Dir. in the U.S., BBC ('76); Asst. Head of Music and Arts, BBC TV ('78); Head of Music Arts, BBC TV ('81).

ACHIEVEMENTS & AWARDS: N.A.

PERSONAL: N.A.

SONNENFELDT, RICHARD W.
Exec. V.P., NBC, Operations and Technical Services

c/o NBC, 30 Rockefeller Plaza, New York, NY 10020

b. July 3, 1923.

EDUCATION: Johns Hopkins University ('49).

CAREER HIGHLIGHTS: Pres. and Chief Exec. Officer, Digitronics ('65); Staff V.P. of New Business Programs, RCA ('70); Chairman of the Board, RCA; Exec. V.P. Operations and Technical Services, NBC ('79).

ACHIEVEMENTS & AWARDS: Holds 30 U.S. patents.

PERSONAL: Three children.

SPAGNOLETTI, LEN
General Sales Mgr., ABC, KABC-TV, Los Angeles

c/o KABC-TV, 4151 Prospect Ave., Los Angeles, CA 90027

b. New York, NY.

EDUCATION: Villanova University, B.A., English.

CAREER HIGHLIGHTS: Media Buyer/Planner, Benton & Bowles, New York; Acct. Exec., Sales, WABC-TV, New York ('70); Acct. Exec., ABC Spot Sales, Los Angeles ('72); Acct. Exec., ABC Spot Sales, Chicago ('74); Natl. Sales Mgr., KGO-TV, San Francisco ('75); General Sales Mgr., KABC-TV, Los Angeles ('81).

ACHIEVEMENTS & AWARDS: N.A.

PERSONAL: N.A.

SPANO, JOE
Actor

c/o "Hill Street Blues," NBC, 3000 W. Alameda Ave., Burbank, CA 91523

b. July 7. San Francisco, CA.

EDUCATION: University of California at Berkeley, B.A.

CAREER HIGHLIGHTS: TV series appearances on "Lou Grant," "Paris," "Trapper John, M.D.," and "Tenspeed and Brownshoe." Feature films include *The Enforcer, American Graffiti,* and *The Incredible Shrinking Woman.* TV series regular on "Hill Street Blues."

ACHIEVEMENTS & AWARDS: N.A.

PERSONAL: Wife, Joan. Resides in Santa Monica, CA.

SPELLING, AARON
Prod.

c/o Burbank Studio, Burbank, CA 91522
b. April 22, 1928. Dallas, TX.

EDUCATION: The Sorbonne (France); University of Paris (France); Southern Methodist University.

CAREER HIGHLIGHTS: Spelling produced "The Mod Squad" and became partners with Danny Thomas ('68) before forming Spelling-Goldberg Productions ('72) to produce "The Rookies," "Starsky and Hutch," "Charlie's Angels," "Family," "Hart to Hart," and "Fantasy Island." Under Spelling Productions, he produced "Vegas," "Aloha Paradise," "Dynasty," "Strike Force," "At Ease," "Hotel" ('83–'84) and "Shooting Stars" ('83–'84). In addition, he shares credit for producing 92 movies of the week for ABC, a record number.

ACHIEVEMENTS & AWARDS: Eugene O'Neill awards ('47, '48); NAACP image award; Man of the Year, Publicists of America ('71); B'nai B'rith Man of the Year ('72).

PERSONAL: Wife, Carole; two children. Resides in Beverly Hills, CA.

SPENCE, JAMES R., JR.
Sr. V.P., ABC, Sports

c/o ABC, 1330 Ave. of the Americas, New York, NY 10019
b. December 20, 1936. Bronxville, NY.

EDUCATION: Dartmouth College, B.A.

CAREER HIGHLIGHTS: Production Asst., Sports Programs, Inc., predecessor of ABC Sports ('60); Asst. to Exec. Prod., "Wide World of Sports" ('63); Coordinating Prod. ('66); V.P., Program Planning, ABC Sports ('70); appointed Sr. V.P., ABC Sports ('78).

ACHIEVEMENTS & AWARDS: Four Emmy awards for work on "Wide World of Sports."

PERSONAL: Resides in Manhattan with wife, Lynn.

SPENCER, SUSAN
Correspondent, CBS, News

c/o CBS, 524 W. 57th St., New York, NY 10019
b. Memphis, TN.

EDUCATION: Michigan State University, B.S. ('68); Columbia University, M.A., Journalism ('69).

CAREER HIGHLIGHTS: Prod., News Dept., WKPC-TV, Louisville, KY ('70); Researcher, WCBS-TV, New York ('71); Reporter/Prod., WCCO-TV, Minneapolis ('72); Reporter, CBS News, Washington, DC ('77); Correspondent, CBS News, Washington, DC ('78).

ACHIEVEMENTS & AWARDS: N.A.

PERSONAL: N.A.

SPENS, WILL
Correspondent, WABC-TV, "Eyewitness News"

c/o WABC-TV, 7 Lincoln Square, New York, NY 10023
b. Bronxville, NY.

EDUCATION: N.A.

CAREER HIGHLIGHTS: Anchor, WCBS-AM, New York; General Assignment Reporter and Weekend Anchor ('76); Morning News Anchor, WNEW-AM Radio ('80); Correspondent, WABC-TV, "Eyewitness News."

ACHIEVEMENTS & AWARDS: N.A.

PERSONAL: N.A.

SPERRY, GEORGE A.
V.P. and General Mgr., Westinghouse Broadcasting Co., Group W Productions TV Syndication Center

c/o Group W Productions TV Syndication Center, 310 Parkway View Dr., Pittsburgh, PA 15205
b. November 9, 1934.

EDUCATION: N.A.
CAREER HIGHLIGHTS: Started as an Announcer, Cameraman, and Dir., before moving into the management area of TV at such stations as WBRE-TV, Wilkes-Barre, PA; WNEP-TV, Scranton, PA; WGR-AM/FM/TV, Buffalo, NY; CKLW-AM/FM/TV, Windsor, Ontario; WDCA-TV, Washington, DC; Promotion Mgr., WKBD-TV, Detroit ('66); V.P., Radio and TV, E. W. Baker Advertising, Detroit ('69); Station Mgr., WKBD-TV, Detroit ('71); Promotion Mgr., Group W Productions, "The Mike Douglas Show" ('76); Dir. of Planning and Administration, Group W Productions ('77); V.P. and General Mgr., Group W Productions TV Syndication Center, Pittsburgh ('78).
ACHIEVEMENTS & AWARDS: N.A.
PERSONAL: Resides in Venetia, PA, with wife, Evelyn.

SPINNEY, CAROLL
Puppeteer/Actor, Children's Television Workshop

c/o Children's Television Workshop, 1 Lincoln Plaza, New York, NY 10023
b. December 26, 1933.

EDUCATION: Art Institute of Boston.
CAREER HIGHLIGHTS: He portrays Big Bird, Oscar the Grouch, and Bruno the Trashman on "Sesame Street." He created a Las Vegas TV show called "Rascal Rabbit" ('55); returned to Boston to become a puppeteer for the show "Judy and Goggle" ('60); joined Boston's "Bozo Show" ('60); portrayed Big Bird and Oscar for "Sesame Street," Children's Television Workshop ('69). He is also a regular guest conductor of such symphony orchestras as the Los Angeles Philharmonic, the Boston Pops, and the Vancouver Symphony Orchestra.

ACHIEVEMENTS & AWARDS: Emmy awards ('74, '75).
PERSONAL: N.A.

SPORER, ANDREA D.
V.P. and General Counsel, United Satellite Communications, Business Affairs

c/o United Satellite Communications, 1345 Ave. of the Americas, New York, NY 10105
b. N.A.

EDUCATION: Tufts University, B.S.; New York University, Law.
CAREER HIGHLIGHTS: Entertainment/Communications Lawyer, Paul Weiss, Rifkind, Wharton & Garrison law firm; V.P., Business Affairs, Warner Amex Satellite Entertainment Co., New York; V.P., Business Affairs, MGM-UA; V.P., Business Affairs and General Counsel, United Satellite Communications, New York.
ACHIEVEMENTS & AWARDS: N.A.
PERSONAL: N.A.

SPRINGFIELD, RICK
Actor

c/o Special Artists Agency, 9155 Sunset Blvd., Suite 7, Los Angeles, CA 90069
b. Sydney, Australia.

EDUCATION: N.A.
CAREER HIGHLIGHTS: Rock and roll songwriter and recording artist. TV actor on "Six Million Dollar Man," "Wonder Woman," "The Rockford Files," and "The Incredible Hulk." Soap star of "General Hospital."
ACHIEVEMENTS & AWARDS: Grammy award as best male rock vocalist for "Jessie's Girl."
PERSONAL: N.A.

SQUIRE, KEN
Sports Broadcaster, CBS, Sports

c/o CBS, 51 W. 52d St., New York, NY 10019
b. Waterbury, VT.

EDUCATION: Boston University.
CAREER HIGHLIGHTS: Worked for his father's radio station WDEV, known as Radio Vermont;

worked as the Public Address Announcer, Daytona Intl. Speedway; joined CBS Sports announcing the network's coverage of auto racing events ('72).

ACHIEVEMENTS & AWARDS: Recipient of the Henry McLemore motorsports award ('76); named Vermont Sportscaster of the Year four times.

PERSONAL: Resides in Vermont with his wife, Susan, and their two children.

STANDER, STEPHEN F.
Managing General Attorney, NBC, Law Dept.

c/o NBC, 30 Rockefeller Plaza, New York, NY 10020
b. New York, NY.

EDUCATION: Columbia College, B.A.; Harvard Law School, LL.B.

CAREER HIGHLIGHTS: Assoc. Attorney, Poletti, Freidin, Prashker, Feldman & Gartner law firm, New York ('69); Attorney, Sabin, Bermant & Blau law firm, New York ('73); Sr. Counsel, NBC, New York ('73); Asst. General Attorney, NBC ('77); Managing General Attorney, NBC ('83).

ACHIEVEMENTS & AWARDS: N.A.

PERSONAL: Resides in Larchmont, NY, with his wife, Janet, and their daughter, Jessica.

STANLEY, BAHNS
Dir., Cable Sales, Weather Channel

c/o Weather Channel, 2840 Wilkinson Parkway, Atlanta, GA 30339
b. January 18, 1953. Martinsville, VA.

EDUCATION: Duke University, B.A., Political Science ('75); University of Virginia, M.B.A., Marketing ('78).

CAREER HIGHLIGHTS: Marketing Analyst, Worrell Newspapers ('78); Publisher, *Sanford Star*, Maine ('79); Publisher, *Princeton Times*, West Virginia ('79); New Ventures Analyst, Landmark Communications ('80); Dir., Cable Sales, Weather Channel ('82).

ACHIEVEMENTS & AWARDS: N.A.

PERSONAL: Resides in Norfolk, VA, with wife, Nancy.

STANLEY, ERIC J.
Dir., Intl. Sales, NBC Intl. Ltd.

c/o NBC, 30 Rockefeller Plaza, New York, NY 10020
b. N.A.

EDUCATION: Colgate University, B.A., Sociology/Anthropology ('73); Columbia University Graduate School of Business, M.B.A., Marketing, Finance and International Business ('78).

CAREER HIGHLIGHTS: Real Estate Broker ('77); Independent Marketing Consultant, NBC ('77); Business Affairs Assoc., NBC News ('78); Sr. Operations Analyst, NBC Corporate Finance Dept. ('79); Mgr., Financial Planning and Evaluation, NBC Enterprises ('80); Mgr., Intl. Sales, NBC Intl. Ltd. ('81); Dir., Intl. Sales, NBC Intl. Ltd. ('83).

ACHIEVEMENTS & AWARDS: N.A.

PERSONAL: Resides in New York City.

STANTON, FRANK
President Emeritus, CBS

c/o CBS, 51 W. 52d St., New York, NY 10019
b. March 20, 1908.

EDUCATION: Ohio State University, Ph.D., Statistical Psychology.

CAREER HIGHLIGHTS: Long one of the most respected and influential executives in commercial broadcasting. After a career in teaching, Stanton joined the CBS research staff ('35) and became a CBS V.P. ('42). As Pres. of CBS ('46–'72), Stanton was influential in shaping the corporation's future. He was active in advocating media access to Congress and the courts, opposing the Equal Time Rule. In '71, he successfully defied a congressional subpoena in the controversy surrounding the CBS News documentary, "The Selling of the Pentagon." After leaving CBS ('73), Stanton served as Chairman of the American Red Cross.

ACHIEVEMENTS & AWARDS: Board Member of the Intl. Herald Tribune; appointed to the President's Committee on the Arts and the Humanities.

PERSONAL: N.A.

STANVILLE, MARTHA PELL
V.P., Affiliate Promotion Services, NBC, Entertainment, West Coast

c/o NBC, 3000 W. Alameda Ave., Burbank, CA 91523
b. Macon, GA.

EDUCATION: Wesleyan College.
CAREER HIGHLIGHTS: Production Asst., WMAZ-TV, Macon, GA ('53); Mgr., Advertising and Promotion Dept., WCCO-TV, Minneapolis ('66); Dir., Advertising and Promotion Dept., WCCO-TV, Minneapolis ('78); V.P., Affiliate Promotion Services, NBC Entertainment, West Coast ('83).
ACHIEVEMENTS & AWARDS: Past Pres. and Chairperson, American Women in Radio and TV ('83) and that organization's convention; YWCA outstanding achievement award for media communication.
PERSONAL: N.A.

STAPLETON, JEAN
Actress

c/o CBS, 7800 Beverly Blvd., Los Angeles, CA 90036
b. January 19, 1925. New York, NY.

EDUCATION: N.A.
CAREER HIGHLIGHTS: As the immortal dingbat herself, Stapleton made Edith Bunker a multi-level acting creation capable of provoking tears or laughter and responsible for TV's most inspired scatterbrained logic since Gracie Allen. Broadway roles in *Damn Yankees, Bells Are Ringing, Juno,* and *Funny Girl.* TV appearances in "Omnibus," "Studio One," "Laugh-In," and "The Carol Burnett Show."

Motion pictures include *Damn Yankees, Bells Are Ringing, Something Wild, Up the Down Staircase, Cold Turkey,* and *Klute.* TV series star of "All in the Family." TV movies include *Aunt Mary, Isabel's Choice,* and *Eleanor Roosevelt: First Lady of the World.*
ACHIEVEMENTS & AWARDS: Two Golden Globe awards as best actress in a comedy for "All in the Family" ('73, '74). Two Emmy awards as best actress in a comedy for "All in the Family" ('70, '71).
PERSONAL: Two children, Pam and John.

STARGER, MARTIN
Independent Prod.

c/o Marstar Productions, 100 Universal City Plaza, University City, CA 91608
b. N.A.

EDUCATION: City College of New York.
CAREER HIGHLIGHTS: V.P., ABC East Coast Programming ('66); V.P., Network Programming, ABC ('69); Pres., ABC Entertainment ('72); Independent Prod. for ABC; Prod. for Lew Grade's Production Co.; Pres. of Marble Arch Productions; Prod., Marstar Productions.
ACHIEVEMENTS & AWARDS: N.A.
PERSONAL: N.A.

STEIN, JAMES
Prod., NBC, "Silver Spoons"

c/o NBC, 3000 W. Alameda Ave., Burbank, CA 91523
b. Chicago, IL.

EDUCATION: University of Southern California.
CAREER HIGHLIGHTS: Writer, "Sanford and Son," "What's Happening," "America 2Night," "Fernwood 2Night," "The Mary Tyler Moore Show," a Tennessee Ernie Ford special, and a Lily Tomlin special; Creator, "Joe and Sons"; Prod., "Flo," "Private Benjamin," and "Silver Spoons."
ACHIEVEMENTS & AWARDS: Two writing Emmy awards for "Lily" ('73) and "The Carol Burnett Show" ('78).
PERSONAL: Single, resides in Los Angeles.

STEIN, MICHAEL H.
Editorial Prod., ABC, "World News Tonight"

c/o ABC, 7 W. 66th St., New York, NY 10023
b. 1935.

EDUCATION: Overland College.
CAREER HIGHLIGHTS: News Dir., WNEW, Metromedia, New York ('61); News Mgr., ABC Entertainment Radio Network ('67); News Mgr., ABC Radio News ('73); Editorial Prod., "ABC World News Tonight" ('78).
ACHIEVEMENTS & AWARDS: Freedom Foundation award.
PERSONAL: N.A.

STENNER, ROBERT D.
Prod., CBS, Sports

c/o CBS, 51 W. 52d St., New York, NY 10019
b. Brooklyn, NY.

EDUCATION: N.A.
CAREER HIGHLIGHTS: One of CBS's best sports producers, Stenner can always be depended on to deliver top-flight coverage of the major events he is assigned to cover. Started at CBS in the Mailroom ('59), quickly working his way up to the Advertising and Sales Dept., CBS Radio. Moved on to the Program Dept., WCBS-TV, New York, and later as Supervisor of Production, where he worked on Frank Gifford's NFL pregame show and New York Giants preseason football games ('66). Prod., New York Yankees baseball telecasts ('70); became a Freelance Prod. on the West Coast before returning to CBS Sports as Prod. His many credits include the Daytona 500, horse racing, boxing, NBA basketball, and NFL football, highlighted by Super Bowls X, XII, and XIV.
ACHIEVEMENTS & AWARDS: N.A.
PERSONAL: Resides in Sherman Oaks, CA.

STERN, CARL
News Correspondent, NBC, News

c/o NBC, 4001 Nebraska Ave., N.W.,
   Washington, DC 20016
b. August 7, 1937. New York, NY.

EDUCATION: Columbia University, B.A., Government ('58) and M.S., Journalism ('59); Cleveland State University, J.D. ('66).
CAREER HIGHLIGHTS: KYW-Radio, Cleveland ('59); KYW-TV News Reporter and Anchor ('61); moved to NBC News as Law Correspondent ('67).
ACHIEVEMENTS & AWARDS: Honorary J.D. from Cleveland State University ('75); New England School of Law ('77). AFTRA George Roberts award for best radio program ('60); Radio-TV Mirror for best radio program, Midwest ('60); American Bar Assn. silver gavel ('69, '74); Peabody award ('74); Emmy nominations, Broadcaster of the Year and outstanding coverage of Watergate ('74); Ted Yates award, Washington, DC Chapter, NATAS ('75); American Bar Assn. certificate of merit ('79). Vice Chairman, American Bar Assn. Criminal Justice Section, Law and the Media ('78); Governor, American Bar Assn., Forum Committee, Communications Law ('80–present).
PERSONAL: Resides in Washington, DC, with wife, Joy Elizabeth, and twin sons, Lawrence and Theodore.

STERN, ROBERT
V.P., 20th Century Fox TV, Finance

P.O. Box 900, Beverly Hills, CA 90213
b. August 13, 1944. Steubenville, OH.

EDUCATION: Miami (Ohio) University, B.S., Accounting.
CAREER HIGHLIGHTS: Business Mgr., Capitol Cities Broadcasting ('72); Business Mgr., Chris Craft Broadcasting ('74); Dir., Planning, Golden West Broadcasters; Dir., Participation, 20th Century Fox Features ('78); V.P., Finance, 20th Century Fox TV ('81).
ACHIEVEMENTS & AWARDS: N.A.
PERSONAL: N.A.

STERN, STEWART
Screenwriter

c/o William Morris Agency, 151 El Camino
   Dr., Beverly Hills, CA 90212
b. 1922. New York.

EDUCATION: University of Iowa ('43); Leighton Rollins Studio School of Theatre.

CAREER HIGHLIGHTS: Began his career as a dialogue director at Eagle-Lion Studios. Impressed with one of his short stories, Fred Zinnemann, MGM director, hired Stern to write a screenplay, which lead to a staff position at MGM. Some of Stern's works include *Rebel Without a Cause* ('55); *The James Dean Story* ('57); *Rachel, Rachel* ('68); and *Sybil* ('77).

ACHIEVEMENTS & AWARDS: Emmy award for *Sybil*.

PERSONAL: Married; resides in Hollywood.

STERNE, PETER B.
V.P., Current Comedy Program Production, CBS, Entertainment

c/o CBS, 6121 Sunset Blvd., Los Angeles, CA 90028
b. N.A.

EDUCATION: University of Southern California, B.A. and M.A., Telecommunications.

CAREER HIGHLIGHTS: Moved up the ranks in programming and production at ABC to the level of Dir., Current Comedy and Variety Programs, ABC Entertainment ('76); V.P., James Komack Co. ('77); Dir., Current Comedy Programming, CBS Entertainment ('79); V.P., Current Comedy Program Production, CBS Entertainment ('82).

ACHIEVEMENTS & AWARDS: N.A.

PERSONAL: Resides in Studio City, CA, with wife, Janis, and daughters, Vicki and Betsy.

STEVENS, JAMES
V.P., Technical Projects, Operations and Technical Services, NBC

c/o NBC, 30 Rockefeller Plaza, New York, NY 10020
b. N.A.

EDUCATION: Columbia University, B.S., Engineering.

CAREER HIGHLIGHTS: Industrial Engineer, Lehn & Fink Products Corp., Montvale, NJ ('51); Designer, Studio Facilities, NBC ('57); Systems Analyst, Management Information Systems, NBC ('60); Mgr., Systems Development, Management Information Systems, NBC ('64); Dir., Systems, Management Information Systems, NBC ('76); V.P., Systems Development, Management Information Systems, NBC ('81); V.P., Technical Projects, Operations and Technical Services, NBC, New York ('83).

ACHIEVEMENTS & AWARDS: N.A.

PERSONAL: Resides in Upper Saddle River, NJ, with wife, Barbara; son, James; daughter, Susan.

STEVENSON, McLEAN
Actor

c/o William Morris Agency, 151 El Camino Dr., Beverly Hills, CA 90212
b. November 14, 1929. Normal, IL.

EDUCATION: Northwestern University.

CAREER HIGHLIGHTS: Guest appearances on "The Defenders" and "'That Was the Week That Was." Writer for "That Was the Week That Was" and "The Smothers Brothers Show." Series regular on "The Doris Day Show," "The Tim Conway Comedy Hour," "M*A*S*H," "The McLean Stevenson Show," "In the Beginning," "Hello Larry," and "Condo."

ACHIEVEMENTS & AWARDS: N.A.

PERSONAL: Resides in Los Angeles.

STEWART, CHUCK
Prod./Dir. (Freelance)

6468 Manor Lane, S. Miami, FL 33143
b. January 21, 1944. Canton, OH.

EDUCATION: University of Miami, B.B.A.

CAREER HIGHLIGHTS: Served as Prod./Dir. in Air Force ('68); worked at WPLG-TV, Miami, as Prod./Dir. ('72–'79); NBC News as freelancer ('80–'81); location sound and VTR on "An American Dream: The Narcs" for NBC ('82); began Stewart Productions while also freelancing for NBC News, "NBC Magazine" and "Today" ('82).

ACHIEVEMENTS & AWARDS: Ohio State University award for directing "Woman, Who Are You" ('76); NAPTE Iris award; best public affairs program director for "Why Johnny Don't Know" ('76); Emmy for outstanding program, Prod./Dir., "The 20 Suns of May" ('76); Emmy for "Lisette and Some Very Special Friends" ('79); AWRT award for best children's program for directing "Arthur and Company" ('79).

PERSONAL: N.A.

STEWART, DON
Actor

c/o "Guiding Light," CBS, 51 W. 52d St.,
New York, NY 10019
b. November 14, 1935. Staten Island, NY.

EDUCATION: Hastings College.

CAREER HIGHLIGHTS: Broadway appearances in *Camelot* and *Anyone Can Whistle*; TV appearances in "The Virginian," "Dragnet," and "Laredo." Soap opera regular on "The Guiding Light."

ACHIEVEMENTS & AWARDS: N.A.

PERSONAL: Married; two children. Resides in New Jersey.

STOCKTON, DICK
Sports Broadcaster, CBS, Sports

c/o CBS, 51 W. 52d St., New York, NY 10019
b. November 22, 1942. Philadelphia, PA.

EDUCATION: Syracuse University.

CAREER HIGHLIGHTS: Started in broadcasting at KYW-AM, Philadelphia ('65); moved to KYW-TV, Philadelphia ('66); Sports Dir., KDKA-TV, Pittsburgh ('67); Host, "The NFL Report," CBS Sports ('67–'73); Sports Dir., WBZ-TV, Boston ('71); Announcer, Boston Celtics basketball games ('72); Play-by-Play Announcer, NFL football telecasts, CBS Sports ('74); Announcer, New York Knicks basketball games ('74); Announcer, Boston Red Sox baseball broadcasts, WSBK-TV ('75); concurrently worked for NBC as a Play-by-Play Announcer, NFL football broadcasts and NCAA basketball games ('76). Rejoined CBS

Sports as a Play-by-Play Announcer, NFL football, NBA basketball, and NCAA basketball telecasts, as well as boxing and figure skating events ('78).

ACHIEVEMENTS & AWARDS: N.A.

PERSONAL: Single, resides in New York City and Boca Raton, FL.

STODDARD, BRANDON
Pres., ABC Motion Pictures

c/o ABC, 2040 Ave. of the Stars, Los Angeles, CA 90067
b. March 31, 1937. Canaan, CT.

EDUCATION: Yale University ('58); Columbia University Law School.

CAREER HIGHLIGHTS: Elevated the quality of ABC's made-for-TV movies and was instrumental in developing *Roots* for ABC, followed by *Rich Man, Poor Man*. Considered one of the most imaginative, literate production executives involved with drama on commercial television, he began with Media Dept., Grey Advertising ('60); promoted to Program Operations Supervisor; Dir. of Daytime Programming; V.P. in charge of TV; V.P. in Charge of Radio and TV Programming ('60–'68). Moved to ABC as Dir. of Daytime Programs ('70); named V.P., Daytime Programs ('72); added responsibility for Children's Programs ('73). Work with motion pictures began as V.P., Motion Pictures for TV, with responsibilities for developing ABC Novels for TV and productions of *Roots, Roots: The Next Generation, Rich Man, Poor Man, Masada, Friendly Fire, The Jericho Mile, Death Be Not Proud, The Shadow Box,* and *Attica*. Promoted to V.P., Dramatic Programs and Motion Pictures for TV ('76); assumed title of Sr. V.P.,

Dramatic Programs, Motion Picures and Novels for TV ('78); appointed Pres., ABC Motion Pictures ('79) while maintaining responsibilities as Sr. V.P., ABC Entertainment.
ACHIEVEMENTS & AWARDS: N.A.
PERSONAL: Resides in Los Angeles.

STOLNITZ, ART
Sr. V.P., Business Affairs, Warner Bros. TV

c/o Warner Bros. TV, 4000 Warner Blvd.,
  Burbank, CA 91522
b. March 13, 1928. Rochester, NY.

EDUCATION: University of Tennessee, LLB.
CAREER HIGHLIGHTS: Joined Legal Dept., William Morris Agency ('53); Dir., Business Affairs, ZIV Productions ('58); Dir., Business Affairs, Selmur Productions ('60); V.P., ABC Pictures ('70); Exec. V.P., Metromedia Producers Corp. ('71); Exec. V.P., Charles Fries Productions ('74); Prod., CBS TV-movie "Foster & Laurie" ('75); Prod., "Grizzly Adams" TV series ('76); Sr. V.P., Business Affairs, Warner Bros. TV ('77).
ACHIEVEMENTS & AWARDS: Won a Golden Halo Award from the Southern California Motion Picture Council for "Grizzly Adams" ('77); Member, Academy of Motion Picture Arts & Sciences; Academy of TV Arts & Sciences; American Film Institute, Phi Alpha Delta Legal Fraternity.
PERSONAL: Resides in Los Angeles, CA; wife, Suzanne; son, Scott.

STONE, EMERSON
V.P., News Practices, CBS, News

c/o CBS, 524 W. 57th St., New York, NY
  10019
b. N.A.

EDUCATION: Yale University ('48).
CAREER HIGHLIGHTS: Joined CBS News ('52), first as a Newswriter and later as an Editor, Assoc. Prod., and Prod. of both TV and Radio News; Prod., "The World Tonight" ('64); Dir., CBS News, Radio ('67); initiated Newsfeed, a closed-circuit material service for CBS affiliates ('68); V.P., CBS News, Radio ('71); V.P., News Practices, CBS ('82).

ACHIEVEMENTS & AWARDS: N.A.
PERSONAL: Resides in Greenwich, CT, with wife, Mary; three daughters.

STONE, JON
Dir. and Creative Consultant, Children's Television Workshop, "Sesame Street"

c/o Children's Television Workshop, 1 Lincoln Plaza, New York, NY 10023
b. April 13, 1931.

EDUCATION: Williams College, B.A.; Yale University, M.F.A.
CAREER HIGHLIGHTS: Head Writer on "Sesame Street" in the program's early years before serving as Prod., Exec. Prod., and Dir. of the show. Also developed other "Sesame Street" specials and worked as a Writer, "John Denver and the Muppets in the Mountains" special.
ACHIEVEMENTS & AWARDS: Five Emmy awards for "Sesame Street."
PERSONAL: N.A.

STONE, KAREN
Co-Anchor/Interviewer, CBS, News

c/o CBS, 524 W. 57th St., New York, NY
  10019
b. Roaring Springs, PA.

EDUCATION: Cornell University, B.A., Communications.
CAREER HIGHLIGHTS: Reporter, *Finger Lakes Times*, Geneva, NY ('71); Anchor/Reporter, WXXI-TV, Rochester, NY ('75); Reporter, for the seven-member station of the Pennsylvania Public TV Network based at WQED-TV, Pittsburgh ('76); Anchor, "New Jersey Nightly News," which aired on WNET-TV and the New Jersey Network of public TV stations ('79); Reporter, CBS News, New York ('81); Reporter, CBS News, Atlanta ('82); Co-Anchor/Interviewer, "CBS News Nightwatch" ('82).
ACHIEVEMENTS & AWARDS: N.A.
PERSONAL: N.A.

STONEY, GEORGE CASHEL
Professor of Film and TV; Pres., George C. Stoney Assoc., New York University, Department of Film/TV

c/o New York University, Dept. of Film/TV, 49
W. Fourth St., New York, NY 10003
b. July 1, 1916. Winston-Salem, NC.

EDUCATION: University of North Carolina,
B.A. ('37); New York University, Journalism
('38); Balliol College, Oxford Social Institutions ('45); University of London Institute of
Education, Media Studies ('48).

CAREER HIGHLIGHTS: One of the most influen-
tial and admired film and video leaders in
America. Writer/Editor/Dir., Southern Educa-
tional Film Production Service, University of
Georgia at Athens; Co-Founder, Potomac
Film Productions, Washington, DC ('53);
Exec. Prod., Challenge for Change Program,
Natl. Film Board of Canada, Montreal ('68);
Co-Founder/Dir., Alternate Media Center,
New York University ('71); Dir., Cable-TV In-
ternship Program, Alternate Media Center
('73); Designer and Co-Dir., the Boston Media
Project ('74). At present a Writer, Dir., and
Prod. of more than 50 documentary films, TV
series, and videotapes such as "How the
Myth Was Made," "Shepherd of the Night
Flock," "Acupuncture and Herbal Therapy,"
"In China, Family Planning Is no Private
Matter," "What's Happening to the Hard
Core?" and "Citicorp." Co-produced the re-
cent award winning "The Weavers: Wasn't
That a Time?"

ACHIEVEMENTS & AWARDS: Among the many
awards his films have won are the Cine Gold-
en Eagle, a Silver Hugo and the Blue Ribbon
at the American Film Festival.

PERSONAL: N.A.

STORY, RALPH
Correspondent/Anchor, KNXT-TV, News

c/o KNXT-TV, 6121 Sunset Blvd., Los
Angeles, CA 90028
b. Kalamazoo, MI.

EDUCATION: Western Michigan University.
CAREER HIGHLIGHTS: Host/Dir., "The Ralph
Story Show," KNX-AM ('48); Correspondent,
CBS Radio News ('53); Host, "The $64,000
Challenge," CBS TV ('56); Reporter, KNXT-
TV ('58); Host, "Ralph Story's Los Angeles,"
KNXT-TV ('63); Correspondent/Anchor,
KNXT-TV ('70).

ACHIEVEMENTS & AWARDS: Golden Mike award
('78, '81); Los Angeles Press Club award ('81);
local Emmy ('81).

PERSONAL: Resides in Los Angeles.

STOSSEL, JOHN
Correspondent, ABC, News

c/o ABC, 7 W. 66th St., New York, NY 10023
b. March 6, 1947.

EDUCATION: Princeton University, B.A., Psychology ('69).

CAREER HIGHLIGHTS: Prod. and Reporter,
KGW-TV, Portland, OR; WCBS-TV Consumer Editor; moved to ABC ('81); contributes investigative reports on consumer issues
to "Good Morning America," "20/20," and
ABC Radio Information Network.

ACHIEVEMENTS & AWARDS: Received 15 Emmy
awards while at WCBS; George Polk Award
for outstanding local radio and TV reporting
('78); consumer journalism award of the Natl.
Press Club ('81); three other Natl. Press Club
awards. Author of Shopping Smart ('82).

PERSONAL: N.A.

STRAIT, GEORGE
Correspondent, ABC News, Washington, DC

c/o ABC, 1330 Ave. of the Americas, New
York, NY 10019
b. Boston, MA.

EDUCATION: Atlanta University, M.S.
CAREER HIGHLIGHTS: Began his broadcasting
career with WQXI-Radio, Atlanta, as a News
Anchor and Board Engineer ('69); Prod.,
Writer, Film Editor, and Reporter, WQXI-TV
('70); General Assignment Reporter and
News Anchor, WPVI-TV, Philadelphia ('72);
Washington, DC, Correspondent, CBS News
('76); Washington, DC, Correspondent, ABC
News ('77); White House Correspondent,
ABC ('79).

ACHIEVEMENTS & AWARDS: AWRT award for
best election coverage ('76); AP State Enterprise journalism award ('74). Co-Founder,
Assn. of Black Journalists.

PERSONAL: N.A.

STRANGIS, GREG
Writer/Prod., Ten-Four Productions

c/o Harry Bloom, 9460 Wilshire Blvd., Beverly Hills, CA 90210
b. January 5, 1951. Los Angeles, CA.

EDUCATION: University of California at Northridge, B.A., Philosophy.
CAREER HIGHLIGHTS: Freelance Writer, Paramount Studio ('69); Story Editor, "Love, American Style" ('72–'74); Exec. Story Editor, Prod., "Eight Is Enough" ('76); Sr. V.P., Ten-Four Productions ('80).
ACHIEVEMENTS & AWARDS: Two People's Choice awards for "Eight Is Enough."
PERSONAL: N.A.

STRANGIS, SAM
Pres., Ten-Four Productions

c/o Ten-Four Productions, Inc., 8271 Melrose Ave., Los Angeles, CA 90046
b. June 19, 1929. Tacoma, WA.

EDUCATION: N.A.
CAREER HIGHLIGHTS: Dir. of various TV shows including several "Batman" episodes. In charge of Production, Greenway Productions; V.P. in Charge of Production, Paramount TV; Prod. of "Nakia," "Six Million Dollar Man." Pres. of Ten-Four Productions.
ACHIEVEMENTS & AWARDS: N.A.
PERSONAL: N.A.

STRASSER, ROBIN
Actress

c/o "One Life To Live," ABC, 1330 Ave. of the Americas, New York, NY 10019
b. May 7, 1945. New York, NY.

EDUCATION: Yale School of Drama.
CAREER HIGHLIGHTS: TV credits include "The Rookies" and "The Paul Sand Show." New York stage appearances in *Chapter Two, Galileo*, and *The Shadow Box*. TV soap star of "Another World," "All My Children," and "One Life To Live."
ACHIEVEMENTS & AWARDS: Emmy award as outstanding actress in a daytime drama for "One Life To Live" ('81).
PERSONAL: N.A.

STRASZEWSKI, TOM
V.P. and General Mgr., NBC, KNBC-TV

c/o KNBC-TV, 3000 W. Alameda Ave., Burbank, CA 91523
b. December 13, 1936. Detroit, MI.

EDUCATION: University of Michigan.
CAREER HIGHLIGHTS: Joined NBC as Sales Promotion Coordinator, WRCV-TV, Philadelphia, which at the time was owned and operated by NBC ('62); Sales Research Analyst, NBC Stations Division, New York ('64); Coordinator, Special Projects ('65); Acct. Exec., NBC Spot Sales; Mgr., Local Sales, KNBC-TV, Los Angeles ('66); General Sales Mgr. ('68); Station Mgr. ('73); V.P. and General Mgr. ('76).
ACHIEVEMENTS & AWARDS: Chairman, Board of the California Broadcasters Assn.; Board of Dirs., Independent Colleges of Southern California; Greater Los Angeles Visitors and Convention Bureau.
PERSONAL: Resides in Westlake Village, CA, with wife, Karin, daughter, Heidi, and son, Tom.

STRINGER, HOWARD
Exec. Prod., CBS, News, "CBS Evening News With Dan Rather"

c/o CBS, 524 W. 57th St., New York, NY 10019
b. Cardiff, Wales.

EDUCATION: University of Oxford, B.A. and M.A.
CAREER HIGHLIGHTS: Production Coordinator, WCBS Radio, New York ('76). Joined CBS News as a Researcher ('68). Named Exec.

Prod., CBS Reports ('76), then Sr. Exec. Prod., CBS Reports ('79). Named Exec. Prod., "CBS Evening News With Dan Rather" ('81).

ACHIEVEMENTS & AWARDS: Overseas Press Club award; Writers Guild award; Emmy awards ('73, '72).

PERSONAL: Wife, Jennifer, a physician. Lives in Manhattan.

STROND, CAROL J.
Dir. of Research, Group W Productions

c/o Group W Productions, 70 Universal City Plaza, Universal City, CA 91608
b. N.A.

EDUCATION: Cornell University; Fairleigh Dickinson University; University of Southern California.

CAREER HIGHLIGHTS: Began as Sales Asst., RKO TV Representatives, New York ('73). Became Dir. of Research, Paramount TV, then Dir. of Research, ABC, KGO-TV, San Francisco ('79). Dir. of Research, Group W Productions, Los Angeles ('82).

ACHIEVEMENTS & AWARDS: Young Career Woman Program citation of honor from the Natl. Federation of Business and Professional Women's Club. Black Achiever in Industry, Harlem Branch, YMCA.

PERSONAL: N.A.

STRUCK, DUKE
Dir., CBS, Sports

c/o CBS, 51 W. 52d St., New York, NY 10019
b. Detroit, MI.

EDUCATION: American University, B.A., English.

CAREER HIGHLIGHTS: First broadcasting job was as Stage Mgr., WTOP-TV, Washington, DC ('61); worked his way up at the station, producing and directing news, sports, and variety programs. While in Washington, DC, Struck also directed "MacNeil/Lehrer Report" for PBS. Joined CBS, as Prod. and Dir., tennis, NBA and NFL games ('69); named Dir., "The NFL Today" ('74); moved to ABC as Dir., "Good Morning America," as well as England's royal wedding, the hostage return, and Pres. Ronald Reagan's inauguration ('79);

rejoined CBS Sports as Dir., "The NFL Today" ('82).

ACHIEVEMENTS & AWARDS: Emmy for direction of a five-part series about Henry Fonda for "Good Morning America" ('81).

PERSONAL: N.A.

STRUTHERS, SALLY
Actress

c/o Creative Artists, 1888 Century Park E., Los Angeles, CA 90067
b. July 28, 1948. Portland, OR.

EDUCATION: Pasadena Playhouse.

CAREER HIGHLIGHTS: TV sitcom land has always had a steady stream of daddy's little girls, but Struthers managed to humanize the stereotype, and her Gloria character continues to generate considerable warmth on her new show. Feature films include *Five Easy Pieces* and *The Getaway*. TV movies include *And Your Name Is Jonah, A Gun in the House, My Husband Is Missing, Intimate Strangers, Aloha Means Goodbye,* and *Hey, I'm Alive*. Series regular on "The Smothers Brothers Summer Show," "The Tim Conway Comedy Hour," "All in the Family," and "Gloria."

ACHIEVEMENTS & AWARDS: Two Emmy awards as best supporting actress in a comedy series for "All in the Family."

PERSONAL: Resides with her daughter in Brentwood, CA.

STUART, MARY
Actress

c/o "Search for Tomorrow," NBC, 30 Rockefeller Plaza, New York, NY 10020
b. July 4. Miami, FL.

EDUCATION: Attended acting school.

CAREER HIGHLIGHTS: Movie credits include *The Hucksters, The Unfinished Dance, Good News,* and *The Adventures of Don Juan.* Soap opera star of "Search for Tomorrow" ('51).

ACHIEVEMENTS & AWARDS: Author of the autobiography *Both of Me.*

PERSONAL: N.A.

SULLIVAN, DAVID
Sportscaster, ESPN

c/o ESPN, ESPN Plaza, Bristol, CT 06010
b. May 13, 1948. Cincinnati, OH.

EDUCATION: University of Kentucky, B.A., Business Administration.

CAREER HIGHLIGHTS: Dir., Sports and News, WVLK AM/FM, Lexington, KY ('69); News Dir., WNOR AM/FM, Norfolk, VA ('71); Sports Dir., WAVY-TV, Norfolk ('72); Weekend Sports Anchor, WXIA-TV, Atlanta ('76); Weekend Sports Anchor, WPXI-TV, Pittsburgh ('79); Sports Anchor, ESPN ('82).

ACHIEVEMENTS & AWARDS: N.A.

PERSONAL: N.A.

SULLIVAN, KATHLEEN
Co-Anchor, ABC, News

c/o ABC, 1717 DeSales St., N.W., Washington, DC 20036
b. Pasadena, CA.

EDUCATION: University of California at Los Angeles, Business Administration and Speech Communications.

CAREER HIGHLIGHTS: Assoc. Prod., KNXT-TV ('77); Anchor and General Assignment Reporter, KTBX, Salt Lake City ('78); Sr. Correspondent and Co-Anchor, "Prime News," Cable News Network ('80); joined ABC as Co-Anchor, "ABC News This Morning" ('82).

ACHIEVEMENTS & AWARDS: N.A.

PERSONAL: Resides in Washington, DC.

SULLIVAN, SUSAN
Actress

c/o "Falcon Crest," CBS, 7800 Beverly Blvd., Los Angeles, CA 90036
b. November 18. New York, NY.

EDUCATION: Hofstra University.

CAREER HIGHLIGHTS: Appearances on the soap operas "A World Apart" and "Another World"; TV guest star on "Switch" and "Taxi." Her TV movies include *Having Babies* and *Rich Man, Poor Man.* Star of the TV series "It's a Living" and "Falcon Crest."

ACHIEVEMENTS & AWARDS: N.A.

PERSONAL: N.A.

SULLIVAN, TIMOTHY
Mgr., Compliance and Practices, NBC, West Coast

c/o NBC, 3000 W. Alameda Ave., Burbank, CA 91523
b. Cleveland, OH.

EDUCATION: Arizona State University, B.A., Fine Arts ('71); Southwestern University School of Law, J.D. ('79).

CAREER HIGHLIGHTS: Began career as an actor before joining NBC as Administrator, Compliance ('79); Mgr., Compliance and Practices, NBC West Coast ('83).

ACHIEVEMENTS & AWARDS: N.A.

PERSONAL: Single, resides in Silverlake, CA.

SULTAN, ARNE
Prod./Writer

c/o ABC, 2040 Ave. of the Stars, Los Angeles, CA 90067
b. June 7, 1925. Brooklyn, NY.

EDUCATION: N.A.
CAREER HIGHLIGHTS: Writer, "The Steve Allen Show" ('59); Exec. Prod./Writer "Get Smart" ('65); Prod. "He and She" ('68); Prod. "The Governor and J.J." ('69); "The Partners" ('71); "The Sandy Duncan Show" ('72); "Barney Miller" ('75). Developed TV projects for Universal Studios ('76); Exec. Prod. "Too Close for Comfort" ('80).
ACHIEVEMENTS & AWARDS: Emmy award for "Get Smart" ('68).
PERSONAL: Single, resides in Studio City, CA.

SUMMERALL, PAT
Broadcaster, CBS, Sports

c/o CBS, 51 W. 52d St., New York, NY 10019
b. 1932.

EDUCATION: University of Arkansas.
CAREER HIGHLIGHTS: A star kicking specialist in the NFL before moving into broadcasting, rising to the top of the ranks of CBS Sports Announcers. Sports Dir., WCBS-AM ('64); signed a network contract ('71), working NFL broadcasts, golf tournaments, and tennis matches. Play-by-Play Announcer, Super Bowl ('76, '78, '80, '82).
ACHIEVEMENTS & AWARDS: Named Sportscaster of the Year by the Natl. Sportscasters and Sportswriters Assn. ('77).
PERSONAL: Resides in Lake City, FL, with wife, Katharine, and their three children, Susan, Jay, and Kyle.

SUNDERLAND, RONALD B.
V.P., Business Affairs and Contracts, ABC

c/o ABC, 4151 Prospect Ave., Los Angeles, CA 90027
b. May 4.

EDUCATION: University of California at Los Angeles; Loyola University School of Law.
CAREER HIGHLIGHTS: Business Affairs Negotiator, William Morris Agency ('62) Business Affairs Negotiator, General Artists Corp.; House Counsel, the Associates and Aldrich Filmmaking Group ('68); Dir., Business Affairs for Records and Motion Pictures, Motown Corp.; V.P. in Charge of Business Affairs, Tandem Productions; Associate Coun-

sel, Hayes & Hume law firm, Beverly Hills, CA; V.P., Business Affairs, ABC, West Coast ('78); V.P., Business Affairs and Contracts, ABC ('80).
ACHIEVEMENTS & AWARDS: N.A.
PERSONAL: N.A.

SUSSKIND, DAVID
Independent Prod./TV Commentator

1350 Ave. of the Americas, New York, NY 10019
b. December 19, 1920. New York, NY.

EDUCATION: N.A.
CAREER HIGHLIGHTS: TV Prod. of such series as "Mr. Peepers," "Play of the Week," "Get Smart," and "East Side, West Side"; TV Prod. of dramatic specials including *The Crucible, The Glass Menagerie,* and *Death of a Salesman;* Host, "Open End" series; Host, "The David Susskind Show"; Head, Talent Assoc., now involved in motion picture and TV productions.
ACHIEVEMENTS & AWARDS: Local New York Emmy ('58); Governor's award ('61); Emmy awards for outstanding drama production ('66, '75, '76).
PERSONAL: N.A.

SWACKHAMER, E. W.
Dir.

c/o Shapiro-Lichtman Agency, 2 Century Plaza, Suite 1320, 2049 Century Park E., Los Angeles, CA 90067
b. N.A.

EDUCATION: N.A.
CAREER HIGHLIGHTS: Dir., episodes of the TV series "McCloud," "McMillan and Wife," "The Rookies," "M*A*S*H," "Switch," "Owen Marshall, Counselor at Law," "The Partridge Family," "Here Come the Brides," "Bewitched," "The New Perry Mason Show," "Love, American Style," "Hazel," and "Hennessey." Dir. of TV movies *SWAT, Ten Speed and Brownshoe, In Name Only, Gidget Gets Married, The Legend of Lorna Love, Death Sentence, Vampire, Night Terror, Amusement Park, Reward, Oklahoma City Dolls, The Dain Curse, Peking Encounter, Cocaine and Blue Eyes, Malibu,* and *Car Pool.*

ACHIEVEMENTS & AWARDS: N.A.

PERSONAL: N.A.

SWAIN, SUSAN
Prod., C-SPAN, On-Air Talent

c/o C-SPAN, Suite 155, 400 N. Capitol N.W.,
  Washington, DC 20001
b. December 23, 1954. Philadelphia, PA.

EDUCATION: University of Scranton, B.A.,
  Communications ('76).
CAREER HIGHLIGHTS: TV Field Reporter, On-Air
  Radio News, WDAU TV-22, Scranton, PA
  ('75); Public Relations, Up With People,
  Tuscon, AZ ('76); Supervisor, Convention
  Dept., Raytheon Co., Cambridge, MA ('78);
  Govt. Relations Asst., Natl. Counsel Assn.,
  Washington, DC ('81); Prod., On-Air Talent,
  C-SPAN ('82).
ACHIEVEMENTS & AWARDS: N.A.
PERSONAL: N.A.

SWANSON, DENNIS
Station Mgr., KABC-TV, Los Angeles

c/o KABC-TV, 4151 Prospect Ave., Los
  Angeles, CA 90027
b. March 15.

EDUCATION: University of Illinois, B.S., Jour-
  nalism ('61); University of Illinois, masters,
  Communications and Political Science ('64).
CAREER HIGHLIGHTS: Reporter, WMT-Radio
  and TV, Cedar Rapids, IA ('64); Assignment
  Editor, WGN ('66); Assignment Editor, NBC
  News, Chicago ('68); News Dir., Channel 7,
  New York ('75); Exec. Prod. for News at
  KABC-TV ('76); News Dir., KABC-TV's "Eye-
  witness News" ('77); Station Mgr., KABC-TV
  ('81).
ACHIEVEMENTS & AWARDS: Peabody award;
  Clarence Darrow Foundation award; Crim-
  inal Courts Bar Assn. award for outstanding
  achievement in reporting; several Emmy
  awards; grand award for best TV reporting
  and best news writing from the Greater Los
  Angeles Press Club.
PERSONAL: Wife, Katherine; three children,

Susan, Eric, and Carol. Resides in La Canada,
CA.

SWENSON, INGA
Actress

c/o "Benson," ABC, 2040 Ave. of the Stars,
  Los Angeles, CA 90067
b. December 29, 1934. Omaha, NE.

EDUCATION: Northwestern University.
CAREER HIGHLIGHTS: Broadway roles in *The
  First Gentlemen, 110 in the Shade,* and *Baker
  Street.* TV credits include "U.S. Steel Hour,"
  "Dupont Show of the Month," "Bonanza,"
  "Dr. Kildare," "Barnaby Jones," and "Soap."
  TV movies include *Before and After, Earth II,*
  and *Ziegfeld: The Man and His Women,* and the
  mini-series *Testimony of Two Men.* Motion pic-
  tures include *Wind River, The Betsy, The Mira-
  cle Worker,* and *Advise and Consent.* Series star
  of "Benson."
ACHIEVEMENTS & AWARDS: N.A.
PERSONAL: Husband, Lowell. Two sons, Mark
  and James. Resides in Los Angeles.

SWETT, RALPH J.
**Pres. and V.P., Times Mirror Cable TV,
Times Mirror Co.**

c/o Times Mirror, 2381 Morse Ave., Irvine,
  CA 92714
b. July 23, 1934.

EDUCATION: University of Illinois, B.S. ('56).
CAREER HIGHLIGHTS: Controller, Beneficial
  Standard Life Insurance ('65); V.P., Opera-
  tions, TM Communications Co. ('69); pro-
  moted to V.P. ('72); named Pres., Times
  Mirror Cable TV ('73); while maintaining pre-
  vious responsibilities, named V.P., Times
  Mirror Co. ('81).
ACHIEVEMENTS & AWARDS: N.A.
PERSONAL: Resides in Mission Viejo, CA; wife,
  Eileen; daughter, Robin; sons, Michael, Tim-
  othy, and Jeffrey.

SWIT, LORETTA
Actress

c/o CBS, 7800 Beverly Blvd., Los Angeles, CA 90036
b. November 4, 1937. Passaic, NJ.

EDUCATION: American Academy of Dramatic Arts.

CAREER HIGHLIGHTS: New York stage appearances in *Any Wednesday* and *Same Time, Next Year*. TV guest star on "Gunsmoke," "Hawaii Five-0," and other major series. TV movies include *Shirts/Skins, Coffeeville, Valentine, Mirror, Mirror, The Walls Came Tumbling Down, They're Playing Our Tape, Cagney and Lacey,* and *Games Mother Never Taught You*. Major films include *S.O.B.* and *Race With the Devil*. Was a series star of "M*A*S*H."

ACHIEVEMENTS & AWARDS: Emmy awards as best supporting actress in a comedy series for "M*A*S*H" ('79, '81).

PERSONAL: N.A.

SYKES, ELIZABETH
Dir., Warner Bros. TV, Network Animation Affairs

240 E. Palisade Ave., Englewood, NJ 07631
b. October 31, 1947. New York, NY.

EDUCATION: Cornell University, B.A., Art History ('69).

CAREER HIGHLIGHTS: Asst. to Pres., Performance Guarantees, Inc. ('75); Dir., Development, David Paradine TV ('76); Dir., Polytel/Polygram ('79); Dir., Network Animation Affairs, Warner Bros. TV ('82).

ACHIEVEMENTS & AWARDS: Judge, international Emmy awards ('82).

PERSONAL: Son, Oliver.

SYKES, JOHN
Dir., Programming, Warner Amex Satellite Entertainment Co., MTV: Music Television

c/o MTV, Warner Amex, 1211 Ave. of the Americas, New York, NY 10036
b. N.A.

EDUCATION: Syracuse University School of Public Communications, B.S.

CAREER HIGHLIGHTS: Asst. to the Dir. for the Saratoga Performing Arts Center ('78); Promotion Mgr., CBS Records, Chicago ('80); Dir., Promotion, MTV: Music Television, New York ('81); Dir., Promotion and Artist Relations, MTV ('82); Dir., Programming, MTV ('82).

ACHIEVEMENTS & AWARDS: N.A.

PERSONAL: N.A.

T

TAFFNER, DON L.
Pres., D.L. Taffner Ltd.

c/o D.L. Taffner Ltd., 31 W. 56th St., New York, NY 10019
b. November 29, 1930, Brooklyn, NY.

EDUCATION: St. John's University, B.A., History ('52)

CAREER HIGHLIGHTS: Secretary and Sub-Agent, William Morris Agency, New York ('52); Agent, William Morris ('55); Acct. Exec., Paramount TV, New York ('59); Pres., D.L. Taffner Ltd. ('63), where he has pioneered trade in importing programming from overseas markets and selling them in the U.S. Among his notable successes are "Three's Company," the American version of Britain's "Man About the House" and "Too Close for Comfort," the Americanized sitcom based on "Keep It in the Family." Taffner has also presented the mini-series *Blood and Honor* and *The Silent Reach*, and his company has achieved enormous sales with the marketing of Thames Television's "Benny Hill Show." Prod., "A Fine Romance," CBS ('83) and "A Foot in the Door," CBS ('83).

ACHIEVEMENTS & AWARDS: Founder and V.P., New World TV Festival.

PERSONAL: Wife, Eleanor; children, Donald Jr. and Karen.

TAGLIAFERRO, JOHN
Pres. and General Mgr., Hughes TV Network and Madison Square Garden Cablevision

c/o Madison Square Garden Network, 4 Pennsylvania Plaza, New York, NY 10001
b. April 26, 1944.

EDUCATION: Yale University, B.A. ('67).

CAREER HIGHLIGHTS: Worked in various management positions with CBS ('67); Dir. of Broadcast Services, Western Union ('75); V.P., Hughes TV Network ('77); Pres., Hughes TV Network, and General Mgr., Madison Square Garden Cablevision ('81).

ACHIEVEMENTS & AWARDS: N.A.

PERSONAL: N.A.

TAIT, ERIC V.
Prod., ABC, News

c/o ABC, 7 W. 66th St., New York, NY 10023
b. December 8, 1939. Canal Zone, Panama.

EDUCATION: Holy Cross College, B.S., English Literature ('61); Stanford University.

CAREER HIGHLIGHTS: General Assignment Editor, ABC News ('70); Foreign Assignment Editor, ABC News ('74); Political Editor, ABC News ('75); Story Line Consultant and Writer, "Outerscope II" segment of "Vegetable Soup" ('77); Foreign Assignment Editor, ABC News ('78); Field Prod., ABC News ('80); Prod., ABC News "20/20" ('82).

ACHIEVEMENTS & AWARDS: N.A.

PERSONAL: Resides in Mount Vernon, NY, with wife, Emily; daughters, Traci and Kathleen; son, Eric.

TARDY, KAREN
Dir. of Sales, Hearst/ABC

c/o Hearst/ABC, 555 Fifth Ave., New York, NY 10019
b. Montreal, Canada.

EDUCATION: Adelphi University.

CAREER HIGHLIGHTS: Marketing Mgr., Group W Productions, New York ('78); District Affiliate Mgr., Showtime Entertainment ('81); Dir. of Sales, Hearst/ABC ('82).

ACHIEVEMENTS & AWARDS: N.A.

PERSONAL: Resides in Rockville Centre, NY, with her two daughters, Lisa and Sabrina.

TARTIKOFF, BRANDON
Pres., NBC, Entertainment

c/o NBC, 3000 W. Alameda Ave., Burbank,
CA 91523
b. January 13, 1949. Long Island, NY.

EDUCATION: B.A., English, Yale University
('70)
CAREER HIGHLIGHTS: Vibrant TV executive
whose rise to the top reads like a success
manual. Writer/Prod. for "Graffiti," WLS-TV,
Chicago ('72); Dir. of Advertising and Promotion, WLS-TV; Mgr., Dramatic Development, ABC ('76); Program Exec. for "Family"
and "The Hardy Boys/Nancy Drew Mysteries" ('76); Program Exec., "Eight Is Enough"
('77); Dir., Comedy Programs, NBC ('77);
V.P., Programs, NBC Entertainment, West
Coast ('78); Pres., NBC Entertainment ('80).
ACHIEVEMENTS & AWARDS: Named one of the
Ten Outstanding Young Men of America,
U.S. Jaycees ('81).
PERSONAL: Resides in Beverly Hills, CA, with
wife, Lily.

TATE, DON C.
**Staff of Corydon B. Dunham, Exec. V.P. and
General Counsel, NBC**

c/o NBC, 4001 Nebraska Ave., N.W.,
Washington, DC 20016
b. Georgia.

EDUCATION: Emory University, B.A. ('66); Uni-
versity of Georgia, J.D. ('69).
CAREER HIGHLIGHTS: Chief Legislative Asst. to
Sen. Herman E. Talmadge of Georgia ('69);
Deputy Asst. to Pres. Carter for Congres-
sional Liaison ('76); V.P., Communications
Development, NBC ('81); Staff of Corydon B.

Dunham, Exec. V.P. and General Counsel,
NBC ('83).
ACHIEVEMENTS & AWARDS: Named one of the
Outstanding Young Men of America ('74).
PERSONAL: Resides in Alexandria, VA, with his
wife, Ruth, and their son, Danny.

TAUBER, JAKE
V.P., Game Programs, NBC, Entertainment

c/o NBC, 3000 W. Alameda Ave., Burbank,
CA 91523
b. Syracuse, NY.

EDUCATION: Wayne State University, B.A.,
Mass Communications.
CAREER HIGHLIGHTS: Began career producing
industrial videotapes and regional commer-
cials before landing a job with Goodson-
Todman Productions as a Writer/Assoc. Prod.
for that company's game shows ('78); V.P.,
Game Programs, NBC Entertainment ('83).
ACHIEVEMENTS & AWARDS: N.A.
PERSONAL: Resides in Los Angeles with his
wife, Karol.

TAYBACK, VIC
Actor

c/o "Alice," CBS, 7800 Beverly Blvd., Los
Angeles, CA 90036
b. January 6. Brooklyn, NY.

EDUCATION: N.A.
CAREER HIGHLIGHTS: Starred in numerous
stage productions, including *The Diary of
Anne Frank*, *Death of a Salesman*, *Of Mice and
Men*, and *Stalag 17*, as well as feature films
including *Bullitt*, *Papillon*, *The Gambler*, and

Alice Doesn't Live Here Anymore. TV credits include "Mission: Impossible," "Star Trek," "The Man From UNCLE," "The Streets of San Francisco," "The Mary Tyler Moore Show," "Switch," "The Blue Knight," "All in the Family," "James at 15," "Supertrain," "The Love Boat," and "Fantasy Island." Has appeared in the TV movies *The Great American Traffic Jam, Honor Thy Father, Getting Married, Portrait of a Stripper,* and *Moviola.* Series regular as Mel on "Alice."

ACHIEVEMENTS & AWARDS: Two Golden Globe awards for his portrayal of Mel on "Alice" ('79, '80).

PERSONAL: Resides in Glendale, CA, with his wife, Sheila; son, Christopher.

TAYLOR, ARTHUR R.
Independent Prod.

1133 Ave. of the Americas, 7th Floor, New York, NY 10036
b. July 6, 1935. Elizabeth, NJ.

EDUCATION: Brown University, B.A. and M.A.

CAREER HIGHLIGHTS: V.P., Dir., First Boston Corp. ('61); Exec. V.P., Chief Financial Officer, Intl. Paper Co. ('70); Pres., Dir., Chief Operating Officer, CBS, Inc. ('72); Chairman and Pres., Arthur Taylor & Co. ('76); Chairman, Pres., and Chief Exec. Officer, RCTV/Entertainment Channel ('81); currently, Independent Prod.

ACHIEVEMENTS & AWARDS: Co-Founder and Pres., New York City Partnership, Inc. ('79–'81).

PERSONAL: N.A.

TAYLOR, EDWARD L.
Pres., Chairman of the Board, Satellite Syndicated Systems, SPN

8252 S. Harvard, Tulsa, OK 74136
b. December 21, 1932.

EDUCATION: Lehigh University, B.S.C.E.

CAREER HIGHLIGHTS: Held several key positions with AT&T, including Sales Mgr., Plant Design Engineer, Satellite Project Engineer, and Construction Engineer ('54–'70). Became Pres., Creative Consultants, satellite communications consulting firm ('70), then Pres.,

United Video ('72). Joined Southern Pacific Communications Co. as Regional V.P. ('75); V.P., Sales and Market Development, Western Union ('75); Founder, Satellite Syndicated Systems and Southern Satellite Systems ('76). Pres., Satellite Syndicated Systems, Chairman of the Board, SPN ('82).

ACHIEVEMENTS & AWARDS: Award for outstanding contributions and achievements in the film and TV industry, presented by Oklahoma Intl. Film Festival ('82).

PERSONAL: Wife, Nancy, children, Edward IV, Stephen, and Suzanne.

TAYLOR, LANCE B.
Dir., ABC, Current Comedy Programs, Entertainment

c/o ABC, 2040 Ave. of the Stars, Los Angeles, CA 90067
b. August 5, 1949. Montclair, NJ.

EDUCATION: San Fernando Valley State College, B.A., Telecommunications and Cinema.

CAREER HIGHLIGHTS: ABC Page ('70); Unit Mgr., ABC TV ('72); Program Administrator, ABC Entertainment ('76); Current Comedy Program Exec. ('77); appointed Dir., Current Comedy Programs ('79).

ACHIEVEMENTS & AWARDS: Member, Governor's Council for Employment of the Handicapped ('82); Guest Lecturer, Camp Marshallmount, Paramount Studios ('82); Guest Lecturer, Sherwood Oaks Experimental College ('82); Guest Lecturer, California State University ('80–'82).

PERSONAL: Wife, Vicki; children, Stoney and Sarah.

TAYLOR, RONALD
V.P., Dramatic Programs, MGM-UA Entertainment, TV

c/o MGM-UA Studios, 10202 W. Washington Blvd., Culver City, CA 90230
b. January 30, 1951. Los Angeles, CA.

EDUCATION: Yale College, B.A., Latin American Studies.

CAREER HIGHLIGHTS: Dir., Broadcast Standards and Practices, ABC ('73); Program Exec., Programming Dept., ABC ('76); Dir., Dramatic

Programs, ABC ('77); V.P., Motion Pictures Made for TV and Mini-Series, ABC ('78); V.P., Current Programs, ABC ('79); Exec. Prod., Motion Pictures Made for TV, ABC ('80); V.P., Dramatic Programs, MGM-UA Entertainment, TV ('81).
ACHIEVEMENTS & AWARDS: N.A.
PERSONAL: N.A.

TAYLOR, RUTH ASHTON
Reporter, KNXT-TV, News

c/o KNXT-TV, 6121 Sunset Blvd., Los
  Angeles, CA 90028
b. N.A.

EDUCATION: Columbia University School of Journalism.
CAREER HIGHLIGHTS: Asst. Dir., Public Affairs, KNXT Radio ('49); joined KNXT-TV ('51) as Co-Host, "Newsmakers" and "Today's Religion," and serves as Reporter and part-time Anchor for the station.
ACHIEVEMENTS & AWARDS: Golden Mike award.
PERSONAL: Married to cameraman Jack Taylor; three children.

TEMPLETON, JOE
Correspondent, ABC, News

c/o ABC, 1717 DeSales St., N.W.,
  Washington, DC 20036
b. Jamestown, NY.

EDUCATION: Northwestern University.
CAREER HIGHLIGHTS: Reporter/Late Night Anchor, WFAA-TV, Dallas ('57); Anchor, WTVJ-TV, Miami ('59); Anchor, WJZ-TV, Baltimore ('63); Anchor, WLS-TV, Chicago ('66); Correspondent, ABC News, Washington, DC ('68); while continuing his Correspondent duties, named Anchor for the ABC Radio Information Network's morning news broadcasts ('80); currently doing ABC newsbreaks as TV Correspondent.
ACHIEVEMENTS & AWARDS: Sylvania award ('58); Peabody award ('62).
PERSONAL: Resides in Washington, DC, with his wife, Eleanor; three children.

TENENBAUM, HENRY
Anchor/Reporter, WRC-TV, Washington, DC, News

c/o WRC-TV, 4001 Nebraska Ave., N.W.,
  Washington, DC 20016
b. N.A.

EDUCATION: University of Buffalo, B.A., English Literature, M.A., Educational Communications.
CAREER HIGHLIGHTS: News Writer, WKBW-TV, Buffalo, NY; Reporter, WKBW-TV, Buffalo, WTOP-TV, Washington, DC ('74); Asst. News Dir., WTOP-TV ('76); Host, "PM Magazine," WTOP-TV ('79); News Correspondent, NBC, Washington, DC; Anchor/Reporter, WRC-TV, Washington, DC ('82).
ACHIEVEMENTS & AWARDS: Three Washington, DC, area Emmy awards.
PERSONAL: N.A.

TESH, JOHN
Reporter, CBS, Sports

c/o CBS, 51 W. 52d St., New York, NY 10019
b. N.A.

EDUCATION: North Carolina State University; Juilliard School.
CAREER HIGHLIGHTS: Worked as Anchor, Reporter, and Prod., in Raleigh, NC, Orlando, FL, and Nashville; Correspondent, WCBS-TV, New York ('76); Reporter, CBS Sports, including the U.S. Open, "CBS Sports Saturday/Sunday" ('81–'83).
ACHIEVEMENTS & AWARDS: Two local Emmy awards while at WCBS-TV.
PERSONAL: Has run in the New York City Marathon.

THOMAS, BETTY
Actress

c/o "Hill Street Blues," NBC, 3000 W.
  Alameda Ave., Burbank, CA 91523
b. July 27. St. Louis, MO.

EDUCATION: Ohio University.
CAREER HIGHLIGHTS: Feature films include *Tunnelvision, Used Cars,* and *Jackson County Jail;* has appeared on the game show "Fun Fac-

tory" and is a series regular on "Hill Street Blues."
ACHIEVEMENTS & AWARDS: N.A.
PERSONAL: Single, resides in Studio City, CA.

THOMAS, C. ANTHONY (Tony Thomas)
Exec. Prod., ABC

1888 Century Park E., Suite 1400, Los Angeles, CA 90067
b. December 7, 1948. Los Angeles, CA.

EDUCATION: University of San Diego.
CAREER HIGHLIGHTS: Asst. to the Prod., "Young Rebels" series, Screen Gems ('68); Assoc. Prod., "The Sheriff," *Brian's Song*, "Getting Together" series, Screen Gems ('69); Prod., *Blood Sport* ('72); Prod., "The Practice" series ('73); Prod., "Soap" ('75); Prod., "It Takes Two" ('82); and "Just Married" ('83).
ACHIEVEMENTS & AWARDS: N.A.
PERSONAL: Father is comedian Danny Thomas and sister is actress Marlo Thomas.

THOMAS, FRED
Newsman/Public Affairs Show Host, WRC-TV

c/o WRC-TV, 4001 Nebraska Ave., N.W., Washington, DC 20016
b. July 11, 1938.

EDUCATION: University of Maryland; Brooklyn College.
CAREER HIGHLIGHTS: Page and Desk Asst., NBC News, New York ('61); participated in an NBC TV training program ('65–'66); Writer and Reporter, WMAQ-TV, NBC, Chicago ('66–'70); joined WRC-TV ('75). In addition to reporting features regularly on "Channel 4 News Live," Thomas is currently the Host, of the weekday public affairs program "Fred Thomas in the Morning."
ACHIEVEMENTS & AWARDS: N.A.
PERSONAL: N.A.

THOMAS, JIM
Reporter, KNBC-TV, News

c/o KNBC-TV, 3000 W. Alameda Ave., Burbank, CA 91523
b. Atlanta, GA.

EDUCATION: University of Georgia, B.A., TV Journalism ('78).
CAREER HIGHLIGHTS: Sports Dir., WYEA-TV, Columbus, GA ('78); Prod./Anchor, WMAZ-TV, Macon, GA ('79); Prod./Anchor/Reporter, WAGA-TV, Atlanta ('80); Anchor, KTTV-TV, Los Angeles ('82); Reporter, KNBC-TV, Los Angeles ('83).
ACHIEVEMENTS & AWARDS: N.A.
PERSONAL: Resides in Redondo Beach, CA.

THOMAS, REGINALD R.
V.P., ESPN, Technical Operations and Engineering

174 Bengeyfield Dr., East Williston, NY 11596
b. May 2, 1934. New York, NY.

EDUCATION: Polytechnic Institute of Brooklyn, BSEE.
CAREER HIGHLIGHTS: Started as Design Engineer, Sperry Rand Corp. ('57), rose to Sr. Staff Engineer, NBC ('67); became Network Dir. Technical Facilities, NBC ('73); V.P., Technical Operations and Engineering, ESPN ('80).
ACHIEVEMENTS & AWARDS: N.A.
PERSONAL: Wife, Dorothy; daughters, Deborah and Dawn; son, Robert.

THOMAS, STANLEY B., JR.
Sr. V.P., Natl. Accts., HBO

c/o HBO, 1271 Ave. of the Americas, New York, NY 10020
b. April 28, 1942.

EDUCATION: Yale University.
CAREER HIGHLIGHTS: Asst. to the Corporate Secretary and Marketing Mgr., Time, Inc. ('64); Deputy Asst. Secretary, Dept. of HEW, Washington, DC ('69); Exec. in the Marketing and Business Planning Group, ITT ('76); Asst. to the Chairman and Chief Exec. Officer, HBO ('79); Dir. of the Natl. Acct. Management Group, HBO ('80); V.P., Natl. Accts., HBO ('81); Sr. V.P., Natl. Accts., HBO ('83).

ACHIEVEMENTS & AWARDS: N.A.

PERSONAL: Resides in Tenafly, NJ, with wife, Elizabeth, and children, Chip and Beth.

THOMOPOULOS, ANTHONY DENIS
Pres., ABC, Broadcast Group

c/o ABC, 1330 Ave. of the Americas, New York, NY 10019

b. February 7, 1938. Mount Vernon, NY.

EDUCATION: Georgetown University, B.S., Foreign Service ('59).

CAREER HIGHLIGHTS: NBC Mailroom ('59); Production and Administrative Depts. of Radio Division ('60); Intl. Division Sales ('61). Left network to serve as Dir., Foreign Sales, Four Star Entertainment Corp. ('64); V.P., Foreign Sales, Four Star ('65); Exec. V.P. ('69). Dir. of Programming, RCA SelectaVision Division ('70); V.P., "Tomorrow Entertainment," TV Marketing ('71). Joined ABC Entertainment as V.P., Primetime Programs, New York ('73); V.P., Primetime TV Creative Operations ('74); V.P., Special Programs ('75); V.P. and Asst. to Pres., ABC TV ('76). Appointed Pres., ABC Entertainment ('78); added responsibilities for Business Affairs and On-Air Promotion ('81); Pres. ABC Broadcast Group.

ACHIEVEMENTS & AWARDS: Charter Member, Board of Governors, Southern California Regional Natl. Conference of Christians and Jews ('80); Board of Dirs. Sundance Institute ('81); Board of Dirs., Hollywood Radio and TV Society ('82); honorary Fire Chief, Los Angeles City Fire Dept. ('82).

PERSONAL: Wife, Penny; children, Anne, Dennis, and Mark.

THOMPSON, LEA
Anchor/Reporter, WRC-TV News

c/o WRC-TV, 4001 Nebraska Ave., N.W., Washington, DC 20016

b. July 21, 1945.

EDUCATION: University of Wisconsin at Madison, B.A., Journalism and Marketing.

CAREER HIGHLIGHTS: Acct. Exec. Training Program, J. Walter Thompson advertising agency, New York; Administrator of Editorial Services, WRC-TV ('70–'73); Reporter, NBC News, "Today," "Nightly News" ('70–present).

ACHIEVEMENTS & AWARDS: N.A.

PERSONAL: Resides in Bethesda, MD, with husband, Durke, and two children.

THRELKELD, RICHARD
Correspondent, ABC, News

c/o ABC, 7 W. 66th St., New York, NY 10023

b. November 20, 1937. Cedar Rapids, IL.

EDUCATION: Ripon College, B.A., Political Science and History ('60); Medill School of Journalism, B.S.J. ('61); Columbia University School of International Affairs ('65).

CAREER HIGHLIGHTS: Joined WHAS-TV ('61); Reporter for WMT-TV, Cedar Rapids, IA ('61); Prod./Editor, CBS News ('66); Prod./Correspondent ('66); extensive overseas reporting for four years; Bureau Chief, San Francisco ('70); Co-Anchor, CBS Morning News ('77); Cover Story Correspondent for "CBS Sunday Morning"; joined ABC News as Natl. Correspondent ('82).

ACHIEVEMENTS & AWARDS: Several Emmy awards, including one for work on the CBS documentary "The War Machine" ('82);

Overseas Press Club award. Member, RTN-DA; Sigma Delta Chi; Phi Beta Kappa; Overseas Press Club; Assn. of Radio and TV News Analysts.

PERSONAL: Resides in New York City; daughters, Susan and Julie.

THURM, JOEL
V.P., NBC, Talent

c/o NBC, 3000 W. Alameda Ave., Burbank, CA 91505
b. Brooklyn, NY.

EDUCATION: Hunter College, B.A.; University of Perugia (Italy).

CAREER HIGHLIGHTS: Stage Mgr., Company Mgr., House Mgr., for Music Fair Entertainment ('65); Casting Dir., David Merrick Enterprises ('67); Assoc. Prod. for ABC's "The Pearl Bailey Show" ('70); Prod. Mgr. for the Greek Theater and Huntington Hartford Theater ('71). Joined CBS as Dir. of Casting ('72); Co-Prod., *The Boy in the Plastic Bubble* ('76); Prod., "Angie" for ABC/Paramount ('78); Dir. of Casting, Paramount Pictures and TV ('78); appointed V.P., Talent, NBC ('80).

ACHIEVEMENTS & AWARDS: N.A.

PERSONAL: Single, resides in Hollywood.

TIGHE, MARY ANN (Mary Ann Tighe Hidalgo)
V.P., Program Development, ABC, Video Enterprises

825 Seventh Ave., New York, NY 10019
b. August 24, 1948. New York, NY.

EDUCATION: Catholic University of America, B.A., Arts and Humanities; University of Maryland, M.A., Art History.

CAREER HIGHLIGHTS: Museum Fellow, Natl. Collection of Fine Arts, Smithsonian Institute ('70–'72); teaching and curatorial positions in American and European art history at Georgetown University ('71–'77); Northern Virginia Community College ('71–'73); Catholic University of America ('75); Smithsonian Resident Assoc. ('74–'77). Prod. and Co-Author "Art in America" TV series ('74–'75); Curator of Education, Smithsonian Institute, Hirshorn Museum ('74–'77); Office of the V.P. of the U.S. as Arts Adviser ('77–'78). Deputy Chairman, Natl. Endowment of the Arts ('78–'81); joined ABC Video Enterprises as Prod./Writer ('80); named V.P., Program Development ('81).

ACHIEVEMENTS & AWARDS: University of Maryland Fellow ('71–'72); Alumni of the Year, Government ('80); collaborated on *Art America* with Elizabeth E. Lang ('77); monthly columnist for *House and Garden*.

PERSONAL: N.A.

TILTON, CHARLENE
Actress

c/o "Dallas," CBS, 7800 Beverly Blvd., Los Angeles, CA 90036
b. December 1, 1958. San Diego, CA.

EDUCATION: N.A.

CAREER HIGHLIGHTS: Started professional acting career in the Walt Disney feature *Freaky Friday*, and also appeared in *Big Wednesday* and *Sweater Girls*. Guest roles in "Happy Days," "Eight Is Enough," "Please Stand By," "James at 15," "Police Woman," "The

Love Boat," "Fantasy Island," and "The Bionic Woman" and was a guest host of "Saturday Night Live." TV movie credits include *Diary of a Teenage Hitchhiker* and *The Fall of the House of Usher*. Currently stars as Lucy Ewing in the hit series "Dallas."

ACHIEVEMENTS & AWARDS: N.A.

PERSONAL: Resides in Beverly Hills, CA, with her husband, country singer Johnny Lee.

TIMBERMAN, ELEANOR
Dir., Daytime Program Development, ABC, Entertainment

c/o ABC, 1330 Ave. of the Americas, New York, NY 10019
b. N.A.

EDUCATION: Brandeis University; Columbia University.

CAREER HIGHLIGHTS: Production Exec. for the Allied Artists Movie *Cabaret*; Head of Development, MGM Films; Story Editor, Film Division, Warner Bros.; Program Development, NBC; Dir., Daytime Program Development, ABC Entertainment, New York ('81).

ACHIEVEMENTS & AWARDS: N.A.

PERSONAL: Resides in New York City; two children.

TIMOTHY, RAYMOND J.
Pres., NBC TV Network, NBC

c/o NBC, 30 Rockefeller Plaza, New York, NY 10020
b. March 23, 1932. New York, NY.

EDUCATION: Queens College, B.A., Political Science; Brooklyn Law School, LL.B. ('61).

CAREER HIGHLIGHTS: NBC Tour Guide; Records Clerk ('59); Network Sales ('60); Acct. Exec., NBC Spot Sales ('64); local Sales Mgr. for WKYC-TV, Cleveland ('66); moved to WRC as General Sales Mgr. ('67); Station Mgr., WKYC-TV ('70); V.P. and General Mgr., KNBC ('73); V.P. and General Mgr., WNBC-TV ('76); Exec. V.P., NBC Affiliate Relations ('77); Exec. V.P., NBC TV Network ('79); appointed Pres., NBC TV Network ('81).

ACHIEVEMENTS & AWARDS: N.A.

PERSONAL: Married to the former Kathleen Shanahan; children, Matthew, Patrick, and Luke.

TINKER, GRANT A.
Chairman of the Board and Chief Exec. Officer, NBC, Inc.

c/o NBC, 3000 W. Alameda Ave., Burbank, CA 91523
b. January 11, 1926. Stamford, CT.

EDUCATION: Dartmouth College, B.A.

CAREER HIGHLIGHTS: Because Tinker was one of the prime movers behind the phenomenal success of MTM Enterprises, NBC has pinned high hopes on his ability to alter their also-ran status. As NBC Chief Exec., Tinker's strong suit has been permitting off-beat, sophisticated series such as "Cheers" and "Hill Street Blues" the opportunity to develop a following. Benton & Bowles advertising agency ('58); V.P. Programs, West Coast, NBC ('61); V.P., Programming, NBC, New York ('66); V.P., Universal TV ('68); V.P., 20th Century-Fox TV ('69); Pres. and Chief Exec. Officer, MTM Enterprises ('70); Chairman of the Board and Chief Exec. Officer, NBC, Inc. ('81).

ACHIEVEMENTS & AWARDS: N.A.

PERSONAL: N.A.

TINKER, MARK
Prod. (Freelance)

c/o MTM Enterprises, 4024 Radford Avenue, Studio City, CA 91604
b. 1952. Darien, CT.

EDUCATION: Syracuse University, B.S., Communications ('73).

CAREER HIGHLIGHTS: Learned the business from his father, Grant Tinker, and went on to become an enterprising TV producer. Began as Prod. Asst. with Lorimar, working on "The Waltons" and "Apple's Way" ('73); joined MTM Enterprises as Assoc. Prod. on "Three for the Road" ('75); worked on "The Bob Newhart Show." Prod., TV movie *Thornwell*, series "The White Shadow"; Dir., "The Bob Newhart Show" and "Making the Grade"; Prod., "St. Elsewhere" ('82).

ACHIEVEMENTS & AWARDS: N.A.

PERSONAL: N.A.

TIPPETS, THOMAS
Mgr., Program Operations, West Coast, NBC, Entertainment

c/o NBC, 3000 W. Alameda Ave., Burbank, CA 91523
b. San Diego, CA.

EDUCATION: Brigham Young University, B.A., Communications.
CAREER HIGHLIGHTS: Staff, KBYU-TV, Provo, UT ('71); Staff, KUTV-TV, Salt Lake City ('72); Mail Room Clerk, NBC, Burbank ('73); Clerk, Shipping and Receiving, NBC ('74); Assoc., Film Editing and Video Tape ('75); Film and Tape Coordinator, NBC ('76); Supervisor, Film Exchange ('78); Mgr., Program Operations, West Coast, NBC Entertainment ('80).
ACHIEVEMENTS & AWARDS: N.A.
PERSONAL: Resides in Burbank with wife, Linda, and daughters, Carrie and Anna.

TIRADO, ROBERTO
Weathercaster, WPIX-TV, New York

c/o WPIX-TV, 11 WPIX Plaza, New York, NY 10017
b. October 22, 1945. New York, NY.

EDUCATION: Southern Connecticut State College.
CAREER   HIGHLIGHTS: Weatherman,   WPIX News ('79).
ACHIEVEMENTS & AWARDS: N.A.
PERSONAL: Resides in North Haven, CT.

TISCHLER, BOB
Prod., NBC TV, "Saturday Night Live"

c/o NBC, 30 Rockefeller Plaza, New York, NY 10020
b. New York.

EDUCATION: N.A.
CAREER HIGHLIGHTS: Prod., four National Lampoon comedy albums; Prod., all three Blues Brothers albums; Sound Prod., "Saturday Night Live" comedy album; Consultant, for the second season of "SCTV"; Prod., "National Lampoon Radio Hour." Supervising Prod., "Saturday Night Live" ('81).
ACHIEVEMENTS & AWARDS: N.A.
PERSONAL: N.A.

TJADEN, GAROLD S.
V.P., Cox Cable Communications, Engineering and Technology

c/o Cox Cable Communications, 219 Perimeter Center Pkwy., Atlanta, GA 30346
b. November 1, 1944. Bismarck, ND.

EDUCATION: Johns Hopkins University, Ph.D., Computer Science ('72).
CAREER HIGHLIGHTS: Dir. of Hardware Technology, Sperry Univac ('76); V.P., Engineering and Technology, Cox Cable Communications, Atlanta ('79).
ACHIEVEMENTS & AWARDS: Chairman, Engineering Committee, NCTA.
PERSONAL: N.A.

TOMIZAWA, THOMAS
Sr. Prod., NBC News, "Monitor"

c/o NBC, 30 Rockefeller Plaza, New York, NY 10020
b. September 3, 1928.

EDUCATION: Northwestern University.
CAREER HIGHLIGHTS: Reporter, *Louisville Times* ('54); Asst. City Editor, *Stars and Stripes*, Tokyo ('56); rejoined *Louisville Times* as Reporter ('59); Writer, NBC ('62). Went on to produce numerous documentaries, including "What Is This Thing Called Food?" ('76); "The Last Voyage of the Argo Merchant" ('77), "The Struggle for Freedom," "Kissinger on the Record," "Henry Kissinger: An Interview With David Frost" ('79); Prod./Writer/Dir., "Just Plain Folks: The Billionaire Hunts" ('81); Co-Prod./Writer/Dir., "NBC Reports: Protection for Sale" ('82) and Prod., "NBC Reports: For Every Violence—There Is a Victim."
ACHIEVEMENTS & AWARDS: N.A.
PERSONAL: Wife, Sayoka; four sons. Resides in Jamaica, NY.

TONG, KAITY
Correspondent, Co-Anchor, WABC-TV, Eyewitness News, Weekend Edition

c/o WABC-TV, 7 Lincoln Sq., New York, NY 10023
b. Tsingtao, China.

EDUCATION: Bryn Mawr College, B.A., English Literature (with honors); Stanford University, master's, Chinese and Japanese Literature ('71).

CAREER HIGHLIGHTS: Tong's broadcasting career began with a summer job as Morning Editor/Prod., KCBS All-News Radio, San Francisco ('74); Street Reporter, KPIX-TV, CBS, San Francisco ('75); Co-Anchor, Noon and 6:30 P.M. News Telecasts, KCRA-TV, Sacramento, CA ('77); Co-Anchor, Early and Late Nightly Newscasts, KCRA-TV ('79); Correspondent, Co-Anchor, WABC-TV, New York ('81).

ACHIEVEMENTS & AWARDS: N.A.

PERSONAL: Married, resides in Manhattan.

TOROKVEI, PETER JOHN
Actor/Writer/Prod., Comworld Productions, Development

c/o APA, 9000 Sunset Blvd., Los Angeles, CA 90069
b. March 19, 1951. Toronto, Canada.

EDUCATION: York University, B.A.; Osgoode Hall Law School.

CAREER HIGHLIGHTS: Story Editor/Writer, "WKRP in Cincinnati" ('79); Prod./Writer, "WKRP in Cincinnati" ('80–'82); Creator/Writer/Prod., "The Martin Mull Show," Universal TV ('82); Exec. Prod./Writer, Comworld Productions ('82); Exec. Prod./Writer, Comworld Productions ('83).

ACHIEVEMENTS & AWARDS: Humanitas award as producer of "WKRP in Cincinnati" ('81).

PERSONAL: Wife, Andrea; daughter, Caitlin. Resides in Encino, CA.

TOWNLEY, RICHARD
Anchor, "The Wall Street Journal Report"

220 E. 42d St., New York, NY 10017
b. December 17, 1935.

EDUCATION: Odessa College.

CAREER HIGHLIGHTS: Speech Writer for Sargent Shriver; Freelance Writer, *TV Guide* and *Columbia Journalism Review*; covered civil rights stories, NBC TV; Staff Reporter, WDSU-TV, New Orleans; Prod., documentaries; Investigative/Political/Economic Reporter.

ACHIEVEMENTS & AWARDS: Ohio State University award; San Francisco State media award; UPI, AP, New York State Broadcasters, and American Bar Assn. awards. Founding Member and first Chairman, UPI Broadcasters Assn., New York.

PERSONAL: N.A.

TOYOTA, TRITIA
Co-Anchor, KNBC, "News 4 LA"

c/o KNBC, 3000 W. Alameda Ave., Burbank, CA 91523
b. Oregon.

EDUCATION: Oregon State University, B.S.; University of California at Los Angeles, Journalism ('70).

CAREER HIGHLIGHTS: Action Reporter, CBS/KNX Radio, Hollywood; General News Reporter, KNBC ('72); hosted KNBC public affairs programs; Co-Anchor, KNBC ('82).

ACHIEVEMENTS & AWARDS: N.A.

PERSONAL: N.A.

TRABERT, TONY
Sports Broadcaster, CBS

c/o CBS, 7800 Beverly Blvd., Los Angeles, CA 90036
b. August 16, 1930. Cincinnati, OH.

EDUCATION: N.A.

CAREER HIGHLIGHTS: Trabert's impressive tennis career includes capturing the doubles at the Italian, U.S. Hardcourts, and French Championships ('50), and being a member of the U.S. Davis Cup Team ('50–'55). He is in his 11th year as Analyst, CBS Sports coverage of major tennis events broadcast on the CBS TV network and has been a Commentator, for coverage of professional golf, including the Westchester Classic.

ACHIEVEMENTS & AWARDS: Elected to the Natl. Tennis Hall of Fame ('70).

PERSONAL: Wife, Emeryl. Resides in Rancho Mirage, CA.

TRAUM, RICK
Dir., Program Development and Production, NBC Enterprises

c/o NBC, 3000 W. Alameda Blvd., Burbank, CA 91523
b. New York, NY.

EDUCATION: New York University, B.S., Business Management.
CAREER HIGHLIGHTS: Began as a Page with NBC, New York ('66); Assoc. Commercial Prod., "The Tonight Show Starring Johnny Carson" ('67); Administrator, Financial Analysis, NBC Business Affairs Dept. ('74); General Program Exec. assigned to "Saturday Night Live" ('76); Mgr., Administration, NBC Programming Dept. ('76); Dir., Late Night Programs and Administration, NBC TV ('78); formed his own independent production company ('80); Dir., Program Development and Production, NBC Enterprises ('83).
ACHIEVEMENTS & AWARDS: N.A.
PERSONAL: Resides in New York City with his wife, Deborah.

TRAVANTI, DANIEL J.
Actor

c/o "Hill Street Blues," NBC, 3000 W. Alameda Ave., Burbank, CA 91523
b. Kenosha, WA.

EDUCATION: University of Wisconsin; Yale School of Drama; Loyola-Marymount University.
CAREER HIGHLIGHTS: Brought uncommon depth to TV police work with a new kind of primetime hero who is intelligent and compassionate, yet able to protect his principles with as much determination and force as his opponents. Stage credits include *Twigs* and *Othello*, and he appeared in the TV programs "Kojak," "The FBI," "The Mod Squad," "Barnaby Jones," "Hart to Hart," and "Knots Landing." Served as a guest host of "Saturday Night Live," and had a recurring role in the soap opera "General Hospital." Now stars as Capt. Frank Furillo in "Hill Street Blues."
ACHIEVEMENTS & AWARDS: Two Emmy awards as best actor in a drama series for "Hill Street Blues"; Golden Globe award as best actor in a drama series for "Hill Street Blues."
PERSONAL: Single, resides in Venice, CA.

TREBEK, ALEX
Game Show Host, NBC, "The New Battlestars"

c/o NBC, 3000 W. Alameda Ave., Burbank, CA 91523
b. July 22, 1940. Sudbury, Ontario.

EDUCATION: University of Ottawa.
CAREER HIGHLIGHTS: Began career as a Master of Ceremonies in his native Canada with the "Stars on Ice" variety show and later "Championship Horse Racing" and "Championship Sports." As a Game Show Host, Trebek has been at the helm of such shows as "Reach for the Top," "The $128,000 Question," "Wizard of Odds," "High Rollers," "Battlestars," "Pitfall," and "The New Battlestars."
ACHIEVEMENTS & AWARDS: N.A.
PERSONAL: Resides in Beverly Hills, CA, with his wife, Elaine.

TRIAS, JENNIE
Dir., Children's Programs, West Coast, ABC, Entertainment

c/o ABC, 2040 Ave. of the Stars, Los Angeles, CA 90067
b. N.A.

EDUCATION: Marquette University.
CAREER HIGHLIGHTS: Production Asst., ABC Circle Films and Filmation Studios ('76); Program Coordinator, ABC Entertainment ('78); Supervisor, Current Children's Programs, ABC ('80); Mgr., Children's Programs, West Coast, ABC Entertainment, Los Angeles ('81);

Dir., Children's Programs, West Coast, ABC Entertainment ('83).
ACHIEVEMENTS & AWARDS: N.A.
PERSONAL: Resides in Sherman Oaks, CA.

TROTTA, LIZ
Correspondent, CBS, News

c/o CBS, 524 57th St., New York, NY 10019
b. March 28, 1937. New Haven, CT.

EDUCATION: Boston University, B.A.; Columbia University Graduate School of Journalism, M.S.
CAREER HIGHLIGHTS: NBC News Correspondent ('65); Investigative Reporter ('75); News Correspondent, CBS ('79).
ACHIEVEMENTS & AWARDS: AP broadcasters award; two national and one local Emmy awards; Overseas Press Club award; Front Page award for reporting; Ohio State University award for radio reporting. First American woman in TV news to become a full-time foreign correspondent.
PERSONAL: N.A.

TROUTE, DENNIS
Correspondent, ABC, News

c/o ABC, 7 W. 66th St., New York, NY 10023
b. N.A.

EDUCATION: University of San Francisco, B.A., History.
CAREER HIGHLIGHTS: Freelance Reporter, NBC News, Saigon, South Vietnam ('71); Correspondent, NBC News, Saigon ('73); Freelance Reporter for both KNXT-TV, Los Angeles, and KQED-TV, San Francisco ('75); Reporter/Documentary Prod., WFAA-TV, Dallas ('77); Correspondent, Cable News Network, Rome ('80); Diplomatic Correspondent, Cable News Network, Washington, DC ('81); Correspondent, ABC News, Dallas ('82).
ACHIEVEMENTS & AWARDS: N.A.
PERSONAL: N.A.

TUNNELL, DOUG
Correspondent, CBS, News

c/o CBS, 524 W. 57th St., New York, NY 10019
b. November 13, 1949.

EDUCATION: Lewis and Clark College, B.A. (cum laude, '72); Columbia University School of Journalism, M.S. ('75).
CAREER HIGHLIGHTS: Reporter, Copley News Service, in Beirut and Saudi Arabia ('73); Freelance Reporter, CBS News, Beirut ('75); Staff Reporter, CBS News ('76); Correspondent, CBS News ('77); Correspondent, CBS News, London ('79).
ACHIEVEMENTS & AWARDS: Overseas Press Club award; Sigma Delta Chi distinguished service award.
PERSONAL: N.A.

TURNER, ED
News Dir., Exec. Prod., V.P., Cable News Network, News

c/o Cable News Network, 1050 Techwood Dr., N.W., Atlanta, GA 30318
b. September 25, 1935. Bartlesville, OK.

EDUCATION: University of Oklahoma, B.A., Journalism.
CAREER HIGHLIGHTS: Reporter/Anchor, KWTV, Oklahoma City ('59); Press Sec., for Bud Wilkinson's bid for the U.S. Senate ('64); News Dir., WTTG-TV, Washington DC ('66); V.P., UPITN ('74); Prod., "CBS Morning News" ('74); V.P. and News Dir., KWTV ('78); News Dir., Exec. Prod., V.P., Cable News Network ('80).
ACHIEVEMENTS & AWARDS: Cannes Film Festival award for best educational documentary ('59); six UPI awards for best reporting ('60–'64); seven Emmy awards while at WTTG.
PERSONAL: Wife, Beth; son, Chris.

TURNER, TED
Chairman of the Board and Pres., Turner Broadcasting System and Cable News Network

c/o Turner Broadcasting System, 1050 Techwood Dr., N.W., Atlanta, GA 30318
b. November 19, 1938. Cincinnati, OH.

EDUCATION: Brown University.
CAREER HIGHLIGHTS: Visionary, provocative broadcast executive who developed the idea of "SuperStations," merging a regular broad-

cast signal with national cable distribution. Against great economic odds, he conceived and developed the first all-news cable network—the Cable News Network. Began his business career as an Acct. Exec., Turner Advertising Co., Savannah, GA. Became General Mgr., Turner Advertising, Macon, GA ('60); Pres. and Chief Exec. Officer of the various Turner companies ('63), with offices in Atlanta. Turner Broadcasting System owns and operates SuperStation WTBS, Cable News Network, Headline News, Turner Program Sales, and the Atlanta Braves baseball team, and has a partnership in the Atlanta Hawks. He also purchased the Satellite News Channel ('83).

ACHIEVEMENTS & AWARDS: Outstanding Entrepreneur of the Year, *Sales Marketing and Management* magazine ('79); president's award, Natl. Cable TV Assn. ('79); Intl. Communicator of the Year, Sales and Marketing Execs. ('81); sponsor recognition award, the American Council for Better Broadcasts ('81); Business Leader of the Year, 1982, Sigma Delta Pi and the Georgetown University School of Business Administration; Man of the Year, Harvard Business School Communications Chapter ('82).

PERSONAL: N.A.

TURNEY, ED
News Reporter, WJLA-TV

c/o WJLA-TV, 4461 Connecticut Ave., N.W., Washington, DC 20008
b. N.A.

EDUCATION: N.A.
CAREER HIGHLIGHTS: Reporter, KSBW-TV, California; Disc Jockey, WDON-AM, WASH-FM, WMLP, and WJBF; News Reporter, WJLA-TV ('62).
ACHIEVEMENTS & AWARDS: Emmy awards for reporting.
PERSONAL: Married, three daughters. Resides in Silver Spring, MD.

TUSH, BILL
Co-Host, WTBS, "The Lighter Side"

c/o WTBS, 1050 Techwood Dr., N.W., Atlanta, GA 30318
b. N.A.

EDUCATION: N.A.
CAREER HIGHLIGHTS: Joined WTRA-Radio, Latrobe, PA; Traffic Reporter; WEIR Radio in Weirton, WV; News Dir., WEDO-Radio, Pittsburgh ('68); Newscaster, ABC-owned KQV-Radio, Pittsburgh; Program Dir., WEDO; "Afternoon Man," then News Anchor, WGST-Radio ('74); Host, "Academy Award Theater" and Saturday "Hollywood Classics" at WTBS; member of Turner Broadcasting family WTCG, now WTBS, News Dir. and Anchor ('74); Anchor, "Early in the Morning News Show" ('76); WTBS one-hour comedy show, "Tush" ('80–'81); Host, "Atlantic City Alive" ('80–'81); Host, "The Lighter Side" and Cable News Network's "People Now."
ACHIEVEMENTS & AWARDS: Georgia Emmy for outstanding achievement: individual excellence as a performer."
PERSONAL: N.A.

TWIBELL, ROGER C.
Sportscaster, ESPN

c/o ESPN, ESPN Plaza, Bristol, CT 06010
b. October 17, 1949. Kansas City, MO.

EDUCATION: University of Kansas, B.S., Radio/TV Journalism ('72).
CAREER HIGHLIGHTS: Sports Dir., KGUN-TV, Tucson, AZ ('72); Sports Dir., KATU-TV, Portland, OR ('73); Sports Dir., KDFW-TV, Dallas ('75); Sportscaster, WTVJ-TV Miami ('76); Sports Dir., WBZ-TV, Boston ('78);

Sportscaster, PBP Announcer, ESPN, Bristol, CT ('82).

ACHIEVEMENTS & AWARDS: Best play-by-play announcer in New England, AP; New England Emmy for best play-by-play; Syracuse University's Phillips award for best nightly sportscaster.

PERSONAL: Wife, Sarah.

ULASEWICZ, JOSEPH P.
V.P., NBC, West Coast, Operations and Technical Services

c/o NBC, 3000 W. Alameda Ave., Burbank, CA 91523
b. New York, NY.

EDUCATION: Rensselaer Polytechnic Institute, B.S., Electrical Engineering.
CAREER HIGHLIGHTS: Management Trainee, RCA, Camden, NJ ('47); continued at RCA in TV Broadcast Engineering; then in Sales; became Equipment Field Sales Representative ('54); Mgr., Antenna Merchandising ('63); Mgr., Broadcast and Communications Product Marketing ('65); Mgr., Intl. Sales Dept. ('67); Division V.P., Intl. Operations ('71); Division V.P., Product Operations ('75); V.P., Operations and Technical Services, NBC West Coast ('80).
ACHIEVEMENTS & AWARDS: N.A.
PERSONAL: N.A.

ULRICH, STEPHEN
Mgr., Talent and Promotion, NBC, Sports

c/o NBC, 30 Rockefeller Plaza, New York, NY 10020
b. Lockport, NY.

EDUCATION: University of Rochester, B.A., Economics ('78).
CAREER HIGHLIGHTS: Chief Researcher for 1980 Olympic Games, NBC Sports ('78); Production Assoc., NBC Sports ('80); Administrator, Program Planning and Development ('80); Mgr., Talent and Promotion, NBC Sports ('83).
ACHIEVEMENTS & AWARDS: N.A.
PERSONAL: Single, resides in New York City.

UNGER, ARTHUR
TV Critic, *Christian Science Monitor*

c/o *Christian Science Monitor*, Suite 3006, 220 E. 42d St., New York, NY 10017
b. March 29, 1924. New York, NY.

EDUCATION: University of Missouri School of Journalism, B.J.
CAREER HIGHLIGHTS: One of the most perceptive newspaper TV critics. Editorial Dir., Great American Publications ('55); Editor and Publisher, Young World Press ('60); Entertainment Editor, *Ingenue* magazine ('70). TV Critic, *Christian Science Monitor*.
ACHIEVEMENTS & AWARDS: N.A.
PERSONAL: N.A.

UPSHAW, JAMES
Reporter, NBC

c/o NBC, Japan NTV, Yonban Cho, Bekkan Bldg. 5-6, Yonban Cho-Chiyoda-ku, Tokyo, Japan
b. N.A.

EDUCATION: N.A.
CAREER HIGHLIGHTS: Reporter for *Union Tribune*, San Diego, CA, *Tampa Times*, and *San Jose Mercury*; Science/Technology Writer, Lockheed Missiles and Space Co. ('67); Prod., KTVU-TV, Oakland, CA ('70); Writer, Prod., and Reporter, KNBC-TV, Burbank ('71); Reporter/Anchor, KMGH-TV, Denver ('73); General Assignment Reporter, WRC-TV ('74); NBC News Correspondent assigned to Tokyo ('82).
ACHIEVEMENTS & AWARDS: Emmy award.
PERSONAL: Wife, Joan; two daughters. Resides in McLean, VA.

VALENTE, RENEE
Prod.

c/o Lou Pitt, ICM, 8899 Beverly Blvd., Los
Angeles, CA 90048
b. July 15. New York, NY.

EDUCATION: New York University.
CAREER HIGHLIGHTS: V.P., Exec. Dir of Talent,
Columbia Pictures ('68); Exec. Prod., V.P.,
Movies for TV, Columbia Pictures ('75);
formed Renee Valente Productions, Prod.,
Blind Ambition, Swan Song ('78); joined 20th
Century Fox as Ind. Prod. ('80). Exec. Prod.,
"Masquerade," an ABC series ('83–'84).
ACHIEVEMENTS & AWARDS: Emmy award ('60);
Woman of the Year, Conference of Personal
Mgrs. ('72); NOSOTROS award ('74); Los An-
geles achievement award in communications,
City of Hope ('75).
PERSONAL: Husband, Buzz Smidt.

VALENTI, JACK
Pres., Motion Picture Assn. of America;
Motion Picture Export Assn. of America;
Chairman, Alliance of Motion Picture and
TV Producers

525 Fifth Ave., New York, NY
b. September 5, 1921.

EDUCATION: University of Houston, B.A. ('46);
Harvard University, M.B.A. ('48).
CAREER HIGHLIGHTS: Co-founder, Weekley &
Valenti advertising and political consulting
agency ('52). Special Asst. to the Pres. of the
U.S. ('63–'66). Also Pres., Motion Picture
Assn. of America; Pres., Motion Picture Ex-
port Assn. of America; and Chairman, Alli-
ance of Motion Picture Producers.
ACHIEVEMENTS & AWARDS: Member, Board of
Dirs., TWA and Riggs Natl. Bank of Washing-
ton, DC; member, Board of Trustees, Ken-
nedy Center for the Performing Arts and the
American Film Institute. Author, *The Bitter
Taste of Glory, A Very Human President*, and
*Speak Up With Confidence: How To Prepare,
Learn and Deliver an Effective Speech.* Adjunct
Professor of Government and Public Admin-
istration, American University ('77).
PERSONAL: N.A.

VALERIANI, RICHARD
Correspondent, NBC, News

c/o NBC, 4001 Nebraska Ave., N.W.,
Washington, DC 20016
b. August 29, 1932. Camden, NJ.

EDUCATION: Yale University, B.A., English
('53).
CAREER HIGHLIGHTS: Reporter, *The Trentonian*
('57); AP Reporter, New York and Havana
('57); NBC News Correspondent, Miami Bureau ('61); NBC Midwest Correspondent
('62); Washington, DC, Correspondent ('64);
White House Correspondent ('69); State
Dept. Correspondent ('70); Diplomatic Correspondent ('73); "Today" Correspondent ('80);
Pentagon Correspondent ('82).
ACHIEVEMENTS & AWARDS: Peabody citation,
"American Revolution" ('63); Overseas Press
Club award for best radio reporting from
abroad ('65).

PERSONAL: Resides in Washington, DC, with wife, Kathie, daughter, Kimberly.

VALLIER, JEAN
Chief Exec. Officer, Dir. of Programming, TeleFrance USA Ltd.

c/o TeleFrance USA Ltd., 1966 Broadway, New York, NY 10023
b. 1932. France.

EDUCATION: University of Grenoble (France).
CAREER HIGHLIGHTS: Founded the Cine Club of the Alliance Francaise ('64) and screened films which included the complete works of Jean Renoir, Jean Cocteau, Jean-Luc Godard, Francois Truffaut and Louis Malle. He moved to the U.S. ('62) to become Dir., Alliance Francaise, which merged with the French Institute ('71). He has been involved in promoting French theater in the U.S. and has sponsored such troupes as La Comedie Francaise, the Renaud-Barrault Co., and Theatre de la Ville. He joined TeleFrance USA as Chief Exec. Officer and Dir. of Programming ('81).
ACHIEVEMENTS & AWARDS: N.A.
PERSONAL: N.A.

VAN AMBURG, THOMAS K.
V.P. and General Mgr., ABC, KABC-TV, Los Angeles

c/o ABC, 4151 Prospect Ave., Los Angeles, CA 90027
b. May 25. Fresno, CA.

EDUCATION: San Jose State University.
CAREER HIGHLIGHTS: Acct. Exec., KGO-TV, San Francisco ('67); Sales Mgr., KGO-TV ('73);

General Sales Mgr., KABC-TV, Los Angeles ('74); Programming Dir., KABC-TV ('80); V.P., ABC TV, and General Mgr., KABC-TV, Los Angeles ('81).
ACHIEVEMENTS & AWARDS: N.A.
PERSONAL: Resides in Los Angeles with wife, Mary; daughter, Arden; sons, Christopher and Zackary.

VANDOR, CINDY
Anchor, "The Wall Street Journal Report"

220 E. 42d St., New York, NY 10017
b. May 11, 1955.

EDUCATION: Northwestern University, Journalism.
CAREER HIGHLIGHTS: Reporter/Prod., Independent TV News Assn., Washington, DC; Exec. Prod., "News at Noon," NBC Radio Network; Member of Prod. Staff, "Today Show," "NBC Nightly News," "NBC News Update"; Chicago Bureau Chief, Cable News Network; Anchor, "The Wall Street Journal Report."
ACHIEVEMENTS & AWARDS: N.A.
PERSONAL: N.A.

VAN DYKE, DICK
Actor

CBS, 7800 Beverly Blvd., Los Angeles, CA 90036
b. December 18, 1925. West Plains, MO.

EDUCATION: N.A.
CAREER HIGHLIGHTS: This accomplished "physical" comedian can also handle dialogue with flair, and he keeps his comic balance whether tossing out quips or taking pratfalls. TV appearances on "The Merry Mute Show," "Cartoon Theater" and "The Carol Burnett Show." Major motion pictures include *Mary Poppins, Bye Bye Birdie, The Runner Stumbles, Cold Turkey,* and *The Comics.* TV series star of "The Dick Van Dyke Show" and "The New Dick Van Dyke Show." TV movies include *The Morning After* and *The Wrong Way, Kid.*
ACHIEVEMENTS & AWARDS: Three Emmy awards for "The Dick Van Dyke Show" ('63, '64, '65).
PERSONAL: N.A.

VANE, EDWIN T.
Pres. and Chief Exec. Officer, Group W Productions

c/o Group W Productions, 70 Universal City Plaza, Universal City, CA
b. April 29, 1927. New York, NY.

EDUCATION: New York University, M.B.A.
CAREER HIGHLIGHTS: Began broadcasting career as a page at NBC TV. Became Mgr. of Daytime Programs, East Coast, NBC TV ('61). Developed "Concentration" and "Jeopardy." Joined ABC-TV ('64) as Dir. of Daytime Programs, East Coast; promoted to V.P., Daytime Programs ('66). Introduced "The Dating Game," "The Newlywed Game," "One Life To Live," and "Dark Shadows." Became V.P., Natl. Program Dir., for ABC-TV, introducing "Good Morning, America," "Family Feud," ABC weekend specials, and the Barry Manilow and John Denver specials. Contributed to the ABC Theater Presentations, and highly praised programs included *Missiles of October, Eleanor and Franklin, Pueblo, Mary White*, and *The Gathering*. Currently Pres. and Chief Exec. Officer, Group W Productions ('79).
ACHIEVEMENTS & AWARDS: N.A.
PERSONAL: Wife, Claire; four sons.

VAN HORNE, HARRIET
Journalist, New York Times Syndicate

c/o New York Times Syndicate, 200 Park Ave., New York, NY 10017
b. May 17. Syracuse, NY.

EDUCATION: University of Rochester, B.A.
CAREER HIGHLIGHTS: Started as a columnist for the *N.Y. World Telegram*, then the *N.Y. Post*, and is now syndicated through the *N.Y. Times*. A noted lecturer, TV panelist and radio news analyst.
ACHIEVEMENTS & AWARDS: Trustee, Strange Preventive Medicine Institute; Author, *Never Go Anywhere Without a Pencil* ('72).
PERSONAL: Resides in New York City. Widow of documentary filmmaker David Lowe.

VAN LOAN, JOSEPH
V.P., Viacom Cable, Engineering

c/o Viacom Cable, P.O. Box 13, Pleasanton, CA 94566
b. February 25, 1942. New Underwood, SD.

EDUCATION: California State Polytechnic University, BSEE ('70).
CAREER HIGHLIGHTS: Transmitter Engineer, Duhamel Broadcasting Enterprises ('60–'66); U.S. Army Signal Corps ('66); Dir. of Engineering, Transmission, Nebraska ETV Network ('70); V.P., Engineering, Cable Dynamics ('73); Dir. of Engineering, Viacom Cable ('76); V.P., Engineering, Viacom Cable ('79).
ACHIEVEMENTS & AWARDS: N.A.
PERSONAL: Wife, Linda.

VANOCUR, SANDER
Correspondent, ABC, News

c/o ABC, 1717 DeSales St., N.W., Washington, DC 20036
b. January 8, 1928. Cleveland, OH.

EDUCATION: Northwestern University, B.A., Political Science; London School of Economics (England).
CAREER HIGHLIGHTS: Began as Reporter for London's *Manchester Guardian*; BBC Commentator and CBS News Stringer; General Assignment Reporter, *N.Y. Times*; joined NBC News ('57); three years as White House Correspondent, then Natl. Political Correspondent, also served as Washington, DC, Correspondent for "Today," Contributing Editor for "The Huntley-Brinkley Report" and host of "First Tuesday"; Sr. Correspondent for PBS Natl. Public Affairs Center for TV ('71); Consultant to Center for the Study

of Democratic Institutions and Professor at Duke University ('73); TV Editor and Critic, *Washington Post* ('75); joined ABC News ('77) covering political campaigns and conventions; Sr. Correspondent, Buenos Aires; named Chief Diplomatic Correspondent assigned to State Dept. ('81).

ACHIEVEMENTS & AWARDS: N.A.

PERSONAL: Resides in Washington, DC, with wife, Virginia, and three children.

VAN VALKENBURG, DAVID R.
Exec. V.P., Cox Cable Communications, Operations

c/o Cox Cable Communications, 219 Perimeter Center Pkwy., Atlanta, GA 30346
b. May 19, 1942. Tecumseh, MI.

EDUCATION: Malone College, B.A., Science ('64); University of Kansas, M.S., Radiation Biophysics ('66); Harvard University Graduate School of Business Administration, M.B.A. ('69).

CAREER HIGHLIGHTS: V.P., Plant and Facilities Division, American Television and Communications Corp., Denver ('79); Exec. V.P. and Chief Exec. Officer, United Cable TV, Denver ('80); Exec. V.P., Operations, Cox Cable Communications ('82).

ACHIEVEMENTS & AWARDS: Cable TV Advertising Bureau Board of Dirs.; Malone College Board of Trustees.

PERSONAL: N.A.

VARNEY, NORM (Norman A. Varney)
Sr. V.P., J. Walter Thompson USA

466 Lexington Ave., New York, NY 10017
b. January 18, 1922. Boston, MA.

EDUCATION: Duke University, B.A., Economics ('43).

CAREER HIGHLIGHTS: U.S. Navy ('43); J. Walter Thompson ('45); Sr. V.P., J. Walter Thompson USA.

ACHIEVEMENTS & AWARDS: N.A.

PERSONAL: Married; three children.

VAUGHN, ROBERT
Actor

c/o CBS, 7800 Beverly Blvd., L.A., CA 90036
b. 1932. New York, NY.

EDUCATION: University of Southern California, Ph.D., Mass Communications.

CAREER HIGHLIGHTS: TV series credits include "The Man From UNCLE" and the mini-series *Backstairs at the White House, Washington Behind Closed Doors*, and *Centennial*. TV movies include *Return of the Man From UNCLE, Kiss Me, Kill Me, Captains and Kings*, and *The Rebels*. Major motion pictures include *The Young Philadelphians, The Magnificent Seven, Bullitt, The Bridge at Remagen, Julius Caesar*, and *S.O.B.*

ACHIEVEMENTS & AWARDS: N.A.

PERSONAL: N.A.

VENTURI, KEN
Sports Broadcaster, CBS, Sports

c/o CBS, 51 W. 52d St., New York, NY 10019
b. May 15, 1931. San Francisco, CA.

EDUCATION: San Jose State College.

CAREER HIGHLIGHTS: A former U.S. Open golf champion ('64), Venturi has provided expert commentary for CBS Sports coverage of golf events since '68, when, along with Jack Whitaker he co-hosted the "CBS Golf Championship" and "CBS Golf Classic." He has also broadcast the Masters Tournament for seven years.

ACHIEVEMENTS & AWARDS: PGA Player of the Year award ('64).

PERSONAL: Wife, Beau; two children. Resides in Marco Island, FL.

VENZA, JAC
Dir. of Performance Programs, PBS WNET/13

356 W. 58th St., New York, NY 10019
b. December 23, 1926. Chicago, IL.

EDUCATION: Goodman School of Theater and Design.

CAREER HIGHLIGHTS: Designer for theater, opera, and ballet ('50–'64); Prod., Assoc. Prod., Designer, CBS, New York ('50–'64); Exec. Prod. for Cultural Programs, NET New

York ('64); Exec. Prod. for Drama, NET New York ('69–'73); currently Dir. of Performance Programs, PBS WNET/13, New York, responsible for developing, funding, and producing original primetime drama, music, and dance series and specials, creating programs around the U.S. and abroad. Develops international co-production and supervises foreign acquisitions.

ACHIEVEMENTS & AWARDS: Emmy; Peabody awards; Prix Italia; TV Critics Circle awards; San Francisco Intl. Film Festival participation award; American Film Festival, blue ribbon award, Chicago Intl. Film Festival certificate of Merit; Christopher awards; Natl. Dance Week award for "Dance in America."

PERSONAL: N.A.

VERMEIL, DICK
Commentator/Analyst, CBS, Sports

c/o CBS, 51 W. 52d St., New York, NY 10019
b. October 30, 1936. Calistoga, CA.

EDUCATION: Napa Junior College; San Jose State University, M.A.

CAREER HIGHLIGHTS: A career dedicated to football began as coach of a high school team. He moved on to the coaching staffs of Stanford University and the Los Angeles Rams. Received wide recognition as Head Coach of the University of California at Los Angeles ('74–'75), he coached the Pacific 10, Rose Bowl champion UCLA Bruins ('76). Head Coach, the Philadelphia Eagles ('76–'82), won the NFC Championship ('80). Hired by CBS Sports as Expert Analyst ('83).

ACHIEVEMENTS & AWARDS: NFL Coach of the Year, *Football Digest* ('79); NFC Coach of the Year, the Professional Football Writers Assn. of America ('79); NFL Coach of the Year, Washington, D.C., Touchdown Club ('80).

PERSONAL: Resides in Bryn Mawr, PA, with wife, Carolyn; three children, Richard, David, and Nancy.

VICTOR, DAVID
Writer/Prod., Universal City Studios

c/o Universal City Studios, 100 Universal City Plaza, Universal City, CA 91608
b. Odessa, USSR.

EDUCATION: Columbia University.

CAREER HIGHLIGHTS: Victor has written scripts for "Gunsmoke," "Playhouse 90," "Junior Miss," and "Lux Radio Theater." In his producing career, his credits as Exec. Prod., Prod., Writer, or Creator, include "The Rebel," "Dr. Kildare," "The Man From UNCLE," "The Name of the Game," "Marcus Welby, M.D.," and "Lucas Tanner."

ACHIEVEMENTS & AWARDS: Writers Guild awards, Producers Guild awards, an Emmy, two Christopher awards, two Golden Globe awards, a Silver Gavel, the Intl. Silver Dove of Monte Carlo, and the Abe Lincoln award.

PERSONAL: N.A.

VILLECHAIZE, HERVE
Actor

c/o ABC, 2040 Ave. of the Stars, Los Angeles, CA 90067
b. April 23, 1943. Paris, France.

EDUCATION: Beaux Arts School (France).

CAREER HIGHLIGHTS: TV's smallest cult figure managed to make his pronouncement "The plane, Boss, the plane" take its rightful place in the TV trivia hall of fame. Major films include *Hot Tomorrow, Man With the Golden Gun, The One and Only,* and *The Gang That Couldn't Shoot Straight.* TV movies include *Fantasy Island* and *Return to Fantasy Island.* TV series star of "Fantasy Island" for several seasons.

ACHIEVEMENTS & AWARDS: N.A.

PERSONAL: Resides in Los Angeles.

VINSON, PHYLLIS TUCKER
V.P., Children's Programs, NBC, Entertainment

c/o NBC, 3000 W. Alameda Ave., Burbank, CA 91523
b. N.A.

EDUCATION: California State University at Los Angeles, B.A., Child Development.

CAREER HIGHLIGHTS: Joined the NBC Research Dept. ('72); Administrative Specialist, NBC Research ('73); Jr. Research Assoc. ('76); Mgr. Variety Programs, West Coast ('77); Mgr., Current Drama Programs ('78); Dir., Children's Programs ('79); V.P., Children's Programs, NBC Entertainment ('82).

ACHIEVEMENTS & AWARDS: N.A.

PERSONAL: Resides in Los Angeles with husband, Josef, Prod., KNBC-TV, Los Angeles; daughter, Amani, and son, Nye.

VON FREMD, MICHAEL
Correspondent, ABC, News

c/o ABC, 1717 DeSales St., N.W.,
   Washington, DC 20036
b. Washington, DC.

EDUCATION: University of Maryland, B.A., History ('74).

CAREER HIGHLIGHTS: Prod., "CBS Morning News" and weekend news, Prod. for "Evening News" and Asst. Dir., CBS Sports ('74); ABC Evening News Prod.; ABC Reporter in Washington, DC, and Chicago; ABC News Senate Correspondent ('80); named ABC White House Correspondent ('81).

ACHIEVEMENTS & AWARDS: N.A.

PERSONAL: N.A.

WAGNER, ALAN
Pres., Disney Channel

c/o Walt Disney Productions, 500 S. Buena Vista, Burbank, CA 91505
b. October 1, 1931.

EDUCATION: Columbia University, B.A. ('51).
CAREER HIGHLIGHTS: Worked in Network Program Dept., Benton & Bowles ('57); CBS Programming Dept.; V.P., CBS Programs from New York and Europe; Pres., Disney Channel.
ACHIEVEMENTS & AWARDS: N.A.
PERSONAL: N.A.

WAGNER, ROBERT
Actor

c/o "Hart to Hart," ABC, 2040 Ave. of the Stars, Los Angeles, CA 90067
b. February 10, 1930. Detroit, MI.

EDUCATION: N.A.
CAREER HIGHLIGHTS: TV movies include *City Beneath the Sea*, *Killer by Night*, *Madame Sin*, *The Affair*, *Switch*, *Cat on a Hot Tin Roof*, *The Critical List*, and *Pearl*. Motion pictures include *With a Song in My Heart*, *Broken Lance*, *Harper*, *The Pink Panther*, and *Banning*. TV series star of "It Takes a Thief," "Switch," and "Hart to Hart."

ACHIEVEMENTS & AWARDS: People's Choice award as favorite male performer in a new TV program.
PERSONAL: Three daughters; resides in Beverly Hills.

WALD, RICHARD C.
Sr. V.P., ABC, News

c/o ABC, 7 W. 66th St., New York, NY 10023
b. March 19, 1931. New York, NY.

EDUCATION: Columbia College, B.A. ('52); Columbia University, M.A. ('53); Clare College (England), B.A. ('55).
CAREER HIGHLIGHTS: Columbia College Correspondent, *N.Y. Herald Tribune* ('50); Religion Editor, Political Reporter, Foreign Correspondent in London and Bonn; Assoc. Editor and finally Managing Editor; Exec. V.P., Whitney Communications ('66); various executive positions, NBC News ('68); Pres., NBC News ('73); Asst. to the Chairman of the Board, Times-Mirror Co. ('78); joined ABC News as Sr. V.P. ('78); with responsibilities for overseeing all news operations including "World News Tonight," political primaries and conventions, and election coverage.
ACHIEVEMENTS & AWARDS: First Harry J. Carman Fellow, Columbia University; Kellett Fellow, Clare College; Chairman of the Board, *Columbia Spectator*; Nieman Advisory Committee, Nieman Foundation for Journalism, Harvard University; represents ABC News on Board of Dirs. of Satellite News Channels.
PERSONAL: Resides in Larchmont, NY, with wife, Edith; children, Matthew, Elizabeth, and Jonathan.

WALKER, HAL
Correspondent, ABC, News

c/o ABC, 7 W. 66th St., New York, NY 10023
b. Darlington, SC.

EDUCATION: Dennison University, B.A., English and Theater; Syracuse University; New York State University.

CAREER HIGHLIGHTS: Reporter, WTOP-TV, now WDVM-TV, Washington, DC ('63); Reporter, CBS News, Washington, DC ('66); Correspondent, CBS News, Washington, DC ('69); Correspondent, CBS News, Bonn ('77); Correspondent, ABC News, Bonn ('80).

ACHIEVEMENTS & AWARDS: Award for excellence in journalism from Frontiers Intl. ('65); a special Emmy; the Ted Yates award of the Washington, DC, Chapter, NATAS; the Capitol Press Club award for the report "A Dialogue With Whitey" ('68).

WALKER, JAMES
Correspondent, ABC, News

c/o ABC, 7 W. 66th St., New York, NY 10023
b. N.A.

EDUCATION: University of Hartford, B.A.
CAREER HIGHLIGHTS: Desk Asst., CBS News; Management Trainee, Westinghouse Broadcasting; assigned to WBZ-TV as Assignment Editor, Writer, and Asst. Prod.; Washington Bureau Reporter, Westinghouse ('67); WHAS-TV, Louisville, KY; WCAU-TV ('73); joined ABC News as General Correspondent; named to cover stories exclusively for "Nightline" ('82).

ACHIEVEMENTS & AWARDS: Ohio State University award for "Louisville: Open City" ('71–'72); Natl. Award of Merit, American Trial Lawyers Assn.; Sigma Delta Chi award for "The Junk Man" ('74).

PERSONAL: Resides in Bronxville, NY, with wife, Vandy, and children, Loulie and Anne.

WALKINGSHAW, M. JAY
Sr. V.P., Chief Financial Officer, Columbia Pictures

c/o Columbia Pictures, 711 Fifth Ave., New York, NY 10022
b. February 10.

EDUCATION: Williams College; Dartmouth College, M.B.A.

CAREER HIGHLIGHTS: V.P., Finance, Computer TV; V.P., Program Operations, HBO; V.P., Corporate Development, HBO; V.P., Finance and Administration, Time-Life Films; V.P. and Controller, Group W Cable; Sr. V.P., Finance and Administration, Warner Amex ('82); Sr. V.P., Chief Financial Officer, Columbia Pictures.

ACHIEVEMENTS & AWARDS: N.A.
PERSONAL: N.A.

WALLACE, CHRIS
Correspondent, NBC, News

c/o NBC, 4001 Nebraska Ave., N.W., Washington, DC 20016
b. October 12, 1947. Chicago, IL.

EDUCATION: Harvard University, B.A., History.

CAREER HIGHLIGHTS: Reporter, *Boston Globe* ('69); Reporter, WNBC-TV, New York ('73), headed Investigative Unit ('75); assigned to Washington, DC for NBC News ('78); joined "Prime Time Sunday" at its inception ('79); Washington, DC, Correspondent, "Special Segment" reports ('80); appointed Washington, DC, Co-Anchor on "Today"; named White House Correspondent ('82).

ACHIEVEMENTS & AWARDS: New York State AP broadcasters award for best enterprise reporting ('77); Overseas Press Club, Humanitas, and Emmy awards for the documentary "NBC Reports: The Migrants ('80).

PERSONAL: Son of CBS News's Mike Wallace of "60 Minutes." Resides in Washington, DC, with his wife, Elizabeth, and their two children.

WALLACE, MIKE
Co-Editor, CBS, "60 Minutes"

c/o CBS, 51 W. 52d St., New York, NY 10019
b. May 9, 1918. Brookline, MA.

EDUCATION: University of Michigan.
CAREER HIGHLIGHTS: The tough, relentless interrogator of "60 Minutes" established the combative, confrontational interview as his trademark. He began his career as Radio News Writer and Broadcaster, *Chicago Sun*; News Reporter, WMAQ, Chicago; News Feature and Entertainment Reporter, CBS TV Network ('51–'55); CBS News Correspondent ('63); reported every national political convention ('64–'76); anchored Eastern Regional Desk for election night coverage ('68–'74); anchored morning news and midday news ('63–'66); Co-Editor, "60 Minutes" ('68).
ACHIEVEMENTS & AWARDS: Emmy, Dupont-Columbia, and Peabody awards. Robert E. Sherwood awards; distinguished achievement award from the University of Southern California School of Journalism; Preceptor award; first annual Hall of Fame award; elected Fellow of Sigma Delta Chi; doctor of humane letters, honoris causa, University of Massachusetts.
PERSONAL: Wife, Lorraine. Father of NBC correspondent Chris Wallace. Resides in Manhattan.

WALLACE, ROB
Prod./Editor, ABC, News

c/o ABC, 7 W. 66th St., New York, NY 10023
b. April 25, 1953. Yukon, Canada.

EDUCATION: Waterloo University; Conestoga College.

CAREER HIGHLIGHTS: Freelance Film Editor/Prod., New York ('75); Freelance Editor, ABC News "20/20" ('78); Freelance Prod./Editor, ABC News "20/20" ('79).
ACHIEVEMENTS & AWARDS: N.A.
PERSONAL: Resides in Oceanport, NJ, with wife, Janet; son, Christopher.

WALSH, ROBERT S.
Pres., NBC TV Stations/Radio, and Group Exec. V.P., NBC

c/o NBC, 30 Rockefeller Plaza, New York, NY 10020
b. February 24, 1929. Chicago, IL.

EDUCATION: Northern Illinois University, B.S.
CAREER HIGHLIGHTS: Salesman for NBC Radio Spot Sales, Chicago, ('62); TV Sales ('64); Mgr., NBC TV Spot Sales ('67); Mgr., WMAQ-TV Local Sales ('68); Sales Mgr., Chicago Station ('70); Station Mgr., WMAQ-TV, NBC in Chicago ('73); V.P. and General Mgr., WRC-TV, Washington, DC ('76); V.P., General Mgr., WMAQ-TV, Chicago ('78); Exec. V.P., NBC TV Stations ('79); Pres., NBC TV Stations/Radio ('82); added responsibilities as Group Exec. V.P., NBC ('82).
ACHIEVEMENTS & AWARDS: Member, Board of Dirs., TV Bureau of Advertising, and Ad Council.
PERSONAL: Wife, Marion; three children.

WALTERS, BARBARA
On-Air Personality and Correspondent, ABC

c/o ABC, 7 W. 66th St., New York, NY 10023
b. September 25, 1931. Boston, MA.

EDUCATION: Sarah Lawrence College, B.A.

CAREER HIGHLIGHTS: As the first woman to co-host NBC's "Today" show and the first woman to co-anchor a network news program, Walters paved the way for women broadcasters. Throughout her career, she has continually demonstrated a talent for insightful and provocative interviewing that has earned her a well-deserved reputation in broadcast journalism. Began as Prod., WNBC-TV, New York; moved to NBC News as Writer for "Today" ('61); promoted to Reporter-at-Large ('62); made Co-Host ('74). Hosted syndicated series "Not for Women Only" ('70–'76); contributed to NBC Radio Network regularly. Joined ABC as Co-Anchor on evening news ('76); contributes reports and interviews to "World News Tonight," "20/20," and "Issues and Answers," as well as periodic "Barbara Walters Specials" interview programs, in which she has displayed a definite talent for inducing privacy-loving celebrities to go public. She arranged the first primetime interview with Fidel Castro, the first joint interview between the late Anwar Sadat and Menachem Begin, and conducted the first TV interview with Patty Hearst following her release from prison.

ACHIEVEMENTS & AWARDS:· Appeared on cover of *Newsweek* ('74, '76); listed in *Time* among 100 most influential leaders in America; Broadcaster of the Year, IRTS ('75); Emmy award ('75); named among 10 Women of the Decade by *Ladies' Home Journal* ('79); TWIN award (Tribute to Women in Industry, '81). She published *How To Talk With Practically Anyone About Practically Anything*.

PERSONAL: Daughter of impresario Lou Walters; resides in Manhattan with daughter, Jacqueline.

WARING, PAUL C.
V.P., Cox Cable Communications, Corporate Development

c/o Cox Cable Communications, 219 Perimeter Center Pkwy., Atlanta, GA 30346
b. December 30, 1943. Boston, MA.

EDUCATION: Boston College, B.A., English.

CAREER HIGHLIGHTS: Mgr., Marketing Communications, General Electric Apparatus Service, Schenectady, NY ('71); Pres., Waring

Communications, Detroit ('76); Mgr., Business Development, General Electric Cablevision, Schenectady, NY ('78); V.P., Corporate Development, Cox Cable Communications ('80).

ACHIEVEMENTS & AWARDS: N.A.

PERSONAL: N.A.

WARREN, ALBERT
Editor and Publisher, *Television Digest*

c/o *Television Digest*, 1836 Jefferson Place, N.W., Washington, DC 20036
b. May 18, 1920. Warren, OH.

EDUCATION: Ohio State University.

CAREER HIGHLIGHTS: Joined *Television Digest* as Reporter ('45). Promoted to Assoc. Editor, Sr. Editor, Chief of Washington Bureau. Acquired control of *Television Digest* ('61), serving as Editor and Publisher since that time.

ACHIEVEMENTS & AWARDS: Co-Founder ('62), Independent Newsletter Assn.

PERSONAL: Wife, Margaret; six children.

WARREN, MICHAEL
Actor

c/o "Hill Street Blues," NBC, 3000 W. Alameda Ave., Burbank, CA 91523
b. March 5, 1946. South Bend, IN.

EDUCATION: University of California at Los Angeles, B.A.

CAREER HIGHLIGHTS: Guest appearances on such series as "The White Shadow," "Lou Grant," "Adam-12," and "Police Story." Co-star of the series "Sierra" and "Paris." Motion

pictures include *Fast Break* and *Norman Is That You?* Series regular on "Hill Street Blues."
ACHIEVEMENTS & AWARDS: N.A.
PERSONAL: Wife, Susie; two children. Resides in Los Angeles.

WARRICK, RUTH
Actress

c/o "All My Children," ABC, 1330 Ave. of the Americas, New York, NY 10019
b. June 29, 1915. St. Joseph, MO.

EDUCATION: N.A.
CAREER HIGHLIGHTS: Broadway appearances in *Take Me Along, Pal Joey,* and *Irene.* Motion pictures include *Citizen Kane, Journey Into Fear,* and *Forever and a Day.* TV series regular on "Peyton Place" and "Father of the Bride." Soap opera star of "As the World Turns" and "All My Children."
ACHIEVEMENTS & AWARDS: N.A.
PERSONAL: Resides in Manhattan.

WASSERMAN, BERT
Member of the Office of the Pres., Warner Communications

c/o Warner Communications, 75 Rockefeller Plaza, New York, NY 10019
b. December 25.

EDUCATION: Brooklyn Law School, law degree.
CAREER HIGHLIGHTS: Joined Warner Communications ('66) as Exec. V.P. of Kinney Rent-a-Car. Member of the Office of the Pres. ('81). Also serves as Chief Financial Officer and a member of the company's Board of Dir.
ACHIEVEMENTS & AWARDS: N.A.
PERSONAL: Married; three children.

WASSERMAN, LEW R.
Pres., Chief Exec. Officer, and Chairman of the Board, MCA

c/o MCA, 100 Universal City Plaza, Universal City, CA 91608
b. March 15, 1913. Cleveland, OH.

EDUCATION: N.A.
CAREER HIGHLIGHTS: Joined MCA ('36); named Pres. and Chief Exec. Officer ('46); elected Chairman of the Board ('73). One of the most brilliant and influential executives in the history of commercial TV. Because of his top role at MCA for almost 40 years, Wasserman has also been very influential in theatrical films. Started as a talent agent, where his acumen and negotiating skills became quickly apparent. MCA has produced more TV series, on all three commercial networks, than any other production company in Hollywood.
ACHIEVEMENTS & AWARDS: Jean Hersholt Humanitarian Award, NATAS ('73); Trustee, California Institute of Technology, Lyndon B. Johnson Foundation, Kennedy Center for the Performing Arts, Natl. Urban League, Jet Propulsion Lab, Jules Stein Eye Institute. Honorary Chairman of the Board, Center Theater Group of Los Angeles; Treasurer, Music Center Foundation; Member, Radio Free Europe Committee; Pres. and Trustee, Hollywood Canteen Foundation; Pres. and Board Member, Research to Prevent Blindness; Member, Natl. Committee of Lyndon B. Johnson Memorial Grove of the Potomac.
PERSONAL: Resides in Beverly Hills with wife, Edie. Daughter, Lynne Myers; grandchildren, Carole and Casey.

WATERS, LOU (Lou Riegert)
Anchor, Cable News Network

8030 Meadowsweet Trace, Roswell, GA 30076
b. July 7, 1938. Minneapolis, MN.

EDUCATION: University of Minnesota.
CAREER HIGHLIGHTS: Radio Reporter, KDWB, Minneapolis ('59); Radio Reporter, WWTC, Minneapolis ('64); Radio Reporter, WCBS-TV, New York ('69); Reporter/Anchor, KVOA-TV, Tucson, AZ ('70); News Dir./Anchor, KCST-TV, San Diego, CA ('73); News Dir./Anchor, KVOA and KOLD-TV, Tucson ('77); Anchor, Cable News Network.

ACHIEVEMENTS & AWARDS: Golden Microphone reporting award ('73); news programming award ('74); Emmy for live coverage spot news ('78).

PERSONAL: Wife, Mardy; son, Scott.

WATSON, ARTHUR A.
Pres., NBC, Sports

c/o NBC, 30 Rockefeller Plaza, New York, NY 10020

b. May 4, 1930. Brooklyn, NY.

EDUCATION: Fordham University, B.S., Accounting.

CAREER HIGHLIGHTS: NBC Financial Analyst ('56); moved to WRCV/WRCV-TV as Business Mgr. ('59); Station Mgr. ('61); General Manager ('65); WKYC/WKYC-TV as V.P./General Mgr. ('65); returned to NBC as Pres., NBC Radio ('69); WNBC/WNBC-TV as Exec. V.P. and General Mgr. ('71); Exec. V.P., NBC Owned Stations ('76); Exec. V.P., NBC TV Network ('79); appointed Pres., NBC Sports ('79).

ACHIEVEMENTS & AWARDS: Member, Board of Dirs., Advertising Council; IRTS; Member, Board of Governors, Bedside Network; CARTA.

PERSONAL: Resides in Saddle River, NJ, with wife, Maryalesia; children, Arthur Jr., Keith, Lisa, and Scott.

WATSON, BARBARA L.
General Mgr., NBC, Teletext

c/o NBC, 30 Rockefeller Plaza, New York, NY 10020

b. December 18, 1944.

EDUCATION: Marquette University, B.A., English Literature and Political Science (magna cum laude, '66); Harvard Business School, M.B.A. ('78).

CAREER HIGHLIGHTS: Data Processor, IBM ('67); Advisory Systems Engineer, IBM ('72); Systems Engineer, IBM; Management Consultant, Booz, Allen, & Hamilton; General Mgr., NBC Teletext, New York ('83).

ACHIEVEMENTS & AWARDS: N.A.

PERSONAL: Resides in Brooklyn Heights, NY.

WATSON, DOUGLASS
Actor

c/o "Another World," NBC, 30 Rockefeller Plaza, New York, NY 10020

b. Jackson, GA.

EDUCATION: N.A.

CAREER HIGHLIGHTS: Appeared on Broadway in *Antony and Cleopatra, Over Here,* and *The Iceman Cometh.* Has also starred in the PBS special *King Lear* and the daytime dramas "Search for Tomorrow" and "Love of Life." Currently stars as Mac Cory on "Another World."

ACHIEVEMENTS & AWARDS: New York Drama Desk award and Clarence Derwent award for his stage work; two Emmy awards as best actor in a daytime drama ('80, '81).

PERSONAL: Married.

WATSON, GEORGE
V.P., ABC, News

c/o ABC, 1330 Ave. of the Americas, New York, NY 10019

b. July 27, 1936. Birmingham, AL.

EDUCATION: Harvard University, B.A.; Columbia University, M.S.

CAREER HIGHLIGHTS: Reporter for *Detroit News* ('59); moved to *Washington Post* ('60); ABC News Writer and Assignment Editor ('62); Correspondent, ABC News ('66); Moscow Bureau Chief ('66); London Bureau Chief ('66); White House Correspondent ('75). Appointed V.P., ABC News, and Washington Bureau Chief ('76); moved to Cable News Network as V.P. and Managing Editor ('80); returned to ABC as V.P., News ('81).

ACHIEVEMENTS & AWARDS: Overseas Press Club

award for best foreign affairs documentary ('71); Overseas Press Club citation for excellence ('74); Peabody award ('81). Pres., American Assn. of Correspondents in London ('75); Board of Dirs., Committee to Protect Journalists ('82).

PERSONAL: Resides in Bronxville, NY, with wife, the former Emily Bradley; son, George.

WATSON, MARIAN ETOILE
Arts Editor, WNEW-TV, "Black News"

c/o Metromedia, 205 E. 67th St., New York, NY 10021
b. N.A.

EDUCATION: A.M. and N. College, B.S., Music.
CAREER HIGHLIGHTS: Prod./Host, WABC-TV's "Like It Is" and WNEW's "Midday." Admin. Prod., WFIL-TV, Philadelphia; Assoc. Prod./Host, "Inside Bedford Stuyvesant," first all-black produced show in the U.S. Arts Editor, WNEW-TV's "Black News."
ACHIEVEMENTS & AWARDS: N.A.
PERSONAL: N.A.

WEAVER, PAT (Sylvester L. Weaver)
Pres., Weaver Productions

818 Deerpath Rd., Santa Barbara, CA 93108
b. December 21, 1908. Los Angeles, CA.

EDUCATION: Dartmouth University ('30).
CAREER HIGHLIGHTS: Important and much-admired executive during the early and mid-fifties before being eased out of his position as Chairman of NBC. Largely responsible for the creation and early success of "The Today Show" and "The Tonight Show," and the innovative "Wide Wide World" series. He was also involved in early efforts to develop pay TV in California, but a court ruling, later overturned, ended this venture. He began his career as Writer/Prod., CBS Radio ('30s); V.P., Radio and TV, Young & Rubicam ('40s); Pres., NBC ('53–'55); Advertising Exec., McCann-Erickson ('50s); Head of Subscription TV, Inc. ('63–'66); Advertising Consultant for Wells, Rich, Greene; Pres., Weaver Communications.
ACHIEVEMENTS & AWARDS: Member, Phi Beta

Kappa. *TV Guide* Life Achievement award ('81). Outlined concept of TV "spectaculars" ('50); originated the TV magazine concept used in "Today" and the rotating-star system used in "The Colgate Comedy Hour" and "All Star Revue." NATAS trustees award ('66).

PERSONAL: Wife, Desiree Mary; three children, including actress Sigourney Weaver.

WEBER, CHARLES J.
Independent Prod.

c/o Embassy Communications, 1901 Ave. of the Stars, Los Angeles, CA 90067
b. April 1, 1943. New York, NY.

EDUCATION: Manhattan College, B.S., Accounting; Hofstra University, M.B.A., Finance and Administration.
CAREER HIGHLIGHTS: Had various positions with GM Overseas Operations ('65); Mgr. of Financial Planning and Analysis, Celanese Corp. ('68); V.P., Celanese Real Estate Corp. ('71); V.P., Finance and Administration, Real Estate Technology, Inc. ('72); Exec. V.P., Income Equities Corp. ('74); Sr. V.P. and Chief Exec. Officer, Sonnenblick/Goldman ('76); Pres. and Chief Exec. Officer, Lucasfilm Ltd. ('78); Pres. and Chief Exec. Officer, Embassy Communications ('81); Independent Prod. ('83).
ACHIEVEMENTS & AWARDS: Member, Academy of Motion Picture Arts and Sciences; Board of Trustees, Filmex; Board of Trustees, Crossroads School.
PERSONAL: Wife, Elizabeth; daughter, Elizabeth; son, Thomas.

WEBSTER, DAVID
Dir., U.S., BBC

c/o BBC, 630 Fifth Ave., New York, NY 10111
b. January 11, 1931. Somerset, England.

EDUCATION: University of Oxford (England).
CAREER HIGHLIGHTS: External Services News Dept., BBC ('53); Asst. Prod., "Face to Face" and "Lifeline" ('59); Prod., "Panorama" ('59); Prod., "Enquiry" and "Encounter" ('64); Deputy Editor, "Panorama" ('66); Editor,

"Panorama" ('67); Exec. Editor, Current Affairs Group, BBC ('69); Asst. Head, Current Affairs Group, BBC ('70); BBC Representative in the U.S. ('71); Controller of Information Services, BBC ('76); Dir., of Public Affairs, BBC ('77); Dir., U.S., BBC ('81).

ACHIEVEMENTS & AWARDS: Chairman, Intl. Council, NATAS ('74–'75); Member, Programme Committee of the Ditchley Foundation ('77–present).

PERSONAL: Married to Washington, DC-based political writer and broadcaster Elizabeth Drew.

WEBSTER, SKIP
Prod./Writer

c/o Eiisenbach-Greene, 760 N. LaCienega Blvd., Los Angeles, CA 90069
b. Detroit, MI.

EDUCATION: University of California at Los Angeles, B.A.

CAREER HIGHLIGHTS: Writer for various TV shows ('65–'72); Prod./Writer, "The Rookies" ('72); Prod./Writer/Exec. Script Consultant, "Fantasy Island" ('77); Exec. Script Consultant, "Matt Houston" ('82).

ACHIEVEMENTS & AWARDS: N.A.

PERSONAL: N.A.

WEDECK, DAVID
V.P., Programs East Coast, NBC

c/o NBC, 30 Rockefeller Plaza, New York, NY 10020
b. New York.

EDUCATION: Columbia School of Business, M.S.

CAREER HIGHLIGHTS: Principal Prod. at Focus ('68–'78); V.P., Assoc. Media Dir./Programming Dir., Benton & Bowles; Acct. Exec. in Network Sales, CBS TV ('78–'82); V.P., Program Scheduling, NBC Entertainment ('79); V.P., Programs East Coast, NBC.

ACHIEVEMENTS & AWARDS: N.A.

PERSONAL: Wife, Diane; sons, Andrew and Douglas. Resides in Teaneck, NJ.

WEIK, GARY G.
V.P., General Mgr., Cox Cable Communications, Development Division

c/o Cox Cable Communications, 219 Perimeter Center Pkwy., Atlanta, GA 30346
b. March 21, 1946. Nebraska City, NE.

EDUCATION: University of Nebraska, B.A., Journalism/Radio/TV.

CAREER HIGHLIGHTS: Marketing Mgr., TV Transmission, Lincoln, NE ('73); V.P., Marketing, Mission Cable, San Diego, CA ('78); V.P., Marketing, Cox Cable Communications, Atlanta ('80); V.P./General Mgr., Western Division, Cox Cable Communications ('81); V.P./General Mgr., Development Division, Cox Cable Communications ('82).

ACHIEVEMENTS & AWARDS: CTAM, Board of Dirs.; CCTA, Board of Dirs.

PERSONAL: N.A.

WEIL, SUZANNE
Sr. V.P., PBS, Programming

c/o PBS, 475 L'Enfant Plaza, S.W., Washington, DC 20024
b. June 22, 1933. Minneapolis, MN.

EDUCATION: University of Minnesota; Harvard University Institute for Arts Administration.

CAREER HIGHLIGHTS: Coordinator of Performing Arts, Walker Art Center, Minneapolis ('69); Dir., Dance Program, Natl. Endowment for the Arts, Washington, DC ('76); Dir., Arts and Humanities Programming, PBS, Washington, DC ('78); Sr. V.P., Programming, PBS, Washington, DC ('80).

ACHIEVEMENTS & AWARDS: N.A.

PERSONAL: Resides in Washington, DC, and

Minnetonka, MN, with husband, Fred; daughter, Peggy.

WEINBLATT, MIKE (Myron Weinblatt)
Pres., Showtime Entertainment and Movie Channel

c/o Showtime, 1633 Broadway, New York, NY 10019
b. June 10, 1929. Perth Amboy, NJ.

EDUCATION: Syracuse University, B.S. ('51).
CAREER HIGHLIGHTS: Joined NBC ('57); Mgr., Business Affairs, Facilities Operations ('58); Mgr., Planning and Financial Evaluation, TV Network Business Affairs ('59); Dir., Pricing and Financial Services ('62); Mgr., Participating Program Sales ('62); Dir. of Dept. ('64); V.P., Eastern Sales, NBC TV ('68). Named V.P., Talent and Program Administration ('68); V.P., Sales; Exec. V.P., NBC TV; Exec. V.P. and General Mgr., NBC TV Network ('77); first Pres. of NBC Entertainment ('78); Pres., NBC Enterprises Division ('80); joined Showtime as Pres. ('80); Pres., Movie Channel.
ACHIEVEMENTS & AWARDS: N.A.
PERSONAL: Resides in New Jersey with wife, Annie, and two sons.

WEINER, BRUCE
V.P., Affiliate Advertising and Promotion, CBS, Entertainment

c/o CBS, 51 W. 52d St., New York, NY 10019
b. N.A.

EDUCATION: University of Bridgeport ('64).
CAREER HIGHLIGHTS: Promotion Writer, CBS Radio Network ('67); Mgr., Sales Promotion, CBS TV Stations Natl. Sales ('68); Mgr., Advertising and Press Information, CBS TV Stations Division, New York ('71); Dir., Promotion and Information Services, WCAU-TV, Philadelphia ('72); Dir., Affiliate Advertising and Promotion, CBS Entertainment, New York ('82).
ACHIEVEMENTS & AWARDS: N.A.
PERSONAL: Resides in Larchmont, NY, with wife, Penny, son, Jeffrey, and daughter, Sari.

WEINHEIMER, STEPHEN
Mgr., Print Planning, Advertising and Promotion, NBC, Media Planning

c/o NBC, 3000 W. Alameda Ave., Burbank, CA 91523
b. New York, NY.

EDUCATION: State University of New York at New Paltz, B.A., Communications ('76).
CAREER HIGHLIGHTS: First joined NBC as a Page on the Guest Relations Staff, New York ('78); Coordinator, On-Air Promotion ('79); Promoted to Mgr., Operations, On-Air Promotion ('79); Mgr., Operations, On-Air Promotion, NBC, Burbank ('81); Mgr., Print Planning, Advertising and Promotion ('83).
ACHIEVEMENTS & AWARDS: N.A.
PERSONAL: Resides in Santa Monica, CA.

WEINSTEIN, CARL D.
Pres., Eastman CableRep

c/o Eastman CableRep, 1 Rockefeller Plaza, New York, NY 10020
b. N.A.

EDUCATION: Columbia University, M.B.A.
CAREER HIGHLIGHTS: Acct. Exec., Petry TV; V.P., Sales, Righter & Parsons; Founder and Pres., Eastman CableRep ('80).
ACHIEVEMENTS & AWARDS: N.A.
PERSONAL: N.A.

WEINTRAUB, LLOYD W.
V.P., Movies and Mini-Series, MGM-UA Entertainment

c/o MGM-UA, 10202 W. Washington Blvd., Culver City, CA 90230
b. June 30, 1952. Brooklyn, NY.

EDUCATION: Brooklyn College, B.A.; City University of New York, M.F.A.

CAREER HIGHLIGHTS: Theatrical Agent, FiFi Oscard Assoc., New York ('74); Theatrical Agent, Hesseltine Baker & Assoc., New York ('76); Theatrical Agent, Agency for the Performing Arts, Los Angeles ('78); Dir. of Creative Affairs, Bud Austin Productions, Los Angeles ('80); Dir., Movies and Mini-Series, MGM Film Co. ('82); V.P., Movies and Mini-Series, MGM-UA Entertainment ('83).

ACHIEVEMENTS & AWARDS: N.A.

PERSONAL: Wife, Sherry; sons, Ian and Matthew.

WEISBARTH, MICHAEL R.
Sr. V.P., Dramatic Program Development, Embassy Communications

c/o Embassy Communications, 1901 Ave. of the Stars, Los Angeles, CA 90067
b. April 22. Queens, NY.

EDUCATION: Queens College, B.A.; University of Michigan, M.A.

CAREER HIGHLIGHTS: V.P., Sales, Vidtronics Co. ('71); V.P., Production, Tandem/TAT ('76); Prod., "Palmerstown" series on CBS ('80); Supervising Prod., *First Lady of the World: Eleanor Roosevelt*, CBS TV movie ('82); Sr. V.P., Dramatic Program Development, Embassy Communications ('80), served as Exec. Prod. for ABC TV movie *Grace Kelly* ('83).

ACHIEVEMENTS & AWARDS: N.A.

PERSONAL: Wife, Susan; daughters, Kim and Brooke.

WEISMAN, MICHAEL
Exec. Prod., NBC, Sports

c/o NBC, 30 Rockefeller Plaza, New York, NY 10020
b. N.A.

EDUCATION: University of North Carolina; Queens College.

CAREER HIGHLIGHTS: A talented and creative sports producer who rose to the top of his profession in record time. Started as an NBC Page ('71); moved into NBC Sports ('72); named Assoc. Prod. ('74); Prod. ('77); Coordi-

nating Prod. ('79); and Exec. Prod. ('83). Some of his major sports production credits include major league baseball's championship series ('77, '79, '81); World Series ('78, '80, '82); the Orange Bowl ('78–'83); college basketball; boxing; and numerous NFL telecasts, including playoff games and Super Bowl XIII.

ACHIEVEMENTS & AWARDS: Emmy award for his work as a replay producer on Super Bowl XIII ('79).

PERSONAL: Resides in New York City with wife, Carol, and daughter, Brett.

WEISS, DANIEL S.
Dir., Affiliate Promotion, NBC, Entertainment

c/o NBC, 3000 W. Alameda Ave., Burbank, CA 91523
b. Los Angeles, CA.

EDUCATION: University of California at Los Angeles, B.A., Motion Picture and TV Production ('74).

CAREER HIGHLIGHTS: Asst. Dir. of Public Relations, Consolidated Film Industries, Los Angeles ('74); Copywriter, N.W. Ayer advertising agency, San Francisco ('75); Prod. of Promotions and On-Air Consumer Reporter for weekly magazine show, KRON-TV, San Francisco ('77); Prod., "SFO" for KRON-TV ('80); Writer/Prod., On-Air Promotion Dept., NBC, Los Angeles ('82); Dir., Affiliate Promotion, NBC Entertainment, Burbank ('83).

ACHIEVEMENTS & AWARDS: N.A.

PERSONAL: Resides in Burbank.

WEITZ, BRUCE
Actor

c/o "Hill Street Blues," NBC, 3000 W. Alameda Ave., Burbank, CA 91523
b. May 27. Norwalk, CT.

EDUCATION: Carnegie Tech, B.A. and M.F.A.

CAREER HIGHLIGHTS: Broadway credits include *Norman Is That You?* and *The Basic Training of Pavlo Hummel*. Guest star on the series "Quincy," "The Rockford Files," and "Happy Days." TV movies include *Death of a Centerfold*. Series regular on "Hill Street Blues."

ACHIEVEMENTS & AWARDS: N.A.
PERSONAL: N.A.

WEITZMAN, BERNARD
Pres., Acquisition Division, Lorimar Productions

c/o Lorimar Productions, 3970 Overland Ave., Culver City, CA 90230
b. Springfield, MA.

EDUCATION: University of Alabama; University of Southern California; Southwestern University School of Law.
CAREER HIGHLIGHTS: Prod. Exec., CBS TV ('48); Dir., Business Affairs, CBS ('52); V.P., Desilu Productions ('54); V.P. and General Mgr., Universal Studios ('67); V.P., Business Affairs, MGM Studios ('74); V.P., Lorimar Productions ('77); Pres., Lorimar Acquisition Division ('80).
ACHIEVEMENTS & AWARDS: N.A.
PERSONAL: N.A.

WELKER, CHRISTY
V.P., Novels and Limited Series for TV, ABC, Entertainment

c/o ABC, 4151 Prospect Ave., Los Angeles, CA 90027
b. N.A.

EDUCATION: Stephens College, B.S., TV and Film.
CAREER HIGHLIGHTS: Prod. Asst., Children's Programming, NBC ('71); worked in various positions for independent TV production and packaging; Program Exec., Special Programs, CBS Entertainment ('75); Dir., Daytime Program Development ('78); Exec. Prod. of Novels and Limited Series, ABC Entertainment ('80); V.P., Novels and Limited Series for TV, ABC Entertainment ('82).
ACHIEVEMENTS & AWARDS: Resides in Los Angeles.

WELLS, WILLIAM
Mgr., Dramatic Program Development, CBS, Entertainment

c/o CBS, 51 W. 52d St., New York, NY 10019
b. May 26, 1950.

EDUCATION: Middlebury College, B.A.
CAREER HIGHLIGHTS: Project Dir., ASI Market Research; Special Units Coordinator, Advertising Dept., Peterson Publishing Co.; Sr. Reader, Story Dept., CBS ('78); Program Exec., Dramatic Program Development, CBS Entertainment ('81); Mgr., Dramatic Program Development, CBS Entertainment ('82).
ACHIEVEMENTS & AWARDS: N.A.
PERSONAL: N.A.

WELTMAN, WALLY
V.P., ABC, Daytime Programs, West Coast

c/o ABC, 2040 Ave. of the Stars, Los Angeles, CA 90067
b. August 9, 1927. New York, NY.

EDUCATION: New York University, B.S., Marketing and Journalism.
CAREER HIGHLIGHTS: Production Supervisor for CBS, working on all daytime serials ('60); CBS News Special Events Unit, working on space programs and major news events; CBS Sports on all events; worked on Steve Lawrence variety specials and Merv Griffin shows. named Dir., Design and Production, for CBS TV ('71); Dir., ABC Late Night Programming, East Coast ('72); transferred to West Coast in same position ('74); Dir., Late Night Programs and "Good Morning America," West Coast ('75). Dir., Daytime Programs, West Coast ('76); V.P., Daytime Programs, overseeing "General Hospital" and "Family Feud" ('81).
ACHIEVEMENTS & AWARDS: Guest Lecturer, the New School, and the University of Southern California.
PERSONAL: Resides in Hancock Park, Los Angeles; daughter, Eden.

WENDELL, E. W. (Bud)
Chairman of the Board, Pres., and Chief
Exec. Officer, WSM

c/o Nashville Network, 2806 Opryland Dr.,
Nashville, TN 37214
b. N.A.

EDUCATION: Wooster College.
CAREER HIGHLIGHTS: V.P., WSM, and General
Mgr. of the Grand Ole Opry and Opryland
('74–'77); Chairman of the Board, Pres. and
Chief Exec. Officer, WSM ('78).
ACHIEVEMENTS & AWARDS: Metronome award
from the mayor of Nashville ('73).
PERSONAL: N.A.

WENHAM, BRIAN
Dir. of Programmes, BBC

c/o BBC, 12 Cavendish Place, London,
England W1
b. February 9, 1937. London, England.

EDUCATION: St. John's College.
CAREER HIGHLIGHTS: Prod., ITN ('62); Prod.,
"The Struggle for Peace" and "The Power of
the Dollar" for ABC ('65); Editor, "Pano-
rama," BBC ('69); Head of Current Affairs,
BBC-TV ('71); Controller, BBC-2 ('78); Dir. of
Programmes, BBC ('83).
ACHIEVEMENTS & AWARDS: N.A.
PERSONAL: N.A.

WENNER, KATE
Prod., ABC, News, "20/20"

c/o ABC, 77 W. 66th St., New York, NY 10023
b. November 17, 1947. San Francisco, CA.

EDUCATION: Radcliffe College, B.A. ('70).
CAREER HIGHLIGHTS: Freelance Writer, *N.Y.
Times, Village Voice, Soho Weekly News,* and
book projects ('72–'79); Managing Editor,
Rolling Stone College Papers ('79); Prod., ABC
News, "20/20" ('81).
ACHIEVEMENTS & AWARDS: Michael Rockefeller
Memorial Fellowship for travel and study in
Peru ('70); Business and Professional
Women's Foundation grant ('75); New York
State Community Artists Program Grant for
fiction ('77).
PERSONAL: N.A.

WERGELES, JIM
V.P., Madison Square Garden Network,
Public Relations

c/o Madison Square Garden Network, 4
Pennsylvania Plaza, New York, NY 10001
b. December 15, 1922.

EDUCATION: N.A.
CAREER HIGHLIGHTS: Business Mgr., New York
Knicks basketball team; Dir., Public Rela-
tions, Madison Square Garden Network;
V.P., Public Relations, Madison Square Gar-
den Network.
ACHIEVEMENTS & AWARDS: N.A.
PERSONAL: N.A.

WERNER, JOYCE
Mgr., Project Control and Visibility,
Westinghouse Broadcasting and Cable,
Group W Cable

c/o Group W Cable, 888 Seventh Ave., New
York, NY 10016
b. N.A.

EDUCATION: Pennsylvania State University,
B.A., Speech/Broadcasting ('75); Syracuse
University, M.A., Media Administration
('79).
CAREER HIGHLIGHTS: Asst. to the Pres., Tele-
prompter Manhattan Cable TV ('79); Regional
Exec. Dir., New Markets Development,
Group W Cable ('81); Mgr., Project Control
and Visibility, Group W Cable ('83).
ACHIEVEMENTS & AWARDS: Dir., New York
State Cable TV Assn.; Member, Women in
Cable and NATAS.
PERSONAL: N.A.

WERNER, ROBERT L., JR.
Sr. V.P., ESPN, Marketing and Finance

c/o ESPN, ESPN Plaza, Bristol, CT 06010
b. January 19, 1950. Chicago, IL.

EDUCATION: Trinity College, B.A. ('72); University of Virginia, M.B.A. ('77).
CAREER HIGHLIGHTS: Product Dir., Richardson-Vicks ('77); Engagement Mgr., McKinsey & Co. ('79); Sr. V.P., Marketing and Finance, ESPN ('82).
ACHIEVEMENTS & AWARDS: N.A.
PERSONAL: Resides in Rowayton, CT.

WERSHBA, JOSEPH
Prod., CBS, News, "60 Minutes"

c/o CBS, 524 W. 57th St., New York, NY 10019
b. August 19, 1920. New York, NY.

EDUCATION: Brooklyn College.
CAREER HIGHLIGHTS: One of the finest TV news and documentary producers. Worked closely with Edward R. Murrow and Fred W. Friendly during their early TV news work at CBS. Began as Radio News Writer, CBS Radio News, New York ('44); Editor and News Dir., WCBS-AM ('46); Correspondent, CBS News, Washington, DC ('48); Prod. of the "Hear It Now" radio series and the "See It Now" TV series, CBS News; Reporter/Columnist, N.Y. Post ('58); Prod., CBS News, concentrating on documentaries ('64); Prod., CBS News "60 Minutes" ('68).
ACHIEVEMENTS & AWARDS: Golden Gavel Award; Hillman Foundation Award; Silver Gavel award; two Emmy awards for reports on "60 Minutes" ('71–'78).
PERSONAL: Resides in New Hyde Park, NY, with his wife, Shirley; two children.

WERSHBA, SHIRLEY
Prod., CBS, News

c/o CBS, 524 W. 57th St., New York, NY 10019
b. July 7.

EDUCATION: Brooklyn College.
CAREER HIGHLIGHTS: Worked for ABC News and "The MacNeil/Leher Report" before joining CBS News as Prod. for Diane Sawyer.

ACHIEVEMENTS & AWARDS: N.A.
PERSONAL: Married to "60 Minutes" producer Joseph Wershba.

WEST, JOELLA
Assoc. Dir., Business Affairs, Motion Pictures for TV and Mini-Series, CBS, Entertainment, West Coast

c/o CBS, 7800 Beverly Blvd., Los Angeles, CA 90036
b. N.A.

EDUCATION: Mid-Valley College (magna cum laude, '77).
CAREER HIGHLIGHTS: Advertising Mgr., Los Angeles Philharmonic Assn. ('76); Assoc., Hayes & Hume law firm, Los Angeles ('78); Assoc. Dir., Talent and Program Negotiations, CBS ('81); Assoc. Dir., Business Affairs, Motion Pictures for TV and Mini-Series, CBS Entertainment, West Coast ('82).
ACHIEVEMENTS & AWARDS: N.A.
PERSONAL: N.A.

WEST, MARY JO
Co-Anchor/Interviewer, CBS, News, "CBS News Nightwatch"

c/o CBS, 524 W. 57th St., New York, NY 10019
b. Atlanta, GA.

EDUCATION: University of Georgia, B.A., Journalism ('73); Florida State University.
CAREER HIGHLIGHTS: Reporter, WCTV-TV, Tallahassee, FL ('73); Prod./ Public Affairs Program Host, WFSU-TV, Tallahasse ('74); Prod./ Public Affairs Program Host, KAET-TV, Tempe, AZ ('75); Co-Anchor, WSTP-TV, Minneapolis ('76); Co-Anchor, Interviewer, "CBS News Nightwatch" ('82).
ACHIEVEMENTS & AWARDS: Ten Arizona Press Club awards; Golden Gavel award; Arizona AP Broadcasters Assn. award.
PERSONAL: N.A.

WESTFELDT, WALLACE
Prod., ABC, News

c/o ABC, 1330 Ave. of the Americas, New
  York, NY 10019
b. September 23, 1923.

EDUCATION: Columbia Graduate School of Po-
litical Science and International Relations.
CAREER HIGHLIGHTS: Correspondent, Time-
Life; Reporter, *Nashville Tennessean;* Writer/
Prod., NBC News; Exec. Prod., "NBC Night-
ly News" ('69); Exec. Prod., NBC Documen-
taries ('73); Exec. Prod. of Public Affairs for
WETA, Washington, DC; Prod., ABC News
('77).
ACHIEVEMENTS & AWARDS: Emmy awards for
outstanding achievement ('69, '70).
PERSONAL: N.A.

WESTHEIMER, RUTH
Host, WNEW-TV, "Dr. Ruth"

c/o Metromedia, 205 E. 67th St., New York,
  NY 10021
b. N.A.

EDUCATION: Columbia University, Ed.D.
CAREER HIGHLIGHTS: Psychosexual Therapist;
Adjunct Assoc. Professor, Cornell University
Dept. of Psychiatry; hosts radio show "Sexu-
ally Speaking" on WYNY-FM; hosts half-
hour TV show on relationships entitled "Dr.
Ruth."
ACHIEVEMENTS & AWARDS: N.A.
PERSONAL: N.A.

WESTIN, AV
Exec. Prod and V.P., ABC, News

c/o ABC, 7 W. 66th St., New York, NY 10023
b. July 29, 1929. New York, NY.

EDUCATION: New York University, B.A., Russian; and M.A., East European Studies.
CAREER HIGHLIGHTS: Instrumental in shaping
the content and style of network news, Westin conceived new visual effects and introduced short promo headlines on "ABC Evening News," which changed the look of news
presentations. He succeeded in pulling "ABC
Evening News" from third place to a strong
second during the 1969 season, and was responsible for the 1982 success of "20/20,"
which was nominated for 22 Emmy awards
and won 11, far more than any other program
of its genre. Following extensive work with
CBS as Radio Reporter and TV Prod., Exec.
Prod., and Dir. of coverage of major news
events in Europe and "CBS Morning News"
('60), he joined Public Broadcast Library as
Exec. Dir. and Exec. Prod. of Sunday evening
TV magazine programs ('68). Joined ABC as
Exec. Prod. of "ABC Evening News" ('69);
named V.P. and Dir., TV Documentaries
('73); left ABC to produce independent news
documentaries ('76). Returned to ABC as V.P.
and Exec. Prod. of "World News Tonight"
('78); named Exec. Prod., "20/20," and V.P.,
ABC News Program Development ('79); added responsibilities for late night newscast
('82).
ACHIEVEMENTS & AWARDS: Peabody awards
('58, '60, '73, '74); Dupont award ('74); George
Polk award; Sylvania award; several Emmy
awards, including those for "Crisis in the
Cities" ('68) and "The Population Explosion"
('60).
PERSONAL: Resides in Manhattan.

WESTON, ELLEN
**V.P., Business Affairs, Contract
Negotiations, CBS, Theatrical Films**

c/o CBS, 7800 Beverly Blvd., Los Angeles, CA
90036

EDUCATION: Whittier College School of Law.
CAREER HIGHLIGHTS: Professional Actress; Dir.,
Business Affairs, CBS Theatrical Films ('81);
V.P., Business Affairs, Contract Negotia-
tions, CBS Theatrical Films ('83).
ACHIEVEMENTS & AWARDS: N.A.
PERSONAL: N.A.

WESTON, RICHARD
Sr. V.P., Paramount TV, Business Affairs

5451 Marathon St., Hollywood, CA 90038
b. New York, NY.

EDUCATION: City College of New York; Brooklyn Law School.
CAREER HIGHLIGHTS: V.P., Merchandising and Licensing Division, Paramount Pictures ('77); V.P., Business Affairs, TV Prod. Division, Paramount ('79); Sr. V.P., Business Affairs, Paramount TV ('80).
ACHIEVEMENTS & AWARDS: N.A.
PERSONAL: N.A.

WHEELER, THOMAS E.
Pres., Natl. Cable TV Assn.

c/o Natl. Cable TV Assn., 1724 Massachusetts Ave., N.W., Washington, DC 20036
b. N.A.

EDUCATION: Ohio State University.
CAREER HIGHLIGHTS: V.P., Grocery Manufacturers of America; Exec. V.P., Natl. Cable TV Assn., Pres., Natl. Cable TV Assn., Washington, DC.
ACHIEVEMENTS & AWARDS: N.A.
PERSONAL: N.A.

WHELDON, HUW P.
Prod./Exec.

120 Richmond Hill, Richmond, Surrey, England
b. May 7, 1916.

EDUCATION: Bangor and London School of Economics.

CAREER HIGHLIGHTS: Prod., BBC ('53); Head of Documentary Programmes, BBC ('62); Head of Music and Documentary Programmes, BBC ('63); Controller of Programmes, BBC ('65); Managing Dir., TV, BBC ('69); Special Adviser, BBC ('75); Consultant, NBC ('77); Chairman, Court of Governors, L.S.E. and Member of the Committee of Free World.
ACHIEVEMENTS & AWARDS: TV Producers Guild award for best British documentary; Ford Foundation award; TV Society gold medal.
PERSONAL: Married, three children.

WHITAKER, JACK
News and Sports Commentator, ABC, News and Sports

c/o ABC, 1330 Ave. of the Americas, New York, NY 10019
b. May 18, 1924. Philadelphia, PA.

EDUCATION: St. Joseph's University.
CAREER HIGHLIGHTS: Sportscaster, WCAU-TV, Philadelphia ('50); Sports Announcer/Studio Host/Commentator, CBS Sports covering NFL football, track and field events, horse racing, golf tournaments, boxing, and tennis ('61). Also served as Host, "The Verdict Is Yours" ('62); Commentator for ABC News and Sports (82).
ACHIEVEMENTS & AWARDS: Engelhard award ('73); Emmy as outstanding sports personality ('79).
PERSONAL: Resides in Bridgehampton, NY; six children.

WHITE, LAWRENCE
Exec. V.P., Columbia Pictures TV

c/o Columbia Pictures TV, 300 Colgems Sq., Burbank, CA 91505
b. July 31, 1926.

EDUCATION: Syracuse University.
CAREER HIGHLIGHTS: Prod./Dir., Dumont Network ('48); Dir. of Programming, Benton & Bowles ('51); Exec. Prod. for "The Edge of Night"; V.P., Daytime Programming, CBS ('59); Exec., Goodson-Todman Productions; Dir. of Program Development, CBS; V.P., Daytime Programs, NBC ('65); Program

Chief, NBC ('75); Exec. V.P., Columbia Pictures TV.
ACHIEVEMENTS & AWARDS: N.A.
PERSONAL: N.A.

WHITE, LYNNE
Weathercaster, Metromedia, WNEW-TV, New York

c/o WNEW-TV, 205 E. 67th St., New York, NY 10021
b. Elizabeth, NJ.

EDUCATION: Simmons College; University of Illinois.
CAREER HIGHLIGHTS: Reporter, WICS-TV, St. Louis; Assoc. Prod., "North Jersey Weekly," WNET-TV, Newark, NJ; Reporter, Co-Anchor, "Black News," also serving as Weekend Weathercaster, WNEW-TV ('80); named Weathercaster, "10 O'Clock News," WNEW-TV, New York ('82).
ACHIEVEMENTS & AWARDS: N.A.
PERSONAL: N.A.

WHITE, STEPHEN
Supervisor, ABC, Motion Pictures for TV

c/o ABC, 2040 Avenue of the Stars, Los Angeles, CA 90067
b. 1947. New York, NY.

EDUCATION: University of California at Los Angeles, B.A.
CAREER HIGHLIGHTS: Agent Trainee with Ashley Famous ('66); Production Head of Zoetrope Studios ('68); Story Analyst, UA, 20th Century Fox, and Paramount ('69); Freelancer ('70–'73); Staff Writer for Bob Hope ('73–'75); wrote for Merv Griffin ('76); wrote and performed on "Fernwood 2Night" ('77); literary agent for Major Talent Agency ('77–'80). Currently, Supervisor, Motion Pictures for TV, ABC.
ACHIEVEMENTS & AWARDS: N.A.
PERSONAL: Resides in Los Angeles.

WICK, C. Z.
Dir., ABC, Dramatic Series Development

c/o ABC, 2040 Ave. of the Stars, Los Angeles, CA 90067
b. October 30, 1952. New York, NY.

EDUCATION: University of California at Los Angeles, B.A., English; University of Southern California, J.D.
CAREER HIGHLIGHTS: Staff Member, Democratic Natl. Committee ('75); Speechwriter for 1976 convention ('76); Special Asst., Public Affairs, Dept. of HUD ('78). Supervisor, Dramatic Series Development, ABC ('79); Program Exec., Current Comedy Programs ('80); named Dir., Dramatic Series Development ('81).
ACHIEVEMENTS & AWARDS: N.A.
PERSONAL: N.A.

WICKERSHAM, ELIZABETH (Liz)
Co-host, SuperStation WTBS, News

c/o WTBS, 1050 Techwood Drive, N.W., Atlanta, GA 30318
b. Orange, TX.

EDUCATION: University of Texas, Speech and Drama.
CAREER HIGHLIGHTS: Wickersham won the title of Miss Georgia ('76) and became a finalist in the "Miss USA Pageant." She signed with the Ford Agency and became a top model; joined Turner Broadcasting family as Co-Host, "The Lighter Side on WTBS," a weekly, half-hour program highlighting the lighter side of national and international events with news, feature stories, and guest stars. She has appeared on daytime TV's "One Life To Live" and "The Edge of Night," and primetime's "B.J. and the Bear," "Magnum, P.I.," and *Mickey Spillane–Mike Hammer, Margin for Murder*. Her photographs have appeared in *Glamour, Mademoiselle,* and *Cosmopolitan.* She has also appeared on the cover of *Playboy.*
ACHIEVEMENTS & AWARDS: N.A.
PERSONAL: Wickersham is an avid sportswoman.

WICKLEIN, JOHN
Assoc. Dir. for News and Public Affairs Programs, Corp. for Public Broadcasting

5419 Linden Ct., Bethesda, MD 20814
b. July 20, 1924. Reading, PA.

EDUCATION: Columbia University; Rutgers University; University of Pennsylvania; Harvard University.
CAREER HIGHLIGHTS: Reporter/Editor, *N.Y. Times*; Mgr., TV News, WNET-TV, WCBS-TV, and WABC-TV, New York; Washington, DC, Bureau Chief, Public Broadcast Library of NET; Prod., numerous network documentaries including "Free at Last"; Dean, Boston University School of Public Communications. Currently serves as Assoc. Dir. for News and Public Affairs Programs, Corp. for Public Broadcasting, in charge of grants for news and public affairs programs.
ACHIEVEMENTS & AWARDS: George Polk award. Author, *Electronic Nightmare: The New Communications and Freedom*. Member, Advisory Board of the Telecommunications Research and Action Center.
PERSONAL: Wife, Myra; children, Elizabeth, Peter, and Joanna.

WILDE, KIRSTIE
Field Anchor, KNBC, "News 4 LA"

c/o KNBC, 3000 W. Alameda Ave., Burbank, CA 91523
b. Tucson, AZ.

EDUCATION: Stanford University, B.S., Communications.
CAREER HIGHLIGHTS: Studio Dir., KGW-TV, Portland, OR ('72); Reporter, KCST-TV and KGTV, San Diego, CA, and KRON, San Francisco ('74); Co-Anchor, WHAS-TV, Kentucky ('79); general assignment Reporter/Anchor, KNBC ('82).
ACHIEVEMENTS & AWARDS: Two Golden Mike awards; criminal justice award from San Diego State University; award for best documentary from the San Francisco Press Club ('78); AP silver award for best documentary and best investigative report ('78, '79).
PERSONAL: Resides in Toluca Hills, CA.

WILDER, JOHN (Keith Merrill Magaurn)
Prod./Writer (Freelance)

c/o Nightwatch Productions, 4024 Radford, Studio City, CA 91604
b. 1936. Tacoma, WA.

EDUCATION: University of California at Los Angeles, B.A.
CAREER HIGHLIGHTS: Began career at age 8 under the name John McGovern, performing on Lux Radio theater ('44); Story Editor for "Branded" ('65); churned out 134 episodes of "Peyton Place" ('66–'69). Joined QM Productions ('71), Prod., "The Streets of San Francisco" ('73–'75); "Most Wanted" pilot ('76) and "Quinn Martin's Tales of the Unexpected" ('77). Exec. Prod., *The Bastard*, Operation Prime Time ('78) and Exec. Prod./Writer of the 25-hour TV adaptation of James Michener's *Centennial* ('79).
ACHIEVEMENTS & AWARDS: Writers Guild nomination for outstanding teleplay for "The Streets of San Francisco" ('73); Emmy award nominations for producing outstanding dramatic series, "The Streets of San Francisco" ('74, '75).
PERSONAL: Resides in Sherman Oaks, CA, with wife Carolyn; children, Michelle Colleen, Victoria Lynn, Meredith Christine, and Sean Kevin.

WILHITE, THOMAS L.
V.P., Production, Walt Disney Productions

c/o Disney Studios, 500 S. Buena Vista St., Burbank, CA 91521
b. 1952. Keswick IA.

EDUCATION: Iowa State University, B.A.
CAREER HIGHLIGHTS: Press Agent, Rogers &

Cowan ('74); Dir., Publicity, Walt Disney Productions ('77); Dir., Creative Affairs, and Asst. to the Press., Walt Disney Productions ('80); V.P., Production, Walt Disney Productions ('81).

ACHIEVEMENTS & AWARDS: N.A.

PERSONAL: Resides in San Fernando Valley, CA.

WILKERSON, JAMES
Anchor, Cable News Network

c/o Cable News Network, 1050 Techwood Dr., N.W., Atlanta, GA 30318
b. February 5, 1939. Phoenix, AZ.

EDUCATION: University of Southern California, B.A., Telecommunications.

CAREER HIGHLIGHTS: Began career while in the army, broadcasting on the Armed Forces Network ('57); joined KRUX-AM, Phoenix ('61); KFI-AM, Los Angeles ('68); News Anchor for the ABC Radio Network, ('70); KHJ-AM, Los Angeles ('71); KTAR-AM, Phoenix ('72); Sports Anchor, KOA-TV, Denver ('73); KOB-TV, Albuquerque, as Anchor/Reporter ('77); joined Cable News Network as Anchor ('81).

ACHIEVEMENTS & AWARDS: Red Cross service award for series of reports on a blood crisis ('79).

PERSONAL: Wife, Beverly; two children.

WILKINSON, CHARLES (Bud)
Color Commentator/Pregame Analyst, ESPN, College Football

Pebsco, 400 Mansion House Center #2510, St. Louis, MO 63102
b. April 23, 1916. Minneapolis, MN.

EDUCATION: University of Minnesota, B.A. ('37); Syracuse University, M.A. ('40).

CAREER HIGHLIGHTS: NCAA college football ('65); ABC college football and pregame shows ('65–'77); ESPN college football and weekly "College Football Preview" ('80).

ACHIEVEMENTS & AWARDS: Author of *Oklahoma Split-T Football* ('52); *Modern Defensive Football* ('58); *Modern Physical Fitness* ('66). College Football Coach of the Year; Pres., College Football Coaches Assn.; Member, College Football Hall of Fame.

PERSONAL: N.A.

WILL, GEORGE F.
Political Analyst, ABC, News

c/o ABC, 1717 DeSales St., Washington, DC 20007
b. 1941. Champaign, IL.

EDUCATION: Trinity College; University of Oxford (England); Princeton University, Ph.D.

CAREER HIGHLIGHTS: Professor of Political Philosophy, Michigan State University and the University of Toronto; Staff of Sen. Gordon Allott of Colorado ('70); Chairman, Republican Policy Committee ('72); Washington Editor, *National Review* magazine ('73); started a syndicated newspaper column on politics which now appears in more than 300 newspapers ('74); Contributing Editor, *Newsweek* ('76). In addition to writing his newspaper and *Newsweek* columns, Will serves as a regular panelist on "Agronsky and Company" on PBS and "This Week With David Brinkley" on ABC, with occasional appearances on ABC's "Nightline."

ACHIEVEMENTS & AWARDS: Selected as one of the leaders of tomorrow by *Time* magazine ('74). Author, *The Pursuit of Happiness and Other Sobering Thoughts* ('78); *The Pursuit of Virtue and Other Tory Notions* ('81); *Statecraft as Soulcraft* ('83).

PERSONAL: N.A.

WILLENSON, SETH
V.P., United Satellite Communications, Program Development

c/o United Satellite Communications, 1345 Ave. of the Americas, New York, NY 10105
b. June 12, 1947.

EDUCATION: Cornell University, B.S.

CAREER HIGHLIGHTS: V.P., Programming and Business Affairs, RCA Selectavision; V.P., Program Development, United Satellite Communications, New York.

ACHIEVEMENTS & AWARDS: N.A.

PERSONAL: N.A.

WILLIAMS, CHEE CHEE
Reporter, WABC-TV, New York, News

c/o WABC-TV, 7 Lincoln Sq., New York, NY 10023
b. Kansas City, MO.

EDUCATION: College of Emporia, B.A., Political Science and Public Speaking; Columbia University Summer Program in Broadcast Journalism.

CAREER HIGHLIGHTS: News Production Asst., KMBC-TV, Kansas City, MO ('70); Newswriter, KCMO-TV, Kansas City ('71); Anchor, KMBC-TV, Kansas City ('72); Reporter, WABC-TV, New York ('77).

ACHIEVEMENTS & AWARDS: N.A.

PERSONAL: Resides in New Jersey with her husband, Don, and their daughter, Samantha.

WILLIAMS, DONALD O.
Sr. V.P., Operations, Times Mirror Cable TV

c/o Times Mirror Cable TV, 2381 Morse Ave., Irvine, CA 92714

b. May 20, 1932. Wichita Falls, TX.

EDUCATION: San Diego College, B.A. ('59).

CAREER HIGHLIGHTS: V.P., Cox Cable Communications ('66); named Exec. V.P. ('79); Sr. V.P., Oak Communications ('80); Sr. V.P., Operations, Times Mirror Cable TV ('81).

ACHIEVEMENTS & AWARDS: N.A.

PERSONAL: N.A.

WILLIAMS, EDWARD D.
V.P., ABC, Management Information Systems

c/o ABC, 1330 Ave. of the Americas, New York, NY 10019

b. N.A.

EDUCATION: Hofstra University, B.S., Industrial Management; Fairleigh Dickinson University, M.B.A.

CAREER HIGHLIGHTS: Has held numerous consulting and management positions with such companies as Republic Aviation, General Electric, McCormick and Paget, Cresap, Union Carbide, and Western Union. Joined ABC as Dir. of Systems and Data Processing; V.P., Management Information Systems, ABC.

ACHIEVEMENTS & AWARDS: N.A.

PERSONAL: Resides in Franklin Lakes, NJ, with his wife, Natalie, and their two daughters, Denise and Claudia.

WILLIAMS, MARY ALICE
V.P./Anchor, Cable News Network, New York Bureau

c/o Cable News Network, 1050 Techwood Dr., N.W., Atlanta, GA 30318

b. March 12, 1949. Minneapolis, MN.

EDUCATION: Creighton University, B.A., English and Mass Communications.

CAREER HIGHLIGHTS: Reporter, KSTP-TV ('68); Prod., Exec. Prod. KSTP-Minneapolis ('71); Exec. Prod., WPIX-TV ('73); Correspondent, Anchor, Network Correspondent, Education Reporter, and Morning Anchor, WNBC-TV ('74); New York Bureau Chief, New York Anchor, V.P., Cable News Network ('80).

ACHIEVEMENTS & AWARDS: New York Press Club byline award ('77); Natl. Council of Women achievement award ('80).

PERSONAL: Husband, Scott Latham.

WILLIAMS, PALMER
Former Managing Editor, CBS, "60 Minutes"

c/o CBS, 524 W. 57th St., New York, NY 10019

b. October 7, 1916. Englewood, NJ.

EDUCATION: Wooster Prep School.

CAREER HIGHLIGHTS: One of the best news production executives in the history of TV. Played a large role in the success of "60 Minutes." Production Mgr. and Prod., "See It Now" series on CBS ('51); Dir. of Broadcast operations, CBS News ('64); Prod., "CBS Reports" ('65); Sr. Prod., "60 Minutes" ('68); Managing Editor, "60 Minutes" ('80).

ACHIEVEMENTS & AWARDS: N.A.

PERSONAL: Resides in New York City with wife, Barbara; four children.

WILLIAMS, ROBIN
Actor

c/o Paramount TV, Miller-Milkis-Boyett Productions, 5555 Melrose Ave., Los Angeles, CA 90038

b. July 21. Edinburgh, Scotland.

EDUCATION: Claremont Men's College; College of Marin; Juilliard School.

CAREER HIGHLIGHTS: The worthiest proponent

of the Jonathan Winters school of comedy—nonsenical sound effects mixed with a wonderfully zany comic vision. It's only fitting that Williams and Winters ended up on "Mork and Mindy" together. Williams displays dazzling technique and range as a comedy performer, and attained instant huge success as Mork. Stand-up comedian with guest roles on "Laugh-In," "The Richard Pryor Show," and "Happy Days." Motion pictures include *Popeye* and *The World According to Garp*. Series star of "Mork and Mindy." Star of comedy specials on HBO.

ACHIEVEMENTS & AWARDS: N.A.

PERSONAL: Wife, Valerie.

WILLMORE, JOSEPH X.
Prod., CBS, "The Guiding Light"

c/o CBS, 51 W. 52d St., New York, NY 10019

b. June 11, 1942. New York, NY.

EDUCATION: Manhattan College, B.S.

CAREER HIGHLIGHTS: Began at CBS as an usher ('60); moved up the ranks in the company as an Admin. Asst. ('63); Production Supervisor ('65); Assoc. Prod., "As the World Turns" ('70); Prod., "As the World Turns" ('73); Exec. Prod., "As the World Turns" ('77); Prod., "Another World" ('78); Prod., "The Guiding Light" ('78).

ACHIEVEMENTS & AWARDS: Two Emmy awards for work on "The Guiding Light" ('80, '82).

PERSONAL: Resides in Union, NJ, with wife, Joanne, and sons, Joseph, James, and John.

WILSON, WARREN
Reporter, KNBC

c/o KNBC, 3000 W. Alameda Ave., Burbank, CA 91523

b. Greenville, NC.

EDUCATION: West Los Angeles School of Law.

CAREER HIGHLIGHTS: Only black reporter for a major news agency to work behind police lines during the Watts riots ('65). Reporter for KABC-Radio, KFWB-Radio, City News Service, and UPI. Investigative Reporter, KNBC ('69).

ACHIEVEMENTS & AWARDS: Emmy from the Los Angeles ATAS for his investigative report

"Children of the Night" ('79). Received the Natl. Headliner award; special award of the Natl. Assn. of Media Women, and the Greater Los Angeles Press Club award for best TV news reporting ('74).

PERSONAL: N.A.

WINANT, ETHEL
Sr. V.P., Metromedia Producers Corp., Creative Affairs

5746 Sunset Blvd., Hollywood, CA 90028

b. Worcester, MA.

EDUCATION: University of California at Berkeley; Whittier College.

CAREER HIGHLIGHTS: Began backstage in production of Broadway's *A Streetcar Named Desire*, *Death of a Salesman*, and *Summer and Smoke*. Moving to TV, became casting head for Talent Associates ('53). CBS TV Dir. of Casting for nine years, then V.P., Talent and Casting. Joined NBC as V.P., Talent ('78), then joined Metromedia Producers Corp. ('82) as Sr. V.P., Creative Affairs.

ACHIEVEMENTS & AWARDS: California Community and Junior College Assn. distinguished alumni award for Women in Film.

PERSONAL: Three sons; resides in Los Angeles.

WINFREY, LEE
TV Critic, *Philadelphia Inquirer*

c/o *Philadelphia Inquirer*, 400 N. Broad St., Philadelphia, PA 19101

b. July 7, 1932. Knoxville, TN.

EDUCATION: University of Tennessee, B.S. ('66); University of Iowa, M.F.A. ('68).

CAREER HIGHLIGHTS: Reporter, *Nashville Tennessean* ('57); *Knoxville News-Sentinel* ('58); UPI Miami Bureau ('60); Reporter, *Miami Herald* ('62); Reporter based in Washington, DC, for the Knight-Ridder Newspapers ('63); Reporter, *Detroit Free Press* ('66); Reporter, *Philadelphia Inquirer* ('72); TV Critic, *Philadelphia Inquirer* ('74).

ACHIEVEMENTS & AWARDS: Author, *Kent State Report: The President's Commission on Campus Unrest* ('70).

PERSONAL: N.A.

WINKLER, HENRY
Actor

c/o "Happy Days," ABC, 2040 Ave. of the
Stars, Los Angeles, CA 90067
b. October 30, 1946. New York, NY.

EDUCATION: Yale School of Drama, B.A.

CAREER HIGHLIGHTS: Fonzie started out as a
supporting character and became the focal
point of the long-running series "Happy
Days." Motion pictures include *The One and
Only, Heroes, Night Shift,* and *Lords of Flatbush.*
Produced the afterschool special "Run, Don't
Walk" and *Who Are the Debolts and Where Did
They Get 19 Kids?* Guest appearances on "The
Mary Tyler Moore Show," "Laverne and Shir-
ley," "Rhoda," and "The Bob Newhart
Show." TV movies include *An American
Christmas Carol* and *Katherine.*

ACHIEVEMENTS & AWARDS: Two Golden Globe
awards as best actor in a comedy series.
Hollywood Radio and TV Society Man of the
Year. Natl. Epilepsy Foundation distinguished service award ('82).

PERSONAL: Wife, Stacey.

WINSTON, BRIAN NORMAN
**Professor, New York University, Tisch School
of the Arts**

2 Washington Sq. Village, New York, NY
10012
b. N.A.

EDUCATION: N.A.

CAREER HIGHLIGHTS: One of the most brilliant
young academics teaching film and TV.
Course Dir., Mass Communications, Rockland College ('71); Course Dir., Video, Bradford College of Art ('72); Dir. of Media Studies

Group, Dept. of Sociology, University of
Glasgow ('74); Head of General Studies, Natl.
Film School of Great Britain ('73); Professor,
Dept. of Undergraduate Film, TV and Radio
Production, New York University ('79); Chair,
Dept. of Cinema Studies, Tisch School of the
Arts, New York University ('81).

ACHIEVEMENTS & AWARDS: Author of many articles for English and American publications.

PERSONAL: Wife, Adele, one child.

WINSTON, CAROLINE
**V.P., Showtime Entertainment, Program
Development, East Coast**

c/o Showtime, 1211 Ave. of the Americas,
New York, NY 10036
b. March 10, 1948.

EDUCATION: St. John's College, B.S. ('73).

CAREER HIGHLIGHTS: Production Unit Mgr.,
ABC Sports ('74); Production Unit Mgr., ABC
Entertainment ('77); Programming Exec.,
Showtime Entertainment ('80); Dir. of Production, Showtime ('81); V.P., Program Development, East Coast, Showtime Entertainment ('81).

ACHIEVEMENTS & AWARDS: N.A.

PERSONAL: N.A.

WINSTON, SUSAN
Exec. Prod., ABC

c/o "Good Morning America," ABC, 1 Lincoln
Plaza, New York, NY 10023
b. N.A.

EDUCATION: University of Pennsylvania, B.A.,
American Literature.

CAREER HIGHLIGHTS: WCAU-TV Prod. of chil-
dren's specials, Writer/Researcher for special
productions and daily one-hour talk show,
"Morningside"; "The Mike Douglas Show"
Researcher ('75); Talent Coordinator and
Assoc. Prod. ('76); NBC TV Coordinating
Prod., "America Alive" ('76); left for ABC's
"Good Morning America" as Line Prod. ('79);
named Exec. Prod. ('81).

ACHIEVEMENTS & AWARDS: N.A.

PERSONAL: Resides in Manhattan and is a private airplane pilot.

WINTER, PETER M.
Pres., Digital Applications Intl.

624 Ironwood, Elk Grove Village, IL 60007
b. September 19, 1949. Lower Hutt, New
    Zealand.

EDUCATION: Victoria University, New Zeal-
    and, B.A. and M.A.
CAREER HIGHLIGHTS: Sub-Editor, Teletext Sys-
    tem, CEEFAX ('77); Managing Editor, Field
    Electronic Publishing ('81); Exec. Editor, Key-
    com Electronic Publishing ('82); Pres. Digital
    Applications Intl. ('83).
ACHIEVEMENTS & AWARDS: N.A.
PERSONAL: N.A.

WINTERS, RICHARD J.
**Exec. Dir., Paramount TV, Publicity,
    Advertising, and Promotion**

5451 Marathon St., Hollywood, CA 90038
b. October 3, 1928.

EDUCATION: Columbia University.
CAREER HIGHLIGHTS: Prod. Publicity, Para-
    mount Pictures ('65); Prod. Publicity, MGM
    ('68); Natl. Dir. of Publicity, Columbia Pic-
    tures, New York ('69); Natl. Dir. of Publicity,
    MGM Pictures, New York ('71); Natl. Dir. of
    Advertising, Publicity, and Promotion, Para-
    mount TV ('73); Exec. Dir., Publicity, Adver-
    tising, and Promotion, Paramount TV ('77).
ACHIEVEMENTS & AWARDS: N.A.
PERSONAL: Married, resides in Los Angeles.

WIRTH, TIMOTHY ENDICOTT
**Congressman, U.S. Government,
    Telecommunications and Consumer
    Protection and Finance Committee**

2454 Rayburn House Office Bldg.,
    Washington, DC 20515
b. September 22, 1939. Santa Fe, NM.

EDUCATION: Harvard University, B.A. and
    M.A.; Stanford University, Ph.D.
CAREER HIGHLIGHTS: Asst. to Chairman, Natl.
    Urban Coalition, Washington, DC ('68); Dep-
    uty Asst. Secretary for Education ('69); V.P.,
    Great Western United Corp., Denver ('70);
    Mgr., Rocky Mountain Office, Arthur D. Lit-
    tle, Inc. ('71); elected to the House of Repre-

sentatives, 2d Congressional District, Colo-
    rado ('74).
ACHIEVEMENTS & AWARDS: Recipient of dis-
    tinguished service award, Dept. of Health,
    Education and Welfare ('69); Member, White
    House Fellows Assn.
PERSONAL: Wife, Wren; children, Christopher
    and Kelsey.

WISEMAN, FREDERICK
Independent Filmmaker

54 Lewis Wharf, Boston, MA 02110
b. January 1, 1930.

EDUCATION: Williams College, B.A. ('51); Yale
    Law School, LL.B. ('54).
CAREER HIGHLIGHTS: One of the most influ-
    ential documentary filmmakers in the sixties
    and seventies, this independent pioneering
    figure introduced TV documentaries without
    an on-camera narrator or correspondent. His
    career began as a physician in private prac-
    tice, Paris ('56); Instructor in Legal Medicine,
    Boston University Law-Medicine Institute
    ('58); Lecturer in Law, Boston University Law
    School ('59); Research Assoc., Brandeis Uni-
    versity, Dept. of Sociology ('63); Treasurer,
    Organization for Social and Technical Inno-
    vation ('66); Independent Filmmaker, Zip-
    porah Films, Visiting Lecturer ('67).
ACHIEVEMENTS & AWARDS: MacArthur Prize
    Fellowship ('82); honorary mention, *Seraph-
    ita's Diary*, Festival Dei Popoli ('82); *Manoevre*,
    best documentary, Festival Intl. de Cinema,
    Portugal ('80); *Canal Zone*, golden Athena
    award for best feature, Athens Intl. Festival
    ('78); *Hospital*, Emmy awards, best news doc-
    umentary and best director, Catholic Film-
    makers award, Dupont award for excellence

in broadcast journalism ('70); "Law and Order," Emmy award, best news documentary award for exceptional merit, Philadelphia Intl. Festival ('69).
PERSONAL: N.A.

WITKER, KRISTI
Reporter, Independent Network News and WPIX-TV

c/o WPIX-TV, 11 WPIX Plaza, New York, NY 10017
b. N.A.

EDUCATION: N.A.
CAREER HIGHLIGHTS: Covered Senator Robert F. Kennedy's campaign ('68); Co-Author of *Bobby* and *RFK: His Life and Death*. Contributing Editor, *The Horizon Book of Great Cathedrals* ('69); *How To Become a Super Salesman* ('70), *How To Be an Absolutely Smashing Public Speaker Without Saying Anything* ('70), *The American Heritage History of American People* ('71), *The Horizon History of China* ('72). Author, *How To Lose Everything in Politics* ('74). Correspondent for ABC-TV News ('78); Reporter for WABC-TV's "Eyewitness News" ('78); Covered the Jean Harris trial ('81–'82). Reporter, Independent Network News, WPIX-TV.
ACHIEVEMENTS & AWARDS: *Newsweek* prize for excellence in campaign photography ('72).
PERSONAL: N.A.

WITT, PAUL JUNGER
Prod./Writer/Dir., Witt/Harris/Thomas Productions,

c/o Creative Artists Agency, 1888 Century Park E., Los Angeles, CA 90067
b. March 20, 1941. New York, NY.

EDUCATION: University of Virginia, B.A. ('63)
CAREER HIGHLIGHTS: Assoc. Prod./Dir., Screen Gems ('65); Prod./Dir., Screen Gems ('68); Prod., "The Partridge Family" ('70); Prod., *Brian's Song* ('71); Prod., Spelling/Goldberg Productions ('72); Prod., "The Rookies" ('72); Pres./Exec. Prod., Danny Thomas Productions ('73); Prod., *Blood Sport* ('73); Prod., "The Practice" ('74); Co-Founder/Exec. Prod., Witt/Harris/Thomas Productions ('75); Exec.

Prod., *Griffin Loves Phoenix* ('75); Exec. Prod., "Soap" ('77); Exec. Prod., "Benson" ('79); Exec. Prod., "It's a Living" ('80); Exec. Prod., "I'm a Big Girl Now" ('80); Exec. Prod., "It Takes Two" ('82); Exec. Prod., "Condo" ('83); Exec. Prod., "Just Married" ('83).
ACHIEVEMENTS & AWARDS: Emmy award for *Brian's Song* ('71); Black Image award for "The Rookies" ('72).
PERSONAL: Children, Christopher, Anthony, and Genevieve.

WOLCOTT, JAMES
TV Critic, *New York* Magazine

c/o *New York* Magazine, 755 Second Ave., New York, NY 10017
b. N.A.

EDUCATION: Frostburg State College.
CAREER HIGHLIGHTS: Erudite and witty, Wolcott is one of the best young critics and essayists. Prior to writing for *New York*, Wolcott wrote a TV column for the *Village Voice*. He also writes a literary column for *Harper's*, a film column for *Texas Monthly*, and essays for *Vogue* and the *New York Review of Books*.
ACHIEVEMENTS & AWARDS: N.A.
PERSONAL: Single, resides in Manhattan.

WOLFE, DONNA
V.P./Assoc. Dir., Ted Bates Advertising, Network and Cable TV Negotiations

c/o Ted Bates Advertising, 1515 Broadway, New York, NY 10036
b. August 7, 1951. Brooklyn, NY.

EDUCATION: Baruch College, B.B.A. ('73).
CAREER HIGHLIGHTS: Began as Research Analyst ('73) and rose to current position as V.P./Assoc. Dir., Ted Bates Advertising, Network and Cable TV Negotiations.
ACHIEVEMENTS & AWARDS: N.A.
PERSONAL: Husband, Michael.

WOLFF, PERRY
Exec. Prod., CBS, News, Specials

c/o CBS, 524 W. 57th St., New York, NY 10019
b. June 12, 1921. Chicago, IL.

EDUCATION: University of Wisconsin.

CAREER HIGHLIGHTS: Joined CBS's Chicago affiliate as a reporter ('47). Created documentary series "Adventure" and then joined "Air Power" ('56). Independent Documentary Prod. ('57–'61); Documentary Writer and Prod. for CBS ('61–'75), including "A Tour of the White House With Mrs. John F. Kennedy" ('62), "Of Black America" ('68). "A Black View of South Africa" ('70), and "The Selling of the Pentagon" ('71). Exec. Prod. of "CBS Reports" ('75); Exec. Prod. of CBS News Specials ('76). His total body of documentary films represent many of the best documentaries aired on CBS for nearly three decades.

ACHIEVEMENTS & AWARDS: Academy Award, several Emmy awards, eight Peabody awards, and three Writers Guild awards.

PERSONAL: Resides in Manhattan.

WOLFSON, LOUIS
V.P., Operations, and Dir., Wometco Cable TV

c/o Wometco Cable TV, 400 N. Miami Ave.
  Miami, FL 33128
b. November 25, 1953.

EDUCATION: Stetson University.

CAREER HIGHLIGHTS: Supervisor, Wometco Enterprises, South Carolina ('76); Operations Mgr., Georgia Vending Division, Wometco Enterprises, Georgia ('78); General Mgr., Wometco Arkansas Vending Operation, Wometco Enterprises, Arkansas ('79); Construction Coordinator, Wometco Cable TV ('80); V.P., Operations, and Dir., Wometco Cable TV ('82).

ACHIEVEMENTS & AWARDS: N.A.

PERSONAL: N.A.

WOLLOCK, EDWARD
V.P. and Sales Mgr., ABC TV, Central Division

c/o ABC, 190 N. State St., Chicago, IL 60601
b. Chicago, IL.

EDUCATION: Roosevelt University, B.S. and B.A., Marketing and Advertising; University of Iowa.

CAREER HIGHLIGHTS: Assoc., Daniel J. Edelman Public Relations Firm; Asst. to the Dir., Sales Service, ABC, Chicago ('69); Dir., Sales Service, ABC, Chicago ('70); Dir., Sales Planning, ABC, Chicago ('71); Acct. Exec., ABC, Chicago ('73); Acct. Exec., ABC, New York ('79); Sales Mgr., ABC TV, Central Division, Chicago ('80); V.P. and Sales Mgr., ABC TV, Central Division, Chicago ('83).

ACHIEVEMENTS & AWARDS: N.A.

PERSONAL: Resides in Winnetka, IL, with his wife, Janet, and their two sons, Joshua and Jake.

WOLPER, DAVID
Independent Prod.

c/o Wolper Organization, 4000 Warner Blvd.,
  Burbank, CA 91523
b. January 11, 1928. New York, NY.

EDUCATION: Drake University; University of Southern California.

CAREER HIGHLIGHTS: After a distinguished career in documentaries, Wolper transferred his considerable talent and energy to phenomenally successful mini-series. He began his career as V.P., Flamingo Films and Associated Artists, then became Pres., Wolper Productions and Dawn Productions; and served on the board of Metromedia before becoming Pres., Wolper Pictures; and Pres. and Chairman of the Board, Wolper Organization. His numerous documentaries include *Race for Space* ('58); *The Rafer Johnson Story* ('60); *The Story of Hollywood and the Stars* ('63); *The Legend of Marilyn Monroe* ('64); National Geographic specials for CBS ('64); "The Undersea World of Jacques Cousteau"; "The Making of the President." Co-Prod. in the seventies of "Welcome Back Kotter" and "Chico and the Man"; Prod., the TV mini-series *Roots* ('77), *Roots: The Next Generation* ('79), and *The Thorn Birds* ('83). His theatrical films include *Willy*

Wonka and the Chocolate Factory and *The Hellstrom Chronicle.*

ACHIEVEMENTS & AWARDS: Received 28 Emmy awards; Peabody award ('63); Academy Award ('71); Cannes Film Festival award.

PERSONAL: Wife, Margaret; children, Mark, Michael, and Leslie. Resides in Bel Air, CA.

WOLYNSKI, MARA
Reporter, WABC-TV, News, New York, NY

c/o WABC-TV, 7 Lincoln Sq., New York, NY 10023
b. New York, NY.

EDUCATION: New York University, B.A., Journalism/English Literature ('74).

CAREER HIGHLIGHTS: Freelance Writer, *Village Voice, Vogue, Mademoiselle, Newsweek* and the *American Journal;* Commentator, WKTU-FM, New York ('80); Reporter, WABC-TV, New York ('81).

ACHIEVEMENTS & AWARDS: N.A.

PERSONAL: Resides in New York City.

WOLZIEN, THOMAS R.
Exec. Prod., NBC, News

c/o NBC, 30 Rockefeller Plaza, New York, NY 10020
b. February 26, 1947. Washington, DC

EDUCATION: University of Denver, B.A., History/Mass Communications.

CAREER HIGHLIGHTS: Reporter/Photographer, KLZ/KMGH-TV, Denver ('68); News Prod., WLUK-TV, Green Bay, WI ('73)News Prod., KMOX, St. Louis ('73); Asst. News Dir., KSD-TV, St. Louis ('75). Joined NBC News as Field Prod., White House ('76); named Dir., News Operations, New York ('77); Sr. Prod., "Special Segment" of "NBC Nightly News" ('79); Exec. Prod., "NBC Magazine" ('81); appointed Exec. Prod., "NBC Nightly News" weekend editions.

ACHIEVEMENTS & AWARDS: N.A.

PERSONAL: N.A.

WOOD, ROBERT D.
Pres., Metromedia Producers Corp.

5746 Sunset Blvd., Hollywood, CA 90028
b. April 17, 1925. Boise, ID

EDUCATION: University of Southern California.

CAREER HIGHLIGHTS: CBS Station Management and Sales; General Sales Mgr. for KNXT ('55); General Mgr. of KNXT; Exec. V.P., CBS TV Stations ('66); Pres., CBS TV ('69). As CBS Pres., he gained prominence when he championed the cause of Norman Lear and his then-controversial "All in the Family" series. Also initiated the series "The Mary Tyler Moore Show," "M*A*S*H," "The Waltons," "The Jeffersons," and "Kojak" and the TV movies *The Autobiography of Miss Jane Pittman, Queen of the Stardust Ballroom, I Heard the Owl Call My Name,* and *Dummy.* Pres., Metromedia Producers Corp. ('79).

ACHIEVEMENTS & AWARDS: University of Southern California School of Business Administration award for outstanding alumni achievement ('71); humanitarian award of the Natl. Assn. of Christians and Jews ('75); honorary doctor of laws degree.

PERSONAL: Resides in Hollywood.

WOODROW, DAVID M.
Dir., Cox Cable Communications, INDAX Market Development

c/o Cox Cable Communications, 219 Perimeter Center Pky., Atlanta, GA 30346
b. March 18, 1946. Norwalk, CT.

EDUCATION: University of Connecticut, M.B.A. ('75).

CAREER HIGHLIGHTS: Sr. Product Planner; Product Planner; Planning Analyst; Application Engineer, Pitney Bowes, Stamford, CT ('71); Planning Mgr., Tech. Comp. Group, Exxon Enterprises; Venture Dept. Mgr., Office Systems, Exxon Enterprises, New York ('76); Dir., INDAX Market Development, Cox Cable Communications, Atlanta ('82).

ACHIEVEMENTS & AWARDS: Tau Beta Pi; Pi Tau Sigma; Distinguished Student Award from Purdue University.

PERSONAL: N.A.

WOODRUFF, JUDY
Network Correspondent, NBC, News

c/o NBC, 4001 Nebraska Ave., N.W.,
Washington, DC 20016
b. November 20. Tulsa, OK.

EDUCATION: Richmond Academy; Meredith College; Duke University, B.A.
CAREER HIGHLIGHTS: Began at WQXI-TV, Atlanta, as Newsroom Secretary ('68); worked her way up to Asst. and Researcher ('69); moved to WAGA-TV, Atlanta, as Reporter and Anchor ('70); joined NBC as Southeastern Bureau News Correspondent ('75); named NBC White House Correspondent ('77); Sr. White House Correspondent ('82); Washington, DC, Correspondent "Today" show ('82).
ACHIEVEMENTS & AWARDS: Member, Board of Governors, White House Correspondents ('80–present; V.P., '82); Board of Visitors, Wake Forest University ('82–'83); Board of Advisors, Duke University, School of Public Policy ('82–'83). Co-Author, *This Is Judy Woodruff at the White House* ('82).
PERSONAL: Married to Albert Hunt; son, Jeffrey.

WOOL, BRIDGET POTTER
Senior V.P., HBO, Original Programming

c/o HBO, 1271 Ave. of the Americas, New York, NY 10020
b. August 21, 1943. England.

EDUCATION: American Theater Wing.
CAREER HIGHLIGHTS: Assoc. Prod., "The Dick Cavett Show"; Prod., Palomar Pictures Intl. ('74); Dir. of Program Development, ABC TV ('76); V.P. in Charge of Prime Time Program Development, Mini-Series and Movies for TV, East Coast; V.P., Lorimar Productions ('80); joined HBO as V.P., Original Programming ('82); Senior V.P., HBO, Original Programming ('83).
ACHIEVEMENTS & AWARDS: N.A.
PERSONAL: N.A.

WOON, PETER
Editor, BBC, News

c/o BBC, 12 Cavendish Place, London, England W1
b. December, 1931. Bristol, England.

EDUCATION: N.A.
CAREER HIGHLIGHTS: Reporter, *Bristol Evening Post* ('49); Correspondent, *Daily Express;* Reporter, BBC News ('61); Asst. Editor, BBC TV News ('66); Editor, BBC Radio News ('69); Head of Publicity and Information, BBC ('76); Head of Information, BBC ('77); Editor, News and Current Affairs, BBC Radio ('78); Editor, BBC TV News ('80).
ACHIEVEMENTS & AWARDS: N.A.
PERSONAL: Married, two children.

WOOTEN, JAMES
Correspondent, ABC, News

c/o ABC, 7 W. 66th St., New York, NY 10023
b. Detroit, MI.

EDUCATION: N.A.
CAREER HIGHLIGHTS: Wrote for various newspapers and at WHDM-Radio and WGLN; six years as Reporter and then Atlanta Bureau Chief for *N.Y. Times;* War Correspondent, *Philadelphia Inquirer* ('73); Natl. Correspondent, *N.Y. Times* ('74); Roving Editor, *Esquire* ('78); joined ABC News and served as Chief Political "Overview" Correspondent for Republican campaigns ('80); named Natl. Correspondent ('81) and has contributed to "This Week With David Brinkley" since its premiere ('81).
ACHIEVEMENTS & AWARDS: Ernie Pyle memorial award for combat reportage of Arab-Israeli War ('73); blue pencil award for journalistic excellence, Columbia University Graduate School of Journalism ('78).
PERSONAL: Four daughters.

WRIGHT, BEN
Golf Broadcaster, CBS, Sports

c/o CBS, 51 W. 52d St., New York, NY 10019
b. N.A.

EDUCATION: Felsted School (England); London University (England).
CAREER HIGHLIGHTS: Correspondent, *London Daily Mirror;* Correspondent, *London Observer;* Correspondent, *Sunday Times;* Golf Correspondent, *Financial Times* ('66); Broadcaster, British Commercial Network ('67); Golf Commentator, CBS Sports ('72).

ACHIEVEMENTS & AWARDS: N.A.
PERSONAL: N.A.

WRIGHT, BOB
Dir., ABC, West Coast Public Relations

c/o ABC, 2040 Ave. of the Stars, Los Angeles,
  CA 90067
b. May 21, 1937. Leicester, England.

EDUCATION: Transylvania University, B.A., Li-
  beral Arts.
CAREER HIGHLIGHTS: Joined ABC as Apprentice
  Publicist ('65); promoted through the ranks to
  Publicist, Newspaper Plant, Mgr. of Business
  Information; named Dir., Public Relations,
  ABC TV, West Coast ('78).
ACHIEVEMENTS & AWARDS: N.A.
PERSONAL: Resides in Hollywood.

WRIGHT, ROBERT C.
Pres., Cox Cable Communications

c/o Cox Cable Communications, 219 Perimeter
  Center Pkwy., Atlanta, GA 30346
b. April 23, 1943. Rockville Centre, NY.

EDUCATION: Holy Cross, B.A. ('65); University
  of Virginia, LL.B. ('68).
CAREER HIGHLIGHTS: Law Secretary to Chief
  Judge of the U.S. District Court for New Jer-
  sey ('70); Private Law Practice, Newark, NJ
  ('71); Counsel, General Electric ('73); Mgr.
  and General Mgr., Products Division, Gen-
  eral Electric ('74); General Mgr. Plastics Sales
  Dept., General Electric ('78); Pres., Cox Cable
  Communications Atlanta ('80).
ACHIEVEMENTS & AWARDS: Member, NCTA
  Public Policy Planning Committee; Chair-
  man, NCTA Enhanced Services Committee.
PERSONAL: N.A.

WUSSLER, ROBERT J.
Exec. V.P. and Pres., Turner Broadcasting System, WTBS-TV

c/o Turner Broadcasting System, 1050
  Techwood Dr., N.W., Atlanta, GA 30318
b. September 8, 1936. Newark, NJ.

EDUCATION: Seton Hall University, B.A., Communication Arts ('57).

CAREER HIGHLIGHTS: Mailroom Clerk, CBS
  ('57); Production Asst., CBS News ('57); Assoc. Prod., CBS News ('59); Prod., CBS News
  ('61); Head of the CBS News Election Unit
  ('62); Exec. Prod. and Dir. of Special Events,
  CBS News ('65); V.P. and General Mgr.,
  WBBM-TV, Chicago ('72); V.P., CBS Sports
  ('74); Pres., CBS TV ('76); Pres., CBS Sports
  ('77); formed own production company, Pyr-
  amid Enterprises LTD., New York ('78); Exec.
  V.P., Turner Broadcasting System, and Pres.,
  WTBS-TV, Atlanta ('83).
ACHIEVEMENTS & AWARDS: Four national Emmy
  awards; two international sports awards;
  Member, Advisory Board, Writers Guild,
  East, Foundation; former Chairman, NATAS.
PERSONAL: N.A.

WYATT, WILL
Head of Documentary Features, BBC-TV

c/o BBC, 12 Cavendish Place, London,
  England, W1
b. 1942. Oxford, England.

EDUCATION: Magdalen College School, Uni-
  versity of Oxford (England); Emmanuel Col-
  lege, University of Cambridge (England).
CAREER HIGHLIGHTS: Staff, *Sheffield Morning
  Telegraph* ('64); BBC Radio News ('65); Prod.,
  BBC TV ('68); Head of Presentation Pro-
  grammes, BBC TV ('77); Head of Documen-
  tary Features, BBC TV ('81).
ACHIEVEMENTS & AWARDS: Author, *The Man
  Who Was B. Traven.*
PERSONAL: N.A.

WYLER, CATHERINE
Dir., PBS, Children's and Cultural Programming

c/o PBS, 475 L'Enfant Plaza, S.W.,
  Washington, DC 20024
b. Los Angeles, CA.

EDUCATION: Stanford University, B.A.
CAREER HIGHLIGHTS: Asst. Librarian, American
  Heritage ('62); Literary/Theatrical Agent,
  Robert Lantz Agency ('65); Story Editor, Ras-
  tar Productions ('68); Story Editor, Avco Embassy Pictures ('69); Literary/Theatrical Agent
  ('74); Mgr., Network Relations, Warner Bros.

TV, New York ('75); Asst. Dir., Media Arts, Natl. Endowment for the Arts ('76–'81); Dir., PBS, Children's and Cultural Programming.

ACHIEVEMENTS & AWARDS: N.A.

PERSONAL: Daughter of Academy Award-winning movie director William Wyler.

WYMAN, JANE
Actress

c/o "Falcon Crest," CBS, 51 W. 52d St., New York, NY 10019
b. January 4, 1914. St. Joseph, MO.

EDUCATION: N.A.

CAREER HIGHLIGHTS: Wyman exhibited her versatility with the many heroine roles she played in her drama series in the fifties. Today, her unexpected venture into TV villainy finds her clawing the scenery in "Falcon Crest," and she meets the challenge admirably. Her motion pictures include *The Lost Weekend, The Yearling, The Blue Veil, Magnificent Obsession, The Glass Menagerie, Just for You, So Big, Stage Fright, Pollyanna, Here Comes the Groom,* and *All That Heaven Allows.* TV movies include *The Failing of Raymond* and *The Incredible Journey of Dr. Meg Laurel.* Star of "Fireside Theater," "Jane Wyman Theater," and "Falcon Crest."

ACHIEVEMENTS & AWARDS: Academy Award as best actress for *Johnny Belinda* ('48).

PERSONAL: Two children; resides in Los Angeles. Formerly married to Ronald Reagan.

WYMAN, THOMAS H.
Pres. and Chairman of the Board, CBS

c/o CBS, 51 W. 52d St., New York, NY 10019
b. November 30, 1929. St. Louis, MO.

EDUCATION: Phillips Academy; Amherst College, B.A., English (magna cum laude, '51).

CAREER HIGHLIGHTS: Nestle Co. as a Salesman, then rose to Asst. to the Pres.; moved to Europe for Nestle as Asst. to Managing Dir.; promoted to V.P. of parent company (55–'65); joined Polaroid Corp. as V.P., rising to Sr. V.P., Gen. Mgr. and Chairman of the Management Exec. Committee ('65–'75); Pres. and Chief Exec. Officer, Green Giant Co. ('75–'79); Vice Chairman of Pillsbury when it acquired Green Giant Co. ('79); named Pres., Chief Exec. Officer, and a Dir. of CBS, Inc. ('80). Became Pres. and Chairman of the Board, CBS, following William Paley's retirement ('83)

ACHIEVEMENTS & AWARDS: Member, Board of Dirs., AT&T; Lincoln Center for the Performing Arts; Natl Exec. Service Corps; United Negro College Fund. Member, Pres. Task force on Private Sector Initiatives; Council on Foreign Relations; Business Committee for the Arts. Trustee, Amherst College; Phillips Academy; Museum of Broadcasting; the Economic Club of New York.

PERSONAL: Married, four children.

WYNN, ROBERT H.
Pres., Mellodan Productions

3115 West Olive Ave., Burbank, CA 91505
b. September 2, 1932. St. Louis, MO.

EDUCATION: N.A.

CAREER HIGHLIGHTS: Began as Sports Announcer, WKOC, Missouri ('51); Sports Announcer, WPAD, Kentucky ('52); Staff Announcer, WFIE-TV, Evansville, IN ('53); Prod./Dir., McCann Erickson ('56); Assoc. Prod., "The Andy Williams Show," "The Bing Crosby Show" ('61); Unit Mgr., "The Judy Garland Show," "The Danny Kaye Show" ('62); Prod., "The Bing Crosby Show" ('62), Prod., Danny Thomas specials, "Alice Through the Looking Glass," "Jimmy Durante Meets the Lively Arts" ('65); Prod., "Carol Channing and 101 Men" ('68); Prod., "The Petula Clark Show" ('69); Prod., Tennessee Ernie Ford specials ('71); Prod., "ABC Mystery Movies," "Saturday Night Live" ('75); Prod., "The Great American Celebration" ('76); Dir., "Vice Presidential Debate" ('76); Prod., "Annual Rock Music Awards"

('76); Prod., "Inaugural Eve Gala Perfor-mance—President Carter" ('77); Dir., "Gold-en Globe Awards" ('78); Dir., "Tribute to Neil Simon," "Happy Birthday Bob Hope" ('78); Prod., "Hello, Here Is Berlin," "Bob Hope on the Road to China" ('79); Prod., "Real People" ('79–'82); Pres., Mellodan Productions.
ACHIEVEMENTS & AWARDS: N.A.
PERSONAL: N.A.

WYNNE, JOHN O.
Pres., Broadcasting and Video Enterprises, Landmark Communications

c/o Landmark Communications, 150 W. Brambleton Ave., Norfolk, VA
b. July 6, 1945. Norfolk, VA.

EDUCATION: Princeton University, B.A.
CAREER HIGHLIGHTS: Attorney, Wilcox, Savage, Lawrence, Dickson & Spindle, in Norfolk, VA. Joined Landmark Communications, be-came Pres., Broadcasting and Video Enter-prises, Landmark Communications ('80). As Pres., responsible for KNTV, San Jose, CA; KLAS-TV, Las Vegas; and WTAR-AM and WLTY-FM, Norfolk, as well as the Weather Channel. He is also responsible for develop-ing new video enterprises for Landmark.
ACHIEVEMENTS & AWARDS: N.A.
PERSONAL: Wife, Susan; sons, John, Lee, and Brad. Resides in Virginia Beach, VA.

YABLANS, FRANK
Vice Chairman and Chief Operating Officer, MGM-UA

c/o MGM-UA, 10202 W. Washington Blvd., Culver City, CA 90230
b. August 27, 1935. New York, NY.

EDUCATION: N.A.

CAREER HIGHLIGHTS: Booked films for Warner Bros. ('57); Head of Distribution and Marketing, Paramount; Pres., Paramount Pictures Corp. ('71). Produced major films including *North Dallas Forty, Silver Streak, The Fury, Mommie Dearest, The Other Side of Midnight, Monsignor, Octopussy,* and *WarGames.* Currently Vice Chairman and Chief Operating Officer, MGM/UA.

ACHIEVEMENTS & AWARDS: N.A.

PERSONAL: N.A.

YATES, WILLIAM R.
V.P., Exec. Prod., TV, Walt Disney Productions

c/o Walt Disney Productions, 500 S. Buena Vista St., Burbank, CA 91521
b. October 4, 1929. Los Angeles, CA.

EDUCATION: University of Illinois; Columbia University Law School.

CAREER HIGHLIGHTS: Reporter, *N.Y. Daily News* ('51); worked as a Press Agent in Hollywood ('55); Story Editor, "Studio One" ('58); Story Editor, "Camera Three" ('59); Dir., Program Development, ABC, New York ('61); Prod., "Repertoire Workshop" ('63); Lawyer, Attorney's Office, Los Angeles ('64); Story Consultant, "Combat" ('66); Story Consultant, "Garrison's Guerrillas" ('67); Writer, "The Wonderful World of Disney" ('71); Prod./Writer/Story Consultant, "The Streets of San Francisco" ('73); Prod., "The Tales of the Unexpected" ('77); Prod., "The Runaways" ('78); V.P., Exec. Prod., TV, Walt Disney Productions ('79).

ACHIEVEMENTS & AWARDS: N.A.

PERSONAL: Resides in Long Beach, CA, with wife, Joann; sons, James and Douglas.

YORKIN, BUD
Prod., Tandem Productions

c/o Tandem Productions, 100 Universal City Plaza, Universal City, CA 91608
b. February 22, 1926. Washington, PA.

EDUCATION: Carnegie-Mellon University, B.S.; Columbia University, M.A.

CAREER HIGHLIGHTS: With partner Norman Lear, Yorkin has been a major producer and director of outstanding TV shows for three decades. In the fifties, TV Dir. for Dinah Shore, Ernie Ford and George Gobel shows, as well as for "The Colgate Comedy Hour." Partner in Tandem Productions ('59); Exec. Prod., "All in the Family" ('69); Exec. Prod., "Sanford and Son" ('71). Co-Prod., "Maude," "Good Times," "What's Happening." Major motion pictures he directed include *Never Too Late, Divorce American Style,* and *The Thief Who Came To Dinner.*

ACHIEVEMENTS & AWARDS: Six Emmy awards; Peabody, Sylvania, and Directors Guild awards.

PERSONAL: N.A.

YOUMAN, ROGER
Editor, Local Sections, *TV Guide*

c/o *TV Guide,* Radnor, PA 19088
b. February 25, 1932. New York, NY.

EDUCATION: Swarthmore College, B.A.
CAREER HIGHLIGHTS: Desk Asst., CBS News ('53); various editorial positions, *TV Guide* ('54); Assoc. Editor, *TV Guide* ('60); Asst. Managing Editor, *TV Guide* ('65); Managing Editor ('72); Exec. Editor ('76); Editor, *Panorama Magazine* ('79); Exec. Editor. *TV Guide* ('80); Editor, Local Sections *TV Guide.*
ACHIEVEMENTS & AWARDS: Co-Author, *How Sweet It Was* and *The Television Years.*
PERSONAL: N.A.

YOUNG, ELIZABETH L.
Pres., Services by Satellite

c/o Services by Satellite, 1660 L St., N.W., Suite 906, Washington, DC 20036
b. N.A.

EDUCATION: Columbia University, Ph.D.
CAREER HIGHLIGHTS: Serves as Pres., Services by Satellite (SatServ) and its parent organization, the Public Service Satellite Consortium (PSSC). Before joining PSSC ('79), Young was Dir., Ohio State University Telecommunications Center, Columbus, OH. She was previously Exec. Dir., Kansas Public TV, Topeka; Dir., Station Relations, Natl. Public Radio, Washington, DC, and had held adjunct faculty status at American University and Ohio State University.
ACHIEVEMENTS & AWARDS: N.A.
PERSONAL: N.A.

YOUNG, LOUIS
Correspondent, WABC-TV, "Eyewitness News"

c/o WABC-TV, 7 Lincoln Sq., New York, NY 10023
b. New York.

EDUCATION: University of Florida, B.S., Broadcasting.
CAREER HIGHLIGHTS: Sr. Prod., WNET ('79); Reporter, WTVT, Tampa, FL ('80); Correspondent, WABC-TV "Eyewitness News" ('81).
ACHIEVEMENTS & AWARDS: N.A.
PERSONAL: Resides in New York City.

YOUNG, ROGER
Dir.

c/o Broder/Kurland Agency, 9046 Sunset Blvd., Los Angeles, CA 90069
b. May 13, 1942. Champaign, IL.

EDUCATION: University of Illinois, M.S.
CAREER HIGHLIGHTS: Cameraman, WILL-TV, Champaign, IL ('62); Dir., WCIA-TV, Champaign ('63); Instructor, TV Dept., Ball State University ('66); Prod./Dir., WFBM-TV, Indianapolis ('67); Prod., Natl. Commercials, Foote, Cone & Belding advertising ('71); Dir., Lippert/Saviano ('72); Dir., Topel & Assoc. ('73); Pres., Young & Co. ('74); Assoc. Prod., *Something for Joey* ('76), *Critical List* ('77), and "Lou Grant" ('77); Dir., "Lou Grant" ('79), "Magnum, P.I." pilot ('80), *Bitter Harvest* ('80), *An Innocent Love* ('81), *Dreams Don't Die* ('81), and *Two of a Kind* ('82).
ACHIEVEMENTS & AWARDS: Directors Guild awards for "Lou Grant" ('79, '80); Christopher award for *Bitter Harvest* ('81).
PERSONAL: Wife, Rita; stepchildren, Leland and Bridget.

ZACHARY, TED
Sr. V.P., MGM-UA, TV Production

c/o MGM-UA, 10202 W. Washington Blvd.,
  Culver City, CA 90230
b. October 30, 1937. New York, NY.

EDUCATION: New York University, B.S. ('58).

CAREER HIGHLIGHTS: Prod., Prod. Exec, UPI
  Productions, New York ('61–'66); Freelance
  Prod. Mgr. and Asst. Dir. ('66–'76). Features
  include *The Swimmer, Loving, Shaft, Shamus,
  The Hot Rock, The Gambler, The Seven Ups,* and
  Lenny. Prod. Mgr., CBS TV ('76); V.P., Prod.,
  Viacom Productions ('77–'82); Sr. V.P.,
  MGM-UA TV Production.

ACHIEVEMENTS & AWARDS: Directors Guild
  award nominee for *Lenny* ('74).

PERSONAL: Wife, Marian; sons, Marc and
  Alan.

ZADEH, STELLA
Managing Editor, CBS Teletext Project

c/o CBS Teletext Project, 6255 Sunset Blvd.,
  #2206, Hollywood, CA 90028
b. July 27, 1947. New York, NY.

EDUCATION: University of California at Los Angeles; Harvard University.

CAREER HIGHLIGHTS: Considered one of the
  most talented young executives in the new
  field of electronic publishing. Acting News
  Planning Mgr, KNXT ('80); Dir., CBS, Alameda ('81); Managing Editor, CBS Teletext
  Project ('81).

ACHIEVEMENTS & AWARDS: N.A.

PERSONAL: Single, resides in Los Angeles.

ZEIDMAN, LEE
Anchor, Cable News Network, Sports

c/o Land & Newlin, Suite 620, 5 Piedmont
  Center, Atlanta, GA 30305
b. July 6, 1956. Washington, DC.

EDUCATION: University of Maryland, B.S.,
  Broadcast Journalism.

CAREER HIGHLIGHTS: Sports Dir., WCIV-TV,
  Charleston, SC ('78); Sports Reporter/
  Weekend Anchor, WJLA-TV, Washington,
  DC ('79); Sports Anchor, Cable News Net-
  work ('80).

ACHIEVEMENTS & AWARDS: Emmy and Dupont
  awards for participation on a WJLA documentary.

PERSONAL: N.A.

ZIMBALIST, STEPHANIE
Actress

c/o "Remington Steele," NBC, 3000 W.
  Alameda Ave., Los Angeles, CA 90067
b. October 6, 1956. Encino, CA.

EDUCATION: N.A.

CAREER HIGHLIGHTS: TV films and mini-series
  include *The Golden Moment, Centennial,* and
  The Gathering. Guest star on "The Love Boat."
  Series lead in "Remington Steele."

ACHIEVEMENTS & AWARDS: N.A.

PERSONAL: Single, resides in North Holly-wood, CA. Father is actor Efrem Zimbalist, Jr.

ZIMMERMAN, BILL
Anchor, Cable News Network

c/o Cable News Network, 1050 Techwood Dr., N.W., Atlanta, GA 30318
b. April 5, 1940. Washington, DC.

EDUCATION: National Academy of Broadcasting.

CAREER HIGHLIGHTS: Started broadcasting career at WFAN-AM, Washington, DC ('60); News Dept., WTVR-AM/FM/TV ('61); Reporter, Talk Show Host, WKBN-TV, Youngstown, OH ('63); Reporter, WTOP-TV, Washington, DC ('64); Reporter, WHDH-TV, now WCVB, Boston ('69); Correspondent, ABC News, Washington, DC, and Vietnam ('71); named Bureau Chief, ABC News, Beirut ('75); Bureau Chief, ABC News, Rome ('76); Political Correspondent, ABC News, Washington, DC ('77); Anchor, Cable News Network ('80).

ACHIEVEMENTS & AWARDS: Virginia UPI award for documentary on John Glenn's space flight ('62).

PERSONAL: Married, four children.

ZINBERG, MICHAEL
Dir.

c/o Bob Broder, Broder-Kurland Agency, 9046 Sunset Blvd., Los Angeles, CA 90069
b. San Antonio, TX.

EDUCATION: University of Texas.

CAREER HIGHLIGHTS: Started with James Garner's Cherokee Productions, moved to Talent Associates, then joined MTM Enterprises ('70). He supervised film production, wrote for "The Mary Tyler Moore Show," "The Bob Newhart Show," "Rhoda," "The Tony Randall Show," and "Phyllis." He became Exec. Prod., "The Bob Newhart Show," and then joined NBC as V.P., Comedy Development ('79) before freelancing as Dir. ('82). Dir: "Yellow Rose." NBC ('83–'84)

ACHIEVEMENTS & AWARDS: N.A.

PERSONAL: Married; one son. Resides in the San Fernando Valley, CA.

ZORNOW, EDITH
Film Prod., Children's Television Workshop

c/o Children's Television Workshop, 1 Lincoln Plaza, New York, NY 10023
b. March 21.

EDUCATION: St. John's University, B.B.A.

CAREER HIGHLIGHTS: Directed the Film Division of Grove Press and for 10 years was Dir., Film Distribution and Acquisition, Brandon Films. Now produces all the animation for "Sesame Street" and served in the same capacity for the Children's Television Workshop's "The Electric Company."

ACHIEVEMENTS & AWARDS: Emmy, for producing the series "The Art of Film," with critic Stanley Kauffmann on WNET-TV ('64).

PERSONAL: N.A.

ZRAKE, JIM
Exec. Prod., USA Network, Sports

c/o USA Network, 208 Harristown Rd., Glen Rock, NJ 07452
b. N.A.

EDUCATION: University of California at Los Angeles.

CAREER HIGHLIGHTS: Writer, Dir., KTLA-TV, Los Angeles ('70); joined Golden West Video Tape as Unit Mgr. for a number of TV series ('75); Assoc. Prod., the Donny and Marie Osmond series ('78). Returned to Los Angeles ('79) to produce a variety of sports and entertainment specials. Included in this series has been coverage of University of Southern California football and basketball games, in addition to numerous assignments for "On-TV" in Los Angeles and for the USA Network.

ACHIEVEMENTS & AWARDS: N.A.

PERSONAL: N.A.

CORPORATION INDEX

ABC

AARON, BETSY
Correspondent

ABERNATHY, JAMES L.
V.P., Corporate Affairs

AGREE, ARNOLD
V.P., Taxes

AMLEN, SEYMOUR
V.P.

ARCHER, NICHOLAS
(Nicholas Occiogrosso)
V.P., TV News Services

ARLEDGE, ROONE
Pres., News

ARMEL, PAULA
Dir., Affiliate Services
Hearst/ABC Video Services

ARTHUR, BEATRICE
Actress

ASTIN, PATTY DUKE
Actress

AUG, STEPHEN
Correspondent

BARNATHAN, JULIUS
Pres.

BARRETT, PETE
(Paul W. Barrett)
V.P.

BARRY, MIKE
Sports Reporter
WABC-TV, New York, NY

BEESEMEYER, RICHARD L.
V.P. & General Mgr.

BELL, STEVE
Anchor

BENTON, JOE
Correspondent

BERADINO, JOHN
Actor

BERG, ILENE AMY
Exec. Prod., Motion Pictures for
Television

BERGER, MARILYN
Correspondent

BERGMAN, JULES
Science Editor

BERKOWITZ, BOB
Correspondent

BERNSTEIN, CARL
Prod., Principal Correspondent

BERNSTEIN, INA
V.P., Casting, Motion Pictures

BEUTEL, BILL
Anchor
WABC-TV, New York, NY

BLACK, MAXENE
Correspondent
WABC-TV

BLAKEMORE, BILL
Bureau Chief, News

BLANCHARD, BOB
Consumer Reporter
WABC-TV

BLANK, BEN
Dir.

BLOOMBERG, STUART JAMES
V.P., Variety Series, Specials, and
Late-Night Program Develop-
ment

BOMBECK, ERMA
On-Air Personality

BONANNI, JACK
(John S. Bonanni)
V.P., Station Mgr.
WABC-TV

BOYER, PHILIP B.
V.P. and General Manager
ABC-Owned TV Stations

BRANDT, YANNA KROYT
Prod., Writer, Dir.

BRINKLEY, DAVID
Anchor "This Week with David
Brinkley"

BROOKMAN, MICHAEL S.
Consultant

BROWER, STUART
V.P., On-Air Promotion

BROWN, HILARY
Correspondent

BUCHIN, JOHN
Correspondent
WABC-TV

BURKE, DAVID W.
V.P. and Asst. to Pres.

BURKE, DENISE W.
Dir.

BURKE, VINCENT
V.P.

BURKS, RUPERT
Dir. of Systems
Video Enterprises

BUTCHER, TED
V.P., Film Production

CARAS, ROGER
Correspondent, News

CAREY, PHILIP
Actor

CASO, PATRICIA
Exec. Prod.
WABC-TV, New York

CHALOM, MARC
V.P., Production and Operations
and Exec. Dir., DAYTIME

CHASE, REBECCA
Correspondent

CHASE, SYLVIA
Correspondent

CHILD, JULIA
On-Air Personality

CHRISTIAN, SPENCER
Weathercaster/Sportscaster/
Reporter
WABC-TV

CLARK, BOB
Correspondent

COHEN, MARK H.
Sr. V.P.

COLLINS, JOAN
Actress

WILLIAMS, ROBIN
Actor
WINKLER, HENRY
Actor
WINSTON, SUSAN
Exec. Prod.

WOLLOCK, EDWARD
V.P. and Sales Mgr.
WOLYNSKI, MARA
Reporter
WABC-TV
WOOTEN, JAMES

Correspondent
WRIGHT, BOB
Dir.
YOUNG, LOUIS
Correspondent
WABC-TV

CBS

ADAMS, JACQUELINE
Correspondent
AGUILAR, CARLOS
Reporter
ARONSON, HERMAN
V.P., Operations and Creative
   Services, Advertising and
   Promotion, East Coast
BACH, CATHERINE
Actress
BAER, J.A. (Ted)
V.P., Business Affairs, Talent and
   Program Acquisitions
BAKER, MARGERY CLAIRE
Sr. Broadcast Prod., News
BARKER, BOB
Host
BARONE, JOAN S.
Prod.
BARR, TONY
V.P., Current Dramatic Program
   Production
BARTON, GARY
Dir., Casting, Motion Pictures
   for Television
BAUER, CHARITA
Actress
BAUER, JAMES L.
Dir., Venture One
BECKER, ARNOLD
V.P., Broadcast Group
BEL GEDDES, BARBARA
Actress
BENJAMIN, BURTON
V.P., News
BENSLEY, RUSS
Executive Prod.
BERGER, RICK
Program Exec., Motion Pictures
   for Television
BERGMANN, DOUGLASS
Assoc. Dir., Talent and Program
   Acquisitions, Business Affairs

BERMAN, STEVE
Dir., Comedy Program
   Development
BERNAU, CHRISTOPHER
Actor
BERNTSEN, GEORGE J.
V.P., Feature Films and Late
   Night Programming
BERTINELLI, VALERIE
Actress
BLACKSTONE, JOHN
Correspondent
BLESSINGTON, JOHN
V.P.
BOGROW, PAUL
Dir.
BOOKE, SORRELL
Actor
BOWEN, JERRY
Correspondent
BRADLEY, ED
Co-Editor, "60 Minutes"
BRADY, RAY
Correspondent
BRAVER, RITA
Reporter
BRAYTON, MARIAN
V.P., Dramatic Specials
BROCKMAN, MICHAEL S.
V.P., Daytime and Children's
   Programs
BROKAW, JOANNE
V.P., Educational and
   Community Services
BROOKSHIER, TOM
Sports Broadcaster
BROWN, PHYLLIS GEORGE
Co-Host, "NFL Today"
BROWNE, L. VIRGINIA
Writer
BUCHANAN, MICHAEL A.
V.P., CBS Entertainment
BUCK, JACK

Commentator
BUNIM, MARY-ELLIS
Exec. Prod.
Proctor & Gamble Productions
CAPPLEMAN, CHARLES
V.P.
CASO, LAURENCE
Dir., Daytime
CASSUTT, MICHAEL
Dir., Prime Time
CESLIK, CAROLYN
Dir., Children's Programs
CHANDLER, ROBERT
V.P., News
COLLINGWOOD, CHARLES
Correspondent
COLLOFF, ROGER
V.P., Television Stations
CONVY, BERT
Host
COOPER, KAREN
Program Exec.
CRANE III, ALBERT H.
V.P., Teletext
CRILE III, GEORGE
Correspondent/Prod.
CRONKITE, WALTER
Special Correspondent
CULHANE, DAVID
Correspondent
CULLETON, KATHLEEN
Dir., Administration, Advertising
   and Promotion
DALY, ROBERT
Pres.
DEAN, MORTON
Anchor, CBS Evening News;
   Newsbreak
DERROUGH, NEIL E.
Pres.
Television Stations Division
DESMONI-HORNE, MADDY
Program Exec., Motion Pictures

LAMOREAUX III, E.S. (Bud)
Exec. Prod.
LANDAY, JERRY M.
News Correspondent
LAVIN, LINDA
Actress
LEAHY, THOMAS F.
Exec. V.P.
LEE, MICHELE
Actress
LEISER, ERNEST
Prod. & V.P.
LEM, CAROL
Dir., Program Planning
LEONARD, BILL
Prod.
LEVIN, ALAN
V.P.
LeMASTERS, KIM (Earle H.
   LeMasters)
V.P., Program Development and
   Production
LUND, PETER A.
V.P. & General Mgr.
LYNCH, BILL
Correspondent
LYONS, SIDNEY
V.P., Business Affairs, Motion
   Pictures for Television and
   Mini-Series
McCORKLE, PAULA
Dir. of Communications
WCBS-TV
McDANIEL, JAN
News Assignment Mgr.
McGOWAN, JAMES F.
V.P.
McLAGLEN, ANDREW
Dir./Entertainment
McLAUGHLIN, BILL
Correspondent
McNAMARA, ROBERT
Correspondent
McNEILL, DONALD
Correspondent
MADDEN, JOHN
Broadcaster, Sports Commentary
MALARA, ANTHONY C.
Pres.
MARDEN, MICHAEL
Dir.
MARKELL, ROBERT
V.P., Mini-Series
MARTIN, DAVID
Correspondent
MASUCCI, TONY
Dir., Mini-Series

MATER, GENE PAUL
Sr. V.P., Policy
MAYNOR, ASA
Producer
MENDELSON, NANCY
Creative Director
MEREDITH, BURGESS
Actor
MERLIS, GEORGE
Exec. Prod.
MILLS, DONNA
Actress
MILLS, STEVE
V.P., Motion Pictures for
   Television and Mini-Series
MILTON, CHARLES H.
Sr. Prod.
MITCHELL, JANE
Correspondent
Channel 2 News, WCBS-TV
MORFOGEN, ANN
Dir., Communications
MORGAN, HARRY
Actor
MOSES, HARRY
Prod.
MOYERS, BILL
Correspondent
MUSBURGER, BRENT
Host and Managing Editor
MYLES, STAN
Program Exec., Motion Pictures
   for Television
NELSON, LINDSEY
Sports Commentator
NEWHART, BOB
Actor
NORTHSHIELD, ROBERT
   (Shad)
Senior Executive Prod.
NORVET, ROBERT
V.P., Production Facilities,
   Hollywood
OBER, ERIC
V.P. & General Mgr.
O'CONNOR, CARROLL
Actor
OGIENS, MICHAEL
V.P.
Entertainment
O'NEIL, TERRY
Exec. Prod., NFL Football
OSERANSKY, BERNARD
V.P.
OSGOOD, CHARLES
Correspondent
News

PALEY, WILLIAM
Founder, Chairman
PAPPAS, IKE
Correspondent
PERCELAY, DAVID
V.P./Asst. to the Pres.
PILSON, NEAL H.
Exec. V.P., Sports and Radio Div
Sports
POLING, DOUG
Correspondent
Radio Network News
POLLACK, MORTON J.
V.P., Advertising and Promotion
POSTON, TOM
Actor
POWELL, NORMAN S.
Dir., Motion Pictures for
   Television
PRINCIPAL, VICTORIA
Actress
QUINN, JANE BRYANT
Commentator
RABEL, ED
Correspondent
RANDALL, ELIZABETH
V.P., Print Advertising, West
   Coast
RATHER, DAN
Anchor and Managing Editor
REASONER, HARRY
Co-Editor, "60 Minutes"
REDGRAVE, LYNN
Actress
RENICK, JEANE
V.P.
REVARD, JAMES
Dir.
RICHARDSON, BARRIE
V.P., Press Information
RICHMAN, JOAN
V.P. and Dir., Special Events
ROBERTS, PERNELL
Actor
RODGERS, JONATHAN
Exec. Prod., "CBS News
   Nighwatch"
ROONEY, ANDY
Writer, Prod.
ROSENFELD, JAMES H.
Sr. Exec. V.P.
ROSENTHAL, JANE
Dir., Motion Pictures for
   Television
ROTH, RICHARD
Correspondent
ROZENZWEIG, BARNEY

Exec. Prod.
RYAN, TIM
Sports Broadcaster
SAFER, MORLEY
Co-Editor
SAND, LAURA JOY
Dir., Late Night Development
SANDERS, MARLENE
Correspondent/Prod.
SANFORD, ISABEL
Actress
SAUTER, VAN GORDON
Exec. V.P., Broadcast Group
SAWYER, DIANA
Co-Anchor
SCHIEFFER, BOB
Anchor/Correspondent
SCHWARTZ, DOROTHY
V.P., Primetime Sales
SELF, WILLIAM
Pres.
Theatrical Films
SELLECK, TOM
Actor
SEVAREID, ERIC
Commentator/Consultant
SHAKER, TED
Exec. Prod.
SHEAHAN, JOHN
Correspondent
SHEPARD, GARY
Correspondent
SHEPHARD, HARVEY
Sr. V.P., Programs
SIDEL, ELLY
Dir. of Special Projects, Motion
    Pictures for Television and
    Mini-Series
SEIBERT, CHARLES
Actor
SILBERLING, ROBERT M.
V.P., Motion Pictures for
    Television
SINGER, CARLA
V.P., Dramatic Program Devel-

opment
SMITH, HARRY E.
V.P., New Venture Development
SNYDER, JIMMY ("The Greek")
Sports Analyst
SPENCER, SUSAN
Correspondent
SQUIRE, KEN
Sports Broadcaster
STANTON, FRANK
President Emeritus
STENNER, ROBERT D.
Prod.
STERNE, PETER B.
V.P., Current Comedy Program
    Production
STEWART, DON
Actor
STOCKTON, DICK
Sports Broadcaster
STONE, EMERSON
V.P., News Practices
STONE, KAREN
Co-Anchor/Interviewer
STRINGER, HOWARD
Exec. Prod.
STRUCK, DUKE
Dir.
STRUTHERS, SALLY
Actress
SULLIVAN, SUSAN
Actress
SUMMERALL, PAT
Broadcaster
SWIT, LORETTA
Actress
TAYBACK, VIC
Actor
TESH, JOHN
Reporter, Sports
TILTON, CHARLENE
Actress
TRABERT, TONY
Sports Broadcaster

TROTTA, LIZ
Correspondent
TUNNELL, DOUG
Correspondent
VAUGHN, ROBERT
Actor
VENTURI, KEN
Sports Broadcaster
VERMEIL, DICK
Commentator/Analyst
WALLACE, MIKE
Co-Editor/Anchor
WEINER, BRUCE
V.P., Affiliate Advertising and
    Promotion
WELLS, WILLIAM
Mgr., Dramatic Program
    Development
WERSHBA, JOSEPH
Prod./News
WERSHBA, SHIRLEY
Prod.
WEST, JOELLA
Assoc. Dir., Business Affairs,
    Motion Pictures for Television
    and Mini-Series
WEST, MARY JO
Co-Anchor/Interviewer
WESTON, ELLEN
V.P., Business Affairs
WILLIAM, PALMER
Managing Editor, "60 Minutes"
WILLMORE, JOSEPH X.
Prod.
WOLFF, PERRY
Prod., News
WRIGHT, BEN
Golf Broadcaster
WYMAN, JANE
Actress
WYMAN, THOMAS H.
Pres. and COB
ZADEH, STELLA
Managing Editor
Teletext Project

NBC

AAGAARD, KENNETH J.
V.P.
ABERNATHY, ROBERT
Correspondent

AGRESS, ELLEN SHAW
V.P., Business Planning
ALLEN, DEBBIE
Actress

ALLISON, CYNTHIA
Co-Anchor
KNBC
ALTEMEYER, PAUL

Prod.
News

AMSTER, LINDA
V.P.

ANCIER, GARTH RICHARD
Dir., Current Comedy Programs

ANCONA JR., EDWARD
Dir., Film and Tape Production

ANDERSON, BONNIE MARIE
News Correspondent

ANGOTTI, JOSEPH
General Mgr.

ARRANTS, ROD
Actor

ASSENZIO, RICHARD
Administrator, Sports Program
Planning

AXTHELM, PETE
Sportscaster

BAERWALD, SUSAN
Dir., Mini-Series

BAFFICO, JIM
Prod.

BAIN, CONRAD
Actor

BAKER, WARREN
Dir., Programs

BARNETT, JOAN
V.P.

BARTELME, JOE
Dir., Domestic News

BAZELL, ROBERT
Science Correspondent

BEARD, JOHN
Co-Anchor
KNBC-TV

BERK, ANN
V.P., Advertising, Promotion and
Publicity

BERRESFORD, THOMAS
Treasurer

BETZ, PAT
V.P., Story Dept.

BIVKINS, DAVID K.
V.P., Finance and Administration

BLACKBURN, DAN
Correspondent
News

BLACKMORE, ROBERT
V.P.
Television Network

BLAKE, CHARLES
Director of Design

BLOCK, CURT
V.P.

BOCHCO, STEVEN
Prod.

BODE, KEN
News Correspondent

BOURGHOLTZER, FRANK
Correspondent

BREWSTER, ALLEN
Mgr., Recording and
Post-Production

BRIGGS, FRED
Correspondent

BROCKINGTON, JACKIE
General Assignment Weather
Reporter

BROKAW, TOM
Anchor

BROOKS, TIMOTHY H.
Dir., Program Research

BROWN, JIM
Entertainment Editor

BRUSTIN, MICHELE
V.P., Drama Development

BURKE, DAVID
Prod.
News

BURKE, KELLY
General Assignment Reporter
WRC-TV 4

BURNS, ERIC
Midwest Correspondent

BURRINGTON, DAVID
Correspondent

CAFFERTY, JACK
Reporter/Anchor/Host
WNBC-TV

CALABRESE, PETER ROBERT
V.P.

CANDIDO, JOSEPH
Dir., Compliance and Practices

CAREY, CARL "BUD"
V.P., General Mgr.
WNBC-TV

CAREY, MacDONALD
Actor

CARSWELL, DONALD
V.P., Finance & Administration

CERVAMI, ANTHONY
V.P., Planning/Affiliate Services

CHANCELLOR, JOHN
News Correspondent

CHEATHAM, MARIE
Actress

CICERO, JOSEPH S.
V.P., Financial Administration
and Control

CLOUD II, HAMILTON S.
V.P.

COATES-WEST, CAROLE
Dir., Current Drama Programs

COCHRAN, JOHN
Correspondent

COLEMAN, CHARLES E.
Dir., Financial Planning and
Control

COMPTON, JAMES M.
Correspondent

CONRAD, MICHAEL
Actor

CONWAY. ELAINE
Dir., Talent Relations and
Creative Services

CORNET, ROBERT J.
V.P.

CORPORA, THOMAS
Atlanta Bureau Chief

CORWIN, M.J.
V.P., Program Production
Operations

COYLE, HARRY
Dir.

CRAIG, DEAN K.
Dir., Program Preparation

CRIQUI, DON
Sportscaster

CRUZ, FRANK
Co-Anchor

CRYSTAL, LESTER M.
V.P.

CURRLIN, LEE
V.P., Entertainment

CURTAN, DEBORAH A.
Mgr., Casting

DANCY, JOHN
Correspondent

DANIELS, RALPH
V.P., Broadcast Standards

DANNHAUSER, WILLIAM
Dir., Special Programs

DAVIS, SID
V.P., News

DAWSON, LEN
Sportscaster

DE CORDOVA, FREDERICK
Prod.

DELANEY, STEVE
Correspondent

DEMARCO, FRED
Station Mgr.

DISHELL, WALTER D., M.D.,
F.A.C.S.
Health and Medical Reporter
KNBC

DOBYNS, LLOYD
Anchor, News

DODD, KIRK
V.P., Entertainment

DOTSON, BOB
Correspondent
DUKE, ROBIN
Repertory Player
DUNHAM, CORYDON B.
Exec. V.P. and General Counsel
deVARONA, DONNA
Commentator
EATON, BOB
Los Angeles Bureau Chief
News
ELLERBEE, LINDA
News Anchor/Correspondent
ENBERG, DICK
Sportscaster
ENGLER, NOEL M.
V.P., Advertising and Promotion
ENRIQUEZ, RENE
Actor
ERBE, BONNIE G.
Correspondent
ERICKSON, LAUREL M.
Reporter
KNBC
ESKRIDGE, MICHAEL
Exec. V.P.
EUBANKS, BOB
Host
FELL, NORMAN
Actor
FIELD, DR. FRANK
Health and Science Editor
WNBC
FINKEL, GEORGE
Sports Prod.-Dir.
FLAHERTY, JOE
Writer-Performer
FLETCHER, MARTIN
Prod./Correspondent
FLYNN, JOHN P.
Mgr. Broadcast Technical
   Training
FLYNN, STEPHEN
V.P., Sales Service
FRANCIS, FRED
Correspondent
FRANCIS, GENIE ANN
Actress
FRANK, REUVEN
Former Pres., News
FRAZIER, STEPHEN
Correspondent
FRIEDMAN, STEVE
Exec. Prod.
FRONS, BRIAN
V.P., Daytime Programs
FURNESS, BETTY

Consumer Reporter
GARAGIOLA, JOE
Sportscaster
GARNER, JAMES
Actor
GARRETT, EDWARD
V.P.
GELINE, ROBERT J.
Dir., Teletext
GERALDI, JOSEPH M.
Dir., Advertising Operations
GERSON, ALAN H.
V.P.
GIGANTE, PAULA M.
Regional Dir.
GIGGANS, JIM
Reporter
KNBC-TV, Los Angeles
GILBERT, MELISSA
Actress
GILMOUR, SANDY
Correspondent
GITTER, RICHARD P.
V.P.
GOLDSTEIN, CHARLES A.
V.P.
GOODMAN, MAURICE
V.P.
GOSSETT JR., LOUIS
Actor
GOULD, CHERYL
Sr. Prod.
GREENBERG, PAUL W.
Exec. Prod.
GREENWALD, SHELLEY
Sr. Attorney
GROSS, MARY
Repertory Player
GROSSMAN, LARRY
Pres., NBC News
GUMBEL, BRYANT C.
On-Air Personality, Co-Anchor
   "Today"
HAID, CHARLES
Actor
HAINES, LARRY
Actor
HALL, DEIDRE
Actress
HALPERT, SAUL
Political Editor/Reporter
KNBC
HAMBRICK, JOHN
Reporter/Anchor
WNBC-TV
HAMEL, VERONICA
Actress

HAMNER, EARL JR.
Atlanta Bureau Chief
HANSON, JANE
Reporter
WNBC-TV
HART, JOHN
Correspondent
HASSELHOFF, DAVID
Actor
HAYES, BILL
Actor
HAYES, SUSAN SEAFORTH
Actress
HEKTOEN, JEANNETTE
Dir.
HENDREN, RON
Reporter, "Observer"; Co-Host,
   "Entertainment Tonight"
KNBC
HENINBURG, GUSTAV
Co-Host
WNBC-TV
HENNER, MARILU
Actress
HIRSCH, JUDD
Actor
HOFFMANN, BETTYE K.
V.P.
HOPE, BOB
Comedian
HOROWITZ, DAVID
Consumer Advocate/Reporter
KNBC News
HUDSON, BETTY
V.P.
HUNTER, NATALIE
V.P., Strategic Planning,
   Corporate Planning and
   Business Development
JAMIESON, BOB
News Correspondent
JENSEN, MIKE (Michael C.
   Jensen)
News Correspondent
JEROME, ALBERT
Exec. V.P.
JOHNSON, DEBORAH
Exec. Prod.
JOHNSON, LUCY ANTEK
V.P.
JONES, CHARLIE
Sportscaster
JONES, KENLEY
Correspondent
KALB, BERNARD
Correspondent
KALB, MARVIN
Correspondent

NEWMAN, MONTELLE G.
V.P., & General Mgr.
NYKANEN, MARK
News Correspondent
O'CONNELL, KEVIN
Weather Reporter
O'CONNELL, RAYMOND T.
V.P.
O'CONNOR, DANIEL P.
Managing Dir., Documentaries
O'HARA, CATHERINE
Writer/Performer
OHLMEYER, DON
Prod. Sports
OKIE, RICHARD C.
Dir., Current Drama Programs
OLIVER, DON
Correspondent
OLSEN, MERLIN
Actor/Sports Broadcaster
O'NEIL, ROGER
Correspondent
OVADIA, AL
Dir., Affiliate Creative Services
PALMER, JOHN
Anchor/Correspondent
PARDI, KATHLEEN
Mgr., On-Air Promotion
  Operations
PARKER, JEANNE A.
Mgr., Art Services
PARKIN, JUDD
Mgr., Mini-Series and Novels for
  Television
PAULEY, JANE
Co-Anchor
PEARLMAN, SY
Exec. Prod., News
PELGRIFT, KATHRYN C.
V.P., Corporate Planning and
  Business Development
PEPPER, PETE
Reporter
PERKINS, JACK
Co-Anchor
KNBC
PETERSON, SUSAN
Correspondent
News
PETINA, DOMINIC A.
Dir., On-Air Production
  Operations
PETIT, TOM
Exec. V.P.
PIERCE, PONCHITTA
Host and Co-Producer
WNBC-TV

PINTAURO, FRANCIS N.
V.P.
PISCOPO, JOE
Repertory Player
PLANTE, JAMES F.
Director of News Services
POLK, JAMES
Correspondent
POOR, PETER
Sr. Prod., News
PRESSMAN, GABE
General Assignment Reporter
WNBC-TV
QUARLES, NORMA
Correspondent
RAE, CHARLOTTE
Actress
RANDALL, TONY
Actor
RETTIG, RICHARD
Dir., Administration, Advertising
  and Creative Services
RICH, TRACY S.
Sr. General Attorney
RINTELS, DAVID W.
Prod./Writer
RODMAN, DR. ELLEN
Dir.
ROGGIN, FRED
Reporter
KNBC
ROSS, BRIAN
Correspondent
RUBENS, WILLIAM S.
V.P.
RUKEYSER, JR., BUD (M.S.
  Rukeyser, Jr.)
Exec. V.P.
RUNGE, BLANCHE
Dir., Administration
RYDER, JEFFREY C.
V.P.
Daytime Programs
SABINSON, ALLEN C.
V.P.
Entertainment
SAGANSKY, JEFFREY
V.P., Series Development
SALANT, RICHARD
Vice Chairman, Board of
  Directors
SAND, BARRY
Prod.
SASSER, II, DUFFY A.
V.P.
SCARBOROUGH, CHUCK
Co-Anchor
WNBC-TV

SCHANZER, KENNETH D.
Exec. V.P., Sports
SCHECHNER, WILLIAM
Co-Anchor
SCHUBECK, JOHN
Co-Anchor
KNBC
SCOTT, JR., WILLARD H.
On-Air Personality
SCULLY, VIN
Sportscaster
SEAMANS, IKE
News Correspondent
SEGELSTEIN, IRWIN B.
Vice Chairman
SEVERINSEN, DOC
Music Dir.
SHALIT, GENE
On-Air Personality
SHERLOCK, MICHAEL J.
Exec. V.P.
SIKKING, JAMES B.
Actor
SIMMONS, SUE
Reporter/Anchor
WNBC-TV
SIMONS, SUSAN
Mgr., Daytime Programs
SOBEL, REBECCA
Correspondent
SOHMER, STEVE (Stephen T.
  Sohmer)
V.P.
SONNENFELDT, RICHARD W.
Exec. V.P.
SPANO, JOE
Actor
STANDER, STEPHEN F.
Managing General Attorney
STANLEY, ERIC J.
Dir., Int'l Sales
STANVILLE, MARTHA PELL
V.P., Affiliate Promotion Services
STEIN, JAMES
Prod.
STERN, CARL
News Correspondent
STEVENS, JAMES
V.P., Technical Projects,
  Operations and Technical
  Services
STEVENSON, McLEAN
Actor
STRASZEWSKI, TOM
V.P. & General Mgr.
STUART, MARY
Actress

SULLIVAN, TIMOTHY
Mgr., Compliance and Practices
TARTIKOFF, BRANDON
Pres.
TATE, DON
Assistant to Gen. Counsel
THOMAS, BETTY
Actress
THOMPSON, LEA
Anchorwoman/Reporter
WRC-TV
THURM, JOEL
V.P.
Entertainment
TIMOTHY, RAYMOND J.
Pres., NBC TV Network
NBC
TINKER, GRANT A.
C.O.B. and C.E.O.
TIPPETS, THOMAS
Mgr., Program Operations,
   West Coast
TISCHLER, BOB
Prod.
TOMIZAWA, THOMAS
Sr. Prod.

TOYOTA, TRITIA
Co-Anchor
KNBC
TRAUM, RICK
Dir., Program Development and
   Production
TRAVANTI, DANIEL J.
Actor
TREBEK, ALEX
Game Show Host
ULASEWICZ, JOSEPH P.
V.P., West Coast
ULRICH, STEPHEN
Mgr., Talent and Promotion
VALERIANI, RICHARD
Correspondent
VINSON, PHYLLIS TUCKER
V.P., Children's Programs
WALLACE, CHRIS
Correspondent
WALSH, ROBERT S.
Pres. T.V. Stations/Radio and
   Group Exec. V.P.
WARREN, MICHAEL
Actor
WATSON, ARTHUR A.

Pres., NBC Sports
WATSON, BARBARA L.
General Mgr.
WATSON, DOUGLASS
Actor
WEDECK, DAVID
V.P.
Entertainment
WEINHEIMER, STEPHEN
Mgr., Print Planning, Advertising
   and Promotion
WEISMAN, MICHAEL
Exec. Prod.
WEITZ, BRUCE
Actor
WILDE, KIRSTIE
Field Anchor
KNBC
WILSON, WARREN
Reporter
KNBC
WOLZIEN, THOMAS R.
Exec. Prod., NBC News
WOODRUFF, JUDY
Network Correspondent
ZIMBALIST, STEPHANIE
Actress

BBC

CAPRON, CHRISTOPHER
Head of Current Affairs
   Programmes, Television
CHECKLAND, MICHAEL
Dir. of Resources, Television
COTTON, BILL
Managing Dir.
DAVIES, JOHN HOWARD
Head of Light Entertainment
   Group, Television
GOODCHILD, PETER
Head of Science Features Dept.,
   Television
HART, ALAN

Controller BBC-1
LAUGHTON, ROGER
Head of Network Features
McDONALD, GRAEME
Controller BBC 2
MILNE, ALASDAIR
Dir.-General
MORGAN, CLIFF
Head of Outside Broadcasts
   Group, Television
PARKIN, BRYON
Managing Dir.
BBC Enterprises, Ltd.
REYNOLDS, JOHN

General Mgr., Co-Productions
SINGER, AUBREY
Managing Dir.
SOMERSET-WARD, RICHARD
Head of Music and Arts
WEBSTER, DAVID
Dir., United States
WENHAM, BRIAN
Dir. of Programmes
WOON, PETER
Editor
WYATT, WILL
Head of Documentary Features

COLUMBIA PICTURES TELEVISION

CHASIN, ROBERT
V.P. in Charge of Business
   Affairs
CHERNIN, PETER
V.P., Program Development
CLAIBORNE, JIM

V.P. of Financial Analysis
CONLIN, NOREEN, P.
V.P., Daytime
DUITSMAN, DOUG
V.P., Publicity and Promotion
FISCHER, WILLIAM P.

V.P., Live Tape Production
FREIDMAN, SEYMOUR
Sr. V.P.
GIRARD, STEPHEN
Sr. V.P., Creative Affairs
GROSSMAN, MICHAEL J.

V.P. in Charge of Business
  Affairs
HILL, ANDREW

V.P. in Charge of Movies and
  Mini-Series
HUSKY, RICK

Prod./Writer
ONORATO, AL
V.P., Casting

COX CABLE COMMUNICATIONS

BENNETT, BRUCE R.
V.P., General Mgr.
BURNHAM, BRUCE N.
V.P.
DALVI, AJIT
Dir. of Marketing
DAVENPORT, GEORGE LEWIS
V.P.
DWYER, ARTHUR A.
V.P.

HOCKEMEIR, J. CURT
Dir.
LAFFERTY, MARTIN C.
Dir.
TJADEN, GAROLD S.
V.P.
VAN VALKENBURG, DAVID R.
Exec. V.P.

WARING, PAUL C.
V.P.
WEIK, GARY G.
V.P., G.M.
WOODROW, DAVID M.
Dir.
WRIGHT, ROBERT C.
Pres.

EMBASSY COMMUNICATIONS

BROGLIATTI, BARBARA
  SPENCER
V.P., World Wide Publicity,
  Promotion, and Advertising
BURTON, AL
Exec. V.P., Creative Affairs

GRADE, MICHAEL
Pres., Embassy T.V.
HORN, ALAN
Independent Producer
LEAR, NORMAN
Writer/Producer/Director

LIEBERTHAL, GARY B.
Sr. V.P., Syndication
WEISBARTH, MICHAEL R.
Sr. V.P., Dramatic Program
  Development

ESPN

BERMAN, CHRIS
Sports Anchor
BRILLIANT, ANDREW P.
V.P. & General Counsel
CAVAZZINI, JAMES J.
V.P.
CONNAL, SCOTTY (Allan B.
  Connal)
Exec. V.P. & Chief Operating
  Officer
GRANDE, GEORGE

Sr. Announcer
GRIMES, J. WILLIAM
Pres. & C.E.O.
GUMBEL, GREG
Sportscaster
GUTKOWSKI, ROBERT M.
V.P., Programming
LEY, ROBERT
Anchor
MARCHIANO, SAL
Sportscaster

PRESBREY, MICHAEL O.
Sr. V.P., Advertising Sales
SANDERS, DAVE
Sportscaster
SIMPSON, JIM
Sportscaster
SULLIVAN, DAVID
Sportscaster
WERNER JR., ROGER L.
Sr. V.P.

GROUP W WESTINGHOUSE

BAKER, WILLIAM F.
Pres. & Chairman
COSGROVE, DANIEL J.
V.P., Media Sales
FOSTER, CHRISTINE
V.P., Program Development
GIARRAPUTO, LEONARD T.

V.P., Sales
HAMILTON, NANCY E.
Dir. of Operations
HAYES, JONATHAN
Pres.
LISWOOD, LAURA
District Mgr.

MILLER, FRANK R.
V.P., Marketing
RESING, GEORGE
Sr. V.P.
RITCHIE, DANIEL
Chairman, CEO
RUBIN, ROBERT H.

V.P., Programming for Cable

SPERRY, GEORGE A.
V.P. & General Mgr.

STROND, CAROL J.
Dir. of Research

VANE, EDWIN T.

Pres., CEO

WERNER, JOYCE
Mgr. of Project Control and
Visibility

HBO

ABRAHAM, SETH
V.P.
ANDERSON, DONALD E.
V.P. & General Mgr.
BEAHRS, DICK
V.P., Marketing Services,
Information & Analysis
BILLOCK, JOHN
V.P., Marketing
BIONDI JR., FRANK J.
Exec. V.P.
BLANK, MATTHEW
V.P., Marketing
BRADY, PAMELA
Dir., Subscriber Information
Services
CARLSON, LARRY
V.P.
COHEN, FRED
V.P.
COX, TONY (Winston H. Cox)
Pres., HBO Network Group
deBOER, LEE
V.P.
DEKNATEL, JANE
V.P.
DUGOW, IRIS
V.P.
FRAME, PETER W.
V.P.

FRANSECKY, ROGER
V.P., Corporate Affairs
FUCHS, MICHAEL J.
Pres., HBO Entertainment
Group
GARCHER, DENNIS
V.P. and General Mgr.
GRUMBLES, WILLIAM H.
V.P. and General Mgr.
HEYWORTH, JIM (James O.
Heyworth)
Pres. and CEO
HOOKS, WILLIAM G.
Sr. V.P.
HOROWITZ, EDWARD D.
V.P., Studio and Network
Operations
KING, JOE
Regional Dir.
KREEK, BOB
V.P.
LEVIN, GERALD MANUEL
Group V.P. Video
LEVY, ALAN
Mgr. of Corporate Public
Relations
LITVACK, NEAL
Marketing Dir.
LONG, JANET
Regional Dir.

MAXWELL, ROBERT
V.P., Research
MEISTER, DAVID L.
Sr. V.P.
MYERS, BARBARA
Marketing Dir.
PERAGINE, FRANCES
Dir. of Programming
PERRYMAN, MACK
V.P.
REDPATH JR, JOHN
Sr. V.P. & General Counsel
SCHEFFER, STEPHEN J.
Exec. V.P.
SENIE, KEVIN D.
Sr. V.P. and Treasurer
SERIO, DOM
V.P. & General Mgr. of Studio
Production and Operations
SERMERSHEIM, GAIL
V.P. & General Mgr.
SHENKER, NEIL
Dir.
SINGER, MAURICE
V.P.
THOMAS JR., STANLEY B.
Sr. V.P., Nat'l Accounts
WOOL, BRIDGET POTTER
V.P.

MGM/UA

BLAUG, GEORGE
V.P., Director of Distribution,
International Operations
CORONA, ROBERT J.
Division Manager, Distribution
Sales
GERSHMAN, JEAN V.
Director of Marketing Research
GOTTLIEB, JEROME

Executive V.P.
LEARY, MARIAN CLAASSEN
Manager of Marketing Research
REISBERG, RICHARD
Pres.
SIEGEL, ANDREW M.
Sr. V.P., Creative Affairs
SMITH, SUKI

Advertising/Sales Promotion
Manager
TAYLOR, RONALD
V.P., Television
WEINTRAUB, LLOYD W.
V.P. Movies and Mini-Series
YABLANS, FRANK
Vice Chairman and COO

PARAMOUNT TELEVISION

BANTA, GLORIA
V.P., Comedy Development
GOLDBERG, GARY D.
Producer/Writer
KEEPER, GARY
Dir. of Comedy Development

NARDINO, GARY
Pres.
OVITZ, MARK
Sr. V.P., Creative Affairs
SCHEINFELD, JOHN
Mgr., Dramatic Development

WESTON, RICHARD
Sr. V.P., Business Affairs

WINTERS, RICHARD J.
Exec. Dir. of Publicity,
Advertising and Promotion

SHOWTIME

CATLIN, ROBERT L.
Senior V.P.
CLARK, MICHAEL J.
V.P., Program Development
DENISON, SUSAN
V.P., Marketing
ENGLISH, JIM
V.P., Program Planning

LAFFERTY, STEVE
V.P., Business Affairs
MARSH, EARLE F.
V.P., Research
MILLER, JIM
V.P., Program Planning and
Feature Films
NATHANSON, GREG

Sr. V.P., Programming
SCHULTE, STEPHEN WM.
V.P., Operations and Production
Services
SIE, JOHN J.
Sr. V.P. Sales and Planning
WEINBLATT, MIKE
Pres.

TIME, INC.

BEDELL, J. ROBERT
Dir., Affiliate Relations and
Marketing
Time, Inc.

CHERTOK, HARVEY
V.P.
Time Life TV

GROSS, PETER A.
Pres.
Time, Inc. Video Group

HEYWORTH, JIM

Deputy V.P., Video Group,
Time Inc.
LABICH, RICHARD A.
Associate Publisher
Time, Inc.
LEVIN, GERALD M.
Group V.P.-Video
Time, Inc.
LOPINTO, JOHN
Dir. of Technology Development
Time Video Information Services
McCARTHY, SEAN J.

Pres.
Time Video Information Services
PFISTER, LARRY
V.P.
Time Video Information Services

SCHWARTZ, MICHAEL
Dir. of Marketing Services
Time Video Information Services

SIDER, DON
Managing Editor/V.P.
Time Video Information Services

TURNER BROADCASTING CO.

BURGESS, CHET
News Anchor and Reporter
CAIN, BOB (Robert O. Cain)
News Correspondent/Anchor
CARPER, JEAN
Health Reporter
CHARLES, NICK
Sportscaster, Reporter
CHASE, CHRIS
Host, "TV Tonight"
CHRISTOPHER, KEVIN
Host
CURLE, CHRIS
Broadcast Journalist/Newsanchor

DESPAIN, DAVE
Managing Editor/Host
DOLAN, PATRICK FRANCIS
Correspondent
DOUTHIT, RANDALL
Exec. Prod.
ELLIOTT, BUD (R. Elliott
Stambaugh)
Prod./Anchor
FARMER, DON (Donald E.)
Anchor
FLOCK, JEFF
Chief Midwest Correspondent
FORD, PETER SHANN

Anchor/Correspondent
FRICKE, JOHN
Anchor
GILLESPIE, HENRY
Corp. V.P.
GREGORY, NICK
Meteorologist
HACKEL, DAN
Anchor
HANSON, TERRY
Exec. Prod.
HEADLINE, WILLIAM
Washington Bureau Chief
HOGAN, GERALD

V.P.
HOLLIMAN, JOHN
White House Correspondent
HUMI, PETER JOHN
Prod./Correspondent
Rome
KANDLE, MYRON
Financial Editor
KAVANAU, TED
Exec. V.P.
KENYON, SANDY
Entertainment Correspondent
KURTZ, BOB
Sportscaster
LADENDORFF, MARCIA
News Anchor
LECLAIR, DENISE
Anchor

LOUGHLIN, MARY ANNE
Prod. and Show Host
MacPHAIL, WILLIAM C.
V.P.
McDERMOTT, ANNE
Reporter
McGUIRK, TERENCE F.
V.P.
MOORE, RICK
News Anchor
MOOS, JEANNE
Reporter
SCHORR, DANIEL
Senior Washington
Correspondent
SEGURA, DEBI
Anchor
SEIDEL, ERIC M.

Correspondent
SHAW, BERNARD
Anchor/Correspondent
TURNER, ED
News Dir., Exec. Prod., V.P.
TURNER, TED
C.O.B., Pres.
TUSH, BILL
Co-Host
WATERS, LOU (Lou Riegert)
Anchorman
WICKERSHAM, ELIZABETH
("Liz")
Co-Host
WILKERSON, JAMES
Anchor
WILLIAMS, MARY ALICE
Vice Pres., Anchor

TURNER BROADCASTING INC.

BARNES, GORDON
Meteorologist
BATTISTA, BOBBIE (Barbara
Battista)
Anchor
BEADLE, DAVID
Weekend Anchor
BECKMAN, PAUL D.
V.P. & Controller
BEGLEITER, RALPH J.
Washington Correspondent
(State Dept.)
BIERBAUER, CHARLES J.
Defense Correspondent
BISSONETTE, PAUL A.
V.P.
BLYSTONE, RICHARD M.
Correspondent

BRADEN, THOMAS W.
Co-Host
BROWN, RICK
Anchor
BUCHANAN, PATRICK
JOSEPH
Co-Host
MUSE, REYNELDA W.
News Anchor/Reporter
OLBERMANN, KEITH
Nat'l Sports Correspondent
O'NEIL, CAROLYN A.
Prod./Reporter for "Nutrition
News"
PETRICK, JACK
Dir. of Programming
PIKE, SIDNEY
Pres.

QUIRT, JOHN
Chief Economics Correspondent
RAINES, DALLAS D.
Meteorologist
RINGO, MARILYN
News Dir./Prod.
RUCKER, BOB
Correspondent
RUTZ, DANIEL C.
Medical News Correspondent
SAGER, CRAIG
Anchor
WUSSLER, ROBERT J.
Exec. V.P. and Pres.
ZEIDMAN, LEE
Anchor
ZIMMERMAN, BILL
Anchor

20th CENTURY FOX TELEVISION

GLICKSMAN, FRANK
Executive Producer
GRAD, PETER
Sr. V.P., Development
GRADINGER, EDWARD
BARRY
COO

KATLEMAN, HARRIS L.
COB & COE
KAUFMAN, ARVIN
Dir. of TV Movies and
Mini-Series
RICE, ALLAN LEONARD
V.P. Network Business Affairs

SCHADLOW, JEFFREY H.
V.P. Marketing and Research
SNOW, RONALD
Writer/Producer, On-Air
Promotion
STERN, ROBERT
V.P., Finance

USA NETWORK

FRIEDMAN, DR. SONYA
Host
JOBLIN, MONIA B.
Mgr.
KENIN, DAVID
V.P.
KOPLOVITZ, KAY
Pres.

LAWENDA, JEFFREY B.
V.P. of Advertising Sales and
  Commercial Program
  Development
LELAND, JON
Mgr., On-Air Promotion
ROSENTHAL, ARNIE
Exec. V.P.

Telefrance USA, Ltd.
ROSS, RICHARD
Dir.
VALLIER, JEAN
CEO, Dir. of Programming
Telefrance USA, Ltd.
ZRAKE, JIM
Exec. Prod.

VIACOM

BARUCH, RALPH M.
Chairman, CEO
Viacom International Inc.
BIAS, FRANK
V.P., Science and Technology
Viacom International Inc.
BLOCK, WILLARD
Pres.
Viacom World Wide Ltd.
DREILINGER, DAVID A.
V.P., General Counsel and
  Secretary
Viacom International Inc.
ELKES, TERRENCE A.
Pres.
Viacom International Inc.
FABER, GEORGE D.
Director of Communications
Viacom Ent. West Coast
GERBER, MICHAEL H.
V.P., Business Affairs
Viacom Ent.

GILLMAN, BRUCE
V.P., Human Resources
Viacom Cable
GIRVAN, GARRETT J.
Chief Financial Officer
Viacom Cable
GLASER, ROBERT L.
Pres.
Viacom Ent.
GORMAN, KENNETH F.
Pres.
Viacom Entertainment Group
HAIMOVITZ, JULES
V.P.
Viacom International
KAUFER, JERRY
V.P., Creative Services
Viacom International
KINLEY, DAVID D.
Sr. V.P.
Viacom Cable

LIGHTSTONE, RONALD
V.P., Corporate Affairs
Viacom International
McHUGH, NEIL R.
V.P. and General Manager
Viacom World Wide
ROSEMONT, NORMAN
Producer
Viacom
SALKOWITZ, SY
Pres.
Viacom Productions
SCHNEIER, FREDERICK
Sr. V.P., Program Aquisitions and
  Motion Pictures
Viacom Ent.
STE. MARIE, STEPHEN B.
V.P., Marketing
Viacom Cable
VAN LOAN, JOSEPH
V.P., Engineering
Viacom Cable

WARNER AMEX

BLACKWOOD, NINA
Video Jockey
Warner Amex Satellite
  Entertainment Company
COHEN, HARVEY
Dir.
Warner Amex Satellite
  Entertainment Company
COHEN, MARSHALL
V.P., Warner Amex Satellite
  Entertainment Company
COYLE, WILLIAM
V.P., Operations
Warner Amex Cable
  Communications Inc.
FOWLER, JOHN

Exec. V.P.
Warner Amex Cable
  Communications Inc.
GOODMAN, MARK
Video Jockey
Warner Amex Satellite
  Entertainment Company
HOBAN, BRUCE
Dir., Research
Warner Amex Cable
  Communications
HUNTER, ALAN
Video Jockey
Warner Amex Satellite
  Communications Company
JACKSON, J.J.

Video Jockey
Warner Amex Satellite
  Entertainment Company
McDEVITT, F. RAYMOND
Sr. V.P., Technical Operations
Warner Amex Cable
  Communications, Inc.
McGROARTY, ROBERT G.
Sr. V.P., Advertising Sales
Warner Amex Satellite
  Entertainment Company
PITTMAN, ROBERT W.
Sr. V.P., Programming
Warner Amex Satellite
  Entertainment Company
QUINN, MARTHA

Video Jockey
Warner Amex Satellite
  Entertainment Company
SCHNEIDER, JOHN
Pres.
Warner Amex Satellite
  Entertainment Corp.
SCHNEIDER, JOHN A.
Pres. & C.E.O.
Warner Communications,
  American Express Co.

SIMON, ARTHUR
Dir., Marketing
Warner Amex Cable
  Communications, Inc.

SMITH, JOE
Pres. & C.E.O.
Warner Amex Cable
  Communications, Inc.

SYKES, JOHN
Dir., Programming

Warner Amex Satellite
  Entertainment Company
WALKINGSHAW, M. JAY
Sr. V.P., Finance and
  Administration
Warner Amex Satellite
  Entertainment Company
WASSERMAN, BERT
Member of the Office of the
  Pres.
Warner Communications Inc.

WARNER BROS. TELEVISION

BRUNNER, BOB
Prod.
CALMAN, JEFFREY
Dir. Sales Development
CREDLE, GARY
V.P. Production
DALY, ROBERT

CMgr.
McLAIN, CHUCK
V.P.
MEYER, BARRY
Exec. V.P.
SHAYNE, ALAN
Pres. TV Programming

SOLSON, STANLEY
V.P. Pay-TV Marketing

STOLNITZ, ART
Sr., V.P. Business Affairs

SYKES, ELIZABETH
Dir. Network Animation Affairs

INDEX BY JOB TITLE OR POSITION

CHAIRMEN OF THE BOARD AND CHIEF EXECUTIVE OFFICERS

ADELSON, MERV
COB, Lorimar

ASHLEY, TED
Vice Chairman, Warner
    Communications

BACKE, JOHN
COB, Universal
    Communications

BARUCH, RALPH
Chairman and CEO, Viacom
    Intl.

BLYTON, JOHN
CEO, RKO Nederlander
    International Division

BRADSHAW, THORNTON
COB, CEO, RCA Corp.

BRESNAN, WILLIAM
Chairman and CEO, Group W
    Cable

BAUM, ROBERT
CEO, Cablentertainment

DALY, ROBERT
Co-Chairman and CEO,
    Warner Bros.

DOLAN, CHARLES
Chairman and Founder,
    Cablevision

DAWSON, FREDERIC
COB, CEO, Diaspora Comm.

FOWLER, MARK
Chairman, FCC

GOLDENSON, LEONARD
COB, CEO, ABC

GRINKER, CHARLES
Vice-Chairman, Corporation
    for Entertainment and
    Learning

HUBERT, DICK
Chairman, Gateway
    Productions

ISAACS, JEREMY
CEO, Channel Four TV,
    London

KATLEMAN, HARRIS
COB, 20th Century Fox

KLUGE, JOHN
Chairman and President,
    Metromedia, Inc.

KOPLIN, MERT
COB, Corporation for
    Entertainment and Learning

LEWIS, DREW
CEO, Warner Amex

McGOWAN, WILLIAM
Chairman and CEO,

MCI Corp.

NEDERLANDER, JAMES
COB, Nederlander Corp.

PALEY, WILLIAM
Founder/Chairman, CBS

RITCHIE, DANIEL
Chairman, CEO, Westinghouse
    Broadcasting Co.

SALANT, RICHARD
President and CEO, National
    News Council

TINKER, GRANT
COB and CEO, NBC Inc.

VALLIER, JEAN
CEO, Telefrance, Ltd.

WASSERMAN, LEW
CEO, COB and President,
    MCA

WENDELL, E.W.
COB and President, WSM Inc.

WINSTON, BRIAN
Chairman Cinema Studies, NYU

WYMAN, THOMAS
COB, CEO and President,
    CBS Inc.

YABLANS, FRANK
CEO and Vice-Chairman,
    MGM-UA

PRESIDENTS

ALTER, ROBERT H.
Pres. Cabletelevision Advertising
    Bureau

ANNENBERG, WALTER H.
Pres. TV Guide

ANTONOWSKY, MARVIN
Pres. Mktg. and Research,
    Columbia Pictures

ARLEDGE, ROONE
Pres. ABC News and Sports

ARLEN, GARY H.

Pres. Arlen Communications

BACKE, JOHN D.
Pres. Tomorrow Entertainment
    Corp.

BAER JR., ARTHUR H.
Pres. Rainbow Inc.

BAKER, WILLIAM F.
Pres. Westinghouse Broadcasting
    and Cable Inc.

BANNER, JONATHAN
Pres. View Magazine

BARNATHAN, JULIUS
Pres. ABC, Broadcast Operations
    & Engineering

BATSCHA, ROBERT
Pres. Museum of Broadcasting

BAUM, ROBERT
Pres. Cablentertainment

BENNETT, ROBERT MARTIN
Pres. Boston Broadcasters

BERGER, RICHARD L.
Pres. Walt Disney Productions
    (Subsidiary)

MULHOLLAND, ROBERT E.
Pres. NBC

MYERS, VAN
Pres. WOMETCO Enterprises
Inc.

NARDINO, GARY
Pres. Paramount TV

NEDERLANDER, ROBERT E.
Pres. The Nederlander
Organization Inc.

PAISNER, BRUCE
Pres. King Features

PATTERSON, V.L. "PAT"
Pres. Cardiff Cablevision Inc.

PERKINS, JAMES N.
Pres. Perkins-Washburn Inc.

PFISTER, EDWARD J.
Pres. Corporation for Public
Broadcasting

PIERCE, FREDERICK
Pres. and COO ABC Inc.

PIKE, SIDNEY
Pres. Turner Broadcasting
Systems

PILSON, NEAL H.
Exec. V.P. CBS Sports and Radio

POMPADUR, MARTIN
Pres. Ziff-Davis Publishing

POOLE, MARCUS LLOYD
Pres. DIASPORA

POPE, LEAVITT J.
Pres. WPIX Inc.

REISBERG, RICHARD
Pres. MGM-UA-TV

REISS, JEFFREY C.
Pres. Cable Health Network

RICE, MICHAEL
Pres. Michael Rice Media Inc.

RICH, LEE
Pres. Lorimar Inc.

ROBERTSON, PAT (Marion
Gordon Robertson)
Pres. Christian Broadcasting
Network

ROSENCRANS, ROBERT
Pres. Rogers UA Cablesystems

RUSH, HERMAN
Pres. Columbia Pictures TV

SALKOWITZ, SY
Pres. Viacom Productions

SCHAPIRO, ANGELA
Pres. Angela Schapiro Assoc.

SCHNEIDER, JOHN
Pres. Warner Amex Satellite
Entertainment Co.

SEARLE, ROBERT A.
Pres. Cardiff Communications

SELF, WILLIAM
Pres. CBS Theatrical Films

SEVERINO, JOHN C.
Pres. ABC TV

SHAYNE, ALAN
Pres. Warner Bros TV
Programming

SMALL, WILLIAM J.
Pres. UPI

SMITH, JOE
Pres. Warner Amex Cable
Communications Inc.

SMITH, RICHARD B.
Pres. SPN

STANTON, FRANK
President Emeritus, CBS

STODDARD, BRANDON
Pres. ABC Motion Pictures

STRANGIS, SAM
Pres. Ten-Four Productions

SWETT, RALPH J.
Pres. Times Mirror Cable TV

TAFFNER, DON
Pres. D.L. Taffner Ltd.

TAGLIAFERRO, JOHN
Pres. Hughes Television Network

TARTIKOFF, BRANDON
Pres. NBC Entertainment

TAYLOR, EDWARD L.
Pres. Satellite Syndicated
Systems, SPN

THOMOPOULOS, ANTHONY
Pres. ABC Broadcast Group

TIMOTHY, RAYMOND J.
Pres. NBC-TV Network

TURNER, TED
Pres. Turner Broadcasting
System

VALENTI, JACK
Pres. MPAA, MPEAA Inc.

VANE, EDWIN T.
Pres. Group W Productions

WAGNER, ALAN
Pres. Disney Channel

WALSH, ROBERT S.
Pres. and Group Exec. V.P. NBC
TV/Stations/Radio

WASSERMAN, LEW R.
Pres. MCA

WATSON,, ARTHUR A.
Pres. NBC Sports

WEAVER, PAT (Sylvester L.)
Pres. Weaver Prod.

WEINBLATT, MIKE (Myron
Weinblatt)
Pres. Showtime Entertainment

WEINSTEIN, CARL D.
Pres. Eastman Cablerep

WEITZMAN, BERNARD
Pres.

WENDELL, E.W. (Bud)
Pres. WSM Inc.

WHEELER, THOMAS E.
Pres. National Cable TV Assn.

WINTER, PETER
Pres. Digital Applications
International

WOOD, ROBERT D.
Pres. Metromedia Producers
Corp.

WRIGHT, ROBERT C.
Pres. Cox Cable

WUSSLER, ROBERT J.
Pres. and Exec. V.P. Turner
Broadcasting Inc.

WYNN, ROBERT
Pres. Mellodan Prod.

WYNNE, JOHN O.
Pres. Landmark Communications

YOUNG, ELIZABETH L.
Pres. Services by Satellite Inc.

V.P.'s

AAGAARD, KENNETH J.
V.P. Sports Operations

ABERNATHY, JAMES L.
V.P., Corporate Affairs

ABRAHAM, SETH
V.P., Sports Programming and

Programming Operations

AGREE, ARNOLD
V.P., Taxes

AGRESS, ELLEN SHAW
V.P., Business Planning

AMES, BOB

V.P., Accounting

AMLEN, SEYMOUR
V.P., Entertainment

AMSTER, LINDA
V.P., Sales

ANDERSON, DONALD E.

V.P.

SCHNEIER, FREDERICK
Sr. V.P., Program Acquisitions
and Motion Pictures

SCHWAB, SHELLY
Sr. V.P., Marketing

SCHWARTZ, DOROTHY
V.P., Primetime Sales

SEARLE, ROBERT A.
V.P.

SEGAL, JOEL M.
Sr. V.P., Advertising

SENIE, KEVIN D.
V.P., Finance and Administration

SEPKOWITZ, IRV
Sr. V.P., Business Affairs

SERIO, DOM
V.P. of Studio Production and
Operations

SERMERSHEIM, GAIL
V.P.

SHEPHARD, HARVEY
Sr. V.P., Programs

SHERLOCK, MICHAEL
V.P., Finance and Administration,
Exec. V.P.

SIDER, DON
V.P., Information Services

SIE, JOHN J.
Sr. V.P., Sales and Planning

SIEGEL, ANDREW M.
Sr. V.P., Creative Affairs

SIEGENTHALER, ROBERT
V.P., Special Events Coverage

SIEGLER, SCOTT MERRILL
Sr. V.P., Creative Affairs

SILBERLING, ROBERT M.
V.P., Motion Pictures for
Television

SILVESTRI, JOHN
V.P., Sales

SIMON, ALBERT J.
V.P., Tape Production

SINGER, MAURICE
V.P., Pre-Production Acquisition

SISK, JOHN
Sr. V.P. Network Negotiations

SKAGGS, CALVIN
V.P.

SLAKOFF, MORTON A.
V.P., Creative Services

SLATER, GERALD
Exec. V.P.

SMILEY JR., CHARLES A.
V.P.

SMITH, DOW C.
V.P.

SMITH, HARRY E.
V.P., New Venture Development

SMITH, JACQUELINE
V.P., Daytime
Programs-Entertainment

SMITH, JERRY
Exec. V.P., Marketing

SMYLIE, BEN B.
V.P.

SNOWDEN, GEORGE
V.P., Programming

SOHMER, STEVE (Stephen T.
Sohmer)
V.P., Advertising and Creative
Services

SOLSON, STANLEY J.
V.P., Pay-TV Marketing

SONNENFELDT, RICHARD W.
Exec. V.P., Operations and
Technical Services

SPENCE JR., JAMES R.
Sr. V.P., Sports

SPERRY, GEORGE A.
V.P.

SPORER, ANDREA D.
V.P.

ST. JOHNS, KATHLEEN
V.P., Creative Affairs

STANVILLE, MARTHA PELL
V.P., Affiliate Promotion Services

STE. MARIE, STEPHEN B.
V.P., Marketing

STERN, ROBERT
V.P., Finance

STERNE, PETER B.
V.P., Current Comedy Program
Production

STEVENS, JAMES
V.P., Technical Projects,
Operations and Technical
Services

STOLNITZ, ART
Sr. V.P., Business Affairs

STONE, EMERSON
V.P., News Practices

STRASZEWSKI, TOM
V.P.

SUNDERLAND, RONALD B.
V.P., Business Affairs and
Contracts

SWETT, RALPH J.
V.P.

TAYLOR, RONALD
V.P., Dramatic Programs

THOMAS JR., STANLEY B.
Sr. V.P., Nat'l Accounts

THURM, JOEL
V.P., Talent

TIGHE, MARY ANN (Mary Ann
Tighe Hidalgo)
V.P., Program Development

TIMOTHY, RAYMOND J.
Group Exec. V.P.

TJADEN, GAROLD S.
V.P., Engineering and
Technology

TURNER, ED
V.P.

ULASEWICZ, JOSEPH P.
V.P., Operations and Technical
Services

VAN AMBURG, THOMAS K.
V.P.

VAN LOAN, JOSEPH
V.P., Engineering

VAN VALKENBURG, DAVID R.
Exec. V.P., Operations

VINSON, PHYLLIS TUCKER
V.P., Children's Programs

WALD, RICHARD S.
Sr. V.P., News

WALKINGSHAW, M. JAY
Sr. V.P., Chief Financial Officer

WALSH, ROBERT S.
Group Exec. V.P.

WARING, PAUL C.
V.P., Corporate Development

WATSON, GEORGE
V.P., News

WEDECK, DAVID
V.P., Program Scheduling

WEIK, GARY G.
V.P., Development Division

WEIL, SUZANNE
Sr. V.P., Programming

WEINER, BRUCE
V.P., Affiliate Advertising and
Promotion

WEINTRAUB, LLOYD W.
V.P., Movies & Mini-Series

WEISBARTH, MICHAEL R.
Sr. V.P., Dramatic Program
Development

WELKER, CHRISTY
V.P., Novels and Limited Series
for Television

WELTMAN, WALLY
V.P., Daytime Programs

WERGELES, JIM
V.P., Public Relations

WERNER, MICHAEL
Sr. V.P.

WERNER JR., ROGER L.
Sr. V.P. Marketing and Finance

WESTIN, AV
V.P.

WESTON, ELLEN
V.P., Business Affairs
WESTON, RICHARD
Sr. V.P., Business Affairs
WILHITE, THOMAS L.
V.P., Production
WILLENSON, SETH
V.P., Program Development
WILLIAMS, DONALD O.
Sr. V.P., Operations

WILLIAMS, MARY ALICE
V.P.
WINANT, ETHEL
Sr. V.P., Creative Affairs
WINSTON, CAROLINE
V.P.
WOLFE, DONNA
V.P.
WOLFSON, LOUIS

V.P., Operations and Dir.
WOLLOCK, EDWARD
V.P.
WOOL, BRIDGET POTTER
V.P., Original Programming
WUSSLER, ROBERT J.
Exec. V.P.
YATES, WILLIAM R.
V.P., Television

COMPANY DIRECTORS

ANCIER, GARTH RICHARD
Dir., Current Comedy Programs
ANCONA JR., EDWARD
Dir., Film and Tape Production
ARMEL, PAULA
Dir., Affiliate Services
BAERWALD, SUSAN
Dir., Mini-Series
BAKER, WARREN
Dir., Programs
BARRET, EARL
Dir.
BARRETT, MARVIN GALBRAITH
Dir.
BARTELME, JOE
Dir., Domestic News
BARTON, GARY
Dir., Casting, Motion Pictures
for Television
BAUER, JAMES L.
Dir. Business Development
BEDELL, J. ROBERT
Dir., Affiliate Relations and
Marketing
BENNETT, ROBERT MARTIN
Pres., Dir.
BERGMANN, DOUGLASS
Assoc. Dir., Talent and Program
Acquisitions, Business Affairs
BERMAN, STEVE
Dir., Comedy Program
Development
BESCH, ANDREW
Dir. of Marketing
BLANK, BEN
Dir. Graphics
BLAUG, GEORGE
V.P., Dir.
BOGROW, PAUL
Dir. Program Practices
BOLEN, LIN
Head of Creative Affairs

BRADY, PAMELA
Dir., Subscriber Information
Services
BRANT, TIM
Sports Dir.
BRONSON, MICHAEL
Dir., Media Dept.
BROOKS, TIMOTHY H.
Dir., Program Research
BURKE, DENISE W.
Dir. Awards and Special Projects
BURKS, RUPERT
Dir. of Systems
BURNS, RED
Dir., Alternate Media Ctr.
BURROWS, JAMES
Exec. Prod./Dir.
CALMAN, JEFFREY
Dir. Sales Development
CANDIDO, JOSEPH
Dir., Compliance and Practices
CASSUTT, MICHAEL
Dir., Prime Time
CESLIK, CAROLYN
Dir., Children's Programs
CHALOM, MARC
V.P., Production and Operations
and Exec. Dir., DAYTIME
CHAMBERS, EVERETT
Dir.
COATES-WEST, CAROLE
Dir., Current Drama Programs
COHEN, HARVEY
Dir., Management Information
Systems
COLEMAN, CHARLES E.
Dir., Financial Planning and
Control
COLLINS, BRUCE D.
Dir. of Operations
CONWAY, ELAINE
Dir., Talent Relations and

Creative Services
COYLE, HARRY
Dir. Sports
CRAIG, DEAN K.
Dir., Program Preparation
CROFOOT, TERRY
Dir., News
CULLETON, KATHLEEN
Dir., Administration, Advertising
and Promotion
CURRAN, JOHN
Sr. V.P., Dir. of Network Buying
and Programming
DALVI, AJIT
Dir. of Marketing
DANNHAUSER, WILLIAM
Dir., Special Programs
DARION, SIDNEY
Dir., Cultural Affairs
DAVIS, CURTIS
Dir. Programs
DREXLER, MICHAEL
Exec. V.P., Dir. of Media and
Programming
ENGLUND, GEORGE
Dir.
ESCHELBACHER, DAVID
Dir., TV Production
FABER, GEORGE
Dir. of Communications
FITZGERALD, GLEN
Dir. Affiliate Advertising
FLEMING, PAMELA S.
Program Dir.
FRANKEL, ERIC C.
Dir., Pay-TV Marketing
FRANKOVICH, PETER
Dir., Motion Pictures for
Television
FRONS, BRIAN S.
Dir., Daytime Programs
GALBRAITH, BILL
Dir., News Operations

GARTIN, SANDY RUSSEL
Dir. Children's Programming

GELINE, ROBERT J.
Dir., Teletext

GELLER, HENRY
Dir., Wash. Ctr. for Pub. Policy

GERALDI, JOSEPH M.
Dir., Advertising Operations

GIGANTE, PAULA M.
Regional Dir.

GILBERT, JON C.
Assoc. Dir. of Labor Relations

GLUCKSMAN, MARGIE
Dir., Talent and Casting

GOLDBERG, JEAN V.
Dir., Marketing Research

GOLDEN-GOTTLIEB, PHYLLIS
Dir., Comedy Development

GOLDSTEIN, MORTON N.
Dir. Production Tape Shows

GROSSMAN, SANDY
Dir., Sports

HALEY, JACK, JR.
Exec. Prod./Dir.

HAMILTON, NANCY E.
Dir. of Operations

HARBERT, TED (Edward W.
    Harbert III)
Dir. Program Planning and
    Scheduling

HEKTOEN, JEANNETTE
Dir., Guest Relations

HERZOG, FRANK
Sports Dir.

HEWITT, STEVEN W.
Dir., Special Programs

HOBAN, BRUCE
Dir., Research

HOCKEMEIR, J. CURT
Dir., Market Development
    Operations

HOUGH, STANLEY
Dir., Motion Pictures

HULL, RON
Dir., Program Fund

HUSTED, AL
Dir. Public Relations

IGER, ROBERT
Dir., Program Planning

JACOBS, RICK
Dir., Talent and Casting

JOHNSON, LUCY ANTEK
Dir. Daytime Children's Project

KAATZ, RONALD B.
Sr. V.P., Dir. of Media Resources
    & Research

KANE, PETER

Assoc. Dir., Business Affairs,
    Talent and Program
    Acquisition

KAUFMAN, ARVIN
Dir. of Network Movies &
    Mini-Series for Television

KAUFMAN, SID
Dir., Technical Planning and
    Labor Affairs

KEEPER, GARY
Dir., Comedy Development

KING, JOE
Regional Dir.

KLEIN, MALCOM
Sr. V.P., Managing Dir.

KLEINE, JOHN
Dir., Financial Affairs

KOPELAN, AMY DORN
Dir. Early Morning Programming

KORDA, RONALD
Dir., Program Scheduling and
    Theatrical Acquisitions

LABUNSKI, STEPHEN
Exec. Dir.

LACHER, RICHARD S.
Dir., Financial Administration

LAMONT, PEGGY
Dir. of Program Development

LEM, CAROL
Dir., Program Planning

LEVINE, ELLEN
Dir., Pricing

LEVINE, MICHAEL A.
Dir., Current Drama Programs

LEVINSOHN, ROANN KIM
Dir. Public Relations

LeWINTER, RANDI
Dir. Daytime Programs

LEWIS, JOHN M.
Pres. & Dir.

LITVACK, NEAL
Marketing Dir.

LOPINTO, JOHN
Dir. of Technology Development

LORD, ARTHUR
Dir. of Special Operations

LOW, RICHARD H.
Exec. V.P./Dir.

LOXTON, DAVID
Dir., TV/Lab

LUMA, JOHN C.
Dir., On-Air Promotion

LUXENBERG, LEON
Sr. V.P., Dir., Network Relations

MAAS, JOHN
Dir. Programs

MARAZZI, JOSEPH

Dir., Affiliate Marketing and
    Planning

MARDEN, MICHAEL
Dir., Motion Pictures for TV and
    Mini-Series

MARLAND, DOUGLAS
Dir.

MARKS, KENNETH
Dir., Marketing

MASUCCI, TONY
Dir., Mini-Series

McCORKLE, PAULA
Dir. of Communications

McGUINESS, JOHN P.
Associate Nat'l Dir. of Credit and
    Collections

MEANEY, DONALD
Managing Dir. of Affiliate and
    Int'l Liaison

MELTZER, BARBARA
Dir., Network Creative Services

MENDELSON, NANCY
Creative Dir.

MOGUL, LAURA
Dir. of Advertising

MOONEY, ELIZABETH WILDE
Dir., Regional Affiliate Relations

MORRIS, DELORES
Dir., Children's Programming,
    East Coast

MYERS, BARBARA
Marketing Dir.

MYERS, VAN
Pres., CEO, Dir.

NAHAN, STU
Dir. of Sports

NEDERLANDER, ROBERT E.
Pres./Dir.

NENNO, STEPHEN K.
Dir., Program Administration

NERENBERG, SUSAN A.
Dir., Prime Time Program
    Development, East Coast

NEUMEISTER, FRANK
Dir., Sales Service, West Coast

NEWMAN-MINSON, LAUNA
Dir., Special Programs

O'CONNOR, DANIEL P.
Managing Dir., Documentaries

OKIE, RICHARD C.
Dir., Current Drama Programs

OPOTOWSKY, STAN
Dir., Political Operations

OVADIA, AL
Dir., Affiliate Creative Services

PAGE, GEORGE H.
Dir., Program Development

CORPORATE MANAGERS

ANDERSON, DONALD E.
General Mgr.

ANGOTTI, JOSEPH
General Mgr.

BEESEMEYER, RICHARD L.
General Mgr.

BENNETT, BRUCE R.
General Mgr.

BENNETT, JAMES S.
General Mgr.

BONANNI, JACK
(John S. Bonanni)
Station Mgr.

BREWSTER, ALLEN
Mgr., Recording and Post-
   Production

CAREY, CARL "BUD"
General Mgr.

CARTER, SPENCER P.
Mgr. of Employee Relations

CICHOCKI, RONALD
General Mgr.

COATES-WEST, CAROLE
Mgr., Drama Development

COHEN, BARBARA
Mgr., Pol. Coverage

CORONA, ROBERT J.
Division Mgr.

CURTAN, DEBORAH A.
Mgr., Casting

DEMARCO, FRED
Station Mgr.

EATON, HUGH MITCHELL, JR.
General Mgr.

EVEY, STUART W.
General Mgr.

FLYNN, JOHN P.
Mgr., Broadcast Technical Training

FYFFE, WILIAM C.
General Mgr.

GARCHER, DENNIS
General Mgr.

GRUMBLES, WILLIAM H.
General Mgr.

HALL, DAVID
General Mgr.

HERRLING, ANTHONY C.
Mgr., Public Relations

HOLLY, JAMES
General Mgr.

JOBLIN, MONIA B.
Mgr.

KATER, DAN
General Mgr.

LEARY, MARIAN CLAASSEN
Mgr.

LEIBERT, PHYLLIS R.
Mgr., Daytime Research

LELAND, JON
Mgr., On-Air Promotion

LEVY, ALAN
Mgr. of Corporate Public Relations

LISWOOD, LAURA
District Mgr.

LOBO, RICHARD
Station Mgr.

LOMOND, DIANE
Mgr.

LUDWIG, FORREST
Production Mgr.

LUND, PETER A.
General Mgr.

MacCURDY, JEAN H.
General Mgr.

McDANIEL, JAN
News Assignment Mgr.

McGANNON, LAURA L.
Design Mgr.

McHUGH, NEIL R.
General Mgr.

MALARA, ANTHONY C.
General Mgr.

MILLER, SCOTT W.
Design Mgr.

MORING, JO
General Mgr., Affiliate News
   Services

NEWMAN, MONTELLE G.
General Mgr.

OBER, ERIC
General Mgr.

PARDI, KATHLEEN
Mgr., On-Air Promotion Operations

PARKER, JEANNE A.
Mgr., Art Services

PARKIN, JUDD
Mgr., Mini-Series and Novels for
   Television

REDA, LOUIS J.
Personal Mgr.

RODGERS, JONATHAN
Station Mgr.

ROHRBECK, JOHN H.

General Mgr.

SCHEINFELD, JOHN
Mgr. Dramatic Development

SERIO, DOM
General Mgr. of Studio Production and Operations

SERMERSHEIM, GAIL
General Mgr.

SHEA, TIMOTHY M.
Project Mgr.

SIMONS, SUSAN
Mgr., Daytime Programs

SMITH, DOW C.
Station Mgr.

SMITH, SUKI
(Sue Laniado Smith)
Sales Promotion Mgr.

SPAGNOLETTI, LEN
General Sales Mgr.

SPERRY, GEORGE A.
General Mgr.

STANDER, STEPHEN
Managing Gen. Atty.

STRASZEWSKI, TOM
General Mgr.

SULLIVAN, TIMOTHY
Mgr., Compliance and Practices

SWANSON, DENNIS
Station Mgr.

TAGLIAFERRO, JOHN
General Mgr.

TIPPETS, THOMAS
Mgr., Program Operations, West
   Coast

ULRICH, STEPHEN
Mgr., Talent and Promotion

VAN AMBURG, THOMAS K.
General Mgr.

WATSON, BARBARA L.
General Mgr.

WEINHEIMER, STEPHEN
Mgr., Print Planning, Advertising
   and Promotion

WELLS, WILLIAM
Mgr., Dramatic Program Development

WERNER, JOYCE
Mgr. of Project Control and
   Visibility

WOLLOCK, EDWARD
Sales Mgr.

ZADEH, STELLA
Managing Editor, TELETEXT

PRODUCERS

AARON, CHLOE
Prod.

ADATO, PERRY MILLER
Prod.

ALLEN, IRWIN
Prod.

ALTEMEYER, PAUL
Prod.

ARNAZ, DESI
Prod.

ARNOLD, DANNY
Prod.

AUBREY, JAMES
Independent Prod.

AZEVEDO, HELEN
Prod.

BABBIN, JAQUELINE
Prod.

BAFFICO, JIM
Prod.

BAKER, MARGERY CLAIRE
Sr. Broadcast Prod.

BALDWIN, GERALD
Prod.

BALKAN, DAVID H.
Prod.

BANNER, BOB
Independent Prod.

BARBERA, JOSEPH R.
Prod.

BARKLEY, DEANNE
Prod.

BARONE, JOAN S.
Prod.

BARRET, EARL
Prod.

BARRIS, CHUCK
Prod.

BARRY, JACK
Prod.

BASKIN, JOHN
Prod.

BELL, DALE
Exec. Prod.

BELLISARIO, DONALD P.
Prod.

BENDIK, ROBERT
TV Prod.

BENJAMIN, BURTON
Sr. Exec. Prod.

BENSLEY, RUSS
Executive Prod.

BENSON, HUGH
Prod.

BERG, ILENE AMY
Exec. Prod.

BERNSTEIN, CARL
Prod.

BINBERG, MICHAEL
Prod.

BOCHCO, STEVEN
Prod.

BRAND, JOSHUA
Prod.

BRANDT, YANNA KROYT
Prod.

BRODER, DICK
Prod.

BRODKIN, HERBERT
Prod.

BROOKS, JAMES
Prod.

BRUNNER, BOB
Prod.

BUNIM, MARY-ELLIS
Exec. Prod.

BURKE, DAVID
Prod.

BURNS, ALAN
Prod.

BURROWS, JAMES
Exec. Prod.

BYRNES, JIM
Prod.

CAMPANELLA JR., ROY
Prod./Dir.

CANNELL, STEPHEN J.
Prod.

CAPICE, PHILIP
Exec. Prod.

CARDEA, FRANK
Co-Exec. Prod.

CARR, MARTIN
Exec. Prod.

CARROLL JR., BOB
Prod.

CARSEY, MARCIA
Independent Prod.

CASO, PATRICIA
Exec. Prod.

CATES, GILBERT
Prod.

CATES, JOSEPH
Prod.

CHAMBERS, ERNEST
Prod.

CHAMBERS, EVERETT
Prod.

CHARLES, GLEN
Exec. Prod.

CHARLES, LES
Exec. Prod.

CHASE, DAVID
Prod.

CHERMAK, CY
Prod.

CLANCY, MARTIN
Prod.

CLARK, DICK
Prod.

CLAXTON, WILLIAM
Prod.

COHEN, ALEXANDER H.
Broadway Theatre and TV Prod.

COHEN, ELLIS
Prod.

COLLINS, CARRIE
Assoc. Prod.

COLMAN, HENRY
Prod.

CONBOY, JOHN
Exec. Prod.

CONRAD, WILLIAM
Prod.

COOPER, HAL
Prod.

COOPERMAN, ALVIN
Prod.

COWGILL, BRIAN
Prod. Exec.

COX, NELL
Prod.

CRAMER, DOUGLAS
Prod.

CRILE III, GEORGE
Prod.

CRYSTAL, LESTER
Prod.

CURTIS, DAN
Prod.

DAVIS, DAVID
Prod.

DAVIS, MADELYN
Prod.

DAVIS, PETER
Prod.

DE CORDOVA, FREDERICK
Prod.

DE GUERE, PHILIP
Prod.

DIAMOND, JEFFREY
Prod.

DIEKHAUS, GRACE
Prod.
DOUTHIT, RANDALL
Exec. Prod.
DWYER, MARY ALICE
Exec. Prod.
EDWARDS, RALPH
Prod.
ELLIOTT, BUD
Prod.
ENGLUND, GEORGE
Exec. Prod.
ENTELIS, AMY R.
Prod.
EPSTEIN, JON
Exec. Prod.
FILERMAN, MICHAEL
Prod.
FINE, DELIA
Prod.
FINELL, ALYCE
Prod.
FINNEGAN, BILL
Prod.
FINNEGAN, PAT
Prod.
FLETCHER, MARTIN
Prod.
FOX, SONNY
Prod.
FREEDMAN, LEWIS
Prod.
FRIEDMAN, PAUL
Prod.
FRIEDMAN, STEVE
Exec. Prod.
FRIENDLY, ANDREW
Prod.
FRIENDLY, ED
Prod.
FRYE, ROBERT
Exec. Prod.
GAFFNEY, RICKIE
Prod.
GANZ, LOWELL
Prod.
GELLER, ROBERT
Exec. Prod.
GERBER, DAVID
Exec. Prod.
GETZ, ROBERT
Prod.
GLEASON, MICHAEL
Exec. Prod.
GLICKSMAN, FRANK
Exec. Prod.

GOLDBERG, GARY D.
Prod.
GOLDBERG, LEONARD
Prod.
GOLDIN, MARION
Sr. Prod.
GOODSON, MARK
Prod.
GOULD, CHERYL
Sr. Prod.
GRALNICK, JEFF
Executive Prod.
GRAUMAN, WALTER
Prod.
GREEN, JAMES
Exec. Prod.
GREENBERG, PAUL W.
Exec. Prod.
GREENBURG, EARL
Prod.
HABER, LES
Exec. Prod.
HALEY JR., JACK
Exec. Prod.
HAMILTON, JOE
Prod.
HANNA, WILLIAM
Prod.
HANSON, TERRY
Exec. Prod.
HECHT, KEN
Prod.
HELLER, JOEL
Exec. Prod.
HEMION, DWIGHT
Prod.
HENSON, JIM
Prod.
HEWITT, DON
Executive Prod.
HILL, PAMELA
Exec. Prod.
HORGAN, SUSAN BEDSOW
Prod.
HORN, ALAN
Prod.
HUMI, PETER JOHN
Prod.
HUSKY, RICK
Prod.
ILLES, ROBERT
Prod.
ILSON, SAUL
Prod.
INGALLS, DON
Prod.

ISENBERG, GERALD
Prod.
JACOBS, DAVID
Prod.
JAFFE, HENRY
Prod.
JAFFE, STEPHEN (Steve)
Prod.
JARVIS, LUCY
Documentary Prod.
JOHNSON, DEBORAH
Exec. Prod.
JOHNSON, KENNETH
Prod.
KANE, ARNOLD
Prod.
KANTER, HAL
Prod.
KAUFMAN, LEONARD B.
Prod.
KAYDEN, WILLIAM
Prod.
KENNEY, H. WESLEY
Prod.
KEYES, PAUL WILLIAM
Prod.
KIBBEE, ROLAND
Prod.
KLEINERMAN, ISAAC
Prod.
KOBE, GAIL
Exec. Prod.
KOMACK, JAMES
Prod.
KOTLOWITZ, ROBERT
Exec. Prod.
KWARTIN, LESLIE
Prod.
LACHMAN, BRAD
Prod.
LACHMAN, MORT
Prod.
LACK, ANDREW
Exec. Prod.
LAFFERTY, MARTIN C.
Prod.
LAIBSON, MICHAEL
Prod.
LAMOREAUX III, E.S. (Bud)
Exec. Prod.
LANDERS, HAL
Prod.
LANDSBURG, ALAN
Exec. Prod.
LARSON, GLEN A.
Exec. Prod.

LASALLY, PETER
Prod.
LAW, LINDSAY E.
Exec. Prod.
LEAR, NORMAN
Prod.
LEE, JOANNA
Exec. Prod.
LEISER, ERNEST
Prod.
LENZ, PETER G.
Exec. Prod.
LEONARD, BILL
Prod.
LERNER, KAREN
Sr. Prod.
LEVIN, ALAN M.
Independent Prod.
LEVINE, DEBORAH JOY
Prod.
LEVINE, KEN
Prod.
LEVINSON, RICHARD L.
Prod.
LEVY, FRANKLIN
Exec. Prod.
LEWIS, ARTHUR BERNARD
Prod.
LEWIS, RICHARD
Exec. Prod.
LINK, WILLIAM
Prod.
LOLLOS, JOHN S.
Prod.
LORD, WILLIAM E.
Exec. Prod.
LOUGHLIN, MARY ANNE
Prod.
LOVULLO, SAM
Prod.
LYNCH, PATRICIA
Prod.
MADDEN, JERRY
(Malcolm E. Madden)
Prod.
MANN, ABBY
Prod.
MANULIS, MARTIN
Prod.
MARCH, ALEX
Prod.
MARGULIES, STAN
Exec. Prod.
MARKELL, ROBERT
Drama Prod.
MARMOR, HELEN

Exec. Prod.
MARSHALL, GARRY KENT
Exec. Prod.
MARTIN, QUINN
Prod.
MASON, GEOFF
Prod.
McMAHON, JENNA
Prod.
MELNICK, DANIEL
Prod.
MERLIS, GEORGE
Prod.
METCALFE, BURT
Prod.
MICHAELS, LORNE
Prod.
MILKIS, EDWARD
Prod.
MILTON, CHARLES H.
Sr. Prod.
MIZIKER, RON
Prod.
MONTY, GLORIA
Prod.
MOORE, THOMAS
Prod.
MOSES, HARRY
Prod.
NEUFELD, MACE
Prod.
NICHOLSON, NICK
Prod.
NIXON, AGNES
Prod.
NOBLE, GIL
Prod.
NOBLE, PAUL
Exec. Prod.
NORTHSHIELD, ROBERT
(Shad)
Senior Executive Prod.
OHLMEYER, DON
Prod. Sports
O'NEIL, CAROLYN A.
Prod.
O'NEIL, TERRY
Exec. Prod., NFL Football
O'NEIL, ROBERT F.
Prod.
PALTROW, BRUCE
Exec. Prod.
PARKINSON, BOB
Prod.
PARIS, JERRY
Prod.

PARRIOTT, JAMES
Prod.
PEARLMAN, SY
Exec. Prod.
PERLMUTTER, ALVIN
Prod.
PICARD, PAUL
Prod.
PIFER, ALICE
Prod.
POOR, PETER
Sr. Prod.
PORGES, WALTER
Sr. News Prod.
POTTER, ALLEN M.
Exec. Prod.
RAPPAPORT, JOHN H.
Prod.
RASKY, HARRY
Prod.
RAUCH, PAUL
Prod.
REDA, LOUIS J.
Prod.
REO, DON
Prod.
REYNOLDS, GENE
Prod.
RICHARDSON, LINDA
Prod.
RICHTER, RICHARD
Sr. Prod.
RICHTER, ROBERT
Documentary Producer
RIISNA, ENE
Prod.
RINGO, MARILYN
Prod.
RINTELS, DAVID W.
Prod.
RISSIEN, EDWARD L.
Independent Prod.
ROBINS, DEBBIE
Prod.
RODGERS, JONATHAN
Exec. Prod., "CBS News Night-
   watch"
ROONEY, ANDY
Prod.
ROSEMONT, NORMAN
Prod.
ROSENBERG, META
Prod.
ROSNER, RICK
Prod.
ROSS, MICHAEL

Prod.
ROZENZWEIG, BARNEY
Exec. Prod.
RUSSIN, JOSEPH
Sr. Prod.
SALLAN, BRUCE
Exec. Prod., Motion Pictures for
Television
SAND, BARRY
Prod.
SANDERS, MARLENE
Prod.
SCHAEFER, GEORGE
Prod.
SCHAFFNER, FRANKLIN
JAMES
Prod.
SCHENCK, GEORGE
Prod.
SCHERICK, EDGAR J.
Prod.
SCHICK, ELLIOTT
Prod.
SCHILLER, LAWRENCE
Prod.
SCHLATTER, GEORGE H.
Exec. Prod., Prod.
SCHNEIDER, DICK
Prod.
SCHNURMAN, NED
Exec. Prod.
SHAKER, TED
Exec. Prod.
SHERMAN, HARRY R.
Prod.
SIEGENTHALER, ROBERT
Exec. Prod., Special Events
Coverage
SILVERMAN, FRED
Exec. Prod.
SILVERMAN, PETE
Exec. Prod.
SINGER, DULCY
Exec. Prod.
SKAGGS, CALVIN
Prod.
SKLOVER, THEODORA
Prod.
SMITH, APRIL

Prod.
SMITH, DORRANCE
Exec. Prod.
SMITH, GARY
Prod.
SMITH, PATRICIA FALKEN
Prod./Writer
SNOW, RONALD
Prod. On-Air Promotion
SOLOMON, MARK
Prod.
SPELLING, AARON
Prod.
STARGER, MARTIN
Prod.
STEIN, JAMES
Prod.
STEIN, MICHAEL H.
Editorial Prod.
STENNER, ROBERT D.
Prod.
STONEY, GEORGE
Prod.
STRINGER, HOWARD
Exec. Prod.
SULTAN, ARNE
Prod.
SUSSKIND, DAVID
Prod.
SWAIN, SUSAN
Prod.
TAIT, ERIC V.
Prod.
TAYLOR, ARTHUR
Prod.
THOMAS, C. ANTHONY
(Tony Thomas)
Exec. Prod.
TINKER, MARK
Prod.
TISCHLER, BOB
Prod.
TOMIZAWA, THOMAS
Sr. Prod.
TOROKVEI, PETER JOHN
Prod.
TURNER, ED
Exec. Prod.

VALENTE, RENE
Prod.
VERTUE, BERYL
Prod.
VICTOR, DAVID
Prod.
WALLACE, ROB
Prod.
WEBER, CHARLES
Prod.
WEBSTER, SKIP
Prod.
WEISMAN, MICHAEL
Exec. Prod.
WERSHBA, JOSEPH
Prod.
WERSHBA, SHIRLEY
Prod.
WESTFELDT, WALLACE
Broadcast Exec.
WESTIN, AV
Prod.
WHELDON, SIR HUW
British Prod.
WILDER, JOHN
Prod.
WILLMORE, JOSEPH X.
Prod.
WINSTON, SUSAN
Exec. Prod.
WISEMAN, FREDERICK
Prod./Documentarian
WITT, PAUL JUNGER
Prod.
WOLFF, PERRY
Prod.
WOLPER, DAVID
Independent Prod.
WOLZIEN, THOMAS R.
Exec. Prod., NBC News
YATES, WILLIAM R.
Exec. Prod.
YORKIN, BUD
Prod.
ZORNOW, EDITH
Film Prod.
ZRAKE, JIM
Exec. Prod.

ACTORS AND ACTRESSES

ADAMS, EDIE
Actress

ALDA, ALAN
Actor

ALLEN, DEBBIE
Actress

ARDEN, EVE
Actress

ARNAZ, DESI
Actor

ARRANTS, ROD
Actor

ARTHUR, BEATRICE
Actress

ASNER, ED
Actor

ASTIN, PATTY DUKE
Actress

BACH, CATHERINE
Actress

BACKUS, JIM
Actor

BAIN, CONRAD
Actor

BALL, LUCILLE
Actress

BALSAM, MARTIN
Actor

BAUER, CHARITA
Actress

BAXTER BIRNEY, MEREDITH
Actress

BEL GEDDES, BARBARA
Actress

BERADINO, JOHN
Actor

BERLE, MILTON
Actor

BERNAU, CHRISTOPHER
Actor

BERRY, KEN
Actor

BERTINELLI, VALERIE
Actress

BIRNEY, DAVID
Actor

BIXBY, BILL
Actor

BLACQUE, TAUREAN
Actor

BLAKE, ROBERT
Actor

BLANC, MEL
Voice Specialist

BONERZ, PETER
Actor

BOOKE, SORRELL
Actor

BOSSON, BARBARA
Actress

BURNETT, CAROL
Actress

BURNS, GEORGE
Actor

BURR, RAYMOND
Actor

CAREY, MacDONALD
Actor

CAREY, PHILIP
Actor

CARTER, NELL
Actress

CHAMBERLAIN, RICHARD
Actor

CHEATHAM, MARIE
Actress

CHRISTOPHER, WILLIAM
Actor

COCA, IMOGENE
Actress

COLEMAN, DABNEY
Actor

COLEMAN, GARY
Actor

COLLINS, JOAN
Actress

COLLINS, STEPHEN
Actor

COMPTON, FORREST
Actor

CONRAD, MICHAEL
Actor

CONRAD, ROBERT
Actor

COSBY, BILL
Actor

CRENNA, RICHARD
Actor

CROTHERS, JOEL
Actor

CULP, ROBERT
Actor

CURTIN, VALERIE
Actress

DAILEY, IRENE
Actress

DALY, TYNE
Actress

DAMON, STUART
Actor

DANIELS, WILLIAM
Actor

DANZA, TONY
Actor

DAVIS JR., SAMMY
Entertainer

DE VITO, DANNY
Actor

DE WITT, JOYCE
Actress

DICKINSON, ANGIE
Actress

DOBSON, KEVIN
Actor

DUFFY, PATRICK
Actor

DUKE, ROBIN
Comedienne

DUSSAULT, NANCY
Actress

ENRIQUEZ, RENE
Actor

ESTRADA, ERIK
Actor

EVANS, LINDA
Actress

FABRAY, NANETTE
Actress

FARRELL, MIKE
Actor

FARR, JAMIE
Actor

FELL, NORMAN
Actor

FIELD, SALLY
Actress

FLOOD, ANN
Actress

FORSYTHE, HENDERSON
Actor

FORSYTHE, JOHN
Actor

FOSTER, PHIL
Actor

FRANCIS, GENIE ANN
Actress

FRANKLIN, BONNIE
Actress

FREEMAN JR., AL
Actor

FULTON, EILEEN
Actress

RAMBO, DACK
Actor
RANDALL, TONY
Actor
RAYE, MARTHA
Actress
REDGRAVE, LYNN
Actress
RITTER, JOHN
Actor
ROBERTS, PERNELL
Actor
ROSS, MARION
Actress
SANFORD, ISABEL
Actress
SELLECK, TOM
Actor
SHATNER, WILLIAM
Actor
SIEBERT, CHARLES
Actor
SIKKING, JAMES B.
Actor
SMITH, JACLYN
Actress
SOMERS, SUZANNE
Actress

SPANO, JOE
Actor
SPINNEY, CARROLL
Actor
SPRINGFIELD, RICK
Actor
STAPLETON, JEAN
Actress
STEVENSON, McLEAN
Actor
STEWART, DON
Actor
STRASSER, ROBIN
Actress
STRUTHERS, SALLY
Actress
STUART, MARY
Actress
SULLIVAN, SUSAN
Actress
SWENSON, INGA
Actress
SWIT, LORETTA
Actress
TAYBACK, VIC
Actor
THOMAS, BETTY
Actress

TILTON, CHARLENE
Actress
TRAVANTI, DANIEL J.
Actor
VAN DYKE, DICK
Actor
VAUGHN, ROBERT
Actor
VILLECHAIZE, HERVE
Actor
WAGNER, ROBERT
Actor
WARREN, MICHAEL
Actor
WARRICK, RUTH
Actress
WATSON, DOUGLASS
Actor
WEITZ, BRUCE
Actor
WILLIAMS, ROBIN
Actor
WINKLER, HENRY
Actor
WYMAN, JANE
Actress
ZIMBALIST, STEPHANIE
Actress

TV HOSTS AND ANNOUNCERS

ALLEN, STEVE
BARKER, BOB
BARRIS, CHUCK
BARRY, JACK
BLACKWOOD, NINA
BOGGS, BILL
BOMBECK, ERMA
CARSON, JOHNNY
CAVETT, DICK
CHILDS, JULIA
CLARK, DICK
CONVY, BERT
COSSELL, HOWARD
CULLEN, BILL
DAVIDSON, JOHN
DAWSON, RICHARD
DONAHUE, PHIL
DOUGLAS, MIKE
DOWNS, HUGH
EDWARDS, STEVE
EUBANKS, BOB

FRANKLIN, JOE
FRANCIS, ARLENE
FRIEDMAN, DR. SONYA
GARAGIOLA, JOE
GARVEY, CYNDY
GIFFORD, FRANK
GOODMAN, MARK
GOWDY, CURT
GRIFFIN, MERV
HALL, MONTY
HARTMAN, DAVID
HARTZ, JIM
HENDREN, RON
HENINBURG, GUSTAV
HUNTER, ALAN
JACKSON, J.J.
KELLY, KATIE
KLEIN, STEWART
LETTERMAN, DAVID
LUNDEN, JOAN
McKAY, JIM

McMAHON, ED
MARSHALL, PETER
MARTIN, MARY
MUSBURGER, ED
PHILBEN, REGIS
POWERS, RON
QUINN, MARTHA
RAYBURN, GENE
RIVERS, JOAN
ROGERS, FRED
ROGERS, MELODY
RUKEYSER, LOUIS
SAGAN, DR. CARL
SCOTT, WILLARD
SHALIT, GENE
SIEGEL, JOEL
SIMMONS, RICHARD
THOMAS, FRED
TREBEK, ALEX
TUSH, BILL
WALTERS, BARBARA

TV MOVIE, SPECIAL AND SERIES DIRECTORS

ADATO, PERRY MILLER
ALDA, ALAN
BAXTER, ELLEN
BINDER, STEVE
BOWAB, JOHN
BRANDT, YANNA KROYT
BRAVERMAN, CHUCK
BURROWS, JAMES
BUTLER, ROBERT
CASTELLI, LOUIS P.
CATES, GILBERT
CATES, JOSEPH
CHAMBERS, EVERETT
CHARNIN, MARTIN
CHOMSKY, MARVIN
CLAXTON, WILLIAM
CONRAD, WILLIAM
COOK, FIELDER
COX, NELL
DAMSKI, MEL

FENADY, GEORG J.
FLICKER, THEODORE
FRANKENHEIMER, JOHN
GRAUMAN, WALTER
GREENE, DAVID
HAINES, RANDA
HARDY, JOE
HEMION, DWIGHT
JOHNSON, KENNETH
KENNEY, WESLEY H.
KIBBEE, ROLAND
KOMACK, JAMES
LACHMAN, MORT
LARGE, BRIAN
LEAR, NORMAN
McEVEETY, BERNARD
McLAGLEN, ANDREW
MANN, DELBERT
MARCH, ALEX
MASUCCI, TONY

MYERSON, ALAN
MYHRUM, ROBERT G.
PARIS, JERRY
PASETTA, MARTIN A.
PRESSMAN, DAVID
RICH, JOHN
ROSS, MICHAEL
SANDRICH, JAY
SARGENT, JOSEPH
SCHAEFER, GEORGE
SCHAFFNER, FRANKLIN
SCHLATTER, GEORGE H.
SINGER, ALEXANDER
STEWART, CHUCK
STONEY, GEORGE
SWACKHAMER, E.W.
WISEMAN, FREDERICK
WITT, PAUL JUNGER
YOUNG, ROGER
ZINBERG, MICHAEL

WRITERS

ALDA, ALAN
Writer
ALLEN, STEVE
Writer
BAILEY, JOSEPH
Writer
BALKAN, DAVID H.
Writer
BARRET, EARL
Writer
BASKIN, JOHN
Writer
BELLISARIO, DONALD P.
Writer
BLINN, WILLIAM
Writer
BOCHCO, STEVEN
Writer
BRAND, JOSHUA
Writer
BRANDT, YANNA KROYT
Writer
BROOKS, JAMES
Writer
BROWNE, L. VIRGINIA
Writer
BURNS, ALAN
Writer

BYRNES, JIM
Writer
CANDY, JOHN
Writer
CANNELL, STEPHEN J.
Writer
CARDEA, FRANK
Writer
CARROLL JR., BOB
Writer
CASTELLI, LOUIS P.
Writer
CHAMBERS, ERNEST
Writer
CHAMBERS, EVERETT
Writer
CHARLES, GLEN
Writer
CHARLES, LES
Writer
CHASE, DAVID
Writer
COHEN, ELLIS
Exec. Writer
COLMAN, HENRY
Writer
COOPER, HAL
Writer

COX, NELL
Writer
CURTIN, VALERIE
Writer
DAVIS, MADELYN
Writer
DAVIS, PETER
Writer
DENOFF, SAM
Writer
DUCLON, DAVID W.
Writer
FIELDER, RICHARD
Writer
FINELL, ALYCE
Writer
FLAHERTY, JOE
Writer
FLICKER, THEODORE
Writer
GAFFNEY, RICKIE
Writer
GAY, JOHN
Writer
GEISS, TONY
Writer
GELBART, LARRY
Writer

GLEASON, MICHAEL
Writer

GOLDBERG, GARY D.
Writer

HUSKY, RICK
Writer

ILLES, ROBERT
Writer

ILSON, SAUL
Writer

INGALLS, DON
Writer

ISAACS, DAVID
Writer

JOHNSON, KENNETH
Writer

KANE, ARNOLD
Writer

KANTER, HAL
Comedy Writer

KAUFMAN, LEONARD B.
Writer

KAYDEN, WILLIAM
Writer

KAZURINSKY, TIM
Writer

KEYES, PAUL WILLIAM
Writer

KIBBEE, ROLAND
Writer

KINOY, ERNEST
Writer

KOMACK, JAMES
Writer

LACHMAN, MORT
Writer

LEAR, NORMAN
Writer

LEVINE, KEN
Writer

LEVINSON, RICHARD L.
Writer

LEVY, EUGENE
Writer

LEWIS, ARTHUR BERNARD
Writer

LINK, WILLIAM
Writer

McMAHON, JENNA
Writer

MANN, ABBY
Writer

MARCUS, ANN
Writer

MARLAND, DOUGLAS
Writer

MARSHALL, GARRY KENT
Writer

MARTIN, ANDREA
Writer

MASIUS, JOHN W.
Writer

MAYER, JERRY
Writer

MICHAELS, LORNE
Writer

MILLER, J.P.
Writer

MOSS, JEFFREY
Writer

NIXON, AGNES
Writer

O'HARA, CATHERINE
Writer

OLIANSKY, JOEL
Writer

PARRIOTT, JAMES D.
Writer

PERSKY, BILL
Writer

RAPPAPORT, JOHN H.
Writer

RASKY, HARRY
Writer

REO, DON
Writer

RINTELS, DAVID W.
Writer

ROONEY, ANDY
Writer

ROSE, REGINALD
Writer

ROSENBERG, META
Writer

ROSS, MICHAEL
Writer

SARGENT, HERB
Writer

SAGAN, DR. CARL
Writer

SCHENCK, GEORGE
Writer

SCHLATTER, GEORGE H.
Writer

SHULMAN, ROGER
Writer

SMITH, APRIL
Writer

SMITH, PAT FALKEN
Writer

STERN, STEWART
Writer

STONEY, GEORGE
Writer

STRANGIS, GREG
Writer

SULTAN, ARNE
Writer

TOROKVEI, PETER JOHN
Writer

VICTOR, DAVID
Writer

WEBSTER, SKIP
Writer

WILDER, JOHN
Writer

WITT, PAUL JUNGER
Writer

ANCHORS

ALLISON, CYNTHIA
Co-Anchor

ANASTOS, ERNIE
Anchor

BEARD, JOHN
Co-Anchor

BELL, STEVE

Anchor

BERMAN, CHRIS
Sports Anchor

BERRY, JIM
Weekend News Anchor

BEUTEL, BILL
Anchor

BRINKLEY, DAVID
Anchor "This Week with David Brinkley"

BROKAW, TOM
Anchor

BROWN, RICK
Anchor

BURGESS, CHET
News Anchor
CAFFERTY, JACK
Anchor
CARTER III, HODDING
Anchor
CHAPMAN, ROBIN
Co-Anchor
CHUNG, CONNIE
Anchor
DEAN, MORTON
Anchor, CBS Evening News;
    Newsbreak
DOBYNS, LLOYD
Anchor
DOW, HAROLD
Co-Anchor
DUNPHY, JERRY
Anchor
EDWARDS, DOUGLAS
Anchor
ELLERBEE, LINDA
News Anchor
FARMER, DON (Donald E.)
Anchor
FIELD, STORM
Anchor
FRICKE, JOHN
Anchor
GLENN, CHRISTOPHER
Anchor
GORDON, CHRIS
Co-Anchor
GRIMSBY, ROGER
Anchor
GUMBEL, BRYANT C.
Co-Anchor "Today"
HACKEL, DAN
Anchor
HAMBRICK, JOHN
Anchor
HARPER, PAT
Co-Anchor
HARRISON, BARBARA
Co-Anchor
HARTER, JOHN
Co-Anchor
HENRY, CHUCK
Anchor
JENNINGS, PETER
Anchor
JETER, FELICIA
Anchor

JOHNSON, JOHN
Part-Time Anchor
JORGENSEN, BILL
Anchor
KOPPEL, TED
Anchor
KROENCKE, MARY
Anchor
KURALT, CHARLES
News Anchor
KURTIS, BILL
Co-Anchor
LADENDORFF, MARCIA
News Anchor
LECLAIR, DENISE
Anchor
LEHRER, JIM
Co-Anchor
LEY, ROBERT
Anchor
LITTLE, TAWNY GODIN
Anchor
LUND, CHRISTINE
Co-Anchor
McBRIDE, BOB
Anchor
McCREARY, BILL
Co-Anchor
MacNEIL, ROBERT
Co-Anchor
MARLOW, JESS
Co-Anchor
MOORE, RICK
News Anchor
MOYER, PAUL
Anchor
MUDD, ROGER
Anchor
PALMER, JOHN
Anchor
PAULEY, JANE
Co-Anchor
PERKINS, JACK
Co-Anchor
RATHER, DAN
Anchor
REASONER, HARRY
Anchor
ROBINSON, MAX
Anchor
ROLAND, JOHN
Anchor
SAFER, MORLEY

Anchor
SAGER, CRAIG
Anchor
SCAMARDELLA, ROSE ANN
Anchor
SCARBOROUGH, CHUCK
Co-Anchor
SCHECHNER, WILLIAM
Co-Anchor
SCHIEFFER, BOB
Anchor
SCHUBECK, JOHN
Co-Anchor
SCOTT, MARVIN
Co-Anchor
SEGURA, DEBI
Anchor
SHAW, BERNARD
Anchor
SIMMONS, SUE
Anchor
SNYDER, TOM
Anchor
STONE, KAREN
Co-Anchor
STORY, RALPH
Co-Anchor
SULLIVAN, KATHLEEN
Co-Anchor
THOMPSON, LEA
Anchor
TONG, KAITY
Co-Anchor
TOWNLEY, RICHARD
Anchor
TOYOTA, TRITIA
Co-Anchor
VANDOR, CINDY
Anchor
WALLACE, MIKE
Anchor
WATERS, LOU (Lou Riegert)
Anchor
WEST, MARY JO
Co-Anchor
WILDE, KIRSTIE
Field Anchor
WILKERSON, JAMES
Anchor
ZEIDMAN, LEE
Anchor
ZIMMERMAN, BILL
Anchor

CORRESPONDENTS

AARON, BETSY
Correspondent

ABERNATHY, ROBERT
Correspondent

ADAMS, JACQUELINE
Correspondent

AGRONSKY, MARTIN
Correspondent/Doc. Prod.

ANDERSON, BONNIE MARIE
News Correspondent

AUG, STEPHEN
Correspondent

BAZELL, ROBERT
Science Correspondent

BEGLEITER, RALPH J.
Washington Correspondent
 (State Dept.)

BENTON, JOE
Correspondent

BERGER, MARILYN
Correspondent

BERKOWITZ, BOB
Correspondent

BERNSTEIN, CARL
Principal Correspondent

BIERBAUER, CHARLES J.
Defense Correspondent

BLACK, MAXENE
Correspondent

BLACKBURN, DAN
Correspondent

BLACKSTONE, JOHN
Correspondent

BLYSTONE, RICHARD M.
Correspondent

BODE, KEN
Correspondent

BOURGHOLTZER, FRANK
Correspondent

BOWEN, JERRY
Correspondent

BRADY, RAY
Correspondent

BRIGGS, FRED
Correspondent

BROWN, HILARY
Correspondent

BUCHIN, JOHN
Correspondent

BURNS, ERIC
Midwest Correspondent

BURRINGTON, DAVID
Correspondent

CARAS, ROGER
Correspondent

CHANCELLOR, JOHN
Correspondent

CHASE, REBECCA
Correspondent

CHASE, SYLVIA
Correspondent

CLARK, BOB
Correspondent

COCHRAN, JOHN
News Correspondent

COLLINS, PETER
Correspondent

COMPTON, ANN
Correspondent

COMPTON, JAMES M.
Correspondent

CONNOR, MICHAEL
Correspondent

CRILE III, GEORGE
Correspondent

CRONKITE, WALTER
Special Correspondent

CULHANE, DAVID
Correspondent

DALE, AL
Correspondent

DANCY, JOHN
News Correspondent

DELANEY, STEVE
Correspondent

DICK, DAVID
Correspondent

DOBBS, GREG
Correspondent

DOLAN, PATRICK FRANCIS
Correspondent

DONALDSON, SAM
Correspondent

DONVAN, JOHN
News Correspondent

DOTSON, BOB
Correspondent

DOW, DAVID
Correspondent

DOW, HAROLD
Correspondent

DRINKWATER, TERRY
Correspondent

DUNNING, BRUCE
Correspondent

DUNSMORE, BARRIE
Correspondent

ECKHERT, JULIE
Correspondent

EGAN, TRACY
Correspondent

ELLERBEE, LINDA
Correspondent

ERBE, BONNIE G.
Correspondent

FAW, BOB
Correspondent

FLETCHER, MARTIN
Correspondent

FLOCK, JEFF
Chief Midwest Correspondent

FOX, STEVE
Correspondent

FRANCIS, FRED
Correspondent

FRAZIER, STEPHEN
Correspondent

GARCIA, DAVID
Correspondent

GARRELS, ANNE
Correspondent

GEER, STEPHEN
Correspondent

GIBSON, CHARLES
Correspondent

GILMOUR, SANDY
Correspondent

GLASS, CHARLES
Correspondent

GOLDBERG, BERNARD
Correspondent

GOMEZ, CHARLES
Correspondent

GRAHAM, FRED
Law Correspondent

GREENE, BOB
Contributing Correspondent

GREENFIELD, JEFF
Special Correspondent

GREENWOOD, BILL
Correspondent

GREGORY, BETTINA
Correspondent

GRENIER, JACQUES
Correspondent

GROTH, ROBIN
Correspondent

HAINES, MARK
Correspondent

HALL, BRUCE
Correspondent

HARPER, CHRIS
Correspondent

HART, JOHN
Correspondent
HERMAN, GEORGE
Moderator & Economics
 Correspondent
HICKEY, JIM
Correspondent
HOLLIMAN, JOHN
White House Correspondent
HOTTELET, RICHARD C.
U.N. Correspondent
HUME, BRIT
Correspondent
HUMI, PETER JOHN
Correspondent
INDERFURTH, RICK
Correspondent
JARRIEL, TOM
Correspondent
JENSEN, MIKE (Michael C.
 Jensen)
NBC News Correspondent
JETER, FELICIA
Correspondent
JOHNSON, DOUG
Correspondent
JOHNSON, JOHN
Correspondent
JONES, KENLEY
Correspondent
JONES, PHIL
News Correspondent
JOSELOFF, GORDON
Correspondent
KALB, BERNARD
Correspondent
KALB, MARVIN
Correspondent
KAPLOW, HERBERT
News Correspondent
KASHIWAHARA, KEN
Correspondent
KELLEY, CHRIS
Correspondent
KENNEDY, ROYAL
Correspondent
KENT, ART
Correspondent
KENYON, SANDY (Alexander
 Vicary Low Kenyon)
Entertainment Correspondent
KIKER, DOUGLAS
Correspondent
KING, EMERY
Correspondent
KLADSTRUP, DON
Correspondent

KRAUSS, MITCHELL
Correspondent
KROFT, STEVE
Correspondent
KUR, BOB
Network News Correspondent
KURALT, CHARLES
Correspondent
LANDY, JERRY M.
News Correspondent
LAURENCE, JOHN
Correspondent
LEE, MIKE
Correspondent
LEVINE, IRVING R.
Network News Correspondent
LEWIS, MILTON
Correspondent
LICHT, JUDY
Correspondent, "Eyewitness
 News"
LITKE, MARK
Correspondent
LLOYD, ROBIN
News Correspondent
LYNCH, BILL
Correspondent
McCARTHY, SHERYL
Correspondent
McCOURT, MICHAEL
Correspondent and Bureau Chief
McLAUGHLIN, BILL
Correspondent
McMILLON, DORIS
Correspondent
McNAMARA, ROBERT
Correspondent
McNEILL, DONALD
Correspondent
McWETHY, JOHN F.
Chief Pentagon Correspondent
MARTIN, DAVID
Correspondent
MARTIN, JOHN
Correspondent
MILLER, RON
Correspondent
MITCHELL, ANDREA
Correspondent
MITCHELL, JANE
Correspondent
MONROE, BILL (William B., Jr.)
News Correspondent
MOYERS, BILL
Correspondent
MYERS, LISA MERRYMAN
Correspondent

NEWMAN, EDWIN
Correspondent
NOBLE, GIL
Correspondent
NUNN, RAY
Correspondent
NYKANEN, MARK
News Correspondent
O'BRIEN, TIM
Correspondent
OLBERMANN, KEITH
Nat'l Sports Correspondent
OLIVER, DON
Correspondent
O'NEIL, ROGER
Correspondent
OSGOOD, CHARLES
Correspondent
PALMER, JOHN
Correspondent
PAPPAS, IKE
Correspondent
PETERSON, ROGER
Correspondent
PETERSON, SUSAN
Correspondent
POLING, DOUG
Correspondent
POLK, JAMES
Correspondent
POTTER, MARK
Correspondent
QUARLES, NORMA
Correspondent
QUINONES, JOHN
Correspondent
QUIRT, JOHN
Chief Economics Correspondent
RABEL, ED
Correspondent
RATNER, VIC
Correspondent
REDEKER, BILL
Correspondent
ROJAS, GLORIA
Correspondent
ROLLIN, BETTY
Correspondent
ROSE, JUDD
Correspondent
ROSS, BRIAN
Correspondent
ROTH, RICHARD
Correspondent
RUCKER, BOB
Correspondent

RUDD, HUGHES
Correspondent
RUTZ, DANIEL C.
Medical News Correspondent
SANDERS, MARLENE
Correspondent
SARGENT, TONY
Correspondent
SCALI, JOHN
Sr. Correspondent
SCHAAP, DICK
Sports Correspondent
SCHADLER, JAY
Correspondent
SCHELL, TOM
Correspondent
SCHIEFFER, BOB
Correspondent
SCHOENBRUN, DAVID
News Analayst
SCHORR, DANIEL
Senior Washington
    Correspondent
SCHOUMACHER, DAVID
Correspondent
SCOTT, DREW
Correspondent
SEAMANS, BILL
Correspondent
SEAMANS, IKE
News Correspondent
SEIDEL, ERIC M.
Correspondent
SERAFIN, BARRY

Correspondent
SEVAREID, ERIC
Consultant
SHARP, ROGER
Correspondent
SHAW, BERNARD
Correspondent
SHEAHAN, JOHN
Correspondent
SHEPARD, GARY
Correspondent
SHEPARD, STEVE
Correspondent
SHERR, LYNN
Correspondent
SIMPSON, CAROLE
Correspondent
SIRKIN, BOB
Correspondent
SLATTERY, JOHN
Correspondent
SMITH, HOWARD K.
Correspondent
SOBEL, REBECCA
Correspondent
SPENCER, SUSAN
Correspondent
SPENS, WILL
Correspondent
STERN, CARL
News Correspondent
STOSSEL, JOHN
Correspondent
STRAIT, GEORGE

Correspondent
TEMPLETON, JOE
Correspondent
THRELKELD, RICHARD
Correspondent
TONG, KAITY
Correspondent
TROTTA, LIZ
Correspondent
TROUTE, DENNIS
Correspondent
TUNNELL, DOUG
Correspondent
VALERIANI, RICHARD
Correspondent
VANOCUR, SANDER
Correspondent
Von FREMD, MICHAEL
Correspondent
WALKER, HAL
Correspondent
WALKER, JAMES
Correspondent
WALLACE, CHRIS
Correspondent
WALTERS, BARBARA
Correspondent
WOODRUFF, JUDY
Network Correspondent
WOOTEN, JAMES
Correspondent
YOUNG, LOUIS
Correspondent

REPORTERS

AGRONSKY, MARTIN
Reporter
AGUILAR, CARLOS
Reporter
AXTHELM, PETE
Sportscaster
BARNES, GORDON
Meteorologist
BARRETT, RONA
TV Gossip Reporter
BARRY, MIKE
Sports Reporter
BERGMAN, JULES
Science Editor
BERRY, JIM
Reporter
BLANCHARD, BOB
Consumer Reporter

BRAVER, RITA
Reporter
BROCKINGTON, JACKIE
General Assignment Weather
    Reporter
BROOKSHIER, TOM
Sports Broadcaster
BURGESS, CHET
Reporter
BURKE, KELLY
General Assignment Reporter
CAFFERTY, JACK
Reporter
CAMPBELL, ARCH
Feature Reporter
CARPER, JEAN
Health Reporter
CASEY, FRANK

Newscaster
CHARLES, NICK
Reporter
CHRISTIAN, SPENCER
Reporter
CLARK, SCOTT
Sportscaster
CLARK, SUSAN
General Assignment Reporter
CLARKE, JIM
Investigative Reporter
CLOHERTY, JACK
Reporter
COLLINS, PAT
Reporter
CORCORAN, JOHN
Entertainment Reporter
DANDRIDGE, PAUL

WILKINSON, CHARLES
Pre-Game Analyst
WILL, GEORGE F.
Reporter
WILLIAMS, CHEE CHEE
Reporter

WILSON, WARREN
Reporter
WITKER, KRISTI
Reporter

WOLYNSKI, MARA
Reporter
WRIGHT, BEN
Broadcaster

TV JOURNALISTS AND PUBLISHERS

ANDERSON, JON STEPHEN
Writer
ARLEN, MICHAEL
Writer
BANNER, JONATHAN
President and Publisher
BEDELL, SALLY
TV and Cultural Reporter
BURGHEIM, RICHARD
Publisher
CLARK, KEN
National Media Reporter
COOK STANTON
Publisher
CRIST, JUDITH
TV Critic
COSTELLO, MARJORIE
Editor
FEDER, ROBERT
Reporter
GOODMAN, WALTER
Media Critic
GORDON, JANE

Editor
HICKEY, NEIL
N.Y. Bureau Chief
JAFFE, AL
Editor
KITMAN, MARVIN
TV Critic
LABICH, RICHARD
Associate Publisher
LARSON, ERIC
Publisher
MARGULIES, LEE
Staff Writer
O'CONNOR, JOHN J.
TV Critic
PANITT, MERRILL
Editorial Director
PAUL, SOL
Publisher
PRESTON, MARILYN
TV Columnist
ROSENBERG, HOWARD
TV Columnist

RUBIN, JAY
Editor
SENDLER, DAVID ALAN
Co-Editor
SHALES, TOM
TV Critic
SMITH, ROBERT C.
Managing Editor
SMITH BROWNSTEIN,
  ELIZABETH
Editorial Director
UNGER, ARTHUR
TV Critic
VAN HORNE, HARRIET
TV Reporter
WARREN, ALBERT
Editor and Publisher
WINFREY, LEE
TV Reporter
WOLCOTT, JAMES
TV Critic
YOUMAN, ROGER
Editor

TV/COMMUNICATIONS LAWYERS

ABRAMS, FLOYD
Attorney, Cahill, Gordon, Reindel
FERRIS, CHARLES DANIEL
Lawyer

HAMBURG, MORTON
Lawyer, Netter, Dowd and Alfieri
MOORE, EARLE
Lawyer

NEUSTADT, RICHARD
Partner, Wiley, Johnson and Rein
STANDER, STEPHEN
Managing Gen. Atty., NBC

TV/COMMUNICATIONS POLITICAL FIGURES

DAWSON, MIMI WEYFORTH
Commissioner, FCC
DOUGAN, DIANA LADY
Coordinator for Int'l Commun.
  and Information Policy, U.S.
  State Dept.

FOGARTY, JOSEPH
Commissioner, FCC
QUELLO, JAMES
Commissioner, FCC
RIVERA, HENRY

Commissioner, FCC
WIRTH, TIMOTHY
U.S. Representative,
  Telecommunications and
  Consumer Protection and
  Finance Comm.

TV/COMMUNICATIONS PROFESSORS

ABEL, ELLIE
Professor of Communications,
  Stamford
DAY, JAMES

TV Consultant/Professor,
  Brooklyn College
GERBNER, GEORGE
Professor of Communications,

U. of Pa.

WINSTON, BRIAN
Professor, NYU

TV PERSONNEL AGENTS

BARISH, SHERLEE
Pres., Broadcast Personnel

HOOKSTRATTEN, ED
Attorney/Agent

LEIBNER, RICHARD
Talent Agent for the News

OTHER TV-RELATED OCCUPATIONS

CARPENTER, TED
Editor, Telekey
FRITZ, ALLEN
Treasurer, Cablentertainment
GIRVAN, GARRETT
Chief Financial Officer, Viacom
GOLDEN, STAN
Distributor-Alan Landsburg
  Productions
JONES, CHUCK

Animator
LOPER, JAMES
Independent Telecommunications
MIDGLEY, LESLIE
TV Consultant
O'LEARY, RICHARD
TV Consultant
RUSSELL, MICHAEL
Publicist, Disney Prod.
SCHEIMER, LOU

Animated Cartoon Exec.
SIMON, RONALD
Curator, Museum of
  Broadcasting
WASSERMAN, BERT
Member of Office of Pres.
  Warner Comm.
WHITE, STEPHEN
Supervisor, ABC Motion
  Pictures for TV